T0145373

Lecture Notes in Computer Science 10862

Commenced Publication in 1973
Founding and Former Series Editors:
Gerhard Goos, Juris Hartmanis, and Jan van Leeuwen

More information about this series at http://www.springer.com/series/7407

Yong Shi · Haohuan Fu
Yingjie Tian · Valeria V. Krzhizhanovskaya
Michael Harold Lees · Jack Dongarra
Peter M. A. Sloot (Eds.)

Computational Science – ICCS 2018

18th International Conference
Wuxi, China, June 11–13, 2018
Proceedings, Part III

 Springer

Editors
Yong Shi
Chinese Academy of Sciences
Beijing
China

Haohuan Fu
National Supercomputing Center in Wuxi
Wuxi
China

Yingjie Tian
Chinese Academy of Sciences
Beijing
China

Valeria V. Krzhizhanovskaya (iD)
University of Amsterdam
Amsterdam
The Netherlands

Michael Harold Lees
University of Amsterdam
Amsterdam
The Netherlands

Jack Dongarra
University of Tennessee
Knoxville, TN
USA

Peter M. A. Sloot (iD)
University of Amsterdam
Amsterdam
The Netherlands

ISSN 0302-9743   ISSN 1611-3349 (electronic)
Lecture Notes in Computer Science
ISBN 978-3-319-93712-0   ISBN 978-3-319-93713-7 (eBook)
https://doi.org/10.1007/978-3-319-93713-7

Library of Congress Control Number: 2018947305

LNCS Sublibrary: SL1 – Theoretical Computer Science and General Issues

Printed on acid-free paper

This Springer imprint is published by the registered company Springer International Publishing AG
part of Springer Nature
The registered company address is: Gewerbestrasse 11, 6330 Cham, Switzerland

Preface

Welcome to the proceedings of the 18th Annual International Conference on Computational Science (ICCS: https://www.iccs-meeting.org/iccs2018/), held during June 11–13, 2018, in Wuxi, China. Located in the Jiangsu province, Wuxi is bordered by Changzhou to the west and Suzhou to the east. The city meets the Yangtze River in the north and is bathed by Lake Tai to the south. Wuxi is home to many parks, gardens, temples, and the fastest supercomputer in the world, the Sunway TaihuLight. ICCS 2018 was jointly organized by the University of Chinese Academy of Sciences, the National Supercomputing Center in Wuxi, the University of Amsterdam, NTU Singapore, and the University of Tennessee.

The International Conference on Computational Science is an annual conference that brings together researchers and scientists from mathematics and computer science as basic computing disciplines, researchers from various application areas who are pioneering computational methods in sciences such as physics, chemistry, life sciences, and engineering, as well as in arts and humanitarian fields, to discuss problems and solutions in the area, to identify new issues, and to shape future directions for research.

Since its inception in 2001, ICCS has attracted increasingly higher quality and numbers of attendees and papers, and this year was no an exception, with over 350 expected participants. The proceedings series have become a major intellectual resource for computational science researchers, defining and advancing the state of the art in this field.

ICCS 2018 in Wuxi, China, was the 18th in this series of highly successful conferences. For the previous 17 meetings, see: http://www.iccs-meeting.org/iccs2018/previous-iccs/.

The theme for ICCS 2018 was "Science at the Intersection of Data, Modelling and Computation," to highlight the role of computation as a fundamental method of scientific inquiry and technological discovery tackling problems across scientific domains and creating synergies between disciplines. This conference was a unique event focusing on recent developments in: scalable scientific algorithms; advanced software tools; computational grids; advanced numerical methods; and novel application areas. These innovative novel models, algorithms, and tools drive new science through efficient application in areas such as physical systems, computational and systems biology, environmental systems, finance, and others.

ICCS is well known for its excellent line up of keynote speakers. The keynotes for 2018 were:

- Charlie Catlett, Argonne National Laboratory|University of Chicago, USA
- Xiaofei Chen, Southern University of Science and Technology, China
- Liesbet Geris, University of Liège|KU Leuven, Belgium
- Sarika Jalan, Indian Institute of Technology Indore, India
- Petros Koumoutsakos, ETH Zürich, Switzerland
- Xuejun Yang, National University of Defense Technology, China

This year we had 405 submissions (180 submissions to the main track and 225 to the workshops). In the main track, 51 full papers were accepted (28%). In the workshops, 97 full papers (43%). A high acceptance rate in the workshops is explained by the nature of these thematic sessions, where many experts in a particular field are personally invited by workshop organizers to participate in their sessions.

ICCS relies strongly on the vital contributions of our workshop organizers to attract high-quality papers in many subject areas. We would like to thank all committee members for the main track and workshops for their contribution toward ensuring a high standard for the accepted papers. We would also like to thank Springer, Elsevier, Intellegibilis, Beijing Vastitude Technology Co., Ltd. and Inspur for their support. Finally, we very much appreciate all the local Organizing Committee members for their hard work to prepare this conference.

We are proud to note that ICCS is an ERA 2010 A-ranked conference series.

June 2018

Yong Shi
Haohuan Fu
Yingjie Tian
Valeria V. Krzhizhanovskaya
Michael Lees
Jack Dongarra
Peter M. A. Sloot
The ICCS 2018 Organizers

Organization

Local Organizing Committee

Co-chairs

Yingjie Tian	University of Chinese Academy of Sciences, China
Lin Gan	National Supercomputing Center in Wuxi, China

Members

Jiming Wu	National Supercomputing Center in Wuxi, China
Lingying Wu	National Supercomputing Center in Wuxi, China
Jinzhe Yang	National Supercomputing Center in Wuxi, China
Bingwei Chen	National Supercomputing Center in Wuxi, China
Yuanchun Zheng	University of Chinese Academy of Sciences, China
Minglong Lei	University of Chinese Academy of Sciences, China
Jia Wu	Macquarie University, Australia
Zhengsong Chen	University of Chinese Academy of Sciences, China
Limeng Cui	University of Chinese Academy of Sciences, China
Jiabin Liu	University of Chinese Academy of Sciences, China
Biao Li	University of Chinese Academy of Sciences, China
Yunlong Mi	University of Chinese Academy of Sciences, China
Wei Dai	University of Chinese Academy of Sciences, China

Workshops and Organizers

Advances in High-Performance Computational Earth Sciences: Applications and Frameworks – IHPCES 2018
Xing Cai, Kohei Fujita, Takashi Shimokawabe

Agent-Based Simulations, Adaptive Algorithms, and Solvers – ABS-AAS 2018
Robert Schaefer, Maciej Paszynski, Victor Calo, David Pardo

Applications of Matrix Methods in Artificial Intelligence and Machine Learning – AMAIML 2018
Kourosh Modarresi

Architecture, Languages, Compilation, and Hardware Support for Emerging Manycore Systems – ALCHEMY 2018
Loïc Cudennec, Stéphane Louise

Biomedical and Bioinformatics Challenges for Computer Science – BBC 2018
Giuseppe Agapito, Mario Cannataro, Mauro Castelli, Riccardo Dondi, Rodrigo Weber dos Santos, Italo Zoppis

Computational Finance and Business Intelligence – CFBI 2018
Shouyang Wang, Yong Shi, Yingjie Tian

Computational Optimization, Modelling, and Simulation – COMS 2018
Xin-She Yang, Slawomir Koziel, Leifur Leifsson, T. O. Ting

Data-Driven Computational Sciences – DDCS 2018
Craig Douglas, Abani Patra, Ana Cortés, Robert Lodder

Data, Modeling, and Computation in IoT and Smart Systems – DMC-IoT 2018
Julien Bourgeois, Vaidy Sunderam, Hicham Lakhlef

Mathematical Methods and Algorithms for Extreme Scale – MATH-EX 2018
Vassil Alexandrov

Multiscale Modelling and Simulation – MMS 2018
Derek Groen, Lin Gan, Valeria Krzhizhanovskaya, Alfons Hoekstra

Simulations of Flow and Transport: Modeling, Algorithms, and Computation – SOFTMAC 2018
Shuyu Sun, Jianguo (James) Liu, Jingfa Li

Solving Problems with Uncertainties – SPU 2018
Vassil Alexandrov

Teaching Computational Science – WTCS 2018
Angela B. Shiflet, Alfredo Tirado-Ramos, Nia Alexandrov

Tools for Program Development and Analysis in Computational Science – TOOLS 2018
Karl Fürlinger, Arndt Bode, Andreas Knüpfer, Dieter Kranzlmüller, Jens Volkert, Roland Wismüller

Urgent Computing – UC 2018
Marian Bubak, Alexander Boukhanovsky

Program Committee

Ahmad Abdelfattah
David Abramson
Giuseppe Agapito
Ram Akella
Elisabete Alberdi
Marco Aldinucci
Nia Alexandrov
Vassil Alexandrov
Saad Alowayyed
Ilkay Altintas
Stanislaw
    Ambroszkiewicz

Ioannis Anagnostou
Michael Antolovich
Hartwig Anzt
Hideo Aochi
Tomasz Arodz
Tomàs Artés Vivancos
Victor Azizi Tarksalooyeh
Ebrahim Bagheri
Bartosz Balis
Krzysztof Banas
Jörn Behrens
Adrian Bekasiewicz

Adam Belloum
Abdelhak Bentaleb
Stefano Beretta
Daniel Berrar
Sanjukta Bhowmick
Anna Bilyatdinova
Guillaume Blin
Nasri Bo
Marcel Boersma
Bartosz Bosak
Kris Bubendorfer
Jérémy Buisson

Aleksander Byrski
Wentong Cai
Xing Cai
Mario Cannataro
Yongcan Cao
Pedro Cardoso
Mauro Castelli
Eduardo Cesar
Imen Chakroun
Huangxin Chen
Mingyang Chen
Zhensong Chen
Siew Ann Cheong
Lock-Yue Chew
Ana Cortes
Enrique
   Costa-Montenegro
Carlos Cotta
Jean-Francois Couchot
Helene Coullon
Attila Csikász-Nagy
Loïc Cudennec
Javier Cuenca
Yifeng Cui
Ben Czaja
Pawel Czarnul
Wei Dai
Lisandro Dalcin
Bhaskar Dasgupta
Susumu Date
Quanling Deng
Xiaolong Deng
Minh Ngoc Dinh
Riccardo Dondi
Tingxing Dong
Ruggero Donida Labati
Craig C. Douglas
Rafal Drezewski
Jian Du
Vitor Duarte
Witold Dzwinel
Nahid Emad
Christian Engelmann
Daniel Etiemble

Christos
   Filelis-Papadopoulos
Karl Frinkle
Haohuan Fu
Karl Fuerlinger
Kohei Fujita
Wlodzimierz Funika
Takashi Furumura
David Gal
Lin Gan
Robin Gandhi
Frédéric Gava
Alex Gerbessiotis
Carlos Gershenson
Domingo Gimenez
Frank Giraldo
Ivo Gonçalves
Yuriy Gorbachev
Pawel Gorecki
George Gravvanis
Derek Groen
Lutz Gross
Kun Guo
Xiaohu Guo
Piotr Gurgul
Panagiotis Hadjidoukas
Azzam Haidar
Dongxu Han
Raheel Hassan
Jurjen Rienk Helmus
Bogumila Hnatkowska
Alfons Hoekstra
Paul Hofmann
Sergey Ivanov
Hideya Iwasaki
Takeshi Iwashita
Jiří Jaroš
Marco Javarone
Chao Jin
Hai Jin
Zhong Jin
Jingheng
David Johnson
Anshul Joshi

Jaap Kaandorp
Viacheslav Kalashnikov
George Kampis
Drona Kandhai
Aneta Karaivanova
Vlad Karbovskii
Andrey Karsakov
Takahiro Katagiri
Wayne Kelly
Deepak Khazanchi
Alexandra Klimova
Ivan Kondov
Vladimir Korkhov
Jari Kortelainen
Ilias Kotsireas
Jisheng Kou
Sergey Kovalchuk
Slawomir Koziel
Valeria Krzhizhanovskaya
Massimo La Rosa
Hicham Lakhlef
Roberto Lam
Anna-Lena Lamprecht
Rubin Landau
Johannes Langguth
Vianney Lapotre
Jysoo Lee
Michael Lees
Minglong Lei
Leifur Leifsson
Roy Lettieri
Andrew Lewis
Biao Li
Dewei Li
Jingfa Li
Kai Li
Peijia Li
Wei Li
I-Jong Lin
Hong Liu
Hui Liu
James Liu
Jiabin Liu
Piyang Liu

Weifeng Liu
Weiguo Liu
Marcelo Lobosco
Robert Lodder
Wen Long
Stephane Louise
Frederic Loulergue
Paul Lu
Sheraton M. V.
Scott MacLachlan
Maciej Malawski
Michalska Malgorzatka
Vania
    Marangozova-Martin
Tomas Margalef
Tiziana Margaria
Svetozar Margenov
Osni Marques
Pawel Matuszyk
Valerie Maxville
Rahul Mazumder
Valentin Melnikov
Ivan Merelli
Doudou Messoud
Yunlong Mi
Jianyu Miao
John Michopoulos
Sergey Mityagin
K. Modarresi
Kourosh Modarresi
Jânio Monteiro
Paulo Moura Oliveira
Ignacio Muga
Hiromichi Nagao
Kengo Nakajima
Denis Nasonov
Philippe Navaux
Hoang Nguyen
Mai Nguyen
Anna Nikishova
Lingfeng Niu
Mawloud Omar
Kenji Ono
Raymond Padmos

Marcin Paprzycki
David Pardo
Anna Paszynska
Maciej Paszynski
Abani Patra
Dana Petcu
Eric Petit
Serge Petiton
Gauthier Picard
Daniela Piccioni
Yuri Pirola
Antoniu Pop
Ela Pustulka-Hunt
Vladimir Puzyrev
Alexander Pyayt
Pei Quan
Rick Quax
Waldemar Rachowicz
Lukasz Rauch
Alistair Rendell
Sophie Robert
J. M. F Rodrigues
Daniel Rodriguez
Albert Romkes
James A. Ross
Debraj Roy
Philip Rutten
Katarzyna Rycerz
Alberto Sanchez
Rodrigo Santos
Hitoshi Sato
Robert Schaefer
Olaf Schenk
Ulf D. Schiller
Bertil Schmidt
Hichem Sedjelmaci
Martha Johanna
    Sepulveda
Yong Shi
Angela Shiflet
Takashi Shimokawabe
Tan Singyee
Robert Sinkovits
Vishnu Sivadasan

Peter Sloot
Renata Slota
Grażyna Ślusarczyk
Sucha Smanchat
Maciej Smołka
Bartlomiej Sniezynski
Sumit Sourabh
Achim Streit
Barbara Strug
Bongwon Suh
Shuyu Sun
Martin Swain
Ryszard Tadeusiewicz
Daisuke Takahashi
Jingjing Tang
Osamu Tatebe
Andrei Tchernykh
Cedric Tedeschi
Joao Teixeira
Yonatan Afework
    Tesfahunegn
Andrew Thelen
Xin Tian
Yingjie Tian
T. O. Ting
Alfredo Tirado-Ramos
Stanimire Tomov
Ka Wai Tsang
Britt van Rooij
Raja Velu
Antonio M. Vidal
David Walker
Jianwu Wang
Peng Wang
Yi Wang
Josef Weinbub
Mei Wen
Mark Wijzenbroek
Maciej Woźniak
Guoqiang Wu
Jia Wu
Qing Wu
Huilin Xing
Wei Xue

Chao-Tung Yang
Xin-She Yang
He Yiwei
Ce Yu
Ma Yue
Julija Zavadlav
Gábor Závodszky

Peng Zhang
Yao Zhang
Zepu Zhang
Wenlai Zhao
Yuanchun Zheng
He Zhong
Hua Zhong

Jinghui Zhong
Xiaofei Zhou
Luyao Zhu
Sotirios Ziavras
Andrea Zonca
Italo Zoppis

Contents – Part III

Track of Solving Problems with Uncertainties

Track of Teaching Computational Science

Poster Papers

Track of Simulations of Flow and Transport: Modeling, Algorithms and Computation

Simulations of Flow and Transport: Modeling, Algorithms and Computation

Shuyu Sun[1] (iD), Jiangguo Liu[2] (iD), and Jingfa Li[1,3] (iD)

[1] Computational Transport Phenomena Laboratory, Division of Physical Science and Engineering, King Abdullah University of Science and Technology, Thuwal 23955-6900, Saudi Arabia
shuyu.sun@kaust.edu.sa
[2] Department of Mathematics, Colorado State University, Fort Collins, CO 80523-1874, USA
[3] School of Mechanical Engineering, Beijing Institute of Petrochemical Technology, Beijing 102617, China

Abstract. We first briefly discuss the significance of flow and transport simulation that motivates the international workshop on "Simulations of Flow and Transport: Modeling, Algorithms and Computation" within the International Conference on Computational Science. We then review various works published in the proceedings of our workshop in 2018. Based on the works presented in this workshop in recent years, we also offer our observations on the general trends of the research activities in flow and transport simulations. We discuss existing challenges, emerging techniques, and major progress.

Keywords: Algorithms · Flow and transport · Modeling
Numerical simulations

Introduction

Most processes in natural and engineered systems inherently involve flow and transport. Thus simulations of flow and transport are extremely important for a wide range of scientific and industrial applications at various spatial and temporal scales. In this year's international workshop on "Simulations of Flow and Transport: Modeling, Algorithms and Computation" (SOFTMAC) within International Conference on Computational Science (ICCS), we focus on the recent advances in mathematical modeling, numerical algorithms, scientific computation, and other computational aspects of flow and transport phenomena. We have received 26 active submissions from China, Japan, Russia, Saudi Arabia, Singapore, and United States of America. After a strict peer review process, a total of 19 papers in this SOFTMAC workshop have been accepted for publication in the Proceeding of ICCS 2018.

It is worth noting that the SOFTMAC workshop has been held within the ICCS for seven years since 2011. A brief overview of our workshop is presented in Table 1. As one of the important sessions within ICCS, it has successfully attracted attention from worldwide researchers and scientists in the field of flow and transport. The workshop provides a great platform for bringing together scholars in this field annually to report

Table 1. Overview of our international workshop within the ICCS

No.	Our workshop	ICCS theme	Time and location
1	Flow and Transport: Computational Challenges	The Ascent of Computational Excellence	Nanyang Technological University, Singapore, 1–3 June, 2011
2	Flow and Transport: Modeling, Simulations and Algorithms	Empowering Science through Computing	Omaha, Nebraska, USA, 4–6 June, 2012
3	Flow and Transport: Modeling, Simulations and Algorithms	Computation at the Frontiers of Science	Barcelona, Spain, 5–7 June, 2013
4	Computational Flow and Transport: Modeling, Simulations and Algorithms	Computational Science at the Gates of Nature	Reykjavík, Iceland, 1–3 June, 2015
5	Computational Flow and Transport: Modeling, Simulations and Algorithms	Data through the Computational Lens	San Diego, California, USA, 6–8 June, 2016
6	Simulations of Flow and Transport: Modeling, Algorithms and Computation	The Art of Computational Science. Bridging Gaps – Forming Alloys	Zürich, Switzerland, 12–14 June, 2017
7	Simulations of Flow and Transport: Modeling, Algorithms and Computation	Science at the Intersection of Data, Modelling and Computation	Wuxi, China, 11–13 June, 2018

their research progresses in both theory and methods, to exchange new ideas for research, and to promote further collaborations.

Overview of Work Presented in This Workshop Proceeding

The list of papers published in this workshop covers state-of-the-art simulations of flow and transport problems. These papers represent ongoing research projects on various important topics relevant to the modeling, algorithms and computation of flow and transport. Here the workshop papers may be classified into five groups as follows.

The first group consists of seven papers that devoting to various issues and applications in the area of fluid flow and heat transfer. P. Sun et al. studied a dynamic fluid-structure interaction (FSI) problem involving a rotational elastic turbine by using the arbitrary Lagrangian-Eulerian (ALE) approach in the paper entitled "*ALE method for a rotating structure immersed in the fluid and its application to the articial heart pump in hemodynamics*". S. Ishihara et al. investigated the influence of depth from the free surface of the fish and turning motion via the moving-grid finite volume method and moving computational domain method with free surface height function in the paper entitled *"Free Surface Flow Simulation of Fish Turning Motion"*. In the paper entitled *"Circular Function-Based Gas-kinetic Scheme for Simulation of Viscous Compressible Flows"*, Z. Meng et al. simplified the integral domain of Maxwellian distribution function and proposed a stable gas-kinetic scheme based on circular function for the simulation of viscous compressible flows. J. Li et al presented an N-parallel FENE-P constitutive model for viscoelastic incompressible non-Newtonian fluids based on the idea of multiple relaxation times in the paper entitled *"Study on an N-parallel FENE-P constitutive model based on multiple relaxation times for viscoelastic fluid"*. Moreover, in another paper entitled *"LES study on high Reynolds turbulent drag-reducing flow of viscoelastic fluids based on multiple relaxation times constitutive model and mixed subgrid-scale model"*, J. Li et al. further revealed the drag-reduction mechanism of high Reynolds viscoelastic turbulent flow and addressed the different phenomena occurring in high and low Reynolds turbulent drag-reducing flows. A coupled LBGK scheme, constituting of two independent distribution functions describing velocity and temperature respectively, was established by T. Zhang and S. Sun in the paper entitled *"A Compact and Efficient Lattice Boltzmann Scheme to Simulate Complex Thermal Fluid Flows"*. The complex Rayleigh-Benard convection was studied and various correlations of thermal dynamic properties were illustrated. In the last paper of this group entitled *"A new edge stabilization method"*, H. Duan and Y. Wei theoretically and numerically studied a new edge stabilization method for the finite element discretization of the convection-dominated diffusion-convection equations.

The second group of papers concerns the modeling and simulation of multiphase flow and the flow and transport in porous media. In the paper entitled *"A novel energy stable numerical scheme for Navier-Stokes-Cahn-Hilliard two-phase flow model with variable densities and viscosities"*, X. Feng et al. constructed a novel numerical scheme for the simulation of coupled Cahn-Hilliard and Navier-Stokes equations considering the variable densities and viscosities. And the accuracy and robustness of this novel scheme were validated by the benchmark bubble rising problem. Z. He et al. studied linearly first and second order in time, uniquely solvable and unconditionally energy stable numerical schemes to approximate the phase field model of solid-state dewetting problems based on the novel scalar auxiliary variable (SAV) approach in the paper entitled *"Efficient Linearly and Unconditionally Energy Stable Schemes for the Phase Field Model of Solid-State Dewetting Problems"*. Y. Wang et al in their paper *"Study on Numerical Methods for Gas Flow Simulation Using Double-Porosity Double-Permeability Model"* first investigated the numerical methods for gas flow simulation in dual-continuum porous media by using the mass balance technique and local linearization of the nonlinear source term. The paper of G. Harper et al., *"A Two-field Finite Element Solver for Poroelasticity on Quadrilateral Meshes"*, focused on a finite element solver for linear poroelasticity problems on quadrilateral meshes based on the displacement-pressure two-field model. This new solver combined the Bernardi-Raugel element for linear elasticity and a weak Galerkin element for Darcy flow through the backward Euler temporal discretization. In the paper entitled *"Coupling multipoint flux mixed finite element methods with discontinuous Galerkin methods for incompressible miscible displacement equations in porous media"*, J. Chen studied the numerical approximation of the incompressible miscible displacement equations on general quadrilateral grids in two dimensions with the multipoint flux mixed finite element method and discontinuous Galerkin method.

The third group is related to applications in petroleum engineering. In the paper entitled "*Computational Studies of an Underground Oil Recovery Model*", Y. Wang deeply studied the underground oil recovery model, and extended the second and third order classical central schemes for the hyperbolic conservation laws to solve the modified Buckley-Leverett (MBL) equation. J. Shi, et al. conducted the grand canonical Monte Carlo (GCMC) simulation to investigate the displacement of methane in shale by injection gases and employed the molecular dynamics (MD) simulation to investigate the adsorption occurrence behavior of methane in different pore size in the article entitled "*Molecular Simulation of Displacement of Methane by Injection Gases in Shale*". P. Wang et al. developed a pipeline network topology-based method to identify vulnerability sources of the natural gas pipeline network based on the network evaluation theory in the paper entitled "*Study on topology-based identification of sources of vulnerability for natural gas pipeline networks*".

The fourth group, which consists of two articles, is focusing on the traffic flow problems. In the first paper entitled "*Data Fault Identification and Repair Method of Traffic Detector*", X. Li et al. combined the wavelet packet energy analysis and principal component analysis (PCA) to achieve the traffic detector data fault identification. D. Liu et al. proposed three different methods for node importance measurement of urban road network based on a spatially weighted degree model, the Hansen Index and h-index in the paper entitled "*Method of Node Importance Measurement in Urban Road Network*". Moreover, the topological structure, geographic information and traffic flow characteristics of urban road network were considered.

The last group addresses some numerical issues to tackle challenges in flow and transport simulations. A method to calculate intersections of two admissible general quadrilateral mesh of the same logically structure in a planar domain was presented by X. Xu and S. Zhu in the paper entitled "*Symmetric Sweeping Algorithms for overlaps of Two Quadrilateral Mesh of the same connectivity*". G. Jr. et al. improved the efficiency of preprocessing phase of the ALT algorithm through parallelization technique which could cut the landmark generation time significantly in the paper entitled "*Preprocessing parallelization for the ALT-algorithm*".

Observations of General Trends in Flow and Transport Simulations

The past decade has seen remarkable advances in the simulations of flow and transport phenomena because of its significance to understand, predict, and optimize various scientific and industrial flow and transport processes. Nevertheless, accurate, efficient and robust numerical simulations of flow and transport still remain challenging. Below we give a brief overview on the general trend of flow and transport simulations.

(1) *"Multi"-modeling*: With the increased complexity of the flow and transport phenomena, the modeling tends to be more complex. For instance, multiphase flow especially in porous media and with the partial miscibility of different phases provides more challenges and opportunities now. Multicomponent transport with reaction, such as computational thermodynamics of fluids, especially hydrocarbon and other oil reservoir fluids, and its interaction with flow and transport still remain to be further explored. From the aspect of computational scale, coupling of flow and transport in different scales is also a research hotspot, such as transport in molecular scale, pore scale, lab scale, and field scale, flow from Darcy scale to pore-scale, etc.

(2) *Advanced "multi"-algorithms*: The increasing complexity of flow and transport simulations demands the algorithms to be multi-scale, multi-domain, multi-physics and multi-numerics. For the complex flow and transport phenomena, the mathematical models usually with possibly rough and discontinuous coefficients, and the solutions are often singular and discontinuous. Thus, the advanced discretization methods should be applied to discretize the governing equations. Local mass conservation and compatibility of numerical schemes are often necessary to obtain physical meaningful solutions. In addition, the design of fast and accurate solvers for the large-scale algebraic equation systems should be addressed. Solution techniques of interest include mesh adaptation, model reduction (such as MsFEM, upscaling, POD, etc.), multiscale algorithms (such as coupling of LBM and MD, etc.), parallel algorithms (such as CPU parallel, GPU parallel, etc.), and others.

(3) *Heterogeneous parallel computing with "multi"-hardware:* Today flow and transport simulations are becoming more and more computationally demanding, more than one kind of processors or cores are preferred to be used to gain a better computational performance or energy efficiency. Thus the "multi"-hardware for the heterogeneous parallel computing is a clear trend. Especially the heterogeneous parallel computing coupled with tensor processing unit (TPU), graphics processing unit (GPU) and cloud computing should be paid more attentions. The TPU parallel, GPU parallel and cloud computing provide completely new possibilities for significant cost savings because simulation time can be reduced on hardware that is often less expensive than server-class CPUs.

(4) *"Multi"-application*: The interaction of flow and transport with other physical, chemical, biological, and sociological processes, etc. is gaining more attentions from the global researchers and scientists, and application areas of flow and transport have been widened largely in recent years. It includes but not limited to the fields of earth sciences (such as groundwater contamination, carbon sequestration, petroleum exploration and recovery, etc.), atmospheric science (such as air pollution, weather prediction, etc.), chemical engineering (such as chemical separation processes, drug delivery, etc.), biological processes (such as biotransport, intracellular protein trafficking, etc.), traffic flow (such as traffic networks, material flow in supply chain networks, etc.), material design, natural disaster assessments, information flow and many others.

Concluding Remarks

In conclusion, this workshop proceeding presents and highlights new applications and new (or existing) challenges in five different important research areas of flow and transport mainly from the aspects of modeling, algorithms and computation. The workshop proceeding is not intended to be an exhaustive collection nor a survey of all of the current trends in flow and transport research. Many additional significant research areas of flow and transport still exist and remain to be explored further, but "multi"-modeling, advanced "multi"-algorithms, heterogeneous parallel computing with "multi"-hardware and "multi"-application are clear trends.

Acknowledgments. The authors would like to thank all the participants of this workshop for their inspiring contributions and the anonymous reviewers for their diligent work, which led to the high quality of the workshop proceeding. The authors also express their sincere gratitude to the ICCS organizers for providing a wonderful opportunity to hold this workshop. The workshop chair S. Sun and co-chair J. Li would like to acknowledge the research funding from King Abdullah University of Science and Technology (KAUST) through the grants BAS/1/1351-01, URF/1/2993-01 and REP/1/2879-01. J. Liu would like to acknowledge the funding support from US National Science Foundation (NSF) under grant DMS-1419077.

ALE Method for a Rotating Structure Immersed in the Fluid and Its Application to the Artificial Heart Pump in Hemodynamics

Pengtao Sun[1]($\boxtimes$), Wei Leng[2], Chen-Song Zhang[2], Rihui Lan[1], and Jinchao Xu[3]

[1] Department of Mathematical Sciences, University of Nevada, Las Vegas,
4505 Maryland Parkway, Las Vegas, NV 89154, USA
{pengtao.sun,rihui.lan}@unlv.edu
[2] LSEC & NCMIS, Academy of Mathematics and System Science,
Chinese Academy of Sciences, Beijing, China
{wleng,zhangcs}@lsec.cc.ac.cn
[3] Department of Mathematics, Pennsylvania State University,
University Park, PA 16802, USA
xu@math.psu.edu

Abstract. In this paper, we study a dynamic fluid-structure interaction (FSI) problem involving a rotational elastic turbine, which is modeled by the incompressible fluid model in the fluid domain with the arbitrary Lagrangian-Eulerian (ALE) description and by the St. Venant-Kirchhoff structure model in the structure domain with the Lagrangian description, and the application to a hemodynamic FSI problem involving an artificial heart pump with a rotating rotor. A linearized rotational and deformable structure model is developed for the rotating rotor and a monolithic mixed ALE finite element method is developed for the hemodynamic FSI system. Numerical simulations are carried out for a hemodynamic FSI model with an artificial heart pump, and are validated by comparing with a commercial CFD package for a simplified artificial heart pump.

Keywords: Arbitrary Lagrangian-Eulerian (ALE) finite element method · Fluid-structure interactions (FSI) · Artificial heart pump

P. Sun and R. Lan were supported by NSF Grant DMS-1418806. W. Leng and C.-S. Zhang were supported by the National Key Research and Development Program of China (Grant No. 2016YFB0201304), the Major Research Plan of National Natural Science Foundation of China (Grant Nos. 91430215, 91530323), and the Key Research Program of Frontier Sciences of CAS. W. Leng was also partially supported by Grant-in-aid for scientific research from the National Natural Science Foundation for the Youth of China (Grant No. 11501553). J. Xu was supported by NSF Grant DMS-1522615 and DOE DE-SC0014400.

© Springer International Publishing AG, part of Springer Nature 2018
Y. Shi et al. (Eds.): ICCS 2018, LNCS 10862, pp. 9–23, 2018.
https://doi.org/10.1007/978-3-319-93713-7_1

1 Introduction

Fluid-structure interaction (FSI) problems remain among the most challenging problems in computational mechanics and computational fluid dynamics. The difficulties in the simulation of these problems stem from the fact that they rely on the coupling of models of different nature: Lagrangian in the solid and Eulerian in the fluid. The so-called Arbitrary Lagrangian Eulerian (ALE) method [7,9] copes with this difficulty by adapting the fluid solver along the deformations of the solid medium in the direction normal to the interface. These methods allow us to accurately account for continuity of stresses and velocities at the interface, where the body-fitted conforming mesh is used and the surface mesh is accommodated to be shared between the fluid and solid, and thus to automatically satisfy the interface kinematic condition. In this paper, we use the ALE method to reformulate and solve fluid equations on a moving fluid mesh which moves along with structure motions through the interface.

In contrast to a large amount of FSI literatures which are dedicated to either a rigid structure [8,11], or a non-rotational structure [4,7], or a stationary fluid domain (thus the interface) [5,13], few works are contributed to FSI problems with a rotational and deformable structure. This is mainly due to the fact that the corresponding mathematical and mechanical model is lacking. Some relevant models arise from the field of graphics and animation applications for the co-rotational linear elasticity [14], but still far away from our need. To simulate such a FSI problem with a more realistic operating condition, we first derive a linearized constitutive model of structure combining the elastic deformation with the rotation, then present its weak formulation and develop a specific ALE mapping technique to deal with the co-rotational fluid and structure. Furthermore, we describe an efficient monolithic iterative algorithm and ALE-type mixed finite element method to solve the hydrodynamic/hemodynamic FSI problem.

The application of our developed monolithic ALE finite element method in this paper is to study the numerical performance of an artificial heart pump running in the hemodynamic FSI system. It has been always significant to study efficient and accurate numerical methods for simulating hemodynamic FSI problems in order to help patients being recovered from a cardiovascular illness, especially from a heart failure. The statistical data tell us about 720,000 people in the U.S. suffer heart attacks each year, in which about 2,000–2,300 heart transplants are performed annually in the United States [1]. The vast majority of these patients are unsuitable to take the heart transplantation, or, are waiting for the proper human heart to transplant. Under such circumstance, the artificial heart pump is thus the only choice to sustain their lives. Since 1980s, the left ventricle auxiliary device (LVAD), also usually called the artificial heart pump, has become an effective treatment by breaking the vicious cycle of heart failure. Currently, although a massive amount of heart failure patients need the artificial heart to assistant their treatment, an individually designed artificial heart for a specially treated patient is still lacking since such individual design heavily relies on an accurate modeling and solution of the artificial heart-bloodstream-vascular interactions, which may tell the doctors the accurate shape and size of the artificial heart pump to be manufactured, and the exact location to implant it into the cardiovascular system in order to help on saving the patients' lives from their heart failure illnesses [2].

The goal of this paper is to develop advanced modeling and novel numerical techniques for hemodynamic FSI problems in order to effectively perform stable, precise and state of the art simulation for the cardiovascular interactions between the artificial heart pump and blood flow. In our case, the artificial heart pump is equipped with a rotating impeller that may bear a small deformation under the bloodstream impact but large rotations, simultaneously, interacting with the incompressible blood flow through the interface transmissions.

2 Model Description of FSI Problems

Let us consider a deformable elastic structure in Ω_s that is immersed in an incompressible fluid domain Ω_f. $\Omega_f \cup \Omega_s = \Omega \in R^d$, $\Omega_f \cap \Omega_s = \emptyset$. The interface of fluid and structure is $\Gamma = \partial \Omega_s$. As shown in Fig. 1, the Eulerian coordinates in the fluid domain are described with the time invariant position vector $\boldsymbol{x}$; the solid positions in the initial configuration $\hat{\Omega}_s$ and the current configuration Ω_s are represented by $\boldsymbol{X}$ and $\boldsymbol{x}(\boldsymbol{X}, t)$, respectively. We use $\boldsymbol{v}_f$ to denote the velocity of fluid, p_f the pressure of fluid, $\boldsymbol{v}_s$ the velocity of solid structure, and $\boldsymbol{u}_s$ the displacement of structure. Thus, $\boldsymbol{u}_s(\boldsymbol{x}(\boldsymbol{X}, t), t) = \hat{\boldsymbol{u}}_s(\boldsymbol{X}, t) = \boldsymbol{x} - \boldsymbol{X}$, and $\boldsymbol{v}_s = \frac{d\boldsymbol{x}}{dt} = \frac{\partial \boldsymbol{u}_s}{\partial t}$. The Jacobian matrix $\boldsymbol{F} = \frac{\partial \boldsymbol{x}}{\partial \boldsymbol{X}}$ describes the structure deformation gradient.

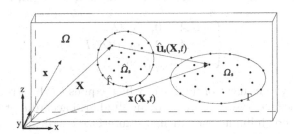

Fig. 1. Schematic domain of FSI problem.

Fluid Motion in Eulerian Description

$$\rho_f \left(\frac{\partial \boldsymbol{v}_f}{\partial t} + \boldsymbol{v}_f \cdot \nabla \boldsymbol{v}_f \right) = \nabla \cdot \boldsymbol{\sigma}_f + \rho_f \boldsymbol{f}_f, \quad \text{in } \Omega_f \tag{1}$$

$$\nabla \cdot \boldsymbol{v}_f = 0, \quad \text{in } \Omega_f \tag{2}$$

$$\boldsymbol{\sigma}_f = -p_f \boldsymbol{I} + \mu_f \left(\nabla \boldsymbol{v}_f + (\nabla \boldsymbol{v}_f)^T \right), \tag{3}$$

$$\boldsymbol{v}_f = \boldsymbol{v}_B, \quad \text{on } \partial \Omega \tag{4}$$

$$\boldsymbol{v}_f(\boldsymbol{x}, 0) = \boldsymbol{v}_{f0}, \quad \text{in } \Omega_f \tag{5}$$

Solid Motion in Lagrangian Description

$$\rho_s \frac{\partial^2 \hat{u}_s}{\partial t^2} = \nabla \cdot (J \sigma_s F^{-T}) + \rho_s \hat{f}_s, \quad \text{in } \hat{\Omega}_s \tag{6}$$

$$\hat{u}_s(X, 0) = \hat{u}_{s0}, \text{ and } \frac{\partial \hat{u}_s}{\partial t}(X, 0) = \hat{v}_{s0}, \quad \text{in } \hat{\Omega}_s \tag{7}$$

where the stress tensor σ_s in the reference configuration X, denoted by $\hat{\sigma}_s$, is defined by the first Piola-Kirchhoff stress tensor, P, as $\hat{\sigma}_s = P = J\sigma_s F^{-T} = FS$, where $S = JF^{-1}\sigma_s F^{-T}$ denotes the second Piola-Kirchhoff stress tensor. For a compressible St. Venant-Kirchhoff (STVK) material [10], $\sigma_s(x) = \frac{1}{J} F(2\mu_s E + \lambda_s(trE)I)F^T$, thus $S = 2\mu_s E + \lambda_s(trE)I$, where E is the Green-Lagrangian finite strain tensor, defined as $E = (F^T F - I)/2 = [\nabla_X u_s + (\nabla_X u_s)^T + (\nabla_X u_s)^T \nabla_X u_s]/2$. λ_s, μ_s are the Lamé's constants.

Interface Conditions

$$v_f = v_s, \qquad \text{on } \Gamma \tag{8}$$

$$\sigma_f \cdot n = \sigma_s \cdot n, \quad \text{on } \Gamma \tag{9}$$

which are called the kinematic and dynamic lateral interface conditions, respectively, describing the continuities of velocity and of normal stress.

ALE Mapping Technique. Define $\mathcal{A}(\cdot, t) = \mathcal{A}_t : \hat{\Omega}(X) \mapsto \Omega(x)$ is an arbitrary diffeomorphism, satisfying the following conventional ALE (harmonic) mapping:

$$\begin{cases} -\Delta \mathcal{A} = 0, & \text{in } \hat{\Omega}_f, \\ \mathcal{A} = 0, & \text{on } \partial \hat{\Omega}_f \backslash \hat{\Gamma}, \\ \mathcal{A} = \hat{u}_s, & \text{on } \hat{\Gamma}, \end{cases} \tag{10}$$

where $\mathcal{A}$ is the displacement of fluid grid which equals to the structure displacement on the interface, resulting in a moving fluid grid according to the structure motion and further fulfilling the kinematic interface condition.

Fluid Motion in ALE Description. The momentum equation of fluid motion (1) in ALE description is given as

$$\rho_f \partial_t^{\mathcal{A}} v_f + \rho_f((v_f - w) \cdot \nabla)v_f = \nabla \cdot \sigma_f + \rho_f f_f, \tag{11}$$

where $w = \frac{\partial \mathcal{A}}{\partial t} \circ \mathcal{A}_t^{-1}$ denotes the velocity of fluid grid and

$$\partial_t^{\mathcal{A}} v_f |_{(x,t)} := \frac{\partial [v_f(\mathcal{A}(X,t),t)]}{\partial t} \bigg|_{(X,t)=(\mathcal{A}_t^{-1}(x),t)} = \frac{\partial v_f}{\partial t} + (w \cdot \nabla)v_f$$

is the ALE time derivative. For the simplicity of notation, in what follows, we suppose $f_f = f_s = 0$ by assuming no external force is acted on fluid and structure.

3   A Monolithic Weak Formulation of FSI

Introduce $\hat{V}_s = \{\hat{v}_s \in (H^1(\hat{\Omega}_s))^d | \hat{v}_s(X) = v_f(x(X, t)) \circ \mathcal{A}$ on $\hat{\Gamma}\}$, $V_f = \{v_f \in (H^1(\Omega_f))^d | v_f = v_B$ on $\partial\Omega\}$, $W_f = L^2(\Omega_f)$, $\hat{Q}_f = \{\mathcal{A} \in (H^1(\hat{\Omega}_f))^d | \mathcal{A} = 0$ on $\partial\hat{\Omega}_f \cap \partial\hat{\Omega}$, and $\mathcal{A} = \hat{u}_s$ on $\hat{\Gamma}\}$, we define a monolithic ALE weak formulation of FSI model as follows: find $(\hat{v}_s, v_f, p, \mathcal{A}) \in (\hat{V}_s \oplus V_f \oplus W_f \oplus \hat{Q}_f) \times L^2([0, T])$ such that

$$
\begin{cases}
\left(\rho_s \dfrac{\partial \hat{v}_s}{\partial t}, \phi\right) + \left(\hat{\sigma}_s \left(\hat{u}_s^0 + \displaystyle\int_0^t \hat{v}(\tau)\, d\tau\right), \varepsilon(\phi)\right) \\
+ \left(\rho_f \partial_t^{\mathcal{A}} v_f, \psi\right) + \left(\rho_f (v_f - w) \cdot \nabla v_f, \psi\right) + \left(\sigma_f, \varepsilon(\psi)\right) = 0, \\
\hspace{6cm} (\nabla \cdot v_f, q) = 0, \\
\hspace{6cm} (\nabla\mathcal{A}, \nabla\xi) = 0, \\
\forall \phi \in \hat{V}_s,\ \psi \in V_f,\ q \in W_f,\ \xi \in \hat{Q}_f,
\end{cases}
\tag{12}
$$

where $\varepsilon(u) = \frac{1}{2}\left(\nabla u + (\nabla u)^T\right)$. The boundary integrals that arise from the integration by parts for fluid and structure equations are cancelled due to the continuity of normal stress condition (9). To efficiently implement the kinematic condition (8), we employ the master-slave relation technique, namely, two sets of grid nodes are defined on the interface, one belongs to the fluid grid and the other one belongs to the structure grid, both share the same position and the same degrees of freedom of velocity on the interface. The usage of structure velocity $\hat{v}_s$ instead of the displacement $\hat{u}_s$ as the principle unknown in (12) has an advantage to precisely apply the master-slave relation, where, $\hat{v}_s = \frac{\partial \hat{u}_s}{\partial t}$ or $\hat{u}_s = \hat{u}_s^0 + \int_0^t \hat{v}_s(\tau) d\tau$, then (8) becomes $\hat{v}_s(X) = v_f(x(X, t)) \circ \mathcal{A}$ on $\hat{\Gamma}$.

4   FSI Problem Involving a Rotating Elastic Structure

Based on the constitutive law of STVK material, we rewrite the structure equation in Lagrangian description (6) as follows

$$
\rho_s \frac{\partial^2 \hat{u}_s}{\partial t^2} = \nabla \cdot \left(\lambda_s (tr E) F + 2\mu_s F E\right).
\tag{13}
$$

Suppose X_0 is the structure centroid in statics, but the center of mass in dynamics, we define the structure displacement with regard to X_0 as [6]

$$
x - X_0 = R(X + \hat{u}_d - X_0),
\tag{14}
$$

where $\hat{u}_d$ is the deformation displacement in the local coordinate system whose origin is X_0, R is the rotator from the base configuration $\mathcal{C}^0$ to the corotated configuration $\mathcal{C}^R$, given by $R = T_R T_0^T$, here T_0 and T_R are the global-to-local displacement transformations [6]. T_R, T_0 and R are all orthogonal matrices. We specialize one case of which the rotation of axis is Z-axis, resulting in

$$
R(\theta) = \begin{pmatrix} \cos(\theta - \theta_0) & -\sin(\theta - \theta_0) & 0 \\ \sin(\theta - \theta_0) & \cos(\theta - \theta_0) & 0 \\ 0 & 0 & 1 \end{pmatrix},
\tag{15}
$$

where θ_0 is a fixed initial angle from the globally-aligned configuration $\mathcal{C}^G$ in $\mathcal{C}^0$ and $\theta = \theta(t)$ is a time-dependent angle from $\mathcal{C}^G$ in $\mathcal{C}^R$. Without loss of generality, we let $\theta_0 = 0$. Hence, the total structure displacement, $\hat{u}_s$, can be defined as

$$\hat{u}_s = x - X = (R - I)(X - X_0) + R\hat{u}_d = \hat{u}_\theta + R\hat{u}_d, \tag{16}$$

where $\hat{u}_\theta = (R - I)(X - X_0)$ is the rotational displacement of the structure.

From (14), we obtain $F = R(I + \Phi)$, where $\Phi = \nabla\hat{u}_d$. Then, $E = (F^T F - I)/2 = (\Phi + \Phi^T + \Phi^T\Phi)/2$. Thus, the first Piola-Kirchhoff stress $P = F(\lambda_s(trE) + 2\mu_s E)$, leading to a function of Φ as follows

$$P(\Phi) = R(I + \Phi)\left[\frac{1}{2}\lambda_s\left(tr\Phi + tr\Phi^T + tr\left(\Phi^T\Phi\right)\right) + \mu_s\left(\Phi + \Phi^T + \Phi^T\Phi\right)\right].$$

The following linear approximation is then derived by Taylor expansion at $\Phi = 0$,

$$P \approx \frac{1}{2}\lambda_s R\left(tr\Phi + tr\Phi^T\right) + \mu_s R\left(\Phi + \Phi^T\right) = R\left(\lambda_s tr\left(\varepsilon\left(\hat{u}_d\right)\right)I + 2\mu_s\varepsilon\left(\hat{u}_d\right)\right),$$

where $\varepsilon(\hat{u}_d) = \frac{1}{2}(\nabla\hat{u}_d + (\nabla\hat{u}_d)^T)$ is the linear approximation of $E(\hat{u}_d)$. We may equivalently rewrite $\hat{\sigma}_s = RD\varepsilon(\hat{u}_d)$, where D denotes the constitutive matrix in terms of the Young's modulus E and Poisson's ratio ν [3]. Thus, (13) is approximated by the following co-rotational linear elasticity model

$$\rho_s\frac{\partial^2\hat{u}_s}{\partial t^2} = \nabla \cdot \left(RD\varepsilon\left(\hat{u}_d\right)\right). \tag{17}$$

The weak formulation of (17) is defined as: find $\hat{u}_s \in L^2([0, T]; \hat{V}_s)$ such that

$$\left(\rho_s\frac{\partial^2\hat{u}_s}{\partial t^2}, \phi\right) + \left(D\varepsilon\left(\hat{u}_d\right), \varepsilon\left(R^T\phi\right)\right) = \int_{\partial\Omega_s} \sigma_s n_s\phi\, ds, \quad \forall\phi \in \hat{V}_s. \tag{18}$$

Due to (16), we have $R\hat{u}_d = \hat{u}_s - \hat{u}_\theta$, thus $\varepsilon(\hat{u}_d) = \varepsilon(R^T\hat{u}_s) - \varepsilon(R^T\hat{u}_\theta)$. Note that $\hat{u}_\theta = (R - I)(X - X_0)$, then $D\varepsilon(R^T\hat{u}_\theta) = D\varepsilon((I - R^T)(X - X_0))$. Therefore, (18) is rewritten as

$$\left(\rho_s\frac{\partial^2\hat{u}_s}{\partial t^2}, \phi\right) + \left(D\varepsilon\left(R^T\hat{u}_s\right), \varepsilon\left(R^T\phi\right)\right) = \left(D\varepsilon((I - R^T)(X - X_0)), \varepsilon(R^T\phi)\right)$$

$$+ \int_{\partial\Omega_s} \sigma_s n_s\phi\, ds, \forall\phi \in \hat{V}_s, \tag{19}$$

where, the stiffness term on the L.H.S. is symmetric positive definite, the first term on the R.H.S. is the body force contribution from the rotation, the boundary integral term shall be canceled later due to the continuity condition of normal stress (9). The remaining unknown quantity in (19) is the rotational matrix R if the structure rotation is passive. In the following we introduce two propositions to the computation of R by means of the structure velocity $\hat{v}_s$, both proofs are relatively easy and thus are omitted here.

Proposition 1. *The angular velocity $\omega(t) = (\omega_1, \omega_2, \omega_3)^T$ satisfies*

$$I\omega = \int_{\Omega_{\mathrm{s}}} \rho_{\mathrm{s}} \boldsymbol{r} \times \hat{\boldsymbol{v}}_{\mathrm{s}} \, d\boldsymbol{X}, \tag{20}$$

where, $I = \int_{\Omega_{\mathrm{s}}} \rho_{\mathrm{s}} \boldsymbol{r}^2 \, d\boldsymbol{X}$ is the inertia, $\boldsymbol{r}$ is the position vector to the rotation of axis which has the following relation with ω

$$\frac{d\boldsymbol{r}}{dt} = \omega \times \boldsymbol{r} = \tilde{\omega}\boldsymbol{r} = \begin{pmatrix} 0 & -\omega_3 & \omega_2 \\ \omega_3 & 0 & -\omega_1 \\ -\omega_2 & \omega_1 & 0 \end{pmatrix} \begin{pmatrix} r_1 \\ r_2 \\ r_3 \end{pmatrix}, \quad and \quad \hat{\boldsymbol{v}}_{\mathrm{s}} = \frac{\partial \hat{\boldsymbol{u}}_{\mathrm{s}}}{\partial t} = \frac{d\boldsymbol{r}}{dt}. \tag{21}$$

Proposition 2. *$\boldsymbol{R}$ satisfies the following O.D.E.*

$$\frac{d\boldsymbol{R}}{dt} = \tilde{\omega}\boldsymbol{R}, \quad and \quad \boldsymbol{R}(0) = \boldsymbol{R}_0. \tag{22}$$

Now, by iteratively solving (19), (20), and (22) together, we are able to sequentially obtain the structure velocity $\hat{\boldsymbol{v}}_{\mathrm{s}}$, the angular velocity ω, then the rotational matrix $\boldsymbol{R}$, further, the structure displacement $\hat{\boldsymbol{u}}_{\mathrm{s}}$.

5   Algorithm Description

We first split $\Omega_{\mathrm{f}} = \Omega_{\mathrm{sf}} \cup \Omega_{\mathrm{rf}}$, where Ω_{rf} is an artificial buffer zone containing the rotating elastic structure inside, which could be a disk in 2D or a cylinder in 3D, as shown in Fig. 2. And, the size of Ω_{rf} which is characterized by the radius of its cross section is usually taken as the middle between the outer boundary of the flow channel and the rotating structure in order to guarantee the mesh quality inside and outside of the artificial buffer zone Ω_{rf}. Both Ω_{rf} and Ω_{s} suppose to rotate about the same rotation of axis with the same angular velocity under the circumstance of a small strain arising from the structure. Suppose all the necessary solution data from the last time step are known: $\boldsymbol{v}_{\mathrm{f}}^{n-1}$, $\hat{\boldsymbol{v}}_{\mathrm{s}}^{n-1}$, $\hat{\boldsymbol{u}}_{\mathrm{s}}^{n-1}$, $\boldsymbol{R}^{n-1}$, w^{n-1}, $\mathcal{A}^{n-1}$, and the mesh on the last time step, $\mathbb{T}_h^{n-1} = \mathbb{T}_{\mathrm{sf},h} \cup \mathbb{T}_{\mathrm{rf},h}^{n-1} \cup \hat{\mathbb{T}}_{\mathrm{s},h}$, where $\hat{\mathbb{T}}_{\mathrm{s},h}$ is the Lagrangian structure mesh in $\hat{\Omega}_{\mathrm{s}}$ which is always fixed, $\mathbb{T}_{\mathrm{sf},h}$ is the mesh in the stationary fluid domain Ω_{sf} which is also fixed, and $\mathbb{T}_{\mathrm{rf},h}$ is the mesh in the rotational fluid domain Ω_{rf} which needs to be computed all the time. Thus, we decompose the displacement of the rotational fluid mesh $\mathbb{T}_{\mathrm{rf},h}$ to two parts: the rotational part $\boldsymbol{u}_\theta$ and the deformation part $\mathcal{A}$ which is attained from a specific ALE mapping defined in (26), where $\mathcal{A}$ is only subject to a structure deformation displacement $\hat{\boldsymbol{u}}_{\mathrm{s}} - \boldsymbol{u}_\theta$ on $\hat{\Gamma}$, and the local adjustment of the mesh nodes on $\partial\Omega_{\mathrm{rs}} = \partial\Omega_{\mathrm{rf}} \cap \partial\Omega_{\mathrm{sf}}$ for the sake of a conforming fluid mesh across $\partial\Omega_{\mathrm{rs}}$. Such specific ALE mapping always guarantees a shape-regular fluid mesh in Ω_{rf}, and still conforms with the stationary fluid mesh in Ω_{sf} through $\partial\Omega_{\mathrm{rs}}$.

In the following, we define an implicit relaxed fixed-point iterative scheme for the FSI simulation at the current n-th time step, i.e., we first iteratively solve the implicit nonlinear momentum equations of both fluid and structure on a known fluid mesh $\mathbb{T}_{\mathrm{f},h}$ obtained from the previous step and the fixed structure mesh

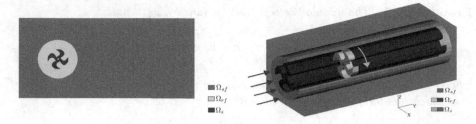

Fig. 2. An illustration of the rotational part (a buffer zone) of the fluid (green) separates the structure (blue) from the stationary part of the fluid (red) in 2D & 3D. (Color figure online)

$\hat{\mathbb{T}}_{s,h}$ until the convergence, then compute a new fluid mesh $\mathbb{T}_{f,h}$ based on the newly obtained structure velocity, and start another inner iteration to solve the momentum equations on the new fluid mesh. Continue this fixed-point iteration until the fluid mesh is converged, then march to the next time step. The detailed algorithms are described in Algorithms 1–3.

Algorithm 1. ALE method for FSI:

On the n-th time step, let $\boldsymbol{w}^{n,0} = \boldsymbol{w}^{n-1}$, $\boldsymbol{R}^{n,0} = \boldsymbol{R}^{n-1}$, $\mathbb{T}_{f,h}^{n,0} = \mathbb{T}_{f,h}^{n-1}$.

For $j = 1, 2, \cdots$ until convergence, do

1. $(\boldsymbol{v}_f^{n,j}, p^{n,j}, \hat{\boldsymbol{v}}_s^{n,j}, \hat{\boldsymbol{u}}_s^{n,j}) \leftarrow \text{Momentum}(\boldsymbol{v}_f^{n-1}, \hat{\boldsymbol{v}}_s^{n-1}, \boldsymbol{w}^{n,j-1}, \boldsymbol{R}^{n,j-1}, \hat{\boldsymbol{u}}_s^{n-1}, \mathbb{T}_{f,h}^{n,j-1})$

2. $(\boldsymbol{w}^{n,j}, \boldsymbol{R}^{n,j}, \mathcal{A}^{n,j}, \mathbb{T}_{f,h}^{n,j}) \leftarrow \text{Mesh}(\hat{\boldsymbol{v}}_s^{n,j}, \hat{\boldsymbol{u}}_s^{n,j}, \boldsymbol{R}^{n-1}, \mathcal{A}^{n-1}, \boldsymbol{w}^{n-1})$

Algorithm 2. Momentum Solver:

$(\boldsymbol{v}_f^{n,j}, p^{n,j}, \hat{\boldsymbol{v}}_s^{n,j}, \hat{\boldsymbol{u}}_s^{n,j}) \leftarrow \text{Momentum}(\boldsymbol{v}_f^{n-1}, \hat{\boldsymbol{v}}_s^{n-1}, \boldsymbol{w}^{n,j-1}, \boldsymbol{R}^{n,j-1}, \hat{\boldsymbol{u}}_s^{n-1}, \mathbb{T}_{f,h}^{n,j-1})$

1. Find $(\boldsymbol{v}_f^{n,j}, p^{n,j}, \hat{\boldsymbol{v}}_s^{n,j}) \in \boldsymbol{V}_f \oplus \boldsymbol{W}_f \oplus \hat{\boldsymbol{V}}_s$ such that

$$\begin{cases} \left(\rho_f \dfrac{\boldsymbol{v}_f^{n,j} - \boldsymbol{v}_f^{n-1}}{\Delta t}, \psi\right) + \left(\rho_f(\boldsymbol{v}_f^{n,j} - \boldsymbol{w}^{n,j-1}) \cdot \nabla \boldsymbol{v}_f^{n,j}, \psi\right) + \left(\mu_f \varepsilon(\boldsymbol{v}_f^{n,j}), \varepsilon(\psi)\right) \\ - (p^{n,j}, \nabla \cdot \psi) + \left(\rho_s \dfrac{\hat{\boldsymbol{v}}_s^{n,j} - \hat{\boldsymbol{v}}_s^{n-1}}{\Delta t}, \phi\right) + \dfrac{\Delta t}{2}\left(\boldsymbol{D}\varepsilon((\boldsymbol{R}^{n,j-1})^T \hat{\boldsymbol{v}}_s^{n,j}), \varepsilon((\boldsymbol{R}^{n,j-1})^T \phi)\right) \\ = -\dfrac{\Delta t}{2}\left(\boldsymbol{D}\varepsilon((\boldsymbol{R}^{n,j-1})^T \hat{\boldsymbol{v}}_s^{n-1}), \varepsilon((\boldsymbol{R}^{n,j-1})^T \phi)\right) - \left(\boldsymbol{D}\varepsilon((\boldsymbol{R}^{n,j-1})^T \hat{\boldsymbol{u}}_s^{n-1}), \right. \\ \left. \varepsilon((\boldsymbol{R}^{n,j-1})^T \phi)\right) + \left(\boldsymbol{D}\varepsilon((\boldsymbol{I} - (\boldsymbol{R}^{n,j-1})^T)(\boldsymbol{X} - \boldsymbol{X}_0)), \varepsilon((\boldsymbol{R}^{n,j-1})^T \phi)\right), \\ (\nabla \cdot \boldsymbol{v}_f^{n,j}, q) = 0, \qquad\qquad \forall \phi \in \hat{\boldsymbol{V}}_s, \ \psi \in \boldsymbol{V}_f, \ q \in \boldsymbol{W}_f, \end{cases}$$

$$\tag{23}$$

where the convection term $(\rho_f \boldsymbol{v}_f^{n,j} \cdot \nabla \boldsymbol{v}_f^{n,j}, \psi)$ can be linearized by Picard's or Newton's method.

2. $\hat{\boldsymbol{u}}_s^{n,j} \leftarrow \hat{\boldsymbol{u}}_s^{n-1} + \dfrac{\Delta t}{2}(\hat{\boldsymbol{v}}_s^{n,j} + \hat{\boldsymbol{v}}_s^{n-1})$.

In Algorithm 2, the ALE time derivative, $\partial_t^A \boldsymbol{v}_f$, is discretized as

$$\partial_t^A \boldsymbol{v}_f \approx \frac{\boldsymbol{v}_f(\boldsymbol{x}, t_n) - \boldsymbol{v}_f(\mathcal{A}_{n-1} \circ \mathcal{A}_n^{-1}(\boldsymbol{x}), t_{n-1})}{\Delta t}, \tag{24}$$

where $\mathcal{A}_{n-1} \circ \mathcal{A}_n^{-1}(\boldsymbol{x})$ is on the corresponding grid node at $t = t_{n-1}$ as long as $\boldsymbol{x}$ is on one grid node at $t = t_n$. Thus the interpolation between different time levels is avoided due to the mesh connectivity that is guaranteed by the ALE mapping.

Algorithm 3. Mesh Update:
$(\boldsymbol{w}^{n,j}, \boldsymbol{R}^{n,j}, \mathcal{A}^{n,j}, \mathbb{T}_{f,h}^{n,j}) \leftarrow \text{Mesh}(\hat{\boldsymbol{v}}_s^{n,j}, \hat{\boldsymbol{u}}_s^{n,j}, \boldsymbol{R}^{n-1}, \mathcal{A}^{n-1}, \boldsymbol{w}^{n-1})$

1. Calculate $I\omega = \int_{\Omega_s} \rho \boldsymbol{r} \times \hat{\boldsymbol{v}}_s^{n,j} \, d\boldsymbol{X}$ for ω then obtain $\tilde{\omega}$.
2. Solve $(\boldsymbol{I} - \frac{\Delta t}{2}\tilde{\omega})\boldsymbol{R}^{n,j} = (\boldsymbol{I} + \frac{\Delta t}{2}\tilde{\omega})\boldsymbol{R}^{n-1}$ for $\boldsymbol{R}^{n,j}$, which is the Crank-Nicolson scheme of (22), and preserves the orthogonality of $\boldsymbol{R}^{n,j}$.
3. $\hat{\boldsymbol{u}}_\theta^{n,j} \leftarrow (\boldsymbol{R}^{n,j} - \boldsymbol{I})(\boldsymbol{X} - \boldsymbol{X}_0)$ and $\mathbb{T}_{rf,h}^{n,j} \leftarrow \boldsymbol{X} + \hat{\boldsymbol{u}}_\theta^{n,j}$.
4. By locally moving the mesh nodes of $\mathbb{T}_{rf,h}^n$ on $\partial\Omega_{rs}$ to match with the mesh nodes of $\mathbb{T}_{sf,h}^n$ on $\partial\Omega_{rs}$, find the extra fluid mesh displacement $\hat{\boldsymbol{u}}_m^{n,j}$ on $\partial\Omega_{rs}$ other than the rotational part $\hat{\boldsymbol{u}}_\theta^{n,j}$.
5. Update the displacements on the interface position by relaxation:

$$\hat{\boldsymbol{u}}_{s,*}^{n,j} = (1-\omega)\hat{\boldsymbol{u}}_s^{n,j-1} + \omega\hat{\boldsymbol{u}}_s^{n,j}, \quad \text{on } \hat{\Gamma}, \tag{25}$$

$$\hat{\boldsymbol{u}}_{\theta,*}^{n,j} = (1-\omega)\hat{\boldsymbol{u}}_\theta^{n,j-1} + \omega\hat{\boldsymbol{u}}_\theta^{n,j}, \quad \text{on } \hat{\Gamma},$$

where, $\omega \in [0,1]$ is the relaxation number that is tuned based upon the performance of nonlinear iteration: if the iterative errors are smoothly decreasing, then the value of ω is taken closer to 1; otherwise, if the iterative errors are not dramatically decreasing but keep oscillating, then the value of ω shall be closer to 0.

6. Solve the following ALE mapping for $\mathcal{A}^{n,j}$

$$\begin{cases} -\Delta\mathcal{A}^{n,j} = 0, & \text{in } \hat{\Omega}_{rf}, \\ \mathcal{A}^{n,j} = \hat{\boldsymbol{u}}_{s,*}^{n,j} - \hat{\boldsymbol{u}}_{\theta,*}^{n,j}, & \text{on } \hat{\Gamma}, \\ \mathcal{A}^{n,j} = \hat{\boldsymbol{u}}_m^{n,j}, & \text{on } \partial\hat{\Omega}_{rs}. \end{cases} \tag{26}$$

7. $\hat{\boldsymbol{u}}_f^{n,j} \leftarrow \hat{\boldsymbol{u}}_{\theta,*}^{n,j} + \mathcal{A}^{n,j}$, $\mathbb{T}_{rf,h}^{n,j} \leftarrow \boldsymbol{X} + \hat{\boldsymbol{u}}_f^{n,j}$.
8. $\boldsymbol{w}^{n,j} \leftarrow \frac{\boldsymbol{u}_f^{n,j} - \boldsymbol{u}_f^{n-1}}{\Delta t}$.

---

6   Application to the Artificial Heart Pump

To test our model and numerical method, in this section we study the hemodynamic interaction of blood flow with an artificial heart pump which is embedded into the blood vessel and immersed in the blood flow. The artificial heart pump to be studied in this paper consists of three parts: the rotating rotor in the middle and the unmoving head guide and tail guide on two terminals. It locates close to the inlet of the vascular lumen and its rotation of axis is fixed, as illustrated in Fig. 3. In principle, the pump rotor plays a role of impeller to increase the blood pressure when the blood flows through it, the head/tail guides are used to stabilize the incoming and outgoing blood flow, altogether helping the failing human heart to propel a stable blood flow through the entire human body.

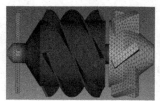 

Fig. 3. Computational meshes – Left: the artificial heart pump (3 parts from the left end to the right end: head guide, rotor and tail guide); Right: the blood flow mesh in a vascular lumen, where the rotational part that immerses the pump rotor is separated from the stationary part by two discs between the pump rotor and the tail/head guide of the pump. The meshes on two discs are shown in Fig. 4.

To apply our ALE finite element method to the above specific artificial heart pump, we need to separate the entire computational domain shown on the right of Fig. 3 to three parts: the rotational part containing the pump rotor and the surrounding fluid area, and two stationary parts including the unmoving head/tail guide of the pump and surrounding fluid regions. Two discs with particular meshes shown in Fig. 4 are made between the head/tail guide and the rotor to fulfill this purpose. The mesh on each disc is made along a series of concentric circles, by which the local adjustment of the mesh motion on the interface of the rotational fluid region (Ω_{rf}) and the stationary fluid region (Ω_{sf}), $\partial\Omega_{\mathrm{rs}}$, can then be easily calculated.

To start the artificial heart pump, the rotor is always given an initial angular velocity, ω, in the unit of revolution per minute (rpm), starting from $\omega = 1000$ rpm then running up to $\omega = 8000$ rpm to work as an impeller of the blood flow by increasing the blood pressure to normal level. In turn, the artificial heart pump itself bears a relatively tiny deformation due to its nearly rigid structure material (the Young's modulus is up to 1.95×10^{11} Pa), thus the developed co-rotational linear elasticity model (17) works well for the artificial heart pump. We will simulate such a hemodynamic FSI process by carrying out Algorithms 1–3 with a stable Stokes-pair (e.g. P^2P^1 or MINI mixed finite element) or a stabilized scheme (e.g. P^1P^1 mixed element with pressure-stabilization).

It is worth mentioning that our numerical simulations are carried out on Tianhe-1A which locates in the National Supercomputing Center, Tianjin, China, and each node of which has two Intel Xeon X5670 CPUs of six cores

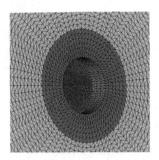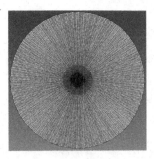

Fig. 4. Interface meshes on $\partial\Omega_{\mathrm{rs}}$ between the stationary fluid and the rotational fluid regions.

and 24 GB memory. The mesh we used in the computation has 473,403 vertices, 2,614,905 cells, and 10 boundary layers are attached on the rotor blades and the wall near them. With P^2P^1 mixed finite element, the total number of DOFs is 11,296,137. The time step is chosen to be 5×10^{-5} s to reach a rotational steady state at t = 0.13 s. The linear system is solved by the additive Schwartz method, and on each processor, the local linear system is solved with the direct solver MUMPS. As for the timing issue, 1024 cores is used in our computation, and each time step cost about 47 s, the total time of the simulation cost about 33 h.

Considering the Reynolds number of blood flow near the high-speed rotating rotor surface is higher than elsewhere, behaving like a turbulence flow, we then also employ the Reynolds-Averaged Simulation (RAS) turbulence model [12] to replace the laminar fluid model in (1) if $\omega > 4000$ rpm. We conduct a comparison computation and show a large difference between the RAS model and the laminar model, as elucidated in Fig. 5, the convergence history of the pressure drop from the inlet to the outlet obtained by the RAS model is much stabler while the result of laminar model is oscillatory. Under a prescribed angular velocity $\omega = 6000$ rpm of the rotor and the incoming flow velocity 3 L/min (about 0.2 m/s) at the inlet, we obtain numerical results as shown in Figs. 6 and 7 for the artificial heart pump simulation with both rotating rotor and unmoving guides are interacting with the surrounding blood flow. We can see that the pressure is greatly increased after the blood flow passes through the pump, inducing the blood flow being propelled further forward along with the time marching as shown in Fig. 7 with a reasonable velocity vector field near and behind the high-speed rotating pump rotor.

To validate our numerical results, we attempt to rebuild the above FSI simulation in a commercial CFD package (Star-CCM+), and compare the obtained numerical results with ours. However, the commercial CFD package cannot deal with the fluid-rotating structure interaction problem with the co-existing rotational fluid/structure regions and stationary fluid/structure regions, which is incomparable with our developed numerical method. In order to compare with the commercial CFD package, we therefore simplify the original setup of the artificial heart pump to let it consist of the rotor only, and remove all

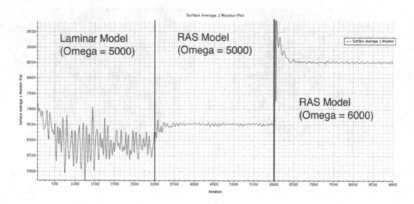

Fig. 5. Comparison of convergence history of pressure drop between RAS turbulence model and the laminar model with higher angular velocity ω.

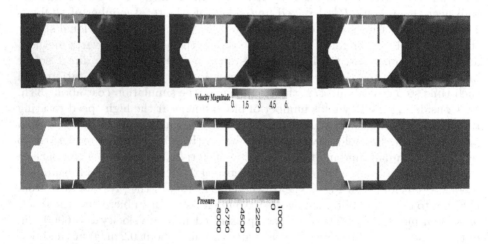

Fig. 6. Cross-sectional results of velocity magnitude and pressure in flow direction developing at 0.02 s, 0.09 s and 0.13 s from the left to the right.

Fig. 7. The velocity vector field.

Fig. 8. Comparisons of velocity magnitude (top) and pressure (bottom) between our method (left) and the commercial package (right).

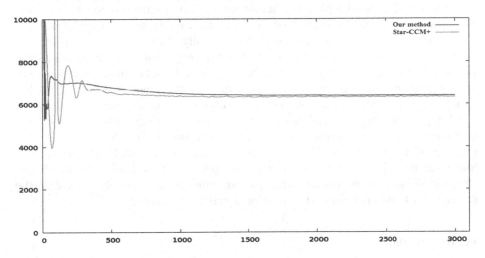

Fig. 9. Comparison of convergence history of pressure drop vs iteration steps between our method and the commercial package (Star-CCM+).

unmoving parts of the pump. Then, we let the blood flow inside the entire vascular lumen rotates together with the pump rotor. Figure 8 illustrates that numerical results obtained from both the commercial package and our method are comparable in regard to the profile and the value range of the velocity magnitude and the pressure. Though, a detailed observation over Fig. 8 shows a slight difference between the results of our method and the commercial package, e.g., our velocity is smaller near the head guide and tail guide but larger near the rotor, our pressure is a bit larger near the head guide. That is because some numerical techniques used in our method are still different from the commercial CFD package in many ways. For instance, we use the streamline-diffusion finite element method versus the upwind finite volume method in the CFD package, and a different way to generate the boundary layer meshes, etc.

In addition, we also compare the convergence history of the pressure-drop field with the commercial CFD package, the comparison is shown in Fig. 9 which illustrates that our result matches well with that of the commercial package, moreover, our method even shows a smoother and stabler convergence process. On the other hand, considering that our ALE finite element method is also able to deal with a realistic artificial heart pump that contains both rotating rotor and unmoving head/tail guide and their surrounding blood flow which, however, the commercial CFD package cannot do, we can say that our well developed method is more capable and more powerful in realistic applications to many kinds of fluid-rotating structure interaction problems.

7   Conclusions

We build a Eulerian-Lagrangian model for fluid-structure interaction problem with the rotating elastic body based on the arbitrary Lagrangian-Eulerian approach. The kinematic interface condition is easily dealt with by adopting the velocity as the principle unknown of structure equation and the master-slave relation technique. The dynamic interface condition vanishes in the finite element approximation of a monolithic scheme. Our well developed iterative algorithm demonstrates a satisfactory numerical result for a hemodynamic FSI problem involving a rotating artificial heart pump, where, the RAS turbulence model is employed in our FSI simulation to tackle the turbulent flow behavior near the high-speed rotating rotor. Comparisons with the commercial CFD package validate our numerical results and further our numerical methods, also illustrates that the developed numerical techniques are efficient and flexible to explore the interaction between fluid and a rotational elastic structure.

References

1. CDC.gov - Heart Disease Facts American Heart Association: Heart Disease and Stroke Update. compiled by AHA, CDC, NIH and Other Governmental Sources (2015)
2. Ferreira, A., Boston, J.R., Antaki, J.F.: A control system for rotary blood pumps based on suction detection. IEEE Trans. Bio-Med. Eng. **56**, 656–665 (2009)
3. Bathe, K.J.: Finite Element Procedures, 2nd edn. Prentice Hall Professional Technical Reference, Englewood Cliffs (1995)
4. Belytschko, T., Kennedy, J., Schoeberle, D.: Quasi-Eulerian finite element formulation for fluid structure interaction. J. Pressure Vessel Technol. **102**, 62–69 (1980)
5. Du, Q., Gunzburger, M., Hou, L., Lee, J.: Analysis of a linear fluid-structure interaction problem. Discrete Continuous Dyn. Syst. **9**, 633–650 (2003)
6. Felippa, C., Haugen, B.: A unified formulation of small-strain corotational finite elements: I. Theory. Comput. Methods Appl. Mech. Eng. **194**, 2285–2335 (2005)
7. Hirt, C., Amsden, A., Cook, J.: An arbitrary Lagrangian-Eulerian computing method for all flow speeds. J. Comput. Phys. **14**, 227–253 (1974)

8. Hu, H.: Direct simulation of flows of solid-liquid mixtures. Int. J. Multiphase Flow **22**, 335–352 (1996)
9. Nitikitpaiboon, C., Bathe, K.: An arbitrary Lagrangian-Eulerian velocity potential formulation for fluid-structure interaction. Comput. Struct. **47**, 871–891 (1993)
10. Richter, T.: A fully Eulerian formulation for fluid-structure-interaction problems. J. Comput. Phys. **233**, 227–240 (2013)
11. Sarrate, J., Huerta, A., Donea, J.: Arbitrary Lagrangian-Eulerian formulation for fluid-rigid body interaction. Comput. Methods Appl. Mech. Eng. **190**, 3171–3188 (2001)
12. Wilcox, D.: Turbulence Modeling for CFD. DCW Industries, Incorporated (1994). https://books.google.com/books?id=VwlRAAAAMAAJ
13. Zhang, L., Guo, Y., Wang, W.: Fem simulation of turbulent flow in a turbine blade passage with dynamical fluid-structure interaction. Int. J. Numer. Meth. Fluids **61**, 1299–1330 (2009)
14. Zhu, Y., Sifakis, E., Teran, J., Brandt, A.: An efficient multigrid method for the simulation of high-resolution elastic solids. ACM Trans. Graph. **29**, 16 (2010)

Free Surface Flow Simulation of Fish Turning Motion

Sadanori Ishihara[1]([✉]), Masashi Yamakawa[1], Takeshi Inomono[1],
and Shinichi Asao[2]

[1] Kyoto Institute of Technology, Matsugasaki, Sakyo-ku, Kyoto, Japan
sada.ishihara@gmail.com
[2] College of Industrial Technology, 1-27-1, Nishikoya, Amagasaki
Hyogo, Japan

Abstract. In this paper, the influence of depth from the free surface of the fish and turning motion will be clarified by numerical simulation. We used Moving-Grid Finite volume method and Moving Computational Domain Method with free surface height function for numerical simulation schemes. Numerical analysis is performed by changing the radius at a certain depth, and the influence of the difference in radius is clarified. Next, analyze the fish that changes its depth and performs rotational motion at the same rotation radius, and clarify the influence of the difference in depth. In any cases, the drag coefficient was a positive value, the side force coefficient was a negative value and the lift coefficient was a smaller value than drag. Analysis was performed with the radius of rotation changed at a certain depth. The depth was changed and the rotational motion at the same rotation radius was analyzed. As a result, it was found the following. The smaller radius of rotation, the greater the lift and side force coefficients. The deeper the fish from free surface, the greater the lift coefficient. It is possible to clarify the influence of depth and radius of rotation from the free surface of submerged fish that is in turning motion on the flow.

Keywords: Free surface · Turning motion · Moving fish
Computational fluid dynamics

1 Introduction

Free surface flows [1] are widely seen in industries. For example, sloshing in the tank [2], mixing in the vessel [3], droplets from the nozzle [4], resin in the injection molding [5] are free surface flows with industrial applications. Focusing, on moving submerged objects, wave power generator [6], moving fish [7–9], fish detection in ocean currents are attractive application.In particular, since fish are familiar existence and application to fish robots can be considered in the future, many research has been reported on the flow of free surface with fish [7–9]. In general, fish are not limited to linear motion, but always move three-dimensionally including curvilinear motion. Also, when fish escape from enemies, it is known to change the direction of moving by deforming the shape of the fish [7]. In other words, the surface shape change on the fish itself has some influence on the flow fields. Furthermore, for fish swimming near the surface of the water, the movement may influence the free surface as water surface, or the interaction such as the influence on the fish due to the large wave may considered. In other words, when analyzing the swimming phenomenon of fish, it is necessary to simultaneously consider the three-dimensional curved movement, the change of the surface shape of the fish and the shape of the water at the same time, various researches are done. Numerical simulation approaches to these studies can be also be found in several papers. Focusing on what does not consider the influence of the free surface, Yu et al. carried out a three-dimensional simulation to clarify the relationship between how to move fish fins and surrounding flow field [8]. In addition, Kajtar simulates fish with a rigid body connected by a link, and reveals a flow near a free surface of two dimensions by a method of moving a rigid body [9]. However, as far as the authors know, these numerical researches have only studies that do not consider the influence of free surfaces or only one-way motion to fish.

In the view of these backgrounds, it can be said that calculation of curved rotational motion is indispensable in addition or free surface in order to capture more accurate motion of fish near the water surface, but in the past this case is not, we focused on t part and carried out the research. In such free surface flow with moving submerged object, a method for tracking a free surface is important. Among them, the height function method [10] has high computational efficiency. Generally, in free surface flow, there are cases where complicated phenomena such as bubble, droplet and wave entrainment are sometimes presented, which is one of major problems. However, in this paper, we will not consider the influence of breaking in order to make the expression of motion of fish with high flexibility and expansions of analysis area top priority. In simulating such a free surface with fish, since the computational grid moves and deforms according to the change of the free surface and the movement, a method suitable for a computational grid which moves and deforms with time is necessary. Among them, Moving-Grid Finite volume method [11] that strictly satisfies the Geometric Conservation Law, and it was considers suitable. The Moving-Grid Finite volume method has been proposed as a computational scheme suitable for moving grid and has been successfully applied to various unsteady flow problems. For example, this method was applied to the flows with the falling spheres in long pipe [12–14] and fluid-rigid bodies interaction problem [15, 16]. Furthermore, using Moving Computational Domain Method (MCD) [17], it is possible to analyze the flow while moving the object freely by moving the entire computational domain including the object.

The purpose of this paper is to perform hydrodynamic analysis when the fish shape submerged objects rotates using the height function method, the Moving-Grid Finite volume method and the Moving Computational Domain method. In this paper, we pay attention to the difference in flow due to the difference in exercise. Therefore, the fish itself shall not be deformed. In this paper, we will clarify the influence of depth from the free surface of the free surface and rotating radius of motion. For this reason, analysis is performed by changing the radius at a certain depth, and the influence of the difference in radius is clarified. Next, analyze the fish that changes its depth and performs rotational motion at the same rotation radius, and clarify the influence of the difference in depth. Based on the finally obtained results, we will state the conclusion.

2 Governing Equations

In this paper, three-dimensional continuity equation and Navier-Stokes equations with gravity force are used as governing equations. Nondimensionalized continuity equation and Navier-Stokes equations are

$$\frac{\partial u}{\partial x} + \frac{\partial v}{\partial y} + \frac{\partial w}{\partial z} = 0, \tag{1}$$

$$\frac{\partial q}{\partial t} + \frac{\partial E}{\partial x} + \frac{\partial F}{\partial y} + \frac{\partial G}{\partial z} + \frac{\partial P_1}{\partial x} + \frac{\partial P_2}{\partial y} + \frac{\partial P_3}{\partial z} = H, \tag{2}$$

where, x, y, z are coordinates, t is time. u, v, w are velocity in x, y, z coordinates, respectively, q is velocity vector, $q = [u, v, w]^T$. E, F, G are flux vectors in x, y, z direction, respectively. H is force term including gravity, $H = [0, 0, -1/\mathrm{Fr}^2]^T$, Fr is Froude number. P_1, P_2, P_3 are pressure gradient vectors in x, y, z directions, respectively. Where, flux vectors are

$$E = E_a - E_v, F = F_a - F_v, G = G_a - G_v, \tag{3}$$

where, E_a, F_a, G_a are inviscid flux vectors in x, y, z directions, E_v, F_v, G_v are viscid flux vectors, respectively. These vectors are

$$\begin{aligned} E_a &= [u^2, uv, uw]^T, & F_a &= [vu, v^2, vw]^T, & G_a &= [wu, wv, w^2]^T, \\ E_v &= \tfrac{1}{\mathrm{Re}}[u_x, v_x, w_x]^T, & F_v &= \tfrac{1}{\mathrm{Re}}[u_y, v_y, w_y]^T, & G_v &= \tfrac{1}{\mathrm{Re}}[u_z, v_z, w_z]^T, \\ P_1 &= [p, 0, 0]^T, & P_2 &= [0, p, 0]^T, & P_3 &= [0, 0, p]^T, \end{aligned} \tag{4}$$

where, p is pressure, Re is Reynolds number, the subscript x, y, z means velocity difference in x, y, z directions. The relational expression of nondimensionalization are

$$x = \frac{\bar{x}}{\bar{L}_0}, y = \frac{\bar{y}}{\bar{L}_0}, z = \frac{\bar{z}}{\bar{L}_0}, u = \frac{\bar{u}}{\bar{U}_0}, v = \frac{\bar{v}}{\bar{U}_0}, w = \frac{\bar{w}}{\bar{U}_0}, p = \frac{\bar{p}}{\bar{\rho}\bar{U}_0^2}, t = \frac{\bar{t}}{\bar{L}_0/\bar{U}_0}, \tag{5}$$

where, $^-$ means dimensional number, $\bar{L}_0, \bar{U}_0, \bar{\rho}$ are characteristic length, characteristic velocity and density. $\mathrm{Re} = \bar{U}_0\bar{L}_0/\bar{v}$, $\mathrm{Fr} = \bar{U}_0 / \sqrt{\bar{g}\bar{L}_0}$, where $\bar{v}$ is kinetic viscosity and $\bar{g}$ is gravitational acceleration.

3 Discretization Method

In discretization method, Moving-Grid Finite volume method [11] was used. This method is based on cell centered finite volume method. In three dimensional flow, space-time unified four dimensional control volume is used.

In this paper, moving grid finite volume method with fractional step method [18] was used for incompressible flows. In this method, there are two computational step and pressure equation. In first step, intermediate velocity is calculated. Pressure is calculated from pressure Poisson equation. In the second step, velocity is corrected from the pressure.

Figure 1 shows schematic drawing of structured four dimensional control volume in space-time unified domain. $\boldsymbol{R}$ is grid position vector, $\boldsymbol{R} = [x, y, z]^T$, where superscript n shows computational step and subscript i, j, k show structured grid point indexes. The red region is computational cell at n computational step, blue region is computational cell at $n + 1$ computational step. The control volume Ω is four dimensional polyhedron and formed between the computational cell at n computational step and computational cell at $n + 1$ computational step.

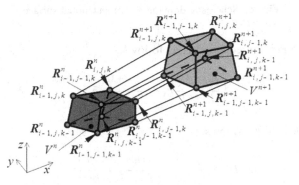

Fig. 1. Schematics drawing of control volume. (Color figure online)

The Moving-Grid finite volume method was adapted to Eq. (2), the first step is

$$
\boldsymbol{q}^* V^{n+1} - \boldsymbol{q}^n V^n + \frac{1}{2} \sum_{l=1}^{6} \left\{ (\boldsymbol{E}^* + \boldsymbol{E}^n)\tilde{n}_x + (\boldsymbol{F}^* + \boldsymbol{F}^n)\tilde{n}_y + (\boldsymbol{G}^* + \boldsymbol{G}^n)\tilde{n}_z \right.
$$
$$
\left. + (\boldsymbol{q}^* + \boldsymbol{q}^n)\tilde{n}_t \right\}_l \tilde{S}_l = V_\Omega \boldsymbol{H}, \tag{6}
$$

where V_Ω is volume of four dimensional control volume. The superscript index n is computational step, $*$ is sub-iteration step. The $\tilde{n}_x, \tilde{n}_y, \tilde{n}_y, \tilde{n}_t$ are the components of outward unit normal vectors in x, y, z, t coordinate of four dimensional control volume. The subscript l index means computational surface. The $l = 1, 2, \dots, 6$ surface are the surface from n step computational cell and $n + 1$ step computational cell. For example, Fig. 2 shows the computational surface at $l = 2$. The $\tilde{S}_l$ is length of normal vector $\tilde{n}$.

The second step is as follows.

$$
(\boldsymbol{q}^{n+1} - \boldsymbol{q}^*)V^{n+1} + \sum_{l=1}^{6} \left(\boldsymbol{P}_1^{n+1/2}\tilde{n}_x + \boldsymbol{P}_2^{n+1/2}\tilde{n}_y + \boldsymbol{P}_3^{n+1/2}\tilde{n}_z \right)_l \tilde{S}_l = \boldsymbol{0}. \tag{7}
$$

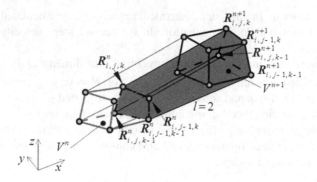

Fig. 2. Schematic drawing of computational surface.

The pressure Poisson equation is as follows.

$$-D^* V^{n+1} + \sum_{l=1}^{6} \left(\frac{\partial p^{n+1/2}}{\partial x^{n+1}} \tilde{n}_x + \frac{\partial p^{n+1/2}}{\partial y^{n+1}} \tilde{n}_y + \frac{\partial p^{n+1/2}}{\partial z^{n+1}} \tilde{n}_z \right)_l \tilde{S}_l = 0. \qquad (8)$$

The D^* is defined as follows.

$$D^* = \frac{\partial u^*}{\partial x^{n+1}} + \frac{\partial v^*}{\partial y^{n+1}} + \frac{\partial w^*}{\partial z^{n+1}}. \qquad (9)$$

The computational step is as follows. In the first step, the intermediate velocity q^* is solved from Eq. (6). The pressure $p^{n+1/2}$ is solved from Eq. (8). In the second step, velocity q^{n+1} is solved from Eq. (7).

4 Numerical Schemes

Numerical schemes are as follows. Equation (2) was divided from fractional step method [18]. The intermediate velocity was calculated using LU-SGS [19] iteratively. The inviscid flux term E_a, F_a, G_a and moving grid term $q\tilde{n}_t$ were evaluated using QUICK [20]. In our computation results, there were not unphysical results or divergence. The viscous term E_v, F_v, G_v and pressure gradient term $P_1^{n+1/2}, P_2^{n+1/2}, P_3^{n+1/2}$ were evaluated using centred difference scheme. The pressure Poisson equation Eq. (8) was calculated using Bi-CGSTAB [21] iteratively.

5 Surface Tracking Method

In this paper, the surface height function is used for free surface tracking. Figure 3 shows schematic drawing of free surface height function h. In time step n, the function h are free surface, h is assumed free surface in the next time step $n + 1$.

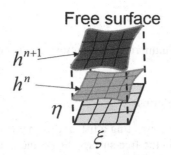

Fig. 3. Schematic drawing of free surface height function.

The surface height equation is

$$\frac{\partial h}{\partial t} + (u - u_G)\frac{\partial h}{\partial x} + (v - v_G)\frac{\partial h}{\partial y} = w, \tag{10}$$

where u_G, v_G means the moving velocity in x, y directions respectively. In addition, general coordinate transformation is used. When ξ, η are defined as $\xi = \xi(x, y)$, $\eta = \eta(x, y)$,

$$\xi_x = \frac{y_\eta}{J}, \xi_y = -\frac{x_\eta}{J}, \eta_x = -\frac{y_\xi}{J}, \eta_y = \frac{x_\xi}{J}, \tag{11}$$

where the subscript indexes x, y, ξ, η are the derivatives in x, y, ξ, η directions, respectively. J means Jacobian, $J = x_\xi y_\eta - x_\eta y_\xi$.

The Eq. (10) is transformed as

$$\frac{\partial h}{\partial t} + (U - U_G)\frac{\partial h}{\partial \xi} + (V - V_G)\frac{\partial h}{\partial \eta} = w, \tag{12}$$

$$U = \frac{1}{J}\left(uy_\eta - vx_\eta\right), V = \frac{1}{J}\left(-uy_\xi + vx_\xi\right), \\ U_G = \frac{1}{J}\left(u_G y_\eta - v_G x_\eta\right), V_G = \frac{1}{J}\left(-u_G y_\xi + v_G x_\xi\right). \tag{13}$$

The Eq. (12) is not conservation form. For solving this equation, finite difference method is used. The advection term $(U - U_G)h_\xi, (V - V_G)h_\eta$ are evaluated by 1st order upwind difference. The 1st order upwind method has low accuracy. When high order scheme is used, free surface shape tends to be sharp, which causes calculation instability. The 1st order upwind method is used to prevent this phenomenon. The moving velocity components u_G, v_G are evaluated by moving grid velocity at grid points. In this paper, surface tension is omitted. The pressure at free surface is fixed by 0.

6 Numerical Results

In this section, we present numerical simulation results for moving submerged fish along a curved path.

6.1 Computational Conditions

This case is to create a shape simulating a fish and to make it rotate. The purpose of this case is to see the difference in the free surface shape and the force acting on the fish by changing the depth from the initial free surface and the radius of rotation of the fish.

Figure 4 shows schematics of computational domain. Figure 5 shows shape of fish. The characteristic length of fish is L. The length of fish is 1, the width is 0.5 and the height is 0.5. The length of computational domain is 60, the width is 20 and the height is 4 or 3.5. The fish position is 20L from forward boundary, centered at width. When the height of computational domain height is 4, the fish position from initial free surface is 2. When the height of computational domain height is 3.5, the fish position from initial free surface is 1.5.

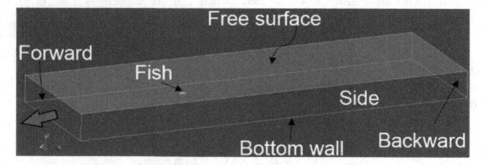

Fig. 4. Schematics of computational domain.

Fig. 5. Shape of fish.

The Reynolds number is 5000, the Froude number is 2, and the time step is 0.002. The grid points are 121(Length) × 81(Width) × 81(Height). The grid points at the fish surface are 21 × 21 × 21.

Table 1 shows the comparison of our computational cases. The cycle of rotation of fish are 50 and 75. The initial fish depth from free surface is 2 or 1.5. Therefore, four cases were analyzed.

Table 1. Computational conditions.

Case name	Cycle of rotation	Radius of rotation	Depth from free surface
Case (a)	50	7.96	2
Case (b)	75	11.9	2
Case (c)	50	7.96	1.5
Case (d)	75	11.9	1.5

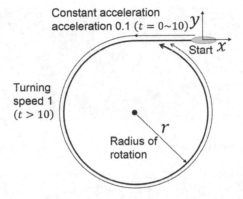

Fig. 6. Schematics of fish motion.

Figure 6 shows schematics of fish motion. It is assumed that the motion condition is linear motion of constant acceleration with acceleration 0.1 up to dimensionless time 10 in the negative direction of the x axis, and then to rotate at speed 1 thereafter. The cycle of rotation is 50 or 75. When the cycle of rotation is 50, the radius of rotation is about 7.96. When the cycle of rotation is 75, the radius of rotation is about 11.9. The Moving Computational Domain method [17] was used, the simulation was performed by moving the entire computational domain including the fish.

Initial conditions of velocity is $u = v = w = 0$ and pressure is given as a function of height considering hydrostatic pressure.

Boundary conditions are as follows. At the forward boundary, velocity is $u = v = w = 0$, pressure is Neumann boundary condition. Free surface height is fixed by initial free surface height. At the backward boundary, velocity is linear extrapolated, pressure is Neumann boundary condition. Free surface height is Neumann boundary condition. At the fish boundary, velocity is no-slip condition, pressure is Neumann boundary condition. At the bottom wall, velocity is slip condition, pressure is Neumann boundary condition. At the side boundary, velocity is outflow condition, pressure is Neumann boundary condition. Free surface height is Neumann boundary condition. At the free surface boundary, free surface shape is calculated from surface height function equation, velocity is extrapolated, pressure is fixed by $p = 0$.

6.2   Numerical Results

In this section, numerical results are shown. First, we will explain the flow fields.

Figure 7 shows the isosurface where the vorticity magnitude is 5 and free surface shape in Case (a). As for the shape of the free surface, the amount of change from the initial height is emphasized 50 times and displayed. Figure 7(a) shows the results at $t = 10$, deformed with moving. Figures 7(b)–(f) show the results at $t = 15 - 35$, respectively. In these figures, it is understood that there is a region with large vorticity around the fish. From the viewpoint if the free surface shape, there is a region where the free surface rises at the top of the fish, and it is recessed behind. Furthermore, it can be seen that the shape of the free surface behind the fish.

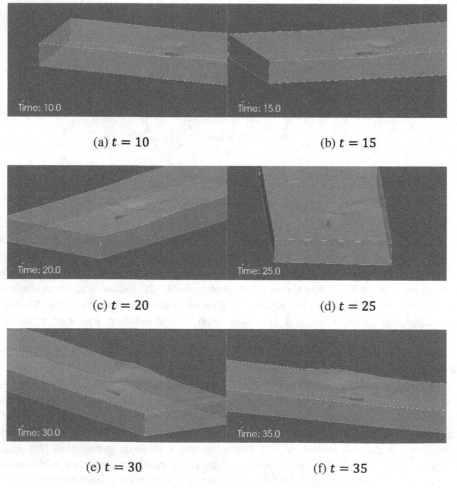

(a) $t = 10$ (b) $t = 15$

(c) $t = 20$ (d) $t = 25$

(e) $t = 30$ (f) $t = 35$

Fig. 7. Isosurface of vorticity magnitude and free surface shape (Case (a)).

In the next, we describe the drag, side force and lift acting on the surface of the fish. In this paper, the force acting in the direction opposite to the travelling direction of the fish is defined as a drag force, the force acting in the vertical direction on the motion path is defined as a side force, and the force acting in the depth direction is defines as a lift force. Also, each nondimensionalization one is called a drag coefficient (Cd), a side force coefficient (Cs) and a lift coefficient (Cl). When calculating the lift coefficient, the pressure excluding the influence of gravity are used for calculation.

Figure 8 shows the time history of the drag, side and lift coefficient. As an example, the results of Case (a) are shown, but in all other cases the overall trend was similar. The horizontal axis shows nondimensionalized time, the vertical axis shows the coefficients (Cd, Cs and Cl). Since the rotational motion is started after the dimensionless time 10, it is indicated by the dimensionless time 50 for one cycle from the dimensionless time 10. From Fig. 8, the Cd is always positive value, it is understood that the fish receives the force from the direction of motion. Also the Cl is always a negative value, it is understood that the fish receives the force in the direction of the center of rotation. Furthermore, the Cl is smaller than the other coefficients, and it can be seen that the free surface is less affected by the farther from the fish. It is also understood that these coefficients hardly change with time.

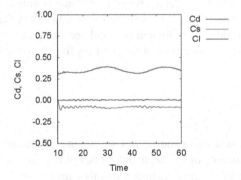

Fig. 8. Time history of coefficient of drag, side force and lift (Case (a)).

Table 2. Comparisons of coefficients of drag, side force and lift.

Case name	Cd(Drag)	Cs(Side force)	Cl(Lift)
Case (a)	0.348	−0.0791	0.00365
Case (b)	0.325	−0.0503	0.00124
Case (c)	0.340	−0.0780	0.00802
Case (d)	0.316	−0.0487	0.00409

Next, average values of coefficients in cases are shown. Table 2 shows the average values of Cd, Cs and Cl in these cases respectively. The average is the time when the fish has rotated by one cycle. Therefore, Case (a) and (c) are time averaged with dimensionless time 50, and Case (b) and (d) are time averaged by dimensionless time 75.

First, from Table 2, it can be seen that the lift coefficient Cl is smaller than the absolute values of the drag coefficient Cd and the side force coefficient Cs. Next, from Table 2, we will consider the influence due to the difference in the cycle of rotation. Cases (a) and (b) are cases with the depth 2, and Case (c) and (d) when the depth is 1.5 when the cycle of rotation only differs. When comparing Case (a) and (b), both coefficients are smaller in Case (b) than in Case (a). This is considered to be due to the fact that the cycle of rotation of Case (b) is longer than the cycle of rotation of Case (a), that is, the radius of rotation is large, so the influence of rotation is reduced in Case (b). Case (c) and Case (d) have the same tendency.

Next, consider the influence of the depth of the fish from the free surface. Case (a) and (c), Case (b) and (d), are cases with the same cycle of rotation. When comparing Case (a) and (c), the lift coefficient is larger in Case (c). In addition, the drag coefficient and the side force coefficient hardly change. This seems to be because Case (c) is more likely to have fish than free surface than Case (a), and Case (c) has greater influence on the lift coefficient. Since the motion path in the same, it is considered that the drag coefficient and the side force coefficient did not change so much. Case (b) and Case (d) have the same tendency.

In conclusion, focusing on the lift coefficient, the lift coefficient is greatly influenced by the radius of rotation and the depth from free surface. When the radius of rotation is small, and when the depth from free surface is small, the lift coefficient is large. The absolute value of the lift coefficient is smaller than the drag and lift coefficients, this is because the lift coefficient is calculated using the pressure excluding the influence of gravity. The computational required for the computation of dimensionless time 10 was 13 h.

7 Conclusions

In this paper, a simulation was conducted with varying depth and radius of rotation in order to clarify the influence of the depth and radius of rotation from the free surface of submerged fish in the low. The conclusion of this paper is summarized below.

- Analysis was performed with the radius of rotation changed at a certain depth. The smaller radius of rotation, the greater the side force and the lift coefficients.
- The depth was changed and the rotational motion at the same rotation radius was analyzed. It was found that the deeper the depth from free surface, the greater the lift coefficient.
- It is possible to clarify the influence of depth from the free surface and radius of rotation of submerged fish that is in rotational motion on the flow.

This work was supported by JSPS KAKENHI Grant Numbers 16K06079, 16K21563.

References

1. Scardovelli, R., Zaleski, S.: Direct numerical simulation of free-surface and interfacial flow. Ann. Rev. Fluid Mech. **31**, 567–603 (1999)
2. Okamoto, T., Kawahara, M.: Two-dimensional sloshing analysis by Lagrangian finite element method. Int. J. Numer. Meth. Fluids **11**(5), 453–477 (1990)
3. Brucato, A., Ciofalo, M., Grisafi, F., Micale, G.: Numerical prediction of flow fields in baffled stirred vessels: a comparison of alternative modelling approaches. Chem. Eng. Sci. **53**(321), 3653–3684 (1998)
4. Eggers, J.: Nonlinear dynamics and breakup of free-surface flows. Rev. Mod. Phys. **69**(3), 865–929 (1997)
5. Chang, R.-y., Yang, W.-h.: Numerical simulation of mold filling in injection molding using a three-dimensional finite volume approach. Int. J. Numer. Methods Fluids **37**(2), 125–148 (2001)
6. Drew, B., Plummer, A.R., Sahinkaya, M.N.: A review of wave energy converter technology. Proc. Inst. Mech. Eng. Part A J. Power Energy **223**(8), 887–902 (2009)
7. Triantafyllou, M.S., Weymouth, G.D., Miao, J.: Biomimetic survival hydrodynamics and flow sensing. Ann. Rev. Fluid Mech. **48**, 1–24 (2016)
8. Yu, C.-L., Ting, S.-C., Yeh, M.-K., Yang, J.-T.: Three-dimensional numerical simulation of hydrodynamic interactions between pectoral fin vortices and body undulation in a swimming fish. Phys. Fluids **23**, 1–12 (2012). No. 091901
9. Kajtar, J.B., Monaghan, J.J.: On the swimming of fish like bodies near free and fixed boundaries. Eur. J. Mech. B/Fluids **33**, 1–13 (2012)
10. Lo, D.C., Young, D.L.: Arbitrary Lagrangian-Eulerian finite element analysis of free surface flow using a velocity-vorticity formulation. J. Comput. Phys. **195**, 175–201 (2004)
11. Matsuno, K.: Development and applications of a moving grid finite volume method. In: Topping, B.H.V., et al. (eds.) Developments and Applications in Engineering Computational Technology, Chapter 5, pp. 103–129. Saxe-Coburg Publications (2010)
12. Asao, S., Matsuno, K., Yamakawa, M.: Simulations of a falling sphere with concentration in an infinite long pipe using a new moving mesh system. Appl. Therm. Eng. **72**, 29–33 (2014)
13. Asao, S., Matsuno, K., Yamakawa, M.: Parallel computations of incompressible flow around falling spheres in a long pipe using moving computational domain method. Comput. Fluids **88**, 850–856 (2013)
14. Asao, S., Matsuno, K., Yamakawa, M.: Simulations of a falling sphere in a long bending pipe with Trans-Mesh method and moving computational domain method. J. Comput. Sci. Technol. **7**(2), 297–305 (2013)
15. Asao, S., Matsuno, K., Yamakawa, M.: Parallel computations of incompressible fluid-rigid bodies interaction using Transmission Mesh method. Comput. Fluids **80**, 178–183 (2013)
16. Asao, S., Matsuno, K., Yamakawa, M.: Trans-Mesh method and its application to simulations of incompressible fluid-rigid bodies interaction. J. Comput. Sci. Technol. **5**(3), 163–174 (2011)
17. Watanabe, K., Matsuno, K.: Moving computational domain method and its application to flow around a high-speed car passing through a hairpin curve. J. Comput. Sci. Technol. **3**, 449–459 (2009)
18. Chorin, A.J.: On the convergence of discrete approximations to the Navier-Stokes equations. Math. Comput. **23**, 341–353 (1969)

19. Yoon, S., Jameson, Y.: Lower-upper Symmetric-Gauss-Seidel methods for the euler and Navier-Stokes equations. AIAA J. **26**, 1025–1026 (1988)
20. Leonard, B.P.: A stable and accurate convective modeling procedure based on quadratic interpolation. Comput. Methods Appl. Mech. Eng. **19**, 59–98 (1979)
21. Van Der Vorst, H.: Bi-CGSTAB: a fast and smoothly converging variant of Bi-CG for the solution of nonsymmetric linear systems. SIAM J. Sci. Comput. **13**(2), 631–644 (1992)

Circular Function-Based Gas-Kinetic Scheme for Simulation of Viscous Compressible Flows

Zhuxuan Meng[1], Liming Yang[2], Donghui Wang[1(✉)], Chang Shu[2], and Weihua Zhang[1]

[1] College of Aerospace Science and Engineering, National University of Defense Technology, No. 109 Deya Road, Changsha 410073, China
xxmnudt@163.com
[2] Department of Mechanical Engineering, National University of Singapore, 10 Kent Ridge Crescent, Singapore 119260, Singapore

Abstract. A stable gas-kinetic scheme based on circular function is proposed for simulation of viscous compressible flows in this paper. The main idea of this scheme is to simplify the integral domain of Maxwellian distribution function over the phase velocity and phase energy to modified Maxwellian function, which will integrate over the phase velocity only. Then the modified Maxwellian function can be degenerated to a circular function with the assumption that all particles are distributed on a circle. Firstly, the RAE2822 airfoil is simulated to validate the accuracy of this scheme. Then the nose part of an aerospace plane model is studied to prove the potential of this scheme in industrial application. Simulation results show that the method presented in this paper has a good computational accuracy and stability.

Keywords: Circular function · Maxwellian function · Gas-kinetic scheme
Vicous compressible flows

1 Introduction

With the development of numerical simulation, the computational fluid dynamics (CFD) is becoming more and more important in industrial design of aircraft since its high-fidelity description of the flow field compared to the engineering method. Most numerical schemes are based on directly solving the Euler or N-S equations [1–3]. Whereas, a new method we proposed here is to solve the continuous Boltzmann model at the micro level and N-S equations at macro level. The gas-kinetic scheme (GKS) is commonly used as a continuous Boltzmann model which is based on the solution of Boltzmann equation and Maxwellian distribution function [4–7]. The GKS attracts more researchers' attention during the last thirty years since its good accuracy and efficiency in solving the inviscid and viscous fluxes respectively [8, 9].

The GKS is developed from the equilibrium flux method (EFM) [10] to solve inviscid flows in the very beginning. Then, the Kinetic Flux Vector Splitting (KFVS) [11] scheme is applied to solve collisionless Boltzmann equation. The Bhatnagar Gross

© Springer International Publishing AG, part of Springer Nature 2018
Y. Shi et al. (Eds.): ICCS 2018, LNCS 10862, pp. 37–47, 2018.
https://doi.org/10.1007/978-3-319-93713-7_3

Krook (BGK) gas kinetic scheme was developed by Prendergast et al. [12], Chae et al. [13], Xu [14, 15] and other researchers based on the KFVS scheme. The particle collisions are considered in BGK scheme to improve the accuracy, which contributes great developments and application potential for BGK gas kinetic scheme.

In this work, a stable gas-kinetic scheme based on circular function framework is proposed for simulating the 2-D viscous compressible flows. Most existing GKS are based on Maxwellian function and make it time consuming and complex. Hence, the original Maxwellian function, which is the function of phase velocity and phase energy, is simplified into a function including phase velocity only. The effect of phase energy is contained in the particle inter energy e_p. Then, based on the assumption which all particles are concentrated on a circle, the simplified Maxwellian function can be reduced to a circular function, which makes the original infinite integral to be integrated along the circle. Compressible flow around RAE2822 airfoil is simulated to validate the proposed scheme. Furthermore, the nose part of an aerospace plane model is studied to prove the application potential of this scheme.

2 Methodology

2.1 Maxwellian Distribution Function

Maxwellian distribution function is an equilibrium state distribution of Boltzmann function. The continuous Boltzmann equation based on Bhatnagar Gross Krook (BGK) without external force collision model is shown as Eq. (1):

$$\frac{\partial f}{\partial t} + \xi \cdot \nabla f = \frac{1}{\tau}(f^{eq} - f),$$ (1)

Where f is the gas distribution function and the superscript eq means the equilibrium state approached by f through particle collisions within a collision time scale τ.

The Maxwellian distribution function is

$$f^{eq} = g_M = \rho(\frac{\lambda}{\pi})^{\frac{D+K}{2}} e^{-\lambda \left[\sum_{i=1}^{D}(\xi_i - U_i)^2 + \sum_{j=1}^{K} \zeta_j^2 \right]},$$ (2)

in which U_i is the macroscopic flow velocity in i-direction and $\lambda = m/(2kT) = 1/(2RT)$. The number of phase energy variables is $K = 3 - D + N$. D is the dimension and N is freedom rotational degree number.

The heat ratio γ can be expressed as:

$$\gamma = \frac{b+2}{b} = \frac{K+D+2}{K+D},$$ (3)

in which b represents the freedom degree number of molecules.

Based on Maxwellian function (Eq. (2)), the continuous Boltzmann equation (Eq. (1)) can be recovered to N-S equations by applying Chapman-Enskog expansion analysis [4] with following conservation moments equations:

$$\int g_M d\Xi = \rho, \tag{4a}$$

$$\int g_M \xi_\alpha d\Xi = \rho u_\alpha, \tag{4b}$$

$$\int g_M (\xi_\alpha \xi_\alpha + \sum_{j=1}^{K} \zeta_j^2) d\Xi = \rho(u_\alpha u_\alpha + bRT), \tag{4c}$$

$$\int g_M \xi_\alpha \xi_\beta d\Xi = \rho u_\alpha u_\beta + p\delta_{\alpha\beta}, \tag{4d}$$

$$\int g_M (\xi_\alpha \xi_\alpha + \sum_{j=1}^{K} \zeta_j^2) \xi_\beta d\Xi = \rho[u_\alpha u_\alpha + (b+2)RT]u_\beta, \tag{4e}$$

in which $d\Xi = d\xi_\alpha d\xi_\beta d\xi_\chi d\zeta_1 d\zeta_2 \cdots d\zeta_K$ is the volume element in the phase velocity and energy space. ρ is the density of mean flow, the integral domain for each variable is $(-\infty, +\infty)$.

Due to phase velocity is independent from phase energy space, Eq. (2) can be written as:

$$g_M = g_{M1} \cdot g_{M2}, \tag{5}$$

$$g_{M1} = \rho \left(\frac{\lambda}{\pi}\right)^{\frac{D}{2}} e^{-\lambda \sum_{i=1}^{D}(\xi_i - u_i)^2}, \tag{6}$$

$$g_{M2} = \rho \left(\frac{\lambda}{\pi}\right)^{\frac{K}{2}} e^{-\lambda \sum_{j=1}^{K} \zeta_j^2}. \tag{7}$$

If we define $d\Xi_1 = d\xi_\alpha d\xi_\beta d\xi_\chi$ and $d\Xi_2 = d\zeta_1 d\zeta_2 \cdots d\zeta_K$, then we can get $d\Xi = d\Xi_1 d\Xi_2$. With these definitions, the integral form of g_{M2} can be concluded as:

$$\int g_{M2} d\Xi_2 = \int \left(\frac{\lambda}{\pi}\right)^{\frac{K}{2}} e^{-\lambda \sum_{j=1}^{K} \zeta_j^2} d\zeta_1 d\zeta_2 \cdots d\zeta_K = 1. \tag{8}$$

Substituting Eqs. (5)–(8) to Eq. (4), we have

$$\int g_{M1} d\Xi_1 = \rho, \tag{9a}$$

$$\int g_{M1} \xi_\alpha d\Xi_1 = \rho u_\alpha, \tag{9b}$$

$$\int g_{M1} (\xi_\alpha \xi_\alpha + 2e_p) d\Xi_1 = \rho(u_\alpha u_\alpha + bRT), \tag{9c}$$

$$\int g_{M1} \xi_\alpha \xi_\beta d\Xi_1 = \rho u_\alpha u_\beta + p\delta_{\alpha\beta}, \tag{9d}$$

$$\int g_{M1} (\xi_\alpha \xi_\alpha + 2e_p) \xi_\beta d\Xi_1 = \rho[u_\alpha u_\alpha + (b+2)RT]u_\beta, \tag{9e}$$

in which e_p is particle potential energy, shown as Eq. (10):

$$e_p = \frac{1}{2} \int g_{M2} \sum_{j=1}^{K} \zeta_j^2 d\Xi_2 = \frac{K}{4\lambda} = [1 - \frac{D}{2}(\gamma - 1)]e, \tag{10}$$

where $e = p/[(\gamma - 1)\rho]$ is the potential energy of mean flow. It can be seen from Eqs. (9) and (10) that e_p is independent from phase velocity ξ_i.

2.2   Simplified Circular Function

Suppose that all the particles in the phase velocity space are concentrated on a circle which has center (u_1, u_2) and radius c, shown as:

$$(\xi_1 - u_1)^2 + (\xi_2 - u_2)^2 = c^2, \tag{11}$$

in which c^2 means the mean particle kinetic energy and we have

$$c^2 = \frac{\int \sum_{i=1}^{D} (\xi_i - U_i)^2 g_{M1} d\Xi_1}{\int g_{M1} d\Xi_1} = \frac{D}{2\lambda} = D(\gamma - 1)e. \tag{12}$$

By substituting Eq. (12) into Eq. (9a) we can get Eq. (13), which is the mass conservation form in the cylindrical coordinate system:

$$\rho = \int_0^{2\pi} \int_0^\infty \rho \left(\frac{\lambda}{\pi}\right)^{\frac{D}{2}} e^{-\lambda r^2} \delta(r - c) r dr d\theta = 2\pi c \rho \left(\frac{\lambda}{\pi}\right)^{\frac{D}{2}} e^{-\lambda c^2}. \tag{13}$$

Then we can get the simplified circular function shown as follows:

$$g_C = \begin{cases} \frac{\rho}{2\pi} & (\xi_1 - u_1)^2 + (\xi_2 - u_2)^2 = c^2, \\ 0 & else. \end{cases} \tag{14}$$

All particles are concentrated on the circle and the velocity distribution is shown as

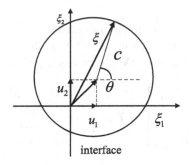

Fig. 1. Configuration of the phase velocity at a cell interface

Fig. 1. Then the phase velocity components in the Cartesian coordinate system can be expressed as:

$$\xi_1 = u_1 + c\cos(\theta), \tag{15a}$$

$$\xi_2 = u_2 + c\sin(\theta). \tag{15b}$$

Substituting Eqs. (14) and (15) to Eq. (9), the conservation forms of moments to recover N-S equations can be expressed as follows:

$$\int g_{M1} d\Xi_1 = \int_0^{2\pi} g_C d\theta = \rho, \tag{16a}$$

$$\int g_{M1} \xi_\alpha d\Xi_1 = \int_0^{2\pi} g_C \xi_\alpha d\theta = \rho u_\alpha, \tag{16b}$$

$$\int g_{M1} (\xi_\alpha \xi_\alpha + 2e_p) d\Xi_1 = \int_0^{2\pi} g_C (\xi_\alpha \xi_\alpha + 2e_p) d\theta = \rho(u_\alpha u_\alpha + bRT), \tag{16c}$$

$$\int g_{M1} \xi_\alpha \xi_\beta d\Xi_1 = \int_0^{2\pi} g_C \xi_\alpha \xi_\beta d\theta = \rho u_\alpha u_\beta + p\delta_{\alpha\beta}, \tag{16d}$$

$$\int g_{M1} (\xi_\alpha \xi_\alpha + 2e_p) \xi_\beta d\Xi_1 = \int_0^{2\pi} g_C (\xi_\alpha \xi_\alpha + 2e_p) \xi_\beta d\theta = \rho[u_\alpha u_\alpha + (b+2)RT]u_\beta. \tag{16e}$$

2.3   Governing Equations Discretized by Finite Volume Method

N-S equation discretized by finite volume method in 2-dimensional can be expressed as:

$$\frac{d\mathbf{W}_I}{dt} = -\frac{1}{\Omega_I}\sum_{j=1}^{N_f} F_{Nj}S_j, \tag{17}$$

in which I represents the index of a control volume, Ω_I is the volume, N_f means the number of interfaces of control volume I and S_j is the area of the interface in this volume. The conservative variables $\mathbf{W}$ and convective flux $\mathbf{F}_n$ can be expressed as:

$$\mathbf{W} = \begin{bmatrix} \rho \\ \rho u_1 \\ \rho u_2 \\ \rho(u_1^2 + u_2^2 + bRT)/2 \end{bmatrix}, \quad \mathbf{F} = \begin{bmatrix} \rho U_n \\ \rho u_1 U_n + n_x p \\ \rho u_2 U_n + n_y p \\ U_n \rho(u_1^2 + u_2^2 + (b+2)RT)/2 \end{bmatrix}. \tag{18}$$

Suppose that cell interface is located on $r = 0$, then the distribution function at cell interface (Eq. (19)) consists two parts, the equilibrium part f^{eq} and the non-equilibrium part f^{neq}:

$$f(0,t) = g_C(0,t) + f^{neq}(0,t) = f^{eq}(0,t) + f^{neq}(0,t). \tag{19}$$

To recover N-S equations by Boltzmann equation from Chapman-Enskog analysis [4, 9, 16–19], the non-equilibrium part $f_i^{neq}(0,t)$ applying Taylor series expansion in time and physics space can be written as:

$$f^{neq}(0,t) = -\tau_0\left[g_C(0,t) - g_C(-\xi\delta t, t - \delta t) + o(\delta t^2)\right]. \tag{20}$$

Substituting Eq. (20) into Eq. (19) and omit the high order error item, then we have

$$f(0,t) \approx g_C(0,t) + \tau_0[g_C(-\xi\delta t, t - \delta t) - g_C(0,t)], \tag{21}$$

in which $g_C(-\xi\delta t, t - \delta t)$ is the distribution function around the cell interface, $\tau_0 = \tau/\delta t = \mu/p\delta t$ is dimensionless collision time. μ is dynamic coefficient of viscosity, δt is the streaming time step which represents the physical viscous of N-S equations. Now convective flux at cell interface can be expressed as:

$$\mathbf{F} = \mathbf{F}^I + \tau_0(\mathbf{F}^{II} - \mathbf{F}^I), \tag{22}$$

in which $\mathbf{F}^I$ represents contribution of equilibrium distribution function $g_C(0,t)$ at cell interface and $\mathbf{F}^{II}$ means equilibrium distribution function $g_C(-\xi\delta t, t - \delta t)$ at surrounding point of the cell interface. Their functions are shown as:

$$\mathbf{F^I} = \begin{bmatrix} \rho u_1 \\ \rho u_1 u_1 + p \\ \rho u_1 u_2 \\ (\rho E + p)u_1 \end{bmatrix}^{face}, \qquad (23)$$

$$\mathbf{F^{II}} = \int \xi_1^{cir} \varphi_a^{cir} g_C^{cir} d\theta, \qquad (24)$$

in which the superscript *face* represents value at $(0, t)$ and *cir* means $(-\xi \delta t, t - \delta t)$.

When $\xi_1 \geq 0$, we have expressions as Eq. (25). The superscript L become R when $\xi_1 < 0$:

$$\xi_1^{cir} = u_1^L - \frac{\partial u_1^L}{\partial x_1}(u_1^+ + c^+ \cos(\theta))\delta t - \frac{\partial u_1^L}{\partial x_2}(u_2^+ + c^+ \sin(\theta))\delta t + c^+ \cos(\theta), \quad (25a)$$

$$\xi_2^{cir} = u_2^L - \frac{\partial u_2^L}{\partial x_1}(u_1^+ + c^+ \cos(\theta))\delta t - \frac{\partial u_2^L}{\partial x_2}(u_2^+ + c^+ \sin(\theta))\delta t + c^+ \sin(\theta), \quad (25b)$$

$$e_p^{cir} = e_p^L - \frac{\partial e_p^L}{\partial x_1}(u_1^+ + c^+ \cos(\theta))\delta t - \frac{\partial e_p^L}{\partial x_2}(u_2^+ + c^+ \sin(\theta))\delta t, \qquad (25c)$$

$$g_C^{cir} = g_C^L - \frac{\partial g_C^L}{\partial x_1}(u_1^+ + c^+ \cos(\theta))\delta t - \frac{\partial g_C^L}{\partial x_2}(u_2^+ + c^+ \sin(\theta))\delta t. \qquad (25d)$$

Substituting Eq. (25) into Eq. (24), the final expression of the equilibrium distribution function at the surrounding points of the cell interface $\mathbf{F^{II}}$ can be calculated by

$$\mathbf{F^{II}}(1) = \int \xi_1^{cir} g_C^{cir} d\theta = \int (a_0 + a_1 r + a_2 s)(g_0 + g_1 r + g_2 s) d\theta, \qquad (26a)$$

$$\mathbf{F^{II}}(2) = \int \xi_1^{cir} \xi_1^{cir} g_C^{cir} d\theta = \int (a_0 + a_1 r + a_2 s)(a_0 + a_1 r + a_2 s)(g_0 + g_1 r + g_2 s) d\theta, \qquad (26b)$$

$$\mathbf{F^{II}}(3) = \int \xi_1^{cir} \xi_2^{cir} g_C^{cir} d\theta = \int (a_0 + a_1 r + a_2 s)(b_0 + b_1 r + b_2 s)(g_0 + g_1 r + g_2 s) d\theta, \qquad (26c)$$

$$\mathbf{F^{II}}(4) = \int \xi_1^{cir} (\frac{1}{2}|\xi^{cir}|^2 + e_p^{cir}) g_C^{cir} d\theta$$

$$= \int (a_0 + a_1 r + a_2 s) \left(\frac{1}{2}((a_0 + a_1 r + a_2 s)^2 + (b_0 + b_1 r + b_2 s)^2) + (e_0 + e_1 r + e_2 s) \right)$$

$$(g_0 + g_1 r + g_2 s) d\theta. \qquad (26d)$$

The operators in Eq. (26) can be expressed as:

$$a_0 = u_1^L - \frac{\partial u_1^L}{\partial x_1} u_1^+ \delta t - \frac{\partial u_1^L}{\partial x_2} u_2^+ \delta t, a_1 = c^+ - \frac{\partial u_1^L}{\partial x_1} c^+ \delta t, a_2 = -\frac{\partial u_1^L}{\partial x_2} c^+ \delta t,$$

$$b_0 = u_2^L - \frac{\partial u_2^L}{\partial x_1} u_1^+ \delta t - \frac{\partial u_2^L}{\partial x_2} u_2^+ \delta t, b_1 = -\frac{\partial u_2^L}{\partial x_1} c^+ \delta t, b_2 = c^+ - \frac{\partial u_2^L}{\partial x_1} c^+ \delta t,$$

$$e_0 = e_p^L - \frac{\partial e_p^L}{\partial x_1} u_1^+ \delta t - \frac{\partial e_p^L}{\partial x_2} u_2^+ \delta t, e_1 = -\frac{\partial e_p^L}{\partial x_1} c^+ \delta t, e_2 = -\frac{\partial e_p^L}{\partial x_2} c^+ \delta t,$$

$$g_0 = g_C^L - \frac{\partial g_C^L}{\partial x_1} u_1^+ \delta t - \frac{\partial g_C^L}{\partial x_2} u_2^+ \delta t, g_1 = -\frac{\partial g_C^L}{\partial x_1} c^+ \delta t, e_2 = -\frac{\partial g_C^L}{\partial x_2} c^+ \delta t,$$

$$(27)$$

in which u_1^+, u_2^+ and c^+ are predictional normal velocity, tangential velocity and particle specific velocity at cell interface. These velocities can be obtained both by Roe average [19] and the value of the former moment at cell interface.

3   Numerical Simulations

To validate the proposed circular function-based gas-kinetic scheme for simulation of viscous compressible flows, the RAE2822 airfoil and nose part of aerospace plane model are discussed.

3.1   Case1: Compressible Flow Around RAE2822 Airfoil

The transonic flow around RAE2822 airfoil is discussed to validate the accuracy of the proposed scheme. The free stream has Mach number of $Ma_\infty = 0.729$ with $2.31°$ angle of attack.

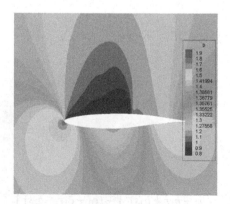

Fig. 2. Pressure contours of presented scheme around RAE2822 airfoil.

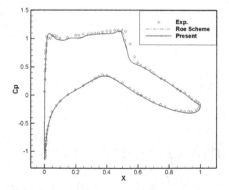

Fig. 3. Pressure coefficient comparison of RAE2822 airfoil surface.

Figure 2 shows the pressure contours obtained by the proposed scheme. Figure 3 shows the comparison between experimental data [20], Roe scheme and the presented scheme. It can be seen clearly that the presented scheme has good accordance with both experimental data and results of Roe scheme.

3.2   Case2: Supersonic Flow Around Nose Part of Aerospace Plane Model

The supersonic flow around the nose part of an aerospace plane model (wind tunnel) is simulated in this section. The model is 290 mm in length, 58 mm in width, the head radius is 15 mm and semi-cone angle is 20°. The free stream has Mach number of $Ma_\infty = 3.6$ with −5, 0 and 5° angle of attack respectively. Figure 4 gives out the pressure contours simulated by the presented scheme at 5° angle of attack, and Fig. 5 is the Mach number contours at the same condition.

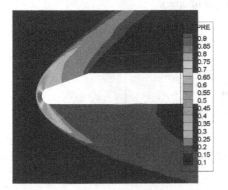 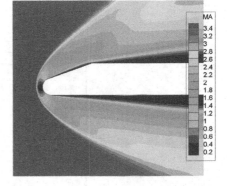

Fig. 4. Pressure contours at 5° angle of attack   **Fig. 5.** Mach number contours at 5° angle of attack

Figure 6 shows comparison of pressure coefficient distribution on upper and lower surface of aerospace plane model at −5 angle of attack, which computed by scheme presented, Roe scheme and Van Leer scheme. It can be seen that the result of present solver has good accordance with other two numerical schemes. Similar conclusions can be obtained according to Figs. 7 and 8. Therefore, the solver presented in this article shows both high computational accuracy and numerical stability. Hence, the circular function-based gas-kinetic scheme shows the potential of future industrial application in flight vehicle research and design.

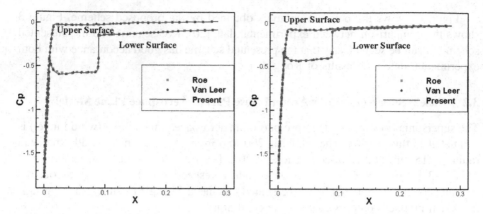

Fig. 6. Pressure coefficient comparison at −5° angle of attack

Fig. 7. Pressure coefficient comparison at 0° angle of attack

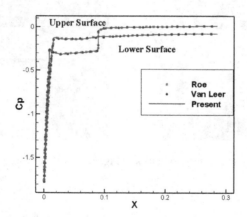

Fig. 8. Pressure coefficient comparison at 5° angle of attack

4 Conclusions

This paper presents a stable gas-kinetic scheme based on circular function. It is focus on improving the calculation efficiency of existing GKS. Firstly, simplifying the original Maxwellian function, which is the function of phase velocity and phase energy, into the function of phase velocity. Furthermore, reducing the simplified function to a circular function. Hence, the original infinite integral can be changed to the integral along the circle.

Transonic flow around RAE2822 airfoil and supersonic flow around the nose part of an aerospace plane model are studied. The results show a good computational accuracy and the potential for future industrial application.

References

1. Anderson, J.D.: Computational Fluid Dynamics: The Basics with Application. McGraw-Hill, New York (1995)
2. Blazek, J.: Computational Fluid Dynamics: Principles and Applications. Elsevier Science, Oxford (2001)
3. Toro, E.F.: Riemann Solvers and Numerical Methods for Fluid Dynamics. Springer, Heidelberg (2009). https://doi.org/10.1007/b79761
4. Yang, L.M., Shu, C., Wu, J.: A hybrid lattice Boltzmann flux solver for simulation of viscous compressible flows. Adv. Appl. Math. Mech. 8(6), 887–910 (2016)
5. Yang, L.M., Shu, C., Wu, J.: A moment conservation-based non-free parameter compressible lattice Boltzmann model and its application for flux evaluation at cell interface. Comput. Fluids 79, 190–199 (2013)
6. Chen, Z., Shu, C., Wang, Y., Yang, L.M., Tan, D.: A simplified lattice Boltzmann method without evolution of distribution function. Adv. Appl. Math. Mech. 9(1), 1–22 (2017)
7. Yang, L.M., Shu, C., Wu, J.: Extension of lattice Boltzmann flux solver for simulation of 3D viscous compressible flows. Comput. Math. Appl. 71, 2069–2081 (2016)
8. Yang, L.M., Shu, C., Wu, J., Zhao, N., Lu, Z.L.: Circular function-based gas-kinetic scheme for simulation of inviscid compressible flows. J. Comput. Phys. 255, 540–557 (2013)
9. Yang, L.M., Shu, C., Wu, J.: A three-dimensional explicit sphere function-based gas-kinetic flux solver for simulation of inviscid compressible flows. J. Comput. Phys. 295, 322–339 (2015)
10. Pullin, D.I.: Direct simulation methods for compressible inviscid ideal-gas flow. J. Comput. Phys. 34, 231–244 (1980)
11. Mandal, J.C., Deshpande, S.M.: Kinetic flux vector splitting for Euler equations. Comput. Fluids 23, 447–478 (1994)
12. Prendergast, K.H., Xu, K.: Numerical hydrodynamics from gas-kinetic theory. J. Comput. Phys. 109, 53–66 (1993)
13. Chae, D., Kim, C., Rho, O.H.: Development of an improved gas-kinetic BGK scheme for inviscid and viscous flows. J. Comput. Phys. 158, 1–27 (2000)
14. Xu, K.: A gas-kinetic BGK scheme for the Navier-Stokes equations and its connection with artificial dissipation and Godunov method. J. Comput. Phys. 171, 289–335 (2001)
15. Xu, K., He, X.Y.: Lattice Boltzmann method and gas-kinetic BGK scheme in the low-Mach number viscous flow simulations. J. Comput. Phys. 190, 100–117 (2003)
16. Guo, Z.L., Shu, C.: Lattice Boltzmann Method and Its Applications in Engineering. World Scientific Publishing, Singapore (2013)
17. Benzi, R., Succi, S., Vergassola, M.: The lattice Boltzmann equation: theory and application. Phys. Rep. 222, 145–197 (1992)
18. Bhatnagar, P.L., Gross, E.P., Krook, M.: A model for collision processes in gases. I: small amplitude processes in charged and neutral one-component systems. Phys. Rev. 94, 511–525 (1954)
19. Roe, P.L.: Approximate Riemann solvers, parameter vectors, and difference schemes. J. Comput. Phys. 43, 357–372 (1981)
20. Slater, J.W.: RAE 2822 Transonic Airfoil: Study #1. https://www.grc.nasa.gov/www/wind/val-id/raetaf/raetaf.html

A New Edge Stabilization Method for the Convection-Dominated Diffusion-Convection Equations

Huoyuan Duan[✉] and Yu Wei

School of Mathematics and Statistics, Wuhan University, Wuhan 430072, China
hyduan.math@whu.edu.cn, 848024931@qq.com

Abstract. We study a new edge stabilization method for the finite element discretization of the convection-dominated diffusion-convection equations. In addition to the stabilization of the jump of the normal derivatives of the solution across the inter-element-faces, we additionally introduce a SUPG/GaLS-like stabilization term but on the domain boundary other than in the interior of the domain. New stabilization parameters are also designed. Stability and error bounds are obtained. Numerical results are presented. Theoretically and numerically, the new method is much better than other edge stabilization methods and is comparable to the SUPG method, and generally, the new method is more stable than the SUPG method.

Keywords: Diffusion-convection equation
Stabilized finite element method · Stability · Error estimates

1 Introduction

When discretizing the diffusion-convection equations by the finite element method, the standard Galerkin variational formulation very often produces oscillatory approximations in the convection-dominated case (cf. [3,14]). As is well-known, this is due to the fact that there lacks controlling the dominating convection in the stability of the method. For obtaining some stability in the direction of the convection, over more than thirty years, numerous stabilized methods have been available. Basically, all the stabilization methods share the common feature: from some residuals relating to the original problem to get the stability in the streamline direction. The stabilization method is highly relevant to the variational multiscale approach [6]: solving the original problem locally (e.g., on

Supported by NSFC under grants 11571266, 11661161017, 91430106, 11171168, 11071132, the Wuhan University start-up fund, the Collaborative Innovation Centre of Mathematics, and the Computational Science Hubei Key Laboratory (Wuhan University).

Y. Shi et al. (Eds.): ICCS 2018, LNCS 10862, pp. 48–60, 2018.
https://doi.org/10.1007/978-3-319-93713-7_4

element level) to find the unresolved component of the exact solution in the standard Galerkin method. Some extensively used stabilization methods are: SUPG (Streamline Upwind/Petrov-Galerkin) method or SD (Streamline Diffusion) method (cf. [7,12]), residual-free bubble method (cf. [15]), GaLS method (cf. [4,9–11,16,22]), local projection method (cf. [2,3]), edge stabilization method (cf. [17,20]), least-squares method (cf. [5,8,23]), etc. All these stabilization methods can generally perform well for the convection-dominated problem, i.e., the finite element solution is far more stable and accurate than that of the standard method. The edge stabilization method is such method, which uses the jump residual of the normal derivatives of the exact solution, $[\![\nabla u \cdot \mathbf{n}]\!] = 0$ across any inter-element-face F. This method is also known as CIP (continuous interior penalty) method [1] for second-order elliptic and parabolic problems. In [17], the edge stabilization method is studied, suitable for the convection-dominated problem. It has been as well proven to be very useful elsewhere (e.g., cf. [18–21], etc.).

In this paper, we study a new edge stabilization method, motivated by the one in [17]. Precisely, letting $\mathcal{F}_h^{int}$ be the set of the interior element faces, and h_F the diameter of element face F, and $\mathcal{F}_h^\partial$ the set of the element faces on $\partial\Omega$, we define the new edge stabilization as follows:

$$\mathscr{J}_h(u,v) = \sum_{F\in\mathcal{F}_h^{int}} \beta\tau_{int,F} \int_F [\![\nabla u \cdot \mathbf{n}]\!][\![\nabla v \cdot \mathbf{n}]\!] + \sum_{F\in\mathcal{F}_h^\partial} \alpha\tau_{\partial,F} \int_F (-\varepsilon\Delta u + \mathbf{b}\cdot\nabla u)(\mathbf{b}\cdot\nabla v).$$

(1.1)

Here α, β are positive constants, and $\tau_{int,F}, \tau_{\partial,F}$ are mesh-dependent parameters, which will be defined later. The role of $\tau_{int,F}, \tau_{\partial,F}$ is approximately the same as h_F^2. The new method is consistent in the usual sense (cf. [13,14]), and it allows higher-order elements to give higher-order convergent approximations, whenever the exact solution is smooth enough. The first stabilization term on the right of (1.1) is essentially the same as [17]. However, the additional second term on the right of (1.1) is crucial. It ensures that the new method can wholly control the term $\mathbf{b} \cdot \nabla u$ on every element and can give the same stability as the SUPG method. Differently, the stabilization in [17] cannot have the same stability. See further explanations later. We analyze the new method, and give the stability and error estimates. Numerical experiments are provided to illustrate the new method, also to compare it with the method in [17] and the SUPG method. As will be seen from the numerical results, in the presence of boundary and interior layers, the new edge stabilization method is much better than the method in [17] and is comparable to the SUPG method. In general, the new edge stabilization is more stable than the SUPG method.

2   Diffusion-Convection Equations

We study the following diffusion-convection problem: Find u such that

$$-\varepsilon \Delta u + \mathbf{b} \cdot \nabla u = f \quad \text{in } \Omega, \quad u = 0 \quad \text{on } \partial\Omega. \tag{2.1}$$

Here $\varepsilon > 0$ denotes the diffusive constant, $\mathbf{b}$ the convection/velocity field, and f the source function. The convection-dominated case means that $\varepsilon \ll \|\mathbf{b}\|_{L^\infty(\Omega)}$; or, the dimensionless quantity *Peclet number*: $Pe = VL/\varepsilon$ is very large. Here V and L are the characteristic velocity and the length scales of the problem. In this paper, we shall use the standard Sobolev spaces [13]. The standard Galerkin variational problem is to find $u \in H_0^1(\Omega)$ such that

$$A(u,v) := \varepsilon(\nabla u, \nabla v)_{L^2(\Omega)} + (\mathbf{b} \cdot \nabla u, v)_{L^2(\Omega)} = (f,v)_{L^2(\Omega)} \quad \forall v \in H_0^1(\Omega). \tag{2.2}$$

From (2.2), the finite element method reads as follows: find $u_h \in U_h \subset H_0^1(\Omega)$ such that

$$A(u_h, v_h) = (f, v_h) \quad \forall v_h \in U_h. \tag{2.3}$$

It has been widely recognized whether (2.3) performs well or not depends on whether the following discrete Peclet number is large or not:

$$Pe_h = \|\mathbf{b}\|_{L^\infty(\Omega)} h/\varepsilon \quad \text{discrete Peclet number}, \tag{2.4}$$

where h is the mesh size of the triangulation $\mathcal{T}_h$ of Ω. We assume that Ω is partitioned into a family of triangles, denoted by $\mathcal{T}_h$ for $h > 0$ and $h \to 0$, such that $\bar{\Omega} = \cup_{T \in \mathcal{T}_h} \bar{T}$. The mesh size $h := \max_{T \in \mathcal{T}_h} h_T$, where h_T denotes the diameter of the triangle element $T \in \mathcal{T}_h$. Concretely, letting P_ℓ denote the space of polynomials of degree not greater than the integer $\ell \geq 1$.

$$U_h = \{v_h \in H_0^1(\Omega) : v_h|_T \in P_\ell(T), \forall T \in \mathcal{T}_h, v_h|_{\partial\Omega} = 0\}. \tag{2.5}$$

3   Edge Stabilization

In this paper, we shall consider a stabilized $A_h(\cdot, \cdot)$ by the residual of the normal derivatives of the exact solution, i.e.,

$$[\![\nabla u \cdot \mathbf{n}]\!] = 0 \quad \forall F \in \mathcal{F}_h^{int}, \tag{3.1}$$

and the residual of the partial differential equation (2.1), i.e.,

$$-\varepsilon \Delta u + \mathbf{b} \cdot \nabla u - f = 0 \quad \forall T \in \mathcal{T}_h. \tag{3.2}$$

Corresponding to the new edge stabilization (1.1), we define the right-hand side as follows:

$$\mathscr{L}_h(v) = \sum_{F \in \mathcal{F}_h^\partial} \alpha \tau_{\partial, F} \int_F f(\mathbf{b} \cdot \nabla v), \tag{3.3}$$

where, denoting by h_F the diameter of F,

$$\tau_{int,F} := \frac{h_F^3 \|\mathbf{b}\|_{L^\infty(F)}^2}{\|\mathbf{b}\|_{L^\infty(F)} h_F + \varepsilon}, \quad \tau_{\partial,F} := \frac{h_F^3}{\|\mathbf{b}\|_{L^\infty(F)} h_F + \varepsilon}. \tag{3.4}$$

The stabilizing parameters $\tau_{\partial,F}$ and $\tau_{int,F}$ are motivated by [9,10,16].

Now, the new edge stabilized finite element method is to find $u_h \in U_h$ such that

$$A_h(u_h, v_h) := A(u_h, v_h) + \mathscr{J}_h(u_h, v_h) = R_h(v_h) := (f, v_h)_{L^2(\Omega)} + \mathscr{L}_h(v_h) \quad \forall v_h \in U_h. \tag{3.5}$$

This method is consistent, i.e., letting u be the exact solution of (2.1), we have

$$A_h(u, v_h) = R_h(v_h) \quad \forall v_h \in U_h. \tag{3.6}$$

4   Stability and Error Estimates

Without loss of generality, we assume that div $\mathbf{b} = 0$.

Define

$$|||u_h|||_h^2 := \varepsilon \|\nabla u_h\|_{L^2(\Omega)}^2 + \sum_{T \in \mathcal{T}_h} \tau_T \|\mathbf{b} \cdot \nabla u_h\|_{L^2(T)}^2$$

$$+ \sum_{F \in \mathcal{F}_h^{int}} \beta \tau_{int,F} \int_F |[\![\nabla u_h \cdot \mathbf{n}]\!]|^2 + \sum_{F \in \mathcal{F}_h^\partial} \alpha \tau_{\partial,F} \int_F |\mathbf{b} \cdot \nabla u_h|^2,$$

where

$$\tau_T = \frac{h_T^2}{\|\mathbf{b}\|_{L^\infty(\Omega)} h_T + \varepsilon}.$$

Now we can prove the following Inf-Sup condition.

Theorem 1. *([27])   The Inf-Sup condition*

$$\sup_{v_h \in U_h} \frac{A_h(u_h, v_h)}{|||v_h|||_h} \geq C |||u_h|||_h \quad \forall u_h \in U_h$$

holds, where the constant C is independent of $h, \varepsilon, \mathbf{b}, u_h$, only depending on Ω and ℓ.

The above result crucially relies on the following Lemma 1.

Denote by $W_h = \{w_h \in L^2(\Omega) : w_h|_T \in P_{\ell-1}(T), \forall T \in \mathcal{T}_h\}$, and let $W_h^c = W_h \cap H_0^1(\Omega) \subset U_h$. Introduce the jump of v across $F \in \mathcal{F}_h$. If $F \in \mathcal{F}_h^{int}$, which is the common side of two elements T^+ and T^-, denoting the both sides of F by F^+ and F^-, we define the jump $[\![v]\!] = (v|_{T^+})|_{F^+} - (v|_{T^-})|_{F^-}$. If $F \in \mathcal{F}_h^\partial$, letting T be such that $F \subset \partial T$, we define the jump $[\![v]\!] = (v|_T)|_F$.

Lemma 1. *For any $w_h \in W_h$, there exists a $w_h^c \in W_h^c$, which can be constructed by the averaging approach from w_h, such that, for all $T \in \mathcal{T}_h$,*

$$||w_h - w_h^c||_{L^2(T)} \le Ch_T^{1/2} \sum_{F \subset \partial T} ||[[w_h]]||_{L^2(F)}.$$

For a linear element, the argument for constructing the finite element function $w_h^c \in W_h^c$ from the discontinuous $w_h \in W_h$ through a nodal averaging approach can be found in [25]. For higher-order elements, we refer to [24] (see Theorem 2.2 on page 2378) for a general nodal averaging approach. An earlier reference is [26], where a similar nodal averaging operator can be found. In [17], a proof is also given to prove a similar result for any $w_h|_T := h_T \mathbf{b} \cdot \nabla u_h$ for all $T \in \mathcal{T}_h$, but there is a fault. In fact, the authors therein made the mistake in those elements whose sides locate on $\partial \Omega$, e.g., for $T \in \mathcal{T}_h$ with three sides F_1, F_2, F_3, letting $F_1 \in \mathcal{F}_h^\partial$ and $F_2, F_3 \in \mathcal{F}_h^{int}$,

$$||w_h^c - w_h||_{L^2(T)} \le Ch_T^{1/2} \sum_{\substack{F \subset \partial T \\ F \in \mathcal{F}_h^{int}}} ||[[w_h]]||_{L^2(F)} = Ch_T^{1/2} \sum_{F_2, F_3} ||[[w_h]]||_{L^2(F)}.$$

This result can hold only for $w_h|_{\partial \Omega} = 0$. In general, it is not necessarily true that $w_h = 0$ on $\partial \Omega$. Of course, for some problems, say, nonlinear Navier-Stokes equations of the no-slip Dirichlet velocity boundary condition, the convection field $\mathbf{b}$ is the velocity itself of the flow, trivially $\mathbf{b}|_{\partial \Omega} = \mathbf{0}$, and consequently, the result of [17] will be correct. Now, it is clear the reason why we introduce the second stabilization on $\partial \Omega$ on the right of (1.1). With this stabilization, we can obtain the result in Lemma 1 to correct the one of [17] and ensure that the new method is still consistent as usual. If the method is consistent, for a higher-order element (applicable when the exact solution is smooth enough), a higher-order convergence can be obtained.

Theorem 2. *([27]) Let u and u_h be the exact solution and finite element solution of (2.1) and (3.6), respectively. Then,*

$$|||u - u_h|||_h \le C \left(\left(\varepsilon^{1/2} h^\ell + (||\mathbf{b}||_{L^\infty(\Omega)} h + \varepsilon)^{1/2} h^\ell \right) |u|_{H^{\ell+1}(\Omega)} \right.$$
$$\left. + (||\mathbf{b}||_{L^\infty(\Omega)} h + \varepsilon)^{-1/2} ||\mathbf{b}||_{L^\infty(\Omega)} h^{\ell+1} |u|_{H^{\ell+1}(\Omega)} + \varepsilon^{1/2} h^{\ell+1} |\Delta u|_{H^\ell(\Omega)} \right).$$

In the case of convection-dominated case, i.e., $Pe_h \gg 1$, or $\varepsilon \ll ||\mathbf{b}||_{L^\infty(\Omega)} h$, we find that

$$|||u - u_h|||_h \le C(\varepsilon^{1/2} h^\ell + ||\mathbf{b}||_{L^\infty(\Omega)}^{1/2} h^{\ell+1/2}) |u|_{H^{\ell+1}(\Omega)} + C\varepsilon^{1/2} h^{\ell+1} |\Delta u|_{H^\ell(\Omega)}.$$

Denote by

$$||v||_{SUPG}^2 := \varepsilon ||\nabla v||_{L^2(\Omega)}^2 + \sum_{T \in \mathcal{T}_h} \tau_T ||\mathbf{b} \cdot \nabla v||_{L^2(T)}^2$$

the norm which is often used in the SUPG method or other methods such as the residual-free bubble method (or which is equivalent to the norms used in the literature for the SUPG method and other methods, at least, in the convection-dominated case of $Pe_h \gg 1$). Using this norm, we restate the above error bounds as follows:

$$||u - u_h||_{\mathrm{SUPG}} \leq (\varepsilon^{1/2}h^\ell + ||\mathbf{b}||_{L^\infty(\Omega)}^{1/2} h^{\ell+1/2})|u|_{H^{\ell+1}(\Omega)} + C\varepsilon^{1/2}h^{\ell+1}|\Delta u|_{H^\ell(\Omega)}.$$

In comparison with the SUPG method, here the error bounds are essentially the same [15], only up to a higher-order error bound $C\varepsilon^{1/2}h^{\ell+1}|\Delta u|_{H^\ell(\Omega)}$. Therefore, the new edge stabilization method in this paper is theoretically comparable to the SUPG method. The numerical results will further show that the new edge stabilization method is comparable to the SUPG method. Moreover, in the new edge stabilization method, we have more stability than the SUPG method, i.e., the stability is measured in the norm $||| \cdot |||_h$, where the jump of the normal derivatives of the solution (including the normal derivatives of the solution on $\partial\Omega$) are controlled. Numerically, for some meshes, the new edge stabilization method is indeed more stable than the SUPG method.

In comparison with the edge stabilization method [17], we have already observed the advantages of the new method in this paper. Theoretical results have confirmed the observations. Numerical results will further give the supports.

5   Numerical Experiments

In this section, we give some numerical results for illustrating the performance of the new edge stabilization method, the SUPG method and the edge stabilization method [17] for solving the convection-dominated diffusion-convection equations with boundary and inner layers.

We study two types of meshes as shown in Fig. 1. In the first case (denoted mesh-1) the square elements are cut into two triangles approximately along the direction of the convection; in the second case (mesh-2) they are cut almost perpendicular to the direction of the convection. We choose domain $\Omega := (0,1)^2$, the convection field $|\mathbf{b}| = 1$ which is constant, $f = 0$, and nonhomogeneous boundary condition $u|_{\partial\Omega} = U$. The geometry, the boundary conditions and the orientation of $\mathbf{b}$ are shown in Fig. 2. At $h = 1/64$ and $\varepsilon = 10^{-5}$ and $\varepsilon = 10^{-8}$, using the linear element, we have computed the finite element solutions using three methods: SUPG method, BH method [17], New method in this paper. For mesh-1, the elevations and contours are given by Figs. 3 and 4. For mesh-2, the elevations and contours are given by Figs. 5 and 6. For mesh-1, from Figs. 3 and 4, we clearly see that the New method is comparable to the SUPG method and is much better than the BH method. For mesh-2, from Figs. 5 and 6, we clearly see that the New method is better than the SUPG method and is still much better than the BH method.

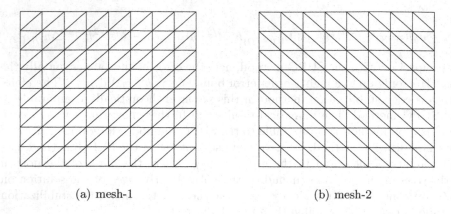

(a) mesh-1   (b) mesh-2

Fig. 1. Meshes

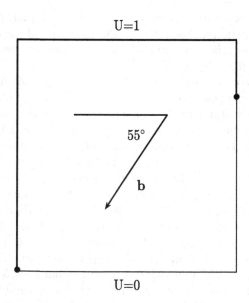

Fig. 2. Boundary conditions and flow orientation: $U = 1$ thick edge and $U = 0$ thin edge.

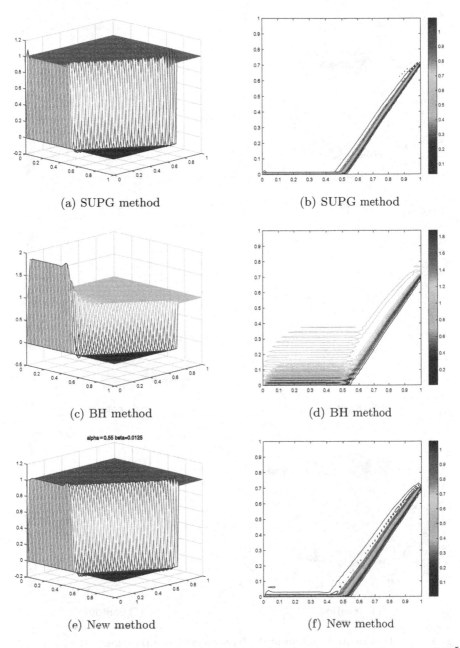

(a) SUPG method

(b) SUPG method

(c) BH method

(d) BH method

(e) New method

(f) New method

Fig. 3. The elevation and contour of the finite element solution, mesh-1, $\varepsilon = 10^{-5}$, $h = 1/64$.

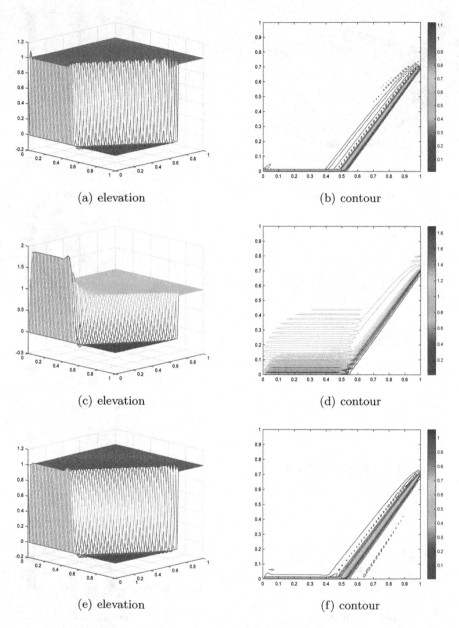

(a) elevation

(b) contour

(c) elevation

(d) contour

(e) elevation

(f) contour

Fig. 4. The elevation and contour of the finite element solution, mesh-1, $\varepsilon = 10^{-8}, h = 1/64$.

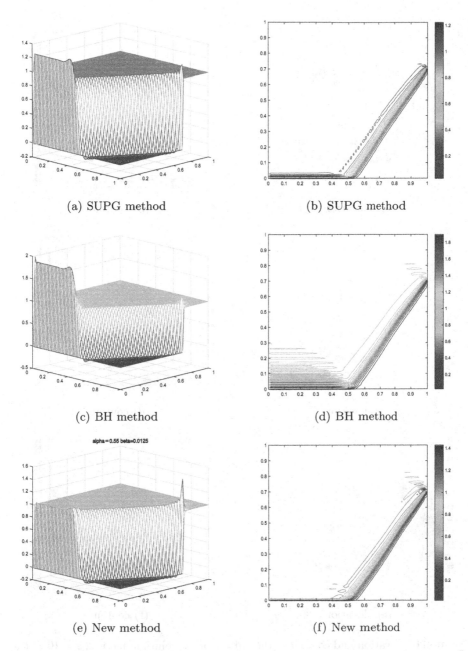

(a) SUPG method

(b) SUPG method

(c) BH method

(d) BH method

(e) New method

(f) New method

Fig. 5. The elevation and contour of the finite element solution, mesh-2, $\varepsilon = 10^{-5}$, $h = 1/64$.

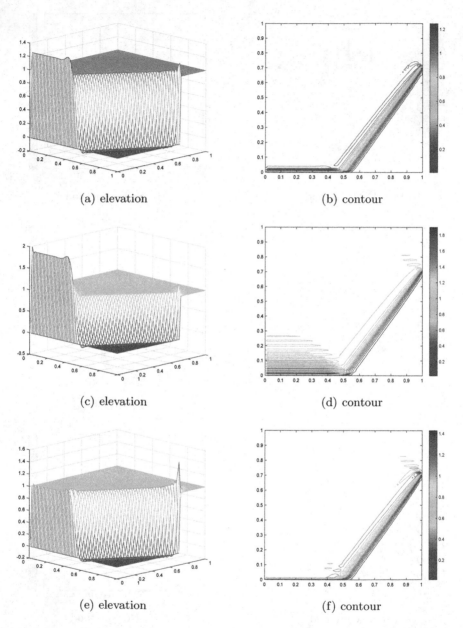

(a) elevation

(b) contour

(c) elevation

(d) contour

(e) elevation

(f) contour

Fig. 6. The elevation and contour of the finite element solution, mesh-2, $\varepsilon = 10^{-8}, h = 1/64$.

References

1. Douglas Jr., J., Dupont, T.: Interior penalty procedures for elliptic and parabolic Galerkin methods. In: Glowinski, R., Lions, J.L. (eds.) Computing Methods in Applied Sciences. LNP, vol. 58, pp. 207–216. Springer, Heidelberg (1976). https://doi.org/10.1007/BFb0120591
2. Knobloch, P., Lube, G.: Local projection stabilization for advection-diffusion-reaction problems: one-level vs. two-level approach. Appl. Numer. Math. **59**, 2891–2907 (2009)
3. Roos, H.-G., Stynes, M., Tobiska, L.: Robust Numerical Methods for Singularly Perturbed Differential Equations: Convection-Diffusion-Reaction and Flow Problems. Springer, Heidelberg (2008). https://doi.org/10.1007/978-3-540-34467-4
4. Franca, L.P., Frey, S.L., Hughes, T.J.R.: Stabilized finite element methods: I. Application to the advective-diffusive model. Comput. Methods Appl. Mech. Eng. **95**, 253–276 (1992)
5. Hsieh, P.-W., Yang, S.-Y.: On efficient least-squares finite element methods for convection-dominated problems. Comput. Methods Appl. Mech. Eng. **199**, 183–196 (2009)
6. Hughes, T.J.R.: Multiscale phenomena: green's functions, the Dirichlet-to-Neumann formulation, subgrid scale models, bubbles and the origins of stabilized methods. Comput. Methods Appl. Mech. Eng. **127**, 387–401 (1995)
7. Hughes, T.J.R., Mallet, M., Mizukami, A.: A new finite element formulation for computational fluid dynamics: II. Beyond SUPG. Comput. Methods Appl. Mech. Eng. **54**, 341–355 (1986)
8. Hsieh, P.-W., Yang, S.-Y.: A novel least-squares finite element method enriched with residual-free bubbles for solving convection-dominated problems. SIAM J. Sci. Comput. **32**, 2047–2073 (2010)
9. Duan, H.Y.: A new stabilized finite element method for solving the advection-diffusion equations. J. Comput. Math. **20**, 57–64 (2002)
10. Duan, H.Y., Hsieh, P.-W., Tan, R.C.E., Yang, S.-Y.: Analysis of a new stabilized finite element method for solving the reaction-advection-diffusion equations with a large recation coefficient. Comput. Methods Appl. Mech. Eng. **247–248**, 15–36 (2012)
11. Hauke, G., Sangalli, G., Doweidar, M.H.: Combining adjoint stabilized methods for the advection-diffusion-reaction problem. Math. Models Methods Appl. Sci. **17**, 305–326 (2007)
12. Johnson, C.: Numerical Solution of Partial Differential Equations by the Finite Element Method. Cambridge University Press, Cambridge (1987)
13. Ciarlet, P.G.: The Finite Element Method for Elliptic Problems. North-Holland Publishing Company, Amsterdam (1978)
14. Quarteroni, A., Valli, A.: Numerical Approximation of Partial Differential Equations. Springer, Heidelberg (1994). https://doi.org/10.1007/978-3-540-85268-1
15. Brezzi, F., Hughes, T.J.R., Marini, D., Russo, A., Suli, E.: A priori error analysis of a finite element method with residual-free bubbles for advection dominated equations. SIAM J. Numer. Anal. **36**, 1933–1948 (1999)
16. Duan, H.Y., Qiu, F.J.: A new stabilized finite element method for advection-diffusion-reaction equations. Numer. Methods Partial Differ. Equ. **32**, 616–645 (2016)
17. Burman, E., Hansbo, P.: Edge stabilization for Galerkin approximations of convection-diffusion-reaction problems. Comput. Methods Appl. Mech. Eng. **193**, 1437–1453 (2004)

18. Burman, E., Hansbo, P.: Edge stabilization for the generalized Stokes problem: a continuous interior penalty method. Comput. Methods Appl. Mech. Eng. **195**, 2393–2410 (2006)
19. Burman, E., Ern, A.: A nonlinear consistent penalty method weakly enforcing positivity in the finite element approximation of the transport equation. Comput. Methods Appl. Mech. Eng. **320**, 122–132 (2017)
20. Burman, E., Ern, A.: Continuous interior penalty hp-finite element methods for advection and advection-diffusion equations. Math. Comput. **76**, 1119–1140 (2007)
21. Burman, E., Schieweck, F.: Local CIP stabilization for composite finite elements. SIAM J. Numer. Anal. **54**, 1967–1992 (2016)
22. Hughes, T.J.R., Franca, L.P., Hulbert, G.: A new finite element formulation for computational fluid dynamics: VIII. The Galerkin/least-squares method for advective-diffusive equations. Comput. Methods Appl. Mech. Eng. **73**, 173–189 (1989)
23. Chen, H., Fu, G., Li, J., Qiu, W.: First order least squares method with weakly imposed boundary condition for convection dominated diffusion problems. Comput. Math. Appl. **68**, 1635–1652 (2014)
24. Karakashian, O.A., Pascal, F.: A posteriori error estimates for a discontinuous Galerkin approximation of second-order elliptic problems. SIAM J. Numer. Anal. **41**, 2374–2399 (2003)
25. Brenner, S.C.: Korn's inequalities for piecewise H1 vector fields. Math. Comput. **73**, 1067–1087 (2004)
26. Oswald, P.: On a BPX-preconditioner for P1 elements. Compututing **51**, 125–133 (1993)
27. Duan, H.Y., Wei, Y.: A new edge stabilization method. Preprint and Report, Wuhan University, China (2018)

Symmetric Sweeping Algorithms for Overlaps of Quadrilateral Meshes of the Same Connectivity

Xihua Xu[1] and Shengxin Zhu[2](✉)

[1] Institute of Applied Physics and Computational Mathematics, Beijing 10088, China
[2] Department of Mathematics, Xi'an Jiaotong-Liverpool University, Suzhou 215123, China
Shengxin.Zhu@xjtlu.edu.cn
https://www.researchgate.net/profile/Shengxin_Zhu

Abstract. We propose a method to calculate intersections of two admissible quadrilateral meshes of the same connectivity. The global quadrilateral polygons intersection problem is reduced to a local problem that how an edge intersects with a *local frame* which consists 7 connected edges. A classification on the types of intersection is presented. By symmetry, an alternative direction sweep algorithm halves the searching space. It reduces more than 256 possible cases of polygon intersection to 34 (17 when considering symmetry) programmable cases of edge intersections. Besides, we show that the complexity depends on how the old and new mesh intersect.

Keywords: Computational geometry · Intersections
Arbitrary Lagrangian Eulerian · Remapping · Quadrilateral mesh

1 Introduction

A remapping scheme for Arbitrary Lagrangian Eulerian(ALE) methods often requires intersections between the old and new mesh [1,2]. The aim of this paper is to articulate the mathematical formulation of this problem. For admissible quadrilateral meshes of the same connectivity, we show that the mesh intersection problem can be reduced to a local problem that how an edge intersects with a *local frame* which consists of 7 edges. According to our classification on the types of intersections, An optimal algorithm to compute these intersections can be applied [3,4]. The overlap area between the new and old mesh, and the union of the fluxing/swept area can be traveled in $O(n)$ time (Theorem 1), where n is the number of elements in the underlying mesh or tessellation. When there is non degeneracy of the overlapped region, the present approach only requires 34 programming cases (17 when considering symmetry), while the classical *Cell Intersection Based Donor Cell* CIB/DC approach requires 98 programming

Xihua Xu's research is supported by the Natural Science Foundation of China (NSFC) (No.11701036). Shengxin Zhu's research is supported by NSFC(No. 11501044), Jiangsu Science and Technology Basic Research Programme (BK20171237) and partially supported by NSFC (No.11571002,11571047,11671049,11671051,61672003).

© Springer International Publishing AG, part of Springer Nature 2018
Y. Shi et al. (Eds.): ICCS 2018, LNCS 10862, pp. 61–75, 2018.
https://doi.org/10.1007/978-3-319-93713-7_5

cases [5,6]. When consider degeneracy, more benefit can be obtained. The degeneracy of the intersection depends on the so called *singular intersection points* and impacts the computational complexity. As far as we known this is the first result on how the computational complexity depends on the underlying problem.

2 Preliminary

A *tessellation* $\mathcal{T} = \{T_j\}_{j=1}^n$ of a domain Ω is a partition of Ω such that $\bar{\Omega} = \cup_{i=1}^N T_i$ and $\dot{T}_i \cap \dot{T}_j = \emptyset$, where $\dot{T}_i$ is the interior of the cell T_j and $\bar{\Omega}$ is the closure of Ω. An *admissible* tessellation has no hanging node on any edge of the tessellation. Precisely, T_i and T_j can only share a common vertex or a common edge. We use the conversional notation as follows:

- $P_{i,j}$, for $i = 1 : M, j = 1 : N$ are the vertices;
- $F_{i+\frac{1}{2},j}$ for $i = 1 : M - 1, j = 1 : N$ and $F_{i,j+\frac{1}{2}}$ for $i = 1 : M, j = 1 : N - 1$ are the edges between vertices $P_{i,j}$ and $P_{i+1,j}$;
- $C_{i+\frac{1}{2},j+\frac{1}{2}}$ stands for the quadrilateral cell $P_{i,j}P_{i,j+1}P_{i+1,j+1}P_{i,j+1}$ for $1 \le i \le M - 1$ and $1 \le j \le N + 1$. $C_{i+\frac{1}{2},j+\frac{1}{2}}$ is an element of $\mathcal{T}$, we denote it as $T_{i,j}$;
- $x_i(t)$ is the piecewise curve which consists all the face of $F_{i,j+\frac{1}{2}}$ for $j = 1 : N - 1$, $y_j(t)$ is the piece wise curve which consists all the faces of $F_{i+\frac{1}{2},j}$ for $i = 1 : M - 1$.

Let $\mathcal{T}^a$ and $\mathcal{T}^b$ be two admissible quadrilateral meshes. The vertices of $\mathcal{T}^a$ and $\mathcal{T}^b$ are denoted as $P_{i,j}$ and $Q_{i,j}$ respectively, if there is a one-to-one map between $P_{i,j}$ and $Q_{i,j}$, then the two tessellations share the same *logical structure* or *connectivity*. We assume the two admissible meshes of the connectivity $\mathcal{T}^a$ and $\mathcal{T}^b$ have the following property:

A1. *Vertex $Q_{i,j}$ of $\mathcal{T}^b$ can only lie in the interior of the union of the cells $C^a_{i\pm\frac{1}{2},j\pm\frac{1}{2}}$ of $\mathcal{T}^a$.*

A2. *Curve $x_i^b(t)$ has at most one intersection point with $y_j^a(t)$, so does for $y_j^b(t)$ and $x_i^a(t)$.*

A3. *The intersection of edges between the old and new meshes lies in the middle of the two edges.*

For convenience, we also introduce the following notation and definition.

Definition 1. *A local patch $\mathbb{P}_{i,j}$ of an admissible quadrilateral mesh consists an element $T_{i,j}$ and its neighbours in $\mathcal{T}$. Take an interior element of $T_{i,j}$ as an example,*

$$\mathbb{P}_{i,j} := \{T_{i,j}, T_{i\pm1,j}, T_{i,j\pm1}, T_{i\pm1,j\pm1}\}. \tag{1}$$

The index set of $\mathbb{P}_{i,j}$ are denoted by $\mathcal{J}_{i,j} = \{(k, s) : T_{k,s} \in \mathbb{P}_{i,j}\}$.

Definition 2. *An invading set of the element $T_{i,j}^b$ with respect to the local patch $\mathbb{P}_{i,j}^a$ is defined as $I_{i,j}^b = (T_{i,j}^b \cap \mathbb{P}_{i,j}^a)\backslash(T_{i,j}^b \cap T_{i,j}^a)$. An occupied set of the element $T_{i,j}^a$ with respect to the local patch $\mathbb{P}_{i,j}^b$ is defined as $O_{i,j}^a = (T_{i,j}^a \cap \mathbb{P}_{i,j}^b)\backslash(T_{i,j}^a \cap T_{i,j}^b)$.*

Definition 3. *A swept area or fluxing area is the area which is enclosed by a quadrilateral polygon with an edge in $\mathcal{T}^a$ and its counterpart edge in $\mathcal{T}^b$. For example, the swept area enclosed by the quadrilateral polygon with edges $F^a_{i+\frac{1}{2},j}$ and $F^b_{i+\frac{1}{2},j}$ are denoted as $\partial F_{i+\frac{1}{2},j}$. $\partial^{b+} F_{k,s}$ stands for boundary of the fluxing/swept area $\partial F_{k,s}$ is ordered such that direction of edges of the cell $T^b_{i,j}$ are counterclockwise in the cell $T^b_{i,j}$. Precisely*

$$\partial^{b+} F_{i+\frac{1}{2},j} = Q_{i,j}Q_{i,j+1}P_{i,j+1}P_{i,j}, \qquad \partial^{b+} F_{i+1,j+\frac{1}{2}} = Q_{i+1,j}Q_{i+1,j+1}P_{i+1,j+1}P_{i+1,j},$$

$$\partial^{b+} F_{i,j+\frac{1}{2}} = Q_{i,j+1}Q_{i,j}P_{i,j}P_{i,j+1}, \qquad \partial^{b+} F_{i+\frac{1}{2},j+1} = Q_{i+1,j+1}Q_{i,j+1}P_{i+1,j+1}P_{i,j+1}.$$

where $Q_{i,j}Q_{i+1,j}Q_{i+1,j+1}Q_{i,j+1}$ are in the counterclockwise order.

The invading set $I^b_{i,j}$ has no interior intersection with the occupied set $O^a_{i,j}$, while the fluxing area associated to two connect edges can be overlapped. The invading and occupied sets consist of the whole intersection between an old cell and a new cell, while corners of a fluxing area may only be part of an intersection between an old cell and a new cell. Figure 1(a), (b) and (c) illustrate such differences. In a local patch, the union of the occupied and invading set is a subset of the union of the swept/fluxing area of a home cell $T^a_{i,j}$. However, the difference (extra corner area), if any, will be self-canceled when summing all the *signed* fluxing area, see the north-west and south-east color region in Fig. 1(b) and (c).

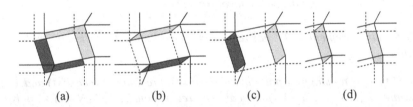

(a)   (b)   (c)   (d)

Fig. 1. (a) the invading set $I^b_{i,j}$ (red) and occupied set $O^a_{i,j}$. (b) the swept/fluxing area $\partial F_{i\pm\frac{1}{2},j}$. (c) The swept/fluxing area $\partial F_{i,j\pm\frac{1}{2}}$. (d) the swept area (left) v.s. the local swap set (right) in a local frame. Solid lines for old mesh and dash lines for new mesh. (Color figure online)

Definition 4. *A local frame consists an edge and its neighbouring edges. Taking the edge $F_{i,j+\frac{1}{2}}$ as an example, $\mathit{lF}_{i,j+\frac{1}{2}} = \{F_{i,j\pm\frac{1}{2}}, F_{i,j+\frac{3}{2}}, F_{i\pm\frac{1}{2},j}, F_{i\pm\frac{1}{2},j+1}\}$.*

Figure 2(b) illustrates the local frame $\mathit{lF}_{i,j+\frac{1}{2}}$.

Definition 5. *The region between the two curves $x^a_i(t)$ and $x^b_i(t)$ in Ω is defined as a vertical swap region. The region between $y^a_j(t)$ and $y^b_j(t)$ is defined as a horizontal swap region. The region enclosed by $x^a_i(t), x^b_i(t), y^b_j(t)$ and $y^b_{j+1}(t)$ is referred to as a local swap region in the local frame $\mathit{lF}_{i,j+\frac{1}{2}}$.*

Definition 6. *The intersection points between $x^a_i(t)$ and $x^b_i(t)$ or $y^a_j(t)$ and $y^b_j(t)$ are referred to as singular intersection points. The total number of singular intersections between $x^a_i(t)$ and $x^a_i(t)$ is denoted as ns_{xx} for $1 \leq i \leq M$, and the total singular intersection points between $y^a_j(t)$ and $y^b_j(t)$ is denoted as ns_{yy}.*

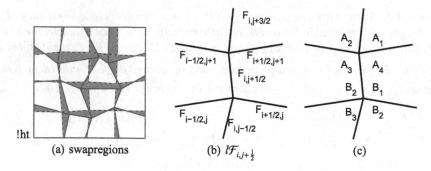

(a) swapregions   (b) $I\!F_{i,j+\frac{1}{2}}$ (c)

Fig. 2. Illustration of the swept/swap region and the local frame

3 Facts and Results

Let $\mathcal{T}^a$ and $\mathcal{T}^b$ be two admissible quadrilateral meshes with the Assumption A1, then the following facts hold

Fact 1 *The element $T^b_{i,j}$ of $\mathcal{T}^b$ locates in the interior of a local patch $I\!P^a_{i,j}$ of $\mathcal{T}^a$.*

Fact 2 *The face $F^b_{i,j+\frac{1}{2}}$ locates in the local frame $I\!F^a_{i,j+\frac{1}{2}}$.*

Fact 3 *An inner element of $\mathcal{T}^b$ has at least 4^4 possible ways to intersect with a local patch in $\mathcal{T}^a$.*

Fact 4 *If there is no singular point in the local swap region between $x^a_i(t)$ and $x^b_i(t)$ in Ω for some $i \in \{2, 3, \ldots, M-1\}$, the local swap region consists of $2(N-1)-1$ polygons. Each singular intersection point in the swap region will bring one more polygon.*

3.1 Basic Lemma

The following results serve as the basis of the CIB/DC and FB/DC methods.

Lemma 1. *Let $\mathcal{T}^a$ and $\mathcal{T}^b$ be two admissible meshes of the same structure. Under the assumption A1, we have*

$$\mu(T^b_{i,j}) = \mu(T^a_{ij}) - \mu(O^a_{i,j}) + \mu(I^b_{i,j}), \tag{2}$$

where $\mu(\cdot)$ is the area of the underlying set, $I^b_{i,j}$ is the invading set of $T^b_{i,j}$ and $O^a_{i,j}$ is the occupied set of $T^a_{i,j}$ in Definition 2.

$$\mu(T^b_{i,j}) = \mu(T^a_{i,j}) + \vec{\mu}(\partial F^{b+}_{i+\frac{1}{2},j}) + \vec{\mu}(\partial^{b+} F_{i+1,j+\frac{1}{2}}) + \vec{\mu}(\partial F^{b+}_{i+\frac{1}{2},j+1}) + \vec{\mu}(\partial^{b+} F_{i,j+\frac{1}{2}}), \tag{3}$$

where $\vec{\mu}$ stands for the signed area calculated by directional line integrals.

Proof. See [1] for details.

Suppose a density function is a piecewise function on the tessellation $\mathcal{T}^a$ of Ω. To avoid the interior singularity, we have to calculate the mass on $T^b_{i,j}$ piecewisely to avoid interior singularity according to

$$\int_{T^b_{i,j}} \rho d\Omega = \sum_{(k,s)\in \mathcal{T}^a_{i,j}} \int_{T^b_{i,j}\cap T^a_{k,s}} \rho d\Omega = \int_{T^a_{i,j}} \rho d\Omega - \int_{I^b_{i,j}} \rho d\Omega - \int_{O^a_{i,j}} \rho d\Omega. \tag{4}$$

The following result is a directly consequence of Lemma 1.

Corollary 1. *Let $\mathcal{T}^a$ and $\mathcal{T}^b$ be two admissible quadrilateral meshes of Ω, and ρ is a piecewise function on $\mathcal{T}^a$, then the mass on each element of $\mathcal{T}^b$ satisfies*

$$m(T^b_{i,j}) = m(T^a_{i,j}) - m(O^a_{i,j}) + m(I^b_{i,j}). \tag{5}$$

and

$$m(T^b_{i,j}) = m(T^a_{i,j}) + \sum_{k,s} m(\partial^{b+} F_{k,s}). \tag{6}$$

where $(k, s) \in \{(i + \frac{1}{2}, j), (i + 1, j + \frac{1}{2}), (i + \frac{1}{2}, j + 1), (i, j + \frac{1}{2})\}$, $m(\partial^{b+} F_{k,s})$ is directional mass, the sign is consistent with the directional area of $\partial^{b+} F_{k,s}$.

The formulas (5) and (6) are the essential formulas for the CIB/DC method and FB/DC method respectively. It is easy to find that $\bigcup_{i,j} O^a_{i,j} = \bigcup_{i,j} I^b_{i,j} = \bigcup_{i,j}(\partial F_{i+\frac{1}{2},j} \cup \partial F_{i,j+\frac{1}{2}})$. This is the total swap region and the fluxing area. Since the swap region is nothing but the union of the the intersections between elements in $\mathcal{T}^a$ and $\mathcal{T}^b$.

Theorem 1. *Let $\mathcal{T}^a$ and $\mathcal{T}^b$ be two admissible quadrilateral meshes of a square in R^2 with the Assumption A1 and A2. ns_{xx} and ns_{yy} be the singular intersection numbers between the vertical and horizonal edges of the two meshes. If there is no common edge in the interior of Ω between $\mathcal{T}^a$ and $\mathcal{T}^b$. Then the swapping region of the two meshes consists of*

$$3(N - 1)(M - 1) - 2((M - 1) + (N - 1)) + 1 + ns_{xx} + ns_{yy}. \tag{7}$$

polygons.

Proof. See [1] for details.

Notice that $(N - 1)(M - 1)$ is the number of the elements of the tessellation of $\mathcal{T}^a$ and $\mathcal{T}^b$. Then (7) implies for the CIB/DC method, the swap region can be computed in $O(n)$ time when every the overall singular intersection points is bounded in $O(n)$, where n is the number of the cells. The complexity depends on the singular intersection points. Such singular intersection points depends on the underlying problem, for example, a rotating flow can bring such singular intersections.

Table 1. Cases of intersections of a vertical edge with a local frame

	Intersection # with horizonal/vertical frames (H#/V#)		
	H0	H1	H2
0	Shrunk	Shifted	Stretched
V1	Diagonally shrunk	Diagonally shifted	Diagonally stretched
V2	–	Shifted	Stretched
V3	–	–	Diagonally stretched

3.2   Intersection Between a Face and a Local Frame

For the two admissible meshes $\mathcal{T}^a$ and $\mathcal{T}^b$, we classify the intersections between a face $F^b_{i,j+\frac{1}{2}}$ and the local frame $l\mathcal{F}^a_{i,j+\frac{1}{2}}$ into six groups according to the relative position of the vertices $Q_{i,j}$ and $Q_{i,j+1}$ in the local frame $l\mathcal{F}^a_{i,j+\frac{1}{2}}$. The point $Q_{i,j+1}$ can locate in A_1, A_2, A_3 and A_4 in the local frame of $l\mathcal{F}_{i,j+\frac{1}{2}}$ in Fig. 2(c), and the point $Q_{i,j}$ can locate in B_1, B_2, B_3 and B_4 region. Compared with the face $F^a_{i,j+\frac{1}{2}}$, the face $F^b_{i,j+\frac{1}{2}}$ can be

- shifted: A_1B_1, A_2B_2, A_3B_3 and A_4, B_4;
- diagonally shifted: A_1B_2, A_2B_1, A_3B_2, and A_4B_3;
- shrunk: A_3B_2 and A_4B_1; diagonally shrunk: A_3B_1 and A_4B_3;
- stretched: A_1B_2 and A_2B_3; diagonally stretched: A_1B_3 and A_2B_4.

And then for each group, we choose one representative to describe the intersection numbers between the face $F^b_{i,j+\frac{1}{2}}$ and the local frame $l\mathcal{F}^a_{i,j+\frac{1}{2}}$. Finally, according to intersection numbers between $F^b_{i,j+\frac{1}{2}}$ and the horizonal/vertical edges in the local frame $l\mathcal{F}^a_{i,j+\frac{1}{2}}$, we classify the intersection cases into six groups in Table 1 and 17 symmetric cases in Fig. 3.

Fact 5 *Let $\mathcal{T}^a$ and $\mathcal{T}^b$ be two admissible quadrilateral meshes of the same structure. Under the assumption A1, A2 and A3, an inner edge $F^b_{i,j+\frac{1}{2}}$ of $\mathcal{T}^b$ has 17 symmetric ways to intersect with the local frame $l\mathcal{F}^a_{i,j+\frac{1}{2}}$. A swept/fluxing area has 17 possible symmetric cases with respect to the local frame.*

3.3   Fluxing/Swept Area and Local Swap Region in a Local Frame

For the FB/DC method, once the intersection between $F^b_{i,j+\frac{1}{2}}$ between $l\mathcal{F}^a_{i,j+\frac{1}{2}}$ is determined, then the shape of the swept area $\partial F_{i,j+\frac{1}{2}}$ will be determined. There are 17 symmetric cases as shown in Fig. 3. On contrast, the local swap region requires additional effort to be identified. The vertex $Q_{i,j}$ lies on the line segment $y^b_j(t)$, according the Assumption A2, $y^b_j(t)$ can only have one intersection with $x^a_i(t)$. This intersection point is referred to as V_1. The line segment $Q_{i,j}V_1$ can have 0 or 1 intersection with the local frame $l\mathcal{F}_{i,j+\frac{1}{2}}$ except V_1 itself; the intersection point, if any, will be denoted as V_2.

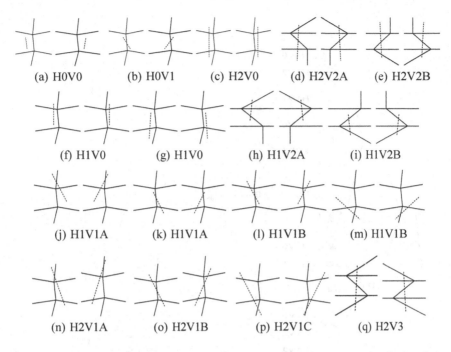

(a) H0V0   (b) H0V1   (c) H2V0   (d) H2V2A   (e) H2V2B

(f) H1V0   (g) H1V0   (h) H1V2A   (i) H1V2B

(j) H1V1A   (k) H1V1A   (l) H1V1B   (m) H1V1B

(n) H2V1A   (o) H2V1B   (p) H2V1C   (q) H2V3

Fig. 3. Intersections between a face (dashed line) and a local frame. (a) shrunk (b) diagonal shrunk, where $H0$ stands for the intersection number with horizontal edges is 0, $V1$ stands for the intersection number between the dash line and the vertical edge is 1.

The north and south boundary of the local swap region therefore can have 1 or 2 intersection with the local frame. Therefore each case in Fig. 3 results up to four possible local swap region. We use the intersection number between the up and south boundary and the local frame to classify the four cases, see Fig. 4 for an illustration. For certain cases, it is impossible for the point $Q_{i,j}V_1$ have two intersection points with the local frame, 98 possible combinations are illustrated in Fig. 5.

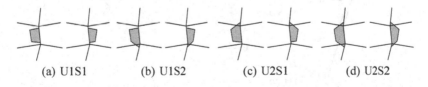

(a) U1S1   (b) U1S2   (c) U2S1   (d) U2S2

Fig. 4. The shapes of local swap region based on the case of H0V0 in Fig. 3, where $U1/U2$ stands for the face $Q_{i,j+1}Q_{i+1,j+1}$ or $Q_{i-1,j+1}Q_{i,j+1}$ has 1/2 intersections with the old local frame, while $S1/S2$ stands for the face $Q_{i,j-1}Q_{i+1,j-1}$ or $Q_{i-1,j-1}Q_{i-1,j}$ has 1/2 intersections with the old local frame.

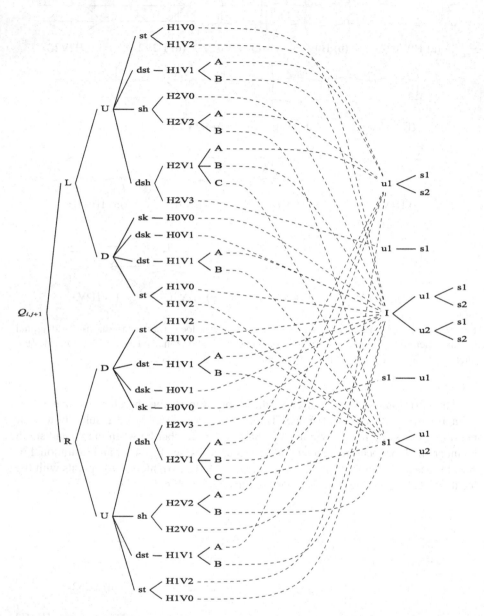

Fig. 5. Classification tree for all possible cases of a local swap region. $Q_{i+1,j+1}$ is on of the vertex of $F_{i,j+1/2}^b$, L, R U and D stand for the relative position of $Q_{i,j}$ in the local frame $\mathit{lF}_{i,j+\frac{1}{2}}^a$. The edge $F_{i,j+\frac{1}{2}}^b$ can be shifted(st), shrunk(sk), stretched(sh), diagonally shifted(dst), diagonally shrunk(dsk), and diagonally stretched(dsh).

Fact 6 *Let $\mathcal{T}^a$ and $\mathcal{T}^b$ be two admissible quadrilateral meshes of the same structure. Under the Assumption A1, A2 and A3, a local swap region has up 98 cases with respect to a local frame.*

Form the Fig. 1 in [6, 7], we shall see that Ramshaw's approach requires at least 98 programming cases. Under the assumption A1, A2 and A3, while the swept region approach requires only 34 programming cases. This is a significant improvement. When the assumption A3 fails, or the so called degeneracy of the overlapped region arises, more benefit can be obtained.

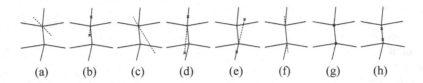

(a)   (b)   (c)   (d)   (e)   (f)   (g)   (h)

Fig. 6. Some degeneracy of the intersections. The swept/fluxing area for (a)–(e) degenerates to be a triangle plus a segment, for (f), (g) and (h), the intersection degenerate to a line segment. While for the swap region, an overlap line segment of a new edge and the old edge can be viewed a degeneracy of a quadrilaterals. A overlap of the horizontal and vertical intersection point can be viewed as the degeneracy of a triangular.

3.4   Degeneracy of the Intersection and Signed Area of a Polygon

The intersection between $T^b_{i,j}$ and $T^a_{k,s}$ for $(k, s) \in \mathcal{J}^a_{i,j}$ can be an polygon, an edge or even only a vertex. The degeneracy of the intersection was believed as one of the difficulty of the challenge of the CIB/DC method [8, p. 273]. In fact, some cases can be handled by the Green formula to calculate the planar polygon with line integrals. Suppose the vertices of a polygon are arranged in counterclockwise, say, $P_1 P_2, \ldots, P_s$, then it area can be calculated by

$$\iint dxdy = \oint_{\overrightarrow{P_1P_2}+\overrightarrow{P_2P_3}+\cdots+\overrightarrow{P_sP_1}} xdy = \frac{1}{2}\sum_{k=1}^{s-1}(x_k y_{k+1} - y_k x_{k+1}), \tag{8}$$

where $P_{s+1} = P_1$. This is due to the fact

$$\int_{\overrightarrow{P_1P_2}} xdy = \int_{x_1}^{x_2} x\frac{y_2 - y_1}{x_2 - x_1}dx = \frac{(y_2 - y_1)(x_1 + x_2)}{2}.$$

The formula (8) can handle any polygon including the degenerate cases: a polygon with $s+1$ vertices degenerate to one with s vertices, a triangle degenerates to a vertex or a quadrilateral polygonal degenerates to a line segment. Such degenerated cases arise when one or two vertices of the face $F^b_{i,j+\frac{1}{2}}$ lic on the local frame $l\mathcal{F}^a_{i,j+\frac{1}{2}}$, or the horizontal intersection points overlap with the vertical intersection points. The later cases bring no difficulty, while the cases when Q_{ij} locates in the vertical lines in the local frame or the face overlaps with partial of the vertical lines in the local frame do bring difficulties. To identify such degeneracies, one need more flags to identify whether such cases happens when calculating the intersections between face $F^b_{i,j+\frac{1}{2}}$ and $F^a_{i,j\pm\frac{1}{2}}$ and $F^a_{i,j+\frac{3}{2}}$.

Algorithm 1. Assign current new vertex to an old cell

    Compute A_1
    if $A_1 \geq 0$ **then**
        Compute A_2
        if $A_2 \leq 0$ **then**
            return flag='RU';   ▷ $Q_{i,j} \in C_{i+\frac{1}{2},j+\frac{1}{2}}$
        else
            Compute A_3
            if $A_3 \geq 0$ **then**
                return flag='LU';   ▷ $Q_{i,j} \in C_{i-\frac{1}{2},j+\frac{1}{2}}$
            else
                return flag='LD';   ▷ $Q_{i,j} \in C_{i-\frac{1}{2},j-\frac{1}{2}}$
            end if
        end if
    else
        Compute A_4
        if $A_4 \leq 0$ **then**
            return flag='RD';   ▷ $Q_{i,j} \in C_{i+\frac{1}{2},j-\frac{1}{2}}$
        else
            Compute A_3
            if $A_3 < 0$ **then**
                return flag='LD';   ▷ $Q_{i,j} \in C_{i-\frac{1}{2},j-\frac{1}{2}}$
            else
                return flag='LU';   ▷ $Q_{i,j} \in C_{i-\frac{1}{2},j+\frac{1}{2}}$
            end if
        end if
    end if

3.5 Assign a New Vertex to an Old Cell

As shown in Fig. 5, the relative position of a new vertex in an old local frame is the basis to classify all the intersections. This can also be obtained by the Green formula for the singed area of a polygon. We denote the signed area of $P_{i,j}P_{i+1,j}Q_{i,j}$ as A_1, $P_{i,j}P_{i,j+1}Q_{i,j}$ as A_2, $P_{i-1,j}P_{i,j}Q_{i,j}$ as A_3 and $P_{i,j-1}P_{i,j}Q_{i,j}$ as A_4. Then the vertex $Q_{i,j}$ can be assigned according to Algorithm 1. This determines the first two level (left) of branches of the classification tree in Fig. 5.

3.6 Alternative Direction Sweeping

To calculate all intersections in the swap area and swept/fluxing area, we can apply the alternative direction idea: view the union of the swap area between two admissible quadrilateral meshes of a domain as the union of (logically) vertical strips (shadowed region in Fig. 7(b)) and horizontal strips (shadowed area in Fig. 7(c)). One can alternatively sweep the vertical and horizontal swap strips. Notice that the horizontal strips can

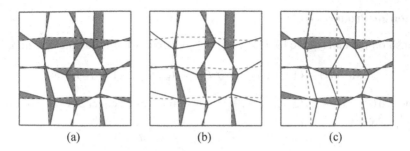

(a)	(b)	(c)

Fig. 7. Illustration for the vertical and horizontal swap and swept regions.

be viewed as the vertical strip by exchanging the x-coordinates and the y-coordinates. Therefore, one can only program the vertical sweep case. Each sweep calculate the intersections in the vertical/horizontal strips chunk by chunk. For the CIB/DC method, each chunk is a local swap region, while the FB/DC method, each chunk is a fluxing/swept area.

For the CIB/DC method, one can avoid to repeat calculating the corner contribution by thinning the second sweeping. The first vertical sweep calculate all the intersection areas in the swap region. The second sweep only calculates the swap region due to the intersection $T_{i,j}^b \cap T_{i,j\pm1}^a$. On contrast, in the FB/DC methods, the two sweep is totaly symmetric, repeat calculating the corner contribution is necessary.

4   Examples

The following examples is used to illustrated the application background. Direct apply the implementation of the result results a first order remapping scheme. We consider the following two kinds of grids.

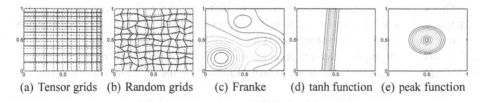

| (a) Tensor grids | (b) Random grids | (c) Franke | (d) tanh function | (e) peak function |

Fig. 8. Illustration of the tensor grids (a) and the random grids (b). The franke test function (c), the tanh function(d) and the peak function(e).

4.1 Tensor Product Grids

The mesh on the unit square $[0, 1] \times [0, 1]$ is generated by the following function

$$x(\xi, \eta, t) = (1 - \alpha(t))\xi + \alpha(t)\xi^3, \quad y(\xi, \eta, t) = (1 - \alpha(t))\eta^2, \tag{9}$$

where $\alpha(t) = \sin(4\pi t)/2, \xi, \eta, t \in [0, 1]$. This produces a sequence of tensor product grids $x_{i,j}^n$ given by

$$x_{i,j}^n = x(\xi_i, \eta_i, t^n), \quad y_{i,j}^n = y(\xi_i, \eta_j, t^n). \tag{10}$$

where ξ_i and η_j are nx and ny equally spaced points in $[0, 1]$. For the old grid, $t_1 = 1/(320 + nx)$, $t_2 = 2t_1$. We choose $nx = ny = 11, 21, 31, 41, \ldots, 101$.

4.2 Random Grids

A random grid is a perturbation of a uniform grid, $x_{ij}^n = \xi_i + \gamma r_i^n h$, and $y_{ij}^n = \eta_j + \gamma r_j^n h$. where ξ_i and η_j are constructed as that in the above tensor grids. $h = 1/(nx - 1)$. We use $\gamma = 0.4$ as the old grid and $\gamma = 0.1$ as the new grid, $nx = ny$.

4.3 Testing Functions

We use three examples as density functions, the franke function in Matlab (Fig. 8(c)), a shock like function (Fig. 8(d)) defined by

$$\rho_2(x, y) = \tanh(y - 15x + 6) + 1.2. \tag{11}$$

and the peak function (Fig. 8(e)) used in [8]

$$\rho_3(x, y) = \begin{cases} 0, & \sqrt{(x - 0.5)^2 + (y - 0.5)^2} > 0.25; \\ \max\{0.001, 4(0.25 - r)\}, & \sqrt{(x - 0.5)^2 + (y - 0.5)^2} \leq 0.25. \end{cases} \tag{12}$$

The initial mass of on the old cell is calculated by a fourth order quadrature, the remapped density function is calculated by the exact FB/DC method: the swept region is calculated exactly. The density are assumed to be a piecewise constant on each old cell. Since the swept/flux area are calculated exactly. The remapped error only depends on the approximation scheme to the density function on the old cell. The L_∞ norm

$$\|\rho^* - \rho\|_\infty = \max_{ij} |\rho_{i+\frac{1}{2}, j+\frac{1}{2}}^h - \rho(x_{i+\frac{1}{2}, j+\frac{1}{2}})| \tag{13}$$

is expected in the order of $O(h)$ for piecewise constant approximation to the density function on the old mesh. While the L_1 norm

$$\|m^* - m\|_\infty = \max_{i,j} |(\rho_{i+\frac{1}{2}, j+\frac{1}{2}}^h - \rho(x_{i+\frac{1}{2}, j+\frac{1}{2}}))\mu(C_{i+\frac{1}{2}, j+\frac{1}{2}})|.$$

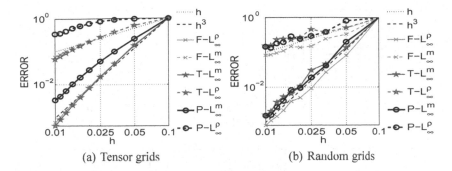

(a) Tensor grids (b) Random grids

Fig. 9. Convergence of the error between the remapped density functions and the true density functions. F: the Franke function, P: the peak function, and T: tanh function. The error are scaled by the level on the coarse level.

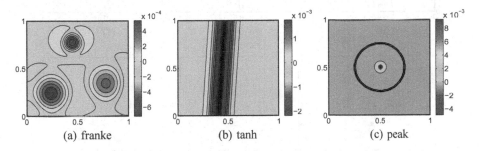

(a) franke (b) tanh (c) peak

Fig. 10. Remapped error of the density function on 101×101 tensor grids.

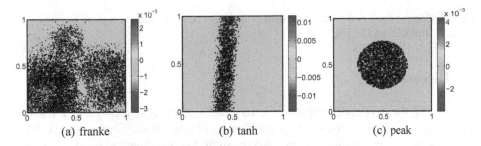

(a) franke (b) tanh (c) peak

Fig. 11. Remapped error of the density function on 101×101 random grinds.

is expected to be in the order of $O(h^3)$. We don't use the L_1 normal like in other publications, because when plot the convergence curve in the same figure, the L_1 norm and the L_∞ norm for the density function converges also the same rate. Figure 9 demonstrates the convergence of the remmapping error based on the piecewise constant reconstruction of the density function in the old mesh.

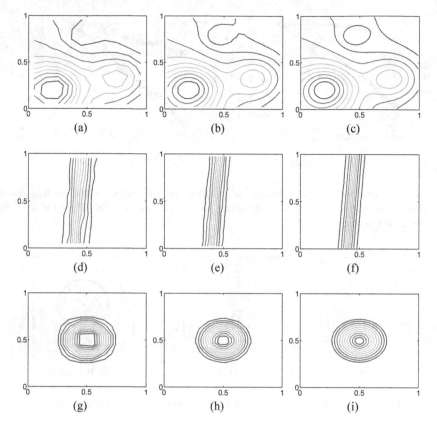

Fig. 12. Contour lines of the remapped density functions on $nx \times ny$ random grids. $nx = ny = 11$ (left), 21 (middle) and 51 (right).

5   Discussion

Computing the overlapped region of a Lagrangian mesh (old mesh) and a rezoned mesh(new mesh) and reconstruction (the density or flux) on the Lagrangian mesh are two aspects of a remapping scheme. According to the way how the overlapped (vertical) strips are divided, a remmapping scheme can be either an CIB/DC approach or an FB/DC approach. Both approaches are used in practice. The CIB/DC methods is based on pure geometric or set operation. It is conceptually simple, however, it is non trial even for such a simple case of two admissible meshes of the same connectively. The CIB/DC approach requires 98 programming cases for the non-degenerate intersections to cover all the possible intersection cases which are more than 256. On contrast, the FB/DC method, only requires 34 programming cases for the non-degenerate intersections. This approach is attractive for the case when the two meshes share the same connectivity. Here we present method to calculate fluxing/swept area or the local swap area. They are calculated exact. The classification on the intersection types can help us to identify the possible degenerate cases, this is convenient when develop a robust remapping procedure. Based on the Fact 3, we know there are at least 256 possible ways for a new cell to intersect with an old tessellation. But according to Fig. 3, we can tell there are more cases than 256. What is the exactly possibilities? This problem remains open as far as we know.

References

1. Xu, X., Zhu, S.: Computing overlaps of two quadrilateral mesh of the same connectivity. axXiv:1605.00852v1
2. Liu, J., Chen, H., Ewing, H., Qin, G.: An efficient algorithm for characteristic tracking on two-dimensional triangular meshes. Computing **80**, 121–136 (2007)
3. Balaban, I.J.: An optimal algorithm for finding segments intersections. In: Proceedings of the Eleventh Annual Symposium on Computational Geometry, pp. 211–219 (1995)
4. Chazelle, B., Edelsbrunner, H.: An optimal algorithm for intersecting line segments in the plane. J. Assoc. Comput. Mach. **39**(1), 1–54 (1992)
5. Ramshaw, J.D.: Conservative rezoning algorithm for generalized two-dimensional meshes. J. Comput. Phys. **59**(2), 193–199 (1985)
6. Ramshaw, J.D.: Simplified second order rezoning algorithm for generalized two-dimensional meshes. J. Comput. Phys. **67**(1), 214–222 (1986)
7. Dukowicz, J.K.: Conservative rezoning (remapping) for general quadrilateral meshes. J. Comput. Phys. **54**, 411–424 (1984)
8. Margolin, L., Shashkov, M.: Second order sign preserving conservative interpolation (remapping) on general grids. J. Comput. Phys. **184**(1), 266–298 (2003)

A Two-Field Finite Element Solver for Poroelasticity on Quadrilateral Meshes

Graham Harper, Jiangguo Liu, Simon Tavener, and Zhuoran Wang[✉]

Colorado State University, Fort Collins, CO 80523, USA
{harper,liu,tavener,wangz}@math.colostate.edu

Abstract. This paper presents a finite element solver for linear poroelasticity problems on quadrilateral meshes based on the displacement-pressure two-field model. This new solver combines the Bernardi-Raugel element for linear elasticity and a weak Galerkin element for Darcy flow through the implicit Euler temporal discretization. The solver does not use any penalty factor and has less degrees of freedom compared to other existing methods. The solver is free of nonphysical pressure oscillations, as demonstrated by numerical experiments on two widely tested benchmarks. Extension to other types of meshes in 2-dim and 3-dim is also discussed.

Keywords: Bernardi-Raugel elements · Locking-free · Poroelasticity
Raviart-Thomas spaces · Weak Galerkin (WG)

1 Introduction

Poroelasticity involves fluid flow in porous media that are elastic and can deform due to fluid pressure. Poroelasticity problems exist widely in the real world, e.g., drug delivery, food processing, petroleum reservoirs, and tissue engineering [6,7,19] and have been attracting attention from the scientific computing community [10,16,17,23] (and references therein). Some recent work can be found in [9–11,20,24].

Mathematically, poroelasticity can be modeled by coupled Darcy and elasticity equations as shown below

$$\begin{cases} -\nabla \cdot (2\mu\varepsilon(\mathbf{u}) + \lambda(\nabla \cdot \mathbf{u})\mathbf{I}) + \alpha\nabla p = \mathbf{f}, \\ \partial_t \left(c_0 p + \alpha\nabla \cdot \mathbf{u}\right) + \nabla \cdot (-\mathbf{K}\nabla p) = s, \end{cases} \tag{1}$$

where $\mathbf{u}$ is the solid displacement, $\varepsilon(\mathbf{u}) = \frac{1}{2}\left(\nabla\mathbf{u} + (\nabla\mathbf{u})^T\right)$ is the strain tensor, λ, μ (both positive) are Lamé constants, $\mathbf{f}$ is a body force, p is the fluid pressure,

G. Harper, J. Liu, and Z. Wang were partially supported by US National Science Foundation under grant DMS-1419077.

$\mathbf{K}$ is a permeability tensor (that has absorbed fluid viscosity for notational convenience), s is a fluid source or sink (treated as negative source), α (usually close to 1) is the Biot-Williams constant, $c_0 \geq 0$ is the constrained storage capacity. Appropriate boundary and initial conditions are posed to close the system.

An early complete theory about poroelasticity was formulated in Biot's consolidation model [3]. A more recent rigorous mathematical analysis was presented in [18]. It is difficult to obtain analytical solutions for poroelasticity problems. Therefore, solving poroelasticity problems relies mainly on numerical methods.

According to what variables are being solved, numerical methods for poroelasticity can be categorized as

- *2-field*: Solid displacement, fluid pressure;
- *3-field*: Solid displacement, fluid pressure and velocity;
- *4-field*: Solid displacement and stress, fluid pressure and velocity.

The simplicity of the 2-field approach is always attractive and hence pursued by this paper.

Continuous Galerkin (CG), discontinuous Galerkin (DG), mixed, nonconforming, and weak Galerkin finite element methods all have been applied to poroelasticity problems. A main challenge in all these methods is the *poroelasticity locking*, which often appears in two modes [24]: (i) *Nonphysical pressure oscillations* for low permeable or low compressible media [8,15], (ii) Poisson locking in elasticity.

Based on the displacement-pressure 2-field model, this paper presents a finite element solver for linear poroelasticity on quadrilateral meshes. The rest of this paper is organized as follows. Section 2 discusses discretization of planar linear elasticity by the 1st order Bernardi-Raugel elements on quadrilaterals. Section 3 presents discretization of 2-dim Darcy flow by the novel weak Galerkin finite element methods, in particular, $\mathrm{WG}(Q_0, Q_0; RT_{[0]})$ on quadrilateral meshes. In Sect. 4, the above two types of finite elements are combined with the first order implicit Euler temporal discretization to establish a solver for poroelasticity on quadrilateral meshes, which couples the solid displacement and fluid pressure in a monolithic system. Section 5 presents numerical tests for this new solver to demonstrate its efficiency and robustness (locking-free property). Section 6 concludes the paper with some remarks.

2 Discretization of Elasticity by Bernardi-Raugel (BR1) Elements

In this section, we consider linear elasticity in its usual form

$$\begin{cases} -\nabla \cdot \sigma = \mathbf{f}(\mathbf{x}), & \mathbf{x} \in \Omega, \\ \mathbf{u}|_{\Gamma^D} = \mathbf{u}_D, & (-\sigma\mathbf{n})|_{\Gamma^N} = \mathbf{t}_N, \end{cases} \tag{2}$$

where Ω is a 2-dim bounded domain occupied by a homogeneous and isotropic elastic body, $\mathbf{f}$ is a body force, $\mathbf{u}_D, \mathbf{t}_N$ are respectively Dirichlet and Neumann data, $\mathbf{n}$ is the outward unit normal vector on the domain boundary $\partial\Omega = \Gamma^D \cup \Gamma^N$. As mentioned in Sect. 1, $\mathbf{u}$ is the solid displacement,

$$\varepsilon(\mathbf{u}) = \frac{1}{2}\left(\nabla\mathbf{u} + (\nabla\mathbf{u})^T\right) \tag{3}$$

is the strain tensor, and

$$\sigma = 2\mu\,\varepsilon(\mathbf{u}) + \lambda(\nabla\cdot\mathbf{u})\mathbf{I}, \tag{4}$$

is the Cauchy stress tensor, where $\mathbf{I}$ is the order two identity matrix.

Note that the Lamé constants λ,μ are given by

$$\lambda = \frac{E\nu}{(1+\nu)(1-2\nu)}, \qquad \mu = \frac{E}{2(1+\nu)}, \tag{5}$$

where E is the elasticity modulus and ν is Poisson's ratio.

In this section, we discuss discretization of linear elasticity using the first order Bernardi-Raugel elements (BR1) on quadrilateral meshes. The Bernardi-Raugel elements were originally developed for Stokes problems [2]. They can be applied to elasticity problems when combined with the "reduced integration" technique [4,5,24]. In this context, it means use of less quadrature points for the integrals involving the divergence term. The BR1 element on a quadrilateral can be viewed as an enrichment of the classical bilinear Q_1^2 element, which suffers Poisson locking when applied directly to elasticity.

Let E be a quadrilateral with vertices $P_i(x_i, y_i)(i = 1, 2, 3, 4)$ starting at the lower-left corner and going counterclockwise. Let $e_i(i = 1, 2, 3, 4)$ be the edge connecting P_i to P_{i+1} with the modulo convention $P_5 = P_1$. Let $\mathbf{n}_i(i = 1, 2, 3, 4)$ be the outward unit normal vector on edge e_i. A bilinear mapping from $(\hat{x}, \hat{y})$ in the reference element $\hat{E} = [0, 1]^2$ to (x, y) in such a generic quadrilateral is established as follows

$$\begin{cases} x = x_1 + (x_2 - x_1)\hat{x} + (x_4 - x_1)\hat{y} + ((x_1 + x_3) - (x_2 + x_4))\hat{x}\hat{y}, \\ y = y_1 + (y_2 - y_1)\hat{x} + (y_4 - y_1)\hat{y} + ((y_1 + y_3) - (y_2 + y_4))\hat{x}\hat{y}. \end{cases} \tag{6}$$

On the reference element $\hat{E}$, we have four standard bilinear functions

$$\begin{array}{ll} \hat{\phi}_4(\hat{x}, \hat{y}) = (1 - \hat{x})\hat{y}, & \hat{\phi}_3(\hat{x}, \hat{y}) = \hat{x}\hat{y}, \\ \hat{\phi}_1(\hat{x}, \hat{y}) = (1 - \hat{x})(1 - \hat{y}), & \hat{\phi}_2(\hat{x}, \hat{y}) = \hat{x}(1 - \hat{y}). \end{array} \tag{7}$$

After the bilinear mapping defined by (6), we obtain four scalar basis functions on E that are usually rational functions of x, y:

$$\phi_i(x, y) = \hat{\phi}_i(\hat{x}, \hat{y}), \quad i = 1, 2, 3, 4. \tag{8}$$

These lead to eight node-based local basis functions for $Q_1(E)^2$:

$$\begin{bmatrix} \phi_1 \\ 0 \end{bmatrix}, \begin{bmatrix} 0 \\ \phi_1 \end{bmatrix}, \begin{bmatrix} \phi_2 \\ 0 \end{bmatrix}, \begin{bmatrix} 0 \\ \phi_2 \end{bmatrix}, \begin{bmatrix} \phi_3 \\ 0 \end{bmatrix}, \begin{bmatrix} 0 \\ \phi_3 \end{bmatrix}, \begin{bmatrix} \phi_4 \\ 0 \end{bmatrix}, \begin{bmatrix} 0 \\ \phi_4 \end{bmatrix}. \tag{9}$$

Furthermore, we define four edge-based scalar functions on $\hat{E}$:

$$\hat{\psi}_1(\hat{x}, \hat{y}) = (1 - \hat{x})\hat{x}(1 - \hat{y}), \quad \hat{\psi}_2(\hat{x}, \hat{y}) = \hat{x}(1 - \hat{y})\hat{y},$$
$$\hat{\psi}_3(\hat{x}, \hat{y}) = (1 - \hat{x})\hat{x}\hat{y}, \qquad \hat{\psi}_4(\hat{x}, \hat{y}) = (1 - \hat{x})(1 - \hat{y})\hat{y}. \tag{10}$$

They become univariate quadratic functions on respective edges of $\hat{E}$. For a generic convex quadrilateral E, we utilize the bilinear mapping to define

$$\psi_i(x, y) = \hat{\psi}_i(\hat{x}, \hat{y}), \quad i = 1, 2, 3, 4. \tag{11}$$

Then we have four edge-based local basis functions, see Fig. 1 (left panel):

$$\mathbf{b}_i(x, y) = \mathbf{n}_i \, \psi_i(x, y), \quad i = 1, 2, 3, 4. \tag{12}$$

Finally the BR1 element on a quadrilateral is defined as

$$BR1(E) = Q_1(E)^2 + \mathrm{Span}(\mathbf{b}_1, \mathbf{b}_3, \mathbf{b}_3, \mathbf{b}_4). \tag{13}$$

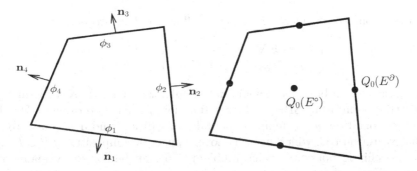

Fig. 1. *Left panel*: Four edge bubble functions needed for the 1st order Bernardi-Raugel element on a quadrilateral; *Right panel*: WG($Q_0, Q_0; RT_{[0]}$) element on a quadrilateral.

On each quadrilateral, there are totally twelve vector-valued basis functions. Their classical gradients are calculated *ad hoc* and so are the strains. Clearly, their classical divergences are not constants. The elementwise averages of divergence or the local projections into the space of constants are calculated accordingly.

Let $\mathbf{V}_h$ be the space of vector-valued shape functions constructed from the BR1 elements on a shape-regular quadrilateral mesh $\mathcal{E}_h$. Let $\mathbf{V}_h^0$ be the subspace of $\mathbf{V}_h$ consisting of shape functions that vanish on Γ^D. Let $\mathbf{u}_h \in \mathbf{V}_h$ and $\mathbf{v} \in \mathbf{V}_h^0$. Then the bilinear form in the strain-div formulation utilizing the Bernardi-Raugel elements reads as

$$A_h^{SD}(\mathbf{u}_h, \mathbf{v}) = \sum_{E \in \mathcal{E}_h} 2\mu\Big(\varepsilon(\mathbf{u}_h), \varepsilon(\mathbf{v})\Big)_E + \lambda(\overline{\nabla \cdot \mathbf{u}_h}, \overline{\nabla \cdot \mathbf{v}})_E, \tag{14}$$

where the overline bar indicates the elementwise averages of divergence. The linear form for discretization of the body force is simply

$$\mathcal{F}_h(\mathbf{v}) = \sum_{E \in \mathcal{E}_h} (\mathbf{f}, \mathbf{v})_E, \quad \forall \mathbf{v} \in \mathbf{V}_h^0. \tag{15}$$

Now there are two sets of basis functions: node-based and edge-based. Compatibility among these two types of functions needs to be maintained in enforcement or incorporation of boundary conditions.

(i) For a Dirichlet edge, one can directly enforce the Dirichlet condition at the two end nodes and set the coefficient of the edge bubble function to zero;
(ii) For a Neumann edge, integrals of the Neumann data against the three basis functions (two linear polynomials for the end nodes, one quadratic for the edge) are computed and assembled accordingly.

3   Discretization of Darcy Flow by WG($Q_0, Q_0; RT_{[0]}$) Elements

In this section, we consider a 2-dim Darcy flow problem prototyped as

$$\begin{cases} \nabla \cdot (-\mathbf{K} \nabla p) + cp = f, & \mathbf{x} \in \Omega, \\ p|_{\Gamma^D} = p_D, \quad ((-\mathbf{K} \nabla p) \cdot \mathbf{n})|_{\Gamma^N} = u_N, \end{cases} \tag{16}$$

where Ω is a 2-dim bounded domain, p the unknown pressure, $\mathbf{K}$ a conductivity matrix that is uniformly SPD, c a known function, f a source term, p_D a Dirichlet boundary condition, p_D a Neumann boundary condition, and $\mathbf{n}$ the outward unit normal vector on $\partial\Omega$, which has a nonoverlapping decomposition $\Gamma^D \cup \Gamma^N$.

As an elliptic boundary value problem, (16) can be solved by many types of finite element methods. However, *local mass conservation* and *normal flux continuity* are two most important properties to be respected by finite element solvers for Darcy flow computation. In this regard, continuous Galerkin methods (CG) are usable only after postprocessing. Discontinuous Galerkin methods (DG) are locally conservative by design and gain normal flux continuity after postprocessing. The enhanced Galerkin methods (EG) [21] are also good choices. The mixed finite element methods (MFEM) have both properties by design but result in indefinite discrete linear systems that need specially designed solvers. The recently developed weak Galerkin methods [12,22], when applied to Darcy flow computation, have very attractive features in this regard: They possess the above two important properties and result in symmetric positive linear systems that are easy to solve [12–14].

The weak Galerkin methods [22] rely on novel concepts to develop finite elements for differential equations. Discrete weak basis functions are used separately in element interiors and on interelement boundaries (or mesh skeleton). Then discrete weak gradients of these basis functions are computed via integration by parts. These discrete weak gradients can be established in certain known spaces, e.g., the local Raviart-Thomas spaces RT_0 for triangles, the standard $RT_{[0]}$ for rectangles, and the unmapped $RT_{[0]}$ for quadrilaterals [14]. These discrete weak gradients are used to approximate the classical gradient in variational forms.

Recall that for a quadrilateral element E, the local unmapped Raviart-Thomas space has dimension 4 and can be generated by these four basis functions

$$RT_{[0]}(E) = \text{Span}(\mathbf{w}_1, \mathbf{w}_2, \mathbf{w}_3, \mathbf{w}_4), \tag{17}$$

where

$$\mathbf{w}_1 = \begin{bmatrix} 1 \\ 0 \end{bmatrix}, \quad \mathbf{w}_2 = \begin{bmatrix} 0 \\ 1 \end{bmatrix}, \quad \mathbf{w}_3 = \begin{bmatrix} X \\ 0 \end{bmatrix}, \quad \mathbf{w}_4 = \begin{bmatrix} 0 \\ Y \end{bmatrix}, \tag{18}$$

and $X = x - x_c$, $Y = y - y_c$ are the normalized coordinates using the element center (x_c, y_c).

For a given quadrilateral element E, we consider 5 discrete weak functions $\phi_i (0 \le i \le 4)$ as follows:

- ϕ_0 for element interior: It takes value 1 in the interior E° but 0 on the boundary E^∂;
- $\phi_i (1 \le i \le 4)$ for the four sides respectively: Each takes value 1 on the i-th edge but 0 on all other three edges and in the interior.

Any such function $\phi = \{\phi^\circ, \phi^\partial\}$ has two independent parts: ϕ° is defined in E°, whereas ϕ^∂ is defined on E^∂. Then its discrete weak gradient $\nabla_{w,d}\phi$ is specified in $RT_{[0]}(E)$ via integration by parts [22] (implementation wise solving a size-4 SPD linear system):

$$\int_E (\nabla_{w,d}\phi) \cdot \mathbf{w} = \int_{E^\partial} \phi^\partial (\mathbf{w} \cdot \mathbf{n}) - \int_{E^\circ} \phi^\circ (\nabla \cdot \mathbf{w}), \quad \forall \mathbf{w} \in RT_{[0]}(E). \tag{19}$$

When a quadrilateral becomes a rectangle $E = [x_1, x_2] \times [y_1, y_2]$, we have

$$\begin{cases} \nabla_{w,d}\phi_0 = & 0\mathbf{w}_1 + & 0\mathbf{w}_2 + & \frac{-12}{(\Delta x)^2}\mathbf{w}_3 + & \frac{-12}{(\Delta y)^2}\mathbf{w}_4, \\ \nabla_{w,d}\phi_1 = & \frac{-1}{\Delta x}\mathbf{w}_1 + & 0\mathbf{w}_2 + & \frac{6}{(\Delta x)^2}\mathbf{w}_3 + & 0\mathbf{w}_4, \\ \nabla_{w,d}\phi_2 = & \frac{1}{\Delta x}\mathbf{w}_1 + & 0\mathbf{w}_2 + & \frac{6}{(\Delta x)^2}\mathbf{w}_3 + & 0\mathbf{w}_4, \\ \nabla_{w,d}\phi_3 = & 0\mathbf{w}_1 + & \frac{-1}{\Delta y}\mathbf{w}_2 + & 0\mathbf{w}_3 + & \frac{6}{(\Delta y)^2}\mathbf{w}_4, \\ \nabla_{w,d}\phi_4 = & 0\mathbf{w}_1 + & \frac{1}{\Delta y}\mathbf{w}_2 + & 0\mathbf{w}_3 + & \frac{6}{(\Delta y)^2}\mathbf{w}_4, \end{cases} \tag{20}$$

where $\Delta x = x_2 - x_1, \Delta y = y_2 - y_1$.

Let $\mathcal{E}_h$ be a shape-regular quadrilateral mesh. Let Γ_h^D be the set of all edges on the Dirichlet boundary Γ^D and Γ_h^N be the set of all edges on the Neumann boundary Γ^N. Let S_h be the space of discrete shape functions on $\mathcal{E}_h$ that are degree 0 polynomials in element interiors and also degree 0 polynomials on edges. Let S_h^0 be the subspace of functions in S_h that vanish on Γ_h^D. For (16), we seek $p_h = \{p_h^\circ, p_h^\partial\} \in S_h$ such that $p_h^\partial|_{\Gamma_h^D} = Q_h^\partial(p_D)$ (the L^2-projection of Dirichlet boundary data into the space of piecewise constants on Γ_h^D) and

$$\mathcal{A}_h(p_h, q) = \mathcal{F}(q), \quad \forall q = \{q^\circ, q^\partial\} \in S_h^0, \tag{21}$$

where

$$\mathcal{A}_h(p_h, q) = \sum_{E \in \mathcal{E}_h} \int_E \mathbf{K} \nabla_{w,d} p_h \cdot \nabla_{w,d} q + \sum_{E \in \mathcal{E}_h} \int_E c p q \qquad (22)$$

and

$$\mathcal{F}(q) = \sum_{E \in \mathcal{E}_h} \int_E f q^\circ - \sum_{\gamma \in \Gamma_h^N} \int_\gamma u_N q^\partial. \qquad (23)$$

As investigated in [14], this Darcy solver is easy to implement and results in a symmetric positive-definite system. More importantly, it is locally mass-conservative and produces continuous normal fluxes.

4   Coupling BR1 and WG$(Q_0, Q_0; RT_{[0]})$ for Linear Poroelasticity on Quadrilateral Meshes

In this section, the Bernardi-Raugel elements (BR1) and the weak Galerkin WG$(Q_0, Q_0; RT_{[0]})$ elements are combined with the implicit Euler temporal discretization to solve linear poroelasticity problems.

Assume a given domain Ω is equipped with a shape-regular quadrilateral mesh $\mathcal{E}_h$. For a given time period $[0, T]$, let

$$0 = t^{(0)} < t^{(1)} < \ldots < t^{(n-1)} < t^{(n)} < \ldots < t^{(N)} = T$$

be a temporal partition. Denote $\Delta t_n = t^{(n)} - t^{(n-1)}$ for $n = 1, 2, \ldots, N$.

Let $\mathbf{V}_h$ and $\mathbf{V}_h^0$ be the spaces of vector-valued shape functions constructed in Sect. 2 based on the first order Bernardi-Raugel elements. Let S_h and S_h^0 be the spaces of scalar-valued discrete weak functions constructed in Sect. 3 based on the WG$(Q_0, Q_0; RT_{[0]})$ elements. Let $\mathbf{u}_h^{(n)}, \mathbf{u}_h^{(n-1)} \in \mathbf{V}_h$ be approximations to solid displacement at time moments $t^{(n)}$ and $t^{(n-1)}$, respectively. Similarly, let $p_h^{(n)}, p_h^{(n-1)} \in S_h$ be approximations to fluid pressure at time moments $t^{(n)}$ and $t^{(n-1)}$, respectively. Note that the discrete weak trail function has two pieces:

$$p_h^{(n)} = \{p_h^{(n),\circ}, p_h^{(n),\partial}\}, \qquad (24)$$

where $p_h^{(n),\circ}$ lives in element interiors and $p_h^{(n),\partial}$ lives on the mesh skeleton.

Applying the implicit Euler discretization, we establish the following time-marching scheme, for any $\mathbf{v} \in \mathbf{V}_h^0$ and any $q \in S_h^0$,

$$\begin{cases} 2\mu\left(\varepsilon(\mathbf{u}_h^{(n)}), \varepsilon(\mathbf{v})\right) + \lambda(\overline{\nabla \cdot \mathbf{u}_h^{(n)}}, \overline{\nabla \cdot \mathbf{v}}) - \alpha(p_h^{(n),\circ}, \overline{\nabla \cdot \mathbf{v}}) = (\mathbf{f}^{(n)}, \mathbf{v}), \\ c_0\left(p_h^{(n),\circ}, q^\circ\right) + \Delta t_n \left(\mathbf{K}\nabla p_h^{(n)}, \nabla q\right) + \alpha(\overline{\nabla \cdot \mathbf{u}_h^{(n)}}, q^\circ) \\ \qquad = c_0\left(p_h^{(n-1),\circ}, q^\circ\right) + \Delta t_n \left(s^{(n)}, q^\circ\right) + \alpha(\overline{\nabla \cdot \mathbf{u}_h^{(n-1)}}, q^\circ), \end{cases} \qquad (25)$$

for $n = 1, 2, \ldots, N$. The above two equations are further augmented with appropriate boundary and initial conditions. This results in a large monolithic system.

This solver has two displacement degrees of freedom (DOFs) per node, one displacement DOF per edge, one pressure DOF per element, one pressure DOF per edge. Let N_d, N_e, N_g be the numbers of nodes, elements, and edges, respectively, then the total DOFs is

$$2 * N_d + N_e + 2 * N_g, \tag{26}$$

which is less than that for many existing solvers for poroelasticity.

5   Numerical Experiments

In this section, we test this novel 2-field solver on two widely used benchmarks. In these test cases, the permeability is $\mathbf{K} = \kappa \mathbf{I}$, where κ is a piecewise constant over the test domain. Finite element meshes align with the aforementioned pieces. Rectangular meshes (as a special case of quadrilateral meshes) are used in our numerics.

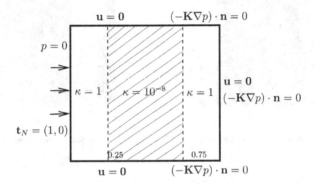

Fig. 2. Example 1: A sandwiched low permeability layer.

Example 1 (A sandwiched low permeability layer). This problem is similar to the one tested in [8,9], the only difference is the orientation. The domain is the unit square $\Omega = (0,1)^2$, with a low permeability material ($\kappa = 10^{-8}$) in the middle region $\frac{1}{4} \leq x \leq \frac{3}{4}$ being sandwiched by the other material ($\kappa = 1$). Other parameters are $\lambda = 1$, $\mu = 1$, $\alpha = 1$, $c_0 = 0$. Listed below are the boundary conditions.

– *For solid displacement*:
   For the left side: Neumann (traction) $-\sigma \mathbf{n} = \mathbf{t}_N = (1,0)$;
   For the bottom-, right-, and top-sides: homogeneous Dirichlet (rigid) $\mathbf{u} = \mathbf{0}$;
– *For fluid pressure*:
   For the left side: homogeneous Dirichlet (free to drain) $p = 0$;
   For 3 other sides: homogeneous Neumann (impermeable) $(-\mathbf{K}\nabla p) \cdot \mathbf{n} = 0$.

The initial displacement and pressure are assumed to be zero. See Fig. 2 for an illustration.

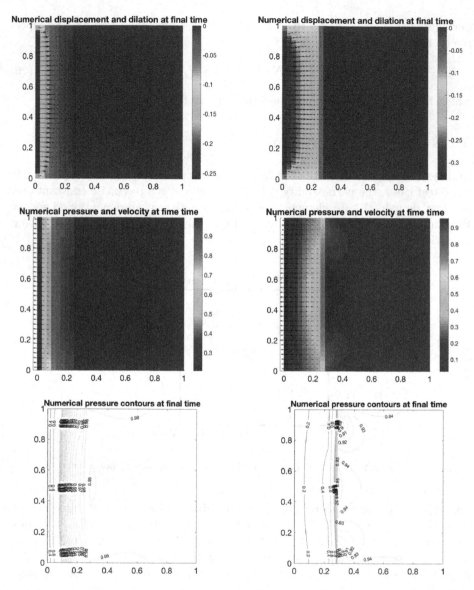

Fig. 3. Sandwiched low permeability layer: Numerical displacement and dilation, numerical pressure and velocity, numerical pressure contours for $h = 1/32$ and $\Delta t = 0.001$. Left column for time $T_1 = 0.001$; Right column for time $T_2 = 0.01$. Further shrinking in solid, drop of maximal fluid pressure, and pressure front moving are observed.

For this problem, we examine more details than what is shown in the literature. We use a uniform rectangular mesh with $h = 1/32$ for spatial discretization and $\Delta t = 0.001$ for temporal discretization. This way, $\Delta t \approx h^2$. Shown in Fig. 3

are the numerical displacement and dilation (div of displacement), the numerical pressure and velocity, and the numerical contours at time $T_1 = 0.001$ and $T_2 = 0.01$, respectively. As the process progresses and the fluid drains out from the left side ($x = 0$), it is clearly observed that

(i) The maximal pressure is dropped from around 0.9915 to around 0.9570;
(ii) The pressure front moves to the right and becomes more concentrated around the interface $x = 0.25$;
(iii) The solid is further shrunk: maximal shrinking (negative dilation) magnitude increases from around 0.2599 to around 0.3385.

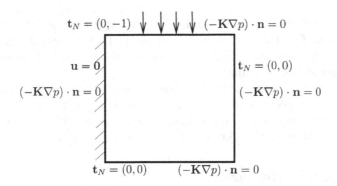

Fig. 4. Example 2: Cantilever bracket problem.

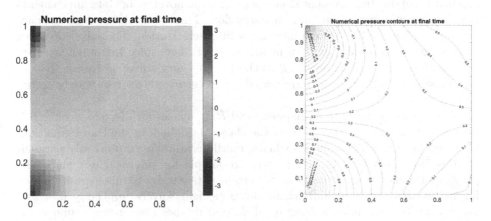

Fig. 5. Example 2: Cantilever bracket problem. Numerical pressure at time $T = 0.005$ is obtained by combining Bernardi-Raugel and weak Galerkin elements through the implicit Euler discretization with $\Delta t = 0.001$, $h = 1/32$.

Example 2 (Cantilever bracket problem). This benchmark is often used to test spurious pressure oscillations [1,17,24]. The domain is the unit square $\Omega = (0,1)^2$. A no-flux (Neumann) condition is prescribed on all four sides for the fluid pressure. The left side is clamped, that is, a homogeneous Dirichlet condition $\mathbf{u} = \mathbf{0}$ is posed for the solid displacement for $x = 0$. A downward traction (Neumann condition) $-\sigma\mathbf{n} = \mathbf{t}_N = (0,-1)$ is posed on the top side, whereas the right and bottom sides are traction-free. The initial displacement and pressure are assumed to be zero. See Fig. 4.

Here we follow [1,24] to choose the following parameter values

$$E = 10^5, \quad \nu = 0.4, \quad \kappa = 10^{-7}, \quad \alpha = 0.93, \quad c_0 = 0.$$

We set $\Delta t = 0.001, h = 1/32$. Shown in Fig. 5 are the numerical pressure profile and contours at $T = 0.005$, obtained from using the Bernardi-Raugel elements and weak Galerkin elements. Clearly, the numerical pressure is quite smooth and there is no nonphysical oscillation.

This new finite element solver has been added to our `Matlab` code package `DarcyLite`. The implementation techniques presented in [13] are used.

It is demonstrated in [24] that nonphysicial pressure oscillations occur when the classical continuous Galerkin method is used for elasticity discretization.

6   Concluding Remarks

In this paper, we have developed a finite element solver for linear poroelasticity on quadrilateral meshes based on the two-field model (solid displacement and fluid pressure). This solver relies on the Bernardi-Raugel elements [2] for discretization of the displacement in elasticity and the novel weak Galerkin elements [14] for discretization of pressure in Darcy flow. These spatial discretizations are combined with the backward Euler temporal discretization. The solver does not involve any nonphysical penalty factor. It is efficient, since less unknowns are used, compared to other existing methods. This new solver is robust, free of poroelasticity locking, as demonstrated by experiments on two widely tested benchmarks.

This paper utilizes the unmapped local $RT_{[0]}$ spaces for discrete weak gradients, which are used to approximate the classical gradient in the Darcy equation. Convergence can be established when quadrilateral are asymptotically parallelograms [14]. This type of new solvers are simple for practical use, since any polygonal domain can be partitioned into asymptotically parallelogram quadrilateral meshes. Efficient and robust finite element solvers for Darcy flow and poroelasticity on general convex quadrilateral meshes are currently under our investigation and will be reported in our future work.

Our discussion focuses on quadrilateral meshes, but the ideas apply to other types of meshes. For triangular meshes, one can combine the Bernardi-Raugel elements on triangles for elasticity [2] and the weak Galerkin elements on triangles for Darcy [12]. This combination provides a viable alternative to the three-field solver investigated in [24]. Similar 2-field solvers can be developed for tetrahedral and cuboidal hexahedral meshes. This is also a part of our current research efforts for developing efficient and accessible computational tools for poroelasticity.

References

1. Berger, L., Bordas, R., Kay, D., Tavener, S.: Stabilized lowest-order finite element approximation for linear three-field poroelasticity. SIAM J. Sci. Comput. **37**, A2222–A2245 (2015)
2. Bernardi, C., Raugel, G.: Analysis of some finite elements for the stokes problem. Math. Comput. **44**, 71–79 (1985)
3. Biot, M.: General theory of three-dimensional consolidation. J. Appl. Phys. **12**, 155–164 (1941)
4. Brenner, S., Sung, L.Y.: Linear finite element methods for planar linear elasticity. Math. Comput. **59**, 321–338 (1992)
5. Chen, Z., Jiang, Q., Cui, Y.: Locking-free nonconforming finite elements for planar linear elasticity. In: Discrete and Continuous Dynamical Systems, pp. 181–189 (2005)
6. Cheng, A.H.-D.: Poroelasticity. TATPM, vol. 27. Springer, Cham (2016). https://doi.org/10.1007/978-3-319-25202-5
7. Cowin, S., Doty, S.: Tissue Mechanics. Springer, New York (2007). https://doi.org/10.1007/978-0-387-49985-7
8. Haga, J., Osnes, H., Langtangen, H.: On the causes of pressure oscillations in low permeable and low compressible porous media. Int. J. Numer. Aanl. Meth. Geomech. **36**, 1507–1522 (2012)
9. Hu, X., Mu, L., Ye, X.: Weak Galerkin method for the Biot's consolidation model. Comput. Math. Appl. (2018, in press)
10. Hu, X., Rodrigo, C., Gaspar, F., Zikatanov, L.: A nonconforming finite element method for the Biot's consolidation model in poroelasticity. J. Comput. Appl. Math. **310**, 143–154 (2017)
11. Lee, J., Mardal, K.A., Winther, R.: Parameter-robust discretization and preconditioning of Biot's consolidation model. SIAM J. Sci. Comput. **39**, A1–A24 (2017)
12. Lin, G., Liu, J., Mu, L., Ye, X.: Weak galerkin finite element methdos for Darcy flow: anistropy and heterogeneity. J. Comput. Phys. **276**, 422–437 (2014)
13. Liu, J., Sadre-Marandi, F., Wang, Z.: Darcylite: a matlab toolbox for darcy flow computation. Proc. Comput. Sci. **80**, 1301–1312 (2016)
14. Liu, J., Tavener, S., Wang, Z.: The lowest-order weak Galerkin finite element method for the Darcy equation on quadrilateral and hybrid meshes. J. Comput. Phys. **359**, 312–330 (2018)
15. Phillips, P.: Finite element methods in linear poroelasticity: theoretical and computational results. Ph.D. thesis, University of Texas at Austin (2005)
16. Phillips, P., Wheeler, M.: A coupling of mixed with discontinuous Galerkin finite element methods for poroelasticity. Comput. Geosci. **12**, 417–435 (2008)
17. Phillips, P.J., Wheeler, M.F.: Overcoming the problem of locking in linear elasticity and poroelasticity: an heuristic approach. Comput. Geosci. **13**, 5–12 (2009)
18. Showalter, R.: Diffusion in poro-elastic media. J. Math. Anal. Appl. **251**, 310–340 (2000)

19. Støverud, K., Darcis, M., Helmig, R., Hassanizadeh, S.M.: Modeling concentration distribution and deformation during convection-enhanced drug delivery into brain tissue. Transp. Porous Med. **92**, 119–143 (2012)
20. Sun, M., Rui, H.: A coupling of weak Galerkin and mixed finite element methods for poroelasticity. Comput. Math. Appl. **73**, 804–823 (2017)
21. Sun, S., Liu, J.: A locally conservative finite element method based on piecewise constant enrichment of the continuous Galerkin method. SIAM J. Sci. Comput. **31**, 2528–2548 (2009)
22. Wang, J., Ye, X.: A weak Galerkin finite element method for second order elliptic problems. J. Comput. Appl. Math. **241**, 103–115 (2013)
23. Wheeler, M., Xue, G., Yotov, I.: Coupling multipoint flux mixed finite element methods with continuous Galerkin methods for poroelasticity. Comput. Geosci. **18**, 57–75 (2014)
24. Yi, S.Y.: A study of two modes of locking in poroelasticity. SIAM J. Numer. Anal. **55**, 1915–1936 (2017)

Preprocessing Parallelization
for the ALT-Algorithm

Genaro Peque Jr.[(✉)], Junji Urata, and Takamasa Iryo

Department of Civil Engineering, Kobe University, Kobe, Japan
gpequejr@panda.kobe-u.ac.jp, urata@person.kobe-u.ac.jp,
iryo@kobe-u.ac.jp

Abstract. In this paper, we improve the preprocessing phase of the ALT algorithm through parallelization. ALT is a preprocessing-based, goal-directed speed-up technique that uses **A*** (A star), **L**andmarks and **T**riangle inequality which allows fast computations of shortest paths (SP) in large-scale networks. Although faster techniques such as arc-flags, SHARC, Contraction Hierarchies and Highway Hierarchies already exist, ALT is usually combined with these faster algorithms to take advantage of its goal-directed search to further reduce the SP search computation time and its search space. However, ALT relies on landmarks and optimally choosing these landmarks is NP-hard, hence, no effective solution exists. Since landmark selection relies on constructive heuristics and the current SP search speed-up is inversely proportional to landmark generation time, we propose a parallelization technique which reduces the landmark generation time significantly while increasing its effectiveness.

Keywords: ALT algorithm · Shortest path search
Large-scale traffic simulation

1 Introduction

1.1 Background

The computation of shortest paths (SP) on graphs is a problem with many real world applications. One prominent example is the computation of the shortest path between a given origin and destination called a single-source, single-target problem. This problem is usually encountered in route planning in traffic simulations and is easily solved in polynomial time using Dijkstra's algorithm [1] (assuming that the graph has non-negative edge weights). Indeed, road networks can easily be represented as graphs and traffic simulations usually use edge (road) distances or travel times as edge weights which are always assumed positive.

In large-scale traffic simulations where edge weights are time-dependent, one is normally interested in computing shortest paths in a matter of a few milliseconds. Specifically, the shortest path search is one of the most computationally intensive parts of a traffic simulation due to the repeated shortest path calculation of each driver departing at a specific time. This is necessary because a driver needs to consider the

© Springer International Publishing AG, part of Springer Nature 2018
Y. Shi et al. (Eds.): ICCS 2018, LNCS 10862, pp. 89–101, 2018.
https://doi.org/10.1007/978-3-319-93713-7_7

effects of the other drivers who departed earlier in his/her route's travel time. However, faster queries are not possible using only Dijkstra or A* (A star) search algorithms. Even the most efficient implementation of Dijkstra or A* isn't sufficient to significantly reduce a simulation's calculation time. Thus, speed-up techniques that preprocess input data [2] have become a necessity. A speed-up technique splits a shortest path search algorithm into two phases, a preprocessing phase and a query phase. A *preprocessing phase* converts useful information on the input data, done before the start of the simulation, to accelerate the *query phase* that computes the actual shortest paths. There are many preprocessing based variants of Dijkstra's algorithm such as the ALT algorithm [3], Arc-Flags [4], Contraction Hierarchies [5], Highway Hierarchies [6] and SHARC [7] among others. These variants are normally a combination of different algorithms that can easily be decomposed into the four basic ingredients that efficient speed-up techniques belong to [8], namely, Dijkstra's algorithm, landmarks [3, 9], arc-flags [10, 11] and contraction [6]. The combination is usually with a goal-directed search algorithm such as the ALT algorithm that provides an estimated distance or travel time from any point in the network to a destination at the cost of additional preprocessing time and space. A few examples are the (i) L-SHARC [8], a combination of landmarks, contraction and arc-flags. L-SHARC increases performance of the approximate arc-flags algorithm by incorporating the goal-directed search, (ii) Core-ALT [12], a combination of contraction and ALT algorithm. Core-ALT reduces the landmarks' space consumption while increasing query speed by limiting landmarks in a specific "core" level of a contracted network, and the (iii) Highway Hierarchies Star (HH*) [13], a combination of Highway Hierarchies (HH) and landmarks which introduces a goal-directed search to HH for faster queries at the cost of additional space.

The ALT algorithm is a goal-directed search proposed by Golberg and Harrelson [3] that uses the A* search algorithm and distance estimates to define node potentials that direct the search towards the target. The A* search algorithm is a generalization of Dijkstra's algorithm that uses node coordinates as an input to a potential function to estimate the distance between any two nodes in the graph. A good potential function can be used to reduce the search space of an SP query, effectively. In the ALT algorithm, a potential function is defined through the use of the triangle inequality on a carefully selected subset of nodes called landmark nodes. The distance estimate between two nodes is calculated using the landmark nodes' precomputed shortest path distances to each node using triangle inequality. The maximum lower bound produced by one of the landmarks is then used for the SP query. Hence, ALT stands for *A*, L*andmarks and *T*riangle inequality. However, a major challenge for the ALT algorithm is the landmark selection. Many strategies have been proposed such as *random, planar, Avoid, weightedAvoid, advancedAvoid, maxCover* [3, 9, 13, 14] and as an integer linear program (ILP) [15]. In terms of the landmark generation times of these proposed strategies, *random* is the fastest while ILP is the slowest, respectively. For query times using the landmarks produced by these strategies, *random* is the slowest while ILP is the fastest, respectively. The trend of producing better landmarks at the expense of additional computation times have always been true. Moreover, the aforementioned landmark selection strategies weren't designed to run in parallel. The question is whether a parallel implementation of a landmark selection algorithm can increase landmark efficiency while only slightly increasing its computation cost.

Our aim is to use the ALT algorithm in the repeated calculation of drivers' shortest paths in a large-scale traffic simulation. The traffic simulator is implemented in parallel using a distributed memory architecture. By reducing the preprocessing phase through parallelization, we are able to take advantage of the parallelized implementation of the traffic simulator and the architecture's distributed memory. Additionally, if we can decrease the landmark generation time, it would be possible to update the landmark lower bounds dynamically while some central processing units (CPUs) are waiting for the other CPUs to finish.

1.2 Contribution of This Paper

Since the ALT algorithm is commonly combined with other faster preprocessing techniques for additional speed-up (i.e. goal-directed search), we are motivated in studying and improving its preprocessing phase. Our results show that the parallelization significantly decreased the landmark generation time and SP query times.

1.3 Outline of This Paper

The paper is structured as follows. In the following section, the required notation is introduced. Additionally, three shortest path search algorithms, namely, Dijkstra, A* search and the ALT algorithm, are presented. Section 3 is dedicated to the description of the landmark preprocessing techniques, our proposed landmark generation algorithm and its parallel implementation. In Sect. 4, the computational results are shown where our conclusions, presented in Sect. 5, are drawn from.

2 Preliminaries

A graph is an ordered pair $G = (V, E)$ which consists of a set of vertices, V, and a set of edges, $E \subset V \times V$. Sometimes, $(u, v) \in E$, will be written as $e \in E$ to represent a link. Additionally, vertices and edges will be used interchangeably with the terms nodes and links, respectively. Links can either be composed of an unordered or ordered pairs. When a graph is composed of the former, it is called an undirected graph. If it composed of the latter, it is called a directed graph. Throughout this paper, only directed graphs are studied. For a directed graph, an edge $e = (u, v)$ leaves node u and enters node v. Node u is called the tail while the node v is called the head of the link and its weight is given by the cost function $c: E \rightarrow \mathbb{R}^+$. The number of nodes, $|V|$, and the number of links, $|E|$, are denoted as n and m, respectively.

A path from node s to node t is a sequence, $(v_0, v_1, \ldots, v_{k-1}, v_k)$, of nodes such that $s = v_0, t = v_k$ and there exists an edge $(v_{i-1}, v_i) \in E$ for every $i \in \{1, \ldots, k\}$. A path from s to t is called simple if no nodes are repeated on the path. A path's cost is defined as,

$$dist(s, t) := \sum_{i=1}^{k} c_{(v_{i-1}, v_i)}. \tag{1}$$

A path of minimum cost between nodes s and t is called the $(s, t)-$ shortest path with its cost denoted by $dist^*(s, t)$. If no path exists between nodes s and t in G, $dist(s, t) := \infty$. In general, $c(u, v) \neq c(v, u)$, $\forall(u, v) \in E$ so that $dist(s, t) \neq dist(t, s)$. One of the most well-known algorithms used to find the path and distance between two given nodes is the Dijkstra's algorithm.

2.1 Dijkstra's Algorithm

In Dijkstra's algorithm, given a graph with non-negative edge weights, a source (origin) and a target (destination), the shortest path search is conducted in such a way that a "Dijkstra ball" slowly grows around the source until the target node is found.

More specifically, Dijkstra's algorithm is as follows: during initialization, all node costs (denoted by g) from the source, s, to all the other nodes are set to infinity (i.e. $g(w) = \infty$, $\forall w \in V \backslash \{s\}$). Note that $g(s) = 0$. These costs are used as *keys* and are inserted into a minimum-based priority queue, PQ, which decides the order of each node to be processed. Take $w = argmin_{u \in PQ} g(u)$ from the priority queue. For each node $v \in PQ$ subject to $(w, v) \in E$, if $g(v) > g(w) + c(w, v)$, set $g(v) = g(w) + c(w, v)$. Repeat this process until either the target node is found or PQ is empty. This means that the algorithm checks all adjacent nodes of each processed node, starting from the source node, which is the reason for the circular search space or "Dijkstra ball".

Although Dijkstra's algorithm can calculate the shortest path from s to t, its search speed can still be improved by using other network input data such as node coordinates. This is the technique used by the A* algorithm described in the next subsection.

2.2 A* (A Star) Search Algorithm

The A* search algorithm is a generalization of Dijkstra's algorithm. A* search algorithm uses a potential function, $\pi_t : V \rightarrow \mathbb{R}^+$, which is an estimated distance from an arbitrary node to a target node.

Consider the shortest path problem from a source node to a target node in the graph and suppose that there is a potential function, π_t, such that $\pi_t(u)$ provides an estimate of the cost from node u to a given target node, t. Given a function $g : V \rightarrow \mathbb{R}^+$ and a priority function, PQ, defined by $PQ(u) = g(u) + \pi_t(u)$, let $g^*(u)$ and $\pi_t^*(u)$ represent the length of the $(s, u)-$ shortest path and $(u, t)-$ shortest path, respectively. Note that $g^*(u) = dist^*(s, u)$ and $\pi_t^*(u) = dist^*(u, t)$, so that $PQ^*(u) = g^*(u) + \pi_t^*(u) = dist^*(s, t)$. This means that the next node that will be taken out of PQ belongs to the $(s, t)-$ shortest path. If this holds true for the succeeding nodes until the target node is reached, its search space starting at node u will only consist of the shortest path nodes. However, if $PQ(u) = g^*(u) + \pi_t(u) = dist(s, t)$ for some u, then its search space will increase depending on how bad the estimates for each node is, $\pi_t(u)$.

In the A* search algorithm, the value used for the potential function is the Euclidean or Manhattan distance based on the nodes' coordinates. Given π_t, the reduced link cost is defined as $c_{e,\pi_t} = c(u,v) - \pi_t(u) + \pi_t(v)$. We say that π_t is feasible if $c_{e,\pi_t} \geq 0$ for all $e \in E$. The feasibility of π_t is necessary for the algorithm to produce a correct solution. A potential function, π, is called valid for a given network if the A* search algorithm outputs an (s,t)– shortest path for any pair of nodes.

The potential function can take other values coming from the network input data. The algorithm described in the next subsection takes preprocessed shortest path distances to speed-up the SP search.

2.3 ALT Algorithm

The ALT algorithm is a variant of the A* search algorithm where landmarks and the triangle inequality are used to compute for a feasible potential function. Given a graph, the algorithm first preprocesses a set of landmarks, $L \subset V$ and precomputes distances from and to these landmarks for every node $w \in V$. Let $L = \{l_1, \ldots, l_{|L|}\}$, based on the triangle inequality, $|x + y| \leq |x| + |y|$, two inequalities can be derived, $dist^*(u,v) \geq dist^*(l,v) - dist^*(l,u)$ (see Fig. 1) and $dist^*(u,v) \geq dist^*(u,l) - dist^*(v,l)$ for any $u,v,l \in V$. Therefore, potential functions denoted as,

$$\pi_t^+(v) = dist^*(v,l) - dist^*(t,l), \tag{2}$$

$$\pi_t^-(v) = dist^*(l,t) - dist^*(l,v), \tag{3}$$

can be defined as feasible potential functions.

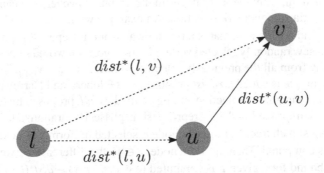

Fig. 1. A triangle inequality formed by a landmark l and two arbitrary nodes u and v

To get good lower bounds for each node, the ALT algorithm can use the maximum potential function from the set of landmarks, i.e.,

$$\pi_t(v) = \max_{l \in L} \{\pi_t^+(v), \pi_t^-(v)\} \tag{4}$$

A major advantage of the ALT algorithm over the A* search algorithm in a traffic simulation is its potential function's input flexibility. While the A* search algorithm can only use node coordinates to estimate distances, the ALT algorithm accepts either travel time or travel distance as a potential function input which makes it more robust with respect to different metrics [12]. This is significant because traffic simulations usually use travel times as edge weights where a case of a short link length with a very high travel time and a long link length with a shorter travel time can occur. Moreover, the ALT algorithm has been successfully applied to social networks [16, 17] where most hierarchal, road network oriented methods would fail.

One disadvantage of the ALT algorithm is the additional computation time and space required for the landmark generation and storage, respectively.

3   Preprocessing Landmarks

Landmark selection is an important part of the ALT algorithm since good landmarks produce good distance estimates to the target. As a result, many landmark selection strategies have been developed to produce good landmark sets. However, as the landmark selection strategies improved, the preprocessing time also increased. Furthermore, this increase in preprocessing time exceeds the preprocessing times of faster shortest path search algorithms to which the ALT algorithm is usually combined with [13]. Thus, decreasing the landmark selection strategy's preprocessing time is important.

3.1   Landmark Selection Strategies

Finding a set, k, of good landmarks is critical for the overall performance of the shortest path search. The simplest and most naïve algorithm would be to select a landmark, uniformly at random, from the set of nodes in the graph. However, one can do better by using some criteria for landmark selection. An example would be to randomly select a vertex, $\hat{v}_1$, and find a vertex, v_1, that is farthest away from it. Repeat this process k times where for each new randomly selected vertex, $\hat{v}_i$, the algorithm would select a the vertex, v_i, farthest away from all the previously selected vertices, $\{v_1, \ldots, v_{i-1}\}$. This landmark generation technique is called *farthest* proposed by Goldberg and Harrelson [3].

In this paper, a landmark selection strategy called *Avoid*, proposed by Goldberg and Werneck [9], is improved and its preprocessing phase is parallelized. In the *Avoid* method, a shortest path tree, T_r, rooted at node r, selected uniformly at random from the set of nodes, is computed. Then, for each node, $v \in V$, the difference between $dist^*(r, v)$ and its lower bound for a given L is computed (e.g. $dist^*(r, v) - dist^*(l, v) + dist^*(l, r)$). This is the node's weight which is a measure of how bad the current cost estimates are. Then, for each node v, the size is calculated. The size, $size(v)$, depends on T_v, a subtree of T_r rooted at v. If T_v contains a landmark, $size(v)$ is set to 0, otherwise, the $size(v)$ is calculated as the sum of the weights of all the nodes in T_v. Let w be the node of maximum size, traverse T_w starting from w and always follow the child node with the largest size until a leaf node is reached. Make this leaf a new landmark (see Fig. 2). This process is repeated until a set with k landmarks is generated.

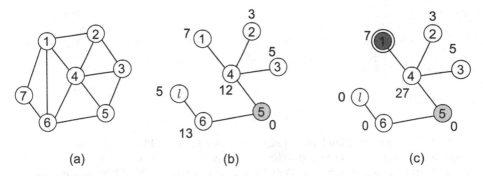

Fig. 2. The *Avoid* method. (a) A sample network with 7 nodes is shown. In (b), node 5 is randomly selected and a shortest path tree, T_5, is computed. Then, the distance estimate is subtracted by the shortest path cost for each node. These are the nodes' weights (shown in red). In (c), node sizes are computed. Since node 7 is a landmark and the subtree, T_6, has a landmark, both sizes are set to 0. Starting from the node with the maximum size (node 4), traverse the tree deterministically until a leaf is reached (node 1) and make this a landmark (Color figure online)

A variant of *Avoid* called the *advancedAvoid* was proposed to try to compensate for the main disadvantage of *Avoid* by probabilistically exchanging the initial landmarks with newly generated landmarks using *Avoid* [13]. It had the advantage of producing better landmarks at the expense of an additional computation cost. Another variant called *maxCover* uses *Avoid* to generate a set of $4k$ landmarks and uses a scoring criterion to select the best k landmarks in the set through a local search for $\lfloor \log_2 k + 1 \rfloor$ iterations. This produced the best landmarks at the expense of an additional computation cost greater than the additional computation cost incurred by *advancedAvoid*.

We improve *Avoid* by changing the criteria of the shortest path tree to traverse deterministically. Rather than just consider the tree with the maximum size, T_w, the criteria is changed to select the tree with the largest value when size is multiplied by the number of nodes in the tree, i.e. $size(v) \times |T_v|$, where $|T_v|$ denotes the number of nodes in the tree T_v [15]. This method prioritizes landmarks that can cover a larger region without sacrificing much quality. Additionally, following the *advancedAvoid* algorithm, after k landmarks are generated, a subset $\hat{k} \subset k$ is removed uniformly at random and the algorithm then continues to select landmarks until k landmarks are found.

To increase landmark selection efficiency without drastically increasing the computation time, the algorithm, which we call *parallelAvoid*, is implemented in parallel using the C++ Message Passing Interface (MPI) standard. In *parallelAvoid*, each CPU, p_j, generates a set of k landmarks using the method outlined in the previous paragraph. These landmark sets are then evaluated using a scoring criterion that determines the effectiveness of the landmark set. The score determined by each CPU is sent to a randomly selected CPU, p_k, which then determines the CPU with the maximum score, $\hat{p}_j$. The CPU p_k sends a message informing $\hat{p}_j$ to broadcast its landmark set to all the other CPUs including p_k (see Fig. 3).

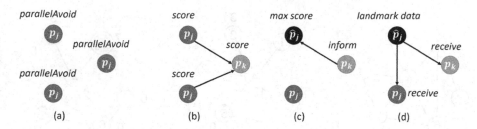

Fig. 3. The *parallelAvoid* landmark strategy algorithm. (a) The CPUs, p_j, generates landmarks using the *parallelAvoid* algorithm. (b) The score for each landmark set is sent to CPU p_k where the maximum score is determined. (c) The CPU p_k then informs the CPU with the maximum score, $\hat{p}_j$, to send its landmark data to all the other CPUs. (d) The CPU, $\hat{p}_j$, sends its landmark data to all the other CPUs

Hence, in terms of the query phase calculation time, the hierarchy of the landmark generation algorithms introduced above are as follows,

$$Avoid > advancedAvoid > parallelAvoid \geq maxCover > ILP, \qquad (5)$$

There can be a case where *parallelAvoid* produces better landmarks, thus better query times, than *maxCover*. This case happens when the CPUs used to generate landmarks significantly exceed the $\lfloor \log_2 k + 1 \rfloor$ iterations used by the *maxCover* algorithm.

For the landmark preprocessing phase calculation time, the hierarchy of the same landmark generation algorithms are as follows,

$$Avoid < advancedAvoid \leq parallelAvoid < maxCover < ILP. \qquad (6)$$

3.2   Landmark Set Scoring Function

In order to measure the quality of the landmarks generated by the different landmark generation algorithms, a modified version of the maximum coverage problem [14] is solved and its result is used as the criterion to score the effectiveness of a landmark set.

The maximum coverage problem is defined as follows: Given a set of elements, $\{a_1, \ldots, a_r\}$, a collection, $S = \{S_1, \ldots, S_p\}$, of sets where $S_i \subset \{a_1, \ldots, a_r\}$ and an integer k, the problem is to find a subset $S^* \subset S$ with $|S^*| \leq k$ so that a maximum number of elements a_i covered is maximal, i.e., $\max \bigcap_{S_i \in S^*} S_i$. Such a set S^* is called a set of maximum coverage.

In order to find the maximum coverage, a query of selected source and target pairs are carried out using Dijkstra's algorithm. A $|V|^3 \times |V|$ matrix with one column for each node in each search space of the Dijkstra query and one row for each node, $v \in V$, interpreted as a potential landmark, l_i, is initialized with zero entries. The ALT algorithm is carried out on the same source and target pairs queried by the Dijkstra's algorithm. Then for each node in the Dijkstra algorithm's search space, if the ALT algorithm doesn't visit the node, v, using l_i (i.e. l_i would exclude v from the search space), the entry for the column assigned to the node v is set to 1 (see Fig. 4). Selecting k rows so that a maximum number of columns are covered is equivalent to the maximum coverage problem.

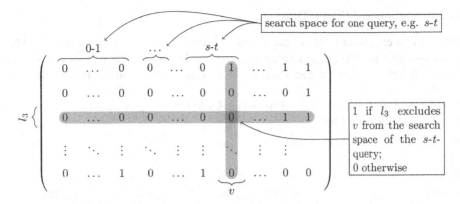

Fig. 4. The matrix for the landmark selection problem interpreted as a maximum coverage problem [14]

For our case, the maximum coverage problem is modified to only consider a subset of the origin-destination pairs used in the traffic simulation for the $(s, t)-$ query. Additionally, each row is composed of the k landmarks found by *parallelAvoid* rather than all the nodes in the node set. The modified maximum coverage problem is then defined as the landmark set that has the maximum number of columns in the matrix that is set to 1. Furthermore, the number of columns set to 1 are summed up and then used as the score of the landmark set. In this modified maximum coverage problem, the landmark set with the highest score is used for the shortest path search.

4   Computational Results

The network used for the computational experiments is the Tokyo Metropolitan network which is composed of 196,269 nodes, 439,979 links and 2210 origin-destination pairs. A series of calculations were carried out and averaged over 10 executions for the *Avoid*, *advanceAvoid*, *maxCover* and *parallelAvoid* algorithms using Fujitsu's K computer. A landmark set composed of $k = 4$ landmarks with $\hat{k} = 2$ and $\hat{k} = 0$ for the *advanceAvoid* and *parallelAvoid*, respectively, were generated for each landmark selection strategy.

The K computer is a massively parallel CPU-based supercomputer system at the Advanced Institute of Computational Science, RIKEN. It is based on a distributed memory architecture with over 80,000 compute nodes where each compute node has 8 cores (SPARC64™ VIIIfx) and 16 GB of memory. Its node network topology is a 6D mesh torus network called the tofu (**torus fu**sion) interconnect.

The performance measures used are the execution times of the algorithms and the respective query times of its SP searches using the landmark sets that each of the algorithms have generated. For *parallelAvoid*, its parallel implementation was also measured using different number of CPUs for scalability.

4.1   Execution and Query Times

The average execution times of the *Avoid* (A), *advanceAvoid* (AA), *maxCover* (MC) and *parallelAvoid* (PA) algorithms generating 4 landmarks and the average query times of each SP search using the generated landmarks are presented in the Table 1 below.

Table 1. Averaged execution times of the landmark selection strategies and averaged query times of each SP searches in seconds.

Number of CPUs	A	AA	MC	PA	Query time
1 (A)	124.270	——	——	——	0.1382
1 (AA)	——	180.446	——	——	0.1253
1 (MC)	——	——	521.602	——	0.1081
2 (PA)	——	——	——	133.829	0.1390
4 (PA)	——	——	——	134.515	0.1282
8 (PA)	——	——	——	140.112	0.1128
16 (PA)	——	——	——	143.626	0.1102
32 (PA)	——	——	——	157.766	0.1078
64 (PA)	——	——	——	160.941	0.1044
128 (PA)	——	——	——	163.493	0.1022
256 (PA)	——	——	——	169.606	0.1004
512 (PA)	——	——	——	178.278	0.0998
1024 (PA)	——	——	——	180.661	0.0986

The table above shows that algorithms took at least 30 s to select a landmark. The *advanceAvoid* algorithm took a longer time as it selected 6 landmarks (i.e. $k = 4$ and $\hat{k} = 2$). The *maxCover* algorithm took the longest time as it generated 16 landmarks and selected the best 4 landmarks through a local search. The local search was executed $\lfloor \log_2 k + 1 \rfloor$ which is equal to 2 in this case. The *parallelAvoid* algorithm's execution (landmark generation) time slowly increased because of the increasing number of CPUs that the CPU, $\hat{p}_j$, had to share landmark data with.

In terms of query times, the algorithms follow Eq. (5) up to 16 CPUs. At 32 CPUs, *parallelAvoid*'s query performance is better than *maxCover*'s query performance. Note that 32 CPUs mean that 32 different landmark sets were generated by *parallelAvoid* which is twice the number of landmarks generated by the *maxCover* algorithm. Moreover, the table also shows that the number of CPUs is directly proportional to the landmark generation time and inversely proportional to the query time. The former is due to the overhead caused by communication which is expected. As the number of communicating CPUs increase, the execution time of the algorithm also increases. While for the latter, as the number of CPUs increase the possibility of finding a better solution also increases which produces faster query times.

4.2 Algorithm Scalability

A common task in high performance computing (HPC) is measuring scalability of an application. This measurement indicates the application's efficiency when using an increasing number of parallel CPUs.

The *parallelAvoid* algorithm belongs to the weak scaling case where the problem size assigned to each CPU remains constant (i.e. all CPUs will generate a set of landmarks which consumes a lot of memory). This is very efficient when used with the K computer's distributed memory architecture. In the Fig. 5 above, a major source of overhead is data transfer. The data transfer overhead is caused by the transfer of landmark data from CPU, $\hat{p}_j$, to all the other CPUs. This was implemented using the MPI_Bcast command which has a tree-based structure that has a logarithmic complexity. Hence, it can be noticed that by using a logarithmic scale on the x-axis, the weak scaling is significantly affected by the data transfer overhead.

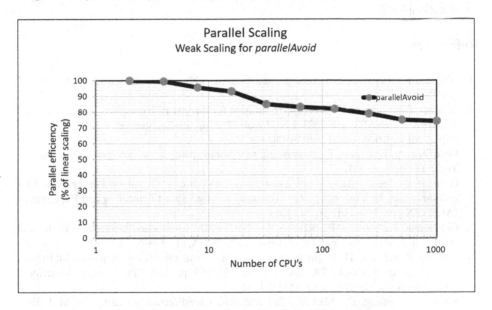

Fig. 5. Weak scaling for the *parallelAvoid* algorithm.

5   Conclusions

In this paper, we have presented a parallelized ALT preprocessing algorithm called the *parallelAvoid*.

We have shown that this algorithm can increase the landmark's efficiency while significantly accelerating the preprocessing time using multiple CPUs. By using many CPUs, it is possible to obtain a better landmark set in a significantly lesser amount of time which produces faster query times. Compared to the *maxCover* algorithm, it is limited only to the number of CPUs rather than the number of local search iterations. This is important since the ALT algorithm is usually combined with other preprocessing algorithms to take advantage of its goal-directed search. Moreover, the parallelization technique doesn't sacrifice landmark quality in exchange for preprocessing speed unlike the ALP (A*, landmarks and polygon inequality) algorithm [18, 19], a generalization of the ALT algorithm or the *partition-corners* method used in [20, 21].

Additionally, results show that the major cause of overhead is the landmark data transfer. This is because the data transfer of the landmark data from the CPU with the highest score to the other CPUs use a tree-like structure which has a logarithmic complexity.

Acknowledgement. This work was supported by Post K computer project (Priority Issue 3: Development of Integrated Simulation Systems for Hazard and Disaster Induced by Earthquake and Tsunami).

This research used computational resources of the K computer provided by the RIKEN Advanced Institute for Computational Science through the HPCI System Research Project (Project ID: hp170271).

References

1. Dijkstra, E.: A note on two problems in connexion with graphs. Numer. Math. **1**, 269–271 (1959)
2. Wagner, D., Willhalm, T.: Speed-up techniques for shortest-path computations. In: Thomas, W., Weil, P. (eds.) STACS 2007. LNCS, vol. 4393, pp. 23–36. Springer, Heidelberg (2007). https://doi.org/10.1007/978-3-540-70918-3_3
3. Goldberg, A., Harrelson, C.: Computing the shortest path: A* search meets graph theory. Technical report (2004)
4. Gutman, R.: Reach-based routing: a new approach to shortest path algorithms optimized for road networks. In: Proceedings 6th Workshop on Algorithm Engineering and Experiments (ALENEX), pp. 100–111. SIAM (2004)
5. Geisberger, R., Sanders, P., Schultes, D., Delling, D.: Contraction hierarchies: Faster and simpler hierarchical routing in road networks. In: WEA, pp. 319–333 (2008)
6. Sanders, P., Schultes, D.: Highway hierarchies hasten exact shortest path queries. In: Brodal, G.S., Leonardi, S. (eds.) ESA 2005. LNCS, vol. 3669, pp. 568–579. Springer, Heidelberg (2005). https://doi.org/10.1007/11561071_51
7. Bauer, R., Delling, D.: SHARC: fast and robust unidirectional routing. ACM J. Exp. Algorithmics **14** (2009)
8. Delling, D., Wagner, D.: Pareto paths with SHARC. In: Vahrenhold, J. (ed.) SEA 2009. LNCS, vol. 5526, pp. 125–136. Springer, Heidelberg (2009). https://doi.org/10.1007/978-3-642-02011-7_13
9. Goldberg, A., Werneck, R.: Computing point-to-point shortest paths from external memory. In: Proceedings Workshop on Algorithm Engineering and Experiments (ALENEX 2005). SIAM (2005)
10. Köhler, E., Möhring, R.H., Schilling, H.: Acceleration of shortest path and constrained shortest path computation. In: Nikoletseas, S.E. (ed.) WEA 2005. LNCS, vol. 3503, pp. 126–138. Springer, Heidelberg (2005). https://doi.org/10.1007/11427186_13
11. Lauther, U.: An extremely fast, exact algorithm for finding shortest paths in static networks with geographical background. In: Geoinformation und Mobilitat - von der Forschung zur praktischen Anwendung, vol. 22, pp. 219–230. IfGI prints (2004)

12. Bauer, R., Delling, D., Sanders, P., Schieferdecker, D., Schultes, D., Wagner, D.: Combining hierarchical and goal-directed speed-up techniques for Dijkstra's algorithm. In: McGeoch, C.C. (ed.) WEA 2008. LNCS, vol. 5038, pp. 303–318. Springer, Heidelberg (2008). https://doi.org/10.1007/978-3-540-68552-4_23
13. Delling, D., Sanders, P., Schultes, D., Wagner, D.: Highway hierarchies star. In: 9th DIMACS Implementation Challenge (2006)
14. Peque Jr., G., Urata, J., Iryo, T.: Implementing an ALT algorithm for large-scale time-dependent networks. In: Proceedings of the 22nd International Conference of Hong Kong Society for Transport Studies, 9–11 December 2017
15. Fuchs, F.: On Preprocessing the ALT Algorithm. Master's thesis, University of the State of Baden-Wuerttemberg and National Laboratory of the Helmholtz Association, Institute for Theoretical Informatics (2010)
16. Mehlhorn, K., Sanders, P.: Algorithms and Data Structures: The Basic Toolbox. Springer, Heidelberg (2008). https://doi.org/10.1007/978-3-540-77978-0
17. Tretyakov, K., Armas-Cervantes, A., García-Bañuelos, L., Vilo, J., Dumas, M.: Fast fully dynamic landmark-based estimation of shortest path distances in very large graphs. In: Proceedings 20th CIKM Conference, pp. 1785–1794 (2011)
18. Campbell Jr., N.: Computing shortest paths using A*, landmarks, and polygon inequalities. arXiv:1603.01607 [cs.DS] (2016)
19. Campbell Jr., N.: Using quadrilaterals to compute the shortest path. arXiv:1603.00963 [cs.DS] (2016)
20. Efentakis, A., Pfoser, D.: Optimizing landmark-based routing and preprocessing. In: Proceedings of the Sixth ACM SIGSPATIAL International Workshop on Computational Transportation Science (IWCTS 2013), New York, pp. 25–30, November 2013
21. Efentakis, A., Pfoser, D., Vassiliou, Y.: SALT. A unified framework for all shortest-path query variants on road networks. arXiv:1411.0257 [cs.DS] (2014)

Efficient Linearly and Unconditionally Energy Stable Schemes for the Phase Field Model of Solid-State Dewetting Problems

Zhengkang He[1], Jie Chen[1](✉), and Zhangxin Chen[1,2]

[1] School of Mathematics and Statistics, Xi'an Jiaotong University,
Shaanxi 710049, People's Republic of China
chenjiexjtu@mail.xjtu.edu.cn

[2] Schulich School of Engineering, University of Calgary, 2500 University Drive NW,
Calgary, AB T2N 1N4, Canada

Abstract. In this paper, we study linearly first and second order in time, uniquely solvable and unconditionally energy stable numerical schemes to approximate the phase field model of solid-state dewetting problems based on the novel approach SAV (scalar auxiliary variable), a new developed efficient and accurate method for a large class of gradient flows. The schemes are based on the first order Euler method and the second order backward differential formulas(BDF2) for time discretization, and finite element methods for space discretization. It is shown that the schemes are unconditionally stable and the discrete equations are uniquely solvable for all time steps. We present some numerical experiments to validate the stability and accuracy of the proposed schemes.

Keywords: Phase field models · Solid-state dewetting · SAV
Energy stability · Surface diffusion · Finite element methods

1 Introduction

Solid-state dewetting of thin films plays an important role in many engineering and industrial applications, such as microelectronics processing, formation of patterned silicides in electronic devices, production of catalysts for the growth of carbon and semiconductor nanowires [2,4–6]. In general, solid-state dewetting can be modeled as interfacial dynamic problems where the morphological evolution is controlled by the surface diffusion. However, during the evolution, the interface may experience complicated topological changes such as pinch-off, splitting and fattening. All of them make great difficulties in the simulation of this interface evolution problem. The phase field model of solid-state dewetting problems presented in [1] can naturally capture topological changes that occur during the morphological evolution and can be easily extended to high dimension spaces. The idea of phase field approach dates back to the pioneering work

© Springer International Publishing AG, part of Springer Nature 2018
Y. Shi et al. (Eds.): ICCS 2018, LNCS 10862, pp. 102–112, 2018.
https://doi.org/10.1007/978-3-319-93713-7_8

of [12, 16], which use an auxiliary variable ϕ (phase field function) to localize the phases and describe the interface by a layer of small thickness. Now, the phase field method becomes one of the major modeling and computational tools for the study of interfacial phenomena (cf. [3, 7, 10, 11, 17]), and the references therein).

From the numerical perspective, for phase field models, one main challenge in the numerical approximation is how to design unconditionally energy stable schemes which keep the energy dissipative in both semi-discrete and fully discrete forms. The preservation of the energy dissipation law is particularly important, and is critical to preclude the non-physical numerical solutions. In fact, it has been observed that numerical schemes which do not respect the energy dissipation law may lead to large numerical errors, particular for long time simulation, so it is specially desirable to design numerical schemes that preserve the energy dissipation law at the discrete level [7, 8]. Another focus of developing numerical schemes to approximate the phase field models is to construct higher order time marching schemes. Under the requests of some degree of accuracy, higher order time marching schemes are usually preferable to lower order time marching schemes when we want to use larger time marching steps to achieve long time simulation [9–11]. This fact motivates us to develop more accurate schemes. Moreover, it goes without saying that linear numerical schemes are more efficient than the nonlinear numerical schemes because the nonlinear scheme are expensive to solve.

In this paper, we study linearly first and second order accurate in time, uniquely solvable and unconditionally energy stable numerical schemes for solving the phase field model of solid-state dewetting problems based on the SAV (scalar auxiliary variable) approach which are applicable to a large class of gradient flows [13, 14]. The essential idea of the SAV approach is to split the total free energy $\mathcal{E}(\phi)$ of gradient flows into two parts, written as

$$\mathcal{E}(\phi) = \frac{1}{2}(\phi, \mathcal{L}\phi) + \mathcal{E}_1(\phi), \tag{1}$$

where $\mathcal{L}$ is a symmetric non-negative linear operator contains the highest linear derivative terms in $\mathcal{E}$, and $\mathcal{E}_1(\phi) \geq C > 0$ is the nonlinear term but with only lower order derivative than $\mathcal{L}$. Then the SAV approach transform the nonlinear term $\mathcal{E}_1$ into quadratic form by only introduce a scalar variable $r = \sqrt{\mathcal{E}_1}$ and the total free energy $\mathcal{E}$ can be written as

$$\mathcal{E}(\phi, r) = \frac{1}{2}(\phi, \mathcal{L}\phi) + r^2. \tag{2}$$

The rest of the paper is organized as follows. In Sect. 2, we describe the phase field model of solid-state dewetting problems and the associated energy law. In Sect. 3, we develop linear numerical schemes with first order and second order accuracy in time for simulating the model, and prove their unconditional energy stabilities and unconditionally unique solvability. In Sect. 4, some numerical experiments are performed to validate the accuracy and energy stability of the proposed schemes. Finally, some concluding remarks are given in Sect. 5.

2   The Governing System and Energy Law

We now give a brief introduction to the phase field model as is proposed in
[1] that simulates the solid-state dewetting phenomenon of thin films and the
morphological evolution of patterned islands on a solid substrate. If we consider
that the free interface (surface between thin film phase and vapor phase) energy
is isotropic, then the total free energy of the system is defined as follows

$$\mathcal{E}(\phi) = \mathcal{E}_{FV}(\phi) + \mathcal{E}_w(\phi) = \int_\Omega f_{FV}(\phi)\mathrm{d}\mathbf{x} + \int_{\Gamma_w} f_w(\phi)\mathrm{d}s \qquad (3)$$

here Ω is a bounded domain in $\mathbb{R}^2$, with boundary $\partial\Omega$ that has an outward-
pointing unit normal $\mathbf{n}$. $\Gamma_w \subseteq \partial\Omega$ represents the solid surface (solid substrate)
to where the thin film adhere, called as wall boundary. $\mathcal{E}_{FV}$ represents the free
interface energy of two phases (thin film phase and vapor phase), $\mathcal{E}_w$ represents
the combined energy on the solid surface called wall energy, and f_{FV} and f_w are
the corresponding energy densities, respectively, defined as follows

$$f_{FV}(\phi) = F(\phi) + \frac{\varepsilon^2}{2}|\nabla\phi|^2 \qquad (4)$$

$$f_w(\phi) = \frac{\varepsilon(\phi^3 - 3\phi)}{3\sqrt{2}}\cos\theta_s. \qquad (5)$$

where $F(\phi) = \frac{1}{4}(\phi^2 - 1)^2$ is the well-known Ginzburg-Landau double-well potential, ε is a positive constant related to the interface width, and θ_s is the prescribed
contact angle between the free interface and the solid surface.

The governing equations of the system is defined as follows

$$\frac{\partial\phi}{\partial t} = \nabla \cdot (M(\phi)\nabla\mu), \qquad \text{in } \Omega \qquad (6)$$

$$\mu = \frac{\delta\mathcal{E}}{\delta\phi} = \phi^3 - \phi - \varepsilon^2\Delta\phi, \qquad \text{in } \Omega \qquad (7)$$

with the following boundary conditions

$$\varepsilon^2\frac{\partial\phi}{\partial\mathbf{n}} + f'_w = 0, \qquad \frac{\partial\mu}{\partial\mathbf{n}} = 0, \qquad \text{on } \Gamma_w \qquad (8)$$

$$\frac{\partial\phi}{\partial\mathbf{n}} = 0, \qquad \frac{\partial\mu}{\partial\mathbf{n}} = 0, \qquad \text{on } \partial\Omega\backslash\Gamma_w \qquad (9)$$

The above system can be derived as a gradient flow of the total free energy
functional $\mathcal{E}(\phi)$ with the dissipation mechanism $\nabla \cdot (M(\phi)\nabla\mu)$, where $M(\phi) = 1 - \phi^2$ is the mobility function chosen in [1] and μ is the first variational derivative
of the total free energy $\mathcal{E}$ with respect to the phase field variable ϕ called the
chemical potential. The boundary condition $\frac{\partial\mu}{\partial\mathbf{n}} = 0$ implies that the total mass
is conservative:

$$\frac{d}{dt}\int_\Omega \phi\mathrm{d}\mathbf{x} = \int_\Omega \phi_t\mathrm{d}\mathbf{x} = \int_\Omega \nabla \cdot (M(\phi)\nabla\mu)\mathrm{d}\mathbf{x} = -\int_\Omega M(\phi)\frac{\partial\mu}{\partial\mathbf{n}}\mathrm{d}s = 0. \qquad (10)$$

Moreover, the total free energy functional $\mathcal{E}(t)$ is dissipative:

$$\frac{d}{dt}\mathcal{E}(t) = \int_\Omega F'(\phi)\phi_t + \varepsilon^2 \nabla\phi \cdot \nabla\phi_t \mathrm{dx} + \int_{\Gamma_w} f'_w(\phi)\phi_t \mathrm{ds}$$

$$= \int_\Omega \mu\phi_t \mathrm{dx} + \int_{\Gamma_w} \left(\varepsilon^2 \frac{\partial\phi}{\partial\mathbf{n}} + f'_w(\phi)\right)\phi_t \mathrm{ds} = \int_\Omega \mu M \triangle\mu \mathrm{dx}$$

$$= -\int_\Omega M\nabla\mu \cdot \nabla\mu \mathrm{dx} + \int_{\partial\Omega} \mu M \frac{\partial\mu}{\partial\mathbf{n}} \mathrm{ds}$$

$$= -\int_\Omega M|\nabla\mu|^2 \mathrm{dx} \leq 0 \tag{11}$$

3   Numerical Schemes and Energy Stability

In this section, we construct several fully discrete numerical schemes for solving the dewetting problems, and prove their energy stabilities and unique solvability.

We aim to obtain some effective numerical schemes, in particular, the linear schemes. Inspired by the SAV approach, we split the total free energy $\mathcal{E}$ as follows,

$$\mathcal{E}(\phi) = \frac{\varepsilon^2}{2}(\nabla\phi, \nabla\phi) + \frac{1}{4}\int_\Omega (\phi^2 - 1)^2 \mathrm{dx} + \int_{\Gamma_w} \frac{\phi^3 - 3\phi}{3\sqrt{2}}\varepsilon\cos\theta_s \mathrm{ds}$$

$$= \frac{\varepsilon^2}{2}(-\triangle\phi, \phi) + \frac{\varepsilon^2}{2}\int_{\partial\Omega}\frac{\partial\phi}{\partial\mathbf{n}}\phi \mathrm{ds} + \frac{\beta}{2}\int_\Omega \phi^2 \mathrm{dx} + \frac{1}{4}\int_\Omega (\phi^2 - 1 - \beta)^2 \mathrm{dx}$$

$$+ \int_{\Gamma_w}\frac{\phi^3 - 3\phi}{3\sqrt{2}}\varepsilon\cos\theta_s \mathrm{ds} - \frac{1}{4}\int_\Omega \beta^2 + 2\beta \mathrm{dx}$$

$$= \frac{1}{2}(\phi, \mathcal{L}\phi) + \mathcal{E}_1(\phi) - \frac{1}{4}\int_\Omega \beta^2 + 2\beta \mathrm{dx} \tag{12}$$

where β is a positive constant to be chosen, and

$$(\phi, \mathcal{L}\phi) = \varepsilon^2(-\triangle\phi, \phi) + \varepsilon^2 \int_{\partial\Omega}\frac{\partial\phi}{\partial\mathbf{n}}\phi \mathrm{ds} + \beta\int_\Omega \phi^2 \mathrm{dx} = \varepsilon^2(\nabla\phi, \nabla\phi) + \beta(\phi, \phi)$$

$$\mathcal{E}_1(\phi) = \frac{1}{4}\int_\Omega (\phi^2 - 1 - \beta)^2 \mathrm{dx} + \int_{\Gamma_w}\frac{\phi^3 - 3\phi}{3\sqrt{2}}\varepsilon\cos\theta_s \mathrm{ds}.$$

We drop the constant $-\frac{1}{4}\int_\Omega \beta^2 + 2\beta \mathrm{dx}$ in the total free energy $\mathcal{E}(\phi)$, then the total free energy becomes as

$$\mathcal{E}(\phi) = \frac{1}{2}(\phi, \mathcal{L}\phi) + \mathcal{E}_1(\phi), \tag{13}$$

and the gradient flow Eqs. (6) and (7) can be written as

$$\frac{\partial\phi}{\partial t} = \nabla \cdot ((1 - \phi^2)\nabla\mu), \tag{14}$$

$$\mu = \mathcal{L}\phi + U(\phi), \tag{15}$$

where,

$$U(\phi) = \frac{\delta \mathcal{E}_1}{\delta \phi} \tag{16}$$

is the first variational derivative of the free energy $\mathcal{E}_1$ with respect to the phase field variable ϕ.

As in [13,14], a scalar auxiliary variable $r = \sqrt{\mathcal{E}_1}$ is introduced, then we rebuild the total free energy functional (12) as

$$\mathcal{E}(\phi, r) = \frac{1}{2}(\phi, \mathcal{L}\phi) + r^2, \tag{17}$$

and accordingly we can rewrite the gradient flow Eqs. (14) and (15) as follows

$$\frac{\partial \phi}{\partial t} = \nabla \cdot ((1 - \phi^2)\nabla \mu), \tag{18}$$

$$\mu = \mathcal{L}\phi + \frac{r}{\sqrt{\mathcal{E}_1(\phi)}} U(\phi), \tag{19}$$

$$r_t = \frac{1}{2\sqrt{\mathcal{E}_1(\phi)}} \langle U(\phi), \phi_t \rangle. \tag{20}$$

where,

$$\langle U(\phi), \psi_t \rangle = \int_\Omega (\phi^3 - \phi - \beta\phi)\psi_t \mathrm{d}\mathbf{x} + \int_{\Gamma_w} \frac{\sqrt{2}}{2}(\phi^2 - 1)\varepsilon \cos\theta_s \psi_t \mathrm{d}s. \tag{21}$$

The boundary conditions are also (8) and (9), and the initial conditions are

$$\phi(x, y, 0) = \phi_0, r(0) = \sqrt{\mathcal{E}_1(\phi_0)} \tag{22}$$

Taking the inner products of the Eqs. (18)–(20) with μ, $\frac{\partial \phi}{\partial t}$ and $2r$ respectively, the new system still follows an energy dissipative law:

$$\frac{d}{dt}\mathcal{E}(\phi, r) = \frac{d}{dt}[(\phi, \mathcal{L}\phi) + r^2] = -(\mu, M(\phi)\mu) \leq 0. \tag{23}$$

Remark: β is a positive number to be chosen.

Since finite element methods have the capability of handling complex geometries, we consider the fully discrete numerical schemes for solving the system (18)–(20) in the framework of finite element methods. Let $\mathcal{T}_h$ be a quasi-uniform triangulation of the domain Ω of mesh size h. We introduce the finite element space S_h to approximate the Sobolev space $H^1(\Omega)$ based on the triangulation $\mathcal{T}_h$.

$$S_h = \{v_h \in C(\Omega) \mid v_h| \in P_r, \forall \in \mathcal{T}_h\}, \tag{24}$$

where P_r is the space of polynomials of degree at most r. Denote the time step by δt and set $t^n = n\delta t$. Firstly, we give the fully discrete scheme of first order.

3.1 The Fully Discrete Linear First Order Scheme

In the framework of finite element space above, we now give the fully discrete semi-implicit first order scheme for the system (18)–(20) based on the backward Euler's method. Assuming that ϕ_h^n and r_h^n are already known, we find $(\phi_h^{n+1}, \mu_h^{n+1}, r_h^{n+1}) \in S_h \times S_h \times \mathbb{R}^+$ such that for all $(\nu_h, \psi_h) \in S_h \times S_h$ there hold

$$\left(\frac{\phi_h^{n+1} - \phi_h^n}{dt}, \nu_h\right) = -\left(\left|1 - (\phi_h^n)^2\right| \nabla \mu_h^{n+1}, \nabla \nu_h\right), \tag{25}$$

$$\left(\mu_h^{n+1}, \psi_h\right) = \left(\mathcal{L}\phi_h^{n+1}, \psi_h\right) + \frac{r_h^{n+1}}{\sqrt{\mathcal{E}_1(\phi_h^{n+1})}} \langle U(\phi_h^n), \psi_h \rangle, \tag{26}$$

$$r_h^{n+1} - r_h^n = \frac{1}{2\sqrt{\mathcal{E}_1(\phi_h^n)}} \langle U(\phi_h^n), \phi_h^{n+1} - \phi_h^n \rangle. \tag{27}$$

where

$$
\begin{aligned}
(\mathcal{L}\phi_h^{n+1}, \psi_h) &= \varepsilon^2(-\Delta\phi_h^{n+1}, \psi) + \varepsilon^2 \int_{\partial\Omega} \frac{\partial\phi_h^{n+1}}{\partial\mathbf{n}} \psi_h ds + \beta \int_\Omega \phi_h^{n+1} \psi_h d\mathbf{x} \\
&= \varepsilon^2(\nabla\phi_h^{n+1}, \nabla\psi_h) + \beta(\phi_h^{n+1}, \psi_h)
\end{aligned} \tag{28}
$$

and

$$
\begin{aligned}
\langle U[\phi_h^{n+1}], \psi_h \rangle &= \int_\Omega \left((\phi_h^{n+1})^3 - \phi_h^{n+1} - \beta\phi_h^{n+1}\right) \psi_h d\mathbf{x} \\
&\quad + \int_{\Gamma_w} \frac{\sqrt{2}}{2}\left((\phi_h^{n+1})^2 - 1\right)\varepsilon\cos\theta_s \psi_h ds.
\end{aligned} \tag{29}
$$

Remark: Taking $\nu_h = 1$ in Eq. (25), we obtain the conservation of the total mass,

$$\int_\Omega \phi_h^{n+1} d\mathbf{x} = \int_\Omega \phi_h^n d\mathbf{x} = \cdots = \int_\Omega \phi_h^0 d\mathbf{x} \tag{30}$$

Theorem 1. *Given* $(\phi_h^n, r_h^n) \in S_h \times \mathbb{R}^+$, *the system (25)–(27) admits a unique solution* $(\phi_h^{n+1}, \mu_h^{n+1}, r_h^{n+1}) \in S_h \times S_h \times \mathbb{R}^+$ *at the time* t^{n+1} *for any* $h > 0$ *and* $\delta t > 0$. *Moreover, the solution satisfies a discrete energy law as follows*

$$\mathcal{E}_{1st}^{n+1} - \mathcal{E}_{1st}^n + \frac{1}{2}(\phi_h^{n+1} - \phi_h^n, \mathcal{L}(\phi_h^{n+1} - \phi_h^n)) + (r_h^{n+1} - r_h^n)^2$$

$$= -\delta t(\left|1 - (\phi_h^n)^2\right| \nabla\mu_h^{n+1}, \nabla\mu_h^{n+1})$$

where $\mathcal{E}_{1st}^{n+1}$ *is the modified energy*

$$\mathcal{E}_{1st}^n = \frac{1}{2}(\phi_h^n, \mathcal{L}\phi_h^n) + (r_h^n)^2. \tag{31}$$

Thus the scheme is unconditionally stable.

Proof. Taking $\nu_h = \mu^{n+1}$ and $\psi_h = (\phi^{n+1} - \phi^n)/\delta t$ in Eqs. (25) and (26) respectively and adding Eqs. (25)–(27) together, we can obtain the discrete energy law, in addition, the schemes (25)–(27) is a linear system, thus there exists a unique solution $(\phi_h^{n+1}, \mu_h^{n+1}, r_h^{n+1})$ at time t^{n+1}.

3.2   The Fully Discrete Linear Second Order Scheme

We now give the fully discrete semi-implicit second order scheme for the system (18)–(20) based on the backward differentiation formula (BDF2). Assuming that ϕ_h^{n-1}, r_h^{n-1}, ϕ_h^n and r_h^n are already known, we find $(\phi_h^{n+1}, \mu_h^{n+1}, r_h^{n+1}) \in S_h \times S_h \times \mathbb{R}^+$ such that for all $(\nu_h, \psi_h) \in S_h \times S_h$ there hold

$$\left(\frac{3\phi_h^{n+1} - 4\phi_h^n + \phi_h^{n-1}}{2\delta t}, \nu_h \right) = -\left(\left| 1 - (\bar\phi_h^{n+1})^2 \right| \nabla \mu_h^{n+1}, \nabla \nu_h \right) \tag{32}$$

$$\left(\mu_h^{n+1}, \psi_h \right) = \left(\mathcal{L}\phi_h^{n+1}, \psi_h \right) + \frac{r_h^{n+1}}{\sqrt{\mathcal{E}_1(\bar\phi_h^{\,n+1})}} \langle U(\bar\phi_h^{n+1}), \psi_h \rangle, \tag{33}$$

$$3r_h^{n+1} - 4r_h^n + r_h^{n-1} = \frac{1}{2\sqrt{\mathcal{E}_1(\bar\phi_h^{n+1})}} \langle U(\bar\phi_h^{n+1}), 3\phi_h^{n+1} - 4\phi_h^n + \phi_h^{n-1} \rangle, \tag{34}$$

where $\bar\phi_h^{n+1} = 2\phi_h^n - \phi_h^{n-1}$,

$$(\mathcal{L}\phi_h^{n+1}, \psi_h) = \varepsilon^2(-\Delta\phi_h^{n+1}, \psi) + \varepsilon^2 \int_{\partial\Omega} \frac{\partial\phi_h^{n+1}}{\partial \mathbf{n}} \psi_h \mathrm{d}s + \beta \int_\Omega \phi_h^{n+1}\psi_h \mathrm{d}\mathbf{x}$$

$$= \varepsilon^2(\nabla\phi_h^{n+1}, \nabla\psi_h) + \beta(\phi_h^{n+1}, \psi_h), \tag{35}$$

and

$$\langle U[\bar\phi_h^{n+1}], \psi_h \rangle = \int_\Omega \left((\bar\phi_h^{n+1})^3 - \bar\phi_h^{n+1} - \beta\bar\phi_h^{n+1} \right)\psi_h \mathrm{d}\mathbf{x}$$

$$+ \int_{\Gamma_w} \frac{\sqrt{2}}{2}\left((\bar\phi_h^{n+1})^2 - 1 \right)\varepsilon \cos\theta_s \psi_h \mathrm{d}s. \tag{36}$$

Remark: The second order scheme (32)–(34) is a two step method, we can solve for ϕ_h^1 and r_h^1 through the first order scheme (25)–(27), similarly by taking $\nu_h = 1$ in Eq. (32), we obtain the conservation of the total mass,

$$\int_\Omega \phi_h^{n+1}\mathrm{d}\mathbf{x} = \int_\Omega \phi_h^n\mathrm{d}\mathbf{x} = \cdots = \int_\Omega \phi_h^0\mathrm{d}\mathbf{x} \tag{37}$$

Theorem 2. *Given* $(\phi_h^n, r_h^n) \in S_h \times \mathbb{R}^+$, *the system (32)–(34) admits a unique solution* $(\phi_h^{n+1}, \mu_h^{n+1}, r_h^{n+1}) \in S_h \times S_h \times \mathbb{R}^+$ *at the time* t^{n+1} *for any* $h > 0$ *and* $\delta t > 0$. *Moreover, the solution satisfies a discrete energy law as follows*

$$\mathcal{E}_{2nd}^{n+1,n} - \mathcal{E}_{2nd}^{n,n-1} + \frac{1}{4}\left(\phi_h^{n+1} - 2\phi_h^n + \phi_h^{n-1}, \mathcal{L}(\phi_h^{n+1} - 2\phi_h^n + \phi_h^{n-1}) \right)$$

$$+ \frac{1}{2}(r_h^{n+1} - 2r_h^n + r_h^{n-1})^2 = -\delta t(|1 - (\bar\phi_h^{n+1})^2| \nabla\mu_h^{n+1}, \nabla\mu_h^{n+1})$$

where $\mathcal{E}_{2nd}^{n+1,n}$ *is the modified energy*

$$\mathcal{E}_{2nd}^{n+1,n} = \frac{1}{4}\left((\phi_h^{n+1}, \mathcal{L}\phi_h^{n+1}) + (2\phi_h^{n+1} - \phi_h^n, \mathcal{L}(2\phi_h^{n+1} - \phi_h^n)) + \frac{1}{2}\left((r_h^{n+1})^2 + (2r_h^{n+1} - r_h^n)^2 \right) \right) \tag{38}$$

Proof. Taking $\nu_h = \mu_h^{n+1}$ and $\psi_h = (3\phi_h^{n+1} - 4\phi_h^n + \phi_h^{n-1})/\delta t$ in Eqs. (32) and (33) respectively integrating the first two equations and applying the following identity:

$$2(3a^{k+1} - 4a^k + a^{k-1}, a^{k+1}) = \left|a^{k+1}\right|^2 + \left|2a^{k+1} - a^k\right|^2 + \left|a^{k+1} - 2a^k + a^{k-1}\right|^2$$
$$- \left|a^k\right|^2 - \left|2a^k - a^{k-1}\right|^2, \tag{39}$$

we can obtain the discrete energy law, in addition, the schemes (32)–(34) is a linear system, thus there exists a unique solution $(\phi_h^{n+1}, \mu_h^{n+1}, r_h^{n+1})$ at time t^{n+1}.

4   Numerical Experiments

In this section, we present some numerical experiments to validate the accuracy and stability of numerical schemes presented in this paper. For simplicity, we use the conforming P_1 finite element in space S_h to approximate ϕ_h and μ_h. For all our experiments in this section, the computational domain is taken as a rectangle $\Omega = [-1, 1] \times [0, 1]$, and the wall boundary Γ_w is the bottom of the rectangle domain, defined as

$$\Gamma_w = \{(x, y)| -1 < x < 1, y = 0\}.$$

The algorithms are implemented in MATLAB using the software library *i*FEM [15].

4.1   Convergence Test

In this subsection, we provide some numerical evidence to show the second order temporal accuracy for the numerical scheme (32)–(34) by the method of Cauchy convergence test as in [17]. We consider the problem with an given initial condition but with no explicit exact solution. The domain Ω is triangulated by a structured mesh with uniform 2^{k+1} grid points in the x direction and uniform 2^k grid points in the y direction, for k from 4 to 8. The final time is taken to be $T = 0.1$ and the time step is taken to be $\delta t = 0.2h$. Since the P_1 finite element approximation is used for the phase field variable ϕ_h, the L^2 norm of the Cauchy difference error $\|\phi_h^k - \phi_h^{k-1}\|$ is expected to converge to zero at the rate of second order $err = O(\delta t^2) + O(h^2) = O(\delta t^2)$. The initial condition of the phase field variable ϕ is taken to be

$$\phi_0(x, y) = \tanh\left(\frac{0.25 - \sqrt{x^2 + y^2}}{\sqrt{2}\varepsilon}\right), \tag{40}$$

We take parameters $\varepsilon = 0.1$, $\beta = 5$ and use five different contact angles $\theta_s = \pi$, $\theta_s = 3\pi/4$, $\theta_s = \pi/2$, $\theta_s = \pi/4$, $\theta_s = 0$ to test the convergence rate respectively, The Cauchy errors and the relative convergence rates are presented in Table 1 which shows the second order convergence for all cases.

Table 1. Cauchy convergence test for the second order linear numerical scheme (32)–(34) with the initial condition (40), parameters are $\varepsilon = 0.1$ and $\beta = 5$, errors are measured in L^2 norm; 2^{k+1} and 2^k grid points in the x and y direction for k from 4 to 8, five different contact angles $\theta_s = \pi$, $\theta_s = 3\pi/4$, $\theta_s = \pi/2$, $\theta_s = \pi/4$, $\theta_s = 0$ are tested respectively

θ	$16 - 32$	Cvg. rate	$32 - 64$	Cvg. rate	$64 - 128$	Cvg. rate	$128 - 256$
π	0.0063	1.9480	0.0016	2.0777	3.8837e-004	2.1738	8.9332e-005
$3\pi/4$	0.0063	1.9505	0.0016	2.0246	3.9578e-004	2.0869	9.4824e-005
$\pi/2$	0.0061	1.9379	0.0016	1.9797	3.9895e-004	1.9978	9.9849e-005
$\pi/4$	0.0066	1.9218	0.0017	1.9882	4.2918e-004	2.0253	1.0596e-004
0	0.0069	1.9084	0.0018	1.9850	4.5246e-004	2.0179	1.1211e-004

4.2   Solid-State Dewetting Simulation in Two Dimension

In this subsection, we present some two-dimensional simulations for the solid-state dewetting problems using the schemes (32)–(34). The initial state of the thin film is taken to be a small rectangle:

$$\phi_0(x, y) = \begin{cases} 1 & \text{if} - 0.5 \le x \le 0.5 \,\text{and}\, 0 \le y \le 0.2 \\ -1 & \text{otherwise}. \end{cases} \tag{41}$$

the computational parameters are taken as $\varepsilon = 0.01$ and $\delta t = 1/128$. Numerical simulations in [18] suggest that in order to accurately capture the interfacial dynamics, at least 4 elements are needed across the interfacial region of thickness

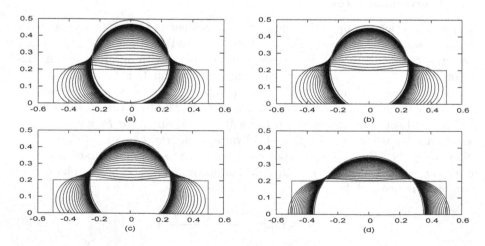

Fig. 1. The evolution of thin film for four different prescribed contact angles: (a) $\theta_s = \pi$, (b) $\theta_s = 5\pi/6$, (c) $\theta_s = 3\pi/4$, (d) $\theta_s = \pi/2$. The film profiles are shown every 2500 time steps (labeled as black lines). The red line and blue line represent the initial and numerical equilibrium states, respectively. (Color figure online)

$\sqrt{2}\varepsilon$. We explore adaptive mesh refinement algorithm of the software library iFEM [15] with the finest element size $h = 1/256$ to improve the computational efficiency. We examine the evolution of thin film under 4 different prescribed contact angles: $\theta_s = \pi$, $\theta_s = 5\pi/6$, $\theta_s = 3\pi/4$, $\theta_s = \pi/2$, respectively. The results are shown in Fig. 1.

We plot dissipative curve of the modified free energy in Fig. 2. Using five different time step of $\delta t = 0.01, 0.05, 0.1, 0.5, 1$ with the prescribed contact angle $\theta_s = \pi/2$. We observe that the energy decreases at all times, which confirms that our algorithm is unconditionally stable, as predicted by the theory.

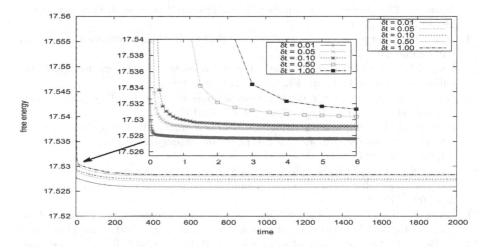

Fig. 2. Time evolution of the free energy functional for five different time steps of $\delta t = 0.01, 0.05, 0.1, 0.5, 1$ with the prescribed contact angle $\theta_s = \pi/2$. The energy curves show the decays for all time steps, which confirms that our algorithm is unconditionally stable.

5 Conclusions

In this paper, we present linearly first and second order in time, uniquely solvable and unconditionally energy stable schemes for solving the solid-state dewetting problems based on the novel SAV approach. We verify numerically that our schemes are up to second order accurate in time. Adaptive strategy is used to improve the efficiency of the algorithm. Numerical examples are presented to illustrate the stability and accuracy of the proposed schemes.

References

1. Jiang, W., Bao, W.: Phase field approach for simulating solid-state dewetting problems. Acta Mater. **60**, 5578–5592 (2012)
2. Mordehai, D., Kazakevich, M.: Nanoindentation size effect in single-crystal nanoparticles and thin films: a comparative experimental and simulation study. Acta Mater. **59**, 2309–2321 (2011)
3. Chen, J., Sun, S., Wang, X.: A numericalmethod for a model of two-phase flow in a coupled free flow and porous media system. J. Comput. Phys. **268**, 1–16 (2014)
4. Jiang, W., Wang, Y.: Solid-state dewetting and island morphologies in strongly anisotropic materials. Scripta Mater. **115**, 123–127 (2016)
5. Jiran, E., Thompson, C.V.: Capillary instabilities in thin films. J. Electron. Mater. **19**, 1153–1160 (1990)
6. Jiran, E., Thompson, C.V.: Capillary instabilities in thin, continuous films. Thin Solid Films **208**, 23–28 (1992)
7. Lee, H.G., Kim, J.: Accurate contact angle boundary conditions for the Cahn-Hilliard equations. Comput. Fluids **44**, 178–186 (2011)
8. Guillengonzalez, F., Tierra, G.: On linear schemes for a Cahn-Hilliard diffuse interface model. J. Comput. Phys. **234**, 140–171 (2013)
9. Han, D., Brylev, A.: Numerical analysis of second order, fully discrete energy stable schemes for phase field models of two-phase incompressible flows. J. Sci. Comput. **70**, 965–989 (2017)
10. Yang, X., Ju, L.: Efficient linear schemes with unconditional energy stability for the phase field elastic bending energy model. Comput. Methods Appl. Mech. Eng. **315**, 691–712 (2017)
11. Yang, X., Han, D.: Linearly first- and second-order, unconditionally energy stable schemes for the phase field crytal model. J. Comput. Phys. **330**, 1116–1134 (2017)
12. Rayleigh, L.: On the theory of surface forces. II. Compressible fluids. Philos. Mag. Ser. 1 **33**(201), 209–220 (1892)
13. Shen, J., Xu, J.: The scalar auxiliary variable (SAV) approach for gradient flows. J. Comput. Phys. **353**, 407–416 (2017)
14. Shen, J., Xu, J.: A new class of efficient and robust energy stable schemes for gradient flows. SIAM Reviews (to appear)
15. Chen, L.: An integrated finite element methods package in matlab, technical report, University of California at Irvine (2009)
16. Der Waals, J.D.: The thermodynamic theory of capillarity under the hypothesis of a continuous variation of density. J. Stat. Phys. **20**(2), 200–244 (1979)
17. Han, D., Wang, X.: A second order in time, uniquely solvable, unconditionally stable numerical scheme for Cahn-Hilliard-Navier-Stokes equation. J. Comput. Phys. **290**, 139–156 (2015)
18. Kim, J., Kang, K.: Conservative multigrid methods for Cahn-Hilliard fluids. J. Comput. Phys. **193**, 511–543 (2004)

A Novel Energy Stable Numerical Scheme for Navier-Stokes-Cahn-Hilliard Two-Phase Flow Model with Variable Densities and Viscosities

Xiaoyu Feng[1] , Jisheng Kou[2] , and Shuyu Sun[3](✉)

[1] National Engineering Laboratory for Pipeline Safety, Beijing Key Laboratory of Urban Oil and Gas Distribution Technology, China University of Petroleum, Beijing 102249, China
[2] School of Mathematics and Statistics, Hubei Engineering University, Xiaogan 432000, China
[3] Computational Transport Phenomena Laboratory, Division of Physical Science and Engineering, King Abdullah University of Science and Technology, Thuwal 23955-6900, Saudi Arabia
shuyu.sun@kaust.edu.sa

Abstract. A novel numerical scheme including time and spatial discretization is offered for coupled Cahn-Hilliard and Navier-Stokes governing equation system in this paper. Variable densities and viscosities are considered in the numerical scheme. By introducing an intermediate velocity in both Cahn-Hilliard equation and momentum equation, the scheme can keep discrete energy law. A decouple approach based on pressure stabilization is implemented to solve the Navier-Stokes part, while the stabilization or convex splitting method is adopted for the Cahn-Hilliard part. This novel scheme is totally decoupled, linear, unconditionally energy stable for incompressible two-phase flow diffuse interface model. Numerical results demonstrate the validation, accuracy, robustness and discrete energy law of the proposed scheme in this paper.

Keywords: Energy stable · Diffuse interface · Two-phase flow

1 Introduction

Two-phase flow is omnipresent in many natural and industrial processes, especially for the petroleum industry, the two-phase flow is throughout the whole upstream production process including oil and gas recovery, transportation and refinery, e.g. [1].

As a critical component in the two-phase fluid system, the interface is usually considered as a free surface, its dynamics is determined by the usual Young-Laplace junction condition in classical interface tracking or reconstruction approaches, such as Level-set [2], volume-of-fluid [3] and even some advanced composite method like VOSET [4].

© Springer International Publishing AG, part of Springer Nature 2018
Y. Shi et al. (Eds.): ICCS 2018, LNCS 10862, pp. 113–128, 2018.
https://doi.org/10.1007/978-3-319-93713-7_9

But when it traced back to 19th century, Van der Waals [5] provided a new alternative point of view that the interface has a diffuse feature, namely non-zero thickness. It can be implicitly characterized by scalar field, namely phase filed, taking constant values in the bulk phase areas and varying continuously but radically across a diffuse front. Within this thin transition domain, the fluids are mixed and store certain quantities of "mixing energy" in this region. Thus, unlike other methods proposed graphically, phase dynamics is derived from interface physics by energy variational approach regardless of the numerical solution, which gives rise to coupled nonlinearly well-posed system at partial differential equation continuous form that satisfies thermodynamically consistent energy dissipation laws. Then there is possibility for us to design numerical scheme preserving energy law in discrete form [6].

The diffuse interface approach excels in some respects of handling two-phase flow among other available methods. Firstly, it is based on the principle of energy minimization. Hence it can deal with moving contact lines problems and morphological changes of interface in a natural way effortlessly, such as droplet coalescence or break-up phenomena. Secondly, we can benefit from the simplicity of formulation, ease of numerical implementation without explicitly tracking or reconstructing interface, also the capability to explore essential physics at the interfacial domain. The accessibility of modeling various material properties or complex interface behaviors directly by introducing appropriate energy functions. Therefore, enforcing certain rheological fluid or modeling polymeric solutions or viscoelastic behaviors would be alluring feature naturally. For these benefits, the diffuse interface model attracted substantial academic attention in recent years, a great number of the advanced and cutting-edge researches are conducted corresponding to partial immiscible multi-components flow based on phase field theory [7] and thermodynamically consistent diffuse interface model for two-phase flow with thermo-capillary [8] et al.

The classical diffuse interface model for cases of two-phase incompressible viscous Newtonian fluids is known as the model H [9]. It has been successfully applied to simulate flows involving incompressible fluids with same densities for both phase components. This model is restricted to the matched density case using Boussinesq approximation. Unlike the matched density case, when it comes to the case with big density ratio, the incompressibility cannot guarantee mass conservation any longer in this model. Therefore, the corresponding diffuse interface model with the divergence free condition no longer preserve an energy law. Thus, a lot of further works have been done by (1998) Lowengrub [10], (2002) Boye [11], (2007) Ding [12], (2010) Shen [13] and most recently Benchmark computations were carried out by (2012) Aland [14].

Generally there are two kinds of approaches to deal with variable densities problem, one is that material derivative of momentum equation written in one kind form that takes density variations into consideration without resorting to mass conservation to guarantee stability of energy proposed by Guermond [15]. Another approach is proposed by Abels [16]. The approach introduces an intermediate velocity to decouple the Cahn-Hilliard equation and Navier-Stokes equation system in Minjeaud's paper [17], and recently this approach is applied in Shen [18] to simulate the model in [16]. However, the schemes proposed in [17, 18] employ the intermediate velocity in the Cahn-Hilliard equation only, imposing the mass balance equation to ensure the discrete energy-dissipation law. Very recently, in Kou [19] the schemes that the intermediate velocity is applied in both mass balance equations and the momentum balance equation are developed to simulate the multi-component diffuse-interface model proposed in [20] to guarantee the consistency between the mass balance and energy dissipation. In this paper, we extend this treatment to the model in [16]. However, this extension is not trivial due to a crucial problem that Cahn-Hilliard equation is not equivalent to mass balance equation. In order to deal with this problem, a novel scheme applying the intermediate velocity in Navier-Stokes equation will be proposed in this paper.

The rest part of this paper is organized as follows. In Sect. 2 we introduce a diffuse interface model for two-phase flow with variable densities and viscosities in detail; In Sect. 3 we propose a brand new numerical scheme for solving the coupled Navier–Stokes and Cahn–Hilliard equation system based on this model; In Sect. 4 some numerical results are demonstrated in this part to validate this scheme comparing with benchmark and to exam the accuracy, discrete energy decaying tendency. Other cases and numerical performances will be investigated to show the robustness of the novel scheme.

2   Mathematical Formulation and Physical Model

The phase field diffuse interface model with variable densities and viscosities can be described through the following Cahn-Hilliard equation coupled with Navier-Stokes equation. An introduced phase field variable ϕ, namely order parameter, defined over the domain, identifies the regions occupied by the two fluids.

$$\phi(\mathbf{x}, t) = \begin{cases} 1 & \textit{fluid 1} \\ -1 & \textit{fluid 2} \end{cases} \tag{1}$$

With a thin smooth transition front of thickness ε bridging two fluids, the microscopic interactions between two kinds of fluid molecules rules equilibrium profiles and configurations of interface mixing layer neighboring level-set $\Gamma_t = \{\phi : (\mathbf{x}, t) = 0\}$. For the situation of isotropic interactions, the following Ginzburg–Landau type of Helmholtz free energy functional is given by the classical self-consistent mean field theory in statistical physics [21]:

$$W(\phi, \nabla\phi) = \lambda \int_\Omega \left(\frac{1}{2} \|\nabla\phi\|^2 + F(\phi) \right) dx \tag{2}$$

The foremost term in right hand side represents the effect of mixing of interactions between the materials, and the latter one implies the trend of separation. Set the Ginzburg–Landau potential in the usual double-well form $F(\phi) - \frac{\phi^2-1}{4\varepsilon^2}$. λ means mixing energy density, ε is the capillary width of interface between two phases. If we focus on one-dimensional interface and assume that total diffusive mixing energy in this domain equals to traditional surface tension coefficient:

$$\sigma = \lambda \int_{-\infty}^{+\infty} \left\{ \frac{1}{2} \left(\frac{d\phi}{dx} \right)^2 + F(\phi) \right\} dx \tag{3}$$

The precondition that diffuse interface is at equilibrium is valid, then we can get the relationship among surface tension coefficient σ, capillary width ε and mixing energy density λ:

$$\sigma = \frac{(2\sqrt{2})}{3} \frac{\lambda}{\varepsilon} \tag{4}$$

The evolution of phase field (ϕ) is governed by the following Cahn-Hilliard equations:

$$\begin{cases} \phi_t + \nabla \cdot (\mathbf{u}\phi) = M\Delta\mu \\ \mu = \frac{\delta W}{\delta \phi} = f(\phi) - \Delta\phi \end{cases} \tag{5}$$

Where μ represents the chemical potential, namely $\frac{\delta W}{\delta \phi}$ that indicates the variation of the energy W with respect to ϕ; the parameter M is a mobility constant related to the diffusivity of bulk phases and $f(\phi) = F'(\phi)$

The momentum equation for the two-phase system is presented as the usual form

$$\begin{cases} \rho(\mathbf{u}_t + (\mathbf{u} \cdot \nabla)\mathbf{u}) = \nabla \cdot \tau \\ \tau = \eta D(\mathbf{u}) - pI + \tau_e \\ \tau_e = -\lambda(\nabla\phi \otimes \nabla\phi) \end{cases} \tag{6}$$

with the identical equation

$$\nabla \cdot (\nabla\mathbf{u} \otimes \nabla\mathbf{u}) = (\Delta\phi - f(\phi)) + \frac{1}{2}\nabla\left(\|\nabla\phi\|^2 + F(\phi)\right) = -\mu\nabla\phi$$
$$+ \frac{1}{2}\nabla\left(\|\nabla\phi\|^2 + F(\phi)\right) = \phi\nabla\mu + \frac{1}{2}\nabla\left(\|\nabla\phi\|^2 + F(\phi) - \phi\mu\right) \tag{7}$$

The second term in Eq. (7) can be merged with the pressure gradient term p, then the pressure of the momentum equation should be a modified pressure p^*, It denotes that: $p^* = p + \frac{1}{2}\nabla\left(|\nabla\phi|^2 + F(\phi) - \phi\mu\right)$. The p is represented the modified one in the following contents for unity.

2.1   Case of Matched Density

The governing equations system:

$$\begin{cases} \phi_t + \nabla \cdot (\mathbf{u}\phi) = M\Delta\mu \\ \mu = f(\phi) - \Delta\phi \\ \mathbf{u}_t + (\mathbf{u} \cdot \nabla)\mathbf{u} = \nabla \cdot \eta D(\mathbf{u}) - \nabla p - \phi\nabla\mu \\ \nabla \cdot \mathbf{u} \end{cases} \tag{8}$$

A set of appropriate boundary condition and initial condition is applied to the above system: no-slip boundary condition for momentum equation and the period boundary condition for the Cahn-Hilliard equation.

$$\mathbf{u}|_{\partial\Omega} = 0 \quad \frac{\partial\phi}{\partial n}\Big|_{\partial\Omega} = 0 \quad \frac{\partial\mu}{\partial n}\Big|_{\partial\Omega} = 0 \tag{9}$$

Also the initial condition:

$$\mathbf{u}|_{t=0} = \mathbf{u}_0 \phi|_{t=0} = \phi_0 \tag{10}$$

If the density contrast of two phases is relatively little, a common approach is to employ the Boussinesq approximation [22], replacing momentum equation in equation system (8) by

$$\rho_0(\mathbf{u}_t + (\mathbf{u} \cdot \nabla)\mathbf{u}) = \nabla \cdot \eta D(\mathbf{u}) - \nabla p - \phi\nabla\mu + \frac{\phi+1}{2}\delta\rho\mathbf{g} \tag{11}$$

Set the background density $\rho_0 = (\rho_1 + \rho_2)$ and term $\frac{\phi+1}{2}\delta\rho\mathbf{g}$ is an additional body force term in charge of the equivalent gravitational effect caused by density difference. Since the density ρ_0 distributed everywhere in this field do not change respect to time. If the divergence of the velocity field $\nabla \cdot \mathbf{u} = 0$ holds. Then basic mass conservation $\rho_t + \nabla \cdot (\rho\mathbf{u}) = 0$ is a natural consequence of incompressibility.

By inner product operation of 1st 2nd and 3rd equation of system (8) with $-\mu$, ϕ_t, $\mathbf{u}$ respectively and summation of these three results, It is easily to conclude that system (8) admits the following energy dissipation law:

$$\frac{d}{dt}\int_\Omega \left(\frac{1}{2}\|\mathbf{u}\|^2 + \frac{\lambda}{2}\|\nabla\phi\|^2 + \lambda F(\phi)\right)dx = -\int_\Omega \left(\frac{\eta}{2}\|D(u)\|^2 + M\|\nabla\mu\|^2\right)dx \tag{12}$$

2.2 Case of Variable Density

Now we consider the case where the density ratio is so large that the Boussinesq approximation is no longer in effect. Here introduced a phase field diffuse interface model for incompressible two-phase flow with different densities and viscosity proposed by Abels [16].

$$\begin{cases} \phi_t + \nabla \cdot (\mathbf{u}\phi) = M\Delta\mu \\ \mu = f(\phi) - \Delta\phi \\ \rho\mathbf{u}_t + (\rho\mathbf{u} + \boldsymbol{J}) \cdot \nabla\mathbf{u} = \nabla \cdot \eta D(\mathbf{u}) - \nabla p - \phi\nabla\mu \\ \nabla \cdot \mathbf{u} = 0 \end{cases} \tag{13}$$

among them

$$\boldsymbol{J} = \frac{\rho_2 - \rho_1}{2} M\nabla\mu \tag{14}$$

The density and viscosity is the function of phase parameter.

$$\rho(\phi) = \frac{\rho_1 - \rho_2}{2}\phi + \frac{\rho_1 + \rho_2}{2} \quad \eta(\phi) = \frac{\eta_1 - \eta_2}{2}\phi + \frac{\eta_1 + \rho\eta_2}{2} \tag{15}$$

The mass conservation property can be derived from Eqs. (14), (15) and (16).

$$\rho_t + \nabla \cdot (\rho\mathbf{u}) + \nabla \cdot \boldsymbol{J} = 0 \tag{16}$$

The NSCH governing system holds thermodynamically consistency and energy law. We can obtain the following energy dissipation law:

$$\frac{d}{dt}\int_\Omega \left(\frac{\rho}{2}\|\mathbf{u}\|^2 + \frac{\lambda}{2}\|\nabla\phi\|^2 + \lambda F(\phi)\right)dx = -\int_\Omega \left(\frac{\eta}{2}\|D(u)\|^2 + \|M\nabla\mu\|^2\right)dx \tag{17}$$

If we add the gravity in this domain, such as modeling topological evolution of a single bubble rising in a liquid column, the total energy must contain the potential energy. Then this energy dissipation law can be expressed as follow:

$$\frac{dE_{tot}}{dt} = \frac{d}{dt}\int_\Omega \left(\frac{\rho}{2}\|\mathbf{u}\|^2 + \frac{\lambda}{2}\|\nabla\phi\|^2 + \lambda F(\phi) - \rho g y\right)dx \leq 0 \tag{18}$$

3   Decoupled Numerical Scheme

3.1   Time Discretization

In matched density case, for simplicity of presentation, we will assume that $\eta_1 = \eta_2 = \eta$. Given initial conditions ϕ^0, $\mathbf{u}^0$, p^0 we compute ϕ^{k+1}, μ^{k+1}, p^{k+1}, $\tilde{\mathbf{u}}^{k+1}$, $\mathbf{u}^{k+1}$ for $n \geq 0$. Here is an additional term to the convective velocity introduced based on the idea from [17]. Then the intermediate velocity term $\hat{\mathbf{u}}^k = \mathbf{u}^k - \delta t \frac{\phi^k \nabla\mu^{k+1}}{\rho^k}$ makes the Cahn-Hilliard equation and the Navier-Stokes equation decoupled fundamentally. The novel scheme can be described as below:

$$\begin{cases} \frac{\phi^{k+1}-\phi^k}{\delta t} + \nabla \cdot (\widehat{\mathbf{u}}^n \phi^{k+1}) = M\Delta\mu^{k+1} \\ \mu^{k+1} = \lambda(f_e(\phi^k) + f_c(\phi^{k+1}) - \Delta\phi^{k+1}).or. \\ \mu^{k+1} = \lambda(f(\phi^k) - \Delta\phi^{k+1}) + \frac{\lambda}{\varepsilon^2}(\phi^{k+1} - \phi^k) \\ \mathbf{n} \cdot \nabla\phi^{k+1}|_{\partial\Omega} = 0 \quad \mathbf{n} \cdot \nabla\mu^{k+1}|_{\partial\Omega} = 0 \end{cases} \qquad (19)$$

We add a stabilizing term $\frac{\lambda}{\varepsilon^2}(\phi^{k+1} - \phi^k)$ or treat the term by convex splitting method $f(\phi) = f_e(\phi) + f_c(\phi)$. Then the time step for computation will not be strictly limited in extreme range by the coefficient Capillary width ε.

$$\begin{cases} \rho_0 \frac{\widetilde{\mathbf{u}}^{k+1}-\mathbf{u}^k}{\delta t} + (\mathbf{u}^k \cdot \nabla)\widetilde{\mathbf{u}}^{k+1} = \nabla \cdot \eta_0 D(\widetilde{\mathbf{u}}^{k+1}) - \nabla p^k - \phi^k \nabla\mu^{k+1} + F_m \\ \widetilde{\mathbf{u}}^{k+1}|_{\partial\Omega} = 0 \end{cases} \qquad (20)$$

Then we can get the pressure by solving a constant coefficient Poisson equation and correct the velocity filed to satisfy divergence free condition.

$$\begin{cases} \rho_0 \frac{\mathbf{u}^{k+1}-\widetilde{\mathbf{u}}^{k+1}}{\delta t} = -\nabla(p^{k+1} - p^k) \\ \nabla \cdot \mathbf{u}^{k+1} = 0 \\ \mathbf{u}^{k+1}|_{\partial\Omega} = 0 \end{cases} \qquad (21)$$

For variable density case, [15, 16] serve as incentive for the novel numerical scheme below. To deal with the variable densities and ensure numerical stability, we have to define a cut-off function $\widehat{\phi}$ for the phase order parameter at first place.

$$\widehat{\phi} = \begin{cases} \phi & |\phi| \leq 1 \\ sign(\phi) & |\phi| > 1 \end{cases} \qquad (22)$$

Given initial conditions $\phi^0, \mathbf{u}^0, p^0, \rho_0, \eta_0$ we compute $\phi^{k+1}, \mu^{k+1}, p^{k+1}\mathbf{u}^{k+1}$, ρ^{k+1}, η^{k+1} for $n \geq 0$. The discretization of the Cahn-Hilliard part is same with the matched density as Eq. (19).

We update the density and viscosity by cut-off function

$$\begin{cases} \rho(\phi^{n+1}) = \frac{\rho_1-\rho_2}{2} \widehat{\phi}^{n+1} + \frac{\rho_1+\rho_2}{2} \\ \eta(\phi^{n+1}) = \frac{\eta_1-\eta_2}{2} \widehat{\phi}^{n+1} + \frac{\eta_1+\rho\eta_2}{2} \end{cases} \qquad (23)$$

For the momentum equation part, we use

$$\begin{cases} \rho^k \frac{\mathbf{u}^{k+1}-\mathbf{u}^k}{\delta t} + (\rho^k\widehat{\mathbf{u}}^k + J^k) \cdot \nabla\mathbf{u}^{k+1} = \nabla \cdot \eta D(\mathbf{u}^{k+1}) - \nabla p^k \\ \qquad -\phi^k\nabla\mu^{k+1} + \frac{1}{2}\left(\frac{\rho_1+\rho_2}{2}\nabla \cdot \widehat{\mathbf{u}}^k\right)\mathbf{u}^{k+1} \\ \mathbf{u}^{k+1}|_{\partial\Omega} = 0 \end{cases} \qquad (24)$$

together with

$$\boldsymbol{J}^k = \frac{\rho_2 - \rho_1}{2} M \nabla \mu^k \tag{25}$$

For saving the computer time consuming and stability, we adopt schemes based on pressure stabilization.

$$\begin{cases} \Delta(p^{k+1} - p^k) = \frac{\theta}{\delta t} \nabla \cdot \mathbf{u}^{n+1} \\ \nabla(p^{k+1} - p^k)|_{\partial\Omega} = 0 \\ \theta = \frac{1}{2}\min(\rho_2, \rho_1) \end{cases} \tag{26}$$

Pressure stabilization at the initial stage might cause velocity without physical meaning because it cannot satisfy solenoidal condition strictly. If we use pressure correction method, we have to face the non-linear Poisson equation. Thus, the solution must cost much more time.

3.2   Spatial Discretization

For 2-D cases, the computational domain is $\Omega = (0, L_x) \times (0, L_y)$, the staggered grid are used for spatial discretization. The cell centers are located on

$$x_i = \left(i - \frac{1}{2}\right)h_x \quad i = 1, \dots, n_x \qquad y_i = \left(j - \frac{1}{2}\right)h_y \quad i = 1, \dots, n_y$$

Where h_x and h_y are grid spacing in x and y directions. n_x, n_y are the number of grids along x and y coordinates respectively. In order to discretize the coupled Cahn-Hilliard and Navier-Stokes system, the following finite volume method is introduced (Fig. 1).

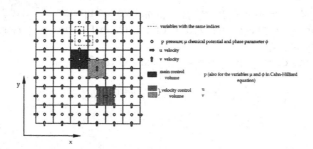

Fig. 1. The staggered grid based on finite volume method

$$U_h = \left(x_{i-\frac{1}{2}}, y_j\right)\Big| i = 1, 2, \ldots, n_x + 1; \quad j = 1, 2, \ldots, n_y$$

$$V_h = \left(x_i, y_{j-\frac{1}{2}}\right)\Big| i = 1, 2, \ldots, n_x; \qquad j = 1, 2, \ldots, n_y + 1$$

$$P_h = \left(x_{i-\frac{1}{2}}, y_j\right)\Big| i = 1, 2, \ldots, n_x; \qquad j = 1, 2, \ldots, n_y$$

Where P_h is cell-centered space, U_h and V_h are edge-center space, $(\phi, \mu, p, \rho, \eta) \in P_h$, $u \in U_h$, $v \in V_h$. Some common differential and averaged operators are used to interpolation of these physical variables from one space to another space which are not discussed in detail here.

4 Numerical Results

4.1 Validation of the Novel Scheme

Case1: A Bubble Rising in Liquid in 2D Domain
There is a rectangular domain $\Omega = (0, 1) \times (0, 2)$ filled with two-phase incompressible fluid and a lighter bubble (with density ρ_1 and dynamic viscosity η_1) in a heavier medium (with density ρ_2 and dynamic viscosity η_2) rises from a fixed position initially. As it described in benchmark test paper [23], the boundary condition imposed on the vertical walls and top wall are replaced by free slip condition. The physical parameters for case 1 follows Table 1.

Table 1. The physical parameters for numerical test case 1.

Case	ρ_1	ρ_2	η_1	η_2	g	σ	M
1	1000	100	10	1	0.98	24.5	1×10^5

The initial bubble is perfect round with radius r = 0.25 and its center is set at the point $(x_0, y_0) = (0.5, 1)$. The initial profile of ϕ is set as

$$\phi(x, y) = -\tanh\left(\frac{1}{\sqrt{2}\varepsilon}\left(\sqrt{(x - x_0)^2 + (y - y_0)^2} - r\right)\right) \qquad (27)$$

We must note these parameters have been through the non-dimensionalization. Mobility coefficient is an additional numerical parameter, which is not appeared in the sharp interface model. The value is chosen in a rational range for comparison of different spatial step and interface thickness. Furthermore, the interface thick ε is chosen proportional to h. The energy density parameter λ can be calculated by the surface tension coefficient σ through the Eq. (4). The time step $\delta t = 0.0001$ (Fig. 2).

The bubble shape at the time point $t = 3.0$ calculated by the novel scheme is compared with the solution from the benchmark paper by the level-set method [23] and the diffuse interface method [14] in Fig. 3(a). Different bubble shapes at the time $t = 3.0$ are compared from the coarsest grid ($h = 1/50$, $\varepsilon = 0.02$) to the finest grid ($h = 1/200$, $\varepsilon = 0.005$).

122   X. Feng et al.

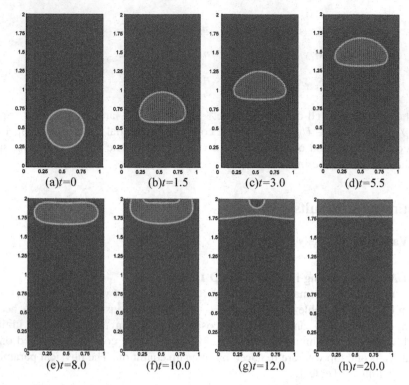

Fig. 2. Snapshots of the bubble evolution with velocity vector field (computed on $h = 1/150$ grid).

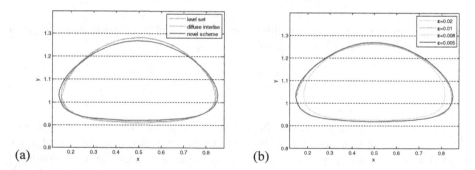

Fig. 3. Bubble shapes at $t = 3$ for the novel scheme comparing with the level-set and diffuse interface benchmark results provided in [14, 23] (a); bubble shapes at $t = 3$ solved by grid with different refinement level and different interface thickness (b).

The shapes of bubble differ distinctly for different values of interface thickness ε. But they seem to be convergent so that there is no significant differences for the finest grid and the case with $\varepsilon = 0.008$. We can also remark that the bubble shape from novel scheme is quite approximate to the benchmark level-set and diffuse interface results. But it is clearly not sufficient to only look at the bubble shapes, therefore we use some previously defined benchmark quantities to validate the new scheme rigorously.

I. Center of the Mass:
Various positions of points can be used to track the motion of bubbles. The most common way is to use the center of mass defined by

$$y_c = \frac{\int_{\phi > 0} y dx}{\int_{\phi > 0} 1 dx} \tag{28}$$

with y as the vertical coordinate of $\mathbf{x}(x, y)$

II. Rise Velocity
v is the vertical component of the bubble's velocity $\mathbf{u}$. Where $\phi > 0$ denotes the region that bubble occupies. The velocity is volume average velocity of bubble.

$$v_c = \frac{\int_{\phi > 0} v dx}{\int_{\phi > 0} 1 dx} \tag{29}$$

Combining the contours given in Fig. 3 and Figs. 4, 5 and 6 about the mass center and rise velocity of the lighter bubble before $t = 3$, a significant increase in rise velocity can be observed at the initial stage and then the velocity decrease slowly to a constant value when the time advances to $t = 3$ gradually. The shape of bubble will reach to a temporary steady state when the rise velocity keeps constant. The mass center of the bubble could be recognized as a linear function of time asymptotically after it is higher than $y = 0.6$.

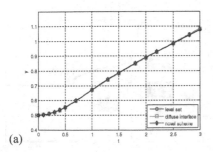 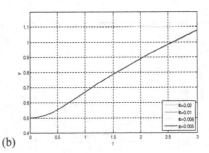

Fig. 4. Center of the mass of the bubble for the novel scheme comparing with the level-set and diffuse interface benchmark result provided in [14, 23] (a); Solutions of center of mass from grids with different refinement level and different interface thickness (b).

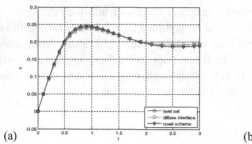 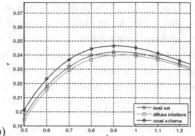

(a)   (b)

Fig. 5. Rise velocity of the bubble for the novel scheme comparing with the level-set and diffuse interface benchmark results (a); close-up of rise velocity at maximum values area (b).

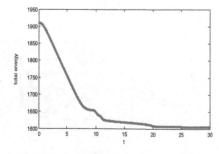 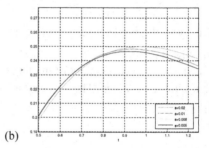

(a)   (b)

Fig. 6. Solutions of rise velocity of the bubble from grids with different refinement level and different interface thickness (a); close-up of rise velocity at maximum values area (b).

Although the difference is visible for the coarsest grid and thickest interface on the velocity plot. It is obvious to see that results become closer and closer to the line corresponding to the computation on the finest grid with refinement. The results calculated by the new scheme shows good agreement with the level-set solution [23] and benchmark diffuse interface method [14].

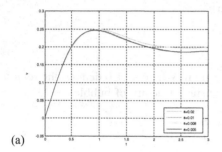 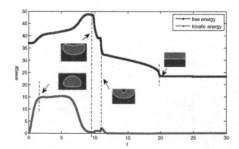

Fig. 7. Energy dissipation of the whole system

Fig. 8. Variation of free energy and kinetic energy of the whole system

The decaying trend of discrete energy in Fig. 7 confirms that the proposed scheme is energy stable. The whole system reaches the equilibrium state at $t = 25$.

Figure 8 gives the evolution of free energy and kinetic energy respectively. At the early stage of bubble rising, kinetic energy and free energy rise dramatically, which come from part of the reduced gravity potential energy. Then the velocity keep constant to some extent at next stage. The bubble shape also change into a relative steady state. When the bubble almost touching the top lid. The kinetic energy gives a considerable decrease to the zero. Then the gas phase will evolve to a stratified state finally under the lead of the diffusion in the Cahn Hilliard equation.

Case2: Novel Scheme for Matched Density with Boussinesq Approximation
In the section, We simulate a physical problem with matched viscosities and a relative low density contrast $(\rho_1 = 1; \rho_2 = 10)$ which ensures the Boussinnesq approximation is applicable. We set 2d bubble diameter $d = 1.0$, $g = 1.0$, $\eta_1 = \eta_2 = 0.1$, $\lambda = 4 \times 10^{-3}$, Mobility = 0.02 and $\varepsilon = 0.008$. The incompressible fluid in a rectangular domain $\Omega = (0, 2) \times (0, 4)$ with initially a lighter bubble center located on $(x_0, y_0) = (1, 1.5)$. These dimensionless parameters are set according to the cases in [13]. The mesh size is 200×400 and the boundary condition at the vertical wall is no-slip boundary condition (Fig. 9).

It is easy to find that the shape of the bubble and the vertical displacement at different time step is pretty similar with the reference contour provided in [13] by GUM/PSM method. The reference only have a contour line at certain ϕ. For a beautiful presentation of the integral contour calculated by the novel scheme here, we adjust interface thickness $\varepsilon = 0.008$. The novel scheme can be employed in the situation.

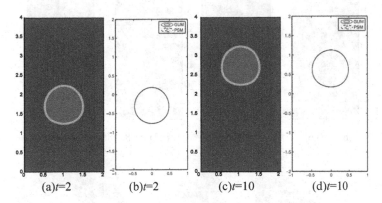

(a)t=2   (b)t=2   (c)t=10   (d)t=10

Fig. 9. The shape and displacement comparison of the bubble calculated by novel scheme with the results presented in [13] for matched density case.

4.2   Robustness Test of the Novel Scheme

Case3: Examining the Performance for Big Density Contrast

We now consider two-phase incompressible fluid with the same initial condition and boundary condition with the case1. But density and viscosity contrast is much more violent in this case (Table 2 and Fig. 10).

Table 2. The physical parameters for numerical test case 3.

Case	ρ_1	ρ_2	η_1	η_2	**g**	σ	M
3	1000	1	10	0.1	0.98	1.96	1×10^5

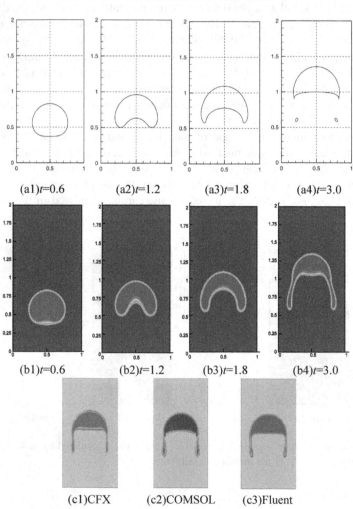

(a1)t=0.6   (a2)t=1.2   (a3)t=1.8   (a4)t=3.0

(b1)t=0.6   (b2)t=1.2   (b3)t=1.8   (b4)t=3.0

(c1)CFX   (c2)COMSOL   (c3)Fluent

Fig. 10. The shapes and displacement comparison of the bubble calculated by novel scheme with the benchmark level-set results and the contours at $t = 3.0$ provided by three common commercial software in [23]

The break-up of bubble happen before the time $t = 3.0$ in the level-set benchmark. So it is not appropriate to compare the results from the new scheme with the contour. But from the results of some common commercial computing software [23]. It's not that difficult to find the shape of bubble and the vertical displacement at $t = 3.0$ solved by our scheme is pretty close to them. Although it could be some slight diffusion on the interface caused by the Cahn-Hilliard system itself. The case shows the robustness of the novel scheme proposed in this paper. It can not only handle an extreme numerical situation with harsh density and viscosity ratio but get reliable results to some extent.

5 Concluding Remark

The numerical simulation and approximation of incompressible and immiscible two-phase flows with matched and variable densities and viscosities is the main topic in this paper. We proposed a brand new scheme for coupled diffuse interface model system with matched and variable densities and viscosities that satisfies the mass conservation and admits an energy law. Plenty of numerical experiments are carried out to illustrate the validation, accuracy compared with sharp interface method by the benchmark problem and to test the robustness of the new scheme for some extreme cases as well.

References

1. Zhang, X.Y., Yu, B., et al.: Numerical study on the commissioning charge-up process of horizontal pipeline with entrapped air pockets. Adv. Mech. Eng. 1–13 (2014)
2. Sussman, M., Osher, S.: A level-set approach for computing solutions to incompressible two-phase flow. J. Comput. Phys. **114**, 146–159 (1994)
3. Hirt, C.W., Nichols, B.D.: Volume of fluid (VOF) method for the dynamics of free boundaries. J. Comput. Phys. **39**, 201–225 (1981)
4. Sun, D.L., Tao, W.Q.: A coupled volume-of-fluid and level-set (VOSET) method for computing incompressible two-phase flows. Int. J. Heat Mass Transfer **53**, 645–655 (2010)
5. van der Waals, J.D., Konink, V.: The thermodynamic theory of capillarity under the hypothesis of a continuous density variation. J. Stat. Phys. Dutch **50**, 3219 (1893)
6. Eyre, D.J.: Unconditionally gradient stable time marching the Cahn-Hilliard equation. In: Computational and Mathematical Models of Microstructural Evolution, Materials Research Society Symposium Proceedings 5, vol. 529, pp. 39–46 (1998)
7. Kou, J.S., Sun, S.Y.: Multi-scale diffuse interface modeling of multi-component two-phase flow with partial miscibility. J. Comput. Phys. **318**(1), 349–372 (2016)
8. Guo, Z., Lin, P.: A thermodynamically consistent phase-field model for two-phase flows with thermo-capillary effects. J. Fluid Mech. **766**, 226–271 (2015)
9. Gurtin, M.E., Polignone, D., Vinals, J.: Two-phase binary fluids and immiscible fluids described by an order parameter. Math. Models Meth. Appl. Sci. **6**, 815–831 (1996)
10. Lowengrub, J., Truskinovsky, L.: Quasi-incompressible Cahn-Hilliard fluids. Proc. R. Soc. Lond. Ser. A **454**, 2617–2654 (1998)
11. Boyer, F.: A theoretical and numerical model for the study of incompressible mixture flows. Comp. Fluids **31**, 41–68 (2002)

12. Ding, H., Shu, C.: Diffuse interface model for incompressible two-phase flows with large density ratios. J. Comput. Phys. **226**(2), 2078–2095 (2007)
13. Shen, J., Yang, X.F.: A phase-field model and its numerical approximation for two-phase incompressible flows with different densities and viscosities. SIAM J. Sci. Comput. **32**(3), 1159–1179 (2010)
14. Aland, S., Voigt, A.: Benchmark computations of diffuse interface models for two-dimensional bubble dynamics. Int. J. Numer. Meth. Fluids **69**, 747–761 (2012)
15. Guermond, J.-L., Quartapelle, L.: A projection FEM for variable density incompressible flows. J. Comput. Phys. **165**, 167–188 (2000)
16. Abels, H., Garcke, H., Grün, G.: Thermodynamically consistent, frame indifferent diffuse interface models for incompressible two-phase flows with different densities. Math. Mod. Meth. Appl. Sic. **22**(3), 1150013-1-40 (2012)
17. Minjeaud, S.: An unconditionally stable uncoupled scheme for a triphasic Cahn-Hilliard/Navier-Stokes model. Numer. Meth. Partial Differ. Eqn. **29**(2), 584–618 (2013)
18. Shen, J., Yang, X.: Decoupled, energy stable schemes for phase-field models of two-phase incompressible flows. SIAM J. Numer. Anal. **53**(1), 279–296 (2015)
19. Kou, J., Sun, S., Wang, X.: Linearly decoupled energy-stable numerical methods for multi-component two-phase compressible flow arXiv:1712.02222 (2017)
20. Kou, J., Sun, S.: Thermodynamically consistent modeling and simulation of multi-component two-phase flow with partial miscibility. Comput. Meth. Appl. Mech. Eng. **331**, 623–649 (2018)
21. Chaikin, P.M., Lubensky, T.C.: Principles of Condensed Matter Physics. Cambridge University Press, Cambridge (1995)
22. Boussinesq, J.: Théorie de l'écoulement tourbillonnant et tumultueux des liquides dans les lits rectilignes a grande section. 1, Gauthier-Villars (1897)
23. Hysing, S., Turek, S., et al.: Quantitative benchmark computations of two-dimensional bubble dynamics. Int. J. Numer. Meth. Fluids **60**, 1259–1288 (2009)

Study on Numerical Methods for Gas Flow Simulation Using Double-Porosity Double-Permeability Model

Yi Wang[1]([∞]) [iD], Shuyu Sun[2] [iD], and Liang Gong[3]

[1] National Engineering Laboratory for Pipeline Safety, MOE Key Laboratory
of Petroleum Engineering, Beijing Key Laboratory of Urban Oil and Gas
Distribution Technology, China University of Petroleum (Beijing),
Beijing 102249, China
wangyi1031@cup.edu.cn
[2] Computational Transport Phenomena Laboratory, Division of Physical Science
and Engineering, King Abdullah University of Science and Technology,
Thuwal 23955-6900, Saudi Arabia
[3] Department of Thermal Energy and Power Engineering, College of Pipeline
and Civil Engineering, China University of Petroleum (Qingdao),
Qingdao 266580, Shandong, China

Abstract. In this paper, we firstly study numerical methods for gas flow simulation in dual-continuum porous media. Typical methods for oil flow simulation in dual-continuum porous media cannot be used straightforward to this kind of simulation due to the artificial mass loss caused by the compressibility and the non-robustness caused by the non-linear source term. To avoid these two problems, corrected numerical methods are proposed using mass balance equations and local linearization of the non-linear source term. The improved numerical methods are successful for the computation of gas flow in the double-porosity double-permeability porous media. After this improvement, temporal advancement for each time step includes three fractional steps: (i) advance matrix pressure and fracture pressure using the typical computation; (ii) solve the mass balance equation system for mean pressures; (iii) correct pressures in (i) by mean pressures in (ii). Numerical results show that mass conservation of gas for the whole domain is guaranteed while the numerical computation is robust.

Keywords: Mass conservation · Numerical method
Double-porosity double-permeability · Fractured porous media
Gas flow

1 Introduction

Fractured reservoirs contain significant proportion of oil and gas reserves all over the world. This proportion is estimated to be over 20% for oil reserves [1] and probably higher for gas reserves [2]. The large proportion of petroleum in fractured reservoirs is a good supplementary to convectional petroleum resource, which cannot solely satisfy energy demands all over the world for oil and gas. Fractured reservoirs are attracting petroleum industry and getting more developments. Despite well understandings and technological accumulations for conventional oil and gas, technologies for explorations in fractured reservoirs are relative immature due to the complicated structures and flow behaviors in fractured reservoirs. Therefore, researches driven by the increasing needs to develop petroleum in fractured reservoirs have been received growing attentions. Efforts on modeling and understanding the flow characteristics in fractured reservoirs have been made continuously [3]. Among the commonly used conceptual models, the double-porosity double-permeability model is probably widely used in petroleum engineering due to its good ability to match many types of laboratory or field data and has been utilized in commercial software [5].

Some numerical simulations [6] and analytical solutions [7, 8] have been proposed for oil flow in dual-continuum porous media. However, analytical solutions can only be obtained under much idealized assumptions, such that slight compressibility, infinite radial flow, homogenization etc., so that their applications are restricted to simplified cases of oil flow. For gas flow, slight compressibility assumption is not held any more. The governing equations are nonlinear and cannot be analytically solved. Numerical computations for gas flow in dual-continuum porous media might be more difficult than oil flow because the strong nonlinearity induced by compressibility of gas. Therefore, it is important to study numerical methods for gas flow in fractured reservoirs based on the dual-continuum model. We also numerically study the effect of the production well on the gas production in a dual-continuum porous medium with non-uniform fracture distribution.

2 Governing Equations and Numerical Methods

2.1 Physical Model and Governing Equations

Figure 1 shows the computational domain. The side length of the domain is L. Other sets can be found in the figure.

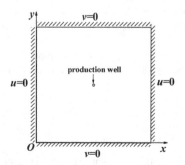

Fig. 1. Physical model

Darcy's law in a dual-continuum system is:

$$u_M = -\frac{k_{xxM}}{\mu}\frac{\partial p_M}{\partial x}, v_M = -\frac{k_{yyM}}{\mu}\frac{\partial p_M}{\partial y} \tag{1}$$

$$u_F = -\frac{k_{xxF}}{\mu}\frac{\partial p_F}{\partial x}, v_F = -\frac{k_{yyF}}{\mu}\frac{\partial p_F}{\partial y} \tag{2}$$

where u_M and v_M are two components of Darcy velocity of gas flow in matrix, u_F and v_F are two components of Darcy velocity of gas flow in fracture, k_{xxM} and k_{yyM} are two components of matrix permeability, k_{xxF} and k_{yyF} are two components of fracture permeability, p_M and p_F are pressures in matrix and fracture respectively. μ is the dynamic viscosity.

Mass conservation equations for gas flow in dual-continuum reservoirs governed by Darcy's law are:

$$\phi_M\frac{\partial p_M}{\partial t} - \frac{\partial}{\partial x}\left(\frac{k_{xxM}}{\mu}p_M\frac{\partial p_M}{\partial x}\right) + \frac{\partial}{\partial y}\left(\frac{k_{yyM}}{\mu}p_M\frac{\partial p_M}{\partial y}\right) - \alpha\frac{k_M}{\mu}p_M(p_M - p_F) \tag{3}$$

$$\phi_F\frac{\partial p_F}{\partial t} = \frac{\partial}{\partial x}\left(\frac{k_{xxF}}{\mu}p_F\frac{\partial p_F}{\partial x}\right) + \frac{\partial}{\partial y}\left(\frac{k_{yyF}}{\mu}p_F\frac{\partial p_F}{\partial y}\right) + \alpha\frac{k_M}{\mu}p_M(p_M - p_F)$$
$$- \delta_w C_w p_F(p_F - p_{bh}) \tag{4}$$

Where ϕ_M and ϕ_F are porosities of matrix and fracture respectively, k_M is the intrinsic permeability of matrix for the matrix-fracture interaction term. α is the shape factor of fracture, taking the form proposed by Kazemi et al. [9]:

$$\alpha = 4\left(\frac{1}{l_x^2} + \frac{1}{l_y^2}\right) \tag{5}$$

Where l_x and l_y are the lengths of fracture spacing in the x and y directions respectively. C_w is a factor of the well:

$$C_w = \frac{2\pi k_F}{\mu h_x h_y \ln(r_e/r_w)} \tag{6}$$

Where k_F is the permeability of fracture at the location of the production well, h_x and h_y are side lengths of the grid containing the well, r_w and r_e are well radius and equivalent radius ($r_e = 0.20788h, h = h_x = h_y$ and $h_x = \Delta x, h_y = \Delta y$ for uniform square grid). C_w is 1 for the grid cell containing the well and 0 for other cells. p_{bh} is the bottom hole pressure.

2.2 Numerical Methods

The above governing equations are similar with those of oil flow in dual-continuum porous media so that we directly apply the numerical methods for oil flow to gas flow at first. Finite difference method is used on staggered grid. Temporal advancement is the semi-implicit scheme to ensure a large time step. Spatial discretization adopts the second-order central difference scheme. Based on these methods, Eqs. (3) and (4) are discretized to:

$$cp_{Mi,j}\, p_{Mi,j}^{(n+1)} = cex_{Mi,j}\, p_{Mi+1,j}^{(n+1)} + cwx_{Mi,j}\, p_{Mi-1,j}^{(n+1)} + cny_{Mi,j}\, p_{Mi,j+1}^{(n+1)} + csy_{Mi,j}\, p_{Mi,j-1}^{(n+1)} + b_{Mi,j}$$

(7)

$$\left(cp_{Fi,j} + \delta_w C_w \Delta t \left(p_{Fi,j}^{(n)} - p_{bh}\right)\right) p_{Fi,j}^{(n+1)} - \Delta t \frac{\alpha k_{Mi,j}}{\mu} p_{Mi,j}^{(n)} p_{Mi,j}^{(n+1)}$$

$$= cex_{Fi,j}\, p_{Fi+1,j}^{(n+1)} + cwx_{Fi,j}\, p_{Fi-1,j}^{(n+1)} + cny_{Fi,j}\, p_{Fi,j+1}^{(n+1)} + csy_{Fi,j}\, p_{Fi,j-1}^{(n+1)} + b_{Fi,j}$$

(8)

Where $cp_{Mi,j} = \phi_M + cwx_{Mi,j} + cex_{Mi,j} + csy_{Mi,j} + cny_{Mi,j} + \Delta t \frac{\alpha k_{Mi,j}}{\mu} p_{Mi,j}^{(n)} \left(1 - \frac{p_{Fi,j}^{(n)}}{p_{Mi,j}^{(n)}}\right)$,

$cp_{Fi,j} = \phi_F + cwx_{Fi,j} + cex_{Fi,j} + csy_{Fi,j} + cny_{Fi,j} + \Delta t \frac{\alpha k_{Mi,j}}{\mu} p_{Mi,j}^{(n)}$,

$b_{Mi,j} = \phi_M p_{Mi,j}^{(n)} + swx_{Mi,j} + sex_{Mi,j} + ssy_{Mi,j} + sny_{Mi,j}$,

$b_{Fi,j} = \phi_F p_{Fi,j}^{(n)} + swx_{Fi,j} + sex_{Fi,j} + ssy_{Fi,j} + sny_{Fi,j}$. Other coefficients are not shown here due to the limitation of the paper.

3   Discussions on Numerical Method

The discretized equations are solved using parameters in Table 1. Computational results show that the well pressure is always negative, which is unphysical, because all pressures must be higher than P_{bh} (2 atm). We further find the difference between initial total mass and computational total mass is increasing (Fig. 2), indicating that gas mass is lost in the computation. This phenomenon demonstrates that current numerical methods cannot automatically ensure the mass conservation, although the computation is based on the mass conservation equation (Eqs. (3) and (4)). Therefore, mass conservation law should be utilized to correct current numerical methods.

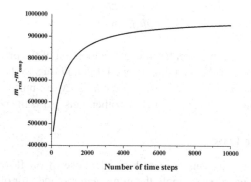

Fig. 2. Difference between real mass and computational mass

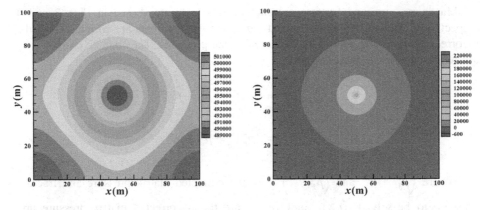

Fig. 3. Matrix pressure after 10000 Δt **Fig. 4.** Fracture pressure after 10000 Δt

Table 1. Computational parameters

Parameter	Value	Unit
ϕ_M	0.5	/
ϕ_F	0.001	/
$p_M(t_0)$	100	atm
$p_F(t_0)$	100	atm
p_{bh}	2	atm
k_{xxF}	100	md
k_{yyF}	100	md
k_{xxM}	1	md
k_{yyM}	1	md
k_M	1	md
W	16	g/mol
R	8.3147295	J/(mol · K)
T	25	$^{\circ}$C
μ	11.067×10^{-6}	Pa · s
nx	101	/
ny	101	/
L	100	m
l_x	20	cm
l_y	20	cm
r_w	20	cm
Δt	0.24	h

*1 atm = 101325 Pa;
1md = $9.8692327 \times 10^{-16}$m^2; t_0
represents initial time.

Matrix pressure and fracture pressure at 10000 Δt are shown in Figs. 3 and 4 respectively. Their distributions indicate that pressure gradients are correct. Thus, the incorrect pressures are caused by the unreal mean pressures. They can be corrected by the real mean pressures as follows:

$$\left(p_M^{(n+1)}\right)_{i,j} = \left(p_M^*\right)_{i,j} - \overline{p_M^*} + \overline{p_M^{real}} \tag{9}$$

$$\left(p_F^{(n+1)}\right)_{i,j} = \left(p_F^*\right)_{i,j} - \overline{p_F^*} + \overline{p_F^{real}} \tag{10}$$

Where $\left(p_M^{(n+1)}\right)_{i,j}$ and $\left(p_F^{(n+1)}\right)_{i,j}$ are the corrected matrix pressure and fracture pressure to be solved, $\left(p_M^*\right)_{i,j}$ and $\left(p_F^*\right)_{i,j}$ are the uncorrected matrix pressure and fracture pressure obtained from the numerical methods in Sect. 2.2, $\overline{p_M^*}$ and $\overline{p_F^*}$ are the unreal mean pressures of matrix and pressure calculated from $\left(p_M^*\right)_{i,j}$ and $\left(p_F^*\right)_{i,j}$, $\overline{p_M^{real}}$ and $\overline{p_F^{real}}$ are the real mean pressures of matrix and fracture which are unknown because they are dependent on $\left(p_M^{(n+1)}\right)_{i,j}$ and $\left(p_F^{(n+1)}\right)_{i,j}$. $\left(p_M^*\right)_{i,j}$, $\left(p_F^*\right)_{i,j}$, $\overline{p_M^*}$ and $\overline{p_F^*}$ can be calculated via the numerical methods in Sect. 2.2 so that they are all known variables for each time step. Thus, the calculation of $\left(p_M^{(n+1)}\right)_{i,j}$ and $\left(p_F^{(n+1)}\right)_{i,j}$ turns to the calculation of unknown $\overline{p_M^{real}}$ and $\overline{p_F^{real}}$. Gas is continuously flowing from matrix to fracture and leaving the dual-continuum system from the well. Therefore, mass balance of matrix in each time step should be:

$$mM^{(n)} - mT^{(n+1)} = mM^{(n+1)} \tag{11}$$

Mass balance of fracture in each time step is:

$$mF^{(n)} + mT^{(n+1)} - Q^{(n+1)} = mF^{(n+1)} \tag{12}$$

Where $mM^{(n)}$ and $mF^{(n)}$ are the masses of gas in matrix and fracture at the beginning moment of each time step, $mM^{(n+1)}$ and $mF^{(n+1)}$ are the masses of gas in matrix and fracture at the ending moment of each time step, $mT^{(n+1)}$ is the mass leaving matrix (i.e. equivalent to the mass entering fracture) at each time step, $Q^{(n+1)}$ is the mass leaving the fracture via the production well at each time step.

Equations (3) and (4) are mass conservation equations in the unit of Pa/s. $\Delta x \Delta y \Delta t \frac{W}{RT}$ should be multiplied to all terms of Eqs. (3) and (4) to obtain the masses in Eqs. (11) and (12):

$$mT^{(n+1)} = \Delta x \Delta y \Delta t \frac{W}{RT} \sum_{j=1}^{ny} \sum_{i=1}^{nx} \left[\alpha \left(\frac{k_M}{\mu}\right)_{i,j} \left(p_M^{(n+1)}\right)_{i,j} \left(\left(p_M^{(n+1)}\right)_{i,j} - \left(p_F^{(n+1)}\right)_{i,j}\right) \right] \tag{13}$$

$$Q^{(n+1)} = \Delta x \Delta y \Delta t \frac{W}{RT} \delta_w C_w p_F^{(n+1)} \left(p_F^{(n+1)} - p_{bh} \right) \tag{14}$$

The masses of gas can be calculated via equation of state:

$$mM^{(n+1)} = \sum_{j=1}^{ny} \sum_{i=1}^{nx} \left(p_M^{(n+1)} \right)_{i,j} \Delta x \Delta y \frac{W}{RT} \tag{15}$$

$$mF^{(n+1)} = \sum_{j=1}^{ny} \sum_{i=1}^{nx} \left(p_F^{(n+1)} \right)_{i,j} \Delta x \Delta y \frac{W}{RT} \tag{16}$$

$$mM^{(n)} = \sum_{j=1}^{ny} \sum_{i=1}^{nx} \left(p_M^{(n)} \right)_{i,j} \Delta x \Delta y \frac{W}{RT} \tag{17}$$

$$mF^{(n)} = \sum_{j=1}^{ny} \sum_{i=1}^{nx} \left(p_F^{(n)} \right)_{i,j} \Delta x \Delta y \frac{W}{RT} \tag{18}$$

Equations (17) and (18) can be used to directly obtain the values of $mM^{(n)}$ and $mF^{(n)}$ in every time step. Equations (13)–(16) are substituted to Eqs. (11) and (12) so that the mass balance equations become:

$$mM^{(n)} - \Delta x \Delta y \Delta t \frac{W}{RT} \sum_{j=1}^{ny} \sum_{i=1}^{nx} \left[\alpha \left(\frac{k_M}{\mu} \right)_{i,j} \left(p_M^{(n+1)} \right)_{i,j} \left(\left(p_M^{(n+1)} \right)_{i,j} - \left(p_F^{(n+1)} \right)_{i,j} \right) \right]$$
$$= \sum_{j=1}^{ny} \sum_{i=1}^{nx} \left(p_M^{(n+1)} \right)_{i,j} \Delta x \Delta y \frac{W}{RT} \tag{19}$$

$$mF^{(n)} + \Delta x \Delta y \Delta t \frac{W}{RT} \sum_{j=1}^{ny} \sum_{i=1}^{nx} \left[\alpha \left(\frac{k_M}{\mu} \right)_{i,j} \left(p_M^{(n+1)} \right)_{i,j} \left(\left(p_M^{(n+1)} \right)_{i,j} - \left(p_F^{(n+1)} \right)_{i,j} \right) \right]$$
$$- \Delta x \Delta y \Delta t \frac{W}{RT} \delta_w C_w p_F^{(n+1)} \left(p_F^{(n+1)} - p_{bh} \right) = \sum_{j=1}^{ny} \sum_{i=1}^{nx} \left(p_F^{(n+1)} \right)_{i,j} \Delta x \Delta y \frac{W}{RT} \tag{20}$$

Equations (9) and (10) are substituted to the above two equations to obtain the following expressions:

$$- \left[\alpha \Delta x \Delta y \Delta t \sum_{j=1}^{ny} \sum_{i=1}^{nx} \left(\frac{k_M}{\mu} \right)_{i,j} \right] \left(\overline{p_M^{real}} \right)^2 + \left[\alpha \Delta x \Delta y \Delta t \sum_{j=1}^{ny} \sum_{i=1}^{nx} \left(\frac{k_M}{\mu} \right)_{i,j} \right] \overline{p_M^{real}} \overline{p_F^{real}}$$

$$- \left[L_x L_y + \alpha \Delta x \Delta y \Delta t \sum_{j=1}^{ny} \sum_{i=1}^{nx} \left(\frac{k_M}{\mu} \right)_{i,j} \left(2 \left(p_M^* \right)_{i,j} - 2 \overline{p_m^*} - \left(p_F^* \right)_{i,j} + \overline{p_F^*} \right) \right] \overline{p_M^{real}}$$

$$+ \left[\alpha \Delta x \Delta y \Delta t \sum_{j=1}^{ny} \sum_{i=1}^{nx} \left(\frac{k_M}{\mu} \right)_{i,j} \left(\left(p_M^* \right)_{i,j} - \overline{p_M^*} \right) \right] \overline{p_F^{real}}$$

$$- \alpha \Delta x \Delta y \Delta t \sum_{j=1}^{ny} \sum_{i=1}^{nx} \left(\frac{k_M}{\mu} \right)_{i,j} \left(\left(p_M^* \right)_{i,j} - \overline{p_M^*} \right) \left(\left(p_M^* \right)_{i,j} - \overline{p_M^*} - \left(p_F^* \right)_{i,j} + \overline{p_F^*} \right) + m M^{(n)} \frac{RT}{W} = 0$$

$$(21)$$

$$\left[\alpha \Delta x \Delta y \Delta t \sum_{j=1}^{ny} \sum_{i=1}^{nx} \left(\frac{k_M}{\mu} \right)_{i,j} \right] \left(\overline{p_M^{real}} \right)^2 - C_w \Delta x \Delta y \Delta t \left(\overline{p_F^{real}} \right)^2 - \left[\alpha \Delta x \Delta y \Delta t \sum_{j=1}^{ny} \sum_{i=1}^{nx} \left(\frac{k_M}{\mu} \right)_{i,j} \right] \overline{p_M^{real}} \overline{p_F^{real}}$$

$$+ \left[\alpha \Delta x \Delta y \Delta t \sum_{j=1}^{ny} \sum_{i=1}^{nx} \left(\frac{k_M}{\mu} \right)_{i,j} \left(2 \left(p_M^* \right)_{i,j} - 2 \overline{p_M^*} - \left(p_F^* \right)_{i,j} + \overline{p_F^*} \right) \right] \overline{p_M^{real}}$$

$$- \left[L_x L_y + \alpha \Delta x \Delta y \Delta t \sum_{j=1}^{ny} \sum_{i=1}^{nx} \left(\frac{k_M}{\mu} \right)_{i,j} \left(\left(p_M^* \right)_{i,j} - \overline{p_M^*} \right) + C_w \Delta x \Delta y \Delta t \left(2 \left(p_F^* \right)_{iW,jW} - 2 \overline{p_F^*} - p_{bh} \right) \right] \overline{p_F^{real}}$$

$$+ \alpha \Delta x \Delta y \Delta t \sum_{j=1}^{ny} \sum_{i=1}^{nx} \left(\frac{k_M}{\mu} \right)_{i,j} \left(\left(p_M^* \right)_{i,j} - \overline{p_M^*} \right) \left(\left(p_M^* \right)_{i,j} - \overline{p_M^*} - \left(p_F^* \right)_{i,j} + \overline{p_F^*} \right)$$

$$- C_w \Delta x \Delta y \Delta t \left(\left(p_F^* \right)_{iW,jW} - \overline{p_F^*} \right) \left(\left(p_F^* \right)_{iW,jW} - \overline{p_F^*} - p_{bh} \right) + m F^{(n)} \frac{RT}{W} = 0$$

$$(22)$$

where iW, jW are the grid numbers of the well in the x and y directions respectively. Equations (21) and (22) are the final expressions of mass balance equations Eqs. (11) and (12). $\overline{p_M^{real}}$ and $\overline{p_F^{real}}$ can be directly solved combining these two equations. Once the combined equations (Eqs. (21) and (22)) are solved, $\overline{p_M^{real}}$ and $\overline{p_F^{real}}$ are obtained so that pressures can be corrected using Eqs. (9) and (10) for every time step.

Well pressure and total mass of gas using the above method considering mass conservation law are shown in Table 2. Well pressure becomes positive. The mass difference is always zero to show the mass conservation is satisfied. However, the well pressure (p_{well}) in Table 2 has an unphysical inverse. This is due to the diagonal dominance cannot be satisfied. It is clear in the governing equations that only the well term $\delta_w C_w \Delta t \left(p_{Fi,j}^{(n)} - p_{bh} \right)$ may cause the diagonal coefficient decreasing. Thus, the non-linear well term ($S = -\delta_w C_w p_F (p_F - p_{bh})$) in Eq. (4) should be transformed to the form of $S = S_c + S_p p_F$ with $S_p \leq 0$ [10]. S_c and S_p can be obtained by the following Taylor expansion:

Table 2. Well pressure and mass difference after improvement

$n_t/100$	1	2	3	...	10	11	12	13	14
p_{well}	3.83	3.63	3.47	...	2.80	2.74	2.69	2.65	2.75
$m_{real} - m_{comp}$	0	0	0	...	0	0	0	0	0

$$S = S^{(n)} + \frac{dS}{dp_F}\bigg|^{(n)} \left(p_F^{(n+1)} - p_F^{(n)} \right)$$

$$= -\delta_w C_w p_F^{(n)} \left(p_F^{(n)} - p_{bh} \right) - \delta_w C_w \left(2p_F^{(n)} - p_{bh} \right)\left(p_F^{(n+1)} - p_F^{(n)} \right) \qquad (23)$$

$$= \delta_w C_w p_F^{(n)2} - \delta_w C_w \left(2p_F^{(n)} - p_{bh} \right) p_F^{(n+1)}$$

Equation (23) is used in the discretization of Eq. (4) instead of $S = -\delta_w C_w p_F(p_F - p_{bh})$ so that Eq. (8) can be modified to be the following form:

$$\left(cp_{Fi,j} + \delta_w C_w \Delta t \left(2p_{Fi,j}^{(n)} - p_{bh} \right) \right) p_{Fi,j}^{(n+1)} - \Delta t \frac{\alpha k_{Mi,j}}{\mu} p_{Mi,j}^{(n)} p_{Mi,j}^{(n+1)}$$

$$= cex_{Fi,j} p_{Fi+1,j}^{(n+1)} + cwx_{Fi,j} p_{Fi-1,j}^{(n+1)} + cny_{Fi,j} p_{Fi,j+1}^{(n+1)} + csy_{Fi,j} p_{Fi,j-1}^{(n+1)} + b_{Fi,j} + \delta_w C_w p_F^{(n)2}$$

$$(24)$$

Figure 5 shows that p_{well} decreases monotonically and is always larger than p_{bh} after this improvement.

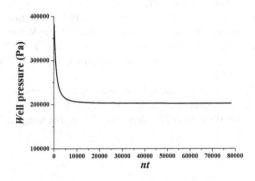

Fig. 5. Improved well pressure using linearization of source term

4 Conclusion

From the above discussions, the proposed numerical methods can be summarized as follows: (1) Governing equations should be discretized into the form of Eqs. (7) and (24) respectively, using linearization of source term; (2) Mass conservation equation (Eqs. (21) and (22)) should be established according to the mass balance of the whole system and solved to obtain real mean pressures of matrix and fracture in every time step; (3) Matrix pressure and fracture pressure should be corrected using the mean pressures obtained in (2). Future computations could be made using field data in engineering.

Acknowledgements. The work presented in this paper has been supported by National Natural Science Foundation of China (NSFC) (No. 51576210, No. 51676208), Science Foundation of China University of Petroleum-Beijing (No. 2462015BJB03), and also supported in part by funding from King Abdullah University of Science and Technology (KAUST) through the grant BAS/1/1351-01-01.

References

1. Firoozabadi, A.: Recovery mechanisms in fractured reservoirs and field performance. J. Can. Petrol. Technol. **39**, 13–17 (2000)
2. Bourbiaux, B.: Fractured reservoir simulation: a challenging and rewarding issue. Oil Gas Sci. Technol. **65**, 227–238 (2010)
3. Wu, Y.S., Di, Y., Kang, Z., Fakcharoenphol, P.: A multiple-continuum model for simulating single-phase and multiphase flow in naturally fractured vuggy reservoirs. J. Pet. Sci. Eng. **78**, 13–22 (2011)
4. Wang, Y., Sun, S., Gong, L., Yu, B.: A globally mass-conservative method for dual-continuum gas reservoir simulation. J. Nat. Gas Sci. Eng. **53**, 301–316 (2018)
5. Wu, Y.S., Lu, G., Zhang, K., Pan, L., Bodvarsson, G.S.: Analyzing unsaturated flow patterns in fractured rock using an integrated modeling approach. Hydrogeol. J. **15**, 553–572 (2007)
6. Presho, M., Wo, S., Ginting, V.: Calibrated dual porosity dual permeability modeling of fractured reservoirs. J. Pet. Sci. Eng. **77**, 326–337 (2011)
7. Huang, C.S., Chen, Y.L., Yeh, H.D.: A general analytical solution for flow to a single horizontal well by Fourier and Laplace transforms. Adv. Water Resour. **34**, 640–648 (2011)
8. Nie, R.S., Meng, Y.F., Jia, Y.L., Zhang, F.X., Yang, X.T., Niu, X.N.: Dual porosity and dual permeability modeling of horizontal well in naturally fractured reservoir. Transp. Porous Media **92**, 213–235 (2012)
9. Kazemi, H., Merrill, L.S., Porterfield, K.L., Zeman, P.R.: Numerical simulation of water-oil flow in naturally fractured reservoirs. SPE J. **16**, 317–326 (1976)
10. Tao, W.Q.: Numerical Heat Transfer, 2nd edn. Xi'an Jiaotong University Press, Xi'an (2002)

Molecular Simulation of Displacement of Methane by Injection Gases in Shale

Jihong Shi[1,3], Liang Gong[1($\boxtimes$)], Zhaoqin Huang[2], and Jun Yao[2]

[1] College of Pipeline and Civil Engineering, China University of Petroleum
(East China), Qingdao 266580, People's Republic of China
lgong@upc.edu.cn
[2] School of Petroleum Engineering, China University of Petroleum (East China),
Qingdao 266580, People's Republic of China
[3] Computational Transport Phenomena Laboratory, Division of Physical Science
and Engineering, King Abdullah University of Science and Technology,
Thuwal 23955-6900, Saudi Arabia

Abstract. Displacement methane (CH_4) by injection gases is regarded as an effective way to exploit shale gas and sequestrate carbon dioxide (CO_2). In our work, the displacement of CH_4 by injection gases is studied by using the grand canonical Monte Carlo (GCMC) simulation. Then, we use molecular dynamics (MD) simulation to study the adsorption occurrence behavior of CH_4 in different pore size. This shale model is composed of organic and inorganic material, which is an original and comprehensive simplification for the real shale composition. The results show that both the displacement amount of CH_4 and sequestration amount of CO_2 see an upward trend with the increase of pore size. The CO_2 molecules can replace the adsorbed CH_4 from the adsorption sites directly. On the contrary, when N_2 molecules are injected into the slit pores, the partial pressure of CH_4 would decrease. With the increase of the pores width, the adsorption occurrence transfers from single adsorption layer to four adsorption layers. It is expected that our work can reveal the mechanisms of adsorption and displacement of shale gas, which could provide a guidance and reference for displacement exploitation of shale gas and sequestration of CO_2.

Keywords: Molecular simulation · Displacement of methane · Shale gas
Injection gases

1 Introduction

Recently, the exploration and development of shale gas have received extensive attention because of the demand for resources and pollution problems [1–3]. Shale gas has gained tremendous attention as an unconventional gas resource [4, 5]. The main component of shale gas is CH_4, which has three states in shale, i.e., adsorbed state, free state and dissolved state [6, 7]. The volume percentage of the adsorbed CH_4 in the shale reservoirs could even account for 20%–85% [8, 9]. Therefore, it is significant to investigate the adsorbed CH_4 in shale reservoirs for shale gas resource evaluation.

Exploration shale gas become very difficult due to the ultralow porosity and permeability shale. Right now, many methods are proposed to boost production of shale

© Springer International Publishing AG, part of Springer Nature 2018
Y. Shi et al. (Eds.): ICCS 2018, LNCS 10862, pp. 139–148, 2018.
https://doi.org/10.1007/978-3-319-93713-7_11

gas, for example, re-fracturing, hydro-fracturing, supercritical CO_2 fracturing, injection gases, etc. Hydro-fracturing, as a method of widely application, is used to enhance permeability of unconventional reservoirs [10–12]. Moreover, this method could waste large amount of water and cause severe environment problems [13–15]. Alternatively, the new method of injection gases is regarded as a good way to improve the recovery efficiency [16–18]. Meanwhile, shale gases are usually stored as adsorption state in silt pore and carbon nanotube. Therefore, investigations about the displacement and diffusion of methane in silt pores are of great significance for estimating and exploiting the shale gas.

Extensive computational studies and experiments on the displacement of CH_4 in shale matrix reported at present. Yang et al. [18] investigated competitive adsorption between CO_2 and CH_4 in Na-montmorillonites by Monto Carlo simulations, and found that the Na-montmorillonite clay shows obviously high adsorption capacity for CO_2, as compared with CH_4. Wu et al. [16] explored the displacement of CH_4 in carbon nanochannels by using molecular dynamics simulations, and found that CO_2 can displace the adsorbed CH_4 directly. Akbarzadeh et al. [19] also performed MD simulations on the mixture of shale gas (methane, ethane and propone) in a nanoscale pore graphite model, and found that the most selectivity (and also recovery) of methane obtains at the methane mole fraction of 0.95. Huo et al. [20] conducted experiments to study the displacement behaviors of CH_4 adsorbed on shales by CO_2 injection, and found that the amount of recovered CH_4 and stored CO_2 increase with CO_2 injection pressure. Huang et al. [21] investigated the adsorption capacities of CH_4, CO_2 and their mixtures on four kerogen models with different maturities by GCMC simulations. And they found that the adsorption capacity of gas molecules is related to the maturity of kerogen.

From the studies mentioned above, most of the shale models are nanosized and simplified. Because some free gases would occupy large pores and adsorbed gases would exist in organic matter and inorganic minerals. For the shale matrix, it is indispensable to simplify the complicated structure of shale matrix to deal with the complex situation. Someone argued that the structure of montmorillonite with some ions could represent the shale. However, this model still did not include the organic matter. At last, it is reasonable and appropriate to construct an all-atom shale model including inorganic silica and organic matter to investigate the displacement and diffusion of CH_4 in gas shale matrix.

In this work, we proposed a modified and generalized shale matrix model including inorganic silica and organic matter. Then, the mechanism of the displacement of CH_4 by injection gases in shale matrix model was investigated through molecular simulations. Finally, some discussion was also addressed. In Sect. 3.1, the occurrence behaviors of CH_4 in different pore size are found to become from one adsorption peak to four adsorption peaks. In Sect. 3.2, CO_2 is injected into shale model to displace the adsorbed CH_4. The displacement efficiency and sequestration amount of CO_2 are investigated. In Sect. 3.3, the displacement CH_4 by CO_2 and N_2 are compared and analyzed.

2   Simulation Models and Methods

2.1   Shale Models

In order to construct the shale model containing inorganic minerals and organic matter, two silica sheets are used to stand for the inorganic mineral. Because the silica's brittleness is favorable for fracture propagation. We can get the initial silica lattice from the structure database of Material Studio software [22]. Along the (1 1 0) crystallo-graphic orientation, we can cleave a repeat unit with the thickness 3.0 nm. Generally, the polycyclic aromatic hydrocarbon is regarded as the major organic component of organic matters, especially for shale gas reservoirs. Therefore, we used methylnaph-thalene molecules to stand for the organic matter in the shale matrix here.

A simulation box was constructed to (32.43 × 39.30 × c $Å^3$), which contains two inorganic layers and two organic layers (see Fig. 1). As mentioned above, the perfect silica sheets were used to represent the inorganic layers. First, two perfect silica sheets were stacked each other in such a way as shown in Fig. 1. Then, methylnaphthalene molecules were absorbed into the interlayer space. The adsorbed methylnaphthalene molecules in slit pores were fixed [23].

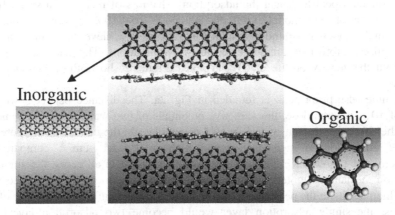

Fig. 1.   The model of shale matrix. Color scheme: yellow, silicon; red, oxygen; white, hydrogen; black, carbon. (Color figure online)

2.2   Methods

GCMC simulations are carried out by SORPTION code in the MATERIAL STUDIO (MS) software developed by Accelrys Inc. The interatomic interactions are described by the force field of condensed-phase optimized molecular potential for atomistic simulation studies (COMPASS), which is a general all-atom force field. First, we took the GCMC method to investigate the displacement of CH_4 by CO_2. The temperature and the pressure of CH_4 were 313 K and 15 MPa respectively. The acceptance or rejection of trial move is set as the Metropolis algorithm. Each equilibration procedure for CO_2 and CH_4 is 2 × 10^6. Next, CO_2 was put into the slit pores with injection pressure from 0 to 110 MPa. We could get the equalized structure until the process of simulation was ended.

In order to adjust the atomic coordinates to reach a stable initial configuration, the equalized structure was minimized by using the conjugate gradient algorithm. Then, we took MD method to study the density profile of adsorbed CH_4. First, the model was relaxed for 2 ns in a NVT ensemble with a time step of 1 fs. The Nose-Hoover thermostat method was used to maintain temperature. When we found that total energy of this model became time-independent, the equilibrium was arrived. In the last stage, this system experienced a simulation process of 2 ns in a NVE ensemble (constant number of atoms, isovolumetric, and constant energy conditions) with a time step of 1 fs, and the data were recorded for analysis. During these simulations, all the atoms of the shale matrix model were fixed as a rigid material.

3 Results and Discussion

3.1 Occurrence Behavior of Methane in Different Pores

The occurrence behaviors of methane in different pores are absolutely different, which is a significant aspect to reveal the adsorption behaviors of methane in shale. In this section, a series of shale model of different size pores from 10 Å to 100 Å are built. All of these shale models have undergone GCMC process to achieve the equilibrium state of adsorption, before they are subjected to MD simulations. Then, we can get some data about the density profile of CH_4 in pores. Figure 2 shows the different density profiles.

A single adsorption peak is founded in Fig. 2a. The distance between two solid walls of 10 Å is very close, the attractive potentials of two walls are strengthened by each other. A large amount of CH_4 would accumulate in the central of the pore. The peak of adsorption layer is the second highest at 0.65 $g \cdot cm^{-3}$, compare with 0.75 $g \cdot cm^{-3}$ at 15 Å. Since the pore size is the narrowest in all cases, the amount of adsorption methane is limited. A small amount of methane molecules absorbed in the pore, which results in the peak of adsorption layer is not the highest. As the size of pore increases, the single adsorption layer would become two adsorption layers. The attractive potentials of two walls become weak or even disappear. Meanwhile, the peaks of adsorption layer are the highest. It can be seen from the Fig. 2b. When the distance of two walls increases to 25 Å, apart from two peaks, a central single layer appears. Two peaks near the walls are lower, around half the figure for H = 15 Å. Four peaks of adsorption layers, including two primary adsorption layers and two secondary, will appear at 40 Å [17]. Figure 2e and f show that the density of bulk phase is all keep in at 0.2 $g \cdot cm^{-3}$ at the pore width of 60–100 Å. This situation illustrates that the central bulk phase will not change with the silt width increases.

In order to show the state of molecular occurrence more intuitively, we give snapshots of the adsorption model in two pore sizes. The pore sizes are set as 25 Å and 60 Å, representing mesopores and macropores respectively. Figure 3a shows that the amount of adsorbed CH_4 next to the walls is much more than the bulk's. So near the walls, two symmetrical peaks appeared. However, the center of the pore is still

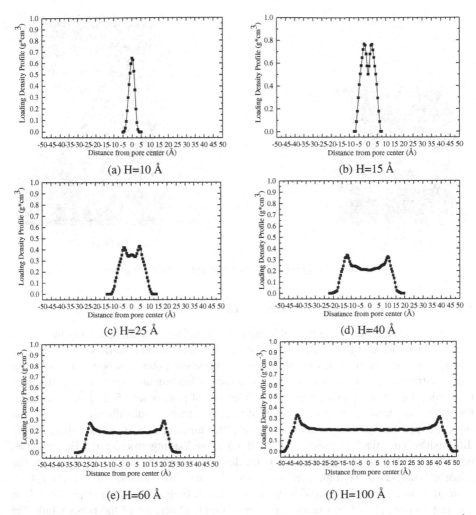

Fig. 2. Loading density profile and adsorption state of methane in different pores. (a) H = 10 Å, single adsorption layer; (b) H = 15 Å, two adsorption layers; (c) H = 25 Å, two adsorption layers and central single layer; (d) H = 40 Å, two adsorption layers and two secondary layers; (e) H = 60 Å, two adsorption layers and middle bulk phase; (f) H = 100 Å, two adsorption layers and middle bulk phase.

adsorbed with a certain amount of CH_4. Correspondingly, a small peak appears in the center of the density profile graph. In contrast to, when the pores become macropores, no more peaks appear in the center of the pores. It can be seen from Fig. 3b. Because in the case of large pore, the density of methane in the central area basically does not change.

(a) 25 Å   (b) 60 Å

Fig. 3. Adsorption occurrence of CH4 in different pores.

3.2 Methane Displacement by Carbon Dioxide in Different Pores

Injection gases has become a high efficient way to exploit the shale gas. CO_2 and N_2 are usually considered ideal gases to displace methane. Some studies find that the adsorption capacity of gases is related to the attractive potentials between gases and shale matrix atoms. Figure 4a shows the changes of loading amount of CH_4 at different CO_2 injection pressure in different pores. The size of pore is set 15–100 Å. Obviously, the downward trend in loading amount of CH_4 is significant at different pores. As the injection pressure of CO_2 increases, the loading amount of CH_4 in the shale model diminishes. For injection pressure of 0–30 MPa, the loading amount of CH_4 decreases quickly. When CO_2 is injected, the molecules can adsorb on the walls to replace the adsorbed methane. At high pressure, there are no more adsorption sites for CO_2 molecules to adsorb. The curve becomes smooth at high CO_2 injection pressure. The loading amount of CH_4 starts to stay stable. With the increase of the pores width, the loading amount of CH_4 at different CO_2 injection pressure increases obviously. Similarly, the sequestration amount of CO_2 rises significantly. For the same width of pore, the figure for sequestration CO_2 grows dramatically, which is shown in the Fig. 4b. Furthermore, the displacement amount of CH_4 at CO_2 injection pressure of 90 MPa is studied. Much more CO_2 is absorbed into the pores with the increase of pore width, causing more methane to be driven out. So Fig. 4c shows that the displacement amount of CH_4 is the highest in the pore size of 100 Å. Correspondingly, the sequestration amount of CO_2 is also the most. It can be seen from Fig. 4d.

3.3 Comparison of Methane Displacement by Nitrogen and Carbon Dioxide

Both N_2 and CO_2 can be used to displace gases. However, our studies find that the displacement mechanisms of these gases is different. The pore width is set 25 Å.

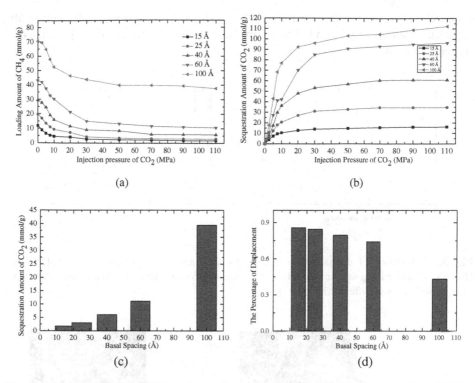

Fig. 4. Displacement of methane by carbon dioxide in different pores. ($T_m = 313$ K, $P_m = 15$ MPa) (a) Loading amount of CH_4 at different CO_2 injection pressure; (b) Sequestration amount of CO_2 at different CO_2 injection pressure; (c) Displacement amount of CH_4 at CO_2 injection pressure of 90 MPa; (d) Sequestration amount of CO_2 at CO_2 injection pressure of 90 MPa.

Figure 5 shows the difference between these two gases. Figure 5a shows the loading amount of CH_4 at different injection pressure. In the case of CO_2 displacing CH_4, the loading amount of methane decreases significantly as the partial pressure of CO_2 increases, compared with the case of N_2 displacing CH_4. Both kinds of gases displacement have led to a sharp decline in loading amount of CH_4. Correspondingly, the sequestration amount of CO_2 has also increased rapidly in the cases of the displacement of methane by CO_2 and N_2. More CO_2 will displace the methane to concentrate in the adsorbed layer, and N_2 will displace less. When CO_2 is added into the pores, the full of this space is filled with CO_2 molecules. Then, CO_2 molecules begin to occupy adsorption sites of CH_4, replacing the adsorbed CH_4 molecules directly. The displaced CH_4 molecules return to free phase. The adsorption capacity of these three gases is sorted as follows: $CO_2 > CH_4 > N_2$. In contrast to, when N_2 is injected, N_2 molecules cannot occupy adsorption sites of CH_4. These N_2 molecules can only adsorb on the vacancies due to the fact that the adsorption capacity of N_2 is weaker than CH_4. N_2 molecules are able to displace CH_4 because they can reduce the partial pressure of CH_4. Once the partial pressure of CH_4 decreases, CH_4 molecules would be desorbed and displaced. Therefore, as CO_2 and N_2 are injected, the loading amount of methane all experiences a downward trend. The screenshots of different displacement processes is shown in Fig. 6.

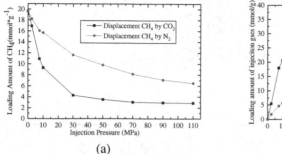 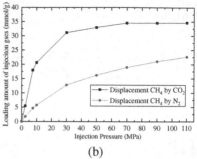

(a)   (b)

Fig. 5. Comparison of methane displacement by CO_2 and N_2. (T_m = 313 K, P_m = 15 MPa, H = 25 Å) (a) Loading amount of CH_4 at different injection pressure; (b) Sequestration amount of injection gases at different injection pressure.

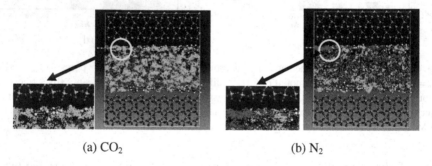

(a) CO_2 (b) N_2

Fig. 6. The adsorption sites snapshots of displacement of CH_4. (P_I = 90 MPa) (a) Displacement of CH_4 by CO_2: red-CH_4; green-CO_2. (b) Displacement of CH_4 by N_2: red-CH_4; green-N_2 (Color figure online)

4   Conclusion

On the basis of adsorption characteristics of CH_4 on the shale model, we built a new shale model by using organic-inorganic composites. Then we used GCMC simulation to study the displacement of shale gas by CO_2 and N_2. The displacement mechanisms of the injection gases are investigated. Next, the occurrence behavior of methane in different pores is investigated by using the MD method. Our conclusions are listed as follows:

1. With the pores width increase, the adsorption occurrence transfers from single adsorption layer to four adsorption layers. In the case of a much wide pore width, the density of the central bulk phase approaches to the same value at 0.2 g·cm^{-3}.

2. To displace the adsorbed CH_4, CO_2 and N_2 are injected and investigated. The results indicate that both of the CO_2 and N_2 molecules can displace the adsorbed shale gas and CO_2 is sequestrated into the shale simultaneously.
3. However, the displacement mechanisms of the injection gases are different. The adsorption capacity of CO_2 is much stronger than that of CH_4. The CO_2 molecules can replace the adsorbed CH_4 from the adsorption sites directly. On the contrary, when the pores are occupied by N_2 molecules, these molecules can decrease the partial pressure of CH_4.

It is expected these results and findings are of great importance for displacement exploitation of shale gas and sequestration of CO_2.

Acknowledgements. This study was supported by the National Natural Science Foundation of China (No. 51676208) and the Fundamental Research Funds for the Central Universities (No. 18CX07012A).

References

1. Arora, V., Cai, Y.: US natural gas exports and their global impacts. Appl. Energy **120**, 95–103 (2014)
2. Howarth, R.W., Santoro, R., Ingraffea, A.: Methane and the greenhouse-gas footprint of natural gas from shale formations. Clim. Change **106**(4), 679 (2011)
3. Li, Y.X., Nie, H.K., Long, P.Y.: Development characteristics of organic-rich shale and strategic selection of shale gas exploration area in China. Nat. Gas. Ind. **29**(12), 115–118 (2009)
4. Bowker, K.A.: Barnett shale gas production, Fort Worth Basin: issues and discussion. AAPG Bull. **91**(4), 523–533 (2007)
5. Caulton, D.R., Shepson, P.B., Santoro, R.L., et al.: Toward a better understanding and quantification of methane emissions from shale gas development. Proc. Natl. Acad. Sci. **111**(17), 6237–6242 (2014)
6. Howarth, R.W., Santoro, R., Ingraffea, A.: Methane and the greenhouse-gas footprint of natural gas from shale formations. Clim. Change **106**(4), 679 (2011)
7. Ji, L., Zhang, T., Milliken, K.L., et al.: Experimental investigation of main controls to methane adsorption in clay-rich rocks. Appl. Geochem. **27**(12), 2533–2545 (2012)
8. Johnson, H.E., Granick, S.: Exchange kinetics between the adsorbed state and free solution: poly (methyl methacrylate) in carbon tetrachloride. Macromolecules **23**(13), 3367–3374 (1990)
9. Curtis, J.B.: Fractured shale-gas systems. AAPG Bull. **86**(11), 1921–1938 (2002)
10. Clark, C., Burnham, A., Harto, C., et al.: Hydraulic fracturing and shale gas production: technology, impacts, and policy. Argonne National Laboratory (2012)
11. Clarkson, C.R., Haghshenas, B., Ghanizadeh, A., et al.: Nanopores to megafractures: current challenges and methods for shale gas reservoir and hydraulic fracture characterization. J. Nat. Gas Sci. Eng. **31**, 612–657 (2016)
12. Chen, H., Carter, K.E.: Water usage for natural gas production through hydraulic fracturing in the United States from 2008 to 2014. J. Environ. Manage. **170**, 152–159 (2016)
13. Jackson, R.E., Gorody, A.W., Mayer, B., et al.: Groundwater protection and unconventional gas extraction: the critical need for field-based hydrogeological research. Groundwater **51**(4), 488–510 (2013)

14. Connor, J.A., Molofsky, L.J., Richardson, S.D., et al.: Environmental issues and answers related to shale gas development. In: SPE Latin American and Caribbean Health, Safety, Environment and Sustainability Conference. Society of Petroleum Engineers (2015)
15. Clarkson, C.R., Solano, N., Bustin, R.M., et al.: Pore structure characterization of North American shale gas reservoirs using USANS/SANS, gas adsorption, and mercury intrusion. Fuel **103**, 606–616 (2013)
16. Wu, H.A., Chen, J., Liu, H.: Molecular dynamics simulations about adsorption and displacement of methane in carbon nanochannels. J. Phys. Chem. C **119**(24), 13652–13657 (2015)
17. Yu, H., Yuan, J., Guo, W., et al.: A preliminary laboratory experiment on coal bed methane displacement with carbon dioxide injection. Int. J. Coal Geol. **73**(2), 156–166 (2008)
18. Yang, N., Liu, S., Yang, X.: Molecular simulation of preferential adsorption of CO2 over CH4 in Na-montmorillonite clay material. Appl. Surf. Sci. **356**, 1262–1271 (2015)
19. Akbarzadeh, H., Abbaspour, M., Salemi, S., et al.: Injection of mixture of shale gases in a nanoscale pore of graphite and their displacement by CO_2/N_2 gases using molecular dynamics study. J. Mol. Liq. **248**, 439–446 (2017)
20. Huo, P., Zhang, D., Yang, Z., et al.: CO_2 geological sequestration: displacement behavior of shale gas methane by carbon dioxide injection. Int. J. Greenhouse Gas Control **66**, 48–59 (2017)
21. Huang, L., Ning, Z., Wang, Q., et al.: Molecular simulation of adsorption behaviors of methane, carbon dioxide and their mixtures on kerogen: effect of kerogen maturity and moisture content. Fuel **211**, 159–172 (2018)
22. Li, X., Xue, Q., Wu, T., et al.: Oil detachment from silica surface modified by carboxy groups in aqueous cetyltriethylammonium bromide solution. Appl. Surf. Sci. **353**, 1103–1111 (2015)
23. Zhang, H., Cao, D.: Molecular simulation of displacement of shale gas by carbon dioxide at different geological depths. Chem. Eng. Sci. **156**, 121–127 (2016)

A Compact and Efficient Lattice Boltzmann Scheme to Simulate Complex Thermal Fluid Flows

Tao Zhang and Shuyu Sun[✉]

Computational Transport Phenomena Laboratory (CTPL), King Abdullah University of Science and Technology (KAUST), Thuwal 23955-6900, Kingdom of Saudi Arabia
shuyu.sun@Kaust.edu.sa

Abstract. A coupled LBGK scheme, constituting of two independent distribution functions describing velocity and temperature respectively, is established in this paper. Chapman-Enskog expansion, a procedure to prove the consistency of this mesoscopic method with macroscopic conservation laws, is also conducted for both lattice scheme of velocity and temperature, as well as a simple introduction on the common used DnQb model. An efficient coding manner for Matlab is proposed in this paper, which improves the coding and calculation efficiency at the same time. The compact and efficient scheme is then applied in the simulation of the famous and well-studied Rayleigh-Benard convection, which is common seen as a representative heat convection problem in modern industries. The results are interesting and reasonable, and meet the experimental data well. The stability of this scheme is also proved through different cases with a large range of Rayleigh number, until 2 million.

Keywords: LBM · Rayleigh-Benard convection · Heat and flow coupling

1 Introduction

LBM, short for Lattice Boltzmann Method, is a numerical approach to simulate fluid flows in mesoscopic level, which is quite popular at present and has been applied to varieties of extensions [1–8]. One main reason of its popularity is the introduction of distribution function, which allows this method to avoid solving directly the common non-linear hydrodynamic equations, e.g. Navier-Stokes equations. The hydraulic flow is modeled by distribution function evolutions, constituted by two stages—collision and streaming process. These two stages represent the general microscopic fluid particles, but not directly model the molecular dynamics. LBM scheme is famous for some feathers, like the natural full parallelism and easy coding, which makes it enhanced and improved from many other classical CFD methods. In the past two decades, plenty of works have been contributed to this area [9, 10], and great success has been obtained in many subsections, including single phase or multiphase flow, isothermal or non-isothermal flow and flow in single tube or porous media.

In original LBM scheme, only mass and momentum conservations are considered, thus it is only applied in isothermal problems. However, as many applications require the investigation of temperature field, it is sometimes important to take the thermal effect into the consideration of fluid flows. For example, in reservoir simulation, phase composition and thermodynamic properties are common needed, which should be calculated under certain temperature evolution. To handle the thermal fluid flows, several models have been developed and the past two decades have seen remarkable progress in this development, with three major classification: the multi-speed (MS) approach [3, 4], the coupled LBGK (CLBGK) approach and multi-distribution function (MDF) [5, 6] approach. The MS approach is limited in a very narrow range of temperature variation, due to its simplicity of distribution function application. It is just a simple and trival extension of the classical isothermal LBGK models, and the thermal effect is only represented by some additional discrete velocities included in the distribution functions. The macroscopic energy conservation is generally reserved by adding higher order velocity terms in the energy distributions. As a result, there is always a severe numerical instability in such models.

To overcome the limitations of both severe instability and narrow temperature range, the MDF model was proposed. With the assumption that pressure effect has been ignored on the heat dissipation and compression process, the fluid flow is the main reason of temperature filed advection and a simpler passive-scaler formula is applied. Compared with MS model, an independent distribution function is introduced in MDF model, which could be computed with LBGK scheme as well. Both the numerical stability and temperature range are improved in MDF model. In the meantime, some disadvantages have been found in this scheme. At present, the Mach number of the flow is restricted to be very slow in MDF model, and the density ratio is assumed to be in a very short range to keep the scheme stable. Besides, these disadvantages are more serious for a turbulent flow, and in such cases some undesired unphysical phenomena may be produced due to the artificial compressibility introduced.

As the recent developments in MDF model have noticed these limitations, some efforts have been made to eliminate such errors. An improved LBGK scheme is proposed to numerically scheme the flow models in steady and unsteady flow conditions. This scheme is further extended in [3] to simulate thermal fluid flows. An additional LBGK equation is introduced and then incorporated with the classical distribution function based on the Boussinesq assumption. This model is called 'coupled LBGK', known as CLBGK. As the multiple distribution functions are applied here, this scheme is similar to MDF, but the lattice in CLBGK used for temperature field can be different compared to that used for velocity field. As a result, this coupling scheme is more flexible and proved to be more numerical efficient.

This paper is organized as follows. First, we introduce the mathematical scheme of the LBGK model as well as the Chapman-Enskog expansion in Sect. 2. The coupling of temperature and velocity is performed in details in Sect. 3. A complex thermal fluid flow phenomena, Rayleigh-Benard heat transfer is simulated in Sect. 4, and results of different Reyleigh number are considered and compared. Finally, in Sect. 5, we make some discussions and conclusions.

2   LBGK Equations

The LBM numerical method is first developed from the Lattice Gas Automata (LGA), which models the microscopic molecular dynamics of gases. During its development, it is founded that it can be derived from original Boltzman equation as well using some discretizations. As a result, LBM is viewed as a special treatment of Boltzmann equation, as well as a mesoscopic model itself. Due to the avoid of solving traditional CFD equations, e.g. NS equations, Lattice Boltzmann Method is often referred as a popular method with easy implementation and coding.

2.1   DnQb LBGK Model

The starting point is the BGK approximation used at Boltzmann equation,

$$\partial_t f + \xi \cdot \nabla_x f = \Omega(f) = -\frac{1}{\tau}(f(x, \xi, t) - f^{eq}(x, \xi, t)), \tag{1}$$

where $f(x, \xi, t)$ is the particle distribution function with x representing space and velocity is symbolled as ξ, which means that the number of particles at time step t, in an area centered at x, with a radius of dx, and velocity varying from ξ to $\xi + d\xi$. τ is called relaxation time and $\frac{1}{\tau}$ represents the collision frequency. The superscript 'eq' means the distribution function has been evolved to the equilibrium state. Macroscopic properties, including density, velocity and internal energy can be obtained through following equations from distribution functions:

$$\rho = \int f d\xi, \rho u = \int \xi f d\xi, \rho e = \int (\xi - u)^2 f d\xi, \tag{2}$$

where total energy E can be derived from $E = \rho e + \frac{1}{2}\rho u^2$. At equilibrium state, the distribution function reaches a Maxwellian equation:

$$f^{eq} = \frac{\rho}{(2\pi RT)^{D/2}} exp\left(-\frac{(\xi - u)^2}{2RT}\right), \tag{3}$$

where $R = k_B/m$ is the gas constant with k_B the Boltzmann constant and m the molecular mass. D is the space dimension. Using Taylor expansion, the continuous distribution function at equilibrium state can be written in terms of the fluid velocity,

$$f^{eq} = \frac{\rho}{(2\pi RT)^{D/2}} exp\left(-\frac{\xi^2}{2RT}\right)\left[1 + \frac{\xi \cdot u}{RT} + \frac{(\xi \cdot u)^2}{2(RT)^2} - \frac{u^2}{2RT}\right] + O(u^3) \tag{4}$$

The velocity space of ξ is then discretized into a finite set of velocities c_i, and to keep the conservation laws, the following quadratures of the expanded equilibrium distribution function should hold exactly,

$$\int \xi^k f^{eq}\left(x, c_i, t\right) d\xi = \sum_i \omega_i c_i^k f^{eq}\left(x, c_i, t\right), \tag{5}$$

where ω_i are the weights and c_i are the points of the numerical quadrature rule. Based on the formulation, the standard LBGK equation can be derived as

$$f_i\left(x + c_i \delta t, t + \delta t\right) - f_i(x, t) = -\frac{1}{\tau}\left(f_i(x, t) - f_i^{eq}(x, t)\right) \tag{6}$$

The LBGK models are the most popular LB method and have been widely applied in variety of complex flows. Among the available models, the group of DnQb (n-dimensional and b-velocities) models proposed by Qian et al. are the most representative ones []. In DnQb models, the discrete equilibrium distribution function can be expressed as

$$f_i^{eq} = \rho \omega_i \left[1 + \frac{c e_i \cdot u}{c_s^2} + \frac{uu:\left(c^2 e_i e_i - c_s^2 I\right)^2}{2c_s^4} \right] \tag{7}$$

The common value used in different DnQb models are listed in Table 1,

Table 1. Parameters of some DnQb models.

Model	Lattice vector e_i	Weight e_i
D1Q3	$0, \pm 1$	$\frac{2}{3}, \frac{1}{6}$
D2Q9	$(0,0), (\pm 1, 0), (0, \pm 1), (\pm 1, \pm 1)$	$\frac{4}{9}, \frac{1}{9}, \frac{1}{36}$
D3Q15	(000)	$\frac{1}{3}, \frac{1}{18}, \frac{1}{36}$
	$(\pm 1, 0, 0), (0, \pm 1, 0), (0, 0, \pm 1)$	
	$(\pm 1, \pm 1, 0), (\pm 1, 0, \pm 1), (0, \pm 1, \pm 1)$	

2.2 Multiscale Chapman-Enskog Expansion

Navier-Stokes equations are common used in computational fluid dynamics, as it can well describe the macroscopic fluid behavior. The Lattice Boltzmann Method focuses on the particle distribution function in a mesoscopic level, higher than the microscopic but less visible than the macroscopic. So it's a necessary step to derive the macroscopic N-S equations from the proposed LB equation formulas, to show the robustness and reliability of our scheme. Such derivation is often processed with the Chapman-Enskog method and it's presented in this paper as well. In the following part, the D2Q9, which is the most popular DnQb model at present, is selected as an example to show the detailed Chapman-Enskog expansion process. By defining the expression of physical properties at different time and space level, the macroscopic variables are automatically separated into the corresponding different scales.

With the basic knowledge of lattice tensor, it is easy to get

$$\sum_i c_i f_i^{eq} = \sum_i c_i f_i = \rho u \tag{8}$$

and for 2nd order,

$$\sum_i c_i c_i f_i^{eq} = c_s^2 \rho I + \rho u u, \tag{9}$$

for 3rd order,

$$\sum_i c_i c_i c_i f_i^{eq} = c_s^2 \rho \Delta \cdot u \tag{10}$$

The distribution function can be expanded in terms of ε as

$$f_i = f_i^{(0)} + \varepsilon f_i^{(1)} + \varepsilon^2 f_i^{(2)} + \cdots \tag{11}$$

Generally, the time **t** and space x are scaled as

$$x = \varepsilon^{-1} x, t_1 = \varepsilon t, t_2 = \varepsilon^2 t, \tag{12}$$

in which, t_1 represents the fast convective scale, while t_2 describes the slow diffusive scale. The above multiscale representation induces a corresponding representation of the differential operators:

$$\frac{\partial}{\partial t} = \varepsilon \frac{\partial}{\partial t_1} + \varepsilon^2 \frac{\partial}{\partial t_2}, \nabla = \varepsilon \nabla_1 \tag{13}$$

Substituting Eqs. (10) and (12) into Eq. (13), we can have

$$\left(\varepsilon \partial t_1 + \varepsilon^2 \partial t_2 + \varepsilon c_i \cdot \nabla_1 \right) \left(f_i^{(0)} + \varepsilon f_i^{(1)} + \varepsilon^2 f_i^{(2)} + \cdots \right) + \frac{\delta t}{2} \left(\varepsilon \partial t_1 + \varepsilon^2 \partial t_2 + \varepsilon c_i \cdot \right.$$
$$\left. \nabla_1 \right)^2 \left(f_i^{(0)} + \varepsilon f_i^{(1)} + \varepsilon^2 f_i^{(2)} + \cdots \right) = -\frac{1}{\tau \delta t} \left(f_i^{(0)} - f_i^{(eq)} + \varepsilon f_i^{(1)} + \varepsilon^2 f_i^{(2)} + \cdots \right) \tag{14}$$

Equating the coefficients of each order of ε, it is easy to obtain that:

$$O(\varepsilon^0): f_i^{(0)} = f_i^{(eq)} \tag{15}$$

$$O(\varepsilon^1): (\partial t_1 + c_i \cdot \nabla_1) f_i^{(0)} = -\frac{1}{\tau \delta t} f_i^{(1)} \tag{16}$$

Furthermore, from Eqs. (14), (15) and (16), the equation at level ε^2 can be written as

$$O(\varepsilon^2): \partial t_2 f_i^{(eq)} + (\partial t_1 + c_i \cdot \nabla_1) \left(1 - \frac{1}{2\iota} \right) f_i^{(1)} = -\frac{1}{\tau \delta t} f_i^{(2)} \tag{17}$$

Take summation over i, it is easy to obtain that

$$O(\varepsilon^1): \partial t_1 \rho + \nabla_1 (\rho u) = 0 \tag{18}$$

$$O(\varepsilon^2){:}\partial_{t_2}\rho = 0 \tag{19}$$

Thus, the macroscopic mass conservation equation can be derived as

$$\partial_t \rho + \nabla \cdot (\rho u) = 0 \tag{20}$$

On the other hand, the equation at 1st and 2nd level can be also written as

$$O(\varepsilon^1){:}\left(\partial_{t_1} + c_i \cdot \nabla_1\right)f_i^{(eq)} = -\frac{1}{\tau \delta t}f_i^{(1)} \tag{21}$$

$$O(\varepsilon^2){:}\partial_{t_2}\rho u = \nabla_1 \cdot \left[\nu\rho\left(\nabla_1 u + \left(\nabla_1 u\right)^T\right)\right], \tag{22}$$

where $\nu = c_s^2\left(\tau - \frac{1}{2}\right)\delta t$. Combining the two scales, it is soon to get the macroscopic momentum conservation equation as

$$\partial_t(\rho u) + \nabla \cdot (\rho uu) = -\nabla p + \nabla \cdot \left[\nu\rho\left(\nabla_1 u + \left(\nabla_1 u\right)^T\right)\right] \tag{23}$$

3   Compact CLBGK Model

It is a common knowledge that the temperature field is passively driven by the fluid flow with advection and a simple advection type equation is enough to model the heat transfer if the viscous heat dissipation and compression work carried out by the pressure are neglected. Thus, it is quite easy to discretize the temperature equation into LBGK model. Meanwhile, as the temperature and velocity field use two independent lattice systems, the implementation and coding can be greatly simplified.

3.1   Lattice BGK Equation for Temperature Field

The general heat transfer equation could be written as

$$\frac{\partial T}{\partial t} + \nabla \cdot (uT) = \mathfrak{D}\nabla^2 T, \tag{24}$$

where $\mathfrak{D}$ is the heat diffusivity. The lattice BGK equation similar as the velocity modeling introduce in previous section can be formed as well for temperature:

$$T_i\left(x + c_i\delta t, t + \delta t\right) - T_i(x, t) = -\frac{1}{\tau'}\left(T_i(x, t) - T_i^{eq}(x, t)\right), \tag{25}$$

where τ is the dimensionless relaxation time, and it could be not the same as the τ in velocity LBGK equation. As the independent distribution function of temperature, the simplest D2Q5 model is applicable here. The temperature distribution function at equilibrium state is given by

$$T_i^{(eq)} = \frac{T}{4}\left[1 + 2\frac{e_i \cdot u}{c}\right], \tag{26}$$

and the macroscopic temperature is the summation of temperature distribution function in all 5 directions:

$$T = \sum_{i=1}^{4} T_i \tag{27}$$

The Chapman-Enskog procedure, a multi-scaling expansion technique to derive macroscopic conservation equations from mesoscopic LBGK equations is shortly introduced for the temperature field here:

Similar with Eq. (11), the temperature is Taylor expanded as

$$T_i = T_i^{(0)} + \varepsilon T_i^{(1)} + \varepsilon^2 T_i^{(2)} + \cdots, \tag{28}$$

where $T_i^{(0)} = T_i^{(eq)}$, and ε is a small parameter proportional to the Knudsen number. Two mesoscopic time scales $t_1 = \varepsilon t$ and $t_1 = \varepsilon^2 t$ and a macroscopic length scale $x_1 = \varepsilon x$ are introduced, thus

$$\frac{\partial}{\partial t} = \varepsilon \frac{\partial}{\partial t_1} + \varepsilon^2 \frac{\partial}{\partial t_2}, \nabla = \varepsilon \nabla_1, \tag{29}$$

which is the same as Eq. (13). Through a Taylor expansion in time and space, the lattice BGK equation can be written in continuous form as

$$D_i T_i + \frac{\Delta t}{2} D_i^2 T_i + O(\Delta t)^2 = -\frac{1}{\tau' \cdot t}(T_i - T_i^{(0)}), \tag{30}$$

where $D_i = \left(\frac{\partial}{\partial t} + ce_i \cdot \nabla\right)$. Substituting Eq. (29) into (30), collecting the terms of order ε and ε^2 respectively, and taking summations of the equations into two scales over i, we can get:

$$\frac{\partial T}{\partial t_1} + \nabla_1 \cdot (uT) = 0 \tag{31}$$

$$\frac{\partial T}{\partial t_2} + \left(1 - \frac{1}{2\tau'}\right)\nabla_1 \cdot \Pi^{(1)} = 0, \tag{32}$$

where $\Pi^{(1)} = \sum_{i=1}^{4} ce_i T_i^{(1)}$. Combining the two levels, it is easy to obtain the following temperature equation as

$$\frac{\partial T}{\partial t} + \nabla \cdot (uT) = \mathfrak{D}\nabla^2 T, \tag{33}$$

to the $O(\Delta t^2)$ order and the diffusivity $\mathfrak{D}$ is determined by

$$\mathfrak{D} = \frac{(2\tau' - 1)}{4} \frac{\Delta x^2}{\Delta t} \tag{34}$$

3.2 The Coupled Lattice BGK Model Using Boussinesq Approximation

The Boussinesq approximation is common seen in the study of natural convection problems, and it's still popular after so many years' development due to the simple treatment of temperature effect on fluid flow. Thus, it is a good method for us to couple temperature and velocity distribution functions. It is assumed common properties cared in fluid flow, including thermal diffusivity, density and viscosity can be treated as a constant, while the temperature effect is only reflected in the body force term. The macroscopic Boussinesq equations can be written as the following form:

$$\nabla \cdot u = 0 \tag{35}$$

$$\frac{\partial u}{\partial t} + \nabla \cdot (uu) = -\nabla p + v\nabla^2 u - g\beta(T - T_0) \tag{36}$$

$$\frac{\partial T}{\partial t} + \nabla \cdot (uT) = \mathfrak{D}\nabla^2 T \tag{37}$$

The coupled LBGK equations in previous section can be used here, and the coupling is established by adding the following term to the right-hand-side of the evolution equation as:

$$f_i = -\frac{1}{2c}\Delta t \alpha_i e_i \cdot g\beta(T - T_0) \tag{38}$$

3.3 The Efficient Coding in Matlab

Previously, LBM is often coded in language Fortran and C, due to the long history and fully developed coding technique in these two. As there are always plenty of iterations in LBM numerical implementations, high-level language, like Matlab, sometimes performs a relatively slow calculation efficiency. To the writer's opinion, the main advantage of language Matlab falls on the sufficient high-level functions included in its library, which benefit a lot in the equation solving and result visualization. Thus, we try to utilize the packaged function in Matlab to speed up the solving of LBM as:

```
for i = 2:9
N(:,i) = reshape(circshift(reshape
(N(:,i),nx,ny),[cx(i),cy(i)]),nx*ny,1); %streaming
end
```

The above codes represent the streaming process. Using the function 'circshift', codes are simplified a lot, compared with a common coding style as a 'traditional Fortran manner':

```
temp=F(:,2);F(:,2)=F(siteNeighbor(:,6),6);F(siteNeighbor(:,6),6)=temp;
temp=F(:,3);F(:,3)=F(siteNeighbor(:,7),7);F(siteNeighbor(:,7),7)=temp;
temp=F(:,4);F(:,4)=F(siteNeighbor(:,8),8);F(siteNeighbor(:,8),8)=temp;
temp=F(:,5);F(:,5)=F(siteNeighbor(:,9),9);F(siteNeighbor(:,9),9)=temp;
```

It is easy to find that the improved coding technique will greatly shorten the codes as well as the CPU time used. In all, the best coding is the codes fit best the features of language.

4   Numerical Cases

Rayleigh–Bénard convection is one of the most commonly studied heat transfer phenomena due to its well-researched analytical and experimental results [11–15]. Applications of R-B type natural convection can be found in many areas, including: the atmosphere and ocean convection on the weather and climate on earth; mantle convection on the plate movement and volcanic formation; nuclear convection to produce the earth's magnetic field; the sun and other stars in the convection heat from the stars inside to the surface; engineering applications convection in heat transfer and heat dissipation; convection in crystal growth and metal preparation; convection in thermonuclear reactor and so on. A general Rayleigh-Benard convection problem can be set as: In a closed convection cell filled with convection medium, the lower guide plate is heated, the upper guide plate is cooled, and the temperature at upper and lower guide plates varies with a constant value. When temperature difference is large enough, the fluid in the cell will exhibit a very complicated random movement pattern, and form turbulent convection. For the fully developed turbulent convection system, there is a very thin temperature boundary layer near the upper and lower guide plates in the convection tank, and hot and cold plumes are generated and separated from the upper and lower temperature boundary layers respectively.

4.1   Results of Different Ra Number

Some important dimensionless number are often used in the establishing and modeling of these convection problems, including Prandtl number (Pr), Rayleigh number (Ra) and Grashof number (Gr). A short introduction is provided as follows to help understand: Grashof number is a dimensionless parameter often applied to approximate the correlation ratio of viscous force and buoyancy effecting the thermal flow. Prandtl number is defined to approximate the correlation effect of thermal diffusivity and momentum diffusivity. Rayleigh number is a dimensionless parameter often used in free convection and natural convection, or sometimes attributed as buoyancy-driven fluid flow. When the Rayleigh number is high enough, heat transfer is always treated as mainly driven by convection, but not conduction. At present, heat convection at high Ra number is of much focus.

For Ra number varying of 5000 and 20000, temperature field and velocity field at steady state are shown as Figs. 1 to 2:

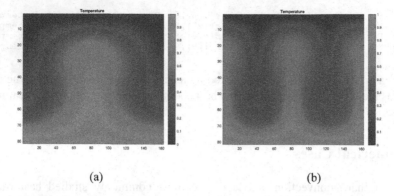

Fig. 1. Temperature field at Ra number equaling (a) 5000 and (b) 20000

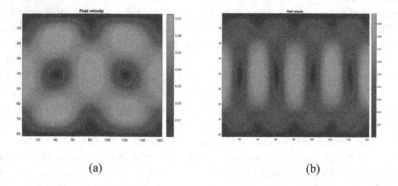

Fig. 2. Velocity field at Ra number equaling (a) 5000 and (b) 20000

From the above two figures, it can be referred that a turbulent flow is driven by temperature difference on two walls and the result is different with Ra numbers.

In the study of circumfluence, the relation of Reynolds number (Re) and Rayleigh Number (Ra) is of special interest. Generally, a positive correlation is assumed, which indicates that a more complex turbulent flow will occur for a larger Ra case. Thus, we expect more intense flow at the steady state driven by the temperature difference in simulation of higher Ra number. Here, a 200000 case is taken as example:

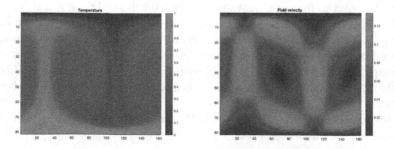

Fig. 3. Temperature and velocity field at Ra number equaling 200000

A different result is shown in Fig. 3 and it is obvious that more complex circumfluence flows occur in the higher Ra situation, with overall higher velocity (seen in color bar). It is a common knowledge that numerical simulation will perform worse for high Re number cases, thus it is always a manner to test the scheme stability. As the positive correlation of Ra and Re number, a Ra equaling 2 million case is performed using our scheme, and we can still get reasonable results (Fig. 4):

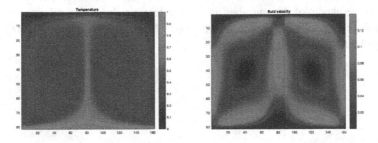

Fig. 4. Temperature and velocity field at Ra number equaling 2000000

4.2 Correlation Between Nu and Ra

In heat transfer problems, the Nusselt number (Nu) is the ratio of convective to conductive heat transfer across (normal to) the boundary. The calculation of Nu number is always calculated by the following equation in the present R-B simulation:

$$\text{Nu} = 1 + \frac{(u_y \cdot \text{T})}{\alpha \cdot \Delta T / H} \tag{39}$$

It is found in previous experimental and numerical investigations that the Nusselt number in Rayleigh–Benard convection can always be represented by a power law: Nu $\propto Ra^r$, in which the power value r varies slightly around 0.282 [11, 12]. In this paper, we also calculate the correlation of Nu and Ra to validate our simulation:

Fig. 5. Correlation of Nu and Ra

As shown in Fig. 5, our simulation results meet well with the empirical data, thus our scheme is validated. Besides, it can be seen that there is slight difference when $Ra \leq 10^4$ and $Ra \gg 10^6$. It can be attributed that such power law is only validated near the turbulence regime, while large Ra will result in large velocity, thus large Mach number will be obtained. However, the stability of LBM scheme is limited in a low Mach condition. Anyway, the robustness of our scheme is proved here as the case with Ra number as high as 2 million can be handled well with acceptable results.

The convergence of Nu number is also a test to show the scheme efficiency. Converging process of Nu number at two cases of Ra numbers equaling 5000, 20000, 200000 and 2000000 are shown here:

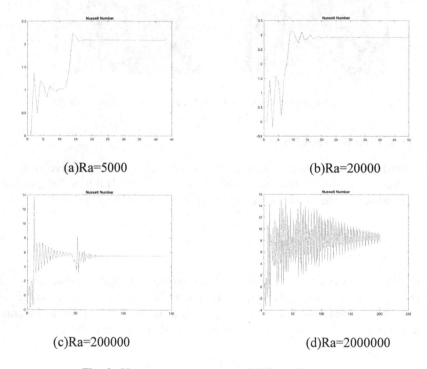

(a)Ra=5000   (b)Ra=20000

(c)Ra=200000   (d)Ra=2000000

Fig. 6. Nu convergence process of different Ra number

It can be seen in Fig. 6 that with the arising of Ra numbers, it will take more time for the Nu number to converge to the steady value. It is reasonable due to the more complex turbulence occurred in a higher Ra number condition. The efficiency of our scheme is validated as in low Ra numbers, it is very fast to see the convergence of Nu number and the iteration steps needed in high Ra number are still acceptable. However, in the case of Ra equaling 2000000, it is very hard to get a steady Nu value, although we could see the obvious convergence trend, which could be attributed that the high Re number resulted from high Ra number is still a high challenging of LBM scheme. For CPU time, only 62.79 s is needed for Ra = 5000 while the Ra = 2000000 case costs more than 200 s to convergence.

5 Conclusion

Complex thermal fluid flows are common seen in modern industry, thus it is very mean-ingful to find an efficient manner to simulate such phenomena. A compact LBGK scheme is generated in this paper, with the coupling of temperature and velocity distribution functions using Boussinesq approximation. As the two distribution functions are inde-pendent to each other, we could treat them in two different lattice systems. In this paper, the D2Q5 model is selected for the temperature field evolution while the D2Q9 model is chosen for velocity distribution function. This treatment will obviously accelerate our simulation. Combined with a more efficient coding style, we can simulate the complex Rayleigh-Benard convection problems under different Rayleigh numbers. The robust-ness of our scheme is validated through the acceptable results obtained at very high Ra number, 2 million. The Nusselt number calculated for different Ra number meet well with the empirical data and the convergence process of Nu is also acceptable and reasonable. The increasing iterations and CPU time needed to get the steady state meet well the arising of Ra numbers.

As this scheme is validated and proved to be compact and efficient, it is a good lattice system based on which we can implement other thermal fluid flows, like the heated oil transfer and Flash calculation with gradient flows.

References

1. Lin, Z., Fang, H., Tao, R.: Improved lattice Boltzmann model for incompressible two-dimensional steady flows. Phys. Rev. E **54**(6), 6323 (1996)
2. Yang, X., Shi, B., Chai, Z.: Generalized modification in the lattice Bhatnagar-Gross-Krook model for incompressible Navier-Stokes equations and convection-diffusion equations. Phys. Rev. E **90**(1), 013309 (2014)
3. Guo, Z., Shi, B., Zheng, C.: A coupled lattice BGK model for the Boussinesq equations. Int. J. Numer. Methods Fluids **39**(4), 325–342 (2002)
4. Qian, Y.H., d'Humières, D., Lallemand, P.: Lattice BGK models for Navier-Stokes equation. EPL (Europhys. Lett.) **17**(6), 479 (1992)
5. Qian, Y.H.: Simulating thermohydrodynamics with lattice BGK models. J. Sci. Comput. **8**(3), 231–242 (1993)
6. Alexander, F.J., Chen, S., Sterling, J.D.: Lattice boltzmann thermohydrodynamics. Phys. Rev. E **47**(4), R2249 (1993)
7. Eggels, J.G.M., Somers, J.A.: Numerical simulation of free convective flow using the lattice-Boltzmann scheme. Int. J. Heat Fluid Flow **16**(5), 357–364 (1995)
8. Zhang, T., Sun, S., Yu, B.: A fast algorithm to simulate droplet motions in oil/water two phase flow. Procedia Comput. Sci. **31**(108), 1953–1962 (2017)
9. El-Amin, M.F., Sun, S., Salama, A.: On the stability of the finite difference based lattice Boltzmann method. Procedia Comput. Sci. **18**, 2101–2108 (2013)
10. Castaing, B., Gunaratne, G., Heslot, F., et al.: Scaling of hard thermal turbulence in Rayleigh-Benard convection. J. Fluid Mech. **204**, 1–30 (1989)
11. Cioni, S., Ciliberto, S., Sommeria, J.: Strongly turbulent Rayleigh-Benard convection in mercury: comparison with results at moderate Prandtl number. J. Fluid Mech. **335**, 111–140 (1997)

12. Calzavarini, E., Lohse, D., Toschi, F., Tripiccione, R.: Rayleigh and Prandtl number scaling in the bulk of Rayleigh-Bénard turbulence. Phys. Fluids **17**(5), 055107 (2005)
13. Silano, G., Sreenivasan, K.R., Verzicco, R.: Numerical simulations of Rayleigh-Bénard convection for Prandtl numbers between 10–1 and 10 4 and Rayleigh numbers between 10 5 and 10 9. J. Fluid Mech. **662**, 409–446 (2010)
14. Puthenveettil, B.A., Arakeri, J.H.: Plume structure in high-Rayleigh-number convection. J. Fluid Mech. **542**, 217–249 (2005)
15. Zhou, Q., Xia, K.Q.: Physical and geometrical properties of thermal plumes in turbulent Rayleigh-Bénard convection. New J. Phys. **12**(7), 075006 (2010)

Study on Topology-Based Identification of Sources of Vulnerability for Natural Gas Pipeline Networks

Peng Wang, Bo Yu[✉], Dongliang Sun, Shangmin Ao, and Huaxing Zhai

Beijing Key Laboratory of Pipeline Critical Technology and Equipment for Deepwater Oil & Gas Development, School of Mechanical Engineering, Beijing Institute of Petrochemical Technology, Beijing 102617, China
yubobox@vip.163.com

Abstract. Natural gas pipeline networks are the primary means of transporting natural gas, and safety is the priority in production operation. Investigating the vulnerability of natural gas pipeline networks can effectively identify weak links in the pipeline networks and is critical to the safe operation of pipeline networks. In this paper, based on network evaluation theory, a pipeline network topology-based natural gas pipeline network method to identify sources of vulnerability was developed. In this process, based on characteristics of actual flow in natural gas pipeline networks, network evaluation indices were improved to increase the accuracy of the identification of sources of vulnerability for natural gas pipeline networks. Based on the improved index, a topology-based identification process for sources of vulnerability for natural gas pipeline networks was created. Finally, the effectiveness of the proposed method was verified via pipeline network hydraulic simulation. The result shows that the proposed method is simple and can accurately identify sources of vulnerability in the nodes or links in natural gas pipeline networks.

Keywords: Natural gas pipeline network · Topology · Pipeline network safety
Vulnerability · Fragile source

1 Introduction

In actual operation, a natural gas pipeline network system is not immune to uncertain internal factors or external hazards such as valve aging or third-party damage [1]. Once a natural gas pipeline network is damaged somewhere and natural gas leaks, the consequences are severe. Therefore, analyzing the weak links or sources of vulnerability in a natural gas pipeline network system and taking relevant control measures is critical to the operational safety of the pipeline network.

The identification of sources of vulnerability belongs to system vulnerability research. Vulnerability is a popular concept in recent years that measures system characteristics such as system disturbance sensitivity, system vulnerability, consequence endurance capability and disaster resiliency. The identification of sources of fragility has been widely adopted in areas such as finance and banking, the electric power grid, network communications, the water supply and drainage systems [2]. In recent years,

© Springer International Publishing AG, part of Springer Nature 2018
Y. Shi et al. (Eds.): ICCS 2018, LNCS 10862, pp. 163–173, 2018.
https://doi.org/10.1007/978-3-319-93713-7_13

some researchers have attempted to apply the identification of sources of vulnerability to safety assurance for natural gas pipeline network systems and have made some achievements. Zhao et al. [3] analyzed damage factors of urban natural gas pipes, proposed a set of indices to describe urban natural gas pipe vulnerability, created a mathematical model to assess the system vulnerability of natural gas pipeline networks and achieved a determination of the vulnerability grade and measured the system vulnerability. Huang et al. [4] analyzed the impact of subjective factors on weight selection, proposed a weight that combined "ANP-based subjective weight" and "entropy-based objective weight" and provided a more objective evaluation of natural gas pipeline network vulnerability. Zhao et al. [5] created the 3D2R oil and gas pipe risk assessment model based on an accident development mechanism, defined the weight for each index based on specifications in the American Petroleum Institute (API) standards and provided a quantitative representation of pipe risk. You et al. [6] analyzed the third-party damage to natural gas pipeline network systems, provided a quantitative calculation of the threat level to the pipeline network system based on a Markov potential effect model and determined the functional deficiency level of pipeline network systems via pipeline network hydraulic calculations. Based on complex network theory, Zhu et al. [7] performed a significant grading and vulnerability analysis for destructive elements in a Mexico oil transport pipeline network, applied this method to a vulnerability analysis for an urban gas pipeline network in Guangdong, China, and proposed an improvement plan to enhance the disaster resistance capability of pipeline networks.

The aforementioned studies show that a pipeline network topology-based pipeline network vulnerability quantitative evaluation method is a method that provides an objective evaluation of node or pipe vulnerability in a pipeline network. Based on this method, weak links in a pipeline network are identified and then protected or enhanced to improve pipeline network safety. However, studies on pipeline network topology-based pipeline network vulnerability analysis are scarce. In addition, the current literature does not provide a detailed process for the identification of sources of vulnerability. Therefore, in this paper, a topology-based natural method for the identification of sources of vulnerability for gas pipeline network is developed.

In this paper, complex network evaluation theory is applied to the identification of sources of fragility for natural gas pipeline networks. Based on a detailed analysis of characteristics of actual flow in a natural gas pipeline network, network performance evaluation indices are improved to increase the accuracy of the identification of sources of fragility of pipeline networks. Then, based on improved evaluation in-dices, the process of identification of sources of fragility is designed, and a topology-based natural method for the identification of sources of fragility for gas pipeline network is developed.

2   Topology-Based Evaluation Index of Natural Gas Pipeline Network Vulnerability

Similar to other networks, natural gas pipeline networks can be abstracted as a set of nodes and links, i.e., a topological graph G (V, E). Elements in set V are nodes in topological graph G; elements in set E are edges or links in topological graph G. Network theory provides various indices to evaluate network topology. In the following section, four commonly used indices are introduced. These indices are the foundation for topology-based identification of natural gas pipeline network vulnerability.

(1) Node degree

Node degree is an essential attribute of nodes in a network. It refers to the total number of links connected to this node, represented as k. Nodes with higher degrees have more connections.

(2) Length of the shortest path

In a topological graph, there are numerous paths with various lengths from node i to node j, and there must be a shortest path. This "shortcut" is called length of the shortest path d_{ij}.

(3) Network efficiency and element vulnerability

Network efficiency means network connectivity and information transmission efficiency, which reflects the efficiency of information transmission in a network at the macroscopic level. Greater value means superior network connectivity.

$$E = \frac{1}{N(N-1)} \sum_{i,j \in V\ (i \neq j)} \frac{1}{d_{ij}} \qquad (1)$$

where, N is the number of nodes in set V, E is the pipeline network efficiency.

In network analysis and measurement, the effect of a network element on network connectivity usually needs to be determined. In general, the element is removed from the network to simulate failure of this element, and then, the change in network efficiency is measured. To facilitate research on element importance to the network, the relative change rate of network efficiency after the removal of element i is defined as element vulnerability $\alpha(i)$. A greater value means this element is more important.

$$\alpha(i) = \left| \frac{E(i) - E}{E} \right| \qquad (2)$$

where, $\alpha(i)$ is the vulnerability of element i in pipeline network, $E(i)$ is the pipeline network efficiency after element i is removed.

(4) Betweenness centrality

Betweenness centrality represents the significance of a node in network as transmission "media". Higher betweenness centrality means this node or link has a higher impact on network. Betweenness centrality is the ratio of the number of shortest paths via a specific node or link versus the total number of shortest paths for all node pairs in the network. There are two types: node betweenness centrality and link betweenness centrality.

The expression for node betweenness centrality is:

$$C_b(k) = \sum_{i,j \in V, i \neq j} \frac{n_{ij}(k)}{n_{ij}} \tag{3}$$

where, n_{ij} is the number of the shortest paths from node i to node j, $n_{ij}(k)$ is the number of the shortest paths from node i to node j via node k, $C_b(k)$ is the node betweenness centrality of node k.

The mathematical expression for link betweenness centrality is:

$$C_b(e) = \sum_{i,j \in V, i \neq j} \frac{n_{ij}(e)}{n_{ij}} \tag{4}$$

where, $n_{ij}(e)$ is the number of the shortest paths from node j to node k via link e, $C_b(e)$ is the link betweenness centrality of link e.

Based on these indices, properties of elements in a natural gas pipeline network and the entire network are evaluated to identify the sources of vulnerability in a natural gas pipeline network and provide guidance for the safe operation of the pipeline network.

3   Improvement of the Vulnerability Evaluation Index for Natural Gas Pipeline Networks

In the network evaluation index calculation process in Sect. 2, by default, there is such an assumption: in topological graphs, there is a bi-directional logic information transmission path between any pair of nodes. This assumption is valid for social networks and transport networks; however, such an assumption does not completely match the actual operation of a natural gas pipeline network. A natural gas pipeline network has the following characteristics: in the pipeline network, flow is not always bi-directional. Pipe in a natural gas pipeline network is bi-directional; however, gas flow is strictly unidirectional. For example, natural gas can only flow from the gas supply source to the pipeline network and then from the pipeline network to the gas demand source. Due to such constraints, the evaluation of natural gas pipeline network vulnerability should consider the operational characteristics of natural gas pipeline networks, such as unidirectional flow and the functional difference between gas sources and demand sources. If the network evaluation indices in Sect. 2 are applied directly to the identification of sources of vulnerability of a natural gas pipeline network, there will be limitations.

Therefore, in this paper, node attributes and flow direction in natural gas pipeline networks are constrained; there is only unidirectional flow from the gas supply source to the gas demand source. When calculating the network efficiency and betweenness centrality, the gas supply source is the starting point of a path and the gas demand source is the end point of a path. A detailed improvement plan for network efficiency and betweenness centrality indices is as follows:

(1) Network efficiency improvement

Improved network efficiency formula is as follows:

$$E = \frac{1}{N_t \times N_s} \sum_{i \in T, j \in S} \frac{1}{d_{ij}}$$

(5)

where, N_t is the number of nodes in set **T**, N_s is the number of nodes in set **S**. **T** is the pipeline network gas supply source node set, **S** is the pipeline network gas demand source node set.

(2) Betweenness centrality improvement

The formulas for improved point betweenness centrality and link betweenness centrality are as follows:

$$C_b(k) = \sum_{i \in T, j \in S} \frac{n_{ij}(k)}{n_{ij}}$$

(6)

$$C_b(e) = \sum_{i \in T, j \in S} \frac{n_{ij}(e)}{n_{ij}}$$

(7)

These formulas improve the key indices of the evaluation of natural gas pipeline network vulnerability in this paper. The improvement process is based on the actual operational characteristics of natural gas pipeline networks. Therefore, improved vulnerability evaluation indices should increase the efficiency of the identification of sources of vulnerability in natural gas pipeline networks.

4 The Process of Identification of Sources of Vulnerability for Natural Gas Pipeline Networks

Based on network theory, network evaluation indices are applied to the identification of sources of vulnerability of natural gas pipeline networks. The procedure is as follows (Fig. 1):

Step 1: Extract the topological graph of a natural gas pipeline network.
Step 2: Classify nodes, i.e., a node is classified into a gas supply source, gas demand source or component connecting point.
Step 3: Determine type of vulnerability. If the source of vulnerability is the node type, then go to step 4. If the source of vulnerability is the pipe type, then go to step 5.
Step 4: Identify source of vulnerability for the node via the following steps:
① Calculate node degrees of all nodes.
② Calculate the network efficiency and network efficiency after a certain node is removed to determine the vulnerability for all nodes.
③ Calculate node betweenness centrality for all nodes.

④ Compare node degree, node vulnerability and betweenness centrality of all nodes. The node with the largest indices is the source of the vulnerability in the pipeline network.

Step 5: Identify source of vulnerability for the pipe via the following steps:

① Calculate the network efficiency and network efficiency after the pipe is removed to determine the link vulnerability for all pipes.

② Calculate the link betweenness centrality for all pipes.

③ Compare the pipe vulnerability and betweenness centrality of all pipes. The pipe with the largest indices is the source of vulnerability in the pipeline network.

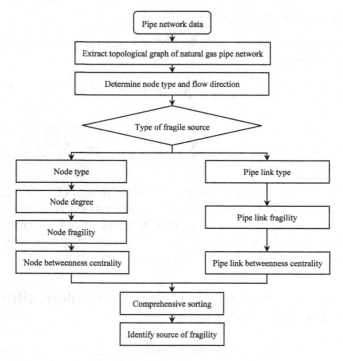

Fig. 1. Natural gas pipeline network topology-based procedure for the identification of sources of vulnerability in a pipeline network

5   Case Analysis

5.1   Identification of Node Fragile Source

In this section, a single gas source simple ring natural gas pipeline network is used as an example to illustrate the process of identifying sources of vulnerability in pipeline network nodes. The hydraulic simulation of pipeline networks is performed to verify the accuracy of the improved network efficiency and betweenness centrality proposed in this paper and verify the effectiveness of the topology-based method for the identification of sources of vulnerability for natural gas pipeline networks designed in this paper.

Case Overview. The simple ring pipeline network consists of 11 nodes and 14 pipes. All pipes are horizontal pipes with an exterior diameter of 200 mm, as shown in Fig. 2. Node 1 is connected to the gas supply source; nodes 2–5 are connected to gas demand sources.

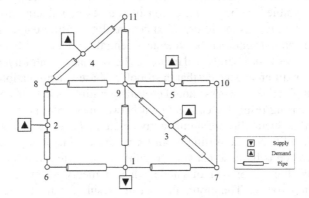

Fig. 2. Topological graph of the ring pipeline network in use case 1

Topology-Based Identification of Sources of Vulnerability for Nodes. In this paper, node degree, node vulnerability and centrality indices of all nodes except those connected to a gas source (i.e., nodes 6–11) are first calculated. Then, comprehensive sorting is performed to identify the sources of vulnerability for nodes in the pipeline network. Node degree, node vulnerability and centrality indices results for nodes 6–11 are listed in Table 1.

Table 1. Calculation results of vulnerability indices of the natural gas pipeline network

Node	Node degree	Node vulnerability	Conventional betweenness centrality	Improved betweenness centrality
6	2	0.170	0.056	0.044
7	3	0.220	0.100	0.056
8	3	0.073	0.211	0.033
9	5	0.280	0.522	0.111
10	2	0.073	0.022	0.022
11	2	0.073	0.067	0.033

Based on each index, the sorting of probability of nodes 6-11 being the source of vulnerability is as follows:

Node degree: node 9 > node 7, 8 > nodes 6, 10, 11
Node vulnerability: node 9 > node 7 > node 6 > node 8, 10, 11

Conventional betweenness centrality: node 9 > node 8 > node 7 > node 11 > node 6 > node 10

Improved betweenness centrality: node 9 > node 7 > node 6 > node 8, 11 > node 10

Table 1 and sorting for indices show that (1) the node degree, network vulnerability and centrality index can balance node vulnerability and importance. Sorting results for different indices have consistent trends. All indices suggest that node 9 is the most important node; nodes 6, 7 and 8 are important nodes; and nodes 10 and 11 are unimportant nodes. This finding indicates that the network evaluation theory-based network measurement is viable for the identification of sources of vulnerability for pipeline networks. (2) Sorting results for different indices are slightly different. In sorting results for node degree and conventional betweenness centrality, node 8 is before node 6; in sorting results for network fragility and improved betweenness centrality, node 8 is after node 6. This slight difference means that the topology-based identification of sources of vulnerability for pipeline networks should consider multiple indices instead of a single index. (3) The sorting result for conventional betweenness centrality and the sorting result for network vulnerability are significantly different; the sorting result for improved betweenness centrality and the sorting result for network vulnerability are similar. This significant difference is because network fragility is calculated from the effect on the pipeline network after the removal of a node, which in theory is a more accurate reflection of node importance. Therefore, the sorting result for improved betweenness centrality is superior to the sorting result for conventional betweenness centrality.

Based on the above sorting results and improved betweenness centrality proposed in this paper, the final sorting for the vulnerability of pipeline network nodes is as follows: node 9 > node 7 > node 6 > node 8 > node 11 > node 10.

Verification of Fragile Source via Natural Gas Pipeline Network Hydraulic Simulation. Hydraulic simulation was performed for the pipeline network when each node loses function. The purpose was to analyze node vulnerability from the perspective of pipeline network operations and to compare that with topology-based sources of vulnerability. In this paper, the hydraulic simulation was based on the international commercial software Stoner Pipeline Simulator (SPS).

The gas supply source was based on pressure control, and all gas demand sources were based on flow control. The comparison of steady state gas supply pressure after failure at each node is listed in Table 2. The decline in pipeline network service capability is reflected by the relative deviation of gas supply pressure change. To evaluate the effect of node failure on the gas supply capability of the entire pipeline network intuitively, the mean deviation of pressure at the gas demand source is listed in Table 3.

Table 2. Mean deviation of pressure at gas demand source

Failure node	Node 6	Node 7	Node 8	Node 9	Node 10	Node 11
Mean deviation of 4 gas demand sources (%)	15.59	15.62	3.90	19.34	0.90	1.56

Table 3. Topological data of the ring pipeline network in case 2

Pipe No.	1	2	3	4	5	6	7	8
Starting point	1	2	3	4	5	6	6	1
End point	2	3	4	5	6	1	4	4

Based on Table 2, the sorting result for node vulnerability in descending order is as follows: node 9 > node 7 > node 6 > node 8 > node 11 > node 10. This sorting result is consistent with the sorting for pipeline network topology-based vulnerability, suggesting that improved vulnerability evaluation indices proposed in this paper generate desirable sorting results for node significance, which also matches the operational simulation result and provides excellent differentiation, helping to identify and providing a reference for sources of fragility for nodes in the pipeline network, as well as a safety evaluation during gas pipeline network design, construction and operation.

5.2 Identification of Pipe Fragile Source

In this section, a single gas source simple ring natural gas pipeline network is used as an example to illustrate the identification of sources of vulnerability in pipes in a pipeline network. A hydraulic simulation of a pipeline network is performed to verify the effectiveness of the topology-based method of identification of sources of vulnerability in natural gas pipeline networks designed in this paper.

Case Overview. The pipeline network consists of 6 nodes and 8 pipes. All pipes are horizontal pipes whose length and exterior diameters are 30 km and 200 mm respectively, as shown in Fig. 3. Node 1 is connected to the gas supply source; the other 5 nodes are connected to gas demand sources. Detailed topological parameters are listed Table 3.

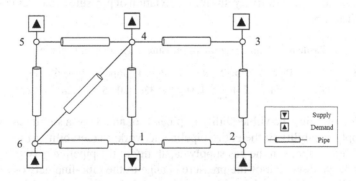

Fig. 3. Topology of the ring pipeline network in case 2

Topology-Based Identification of Sources of Vulnerability of Pipe Type. In the identification of sources of vulnerability for pipes, the pipe vulnerability is listed in Table 4.

Table 4. Network efficiency and vulnerability of each pipe

Pipe No.	1	2	3	4	5	6	7	8
Vulnerability	0.1467	0	0	0	0	0.11	0	0.11

Table 4 shows that after pipe 1 is removed, the network efficiency has the largest decline (0.1467), which is followed by the removal of pipes 6 and 8, with a decline of 0.11; the removal of other pipes has no impact on network efficiency. Next, the fragilities of pipes are differentiated by improved link betweenness centrality. The link betweenness centrality of each pipe in pipeline network is listed in Table 5.

Table 5. Network efficiency and vulnerability of each pipe

Pipe No.	1	2	3	4	5	6	7	8
Improved link betweenness centrality	0.1	0.033	0.033	0.033	0.033	0.1	0	0.133

Table 5 shows that the link betweenness centrality provides desirable differentiation for pipes 6 and 8. Based on the sorting for network effectiveness, the fragilities of pipes are differentiated further, and the sorting for vulnerability is as follows: pipe 1 > pipe 8 > pipe 6 > pipes 2, 3, 4, 5 > pipe 7.

Verification of the Source of Vulnerability via a Hydraulic Simulation of a Natural Gas Pipeline Network. Similar to the identification of sources of vulnerability for nodes, this pipeline network underwent a hydraulic calculation via the international commercial software SPS to verify the effectiveness of the identification of sources of vulnerability for pipes.

The gas source is based on pressure control. All gas demand sources are based on flow control. To evaluate the impact of pipe failure on the gas supply capability of the entire pipeline network intuitively, the mean deviation of pressure at gas demand sources is listed in Table 6.

Table 6. Mean deviation of pressure at gas demand sources

Failed pipe	Pipe 1	Pipe 2	Pipe 3	Pipe 4	Pipe 5	Pipe 6	Pipe 7	Pipe 8
Mean deviation (%)	9.11	2.49	1.31	0.33	0.65	7.24	0.32	7.3

Table 6 shows that the vulnerability of pipes 1, 6, and 8 has a significant impact on the gas supply capability of the entire pipeline network; vulnerability of the other pipe only has a slight impact on the gas supply capability of the pipeline network. Based on the mean relative deviation of the pressure change in the pipe-line network operation, the vulnerability of pipes in descending order is as follows: pipe 1 > pipe 8 > pipe 6 > pipe 2 > pipe 3 > pipe 5 > pipe 4 > pipe 7. It can be seen that the pipeline network topology-based ranking of sources of vulnerability matches the simulation result of the operation, which provides reference for the identification of sources of fragility and safety evaluation during gas pipeline network design, construction and operation.

6   Conclusions

In this paper, network evaluation theory is applied to identify sources of fragility in natural gas pipeline networks. Network performance evaluation indices are improved. The process for the identification of sources of fragility for natural gas pipeline networks is designed. A topology-based method identification of the sources of vulnerability for natural gas pipeline networks is developed. The conclusions are as follows:

(1) Node degree, element fragility and betweenness centrality indices rep-resent the fragility and importance of each node. Therefore, network evaluation theory-based network measurement is viable for the identification of sources of vulnerability for pipeline networks.

(2) Improved network efficiency and centrality index increased the identification efficiency for sources of vulnerability for natural gas pipeline networks. The result of the calculation matches the operational simulation result, which proves the effectiveness of the improvement plan proposed in this paper.

(3) The topology-based method for the identification of sources of vulnerability for natural gas pipeline networks can effectively identify the source of vulnerability for nodes or pipes in a pipeline network.

Acknowledgement. The study is supported by the Project of Construction of Innovative Teams and Teacher Career Development for Universities and Colleges Under Beijing Municipality (No. IDHT20170507), and the Program of Great Wall Scholar (No. CIT&TCD20180313).

References

1. Kim, D.-K., Yoo, H.-R., Cho, S.-H., Koo, S.-J., Kim, D.-K., Yoo, J.-S., Rho, Y.-W.: Inspection of unpiggable natural gas pipelines using in-pipe robot. In: Duy, V.H., Dao, T.T., Kim, S.B., Tien, N.T., Zelinka, I. (eds.) AETA 2016. LNEE, vol. 415, pp. 364–373. Springer, Cham (2017). https://doi.org/10.1007/978-3-319-50904-4_37

2. Efatmaneshnik, M., Bradley, J., Ryan, M.J.: Complexity and fragility in system of systems. Int. J. Syst. Eng. 7(4), 294–312 (2016)

3. Zhao, X., Chai, J.: Study on indicators of vulnerability assessment for city buried gas pipeline system. J. Saf. Sci. Technol. 7(7), 93–94 (2011)

4. Huang, L., Yao, A., Xian, T., et al.: Research on risk assessment method of oil & gas pipeline with consideration of vulnerability. China Saf. Sci. J. 24(7), 93–99 (2014)

5. Zhao, D., Chen, S., Zhao, Z., et al.: Study on oil-gas pipeline risk assessment method based on vulnerability and its application. China Saf. Sci. J. 24(7), 57–62 (2014)

6. You, Q., Zhu, W., Bai, Y., et al.: Vulnerability analysis of external threats for urban gas pipeline network system. Oil Gas Storage Transp. 33(9), 950–955 (2014)

7. Zhu, Y.: Topological Properties and Vulnerability Analysis of Oil and Gas Pipeline Networks. South China University of Technology (2013)

LES Study on High Reynolds Turbulent Drag-Reducing Flow of Viscoelastic Fluids Based on Multiple Relaxation Times Constitutive Model and Mixed Subgrid-Scale Model

Jingfa Li[1,2], Bo Yu[1(✉)], Xinyu Zhang[3], Shuyu Sun[2(✉)], Dongliang Sun[1], and Tao Zhang[2]

[1] School of Mechanical Engineering, Beijing Key Laboratory of Pipeline Critical Technology and Equipment for Deepwater Oil & Gas Development, Beijing Institute of Petrochemical Technology, Beijing 102617, China
yubobox@vip.163.com
[2] Computational Transport Phenomena Laboratory, Division of Physical Science and Engineering, King Abdullah University of Science and Technology, Thuwal 23955-6900, Saudi Arabia
shuyu.sun@kaust.edu.sa
[3] Sinopec International Petroleum Exploration and Production Corporation, Beijing 100029, China

Abstract. Due to complicated rheological behaviors and elastic effect of viscoelastic fluids, only a handful of literatures reporting the large-eddy simulation (LES) studies on turbulent drag-reduction (DR) mechanism of viscoelastic fluids. In addition, these few studies are limited within the low Reynolds number situations. In this paper, LES approach is applied to further study the flow characteristics and DR mechanism of high Reynolds viscoelastic turbulent drag-reducing flow. To improve the accuracy of LES, an N-parallel FENE-P constitutive model based on multiple relaxation times and an improved mixed subgrid-scale (SGS) model are both utilized. DR rate and velocity fluctuations under different calculation parameters are analyzed. Contributions of different shear stresses on frictional resistance coefficient, and turbulent coherent structures which are closely related to turbulent burst events are investigated in details to further reveal the DR mechanism of high Reynolds viscoelastic turbulent drag-reducing flow. Especially, the different phenomena and results between high Reynolds and low Reynolds turbulent flows are addressed. This study is expected to provide a beneficial guidance to the engineering application of turbulent DR technology.

Keywords: Large-eddy simulation · Turbulent drag-reducing flow
Viscoelastic fluid · Constitutive model · Subgrid-scale model

© Springer International Publishing AG, part of Springer Nature 2018
Y. Shi et al. (Eds.): ICCS 2018, LNCS 10862, pp. 174–188, 2018.
https://doi.org/10.1007/978-3-319-93713-7_14

1 Introduction

The phenomenon that adding a little amount of additives into the turbulent flow would induce a significant reduction of turbulent skin frictional drag was called turbulent DR technology [1]. It owns the merits of remarkable DR effect, relative low cost and easy operation, and has been demonstrated to be of great potential in energy saving within the long-distance liquid transportation and circulation systems. To better apply this technique, the turbulent DR mechanism should be investigated intensively. In recent two decades, the rapid development of computer technology brought great changes to the studies on turbulent flow, where numerical simulation has become an indispensable approach. Among the commonly-used numerical approaches for simulation of turbulent flow, the computational workload of LES is smaller than that of direct numerical simulation (DNS) while the obtained information is much more comprehensive and detailed than that of Reynolds-averaged Navier-Stokes (RANS) simulation. It makes a more detailed but time-saving investigation on the turbulent flow with relatively high Reynolds number possible. Therefore, LES has a brilliant prospective in the research of turbulent flow especially with viscoelastic fluids.

Different from the LES of Newtonian fluid, a constitutive model describing the relationship between elastic stress and deformation tensor should be established first for the LES of viscoelastic fluid. An accurate constitutive model that matches the physical meaning is a critical guarantee to the reliability of LES. Up to now most of the constitutive models for viscoelastic fluid, such as generalized Maxwell model [2], Oldroyd-B model [3, 4], Giesekus model [5] and FENE-P model [6], were all built on polymer solutions because the long-chain polymer is the most extensively used DR additive in engineering application. Compared with Maxwell and Oldroyd-B models, the Giesekus model as well as FENE-P model can characterize the shear thinning behavior of polymer solutions much better and thus they are adopted by most researchers. However, it is reported in some studies that the apparent viscosity calculated with Giesekus model and FENE-P model still deviated from experimental data to some extent, indicating an unsatisfactory accuracy [7]. Inspired by the fact that constitutive model with multiple relaxation times can better describe the relaxation-deformation of microstructures formed in viscoelastic fluid, an N-parallel FENE-P model based on multiple relaxation times was proposed in our recent work [8]. The comparison with experimental data shows the N-parallel FENE-P model can further improve the computational accuracy of rheological characteristics, such as apparent viscosity and first normal stress difference.

For the LES of viscoelastic fluid, the effective SGS model is still absent. To the best of our knowledge, only a handful of researches have studied this problem. In 2010, Thais et al. [9] first adopted temporal approximate deconvolution model (TADM) to perform LES on the turbulent channel flow of polymer solutions, in which the filtered governing equation of LES was derived. Wang et al. [10] made a comparison between approximate deconvolution model (ADM) and TADM. It was found that the TADM was more suitable to LES study on viscoelastic turbulent channel flow. In 2015, comprehensively considering the characteristics of both momentum equations and constitutive equations of viscoelastic fluid, Li et al. [11] put forward a mixed SGS model called MCT based on coherent-structure Smagorinsky model (CSM) [12] and TADM. The forced isotropic turbulent flow of polymer solution and turbulent channel flow of surfactant solution were both simulated by using MCT. The calculation results such as turbulent energy spectrum, two-point spanwise correlations, and vortex tube structures agreed well with the DNS database. Although MCT made an important step to the mixed SGS model coupling spatial filtering and temporal filtering altogether, it was still limited by its spatial SGS model—CSM, with which an excessive energy dissipation is observed near the channel wall. In our recent work [13] we improved the CSM and proposed an improved mixed SGS model named MICT based on ICSM and TADM. Simulation results, for instance, DR rate, streamwise mean velocity, two-point spanwise correlations, were compared to demonstrate a better accuracy of MICT than conventional SGS models.

Regarding the turbulent flow itself, due to the intrinsic complexity and limitation of numerical approaches, together with the complicated non-Newtonian behaviors of viscoelastic fluid, the understanding of turbulent DR mechanism is generally limited within flows with relatively low Reynolds number. For the high Reynolds viscoelastic turbulent flows which are commonly seen in industry and engineering, the turbulent DR mechanism is still far from fully understood, which makes the quantitative guidance on engineering application of DR technology inadequate. Therefore, deeper studies need to be performed on the high Reynolds turbulent drag-reducing flows.

With above background and based on our recent studies on the constitutive model and SGS model of viscoelastic fluid, we apply the LES to further explore the turbulent DR mechanism of high Reynolds viscoelastic turbulent flows in this study. The remainder of this paper is organized as follows. In Sect. 2, the N-parallel FENE-P model based on multiple relaxation times and the improved mixed SGS model MICT are briefly introduced. Then the governing equation of LES for viscoelastic turbulent drag-reducing channel flow is presented accordingly. Section 3 of this paper is devoted to describing the LES approach adopted in this paper. In Sect. 4, the flow characteristics and DR mechanism of high Reynolds turbulent drag-reducing channel flow are deeply studied and analyzed. In the final Section the most important findings of this study are summarized.

2 Governing Equation of LES for Viscoelastic Turbulent Drag-Reducing Flows

2.1 The N-Parallel FENE-P Constitutive Model

To improve the computational accuracy of constitutive model needed for LES of viscoelastic turbulent flows, an N-parallel FENE-P model based on multiple relaxation times was proposed in our recent work [8]. As shown in Fig. 1, the core idea of the proposed constitutive model is to connect N FENE-P models, which has single relaxation time, in parallel. With this parallel FENE-P model, stress-strain relationships of different microstructures formed in viscoelastic fluid are more truly modelled compared with the conventional FENE-P model, and it can better characterize the anisotropy of the relaxation-deformation in viscoelastic fluid. Comparative results indicate the N-parallel FENE-P constitutive model can better satisfy the relaxation-deformation process of microstructures, and characterize the rheological behaviors of viscoelastic fluid with much higher accuracy.

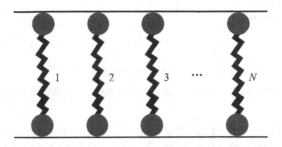

Fig. 1. Schematic of the N-parallel FENE-P model.

2.2   The Improved Mixed SGS Model

In the LES of viscoelastic turbulent drag-reducing flow, different from that of Newtonian fluid, filtering of constitutive equation is needed. However, simulation results show the spatial filtering and spatial SGS model that applicable to Newtonian fluid are not so suitable to constitutive equation. Therefore, an improved mixed SGS model named MICT, proposed in our recent work [13] is adopted for the LES in this study. Figure 2 displays the core idea of MICT, that is, ICSM is employed to perform spatial filtering for the continuity and momentum equations within physical space, and TADM is applied to perform temporal filtering for the constitutive equation within time-domain. It has been proved the MICT has much higher computational accuracy in comparison with the MCT SGS model.

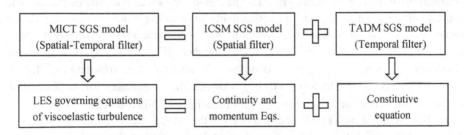

Fig. 2. Core idea of the MICT SGS model.

2.3   LES Governing Equation of Viscoelastic Turbulent Channel Flow

The fully developed turbulent drag-reducing channel flow of viscoelastic fluid [15] is studied in this paper. Sketch map of the computational domain is shown in Fig. 3, where x, y, z represent the streamwise, wall-normal and spanwise directions respectively, the corresponding size of the plane channel is $10h \times 5h \times 2h$, where h denotes the half-height of the plane channel.

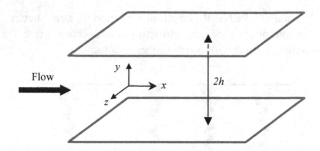

Fig. 3. Sketch map of the computational domain for turbulent channel flow.

Based on the N-parallel FENE-P model, the dimensionless governing equation of turbulent channel flow with viscoelastic fluids in Cartesian coordinate system reads

$$\frac{\partial u_i^+}{\partial x_i^*} = 0 \tag{1}$$

$$\frac{\partial u_i^+}{\partial t^*} + u_j^+ \frac{\partial u_i^+}{\partial x_j^*} = \delta_{1i} - \frac{\partial p^{+'}}{\partial x_i^*} + \frac{1}{Re_\tau} \frac{\partial}{\partial x_j^*}\left(\frac{\partial u_i^+}{\partial x_j^*}\right) + \sum_{m=1}^{N} \frac{\beta_m}{We_{\tau,m}} \frac{\partial\left[f(r_m)c_{ij,m}^+\right]}{\partial x_j^*} \tag{2}$$

$$\frac{\partial c_{ij,m}^+}{\partial t^*} + u_k^+ \frac{\partial c_{ij,m}^+}{\partial x_k^*} - \frac{\partial u_i^+}{\partial x_k^*}c_{kj,m}^+ - \frac{\partial u_j^+}{\partial x_k^*}c_{ik,m}^+ = \frac{Re_\tau}{We_{\tau,m}}\left[\delta_{ij,m} - f(r_m)c_{ij,m}^+\right] \tag{3}$$

where superscript '+' represents the nondimensionalization, $x_i^* = x_i/h$, $t^* = t/(h/u_\tau)$, $u_i^+ = u_i/u_\tau$, $p^+ = p/(\rho u_\tau^2) = \overline{p^+} + p^{+'}$, $\partial\overline{p}/\partial x_i = -\rho u_\tau^2 \delta_{1i}/h$, $u_\tau = \sqrt{\tau_w/\rho}$; u_i^+ represents the velocity component; $p^{+'}$ denotes the pressure fluctuation; β_m is the contribution of the mth branching FENE-P model to zero-shear viscosity of viscoelastic solution, $\beta_m = \eta_{Vm}/\eta_N$, η_{Vm} and η_N respectively refer to the dynamic viscosity of the solute and solvent of viscoelastic solution; Re_τ is the frictional Reynolds number, $Re_\tau = \rho u_\tau h/\eta_N$; $We_{\tau,m}$ is the Weissenberg number, $We_{\tau,m} = \lambda_m \rho u_\tau^2/\eta_N$, λ_m is the relaxation time; $f(r_m)$ denotes nonlinear stretching factor, $f(\overline{r}_m) = (L^2 - 3)/(L^2 - \text{trace}(\mathbf{c}_m^+))$; $c_{ij,m}^+$ denotes the component of conformation tensor; the subscript 'm' represents the mth branching FENE-P model.

In this study, Eqs. (1)–(3) are filtered by the MICT SGS model. The filtered dimensionless LES governing equation of viscoelastic turbulent drag-reducing channel flow reads

$$\frac{\partial \overline{u}_i^+}{\partial x_i^*} = 0 \tag{4}$$

$$\frac{\partial \bar{u}_i^+}{\partial t^*} + \bar{u}_j^+ \frac{\partial \bar{u}_i^+}{\partial x_j^*} = \delta_{1i} - \frac{\partial \bar{p}^{+'}}{\partial x_i^*} + \frac{1}{Re_\tau} \frac{\partial}{\partial x_j^*} \left(\frac{\partial \bar{u}_i^+}{\partial x_j^*} \right) + \sum_{m=1}^{N} \frac{\beta_m}{We_{\tau,m}} \frac{\partial \left[f(\bar{r}_m) \bar{c}_{ij,m}^+ \right]}{\partial x_j^*}$$

$$+ \sum_{m=1}^{N} \frac{\beta_m}{We_{\tau,m}} \frac{\partial R_{ij,m}}{\partial x_j^*} + \frac{\partial \tau_{ij}}{\partial x_j^*} \tag{5}$$

$$\frac{\partial \bar{c}_{ij,m}^+}{\partial t^*} + \bar{u}_k^+ \frac{\partial \bar{c}_{ij,m}^+}{\partial x_k^*} - \frac{\partial \bar{u}_i^+}{\partial x_k^*} \bar{c}_{kj,m}^+ - \frac{\partial \bar{u}_j^+}{\partial x_k^*} \bar{c}_{ik,m}^+ = \frac{Re_\tau}{We_{\tau,m}} \left[\delta_{ij,m} - f(\bar{r}_m) \bar{c}_{ij,m}^+ \right] + P_{ij,m} + Q_{ij,m}$$

$$- \frac{Re_\tau}{We_{\tau,m}} R_{ij,m} + \chi_c \left(\bar{\gamma}_{ij,m} - \bar{c}_{ij,m}^+ \right) \tag{6}$$

where the overbar "—" represents filtering; τ_{ij} is the SGS shear stress in ICSM; $R_{ij,m}$ represents the subfilter term related to nonlinear restoring force; $P_{ij,m}$ and $Q_{ij,m}$ are the subfilter terms induced by stretching of microstructures formed in viscoelastic solution; $\chi_c \left(\bar{\gamma}_{ij,m} - \bar{c}_{ij,m}^+ \right)$ is a second-order regularization term; χ_c denotes dissipative coefficient and is set as 1.0 in this work.

To calculate $P_{ij,m}$, $Q_{ij,m}$, $R_{ij,m}$ and $\chi_c \left(\bar{\gamma}_{ij,m} - \bar{c}_{ij,m}^+ \right)$ in Eqs. (5)–(6), the deconvolution velocity u_i^* for the approximation of unsolved velocity u_i^+, the deconvolution conformation tensor $\phi_{ij,m}$ and $\gamma_{ij,m}$ for the unfiltered conformation tensor $c_{ij,m}^+$ are established respectively as follows

$$u_i^* = \sum_{r=0}^{p} C_r \bar{u}_i^{+(r+1)}, \quad \phi_{ij,m} = \sum_{r=0}^{p} C_r \bar{c}_{ij,m}^{+(r+1)}, \quad \gamma_{ij,m} = \sum_{r=0}^{q} D_r \bar{c}_{ij,m}^{+(r+1)} \tag{7}$$

where p and q refer to the deconvolution degrees, taken $p = 3$ and $q = 2$ in this study; C_r and D_r represent the optimal deconvolution coefficients corresponding to p and q, they can be calculated according to the binomial theorem, $[C_0 \quad C_1 \quad C_2 \quad C_3] = \left[0, \quad \sqrt{6}, \quad \sqrt{4+2\sqrt{6}} - 2\sqrt{6}, \quad 1 - \sqrt{4+2\sqrt{6}} + \sqrt{6} \right]$, $[D_0 \quad D_1 \quad D_2] = [15/8, \quad -15/8, \quad 1/4]$.

Based on Eq. (7), the additional subfilter terms $P_{ij,m}$ and $Q_{ij,m}$ can be calculated as fellows

$$P_{ij,m} = \overline{\frac{\partial u_i^*}{\partial x_k^*} \phi_{kj,m}} - \frac{\partial \bar{u}_i^*}{\partial x_k^*} \bar{\phi}_{kj,m} \tag{8}$$

$$Q_{ij,m} = \overline{\frac{\partial u_j^*}{\partial x_k^*} \phi_{ki,m}} - \frac{\partial \bar{u}_j^*}{\partial x_k^*} \bar{\phi}_{ki,m} \tag{9}$$

Furthermore, $R_{ij,m}$ can be computed by the N-parallel FENE-P model below

$$R_{ij,m} = \overline{\left(f(r_m)\phi_{ij,m} - \delta_{ij}\right)} - \left(f(\bar{r}_m)\bar{\phi}_{ij,m} - \delta_{ij}\right) \tag{10}$$

It is worth noting that the filtering of Eqs. (7)–(10) is carried out on the time-domain. Readers can refer to [11] for the details about the temporal filtering.

3 Numerical Approaches

In this study, the finite difference method (FDM) is applied to discretize the dimensionless governing Eqs. (4)–(6). The diffusion terms are discretized using the second-order central difference scheme and the second-order Adams-Bashforth scheme is adopted for time marching. To obtain high resolution numerical solutions physically and maintain the symmetrically positive definiteness of the conformation tensor, a second-order bounded scheme—MINMOD is applied to discretize the convection term in constitutive Eq. (6).

The projection algorithm [13] is utilized to solve the coupled discrete equations. Within this algorithm, the pressure fluctuation Poisson equation, which is constructed on the continuity equation, is directly solved on staggered mesh. The momentum equation is solved in two steps: (1) Ignore the pressure fluctuation gradient and calculate the intermediate velocities; (2) Substitute the intermediate velocities into the pressure fluctuation Poisson equation to obtain the pressure fluctuation. The finial velocities can be obtained by the summation of intermediate velocities and pressure fluctuation gradient. Considering that it is time-consuming to solve the pressure fluctuation Poisson equation with implicit iterations, the geometric multigrid (GMG) method [14] is employed to speed up the computation. The entire calculation procedures for the projection algorithm are presented as follows

Step1: set the initial fields of velocities, pressure fluctuation and conformation tensor first, and then calculate the coefficients and constant terms in momentum equation and constitutive equation;
Step2: discretize the momentum equation and calculate the intermediate velocities;
Step3: substitute the discrete momentum equation into continuity equation to get the discrete pressure fluctuation Poisson equation;
Step4: adopt the GMG method to solve the discrete pressure fluctuation Poisson equation to obtain the converged pressure fluctuation on current time layer;
Step5: calculate the velocity fields on current time layer with the intermediate velocities and pressure fluctuation;
Step6: discretize the constitutive equation and calculate the conformation tensor field on current time layer;
Step7: advance the time layer and return to Step 2. Repeat the procedures until reach the prescribed calculation time.

4 Study on DR Mechanism of High Reynolds Turbulent Drag-Reducing Flow with Viscoelastic Fluids

4.1 Calculation Conditions

Limited by the computer hardware and numerical approaches, previous studies on turbulent DR mechanism of viscoelastic fluid mainly focused on low Reynolds numbers. In engineering practice, however, the Reynolds number is always up to the order of 10^4. To better provide beneficial guidance to the engineering application of turbulent DR technology, the flow characteristics and DR mechanism in high Reynolds viscoelastic turbulent drag-reducing flow are investigated in present work. To achieve an overall perspective, we design seven test cases in which cases V1–V4 have different Weissenberg numbers while cases V2, V5, V6 have different solution concentrations. The detailed calculation parameters of all test cases are presented in Table 1, where N represents the Newtonian fluid (take water as example) and V denotes the viscoelastic fluid (take surfactant solution as example). In the LES simulation, the double parallel FENE-P model is adopted.

Table 1. Calculation parameters of LES of turbulent drag-reducing channel flow.

Cases	Δt^*	Re_τ	$We_{\tau,1}$	β_1	$We_{\tau,2}$	β_2
N1	0.0005	600	–	–	–	–
V1	0.0001	600	10	0.1	10	0.1
V2	0.0001	600	20	0.1	20	0.1
V3	0.0001	600	30	0.1	30	0.1
V4	0.0001	600	40	0.1	40	0.1
V5	0.0001	600	20	0.15	20	0.15
V6	0.0001	600	20	0.2	20	0.2

For the boundary conditions of the test cases, the periodic boundary is adopted along both the streamwise and spanwise directions, non-slip boundary is imposed on the channel walls. Furthermore, it is essential to give the initial conditions in TADM SGS model. In this paper, the initial conditions are set as the same in [13]. To balance the computational burden and numerical accuracy, a mesh with $32 \times 64 \times 32$ grid points is adopted in LES. The grid independence test can be found in [9, 11, 12] and the mesh has been proved dense enough to sustain the turbulence. It is worth noting that the uniform grid is adopted in streamwise and spanwise directions and non-uniform grid is used in wall-normal direction with denser mesh near the wall due to the 'wall effect'. In the LES the maximum stretching length of the microstructures formed in surfactant solution is set as $L = 100$. The spatial filter width is set as 0.0634 and the temporal filter widths for velocity and conformation tensor are both set as $10 \Delta t^*$.

4.2 Results Analysis and Discussion

(1) **Drag-reduction rate**

Compared with Newtonian fluids, the noticeable characteristic of viscoelastic fluid is DR effect, and it can be described quantitatively with the DR rate. In Table 2, the calculation results including dimensionless mean velocity, Reynolds number, frictional coefficient and DR rate of cases V1–V6 are presented in detail. We can easily observe that when Reynolds number reaches 3×10^4, the turbulent DR effect is very remarkable. For instance, the DR rate can reach up to 51.07% only when $We_{\tau 1}$, β_1, $We_{\tau 2}$, and β_2 are respectively set as 10, 0.1, 10 and 0.1 (case V1).

Table 2. Results of turbulent drag reduction

Cases	U_b^+	Re	$C_f/10^{-3}$	$C_f^D/10^{-3}$	DR/%
V1	27.47	32961	2.651	5.418	51.07
V2	27.74	33287	2.599	5.404	51.91
V3	28.31	33976	2.495	5.377	53.60
V4	28.64	34369	2.438	5.361	54.52
V5	27.02	32427	2.739	5.440	49.65
V6	25.82	30989	2.999	5.502	45.49

Further analyzing the influence of calculation parameters on the DR rate, some extraordinary phenomena in high Reynolds turbulent drag-reducing flow can be found in comparison with low Reynolds turbulent flow. In high Reynolds number situations, DR rate grows with the increase of We_τ under constant β, similarly with low Reynolds number situations. However, the influence from We_τ on DR rate in cases V1–V4 is far less than that in low Reynolds flow. The main reason for this phenomenon lies in that the drag-reducing performance of viscoelastic fluid not only depends on We_τ, but also has close relation with the ratio of elastic effect to viscous effect We_τ/Re_τ. In high Reynolds flow, the variation of We_τ/Re_τ with We_τ is not obvious because the denominator is large, in this way the influence from We_τ on DR rate is weakened. Meanwhile, it is also indicated in cases V5 and V6 that DR rate is not necessarily to increase with the rise of β under constant We_τ. This is because with the increase of solution concentration, the number of microstructures formed in viscoelastic fluid also increases, the elastic resistance induced by the drag additive increases obviously, which can largely offset the DR effect.

(2) **Root-mean-square of velocity fluctuations**

To further clarify the influence from viscoelasticity on characteristics of turbulent drag-reducing flow, it is necessary to analyze the turbulent fluctuation intensity which can be quantified by the root-mean-square (RMS) of dimensionless velocity fluctuation. Figure 4 shows the distributions of velocity fluctuation versus y^+ in cases V1–V4. From the figure it can be obviously seen the RMS of dimensionless streamwise velocity fluctuation is far higher than those of the wall-normal velocity fluctuation and spanwise velocity fluctuation, which indicates that the RMS of dimensionless streamwise velocity fluctuation is dominant. Compared with the Newtonian fluid, the peaks of streamwise, wall-normal and spanwise velocity fluctuations of viscoelastic fluid all move away from the channel wall. However, in high Reynolds flow, the maximum RMS of dimensionless streamwise velocity fluctuation of viscoelastic fluid is almost the same with that of Newtonian fluid, as shown in Fig. 5(a). This phenomenon was also observed in the experiments, it implies the increase of RMS of streamwise velocity fluctuation is not an intrinsic characteristic of turbulent DR. Figure 5(b)–(c) illustrate the dimensionless wall-normal and spanwise velocity fluctuations are suppressed largely by the adding of additive. This trend is more obvious for the dimensionless wall-normal velocity, whose RMS is only 30% of that of Newtonian fluid. The suppression of dimensionless wall-normal velocity fluctuation directly results in the weakening of momentum transfer between turbulence and channel wall, which is one main reason for the DR.

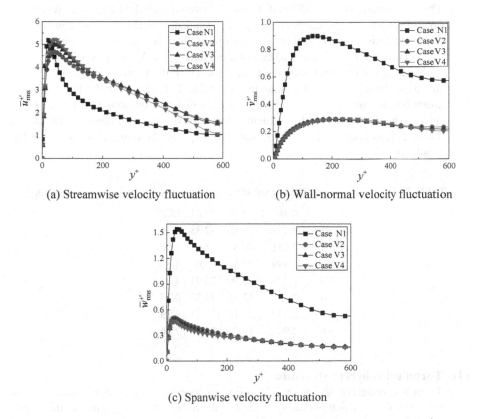

(a) Streamwise velocity fluctuation

(b) Wall-normal velocity fluctuation

(c) Spanwise velocity fluctuation

Fig. 4. Profiles of root-mean-square of dimensionless velocity fluctuation with y^+.

(3) **Contribution of shear stresses on the frictional resistance coefficient**
The balance relationship of shear stresses of viscoelastic fluid is different from that of Newtonian fluid, and different shear stresses have different impacts on turbulent frictional resistance. The contribution of shear stresses on the frictional resistance coefficient of viscoelastic fluid can be derived as follows

$$C_f = \frac{12}{Re_b} + \frac{6}{\left(U_b^+\right)^2} \int_0^1 \left(-\bar{u}^{+\prime}\bar{v}^{+\prime}\right)(1-y^*)dy^* + \frac{6}{\left(U_b^+\right)^2} \int_0^1 \sum_{m=1}^{N} \frac{\beta_m f(\bar{r}_m)\bar{c}_{xy,m}^+}{We_{\tau,m}}(1-y^*)dy^*$$

(11)

where on the right hand side of the equation, the terms from left to right denote influences of viscous stress, Reynolds shear stress and elastic stress on the frictional resistance coefficient, which are named as viscous contribution (VC), turbulent contribution (TC) and elastic contribution (EC), respectively. Especially, elastic contribution is equal to zero in Newtonian fluid.

The proportions of VC, EC and TC to the overall turbulent frictional resistance coefficient for the test cases are presented detailedly in Table 3. We can find the frictional resistance coefficient of Newtonian fluid is much larger than that of viscoelastic fluid under same calculation condition. The VC of viscoelastic fluid is higher than that of Newtonian fluid while the TC of the former is much lower than the later, although TC is dominant in both fluids. Different from the low Reynolds situations, the influence of Weissenberg number is not obvious in high Reynolds flows. This is similar to the influence from Weissenberg number on DR rate in Table 2. However, the EC is more sensitive to β and the larger β is, the larger EC would be.

Table 3. Contributions of different shear stresses on frictional resistance coefficient.

Cases	$C_f/10^{-3}$	VC/%	TC/%	EC/%
N1	3.487	12.15	87.85	–
V1	2.651	20.33	75.61	4.06
V2	2.599	22.16	73.46	4.38
V3	2.495	21.80	73.92	4.28
V4	2.438	22.33	73.32	4.35
V5	2.739	21.14	72.57	6.29
V6	2.999	19.00	73.44	7.56

(4) **Turbulent coherent structure**
Turbulent coherent structure is a series of motions triggered randomly in the turbulent flow, which is closely related to the turbulent burst events. In this work, the following Q method proposed by Hunt et al. [16] is adopted to extract one of coherent structures (vortex tube structure) in the turbulent channel flows

$$Q = \frac{1}{2}\left(\overline{W}_{ij}\overline{W}_{ij} - \bar{S}_{ij}\bar{S}_{ij}\right) > 0 \tag{12}$$

where $\overline{W}_{ij}$ is the filtered vorticity tensor, $\overline{W}_{ij} = \frac{1}{2}\left(\frac{\partial \bar{u}_j}{\partial x_i} - \frac{\partial \bar{u}_i}{\partial x_j}\right)$; $\bar{S}_{ij}$ is the filtered velocity-strain tensor, $\bar{S}_{ij} = \frac{1}{2}\left(\frac{\partial \bar{u}_j}{\partial x_i} + \frac{\partial \bar{u}_i}{\partial x_j}\right)$.

Figure 5 demonstrates the comparison of vortex tube structures at the dimensionless time 80 (the turbulent flow is fully developed) with different Q values in cases N1 and V2. From the figure, it can be seen that the number of vortex tube structures in viscoelastic fluid is less than that in Newtonian fluid. Meanwhile, more vortex tube structures in viscoelastic fluid are in large scale. This indicates that the adding of additive in high Reynolds turbulent channel flow can largely suppress the formation of turbulent coherent structures, which further suppresses the intermittency of turbulent flow. In this way, the frequency and intensity of turbulent burst events are largely weakened, this phenomenon is also similar to the low Reynolds situations.

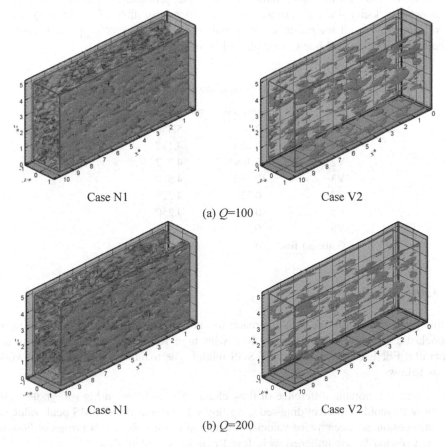

Case N1   Case V2

(a) Q=100

Case N1   Case V2

(b) Q=200

Fig. 5. Comparison of coherent structures (vortex tube structures) in turbulence at the dimensionless time 80

To investigate the intermittency of turbulent flow quantitatively, the skewness factor and flatness factor of streamwise velocity fluctuation are calculated below

$$S(u) = \left\langle \left(\bar{u}^{+\prime}\right)^3 \right\rangle \Big/ \left\langle \left(\bar{u}^{+\prime}\right)^2 \right\rangle^{1.5} \tag{13}$$

$$F(u) = \left\langle \left(\bar{u}^{+\prime}\right)^4 \right\rangle \Big/ \left\langle \left(\bar{u}^{+\prime}\right)^2 \right\rangle^2 \tag{14}$$

Table 4 gives the average skewness factor and flatness factor of the seven test cases. The result of skewness factor indicates the turbulent flow field distributions for Newtonian fluid and viscoelastic fluid are both asymmetrical. However, the absolute value of skewness factor for viscoelastic fluid is larger than that of the Newtonian fluid, which indicates a higher asymmetry and larger deviation from Gaussian field in the viscoelastic fluid. It can also be found the flatness factor of Newtonian fluid is larger than that of viscoelastic fluid, indicating that the probability density function of streamwise velocity in viscoelastic fluid is flatter than that of Newtonian fluid. Therefore, the overall intermittency of turbulent channel flow is suppressed and the turbulent fluctuation and burst events are obviously weakened.

Table 4. Calculation results of average skewness factor and flatness factor.

Cases	Skewness factor	Flatness factor
N1	0.091	5.450
V1	−0.309	4.177
V2	−0.368	4.212
V3	−0.390	4.562
V4	−0.327	4.325
V5	−0.293	4.250
V6	−0.262	3.953
Gaussian field	0	3

5 Conclusions

In this paper, we apply the LES approach to investigate turbulent DR mechanism in viscoelastic turbulent drag-reducing flow with high Reynolds number based on an N-parallel FENE-P model and MICT SGS model. The main conclusions of this work are as follows

(1) There is a notable difference of flow characteristics between high Reynolds and low Reynolds turbulent drag-reducing flows. For instance, the RMS peak value of dimensionless streamwise velocity fluctuation in high Reynolds turbulent flow is not obviously strengthened as in low Reynolds turbulent flow.

(2) The influence of calculation parameters on frictional resistance coefficients in high Reynolds turbulent drag-reducing flow also differs from that in low Reynolds situations. For example, the effect of Weissenberg number exerted to turbulent flow is not obvious while influence of β on elastic contribution is more remarkable.

(3) The number of vortex tube structures in high Reynolds turbulent drag-reducing flow with viscoelastic fluid is much less than that in Newtonian turbulent flow. Compared with the Newtonian fluid, the turbulent flow field of viscoelastic fluid is featured by higher asymmetry and more large-scale motions with low frequency.

Acknowledgements. The study is supported by National Natural Science Foundation of China (No. 51636006), project of Construction of Innovative Teams and Teacher Career Development for Universities and Colleges under Beijing Municipality (No. IDHT20170507) and the Program of Great Wall Scholar (CIT&TCD20180313).

References

1. Savins, J.G.: Drag reductions characteristics of solutions of macromolecules in turbulent pipe flow. Soc. Petrol. Eng. J. **4**(4), 203–214 (1964)
2. Renardy, M., Renardy, Y.: Linear stability of plane couette flow of an upper convected maxwell fluid. J. Nonnewton. Fluid Mech. **22**(1), 23–33 (1986)
3. Oldroyd, J.G.: On the formulation of rheological equations of state. Proc. Roy. Soc. A Math. Phys. Eng. Sci. **200**(1063), 523–541 (1950)
4. Oliveria, P.J.: Alternative derivation of differential constitutive equations of the Oldroyd-B type. J. Nonnewton. Fluid Mech. **160**(1), 40–46 (2009)
5. Giesekus, H.: A simple constitutive equation for polymer fluids based on the concept of deformation-dependent tensorial mobility. J. Nonnewton. Fluid Mech. **11**(1), 69–109 (1982)
6. Bird, R.B., Doston, P.J., Johnson, N.L.: Polymer solution rheology based on a finitely extensible bead-spring chain model. J. Nonnewton. Fluid Mech. **7**(2–3), 213–235 (1980)
7. Wei, J.J., Yao, Z.Q.: Rheological characteristics of drag-reducing surfactant solution. J. Chem. Ind. Eng. **58**(2), 0335–0340 (2007). (in Chinese)
8. Li, J.F., Yu, B., Sun, S.Y., Sun, D.L.: Study on an N-parallel FENE-P constitutive model based on multiple relaxation times for viscoelastic fluid. In: Shi, Y., Fu, H.H., Krzhizhanovskaya, V.V., Lees, M.H., Dongarra, J.J., Sloot, P.M.A. (eds.) ICCS-2018. LNCS, vol. 10862, pp. 610–623. Springer, Heidelberg (2018)
9. Thais, L., Tejada-Martínez, A.E., Gatski, T.B., Mompean, G.: Temporal large eddy simulations of turbulent viscoelastic drag reduction flows. Phys. Fluids **22**(1), 013103 (2010)
10. Wang, L., Cai, W.H., Li, F.C.: Large-eddy simulations of a forced homogeneous isotropic turbulence with polymer additives. Chin. Phys. B **23**(3), 034701 (2014)
11. Li, F.C., Wang, L., Cai, W.H.: New subgrid-scale model based on coherent structures and temporal approximate deconvolution, particularly for LES of turbulent drag-reducing flows of viscoelastic fluids. China Phys. B **24**(7), 074701 (2015)
12. Kobayashi, H.: The subgrid-scale models based on coherent structures for rotating homogeneous turbulence and turbulent channel flow. Phys. Fluids **17**(4), 045104 (2005)
13. Li, J.F., Yu, B., Wang, L., Li, F.C., Hou, L.: A mixed subgrid-scale model based on ICSM and TADM for LES of surfactant-induced drag-reduction in turbulent channel flow. Appl. Therm. Eng. **115**, 1322–1329 (2017)

14. Li, J.F., Yu, B., Zhao, Y., Wang, Y., Li, W.: Flux conservation principle on construction of residual restriction operators for multigrid method. Int. Commun. Heat Mass Transfer **54**, 60–66 (2014)
15. Li, F.C., Yu, B., Wei, J.J., Kawaguchi, Y.: Turbulent Drag Reduction by Surfactant Additives. Higher Education Press, Beijing (2012)
16. Hunt, J.C.R., Wray, A., Moin, P.: Eddies, stream and convergence zones in turbulence flows. Studying Turbul. Numer. Simul. Databases **1**, 193–208 (1988)

Track of Solving Problems with Uncertainties

Statistical and Multivariate Analysis Applied to a Database of Patients with Type-2 Diabetes

Diana Canales$^{(\boxtimes)}$, Neil Hernandez-Gress$^{(\boxtimes)}$, Ram Akella$^{(\boxtimes)}$, and Ivan Perez$^{(\boxtimes)}$

Tecnologico de Monterrey, Mexico City, Mexico
{canalesd,ngress,ivan.perez}@itesm.mx, akella@soe.ucsc.edu
http://tec.mx/en

Abstract. The prevalence of type 2 Diabetes Mellitus (T2DM) has reached critical proportions globally over the past few years. Diabetes can cause devastating personal suffering and its treatment represents a major economic burden for every country around the world. To property guide effective actions and measures, the present study aims to examine the profile of the diabetic population in Mexico. We used the Karhunen-Loève transform which is a form of principal component analysis, to identify the factors that contribute to T2DM. The results revealed a unique profile of patients who cannot control this disease. Results also demonstrated that compared to young patients, old patients tend to have better glycemic control. Statistical analysis reveals patient profiles and their health results and identify the variables that measure overlapping health issues as reported in the database (i.e. collinearity).

Keywords: Type 2 diabetes mellitus · Statistical analysis
Multivariate analysis · Principal component analysis
Dimensionality reduction · Data science · Data mining

1 Introduction

The number of people suffering from diabetes mellitus globally has more than doubled over the past three decades. In 2015, an estimated 415 million people worldwide (representing 8.8% of the population) developed diabetes mellitus; 91% of these people had type 2 diabetes mellitus (T2DM) [1]. Remarkably the International Diabetes Federation estimates that another 193 million individuals with diabetes remain undiagnosed. These individuals are at a great risk of developing health complications. The evidence documenting the large economic burden of treating T2DM has also risen dramatically in the past decade [2]. The causes of the epidemic are embedded in an extremely complex combination of genetic and epigenetic predisposition interacting within an equally complex combination of societal factors that determine behavior and environmental risks [3]. Great efforts have been taken to build a reliable T2DM patients

© Springer International Publishing AG, part of Springer Nature 2018
Y. Shi et al. (Eds.): ICCS 2018, LNCS 10862, pp. 191–201, 2018.
https://doi.org/10.1007/978-3-319-93713-7_15

database and to determine the methodologies and statistical analysis that will allow researchers to identify the variables that best predict outcomes, and inform public health policies to reduce the epidemic and its associated social and economic costs [4]. The rest of the present work is organized as follows. In Sect. 2 we present the methodology used to develop statistical and multivariate analysis to be performed on the database of patients diagnosed with T2DM provided by the Mexican National Nutrition Institute. Results and conclusions are presented in Sects. 3 and 4, respectively.

2   Methods

2.1   Patient Database

The present study reports on an analysis of patient data provided by a third level hospital (i.e. highly specialized) from the National Nutrition Institute in Mexico. The database comprises $p = 40$ health features in $n = 204$ patients diagnosed with T2DM. The age of the patients ranges from 29 to 90 years ($\mu = 61$, $\sigma = 11.7$), with 80% of these patients between the age of 50 and 70 years, and 60% the patients are females. The health features include in this database comprise four socio-demographic features[1], three non-modifiable risk factors[2] and 33 modifiable risk factors[3] that are commonly studied in the context of T2DM [4].

2.2   Multivariate Analysis

For multivariate analysis, we applied the Karhunen-Loève transform which is a form of principal component analysis (PCA) [5]. PCA allows for the identification of variable subsets that are highly correlated and could be measuring the same health indicator, implying dimensionality reduction. The method works through an orthonormal linear transformation constructed with the idea of representing the data as best as possible representation in terms of the least squares technique [6], which converts the set of health features, possibly correlated, into a set of variables without linear correlation called principal components. The components are numbered in such a manner that the first explains the greatest amount of information through their variability, while the last explains the least. The solution of the computation of the principal components is reduced to an eigenvalue-eigenvector problem reflected in a single positive-semidefinite symmetric matrix called the correlation or covariance matrix.

The eigenvectors of the correlation matrix show the direction in a feature space of $p = 40$ dimensions in which the variance is maximized. Each principal component contains the cosine of the projection of the patients to the eigenvector correspond. This is relevant because if a variable can be associated with a

---

[1] Socio-economic strata, residence area, educational levels and occupation.
[2] Age, gender and size.
[3] Weight, HbA_{1c} (measure glycated hemoglobin), triglycerides, etc.

particular principal component, it must point approximately in the same direction of the eigenvector, and their cosine should approach the value 1. If the value of the cosine approaches 0, then the variable points in an orthogonal direction to the principal component and they are not likely associated. The product of each eigenvector by its corresponding eigenvalue will give each vector a magnitude relative to its importance. These scaled vectors are called *Factor Loadings*. The projection of each sample of $n = 204$ patients to each eigenvector is called the *Factor Score*. This will help cluster samples to determine patient profiles.

The principal component analysis method requires a standardized database X for its development, i.e. each of its features have zero mean and variance equal to one.

$$X = \begin{pmatrix} x_{11} & x_{12} & \cdots & x_{1p} \\ x_{21} & x_{22} & \cdots & x_{2p} \\ \vdots & \vdots & & \vdots \\ x_{n1} & x_{n2} & \cdots & x_{np} \end{pmatrix} = \begin{pmatrix} - & x_1 & - \\ - & x_2 & - \\ & \vdots & \\ - & x_n & - \end{pmatrix} = \begin{pmatrix} | & | & & | \\ X_1 & X_2 & \cdots & X_p \\ | & | & & | \end{pmatrix},$$

where $x_i = (x_{i1}, x_{i2}, ..., x_{ip})$ represents the ith patient, and $X_j = (x_{1j}, x_{2j}, ..., x_{pj})^T$ represents the jth health feature, $i = 1, 2, ..., n$ and $j = 1, 2, ..., p$, and $n \geq p$. Geometrically, the n patients represent points in the p-dimensional feature space.

The linear transformation that will take the database to a new uncorrelated coordinate system of features which keeps as much important information as possible and identify if more than one health feature might be measuring the same principle governing the behavior of the patients, will be constructed vector by vector.

Let $v_1 = (v_{11}, v_{21}, ..., v_{p1})^T \neq 0$ be this first vector such that, as the technique least squares [6], the subspace generated by it has the minimum possible distance to all instances. This problem can be represented mathematically as the following optimization problem:

$$\min \sum_{i=1}^{n} ||x_i - y_{i1}||^2,$$

where y_{i1} denote the projection of the ith instance x_i onto the subspace spanned by v_1, and $k_{i1} = \frac{\langle x_i, v_1 \rangle}{||v_1||^2}$, with the usual Euclidean inner product and norm.

Then, by the Pythagoras Theorem $||x_i - y_{i1}||^2 = ||x_i||^2 - ||y_{i1}||^2$, and noting that $||x_i||$ is a constant, the problem turn into $\min \sum_{i=1}^{n} ||x_i - y_{i1}||^2 = \max \sum_{i=1}^{n} ||y_{i1}||^2$. Thus, if $Y_1 = (k_{11}, k_{21}, ..., k_{n1})^T$ then $||Y_1||^2 = \sum_{i=1}^{n} k_{i1}^2 = \sum_{i=1}^{n} ||y_{i1}||^2$ and $\max \sum_{i=1}^{n} ||y_{i1}||^2 = \max \sum_{i=1}^{n} ||Y_1||^2$.

With some simple calculations involving the biased variance estimator, the correlation definition, the Euclidean norm, and the properties of X standardized, we can be concluded that $\frac{1}{n}||Y_1||^2 = Var(Y_1) = v_1^T Corr(X) v_1$, where $Corr(X)$ is the correlation matrix of X. Therefore $\max \sum_{i=1}^{n} ||Y_1||^2 = \max v_1^T Corr(X) v_1$.

Note that, since $Corr(X)$ is a constant, $v_1^T Corr(X)v_1$ increases arbitrarily if $||v_1||$ increases. Thus, the problem turns into the next optimization problem

$$\max_{v_1} \quad v_1^T Corr(X)v_1$$
$$\text{subjet to} \quad ||v_1|| = 1.$$

The Lagrange multiplier technique let conclude that v_1 is the eigenvector of $Corr(X)$ corresponding to the larger eigenvalue λ_1. Then $\max v_1^T Corr(X)v_1 = \max \lambda_1$ solve the problem $\min \sum_{i=1}^{n} ||x_i - y_{i1}||^2 = \max \lambda_1$.

This means that the first vector of the subspace that maintains the minimum distance to all the instances is given by the eigenvector v_1 corresponding to the eigenvalue λ_1 of the correlation matrix of the standardized database, $Corr(X)$. Then, as the correlation matrix is symmetric and positive-defined, by the Principal Axes Theorem, $Corr(X)$ has an orthogonal set of p eigenvectors $\{v_j\}_{j=1}^{p}$ corresponding to p positive eigenvalues $\{\lambda_j\}_{j=1}^{p}$. Which implies that by ordering the eigenvalues $\lambda_1 \geq \lambda_2 \geq \cdots \geq \lambda_p \geq 0$ and following an analysis similar to the previous one, we have that the next searched vector is the eigenvector v_2 corresponding to λ_2, the largest eigenvalue after λ_1, and so on for the following vectors. The Main Axes Theorem and the condition of the Lagrange Multipliers that each v_j must be normal imply that the set of eigenvectors is orthonormal, and $\{Y_j\}_{j=1}^{p}$ are called the set of principal axes. So, $Y_1 = Xv_1$ the first principal component, $Y_2 = Xv_2$ the second principal component, and so on.

In this way, the new coordinate system that is given by the change to the base $\{v_j\}_{j=1}^{p}$, provides the orthonormal linear transformation that takes the standardized database to a new space of uncorrelated features that maintains the greatest amount of information from the original database. This new database is represented by the matrix of principal components $Y = (Y_1, Y_2, ..., Y_p) = X(v_1, v_2, ..., v_p)$. In general terms, what this means is that the projection of the database in the new coordinate system results in a representation of the original database with the property that its characteristics are uncorrelated and where the contribution of the information of the original database that each of them keeps, is reflected in the variances of the main components. This property allows extracting the characteristics that do not provide much information, fulfilling the task of reducing the dimensionality of the base. In addition, this technique allows the original database to identify and relate the characteristics that could be measuring the same principle that governs the behavior of the base contributing a plus to this analysis technique.

3   Results

Our statistical analysis revealed the following interesting trend in the database of T2DM: old patients tend to have good glycemic control. Our analysis also shows that patients with poor glycemic control are commonly young, are overweight or obese (70%), and belong to a low socio-economic strata (85%). Further, patients with poor glycemic control frequently have an educational level lower than the high school level (80%), are unemployed (66%), smoke (80%), and have higher levels of triglycerides and cholesterol. These patients also demonstrate great disease chronicity with a range of complications, such as liver disease (68%), diabetic foot (56%), hypoglycemia (71%), and diabetic Ketoacidosis (82%). They have to undergo insulin (62%) and metformin (52%) treatments. With regard to disease progression, the two glycemic measures (HbA_{1c} and $2ndHbA_{1c}$) were associated with a 47% reduction in glycemic control, while 53% of patients retained the same level of glycemic control or improved, and 69% retained the same level control or worse. Thus, our results demonstrate that patients in the database who were remained in control in most cases. However, if patients had poor control they tended to retain poor control or even get worse.

Correlation analysis demonstrated that the first and second measures of HbA_{1c}, size and gender, and blood urea nitrogen (BUN) and creatinina, were significantly associated with diabetic retinopathy (DR) and nephropathy. Regarding the association with height and gender, it should be noted that on average, men are taller than women. Renal failure is usually measured through BUN and Creatinina. Additionally, DR and nephropathy are both known chronic complications of diabetes mellitus (see Fig. 1).

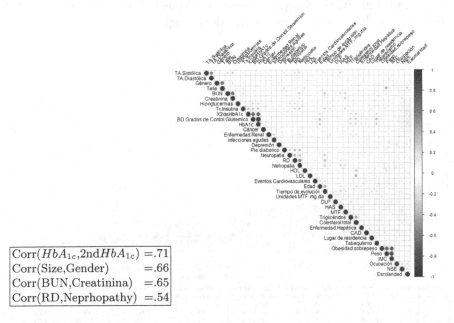

Corr(HbA_{1c},$2ndHbA_{1c}$) = .71
Corr(Size,Gender)   = .66
Corr(BUN,Creatinina)   = .65
Corr(RD,Neprhopathy)   = .54

Fig. 1. The chart shows the upper triangular correlation matrix of the database. Positive correlations are displayed in blue and negative correlations are displayed in red color. Color intensity and the size of the circle are proportional to the correlation coefficients (see legend provided on right). The most highly correlated values are provided ant the top (bottom). (Color figure online)

Figure 2 shows variance, percentage of variation, and the cumulative percentage of variation for each of the ten principal components obtained via the Karhunen-Loève transform. The percentage of variation analysis indicates the amount of information explained by all of the health features in the database. Here, 32.2% of the health features in the database can be explained through the first four principal components. A list of the health features most highly correlated with each of the principal components is provided in Table 1 such that the values represent the correlation between each health feature and the corresponding principal component. For example 0.63 corresponds to the correlation between the first principal component and the health feature Evolution Time. Broadly, this list means that the Evolution Time, Nephropathy, BUN, and DR are interrelated and can together be represented by the first principal component. This principal component explains 10.3% of variance in health features and may reflect the chronicity of diabetes. This principal component suggests that a long evolution time is associated with a great risk of kidney damage and micro-vascular complications such as elevation of BUN and eye damage (DR). The second principal component, which explains 9.0% of the variance in health features, is associated with the degree of glycemic control. The third principal component, which explains 7.1% of the variance, is predominantly associated with weight. Finally, the fourth principal component which explains 5.8% of the variance in health features, measures patient height.

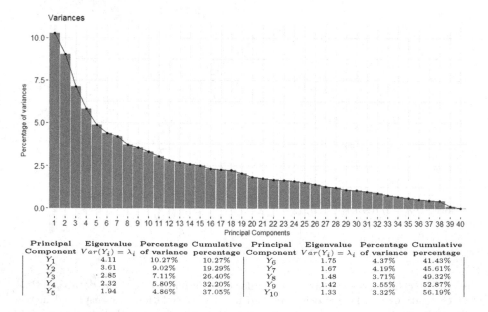

Principal Component	Eigenvalue $Var(Y_i) = \lambda_i$	Percentage of variance	Cumulative percentage	Principal Component	Eigenvalue $Var(Y_i) = \lambda_i$	Percentage of variance	Cumulative percentage
Y_1	4.11	10.27%	10.27%	Y_6	1.75	4.37%	41.43%
Y_2	3.61	9.02%	19.29%	Y_7	1.67	4.19%	45.61%
Y_3	2.85	7.11%	26.40%	Y_8	1.48	3.71%	49.32%
Y_4	2.32	5.80%	32.20%	Y_9	1.42	3.55%	52.87%
Y_5	1.94	4.86%	37.05%	Y_{10}	1.33	3.32%	56.19%

Fig. 2. Top: Percent of variance explained by each of the principal components Y_i, $i = 1, 2, ..., 40$. Bottom: For each component, the percentage variance and cumulative percentage variance is provided.

Figure 3 shows the graphic of the first two lists, the correlation between the principal components Y_1 and Y_2 with each health feature.

Figure 4 depicts plots for Y_1, Y_2, Y_3 and Y_4, arranged in triads. The first graph depicts the plot of the first three principal components, wherein Y_1 is related to chronicity of diabetes through the strong associations with Nephropathy, Evolution Time, BUN and DR, Y_2 is related to glycemic degree control, and Y_3 is related to weight. In each graph, blue points represent patients with high glycemic control (GC), green points represent patients with levels of regular GC (RGC), and yellow points represent patients with bad GC (BGC), and in red points patients in extremely poor GC (EGC). These patient groupings are not retained in the third scatter plot as this plot does not include the second component which determines the degree of GC.

Table 1. Correlation between the principal components and health features.

Y_1 (10.27%)	Y_2 (9.02%)	Y_3 (7.11%)	Y_4 (5.80%)
(.63)Evolution Time	(.72)Glycemic Control Degree	(.87)Weight	(.64)Size
(.62)Nephropathy	(.70)HbA_{1c}	(.77)BMI (Body Mass Index)	(.61)Gender
(.57)BUN (Blood Urea Nitrogen)	(.67)2ndHbA_{1c}	(.66)Overweight / Obesity	
(.53)DR (Diabetic Retinopathy)	(.57)TX Insulin		

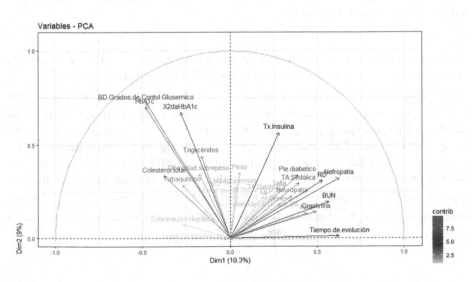

Fig. 3. Correlation between each health feature and components Y_1 and Y_2, i.e. $Corr(Y_i, X_j)$, where $i = 1, 2$ and X_j are the health features, $j = 1, 2, ..., 40$.

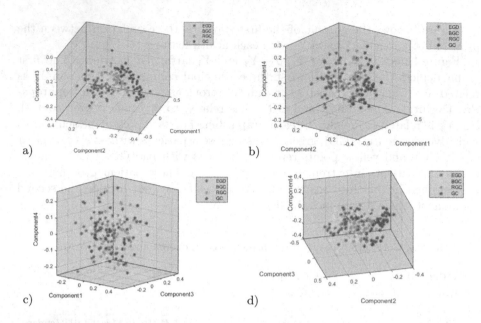

Fig. 4. Comparison of principal components. (a) Displays the first three principal components. (b) Displays the first (Nephropathy, Evolution Time, BUN and DR), second (Control of GC, HbA_{1c}, $2ndHbA_{1c}$ and insulin treatment) and fourth (Height and Gender) principal components. (c) Displays the first (Nephropathy, Evolution Time, BUN and DR), third (Weight, BMI and Overweight/Obesity) and fourth (Size and Gender) principal components. (d) Displays the second (Degree GC, HbA_{1c}, $2ndHbA_{1c}$ and insulin treatment), third (Weight, BMI, and Overweight/Obesity) and fourth (Height and Gender) principal components.

Figure 5, shows the contributions of the health features to the first, second, third and fourth principal components, respectively. Such percentage of contribution is given as follows $C_i = \frac{Corr(Y_i, X_j)^2}{\sum_{j=1}^{40} Corr(Y_i, X_j)^2} \%$, where X_j represents the jth health feature and Y_i represents the ith principal component. In each figure, the red dashed line on the graph above indicates the expected average contribution. If the contribution of the variables were uniform, the expected value would be $\frac{1}{\#variables} = \frac{1}{40} = 2.5\%$. Regarding joint contributions, Fig. 6 shows the contributions of health features to the four principal components. This joint contribution is given by $Cc_4 = \frac{\sum_{i=1}^{4} C_i Var(Y_i)}{\sum_{l=1}^{40} Var(Y_l)}$. The red dashed line in each of these figures indicates the linear combination between the expected average contribution and the percentage of the variance of the principal components, i.e. $\frac{\sum_{i=1}^{4} \frac{1}{40} Var(Y_i)}{\sum_{l=1}^{40} Var(Y_l)} \%$.

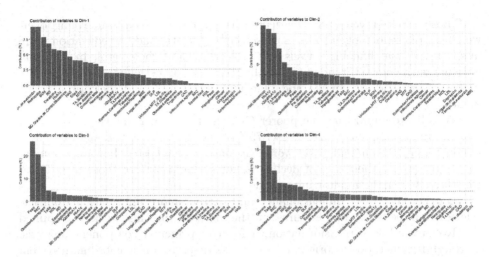

Fig. 5. Percentage of contributions of different health features to principal components 1–4 (i.e. C_1, C_2, C_3 and C_4). (Of note, components 1–4 explained 10.3%, 9.02%, 7.11% and 5.8% of the variance in data, respectively). (Color figure online)

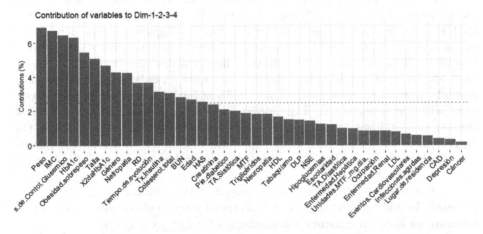

Fig. 6. Graph of Cc_4, the joint contributions of the various health features to the first four principal components. These components explain 32.2% of the variance in the data.

4   Conclusions

The present study examined multivariate patterns of health in a dataset of Mexican T2DM patients. Through statistic analysis, we found that old patients tend to have good GC. Our analysis revealed patient profiles that corresponded to poor GC.

These profiles revealed that patients with poor GC tended to be young, overweight or obese, belonged to low socio-economic strata, had low education, were unemployed, and had high levels of triglycerides and cholesterol. In addition, patients with poor GC tended to have liver disease, diabetic foot, hypoglycemia, diabetic Ketoacidosis, smoke and take undergo insulin and metformin treatments.

Overall, we found that the poorer GC, the harder it is for them to stay in and the more they tend to get worse: 79% of those who have bad and extremely uncontrol GC remain bad or get worse. In contrast, the better they are, the more they stay in and their rate of decline is not so high: 66% of those in GC and Regular GC remain good or improve it.

In order to reduce dimensionality and extract more information from the relationship between the features of the dataset, in this work we applied the Karhunen-Loéve transformation, a form of principal component analysis. Through this method the original dataset was taken to a new coordinate system of 20 dimensions under the least squares principle, with the property that its features (principal components) are not correlated and keep 80.43 % of the information of the original dataset, facilitating the handle and study of the dataset information. In addition, this technique allowed the original dataset to identify and relate the features that could be measuring the same principle that governs the behavior of the dataset through their principal components. Thus, we found that the first principal component, which has the highest amount of variance in the data, explained 10.3% of the health features and was related to diabetes chronicity. This component suggests that along disease evolution time is associated with a great risk of kidney damage and microvascular complications. The second principal component explained 9.0% of health features and was associated with the level of GC. The third principal component explained 7.1% of the variance and was predominantly associated with patient weight. Finally, the fourth principal component, which explained 5.8% of the variance, was associated with patients height. The remaining principal components did not reveal relevant information.

Future research should examine dataset that include a larger number of patients. In addition, we expect the advanced statistical analysis and machine learning tools and techniques will promote a further great discovery.

References

1. Seuring, T., Archangelidi, O., Suhrcke, M.: International Diabetes Federation, 7th edn. Diabetes Atlas. International Diabetes Federation (2015)
2. Seuring, T., Archangelidi, O., Suhrcke, M.: The economic costs of type 2 diabetes: a global systematic review. Pharmaco Econ. **33**(8), 811–831 (2015)
3. Chen, L., Magliano, D.J., Zimmet, P.Z.: The worldwide epidemiology of type 2 diabetes mellitus-present and future perspectives. Nat. Rev. Endocrinol **8**, 228–236 (2012)

4. Hernandez-Gress, N., Canales, D.: Socio-demographic factors and data science methodologies in type 2 diabetes mellitus analysis. In: 2016 IEEE International Conference on Computational Science and Computational Intelligence, pp. 1380–1381. IEEE (2016)
5. Jolliffe, I.T.: Principal Component Analysis. Springer, New York (2002). https://doi.org/10.1007/b98835
6. Wolberg, J.: Data Analysis Using the Method of Least Squares: Extracting the Most Information From Experiments. Springer Science & Business Media, Heidelberg (2006). https://doi.org/10.1007/3-540-31720-1

Novel Monte Carlo Algorithm for Solving Singular Linear Systems

Behrouz Fathi Vajargah[1]([✉]), Vassil Alexandrov[2], Samaneh Javadi[3], and Ali Hadian[4]

[1] Department of Statistics, University of Guilan, P. O. Box 1914, Rasht, Iran
fathi@guilan.ac.ir
[2] ICREA-Barcelona Supercomputing Centre, Barcelona, Spain
vassil.alexandrov@bsc.es
[3] Faculty of Technology and Engineering, East of Guilan, University of Guilan, 44891-63157 Roudsar, Iran
s.javadi62@gmail.com
[4] Department of Mathematics, University of Guilan, P. O. Box 1914, Rasht, Iran
ahg.info2003@gmail.com

Abstract. A new Monte Carlo algorithm for solving singular linear systems of equations is introduced. In fact, we consider the convergence of resolvent operator R_λ and we construct an algorithm based on the mapping of the spectral parameter λ. The approach is applied to systems with singular matrices. For such matrices we show that fairly high accuracy can be obtained.

Keywords: Monte Carlo · Markov chain · Resolvent operator

1 Introduction

Consider the linear system $Tx = b$ where $T \in \mathbb{R}^{n \times n}$ is a nonsingular matrix and b, T are given. If we consider $L = I - T$, then

$$x = Lx + b. \tag{1}$$

The iterative form of (1) is $x^{(k+1)} = Lx^{(k)} + b, k = 0, 1, 2....$ Let us have now $x^0 = 0, L^0 = I$, we have

$$x^{(k+1)} = \Sigma_{m=0}^{k} L^m b. \tag{2}$$

If $\|L\| < 1$, then $x^{(k)}$ tends to the unique solution x [7]. In fact, the solution of (1) can be obtained by using the iterations

$$\lim_{k \to \infty} x^{(k)} = \lim_{k \to \infty} \Sigma_{m=0}^{k} L^m b = (I - L)^{-1} b = T^{-1} b = x. \tag{3}$$

We consider the stochastic approach. Suppose that we have a Markov chain given by:

$$\alpha_0 \to \alpha_1 \to ... \to \alpha_k$$

© Springer International Publishing AG, part of Springer Nature 2018
Y. Shi et al. (Eds.): ICCS 2018, LNCS 10862, pp. 202–206, 2018.
https://doi.org/10.1007/978-3-319-93713-7_16

where α_i, $i = 0, 1, 2, 3..., k$ belongs to the state space $\{1, 2, ..., n\}$. Then α, $\beta \in \{1, 2..., n\}$, $p_\alpha = P(\alpha_0 = \alpha)$ is the probability that the Markov chain starts at state α and $p_{\alpha\beta} = P(\alpha_{i+1} = \beta | \alpha_i = \alpha)$ is the transition probability from state α to β. The set of all probabilities $p_{\alpha\beta}$ defines a transition probability matrix $[p_{\alpha\beta}]$. We say that the distribution $[p_1, p_2 ..., p_n]^t$ is acceptable for a given vector h, and the distribution $p_{\alpha\beta}$ is acceptable for matrix L, if $p_\alpha > 0$ when $h_\alpha \neq 0$, and $p_\alpha \geq 0$ when $h_\alpha = 0$, and $p_{\alpha\beta} > 0$ when $l_{\alpha\beta} \neq 0$ and $p_{\alpha\beta} \geq 0$ when $l_{\alpha\beta} = 0$ respectively. We assume

$$\Sigma_{\alpha=1}^n p_\alpha = 1, \quad \Sigma_{\beta=1}^n p_{\alpha\beta} = 1$$

for all $\alpha = 1, 2 ..., n$. The random variable whose mathematical expectation is equal to $\langle x, h \rangle$ is given by the following expression

$$\theta(h) = \frac{h_{\alpha_0}}{p_{\alpha_0}} \Sigma_{j=0}^\infty W_j b_{\alpha_j} \tag{4}$$

where $W_0 = 1, W_j = W_{j-1} \frac{l_{\alpha_{j-1}\alpha_j}}{p\alpha_{j-1}\alpha_j}, j = 1, 2, 3....$ We use the following notation for the partial sum:

$$\theta_i(h) = \frac{h_{\alpha_0}}{p_{\alpha_0}} \Sigma_{j=0}^i W_j b_{\alpha_j} \tag{5}$$

It is shown that $E(\theta_i(h)) = \langle h, \Sigma_{m=0}^i L^m b \rangle = \langle h, x^{(i+1)} \rangle$ and $E(\theta_i(h))$ tends to $\langle x, h \rangle$ as $i \to \infty$ [7]. To find r^{th} component of x, we put

$$h = (\underbrace{0, 0..., 1}_{r}, 0, ..., 0).$$

It follows that

$$\langle h, x \rangle = x_r.$$

The number of Markov chain is given by $N \geq (\frac{0.6745}{\epsilon} \frac{\|b\|}{(1-\|L\|)})^2$. With considering N paths $\alpha_0^{(m)} \to \alpha_1^{(m)} \to ... \to \alpha_k^{(m)}$, $m = 1, 2, 3..., N$, on the coefficient matrix, we have the Monte Carlo estimated solution by

$$\Theta_i(h) = \frac{1}{N} \Sigma_{m=1}^N \theta_i^{(m)}(h) \simeq \langle h, x^{(i+1)} \rangle.$$

The condition $\|L\| \leq 1$ is not very strong. In [9,10], it is shown that, it is possible to consider a Monte Carlo algorithm for which the Neumann series does not converge.

In this paper, we continue research on resolvent Monte Carlo algorithms presented in [4] and developed in [2,3,5]. We consider Monte Carlo algorithms for solving linear systems in the case when the corresponding Neumann series does not necessarily converge. We apply a mapping of the spectral parameter λ to obtain a convergent algorithm. First, sufficient conditions for the convergence of the resolvent operator are given. Then the Monte Carlo algorithm is employed.

2   Resolvent Operator Approach

2.1   The Convergence of Resolvent Operator

We study the behaviour of the equation

$$x - \lambda L x = b$$

depending on the parameter λ. Define nonsingular values of L by

$$\pi(L) = \{\lambda \mid x - \lambda L x = b \text{ has a unique solution}\}.$$

$\chi(L) = (\pi(L))^c$ is called the characteristic set of L. Let X and Y be Banach spaces and let $U = \{x \in X : \|x\| \leq 1\}$. An operator $L : X \to Y$ is called compact if the closure of $L(U)$ is compact. By Theorem 4.18 in [8], if dimension the rang of L is finite, then L is compact. The statement that $\lambda \in \pi(L)$ is equivalent to asserting the existence of the two-sided inverse operator $(I - \lambda L)^{-1}$. It is shown that for compact operators, λ is a characteristic point of L if and only if $\frac{1}{\lambda}$ is an eigenvalue of L. Also, it is shown that for every $r > 0$, the disk $|\lambda| < r$ contains at most a finite number of characteristic values.

The operator R_λ defined by $R_\lambda = (I - \lambda L)^{-1}$ is called the resolvent of L, and

$$R_\lambda = I + L + \lambda L^2 + \ldots + \lambda^n L^{n+1} + \ldots$$

The radius of convergence r of the series is equal to the distance r_0 from the point $\lambda = 0$ to the characteristic set $\chi(L)$. Let $\lambda_1, \lambda_2, \ldots$ be the characteristic values of L that $|\lambda_1| \leq |\lambda_2| \leq \ldots$. The systematic error of the above presentation when m terms are used is

$$O((\frac{|\lambda|}{|\lambda_1|})^{m+1} m^{\rho-1})$$

where ρ is multiplicity of roots λ_1. This follows that when $|\lambda| \geq |\lambda_1|$ the series does not converge. In this case we apply the analytical method in functional analysis. The following theorem for the case of compact operators has been proved in [6].

Theorem 1. *Let λ_0 be a characteristic value of a compact operator L. Then, in a sufficiently small neighbourhood of λ_0, we have the expansion*

$$R_\lambda = \ldots + \frac{L_{-r}}{(\lambda - \lambda_0)^r} + \ldots + \frac{L_{-1}}{(\lambda - \lambda_0)} + L_0 + L_1(\lambda - \lambda_0) + \ldots + L_n(\lambda - \lambda_0)^n + \ldots \quad (6)$$

Here r is the rank of characteristic value λ_0, the operators $L_{-r}, \ldots, L_{-1}$ are finite dimensional and $L_{-r} \neq 0$. The series on the right-hand side of (6) is convergent in the space of operators $B(X, X)$.

3   The Convergence of Monte Carlo Method

Let $\lambda_1, \lambda_2, ..$ be real characteristic values of L such that $\lambda_k \in (-\infty, -a]$. In this case we may apply a mapping of the spectral parameter λ. We consider a domain Ω lying inside the definition domain of R_λ as a function of λ such that all characteristic values are outside of Ω, $\lambda_* = 1 \in \Omega$, $0 \in \Omega$. Define $\psi(\alpha) = \frac{4a\alpha}{(1-\alpha)^2}$, $(|\alpha| < 1)$, which maps $\{\alpha : |\alpha| < 1\}$ to Ω described in [1]. Therefore the resolvent operator can be written in the form

$$R_\lambda b \simeq \Sigma_{k=1}^m b_k \alpha^k = \Sigma_{k=1}^m \Sigma_{i=1}^k d_i^{(k)} c_i \alpha^k$$
$$= \Sigma_{k=1}^m \Sigma_{j=k}^m d_k^{(j)} \alpha^j c_k = \Sigma_{k=1}^m g_k^{(m)} c_k$$

where $g_k^{(m)} = \Sigma_{j=k}^m d_k^{(j)} \alpha^j$ and $c_k = L^{k+1}b$. In [1], it is shown that $d_k^{(j)} = (4a)^k C_{k+j-1}^{2k-1}$. All in all, in the following theorem, it is shown that the random variable whose mathematical expectation is equal to $\langle h, \Sigma_{k=0}^m L^k \rangle$, is given by the following expression:

$$\Theta_m^*(h) = \frac{h_{\alpha_0}}{p_{\alpha_0}} \Sigma_{\nu=0}^m g_\nu^{(m)} W_\nu b_{\alpha_\nu}$$

where $W_0 = 1, W_j = W_{j-1} \frac{l_{\alpha_{j-1}\alpha_j}}{p_{\alpha_{j-1}\alpha_j}}, j = 1, 2, 3..., g_0^{(m)} = 1$ and $\alpha_0, \alpha_1, ...$ is a Markov chain with initial probability p_{α_0} and one step transition probability $p_{\alpha_{\nu-1}\alpha_\nu}$ for choosing the element $l_{\alpha_{\nu-1}\alpha_\nu}$ of the matrix L [1].

Theorem 2. *Consider matrix L, whose Neumann series does not necessarily converge. Let $\psi(\alpha) = \frac{4a\alpha}{(1-\alpha)^2}$ be the required mapping, so that the presentation $g_k^{(m)}$ exists. Then*

$$E\{ \lim_{m \to \infty} \frac{h_{\alpha_0}}{p_{\alpha_0}} \Sigma_{\nu=0}^m g_\nu^{(m)} W_\nu b_{\alpha_\nu} \} = \langle h, x \rangle$$

In [5], authors have analysed the robustness of the Monte Carlo algorithm for solving a class of linear algebra problems based on bilinear form of matrix powers $\langle h, L^k b \rangle$. In [5], authors have considered real symmetric matrices with norms smaller than one. In this paper, results are extended considerably compared to cases [3,5]. We consider singular matrices. For matrices that are stochastic matrices the accuracy of the algorithm is particularly high.

3.1   Numerical Tests

In this section of paper we employed our resolvent Monte Carlo algorithm for solving systems of singular linear algebraic equations. The test matrices are randomly generated. The factor of the improvement of the convergence depends on parameter α. An illustration of this fact is Table 1. We consider randomly generated matrices of order 100, 1000 and 5000. But more precise consideration shows that the error decreases with the increasing of the matrix size.

Table 1. Resolvent Monte Carlo results (number of trajectories $N = 10^5$)

Size n	Error
n = 100	6.7668×10^{-4}
n = 500	2.3957×10^{-5}
n = 1000	1.1487×10^{-5}
n = 2000	6.3536×10^{-6}
n = 3000	3.8250×10^{-6}
n = 4000	3.0871×10^{-6}
n = 5000	2.2902×10^{-6}
n = 6000	2.0030×10^{-6}

4 Conclusion

A new Monte Carlo algorithm for solving singular linear systems of equations is presented in this paper. The approach is based on the resolvent operator R_λ convergence. In fact we construct an algorithm based on the mapping of the spectral parameter λ. The approach is applied to systems with singular matrices. The initial results show that for such matrices a fairly high accuracy can be obtained.

References

1. Dimov, I.T.: Monte Carlo Methods for Applide Scientists. World Scientific Publishing, Singapore (2008)
2. Dimov, I., Alexandrov, V.: A new highly convergent Monte Carlo method for matrix computations. Mathe. Comput. Simul. **47**, 165–181 (1998)
3. Dimov, I., Alexandrov, V., Karaivanova, A.: Parallel resolvent Monte Carlo algorithms for linear algebra problems. Monte Carlo Method Appl. **4**, 33–52 (1998)
4. Dimov, I.T., Karaivanova, A.N.: Iterative monte carlo algorithms for linear algebra problems. In: Vulkov, L., Waśniewski, J., Yalamov, P. (eds.) WNAA 1996. LNCS, vol. 1196, pp. 150–160. Springer, Heidelberg (1997). https://doi.org/10.1007/3-540-62598-4_89
5. Dimov, I.T., Philippe, B., Karaivanova, A., Weihrauch, C.: Robustness and applicability of Markov chain Monte Carlo algorithms for eigenvalue problems. Appl. Math. Model. **32**, 1511–1529 (2008)
6. Kantorovich, L.V., Akilov, G.P.: Functional Analysis. Pergamon Press, Oxford (1982)
7. Rubinstein, R.Y.: Simulation and the Monte Carlo Method. Wiley, New York (1981)
8. Rudin, W.: Functional Analysis. McGraw Hill, New York (1991)
9. Sabelfeld, K.K.: Monte Carlo Methods in Boundary Value Problems. Springer, Heidelberg (1991)
10. Sabelfeld, K., Loshchina, N.: Stochastic iterative projection methods for large linear systems. Monte Carlo Methods Appl. **16**, 1–16 (2010)

Reducing Data Uncertainty in Forest Fire Spread Prediction: A Matter of Error Function Assessment

Carlos Carrillo$^{(\boxtimes)}$, Ana Cortés, Tomàs Margalef, Antonio Espinosa, and Andrés Cencerrado

Computer Architecture and Operating Systems Department,
Universitat Autònoma de Barcelona, Barcelona, Spain
{carles.carrillo,ana.cortes,tomas.margalef,antoniomiguel.espinosa,
andres.cencerrado}@uab.cat

Abstract. Forest fires are a significant problem that every year causes important damages around the world. In order to efficiently tackle these hazards, one can rely on forest fire spread simulators. Any forest fire evolution model requires several input data parameters to describe the scenario where the fire spread is taking place, however, this data is usually subjected to high levels of uncertainty. To reduce the impact of the input-data uncertainty, different strategies have been developed during the last years. One of these strategies consists of adjusting the input parameters according to the observed evolution of the fire. This strategy emphasizes how critical is the fact of counting on reliable and solid metrics to assess the error of the computational forecasts. The aim of this work is to assess eight different error functions applied to forest fires spread simulation in order to understand their respective advantages and drawbacks, as well as to determine in which cases they are beneficial or not.

Keywords: Error function · Wild fire · Prediction · Data uncertainty

1   Introduction

As it is known, forest fires are one of the most destructive natural hazards in the Mediterranean countries because of their significant impact on the natural environment, human beings and economy. For that reason, scientific community has invested lots of efforts in developing forest fire propagation models and computational tools that could help firefighter and civil protection to tackle those phenomena in a smart way in terms of resources allocation, extinguish actions and security. The quality results of these models depend not only on the propagation equations describing the behaviour of the fire, but also on the input data required to initialize the model. Typically, this data is subjected to a high

© Springer International Publishing AG, part of Springer Nature 2018
Y. Shi et al. (Eds.): ICCS 2018, LNCS 10862, pp. 207–220, 2018.
https://doi.org/10.1007/978-3-319-93713-7_17

degree of uncertainty and variability during the evolution of the event due to the dynamic nature of some of them such as meteorological conditions or moisture contents in the vegetation. Any strategy oriented to reduce this input data uncertainty requires a quality measure of the results to determine the goodness of the proposed strategy. Typically, on the forest fire spread prediction field, this assessment relies on a fitness/error function that must evaluate how well the prediction system reproduces the real behaviour of the fire. In order to speed up the process of finding good estimations of certain input parameters, the prediction systems tend to include a calibration stage prior to perform the forest fire spread prediction (prediction stage) [4]. In particular, we focus on a well know two-stage methodology, which is based on Genetic Algorithms (GA). In this scheme, the calibration stage runs a GA to reduce input data uncertainty. To do that, the GA generates an initial population (set of individuals) where each individual consists of a particular configuration of the input parameters from which reducing their uncertainty implies an improvement in terms of quality results. This initial population will evolve using the so called genetic operators (elitism, mutation, selection, crossover) to obtain an improved set of individuals that better reproduces the observed past behaviour of the fire. After several iterations of the GA, the best individual will be selected to predict the near future (prediction stage). A key point in all this process is the error function applied to determine the prediction quality of each individual. This function drives the GA's evolution process, consequently, to establish an appropriate level of confidence in the way that the error function is assessed is crucial in the system, [2].

The goal of this work is to study and test eight different error functions to assess the simulation error in the case of forest fire spread prediction.

This paper is organized as follows. In Sect. 2 the data uncertainty problem when dealing with forest fires spread prediction and how it can be minimize with an appropriate error function selection is introduced. Section 3 details an analysis of the different proposed functions to compute the simulation error. Section 4 presents the experimental results and, finally, Sect. 5 summarizes the main conclusions and future work.

2   Reducing Input Data Uncertainty

In order to minimize the uncertainty in the input data when dealing with forest fire spread prediction, we focus on the Two-Stage prediction scheme [1]. The main goal of this approach is to introduce an adjustment stage previous to the prediction stage to better estimate certain input parameters according to the observed behaviour of the forest fire. The main idea behind this strategy is to extract relevant information from the recent past evolution of the fire that could be used to reduce data uncertainty in the near future forecast. As it has previously mentioned, this scheme relies on a GA. Each individual of the GA population consists of a particular input parameter setting that will be fed into the underlying forest fire spread simulator. In this work, the forest fire spread simulator used is FARSITE [7], however, the methodology described would be

reproduced for any other simulator. Each simulation generates a forest fire propagation that must be compared to the real evolution of the fire. According to
the similarity in terms of shape and area among the simulated propagation and
the real fire behaviour, the corresponding input parameters set is scored with an
error value. Typically, low errors indicates that the provided forecast is closer
to the reality, meanwhile higher errors indicate certain degree of mismatching
between the two propagations.

There are several metrics to compare real and simulated values and each one
weighs the events involved differently, depending on the nature of the problem
[2]. In the forest fire spread case, the map of the area where the fire is taking
place is represented as a grid of cells. Each cell is labeled to know if it has
been burnt or not in both cases: the real propagation map and the simulated
fire spread map. Then, if one compare both maps cell by cell, we came up with
different possibilities: cells that were burnt in both the actual and simulated
spread *(Hits)*, cells burnt in the simulated spread but not in the reality *(False
Alarms)*, cells burnt in the reality but not in the simulated fire *(Misses)* and cells
that were not burnt in any case *(Correct negatives)* [6,8]. These four possibilities
are used to construct a 2×2 contingency table, as is shown in Fig. 1.

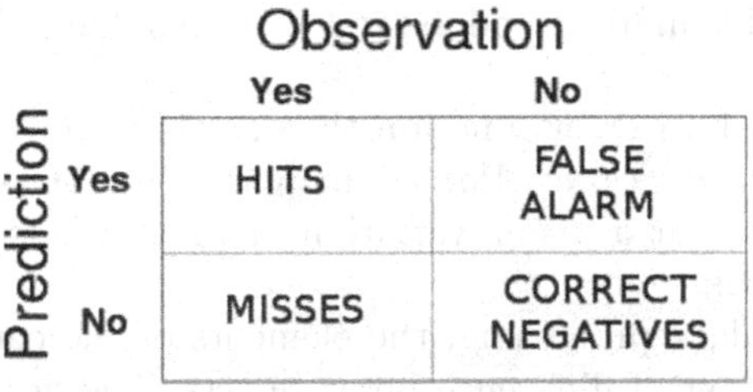

Fig. 1. Standard structure of a contingency table.

Nevertheless, at the time to put a prediction system into practice, it is important to consider what a *good forecast* actually means, according to the underlying phenomena we are dealing with, since there are many factors that models do
not take into account. In our case, when a fire is simulated, a free fire behavior
is considered, without including human intervention (firefighters). Under this
hypothesis, the simulations should overestimate the burnt area. For this reason,
when a simulation produces an underestimated perimeter (front of the fire), it
is considered a bad result. Because of this, we are interested in those error functions that minimize the impact of *False Alarms* above the impact of *Misses*.
Let's imagine two hypothetical forest fire spread predictions where the number
of FA in one of them is the same value that the number of Misses in the other
one. Under this assumption, we would expect that the error function provides a
lower error in the first case than in the second case.

In addition, for the particular case of forest fire spread forecast, the cells
labeled as correct negatives are ignored because the area of the map to be

simulated may vary independently of the fire perimeter, so they may distort the measurement of the error. In the following section, a description of the different error functions analyzed in this work is done.

3   Error Function Description

We propose the analysis of eight different functions that are potential candidates to be used as error metric in the Calibration Stage of a forest fire spread forecast system. To study their strengths and lacks, we carried out a preliminary study to *artificially* compute the error of each function depending on its *Hits*, *False Alarms* and *Misses*. For this purpose, we consider a sample map with a number of real burnt cells equal to 55 (*RealCell* = 55). A simple and intuitive, way to test the behavior of a given error function consists of evaluating its value for all configurations of *Hits*, *Misses* and *False Alarms* when their values varies within the range [0 to 55]. With the computed errors we build a color map representation where the behavior of the Error function with regard to the *False Alarms* and the *Misses* is shown. On the right side of the color map, the legend will show a color scale for the error function values where blue color represents lowest errors, while red colour represents highest errors. In this section, we will use the described color map to understand the behaviour of all described error functions.

Our goal is to find an error function that grows faster as *Misses* increases rather than doing so as *False Alarms* increase, that is, solid error function candidates should present a *faster* variation along the *Misses* axis than along the *False Alarms* axis.

To facilitate the data processing, the elements of the contingency table are expressed in the context of difference between sets. The description of the conversion of these metrics is showed in the Table 1. Using this notation, in the subsequent sections, we shall describe different error functions that have been deployed in the above described Calibration Stage, and the advantages and drawbacks of each one are reported.

3.1   Bias Score or Frequency Bias (BIAS)

The *BIAS* score is the ratio of the number of correct forecasts to the number of correct observations [8]. Equation 1 describes this error function. This metric represents the normalized symmetric difference between the real map and the simulated map.

$$BIAS = \frac{Hits + FA}{Hits + Misses} \tag{1}$$

However, in the evolutionary process we focus on minimizing the ratio of the frequency of the erroneous simulated events, so we rely on a slight variation of the *BIAS* score. The same Error Function can be expressed in terms of the

Table 1. Elements of the contingency table expressed in the context of difference between sets.

RealCell	$Hits + Misses$	Cells burnt in real fire
SimCell	$Hits + FA$	Cells burnt in simulated fire
UCell	$Hits + Misses + FA$	Union of cells burnt in real fire and simulated one
ICell	$Hits$	Cells burnt in real fire and in simulated fire

difference between sets where the initial fire is considered a point and, therefore, it can be removed from the equation. The obtained formula is shown in Eq. 2.

$$\in = \frac{Misses + FA}{Hits + Misses} = \frac{UCell - ICell}{RealCell} \tag{2}$$

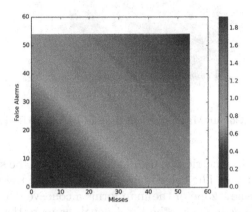

Fig. 2. Colour map representation of BIAS (Eq. 2).

In Fig. 2 the behaviour of the function 2 depending on *False Alarms* and *Misses* is shown. As it can be seen, the computed error grows up slightly faster in the *False Alarms* direction than in the *Misses* direction, this effect means that Eq. 2 lightly penalizes *False Alarms* compared to *Misses*.

3.2 BIAS+False Alarm Rate (BIAS+FAR) ($\in_1$)

This function is a combination of the previous formula (Eq. 2) and the *False Alarm Rate (FAR)*. The *FAR* measures the proportion of the wrong events forecast (see Eq. 3).

$$FAR = FA/(Hits + FA) \tag{3}$$

Since we are interested in penalizing those cases that underestimate the forecast, $\in_1$ combines BIAS and FAR. Equation 4 shows this new Fitness Function in terms of events and difference between cell sets.

$$\begin{aligned} \in_1 &= \frac{1}{2} \cdot \left(\frac{Misses + FA}{Hits + Misses} + \frac{FA}{Hits + FA} \right) \\ &= \frac{1}{2} \cdot \left(\frac{UCell - ICell}{RealCell} + \frac{SimCell - ICell}{SimCell} \right) \end{aligned} \qquad (4)$$

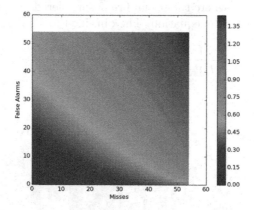

Fig. 3. Colour Map representation of BIAS+FAR (Eq. 4)

The behavior of this metric is shown in Fig. 3. As it can be seen, the variation of the error is not lineal. The color map shows that while the blue part forms a convex curve, the yellow zone of the map forms a concave curve. It means that, while the amount of cells is low, the Eq. 4 penalizes more the $Misses$ than the $False\ Alarms$, whereas with a large number of cells it tends to provide higher error for underestimated areas than for overestimated ones.

3.3   BIAS-False Alarm Rate (BIAS-FAR) ($\in_2$)

The next Error Function is quite similar to the previous equation (Eq. 4), but in this case the FAR is subtracted from the $BIAS$, as it is shown in the Eq. 5. As we said, FAR measures the rate of $False\ Alarms$, so the overestimated simulations have a high value of FAR. So, in this case, we subtract FAR from BIAS in order to provide a better position for those simulations that provide overestimated spread perimeters.

$$\begin{aligned} \in_2 &= \frac{1}{2} \cdot \left(\frac{Misses + FA}{Hits + Misses} - \frac{FA}{Hits + FA} \right) \\ &= \frac{1}{2} \cdot \left(\frac{UCell - ICell}{RealCell} - \frac{SimCell - ICell}{SimCell} \right) \end{aligned} \qquad (5)$$

The behavior of this metric is shown in Fig. 4. This figure shows that this metric presents a not linear behavior. We are able to see how the blue zone (low error) is bigger in the *False Alarms* axis than in the *Misses* one, it means that BIAS-FAR penalizes much more the *Misses* than the *False Alarms*. Moreover, a big green zone is present, where the computed error remains more or less constant. Above this green zone, we can see that the error grows faster in the *False Alarms* direction than in the *Misses* direction.

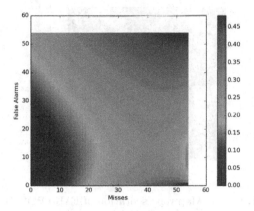

Fig. 4. Colour Map representation of BIAS-FAR (Eq. 5)

The main problem of this function is that for values around *Misses* = 55 and *FalseAlarms* = 10 (see Fig. 4), the error is lower than some simulations with better fitness. So, we cannot be confident about this metric, since it could cause that individuals with a better adjustment are discarded before individuals with a worse adjustment.

3.4 FAR+Probability of Detection of Hit Rate (FAR+POD) ($\in_3$)

The next Fitness Function used is a combination of Eq. 3 and the *Probability of Detection of hits rate (POD)*. The *POD* formula relates the observed events and estimated positively with all ones, Eq. 6. It represents the probability of a phenomenon being detected.

$$POD = \frac{Hits}{Hits + Misses} \tag{6}$$

However, as it was mentioned, we focus on minimizing the ratio of the frequency of the erroneous simulated events, so a slight variant of the *POD* is used, as expressed in formula 7.

$$\in = \frac{Misses}{Hits + Misses} \tag{7}$$

The result of combining Eq. 7 with Eq. 3 is expressed in Eq. 8.

$$\in_3 = \frac{1}{2} \cdot \left(\frac{Misses}{Hits+Misses} + \frac{FA}{Hits+FA} \right)$$

$$= \frac{1}{2} \cdot \left(\frac{RealCell-Icell}{RealCell} + \frac{SimCell-ICell}{SimCell} \right)$$
(8)

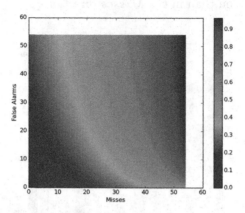

Fig. 5. Colour Map representation of FAR+POD (Eq. 8)

In Fig. 5, we can see that, while *False Alarms* are low, the error grows more slowly in the *Misses* direction than when the amount of *FalseAlarms* is high. In the same way, when the number of *Misses* is low, the error remains more or less constant in the *False Alarms* direction, but when the amount of *Misses* increases, the error grows up very fast in the *False Alarms* direction.

3.5 BIAS+Incorrectness Rate (BIAS+IR) ($\in_4$)

This Error Function was proposed in [3]. Using this function, the individuals that provide overestimated prediction have a better error than those individuals that underestimate the fire evolution. This function is shown in Eq. 9.

$$\in_4 = \frac{1}{2} \cdot \left(\frac{Misses + FA}{Hits + Misses} + \frac{Misses + FA}{Hits + FA} \right)$$

$$= \frac{1}{2} \cdot \left(\frac{UCell - Icell}{RealCell} + \frac{UCell - ICell}{SimCell} \right)$$
(9)

Figure 6 depicts the behaviour of this metric. As it can be seen, it shows a predominance of blue color, which means that the error growths very slowly. This might suggest that the errors obtained are very good in any case, but in the reality what happens is that this function practically treated every case, i.e., overestimated simulations and underestimated ones, in the same way. It is for a large number of cells where equation BIAS+IR provide lower errors for overestimated simulations than for underestimate simulations.

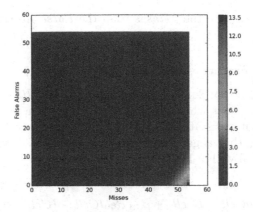

Fig. 6. Colour Map representation of BIAS+IR (Eq. 9)

3.6 Adjustable Incorrectness Aggregation (AIA) ($\in_5$)

As we said, we look for an equation that penalize more the underestimated simulated areas than the overestimated, this implies that *Misses cells* are worse than *False Alarms cells*. In order to penalize more *Misses* than *False Alarms* the Eq. 10 was proposed

$$\in_5 = \alpha \cdot FA + \beta \cdot Misses = \alpha \cdot (SimCell - ICell) + \beta \cdot (RealCell - ICell) \quad (10)$$

with $\alpha = 1$ and $\beta = 2$. This Fitness Function provides very high errors, but, in our case, this is not a problem, because we only want to compare the errors among the individuals but not the absolute value of the error.

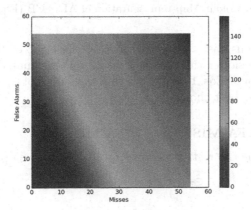

Fig. 7. Colour Map representation of AIA (Eq. 10)

Figure 7 represents the behaviour of this metric. As it can be observed, this metric clearly reproduces the behavior that we were expected. It is easy to see that Eq. 10 penalizes more the *Misses* than the *False Alarms*, which is what we are looking for.

3.7   AIA with Correctness BIAS (AIA+CB) ($\in_6$)

This equation is close to Eq. 10 but, in this case, the *Hits* are removed (see Eq. 11). This implies that when using this error function, negatives values can be obtained but, as it was stated, we do not care about the value of the error but on the final ranking that is generated using it. In this case, the best individual will be the individual with a higher negative value.

$$\in_6 = \alpha \cdot FA + \beta \cdot Misses - \gamma \cdot Hits \qquad (11)$$
$$= \alpha \cdot (SimCell - ICell) + \beta \cdot (RealCell - ICell) - \gamma \cdot ICell$$

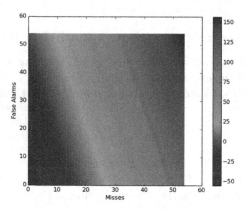

Fig. 8. Colour Map representation of AIA+CB (Eq. 11)

As in the previous case, using this metric, the error of the overestimated predictions increase slower than in the case of underestimated simulations (see Fig. 8). The problem of Eqs. 10 and 11 is that the values of α, β, and γ are fixed and they are not the best choice for all forest fires.

3.8   Ponderated FA-MISS Rate (PFA-MR) ($\in_7$)

In order to overcome the restrictions of Eqs. 10, 12 has been proposed.

$$\in_7 = \alpha \cdot FA + \beta \cdot Misses \qquad (12)$$

with

$$\alpha = \frac{Hits}{Hits + FA} = \frac{ICell}{SimCell} \qquad (13)$$

and

$$\beta = \alpha + \frac{Hits}{Hits + Misses} = \frac{ICell}{SimCell} + \frac{ICell}{RealCell} \qquad (14)$$

Then, the Error Function expressed in context of difference between sets corresponds to Eq. 15.

$$\in_7 = \frac{ICell}{SimCell} \cdot (SimCell - ICell) + \left(\frac{ICell}{SimCell} + \frac{ICell}{RealCell} \right) \cdot (RealCell - ICell)$$

(15)

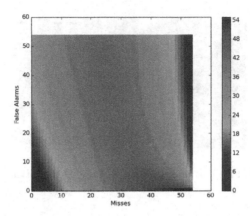

Fig. 9. Color Map representation of PFA-MR (Eq. 11)

In Fig. 9 the behavior of Eq. 15 is shown. As it was expected, it can be seen that this metric penalizes the *Misses* above the *False Alarms*. However, similarly to the case of *BIAS-FAR*, it behaves in a way that, in cases with high values of *Misses* (combined, in this case, with high values of *False Alarms*), it returns low error values. The big orange zone, between 20 and 45 *Misses* value, means that the maximum value of the error is achieved within this area. This implies that a large number of *Misses* can distort the selection of those individuals with a better fitting.

Based on the previous analyses and interpretations of the different proposed Error Functions, in the subsequent section we present an applied test using both synthetic and real results of a large fire that took place in Greece in 2011.

4   Experimental Study and Results

In order to analyze how the use of different error functions affects the prediction of the forest fire spread, we have selected as study case one event stored in the database of EFFIS (*European Forest Fire Information System*) [5]. In particular, we have retrieved the information of a past fire that took place in Greece during the summer season of 2011 in the region of Arkadia. The forest fire began on the

26th of August, and the total burnt area was 1.761 ha. In Fig. 10, it can be seen the fire perimeters at three different time instants: t_0 (August 26th at 09:43am) called *Perimeter 1*, t_1 (August 26th at 11:27am) corresponds to *Perimeter 2* and t_2 (August 27th at 08:49am) is *Perimeter 3*. The Two-Stage predictions strategy based on the Genetic Algorithm has been applied where the *Perimeter 1* was used as initial perimeter (ignition Perimeter), *Perimeter 2* was used in the Calibration Stage and the perimeter to be predicted is *Perimeter 3*.

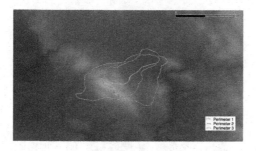

Fig. 10. Fire perimeters corresponding to the Arkadia fire.

Figure 11 shows the forest fire spread obtained using best individual at the end of the Calibration Stage and the forecast delivered using that individual for each error function defined in the previous section. As it can be observed, the fire evolution provided by the best individual at the end of the Calibration Stage is directly related to the Error Function applied. Using the POD+FAR and AIA+CB errors functions, the obtained best individuals fits well enough the bottom of the fire, see Fig. 11(d) and (g), but they overestimate the top very much. This could be a good result because it could happen that human intervention had stopped the real fire spread in that zone. However, the problem is that the corresponding predictions have a high overestimation of the burned area. The worst error formula is the seventh (PFA-MR), because the best individual obtained underestimates the real fire but the simulation in the Prediction stage has a very overestimate burned area.

In this case, the prediction that better fits the burned area is the simulation obtained when BIAS is used in the Calibration Stage (see 11(a)). This function provides the forecast with the highest number of intersection cells, although in some regions the burned area is overestimated. As we can see, the Error Function with the lower number of intersections cells are the AIA equation, Fig. 11(f). The predictions obtained from BIAS+FAR, BIAS-FAR and BIAS+IR, Fig. 11(b), (c) and (e) respectively, have less intersection cells than the prediction using BIAS but, at the same time, it has less *False Alarms*.

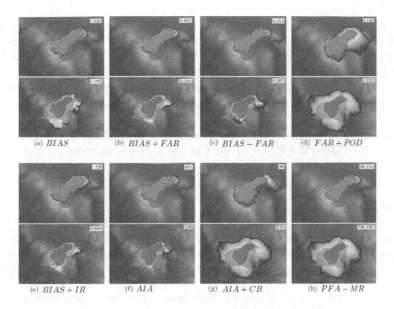

Fig. 11. For each error function (a) to (h), the upper figure shows the forest fire spread obtained using the best individual provided by the Calibration stage and the bottom figure depicts the final forecast delivered using that individual. The error evaluated for each case is also included

5 Conclusions

In the last years, the simulation of complex systems have demonstrated to be a powerful tool to improve the fight against natural hazards. For this reason, an adequate error function to evaluate the fitness of these models is a key issue. In this work, we focus on the specific case of wild fires as one of the most worrisome natural disaster.

In this work, eight equations have been tested in order to evaluate the prediction quality for large forest fires taking into account the factor of overestimated/underestimated predictions compared to the real fire. The results show that different error functions imply different calibration of the parameters and, therefore, different forest fire spread predictions are obtained. After applying the proposed error functions in the Two-Stage methodology, we can conclude that FAR+POD and AIA+CB functions tend to select individuals that provide very overestimated predictions. These functions provide the fittest individual in the Calibration Stage. The problem is, that using the adjusted inputs in these cases, the obtained predictions present very overestimated burnt areas. The function that underestimated more the fire perimeter is the sixth Error function (AIA), using this equation, the obtained prediction is the one with fewer intersection cells. The PFA-MR function is dismissed due to its lack of reliability.

There are a set of three Error Functions which stand out above others. These equations are BIAS, BIAS+FAR and BIAS+IR. As a result of our experimental study, we can observe that we obtain more favorable results with this set of functions than with the rest. However, we are not able to determine undoubtedly which Equation is best for most of the cases. For this reason, our future work will be oriented to differentiate large fires of small fires, or fires with different meteorological conditions (wind prominence, mainly), in order to determine which Error function is more suitable, depending on these aspects.

Acknowledgments. This research has been supported by MINECO-Spain under contract TIN2014-53234-C2-1-R and by the Catalan government under grant 2014-SGR-576.

References

1. Abdalhaq, B., Cortés, A., Margalef, T., Luque, E.: Enhancing wildland fire prediction on cluster systems applying evolutionary optimization techniques. Future Generation Comp. Syst. **21**(1), 61–67 (2005). https://doi.org/10.1016/j.future.2004.09.013
2. Bennett, N.D., et al.: Characterising performance of environmental models. Environ. Model. Software **40**, 1–20 (2013)
3. Brun, C., Cortés, A., Margalef, T.: Coupled dynamic data-driven framework for forest fire spread prediction. In: Ravela, S., Sandu, A. (eds.) DyDESS 2014. LNCS, vol. 8964, pp. 54–67. Springer, Cham (2015). https://doi.org/10.1007/978-3-319-25138-7_6
4. Cencerrado, A., Cortés, A., Margalef, T.: Response time assessment in forest fire spread simulation: an integrated methodology for efficient exploitation of available prediction time. Environ. Model. Software **54**, 153–164 (2014). https://doi.org/10.1016/j.envsoft.2014.01.008
5. Joint Research Centre: European forest fire information system, August 2011. http://forest.jrc.ec.europa.eu/effis/
6. Ebert, B.: Forecast verification: issues, methods and FAQ, June 2012. http://www.cawcr.gov.au/projects/verification
7. Finney, M.A.: FARSITE: fire area simulator-model development and evaluation. FResearch Paper RMRS-RP-4 Revised 236, Research Paper RMRS-RP-4 Revised (1998)
8. Gjertsen, U., Ødegaard, V.: The water phase of precipitation: a comparison between observed, estimated and predicted values, October 2005. https://doi.org/10.1016/j.atmosres.2004.10.030

Analysis of the Accuracy of OpenFOAM Solvers for the Problem of Supersonic Flow Around a Cone

Alexander E. Bondarev$^{(\boxtimes)}$ (ID) and Artem E. Kuvshinnikov (ID)

Keldysh Institute of Applied Mathematics RAS, Moscow, Russia
bond@keldysh.ru, kuvsh90@yandex.ru

Abstract. The numerical results of comparing the accuracy for some Open-FOAM solvers are presented. The comparison was made for the problem of inviscid compressible flow around a cone at zero angle of attack. The results obtained with the help of various OpenFOAM solvers are compared with the known numerical solution of the problem with the variation of cone angle and flow velocity. This study is a part of a project aimed to create a reliable numerical technology for modelling the flows around elongated bodies of rotation (EBR).

Keywords: Flow around a cone · Computational fluid dynamics
OpenFOAM · Accuracy comparison

1 Introduction

In recent years, there has been a fairly frequent situation where it is necessary to calculate the flow of elongated bodies of rotation (EBR) under specific conditions. Such calculations are usually carried out for practical purposes, taking into account all technological features of the body in question. Naturally, for such calculations, there is a desire to apply some of CFD software packages, which have been widely used in recent times. However, when trying to solve practical problems with the help of such packages, there are some difficulties. The catalogs of mathematical models and finite-difference schemes used in such complexes are imperfect. The acceptability of many models for solving complex problems and determining the limits of their applicability are the subject of a separate study. This refers to the problems of flow around the elongated bodies of rotation and the implementation of turbulence simulation methods for them. For a particular class of EBR it is required to carry out a large number of test calculations to show the applicability of the chosen numerical method and the chosen model of turbulence. These methodological studies are often neglected. Therefore, a user of similar software packages encounters the need to specify a variety of variable parameters, which in practice provides an indefinite result.

In this situation, obviously, we need a computational technology that would be a kind of standard for solving the problems of flow around the EBR and would help to regulate the tunable parameters of both numerical methods and models of turbulence in various software packages. In this capacity, it was decided to recreate on the modern level the computational technology developed earlier in the Keldysh Institute of Applied Mathematics. In the late 80's - early 90's this computational technology allowed to make mass industrial computing for a flow around EBR with a high degree of reliability. The error of aerodynamic drag coefficients did not exceed 2–3% in comparison with the experimental results. The essence of this technology was that the aerodynamic drag coefficient Cx, was considered as a sum of three components: Cp – coefficient for inviscid flow, Cf - coefficient for viscous friction and Cd – coefficient for near wake pressure. Such an approach was widely used for industrial analysis of aerodynamic properties of EBR and proved to be very effective. The work presented is a part of the general project to create a similar technology [1, 2]. To calculate the friction coefficient, a computational technique [2] is realized. The technique is based on an approximate semi-empirical model which combines the results of experimental studies and the method of effective length. This computational technology is designed to determine the friction coefficient and estimate the characteristics of the boundary layer for EBR. To calculate the aerodynamic characteristics for inviscid flow around the elongated bodies of rotation, it was proposed to use the OpenFOAM software package (Open Source Field Operation and Manipulation CFD Toolbox) [3]. Open-FOAM is actively used in industry and in science. OpenFOAM contains a number of solvers [4–7] having different computational properties.

Therefore, it is necessary to make methodological calculations that allow to evaluate the effectiveness of these solvers for practical application. This paper presents a comparative analysis of the OpenFOAM solvers accuracy for the problem of inviscid flow around cones with different angles and different flow velocities at zero angle of attack. Tabular solutions [8] are used as an exact solution for comparison. Presented in a tabular form solutions [8] have high accuracy and for many years are used for testing the computational properties of numerical methods. It should be noted that similar comparisons of solvers were carried out in [9, 10]. However, these comparisons do not give full and clear recommendations on the accuracy of solvers.

2   Formulation of the Problem

The statement of the problem is presented in full accordance with [8], where the results of the inviscid flow around cones with different angles at various Mach numbers are considered. We consider the case of a cone placed in a uniform supersonic flow of an ideal gas at zero angle of attack $\alpha = 0°$ with a Mach number of 2 to 7. The body under investigation is a cone with an angle $\beta = 10–35°$ in steps of 5°. Here angle β is a half of cone angle as shown in Fig. 1. The conditions of the input flow are denoted by the index "∞", and at the output by the index ξ, since the solution is self-similar and depends on the dimensionless variable. The Euler equations system is used for the calculation. The system is supplemented by the equation of state of an ideal gas.

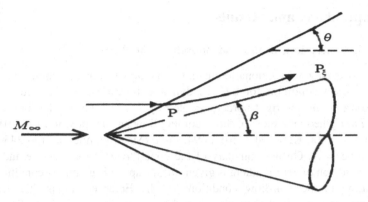

Fig. 1. Flow scheme.

3 OpenFOAM Solvers

For comparison, 4 solvers were selected from the OpenFOAM software package:

RhoCentralFoam is based on a central-upwind scheme, which is a combination of central-difference and upwind schemes [4, 5]. The essence of the central-upwind schemes consists in a special choice of a control volume containing two types of domains: around the boundary points, the first type; around the center point, the second type. The boundaries of the control volumes of the first type are determined by means of local propagation velocities. The advantage of these schemes is that, using the appropriate technique to reduce the numerical viscosity, it is possible to achieve good solvability for discontinuous solutions — shock waves in gas dynamics, and for solutions in which viscous phenomena play a major role.

SonicFoam is based on the PISO algorithm (Pressure Implicit with Splitting of Operator) [6]. The basic idea of the PISO method is that two difference equations are used to calculate the pressure for the correction of the pressure field obtained from discrete analogs of the equations of moments and continuity. This approach is due to the fact that the velocities corrected by the first correction may not satisfy the continuity equation, therefore, a second corrector is introduced which allows us to calculate the velocities and pressures satisfying the linearized equations of momentum and continuity.

RhoPimpleFoam is based on the PIMPLE algorithm, which is a combination of the PISO and SIMPLE (Semi-Implicit Method for Pressure-Linked Equations) algorithms. An external loop is added to the PISO algorithm, thanks to which the method becomes iterative and allows to count with the Courant number greater than 1.

PisoCentralFoam is a combination of a Kurganov-Tadmor scheme [4] with the PISO algorithm [7].

For all solvers the calculations were carried out using the OpenFOAM version 2.3.0. Solver sonicFoam in the standard version does not support dynamic time step change, so the necessary corrections have been made to the code of solver. Also the calculations were made for pimpleCentralFoam solver. This solver exists only for OpenFOAM version 3.0.1 and higher. The results for this solver were similar to the results of pisoCentralFoam, so it was decided not to include these results in the tables below.

4 Computations and Results

4.1 Mesh Generation, Initial and Boundary Conditions

Figure 2 shows the computational domain. On the upper boundary indicated as "top", the zero gradient condition for the gas dynamic functions, is specified. The same conditions are set on the right border, denoted by "*outlet*". On the left border, designated as "*inlet*", the parameters of the oncoming flow are set: pressure P = 101325 Pa, temperature T = 300 K, speed U from 694.5 m/s (Mach number = 2) to 2430.75 m/s (Mach number = 7). On the boundary of the cone ("*cone*") for pressure and temperature, the condition of zero gradient is given, for the speed is given the condition "*slip*", corresponding to the non-flow condition for the Euler equations. To model the axisymmetric geometry in the OpenFoam package, a special "*wedge*" condition is used for the front ("*front*") and back ("*back*") borders. The OpenFoam package also introduces a special "*empty*" boundary condition. This condition is specified in cases when calculations in a given direction are not carried out. In our case, this condition is used for the "*axis*" border.

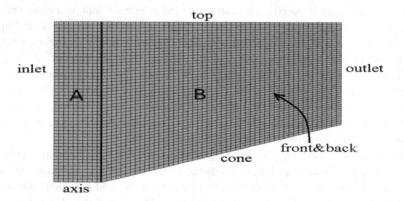

Fig. 2. Computational domain and boundaries.

The number of grid cells is 13200. The initial conditions correspond to the boundary conditions on the inlet edge, that is, the initial conditions are used for the parameters of the oncoming stream. The molar mass M = 28.96 kg/mol and the specific heat at constant pressure C_p = 1004 were also set.

To estimate the effect of the grid partition on the accuracy of calculations, the calculations were carried out on three grids, denoted as *coarse, fine, finest*. The number of cells: *coarse* – 3000, *fine* – 12000, *finest* – 48000.

4.2 Parameters of Solvers

In the OpenFOAM package, there are two options for approximating differential operators: directly in the solver's code or using the fvSchemes and fvSolution configuration files. In order for the comparison to be correct, we used the same parameters where possible. In the fvSchemes file: ddtSchemes – *Euler*, gradSchemes – *Gauss linear*, div-Schemes – *Gauss linear*, laplacianSchemes – *Gauss linear corrected*, interpolationSchemes– *vanLeer*. In the fvSolution file: solver – *smoothSolver*, smoother *symGaussSeidel*, tolerance – 1e−09, nCorrectors – 2, nNonOrthogonalCorrectors – 1.

4.3   Calculation of the Axisymmetric Flow

Figure 3 presents the steady-state flow field for pressure when using the solver rhoCentralFoam. The figure indicates that, as a result of the establishment, a qualitative picture of the flow is obtained that corresponds to the known solutions [8].

Fig. 3. Pressure field for steady flow.

Tables from 1, 2, 3, 4, 5, 6, 7, 8 and 9 show the results of calculations in the form of an analog of the L_2 norm:

$$\sqrt{\sum_m |y_m - y_m^{exact}|^2 V_m} \Big/ \sqrt{\sum_m |y_m^{exact}|^2 V_m} \qquad (1)$$

In Tables 1, 2 and 3 y_m is the velocity U_x, U_y, pressure p and density ρ in the cell, V_m is the cell volume for the cone angle $\beta = 20°$ and the Mach number $M = 2$. These tables show the grid convergence for the variant considered. Grid convergence for all variants was considered similarly.

In Tables 4, 5, 6, 7, 8 and 9 y_m is the pressure p in the cell, V_m is the cell volume for the cone angle $\beta = 10–35°$ in steps of $5°$ and the Mach numbers $M = 2–7$. The minimum values are highlighted in bold. The symbol "x" in the tables means that at a given speed and given cone angle, the solver became unstable. The values of y_m^{exact} are obtained by interpolating tabular values from [8] into grid cells. It should be noted that the authors of the tables [8] indicate the admissibility of interpolation for all parameters and table values. Further we will use abbreviations for solvers. rCF (rhoCentralFoam), pCF (pisoCentralFoam), sF (sonicFoam), rPF (rhoPimpleFoam).

Table 1. Deviation from the exact solution for coarse grid

	rCF	pCF	sF	rPF
U_x	0.009062	0.008929	**0.008366**	0.010155
U_y	**0.043725**	0.050789	0.050932	0.060268
p	**0.024054**	0.027705	0.033429	0.037406
ρ	**0.018327**	0.021848	0.028965	0.033199

Table 2. Deviation from the exact solution for fine grid

	rCF	pCF	sF	rPF
U_x	0.006268	0.006482	**0.005809**	0.007588
U_y	**0.029656**	0.034403	0.033814	0.043562
p	**0.016989**	0.019515	0.022465	0.026656
ρ	**0.012834**	0.015182	0.019085	0.022994

Table 3. Deviation from the exact solution for finest grid

	rCF	pCF	sF	rPF
U_x	0.004372	0.004441	**0.004057**	0.005526
U_y	**0.019862**	0.022855	0.023113	0.030994
p	**0.011611**	0.013269	0.015143	0.018803
ρ	**0.008715**	0.010282	0.012684	0.015810

Table 4. Deviation from the exact solution, U = 2M

Cone angel	rCF	pCF	sF	rPF
10	**0.006090**	0.006973	0.010153	0.010341
15	**0.012654**	0.014446	0.019646	0.020645
20	**0.016623**	0.019353	0.022283	0.024951
25	**0.018678**	0.020948	0.020779	0.025426
30	**0.020695**	0.023130	0.025614	0.023267
35	**0.032486**	0.038658	0.074849	0.043179

Table 5. Deviation from the exact solution, U = 3M

Cone angel	rCF	pCF	sF	rPF
10	**0.015309**	0.019537	0.027152	0.027177
15	**0.024608**	0.030041	0.047813	0.041444
20	**0.030440**	0.035858	0.070564	0.045760
25	**0.032486**	0.038658	0.074849	0.043179
30	**0.034040**	0.040603	0.077408	0.040006
35	**0.026334**	0.029821	0.044853	0.027077

Table 6. Deviation from the exact solution, U = 4M

Cone angle	rCF	pCF	sF	rPF
10	**0.028254**	0.035251	0.058133	0.049334
15	**0.040229**	0.046494	0.106172	0.065384
20	**0.046159**	0.052687	0.126701	0.070649
25	**0.045849**	0.051912	0.134932	0.062785
30	**0.040775**	0.050619	0.109125	x
35	**0.034277**	0.042296	0.069668	x

Table 7. Deviation from the exact solution, U = 5M

Cone angle	rCF	pCF	sF	rPF
10	**0.050834**	0.055133	0.106710	0.075829
15	**0.060069**	0.063293	0.159880	0.090489
20	**0.060174**	0.064675	0.175666	x
25	**0.059900**	0.063284	0.175205	x
30	**0.055975**	0.062637	0.130201	x
35	**0.043288**	0.052737	0.090006	x

Table 8. Deviation from the exact solution, U = 6M

Cone angle	rCF	pCF	sF	rPF
10	**0.061150**	0.063986	0.148118	0.093482
15	0.077744	**0.077303**	0.215881	0.455342
20	**0.076336**	0.078191	0.210225	x
25	**0.073101**	0.075504	0.183841	x
30	**0.063374**	0.067209	0.144629	x
35	**0.052961**	0.062369	0.096355	x

Table 9. Deviation from the exact solution, U = 7M

Cone angle	rCF	pCF	sF	rPF
10	0.076287	**0.074444**	0.191676	0.112744
15	0.090901	**0.089137**	0.247274	0.543143
20	**0.086889**	0.089311	0.215352	x
25	**0.085631**	0.087697	0.188621	x
30	**0.073957**	0.077507	0.140091	x
35	**0.063160**	0.075632	0.111154	x

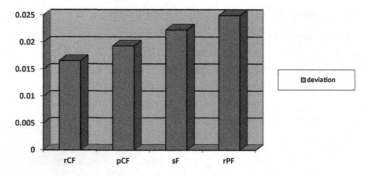

Fig. 4. Deviation from the exact solution for pressure $M = 2$, $\beta = 20$.

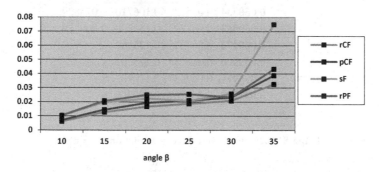

Fig. 5. Change in deviation from the exact solution for pressure depending on the cone angle for all solvers, $M = 2$.

Figure 4 presents a diagram of the deviation from the exact solution in the analogue of the L_2 norm for the pressure for all used solvers by the example of the problem of flow past a cone with a cone angle $\beta = 20°$ with Mach number $M = 2$. The smallest deviation from the exact solution is shown by the solver rhoCentralFoam, the maximum deviation is shown by the solver rhoPimpleFoam.

Figure 5 shows the change in the deviation from the exact solution in the analogue of the L_2 norm for the pressure for all solvers, depending on the cone angle for a fixed Mach number $M = 2$. The smallest deviation from the exact solution is shown by the solver rhoCentralFoam, the largest deviation with an increase in the cone angle is shown by the sonicFoam solver.

Figure 6 shows the dependence of the deviation on the exact solution in the analog of the L_2 norm for the pressure for the solver rhoCentralFoam with the variation of the cone angle and the initial velocity. An increase in the Mach number of the oncoming stream has the greatest effect on the increase in the deviation of the numerical result from the exact solution.

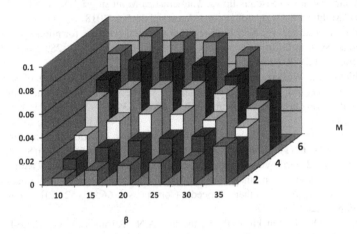

Fig. 6. Change in deviation from the exact solution for pressure depending on the cone angle and the velocity for the solver rhoCentralFoam.

5 Conclusion

Using well-known problem of a supersonic inviscid flow around a cone at zero angle of attack we compared four OpenFoam solvers with the exact solution. Grid convergence was shown for all solvers. According to the results obtained, the solver rhoCentralFoam has minimal error in almost all cases. The only drawback of rhoCentralFoam is the appearance of oscillations near the surface at the head of the cone. Solver pisoCentrlFoam is in second place in accuracy, however, when using this solver, the appearance of oscillations is not observed. The methodical research can serve as a basis for selecting the OpenFoam solver for calculating the inviscid supersonic flow around the elongated bodies of rotation. The results of solvers comparison can also be useful for developers of OpenFoam software content. The results obtained made it possible to get a general idea of the calculation errors for all solvers.

In further studies it is proposed to make a similar comparison of solvers for the problem of flow around a cone with a variation of the angle of attack. It is also proposed to investigate the matrix of mutual errors for solutions obtained by different solvers by constructing elastic maps.

Acknowledgments. This work was supported by grant of RSF № 18-11-00215.

References

1. Bondarev, A.E., Kuvshinnikov, A.E.: Comparative study of the accuracy for OpenFOAM solvers. In: Proceedings of Ivannikov ISPRAS Open Conference (ISPRAS), p. 132. IEEE, Moscow (2017). https://doi.org/10.1109/ispras.2017.00028
2. Bondarev, A.E., Nesterenko, E.A.: Approximate method for estimation of friction forces for axisymmetric bodies in viscous flows. Mathematica Montisnigri **XXXI**, 54–63 (2014)
3. OpenFOAM. http://www.openfoam.org. Accessed 11 Feb 2018
4. Kurganov, A., Tadmor, E.: New high-resolution central schemes for nonlinear conservation laws and convection-diffusion equations. J. Comput. Phys. **160**, 241–282 (2000). https://doi.org/10.1006/jcph.2000.6459
5. Greenshields, C., Wellerr, H., Gasparini, L., Reese, J.: Implementation of semi-discrete, non-staggered central schemes in a colocated, polyhedral, finite volume framework, for high-speed viscous flows. Int. J. Numer. Meth. Fluids **63**(1), 1–21 (2010). https://doi.org/10.1002/fld.2069
6. Issa, R.: Solution of the implicit discretized fluid flow equations by operator splitting. J. Comput. Phys. **62**(1), 40–65 (1986). https://doi.org/10.1016/0021-9991(86)90099-9
7. Kraposhin, M., Bovtrikova, A., Strijhak, S.: Adaptation of Kurganov-Tadmor numerical scheme for applying in combination with the PISO method in numerical simulation of flows in a wide range of Mach numbers. Procedia Comput. Sci. **66**, 43–52 (2015). https://doi.org/10.1016/j.procs.2015.11.007
8. Babenko, K.I., Voskresenskii, G.P., Lyubimov, A.N., Rusanov, V.V.: Three-Dimensional Ideal Gas Flow Past Smooth Bodies. Nauka, Moscow (1964). (in Russian)
9. Karvatskii, A., Pulinets, I., Lazarev, T., Pedchenko, A.: Numerical modelling of supersonic flow around a wedge with the use of free open software code OpenFOAM. Space Sci. Technol. **21**(2), 47–52 (2015). https://doi.org/10.15407/knit2015.02.047. (in Russian)
10. Gutierrez, L.F., Tamagno, J.P., Elaskar, S.A.: High speed flow simulation using OpenFOAM. In: Mecanica Computacional, Salta, Argentina, vol. XXXI, pp. 2939–2959 (2012)

Modification of Interval Arithmetic for Modelling and Solving Uncertainly Defined Problems by Interval Parametric Integral Equations System

Eugeniusz Zieniuk$^{(\boxtimes)}$, Marta Kapturczak, and Andrzej Kużelewski

Faculty of Mathematics and Informatics, University of Bialystok,
Ciolkowskiego 1M, 15-245 Bialystok, Poland
{ezieniuk,mkapturczak,akuzel}@ii.uwb.edu.pl
http://ii.uwb.edu.pl/~zmn/

Abstract. In this paper we present the concept of modeling and solving uncertainly defined boundary value problems described by 2D Laplace's equation. We define uncertainty of input data (shape of boundary and boundary conditions) using interval numbers. Uncertainty can be considered separately for selected or simultaneously for all input data. We propose interval parametric integral equations system (IPIES) to solve so-define problems. We obtain IPIES in result of PIES modification, which was previously proposed for precisely (exactly) defined problems. For this purpose we have to include uncertainly defined input data into mathematical formalism of PIES. We use pseudo-spectral method for numerical solving of IPIES and propose modification of directed interval arithmetic to obtain interval solutions. We present the strategy on examples of potential problems. To verify correctness of the method, we compare obtained interval solutions with analytical ones. For this purpose, we obtain interval analytical solutions using classical and directed interval arithmetic.

Keywords: Interval arithmetic · Interval modeling
Potential boundary value problems
Parametric integral equations system (PIES)

1 Introduction

Classical definition of boundary problems assumes that the shape of the boundary and boundary conditions are precisely (exactly) defined. This is an idealized way. In practice we can obtain measurement errors, for example. The Measurement Theory is widely presented in [1]. Additionally, even differential equations (used to define physical phenomena mathematically) do not model all of the phenomena properties. Therefore, the differential equations, as well as shape of boundary and boundary condition, do not model the phenomenon accurately.

© Springer International Publishing AG, part of Springer Nature 2018
Y. Shi et al. (Eds.): ICCS 2018, LNCS 10862, pp. 231–240, 2018.
https://doi.org/10.1007/978-3-319-93713-7_19

Nevertheless, the methods of solving so-define problems are still being developed. In the most popular techniques the domain or boundary is divided into small parts (elements). On these elements some interpolation functions are defined. Next, to obtain solutions for whole problem, the complex calculations (on so-define numerical model) were carried out.

Above mentioned strategy is used in finite element method (FEM) [2] and in boundary element method (BEM) [3]. The basic problem of such strategy is to ensure proper class of continuity of interpolation functions in points of segment join. However, these methods do not consider the uncertainty of problems. It is impossible to use these methods directly for solving uncertainly defined problems. There is no option to define the uncertainty using traditional mathematical apparatus.

Recently, there is growing number of well known techniques modifications for solving boundary value problems, which use different ways of uncertainty modeling. For example, interval numbers and its arithmetic [4] or fuzzy set theory [5] can be used. In element methods, their development in the form of interval FEM [6] and interval BEM [7] appeared. Unfortunately they inherit disadvantages of classical methods (used with precisely defined boundary value problems), which definitely affect the effectiveness of their application. Description of the boundary shape uncertainty is very troublesome because of discretization process. Moreover, in classical boundary integral equations (BIE), the Lyapunov condition for the shape of boundary should be met [8] and appropriate class of continuity in points of elements join should be ensured. It is significantly troublesome for uncertainly defined boundary value problems.

Contrary to traditional boundary integral equations (BIE), we separate approximation of the boundary shape from the boundary function in parametric integral equations system (PIES). Therefore, we decided to use this method in uncertainly modelled problems. Recently PIES was successfully used for solving boundary value problems defined in precise way [9,10]. PIES was obtained as a result of analytical modification of traditional BIE. The main advantage of PIES is that the shape of boundary is included directly into BIE. The shape could be modeled by curves (used in graphics). Therefore, we can obtain any continuous shape of boundary (using curves control points) directly in PIES. In other words, PIES is automatically adapted to the modified shape of boundary. It significantly improves the way of modeling and solving problems. This advantage is particularly visible in modeling uncertainly defined shape of boundary.

In this paper, for modeling uncertainly defined potential problems (defined using two-dimensional Laplace's equation) we proposed interval parametric integral equations system (IPIES). We obtain IPIES as a result of PIES modification. We include directed interval arithmetic into mathematical formalism of PIES and verify reliability of proposed mathematical apparatus based on examples. It turned out that obtained solutions are different for the same shape of boundary defined in different location in coordinate system. Therefore, to obtain reliable solutions using IPIES, we have to modify applied directed interval arithmetic.

2   Concept of Classical and Directed Interval Arithmetic

Classical interval number $\boldsymbol{x}$ is the set of all real numbers x satisfying the condition [4,12]:

$$\boldsymbol{x} = [\underline{x}, \overline{x}] = \{x \in \mathbb{R} | \underline{x} \leq x \leq \overline{x}\}, \tag{1}$$

where $\underline{x}$ - is infimum and $\overline{x}$ - is supremum of interval number $\boldsymbol{x}$. Such numbers are also called as proper interval numbers. In order to perform calculations on these numbers, the interval arithmetic was developed and generally it was defined as follows [4]:

$$\boldsymbol{x} \circ \boldsymbol{y} = [\underline{x}, \overline{x}] \circ [\underline{y}, \overline{y}] = [min(\underline{x} \circ \underline{y}, \underline{x} \circ \overline{y}, \overline{x} \circ \underline{y}, \overline{x} \circ \overline{y}), max(\underline{x} \circ \underline{y}, \underline{x} \circ \overline{y}, \overline{x} \circ \underline{y}, \overline{x} \circ \overline{y})], \tag{2}$$

where $\circ \in \{+, -, \cdot, /\}$ and in division $0 \notin \boldsymbol{y}$.

The development of different methods of classical interval number applications [13,14] resulted in the detection of some disadvantages of this kind of representation. For example, it is impossible to obtain opposite and inverse element of such numbers. Therefore in the literature, the extension of intervals by improper numbers was appeared. Such extension was called as directed (or extended) interval numbers [15].

Directed interval number $\boldsymbol{x}$ is the set of all ordered real numbers x satisfying the conditions:

$$\boldsymbol{x} = [\underline{x}, \overline{x}] = \{x \in \boldsymbol{x} | \underline{x}, \overline{x} \in \mathbb{R}\}. \tag{3}$$

Interval number $\boldsymbol{x}$ is proper if $\underline{x} < \overline{x}$, degenerate if $\underline{x} = \overline{x}$ and improper if $\underline{x} > \overline{x}$. The set of proper interval numbers is denoted by $\mathbb{IR}$, of degenerated numbers by $\mathbb{R}$ and improper numbers by $\overline{\mathbb{IR}}$. Additionally directed interval arithmetic was extended by new subtraction ($\ominus$) and division ($\oslash$) operators:

$$\boldsymbol{x} \ominus \boldsymbol{y} = [\underline{x} - \underline{y}, \overline{x} - \overline{y}], \tag{4}$$

$$\boldsymbol{x} \oslash \boldsymbol{y} = \begin{cases} [\underline{x}/\underline{y}, \overline{x}/\overline{y}] & \text{for } \boldsymbol{x} > 0, \boldsymbol{y} > 0 \\ [\overline{x}/\overline{y}, \underline{x}/\underline{y}] & \text{for } \boldsymbol{x} < 0, \boldsymbol{y} < 0 \\ [\overline{x}/\underline{y}, \underline{x}/\overline{y}] & \text{for } \boldsymbol{x} > 0, \boldsymbol{y} < 0 \\ [\underline{x}/\overline{y}, \overline{x}/\underline{y}] & \text{for } \boldsymbol{x} < 0, \boldsymbol{y} > 0 \\ [\overline{x}/\underline{y}, \underline{x}/\underline{y}] & \text{for } \boldsymbol{x} \ni 0, \boldsymbol{y} < 0 \\ [\underline{x}/\overline{y}, \overline{x}/\overline{y}] & \text{for } \boldsymbol{x} \ni 0, \boldsymbol{y} > 0 \end{cases}. \tag{5}$$

Such operators allow us to obtain an opposite element ($0 = \boldsymbol{x} \ominus \boldsymbol{x}$) and inverse element ($1 = \boldsymbol{x} \oslash \boldsymbol{x}$). Therefore, it turned out, that direct application of both classical and directed interval arithmetic in modeling the shape of boundary failed. Hence, we try to interpolate the boundary by boundary points using directed interval arithmetic. We define the same shape of boundary in each quarter of coordinate system and, as a result of interpolation, we obtain different shapes of boundary depending on place of its location. Therefore, we propose modification of directed interval arithmetic, where all of arithmetic operations are mapped into positive semi-axis:

$$
x \cdot y = \begin{cases}
x_s \cdot y_s - x_s \cdot y_m - x_m \cdot y_s + x_m \cdot y_m & \text{for } x \leq 0, y \leq 0 \\
x_s \cdot y - x_m \cdot y & \text{for } x > 0, y \leq 0 \\
x \cdot y_s - x \cdot y_m & \text{for } x \leq 0, y > 0 \\
x \cdot y & \text{for } x > 0, y > 0
\end{cases} \tag{6}
$$

where for any interval number $x = [\underline{x}, \overline{x}]$ we define $x_m = \begin{cases} |\overline{x}| & \text{for } \overline{x} > \underline{x} \\ |\underline{x}| & \text{for } \overline{x} < \underline{x} \end{cases}$ and $x_s = x + x_m$, where $x > 0$ means $\underline{x} > 0$ and $\overline{x} > 0$, $x \leq 0$ means $\underline{x} < 0$ or $\overline{x} < 0$ and $(\cdot)$ is an interval multiplication. Finally, application of so-defined modification allow us to obtain the same shapes of boundary independently from the location in coordinate system.

3   Interval Parametric Integral Equations System (IPIES)

PIES for precisely defined problems was applied in [9,10,16]. It is an analytical modification of boundary integral equations. Defining uncertainty of input data by interval numbers, we can present interval form of PIES:

$$
0.5 u_l(s_1) = \sum_{j=1}^{n} \int_{\widehat{s}_{j-1}}^{\widehat{s}_j} \left\{ U_{lj}^*(s_1, s) p_j(s) - P_{lj}^*(s_1, s) u_j(s) \right\} J_j(s) ds, \tag{7}
$$

where $\widehat{s}_{l-1} \leq s_1 \leq \widehat{s}_l, \widehat{s}_{j-1} \leq s \leq \widehat{s}_j$, then $\widehat{s}_{l-1}, \widehat{s}_{j-1}$ correspond to the beginning of l-th and j-th segment, while $\widehat{s}_l, \widehat{s}_j$ to their ends. Function:

$$
J_j(s) = \left[\left(\frac{\partial S_j^{(1)}(s)}{\partial s} \right)^2 + \left(\frac{\partial S_j^{(2)}(s)}{\partial s} \right)^2 \right]^{0.5} \tag{8}
$$

is the Jacobian for segment of interval curve $S_j = [S_j^{(1)}, S_j^{(2)}]$ marked by index j, where $S_j^{(1)}(s) = [\underline{S}_j^{(1)}(s), \overline{S}_j^{(1)}(s)]$, $S_j^{(2)}(s) = [\underline{S}_j^{(2)}(s), \overline{S}_j^{(2)}(s)]$ are scalar components of vector curve S_j and depending on parameter s.

Integral functions $p_j(s) = [\underline{p}_j(s), \overline{p}_j(s)]$, $u_j(s) = [\underline{u}_j(s), \overline{u}_j(s)]$ are interval parametric boundary functions on corresponding interval segments of boundary S_j (on which the boundary was theoretically divided). One of these functions will be defined by interval boundary conditions on segment S_j, then the other one will be searched as a result of numerical solution of IPIES (7).

Interval integrands (kernels) U_{lj}^* and P_{lj}^* are presented in the following form:

$$
U_{lj}^*(s_1, s) = \frac{1}{2\pi} \ln \frac{1}{[\eta_1^2 + \eta_2^2]^{0.5}}, \quad P_{lj}^*(s_1, s) = \frac{1}{2\pi} \frac{\eta_1 n_1(s) + \eta_2 n_2(s)}{\eta_1^2 + \eta_2^2}, \tag{9}
$$

where $\eta_1 = \eta_1(s_1, s)$ and $\eta_2 = \eta_2(s_1, s)$ are defined as:

$$\eta_1(s_1, s) = S_l^{(1)}(s_1) - S_j^{(1)}(s), \quad \eta_2(s_1, s) = S_l^{(2)}(s_1) - S_j^{(2)}(s), \quad (10)$$

where segments S_l, S_j can be defined by interval curves such as: Bézier, B-spline or Hermite, $n_1(s), n_2(s)$ are the interval components of normal vector n_j to boundary segment j. Kernels (9) analytically include in its mathematical formalism the shape of boundary. It is defined by dependencies between interval segments S_l, S_j, where $l, j = 1, 2, 3, ..., n$. We require only a small number of control points to define or modify the shape of curves (created by segments). Additionally, the boundary of the problem is a closed curve and the continuity of C^2 class is easily ensured in points of segments join.

The advantages of precisely defined PIES are more visible in modeling uncertainty of boundary value problem. Inclusion of uncertainly defined shape of the boundary directly in kernels (9) by interval curves is the main advantage of IPIES. Numerical solution of PIES do not require the classical boundary discretization, contrary to the traditional BIE. This advantage in modeling uncertainty of the boundary shape significantly reduces amount of interval input data. Therefore the overestimation is also reduced. Additionally, the boundary in PIES is analytically defined by interval curves. That ensure the continuity in points of segments join.

3.1 Interval Integral Identity for Solutions in Domain

Solving interval PIES (7) we can obtain only solutions on boundary. We have to define integral identity using interval numbers, to obtain solutions in domain. Finally, we can present it as follows:

$$u(x) = \sum_{j=1}^{n} \int_{\widehat{s}_{j-1}}^{\widehat{s}_j} \left\{ \widehat{U}_j^*(x, s) p_j(s) - \widehat{P}_j^*(x, s) u_j(s) \right\} J_j(s) ds, \quad (11)$$

it is right for $x = [x_1, x_2] \in \Omega$.

Interval integrands $\widehat{U}_j^*(x, s)$ and $\widehat{P}_j^*(x, s)$ are presented below:

$$\widehat{U}_j^*(x, s) = \frac{1}{2\pi} \ln \frac{1}{[\overleftrightarrow{r_1}^2 + \overleftrightarrow{r_2}^2]^{0.5}}, \quad \widehat{P}_j^*(x, s) = \frac{1}{2\pi} \frac{\overleftrightarrow{r_1} n_1(s) + \overleftrightarrow{r_2} n_2(s)}{\overleftrightarrow{r_1}^2 + \overleftrightarrow{r_2}^2}, \quad (12)$$

where $\overleftrightarrow{r_1} = x_1 - S_j^{(1)}(s)$ and $\overleftrightarrow{r_2} = x_2 - S_j^{(2)}(s)$.

Interval shape of boundary is included in (12) by expressions: $\overleftrightarrow{r_1}$ and $\overleftrightarrow{r_2}$ that are defined by boundary segments, uncertainly modeled by interval curves $S_j(s) = [S_j^{(1)}(s), S_j^{(2)}(s)]$.

4   Interval Approximation of Boundary Functions

Interval boundary functions $u_j(s)$, $p_j(s)$ are approximated by interval approximation series presented as follows:

$$p_j(s) = \sum_{k=0}^{M-1} p_j^{(k)} f_j^{(k)}(s), \qquad u_j(s) = \sum_{k=0}^{M-1} u_j^{(k)} f_j^{(k)}(s) \qquad (j = 1, ..., n), \quad (13)$$

where $u_j^{(k)}, p_j^{(k)}$ - are searched interval coefficients, M - is the number of terms in the series (13) defined on segment j, $f_j^k(s)$ - are base functions defined in the domain of segment. In numerical tests, we use the following polynomials as base functions in IPIES:

$$f_j^{(k)}(s) = \left\{ P_j^{(k)}(s), H_j^{(k)}(s), L_j^{(k)}(s), T_j^{(k)}(s) \right\}, \qquad (14)$$

where $P_j^{(k)}(s)$ - Legendre polynomials, $H_j^{(k)}(s)$ - Hermite polynomials, $L_j^{(k)}(s)$ - Laguere polynomials, $T_j^{(k)}(s)$ - Chebyshev polynomials of I kind.

In this paper we apply Lagrange interpolation polynomials. When the Dirichlet (or Neumann) interval boundary conditions are defined as analytical function, we can interpolate them by approximation series (14). In case of Dirichlet interval boundary conditions the coefficients $u_j^{(k)}$ are defined, while for Neumann interval conditions $p_j^{(k)}$ ones.

5   Verification of the Concept Reliability

We presented inclusion of the interval numbers and its arithmetic into PIES. Next, we need to verify the strategy on examples to confirm the reliability of IPIES. Firstly, we will test and analyze proposed strategy (application of modified directed interval arithmetic) on simple examples of boundary value problems modeled by Laplace's equation. Solutions obtained by IPIES will be compared with analytical solutions. However, analytical solutions are known only for precisely defined problems. Therefore, we apply interval arithmetic to obtain analytical interval solutions. These solutions will be compared with solutions obtained using IPIES.

5.1   Example 1 - Interval Linear Shape of Boundary and Interval Boundary Conditions

We consider Laplace's equation in triangular domain with interval shape of boundary and boundary conditions. In Fig. 1 we present the uncertainly modeled problem and the cross-section where solutions are searched. The shape is defined by three interval points (P_0, P_1 i P_2) with the band of uncertainty $\varepsilon = 0.0667$.

Interval Dirichlet boundary condition (precisely defined in [17]) are defined as follows:

$$\varphi(x, y) = 0.5(x^2 + y^2). \qquad (15)$$

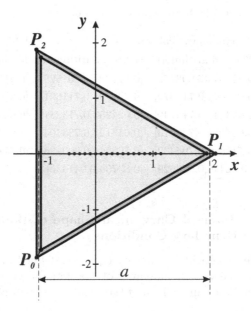

Fig. 1. Example 1 - uncertainty of linear shape of boundary.

So-defined interval boundary condition is defined by interval shape coefficients ($\boldsymbol{x} = [\underline{x}, \overline{x}], \boldsymbol{y} = [\underline{y}, \overline{y}]$) and its uncertainty is caused by uncertainly defined shape of boundary only. Solutions of so-defined problem with uncertainty are obtained in cross-section (Fig. 1) and are presented in Table 1. W decided to compare obtained interval solutions with analytical solution [17], which are presented, with uncertainly defined shape of boundary (interval parameter $\boldsymbol{a}$), as follow:

$$\varphi(\boldsymbol{x}) = \frac{x^3 - 3xy^2}{2a} + \frac{2a^2}{27}, \qquad (16)$$

where $\boldsymbol{a} = [\underline{a}, \overline{a}]$ define interval shape of boundary and the middle value of $\boldsymbol{a}$ was marked as a on Fig. 1.

The analytical solution (defined by intervals) are obtained using interval numbers and their arithmetic. Analytical solutions obtained using classical as well as directed interval arithmetic are compared with IPIES solutions and presented in Table 1. We can notice, that obtained interval analytical solutions are very close to the interval solutions of IPIES. However, classical interval arithmetic solutions (in some points) are wider than in IPIES solutions.

Interval solutions obtained using IPIES are close to analytical solutions obtained using directed interval arithmetic. It confirm reliability of an algorithm. However, for more accurate analysis we decide to consider an example with uncertainly defined curvilinear shape of boundary.

Table 1. Interval solutions in domain.

Cross section		Interval analytical solutions		IPIES
x	y	Directed arithmetic	Classical arithmetic	Modified arithmetic
−0.4	0	[0.61264,0.700817]	[0.611928,0.701529]	[0.611936, 0.701502]
−0.1	0	[0.622802,0.711679]	[0.622791,0.711691]	[0.622783, 0.711675]
0.2	0	[0.624342,0.713142]	[0.624253,0.713231]	[0.624325, 0.713136]
0.5	0	[0.644515,0.732013]	[0.643124,0.733404]	[0.644492, 0.732014]
0.8	0	[0.711239,0.794432]	[0.705544,0.800128]	[0.711213, 0.794441]
1.1	0	[0.852446,0.926529]	[0.83764,0.941335]	[0.852411, 0.926579]

5.2 Example 2 - Interval Curvilinear Shape of Boundary and Interval Boundary Conditions

In the next example we consider Laplace's equation defined in elliptical domain. In Fig. 2 we present the way of modeling of the domain with interval shape of boundary. We defined the same width of the band of uncertainty $\varepsilon = 0.1$ on each segment.

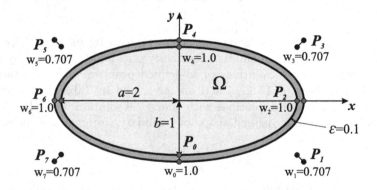

Fig. 2. Uncertainly defined shape of boundary.

The shape of boundary is modeled by interval NURBS curves of second degree. Uncertainty was defined by interval points ($P_0 - P_7$). Interval Dirichlet boundary condition is defined in the same way as in previous example:

$$u(x) = 0.5(x^2 + y^2) \tag{17}$$

Analytical solution for precisely defined problem is presented in [17], therefore it could be define as interval assuming, that the parameters a, b are intervals, i.e.: $a = [\underline{a}, \overline{a}]$ and $b = [\underline{b}, \overline{b}]$:

$$u_a = \frac{x^2 + y^2}{2} - \frac{a^2 b^2 (\frac{x^2}{a^2} + \frac{y^2}{b^2} - 1)}{a^2 + b^2}. \tag{18}$$

Interval solutions in domain of so-define problem with the interval shape of boundary and interval boundary conditions are shown in the Fig. 3. Similarly like in previous example, we obtain interval analytical solutions using classical and directed interval arithmetic. As we can see in Fig. 3, the widest interval is obtained using classical interval arithmetic. Directed interval arithmetic is slightly shifted from IPIES solution, but with similar width.

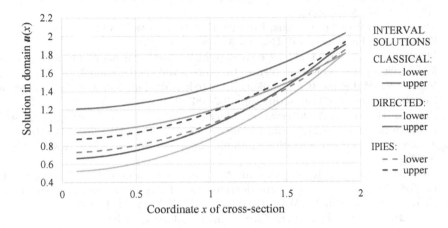

Fig. 3. Comparison between interval analytical solutions and IPIES.

6   Conclusion

In this paper we proposed the strategy of modeling and solving uncertainly defined potential boundary value problems. We modeled uncertainty using interval numbers and its arithmetic. The shape of boundary and boundary conditions were defined as interval numbers. Solutions of so-defined problems are obtained using modified parametric integral equations system. Such generalization includes the directed interval arithmetic into mathematical formalism of PIES. Additionally, we had to modify mentioned arithmetic mapping all of operations into positive semi-axis. Reliability of modeling and solving process of the boundary problems using IPIES was verified on examples with analytical solutions. Applying interval arithmetic to analytical solutions, well known for precisely defined (non-interval) problems, we could easily obtain interval analytical solutions. We used such solutions to verify reliability of proposed algorithm (based on obtained IPIES).

References

1. Potter, R.W.: The Art of Measurement: Theory and Practise. Prentice Hall, Upper Saddle River (2000)
2. Zienkiewicz, O.C., Taylor, R.L.: The Finite Element Method, vol. 1–3. Butter-Worth, Oxford (2000)
3. Brebbia, C.A., Telles, J.C.F., Wrobel, L.C.: Boundary Element Techniques: Theory and Applications in Engineering. Springer, New York (1984). https://doi.org/10.1007/978-3-642-48860-3
4. Moore, R.E.: Interval Analysis. Prentice-Hall, New York (1966)
5. Zadeh, L.A.: Fuzzy sets. Inf. Control **8**, 338–353 (1965)
6. Muhanna, R.L., Mullen, R.L., Rama Rao, M.V.: Nonlinear interval finite elements for structural mechanics problems. In: Vořechovský, M., Sadílek, V., Seitl, S., Veselý, V., Muhanna, R.L., Mullen, R.L., (eds.) 5th International Conference on Reliable Engineering Computing, pp. 367–387 (2012)
7. Piasecka-Belkhayat, A.: Interval boundary element method for transient diffusion problem in two layered domain. J. Theore. Appl. Mech. **49**(1), 265–276 (2011)
8. Jaswon, M.A.: Integral equation methods in potential theory. Proc. Roy. Soc. Ser. A **275**, 23–32 (1963)
9. Zieniuk, E., Szerszen, K., Kapturczak, M.: A numerical approach to the determination of 3D stokes flow in polygonal domains using PIES. In: Wyrzykowski, R., Dongarra, J., Karczewski, K., Waśniewski, J. (eds.) PPAM 2011. LNCS, vol. 7203, pp. 112–121. Springer, Heidelberg (2012). https://doi.org/10.1007/978-3-642-31464-3_12
10. Zieniuk, E., Szerszeń, K.: Triangular Bézier surface patches in modeling shape of boundary geometry for potential problems in 3D. Eng. Comput. **29**(4), 517–527 (2013)
11. Zieniuk, E., Kapturczak, M., Kużelewski, A.: Concept of modeling uncertainly defined shape of the boundary in two-dimensional boundary value problems and verification of its reliability. Appl. Math. Model. **40**(23–24), 10274–10285 (2016)
12. Kearfott, R.B., Nakao, M.T., Neumaier, A., Rump, S.M., Shary, S.P., van Hentenryck, P.: Standarized notation in interval analysis. In: Proceedings XIII Baikal International School-seminar "Optimization Methods and Their Applications", Interval analysis, vol. 4, pp. 106–113 (2005)
13. Dawood, H.: Theories of Interval Arithmetic: Mathematical Foundations and Applications. LAP Lambert Academic Publishing (2011)
14. Zieniuk, E., Kapturczak, M., Kużelewski, A.: Solving interval systems of equations obtained during the numerical solution of boundary value problems. Comput. Appl. Mathe. **35**(2), 629–638 (2016)
15. Markov, S.M.: Extended interval arithmetic involving intervals. Mathe. Balkanica **6**, 269–304 (1992). New Series
16. Zieniuk, E., Kapturczak, M., Sawicki, D.: The NURBS curves in modelling the shape of the boundary in the parametric integral equations systems for solving the Laplace equation. In: Simos, T., Tsitouras, Ch. (eds.) 13th International Conference of Numerical Analysis and Applied Mathematics ICNAAM 2015, AIP Conference Proceedings, vol. 1738, 480100 (2016). https://doi.org/10.1063/1.4952336
17. Hromadka II, T.V.: The Complex Variable Boundary Element Method in Engineering Analysis. Springer, New York (1987). https://doi.org/10.1007/978-1-4612-4660-2

A Hybrid Heuristic for the Probabilistic Capacitated Vehicle Routing Problem with Two-Dimensional Loading Constraints

Soumaya Sassi Mahfoudh[(✉)] and Monia Bellalouna

National School of Computer Science, Laboratory CRISTAL-GRIFT,
University of Manouba, Manouba, Tunisia
soumaya.lsm@gmail.com, monia.bellalouna@gmail.com

Abstract. The Probabilistic Capacitated Vehicle Routing Problem (PCVRP) is a generalization of the classical Capacitated Vehicle Routing Problem (CVRP). The main difference is the stochastic presence of the customers, that is, the number of them to be visited each time is a random variable, where each customer associates with a given probability of presence.

We consider a special case of the PCVRP, in which a fleet of identical vehicles must serve customers, each with a given demand consisting in a set of rectangular items. The vehicles have a two-dimensional loading surface and a maximum capacity.

The resolution of problem consists in finding an a priori route visiting all customers which minimizes the expected length over all possibilities. We propose a hybrid heuristic, based on a branch-and-bound algorithm, for the resolution of the problem. The effectiveness of the approach is shown by means of computational results.

Keywords: Vehicle routing · Bin packing · Probability
Hybrid heuristic · Exact algorithms

1 Introduction

In the last decades, several variants of Vehicle Routing Problem (VRP) have been studied since the initial work of Dantzig and Ramser [9]. In its classical form, the VRP consists in building routes starting and ending at a depot, to satisfy the demand of a given set of customers, with a fleet of identical vehicles.

In particular, the capacitated Vehicle Routing Problem (CVRP) is a well known variation of the VRP [25], defined as follows: we are given a complete undirected graph $G = (V, E)$ in which V is the set of $n+1$ vertexes corresponding to the depot and the n customers. For each vertex v_i is associated a demand d_i. The demand of each customer is generally expressed by a positive integer that represents the weight of the demand. A set of K identical vehicles is available at

© Springer International Publishing AG, part of Springer Nature 2018
Y. Shi et al. (Eds.): ICCS 2018, LNCS 10862, pp. 241–253, 2018.
https://doi.org/10.1007/978-3-319-93713-7_20

the depot. Each vehicle has a capacity Q. The CVRP calls for the determination of vehicles routes with minimal total cost.

Recently, mixed vehicle routing and packing problems have been studied [8,15,16]. This problem is called CVRP with two-dimensional loading constraints (2L-CVRP). In 2L-CVRP, two-dimensional packing problems are considered where all vehicles have a single rectangular loading surface whose width and height are equal to W and H, respectively. Each customer is associated with a set of rectangular items whose total weight is equal to d_i. Solving 2L-CVRP consists in determining the optimal set of vehicles routes of minimal cost to satisfy the demand of the set of customers and without overlapping the loading surface. It is clear that 2L-CVRP is strongly NP-Hard since it generalizes the CVRP (Fig. 1).

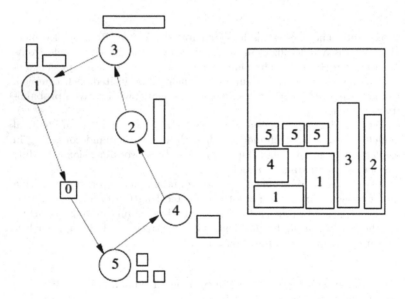

Fig. 1. Example of solution of 2L-CVRP

The 2L-CVRP has an important applications in the fields of logistics or goods distribution. However, in almost all-real world applications, randomness is an inherent characteristic of the problems. For example, in practice whenever a company, in a given day, is faced with only deliveries to a random subset of its usual set of customers, it will not be able to redesign the routes every day since it is not sufficiently important to justify the required effort and cost. Besides, the system's operator may not have the resources for doing so. Even more importantly the operator may have other priorities.

In both cases, the problem of designing routes can very well modeled by introducing a new variant of 2L-CVRP with the above described constraints, denoted as 2L-PCVRP. Among several motivations, 2L-PCVRP is introduced to formulate and analyze models which are more appropriate for real world problems. 2L-PCVRP is characterized by the stochastic presence of the customers. It means that the number of customers to be visited each time is a random variable, where the probability that a certain customer requires a visit is given. This class of problems differs from the Stochastic Vehicle Routing Problem (SVRP) in the sense that here we are concerned only with routing costs without the introduction of additional parameters [3,5,22,23].

2L-PCVRP has not been previously studied in the literature. The only closely related work we are aware of is the deterministic version 2L-CVRP [16] and Probabilistic Vehicle Routing Problem (PVRP) [4].

In fact, compared with the number of studies available on classical CVRP, relatively few papers have been published on optimizing both routing of vehicles and loading constraints. For deterministic 2L-CVRP, Iori et al. [16] presented an exact algorithm for the solution of the problem. The algorithm is making use of both classical valid inequalities from CVRP literature and specific inequalities associated with infeasible loading constraints. The algorithm was evaluated on benchmark instances from the CVRP literature, showing a satisfactory behavior for small-size instances. In order to deal with more larger sized instances, heuristic algorithms have been proposed. Gendereau et al. [13] developed a Tabu search for the 2L-CVRP. The resolution of the routing aspect is handled through the use of Taburoute, a Tabu search heuristic developed by Gendreau et al. [12] for the CVRP. Some improvements were proposed to the above Tabu search, Fuellerer et al. [10] have proposed an Ant Colony Optimization algorithm, as a generalization of savings algorithm by Clarke and Wright [7] through the addition of loading constraints.

Our aim is to develop a hybrid heuristic for the 2L-PCVRP, to solve the perturbation of the initial problem 2L-CVRP, through a combination of sweep heuristic [14] and a branch and bound algorithm [1].

This paper is organized as follows: Sect. 2 exhibits a detailed description of the problem. Section 3 presents the proposed algorithm for the solution of the 2L-PCVRP. In Sect. 4, computational results are discussed and Sect. 5 draws some conclusions.

2   Problem Description

2L-PCVRP is a NP-Hard since it generalizes two NP-Hard problems that have been treated separately 2L-CVRP and PVRP [4]. In fact, 2L-PCVRP belongs to the class of Probabilistic Combinatorial Optimization Problems (PCOP) which was introduced by Jaillet [17] and studied in [1,4,6].

So, 2L-PCVRP is formulated as follows. We consider a complete undirected graph $G = (V, E)$, in which V defines the set of $n + 1$ vertex corresponding to the depot v_0 and the n customers $(v_1, ..., v_n)$. Each customer v_i is associated with a set of m_i rectangular items, whose total weight is equal to his demand d_i, and each having specific width and height equal to w_{il} and h_{il}, $(l = 1, .., m_i)$. A fleet of identical vehicles is available. Each vehicle has a capacity Q and a rectangular loading surface S, for loading operations, whose width and height are respectively equal to W and H.

Let P be the probability distribution defined on the subset of V: $\mathbb{P}(V)$, τ be a given an a priori route through V. Let L_τ be a real random variable defined on, $\mathbb{P}(V)$, which in an a priori route τ and for each S of $\mathbb{P}(V)$, associates the length of the route through S. For each subset $S \subseteq V$, we consider $\mathcal{U}$ a modification method, it consists in erasing from τ the absent vertices by remaining in the same order. The solution of the problem consists on finding an a priori route visiting all points that minimizes the expected length $\mathbb{E}$ of a route τ [4,17] (Fig. 2).

$$\mathbb{E}(L_{\tau,\mathcal{U}}) = \sum_{S \subseteq V} p(S) L_{\tau,\mathcal{U}}(S) \tag{1}$$

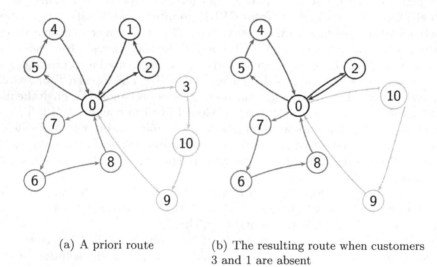

(a) A priori route

(b) The resulting route when customers
3 and 1 are absent

Fig. 2. Example of a priori route for PVRP

In our approach, the priori route is built satisfying the next conditions:

1. Each route starts and ends at the depot.
2. The total customers demands on one route does not exceed vehicle routing capacity Q.
3. All the items of a given customer must be loaded on the same vehicle (each customer is visited once).
4. Items don't have a fixed orientation (a rotation of 90° is allowed).
5. The items delivered on each route must fit within the loading surface S of the vehicle, their total weight should not exceed capacity Q.
6. The loading and unloading surface side of the vehicle is placed at height H.

An alternative approach to define 2L-PCVRP is as a combination of the probabilistic travelling salesman problem (PTSP), with a loading constraints which are closely related to the classical and extensively studied 2BPP [20,21]. The PTSP is the probabilistic version of the well-known problem Travelling salesman problem (TSP), which was introduced by Jaillet [6,17,18]. PTSP calls for the determination of priori route of minimal expected total length and 2BPP occurs in determination of packing the given set of rectangular items into the loading surface of the vehicle.

3   Hybrid Heuristic for 2L-PCVRP

Few papers have proposed methods of resolution for PCOPs [1,4,24], in this section we present a hybrid heuristic for the solution of 2L-PCVRP based on a branch and bound algorithm for PTSP which proved to be a successful technique. The hybrid heuristic proceed in two stages:

1. Sweep Algorithm [14]: we determine clusters (groups of customers) satisfying the six conditions cited above.
2. Each obtained cluster is considered an instance of PTSP, we solve it with the branch and bound algorithm [1].

3.1   Sweep Algorithm

The customers are swept in a clockwise direction around a center gravity which is the depot and assigned to groups. Specifically, the sweep algorithm is the following:

Step 1: Calculate for each customer, his polar coordinate θ_i in relation to the depot. Renumber the customers according to polar coordinates so that:

$$\theta_i < \theta_{i+1}, 1 \leq i \leq n \tag{2}$$

Step 2: Start from the non clustered customer j with smallest angle θ_j construct a new cluster by sweeping consecutive customers $j+1, j+2 \ldots$ until the capacity and the bounding of loading surface constraints will not allow the next customer to be added. This means that each cluster must lead to a feasible packing (items of cluster customers are packed without overlapping the loading surface).

It is clear that it is complex to take into account the 2BPP with the loading of the items into the vehicles, with the additional side constraint that all the items of any given customer must be loaded into the same bin. Concerning the complexity, note that the 2BPP is an NP-hard combinatorial optimization problem (see [11]). To this end, simple packing heuristic Bottom-Left [2] is used to solve 2BPP instances. Bottom-Left consists in packing the current item in the lowest possible position, left justified of open bin; if no bin can allocate it, a new one is initialized. The algorithm has $\mathcal{O}(n^2)$ time complexity.

Step 3: Continue Step 2 until all customers are included in a cluster.

Step 4: Solving each cluster, is tantamount solving an instance of PTSP, where each customer has a probability of presence p_i. The solution consists in finding a priori route visiting the cluster customers which minimizes the expected total length of the route τ.

3.2   Probabilistic Branch and Bound Algorithm

The overall aim is to perform a depth-first traversal of a binary tree by assigning to each branch a probabilistic evaluation. We consider M the distance matrix between the customers. This exact algorithm for solution of the PTSP, is based on the expected length of a route introduced by Jaillet [17]. Let $d(i,j)$ be a distance between the customers $i = \text{ABCD}\cdots = v_1v_2v_3\ldots$, $j = \text{ABCD}\cdots = v_1v_2v_3\ldots$, and $p = P(k) \; \forall k \in \tau$, $q = 1-p$ where p is the probability of presence, the expected length of a route τ is shown by (3) (Table 1).

Table 1. Matrix example

$$M= \begin{array}{c|c|c|c|c} & A & B & C & D \\ \hline A & \infty & d_{AB} & d_{AC} & d_{AD} \\ B & d_{BA} & \infty & d_{BC} & d_{BD} \\ C & d_{CA} & d_{CB} & \infty & d_{CD} \\ D & d_{DA} & d_{DB} & d_{DC} & \infty \end{array}$$

$$E(L_\tau) = p^2 \sum_{r=0}^{n-2} q^r \sum_{i=1}^{n} d(i, T^r(i)) \qquad (3)$$

Where $T^r(i)$ is the successor number r of i in the route τ.

This design takes the form of "Branch and Bound of Little et al. [19]" but in the probabilistic framework, by deriving the equations of the evaluations, in order to direct the search space towards the promising sub-spaces (i.e., the possibility of finding the optimal solution is very likely).

In the same manner of Littel's algorithm for the TSP, we reduce the matrix. The lower bound for the TSP equals Ev_{TSP}, which will help us to calculate the initial evaluation for the PTSP.

$$Ev_{TSP}(n) = \sum_{i=1}^{n} \min R_i + \sum_{j=1}^{n} \min C_j \qquad (4)$$

where R_i is the ith row and C_i is the jth column.

Let $G = (V, E, M)$ be a graph such as $|V| = n$, V is the set of vertices, E the set of edges and M is distance matrix. The probabilistic evaluation $P.E_{PTSP}$: which is defined as follows is considered as a lower evaluation for the PTSP.

$$P.E_\Omega = P.Ev_{PTSP}(n) = Ev_{TSP}(n)(p^2 \sum_{r=0}^{n-2} q^r) = Ev_{TSP}(n)p(1 - q^{n-1}) \qquad (5)$$

This first evaluation associated with the root Ω of the tree shown in Fig. 3. Then, for the next two nodes of the tree, the next two transitional probabilistic evaluations are given due to choice of an arc, according to its effect on the construction of the optimal route. For the arc AB (the same for other arcs):

1. Choose AB: increase the expected length of the route at least by

$$P.Ev_{AB} = P.Ev_{\Omega} + p^2 \sum_{r=1}^{n-2} q^r [\min_{X \neq A}^{(r)} d(A, X)] + p^2 Ev_{TSP_{Next}} \qquad (6)$$

Where $Ev_{TSP_{Next}}$ is the evaluation of resulting matrix for the TSP where row A and column B are removed.

2. Not choose AB: increase the expected length of the route at least by

$$P.Ev_{\overline{AB}} = P.Ev_{\Omega} + p^2 [\min_{K \neq B}^{(1)} d(A, K) + \min_{K \neq A}^{(1)} (d(K, B))] \qquad (7)$$
$$+ p^2 \sum_{r=2}^{n-2} q^r [\min_{X \neq K}^{(r)} d(A, X) + \min_{X \neq B}^{(r)} d(K, X)]$$

$P.Ev_{\overline{AB}}$ represents the probabilistic penalty cost for the arc $\overline{AB}$, $\min^{(i)} d(A, X)$ is the ith minimum of row A, n is the size of the initial matrix. These formulas are valid for all iterations.

The construction starts from the root of the tree, which equals $P.E_{\Omega}$. The problem is divided into two sub-problems with the approach (depth-first, breadth-first) according to the probabilistic penalties cost. After the penalty calculation, it is easily to get the biggest probabilistic penalty cost. So, we separate according to this arc. First remove the row, column and replace the chosen arc by ∞ to prohibiting the parasitic circuits (Table 2).

Table 2. Probabilistic penalties

		A	B	C	D
M=$M_{reduced}$=	A	∞	$(P.Ev_{\overline{AB}})0(P.Ev_{AB})$	-	-
	B	-	∞	-	-
	C	-	-	∞	-
	D	-	-	-	∞

According to this probabilistic penalty calculation, we construct the first branching of the tree, which is shown in Fig. 3.

The search continues until all branches that have been visited are either eliminated or the end of the process is reached. That is, the present evaluation is less than the all evaluations, which are defined by the expected length of each final branch by profiting that the expected length can be calculated in $O(n^2)$ time Jaillet [17].

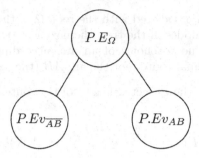

Fig. 3. Branching of the tree for the PTSP

4　Computational Results

In this section, we first compare our method over the benchmark proposed by Iori et al. [16] for the deterministic 2L-CVRP (we suppose that all customers are present). Next, we exhibit the new instances for 2L-PCVRP, before analyzing the performance of the proposed heuristic on those instances. The final results are reported at the end. The algorithm was coded in Java and all tests were performed on a typical PC with i5-5200U CPU (2.2 GHz) under Windows 8 system.

4.1　Comparison on the 2L-CVRP

By assuming that all customers have a probability of occurrence ($p = 1$), deterministic instances of 2L-CVRP are obtained. In this case, our algorithm is only compared to the approach proposed by Iori et al. [16]. The algorithm of Iori was coded in C and was run on a PC with CPU 3 GHz. Because Gendreau et al. [13] and Fuellerer et al. [10] do not solve the problem under the same constraints as we do, direct comparisons with their algorithms can not be made.

To test their algorithm, Iori et al. proposed a benchmark of five classes, for a total of 180 instances. The benchmark presents the coordinates (x_i, y_i), the demand d_i and the items m_i of each customer.

Five classes are considered, which differ in number of customers, number of items, generated items and vehicle capacity. In the first class of instances, each customer has only one item of width and height equal to 1. However, we observed that packing was not constraining so the instances are reduced to the classical CVRP. For the other classes, each customer has 1 to r items in type r ($1 \leq r \leq 5$). The number of items and items dimensions were randomly generated. For all five classes the loading surface of vehicles was fixed to $W = 20$ and $H = 40$. The largest instance have up to 255 customers, 786 items and a fleet of 51 vehicles. Table 3 summarizes the different benchmark classes.

Table 3. Classes used for the generation of items

Class	m_i	w_{il}	h_{il}
1	1	1	1
2	[1,2]	$[\frac{W}{10}, \frac{2W}{10}]$, $[\frac{2W}{10}, \frac{5W}{10}]$, $[\frac{4W}{10}, \frac{9W}{10}]$	$[\frac{4H}{10}, \frac{9H}{10}]$, $[\frac{2H}{10}, \frac{5H}{10}]$, $[\frac{H}{10}, \frac{2H}{10}]$
3	[1,3]	$[\frac{W}{10}, \frac{2W}{10}]$, $[\frac{2W}{10}, \frac{4W}{10}]$, $[\frac{3W}{10}, \frac{8W}{10}]$	$[\frac{3H}{10}, \frac{8H}{10}]$, $[\frac{2H}{10}, \frac{4H}{10}]$, $[\frac{H}{10}, \frac{2H}{10}]$
4	[1,4]	$[\frac{W}{10}, \frac{2W}{10}]$, $[\frac{W}{10}, \frac{4W}{10}]$, $[\frac{2W}{10}, \frac{7W}{10}]$	$[\frac{2H}{10}, \frac{7H}{10}]$, $[\frac{H}{10}, \frac{4H}{10}]$, $[\frac{H}{10}, \frac{2H}{10}]$
5	[1,5]	$[\frac{W}{10}, \frac{2W}{10}]$, $[\frac{W}{10}, \frac{3W}{10}]$, $[\frac{W}{10}, \frac{6W}{10}]$	$[\frac{H}{10}, \frac{6H}{10}]$, $[\frac{H}{10}, \frac{3H}{10}]$, $[\frac{H}{10}, \frac{2H}{10}]$

Table 4 presents the comparison of the two approaches. Since the unloading constrains are not considered in our approach, we only compared the total time spent by routing procedures. In each case, we indicate the number of solved instances by both algorithms as well as the average of routing CPU time in seconds for solving those instances.

Table 4. Comparison of two algorithms for deterministic 2L-CVRP

Type	Solved instances	Iori et al.	Our Hybrid heuristic
		T_{Rout}	T_{Rout}
1	10	38.33	9.49
2	11	620.77	7.30
3	11	1804.50	8.17
4	10	436.91	8.35
5	11	134.38	11.57
Average		624.99	8.79

Overall, our algorithm was able to solve instances with up to 255 customers and 786 items while the algorithm of Iori et al. was limited to maximum of 35 customers and 114 items. For the 53 instances solved by both algorithms, our hybrid heuristic took only few seconds compared to hundreds and thousands for the algorithm of Iori et al. This is a very considerable gain, if we take also into account the different performances of the machines used to run the two algorithms.

4.2   Probabilistic Instances

We exploited the 2L-CVRP benchmark described in the previous section to generate our probabilistic instances. Since packing problems do not occur for the class of type 1, when solving all its instances, so we omit it from tests. For each of the 4 classes, we performed tests on 14 instances that differ in numbers of customers varying in $\{15, 20, 25, 30, 35, 45, 50, 75, 100, 120, 134, 150, 200, 255\}$

Table 5. Summary of final results

n	Q	p	Class 2				Class 3				Class 4				Class 5			
			Inst	T_{clust}	T_{rout}	T_{tot}	Inst	T_{clust}	T_{rout}	T_{tot}	Inst	T_{clust}	T_{rout}	T_{tot}	Inst	T_{clust}	T_{rout}	T_{tot}
15	90	0.1	0102	0.41	0.31	0.73	0103	0.39	0.41	0.80	0104	0.50	0.34	0.84	0105	0.56	0.43	1.00
		0.3		0.42	0.30	0.72		0.40	0.39	0.80		0.51	0.27	0.78		0.57	0.42	0.99
		0.5		0.42	0.29	0.72		0.40	0.38	0.79		0.51	0.20	0.72		0.57	0.41	0.98
		0.7		0.46	0.24	0.71		0.40	0.38	0.78		0.51	0.20	0.72		0.65	0.29	0.95
		0.9		0.45	0.23	0.68		0.39	0.34	0.73		0.46	0.19	0.65		0.56	0.27	0.83
20	85	0.1	0302	0.59	0.35	0.94	0303	0.46	0.67	1.13	0304	0.51	0.70	1.22	0305	0.54	1.18	1.73
		0.3		0.58	0.28	0.86		0.45	0.60	1.05		0.53	0.67	1.20		0.63	0.90	1.54
		0.5		0.56	0.18	0.75		0.45	0.52	0.97		0.50	0.69	1.19		0.94	0.40	1.35
		0.7		0.41	0.19	0.61		0.46	0.43	0.89		0.46	0.70	1.17		0.81	0.35	1.16
		0.9		0.41	0.06	0.48		0.43	0.49	0.92		0.48	0.635	1.11		0.76	0.32	1.08
25	48	0.1	0902	0.47	0.27	0.75	0903	0.48	0.69	1.18	0904	0.51	0.54	1.05	0.90	0.59	0.70	1.30
		0.3		0.45	0.25	0.71		0.46	0.61	1.08		0.54	0.48	1.02		0.60	0.67	1.28
		0.5		0.45	0.25	0.70		0.48	0.51	0.99		0.53	0.45	0.98		0.95	0.21	1.17
		0.7		0.45	0.24	0.69		0.45	0.44	0.90		0.54	0.43	0.98		0.60	0.54	1.15
		0.9		0.45	0.23	0.68		0.46	0.40	0.87		0.55	0.39	0.95		0.70	0.44	1.14
30	68	0.1	1202	0.61	0.37	0.98	1203	0.40	0.95	1.36	1204	0.59	0.59	1.19	1205	0.68	0.98	1.67
		0.3		0.61	0.34	0.95		0.45	0.80	1.25		0.61	0.53	1.14		0.68	0.81	1.50
		0.5		0.60	0.31	0.91		0.43	0.64	1.08		0.58	0.50	1.09		0.67	0.66	1.34
		0.7		0.58	0.29	0.87		0.54	0.37	0.91		0.64	0.40	1.04		0.88	0.29	1.17
		0.9		0.50	0.26	0.76		0.50	0.34	0.84		0.60	0.41	1.02		0.90	0.26	1.16
35	67	0.1	1602	0.43	0.41	0.84	1603	0.51	0.68	1.19	1604	0.88	0.47	1.36	1605	0.95	0.61	1.57
		0.3		0.30	0.35	0.65		0.54	0.56	1.10		0.67	0.57	1.24		0.92	0.45	1.37
		0.5		0.18	0.28	0.46		0.51	0.50	1.02		0.66	0.46	1.12		0.98	0.31	1.29
		0.7		0.11	0.16	0.28		0.65	0.27	0.93		0.79	0.21	1.01		0.90	0.30	1.21
		0.9		0.10	0.17	0.28		0.50	0.41	0.91		0.71	0.25	0.96		0.78	0.24	1.02
45	60	0.1	1702	0.63	0.51	1.15	1703	0.52	0.77	1.29	1704	0.75	0.99	1.74	1705	0.82	0.40	1.23
		0.3		0.58	0.43	1.01		0.48	0.63	1.12		0.73	0.79	1.52		0.91	0.26	1.17
		0.5		0.53	0.34	0.88		0.57	0.36	0.94		0.65	0.65	1.31		0.85	0.17	1.02
		0.7		0.48	0.26	0.74		0.50	0.26	0.76		0.65	0.44	1.10		0.88	0.09	0.98
		0.9		0.23	0.12	0.36		0.22	0.18	0.40		0.62	0.38	1.00		0.74	0.14	0.88
50	160	0.1	1902	0.58	0.56	1.15	1903	0.62	0.79	1.41	1904	0.96	0.38	1.34	1905	0.96	1.24	2.21
		0.3		0.58	0.55	1.13		0.60	0.78	1.38		0.91	0.40	1.31		1.18	0.89	2.07
		0.5		0.64	0.46	1.11		0.67	0.68	1.35		0.92	0.36	1.29		9.85	0.94	1.92
		0.7		0.65	0.43	1.08		0.70	0.62	1.32		0.89	0.39	1.28		1.01	0.77	1.78
		0.9		0.64	0.35	0.99		0.75	0.54	1.29		0.87	0.38	1.26		1.03	0.71	1.75
75	100	0.1	2402	0.70	0.72	1.43	2403	0.73	0.59	1.33	2404	1.22	0.38	1.61	2405	1.29	0.67	1.96
		0.3		0.73	0.53	1.26		0.75	0.57	1.32		1.12	0.44	1.57		1.20	0.72	1.93
		0.5		0.68	0.42	1.10		0.81	0.49	1.30		1.14	0.38	1.53		1.18	0.69	1.89
		0.7		0.69	0.40	1.10		0.76	0.52	1.29		1.01	0.47	1.49		1.19	0.66	1.86
		0.9		0.54	0.39	0.94		0.75	0.50	1.25		1.28	0.19	1.47		1.28	0.51	1.79
100	112	0.1	2702	0.88	0.61	1.49	2703	0.87	1.34	2.22	2704	1.56	0.40	1.96	2705	1.71	0.69	2.41
		0.3		0.87	0.54	1.41		0.89	1.08	1.97		1.65	0.24	1.90		1.95	0.90	2.85
		0.5		0.78	0.54	1.33		0.92	0.81	1.73		1.53	0.29	1.83		1.79	0.50	2.30
		0.7		0.79	0.49	1.24		0.89	0.60	1.49		1.43	0.32	1.76		1.73	0.51	2.24
		0.9		0.73	0.35	1.08		0.92	0.47	1.39		1.34	0.30	1.64		1.75	0.38	2.13
120	200	0.1	2802	0.89	0.60	1.50	2803	1.00	1.74	2.74	2804	1.80	1.74	3.54	2805	2.19	1.17	3.36
		0.3		0.89	0.55	1.44		1.05	1.25	2.31		1.68	1.64	3.33		2.38	0.70	3.08
		0.5		0.88	0.50	1.39		0.96	0.91	1.88		1.62	1.12	2.74		2.38	0.42	2.80
		0.7		0.95	0.38	1.33		1.01	0.43	1.45		2.13	0.39	2.53		2.39	0.13	2.52
		0.9		0.95	0.36	1.32		1.03	0.31	1.34		1.17	0.55	1.73		1.45	0.52	1.97
134	2210	0.1	2902	1.01	0.50	1.51	2903	0.86	0.81	1.68	2904	1.10	2.38	3.49	2905	1.78	1.55	3.34
		0.3		0.96	0.49	1.46		0.92	1.06	1.98		1.34	1.54	2.88		1.71	1.24	2.96
		0.5		0.90	0.51	1.41		0.90	1.32	2.23		1.34	0.93	2.27		1.89	0.69	2.58
		0.7		0.88	0.53	1.41		0.95	1.51	2.47		1.33	0.33	1.66		1.78	0.41	2.20
		0.9		0.87	0.49	1.36		0.95	1.81	2.71		1.26	0.23	1.50		1.54	0.23	1.78
150	200	0.1	3002	0.93	0.64	1.57	3003	0.92	1.35	2.27	3004	1.28	1.72	3.00	3005	1.94	1.39	3.33
		0.3		0.96	0.55	1.52		0.95	1.01	1.96		1.18	1.64	2.83		2.08	1.07	3.15
		0.5		0.87	0.61	1.48		0.96	0.69	1.66		1.25	1.19	2.44		1.97	1.00	2.97
		0.7		0.87	0.61	1.48		0.96	0.71	1.68		1.21	0.82	2.04		2.00	0.97	2.79
		0.9		0.87	0.61	1.49		0.98	0.39	1.38		1.54	0.45	2.00		2.15	0.63	2.79
200	200	0.1	3302	1.06	1.53	2.59	3303	1.24	1.31	2.35	3304	1.63	1.41	3.05	3305	2.25	2.14	4.39
		0.3		1.06	1.39	2.45		1.26	1.05	2.31		1.45	1.44	2.89		2.06	1.93	4.00
		0.5		1.23	1.06	2.29		1.21	1.06	2.27		1.39	1.34	2.74		1.97	1.63	3.60
		0.7		1.20	0.94	2.14		1.25	0.97	2.23		1.56	1.18	2.74		1.97	1.24	3.21
		0.9		1.18	0.84	2.03		1.56	0.44	2.01		1.96	0.62	2.58		2.48	0.59	3.07
255	1000	0.1	3602	1.28	1.65	2.93	3603	1.62	1.21	2.83	3604	1.69	1.55	3.25	3605	2.68	1.93	4.62
		0.3		1.30	1.49	2.80		1.62	1.03	2.66		1.67	1.46	3.14		2.53	1.73	4.26
		0.5		1.31	1.35	2.67		1.39	1.08	2.48		1.59	1.48	3.07		2.46	1.44	3.91
		0.7		1.26	1.27	2.53		1.26	1.04	2.30		1.48	1.52	3.00		2.61	0.95	3.56
		0.9		1.23	1.25	2.49		1.75	0.54	2.29		1.94	0.92	2.87		2.53	1.19	3.72

(255 the largest number of customers in the benchmark). For the $14 * 4 = 56$ instances, we generated 5 different probabilistic instances, for a total of 280, by varying the probability of presence $p \in \{0.1, 0.3, 0.5, 0.7, 0.9\}$.

The computational results are summarized in Table 5. Each instance is represented by a four digits number : the first two digits corresponds to the instance number, while the last two digits identify the instance class. The column denoted "n" represents the number of customers. The table shows T_{clust} representing the CPU time used by the sweep algorithm. T_{rout} gives the CPU time for generating routes to all clusters using the branch and bound algorithm. T_{tot} reports the total CPU time used by the overall heuristic ($T_{tot} = T_{clust} + T_{rout}$). All times are expressed in seconds.

By observing Table 5, we may see that the proposed heuristic was able to solve all instances with up to 255 customers within moderate computing time. We observed that the heuristic is sensitive to the type of items. In fact, T_{clust} arise increasingly from class 2 to class 5 and this is explained by the fact that class 5 is characterized by a large number of items compared to the rest of classes, if we consider the same instance. This is a typical feature of 2BPP.

As matter of fact, T_{clust}, including the CPU time for packing customers items, absorbs a very large part of T_{tot}.

When addressing larger instances of 2L-PCVRP, the complexity of the problem increases consistently. This is, however, not surprising because it is well known that the two problems PTSP and 2BPP are NP-hard. We can observe, for the same probability of presence, an increase of T_{tot} going to a factor of 4 (from 1 s to 4 s).

Table 5 shows that a higher percentage of stochastic customers (low values of probability of presence p) increases the complexity of the problem, as indicated by T_{tot}. For example, when the probability of presence equals 0.1, T_{tot} increases from 166 ms to 1.55 s through all tested instances.

5   Conclusion and Future Work

This paper has introduced a probabilistic variant of 2L-CVRP, where each customer has a probability of presence. 2L-PCVRP combines the well known probabilistic travelling salesman problem and the two-dimensional bin packing problem.

A hybrid heuristic was presented to deal with the new variant, 2L-PCVRP. The heuristic, is consisted of two phases, where in the first phase, the sweep algorithm was used to generate clusters of customers. Each cluster is solved using a branch and bound algorithm.

The proposed heuristic solved successfully all instances derived for 2L-PCVRP, involving up to 255 customers and 786 items. On the deterministic 2L-CVRP, the heuristic outperformed another state-of-the-art of an exact algorithm.

Future work will consider different variants where, for example, stochastic customers and items are considered.

Acknowledgement. Thanks to Mohamed Abdellahi Amar for his contribution to this article. We are grateful for the valuable discussions and for providing the Branch and Bound source code.

References

1. Abdellahi Amar, M., Khaznaji, W., Bellalouna, M.: An exact resolution for the probabilistic traveling salesman problem under the a priori strategy. Procedia Comput. Sci. **108**, 1414–1423 (2017). International Conference on Computational Science, ICCS 2017, 12–14 June 2017, Zurich, Switzerland
2. Baker, B., Coffman, E., Rivest, R.: Orthogonal packing in two dimensions. SIAM J. Comput. **9**(4), 846–855 (1980)
3. Berhan, E., Beshah, B., Kitaw, D., Abraham, A.: Stochastic vehicle routing problem: a literature survey. J. Inf. Knowl. Manage. **13**(3) (2014)
4. Bertsimas, D.: The probabilistic vehicle routing problem. Ph.D. thesis, Sloan School of Management, Massachusetts Institute of Technology (1988)
5. Bertsimas, D.: A vehicle routing problem with stochastic demand. Oper. Res. **40**(3), 574–585 (1992)
6. Bertsimas, D., Jaillet, P., Odoni, A.: A priori optimization. Oper. Res. **38**(6), 1019–1033 (1990)
7. Clarke, G., Wright, J.: Scheduling of vehicles from a central depot to a number of delivery points. Oper. Res. **12**(4), 568–581 (1964)
8. Côté, J., Potvin, J., Gendreau, M.: The Vehicle Routing Problem with Stochastic Two-dimensional Items. CIRRELT, CIRRELT (Collection) (2013)
9. Dantzig, G., Ramser, J.: The truck dispatching problem. Manage. Sci. **6**(1), 80–91 (1959)
10. Fuellerer, G., Doerner, K., Hartl, R., Iori, M.: Ant colony optimization for the two-dimensional loading vehicle routing problem. Comput. Oper. Res. **36**(3), 655–673 (2009)
11. Garey, M., Johnson, D.: Computers and Intractability: A Guide to the Theory of NP-Completeness. W. H. Freeman & Co., New York (1979)
12. Gendreau, M., Hertz, A., Laporte, G.: A tabu search heuristic for the vehicle routing problem. Manage. Sci. **40**(10), 1276–1290 (1994)
13. Gendreau, M., Iori, M., Laporte, G., Martello, S.: A tabu search heuristic for the vehicle routing problem with two-dimensional loading constraints. Networks **51**(1), 4–18 (2008)
14. Gillett, E., Miller, R.: A heuristic algorithm for the vehicle-dispatch problem. Oper. Res. **22**(2), 340–349 (1974)
15. Iori, M., Martello, S.: Routing problems with loading constraints. TOP **18**(1), 4–27 (2010)
16. Iori, M., Salazar-González, J., Vigo, D.: An exact approach for the vehicle routing problem with two-dimensional loading constraints. Transp. Sci. **41**(2), 253–264 (2007)
17. Jaillet, P.: Probabilistic traveling Salesman Problem. Ph.D. thesis, MIT, Operations Research Center (1985)
18. Jaillet, P.: A priori solution of a traveling salesman problem in which a random subset of the customers are visited. Oper. Res. **36**(6), 929–936 (1988)
19. Little, J.D.C., Murty, K.G., Sweeney, D.W., Karel, C.: An algorithm for the traveling salesman problem. Oper. Res. **11**(6), 972–989 (1963)

20. Lodi, A., Martello, S., Monaci, M.: Two-dimensional packing problems: a survey. Eur. J. Oper. Res. **141**(2), 241–252 (2002)
21. Lodi, A., Martello, S., Monaci, M., Vigo, D.: Two-Dimensional Bin Packing Problems, pp. 107–129. Wiley-Blackwell (2014)
22. Oyola, J., Arntzen, H., Woodruff, D.: The stochastic vehicle routing problem, a literature review, part i: models. EURO J. Transp. Logistics (2016)
23. Oyola, J., Arntzen, H., Woodruff, D.: The stochastic vehicle routing problem, a literature review, part ii: solution methods. EURO J. Transp. Logistics **6**(4), 349–388 (2017)
24. Rosenow, S.: Comparison of an exact branch-and-bound and an approximative evolutionary algorithm for the Probabilistic Traveling Salesman Problem. In: Kall, P., Lüthi, H.J. (eds.) Operations Research Proceedings 1998, pp. 168–174. Springer, Heidelberg (1999). https://doi.org/10.1007/978-3-642-58409-1_16
25. Toth, P., Vigo, D.: The vehicle routing problem. In: An Overview of Vehicle Routing Problems, pp. 1–26 (2001)

A Human-Inspired Model to Represent Uncertain Knowledge in the Semantic Web

Salvatore Flavio Pileggi[✉]

School of Systems, Management and Leadership,
University of Technology Sydney, Ultimo, NSW 2007, Australia
SalvatoreFlavio.Pileggi@uts.edu.au

Abstract. One of the most evident and well-known limitations of the Semantic Web technology is its lack of capability to deal with uncertain knowledge. As uncertainty is often part of the knowledge itself or can be inducted by external factors, such a limitation may be a serious barrier for some practical applications. A number of approaches have been proposed to extend the capabilities in terms of uncertainty representation; some of them are just theoretical or not compatible with the current semantic technology; others focus exclusively on data spaces in which uncertainty is or can be quantified. Human-inspired models have been adopted in the context of different disciplines and domains (e.g. robotics and human-machine interaction) and could be a novel, still largely unexplored, pathway to represent uncertain knowledge in the Semantic Web. Human-inspired models are expected to address uncertainties in a way similar to the human one. Within this paper, we (i) briefly point out the limitations of the Semantic Web technology in terms of uncertainty representation, (ii) discuss the potentialities of human-inspired solutions to represent uncertain knowledge in the Semantic Web, (iii) present a human-inspired model and (iv) a reference architecture for implementations in the context of the legacy technology.

1 Introduction

Many systems are experiencing a constant evolution, working on data spaces of an increasing scale and complexity. It leads to a continuous demand for advanced interoperability models, which has pushed the progressive development of the Semantic Web technology [1]. Such a technology, as the name itself suggests, deals with the specification of formal semantics aimed at giving meanings to disparate raw data, information and knowledge. It enables in fact interoperable data spaces suitable to advanced automatic reasoning.

The higher mature level of the Semantic Web infrastructure includes a number of languages (e.g. RDF [2], OWL [3], SWRL [4]) to define ontologies via rich data models capable to specify concepts, relations, as well as the support for automatic reasoning. Furthermore, a number of valuable supporting assets

© Springer International Publishing AG, part of Springer Nature 2018
Y. Shi et al. (Eds.): ICCS 2018, LNCS 10862, pp. 254–268, 2018.
https://doi.org/10.1007/978-3-319-93713-7_21

are available from the community, including reasoners (e.g. Jena [5], Pellet [6], HermiT [7]) and query capabilities (e.g. ARQ [8]). Those components enable a pervasive interaction with the semantic structures. Last but not the least, ontology developers are supported by user-friendly editors (e.g. Protege [9]).

While the major improvements that have defined the second version of the Web [10] focus on aspects clearly visible to the final users (e.g. the socialization of the Web and enhanced multimedia capabilities), the semantic technology is addressing mainly the data infrastructure of the Web, providing benefits not always directly appreciable from a final user perspective. By enriching the meta-data infrastructure, the Semantic Web aims at providing a kind of universal language to define and share knowledge across the Web.

The popularity of the Semantic Web in research is tangible just looking at the massive number of works on the topic currently in literature, as well as at the constant presence of semantic layers or assets in research projects dealing with data, information and knowledge in the context of different domains and disciplines. Although the actual impact in the real world is still to be evaluated, there are significant evidences of application, as recent studies (e.g. [11]) have detected structured or linked data (semantics) over a significant number of websites.

Despite the Semantic Web is unanimously considered a sophisticated environment, it doesn't support the representation of uncertain knowledge, at least considering the "official" technology. In practice, many systems deal with some uncertainty. Indeed, there is a potentially infinite heterogeneous range of intelligible/unintelligible situations which involve imperfect and/or unknown knowledge. Focusing on computer systems, uncertainty can be part of the knowledge itself, as well as it may be inducted as the consequence of adopting a given model (e.g. simplified) or of applying a certain process, mechanism or solution.

Structure of the Paper. The introductory part of the paper continues with two sub-sections that deal, respectively, with a brief discussion of related work and human-inspired models to represent uncertainty within ontology-based systems. The core part of the paper is composed of 3 sections: first the conceptual framework is described from a theoretical perspective (Sect. 2); then, Sect. 3 focuses on the metrics to measure the uncertainty in the context of the proposed framework; finally, Sect. 4 deals with a reference architecture for implementations compatible with the legacy Semantic Web technology. As usual, the paper ends with a conclusions section.

1.1 Related Work

Several theoretical works aiming at the representation of the uncertainty in the Semantic Web have been proposed in the past years. A comprehensive discussion of such models and their limitations is out of the scope of this paper.

Most works in literature are usual to model the uncertainty according to a numerical or quantitative approach. They rely on different theories including, among others, fuzzy logic (e.g. [12]), rough sets (e.g. [13]) and Bayesian models (e.g. [14]). A pragmatic class of implementations is usual to extend the most common languages with the probability theory [15]: Probabilistic RDF [16] extends RDF [2]; Probabilistic Ontology (e.g. [17]) defines a set of possible extensions for OWL [18]; Probabilistic SWRL [19] provides extensions for SWRL [4].

Generally speaking, a numerical approach to uncertainty representation is effective, completely generic, relatively simple and intrinsically suitable to computational environments. However, such an approach assumes that all uncertainties are or can be quantified. Ontologies are rich data models that implement the conceptualisation of some complex reality. Within knowledge-based systems adopting ontologies, uncertainties may depend on underpinning systems and are not always quantified. The representation of uncertainties that cannot be explicitly quantified is one of the key challenges to address.

1.2   Why Human-Inspired Models?

A more qualitative representation of the uncertainty in line with the intrinsic conceptual character of ontological models is the main object of this paper. As discussed in the previous sub-section, considering the uncertainty in a completely generic way is definitely a point. However, in terms of semantics it could represent an issue as, depending on the considered context, different types of uncertainty can be identified. Assuming different categories of uncertainty results in higher flexibility, meaning that different ways to represent uncertainties can be provided for the different categories of uncertainty. At the same time, such an approach implies specific solutions aimed at the representation of uncertainties with certain characteristics, rather than a generic model for uncertainty representation.

As discussed later on in the paper, the proposed framework defines different categories of uncertainty and a number of concepts belonging to each category. The framework is human-inspired as it aims at reproducing the different human understandings of uncertainty in a computational context. The underlying idea is the representation of uncertainties according to a model as similar as possible to the human one.

Human-inspired technology is not a novelty and it is largely adopted in many fields including, among others, robotics [20], human-machine interaction [21], control logic [22], granular computing [23], situation understanding [24], trust modeling [25], computational fairness [26] and evolving systems [27].

2   Towards Human-Inspired Models: A Conceptual Framework

The conceptual framework object of this work (Fig. 1) is a simplification of a possible human perception of uncertain knowledge. It distinguishes three main categories of uncertainty. The first category, referred to as *numerical or quantitative uncertainty*, includes the uncertainties that are or can be quantified; this is intrinsically suitable to a computational context and, indeed, has been object of an extensive research, as briefly discussed in the previous sections. The second category, called *qualitative uncertainty*, includes those uncertainties that cannot be quantified. While a quantitative understanding of uncertainty is typical of human reasoning, it is not obvious within computational environments. The third category considered in the framework, referred to as *indirect uncertainty*, is related to factors external to the knowledge represented by the considered ontology. For example, an ontology could be populated by using the information from different datasets; those datasets could have a different quality, as well as the different providers could be associated with a different degree of reliability. It leads indirectly to an uncertainty. The different categories of uncertainty will be discussed separately in the next sub-sections.

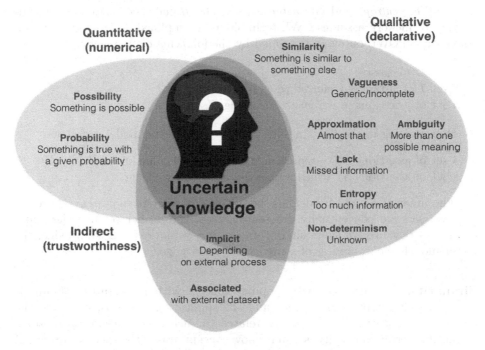

Fig. 1. Conceptual framework.

2.1 Numerical or Quantitative Uncertainty

The quantitative approach relies on the representation of the uncertainty as a numerical value. In a semantic context, it is normally associated with assertions or axioms. As pointed out in the previous sections, such an approach is generic and, in general, effective in a computational context.

On the other hand, it can be successfully adopted within environments in which all uncertainties are or can be quantified. A further (minor) limitation is represented by the interpretation of the "number" associated with the uncertainty that, in certain specific cases, may result ambiguous.

Most numerical approaches are based on the classic concepts of *possibility* or *probability*, as in their common meaning. As quantitative models have been object of several studies and implementations, a comprehensive discussion of those solutions is considered out of the scope of this paper, which rather focuses on qualitative models and indirect uncertainty.

2.2 Qualitative Uncertainty

A non-numerical approach is a major step towards human-inspired conceptualizations of uncertainty. Within the qualitative category, we define a number of concepts, including *similarity, approximation, ambiguity, vagueness, lack of information, entropy* and *non-determinism*. The formal specification of the conceptual framework assumes OWL technology. A simplified abstracted view of a conventional OWL ontology is defined by the following components:

- a set C of classes
- a set I of instances (referred to as individuals) of C
- a set of assertions or axioms S involving C and I

Representing uncertainty implies the extension of the model as follows:

- a set of assertions S^* to represent uncertainty on some knowledge
- a set of assertions S^u which represents lacks of knowledge

The union of S^* and S^u defines the uncertainty in a given system. However, the two sets are conceptually different; indeed, the former set includes those assertions that involve some kind of uncertainty on an existing knowledge; the latter models the awareness of some lack of knowledge.

Similarity. Similarity is a very popular concept within computer systems. It is extensively adopted in a wide range of application domains, in which the elements of a given system can be related to each other, according to some similarity metric. Similarity is a well-know concept also in the specific context of the Semantic Web technology, where *semantic similarity* is normally established on the base of the semantic structures (e.g. [28]).

Unlike most current understandings, where the similarity is associated somehow with knowledge, modeling the uncertainty as a similarity means focusing on the unknown aspect of such a concept [29]. Indeed, the similarity among two concept is not an equivalence.

Given two individuals i and j, and the set of assertion S involving i, a *full similarity* between i and j implies the duplication of all the statements involving i, replacing i with j (Eq. 1a). The duplicated set of axioms is considered an uncertainty within the system.

$$sim(i \in I, j \in I) \Rightarrow \forall s(i, \_) \in S \rightarrow \exists s^*(j, \_) \qquad s^* \in S^* \qquad (1a)$$

$$sim(i \in I, j \in I, S_k \subset S) \Rightarrow \forall s(i, \_) \in S_k \rightarrow \exists s^*(j, \_) \qquad s^* \in S^* \quad \text{(1b)}$$

A full similarity as defined in Eq. 1a is a strong relation, meaning it is conceptually close to a semantic equivalence. The key difference between a semantic equivalence and a full similarity relies in the different understanding of j which, in the latter case, is characterized but also explicitly stated as an uncertainty.

An example of full similarity is depicted in Fig. 2a: a product B is stated similar to a product A in a given context; the two products are produced by different companies; because of the similarity relation, exactly as A, B is recognized to be a soft drink containing caffeine; on the other hand, according to the full similarity model, B is also considered as produced by the same company that produces A, which is wrong in this case.

Partial similarity is a more accurate relation which restricts the similarity and, therefore, the replication of the statements to a subset S_k of specific interest (Eq. 1b). By adopting partial similarity, the previous example may be correctly represented and processed (Fig. 2b): as the similarity is limited at the relations *is* and *contains*, the relation *producedBy* is not affected. *Web of Similarity* [29] provides an implementation of both full and partial similarity. It will be discussed later on in the paper.

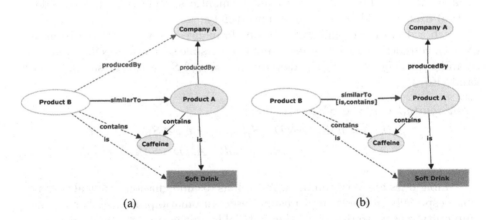

(a)   (b)

Fig. 2. Example of full (a) and partial (b) similarity.

Approximation. Approximation is the natural extension of similarity. Unlike similarity, which applies to instances of classes, the concept of approximation is established among classes (Eq. 2a): a class i which approximates a class j implies each statement involving the members e_i of the class i, replicated to the members e_j of the class j.

$$aprx(i \in C, j \in C) \quad \Rightarrow \quad \forall s(e_i \in i, \_) \rightarrow \exists s^*(e_j \in j, \_)$$
$$s^* \in S^* \quad \text{(2a)}$$

$$aprx(i \in C, j \in C, S_k \subset S) \quad \Rightarrow \quad s(e_i \in i, \_) \in S_k \rightarrow \exists s^*(e_j \in j, \_)$$
$$s^* \in S^* \; (2b)$$

$$aprx(i \in C, j \in C) \quad \Rightarrow \quad \forall e_i \in i \rightarrow e_i \in j$$
$$(e_i \in j) \in S^* \; (2c)$$

As for similarity, we distinguish between a *full approximation* (as in Eq. 2a) and a more accurate variant of the concept (*partial approximation*), for whom the approximation is limited to a set S_k of assertions (Eq. 2b). The semantic of approximation as defined in Eq. 2a and 2b can be considered to be just theoretical, as it is not easy to apply in real contexts. It leads to a much simpler and more pragmatic specification, referred to as *light approximation*, which is defined by Eq. 2c: if the class i approximates the class j, than a member e_i of the class i is also member of the class j.

Ambiguity. According to an intuitive common definition, an ambiguous concept may assume more than one meaning and, therefore, more than one semantic specification. The different possible semantic specifications are considered mutual exclusive. That leads to an uncertainty.

Such a definition of ambiguity can be formalised as an exclusive disjunction (XOR): considering an individual k and two possible semantic specifications of it, S_i and S_j, $ambiguity(k, S_i, S_j)$ denotes that S_i and S_j cannot be simultaneously valid (Eq. 3).

$$ambiguity(k \in I, S_i \in S^*, S_j \in S^*) \Rightarrow$$
$$[S_i(k, \_) = null \quad AND \quad S_j(k, \_) \neq null \in S] \quad XOR$$
$$[S_j(k, \_) = null \quad AND \quad S_i(k, \_) \neq null \in S] \quad (3)$$

Ambiguities are very common. As well as disambiguation is not always possible, especially in presence of unsupervised automatic processes. For instance, ambiguity is usual to rise processing natural language statements. A very simple example of ambiguity is depicted in Fig. 3a: the ambiguity is generated by the homonymy between two football players; each player has his own profile within the system; the link between the considered individual and the profile defines an uncertainty.

The definition of ambiguity as in Eq. 3 allows the correct co-existence of multiple and mutual-exclusive representations.

Lack of Information. A lack of information on a given individual i models those situations in which only a part of the knowledge related to an individual is known. The uncertainty comes from the awareness of a lack of information

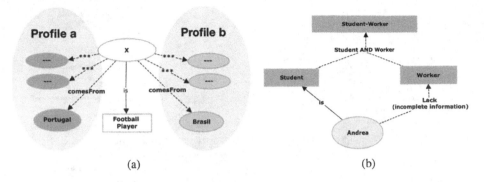

Fig. 3. Example of ambiguity (a) and lack of information (b).

(Eq. 4). The formal specification assumes the existence of a number of unknown assertions (s^u) to integrate the information available S_i.

$$lack(i \in I, S, S^u) \quad \Rightarrow \quad \exists s(i, \_) \in S, \quad \exists s^u(i, \_) \in S^u \tag{4}$$

An example of lack of information is represented in Fig. 3b: considering a database in which people are classified as students or workers, while the information about students is complete, the information about workers presents lacks; it means that a person appearing in the database is definitely recognized as a student if he/she is a student but a person is not always recognized as a worker even if he/she is a worker. That situation produces an evident uncertainty on the main classification; moreover, such an uncertainty is propagated throughout the whole model as it affects the resolution of inference rules (e.g. *student-worker* in the example).

Entropy. Huge amount of complex data may lead to a situation of entropy, meaning a lot of information available but just a small part of it relevant in terms of knowledge in a given context for a certain purpose. Entropic environments are normally not very intelligible and, generally speaking, require important amount of resources to be computed correctly. Within the proposed model, the entropy is a kind of filter for raw data that consider only a subset of statement S_k (Eq. 5).

$$entropy(S, S_k) \quad \Rightarrow \quad S^* = S - S_k \tag{5}$$

In practice, S_k may be defined by considering a restricted number of classes, individuals or relations. An example is shown in Fig. 4a, where a subset of the data space is identified on the base of the relation *contains*. The definition provided is not necessarily addressing an uncertainty. However, in presence of rich data models (ontologies) that include inference rules, the result of a given reasoning might be not completely correct as inference rules apply just to a part of the information. Those situations lead to uncertainties.

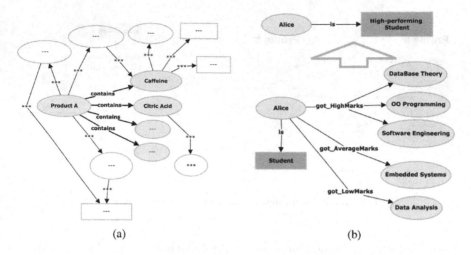

(a)   (b)

Fig. 4. Example of entropy (a) and vagueness (b).

Vagueness. Vagueness is a strongly contextual concept. Within the model, we consider the case in which there is a gap in terms of abstraction between the semantic structure adopted and the reality object of the representation. That kind of circumstance defines an uncertainty as a vagueness.

In order to successfully model vagueness, we first define a supporting operator, *abst*, that measures the abstraction, namely the level of detail, of a given ontological subset. We use this operator to rank sets of assertions as the function of their level of detail. Therefore, $abst(a) > abst(b)$ indicates that the set a and b are addressing a similar target knowledge, with b more detailed (expressive) than a. According to such a definition, a and b are not representing exactly the same knowledge, as a is missing details. Furthermore, we assume there is not an internal set of inference rules that relates a and b.

The formal specification of vagueness (Eq. 6) assumes the representation of a given individual i by using a more abstracted model S_i^a than the required one S_i to address all details.

$$vag(i \in I, S_i, S_i^a) \Rightarrow s(i, \_) \in S_i^a \rightarrow s(i, \_) \in S^*, \quad abst(S_i^a) > abst(S_i) \quad (6)$$

An example is depicted in Fig. 4b: a qualitative evaluation of students' performance assumes their marks belonging to 3 main categories (low, medium and high); a process external to the ontology generates an overall evaluation on the base of the breakdown: in the example Alice got one low score, one average score, as well as three high scores; according to the adopted process, Alice is just classified as an high-performing student without any representation of the data underpinning that statement, as well as of the process adopted; that same statement could reflect multiple configurations providing, therefore, a vague definition due to the lack of detail.

2.3   Indirect Uncertainty

Moving from a quantitative model to a more flexible approach, which integrates qualitative features, is a clear step forward towards richer semantics capable to address uncertain knowledge in the Semantic Web. However, one of the main reasons for the huge gap existing between the human understanding of uncertainty and its representation in computer systems is often the "indirect" and contextual character of the uncertainty. The indirect nature of the uncertainty is an intuitive concept: sometimes an uncertainty is not directly related to the knowledge object of representation, but it can be indirectly associated with some external factor, such as methods, processes and underpinning data.

It leads to a third class of uncertainty, referred to as *indirect uncertainty*, which deals with the uncertainty introduced by external factors and, therefore, with a more holistic understanding of uncertainty.

Associated Uncertainty. As previously mentioned, the uncertainty can have a strongly contextual meaning and could be associated with some external factor or concept. Because of its associative character, this kind of uncertainty is referred to as *associated uncertainty*. A possible formalization of the model is proposed in Eq. 7: an uncertainty related to a certain element u of the knowledge space is associated to an external concept c that is not part of the ontological representation.

$$uncertainty(u, s(u, \_) \in S) \quad \Rightarrow \quad u \leftarrow c \qquad\qquad \nexists \quad s(c, \_) \in S \qquad (7)$$

As an example, we consider the population of an ontology with data from a number of different data sets. The considered data sets are provided by different providers, each one associated with a different degree of reliability. In such a scenario, the reliability of the whole knowledge environment depends on the reliability of the underpinning data. However, a potential uncertainty is introduced in the system because the information is represented indistinctly, although it comes from different data sets associated with a different degree of reliability.

Implicit Uncertainty. *Implicit uncertainty* is a concept similar to the previous one. However, it is not related to underpinning data. It rather focus on the way in which such data is processed to generate and populate the ontological structure (Eq. 8).

$$uncertainty(u, s(u, \_) \in S) \Rightarrow u = f(c) \qquad\qquad \nexists \quad s(c, \_) \in S \qquad (8)$$

The function $f(c)$ in Eq. 8 represents a generic method, process or formalization operating on external information c. Assuming n processes, implicit uncertainty reflects the uncertainty inducted by simplifications, approximations and assumptions in external methods underlying the knowledge base.

3   Measuring and Understanding Uncertainty

Uncertain knowledge assumes the coexistence of knowledge and uncertainty. Despite the qualitative approach allows a non-numerical representation of uncertainty, measuring the uncertainty or, better, the relation between knowledge and uncertainty is a key issue, at both a theoretical and an application level.

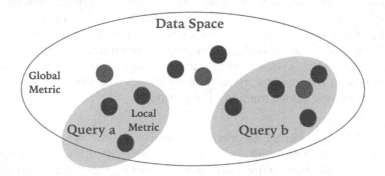

Fig. 5. Global metrics versus local metrics.

We consider two different correlated classes of metrics to quantify and understand the uncertainty in a given context:

- *Global Uncertainty Metric (GUM)* refers to the whole knowledge space and, therefore, is associated with all the knowledge $S \cup S^*$ available (Eq. 9) .

$$GUM(S, S^*) = f(s \in \{S \cup S^*\}) \tag{9}$$

- *Local Uncertainty Metric (LUM)* is a query-specific metric related only to that part of information S_q which is object of the considered query q (Eq. 10).

$$LUM(S, S^*, q \in Q) = f(s \in S_q \subseteq \{S \cup S^*\}) \tag{10}$$

While *GUM* provides a generic holistic understanding of the uncertainty existing in the knowledge space at a given time, *LUM* is a strongly query-specific concept that provides a local understanding of the uncertainty. An effective model of analysis should consider both those types of metrics.

4   Reference Architecture

The reference architecture (Fig. 6) aims at implementations of the proposed framework compatible with the legacy semantic technology. As shown in the figure, we consider the core part of a semantic engine composed of four different functional layers:

– *Ontology layer.* It addresses, as in common meanings, the language to define ontologies; we are implicitly considering ontologies built upon OWL technology. Within the proposed architecture, uncertainties are described according to an ontological approach. Therefore, the key extension of this layer with respect to conventional architectures consists of an ontological support to represent uncertainty.
– *Reasoning layer.* It provides all the functionalities to interact with ontologies, both with reasoning capabilities. The implementation of the framework implies the specification of built-in properties to represent uncertainties, both with the reasoning support to process them. Most existing OWL reasoners and supporting APIs are developed in Java.
– *Query layer.* The conventional query layer, that is usual to provide an interface for an effective interaction with ontologies through a standard query language (e.g. SPARQL [30]), is enriched by capabilities for uncertainty filtering. Indeed, the ideal query interface is expected to retrieve results by considering all uncertainties, considering just a part of them filtered according to some criteria, or, even, considering no uncertainties.
– *Application layer.* The main asset provided at an application level is the set of metrics to measure the uncertainty (as defined in Sect. 3).

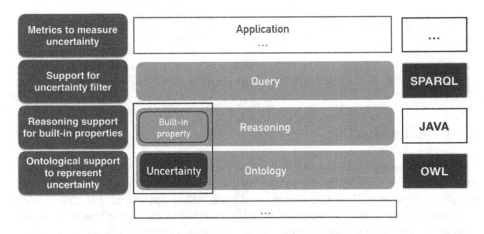

Fig. 6. Reference architecture.

4.1 Current Implementation

The implementation of the framework is currently limited to the concept of uncertainty as a similarity. It is implemented by the *Web of Similarity (WoS)* [29]. WoS matches the reference architecture previously discussed as follows:

- Uncertainty is specified according to an ontological model in OWL.
- The relation of similarity is expressed through the built-in property *similarTo*; WoS implements related reasoning capability.
- The query layer provides filtering capabilities for uncertainty. An example of output is shown in Fig. 7: the output of a query includes two different result sets obtained by reasoning with and without uncertainties; uncertainty is quantified by a global metric.
- The current implementation only includes global metrics to measure uncertainty.

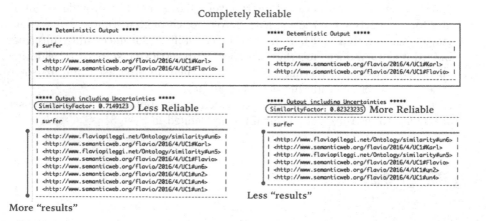

Fig. 7. An example of query result from *Web of Similarity*.

5   Conclusions

This paper proposes a conceptual framework aimed at the representation of uncertain knowledge in the Semantic Web and, more in general, within systems adopting Semantic Web technology and ontological approach. The framework is human-inspired and is expected to address uncertainty according to a model similar to the human one. On one hand, such an approach allows uncertainty representation beyond the common numerical or quantitative approach; on the other hand, it assumes the classification of the different kinds of uncertainty and, therefore, it can miss genericness.

The framework establishes different categories of uncertainty and a set of concepts associated with those categories. Such concepts can be considered either as stand-alone concepts or as part of an unique integrated semantic framework. The reference architecture proposed in the paper aims at implementations of the framework fully compatible with the legacy Semantic Web technology. The current implementation of the framework is limited to the concept of similarity.

References

1. Berners-Lee, T., Hendler, J., Lassila, O., et al.: The semantic web. Sci. Am. **284**(5), 28–37 (2001)
2. Hayes, P., McBride, B.: RDF semantics. W3C recommendation **10** (2004)
3. McGuinness, D.L., Van Harmelen, F., et al.: Owl web ontology language overview. In: W3C recommendation **10**(10) (2004)
4. Horrocks, I., Patel-Schneider, P.F., Boley, H., Tabet, S., Grosof, B., Dean, M., et al.: SWRL: a semantic web rule language combining OWL and RuleML. W3C Member Submission **21**, 79 (2004)
5. Carroll, J.J., Dickinson, I., Dollin, C., Reynolds, D., Seaborne, A., Wilkinson, K.: Jena: implementing the semantic web recommendations. In: Proceedings of the 13th International World Wide Web Conference on Alternate Track Papers & Posters, pp. 74–83. ACM (2004)
6. Sirin, E., Parsia, B., Grau, B.C., Kalyanpur, A., Katz, Y.: Pellet: a practical OWL-DL reasoner. Web Semant. Sci. Serv. Agents World Wide Web **5**(2), 51–53 (2007)
7. Shearer, R., Motik, B., Horrocks, I.: HermiT: a highly-efficient OWL reasoner. In: OWLED, vol. 432, p. 91 (2008)
8. ARQ - A SPARQL processor for Jena. http://jena.apache.org/documentation/query/index.html. Accessed 15 Feb 2018
9. Gennari, J.H., Musen, M.A., Fergerson, R.W., Grosso, W.E., Crubézy, M., Eriksson, H., Noy, N.F., Tu, S.W.: The evolution of protégé: an environment for knowledge-based systems development. Int. J. Hum Comput Stud. **58**(1), 89–123 (2003)
10. Murugesan, S.: Understanding web 2.0. IT professional **9**(4), 34–41 (2007)
11. Guha, R.V., Brickley, D., Macbeth, S.: Schema.org: evolution of structured data on the web. Commun. ACM **59**(2), 44–51 (2016)
12. Straccia, U.: A fuzzy description logic for the semantic web. Capturing Intell. **1**, 73–90 (2006)
13. Kana, D., Armand, F., Akinkunmi, B.O.: Modeling uncertainty in ontologies using rough set. Int. J. Intell. Syst. Appl. **8**(4), 49–59 (2016)
14. da Costa, Paulo Cesar G., Laskey, Kathryn B., Laskey, Kenneth J.: PR-OWL: a Bayesian ontology language for the semantic web. In: da Costa, Paulo Cesar G., d'Amato, Claudia, Fanizzi, Nicola, Laskey, Kathryn B., Laskey, Kenneth J., Lukasiewicz, Thomas, Nickles, Matthias, Pool, Michael (eds.) URSW 2005-2007. LNCS (LNAI), vol. 5327, pp. 88–107. Springer, Heidelberg (2008). https://doi.org/10.1007/978-3-540-89765-1_6
15. Pileggi, S.F.: Probabilistic semantics. Procedia Comput. Sci. **80**, 1834–1845 (2016)
16. Udrea, O., Subrahmanian, V., Majkic, Z.: Probabilistic RDF. In: 2006 IEEE International Conference on Information Reuse & Integration, pp. 172–177. IEEE (2006)
17. Ding, Z., Peng, Y.: A probabilistic extension to ontology language owl. In: Proceedings of the 37th Annual Hawaii international conference on System Sciences, 2004, p. 10. IEEE (2004)
18. Bechhofer, S.: OWL: web ontology language. In: Liu, L., Özsu, M. (eds.) Encyclopedia of Database Systems. Springer, New York (2016). https://doi.org/10.1007/978-1-4899-7993-3
19. Pan, Jeff Z., Stamou, Giorgos, Tzouvaras, Vassilis, Horrocks, Ian: f-SWRL: a fuzzy extension of SWRL. In: Duch, Włodzisław, Kacprzyk, Janusz, Oja, Erkki, Zadrożny, Sławomir (eds.) ICANN 2005. LNCS, vol. 3697, pp. 829–834. Springer, Heidelberg (2005). https://doi.org/10.1007/11550907_131

20. Coradeschi, S., Ishiguro, H., Asada, M., Shapiro, S.C., Thielscher, M., Breazeal, C., Mataric, M.J., Ishida, H.: Human-inspired robots. IEEE Intell. Syst. **21**(4), 74–85 (2006)
21. Moore, R.: PRESENCE: a human-inspired architecture for speech-based human-machine interaction. IEEE Trans. Comput. **56**(9), 1176–1188 (2007)
22. Gavrilets, V., Mettler, B., Feron, E.: Human-inspired control logic for automated maneuvering of miniature helicopter. J. Guid. Control Dyn. **27**(5), 752–759 (2004)
23. Yao, Y.: Human-inspired granular computing. Novel developments in granular computing: applications for advanced human reasoning and soft computation, pp. 1–15 (2010)
24. Liang, Q.: Situation understanding based on heterogeneous sensor networks and human-inspired favor weak fuzzy logic system. IEEE Syst. J. **5**(2), 156–163 (2011)
25. Velloso, Pedro B., Laufer, Rafael P., Duarte, Otto C.M.B., Pujolle, Guy: HIT: a human-inspired trust model. In: Pujolle, Guy (ed.) MWCN 2006. ITIFIP, vol. 211, pp. 35–46. Springer, Boston, MA (2006). https://doi.org/10.1007/978-0-387-34736-3_2
26. de Jong, S., Tuyls, K.: Human-inspired computational fairness. Auton. Agent. Multi-Agent Syst. **22**(1), 103–126 (2011)
27. Lughofer, E.: Human-inspired evolving machines-the next generation of evolving intelligent systems. IEEE SMC Newslett. **36** (2011)
28. Pesquita, C., Faria, D., Falcao, A.O., Lord, P., Couto, F.M.: Semantic similarity in biomedical ontologies. PLoS Comput. Biol. **5**(7), e1000443 (2009)
29. Pileggi, S.F.: Web of similarity. J. Comput. Sci. (2016)
30. Quilitz, Bastian, Leser, Ulf: Querying distributed RDF data sources with SPARQL. In: Bechhofer, Sean, Hauswirth, Manfred, Hoffmann, Jörg, Koubarakis, Manolis (eds.) ESWC 2008. LNCS, vol. 5021, pp. 524–538. Springer, Heidelberg (2008). https://doi.org/10.1007/978-3-540-68234-9_39

Bayesian Based Approach Learning for Outcome Prediction of Soccer Matches

Laura Hervert-Escobar[1]([✉]), Neil Hernandez-Gress[1], and Timothy I. Matis[2]

[1] Instituto Tecnológico y de Estudios Superiores de Monterrey, Monterrey, Mexico
laura.hervert@itesm.mx
[2] Texas Tech University, Lubbock, USA

Abstract. In the current world, sports produce considerable data such as players skills, game results, season matches, leagues management, etc. The big challenge in sports science is to analyze this data to gain a competitive advantage. The analysis can be done using several techniques and statistical methods in order to produce valuable information. The problem of modeling soccer data has become increasingly popular in the last few years, with the prediction of results being the most popular topic. In this paper, we propose a Bayesian Model based on rank position and shared history that predicts the outcome of future soccer matches. The model was tested using a data set containing the results of over 200,000 soccer matches from different soccer leagues around the world.

Keywords: Machine learning · Soccer · Bayesian models
Sport matches · Prediction

1 Introduction

The sport is an activity that the human being performs mainly with recreational objectives. It has become an essential part of our lives as it encourages connivance, and when professionally engaged, it becomes a way to survive. The sport has become one of the big businesses in the world and has shown an important economic growth. Thousands of companies have their main source of income in it. The most popular sport in the world, according to Russell [1], is football soccer. Soccer detonates a great movement of money in bets, sponsorships, attendance to parties, sale of t-shirts and accessories, etc. That is why it has aroused great interest in building predictive and statistical models for it.

Professional soccer has been in the market for quite some time. The sports management of soccer is awash with data, which has allowed the generation of several metrics associated with the individual and team performance. The aim is to find mechanisms to obtain competitive advantages. Machine learning has become a useful tool to transform the data into actionable insights.

Machine Learning is a scientific discipline in the field of Artificial Intelligence that creates systems that learn automatically. Learning in this context means

© Springer International Publishing AG, part of Springer Nature 2018
Y. Shi et al. (Eds.): ICCS 2018, LNCS 10862, pp. 269–279, 2018.
https://doi.org/10.1007/978-3-319-93713-7_22

identifying complex patterns in millions of data. The machine that really learns is an algorithm that reviews the data and is able to predict future behavior. It finds the sort of patterns that are often imperceptible to traditional statistical techniques because of their apparently random nature.

When the scope of data analysis techniques is complemented by the possibilities of machine learning, it is possible to see much more clearly what really matters in terms of knowledge generation, not only at a quantitative level, but also ensuring a significant qualitative improvement. Then researchers, data scientist, engineers and analysts are able to produce reliable, repeatable decisions and results [2].

With data now accessible about almost anything in soccer, machine learning can be applied in a range. However, it has been used mostly for prediction. This type of models are known as multi-class classification for prediction, an it has three classes: win, loss and draw. According to Gevaria, win and loss are comparatively easy to classify. However, the class of draw is very difficult to predict even in real world scenario. A draw is not a favored outcome for pundits as well as betting enthusiasts [3].

In this research we present a new approach for soccer match prediction based on the performance position of the team in the season and the history of matches. The model was tested using a training data set containing the results of over 200,000 soccer matches from different soccer leagues around the world. Details of data set are available at [4].

The remainder of this paper is organized as follows. Section 2 gives a summary of previous work on football prediction. A general description of how the problem is addressed is presented in Sect. 3. Section 4 describes the procedures for preprocessing data, followed by the description of the proposed model. Experiments and results are described in Sects. 6 and 7, respectively. Finally, discussion of the results are in Sect. 8.

2   Related Work

Since soccer is the most popular sport worldwide, and given the amount of data generated everyday, it is not surprising to find abundant amount of research in soccer prediction.

Most of related work is focused on developing models for a specific league or particular event such as world cup. Koning [5] used a Bayesian network approach along with a Monte-Carlo method to estimate the quality of soccer teams. The method was applied in the Dutch professional soccer league. The results were used to assess the change over the time in the balance of the competition.

Rue [6] analyzed skills of all teams and used a Bayesian dynamic generalized linear model to estimate dependency over time and to predict immediate soccer matches.

Falter [7] and Forrest [8] proposed an approach focused more on the analysis of soccer matches rather than on prediction. Falter proposed an updating process for the intra-match winning probability while Forrest computes the uncertainty of the outcome. Both approaches are useful to identify the main decisive elements in a soccer league and use them to compute the probability of success.

Crowder [9] proposed a model using refinements of the independent Poisson model from Dixon and Coles. This model considers that each team has attack and defense strategies that evolves over time according to some unobserved bivariate stochastic process. They used the data from 92 teams in the English Football Association League to predict the probabilities of home win, draw and lost.

Anderson [10] evaluates the performance of the prediction from experts and non-experts in soccer. The procedure utilized was the application of a survey to a 250 participants with different levels of knowledge in soccer. The survey consist on predicting the outcome of the first round of the World Cup 2002. The results shows that a recognition-based strategy seems to be appropriate to use when forecasting worldwide soccer events.

Koning [11] proposed a model based on Poisson parameters that are specific for a match. The procedure combines a simulation and probability models in order to identify the team that is most likely to win a tournament. The results were effective to indicates favorites, and it has the potential to provide useful information about the tournament.

Goddard [12] proposed an ordered probit regression model for forecasting English league football results. This model is able to quantify the quality of prediction along with several explanatory variables.

Rotshtein [13] proposed a model to analyzed previous matches with fuzzy knowledge base in order to find nonlinear dependency patterns. Then, they used genetic and neural optimization techniques in order to tune the fuzzy rules and achieve a acceptable simulations.

Halicioglu [14] analyzed football matches statistically and suggested a method to predict the winner of the Euro 2000 football tournament. The method is based on the ranking of the countries combined with a coefficient of variation computed using the point obtained at the end of the season from the domestic league.

Similar approaches applied to different sports can be found in [15–17]. Their research is focused on the prediction of American football and baseball major league.

Among the existing works, the approach of [18] is most similar to ours. Their system consists of two major components: a rule-based reasoner and a Bayesian network component. This approach is a compound one in the sense that two different methods cooperate in predicting the result of a football match. Second, contrary to most previous works on football prediction they use an in-game time-series approach to predict football matches.

3   General Ideas

Factors such as morale of a team (or a player), skills, coaching strategy, equipment, etc. have a impact in the results for a sport match. So even for experts, it is very hard to predict the exact results of individual matches. It also raises very interesting questions regarding the interaction between the rules, the strategies and the highly stochastic nature of the game itself.

How possible is to have high accuracy prediction by knowing previous results per team? How should be the selection of factors that can be measured and integrated into a prediction model? Are the rules of the league/tournament a factor to consider in the prediction model?

Consider a data set that contains the score results of over 200,000 soccer matches from different soccer leagues around the world. There is no further knowledge of other features such as: importance of the game, skills of the players or rules of the league. In this way and without experience or knowledge on soccer, our hypothesis is that soccer results are influenced by the position rank of the teams during the season as well as the shared history between matched teams.

In general, the methodology proposed decides over two approaches. The first approach consist in finding patterns in the history match of teams that indicates a trend in the results. The second approach considers the given information to rank teams in the current season. Then, based on the ranking position, a Bayesian function is used to compute the probability of win, lose or draw a match.

4   Data Pre-processing and Feature Engineering

The data set contains the results of over 200,000 soccer matches from different soccer leagues around the world. With the information of date, season, team, league, home team, away team, and the score of each game during the season. Details of data set is available at [4].

The main objective in pre-processing the data is to set the initial working parameters for the prediction methodology. Then, the metrics to obtain in this procedure are: the rank position of the teams, the start probabilities for the Bayesian function and the shared history between two teams. Preprocessing procedures were easily implemented using R.

Equations used during the pre-processing data are as follows. Index i refers to team, index t refers to the season of the team playing in the league, finally n refers to total games played by team i during season t.

$$sg_t^i = \sum_n \left(3w_{n,t}^i + d_{n,t}^i\right) \tag{1}$$

Equation (1) describes the computation of the score based on game performance sg. The score computation gives 3 points for each game won (w) during the season, 1 point for a draw (d) and zero points for a lost (l) game. This method is based on the result points from FIFA ranking method. Match status, opposition strength and regional strength are not considered due to the lack of information in the dataset.

$$sb_t^i = \sum_n \left(gf_{n,t}^i - ga_{n,t}^i\right) \tag{2}$$

Equation (2) describes the computation of the score based on the number of goals during the season sb. In this way, the score is given by the number of goals in favor gf minus the number of goals against ga.

$$gs_t^i = sg_t^i + sb_t^i \tag{3}$$

$$score_t^i = \begin{cases} gs_t^i & t = 1 \\ 0.2\left(gs_{t-1}^i\right) + 0.8\left(gs_t^i\right) & t > 1 \end{cases} \tag{4}$$

A partial score given in Eq. (3) is the sum of Eqs. (1) and (2). The total score for each season in given in Eq. (4).

The teams of the league in each season may vary according to promotions or descents derived from their previous performance. As shown in Eq. (4), the previous season has a weight of 20% on the total score. The current season has a weight of 80%. In this way, the ranking process takes into account a previous good/bad performance. But it also gives greater importance to the changes that the team makes in the current season. This measure was designed to have a fair comparison between veteran teams playing and rookie teams in the league. In this way, the history of each team will have an influence on their current rankings (whether positive or not) and rookie teams will have a fair comparison that alleviates league change adjustments.

The rank of the team $rank_i^t$ in Eq. (5) is given by its position according to the total score. Given a collection of M teams, the rank of a team i in season t is the number of teams that precede it.

$$rank_i^t = \left|\{rank_i^t \,|\, rank_i^t < rank_j^t\}\right| \qquad \forall \qquad i \neq j, \qquad i, j \in M_t \tag{5}$$

As expected, not all teams are participating in all seasons. Then, missing teams are not considered in the ranking of the current season.

Equations (6) and (7) are used to obtained start probabilities to be used in the Bayesian function,

$$mrank_i^t = 1 - \frac{rank_i^t}{(Max(rank^t) + 1)}; \tag{6}$$

$$Pstart^t = \frac{mrank_i^t}{\sum_i mrank_i^t} \tag{7}$$

Finally, the shared history of the teams is a list that summarizes the number of cases that the same match has been played. The list also contains the probability of win pRw_{i-j}, lose pRl_{i-j}, and draw pRd_{i-j} a game based on the total matches tg for a given period. See Eq. (8).

$$pRw_{i-j} = \sum_n \left(\frac{w}{tg}\right)_{i-j}; \quad pRd_{i-j} = \sum_n \left(\frac{d}{tg}\right)_{i-j}; \quad pRl_{i-j} = \sum_n \left(\frac{l}{tg}\right)_{i-j} \tag{8}$$

5   Bayesian Algorithm

A pseudo-code for the Bayesian function proposed is given in Algorithm 1. The procedure starts by computing the prior probability of the two teams in the match (step 1). The team with higher probability is labeled as a team, and the team with lower prior probability is subindex as b(step 2). Then, prior probability of the a team is used to generate 1000 random variables using a triangular distribution.

$TD[0, 1, prior_a^t]$ represents a continuous triangular statistical distribution supported over the interval $min = x = max$ and parameterized by three real numbers 0, 1, and $prior_a^t$ (where $0 < prior_a^t < 1$) that specify the lower endpoint of its support, the upper endpoint of its support, and the -coordinate of its mode, respectively. In general, the PDF of a triangular distribution is triangular (piecewise linear, concave down, and unimodal) with a single "peak", though its overall shape (its height, its spread, and the horizontal location of its maximum) is determined by the values of 0, 1, and $prior_a^t$.

Using the random variables, posterior probabilities are computed in step 5. Then, the probability corresponding to mode of posterior is used to compute and adjust measure. The adjust measure is apply to the start probabilities for the next period (step 9). Finally, the probability of win/lose the match in the period $t + 1$, knowing the probabilities of the current period t is given by equations in step 10. This equations correspond to the prior probability based on the adjusted start probability.

The procedure for the soccer prediction using Bayesian function and shared history data is given in Algorithm 2. As the pseudo-code shows. The probability taken for the prediction model is chosen between two options, shared history or ranking. Either choice allows to update results in the Bayesian function.

The procedure starts by checking the shared history of the match to predict. Based on the total matches, the next step is either use history probability or Bayesian probability. The threshold to decide is set at least 10 games of shared history.

Then, if the threshold value is greater or equal to 10, the probability lies on previous results. Otherwise, the probability is given by their rank position in the season-league along with the Bayesian function.

6   Experiments

Procedures were implemented on R statistical free license software. In order to prove the value of the methodology the training data set given by [4] was split in two parts for all leagues. First part contains the results from 2000 to 2015. Second part contains data from 2016–2017 and was used as the matches to predict.

The metric used in the challenge is the ranked probability score (RPS). The RSP helps to determine the error between the actual observed outcome of a match and the prediction. Description of the metric can be found at [4].

Algorithm 1. Pseudocode for probability of win/lose a match game

---

Require:

   $Pstart$: list of start probabilities (See Equation(5))

Ensure: Probability of win/lose the match game $f_m(winteam(a), loseteam(b))$

1: Compute prior probabilities for teams in the match

$$prior_i^t = \frac{Pstart_i^t}{Pstart_i^t + Pstart_j^t}; \qquad prior_j^t = \frac{Pstart_j^t}{Pstart_i^t + Pstart_j^t}$$

2: Set probable winner and loser team

$$prior_a^t = maxPstart_i^t + Pstart_j^t; \qquad prior_b^t = minPstart_i^t + Pstart_j^t$$

3: Continuous triangular prior distribution evaluated at 1000 equally spaced points using prior probability

$$prior^t = TD\{[0, 1, prior_a^t], x\}, \{0, 1, 0.001\}$$

4: Prior discretized into a probability mass function and discretized prior probability masses

$$dprior = \frac{prior}{\sum\limits_{1000} prior}; \qquad probs_i^t = \{i_k = i_{k-1} + 0.001 | i \in [0, 1)\}1 < k < 1000]$$

5: Posterior distribution

$$posterior_i^t = \frac{probs_i^t * dprior_i^t}{\sum\limits_i probs * dprior}$$

6: Probability corresponding to mode of posterior

$$c = \underset{i}{Max}\{posterior_i^t\} \times 0.001$$

7: Adjust probabilities for current rankings

$$adjust = c \times \left(Pstart_a^t - Pstart_b^t\right)$$

8: Update start probabilities

$$Pstart_a^{t+1} = Pstart_a^t + adjust; \qquad Pstart_b^{t+1} = Pstart_a^t - adjust$$

9: Computing final win/lose probabilities

$$pwinteam(a) = \frac{Pstart_a^{t+1}}{Pstart_a^{t+1} + Pstart_b^{t+1}}; ploseteam(b) = \frac{Pstart_b^{t+1}}{Pstart_a^{t+1} + Pstart_b^{t+1}}$$

10:

Two types of outcomes were tested. In a first outcome, the variables xW, xD and xL were defined as binary numbers. In this outcome, the strategy was to check how accurate was the method in order to predict an exact result.

Algorithm 2. Pseudo-code for soccer prediction method

Require:
   $f(winteam(a), loseteam(b))$
   Shared history list
Ensure: Prediction outcome for match xW, xD, xL
 1:
 2: **if** Shared History $\in$ prediction$\{$a,b$\} \geq 10$ **then**
 3:
 4:     $xW = pRW; xD = pRD; xL = pRL$
 5:
 6: **else**
 7: Compute Bayesian Function $f_m(winteam(a), loseteam(b))$
 8: $\Delta = pwinteam(a) - ploseteam(b)$
 9:
10:     **if** $\Delta \leq 0.2$ **then**
11:         $xW = \frac{\Delta}{2}; xD = 1 - \Delta; xL = \frac{\Delta}{2}$
12:     **end if**
13:     $xW = Pstart_a^{t+1}; xD = 1 - Pstart_a^{t+1} + Pstart_b^{t+1}; xL = Pstart_b^{t+1}$
14: **end if**
15: NEXT MATCH

The second approach was to preserve the nature of the computation. Then, the outcome variables xW, xD and xL are in the rank of $[0, 1]$, where the sum is equal to 1.

Additionally, a real prediction was performed based on a call challenge of soccer. Detail of the call can be found at [4].

7   Results

Figure 1 shows the result obtained using both approaches using the training data set. As observed, the RSP improves when nature of the variables are continuous rather than binary. Additionally, the bars indicate the proportion of the training predictions made by history matches and for rank procedure. For the training data set, the RSP has not significant changes related to the prediction method.

As mentioned above, the methodology proposed was tested under the requirements of a call for a challenge soccer. Details results for the challenge soccer can be found at [19]. The results of the prediction for the call of the challenge soccer are shown in Fig. 2. The figure shows the proportion of the prediction defined by history match and for ranking procedure. Additionally, shows the average RSP obtained for each type of prediction. As shown, for leagues where greater proportion of prediction were made by history matches, the average RSP is around 33%, for one league it reaches a desirable 0%. On the other hand, predictions made mainly with rank procedure, the RSP average is over 40%, with one case of 0%.

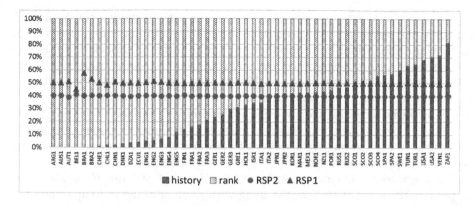

Fig. 1. Prediction results for each league

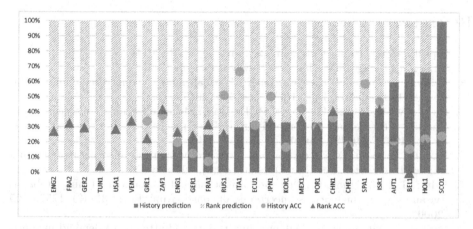

Fig. 2. Results of RSP according to prediction method

8 Conclusions

Main motivation of this work was the chance to participate in the call for the soccer challenge as a way to test a basic Bayesian model along with other techniques to predict the outcome of matches in soccer. Despite the lack of knowledge about soccer in general, we were able to first understand the challenge and then developed a prediction model that is easy to implement. From literature reviewed we learned that each league is driven by different motivations that influence the result of a match game. Then, information based only in the result of matches may no accurate allows to recognize useful patterns for prediction. Most of the time inverted in the process of defining the better way of ranking as well as programming the procedures, trying to make them as efficient as possible.

The methodology proposed is simply an instance of a more general framework, applied to soccer. It would be interesting to try other sports. In this section, we consider the possibilities for extension. Even though the framework can in principle be adapted to a wide range of sports domains, it cannot be used in domains which have insufficient data. Another approach to explore in the future is a Knowledge-based system. This usually require knowledge of relatively good quality while most machine learning systems need a huge amount of data to get good predictions. It is important to understand that each soccer league behaves according to particular environment. Therefore, a better prediction model should include particular features of the match game, such as the importance of the game. Availability of more features that can help in solving the issue of predicting draw class would improve the accuracy.

Future work in this area includes the development of a model that attempt to predict the score of the match, along with more advance techniques and the use of different metrics for evaluating the quality of the result.

References

1. Rusell, B.: Top 10 most popular sports in the world (2013)
2. SAS: Machine learning what it is & why it matters (2016)
3. Vaidya, S., Sanghavi, H., Gevaria, K.: Football match winner prediction. Int. J. Emerg. Technol. Adv. Eng. **10**(5), 364–368 (2015)
4. Dubitzky, W., Berrar, D., Lopes, P., Davis, J.: Machine learning for soccer (2017)
5. Koning, R.H.: Balance in competition in dutch soccer. J. Roy. Stat. Soc. Ser. D (Stat.) **49**(3), 419–431 (2000)
6. Rue, H., Salvesen, O.: Prediction and retrospective analysis of soccer matches in a league. J. Roy. Stat. Soc. Ser. D (Stat.) **49**(3), 399–418 (2000)
7. Falter, J.M., Perignon, C.: Demand for football and intramatch winning probability: an essay on the glorious uncertainty of sports. Appl. Econ. **32**(13), 1757–1765 (2000)
8. Forrest, D., Simmons, R.: Outcome uncertainty and attendance demand in sport: the case of english soccer. J. Roy. Stat. Soc. Ser. D (Stat.) **51**(2), 229–241 (2002)
9. Crowder, M., Dixon, M., Ledford, A., Robinson, M.: Dynamic modelling and prediction of english football league matches for betting. J. Roy. Stat. Soc. Ser. D (Stat.) **51**(2), 157–168 (2002)
10. Andersson, P., Ekman, M., Edman, J.: Forecasting the fast and frugal way: a study of performance and information-processing strategies of experts and non-experts when predicting the world cup 2002 in soccer. In: SSE/EFI Working Paper Series in Business Administration 2003, vol. 9. Stockholm School of Economics (2003)
11. Koning, R.H., Koolhaas, M., Renes, G., Ridder, G.: A simulation model for football championships. Eur. J. Oper. Res. **148**(2), 268–276 (2003). Sport and Computers
12. Goddard, J., Asimakopoulos, I.: Forecasting football results and the efficiency of fixed-odds betting. J. Forecast. **23**(1), 51–66 (2004)
13. Rotshtein, A.P., Posner, M., Rakityanskaya, A.B.: Football predictions based on a fuzzy model with genetic and neural tuning. Cybern. Syst. Anal. **41**(4), 619–630 (2005)
14. Halicioglu, F.: Can we predict the outcome of the international football tournaments: the case of Euro 2000. Doğşu Üniversitesi Dergisi **6**(1) (2005)
15. Martinich, J.: College football rankings: do the computers know best? Interfaces. Interfaces **32**(4), 84–94 (2002)

16. Amor, M., Griffiths, W.: Modelling the behaviour and performance of australian football tipsters. Department of Economics - Working Papers Series 871, The University of Melbourne (2003)
17. Yang, T.Y., Swartz, T.: A two-stage bayesian model for predicting winners in major league baseball. J. Data Sci. **2**(1), 6173 (2004)
18. Min, B., Kim, J., Choe, C., Eom, H., (Bob) McKay, R.I.: A compound framework for sports results prediction: a football case study. Know. Based Syst. **21**(7), 551–562 (2008)
19. Hervert, L., Matis, T.: Machine learning for soccer-prediction results (2017)

Fuzzy and Data-Driven Urban Crowds

Leonel Toledo[1]([✉]), Ivan Rivalcoba[1,2], and Isaac Rudomin[1]

[1] Computer Sciences, Barcelona Supercomputing Center, Barcelona, Spain
{leonel.toledo,isaac.rudomin}@bsc.es, ivan.rivalcoba@gmail.com
[2] Instituto Tecnológico de Gustavo A. Madero, Mexico City, Mexico

Abstract. In this work we present a system able to simulate crowds in complex urban environments; the system is built in two stages, urban environment generation and pedestrian simulation, for the first stage we integrate the WRLD3D plug-in with real data collected from GPS traces, then we use a hybrid approach done by incorporating steering pedestrian behaviors with the goal of simulating the subtle variations present in real scenarios without needing large amounts of data for those low-level behaviors, such as pedestrian motion affected by other agents and static obstacles nearby. Nevertheless, realistic human behavior cannot be modeled using deterministic approaches, therefore our simulations are both data-driven and sometimes are handled by using a combination of finite state machines (FSM) and fuzzy logic in order to handle the uncertainty of people motion.

Keywords: Crowd simulation · Fuzzy logic · Finite state machines
Steering behaviors · Data driven

1 Introduction

The problem of constructing large and complex urban environments for real-time simulations implies several challenges that arise in terms of acquisition and management of large geometric and topological models, real time visualization, and the complexity of the virtual human simulation. This field is increasingly incorporating mathematical and computational tools within the processes of designing urban spaces, consequently there is a need for plausible and realistic crowd simulations in large scale urban environments that can be used by expert designers [1].

Behavior of human crowds in the real world varies significantly depending on time, place, stress levels, the age of the people, and many other social and psychological factors, these variations shown in group behaviors are often characterized by observable traits such as interpersonal space, the fluidity of formation, the level of energy, the uniformity of distribution, the style of interactions, and so on. It is difficult to achieve realistic simulations due to the complex behavior and structures within the crowd.

The aim of the present work is to generate steering behaviors to simulate agents in real scenarios without the need of having a huge amount of data (like

© Springer International Publishing AG, part of Springer Nature 2018
Y. Shi et al. (Eds.): ICCS 2018, LNCS 10862, pp. 280–290, 2018.
https://doi.org/10.1007/978-3-319-93713-7_23

hundreds or even thousands of Mb) and with just a few parameters to adjust. We propose a hybrid method that takes into consideration real data for pedestrian navigation and finite state machines combined with fuzzy logic that help us model variety in each of the individual elements of the crowd, this way characters that share similar profiles might react completely different in the same situation.

2 Related Work

Producing a realistic and useful urban environment requires some steps such as modeling, processing, rendering, animating and displaying heterogeneous set of models [21]. In this section we briefly discuss some of the major work that was considered in the creation of the system.

2.1 Geographic Information Systems

Visualization software such as 3D globe based interfaces, navigation systems presenting a 3D perspective are increasing rapidly due to the recent developments in geographic information systems and data acquisition. This has created a need for the development of algorithms to reconstruct 3D data using 2D objects [15].

The work of Essen [5] describes a method used to produce 3D maps taking as a base a 2D city maps which contains relevant features. We extend this work by using GPS traces that allows us to extract urban and city information to create complex environments using real data and combining it with an interactive crowd.

The work of Thomsen et al. [23] introduces a general approach for modeling topology in 3D GIS, and addresses the problem of using real 3D data in comparison with traditional 2D or 2.5D and how the context of topological abstraction influences the final result, depending on the operations applied to a certain set of data. Using a cell layout hierarchies are created and geometry can have a mesh representation.

2.2 Crowd Visualization

Open world games are massively successful because they grant players absolute freedom in exploring huge, detailed virtual urban environments. The traditional process of creating such environments involves many person-years of work. A potential remedy can be found in procedural modeling using shape grammars. However the process of generating a complete, detailed city the size of Manhattan, which consist of more than 100,000 buildings, can take hours, producing billions of polygons and consuming tera-bytes of storage [13]. Steinberg et al. introduces a parallel architecture system designed for efficient, massively parallel execution on current graphics processing unit (GPU). This work takes into consideration account visibility and different level of detail. This way faster rendering is achieved due to less geometry. An adaptive level of detail is used as well and a dynamic vertex buffer and index buffer that allows geometry to be

generated at any point during grammar derivation on the GPU. It is important
to address that this simulations must run at interactive frame rates (at least
30 frames per second). Thalmann and Boatright [2,22] stated that additional
challenges such as Variety in both appearance and animation and behaviors.
Steering also has a big impact in the creation of realistic simulations [16].

The work of da Silveira et al. [21] presents an approach for real-time generation of 3D virtual cities, providing a generic framework that supports semiautomatic creation, management and visualization of urban complex environments for virtual human simulation. It intends to minimize efforts in modeling
of complex and huge environments.

2.3 Pedestrian Steering Behaviors

Pedestrian steering behaviors or pedestrian motion involves the behavior of an
individual taking into consideration the other members of the crowd. According
to Pettre [16], steering has a big influence as a factor to get a plausible and a
realistic crowd. In order to address steering behavior, researchers have proposed
different approaches. One way is dealing the crowd as macroscopic phenomena
treating the crowd as a whole like Shinohara [20], other authors state that the
movement of a group of pedestrians is driven by physical laws similar to those
valid for dynamics of compressed fluids or gases like the work presented by
Hoogendoorn and Hughes [8,9]. However, these models have problems in simulating complex behaviors [4]. An alternative to the macroscopic approach is
treating every agent in the crowd individually. This approach is called microscopic like vector based [17] and agent based [7,14]. The aforementioned methods
may lead to realistic results for specific situations, in order to do so, many finely
tuned specific rules are required, in some cases up to 24 parameters [10]. As
an alternative, researches have used data-driven techniques [3] by using video
samples to construct a large example database containing the motion of nearby
agents observed in video sequences to determine the moving trajectories of each
simulated agent. The drawback of pure Data-driven is that they usually don't
model social group behaviors and when they do the data base grows significantly.
In other words, data-driven models create very realistic results but require many
examples and large amounts of memory in order to cover the complexity of social
human behavior.

3 Urban Crowd Visualization

As discussed previously, the process of creating a complex urban environment
is not a trivial task, many variables are involved in the process. Computational
resources must be addressed when creating large scenes and memory consumption becomes bigger for every additional element in the given scene. Nevertheless
memory is not the only problem, since these scenarios also consider high density crowds within the simulation processing time is required as well and must
be properly bounded to ensure an acceptable performance. Figure 1 shows an

example of an environment that uses visualization and level of detail techniques in order to have urban scenarios with crowds composed by hundreds of thousands of varied animated characters running at interactive frame rates without compromising visual quality [24].

Fig. 1. Urban environment created using real data.

Rudomin et al. [18,19] state that large scale crowd simulations and visualizations combine aspects from different disciplines, from computer graphics to artificial intelligence and high performance computing. Accordingly, We adapt the mechanism to compute spatio-temporal data such as pedestrians or vehicles, and combine it with map and geometric data used to describe specific places in the world.

Figure 1 shows how we create the urban environment using the previously discussed techniques, we use WRLD3D plug-in which gives us detailed information about geographic locations, in this case we construct the simulation using Barcelona city as a reference. Once the environment is created, we incorporate the crowd into the simulation, our goal is to make the simulations as complex as possible, to reach that goal we consider two different techniques that we combine; first, we collect real data from GPS traces that describe routes that pedestrians take within the city, this trace includes information about the latitude, longitude, elevation and the time when the sample was taken, and our agents can follow the given routes and be animated accordingly. Second, we consider autonomous characters that can navigate the environment. We include simple behaviors such as patrolling, following, avoiding obstacles or pedestrians just to state a few. This behavior is controlled by finite state machines in which each agent has the freedom to decide how to change states accordingly. Nevertheless, pedestrian behavior cannot be modeled realistically using deterministic models, thats why we incorporate fuzzy logic into the simulation, this way we can create different profiles for each character, and work with concepts such as fast or slow inside the simulation, what is true for an agent might not work in the same way for other. To decide whether a character is moving fast or slow and simulate properly we use a shared library of parameters that all characters inherit from, we can manually tweak each of the variables for any given character or randomly assign values. This allows us to create two different profiles for all the elements in the simulation, the first profile is focused in information such as vision range, maximum speed, weight, turn speed, to state some. The second profile is oriented towards how each character understands fuzzy concepts such as fast or slow, this way even if the members of the crowd have the same physical profile they might behave very different according to their fuzzy parameters. One of the main advantages of this method is that all agents have access to this knowledge and without any changes to the script we can achieve a lot of variety in the crowd behavior.

4   Generating Pedestrians Motion

Pedestrian motion is generated by mixing data-driven steering and group social forces. We use trajectories of pedestrians stored as a set of vectors. Those vectors encode the steering motion of real pedestrian interacting with each other in public spaces. This data is used to generate a steering action given a set of states affecting the surroundings of a virtual character. This steering action is complemented by Helbing's social group forces to allow the generation of groups of people usually found on real scenarios [14].

4.1   Trajectories Structure Definition

The dataset of steering actions is conformed by a group of pedestrian trajectories τ of each pedestrian k, formally τ_k which defines a set of N displacements δ_i from position $P_i(x_i, y_i)$ to $P_{i+1}(x_{i+1}, y_{i+1})$. In consequence each displacement δ is given by:

$$\delta_i = (x_{i+1} - x_i, y_{i+1} - y_i) \tag{1}$$

Therefore τ_k is conformed as:

$$\tau_k = \{\delta_0, \delta_1, \cdots, \delta_N\} \tag{2}$$

All the trajectories from the dataset are raw material to create a set of features and actions stored in memory as vectors [11]. We propose a set of 3 features which have strong influence in the steering decision of a pedestrian, those are presented bellow.

– **Goal vector:** The goal vector is defined by Eq. 3.

$$\boldsymbol{goal} = \sum_{i=0}^{N} \delta_i \tag{3}$$

Due to datasets exhibiting a wide range of origins and destinations originated for each pedestrian and this is not desirable, we propose a vector alignment for all vectors of each trajectory in the dataset. To do so, we decided to apply a rotation to the global coordinate system from the original data to one who is always pointing to the "Y" axis. Accordingly given a **goal** vector, We use a vector $\hat{e}_2 = (0,1)$ to get a normalization angle η, which is needed to align the goal with "Y" axis. We call it a normalization angle which is calculated using the following equation:

$$\eta = cos^{-1}\left(\frac{\hat{e}_2 \cdot \mathbf{goal}}{|\hat{e}_2| \cdot |\mathbf{goal}|}\right) \tag{4}$$

Given a vector displacement $\boldsymbol{\delta}$. The normalized version $\boldsymbol{\gamma}$ of that vector according to angle η is given by:

$$\gamma = \left|\begin{matrix} \delta_x * Cos(\eta) - \delta_y * Sin(\eta) \\ \delta_y * Cos(\eta) + \delta_x * Sin(\eta) \end{matrix}\right| \tag{5}$$

- **Velocity:** This factor comprises the rate of change of time, Δt of the displacement of the pedestrian as a function of time. The velocity given by Eq. 6 provides part of the component of behaviors that describe collision avoidance.

$$v_i = \frac{\gamma_{i+1} - \gamma_i}{\Delta t} \tag{6}$$

- **Closeness to goal:** This feature outlines how close (in percentage) the pedestrian is from its current position to the final destination observed in the trajectory dataset. The closeness to goal factor is defined by:

$$\sigma_i = \frac{\gamma_i \cdot \mathbf{goal}_i}{goal_{i_x}^2 + goal_{i_y}^2} \tag{7}$$

- **Obstacle code:** The obstacle code φ is a factor that is calculated by using eight discrete radial regions. This kind of subdivision has been frequently used to capture the influence of the neighborhood in data-driven approaches [25]. Perceptual studies have demonstrated that regions toward the intended direction have a larger radius of influence on the trajectory of pedestrians [12] that fact lead us to introduce a slight difference consisting on incrementing the radius of the section pointing toward the direction of pedestrian's motion (see Fig. 2). The angle of obstruction β of a pedestrian j in the neighborhood of a pedestrian i walking at a velocity v_i is given by:

$$\alpha = atan2\left(e_{i,j_x}, e_{i,j_y}\right) - atan2\left(v_{i_y}, v_{i_x}\right) \tag{8}$$

$$\alpha_1 = \begin{cases} \alpha + 2 * \pi & \alpha < 0 \\ \alpha & \alpha \geq 0 \end{cases} \tag{9}$$

From the Eq. 8, $e_{i,j}$ the vector is pointing from pedestrian i to j. With the angle of obstruction α_1 the next quadrant adjustment is performed:

$$\beta = \begin{cases} \alpha_1 + \frac{\pi}{2} & \alpha_1 < \frac{\pi}{2} \\ -1 & \frac{\pi}{2} \leq \alpha_1 < \frac{3\pi}{2} \\ \alpha - \frac{3\pi}{2} & \alpha_1 \geq \frac{3\pi}{2} \end{cases} \tag{10}$$

Finally the quadrant obstructed by pedestrian j is:

$$\varphi = \lceil \frac{\beta * 8}{\pi} \rceil \tag{11}$$

Fig. 2. The space around the agent is divided into eight regions of radius r. The occupied regions establish the obstacle code φ.

The set of features $v, \sigma, \varphi, A_x, A_y$ define a state vector S (see Eq. 12). In this case A_x and A_y forms a $2D$ the vector defining the motion performed by the pedestrian provides a certain state. All the vectors S which match the same goal $goal_k$ are packed in a look-up table Λ_m see Eq. 13.

$$S_j = \left[\Phi_{ix}, \Phi_{iy}, \sigma, \varphi, A_x, A_y \right] \tag{12}$$

$$\Lambda_m = [S_0, S_1, \ldots, S_N] \tag{13}$$

Therefore table Λ represents our knowledge-base. The input of the knowledge base will be a state s, the system finds the closest match between the incoming state vector inside the knowledge-base. Once we have a match, the system returns the action vector $A = (A_x, A_y)$.

4.2 Social Data Driven Simulation Model

Finally the resulting steering vector of a pedestrian is modeled according to Eq. 14. The A component of the steering force is given by the knowledge base as a function of the pedestrian state presented in the simulation. The rest of the components are given by f_i^{group} which is the last component of the Moussaïd model of group social forces [14]. This fact allowed us to avoid demanding more memory resources to store persistent data related to group formations in the knowledge base. We chose the group force equation presented by Moussaïd because reproduces faithfully the group formations in pedestrians.

$$\frac{dv_i}{dt} = A + f_i^{wall} + \sum_{j \neq i} f_{i,j} + f_i^{group} \tag{14}$$

5   Results

In order to evaluate the simulation of the pedestrian steering motions, we employ a metric based on entropy as a measure of the size of the predicted error. Entropy has proven to be applicable to data generated with small and large number of pedestrians in sparse and dense scenes [6]. The measure of entropy is defined as follows: Given a state of a real scene Z_k the difference between the action vector $A(Z_k)$ and the next state Z_{k+1} is calculated giving an entropy vector. In this case the total entropy for a given path is calculated using Eq. 15. In this case, the smaller the entropy the better the simulation.

$$En = \sum_{k=0}^{N} \|Z_{k+1} - A(Z_k)\| \tag{15}$$

We ran a test measuring the entropy for a single path followed by a pedestrian again different simulation models: vector based, data-driven based and our hybrid model (Fuzzy data-driven with group forces "FDDGF"), the result of this test is presented in Fig. 3. Our system ranked in the second place just slightly above over pure data driven techniques. It is a fact that Data-driven methods closely reflect the behavior of pedestrians in real scenes, but a major drawback in this approach is that they require large amounts of data and scaling sometimes becomes unfeasible. On the other hand, vector-based methods and rule-based methods demand less memory but instead of that they need hard fine tuning parameters that govern agent behaviors, which can be a very demanding task. Our experiments show that mixing data-driven methods with group forces allow us to achieve results comparable to those obtained with data-driven systems but using less memory and avoiding fine tuning parameters jobs.

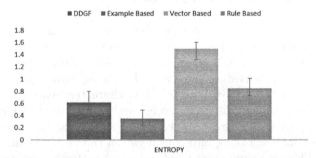

SINGLE AGENT ENTROPY TEST

Fig. 3. We present the measurement of average entropy on the prediction made by vector-based models, data-driven models and our hybrid model (DDFG). Whiskers show the standard error for each sample. The sample size was of fifty random pedestrians walking alone.

For our experiments we executed the simulation and visualization process in a workstation with these characteristics: Intel Core i7-4810MQ CPU @ 2.80 GHz

8, 16 Gb of RAM, GeForce 880M with Gb of video memory. For a simulation in the city (Barcelona) with one thousand characters 4.3 million triangles are needed and 3.1 million vertices. We use 1115 draw calls and 39 batched draw calls. It takes a total of 300 MB of RAM memory, 112 MB of video memory and it takes 28 ms to render each individual frame giving us a 35.71 frame rate. In average each frame has 18000 objects and the total scene is composed by 42767 objects as shown in Fig. 4.

Fig. 4. An example of the system running with the described specs.

6   Conclusions and Future Work

The previously discussed works show a robust approach for urban crowd simulation at interactive frame rates, the system is powerful enough to handle large environments with many agents in real time without compromising visual quality and the simulation of individual behavior. The system proves to be successful in achieving meaningful diversity in terms of how characters react for specific input or situations. Nevertheless this stage can be further optimized by including LOD techniques not only to rendering stages but to simulation, animation, collision avoidance and behavior taking into consideration the viewer position inside the environment. This way simulation overhead could be further reduced.

Applications for virtual city generation range from research and educational purposes such as urban planning and creation of virtual environments for simulation. Movie and game industries have a high demand for quick creation of complex environments in their applications, since they are in constant need for more art assets that form virtual worlds to support interaction, training, evaluation, virtual sets, and other uses. Security, crisis management and virtual training can take advantage of this environments as well.

Acknowledgment. Special thanks to SECITI in Mexico for providing part of the founding for the present research, also we must express our gratitude for all the team that conforms the Barcelona Super Computing Center for facilitate the equipment and the infrastructure for the project.

References

1. Besserud, K., Hussey, T.: Urban design, urban simulation, and the need for computational tools. IBM J. Res. Dev. **55**(1&2), 13–29 (2011). https://doi.org/10.1147/JRD.2010.2097091

2. Boatright, C.D., Kapadia, M., Shapira, J.M., Badler, N.I.: Context-sensitive data-driven crowd simulation. In: Proceedings of the 12th ACM SIGGRAPH International Conference on Virtual-Reality Continuum and Its Applications in Industry - VRCAI 2013, pp. 51–56 (2013). http://dl.acm.org/citation.cfm?doid=2534329.2534332

3. Charalambous, P., Chrysanthou, Y.: The PAG crowd: a graph based approach for efficient data-driven crowd simulation. Comput. Graph. Forum **33**, 95–108 (2014). http://doi.wiley.com/10.1111/cgf.12403

4. Dai, J., Li, X., Liu, L.: Simulation of pedestrian counter flow through bottlenecks by using an agent-based model. Phys. A Stat. Mech. Appl. **392**(9), 2202–2211 (2013). http://linkinghub.elsevier.com/retrieve/pii/S0378437113000265

5. van Essen, R.: Maps Get Real: Digital Maps evolving from mathematical line graphs to virtual reality models. In: van Oosterom, P., Zlatanova, S., Penninga, F., Fendel, E.M. (eds.) Advances in 3D Geoinformation Systems. LNGC, pp. 3–18. Springer, Heidelberg (2008). https://doi.org/10.1007/978-3-540-72135-2_1

6. Guy, S.J., van den Berg, J., Liu, W., Lau, R., Lin, M.C., Manocha, D.: A statistical similarity measure for aggregate crowd dynamics. ACM Trans. Graph. **31**(6), 1 (2012). http://portal.acm.org/citation.cfm?doid=42005.42006dl.acm.org/citation.cfm?doid=2366145.2366209

7. Helbing, D., Molnár, P.: Social force model for pedestrian dynamics. Phys. Rev. E **51**(5), 4282–4286 (1995). http://link.aps.org/doi/10.1103/PhysRevE.51.4282

8. Hoogendoorn, S.P., Bovy, P.H.L.: Normative pedestrian behaviour theory and modelling. In: Proceedings of the 15th International Symposium on Transportation and Traffic Theory, Adelaide, Australia, pp. 219–245 (2002)

9. Hughes, R.L.: The flow of human crowds. Ann. Rev. Fluid Mech. **35**(1997), 169–182 (2003). http://www.annualreviews.org/doi/abs/10.1146/annurev.fluid.35.101101.161136

10. Lakoba, T.I.: Modifications of the Helbing-Molnar-Farkas-Vicsek social force model for pedestrian evolution. Simulation **81**(5), 339–352 (2005). http://sim.sagepub.com/cgi/doi/10.1177/0037549705052772

11. Lee, K., Choi, M., Hong, Q., Lee, J.: Group behavior from video: a data-driven approach to crowd simulation. In: Proceedings of the 2007 ACM, San Diego, California, pp. 109–118 (2007). http://dl.acm.org/citation.cfm?id=1272706

12. Lerner, A., Chrysanthou, Y., Lischinski, D.: Crowds by example. Comput. Graph. Forum **26**, 655–664 (2007)

13. Loviscach, J.: Deformations: wrinkling coarse meshes on the GPU. Comput. Graph. Forum **25**(3), 467–476 (2006)

14. Moussaïd, M., Perozo, N., Garnier, S., Helbing, D., Theraulaz, G.: The walking behaviour of pedestrian social groups and its impact on crowd dynamics. PloS One **5**(4), e10047 (2010). http://www.pubmedcentral.nih.gov/articlerender.fcgi?artid=2850937

15. van Oosterom, P., van Oosterom, P., Zlatanova, S., Penninga, F., Fendel, E.: Advances in 3D Geoinformation Systems, 1st edn. Springer, Heidelberg (2007). https://doi.org/10.1007/978-3-540-72135-2

16. Pettré, J., Ondrej, J., Olivier, A.h., Cretual, A., Donikian, S.: Experiment-based modeling, simulation and validation of interactions between virtual walkers. In: Proceedings of the 2009 ACM SIGGRAPH/Eurographics Symposium on Computer Animation 2009, p. 189 (2009). http://portal.acm.org/citation.cfm?doid=1599470.1599495

17. Reynolds, C.W.: Flocks, herds and schools: a distributed behavioral model. ACM SIGGRAPH Comput. Graph. **21**(4), 25–34 (1987). http://portal.acm.org/citation.cfm?doid=37402.37406

18. Rudomín, I., Hernández, B., De Gyves, O., Toledo, L., Rivalcoba, I., Ruiz, S.: Generating large varied animated crowds in the GPU. In: Proceedings of ISUM 2013, pp. 1–11 (2013)

19. Rudomín, I., Solar, G.V., Oviedo, J.E., Pérez, H., Martini, J.L.Z.: Modelling crowds in urban spaces. Computación y Sistemas (CyS) **21**, 57–66 (2017)

20. Shinohara, K., Georgescu, S.: Modelling adopter behaviour based on the Navier stokes equation. ISRN Mathematical Analysis 2011, pp. 1–10 (2011). http://www.hindawi.com/journals/isrn.mathematical.analysis/2011/894983/

21. da Silveira, L.G., Musse, S.R.: Real-time generation of populated virtual cities. In: Proceedings of the ACM Symposium on Virtual Reality Software and Technology, VRST 2006, pp. 155–164. ACM, New York (2006). http://doi.acm.org/10.1145/1180495.1180527

22. Thalmann, D., Grillon, H., Maim, J., Yersin, B.: Challenges in crowd simulation. In: 2009 International Conference on CyberWorlds, pp. 1–12 (2009). http://ieeexplore.ieee.org/lpdocs/epic03/wrapper.htm?arnumber=5279720

23. Thomsen, A., Breunig, M., Butwilowski, E., Broscheit, B.: Modelling and managing topology in 3D geoinformation systems. In: van Oosterom, P., Zlatanova, S., Penninga, F., Fendel, E.M. (eds.) Advances in 3D Geoinformation Systems. LNGC, pp. 229–246. Springer, Heidelberg (2008). https://doi.org/10.1007/978-3-540-72135-2_14

24. Toledo, L., De Gyves, O., Rivalcoba, I., Rudomn, I.: Hierarchical level of detail for varied animated crowds. Vis. Comput. **30**, 949–961 (2014)

25. Torrens, P., Li, X., Griffin, W.a.: Building agent-based walking models by machine-learning on diverse databases of space-time trajectory samples. Trans. GIS **15**, 67–94 (2011)

Track of Teaching Computational Science

Design and Analysis of an Undergraduate Computational Engineering Degree at Federal University of Juiz de Fora

Marcelo Lobosco$^{(\boxtimes)}$ (iD), Flávia de Souza Bastos(iD), Bernardo Martins Rocha(iD), and Rodrigo Weber dos Santos(iD)

Graduate Program on Computational Modeling, Federal University of Juiz de Fora, Rua José Lourenço Kelmer, s/n, Juiz de Fora, MG 36036-330, Brazil
{marcelo.lobosco,flavia.bastos,bernardo.rocha,rodrigo.weber}@ufjf.edu.br
http://www.ufjf.br/pgmc/

Abstract. The undergraduate program in Computational Engineering at Federal University of Juiz de Fora, Brazil, was created in 2008 as a joint initiative of two distinct departments in the University, Computer Science, located in the Exact Science Institute, and Applied and Computational Mechanics, located in the School of Engineering. First freshmen began in 2009 and graduated in 2014. This work presents the curriculum structure of this pioneering full bachelor's degree in Computational Engineering in Brazil.

Keywords: Curriculum structure · Computational Engineering Undergraduate program

1 Introduction

This work presents the curriculum design of the undergraduate program in Computational Engineering (CE) at Federal University of Juiz de Fora (UFJF), Brazil. The creation of the CE program at UFJF was based in an international trend of creating undergraduate engineering programs with an interdisciplinary background that aims to prepare students to work with formulation, analysis, implementation and application of mathematical models, numerical methods and computational systems to solve modern scientific and engineering problems. These multiple skills are a way of inserting students in new areas of the job market that are dedicated to innovation and technological developments to solve a great diversity of problems.

The CE program at UFJF, due to its intrinsic interdisciplinary nature, was proposed by two distinct units: School of Engineering and the Exact Sciences Institute. The Graduate Program in Computational Modeling, which offers master and doctoral degrees, is also offered by these two units. With a close proximity

Supported by CNPq, FAPEMIG and UFJF.

to the graduate program, the CE program also offers the students to be in contact with a rich scientific research environment. In this way, the students get used to ask and search for new solutions, and to verify and compare them to others, which is certainly an advantage in the job market.

The CE program is offered on a full-time basis. In fact, all CE students are first admitted to the Exact Sciences (ES) program. The ES program was designed in a way that it shares a common core with many distinct programs: Computer Science, Computational Engineering, Electrical Engineering, Mechanical Engineering, Statistics, Physics, Mathematics and Chemistry. An ES student has the opportunity to have contact with these distinct disciplines and, after this first contact, choose the one that he/she is more identified with. Up to 20 ES students can be admitted to the CE program per year, after they finish the third term of the ES program. Another 20 students can enroll at the CE on the very first term of the ES program. This choice is for students that, during the admission process, are confident to proceed directly to CE.

The ES program can be taken as a kind of minor program in which the students receive a full bachelor's degree in ES. After students have concluded the ES program, which occurs after six terms, they are officially admitted in the CE program (or in another program they have chosen).

The fulfillment of requirements to obtain the CE degree should occur, following the suggested curriculum, within 10 terms, including the 6 terms to conclude the ES program. The maximum time allowed for its conclusion is the double of the expected completion time, i.e., 20 terms. The CE program requires at least 3,800 h of courses and activities, in line with the Brazilian law on engineering undergraduate programs.

The remaining of this paper is organized as follows. Section 2 presents the multiple aspects that have been taken into account during the CE curriculum design. Section 3 presents the CE curriculum and discusses some of its main aspects. Section 4 presents the impact of the proximity of the graduate and undergraduate programs. Section 5 presents other CE programs and Sect. 6 presents our conclusions.

2   Curriculum Design

The CE curriculum was designed in order to give a basic formation in a new area of knowledge that has been in consolidation during the last decades, gathering specializations from different fields of engineering and sciences. This interdisciplinary education is present not only in the core courses, but also in a large amount of elective ones.

The advanced topics of the CE curriculum are open, depending on the choices of the student. In other words, the curriculum is flexible to adapt to a variety of students: those that want a breadth or a in depth view of some area. Furthermore, some courses covering themes such as computational modeling, numerical methods and parallel computing are also included for junior and senior students. It is also recommended that junior and senior students choose courses from other sorts of engineering available in the School of Engineering, such as electrical, electronics, telecommunications, mechanics, environmental, among others. The objective is to allow students to improve their skills in modeling problems from other disciplines. In the specific case of our undergraduate CE degree, a large number of courses in structural and computational mechanics fields are available.

Also, a large number of laws in Brazil had to be observed during the CE curriculum design, such as: (a) requirements for bachelor's degree; (b) minimum requirements for engineering programs; (c) syllabus, grading policy; and (d) obligation to include in the curriculum some disciplines, such as Afro-Brazilian and native indigenous history and culture, the Brazilian sign language, and environmental education.

2.1 Objectives and Competencies

The main objective of the curriculum is to prepare the students to be able to formulate, analyze, implement and apply mathematical models, numerical methods and computational systems to solve distinct scientific and engineering problems. To achieve this purpose, many abilities must be developed during the CE undergraduate program:

- Ability to use knowledge from mathematics, physics, computer science, engineering and modern technologies in the development of products and services. The following courses contribute to this goal: Calculus I, II and III; Differential Equations I; Physics I, II and III; Physics Lab; Fundamental Chemistry; Chemistry Lab; Sciences Lab; Calculus of Probability; as well as courses in the area of mechanics and computing;
- Ability to project, implement, test and maintain software for the development of products or services. Algorithms; Data Structures and Data Structures II; Object-Oriented Programming; Programming Lab I and II; Software Modeling; Databases and Software Engineering are courses related to this goal;
- Ability to take advantage of existing techniques and technologies, and to develop and propose new ones. Introduction to Computational Modeling; Transport Phenomena and Mechanics are courses related to this goal;
- Ability to understand the impacts of products and services in the environment. The course Ecology and Environment Preservation is related to this goal;
- Ability to apply the knowledge from numerical methods to solve scientific and engineering problems. The following courses contribute to this goal: Numerical Calculus; Introduction to Computational Modeling and Introduction to Discrete Methods;
- Ability to interact and communicate with engineers and other professionals during the development of projects. Internship; Multidisciplinary Project; Undergraduate Thesis; and the presentation of projects and practical activities in some courses contribute to this goal;
- Ability to keep himself/herself updated with the latest technological trends. This topic is always addressed in courses, specially in Introduction to Computational Engineering and Multidisciplinary Project;

- Ability to act with ethics and integrity in his/her professional activities, evaluating the impacts of his/her professional activities for the society and the environment. Introduction to Computational Engineering and Ecology and Environment Preservation are courses related to this goal;
- Ability to supervise, coordinate, plan, specify, project and implement activities compatible with his/her academic degree. The conclusion of all courses in curriculum contributes to this goal. More specifically, Multidisciplinary Project and Undergraduate Thesis evaluate if the student successfully achieved this ability.

A set of core competencies has been chosen to compose the curriculum. They include, as mandatory courses for all CE students, the following areas: mathematics, science, programming, computer science, numerical methods, and applications (applied and computational mechanics). These competencies were included as mandatory courses for all CE students. Also, a large number of completely unconstrained elective slots are available for students that want to develop, based on their own interests and goals, new skills.

3   Curriculum

The curriculum is divided into eight basic components, following UFJF's and ES's rules, as well as laws in Brazil about Bachelor's degrees: (a) core courses, which are composed of mandatory courses for all CE students; (b) mandatory activity, which is an activity (i.e., there is no grade associated with it, the student is either approved or reproved) mandatory for all CE students; (c) elective courses, which is a pre-selected list of courses on advanced topics, and students can choose some of them to attend to; (d) elective activities, which is a preselected list of activities, such as attend to a conference, workshop, short-term courses and other related activities, as well as additional hours in internships and other hands-on training experiences inside or outside UFJF; (e) optional courses, which can be any course in any area of knowledge that was not listed as an elective course; (f) a mandatory internship; (g) a multidisciplinary project; and (h) undergraduate thesis. Except for the undergraduate thesis, for all other components one hour corresponds to 60 min of lecture class time, activities or internship, so the time spent by students in homeworks and outside class study is not considered. For the undergraduate thesis, the number of hours necessary to develop and implement a computational model, as well as to write the text that describes it, is estimated. Table 1 presents how the total number of hours are divided in these distinct courses and activities. Again, the proposed CE curriculum had to follow some rules and laws in order to define the amount of time for each type of course.

In the proposed curriculum students play a fundamental role in their education through the choice of elective courses that allow to have a breadth view on multiple areas or a in depth view of some area of their particular interest. In fact, the mechanism allows students to trade engineering depth for breadth within a

Table 1. Distribution of the academic load by its basic components. A total of 3, 800 h is required for obtaining the CE Bachelor's degree.

Core Courses	2,520 h
Mandatory Activity	30 h
Elective Courses	420 h
Elective Activities	120 h
Optional Courses	300 h
Internship	170 h
Multidisciplinary Project	60 h
Undergraduate Thesis	180 h

single department (for example, computer science) or breadth among other disciplines (for example, electrical, mechanical and environmental engineering). To achieve this goal, a large number of unconstrained slots are available as elective and optional courses. Although a huge amount of courses can be chosen as optional, the following topics are suggested to those students that may be lost with so many options: (a) scientific method; (b) communication and expression, including foreign languages; (c) administration; (d) economy; (e) humanities, social and environmental sciences. Nevertheless, some students prefer to choose other courses from biology, mathematics, physics, or geology by themselves.

The core courses in the CE curriculum, presented in Table 2, presents the student to fundamental topics of mathematics, physics, programming, numerical methods and structural and computational mechanics, as well as substantial breadth and depth in some topics related to Computer Science, such as digital circuits and computer organization, computer networks, and operating systems. As one can observe, the core courses are scattered across all the curriculum. Some of the courses in the CE curriculum are shared with the ES program, specifically those from the first till the fourth term. Moreover, the focus on structural and computational mechanics is due to the fact that the department in the School of Engineering that supports the program is the Applied and Computational Mechanics Department.

The core courses are approximately distributed in the following way, as Table 3 shows: 19% in Mathematics, 17% in Physics and Chemistry, 14% in Programming, 21% in Computer Science, 12% in Numerical Methods, 12% in Applied and Computational Mechanics, and 5% in other disciplines.

Figure 1 illustrates the basic components of the curriculum, describing how they are distributed along the terms. The term is composed by 15 weeks, so the maximum number of hours a student spend per week in classes is 28 h, in the third, fourth, fifth and sixth terms. Recall that the elective activities are not courses, but external activities such as conferences, short-term courses, and hands-on training experiences. In order to conclude the ES bachelor, it is required that some of the core courses, and all the optional courses and elective activities are concluded. The number of terms suggested to conclude the ES bachelor is

Table 2. CE core courses.

Year	First semester	Hours	Second semester	Hours
1	Calculus I	60	Calculus II	60
	Algorithms	60	Data Structures	60
	Programming Lab	30	Programming Lab II	30
	Introduction to Physical Sciences Lab	30	Introduction to Computational Engineering	30
	Fundamental Chemistry	60	Physics I	60
	Chemistry Lab	30	Physics Lab I	30
	Analytic Geometry and Linear Systems	60	Structures and Transformation Lab	30
			Introduction to Statistics	60
2	Calculus III	60	Differential Equations I	60
	Object-Oriented Programming	60	Data Structures II	60
	Physics II	60	Physics III	60
	Calculus of Probability I	60	Linear Algebra	60
	Graphical Representation and Geometric Modeling	60	Mechanics	60
			Numerical Calculus	60
3	Transport Phenomena	60	Computer Organization	60
	Introduction to Computational Modeling	60	Software Modeling	60
	Graph Theory	60	Solid Mechanics I	60
	Digital Circuits	60	Structural Mechanics	60
	Fundamentals of Structural Mechanics	60	Operational Research	60
	Mechanics of Materials	60		
4	Analysis and Project of Algorithms	60	Formal Languages and Automata Theory	60
	Introduction to Discrete Methods	60	Computer Networks	60
	Databases	60	Introduction to the Finite Element Method	60
	Operating Systems	60		
5	Ecology and Environment Preservation	30		
	Parallel Programming	60		

Table 3. Distribution of core courses by disciplines.

Discipline	Hours
Mathematics	480
Physics/Chemistry	420
Programming	360
Computer Science	540
Numerical Methods	300
Applied and Computational Mechanics	300
Other	120
Total	2,520

six, and for this reason these activities are distributed till the sixth term. Also, due to the fact that elective activities are usually related to advanced topics, they should be attended by junior and senior students. This is a suggestion, since students are free to attend the courses in a distinct way.

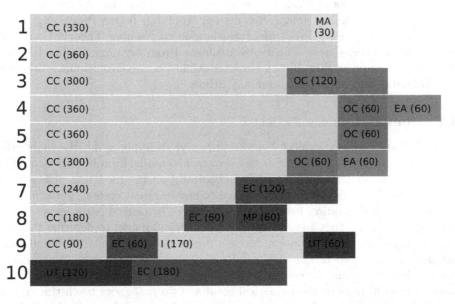

Fig. 1. CE curriculum: basic organization. CC represents core courses, MA mandatory activity, EC elective courses, EA elective activities, OC optional courses, I internship, MP multidisciplinary project and UT Undergraduate Thesis. Each line represents an academic term. Within the parentheses are represented the hourly loads of each components of the curriculum along the term.

Also, as one can observe from Fig. 1 and Table 1, the key attribute of the CE curriculum is its flexibility. In the curriculum 840 h, or 22% of the hours required for obtaining the CE Bachelor's degree, are of free choice of students. If we consider that the theme of the Undergraduate Thesis is usually also chosen by students, the total number of hours in which they decide what to study increases to 1,020, or about 27% of the total. Students have probably thousands of courses to choose as optional, and about 50 to choose as elective ones.

Such a huge number of courses available to choose are exciting for some focused students, but may represent a problem for others. Although the student can count not only on the head of the CE program for advise, but also on other professors and senior colleagues, a group of professors, responsible for the conception, consolidation and continuous updating of the curriculum, decided to group the elective courses into three distinct groups, called thematic groups. These groups are the following: Numerical Methods and Optimization; Applied and Computational Mechanics; and Applied Computational Systems. The idea of the groups is only to guide students in their choices. For example, if a student would like to focus on Numerical Methods and Optimization, he/she can consult the list of elective courses that are related to this topic. Students inclined to be generalists can explore a wider range of courses in these three topics. Examples of courses that are offered as electives are: Numerical Solution of Differential Equations; Scientific Visualization; Fluid Mechanics; Mechanics of Materials II and III; Computational Modeling of Aeroelastic Phenomena; Advanced Topics on Geometric Modeling; Image Processing; Applying Image Processing to the Solution of Engineering Problems; Introduction to Number Theory; Computational Intelligence; Queue Theory; Non-Linear Programming; Artificial Neural Networks; Computer Graphics; Computer Architecture; Evolutionary Computing; Distributed Systems, among many others.

3.1 Multidisciplinary Project

The Multidisciplinary Project has the objective of applying all the knowledge that students have acquired along the program to model a problem proposed by the professors, i.e., a capstone project. Basically all the modeling phases must be observed by students: first, they have to create a real system, perform some experiments and acquire, using sensors, cameras or other instruments, experimental data. Then they have to use a mathematical model to describe the phenomenon under study, and use numerical methods to implement it. Simulations are performed and their numerical results are compared to the experimental ones. Some adjustments may be necessary in this process. Some visualization tools may also be used to present the numerical results. Two professors teach this course, one from the Computer Science Department, and another from the Applied and Computational Mechanics Department. This is done in order to guarantee the multidisciplinary nature of the class. Students are divided in groups to implement the tasks, and each group works on a different task.

The approach used by professors in the course involves a discussion of common issues in the modeling area, such as conceptual models that can not be used to make predictions; the use of projects developed by third-party, and the lack of full control over their operation; the lack of documentation to describe the implementation of a model and its impacts; and especially on the difficulties of fitting parameters and validating models in order to obtain reliable results and predictions.

With respect to project themes, students are led to think, as a way of contextualization, in a complex problem for which the computational modeling is important. Then the student has to associate it with a simpler problem, which one could perform simple laboratory experiments, without the need of sophisticated tools. This is not only due to budget restrictions, but above all the idea that creativity is also necessary for a multidisciplinary training.

The choice of the project theme may take some time, and in the meanwhile some theoretical classes are offered as a way to review important concepts and applications. From this point onwards, materials and methods are proposed by students and the dynamic of meetings changes, so that they assume the leading role. Teachers encourage interaction between groups by asking for systematic presentations of each group's progress, and allowing opinions and suggestions from others, and most of the time they are taken into account.

Students have to describe technical problems and results in a final written report. In addition to the presentation of the reports in classroom, students are also encouraged to produce a video describing the entire project, which is also used to assess their work. Recently, a channel of the course was created in YouTube to store these videos. It is expected that the channel can help other students interested in computational modeling as well as to disseminate the CE program.

4 Participation of Students in a Interdisciplinary Research Environment

An additional advantage of the CE program at UFJF is its proximity to the Graduate Program on Computational Modeling (GPCM). Almost all researchers at GPCM are also professors in the CE program. This proximity is not only important to present the students to the state of art in the research fields of many distinct areas, but also to attract them to work on research.

UFJF funds scholarships to undergraduate students to work on research. This funding program in known as Iniciação Científica (scientific initiation), and offers scholarship from CNPq (the Brazilian Research Council), FAPEMIG (Research Council of the Minas Gerais State) and UFJF. Many of the CE undergraduate students work on interdisciplinary research topics conducted by professors of the GPCM. This research activity may be used by them as an Internship. Also, during the research activity it is usual for students to attend to conferences, workshops, etc., which can be used as part of elective activities. Finally, some of them publish works on conferences, workshops and even in scientific journals, as main authors or coauthors. Part of this research can be presented as the Undergraduate Thesis. As a result, almost all of the CE students choose to enter in a graduate program after graduating. In fact, some of the senior students attend graduate classes while they are finishing the undergraduate, reducing the time to obtain a master degree. Since in UFJF it is mandatory to hold a B.S. degree to be admitted in a graduate program, this is only possible because they finish the ES program after 3 years.

5   Other CE Undergraduate Programs

The SIAM list of undergraduate CSE programs [5] identifies only twelve programs that offer bachelor degrees on Computational Science and Engineering. For sure, this number is out dated. A simple search in the web returns a much large number of colleges and universities that offers distinct types of CSE degrees, and some works [6,13] present an additional list of programs. Basically it is possible to identify distinct ways to structure these programs [6]:

- Full Bachelor degree in CSE;
- Full Bachelor degree in Computational Finance, Computational Physics, Computational Mathematics or Applied Mathematics;
- Emphasis or Concentration in CSE;
- Minor program in CSE.

American University [1] offers a full B.S. in Computational Science, and students can choose distinct application areas, including biology, chemistry, computer science, economics, environmental studies, finance, mathematics, physics, psychology, and statistics. Hood College [4] offers a full B.S. in Computational Science with concentration in four distinct areas: chemistry, ecology, molecular biology and physics. Its Senior Project in Computational Science seems to be very similar to the Multidisciplinary work described in this work: the student uses computational knowledge and skills to investigate a given problem. The same concept is present in the B.S. in Computational Science offered by the Florida State University [2]: in the Practicum in Computational Science course, students are required to work on an ambitious project in computational science. Stanford University [7] offers a full B.S. in Mathematical and Computational Science, and tracks on biology, engineering and statistics are available. The University of Queensland [9] offers a Computational Science and Computer Science Dual Major as part of the Bachelor of Science program. This is similar to the ES undergraduate program, that allow students to have one or more majors in the programs that are part of the ES. Many students that obtained a B.S. in CE have also obtained a B.S. in Computer Science. Many other universities offer full bachelor programs in the CSE field [3,8,10–12].

The undergraduate CE program at UFJF shares common features with these bachelor programs, including mathematics (specially Calculus), programming, and numerical methods. Most CE programs require a capstone project and an industrial internship. Finally, an application area is usually present in most of CE programs. From a design point of view, CE program at UFJF can be distinguished from the other CE programs in the following way: (a) strong emphasis on mathematics and sciences, which corresponds to 900 h of lecture class time; (b) inclusion of courses that are typical of Computer Science, such as Computer

Organization, Databases, Computer Networks and Operating Systems, to show students how computer systems work, and how these systems should be used to improve performance of applications; and (c) the proximity to the graduate program, which helps to attract students to an undergraduate research experience.

6 Conclusions

In this work we presented the curriculum of the undergraduate program in Computational Engineering at Federal University of Juiz de Fora, Brazil. This 5 years full bachelor degree has the focus on mathematics, sciences (physics and chemistry), programming and numerical methods. Moreover, the curriculum also focuses on structural and computational mechanics due to the fact that the department in the School of Engineering that supports the program is the Applied and Computational Mechanics Department. Another key attribute of the CE curriculum is its flexibility: up to 27% of the hours required for obtaining the CE Bachelor's degree are of free choice of students. The program is evaluated frequently by the Brazilian Government, and in its last evaluation it achieved the maximum grade (5 in a scale from 1 to 5).

References

1. American University, Washington, DC: BS Computational Science. https://tinyurl.com/yc2dcnpg
2. Department of Scientific Computing: Computational Science, B.S. https://tinyurl.com/ybza9yh5
3. ETH Zürich: Bachelor rechnergestützte wissenschaften. https://tinyurl.com/ydew5ge9
4. Hood College: Computational Science Major, B.S. https://tinyurl.com/yawgzvvt
5. SIAM: Society for Industrial and Applied Mathematics: Graduate programs in computational science. https://tinyurl.com/yblkxvnt
6. SIAM Working Group on CSE Undergraduate Education and Co-Chairs, P.T., Petzold, L., Shiflet, A., Vakalis, I., Jordan, K., John, S.S.: Undergraduate computational science and engineering education. SIAM Rev. **53**(3), 561–574 (2011)
7. Stanford University: Mathematical and computational science. https://tinyurl.com/y8bhgkeh
8. Technische Universität Chemnitz: Bachelor degree program in computational science. https://tinyurl.com/y82rqjmv
9. The University of Queensland: Computational science and computer science dual major. https://tinyurl.com/yaebpymk
10. University of South Carolina - Beaufort: Computational science. https://tinyurl.com/ya4kqcbk
11. University of Texas in Austin: Bachelor of science in computational engineering. https://tinyurl.com/y8txlm5z
12. University of Texas Rio Grande Valley: Computational science - bachelor of science. https://tinyurl.com/y9dshbyo
13. Yasar, O., Landau, R.H.: Elements of computational science and engineering education. SIAM Rev. **45**(4), 787–805 (2003). https://doi.org/10.1137/S0036144502408075

Extended Cognition Hypothesis Applied to Computational Thinking in Computer Science Education

Mika Letonsaari[1,2(✉)]

[1] University of Helsinki, Helsinki, Finland
mika.letonsaari@helsinki.fi
[2] South-Eastern Finland University of Applied Sciences, Mikkeli, Finland

Abstract. Computational thinking is a much-used concept in computer science education. Here we examine the concept from the viewpoint of the extended cognition hypothesis. The analysis reveals that the extent of the concept is limited by its strong historical roots in computer science and software engineering. According to the extended cognition hypothesis, there is no meaningful distinction between human cognitive functions and the technology. This standpoint promotes a broader interpretation of the human-technology interaction. Human cognitive processes spontaneously adapt available technology enhanced skills when technology is used in cognitively relevant levels and modalities. A new concept technology synchronized thinking is presented to denote this conclusion. More diverse and practical approach is suggested for the computer science education.

Keywords: Computational thinking · Extended cognition
Externalism · Philosophy of mind · Computer science education

1 Introduction

In this article, we study the concept of computational thinking from the viewpoint of the extended cognition hypothesis. Both of these concepts have deep roots in the history of the 20th-century science but they have only very recently made a major impact in the mainstream science.

Computational thinking is a broad term describing the skills needed for solving problems with computers and computational methods. The concept has been popular for about a decade. It has been widely adopted in computer science education and generally made into one of the key concepts in 21st-century skills in education.

Externalism is a school of thought in philosophy. The main idea of externalism is that consciousness and cognition cannot be understood only as the result of the function of the brain or nervous system. The extended cognition hypothesis is an active form of externalism claiming that things external to the

© Springer International Publishing AG, part of Springer Nature 2018
Y. Shi et al. (Eds.): ICCS 2018, LNCS 10862, pp. 304–317, 2018.
https://doi.org/10.1007/978-3-319-93713-7_25

human body function as parts of the human cognitive function. The idea has been widely discussed especially during last two decades, and it has had a prominent contribution to the philosophy of mind, cognitive science, and psychology.

An extensive review of these concepts is out of the scope of this article. Both concepts are introduced here briefly from a practical view of computer science education.

1.1 Computational Thinking

The history of computational thinking is related to the birth of computer science in the early 20th century. Before computer science was accepted as a separate discipline it operated under the disciplines of electric engineering and mathematics. But as the importance of computers and programming grew, there was a need to define what separates computer science from other disciplines.

The distinction between disciplines is often emphasized by the use of different mental processes in the way the disciplines are practiced. This novel way of thinking was called "algorithmizing" by Alan Perlis and it was described as a "general purpose thinking tool" by George Forsythe in the 1960s. In the 1970s Donald Knuth used a term "algorithmic thinking" [1].

For example, Dijkstra discussed the problems of using mathematical proofs in understanding programming in 1974 and observed three differences in the required thinking: construction of new concepts, construction of new notations, and level of abstraction in the terms of semantics [2].

Knuth concluded that the algorithmic thinking is the main difference between mathematics and computer science [3] and later specified practical aspects of algorithmic complexity as the key difference [4]. In the same article Knuth pointed out the use of assignment operator as a distinctive example. The assignment operator in computer programming is often the equals sign of mathematics and equality has often typographically more complex symbol[1].

The term computational thinking was first used by Papert in 1980 [5]. It became widely popular in 2006 when Wing published an essay where she suggested that computational thinking was a beneficial skill set for everyone, not only computer scientists [6].

There are many definitions of the term computational thinking. Wing uses the following definition developed with Jan Cuny, Larry Snyder, and Alfred Aho: "The thought processes involved in formulating problems and their solutions so that the solutions are represented in a form that can be effectively carried out by an information-processing agent" [7,8].

A more specific definition, breaking the term into its constituents in the practical context of education, is developed by the Computer Science Teachers Association (CSTA) and the International Society for Technology in Education (ISTE). According to their definition computational thinking includes the following elements [9]:

---

[1] While there is a traditionally used markup for the assignment, ':=', the equality sign '=' is often used as an assignment operator in computer languages. Equality is tested with double equality sign '==' or functions like 'equals()' or 'is_equal()'.

- formulating problems in a way that enables us to use a computer and other tools to help solve them
- logically organizing and analyzing data
- representing data through abstractions such as models and simulations
- automating solutions through algorithmic thinking (a series of ordered steps)
- identifying, analyzing, and implementing possible solutions with the goal of achieving the most efficient and effective combination of steps and resources
- generalizing and transferring this problem-solving process to a wide variety of problems

There are other definitions and critique of the definition, especially for the vagueness and interpretations of the definition. For a comprehensive review of the subject see Tedre [10].

While no final definition has been achieved for the term, there is a wide consensus that the term computational thinking encapsulates something essential in the deeper understanding of the computer science and the modern technological world. And for this reason, there has been much work to incorporate the ideas of computational thinking into k-9 and k-12 computer science education.

1.2   Extended Cognition Hypothesis

The relationship between human mind and human body has always fascinated artists, scholars of religions, and scientists. Religious scriptures include some of the oldest references to the subject. Parmenides of Elea in Greece in the 5th century BCE, and later Plato, brought the issue to the systematic philosophical discussion [11]. This was followed by probably the most well-known philosophical debate in Western philosophy, the debate between Cartesian dualism, especially defended by René Descartes, and different schools of monism [12].

It was not until late 20th century that technological development in biology, medical imaging, and cognitive science managed to reveal the function of the brain and how cognitive functions arise from neural activity [13]. By the end of the 20th century, there was a significant demand for an explanation of the relationship between human mind and its environment [14]. This demand culminated in the publication of *The Extended Mind* paper in 1998 by Chalmers and Clark where the extended mind hypothesis was presented [15].

Extended cognition hypothesis is a philosophical position that cognitive processes and human mind extend beyond the brain in the environment. As a simple example, one can write things down with a pen and a paper so that one doesn't need to remember them. Or one can use a pocket calculator to perform mathematical calculations.

Using external tools human cognition saves the use of memory and processing capacity. Cognitive processing is extended outside the human body. Extended cognition hypothesis claims that there is no meaningful distinction between internal and external processing for cognitive processes.

According to Rowlands, mental processes of the extended mind can be further classified as embodied, embedded, enacted, and extended processes [16]. The classification describes the relationship of the human neural system, the human body, and the environment, as well as the possible actions of the entities.

These ideas have had a major impact in several disciplines such as cognitive science [17], psychology [18], and biology [19]. In the educational sciences extended cognition hypothesis and especially the concept of enactivism is closely related to constructivist learning theories [20].

In this article, we apply the ideas of the extended cognition hypothesis to the use of computational thinking paradigm in computer science education. For a more complete review of extended mind hypothesis and its applications we refer to textbooks by Rowland [16] and Rupert [21].

2 Analysis

The common denominator for both the computational thinking and the extended cognition is technology, especially the relationship and interaction between human cognition and technology.

From the extended cognition point of view, technology is an integral part of the human cognition. It was built and developed to help humans function in the environment. The human mind actively utilizes these available external features that can be used as cognitive tools and integrates them into cognitive processes.

Quite opposite to the extended cognition point of view, computational thinking approach sees a very strong distinction between the human and the computer. Computers use a different way of logic and technology, something that is not natural for humans. Computational thinking is seen as a tool or a skill to be used to understand and utilize this external technology.

This can be seen for example in the original article by Wing, where she emphasizes that computational thinking is "A way that humans, not computers, think" [6]. The statement can be considered to be actual, at least at the current level of technology, but it still underlines the difference between the human and the machine. This is something that contradicts the external cognition point of view.

To understand better this dichotomy, let us consider some special cases of human-computer relationship.

2.1 Extended Limits of Computational Thinking

From the everyday classroom perspective the adaption of computers may seem like a rapid process. Computational thinking is, therefore, because of this view and for practical reasons, understood and taught using current technology.

But computational systems have had a long history of technological development. Computational systems have existed long before the arrival of digital computers and the development and use of digital computers have seen several extensive revolutions. We may expect that the landscape will not stay stationary in the near future either.

For the extended cognition hypothesis, there is a natural way to expand it to different levels of technology. For example, to remember a phone number:

Without any tools. One has to remember the number using cognitive functions of the brain. This requires the conscious use of chunking techniques to make the number memorable [22]. It also requires recalling the number from memory every now and then to prevent forgetting [23]. In effect, it requires concentration and can result in failure if the person is exposed to cognitive stress or distractions.

A pen and paper. One can write the number down. This eliminates most of the cognitive load caused by the task. The skill required for the task is the ability to write numbers and understand written numbers.

Modern smartphones. The phone number with required contact details are transmitted automatically. Cognitive requirements depend on the usability of the smartphone, but can theoretically be set arbitrarily low.

Future implant technology. Speculative future technology of brain implants is often used as a thought experiment to show ultimate possibilities of how extended cognition might work in the future [15]. A proactive technology anticipates the required action. This could optionally be external agents such as robots or artificial intelligence that serve human needs.

In addition to memory, another example of extended cognition is performing calculations where a pen and a paper, a pocket calculator, or calculator implanted in the human body is used to extend human cognitive capacity.

For computational thinking, such thought experiments using different levels of technology are less often presented. Even though using algorithms to perform mathematical calculations was already used 4000 years ago [24].

Let us consider some tasks where CSTA definition features of computational thinking presented in Sect. 1.1 are used.

Building a house. Building a house requires creating models and organizing plans. Even when human labor is used, repetitive tasks are executed in a rather similar way to which programmable machines work in modern automated factories. Building process also involves problem-solving with technical constraints.

Building a business. Business organizations need multi-level hierarchical organization. Standardized practices and hierarchy create fault tolerance to the system. A highly detailed theory of organizations has been created to help to design and to implement the creation and development of business organizations [25]. All the features of computational thinking are clearly used in governing business organizations.

Building software. Software engineering is the practical side of computer science, and clearly has an affect on how we view computational thinking. But in the same way that we develop analogies to how other engineering and business systems resemble computers, we might also understand computer systems similar to engineering and businesses. Computers just provide us with cheap, tireless workers who need very specific instructions to work.

Building a society. Governing a society and creating an efficient administration for it is a task requiring the solving of many economical and managerial problems. Building, for example, a taxation system or public services requires skills in logic, engineering, and system modeling while the work is also related to social issues and ethics. As just described, this is a non-technical task with high requirements in computational thinking skills as defined by CSTA.

One more good example of human activity closely related to computational thinking without digital computers is many recreational games human play. Rules are created to make a game fair and interesting. The game is executed using humans as the operating agents until the game reaches an objective such as a win or a tie.

Together these two dimensions illuminate the field where human activity is related to computational thinking skills and where the ideas of extended cognition must be applied respectively.

2.2 Levels of Computer Programming

Using the computational thinking term definition by Wing presented in Sect. 1.1, the core idea of the computational thinking is to formulate problems so that they can be solved by information-processing agents such as digital computers. The reasoning is that digital computers can be used to solve problems in many fields and in everyday tasks.

Computer programming is often not considered to be a computational thinking skill by itself. But it is a closely related and often indistinguishable from other computational thinking skills. Let us, therefore, review some computer programming languages and paradigms.

Computer programs were originally hand-coded in binary machine language. It is easy to see how this differs from modern computer programming, with automatic code completion, syntax highlighting, and other convenient features.

More drastic changes have taken place in the application domains. While early computers were isolated machines with little or no user interface, intended for mathematical calculations, modern computers are connected to the Internet, have modern graphical user interfaces and IO devices, and can be used for almost any purpose from computer games and multimedia applications to running network services and social networks.

Let us consider some examples how computer programming has changed from the viewpoint of extended cognition hypothesis.

Low-level language. Primitive languages such as assembler language process information at a very low level. The programmer needs to keep track of the program states in their mind and emulate the execution process.

High-level language. High-level languages hide much of the low-level details in programming and let the programmer concentrate on the programming logic. This allows the building of more complex program for the same cognitive load.

Integrated development environment. When programming is done with a plain text editor, it is the responsibility of the programmer to keep the syntax of the code error free. The programmer also needs to remember or look up the names of variables, functions, etc. Modern integrated development environment (IDE) takes care of these tasks and provide such features as intelligent code completion and help functions to speed up the development process. This frees up cognitive resources for novice programmers and programmers in new coding environments.

Code libraries and frameworks. Modern computers and computing environments including operating systems are highly complex systems. Ready-made code libraries and frameworks are used to create maintainable and scalable programs. This allows the programmer to do work on the higher level of code abstraction.

Internet and social networks. Before the Internet and advanced web services with large user bases, computer programmers were isolated from the programming communities. A programmer needed to read manuals or other literature to learn more about programming topics. Nowadays Google, StackExchange, and other web services provide huge amounts of information. There are ready-made code examples from almost every subject. For the programmer, this allows tools for using alternative problem-solving methods in programming tasks. New skills are needed such as managing and searching large amounts of information and social co-operation skills.

These changes are not independent but they act together. The increasing range of programming paradigms help with problems such as code complexity and re-usability, concurrent programming, and asynchronous code execution. For example, functional programming hides the program execution flow from the user allowing higher level abstraction requiring the use of very different set of cognitive processes.

In the future automatic program generation and artificial intelligence will move computer programming from actual coding to developing technical requirements for the program. Together with artificial intelligence, this will probably move programming away from logic and mathematics, and closer to being a linguistic endeavor.

Another near-future trend in programming is proof systems. The correctness of computer programs can be formally verified using formal methods of mathematics [26]. Using proof systems removes much of the technical details of algorithms from programming, allowing for a higher level of abstraction.

2.3 Modes of Technology

Technology can operate on several fundamentally different modes such as textual, visual, and auditory. In further examination, for example, temporal and metadata level aspects can change the modality of the technology. Let us consider some examples.

Name of a bird species. Naming a bird species is naturally expressed as a text. Symbols needed to present the name can be written down. Either numerical or alphabetical symbols can be used depending on the application.

The visual appearance of a bird. It is possible to sketch the bird on a paper. Even if an exact reproduction is impossible, most prominent features can be drawn so that the image will help in the identification of the bird later.

The sound of the bird. The sound of the bird can be described in words but a direct presentation is difficult without a phonetic script suitable for the task.

A database of features for the identification of birds. Here the second level of abstraction is needed to organize the data meaningfully. Namely, structured metadata is needed to bind together the different modes of features.

From the viewpoint of extended cognition, these examples illustrate how human cognition can be naturally extended by technology in all the modalities we already utilize. The use of technology is not isolated into a certain modality of human existence.

Computational thinking, on the other hand, is very indifferent regarding the modalities. In the way computational thinking is taught, using algorithms and programming, it ignores much of the knowledge of the structure of the world. Dealing with modalities is left to the application level tasks.

Keeping computational thinking insensitive to the modes of technology may seem like a rational choice. This retains the tool used distinct from the subject operated. But according to the extended cognition principle, there is no distinction between what is inside the cognition and what is outside the cognition. This dividing way of thinking separates the human cognition from the technology and undermines their potential efficient cooperation.

From the extended cognition hypothesis we can thus conclude that understanding and internalizing the human-computer interaction using the whole scale of modalities is essential to the efficiency of extended cognition.

One research example of efficiency gained by practicing modalities is the connection between spatial thinking and using 3D computer games. In earlier studies, it has been shown that women do not perform as well as men on some spatial tasks such as mental rotation [27]. Spence et al. showed that fundamentally the learning rate of women is not less than that of men [28]. The difference in skills come from cultural aspects. This has further consequences as spatial thinking is related in learning skills in mathematics and science [29]. If computational thinking in education stresses too much programming logic and understanding algorithms and assumes that data is already in computer processable format, much of the possible interaction is missed.

To improve the situation there are several options. Human-computer interaction (IICI) is a well-established field of science. It is a discipline working together with computer science, cognitive science, psychology. Calderon et al. present a methodology to systematically introduce this topic to students of early age to complement the ideas of computational thinking [30].

In addition to formal HCI methods, human perception should be approached in a systematic way discussing underlying principles of physics, how the human nervous system is stimulated, and how the mind perceives and interprets the sensory information. This provides a more concise view of multimodal interaction with technology.

3 Discussion

Regarding computer science education the main question becomes how to enable efficient use of technology to support cognitive processes in the adoption of skills? What are the technological features that allow us to perform better in these tasks? And how the ideas of extended cognition help us to answer these questions.

Let us revisit the computational thinking definition by CSTA from Sect. 1.1 and consider the interaction of human cognition and technology.

The first claim of the definition says that computational thinking is *"formulating problems in a way that enables us to use a computer and other tools to help solve them"*. From an extended cognition viewpoint, this could be expressed more generally that in education we want students to use technology and solve problems. No special thinking should be required for using technology.

For example, using a calculator to do calculations from very early age gives a different type of thinking that is already adapted to formulating problems adequately. For a person who doesn't have a calculator, large multiplications and divisions are hard problems. With a calculator these calculations are trivial. Doing a large number of calculations is still a hard task even using a calculator but having numbers available digitally and using a spreadsheet program makes this task trivial.

The first claim is closely related to the third claim which states that computational thinking is *"representing data through abstractions such as models and simulations"*. As we saw in Sect. 2.1, computational thinking is not related to digital computers generally. We just use the term often in the context of computer science. Humans already use models and simulations in many activities, such as social relationships, games, economic planning, and in creative tasks, even as simple as cooking or expressing oneself through art.

In many cases, abstract thinking arises spontaneously from using technology. For example, social relationships can be visualized using social media applications such as Facebook [31]. Transactions of a bank account can often be downloaded from an online bank in CSV format. Our mobile phones can track the GPS data of our daily movement.

The deeper understanding of data models is something that does not always arise by itself. But often technology already provides tools to utilize the data. For example different parameters can be calculated and visualizations can be made from GPS data without a deeper understanding. Using the data teaches the properties it possesses. Requirements of use cases define the data models needed for the data. From this point of view, the extended cognition view of thinking encourages declarative and functional thinking versus traditional procedural thinking.

The second claim, one we left without addressing earlier, is that computational thinking includes *"logically organizing and analyzing data"*. From the extended cognition point of view, it is not as necessary to emphasize the logical organizing of the data from the viewpoint that sees human and technology as separated entities. In the extended cognition view, the organization of the data is largely a natural consequence of using technology.

The fourth claim of the definition is that computational thinking is *"automating solutions through algorithmic thinking (a series of ordered steps)"*. Algorithmic thinking as a series of ordered steps expresses the close connection of the definition to the history of computer science and software engineering. Most programming, most notable programming with low-level languages, is procedural programming consisting of series of ordered steps or commands.

While procedural programming is the de facto practical programming paradigm, it should be noted that it is not the only one and might not be cognitively the most natural paradigm. Functional programming is a paradigm that more naturally arises from the use of data and models. There are also automatic code generation and proof systems that allow solving computational tasks without the low-level understanding of programming as mentioned in Sect. 2.2. It is therefore not clear that using technology promotes procedural thinking as expressed in this fourth claim of the definition.

The fifth claim of the definition is that computational thinking is *"identifying, analyzing, and implementing possible solutions with the goal of achieving the most efficient and effective combination of steps and resources"*. The task of optimizing computational efficiency is one of the key differences between mathematics and computer science according to Knuth [4]. It could be argued that while this is one of the key concepts of computer science, from the extended cognition hypothesis point of view, it is more of an auxiliary problem for most of the application domains.

The sixth and final claim of the definition is there should be *"generalizing and transferring this problem-solving process to a wide variety of problems"*. From the extended cognition view of computation, there is an intrinsic means of computational optimization and generalization in that humans can choose from the technology they use. Human cognition is not limited to its natural capacity but there is a drive to find utilize optimal external resources. This is not to dismiss the fifth and sixth claim of the definition but to offer an insight of what is already implied in the adoption of advanced use of technology. The extended cognition view provides a higher level of abstraction in that it is not about algorithmic efficiency but choosing right technological tools and adopting them accordingly to the problem-solving processes.

4   Conclusions

There are many implicit and explicit attributes in the use of the term computational thinking that express the historical constraints of the term. The term comes from software engineering traits and has strong notes of separate human, the programmer or the user, and the computer. Humans need skills to use computers, which are external machines to help humans with their tasks.

This highly contradicts the view of extended cognition where technology is an integral part of the extended human. An example of technological embodiment is the collision of cars. A car is a functional extension of our body and if we are involved in the collision we probably describe the situation as "another car hitting me", and not "another car hitting the car I am in". The same embodiment happens notably in computer games, virtual reality applications, and many other uses of advanced technology.

To understand an efficient computer science education we need deep understanding of what is the relationship between students and technology. We must ask how thinking has changed and how it can be changed by the use of technology. This is the pedagogical content knowledge of 21st-century skills [32].

For this, we suggest the concept *technology synchronized thinking* to complement the idea of computational thinking and to reflect the idea of extended cognition hypothesis that external technology can be seen as part of human cognitive functions.

The idea is that to promote the possibilities of functional extended cognition, a cooperation or synchronization must be developed between the cognitive processes of the mind and the technology. This is achieved using cognitively suitable technologies. It also requires using problem-solving and engineering tasks that adapt the brain for the technological environment.

1. Computation. Traditionally computer programming has been considered something that is created in the human mind and projected onto external computational machines. For example, Alan J. Perlis writes *"Every computer program is a model, hatched in the mind, of a real or mental process. These processes, arising from human experience and thought, are huge in number, intricate in detail, and at any time only partially understood. They are modeled to our permanent satisfaction rarely by our computer programs"* [33]. This one-way interaction is historically related to the low level and compiled programming languages. Instead, programming languages with interactive interpreters are more suitable for creating productive extended cognitive functions. Functional programming paradigm provides a more cognitively compatible way of organizing functions and allows removing strict step-by-step of procedural programming. The compatibility is based on the associative quality of human memory. Much of the low-level information processing in the human mind is done automatically and unconsciously.

2. Models. Almost all the information we use today is digital. This allows easy data processing using computers. Most computer science education approaches this data processing from low-level details such as data formats and low-level algorithms. From the extended cognition point of view higher abstraction level, top-down approaches are preferred. This means that data is processed using practical applications and use cases. Low-level details are not considered at early stages. While details are interesting from many computational aspects, they do not support well the cognitive entanglement of external technology and human cognitive processes.

3. HCI. Traditionally computational thinking and programming are considered as textually expressed symbolic processes. While symbolic presentation allows precise syntax, it doesn't fully utilize human cognitive capacity. As discussed in Sect. 2.3, multimodal and 3D human-computer interfaces provide more integrated experience. This experience allows higher level abstraction in human cognitive processes increasing its capabilities as seen in the example concerning the connection between 3D games and mathematical thinking.

In the teaching of computational thinking, there are many methods that do not use computers or technology but games or other tasks related to the ideas of computational thinking [34,35]. These methods are sometimes called computational thinking unplugged [36,37].

From the extended cognition point of view, it is not advisable to separate computational thinking ideas from technology. This view has some experimental evidence. For example Grover et al. write about computational thinking tools not utilizing computers: *"Noteworthy efforts like CS Unplugged that introduce computing concepts without the use of a computer, while providing valuable introductory activities for exposing children to the nature of CS, may be keeping learners from the crucial computational experiences involved in CTs common practice"* [38].

Peter J. Denning writes also about the value of computer science: *"We are most valued not for our computational thinking, but for our computational doing"* [39]. These views reassert the idea of extended cognition hypothesis that skills needed in using modern digital technology are not separable from the technology itself.

Another aspect related to the extended cognition hypothesis is the socially extended mind hypothesis which extends the cognitive realm to the social domain. The socially extended mind builds on the enactive idea of social affordances. The idea is very strong since human behavior depends greatly on the cultural and the social context. It is impossible to study human behavior meaningfully without considering social and cultural bonds and prospects.

The socially extended mind is an especially current topic as the Internet and social media has changed the way how people interact with each other globally. There is also more intelligent technology for people to interact with, such as commercial online chatbots and personal assistant technology like Apple Siri, Google Assistant, Amazon Alexa, and Microsoft Cortana.

More research is needed on how human social networks and cognitive technology transforms the concept of computational thinking. The phenomenon is bidirectional. The cultural change gives a feedback and guides the technological development. This can lead to subcultures which differ both in technology and in user culture. This makes a single universal skill-set impossible to define in some cases.

References

1. Tedre, M., Denning, P.J.: Shifting identities in computing: from a useful tool to a new method and theory of science. Informatics in the Future, pp. 1–16. Springer, Cham (2017). https://doi.org/10.1007/978-3-319-55735-9_1
2. Dijkstra, E.W.: Programming as a discipline of mathematical nature. Am. Math. Monthly **81**(6), 608–612 (1974)
3. Knuth, D.E.: Computer science and its relation to mathematics. Am. Math. Monthly **81**(4), 323–343 (1974)
4. Knuth, D.E.: Algorithmic thinking and mathematical thinking. Am. Math. Monthly **92**(3), 170–181 (1985)
5. Papert, S.: Mindstorms: Children, computers, and powerful ideas. Basic Books Inc. (1980)
6. Wing, J.M.: Computational thinking. Commun. ACM **49**(3), 33–35 (2006)
7. Wing, J.M.: Research Notebook: Computational Thinking-What and Why? – Carnegie Mellon School of Computer Science. https://www.cs.cmu.edu/link/research-notebook-computational-thinking-what-and-why. Accessed 14 Jan 2018
8. Aho, A.V.: Computation and computational thinking. Comput. J. **55**(7), 832–835 (2012)
9. Stephenson, C., Barr, V.: Defining computational thinking for k-12. Special Issue - Computer Science K-8: Building a Strong Foundation (2012)
10. Tedre, M., Denning, P.J.: The long quest for computational thinking. In: Koli Calling, pp. 120–129 (2016)
11. Palmer, J.: Parmenides. In: Zalta, E.N. (ed.) The Stanford Encyclopedia of Philosophy. Metaphysics Research Lab, Stanford University, Winter 2016 Edn. (2016)
12. Magee, B.: The Great Philosophers: An Introduction to Western Philosophy. Oxford University Press on Demand (2000)
13. Paradiso, M.A., Bear, M.F., Connors, B.W.: Neuroscience: Exploring the Brain. Wolters Kluwe, Philadelphia (2016)
14. Dretske, F.: Phenomenal externalism or if meanings ain't in the head, where are qualia? Philos. Issues **7**, 143–158 (1996)
15. Clark, A., Chalmers, D.: The extended mind. Analysis **58**(1), 7–19 (1998)
16. Rowlands, M.: The New Science of the Mind: From Extended Mind to Embodied Phenomenology. Bradford Books (2016)
17. Arnau, E., Estany, A., González del Solar, R., Sturm, T.: The extended cognition thesis: its significance for the philosophy of (cognitive) science. Philos. Psychol. **27**(1), 1–18 (2014)
18. Wilson, R.A.: Ten questions concerning extended cognition. Philos. Psychol. **27**(1), 19–33 (2014)
19. Mikhael, J.: Philosophy of Bioinformatics: Extended Cognition. Analogies and Mechanisms. ProQuest (2007)
20. Holton, D.L.: Constructivism + embodied cognition= enactivism: theoretical and practical implications for conceptual change. In: AERA 2010 Conference (2010)
21. Rupert, R.D.: Cognitive Systems and the Extended Mind. Oxford University Press (2009)
22. Miller, G.A.: The magical number seven, plus or minus two: some limits on our capacity for processing information. Psychol. Rev. **63**(2), 81 (1956)
23. Altmann, E.M., Gray, W.D.: Forgetting to remember: the functional relationship of decay and interference. Psychol. Sci. **13**(1), 27–33 (2002)

24. Knuth, D.E.: Ancient babylonian algorithms. Commun. ACM **15**(7), 671–677 (1972)
25. Daft, R.L.: Organization theory and design. Cengage Learn. (2015)
26. Chlipala, A., Delaware, B., Duchovni, S., Gross, J., Pit-Claudel, C., Suriyakarn, S., Wang, P., Ye, K.: The end of history? Using a proof assistant to replace language design with library design. In: SNAPL 2017: Proceedings of the 2nd Summit on Advances in Programming Languages, May 2017
27. Voyer, D., Voyer, S., Philip Bryden, M.: Magnitude of sex differences in spatial abilities: a meta-analysis and consideration of critical variables (1995)
28. Spence, I., Yu, J.J., Feng, J., Marshman, J.: Women match men when learning a spatial skill. J. Exp. Psychol. Learn. Mem. Cogn. **35**(4), 1097 (2009)
29. Newcombe, N.S.: Picture this: increasing Math and Science learning by improving spatial thinking. Am. Educ. **34**(2), 29 (2010)
30. Calderon, A.C., Crick, T.: Using interface design to develop computational thinking skills. In: Proceedings of the Workshop in Primary and Secondary Computing Education, pp. 127–129. ACM (2015)
31. Wolfram, S.: Personal analytics for facebook (2012). http://blog.wolframalpha.com/2012/08/30/wolframalpha-personal-analytics-for-facebook/. Accessed 13 Jan 2018
32. Shulman, L.S.: Those who understand: knowledge growth in teaching. Educ. Researcher **15**(2), 4–14 (1986)
33. Abelson, H., Sussman, G.J., Sussman, J.: Structure and Interpretation of Computer Programs. Justin Kelly (1996)
34. Bell, T.C., Witten, I.H., Fellows, M.: Computer science unplugged: off-line activities and games for all ages. Computer Science Unplugged (1998)
35. Bell, T., Alexander, J., Freeman, I., Grimley, M.: Computer science unplugged: school students doing real computing without computers. N. Z. J. Appl. Comput. Inf. Technol. **13**(1), 20–29 (2009)
36. Feaster, Y., Segars, L., Wahba, S.K., Hallstrom, J.O.: Teaching CS unplugged in the high school (with limited success). In: Proceedings of the 16th Annual Joint Conference on Innovation and Technology in Computer Science Education, pp. 248–252. ACM (2011)
37. Curzon, P., McOwan, P.W., Plant, N., Meagher, L.R.: Introducing teachers to computational thinking using unplugged storytelling. In: Proceedings of the 9th Workshop in Primary and Secondary Computing Education, pp. 89–92. ACM (2014)
38. Grover, S., Pea, R.: Computational thinking in k-12: a review of the state of the field. Educ. Researcher **42**(1), 38–43 (2013)
39. Denning, P.J.: The profession of it beyond computational thinking. Commun. ACM **52**(6), 28–30 (2009)

Interconnected Enterprise Systems – A Call for New Teaching Approaches

Bettina Schneider[✉], Petra Maria Asprion[✉],
and Frank Grimberg[✉]

FHNW University of Applied Sciences and Arts Northwestern Switzerland,
4002 Basel, Switzerland
{bettina.schneider, petra.asprion,
frank.grimberg}@fhnw.ch

Abstract. Enterprise Resource Planning Systems (ERPS) have continually extended their scope over the last decades. The evolution has currently reached a stage where ERPS support the entire value chain of an enterprise. This study deals with the rise of a new era, where ERPS is transformed into so-called interconnected Enterprise Systems (iES), which have a strong outside-orientation and provide a networked ecosystem open to human and technological actors (e.g. social media, Internet of Things). Higher education institutions need to prepare their students to understand the shift and to transfer the implications to today's business world. Based on literature and applied learning scenarios the study shows existing approaches to the use of ERPS in teaching and elaborates whether and how they can still be used. In addition, implications are outlined and the necessary changes towards new teaching approaches for iES are proposed.

Keywords: Enterprise Systems · Enterprise Resource Planning
Systems of Engagement · Teaching · Higher education

1 Introduction

1.1 Enterprise Systems

Enterprise Systems (ES) are widely spread in today's businesses [1]. They build a prerequisite for digitizing a variety of essential business processes, stretching from attracting customers, order handling and production up to billing or service activities [2]. ES are packages of software applications that have a shared common database and aim to achieve full connectivity by supporting many, or even most, aspects of enterprises' information needs [3]. The most prominent type of ES are ERPS [4]. Their strength lies in the integration and automation of main operational business processes as to support the operational value chain, from customer inquiry to final payment and from purchase requisition to vendor billing [5].

Today, ES and particularly ERPS are considered commodities in a market that is still growing. According to Gartner [6], the worldwide ERPS sales volume grew overall by 7.1% in 2016. This growth originates on the one hand from small and medium enterprises (SMEs) just starting to adopt ES packages following the efforts of vendors

© Springer International Publishing AG, part of Springer Nature 2018
Y. Shi et al. (Eds.): ICCS 2018, LNCS 10862, pp. 318–331, 2018.
https://doi.org/10.1007/978-3-319-93713-7_26

to provide small scale, less expensive solutions [7]. On the other hand, enterprises with mature ES enhance their existing landscapes with further investments. They acknowledge that technology has advanced tremendously in recent years and have a desire to adapt this progress in a next generation of ES [8].

The implementation of an ES is a high-effort and high-risk endeavor: Enterprises have to make relatively large investments to get the system set up and prepare the workforce to adopt and assimilate to an ES/ERPS [9]. Studies prove that the majority of ERP implementations do not deliver the expected benefits [4]. Instead, very often, they trigger a high potential for conflicts within the workforce [10]. It is, therefore, a prerequisite for an effective adaption that ES users build a thorough understanding of the main principles and concepts [11]. Research confirms that training is one of the key factors to ensure a successful adoption and assimilation [8, 9, 12]. Since the 90 s, universities and other higher educational institutions have incorporated ES into their curricula [13] in order to prepare future managers and IT professionals. To teach the complexity and large scope of ES, numerous teaching approaches exist [14].

1.2 Purpose and Objectives

This study elaborates the need for new teaching approaches following the advancement of ES to a next level. We claim that the traditional ERPS were transformed and are entering a new stage, called 'interconnected ES' (iES). This affects the existing teaching curricula as well as the approaches. To clarify the future developments of ERPS we have expanded Moore´s concept of Systems of Engagement (SoE) [15] in which SoE drive the future evolution of ES towards a networked ecosystem. Our main intention is to provide guidance to lecturers of ES in higher education. The purpose of the study is to (1) elaborate the evolution of ES or rather ERPS towards more collaborative and interactive systems, namely iES and to (2) raise awareness that a shift from an inside-out perspective to an outside-in perspective is in progress and must be taken into account. We aim to (3) delimit and enhance the existing ERPS/ES concepts towards an iES and (4) derive recommendations for new teaching approaches for iES in the current digital age.

1.3 Methodology

To conduct a rigor literature review we used procedural recommendations of Benbasat and Zmud [16] as well as Tranfield et al. [17]. We conducted a structured search in the Web of Science (all journals) and in Google Scholar (top journals). Then, we enriched the matches from scientific literature by adapting practical knowledge from practitioners (see study with ERP professionals conducted by Schneider [18]). The keywords used were among others 'next generation', 'future', 'transformation', 'integrated' combined with 'ERP System', 'Enterprise Resource Planning', 'Enterprise System'. In addition, the keywords were combined with 'teaching', 'higher education', 'training' and 'learning'.

In order to contribute to the discussions on the evolution of ERPS towards iES, we founded our iES-related research on the well-established concept of SoE [15]. This concept is referenced by practitioners [19, 20] and by academia, e.g. to establish a new IT consumerization theory [21, 22] or an ERP transformation model [23].

The remainder of the paper is structured as follows: The next section, Sect. 2, elaborates existing ways to teach ERPS at universities and higher education institutions. In Sect. 3, we outline the evolution of ERPS/ES with the conclusion that a new paradigm from an inside-out to an outside-in perspective is breaking through. In Sect. 4, we assess how lecturers should respond to the enhanced ES concepts. Key factors for teaching the commodity ERPS and the future-oriented iES are presented. In the final section, we draw a conclusion and show areas for further research.

2   Existing Teaching Concepts

2.1   Classification Scheme

The different ways of teaching ERPS can be categorized along two axes. The first axis deals with the decision about how closely the learning process should be connected to a dedicated proprietary ERP product. In the case of hands-on approaches, the learners have direct access to one or more ERP solutions and the understanding is built up in a specific software context. Such a strategy has the advantage that learners take an active part and that they understand a proprietary solution.

However, the selection of an ERP product is not an easy task because there are many products from different large or small vendors available. Education aims to impart the general concepts and principles of a dedicated topic. Using a specific product always comes with the suspicion of privileging a certain vendor. In addition, working with an ES is usually costly. Although many ERP vendors provide free access to their products for universities (e.g. Microsoft, Odoo), the administrative effort for an education facility is substantial. User profiles have to be maintained, an infrastructure for the students has to be provided (hardware, network) and the first steps with the software have to be guided carefully to make sure the students can get accustomed to the user interface. Finally, lecturers need a profound expertise in the selected ERP product in order to use it for teaching and to cope with potential issues.

The complications of choosing a specific ERP solution may be overcome by teaching approaches that do not rely on a particular system access but instead focus on conceptual aspects, core components and principles on a more abstracted level. This can be designated as the indirect approach of teaching ERPS.

The second axis to classify the ways of teaching ERPS relates to the complexity of the chosen scenario. At the lowest end of the scale, the ERPS is embedded into the curriculum in a rather selective manner. At distinct points, related concepts and examples underpin the content to be taught. The lecturer's interventions related to ERPS are rather independent. At the highest end of the scale, teaching approaches aim for comprehensiveness. ERPS are an integral part of the curriculum that builds a broad storyline. Figure 1 shows a classification scheme with the two axes of ERPS usage (vertically) and complexity of the teaching approach (horizontally).

Within the classification scheme there are different teaching approaches arranged; the essential details are described in the following sections.

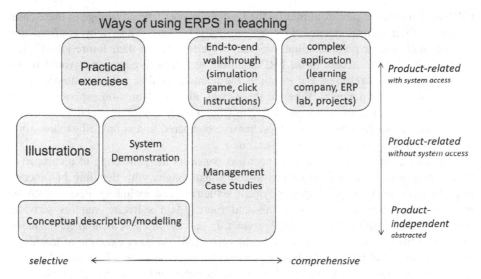

Fig. 1. Classification scheme for teaching ERPS (based on Wilbers [24], Pongratz [14] and Schneider [18])

2.2 Teaching Scenarios

The most straightforward approach are product-independent teaching scenarios; the ERP-related principles are described abstractly without referring to a dedicated ERP product. An example of this teaching strategy can be found in one of Kurbel's books [25]. In order to conceptualize ERP structures and processes, modeling techniques can be applied; an example is the use of notations like business process model and notation (BPMN). This approach allows the lecturers to elaborate ERP content without referencing a dedicated vendor or system. The focus is set on conceptual understanding of ERP main principles and components [18]. Those abstract teaching concepts can be enriched with screenshots from any ERP solution. While illustrations are product-dependent, they help to visualize the theoretical ERP-principles and demonstrate the usage in a real world case.

Instead of showing rather static representations, a more comprehensive approach is the use of live demonstrations from any ERP software. Although the learners will not be able to gain hands-on experience, it makes it possible to show various functionalities in sequence, which represent the (graphical) user-system interaction. A less elaborated version of this learning approach involves the use of videos (e.g. on YouTube) instead of demonstrating the system in a live setting.

An alternative way to teach ERPS is the management case study approach; this one is also without direct system access. In general, a case study refers to a textual representation of a real world scenario. This enables the learner to take on a specific role in which he or she has to deal with certain challenges. As in real life, the situations are not clearly defined but leave room for particular interpretations and various possible solutions [26]. A common case study scenario asks questions regarding a certain ERP architecture during the adoption phase or tackles management challenges during an

ERP implementation (see examples on the-casecenter.org). The advantage of these case studies is their correspondence with realistic ERP projects. Thus, they confront the learners with similar problems that they may have to solve in their future jobs [27].

In case of direct access to an ERP solution, an alternative scenario would be to carry out practical exercises. For example, the learners would create a customer order or process a vendor payment. Whereas these tasks allow for hands-on experience, they only reflect limited steps within the software from a specific user perspective. As such, practical exercises may be more comprehensive compared to a simple illustration, but less encompassing than a live demonstration.

Another comprehensive teaching scenario considers the full scope of a company. One example is the execution of end-to-end walkthroughs with detailing of process steps from customer inquiry up to payment settlement and including aspects such as manufacturing, warehousing, financials and more. Main software vendors provide learning materials related to their ERP product. In the case of SAP, a complete business setting is provided for a (fictive) bicycle enterprise [28]. Another example of teaching, also related to SAP, involves an interactive simulation game, called 'ERPSim'. Various learning scenarios (manufacturing, logistics or distribution) exist that allow the participants to take an active part (e.g. as product manager) and to conduct hands-on tasks within the ERP software. The implications can be perceived thanks to a real-time simulation (solution accessible via https://erpsim.hec.ca/). This way, the students receive a comprehensive overview of the main supported processes in a proprietary ERPS. However, both examples focus on using an existing system and do not emphasize adapting the system to specific needs.

The most sophisticated ERP teaching setup involves complex scenarios that aim to replicate a real world system usage in an advanced manner. An example is the ERP laboratory of a German university in which ERP-related processes and tasks are connected to a physical representation in form of LEGO blocks. When material is withdrawn from the system inventory, the corresponding stock is also removed in the LEGO warehouse. The system processes are reflected in the physical world in form of a LEGO material flow [29]. This setting provides the learners with a comprehensive overview of the ERP capabilities and effects in the real world. In addition, the laboratory offers a platform for enhancing the existing system setup during student projects.

Next to simulations, 'learning enterprises' can also be classified as complex scenarios for ERP teaching. In those scenarios, learners work together in teams and create their own business within a secured setting. The 'business' runs on a real ERPS that applies transactional data and executes process activities [14].

3   Evolution of ERPS

The evolution of ERPS has always been connected to technical progress [7]. Based on the technological advancements enterprises aimed to adapt the existing ERPS to increase their operational effectiveness − a strong inward-looking orientation (inside-out perspective). For the current digital age, we claim that enterprises need to change their mind-set to a new outward-looking oriented paradigm (outside-in perspective).

3.1   Inside-Out: From MRP to ERP II

Long before the label 'ERP' was created, the evolution of ES began. It started in the 1960s with the rise of material requirements planning systems (MRP I). The main achievement was the so-called automated 'explosion' of a finished product into its sub-components. The resulting bill of materials allowed enterprises to plan their material purchases as well as production requirements. Soon in the 1970s, MRP I enlarged its scope and turned into a concept called manufacturing resource planning (MRP II), which included a top-down planning philosophy. On top of the materials perspective, MRP II incorporated the capacity requirements and related financials.

Over the years, the developments continued − with the integration of more processes and functionalities such as sales, management accounting, human resources and security-related functions. As such, the systems started to affect all main organizational entities of an enterprise instead of focusing on one specific functional area. This lead to the creation of a new class of enterprise applications, namely ERPS or later ES [30].

Although academia and practitioners have used and are still using the expression 'ERP system' or its abbreviation ERPS, the products sold by vendors in the 1980s till the 2010s are not comparable to today's state-of-the-art solutions.

Similar to MRP I/II, the ERPS concepts evolved. The original intra-organizational processes extended further and transformed into inter-organizational systems. New names were created like extended ERP or ERP II [31]. With the invention of the internet and service-oriented architecture, new key elements and enhancements were introduced such as web catalogues or business intelligence components [32]. Further valuable extensions were customer relationship management (CRM) and/or supply chain management (SCM) applications [1, 31]. In addition, functionality related to the enterprise's overall ecosystem has been incorporated [8].

Figure 2 shows the evolution from MRPI, MRPII to ERP and ERP II and visualizes the continuous enlargement over time, both in terms of broadening the scope and increasing integration. An important milestone was the expansion to a full enterprise focus. With ERP II, the inside-oriented view was softened and external-oriented functionalities were added. As Fig. 2 illustrates, ERP concepts are continuously expanding, whereas the main imperatives of ERPS were not touched: For years, ERPS have been known for their stability, cost efficiency and secured and integrated database. The broadening of the ERPS scope has led to an opening towards a large user base. Also outside the ERPS, stakeholders were increasingly being connected (mainly customers and suppliers with CRM and SCM functionalities respectively).

3.2   Outside-In: From ERP II Towards SoE

The emergence of digital opportunities also brings many new developments in the context of ERPS. In prior decades, IT innovations usually arose within large enterprises or public institutes and then made their way to SMEs. This sequence is no longer valid: Today, the young generation very often leads innovations, followed by (older) adults as well as SMEs and then large enterprises [33–36].

Moore postulates the 'consumerization of IT' as a highly relevant factor in today's business expressing itself on two significant aspects: The first concerns societal

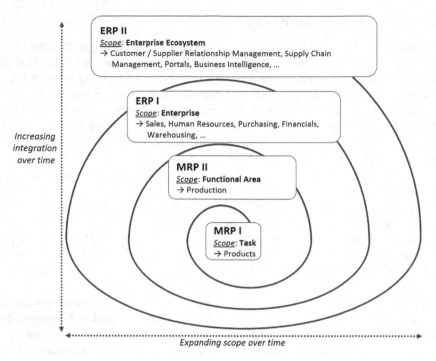

Fig. 2. Expansion from MRP I through to ERP II − an 'inside-out' evolution

changes in relation to the upcoming generation, the digital natives. They are accustomed to communicate and collaborate via mobile devices with web 2.0 functionalities and it is expected, that they will aim for a similar work life experience with e.g. easy-to-use tools and receiving information exactly at the time they need it [37]. The second aspect relates to productivity gains; it is expected that digitalization and thus IT will be the next significant driver for business growth and prosperity.

Accordingly, ERPS can be referred to as 'Systems of Record' (SoR) that paved the way for the automation of processes and outsourcing and led to operating efficiency and tremendous cost savings [15]. In the last decade, SoRs have more or less turned into a commodity, requiring enterprises to concentrate their resources on particular core competences as to differentiate and sharpen their strengths. In the digital age, collaboration between employees, divisions, suppliers and other internal and external parties will be an important success factor for the next wave of productivity.

By utilizing SoE, employees will be enabled to deliver the required conversion in view of the new ways of collaboration. It is expected that the next generation of employees will have the potential to elevate collaboration to a higher level. Significant breakthroughs will take place by applying collaboration tools, which promise easy and user-friendly access and use. The facilitation of the new way of working requires the support of various technical formats such as text, image, audio and video [15]. With regard to Moore's concept, it is crucial to understand that the 'old' ES/ERPS − the SoR − will not disappear but SoE will enhance the existing enterprise IT landscape [15].

Figure 3 shows in the inner circle the expansion starting from MRP I throughout the development phases to ERP II, which is more or less the general concept of ERPS. It represents the layer of SoR, which is based on one central database, focused on repetitive, transactional processing, high availability and comprehensive security mechanisms. The new SoE layer surrounds the SoR; these are systems or services, which are focused on end-user interaction and ease-of-use. They support collaboration and communication across different enterprise levels but are not tied to the inside view. The interactivity can happen between employees, customers and business partners but also between smart products and devices.

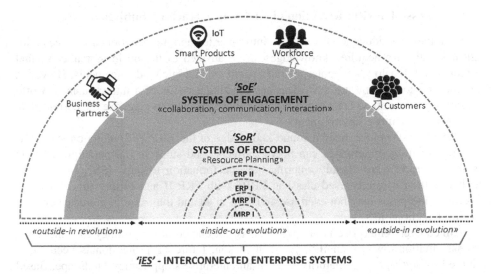

Fig. 3. SoE as a new layer surrounding ES − an outside-in revolution (based on Asprion et al. [23])

This means that instead of a further continuous expansion of ERP II, the iES of the digital age is driven by a new phenomenon: The strong integration and people-centric view, which is following an outside-in paradigm. This evolution is inescapable because user and stakeholder expectations have changed and demand a new level of interactivity across the whole enterprise networked ecosystem. As indicated in Fig. 3, the people-centricity not only enhances the layers of ES, it also opens up to a much larger group of people and devices that are interacting. The classical ERP II setup has already tended to open system boundaries for well-known stakeholders like customers or suppliers. Moving forward, with all the smart products from the Internet of Things (IoT), not only human beings interact with the system, but also devices and products. Overall, instead of only dedicated and named business partners, also unknown stakeholders are in scope of future iES-interactions. However, it is important to stress that the ERPS is not the direct front-end to all these people and devices because this interface is mediated by the SoE layer.

4 Implications for Teaching

Based on the evolution of ERPS towards iES and in particular the mind-shift from an 'inside-out' to an 'outside-in' perspective, we will elaborate the teaching implications of shifting from ES towards iES in networked ecosystems. At first, we justify why the evolution of ERPS (as outlined in Sect. 3) should be a subject of teaching. Next, we focus on existing ways to teach ERPS by suggesting enhancements related to SoE/iES. Finally we argue, that it is important to not only distinguish SoE as an add-on to SoR (or ERPS), but also that new teaching approaches are required.

4.1 Assess Maturity: Evolution of ERPS as a Teaching Subject

Universities and educational institutes introduce learners to new trends and technologies. Ideally, the acquired knowledge can be adapted to the business reality so that graduates will help 'their' enterprise to exploit technological advancements. However, in addition to contributing new ideas and creating a vision of a future business world regarding a networked ecosystem, it is essential to be able to diagnose the current state in a given enterprise environment.

Learners, therefore, need a sound knowledge of the ERPS/ES evolution stages, as the reality in the enterprises can be very diverse and stuck in old paradigms. While some enterprises are already entering the transformation towards iES, others might enhance their currently used classical ERPS with ERP II and further functionalities. Certain enterprises may not even use an ERPS at all and thus require guidance on how to implement an iES.

Since every enterprise is unique, there is not one common strategy to achieve the transformation towards an iES. For that reason, future IT professionals need to be skilled to determine the maturity level of an enterprise's application landscape. Based on that, next steps can be identified to manage the change from an inside-out to an outside-in orientation. Understanding the ERPS/ES evolution from MRP I up to today's iES – as shown in Fig. 2 – serves as an essential prerequisite.

4.2 Inside-Out: Enhancing Existing Ways

ES are complex and it takes a considerable effort to build a thorough understanding of the ERP-related principles and concepts. Therefore, teaching ERPS with a focus on the internal needs of an enterprise is a valid start to enter the topic. Gaining an insight into the processes and structures reflecting an enterprise, helps to build a base for delineating the scope of a classical ERPS.

However, we postulate that existing ways of teaching ES benefit from enhancements towards SoE or rather iES. When talking about classical ES, it is regarded as a commodity. Attracting learners for this topic is challenging, even though the labour market is in need of ERP professionals [38]. Adding some SoE-related engaging elements such as collaborating via social media, connecting to IoT devices or using mobile apps helps to initialize a mind-shift from an inside-out to an outside-in perspective and attracts in particular the new generation of learners.

Few examples exist where teaching already enters the SoE-world. Worth mentioning would be the curricula published by Prifti et al. [39] related to SAP ERP. They adapted the classical approach of end-to-end process execution by embedding it into the context of digital transformation. They start the learning journey with teaching business model innovation and digital innovation management. In addition, content related to IoT and sensor data is employed [39].

4.3 Outside-In: Focus on Interconnection

In order to teach the paradigm shift from an inside-oriented business perspective to an outside-oriented networked enterprise ecosystem, it is not sufficient to add to existing teaching approaches just some 'fancy' elements related to mobility or social media. More than that, a holistic view of iES needs to be established. However, when evaluating the existing approaches for ES/SoR teaching two shortfalls become obvious: First, the approaches show a lack of focus on a networked ecosystem, as it is standard in part already today and definitely will be in the future.

Consider the case of executing an end-to-end business process within an ERP product: In a common scenario, learners use the software to conduct the steps of a process chain such as fulfilling a customer order, starting from the inquiry throughout to the final payment settlement. This procedure helps to understand how a single business activity results in a complete business process serving an external customer. Even though, at some dedicated points within the process chain, the integration to other business functions like implications for the production unit or the purchasing department becomes visible but the whole setup is mainly driven by a straightforward, chronological flow. Some more advanced teaching approaches, such as the ERP simulation game, incorporate some network effects. Nevertheless, the number of participants is restricted and does not reflect the openness of an ecosystem that includes IoT and social media.

The second shortfall relates to the lack of learners to influence the ES setup. The majority of teaching scenarios reduces the complexity by providing a pre-customized system of an imaginary enterprise. Learners move within the boundaries of given processes and interfaces. However, thinking about the future of iES, this scenario is obviously too restrictive. Instead of a closed enterprise perspective with clearly defined interactions (e.g. with customers and suppliers) a more interactive and open solution needs to be chosen. The current trend of classical ES moving towards the cloud will potentially be a key driver to realize such teaching setups (for example using cloud services like the ones based on Microsoft Azure Platform to gain hands-on experience with the interaction of ERP-, IoT- and analytical functionality).

One of the very promising, but also most challenging ways of teaching iES is a 'learning enterprise' scenario as described in Sect. 2.2. It opens space for creativity by working on an own business idea. In the same way, it forces the learners to work from an outside-in perspective. Employees and business partners need to be attracted and supported by engagement and flexible interfaces. This is where SoE come into play. In addition, effectiveness needs to be considered, so that the IoT devices support a higher level of automation. By building an iES in a protected learning environment, learners gather valuable hands-on experience and get the chance to perceive business applications not as closed, unidimensional solutions, but as a means to support an enterprise's business tasks. Research conducted by Schneider [18] emphasizes that this understanding is essential for learners becoming an expert in the area of ERPS towards iES.

5 Conclusions and Outlook

The study has shown that ERPS, and ES in general, are opening their system boundaries. Characteristically, these systems mainly focus on enterprises' internal processes and provide functionality to support interfacing with some dedicated stakeholders. This is the 'classical' inside-out perspective. On the next level, iES will be the standard – based on open and networked platforms – which enables the interaction with a large amount of human and technical actors. Technological advancements like IoT, industry 4.0 or cloud computing are strong enablers, and business decision makers will not fail to incorporate this new generation of ES in their enterprises.

Therefore, the current learners – our future mangers and IT professionals – need to build a deep understanding of ES, in particular ERPS and their evolution towards iES. As the study elaborated, higher educational institutes (can) use a variety of approaches to teach ERPS – they all differ in terms of product/vendor-dependence and comprehensiveness.

We argue that new/adapted curricula are needed, which reflect the networked character of interconnected ES. In particular, the learners should be enabled to actively shape an iES. Curricula should consider customizing iES according to different needs so that learners understand the potential of iES as a means to build a networked business ecosystem.

There is no doubt that the suggested teaching approaches are demanding. However, ERPS vendors are offering their systems as cloud-based solutions, which should facilitate their integration into teaching settings. Nevertheless, using a cloud environment and connecting it with different types of human and technical actors throughout a business network does not only open new potentials, but also comes along with some increased risks. Topics like (cyber) security, data protection as well as compliance requirements must be considered and need to be taught as part of a new era of interconnected enterprise computing.

Future research should go in two directions: firstly, new and challenging curricula and related learning environments should be developed and tested; these should focus on the digital transformation and the associated iES. Secondly, flanking activities should be integrated, such as security aspects, data protection and compliance requirements. Both require new curricula and learning scenarios that need to be developed and tested.

References

1. Chen, C.-S., Liang, W.-Y., Hsu, H.-Y.: A cloud-computing platform for ERP applications. Appl. Soft Comput. **27**, 127–136 (2015). https://doi.org/10.1016/j.asoc.2014.11.009
2. El Kadiri, S., Grabot, B., Thoben, K.-D., Hribernik, K., Emmanouilidis, C., Cieminski, G. von Kiritsis, D.: Current trends on ICT technologies for enterprise information systems. Comput. Ind. **79**, 14–33 (2016)
3. Davenport, T.H.: Mission Critical. Realizing the Promise of Enterprise Systems. Mission Critical: Realizing the Promise of Enterprise Systems. Harvard Business School Press, Cambridge (2000)
4. Morabito, V.: Business Innovation Through Blockchain. The B^3 Perspective. Springer International Publishing, Cham (2017). https://doi.org/10.1007/978-3-319-48478-5
5. Du Plessis, J.-J., Mwalemba, G.: Adoption of emerging technologies into ERP systems landscape: a South African study. In: 2016 IEEE International Conference on Emerging Technologies and Innovative Business Practices for the Transformation of Societies (EmergiTech), Mauritius, pp. 395–399 (2016)
6. Gartner: Market Share: Enterprise Resource Planning, Worldwide 2016 (2017). www.gartner.com/doc/3746919/market-share-enterprise-resource-planning. Accessed 10 Jan 2018
7. Seethamraju, R.: Adoption of software as a service (SaaS) enterprise resource planning (ERP) systems in small and medium sized enterprises (SMEs). Inf. Syst. Front. **17**(3), 475–492 (2015)
8. Elragal, A., Haddara, M.: The future of ERP systems: look backward before moving forward. Procedia Technol. **5**, 21–30 (2012)
9. Asprion, P.M.: Funktionstrennung in ERP-Systemen: Konzepte, Methoden und Fallstudien. Springer Fachmedien Wiesbaden, Wiesbaden (2012). https://doi.org/10.1007/978-3-658-00037-0
10. Asprion, P.M.: ERP-Projekte mit Konfliktklärungskompetenz begleiten. ERP Manag. **12**, 48–51 (2016)
11. Elragal, A.: ERP and big data: the inept couple. Procedia Technol. **16**, 242–249 (2014)
12. Finney, S., Corbett, M.: ERP implementation: a compilation and analysis of critical success factors. Bus. Process Manag. J. **13**(3), 329–347 (2007)
13. Leyh, C.: ERP-System-Einsatz in der Lehre: Ergebnisse einer Umfrage an deutschen Universitäten und Fachhochschulen. In: Mattfeld, D.C., Robra-Bissantz, S. (eds.) Multikonferenz Wirtschaftsinformatik 2012: Tagungsband der MKWI 2012, pp. 513–524. Univ.-Bibl, Berlin, Braunschweig (2012)
14. Pongratz, H.: Integration von ERP-Systemen an beruflichen Schulen als ein umfassendes Projekt der Schulentwicklung. In: Pongratz, H., Tramm, T., Wilbers, K. (eds.) Prozessorientierte Wirtschaftsdidaktik und Einsatz von ERP-Systemen im kaufmännischen Unterricht. Texte zur Wirtschaftspädagogik und Personalentwicklung, vol. 4, pp. 111–180. Shaker Verl, Aachen (2009)
15. Moore, G.: Systems of engagement and the future of enterprise IT: a sea change in enterprise IT (2011). http://info.aiim.org/systems-of-engagement-and-the-future-of-enterprise-it. Accessed 10 Jan 2018
16. Benbasat, I., Zmud, R.W.: Empirical research in information systems: the practice of relevance. MIS Q. **23**(1), 3–16 (1999)
17. Tranfield, D., Denyer, D., Smart, P.: Towards a methodology for developing evidence-informed management knowledge by means of systematic review. Br. J. Manage. **14**(3), 207–222 (2003)

18. Schneider, B.: Unternehmenssoftware als Forschungsfeld ökonomischer Bildung: Eine qualitative Studie zu ERP-Systemen aus der Sicht von Lernenden und Experten. Springer Fachmedien Wiesbaden, Wiesbaden (2017). https://doi.org/10.1007/978-3-658-19083-5

19. Barkol, O., Bergman, R., Kasravi, K., Golan, S., Risov, M.: Enterprise collective: connecting people via content. Tech. Rep. Hewlett-Packard development company. www.hpl.hp.com/techreports/2012/HPL-2012-102.pdf. Accessed 10 Jan 2018

20. Orosco, C.: The future of enterprise IT: an interview with Geoffrey moore (Part 1/2). www.forbes.com/sites/netapp/2015/03/17/geoffrey-moore-part-1/#797ecd287ef1. Accessed 10 Jan 2018

21. Köffer, S., Ortbach, K., Niehaves, B.: Exploring the relationship between IT consumerization and job performance: a theoretical framework for future research. Commun. Assoc. Inf. Syst. **35** (article 14) (2014)

22. Niehaves, B., Köffer, S., Ortbach, K.: The effect of private IT use on work performance - towards an IT consumerization theory. In: Wirtschaftsinformatik Proceedings 2013 11th International Conference on Wirtschaftsinformatik, Leipzig, Germany, 27th February–1st March (2013)

23. Asprion, P.M., Schneider, B., Grimberg, F.: ERP Systems Towards Digital Transformation. In: Dornberger, R. (ed.) Business Information Systems and Technology 4.0. SSDC, vol. 141, pp. 15–29. Springer, Cham (2018). https://doi.org/10.1007/978-3-319-74322-6_2

24. Wilbers, K.: Prozessorientierte Wirtschaftsdidaktik und Einsatz von ERP-Systemen im Unterricht. Hochschultage 2008. Universität Erlangen-Nürnberg, Nürnberg (2008)

25. Kurbel, K.: Enterprise Resource Planning and Supply Chain Management: Functions, Business Processes and Software for Manufacturing Companies. Progress in IS. Springer, Heidelberg (2013). https://doi.org/10.1007/978-3-642-31573-2

26. Ellet, W.: Das Fallstudien-Handbuch der Harvard Business School Press: Business-Cases entwickeln und erfolgreich auswerten. Haupt, Bern, Stuttgart, Wien (2008)

27. Weitz, B.O.: Fallstudien im Ökonomieunterricht. In: Retzmann, T. (ed) Methodentraining für den Ökonomieunterricht I: Mikromethoden Makromethoden, 2nd edn. Ökonomie unterrichten, pp. 101–119. Wochenschau-Verl, Schwalbach/Ts. (2011)

28. Weidner, S., Koch, B., Bernhardt, C.: Introduction to SAP ERP Using Global Bike Inc. 2.40: Course Material (2015). https://performancemanager.successfactors.eu. Accessed 10 Jan 2018

29. Szendrei, D., Teich, T., Unger, K., Militze, J.: Eine integrierte betriebswirtschaftliche Fallstudie mit SAP ERP und deren Einbindung in das SAP LEGO Labor. In: Schumann, M. (ed.) Multikonferenz Wirtschaftsinformatik 2010. Göttingen, Kurzfassungen der Beiträge, pp. 1637–1647. Univ.-Verl. Göttingen, c/o SUB Göttingen, Göttingen, 23–25 February 2010

30. Yazdani Rashvanlouei, K., Thome, R., Yazdani, K.: Functional and technological evolution of enterprise systems: an overview. In: IEEE International Conference on Industrial Engineering and Engineering Management (IEEM) Singapore, pp. 67–72. IEEE (2015)

31. Romero, D., Vernadat, F.: Enterprise information systems state of the art. past, present and future trends. Comput. Indus. **79**, 3–13 (2016). https://doi.org/10.1016/j.compind.2016.03.001

32. Bahssas, D.M., AlBar, A.M., Hoque, R.: Enterprise resource planning (ERP) systems: design, trends and deployment. Int. Technol. Manag. Rev. **5**(2), 72–81 (2015)

33. Koutropoulos, A.: Digital natives: ten years after. J. Online Learn. Teach. **7**(4), 525–538 (2011)

34. Prensky, M.: Digital natives, digital immigrants (part I). Horiz. MCB Univ. Press **9**(5), 1–6 (2001a)

35. Prensky, M.: Digital natives, digital immigrants: do they really think different? (Part II). Horiz. MCB Univ. Press **9**(6), 1–6 (2001)

36. Roberts, G.: Technology and leaning expectations of the net generation. In: Oblinger, D.G., Oblinger, J.L. (eds.) Educating the Net Generation, Edu-cause, pp. 3.1–3.7 (2005)
37. Lemke, C., Brenner, W.: Verstehen des digitalen Zeitalters. Lehrbuch, Lemke C., Brenner, W., Bd. 1. Springer Gabler, Berlin [u.a.] (2015). https://doi.org/10.1007/978-3-662-44065-0
38. Staudt, F.: Hohe Ansprüche im SAP-Arbeitsmarkt, Computerwoche. (2015) www.cowo.de/a/3216120. Accessed 10 Jan 2018
39. Prifti, L., Löffler, A., Knigge, M.: The Digital Transformation of Global Bike. Lecturer Notes (2017). http://dt.sapucc.in.tum.de/. Accessed 10 Jan 2018

Poster Papers

Efficient Characterization of Hidden Processor Memory Hierarchies

Keith Cooper[iD] and Xiaoran Xu[(✉)][iD]

Rice University, Houston, TX 77005, USA
{keith,xiaoran.xu}@rice.edu

Abstract. A processor's memory hierarchy has a major impact on the performance of running code. However, computing platforms, where the actual hardware characteristics are hidden from both the end user and the tools that mediate execution, such as a compiler, a JIT and a runtime system, are used more and more, for example, performing large scale computation in cloud and cluster. Even worse, in such environments, a single computation may use a collection of processors with dissimilar characteristics. Ignorance of the performance-critical parameters of the underlying system makes it difficult to improve performance by optimizing the code or adjusting runtime-system behaviors; it also makes application performance harder to understand.

To address this problem, we have developed a suite of portable tools that can efficiently derive many of the parameters of processor memory hierarchies, such as levels, *effective capacity* and latency of caches and TLBs, in a matter of seconds. The tools use a series of carefully considered experiments to produce and analyze cache response curves automatically. The tools are inexpensive enough to be used in a variety of contexts that may include install time, compile time or runtime adaption, or performance understanding tools.

Keywords: Efficient characterization · Hidden memory hierarchies
Code performance · Portable tool

1 Introduction and Motivation

Application performance on modern multi-core processors depends heavily on the performance of the system's underlying memory hierarchy. The academic community has a history of developing techniques to measure various parameters on memory hierarchies [1–14]. However, as deep, complex, and shared structures have been introduced into memory hierarchies, it has become more difficult to find accurate and detailed information of performance-related characteristics of those hierarchies. What's more, to an increasing degree, large-scale computations are performed on platforms where the actual characteristics of the underlying hardware are hidden. Knowledge of the performance-critical parameters of the underlying hardware can be useful for improving compiled code, adjusting

© Springer International Publishing AG, part of Springer Nature 2018
Y. Shi et al. (Eds.): ICCS 2018, LNCS 10862, pp. 335–349, 2018.
https://doi.org/10.1007/978-3-319-93713-7_27

runtime system behaviors, or understanding performance issues. Specifically, to achieve the best performance on such platforms, the code must be tailored to the detailed memory structure of the target processor. That structure varies widely across different architectures, even for models of the same instruction set architecture (ISA). Thus, performance can be limited by the compiler's ability to understand model-specific differences in the memory hierarchy, to tailor the program's behavior, and to adjust runtime behaviors accordingly. At present, few compilers attempt aggressive model-specific optimization. One impediment to development of such compilers is the difficulty of understanding the relevant performance parameters of the target processor. While manufacturers provide some methods to discover such information, such as Intel's CPUID, those mechanisms are not standardized across manufacturers or across architectures. A standard assumption is that such data can be found in manuals; in truth, details such as the latency of an L1 TLB miss on an Intel Core i7 processor are rarely listed. What is worse, even the listed information may differ from what a compiler really needs for code optimization, such as full hardware capacity vs. *effective capacity*.

Effective capacity is defined as the amount of memory at each level that an application can use before the access latency begins to rise. The effective value for a parameter can be considered an upper bound on the usable fraction of the physical resource. Several authors have advocated the use of effective capacities rather than physical capacities [15–17]. In the best case, *effective capacity* is equal to *physical capacity*. For example, on most microprocessors, L1 data cache's effective and physical capacity are identical, because it is not shared with other cores or instruction cache, and virtually mapped. In contrast, a higher level cache for the same architecture might be shared among cores; contain the images of all those cores' L1 instruction caches or hold page tables, locked into L2 or L3 by hardware that walks the page table. Each of these effects might reduce the *effective cache capacity* and modern commodity processors exhibit all three.

Contribution. This paper presents a set of tools that measure, efficiently and empirically, the *effective capacity* and other parameters of the various levels in the data memory hierarchy, both cache and TLB; that are portable across a variety of systems; that include a robust automatic analysis; and that derive a full set of characteristics in a few seconds. The resulting tools are inexpensive enough to use in a variety of contexts that may include install time, compile time or runtime adaption, or performance understanding tools. Section 4 shows that our techniques produce results with the same accuracy as earlier work, while using a factor of **10x** to **250x** less time, which makes the tools inexpensive enough to be used in various contexts, especially lightweight runtime adaption.

2   Related Work

Many authors describe systems that attempt to characterize the memory hierarchy [1–5,8], but from our perspective, previous systems suffer from several specific flaws: (1) The prior tools are not easily portable to current machines [1–3]. Some rely on system-specific features such as superpages or hardware performance counters to simplify the problems. Others were tested on older systems with shallow hierarchies; multi-level caches and physical-address tags create complications that they were not designed to handle. On contrast, our tools characterize various modern processors using only portable C code and POSIX calls. (2) Some previous tools solve multiple parameters at once [4,5], which is not robust since if the code generates one wrong answer for one parameter, it inevitably causes the failure of all the other parameters. Noisy measurements and new hardware features, such as sharing or victim caches, can also cause these tests to produce inaccurate results. (3) Finally, the time cost of measuring a full set of characteristics by previous tools is very large, e.g. 2–8 min by Sandoval's tool [8] (See Sect. 4). At that cost, the set of reasonable applications for these measurements is limited. For these techniques to find practical use, the cost of measurement and analysis must be much lower.

The other related works have different focuses with ours. P-RAY [6] and SERVET [7] characterized sharing and communication aspects of multi-core clusters. Taylor and Li [9] extended memory characterization techniques to AMD GPUs. Sussman et al. [10] arbitrated between different results produced from different benchmarks. Abel [11] measured physical capacities of caches. SERVET 3.0 [12] improved SERVET [7] by characterizing the network performance degradation. Casas et al. [13,14] quantified applications' utilization of the memory hierarchy.

3   The Algorithms

This section describes three tests we developed that measure the levels, capacity and latency for cache and TLB, along with associativity and linesize for L1 cache. All of the tests rely on a standard C compiler and the POSIX libraries for portability, and timings are taken based on gettimeofday(). All the three algorithms rely on a data structure *reference string*, implemented as a circular chain of pointers, to create a specific pattern of memory references. The reference strings are different for each test to expose different aspects of the memory hierarchy, but their construction, running and timing are shared as presented below.

3.1   Reference Strings

A reference string is simply a series of memory references—in this paper, they are all load operations—that the test uses to elicit a desired response from the memory system. A reference string has a *footprint*, the amount of contiguous virtual address space that it covers. In general, the tests use a specific reference string, in a variety of footprints, to measure memory system response. By constructing, running different footprints and recording the times spent, the test builds up a response curve. Figure 1 shows a typical response curve running on an Intel T9600.

Running a Reference String: The microbenchmarks depend on the fact that we can produce an accurate measurement of the time required to run a reference string, and that we can amortize out compulsory start-up cache misses. To measure the running time for a reference string, the tool must instantiate the string and walk its references enough times to obtain an accurate timing. Our tools instantiate the reference string as an array of pointers whose size equals the footprint of the string. Inside this array, the tools build a circular linked list of the locations. (In C, we use an array of $void **$.) The code to run the reference string is simple as shown in Fig. 2. The actual implementation runs the loop enough times to obtain stable results, where "enough" is scaled by the processor's measured speed. We chose the iteration count by experimentation where the error rate is 1% or less.

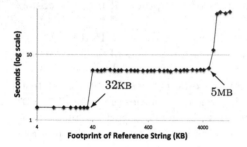

```
loads ← number of accesses
start ← timer()
while loads − − > 0 do
    p ← *p
end while
finish ← timer()
elapsed ← finish − start
```

Fig. 1. Example response curve   **Fig. 2.** Running a reference string

Timing a Reference String: To time a reference string, we insert calls to the POSIX *gettimeofday* routine around the loop as a set of calipers. We run multiple trials of each reference string and record the minimum measured execution time because outside interference will only manifest itself in longer execution times. Finally, we convert the measured times into "cycles", where a cycle is defined as the time of an integer add operation. This conversion eliminates the fractional cycles introduced by amortized compulsory misses and loop overhead.

The basic design and timing of reference strings are borrowed from Sandoval's work [8], since he already showed that these techniques produce accurate timing results across a broad variety of processor architectures and models. Our contribution lies in finding significantly more efficient ways to manipulate the reference strings to detect cache parameters. The L1 cache test provides a good example of how changing the use of the string can produce equivalent results with an order of magnitude less cost (see Sect. 4 for cost and accuracy results). Also, we significantly reduce the measurement time of data while keeping the same accuracy. We repeat each test until we have not seen the minimum time change in the last 25 runs. (The value of 25 was selected via a parameter sweep from 1 to 100. At 25, the error rate for the multi-cache test is 1% or less.)

3.2 L1 Cache

Because the L1 data-cache linesize can be used to reduce spatial locality in the multi-level cache test and the TLB test, we use an efficient, specialized test to discover the L1 cache parameters. Two properties of L1 caches make the test easy to derive and analyze: the lack of sharing at L1 and the use of virtual-address tags. The L1 test relies directly on hardware effects caused by the combination of capacity and associativity. We denote the L1 reference string as a tuple G(n,k,o), where n is the number of locations to access, k is the number of bytes between those locations (the "gap"), and o is an offset added to the start of the last location in the set. The reference string G(n,k,0) generates the following locations:

And $G(n,k,4)$ would move the nth location out another four bytes.

Both X-Ray [4] and Sandoval's [8] "gap" test use a similar reference string. However, they require to iterate k across the full range of cache sizes, and n from 1 to the actual associativity plus one. Our algorithm orders the tests in a different way that radically reduces the number of combinations of n and k that it must try. It starts with the maximum value of associativity, **MaxAssoc**, say 16, and sweeps over the gap size to find the first value that causes significant misses, as shown in the first loop in Fig. 3.

baseline ← time for G(2,LB/2,0)
1. for k ← LB/MaxAssoc to UB/MaxAssoc
   t ← time for G(MaxAssoc+1,k,0)
   if $t > baseline$
      $L1Size = k * MaxAssoc$
      break

2. for n ← $MaxAssoc; n \geq 1; n$ ← $n/2$
   t ← time for G(n+1,L1Size/n,0)
   if $t \leq baseline$
      $L1Assoc = n * 2$
      break

3. for offset ← 1 to pagesize
   t ← time for G(L1Assoc+1,L1Size/L1Assoc,offset)
   if $t \leq baseline$
      L1LineSize = offset
      break

Fig. 3. Pseudo code for the L1 cache test

It sweeps the value of k from LB / MaxAssoc to UB / MaxAssoc, where **LB** and **UB** are the lower and upper bounds of the testing cache. For L1 cache, we choose 1 KB and 4 MB respectively. With $n =$ MaxAssoc $+ 1$ and $o = 0$, the last and the first location will always map to the same cache set location. None of them will miss until $k * MaxAssoc$ reaches the L1 cache size. Figure 4 shows how the string G(33, 1 KB, 0) maps into a 32 KB, 8-way, set-associative cache. With these cache parameters, each way holds 4 KB and all references in G(33, 1 KB, 0) map into sets 0, 16, 32, and 48. The string completely fills those four cache sets, and overflows set 0. Thus, the 33rd reference will always miss in the L1 cache.

The first loop will record uniform (cycle-rounded) times for all iterations, which is called the **baseline** time since all the references hit in L1 cache so far. Until it reaches G(33, 1 KB, 0), at which time it will record a larger time due to the miss on the 33rd element, the larger time causes it to record the cache size and exit the first loop.

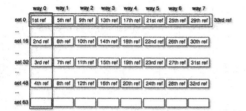

Fig. 4. Running G(33,1 KB,0) on a 32 KB, 8-Way, set-associative cache

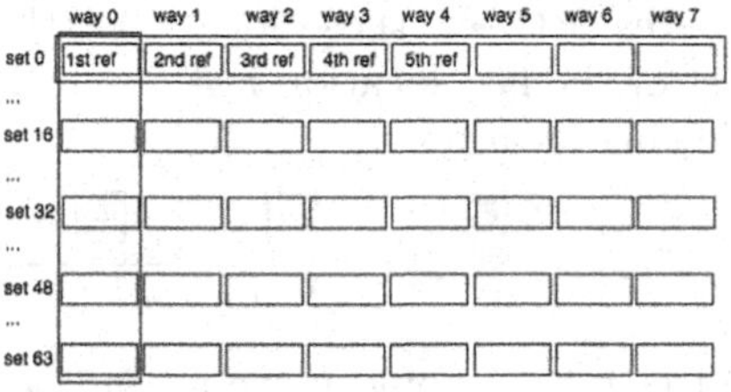

Fig. 5. Running G(5,8 KB,0) on a 32 KB, 8-Way, set-associative cache

The second loop in Fig. 3 finds the associativity by looking at larger gaps (k) and smaller associativities (n). It sweeps over associativity from MaxAssoc + 1 to 2, decreasing n by a factor of 2 at each iteration. In a set-associative cache, the last location in all the reference strings will continue to miss in L1 cache until n is less than the actual associativity. In the example, a 32 KB, 8 way L1 cache, that occurs when n is L1Assoc/2, namely 4, as shown in Fig. 5. At this point, the locations in the reference string all map to the same set and, because there are more ways in the set than references now, the last reference will hit in cache and the time will again match the baseline time.

At this point, the algorithm knows the L1 size and associativity. So the third loop runs a parameter sweep on the value of o, from 1 to pagesize (in words). When o reaches the L1 linesize, the final reference in the string maps to the next set and the runtime for the reference string drops back to the original baseline—the value when all references hit in cache.

3.3   Multilevel Caches

The L1 cache test relies on the fact that it can precisely detect the actual hardware boundary of the cache. We cannot apply the same test to higher level caches for several reasons: higher level caches tend to be shared, either between instruction and data cache, or between cores, or both; higher level caches tend to use physical-address tags rather than virtual ones; operating systems tend to lock page table entries into one of the higher level caches. Each of these factors, individually, can cause the L1 cache test to fail. It works on L1 precisely because L1 data caches are core-private and virtually mapped, without outside interference or page tables.

Our multi-level cache test avoids the weaknesses that the L1 cache test exhibits for upper level caches by detecting cache capacity in isolation from associativity. It uses a reference string designed to expose changes in cache response while isolating those effects from any TLB response. It reuses the infrastructure developed for the L1 cache test to run and time the cache reference string.

The multi-level cache test reference string $C(k)$ is constructed from a footprint k, the OS pagesize obtained from the *Posix* sysconf(), and the L1 cache linesize.[1] Given these values, the string generator builds an array of pointers that spans k bytes of memory. The generator constructs an index set, the column set, that covers one page and accesses one pointer in each L1 cache line on the page. It constructs another index set, the row set, that contains the starting address of each page in the array. Figure 6 shows the cache reference string without randomization; in practice, we randomize the order within each row and the order of the rows to eliminate the impact of hardware prefetching schemes. Sweeping through the page in its randomized order before moving to another page, minimizes the impact of TLB misses on large footprint reference strings.

To measure cache capacity, the test could use this reference string in a simple parameter sweep, for the range from **LB** to **UB**. As we mentioned, **LB** and **UB** are the lower and upper bounds of the testing cache and we choose 1 KB and 32 MB respectively for the whole multi-level cache.

> **for** $k \leftarrow$ Range(LB,UB)
> $\quad t_k \leftarrow$ time for $C(k)$ reference string

The sweep produces a series of values, t_k, that form a piecewise linear function describing the processor's cache response. Recall that Fig. 1 shows the curve from the multi-level cache test on an Intel T9600. The T9600 featured a 32 KB L1 cache and a 6 MB L2 cache, but notice the sharp rise at 32 KB and the softer rise that begins at 5 MB. It's the effect of *effective capacity*.

The implementation of the algorithm, of course, is more complex. Section 3.1 described how to run and time a single reference string. Besides that, the pseudo code given inline above abstracts the choice of sample points into the notation Range(LB,UB). Instead of sampling the whole space uniformly, in both the multi-level cache and the TLB test, we actually only space the points uniformly below 4 KB (we test 1, 2, 3, and 4 KB). Above 4 KB, we test each power of two, along with three points uniformly-spaced in between since sampling fewer points has a direct effect on running time. The pseudo code also abstracts the fact that the test actually makes repeated sweeps over the range from LB to UB. At each size, it constructs, runs, and times a reference string, updating the minimal time for that size, if necessary, and tracking the number of trials since the time was last lowered. Sweeping in this way distributes outside interference, say from an OS daemon or another process, across sizes, rather than concentrating it in a

---

[1] In practice, the L1 linesize is used to accentuate the system response by decreasing spatial locality. Any value greater than $sizeof(void*)$ works, but a value greater than or equal to linesize works better.

small number of sizes. Recreating the reference string at each size and trial allows the algorithm to sample different virtual-to-physical page mappings.

Knocking Out and Reviving Neighbors: Most of the time spent in the multi-level cache test is incurred by running reference strings. The discipline of running each size until its minimum time is "stable"—defined as not changing in the last 25 runs, means that the test runs enough reference strings. (As we mentioned, the value of 25 was selected via a parameter sweep from 1 to 100 and at 25, the error rate for the multi-cache test is 1% or less.)

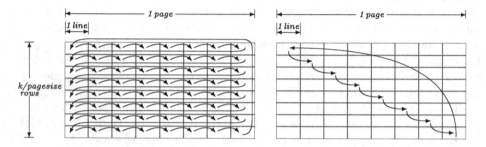

Fig. 6. Cache test reference string   **Fig. 7.** TLB test reference string

In Fig. 1, points that fall in the middle of a level of the memory hierarchy have, as might be expected, similar heights in the graph, indicating similar average latencies. Examining the sweep-by-sweep results, we realized that values in those plateaus quickly reach their minimum values. This is another kind of "stability" of data. To capitalize on this effect, we added a mechanism to knock values out of the testing range when they agree with the values at neighboring sample sizes. As shown in Fig. 8, after every sweep of the reference strings, the knockout phase examines every sample size k in the Range (LB, UB). If t_k, the time of running $C(k)$ string, equals both t_{k-1} and t_{k+1}, then it cautiously asserts k is a redundant sample size and can be knocked out. (It sets the counter for that size that tracks iterations since a new minimum to zero.) In the next sweep of Range (LB, UB), these sample sizes will be omitted.

The knock-out mechanism can eliminate a sample size too soon, e.g. a sample size k and its neighbors have the same inaccurate value. When this occurs, the knockout test may eliminate out k prematurely. To cope with this situation, we added a revival phase. When any point reaches a new minimum, if it has a neighbor that was previously knocked out, it revives that neighbor so that it is again measured in the next sweep of Range (LB, UB).

The knockout-revival optimization significantly reduced the cost of the multi-level cache test, from minutes in earlier work to seconds, as details shown in Sect. 4.

3.4   TLB Test

The TLB test closely resembles the multi-level cache test, except that it uses a reference string that isolates TLB behavior from cache misses. It utilizes the same infrastructure to run reference strings and incorporates the same discipline for sweeping a range of TLB sizes to produce a response curve. It benefits significantly from the knockout-revival mechanism.

The TLB reference string, $T(n,k)$, accesses n pointers in each page of an array with a footprint of k bytes. To construct $T(1,k)$, the generator builds a column index set and a row index set as in the multi-level cache test. It shuffles both sets. To generate the permutation, it iterates over the row set choosing pages. It chooses a single line within the page by using successive lines from the column set, wrapping around in a modular fashion if necessary. The result is a string that accesses one line per page, and spreads the lines over the associative sets in the lower level caches. The effect is to maximize the page footprint, while minimizing the cache footprint. Figure 7 shows $T(1,k)$ without randomization. For $n > 1$, the generator uses n lines per page, with a variable offset within the page to distribute the accesses across different sets in the caches and minimize associativity conflicts. The generator randomizes the full set of references, to avoid the effects of a prefetcher and to successive accesses to the same page.

```
while not all t_k are stable do
    for k ← Range(LB,UB)
        t_k ← time for C(k) reference string
        if t_k is a new minimum && k's neighbors
        have been knocked out
            revive k's neighbors to Range(LB,UB)
    for k ← Range(LB,UB)
        if t_k == t_{k's neighbors}
            knock out k from Range(LB, UB)
```

```
for k ← LB to UB
    t_{1,k} ← time for T(1,k)
    if there's a jump from t_{1,k-1} to t_{1,k}
        for n ← 2, 3, 4
            t_{n,k-1} ← time for T(n,k-1)
            t_{n,k} ← time for T(n,k)
            if there's a jump from t_{n,k-1} to t_{n,k}
            when n=2,3,4
                report a TLB size
```

Fig. 8. Pseudo code for multi-level cache test

Fig. 9. Pseudo code for the TLB test

The multi-level cache test hides the impact of TLB misses by amortizing those misses over many accesses. Unfortunately, the TLB test cannot completely hide the impact of cache misses because any action that amortizes cache misses also partially amortizes TLB misses. When the TLB line crosses a cache boundary, the rise in measured time is indistinguishable from the response to a TLB boundary. However, we could rule out false positives by running $T(2,k)$ reference string and following the rule that if $T(1,k)$ shows a TLB response at x pages, then $T(2,k)$ should show a TLB response at x pages too if x pages is indeed a boundary of TLB. Because $T(2,k)$ uses twice as many lines at x pages as $T(1,k)$, if it's a false positive response caused by the cache boundary in $T(1,k)$, it will appear at a smaller size in $T(2,k)$.

Still, a worst-case choice of cache and TLB sizes can fool this test. If $T(1,k)$ maps into m cache lines at x pages, and $T(2,k)$ maps into $2*m$ cache lines at x pages, and the processor has cache boundaries at m and $2 * m$ lines, both reference strings will discover a suspect point at x pages and the current analysis will report a TLB boundary at x pages even if it's not. Using more tests, e.g., $T(3, k)$ and $T(4, k)$, could eliminate these false positive points.

Sandoval's test [8] ran the higher line-count TLB strings, $T(2, k)$, $T(3, k)$, and $T(4, k)$ exhaustively. We observe that the values for those higher line-count tests are only of interest at points where the code observes a transition in the response curve. Thus, our TLB test runs a series of $T(1, k)$ strings for k from LB to UB. From this data, it identifies potential transitions in the TLB response graph, called "suspect" points. Then it examines the responses of the higher line-count tests at the suspect point and its immediate neighbors as shown in Fig. 9. If the test detects a rise in the $T(1, k)$ response at x pages, but that response is not confirmed by one or more of $T(2, k)$, $T(3, k)$, or $T(4, k)$, then it reports x as a false positive. If all of $T(1, k)$, $T(2, k)$, $T(3, k)$, $T(4, k)$ show a rise at x pages, it reports that transition as a TLB boundary. This technique eliminates almost all false positive results in practice since the situation that all m, $2m$, $3m$, $4m$ cache lines are cache boundaries is extremely unlikely.

Table 1. L1 cache results

Processor	Capacity (KB)	LineSize (B)	Associativity	Latency cycle	Cost secs
Intel Core i3	32	64	8	3	0.49
Intel Core i7	32	64	8	5	0.56
Intel Xeon E5-2640	32	64	8	4	0.49
Intel Xeon E5420	32	64	8	4	0.54
Intel Xeon X3220	32	64	8	3	0.51
Intel Xeon E7330	32	64	8	3	0.52
Intel Core2 T7200	32	64	8	3	0.55
Intel Pentium 4	8	64	4	4	1.71
ARM Cortex A9	32	32	7	4	7.98

Running the higher line-count tests as on-demand confirmatory tests, rather than exhaustively, significantly reduces the number of reference strings run and, thus, the overall time for the TLB test. (See time cost comparison in Sect. 4.)

4   Experimental Validation

To validate our techniques, we ran them on a collection of systems that range from commodity X86 processors through an ARM Cortex A9. All of these systems run some flavor of Unix and support the POSIX interfaces for our tools.

Table 2. Multilevel caches results

Processor	Level	Effective cap. (KB)	Physical cap. (KB)	Latency cycle	Cost (Secs)
Intel Core i3	1	32	32	3	
	2	256	256	13	2.05
	3	**2048**	3072	30	
Intel Core i7	1	32	32	5	
	2	256	256	13	3.70
	3	**3072**	4096	36	
Intel Xeon E5-2640	1	32	32	4	
	2	256	256	13	4.49
	3	**14336**	15360	42	
Intel Xeon E5420	1	32	32	4	4.68
	2	**4096**	6144	16	
Intel Xeon X3220	1	32	32	3	3.92
	2	**3072**	4096	15	
Intel Xeon E7330	1	32	32	3	6.87
	2	**1792**	3072	14	
Intel Core2 T7200	1	32	32	3	5.66
	2	4096	4096	15	
Intel Pentium 4	1	8	8	4	8.03
	2	**384**	512	39	
ARM Cortex A9	1	32	32	4	54.57
	2	1024	1024	11	

Table 1 shows the results of the L1 cache test: the capacity, line size, associativity, and latency, along with the total time cost of the measurements. On most machines, the tests only required roughly half a second to detect all the L1 cache parameters, except for the ARM machine and the Pentium 4. The ARM timings are much slower in all three tests because it is a Solid Run Cubox-i4Pro with a 1.2 GHZ Freescale iMX6-Quad processor. It runs Debian Unix from a commercial SD card in lieu of a disk. Thus, it has a different OS, different compiler base, and different hardware setup than the other systems, which are all off-the-shelf desktops, servers, or laptops. Thus all of the timings from the ARM system are proportionately slower than the other systems. The Intel Pentium 4 system is relatively higher than the other chips, despite its relatively fast clock speed of 3.2 GHZ. Two factors explain this seemingly slow measurement time. The latency of the Pentium 4's last level cache is slow relative to most modern systems. Thus, it runs samples that hit in the cache more slowly than the other modern systems. In addition, its small cache size (384 KB) means that a larger number of samples miss in the last level cache (and run slowly in main memory) than the other tested systems.

The multi-level cache and TLB tests produce noisy data that approximates the piecewise linear step functions that describe the processor's response. We developed an automatic, conservative and robust analysis tool which uses a multi-step process to derive consistent and accurate capacities from that data.[2] The analysis derive for both cache and TLB, the number of levels and the transition point between each pair of levels (*i.e.*, the effective capacity of each level).

Table 2 shows the measured parameters from the multi-level cache test: the number of cache levels, effective capacity, latency, and total time required for the measurement. In addition, the table shows the actual physical capacities for comparison against the effective capacities measured by the tests. The tests are precise for lower-level caches, but typically underestimate the last level of cache—that is, their effective capacities are smaller than the physical cache sizes for the last level of cache. As discussed earlier, if the last level of cache is shared by multiple cores, or if the OS locks the page table into that cache, we would expect the effective capacity to be smaller than the physical capacity. The time costs of the multi-level cache test are all few seconds except for the ARM machine because of the same reasons we explained above.

Table 3. TLB results

Processor	Level	Capacity (KB)	Cost (secs)
Intel Core i3	1	256	0.14
	2	2048	
Intel Core i7	1	256	0.84
	2	4096	
Intel Xeon E5-2640	1	256	0.15
	2	2048	
Intel Xeon E5420	1	64	0.20
	2	1024	
Intel Xeon X3220	1	64	0.18
	2	1024	
Intel Xeon E7330	1	64	0.20
	2	1024	
Intel Core2 T7200	1	64	1.28
	2	1024	
Intel Pentium 4	1	256	3.09
ARM Cortex A9	1	128	8.91
	2	512	

---

[2] The details are omitted due to space limit. Please contact the authors if interested.

Table 3 shows the results of TLB test: the number of levels, effective capacity for each level (*entries × pagesize*), and the time cost of the measurement. From Table 3 we see that, on most systems, the TLB test ran in less than 1 s. As with the multi-level cache test, the Pentium 4 is slower than the newer systems. The same factors come into play. It has a small, one-level TLB with a capacity of 256 KB. The test runs footprints up to 8 MB, so the Pentium 4 generates many more TLB misses than are seen on machines with larger TLB capacities.

The reason why we didn't measure the associativity and linesize for multi-level caches and TLB is that caches above L1 tend to use physical-address tags rather than virtual-address tags, which complicates the measurements. The tools generate reference string that are contiguous in virtual address space; the distance relationships between pages in virtual space are not guaranteed to hold in the physical address space. (Distances within a page hold in both spaces.)

In a sense, the distinct runs of the reference string form distinct samples of the virtual-to-physical address mapping. (Each time a specific footprint is tested, a new reference string is allocated and built.) Thus, any given run at any reasonably large size can show an unexpectedly large time if the virtual-to-physical mapping introduces an associativity problem in the physical address space that does not occur in the virtual address space.

Table 4. Our Tool VS. Sandoval's Tool

Processor	Tools	L1 test cost	Multilevel test cost	TLB test cost
Intel Core i3	Our Tool	0.49	2.05	0.14
	Sandoval's tool	27.02	58.16	36.81
Intel Core i7	Our Tool	0.56	3.70	0.84
	Sandoval's tool	34.75	92.35	94.97
Intel Xeon E5-2640	Our Tool	0.49	4.49	0.15
	Sandoval's tool	33.33	65.42	38.79
Intel Xeon E5420	Our Tool	0.54	4.68	0.20
	Sandoval's tool	28.86	150.43	55.56
Intel Xeon X3220	Our Tool	0.51	3.92	0.18
	Sandoval's tool	28.89	121.54	54.17
Intel Xeon E7330	Our Tool	0.52	6.87	0.20
	Sandoval's tool	35.77	228.13	53.24
Intel Core2 T7200	Our Tool	0.55	5.66	1.28
	Sandoval's tool	34.86	200.82	166.19
Intel Pentium 4	Our Tool	1.71	8.03	3.09
	Sandoval's tool	40.45	227.57	194.37
ARM Cortex A9	Our Tool	7.98	54.57	8.91
	Sandoval's tool	16.76	458.55	42.03

The same effect makes it difficult to determine associativity at the upper level caches. Use of physical addresses makes it impossible to create, reliably, repeatedly, and portably, the relationships required to measure associativity. In addition, associativity measurement requires the ability to detect the **actual**, rather than **effective**, capacity.

The goal of this work was to produce efficient tests. We compare the time cost of our tool and Sandoval's [8] as shown in Table 4. (Other prior tools either cannot run on modern processors or produce wrong answers every now and then.) The savings in measurement time are striking. On the Intel processors, the reformulated L1 cache test is **20** to **70** times faster; the multi-level cache test is **15** to **40** times faster; and the TLB test is **60** to **250** times faster. The ARM Cortex A9 again shows distinctly different timing results: the L1 cache test is 2 times faster, the multi-level cache test is about 8.4 times faster, and the TLB test is about 4.7 times faster.

5   Conclusions

This paper has presented techniques that efficiently measure the *effective capacities* and other performance-critical parameters of a processor's cache and TLB hierarchy. The tools are portable; they rely on a C compiler and the POSIX OS interfaces. The tools are efficient; they take at most a few seconds to discover effective cache and TLB sizes. This kind of data has application in code optimization, runtime adaptation, and performance understanding.

This work lays the foundation for two kinds of future work: (1) measurement of more complex parameters, such as discovering the sharing relationships among hardware resources, or measuring the presence and capacities of features such as victim caches and streaming buffers; and (2) techniques for lightweight runtime adaptation, either with compiled code that relies on runtime-provision of hardware parameters or with lightweight mechanisms for runtime selection from pre-compiled alternative code sequences.

References

1. Saavedra, R.H., Smith, A.J.: Measuring cache and TLB performance and their effect on benchmark runtimes. IEEE Trans. Comput. **44**(10), 1223–1235 (1995)
2. McVoy, L.W., Staelin, C.: Lmbench: portable tools for performance analysis. In: USENIX annual technical conference, pp. 279–294 (1996)
3. Dongarra, J., Moore, S., Mucci, P., Seymour, K., You, H.: Accurate cache and TLB characterization using hardware counters. In: Bubak, M., van Albada, G.D., Sloot, P.M.A., Dongarra, J. (eds.) ICCS 2004. LNCS, vol. 3038, pp. 432–439. Springer, Heidelberg (2004). https://doi.org/10.1007/978-3-540-24688-6_57
4. Yotov, K., Pingali, K., Stodghill, P.: X-ray: a tool for automatic measurement of hardware parameters. In: Proceedings of Second International Conference on the Quantitative Evaluation of Systems 2005, pp. 168–177. IEEE, September 2005
5. Yotov, K., Pingali, K., Stodghill, P.: Automatic measurement of memory hierarchy parameters. ACM SIGMETRICS Perform. Eval. Rev. **33**(1), 181–192 (2005)

6. Duchateau, A.X., Sidelnik, A., Garzarán, M.J., Padua, D.: P-ray: a software suite for multi-core architecture characterization. In: Amaral, J.N. (ed.) LCPC 2008. LNCS, vol. 5335, pp. 187–201. Springer, Heidelberg (2008). https://doi.org/10.1007/978-3-540-89740-8_13

7. González-Domínguez, J., Taboada, G.L., Fragüela, B.B., Martín, M.J., Tourino, J.: Servet: a benchmark suite for autotuning on multicore clusters. In: 2010 IEEE International Symposium on Parallel & Distributed Processing (IPDPS), pp. 1–9. IEEE, April 2010

8. Sandoval, J.A.: Foundations for Automatic, Adaptable Compilation. Doctoral dissertation, Rice University (2011)

9. Taylor, R., Li, X.: A micro-benchmark suite for AMD GPUs. In: 2010 39th International Conference on Parallel Processing Workshops (ICPPW), pp. 387–396. IEEE (2010)

10. Sussman, A., Lo, N., Anderson, T.: Automatic computer system characterization for a parallelizing compiler. In: 2011 IEEE International Conference on Cluster Computing (CLUSTER), pp. 216–224. IEEE (2011)

11. Abel, A.: Measurement-based inference of the cache hierarchy. Doctoral dissertation, Master's thesis, Saarland University (2012)

12. González-Domínguez, J., Martín, M.J., Taboada, G.L., Expósito, R.R., Tourino, J.: The servet 3.0 benchmark suite: characterization of network performance degradation. Comput. Electr. Eng. **39**(8), 2483–2493 (2013)

13. Casas, M., Bronevetsky, G.: Active measurement of memory resource consumption. In: 2014 IEEE 28th International Symposium on Parallel and Distributed Processing, pp. 995–1004. IEEE, May 2014

14. Casas, M., Bronevetsky, G.: Evaluation of HPC applications' memory resource consumption via active measurement. IEEE Trans. Parallel Distrib. Syst. **27**(9), 2560–2573 (2016)

15. Moyer, S.A.: Performance of the iPSC/860 node architecture. Institute for Parallel Computation, University of Virginia (1991)

16. Qasem, A., Kennedy, K.: Profitable loop fusion and tiling using model-driven empirical search. In: Proceedings of the 20th Annual International Conference on Supercomputing, pp. 249–258. ACM, June 2006

17. Luk, C.K., Mowry, T.C.: Architectural and compiler support for effective instruction prefetching: a cooperative approach. ACM Trans. Comput. Syst. **19**(1), 71–109 (2001)

Discriminating Postural Control Behaviors from Posturography with Statistical Tests and Machine Learning Models: Does Time Series Length Matter?

Luiz H. F. Giovanini[1,2(✉)], Elisangela F. Manffra[1,3], and Julio C. Nievola[1,2]

[1] Pontifícia Universidade Católica do Paraná, Curitiba, Paraná, Brazil
{l.giovanini,elisangela.manffra,julio.nievola}@pucpr.br
[2] Programa de Pós-Graduação em Informática, Curitiba, Brazil
[3] Programa de Pós-Graduação em Tecnologia em Saúde, Curitiba, Brazil

Abstract. This study examines the influence of time series duration on the discriminative power of center-of-pressure (COP) features in distinguishing different population groups via statistical tests and machine learning (ML) models. We used two COP datasets, each containing two groups. One was collected from older adults with low or high risk of falling (dataset I), and the other from healthy and post-stroke adults (dataset II). Each time series was mapped into a vector of 34 features twice: firstly, using the original duration of 60 s, and then using only the first 30 s. We then compared each feature across groups through traditional statistical tests. Next, we trained six popular ML models to distinguish between the groups using features from the original signals and then from the shorter signals. The performance of each ML model was then compared across groups for the 30 s and 60 s time series. The mean percentage of features able to discriminate the groups via statistical tests was 26.5% smaller for 60 s signals in dataset I, but 13.5% greater in dataset II. In terms of ML, better performances were achieved for signals of 60 s in both datasets, mainly for similarity-based algorithms. Hence, we recommend the use of COP time series recorded over at least 60 s. The contribution of this paper also include insights into the robustness of popular ML models to the sampling duration of COP time series.

Keywords: Machine learning · Artificial intelligence · Feature extraction
Posture · Posturography · Sampling duration

1 Introduction

Postural control (PC) is essential for the accomplishment of a variety of motor tasks and daily living activities [1]. The decline in this control - usually followed by aging or neurological diseases such as stroke - affects the mobility and independence, thus preventing the person from having a good quality of life. A practical way to characterize PC is through posturography, a technique that uses a device called force plate to record the body sway during quiet standing for a certain amount of time [1]. This sway is

© Springer International Publishing AG, part of Springer Nature 2018
Y. Shi et al. (Eds.): ICCS 2018, LNCS 10862, pp. 350–357, 2018.
https://doi.org/10.1007/978-3-319-93713-7_28

recorded as time series data of the center-of-pressure (COP) displacements of the person over its base of support in both x and y directions [1]. Then, with the help of suitable metrics, COP time series can be parameterized into posturographic features able to work as clinical descriptors for many recognition tasks. Importantly, many widely-used metrics are influenced by the length of the COP time series [2, 3], which depends upon the sampling duration used for data recording. This is a critical point due to the lack of standardization of this acquisition parameter in posturography [4]. Some researchers claim that long durations of at least 120 s are necessary to fully characterize PC [3]. Conversely, some others criticize long durations arguing that factors such as fatigue can confound the results [5]. Hence, short durations are largely observed in the literature, usually around 30 s [2, 4, 5].

Traditionally, discrimination of COP behavior has been performed with statistical tests, where each posturographic feature is analyzed separately. More recently, some studies have successfully replaced such tests by ML models, where the discrimination is achieved by combining multiple features in a more sophisticated fashion. Two ways of COP discrimination are observed in the literature. The first one consists in comparing features from the same population group obtained at different balance tasks, thus helping understand the complexity of such tasks. This is known as intra-group analysis. The second way is the inter-group analysis, where researchers compare features derived from different groups aimed at discriminating them. This allows, for instance, assessing how different pathologies affect the PC.

Many posturographic metrics are influenced by the COP sampling duration, which typically ranges from 30 s to 60 s [4]. To the best of our knowledge, studies have dedicated to examine the sensitivity of such metrics to a variety of short durations for intra-group analyzes [2, 4]; however, similar investigations were not conducted yet for inter-group comparisons. As a first step in this direction, this paper aims at investigating the inter-group discriminative power of features computed from COP data of 30 s and 60 s for the use of both statistical tests and ML models. Since more accurate intra-group features have been reported for 60 s than 30 s [5, 6], we hypothesized that COP data of 60 s can also provide more discriminative inter-group features.

2 Methods

2.1 Datasets

We used two COP datasets, both recorded at quite standing over 60 s at a sample frequency of 100 Hz and filtered at 10 Hz (dual-pass 4th order low-pass Butterworth). Derived from a public database of older adults [7], dataset I has 864 instances (i.e., pairs of COPx and COPy time series), 432 from subjects with high risk of falling (ROF) and 432 from individuals with low ROF. We allocated a time series in the high ROF group when the individual fulfilled at least one of three main risk factors for falls in the elderly [8]: (i) history of falls in the past year; (ii) prevalence of fear of falling; (iii) a score smaller than 16 points at Mini Balance Evaluation Systems Test, which indicates significant balance impairments. Originally collected by [9], dataset II has 114 instances, 57 from post-stroke adults and 57 from healthy individuals. We have permission (no. 991.103) of the Ethics Committee of PUCPR to use such dataset

2.2 Feature Extraction

We implemented a Matlab routine to parameterize pairs of COPx and COPy time series into vectors of 34 features, which are displayed in Table 1. As shown, we included 13 magnitude metrics that derive from the overall size of the COP fluctuations, as well as 6 structural metrics to capture the temporal patterns in the COP dynamics [1, 5]. Out of these 19 metrics, 11 are temporal, 04 are spatial, and 04 are spectral. While temporal and spectral metrics are computed individually from the x and y directions of COP data, spatial metrics derive from both directions simultaneously [1, 5]. As can be seen, there are metrics derived from both displacement (COPd) and velocity (COPv) time series. For more information, including equations and implementation details, please refer to [1, 5]. To investigate our hypothesis, the feature extraction was performed twice for each dataset: firstly, using the original time series of 60 s (6000 data points), and then truncating them in the first 30 s (the first 3000 points).

Table 1. Summary of metrics used for COP parameterization.

Category	Type	Metrics
Magnitude	Temporal	Mean distance, root mean square (RMS) distance, mean velocity, RMS velocity, standard deviation (SD) of velocity
	Spatial	Sway path, length of COP path, excursion area, total mean velocity
	Spectral	Mean frequency, median frequency, Fp% of spectral power (p = 80, 95)
Structural	Temporal	Sample entropy (SE) of distance, SE of velocity, multiscale sample entropy (MSE) of distance, MSE of velocity, scaling exponent of velocity, Hurst exponent of distance

All magnitude features were computed after removing the offset of the COPd signals by subtracting the mean [1]. The spectral features were calculated via Welch's periodogram method with a Hamming window with 50% of overlap [5]. Prior to the SE and MSE analyses, in order to remove nonstationarities and long-range correlations that may confound results, we detrended the COPd signals via Empirical Mode Decomposition method by subtracting from signals the four last Intrinsic Mode Functions of lowest frequency (0.05 Hz to 1 Hz) [10]. Then, we calculated SE taking $N = 2$ and $r = 0.15$ for COPd [10] and $N = 2$ and $r = 0.55$ for COPv [5], where N is the number of data points and r is the tolerance threshold. The scaling exponent (α) and Hurst exponent (H) were computed, respectively, via Detrend Fluctuation Analysis (DFA) and Scaled Windowed Variance (SWV) methods. We computed α from COPv signals only, and H from COPd signals only [11].

2.3 Machine Learning Experiments

For pattern recognition, we considered six popular ML models with specific configurations successfully used by past works to handle COP features [11, 12]: k-Nearest Neighbors (k-NN) with $k = 1, 3, 5, \ldots, 19$; Decision Tree unpruned (DT1) and pruned (DT2); Multilayer Perceptron with 500-epochs training time and 0% validation set size (MLP1), 10 thousand-epochs and 5% validation size (MLP2), and 10 thousand-epochs and 10% validation size (MLP3); Naïve Bayes (NB); Random Forest (RF) with six features used in random selection; Support Vector Machines with 3rd degree RBF kernel and cost 1 (SVM1) and cost 10.0 (SVM2). For each dataset, the input features were normalized to a 0–1 range. Then, using the Weka software, the learning algorithms were trained and tested within 10 repetitions via 10-fold cross-validation for dataset I, and via leave-one-out for dataset II due to the small number of instances. As both datasets are balanced, we adopted the accuracy as performance metric. Each algorithm was trained and tested under each dataset twice: firstly, using the features computed from original COP time series of 60 s, and then using the features calculated from shorter signals of 30 s.

2.4 Statistical Analyses

Firstly, for each dataset, we performed an intra-group analysis where each feature was compared across original (60 s) and shortened (30 s) COP time series using the Wilcoxon test. Next, using the Mann-Whitney U-Test, we conducted an inter-group analysis of each feature for both original and shortened data. Lastly, to analyze the influence of the sampling duration on the ML models, the accuracy of each learning algorithm was compared across 60 s and 30 s features via Mann-Whitney U-Test. Using the same test, we also compared the global mean accuracies computed over all models. The level of confidence adopted was 95%. The normality of all results was verified via Lilliefors test. These analyzes were conducted by using the Matlab R2013b.

3 Results and Discussion

3.1 Intra- and Inter-group Sampling Duration Effects

Table 2 displays the statistical results of our intra-group analysis, where most features have shown to be sensitive to the decreasing of the sampling duration. Similar results were reported by past studies dedicated to address the question of optimal sampling duration for COP data acquisition. For example, after examining COP data recorded over 15, 30, 60, and 120 s from healthy young adults, [6] concluded that longer durations of at least 60 s are necessary to ensure more reliable RMS distance and mean frequency features in an intra-group analysis. A similar conclusion was drafted by [4, 5] based on a variety of magnitude and structural COP features. All these findings corroborate that, when performing either intra- or inter-group analyzes from COP data, comparisons should be limited to features calculated from samples of equal duration, otherwise they may lead to misinterpretations [6].

Table 2. Statistical values obtained in both intra- and inter-group analyzes.

Feature	Intra-group p-values				Inter-group p-values			
	Dataset I		Dataset II		Dataset I		Dataset II	
	High ROF	Low ROF	Stroke	Healthy	60 s	30 s	60 s	30 s
Mean distance	★	★	n.s.	**	n.s.	n.s.	n.s.	n.s.
RMS distance	★	★	n.s.	**	n.s.	*	n.s.	n.s.
Mean velocity	*	**	★	★	n.s.	n.s.	★	★
RMS velocity	*	**	★	★	n.s.	n.s.	★	★
SD of velocity	n.s.	**	**	★	n.s.	n.s.	★	★
Sway path	★	★	★	★	n.s.	n.s.	★	★
Length of COP path	★	★	★	★	n.s.	n.s.	n.s.	n.s.
Excursion area	★	★	n.s.	★	n.s.	n.s.	n.s.	n.s.
Total mean velocity	★	★	★	★	n.s.	n.s.	★	★
Mean frequency	★	★	★	★	*	**	★	**
Median frequency	★	★	★	★	n.s.	**	**	**
F80%	★	★	*	★	*	★	★	**
F95%	★	★	★	★	*	★	★	**
SE of distance	★	★	★	★	n.s.	★	**	*
SE of velocity	★	★	★	★	*	*	n.s.	n.s.
MSE of distance	★	★	★	★	n.s.	★	★	**
MSE of velocity	★	★	★	★	*	★	n.s.	n.s.
Scaling exponent	★	★	★	★	*	★	**	**
Hurst exponent	★	★	★	★	*	★	**	n.s.
Percentage of $p < 0.05$	90.0	92.5	78.1	95.0	17.7	44.2	59.8	46.3

The *, **, and ★ symbols denote, respectively, $p < 0.05$ for COP data in x direction only, y direction only, and both directions. n.s. means not significant ($p \geq 0.05$) for both directions.

Table 2 also shows the statistical results of our inter-group analysis. To the best of our knowledge, this is the first study to report the sampling duration effects on the discriminative power of COP features on older adults with low or high ROF as well as on healthy and post-stroke adults. Surprisingly, our results provided contrasting conclusions for these population groups. While the mean percentage of discriminative features grown 26.5% with the decreasing of the sample duration for dataset I, it decreased 13.5% for dataset II. In other words, the ROF was considerably better recognized from COP time series of 30 s, whereas the contrasts in PC between healthy and post-stroke volunteers were more detectable when using 60 s COP signals. In summary, as these findings allow us accepting our hypothesis for dataset II only, we concluded that the optimal sampling duration in terms of discriminative features depends upon the populations under analysis. Hence, it seems advisable to record COP data over at least 60 s, as argued by other studies [5, 6], and then truncate the signals to examine the optimal sampling duration in each case.

3.2   Sampling Duration Effects on the Machine Learning Results

Table 3 shows the influence of the COP sampling duration on the accuracy of the ML models trained in this work. From a general perspective, the original COP time series yielded slightly better global accuracies than the shortened signals. These results suggest that a sampling duration of 60 s provides more discriminative information than 30 s when distinguishing groups via popular ML models, thus supporting our hypothesis. One should notice, however, that the global accuracies were manly influenced by the performance of k-NN, especially in the case of dataset I. Conversely, some learning algorithms have shown robustness to the COP duration: DT2, MLP2, MLP3, NB, and SVM2. Based on these findings, it is possible to infer that similarity-based ML methods such as k-NN are more sensitive to the sampling duration than other popular models. Thus, they should be avoided in certain situations, for example, when dealing with COP time series recorded over too short durations that prevent good results, or when trying to distinguish populations whose COP data were recorded over different durations. Otherwise, one must be careful to identify how much performance is driven by the PC behaviors under analysis and how much is a function of COP duration.

Table 3.   Machine learning results.

Model	Mean accuracy (%) for dataset I		Mean accuracy (%) for dataset II	
	60 s	30 s	60 s	30 s
1-NN	61.8	61.2	**66.7**	60.5
3-NN	**64.1**	60.3	66.7	66.7
5-NN	**62.8**	60.0	68.4	68.4
7-NN	**63.3**	59.8	72.8	69.3
9-NN	**62.6**	59.9	**71.1**	64.9
11-NN	**63.2**	58.8	**71.1**	65.8
13-NN	**62.8**	59.0	72.8	71.1
15-NN	**62.8**	59.8	71.1	68.4
17-NN	**63.0**	60.1	69.3	69.3
19-NN	**62.3**	60.2	66.7	69.3
DT1	57.0	56.0	57.9	**64.9**
DT2	57.1	56.0	61.4	64.9
MLP1	**61.7**	58.7	65.4	62.8
MLP2	58.7	57.3	63.9	61.6
MLP3	59.0	57.3	64.8	61.8
NB	58.4	58.3	68.4	67.5
RF	**64.9**	61.0	71.9	70.6
SVM1	58.2	57.4	**67.5**	63.2
SVM2	60.1	60.0	71.1	67.5
Global mean	**61.3**	59.0	**67.8**	66.2

Statistically ($p < 0.05$) greater accuracies are marked in bold.

4   Conclusion, Future Work, and Acknowledgment

This paper examined the effects of COP short durations of 30 s and 60 s on the discriminative power of posturographic features in inter-group comparisons using statistical tests and popular ML models. Conclusions are limited to the population groups analyzed here: older adults with high or low ROF, healthy and post-stroke adults. In terms of statistical tests, we concluded that the optimal COP duration changes according to the group under analysis. However, when using ML, COP signals of 60 s have proved to be more discriminative, mainly for similarity-based models. Therefore, we advise one recording COP data over at least 60 s, and then truncating the time series if necessary, depending on the tools to be employed or questions to be investigated. To ensure the repeatability of the experiments performed in this work, we made available to download our COP features and Matlab codes at https://goo.gl/TACWYt. Future work will focus on improving ML performance by testing models of the state-of-the-art for time series classification, such as convolutional and recurrent neural networks.

L. H. F. Giovanini is thankful to PUCPR for his scholarship. We would like to thank NVIDIA Corporation for the donation of a Titan X Pascal GPU.

References

1. Duarte, M., Freitas, S.M.: Revision of posturography based on force plate for balance evaluation. Braz. J. Phys. Ther. **14**, 183–192 (2010)
2. Rhea, C.K., Kiefer, A.W., Wright, W.G., Raisbeck, L.D., Haran, F.J.: Interpretation of postural control may change due to data processing techniques. Gait Posture **41**, 731–735 (2015)
3. van der Kooij, H., Campbell, A.D., Carpenter, M.G.: Sampling duration effects on centre of pressure descriptive measures. Gait Posture **34**, 19–24 (2011)
4. Ruhe, A., Fejer, R., Walker, B.: The test–retest reliability of centre of pressure measures in bipedal static task conditions–a systematic review of the literature. Gait Posture **32**, 436–445 (2010)
5. Kirchner, M., Schubert, P., Schmidtbleicher, D., Haas, C.T.: Evaluation of the temporal structure of postural sway fluctuations based on a comprehensive set of analysis tools. Phys. A **391**, 4692–4703 (2012)
6. Carpenter, M.G., Frank, J.S., Winter, D.A., Peysar, G.W.: Sampling duration effects on centre of pressure summary measures. Gait Posture **13**, 35–40 (2001)
7. Santos, D.A., Duarte, M.: A public data set of human balance evaluations. PeerJ Preprints (2016). https://doi.org/10.7287/peerj.preprints.2162v1
8. Organization WHO global report on falls prevention in older age. World Health Organization (2008)
9. Silva, S.M.: Análise do controle postural de indivíduos pós-acidente vascular encefálico frente a perturbações dos sistemas visual e somatossensorial. PUCPR (2012)
10. Costa, M., et al.: Noise and poise: enhancement of postural complexity in the elderly with a stochastic-resonance–based therapy. EPL (Europhys. Lett.) **77**, 68008 (2007)

11. Giovanini, L.H., Silva, S.M., Manffra, E.F., Nievola, J.C.: Sampling and digital filtering effects when recognizing postural control with statistical tools and the decision tree classifier. Procedia Comput. Sci. **108**, 129–138 (2017)
12. Goh, K.L., et al.: Typically developed adults and adults with autism spectrum disorder classification using centre of pressure measurements. In: Proceedings of 2016 IEEE International Conference on Acoustics, Speech and Signal Processing (ICASSP), pp. 844–848. IEEE (2016)

Mathematical Modelling of Wormhole-Routed x-Folded TM Topology in the Presence of Uniform Traffic

Mehrnaz Moudi[1,2], Mohamed Othman[2(✉)], Kweh Yeah Lun[2],
and Amir Rizaan Abdul Rahiman[2]

[1] Department of Computer Engineering, University of Torbat Heydarieh,
Razavi Khorasan Province, Iran
mehrnazmoudi@gmail.com
[2] Department of Communication Technology and Network,
Universiti Putra Malaysia, 43400 UPM Serdang, Selangor D.E., Malaysia
mothman@upm.edu.my

Abstract. Recently, x-Folded TM topology was introduced as a desirable design in k-ary n-cube networks due to the low diameter and short average distance. In this article, we propose a mathematical model to predict the average network delay for $(k \times k)$ x-Folded TM in the presence of uniform traffic pattern. Our model accurately formulates the applied traffic pattern over network virtual channels based on the average distance and number of nodes. The mathematical results indicate that the average network delay for x-Folded TM topology is reduced when compared with other topologies in the presence of uniform traffic pattern. Finally, the results obtained from simulation experiments confirm that the mathematical model exhibits a significant degree of accuracy for x-Folded TM topology under the traffic pattern even in varied virtual channels.

Keywords: Interconnection networks · x-Folded TM topology
Virtual channel · Mathematical model · Delay

1 Introduction

One of the critical components in a multicomputer is the interconnection network, which significantly influences multicomputer performance. The three significant factors for these network performance are introduced as topology, routing algorithm and switching method. These factors are effectively used to determine network performance. The designs of nodes and the connection to channels are described in the network topology. To select a path between the source and destination, a routing algorithm is employed to select network messages in order to specify the path across the network. Using the switching method, the

© Springer International Publishing AG, part of Springer Nature 2018
Y. Shi et al. (Eds.): ICCS 2018, LNCS 10862, pp. 358–365, 2018.
https://doi.org/10.1007/978-3-319-93713-7_29

allocation of channels and buffer resources for a message across the network is established [1].

A number of studies have disclosed the fact that the advantages of designing variable topologies fall under different traffic patterns. The significant advantage of the mathematical model over simulation is that it can be used to obtain performance results for large systems and behaviour under network configurations and working conditions, which may not be feasible for study using simulation due to the disproportionate computation demands. There are several mathematical models for k-ary n-cubes topologies (n is the dimension and k is the number of nodes in each dimension) under different traffic patterns based on the literature review [3]. In light of this review, this article proposes the mathematical model of the x-Folded TM topology. x-Folded TM [7] is introduced as a low diameter network which can outperform a similar network size in terms of throughput and delay. Using mathematical models in this article, we can see the effect of different topologies and virtual channels on the network performance including the x-Folded TM topology properties and applied traffic patterns. Since a uniform traffic pattern has been used in previous studies and recently non-uniform traffic has been presented [4,5,8,9], unifrom traffic pattern has been employed for evaluation in this study.

2   x-Folded TM Topology

x-Folded TM is a new wormhole-routed topology created by folding the TM topology [10,11] based on the imaginary x-axis when $k \geq 3$ and $n = 2$. The definition of x-Folded TM topology is as follows:

Definition 1. In x-Folded TM, node (x, y) is a valid node if $0 \leq x \leq (k - 1)$ and $0 \leq y \leq (k - 1)$. Along x-axis, the nodes connecting to node (x, y) are: $(x + 1, y)$ if $x < (k - 1)$ and $(x - 1, y)$ if $x > 0$. Along the y-axis, nodes $(x, y + 1)$ if $y < (k - 1)$ and $(x, y - 1)$ if $y > 0$ are connected to node (x, y). Then, node (x, y) is removed from the x-Folded TM if $(x + y) \mod k = 0$ or 1 or ... or $(k - 3)$, where $x > y$ and $(k - 3) \leq x \leq (k - 1)$ and $1 \leq y \leq (k - 2)$. In addition, there is no link between two nodes (x, y) and $(x + 1, y)$ if $x = i$ and $y = i + 1$, when k is even and $i = \frac{k}{2} - 1$.

x-Folded TM topology has a node structure similar to TM topology, except a number of the nodes are shared from top to bottom. Figures 1(a) and (b) show x-Folded TM topology for an $(k \times k)$ interconnection network where k is even and odd respectively. The purple nodes in this figure are representative of the shared nodes between red and blue nodes. Several researchers have proposed mathematical models under different permutations, which have been reported in previous studies. The model developed here uses the main advantages of the proposed model in [8] to derive the mathematical model for the x-Folded TM topology in the presence of uniform and non-uniform traffic patterns.

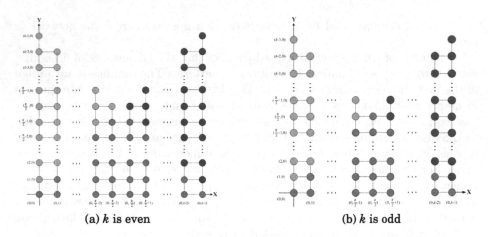

(a) k is even   (b) k is odd

Fig. 1. $(k \times k)$ x-Folded TM Topology

Table 1. Mathematical assumptions.

Parameter	Description
Mean Rate (λ)	The traffic is generated across the network nodes independently and follow a Poisson process with a mean rate
Network size (N)	$N = 8 \times 8$ (k-ary n-cube where $k=8$ and $n=2$)
Message length (L)	The length of a message is L flits (A packet is broken into small pieces called flits which are flow control digits) and each flit is transmitted from source to destination in one cycle across the network
Virtual Channels (VC)	VCs = 2 or 8 are used per physical channel

3   Mathematical Model

This section describes the derivation of the mathematical model based on the introduced assumptions in Table 1.

The model has restricted the attention to x-Folded TM topology, where $n = 2$ is the network dimension and $k \geq 3$ is radix or the number of nodes in each dimension. Generally the relation between dimension, radix and a number of nodes (N) is

$$N = k^n \qquad or \qquad (n = log_k N). \tag{1}$$

In the k-ary n-cube, the average delay is a combination of the average network delay ($\bar{S}$) and the average waiting time ($\bar{W}$) of the source node while the average degree of VCs at each physical channel also influences the average delay and is scaled by a parameter ($\bar{V}$). Thus, the average delay is

$$Average\ Delay = (\bar{S} + \bar{W})\bar{V}. \tag{2}$$

In [2], the average distance along one dimension is defined as AD in that it is multiplied by a number of dimensions, n, for the whole network and is defined $\bar{d}$ as

$$\bar{d} = n \times AD. \tag{3}$$

In order to demonstrate Eq. (3), AD can be obtained according to Theorem 1. Although we need to present Lemma 1 and Proposition 1 before proving Theorem 1.

Lemma 1. *For an x-Folded TM, let $I(i)$ be the number of the nodes that are i nodes away from the source node (0), which can be calculated by using Eq.(4),*

$$I(i) = i + 1 \qquad\qquad \forall 1 \le i \le (k-1). \tag{4}$$

Proof. For $1 \le i \le (k-1)$, $I(i)$ has been defined as the number of the nodes that are i nodes away from node (0). The diagram for (8×8) x-Folded TM topology in Fig. 2 used to show the distance between the assumed source node and the other nodes by dashed lines. For simplicity, all nodes are labelled from 0 to $(k^2\text{-}1)$ in this figure. The node with coordinates $(0, 0)$ has been labelled node (0) and introduced as the assumed source node. For example, $I(1) = 2$, i.e., the number of nodes that are one node away from node (0) is two nodes. In other words, this means that the node (0) has two neighbours. □

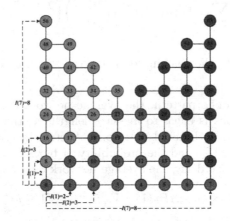

Fig. 2. Illustration of the distance of nodes from node (0) as source node in (8×8) x-Folded TM topology.

Theorem 1. *The average distance of x-Folded TM topology is*

$$AD_k = \begin{cases} 1 & if \quad k = 3, \\ \frac{AD_{k-1} + k(k-1)}{k^2 - 1} & if \quad k \ge 4. \end{cases} \tag{5}$$

Proof. Using Proposition 1, the average distance of the k-ary n-cube topologies is denoted by AD. Substituting Eq. (4) into the average distance of a k-ary n-cube topology along one dimension, the average distance of x-Folded TM topology (AD_k) appears in Eq. (5) for different k. □

Under uniform traffic pattern, messages arrive at network channels at different injection rates. The received injection rate of messages for each channel, λ, is gained by dividing the total channel rates by the total number of channels. The uniform's injection rate, λ_u, can be found using

$$\lambda_u = \frac{1}{2} \cdot (\lambda \times AD_k). \tag{6}$$

Proposition 1. *The number of the nodes for an x-Folded TM can be written as,*

$$N' = a_1 \times N + a_2. \tag{7}$$

It is computed according to a linear model, which has been presented in Eq. (7) where the initial values are $a_1 = 0.8005$, $a_2 = 0.9786$, and $n=2$.

Theorem 2 [8]. *The number of channels that are j nodes away from a given node in a k-ary n-cube topology is*

$$C_j = \sum_{l=0}^{n-1} \sum_{t=0}^{n-1} (-1)^t (n-l) \binom{n}{l} \binom{n-l}{t} \binom{j - t(k-1) - 1}{n - l - 1}. \tag{8}$$

Proof. By referring to the combinatorial theory, this theorem has been proven in [8]. $\square$

Under uniform traffic pattern, the average network delay for each channel in different dimensions is equal to message lengths at the beginning, $\bar{S}_0$. The studies in [8,9] provide the used notation to determine the quantities of the average waiting time, W_{c_i} and the probability of blocking, P_{b_i}, at dimension i. Considering the average delay, the average network delay can be found using

$$\bar{S}_i = \bar{S}_{i-1} + AD_k(1 + W_{c_i} P_{b_i}) \qquad (1 \le i \le n), \tag{9}$$

In addition to computing $\bar{S}$ to develop the mathematical model, the waiting time (W) for a message under uniform traffic pattern is computed as

$$W_j = \frac{\frac{\lambda}{V} S_j^2 (1 + \frac{(S_j - S_{j-1})^2}{S_j^2})}{2(1 - \frac{\lambda}{V} S_j)}. \tag{10}$$

$\bar{W}$ is a function of the average waiting time under different possible values ($1 \le j \le n(k-1)$). $\bar{V}$ is the average degree of VCs under the traffic pattern. It should also be noted that p_{v_j} is the probability used to determine whether the VCs are busy at the physical channel using a Markovian model [9]. The bandwidth is shared between multiple VCs in each physical channel. The average of all the possible values at a given physical channel is computed using

$$\bar{V} = \sum_{j=1}^{n(k-1)} \frac{\sum_{v=1}^{VC} v^2 p_{v_j}}{\sum_{v=1}^{VC} v p_{v_j}}. \tag{11}$$

Consequently, the average network delay between source node and destination node can be written simply as Eq. (2). We presented all of the equations for the mathematical model under uniform traffic pattern to evaluate the x-Folded TM topology performance.

4   Performance Evaluation

The validation results in this section prove that the predictions of the mathematical model with similar assumptions are accurate in terms of the average delay (cycles) with an increase in the packet injection rate (flits/node/cycle). The presented simulation results validate the accuracy of the results obtained from the mathematical model for different topologies. The mathematical model for the x-Folded TM topology has been validated through the discrete-event simulation using the Booksim 2.0 simulator [6].

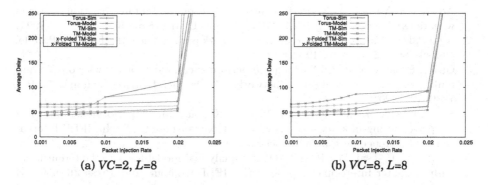

(a) *VC*=2, *L*=8   (b) *VC*=8, *L*=8

Fig. 3. Average delay in the presence of uniform traffic pattern.

The average delay curves for three topologies are illustrated in Fig. 3. The used traffic pattern is uniform to generate destination nodes randomly. Figure 3 reveals the similar saturation time in different numbers of VCs and the effectiveness of x-Folded TM topology on decreasing the average delay compared with the results obtained by Torus and TM under uniform traffic pattern. Figure 3(a) illustrates the predicted results by the mathematical model for different topologies. These have been studied for VCs = 2 and the same packet size. We employ

Torus and TM topologies as benchmarks and represent their mathematical models to show the superiority of x-Folded TM topology on the average delay as a new topology in interconnection networks. Figure 3(b) illustrates the average delay in terms of the packet injection rate in VCs = 8 for different topologies. Both figures reveal the less than average delay for x-Folded TM topology in different numbers of VCs until the saturation time.

5   Conclusion

This article presents a mathematical model for the computation of the average network delay in wormhole-routed Torus, TM and x-Folded TM topologies in the presence of uniform and non-uniform traffic patterns. We explore the mathematical model for x-Folded TM topology to present its novelty by reducing the average delay. This model is validated and deemed accurate by simulation with less than 5% difference in the average delay. We believe that x-Folded TM topology will be applicable for the future studies in high-performance interconnection networks.

Acknowledgment. This research was supported by Malaysian Ministry of Education (FRGS, Ref: FRGS/1/2014/ICT03/UPM/01/1).

References

1. Adve, V.S., Vernon, M.K.: Performance analysis of mesh interconnection networks with deterministic routing. IEEE Trans. Parallel Distrib. Syst. **5**(3), 225–246 (1994)
2. Agarwal, A.: Limits on interconnection network performance. IEEE Trans. Parallel Distrib. Syst. **2**(4), 398–412 (1991)
3. Gajin, S., Jovanovic, Z.: An accurate performance model for network-onchip and multicomputer interconnection networks. J. Parallel Distrib. Comput. **72**(10), 1280–1294 (2012)
4. Sarbazi-Azad, H., Mackenzie, L.M., Ould-Khaoua, M.: A performance model of adaptive routing in k-ary n-cubes with matrix-transpose traffic. In: IEEE International Conference on Parallel Processing (2000)
5. Guan, W.-J., Tsai, W., Blough, D.: An analytical model for wormhole routing in multicomputer interconnection networks. IEEE Comput. Soc. Press **26**, 650–654 (1993)
6. Jiang, N., Becker, D.U., Michelogiannakis, G., Balfour, J., Towles, B., Shaw, D.E., Dally, W.J.: A detailed and flexible cycle-accurate network-on-Chip simulator. In: 2013 IEEE International Symposium on Performance Analysis of Systems and Software (ISPASS), pp. 86–96 (2013)
7. Moudi, M., Othman, M., Lun, K.Y., Abdul Rahiman, A.R.: x-Folded TM: an efficient topology for interconnection networks. J. Netw. Comput. Appl. **73**, 27–34 (2016)
8. Sarbazi-Azad, H., Ould-Khaoua, M., Mackenzie, L.M.: Analytical modelling of wormhole-routed k-Ary n-cubes in the presence of hot-spot traffic. IEEE Trans. Comput. **50**(7), 623–634 (2001)

9. Sarbazi-Azad, H.: A mathematical model of deterministic wormhole routing in hypercube multicomputers using virtual channels. Appl. Math. Model. **27**, 943–953 (2003)
10. Wang, X., Xiang, D., Yu, Z.: TM: a new and simple topology for interconnection networks. J. Supercomput. **66**(1), 514–538 (2013)
11. Wang, X., Xiang, D., Yu, Z.: A cost-effective interconnect architecture for interconnection network. IETE J. Res. **59**(2), 109–117 (2013)

Adaptive Time-Splitting Scheme for Nanoparticles Transport with Two-Phase Flow in Heterogeneous Porous Media

Mohamed F. El-Amin[1]([✉])[ID], Jisheng Kou[2], and Shuyu Sun[3][ID]

[1] College of Engineering, Effat University, Jeddah 21478, Kingdom of Saudi Arabia
momousa@effatuniversity.edu.sa
[2] School of Mathematics and Statistics, Hubei Engineering University,
Xiaogan 432000, Hubei, China
[3] King Abdullah University of Science and Technology (KAUST),
Thuwal 23955–6900, Kingdom of Saudi Arabia

Abstract. In this work, we introduce an efficient scheme using an adaptive time-splitting method to simulate nanoparticles transport associated with a two-phase flow in heterogeneous porous media. The capillary pressure is linearized in terms of saturation to couple the pressure and saturation equations. The governing equations are solved using an IMplicit Pressure Explicit Saturation-IMplicit Concentration (IMPES-IMC) scheme. The spatial discretization has been done using the cell-centered finite difference (CCFD) method. The interval of time has been divided into three levels, the pressure level, the saturation level, and the concentrations level, which can reduce the computational cost. The time step-sizes at different levels are adaptive iteratively by satisfying the Courant-Friedrichs-Lewy (CFL<1) condition. The results illustrates the efficiency of the numerical scheme. A numerical example of a highly heterogeneous porous medium has been introduced. Moreover, the adaptive time step-sizes are shown in graphs.

Keywords: Time-splitting · IMPES · Two-phase flow
Porous media · CFL

1 Introduction

The scheme of IMplicit Pressure Explicit Saturation (IMPES) is a conditionally stable which is usually used to solve the two-phase flow in porous media. In the IMPES scheme, the pressure equation is treated implicitly while the saturation is updated explicitly. Hence it takes a very small time step size, in particular with heterogeneous porous media. The IMPES scheme has been improved in several versions (e.g. [1–3]). The temporal discretization scheme is considered an important factor that affects the efficiency of numerical reservoir simulators.

© Springer International Publishing AG, part of Springer Nature 2018
Y. Shi et al. (Eds.): ICCS 2018, LNCS 10862, pp. 366–378, 2018.
https://doi.org/10.1007/978-3-319-93713-7_30

The application of traditional single-scale temporal scheme is restricted by the rapid changes of the pressure and saturation with capillarity and concentrations if applicable. Applying time splitting strategies has a significant improvement compare to the traditional schemes. Time splitting method has been considered in a number of publications such as [4–10]. For example, in Refs. [9], an explicit sub-timing scheme is provided. On the other hand, an implicit time-stepping scheme have been proposed by Bhallamudi et al. [7] and Park et al. [8].

In the recent years, nanoparticles have been used in many engineering branches including petroleum applications such as enhanced oil recovery. A model of nanoparticles transport in porous media have been established by Ju and Fan [13] based on particle migration in porous media model [14]. El-Amin et al. [15–17] have investigated the problem of nanoparticles transport in porous media. In Ref. [17], they presented an extended model to include mixed relative permeabilities and a negative capillary pressure. Dimensional analysis of the problem of nanoparticles transport in porous media have been presented by El-Amin et al. [18]. The nanoparticles transport in anisotropic porous media have been studied numerically using the multipoint flux approximation by Salama et al. [19]. Also, a numerical simulation of drag reduction effects by hydrophobic nanoparticles adsorption method in water flooding processes has been presented by Chen et al. [20]. The problem of dynamic update of an anisotropic permeability field with nanoparticles transport in porous media has been considering by Chen et al. [21]. In Ref. [22], the authors presented a nonlinear iterative IMPES-IMC scheme to solve the governing system of the nanoparticles transport in subsurface.

In this paper, we propose a time-stepping IMPES-IMC scheme to solve the governing equations of the nanoparticles transport associated with two-phase flow in subsurface. The CCFD method has employed for the spatial discretization. The time-splitting scheme has applied together with the CFL condition to adaptive the time-steps sizes. Finally, some numerical experiments are provided.

2   Modeling and Mathematical Formulation

The mathematical model of the problem under consideration consists of water saturation, Darcy's law, nanoparticles concentration, deposited nanoparticles concentration on the pore-wall, and entrapped nanoparticles concentration in the pore-throat. Moreover, the variations in both porosity and permeability due to the nanoparticles deposition/entrapment on/in the pores have been taken into consideration. In the following we introduce the governing equations briefly, (for details see Refs. [15–19, 21, 22]:

Momentum Conservation (Darcy's Law):

$$\mathbf{u}_\alpha = -\frac{k_\alpha}{\mu_\alpha} \nabla \Phi_\alpha, \qquad \alpha = w, n, \tag{1}$$

where

$$k_\alpha = k_{r\alpha} \mathbf{K}, \quad \Phi_\alpha = p_\alpha + \rho_\alpha g \nabla z, \quad \alpha = w, n,$$

Mass Conservation (Saturation Equations):

$$\phi\frac{\partial s_\alpha}{\partial t} + \nabla \cdot \mathbf{u}_\alpha = q_\alpha, \quad \alpha = w, n, \tag{2}$$

where $s_w + s_n = 1$, ϕ is the porosity, g is the gravitational acceleration, z is the depth. $\mathbf{u}_\alpha$ is the velocity, Φ_α is the pressure potential, p_α is the pressure, μ_α is the viscosity, ρ_α is the density, $k_{r\alpha}$ is the relative permeability, q_α is the external mass flow rate, s_α is the saturation; all of the phase α. $\mathbf{K}$ is the permeability tensor. w stands for the wetting phase (water), and n stands for the non-wetting phase (oil).

Providing the following definitions:

The capillary pressure: $p_c(s_w) = p_n - p_w$.
The total velocity: $\mathbf{u}_t = \mathbf{u}_w + \mathbf{u}_n$.
The flow fraction: $f_w = \lambda_w/\lambda_t$.
The phase mobility: $\lambda_\alpha = k_{r\alpha}/\mu_\alpha$.
The total mobility: λ_t.
The capillary pressure potential: $\Phi_c = p_c + (\rho_n - \rho_w)g\nabla z$.
The total source mass transfer: $q_t = q_w + q_n$.

After some mathematical manipulations and referring to Refs. [11], the pressure equation can be rewritten as,

$$\nabla \cdot \mathbf{u}_t = -\nabla \cdot \lambda_t \mathbf{K}\nabla\Phi_w - \nabla \cdot \lambda_n \mathbf{K}\nabla\Phi_c = q_t. \tag{3}$$

Because this equation contents the capillary pressure which is a function of saturation, it will be coupled with the following saturation equation to calculate the pressure,

$$\phi\frac{\partial s_w}{\partial t} - q_w = -\nabla \cdot \lambda_w \mathbf{K}\nabla\Phi_w. \tag{4}$$

However, the saturation is updated using the following form,

$$\phi\frac{\partial s_w}{\partial t} - q_w = -\nabla \cdot (f_w \mathbf{u}_a). \tag{5}$$

where $\mathbf{u}_w = f_w \mathbf{u}_a$ and $\mathbf{u}_a = -\lambda_t \mathbf{K}\nabla\Phi_w$.

Nanoparticles Transport Model
Assuming that the nanoparticles exist only in the water phase of one size interval. So, The transport equation of the nanoparticles in the water phase is given as [12–19,21,22],

$$\phi\frac{\partial(s_w c)}{\partial t} + \nabla \cdot (\mathbf{u}_w c - D\nabla c) = R + Q_c, \tag{6}$$

Nanoparticles Surface Deposition
The surface deposition is expressed by,

$$\frac{\partial c_{s1}}{\partial t} = \begin{cases} \gamma_d |\mathbf{u}_w| c, & \mathbf{u}_w \le u_r \\ \\ \gamma_d |\mathbf{u}_w| c - \gamma_e |\mathbf{u}_w - u_r| c_{s1}, & \mathbf{u}_w > u_r \end{cases} \tag{7}$$

Nanoparticles Throat Entrapment

The rate of entrapment of the nanoparticles is,

$$\frac{\partial c_{s2}}{\partial t} = \gamma_{pt} |\mathbf{u}_w| c, \tag{8}$$

where c is the nanoparticles concentrations. c_{s1} and c_{s2} are, respectively, the deposited nanoparticles concentration on the pore surface, and the entrapped nanoparticles concentration in pore throats. τ is the tortuosity parameter. Q_c is the rate of change of particle volume belonging to a source/sink term. γ_d is the rate coefficients for surface retention of the nanoparticles. γ_e is the rate coefficients for entrainment of the nanoparticles. u_r is the critical velocity of the water phase. where γ_{pt} is the pore throat blocking constants. The diffusion-dispersion tensor is defined by,

$$D = \phi s_w \tau D_t, \quad D_t = D^{\mathrm{Br}} + D^{\mathrm{disp}} \tag{9}$$

where D^{Br} is the Brownian diffusion and D^{disp} is the dispersion coefficient which is defined by [1],

$$\phi s_w \tau D^{\mathrm{disp}} = d_{t,w} |\mathbf{u}_w| \mathbf{I} + (d_{l,w} - d_{t,w}) \frac{\mathbf{u}_w \mathbf{u}_w^T}{|\mathbf{u}_w|} \tag{10}$$

Thus,

$$D = (\phi s_w \tau D^{\mathrm{Br}} + d_{t,w} |\mathbf{u}_w|) \mathbf{I} + (d_{l,w} - d_{t,w}) \frac{\mathbf{u}_w \mathbf{u}_w^T}{|\mathbf{u}_w|} \tag{11}$$

where $d_{l,w}$ and $d_{t,w}$ are the longitudinal and transverse dispersion coefficients, respectively. R is the net rate of loss of nanoparticles which is defined by,

$$R = \frac{\partial c_{s1}}{\partial t} + \frac{\partial c_{s2}}{\partial t} \tag{12}$$

Initial and Boundary Conditions

The initial conditions are,

$$s_w = s_w^0, \quad c = c_{s1} = c_{s2} = 0 \quad \text{in} \quad \Omega \quad \text{at} \quad t = 0, \tag{13}$$

The boundary conditions are given as,

$$p_w \, (\text{or } p_n) = p^D \quad \text{on} \quad \Gamma_D, \tag{14}$$

$$\mathbf{u}_t \cdot \mathbf{n} = q^N, \quad s_w = S^N, \quad c = c_0, \quad c_{s1} = c_{s2} = 0 \quad \text{on} \quad \Gamma_N. \tag{15}$$

where $\mathbf{n}$ is the outward unit normal vector to $\partial \Omega$, p^D is the pressure on Γ_D and q^N the imposed inflow rate on Γ_N, respectively. Ω is the computational domain such that the boundary $\partial \Omega$ is Dirichlet Γ_D and/or Neumann Γ_N boundaries, i.e. $\partial \Omega = \Gamma_D \cup \Gamma_N$ and $\Gamma_D \cap \Gamma_N = \emptyset$.

3 Multi-scale Time Splitting Method

The concept of time splitting method is to use different time step size for each
equation has a time derivative. In the above-described method, the pressure is
coupled with the saturation in each time-step. The time-step size for the pressure can be taken larger than the those of saturation and nanoparticle concentrations. So, for the pressure the total time interval $[0, T]$ is divided into N_p,
time-steps as $0 = t_0 < t_1 < \cdots < t_{N_p = T}$. Thus, the time-step length assigned
for pressure is, $\Delta t^k = t^{k+1} - t^k$. Since the saturation varies more rapidly than
the pressure, we use a smaller time-step size for the saturation equation. That
is, each interval, $(t^k, t^{k+1}]$, will be divided into $N_{p,s}$ subintervals as $(t^k, t^{k+1}] = \cup_{l=0}^{N_{p,s}-1} (t^{k,l}, t^{k,l+1}]$. On the other hand, as the concentration varies more rapidly
than the pressure (and may be saturation), we also use a smaller time-step size
for the concentration equations. Thus, we partition each subinterval $(t^{k,l}, t^{k,l+1}]$
into $N_{p,s,c}$ subsubintervals as $(t^{k,l}, t^{k,l+1}] = \cup_{m=0}^{N_{p,s,c}-1} (t^{k,l,m}, t^{k,l,m+1}]$. Therefore,
the system of governing equations, (3), (4), (6), (7) and (8), is solved based on
the adaptive time-splitting technique. The backward Euler time discretization
is used for the equations of pressure, saturation, concentration and the two volume concentration. We linearized the capillary pressure function, Φ_c, in terms
of saturation using this formula,

$$\Phi_c \left(s_w^* \right) \cong \Phi_c \left(s_w^k \right) + \Phi_c' \left(s_w^k \right) \left[s_w^{k+1} - s_w^k \right], \tag{16}$$

where Φ_c' is derivative of Φ_c. The quantity, $[s_w^{k+1} - s_w^k]$, can be calculated from
the saturation equation,

$$s_w^{k+1} - s_w^k = \frac{\Delta t^k}{\phi \left(c_{s1}^k, c_{s2}^k \right)} \left[q_w^{k+1} - \nabla \cdot \lambda_t \left(s_w^k \right) \mathbf{K} \left(c_{s1}^k, c_{s2}^k \right) \nabla \Phi_w^{k+1} \right]. \tag{17}$$

In addition to the pressure equation,

$$- \nabla \cdot \lambda_t \left(s_w^k \right) \mathbf{K} \left(c_{s1}^k, c_{s2}^k \right) \nabla \Phi_w^{k+1} - \nabla \cdot \lambda_n \left(s_w^k \right) \mathbf{K} \left(c_{s1}^k, c_{s2}^k \right) \nabla \Phi_c \left(s_w^* \right) = q_t^{k+1}. \tag{18}$$

Then, the above coupled system (16), (17) and (18) is solved implicitly to obtain
the pressure potential. Therefore, the saturation is updated explicitly with using
the upwind scheme for the convection term as,

$$\phi \left(c_{s1}^k, c_{s2}^k \right) \frac{s_w^{k,l+1} - s_w^{k,l}}{\Delta t^l} + \nabla \cdot \left(f_w^k \mathbf{u}_a^{k+1} \right) = q_w^{k,l+1}. \tag{19}$$

Therefore, the nanoparticles concentration, deposited nanoparticles concentration on the pore–walls and entrapped nanoparticles concentration in the pore–
throats are computed implicitly as follow,

$$\phi \left(c_{s1}^k, c_{s2}^k \right) \frac{s_w^{k+1} c^{k,l,m+1} - s_w^k c^{k,l,m}}{\Delta t^m} + \nabla \cdot \left\{ \mathbf{u}_w^{k+1} c^{k,l,m+1} - D \left(s_w^{k+1}, \mathbf{u}_w^{k+1}, c_{s1}^k, c_{s2}^k \right) \right.$$
$$\left. - R \left(\mathbf{u}_w^{k+1}, c_{s1}^k \right) \right\} \nabla c^{k,l,m+1} = Q_c^{k,l,m+1}, \tag{20}$$

$$\frac{c_{s1}^{k,l,m+1} - c_{s1}^{k,l,m}}{\Delta t^m} =$$

$$\begin{cases} \gamma_d |\mathbf{u}_w^{k+1}| c^{k+1}, & \mathbf{u}_w^{k+1} \leq u_r \\ \gamma_d |\mathbf{u}_w^{k+1}| c^{k+1} - \gamma_e |\mathbf{u}_w^{k+1} - u_r| c_{s1}^{k,l,m+1}, & \mathbf{u}_w^{k,l,m+1} > u_r \end{cases} \tag{21}$$

and,

$$\frac{c_{s2}^{k,l,m+1} - c_{s2}^{k,l,m}}{\Delta t^m} = \gamma_{pt} |\mathbf{u}_w^{k+1}| c^{k,l,m+1} \tag{22}$$

Finally, other parameters such as permeability, porosity, $\lambda_w, \lambda_n, \lambda_t$ and f_w are updated each loop.

4   Adaptive Time-Stepping

In our algorithm, we have checked the Courant–Friedrichs–Lewy (CFL) condition to guarantee its satisfactory (i.e. CFL<1). In order to achieve this idea, we have to define the following CFLs,

$$\text{CFL}_{s,x} = \frac{\mathbf{u}_x \Delta t^{k,l}}{\Delta x}, \quad \text{CFL}_{s,y} = \frac{\mathbf{u}_y \Delta t^{k,l}}{\Delta y}, \tag{23}$$

for saturation equation, and,

$$\text{CFL}_{c,x} = \frac{\mathbf{u}_x \Delta t^{k,l,m}}{\Delta x}, \quad \text{CFL}_{c,y} = \frac{\mathbf{u}_y \Delta t^{k,l,m}}{\Delta y}, \tag{24}$$

and for concentration equations. It may be noted that the CFL depends on the ratio $\Delta t / \Delta x$ which can be fixed at larger time-steps and larger mesh-size. Thus, when we use a lager domain (larger mesh size) then we can use larger time step size. In the code, the initial time-step for the saturation equation is taken as the pressure time-step, i.e., $\Delta t^{k,0} = \Delta t^k$, and the initial time-step for the concentration equation is taken as the saturation time-step, i.e., $\Delta t^{k,l,0} = \Delta t^{k,l}$. Then, we check if $\text{CFL}_{s,x} > 1$ or $\text{CFL}_{s,y} > 1$, the saturation time-step will be divided by 2 and the $\text{CFL}_{s,x}$ and $\text{CFL}_{s,y}$ will be recalculated. This procedure will be repeated until satisfying the condition $\text{CFL}_{s,x} < 1$ and $\text{CFL}_{s,y} < 1$, then the final adaptive saturation time-step will be obtained. Similarly, we check if the condition, $\text{CFL}_{c,x} > 1$ or $\text{CFL}_{c,y} > 1$ is satisfied, the concentration time-step will be divided by 2 and therefore, we recalculate both $\text{CFL}_{c,x}$ and $\text{CFL}_{c,y}$. We repeat this procedure to reach the condition $\text{CFL}_{c,x} < 1$ and $\text{CFL}_{c,y} < 1$, then we obtain the final adaptive concentration time-step.

5 Numerical Tests

In order to examine the performance of the current scheme, we introduce some numerical examples in this section. Firstly, we introduce the required physical parameters used in the computations. Then, we study the performance of the scheme by introducing some results for the adaptive time steps based on values of the corresponding Courant–Friedrichs–Lewy (CFL). Then we present some results for the distributions of water saturation and nanoparticles concentrations. In this study, given the normalized wetting phase saturation, $S = (s_w - s_{wr})/(1 - s_{nr} - s_{wr}), 0 \leq S \leq 1$, the capillary pressure is defined as, $p_c = -p_e \log S$, and the relative permeabilities are defined as, $k_{rw} = k_{rw}^0 S^2$, $k_{rn} = k_{rn}^0 (1 - S)^2$, $k_{rw}^0 = k_{rw} (S = 1)$, $k_{rw}^0 = k_{rw} (S = 1)$. p_e is the capillary pressure parameter, s_{wr} is the irreducible water saturation and s_{nr} is the residual oil saturation after water flooding. The values and units of the physical parameters are inserted in Table 1.

In Table 2, some error estimates for water saturation, nanoparticles concentration, and deposited nanoparticles concentration, are provided for various values of the number of time steps k. The reference case ($s_{w,r}^{n+1} = 0.9565$, $c_r^{n+1} = 0.0360$, and $c_{s1,r}^{n+1} = 1.3233 \times 10^{-7}$) is calculated at the point $(0.06, 0.053)$ for non-adaptive dense mesh of 200×150 for 0.6×0.4 m, at 2000 time step. It can be seen from Table 2 that the error decreases as number of number of time steps increases. Table 3 shows the real cost time of running the adaptive scheme for different values of the number of time steps k. One may notice from this table that the real cost time decreases as the number of time steps k increases. It seems more time is needed for the adaptation process.

Table 1. Values of the physical parameters.

Parameter	Value	Units
$\gamma_d, \gamma_{pt}, \gamma_e$	$16, 1.28, 30$	m^{-1}
$\mathbf{u}_r$	4.6×10^{-6}	m/s
c_0	0.1	–
S_{wr}, S_{nr}	0.001	–
ϕ_0	0.3	–
k_f	0.6	–
γ_f	0.01	–
μ_w, μ_n	1, 0.45	$cP = 1.0 \times 10^{-3}$ Pa.s
k_{rw0}, k_{ro0}	1	–
B_c	50	bar $= 1.0 \times 10^5$ Pa
D	4.6×10^{-8}	m^2/s

We use a real permeability map of dimensions 120×50, which is extracted from Ref. [23]. The permeabilities vary in a large scope and are they highly

Table 2. Error estimates for various values of number of time steps k.

k	$\|s_w^{n+1,k+1} - s_{w,r}^{n+1}\|$	$\|c^{n+1,k+1} - c_r^{n+1}\|$	$\|c_{s1}^{n+1,k+1} - c_{s1,r}^{n+1}\|$
500	0.0149	0.0065	1.8701E-05
200	0.0151	0.0065	1.8366E-05
100	0.0166	0.0068	9.9085E-05

Table 3. Real cost time of running the adaptive scheme for different values of the number of time steps k.

k	100	300	500	750
Real time [s]	3215	2307	532	424

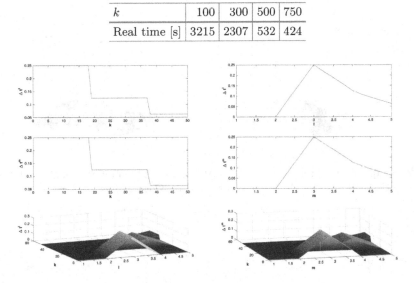

Fig. 1. Adaptive time-step sizes, Δt^l and Δt^m against the number of steps of the outer loop k and the number of the inner loops l and m: Case 1 ($k = 50$).

heterogeneous. We consider a domain of size 40m ×16m which is discretized into 120×50 uniform rectangles grids. The injection rate was 0.01 Pore-Volume-Injection (PVI) and continued the calculation until 0.5 PV. In this example, we choose the number of steps of the outer loop to be: (Case 1, $k = 50$, Fig. 1; Case 1, $k = 100$, Fig. 1; Case 1, $k = 200$, Fig. 3). In these figures, the adaptive time-step sizes, Δt^l and Δt^m are plotted against the number of steps of the outer loop k and the number of the inner loops l and m. It can be seen from these figures (Figs. 1, 2 and 3) that the behavior of adaptive Δt^l and Δt^m are very similar. This may be because the velocity is large and dominate the CFL. Also, both Δt^l and Δt^m start with large values then they gradually become smaller and smaller as k increases. On the other hand, for the first two cases when $k = 50, 100$, Δt^l and Δt^m are small when l and m are small, then they increase to reach a peak, then they are gradually decreasing. However, in the third case

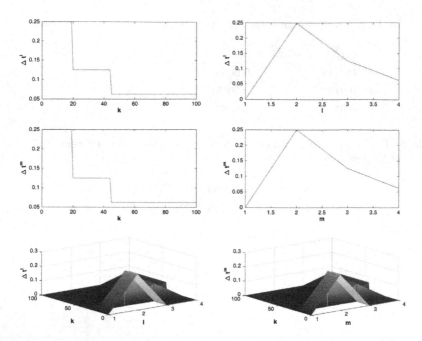

Fig. 2. Adaptive time-step sizes, Δt^l and Δt^m against the number of steps of the outer loop k and the number of the inner loops l and m: Case 2 ($k = 100$).

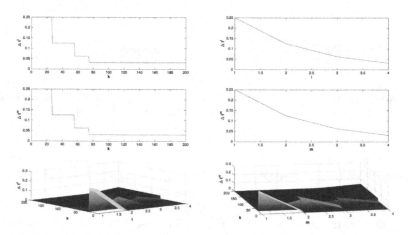

Fig. 3. Adaptive time-step sizes, Δt^l and Δt^m against the number of steps of the outer loop k and the number of the inner loops l and m: Case 3 ($k = 200$).

when $k = 200$, both Δt^l and Δt^m start with large values then they gradually become smaller and smaller as l and m, respectively, increases.

Variations of saturation of the heterogenous permeability are shown in Fig. 4. It is noteworthy that the distribution for water saturation is discontinuous due to the high heterogeneity. Thus, for example, we may note higher water

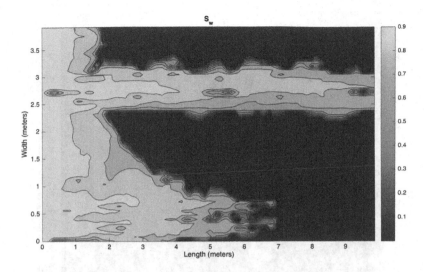

Fig. 4. Variations of saturation of the real heterogenous permeability case.

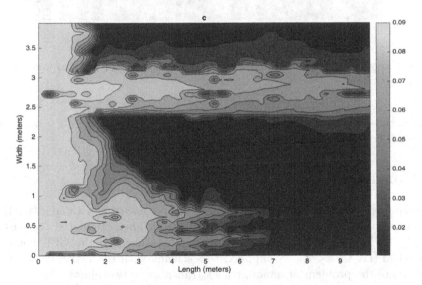

Fig. 5. Variations of nanoparticles concentration of the real heterogenous permeability case.

saturation at higher permeability regions. Similarly, one may observe the discontinuity in the nanoparticles concentration as illustrated in Fig. 5. The contrast of the nanoparticles concentration distribution arisen from the heterogeneity of the medium can also be noted here. Moreover, the contours of the deposited nanoparticles concentration are shown in Fig. 6. The behavior of the entrapped

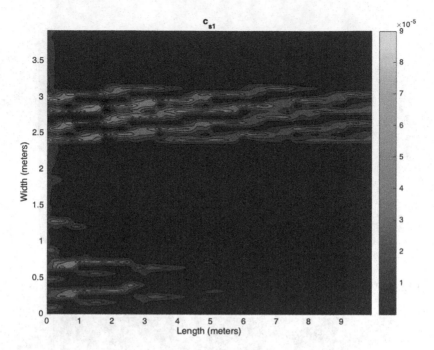

Fig. 6. Variations of deposited nanoparticles concentration of the real heterogenous permeability case.

nanoparticles concentration c_{s2} is very similar to the behavior of c_{s1} because of the similarity in their governing equation.

6   Conclusions

In this paper, we introduce an efficient time-stepping scheme with adaptive time-step sizes based on the CFL calculation. Hence, we have calculated the $\text{CFL}_{s,x}$, $\text{CFL}_{s,y}$, $\text{CFL}_{c,x}$ and $\text{CFL}_{c,y}$ at each substep and check if the CFL condition is satisfied (i.e. CFL< 1). We applied this scheme with the IMES-IMC scheme to simulate the problem of nanoparticles transport in two-phase flow in porous media. The model consists of five differential equations, namely, pressure, saturation, nanoparticles concentration, deposited nanoparticles concentration on the pore-walls, and entrapped nanoparticles concentration in pore–throats. The capillary pressure is linearized and used to couple the pressure and the saturation equations. Then, the saturation equation is solved explicitly to update the saturation at each step. Therefore, the nanoparticles concentration equation is treated implicitly. Finally, the deposited nanoparticles concentration on the pore-walls equation, and entrapped nanoparticles concentration in pore-throats equation are solved implicitly. The CCFD method was used to discretize the governing equations spatially. In order to show the efficiency of the proposed scheme, we presented some numerical experiments. The outer pressure time-step size was selected then the inner ones, namely, the saturation subtime-step and the concentration subtime-step were calculated and adaptive by the CFL condition. We presented three cases with different values of the outer pressure time-step. Moreover, distributions of water saturation, nanoparticles concentration, and deposited nanoparticles concentration on pore-wall are shown in graphs.

References

1. Chen, Z., Huan, G., Ma, Y.: Computational methods for multiphase flows in porous media. SIAM Comput. Sci. Eng (2006). Philadelphia
2. Young, L.C., Stephenson, R.E.: A generalized compositional approach for reservoir simulation. SPE J. **23**, 727–742 (1983)
3. Kou, J., Sun, S.: A new treatment of capillarity to improve the stability of IMPES two-phase flow formulation. Comput. & Fluids **39**, 1923–1931 (2010)
4. Belytschko, T., Lu, Y.Y.: Convergence and stability analyses of multi-time step algorithm for parabolic systems. Comp. Meth. App. Mech. Eng. **102**, 179–198 (1993)
5. Gravouil, A., Combescure, A.: Multi-time-step explicit-implicit method for nonlinear structural dynamics. Int. J. Num. Meth. Eng. **50**, 199–225 (2000)
6. Klisinski, M.: Inconsistency errors of constant velocity multi-time step integration algorithms. Comp. Ass. Mech. Eng. Sci. **8**, 121–139 (2001)
7. Bhallamudi, S.M., Panday, S., Huyakorn, P.S.: Sub-timing in fluid flow and transport simulations. Adv. Water Res. **26**, 477–489 (2003)
8. Park, Y.J., Sudicky, E.A., Panday, S., Sykes, J.F., Guvanasen, V.: Application of implicit sub-time stepping to simulate flow and transport in fractured porous media. Adv. Water Res. **31**, 995–1003 (2008)
9. Singh, V., Bhallamudi, S.M.: Complete hydrodynamic border-strip irrigation model. J. Irrig. Drain. Eng. **122**, 189-197 (1996)
10. Smolinski, P., Belytschko, T., Neal, M.: Multi-time-step integration using nodal partitioning. Int. J. Num. Meth. Eng. **26**, 349–359 (1988)
11. Hoteit, H., Firoozabadi, A.: Numerical modeling of two-phase flow in heterogeneous permeable media with different capillarity pressures. Adv. Water Res. **31**, 56–73 (2008)
12. Gruesbeck, C., Collins, R.E.: Entrainment and deposition of fines particles in porous media. SPE J. **24**, 847–856 (1982)
13. Ju, B., Fan, T.: Experimental study and mathematical model of nanoparticle transport in porous media. Powder Tech. **192**, 195–202 (2009)
14. Liu, X.H., Civian, F.: Formation damage and skin factor due to filter cake formation and fines migration in the Near-Wellbore Region. SPE-27364. In: SPE Symposium on Formation Damage Control, Lafayette, Louisiana (1994)
15. El-Amin, M.F., Salama, A., Sun, S.: Modeling and simulation of nanoparticles transport in a two-phase flow in porous media. SPE-154972. In: SPE International Oilfield Nanotechnology Conference and Exhibition, Noordwijk, The Netherlands (2012)
16. El-Amin, M.F., Sun, S., Salama, A.: Modeling and simulation of nanoparticle transport in multiphase flows in porous media: CO_2 sequestration. SPE-163089. In: Mathematical Methods in Fluid Dynamics and Simulation of Giant Oil and Gas Reservoirs (2012)

17. El-Amin, M.F., Sun, S., Salama, A.: Enhanced oil recovery by nanoparticles injection: modeling and simulation. SPE-164333. In: SPE Middle East Oil and Gas Show and Exhibition held in Manama, Bahrain (2013)
18. El-Amin, M.F., Salama, A., Sun, S.: Numerical and dimensional analysis of nanoparticles transport with two-phase flow in porous media. J. Pet. Sci. Eng. **128**, 53–64 (2015)
19. Salama, A., Negara, A., El-Amin, M.F., Sun, S.: Numerical investigation of nanoparticles transport in anisotropic porous media. J. Cont. Hydr. **181**, 114–130 (2015)
20. Chen, H., Di, Q., Ye, F., Gu, C., Zhang, J.: Numerical simulation of drag reduction effects by hydrophobic nanoparticles adsorption method in water flooding processes. J. Natural Gas Sc. Eng. **35**, 1261–1269 (2016)
21. Chen, M.H., Salama, A., El-Amin, M.F.: Numerical aspects related to the dynamic update of anisotropic permeability field during the transport of nanoparticles in the subsurface. Procedia Comput. Sci. **80**, 1382–1391 (2016)
22. El-Amin, M.F., Kou, J., Salama, A., Sun, S.: An iterative implicit scheme for nanoparticles transport with two-phase flow in porous media. Procedia Comput. Sci. **80**, 1344–1353 (2016)
23. Al-Dhafeeri, A.M., Nasr-El-Din, H.A.: Characteristics of high-permeability zones using core analysis, and production logging data. J. Pet. Sci. Eng. **55**, 18–36 (2007)

Identifying Central Individuals
in Organised Criminal Groups
and Underground Marketplaces

Jan William Johnsen[(✉)] and Katrin Franke

Norwegian University of Science and Technology, Gjøvik, Norway
{jan.w.johnsen,kyfranke}@ieee.org

Abstract. Traditional organised criminal groups are becoming more active in the cyber domain. They form online communities and use these as marketplaces for illegal materials, products and services, which drives the Crime as a Service business model. The challenge for law enforcement of investigating and disrupting the underground marketplaces is to know which individuals to focus effort on. Because taking down a few high impact individuals can have more effect on disrupting the criminal services provided. This paper present our study on social network centrality measures' performance for identifying important individuals in two networks. We focus our analysis on two distinctly different network structures: Enron and Nulled.IO. The first resembles an organised criminal group, while the latter is a more loosely structured hacker forum. Our result show that centrality measures favour individuals with more communication rather than individuals usually considered more important: organised crime leaders and cyber criminals who sell illegal materials, products and services.

Keywords: Digital forensics · Social Network Analysis
Centrality measures · Organised criminal groups
Algorithm reliability

1 Introduction

Traditional Organised Criminal Groups (OCGs) have a business-like hierarchy [10]; with a few leaders controlling the organisation and activities done by men under then, which does most of the criminal activities. OCG are starting to move their operations to the *darknet* [2,6], where they form *digital undergrounds*. These undergrounds serves as meeting places for likeminded people and marketplace for illegal materials, products and services. This also allow the criminal economy to thrive, with little interference from law enforcements [6].

The research leading to these results has received funding from the Research Council of Norway programme IKTPLUSS, under the R&D project "Ars Forensica - Computational Forensics for Large-scale Fraud Detection, Crime Investigation & Prevention", grant agreement 248094/O70.

© Springer International Publishing AG, part of Springer Nature 2018
Y. Shi et al. (Eds.): ICCS 2018, LNCS 10862, pp. 379–386, 2018.
https://doi.org/10.1007/978-3-319-93713-7_31

The transition between traditional physical crime to cyber crime changes how criminals organise. They form a loosely connected network in digital undergrounds [8,11]; where the users can be roughly divided into two distinct groups [6]: a minority and a majority. The division is based on individual's technical skill and capabilities, and the group names reflects how many individuals are found in each group. The minority group have fewer individuals, however, they have higher technical skills and capabilities. They support the majority – without the same level of skills – through the Crime as a Service (CaaS) business model [6]. The consequence is that highly skilled criminals develop tools that the majority group use as a service. This allows entry-level criminals to have greater impact and success in their cyber operations.

The challenge is identifying key actors [12] in digital undergrounds and stopping their activities. The most effective approach is to target those key actors found in the minority group [6]. We represent the communication pattern between individuals as a network, and then use Social Network Analysis (SNA) methods to investigate those social structures. An important aspect of SNA is that it provides scientific and objective measures for network structure and positions of key actors [5]. Key actors – people with importance or greater power – typically have higher centrality scores than other actors [5,12].

We substitute the lack of available datasets of OCG and digital undergrounds with the Enron corpus and Nulled.IO, respectively. The Enron corpus have been extensively studied [3,4,7], where Hardin et al. [7] studied the relationships by using six different centrality measures. While Nulled.IO is a novel dataset for an online forum for distributing cracked software, and trade of leaked and stolen credentials. SNA methods have also been used by Krebs [14] to analyse the network surrounding the airplane highjackers from September 11th, 2001.

The dataset types in these studies are highly varied: ranging from a few individuals to hundreds of them; networks that are hierarchical or are more loosely structured; and complete and incomplete networks. The *no free lunch* theorem [15] states that there is no algorithm that works best for every scenario. The novelty of our work is that we evaluate the results of centrality measures for two dataset with distinctly different characteristics. Our research tries to answer the following research questions: (1) How does centrality measures identify leading people inside networks of different organisational structures and communication patterns? and (2) How good are they to identify people of more importance (i.e. inside the smaller population)? The answers to these questions are particularly important for law enforcement, to enable them to focus their efforts on those key actors whose removal has more effect for disrupting the criminal economy.

2   Materials and Methods

2.1   Datasets

Although the Enron MySQL database dump by Shetty and Adibi [13] is unavailable today, we use a MySQL v5 dump of their original release[1]. The corpus

---

[1] http://www.ahschulz.de/enron-email-data/.

contains 252 759 e-mail messages from 75 416 e-mail addresses. Nulled.IO[2] is an online forum which got their entire database leaked on May 2016. The forum contains details about 599 085 user accounts, 800 593 private messages and 3 495 596 public messages. The distinction between private and public is that private messages are between two individuals, while public messages are forum posts accessible by everyone. These datasets have very different characteristics: Enron is an organisation with strict hierarchical structure, while Nulled.IO is flat and loosely connected network.

The challenge of analysing our datasets are the large amount of information they contain. Every piece of information would be of potential interest in a forensic investigation, however, we limit the information to that which represents individual people and the communication between then. We use this to create multiple *directed graphs* (digraphs), where individuals are modelled as *vertices* and the communication between them as directed *edges*. A digraph G is more formally defined as a set V of vertices and set E of edges, where E contains ordered pairs of elements in V. For example, (v_1, v_2) is an ordered pair if there exists an edge between vertices v_1 and v_2, called *source* and *target* respectively.

2.2 Centrality Measures

Centrality measures are graph-based analysis methods found in SNA, used to identify important and influential individuals within a network. We evaluate five popular centrality measures for digraphs: *in-degree* (C_{deg-}), *out-degree* (C_{deg+}), *betweenness* (C_B), *closeness* (C_C) and *eigenvector* (C_E). They are implemented in well-known forensic investigation tools, such as IBM i2 Analyst's Notebook [1].

The centrality measures differs in their interpretation of what it means to be 'important' in a network [12]. Thus, some vertices in a network will be ranked as more important than others. Figure 1 illustrate how vertices are ranked differently. The number of vertices and edges affects the centrality values. However, normalising the values will counter this effect and allow us to compare vertices from networks of different sizes. Our analysis tool *Networkx* uses a scale to normalise the result to values [0, 1].

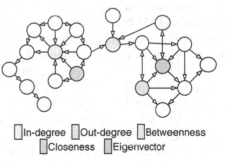

☐In-degree ☐Out-degree ☐Betweenness
☐Closeness ☐Eigenvector

Fig. 1. Highest ranking vertices in a digraph

3 Experiment

We first constructed three weighted digraphs to represent the communication between users in Enron and Nulled.IO. Only a few database (DB) tables and

---

[2] http://leakforums.net/thread-719337 (recently became unavailable).

fields had the necessary information to build the digraphs: *message (sender)* and *recipientinfo (rvalue)* for Enron, and *topics (starter_id)*, *posts (author_id)* and *message_topics (mt_starter_id, mt_to_member_id, mt_to_count, and mt_replies)* for Nulled.IO. The digraph construction method can be generalised as: find the sender and receiver of messages. Represent them as unique vertices in a digraph (if not already exists) and connect them with an edge from sender to receiver. These operations was repeated for every public/private and e-mail message. Finally, edges' weights was initialised once it was first created, and incremented for each message with identical vertices and edge direction. The data extraction and analysis was performed on a desktop computer, with a MySQL server and Python, with packages Networkx v1.11 and PyMySQL v0.7.9.

3.1   Pre-filtering and Population Boundary

The digraph construction included a bit more information than necessary, which have to be removed before the analysis. However, we want to find a balance between reducing the information without removing valuable or relevant information. To analyse the hierarchical structure of Enron (our presumed OCG), we have to remove vertices which does not end with '@enron.com'. Additionally, we removed a few general e-mail addresses which could not be linked to unique Enron employees. A total of 691 vertices was removed by these steps.

We have previously identified user with ID 1 as an administrator account on the Nulled.IO forum [9], used to send out private 'welcome'-messages to newly registered users, which can skew the results. Thus, we only remove edges from ID 1 to other vertices – when its weight equals one – to achieve the goal of information preservation. The private network, that originally had 295 147 vertices and 376 087 edges, was reduced to 33 647 (88.6%) and 98 253 (73.87%), respectively. The public thread communication network did not undergo any pre-processing. From its original 299 702 vertices and 2 738 710 edges, it was reduced to 299 105 (0.2%) and 2 705 578 (1.22%), respectively.

The final pre-processing step was to remove isolated vertices and self-loops. Isolated vertices had to be deleted because they have an infinite distance to every other vertex in the network. Self-loops was also removed because it is not interesting to know a vertex' relation to itself. The reduction in vertices and edges for the Nulled.IO public digraph was a consequence of this final step.

4   Results

The results are found in Tables 1 and 2, sorted in descending order according to vertices' centrality score. Higher scores appear on top and indicates more importance. The results are limited to the top five individuals due to page limitations.

The goal of our research is to identify leaders of OCG or prominent individuals who sell popular services; people whose removal will cause more disruption to the criminal community. To evaluate the success of centrality measures, we first had to identify people's job positions or areas of responsibilities in both Enron and Nulled.IO. We combined information found on LinkedIn profiles, news articles and a previous list[3] to identify Enron employees' position in the hierarchy. For Nulled.IO users we had to manually inspect both private and public messages to estimate their role or responsibility. The total number of possible messages to inspect made it difficult to determine the exact role for each user.

4.1 Enron

sally.beck is within the top three highest ranking individuals in all centrality measures, except for eigenvector centrality. Her role in Enron was being a Chief Operating Officer (COO); responsible for the daily operation of the company and often reports directly to the Chief Executive Officer (CEO). Her result correspond to expectations of her role: a lot of sent and received messages to handle the daily operation.

Table 1. Top ten centrality results Enron

UID	C_{deg-}	UID	C_{deg+}	UID	C_B
louise.kitchen	0.03374	david.forster	0.07393	sally.beck	0.02152
steven.j.kean	0.02900	sally.beck	0.06559	kenneth.lay	0.01831
sally.beck	0.02884	kenneth.lay	0.04982	jeff.skilling	0.01649
john.lavorato	0.02803	tracey.kozadinos	0.04955	j.kaminski	0.01555
mark.e.taylor	0.02685	julie.clyatt	0.04907	louise.kitchen	0.01145
UID	C_C	UID	C_E		
sally.beck	0.39612	richard.shapiro	0.37927		
david.forster	0.38500	james.d.steffes	0.33788		
kenneth.lay	0.38362	steven.j.kean	0.27800		
julie.clyatt	0.38347	jeff.dasovich	0.27090		
billy.lemmons	0.38293	susan.mara	0.25839		

kenneth.lay and *david.forster* are two individuals with high rankings in all centrality measures, except for eigenvector centrality. They are CEO and Vice President, respectively. *kenneth.lay* and his second in command *jeff.skilling* was the heavy hitters in the Enron fraud scandal.

Although there where a few CEOs in the Enron corporation, many of the higher ranking individuals had lower hierarchical positions. Most notably this occurred in eigenvector centrality, however, this is because of how this measure works. Finally, our result also show that centrality measures usually ranks the same individuals as being more important than others.

---

[3] http://cis.jhu.edu/~parky/Enron/employees.

4.2   Nulled.IO

Unique Identifier (UID) 0 in the public digraph appears to be a placeholder for deleted accounts, because the UID does not appear in the member list and the username in published messages are different. UID 4, 6, 8, 15398, 47671 and 301849, among others, provides free cracked software to the community, with most of them being cheats or bots for popular games. While UID 1337 and 1471 appears to be administrators.

Table 2. Top five public and private centrality results

Public centrality results									
UID	C_{deg-}	UID	C_{deg+}	UID	C_B	UID	C_C	UID	C_E
15398	0.23695	1471	0.00393	0	0.00959	1471	0.03564	1337	0.28764
0	0.16282	8	0.00321	15398	0.00855	8	0.03553	0	0.27157
1337	0.06466	193974	0.00294	1337	0.00461	118229	0.03542	15398	0.25494
4	0.05656	47671	0.00273	1471	0.00334	169996	0.03540	334	0.23961
6	0.04276	118229	0.00266	193974	0.00219	47671	0.03520	71725	0.22798
Private centrality results									
UID	C_{deg-}	UID	C_{deg+}	UID	C_B	UID	C_C	UID	C_E
1	0.08412	1	0.42331	1	0.41719	1	0.40665	61078	0.45740
1471	0.05028	51349	0.00773	1471	0.02369	51349	0.28442	51349	0.30353
1337	0.04289	88918	0.00695	334	0.02286	88384	0.28102	1	0.24505
8	0.03970	47671	0.00617	1337	0.02253	10019	0.28080	88918	0.21214
15398	0.03967	334	0.00600	15398	0.02129	61078	0.28043	193974	0.19651

UID 1 in the private digraph is found on top of (almost) all centrality measure. Although this account appear as a key actor, it was mostly used to send out thousands of automatic 'Welcome'-messages, 'Thank you'-letters for donations and support and other server administrative activities.

UIDs 8, 334, 1471, 47671, 51349 and 88918 in the private digraph cracks various online accounts, such as Netflix, Spotify and game-related accounts. They usually go after the 'low hanging fruit' that have bad passwords or otherwise easy to get. Most of the users have low technical skills, however, they are willing to learn to be better and to earn more money from their scriptkid activities. They want to go into software development for economic gains or learn more advanced hacker skills and tools to increase their profit.

5   Discussion and Conclusion

Law enforcement agencies can disrupt the CaaS business model or OCG when they know which key actors to effectively focus their efforts on. However, implementations of centrality measures in forensic investigation tools are given without any explanation or advice for how to interpret the results; which inadvertently can lead to accusation of lesser criminals of being among the leaders of criminal organisations. Although the centrality measures do not perfectly identify individuals highest in the organisation hierarchy, our result show that potential secondary targets can be found via them. Secondary targets are individuals that any leader rely on to effectively run their organisation.

Contemporary centrality measures studies here most often identified individuals with a natural higher frequency of communication, such as administrators and moderators. However, going after forum administrators is only a minor setback, as history has shown a dozen new underground marketplaces took Silk Road's place after it was shut down. Thus, the problem with current centrality measures is that they are affected by the network connectivity rather than actual criminal activities.

Our result demonstrates their weakness, as centrality measures cannot be used with any other definition for their interpretation of 'importance'. There is a lack of good interpretations to current centrality measures that fits for forensic investigations. Interpretations which are able to effectively address the growing problem of cyber crime and the changes it brings. We will continue working on identifying areas where already existing methods are sufficient, in addition to developing our own proposed solutions to address this problem.

References

1. IBM knowledge center - centrality and centrality measures. https://www.ibm.com/support/knowledgecenter/en/SS3J58_9.0.8/com.ibm.i2.anb.doc/sna_centrality.html
2. Choo, K.K.R.: Organised crime groups in cyberspace: a typology. Trends Organ. Crime 11(3), 270–295 (2008). https://doi.org/10.1007/s12117-008-9038-9
3. Diesner, J.: Communication networks from the enron email corpus: it's always about the people. Enron is no different (2005). https://pdfs.semanticscholar.org/875b/59b06c76e3b52a8570103ba6d8d70b0cf33e.pdf
4. Diesner, J., Carley, K.M.: Exploration of communication networks from the enron email corpus. In: SIAM International Conference on Data Mining: Workshop on Link Analysis, Counterterrorism and Security, Newport Beach, CA (2005)
5. Décary-Hétu, D., Dupont, B.: The social network of hackers. Global Crime 13(3), 160–175 (2012). https://doi.org/10.1080/17440572.2012.702523
6. Europol: The internet organised crime threat assessment (iOCTA) (2014). https://www.europol.europa.eu/sites/default/files/documents/europol_iocta_web.pdf
7. Hardin, J.S., Sarkis, G., Urc, P.C.: Network analysis with the enron email corpus. J. Stat. Educ. 23(2) (2015)
8. Holt, T.J., Strumsky, D., Smirnova, O., Kilger, M.: Examining the social networks of malware writers and hackers. Int. J. Cyber Criminol. 6(1), 891–903 (2012)
9. Johnsen, J.W., Franke, K.: Feasibility study of social network analysis on loosely structured communication networks. Procedia Comput. Sci. 108, 2388–2392 (2017). https://doi.org/10.1016/j.procs.2017.05.172
10. Le, V.: Organised crime typologies: structure, activities and conditions. Int. J. Criminol. Sociol. 1, 121–131 (2012)

11. Macdonald, M., Frank, R., Mei, J., Monk, B.: Identifying digital threats in a hacker web forum, pp. 926–933. ACM Press (2015). https://doi.org/10.1145/2808797. 2808878
12. Prell, C.: Social Network Analysis: History, Theory and Methodology. SAGE Publications, London (2012). https://books.google.no/books?id=p4iTo566nAMC
13. Shetty, J., Adibi, J.: The enron email dataset database schema and brief statistical report 4 (2004). http://citeseerx.ist.psu.edu/viewdoc/download?doi=10.1.1. 296.9477&rep=rep1&type=pdf
14. Krebs, V.: Uncloaking terrorist networks. First Monday (2002). http://journals. uic.edu/ojs/index.php/fm/article/view/941
15. Wolpert, D.H., Macready, W.G.: No free lunch theorems for optimization. IEEE Trans. Evol. Comput. **1**(1), 67–82 (1997). http://ieeexplore.ieee.org/abstract/ document/585893/

Guiding the Optimization of Parallel Codes on Multicores Using an Analytical Cache Model

Diego Andrade$^{(\boxtimes)}$, Basilio B. Fraguela, and Ramón Doallo

Universidade da Coruña, A Coruña, Spain
{diego.andrade,basilio.fraguela,ramon.doalllo}@udc.es

Abstract. Cache performance is particularly hard to predict in modern multicore processors as several threads can be concurrently in execution, and private cache levels are combined with shared ones. This paper presents an analytical model able to evaluate the cache performance of the whole cache hierarchy for parallel applications in less than one second taking as input their source code and the cache configuration. While the model does not tackle some advanced hardware features, it can help optimizers to make reasonably good decisions in a very short time. This is supported by an evaluation based on two modern architectures and three different case studies, in which the model predictions differ on average just 5.05% from the results of a detailed hardware simulator and correctly guide different optimization decisions.

1 Introduction

Modern multicore processors, which can execute parallel codes, have complex cache hierarchies that typically combine up to three private and shared levels [2]. There is a vast bibliography on the subject of improving the cache performance of modern multicore systems. Several works have addressed this problem from the energy consumption perspective [6,9]. Other works try to enhance the cache performance in order to improve the overall performance of the system [3,5,8].

The Parallel Probabilistic Miss Equations (ParPME) model, introduced in [1], can estimate the cache performance during the execution of both parallelized and serial loops. In the case of parallelized loops, this model can only estimate the performance of caches that are shared by all the threads that execute the loop. This paper presents the ParPME+ model, an extension of the ParPME model to predict the effect of parallelized loops on private caches as well as in caches shared by an arbitrary number of threads, this ability enables the possibility to model the whole cache hierarchy of a multicore processor. The evaluation shows that the predictions of our model match the performance observed in a simulator, and that it can be an useful tool to guide an iterative optimization process.

The rest of this paper is structured as follows. First, Sect. 2 reviews the existing ParPME model and Sect. 3 describes the ParPME+ model presented

© Springer International Publishing AG, part of Springer Nature 2018
Y. Shi et al. (Eds.): ICCS 2018, LNCS 10862, pp. 387–394, 2018.
https://doi.org/10.1007/978-3-319-93713-7_32

in this paper. Then, Sect. 4 is devoted to the experimental results and finally Sect. 5 presents our conclusions and future work.

2   The Parallel PME Model

The Parallel Probabilistic Miss Equations Model [1] (ParPME) is an extension of the PME model [4] that can predict the behavior of caches during the executions of both parallelized and sequential codes. The scope of application of this model is limited to regular codes where references are indexed using affine functions. The inputs of the ParPME model are the Abstract Syntax Tree (AST) of the source code and a cache configuration. The replacement policy is assumed to be a perfect LRU. This model is built around three main concepts: (1) A **Probabilistic Miss Equation (PME)** predicts the number of misses generated by a given reference within a given loop nesting level. (2) The **reuse distance** is the number of iterations of the currently analyzed loop between two consecutive accesses to the same cache line. (3) The **miss probability** is the probability of an attempt to reuse a cache line associated to a given reuse distance.

Depending on whether the studied reference is affected by a parallelized loop in the current nesting level, the model uses a different kind of PME. The PME for non-parallelized loops, introduced in [4], is valid for both private and shared caches as in both cases all the iterations of the loop are executed by one thread and the corresponding cache lines are loaded in the same cache, no matter if the cache is private to each core or shared among several cores.

The modeling of parallelized loop is much more challenging, as the iterations of this kind of loops are distributed among several threads. In this case, each cache stores the cache lines loaded by the threads that share that cache and one thread can reuse lines loaded previously by the same thread (intra-thread reuse) or a different one (inter-thread reuse). The new PME introduced in the ParPME model [1] only covers the situation where a cache is shared among all the threads involved in the computation. However, current architectures include both private and shared caches. Moreover, many systems include several multicore processors, and thus even if the last level cache of each processor is shared by all its cores, when all the cores in the system cooperate in the parallel execution of a code, each cache is only shared by a subset of the threads.

3   The ParPME Plus Model

This section introduces the main contribution of this paper, the ParPME Plus (ParPME+) model, which extends the existing ParPME model to enable the modeling of all the levels of a multicore cache hierarchy, including both the shared and private ones. Rather than adding more types of PMEs and extending the method to calculate the miss probability, our approach relies on transforming the source code to analyze in order to emulate the behavior of the threads that share a given cache level. Then, the transformed code is analyzed using the original ParPME model.

```
    ...
    #pragma omp for schedule(static,bi)
    for(i=0; i<Mi; i++)

        ...
        array[...][i*k][...];
        ...
```

```
    ...
    #pragma omp for schedule(static,1)
    for(i1=0; i1<tsi; i1++)
        for(i2=0; i2<Mi/(ti*bi); i2++)
            for(i3=0; i<bi; i3++)

                ...
                array[...][i2][i1][i3*k][...];
                ...
```

Fig. 1. Generic transformation to model cache shared among a subset of threads. Original code (top) and transformed code (bottom)

Figure 1, shows the general form of the aforementioned transformation. The top part of the figure shows the original loop, and the bottom part shows the transformed one that is associated to the representation used to analyze the behavior of a cache shared by a subset of ts_i threads. The index variable of the parallel loop that is being modeled can be used in the indexing functions of one or more dimensions of one or several data structures. The first step of the transformation eases the identification of which parts of a data structure are referenced by the iterations assigned to a subset of the threads that share the cache. With this purpose, each dimension of an array that is indexed by the index variable of a parallelized loop i multiplied by a constant value k is split into three dimensions. If the split dimension has size N_i, the three resulting dimensions, defined from the most to the least significant one, have sizes $N_i/(t_i \times b_i \times k)$, ti and $b_i \times k$ respectively, t_i being the number of threads among which the iterations of loop i are distributed and b_i is the block size used to distribute the iterations of the loop among the threads. Since the product of the sizes of these three new dimensions is equal to the size of the original dimension, this modification changes the way the data structure is indexed but not its size or layout. In the case that N_i is not divisible by $t_i \times b_i \times k$, the most significant dimension must be rounded up to $\lceil N_i/(t_i \times b_i \times k) \rceil$, slightly increasing the size of the data structure by up to $t_i \times b_i - 1 \times k$ elements. For big values of N_i this will not affect significantly the accuracy of the predictions.

The second step of the transformation modifies the parallel loops so that (a) indexing functions can be generated for all the new dimensions defined and (b) such indexings give place to access patterns identical to those of the original code in the considered cache. For this latter purpose the transformation of each parallel loop i must take into account a new parameter, ts_i, which is the number of threads that share the cache that is being modeled at this point out of the t_i

threads that participate in the parallelization of the loop. This transformation replaces each considered parallelized loop i of M_i iterations with three different consecutively nested ones of ts_i, $M_i/(t_i \times b_i)$ and b_i iterations respectively, where the first one is the outermost one and the last one the innermost one. Out of them, only the outermost one is parallel, being each one of its ts_i iterations executed in parallel by a different thread, while the two inner ones are executed sequentially by the same thread. This transformation also implies using the loop indexes of these loops for indexing the new dimensions defined in the first step. The mapping is always the same. Namely, the most significant dimension is indexed by the index of the middle loop, the next dimension is indexed by the index of the outermost (and parallel) loop, and the least significant dimension is indexed by the innermost loop.

The new code, or actually, its new representation, is almost equivalent to the original, replicating the same access patterns and work distribution, with a single critical difference. Namely, it only covers the iterations assigned to the subset of ts_i threads of interest, i.e. the ones that share the cache we want to model at this point, instead of all the t_i threads. Notice that this strategy assumes that if several threads share a cache, then they get consecutive chunks of the loop to parallelize. While this may not be always the case, this is a common and very desirable situation, as this tends to increase the potential cache reuse and reduce the overheads in case of false sharing. In those situations in which these benefits do not hold, for example when there is no possible reuse between the data used by different threads, the assumption is irrelevant, as the cache behavior should be the same no matter the sharing threads get consecutive chunks of the loop or not.

4   Experimental Results

The model has been validated on two Intel platforms with very different features: a i7-4790 (with 4 physical cores), and a Xeon 2699 v4 (with 22 cores). The experiments try to prove that the model can accurately predict the cache performance of codes on real cache hierarchies, and that it can guide cache memory optimizations. With this purpose, we have built our experiments around three case studies: (1) The loop **fision** technique is applied to a code (2) The loop **fusion** technique is applied to a code. (3) A matrix multiplication implemented using the 6 possible loop orders (ikj, ijk, jik, jki, kij, kji).

The ParPME+ model is used to predict the number of misses generated by these codes in the different levels of the cache hierarchy. These predictions are used to calculate the memory cost (MemCost) associated to the execution of each given code, that is, the number of cycles it spends due to the cache hierarchy. This calculation has been made using the same approach followed in [3]. The predictions of the model have been compared to the observations made in the SESC cycle-accurate simulator [7] in order to assess their accuracy. The difference between both values is expressed as a relative percentage The average difference across all the experiments is just 5.05%, the accuracy thus being remarkable, from the 0.2% obtained for the **fusion** benchmarks in the Intel i7, to the 11.6% obtained for the **fision** benchmark in the same platform.

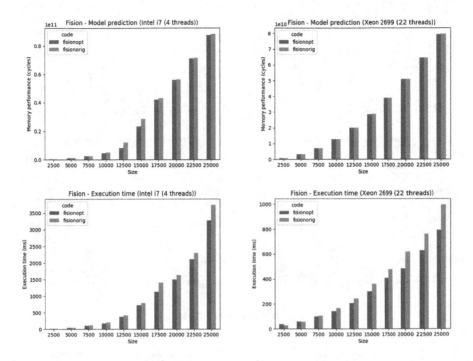

Fig. 2. Results for fision

As a second step, the optimization choices made by the model are compared to those made using the guidance of the actual execution time. Figure 2 summarizes the results for the fision. The figure is composed of two columns with two graphs each. Each column represents the results for one of the two platforms. The number of threads used for the experiments is equal to the number of physical cores available in each platform. We have made sure that each thread is mapped to a different physical core using the affinity feature of OpenMP 4.0. The iterations of the parallel loop have been distributed cyclically among the threads in chunks of 16 iterations. This chunk size has been used in all the experiments of this section. The top graph in each column shows the memory performance predicted by the model for the versions without fision (fisionorig) and with fision (fisionopt) for different problem sizes. The bottom graph of each column make the same comparison using the average execution times of ten executions. These times and the model predictions lead to the same conclusion, this optimization is successful in both the i7 and the Xeon.

The results for the fusion case study are shown in Fig. 3, which has the same structure as Fig. 2. In this case, the model also leads to the right decision, which is to apply the optimization in all the platforms and for all the problem sizes.

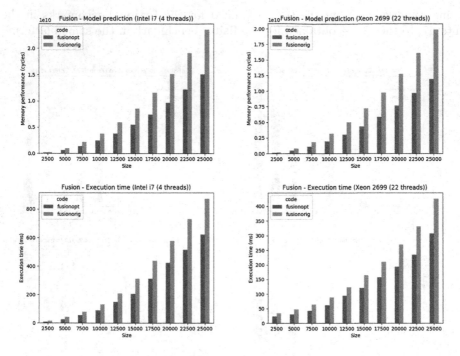

Fig. 3. Results for fusion

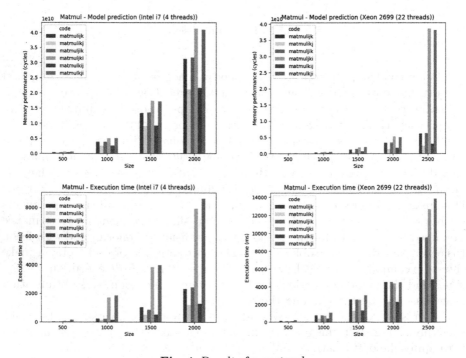

Fig. 4. Results for matmul

The results for the matrix multiplication case study are shown in Fig. 4. In this case, we have to decide the best loop ordering to perform the matrix multiplication. The outermost i or j loop is the one parallelized. The results have the same structure as in the previous cases. According to the actual execution time, the ikj and kij ordering are the best ones, and this decision is accurately taken using the model.

All the predictions of our model have been obtained in less than one second no matter the problem size. However, the execution of the real codes or the simulator took quite longer for the larger problem sizes, ranging from the 3 times longer of **padding** in the Intel i7, to the 30 times longer of **matmul** in the Intel Xeon 2680. This is a crucial characteristic of our model, as we can evaluate several optimization choices in a fraction of the time required to execute the real codes.

5 Conclusions

This paper explores the possibility of using an analytical model of the cache behavior to guide compiler optimizations on parallel codes run on real multicore systems. The existing ParPME model introduced in [1], supported caches shared by all the threads participating in the parallelization. Nevertheless, several architectures present caches that are private to one threads or shared by a subset of the cores/threads participating in the execution of a parallel application. For this reason, a first contribution in this paper, leading to the ParPME+ model, has been the development of a procedure which, by changing the representation of the code to analyze inside the model, allows it to also accurately predict the behavior of this kind of caches. As a result, the model can now analyze the behavior of the complete cache hierarchy of a multicore multiprocessor computer. Our experiments using three case studies and two architectures show that the model is a good guide to choose the most cache friendly optimization choice. This is not surprising, as the predictions of our model only differ by 5.05% on average from the observations of a cycle-accurate simulator. In addition, the model can provide its predictions in less than a second.

In the future, the model can be extended to model any of the missing hardware features present in some processors. It would also interesting to complement it with a CPU model.

Acknowledgment. This research was supported by the Ministry of Economy and Competitiveness of Spain and FEDER funds (80%) of the EU (TIN2016-75845-P), and by the Government of Galicia (Xunta de Galicia) co-founded by the European Regional Development Fund (ERDF) under the Consolidation Programme of Competitive Reference Groups (ED431C 2017/04) as well as under the Centro Singular de Investigación de Galicia accreditation 2016-2019 (ED431G/01). We also acknowledge the Centro de Supercomputación de Galicia (CESGA) for the use of their computers.

References

1. Andrade, D., Fraguela, B.B., Doallo, R.: Accurate prediction of the behavior of multithreaded applications in shared caches. Parallel Comput. **39**(1), 36–57 (2013)
2. Balasubramonian, R., Jouppi, N.P., Muralimanohar, N.: Multi-Core Cache Hierarchies. Synthesis Lectures on Computer Architecture. Morgan & Claypool Publishers, San Rafael (2011)
3. Fraguela, B.B., Carmueja, M.G., Andrade, D.: Optimal tile size selection guided by analytical models. In: Proceedings of Parallel Computing, vol. 33, pp. 565–572 (2005). publication Series of the John von Neumann Institute for Computing (NIC)
4. Fraguela, B.B., Doallo, R., Zapata, E.L.: Probabilistic miss equations: evaluating memory hierarchy performance. IEEE Trans. Comput. **52**(3), 321–336 (2003)
5. Ramos, S., Hoefler, T.: Modeling communication in cache-coherent SMP systems: a case-study with xeon phi. In: 22nd International Symposium on High-Performance Parallel and Distributed Computing, pp. 97–108. ACM (2013)
6. Rawlins, M., Gordon-Ross, A.: A cache tuning heuristic for multicore architectures. IEEE Trans. Comput. **62**(8), 1570–1583 (2013)
7. Renau, J., Fraguela, B., Tuck, J., Liu, W., Prvulovic, M., Ceze, L., Sarangi, S., Sack, P., Strauss, K., Montesinos, P.: SESC simulator, January 2005
8. Schuff, D.L., Kulkarni, M., Pai, V.S.: Accelerating multicore reuse distance analysis with sampling and parallelization. In: 19th International Conference on Parallel Architectures and Compilation Techniques, PACT 2010, pp. 53–64. ACM, New York (2010)
9. Zang, W., Gordon-Ross, A.: A survey on cache tuning from a power/energy perspective. ACM Comput. Surv. (CSUR) **45**(3), 32 (2013)

LDA-Based Scoring of Sequences Generated by RNN for Automatic Tanka Composition

Tomonari Masada[1]([⊠])[iD] and Atsuhiro Takasu[2]

[1] Nagasaki University, 1-14 Bunkyo-machi, Nagasaki-shi, Nagasaki, Japan
masada@nagasaki-u.ac.jp
[2] National Institute of Informatics, 2-1-2 Hitotsubashi, Chiyoda-ku, Tokyo, Japan
takasu@nii.ac.jp

Abstract. This paper proposes a method of scoring sequences generated by recurrent neural network (RNN) for automatic Tanka composition. Our method gives sequences a score based on topic assignments provided by latent Dirichlet allocation (LDA). When many word tokens in a sequence are assigned to the same topic, we give the sequence a high score. While a scoring of sequences can also be achieved by using RNN output probabilities, the sequences having large probabilities are likely to share much the same subsequences and thus are doomed to be deprived of diversity. The experimental results, where we scored Japanese Tanka poems generated by RNN, show that the top-ranked sequences selected by our method were likely to contain a wider variety of subsequences than those selected by RNN output probabilities.

Keywords: Topic modeling · Sequence generation
Recurrent Neural Network · Automatic poetry composition

1 Introduction

Recurrent neural network (RNN) is a class of artificial neural network that has been providing remarkable achievements in many important applications. *Sequence generation* is one among such applications [6,10]. By adopting a special architecture like LSTM [8] or GRU [3,4], RNN can learn dependencies among word tokens appearing at distant positions. When we use sequence generation in realistic situations, we may sift the sequences generated by RNN to obtain only useful ones. Such sifting may give each generated sequence a score representing its usefulness relative to the application under consideration. While an improvement of the generated sequences can also be achieved by modifying the architecture of RNN [5], we here consider a scoring method that can be tuned and applied separately from RNN. In particular, this paper proposes a method achieving a diversity of subsequences appearing in highly scored sequences.

We may score the generated sequences by using their output probabilities in RNN. However, this method is likely to give high scores to the sequences

© Springer International Publishing AG, part of Springer Nature 2018
Y. Shi et al. (Eds.): ICCS 2018, LNCS 10862, pp. 395–402, 2018.
https://doi.org/10.1007/978-3-319-93713-7_33

containing subsequences popular among the sequences used for training RNN. Consequently, the sequences of high score are doomed to look alike and to show only a limited diversity. In contrast, our scoring method uses latent Dirichlet allocation (LDA) [2]. Topic models like LDA can extract diverse topics from training documents. By using the per-topic word probabilities LDA provides, we can assign high scores to the sequences containing many words having a strong relevance to some particular topic. Our scoring method is expected to select the sequences individually being relevant to some particular topic and together being relevant to diverse topics. We performed an evaluation experiment by generating Japanese Tanka poems with RNN. After training RNN under different settings, we chose the best setting in terms of validation perplexity. We then generated random sequences by using RNN under the best setting. The generated sequences were scored by using their output probabilities in RNN or by using our LDA-based method. The results show that our LDA-based method could select more diverse sequences in the sense that a wider variety of subsequences were obtained as the parts of the top-ranked Tanka poems.

2 Method

2.1 Preprocessing of Tanka Poems

Sequence generation is one among the important applications of RNN [6,10]. This paper considers generation of Japanese Tanka poems. We assume that all Tanka poems for training RNN are given in Hiragana characters with no voicing marks. Tanka poems have a 5-7-5-7-7 syllabic structure and thus consist of five subsequences, which are called *parts* in this paper. Here we give an example of Tanka poem taken from *The Tale of Genji*: "mo no o mo hu ni/ta ti ma hu he ku mo/a ra nu mi no/so te u ti hu ri si/ko ko ro si ri ki ya." In this paper, we use *Kunrei-shiki* romanization for Hiraganas. While the first part of the standard syllabic structure consists of five syllables, that of this example consists of six. In this manner, a small deviation from the standard 5-7-5-7-7 structure is often observed. Our preprocessing addresses this kind of deviation.

First, we put a spacing character '_' between each neighboring pair of parts and also at the tail of the poem. Moreover, the first Hiragana character of each of the five parts is "uppercased," i.e., marked as distinct from the same character appearing at the other positions. The above example is then converted to: "MO no o mo hu ni _ TA ti ma hu he ku mo _ A ra nu mi no _ SO te u ti hu ri si _ KO ko ro si ri ki ya _." Second, we represent each Tanka poem as a sequence of *non-overlapping* character bigrams, which are regarded as vocabulary words composing each Tanka poem. However, only to the parts containing an even number of Hiragana characters, we apply an additional modification. The special bigram '(_ _)' is put at the tail of such parts in place of the spacing character '_'. Consequently, the non-overlapping bigram sequence corresponding to the above example is obtained as: "(MO no) (o mo) (hu ni) (_ _) (TA ti) (ma hu) (he ku) (mo _) (A ra) (nu mi) (no _) (SO te) (u ti) (hu ri) (si _) (KO ko) (ro si) (ri ki) (ya _)." Finally, we put a token of the special words 'BOS' and 'EOS' at the head and the tail of each sequence, respectively. The sequences preprocessed in this manner were used for training RNN and also for training LDA.

2.2 Tanka Poem Generation by RNN

We downloaded 179,225 Tanka poems from the web site of International Research Center for Japanese Studies.[1] 3,631 different non-overlapping bigrams were found to appear in this set. Therefore, the vocabulary size was 3,631. Among the 179,225 Tanka poems, 143,550 were used for training both RNN and LDA, and 35,675 were used for validation, i.e., for tuning free parameters. We implemented RNN with PyTorch[2] by using LSTM or GRU modules. RMSprop [11] was used for optimization with the learning rate 0.002. The mini-batch size was 200. The number of hidden layers was three. The dropout probability was 0.5. Based on an evaluation in terms of validation set perplexity, the hidden layer size was set to 600. Since the validation perplexity of GRU-RNN was slightly better than that of LSTM-RNN, GRU-RNN was used for generating Tanka poems.

2.3 LDA-Based Sequence Scoring

This paper proposes a new method of scoring the sequences generated by RNN. We use latent Dirichlet allocation (LDA) [2], the best-known topic model, for scoring. LDA is a Bayesian probabilistic model of documents and can model the difference in semantic contents of documents as the difference in mixing proportions of topics. Each topic is in turn modeled as a probability distribution defined over vocabulary words. We denote the number of documents, the vocabulary size, and the number of topics by D, V, and K, respectively. By performing an inference for LDA via variational Bayesian inference [2], collapsed Gibbs sampling (CGS) [7], etc., over training set, we can estimate the two groups of parameters: θ_{dk} and ϕ_{kv}, for $d = 1, \ldots, D$, $v = 1, \ldots, V$, and $k = 1, \ldots, K$. The parameter θ_{dk} is the probability of the topic k in the document d. Intuitively, θ_{dk} quantifies the importance of each topic in each document. The parameter ϕ_{kv} is the probability of the word v in the topic k. Intuitively, ϕ_{kv} quantifies the relevance of each vocabulary word to each topic. For example, in autumn, people talk about fallen leaves more often than about blooming flowers. Such topic relevancy of each vocabulary word is represented by ϕ_{kv}.

In our experiment, we regarded each Tanka poem as a document. The inference for LDA was performed by CGS, where we used the same set of Tanka poems as that used for training RNN. Therefore, $D = 143,550$ and $V = 3,631$ as given in Subsect. 2.2. K was set to 50, because other values gave no significant improvement. The Dirichlet hyperparameters of LDA were tuned by a grid search [1] based on validation set perplexity. Table 1 gives an example of the 20 top-ranked words in terms of ϕ_{kv} for three among $K = 50$ topics. Each row corresponds to a different topic. The three topics represent blooming flowers,

---

[1] http://tois.nichibun.ac.jp/database/html2/waka/menu.html.

[2] http://pytorch.org/.

autumn moon, and singing birds, respectively from top to bottom. For example, in the topic corresponding to the top row, the words "ha na" (flowers), "ha ru" (spring), "ni ho" (the first two Hiragana characters of the word "ni ho hi," which means fragrance), and "u me" (plum blossom) have large probabilities.

Table 1. An example of topic words obtained by CGS for LDA

(HA na) (ha na) (HA ru) (no _) (hi su) (U ku) (ni _) (YA ma) (hu _)
(sa to) (ru _) (NI ho) (U me) (ha ru) (ta ti) (HU ru) (SA ki) (U no)
(tu ki) (no _) (NA ka) (ni _) (TU ki) (A ka) (KU mo) (te _) (ka ke)
(wo _) (so ra) (ki yo) (ha _) (KA ke) (ka ri) (hi no) (yu ku) (KO yo)
(su _) (to ki) (HO to) (ko ye) (NA ki) (NA ku) (KO ye) (HI to) (ho to)
(ni _) (ni na) (su ka) (ku _) (MA tu) (HA tu) (ku ra) (MA ta) (ya ma)

Our sequence scoring uses the ϕ_{kv}'s, i.e., the per-topic word probabilities, learned by CGS for LDA. Based on the ϕ_{kv}'s learned from the training set, we can estimate the topic probabilities of unseen documents by *fold-in* [1]. In our case, bigram sequences generated by RNN are unseen documents. When the fold-in procedure estimates θ_{dk} for some k as far larger than $\theta_{dk'}$ for $k' \neq k$, we can say that the document d is exclusively related to the topic k. In this manner, LDA can be used to know if a given Tanka poem is exclusively related to some particular topic. By using the fold-in estimation of θ_{dk} for a Tanka poem generated by RNN, we compute the entropy $-\sum_{k=1}^{K} \theta_{dk} \log \theta_{dk}$, which is called *topic entropy* of the Tanka poem. Smaller topic entropies are regarded as better, because smaller ones correspond to the situations where the Tanka poems relate to some particular topic more exclusively. In other words, we would like to select the poems showing a topic consistency. Since LDA can extract a wide variety of topics, our scoring method is expected to select the sequences individually showing a topic consistency and together showing a topic diversity.

3   Evaluation

The evaluation experiment compared our scoring method to the method based on RNN output probabilities. The output probability in RNN can be obtained as follows. We generate a random sequence with RNN by starting from the special word 'BOS' and then randomly drawing words one by one until we draw the special word 'EOS.' The output probability of the generated sequence is the product of the output probabilities of all tokens, where the probability of each token is the output probability at each moment during the sequence generation. Our LDA-based scoring was compared to this probability-based scoring.

We first investigate the difference of the top-ranked Tanka poems obtained by the two compared scoring methods. Table 2 presents an example of the top five Tanka poems selected by our method in the left column and those selected based on RNN output probabilities in the right column. To obtain these top-ranked poems, we first generated 100,000 Tanka poems with the GRU-RNN. Since the number of poems containing grammatically incorrect parts was large, a grammar check was required. However, we could not find any good grammar check tool for archaic Japanese. Therefore, as an approximation, we regarded the poems containing at least one part appearing in no training Tanka poem as grammatically incorrect. After removing grammatically incorrect poems, we assigned to the remaining ones a score based on each method. Table 2 presents the resulting top five Tanka poems for each method.

Table 2. Top five Tanka poems selected by compared methods

(Rank)	Topic entropy	Output probability
1	si ku re yu ku	o ho a ra ki no
	ka tu ra ki ya ma no	mo ri no si ta ku sa
	i ro hu ka ki	ka mi na tu ki
	mo mi ti no i ro ni	mo ri no si ta ku sa
	si ku re hu ri ke ri	ku ti ni ke ru ka na
2	ti ha ya hu ru	hi sa ka ta no
	yu hu hi no ya ma no	ku mo wi ni mi yu ru
	ka mi na hi no	tu ki ka ke no
	mi mu ro no ya ma no	tu ki ka ke wa ta ru
	mo mi ti wo so mi ru	a ma no ka ku ya ma
3	ka he ru ya ma	ti ha ya hu ru
	hu mo to no mi ti ha	ka mo no ka ha na mi
	ki ri ko me te	ta ti ka he ri
	hu ka ku mo mu su hu	ki ru hi to mo na ki
	wo ti no ya ma ka se	a hu sa ka no se ki
4	o ho ka ta mo	ta ka sa ko no
	wa su ru ru ko to mo	wo no he no sa ku ra
	ka yo he to mo	sa ki ni ke ri
	o mo hu ko ko ro ni	mi ne no ma tu ya ma
	o mo hu ha ka ri so	yu ki hu ri ni ke ri
5	u ti na hi ku	ta ka sa ko no
	ko ro mo te sa mu ki	wo no he no sa ku ra
	o ku ya ma ni	na ka mu re ha
	u tu ro hi ni ke ri	a ri a ke no tu ki ni
	a ki no ha tu ka se	a ki ka se so hu ku

Table 2 shows that when we use RNN output probabilities (right column), it is difficult to achieve topic consistency. The fourth poem contains the words "sa ku ra" (cherry blossom) and "yu ki" (snow). The fifth one contains the words "sa ku ra" (cherry blossom) and "a ki ka se" (autumn wind). In this manner, the poems top-ranked based on RNN output probabilities sometimes contain the words expressing different seasons. This is prohibitive for Tanka composition. In contrast, the first poem selected by our method contains the words "si ku re" (drizzling rain) and "mo mi ti" (autumnal tints). Because drizzling rain is a shower observed in late autumn or in early winter, the word "mo mi ti" fits well within this context. In the third poem selected by our method, the words "ya ma" and "hu mo to" are observed. The former means mountain, and the latter means the foot of the mountain. This poem also shows a topic consistency. However, a slight weakness can be observed in the poems selected by our method. The same word is likely to be used twice or more. While refrains are often observed in Tanka poems, some future work may introduce an improvement here.

Table 3. Five most frequent parts observed in the top 200 Tanka poems

Topic entropy	Output probability
hi sa ka ta no (9)	a ri a ke no tu ki no (13)
ko ro mo te sa mu ki (8)	hi sa ka ta no (12)
a ri a ke no tu ki ni (8)	ta ka sa ko no (12)
ho to to ki su (7)	ho to to ki su (11)
a ri a ke no tu ki (6)	a si hi ki no (10)

We next investigate the diversity of selected Tanka poems. We picked up the 200 top-ranked poems given by each method and then split each poem into five parts to obtain 1,000 parts in total. Since the resulting set of 1,000 parts included duplicates, we grouped those parts by their identity and counted duplicates. Table 3 presents the five most frequent parts for each method. When we used RNN output probabilities (right column), "a ri a ke no tu ki no" appeared 13 times, "hi sa ka ta no" 12 times, and so on, among the 1,000 parts coming from the 200 top-ranked poems. In contrast, when we used our LDA-based scoring (left column), "hi sa ka ta no" appeared nine times, "ko ro mo te sa mu ki" eight times, and so on. That is, there were less duplicates for our method. Moreover, we also observed that while only 678 parts among 1,000 were unique when RNN output probabilities were used, 806 were unique when our method was used. It can be said that our method explored a larger diversity.

4   Previous Study

While there already exist many proposals of sequence generation using RNN, LDA is a key component in our method. Therefore, we focus on the proposals using topic modeling. Yan et al. [12] utilize LDA for Chinese poetry composition.

However, LDA is only used for obtaining word similarities, not for exploring topical diversity. The combination of topic modeling and RNN can be found in the proposals not related to automatic poetry composition. Dieng et al. [5] propose a combination of RNN and topic modeling. The model, called TopicRNN, modifies the output word probabilities of RNN by using long-range semantic information of documents captured by an LDA-like mechanism. However, when we generate random sequences with TopicRNN, we need to choose one document among the existing documents as a seed. This means that we can only generate sequences similar to the document chosen as a seed. While TopicRNN has this limitation, it provides a valuable guide for future work. Our method detaches sequence selection from sequence generation. It may be better to directly generate the sequences having some desirable property regarding their topical contents.

5 Conclusions

This paper proposed a method for scoring sequences generated by RNN. The proposed method was compared to the scoring using RNN output probabilities. The experiment showed that our method could select more diverse Tanka poems. In this paper, we only consider the method for obtaining better sequences by screening generated sequences. However, the same thing can also be achieved by modifying the architecture of RNN. As discussed in Sect. 4, Dieng et al. [5] incorporate an idea from topic modeling into the architecture of RNN. It is an interesting research direction to propose an architecture of RNN that can directly generate sequences diverse in topics. With respect to the evaluation, it is a possible research direction to apply evaluations using BLEU [9] or even human subjective evaluations for ensuring the reliability.

Acknowledgments. This work was supported by Grant-in-Aid for Scientific Research (B) 15H02789.

References

1. Asuncion, A., Welling, M., Smyth, P., Teh, Y.W.: On smoothing and inference for topic models. In: Proceedings of the Twenty-Fifth Conference on Uncertainty in Artificial Intelligence (UAI 2009), pp. 27–34 (2009)
2. Blei, D.M., Ng, A.Y., Jordan, M.I.: Latent dirichlet allocation. J. Mach. Learn. Res. **3**, 993–1022 (2003)
3. Cho, K., van Merrienboer, B., Bahdanau, D., Bengio, Y.: On the properties of neural machine translation: encoder-decoder approaches. arXiv preprint, arXiv:1409.1259 (2014)
4. Chung, J., Gulcehre, C., Cho, K., Bengio, Y.: Empirical evaluation of gated recurrent neural networks on sequence modeling. arXiv preprint, arXiv:1412.3555 (2014)
5. Dieng, A. B., Wang, C., Gao, J., Paisley, J.: TopicRNN: a recurrent neural network with long-range semantic dependency. arXiv preprint, arXiv:1611.01702 (2016)
6. Graves, A.: Generating sequences with recurrent neural networks. arXiv preprint, arXiv:1308.0850 (2013)

7. Griffiths, T.L., Steyvers, M.: Finding scientific topics. Proc. Natl. Acad. Sci. USA **101**(Suppl. 1), 5228–35 (2004)
8. Hochreiter, S., Schmidhuber, J.: Long short-term memory. Neural Comput. **9**(8), 1735–1780 (1997)
9. Papineni, K., Roukos, S., Ward, T., Zhu, W.-J.: BLEU: a method for automatic evaluation of machine translation. In: Proceedings of the 40th Annual Meeting on Association for Computational Linguistics (ACL 2002), pp. 311–318 (2002)
10. Sutskever, I., Martens, J., Hinton, G.: Generating text with recurrent neural networks. In: Proceedings of the 28th International Conference on Machine Learning (ICML 2011), pp. 1017–1024 (2011)
11. Tieleman, T., Hinton, G.: Lecture 6.5-RmsProp: divide the gradient by a running average of its recent magnitude. COURSERA Neural Netw. Mach. Learn. **4**, 26–31 (2012)
12. Yan, R., Jiang, H., Lapata, M., Lin, S.-D., Lv, X., Li, X.: I, poet: automatic chinese poetry composition through a generative summarization framework under constrained optimization. In: Proceedings of the 23rd International Joint Conference on Artificial Intelligence (IJCAI 2013), pp. 2197–2203 (2013)

Computing Simulation of Interactions Between $\alpha+\beta$ Protein and Janus Nanoparticle

Xinlu Guo[1,2](✉) ⓘ, Xiaofeng Zhao[1], Shuguang Fang[1], Yunqiang Bian[3], and Wenbin Kang[4]

[1] Jiangsu Research and Development Center of Application Engineering Technology of Wireless Sensor System and School of Internet of Things, Wuxi Vocational Institute of Commerce, Wuxi 214153, China
guoxinlu@wxic.edu.cn
[2] Taihu University of Wuxi, Wuxi 214000, China
[3] Shandong Provincial Key Laboratory of Biophysics, Institute of Biophysics, Dezhou University, Dezhou 253023, China
[4] Bio-X Research Center and Department of Mathmatics and Physics, Hubei University of Medicine, Shiyan 442000, China

Abstract. Janus nanoparticles have surfaces with two or more distinct physical properties, allowing different types of chemical properties to occur on the same particle and thus making possible many unique applications. It is necessary to investigate the interaction between proteins and Janus nanoparticles (NPs), which are two typical building blocks for making bio-nano-objects. Here we computed the phase diagrams for an $\alpha+\beta$ protein(GB1) and Janus NP using coarse-grained model and molecular dynamics simulations, and studied how the secondary structures of proteins, the binding interface and kinetics are affected by the nearby NP. Two phases were identified for the system. In the folded phase, the formation of β-sheets are always enhanced by the presence of NPs, while the formation of α-helices are not sensitive to NPs. The underlying mechanism of the phenomenon was attributed to the geometry and flexibility of the β-sheets. The knowledge gained in this study is useful for understanding the interactions between proteins and Janus NP which may facilitate designing new bio-nanomaterials or devices.

Keywords: Janus nanoparticles · Computing simulation
Protein secondary structure · Phase diagram

1 Introduction

Nanomaterials have attracted attentions from different branches of science and technology, such as physics, chemistry, biology and medicine. Nanomaterials are different from their bulk counterparts in that they have tiny size and high volume to surface ratio, which lead to special chemical, electrical, optical properties, high catalyst efficiencies, and some other intriguing features [1–3]. Of the

© Springer International Publishing AG, part of Springer Nature 2018
Y. Shi et al. (Eds.): ICCS 2018, LNCS 10862, pp. 403–415, 2018.
https://doi.org/10.1007/978-3-319-93713-7_34

same importance and interest are the bio-materials formed of such as polymers, peptides, proteins, or nucleic acids. Biomaterials are easy to be designed at molecular level and able to self- or co-assemble into highly organized structures [2]. Nowadays, it has become a thriving research area to combine nanomaterials and biomaterials and make novel functional materials or tiny devices for drug delivery, bioimaging, sensing, diagnosing, or more speculatively, nanomachines and nanorobots [4–6]. Among all of the possible building blocks for such purposes, proteins represent excellent ones for they have sophisticated structures at nanoscale dimensions, rich chemistry and versatile enzymatic activities. Therefore, it is necessary to study how proteins interact with nanomaterials such as small nanoparticles (NPs).

Early studies of NPs are mainly concerned with the effects of the physical properties of NPs, such as size and shape, on the structure of protein [7–9]. For example, Shang et al. [8] studied the changes in the thermodynamic stability of the ribonuclease A when it adsorbed on the silicon NPs. The results show that the larger the size of the NPs, the greater the effect on the thermodynamic stability of the protein. Gagner et al. [9], studied the influence of protein structure by the shape of NPs when the protein adsorbed on gold NPs. The NPs used in the experiment were spherical gold NPs (diameter 10.6 ± 1 nm) and columnar gold NPs (bottom diameter 10.3 ± 2 nm), respectively, and the proteins were lysozyme and chymotrypsin. The results show that the concentration of protein molecules adsorbed on the surface of the columnar gold NPs is higher for the allogeneic protein. After that, the researchers found that the surface chemical properties of the NPs could produce a more abundant effect. For example, Rocha et al. [10] studied the effects of fluorinated NPs and hydrogenated NPs on the aggregation of $A\beta$ protein The results show that fluorinated NPs could induce the transformation of β-sheets to α-helix, thus inhibiting aggregation, while hydrogenated NPs could induce random curling to form β-sheets, thereby promoting the occurrence of aggregation.

With the development of research, it has been found that one NP with different surface characteristics can play a variety of functions and have wider application value [11–15]. Roh et al. [16] designed a Janus NP, which was synthesized by two different materials. Half of the material emitted green fluorescence after adding fluorescein isothiocyanate labeled dextran, and the other half of the material emitted red fluorescence after adding rhodamine B labeled dextran. The experimental results show that after the mixture of two different modal molecules and Janus NPs, half of the NPs emitted green fluorescence and half of them emitted red fluorescence, that is, the two molecules could combine with the surface of particles with different properties respectively. This indicates that Janus NPs can indeed carry different molecules, which can be applied to molecular detection or drug transport. Further experiments show that the surface of Janus NPs can be selectively modified by using the characteristics of the interaction between Janus NPs and different molecules, so as to design more kinds of NPs. Honegger et al. [17] synthesized gold NPs with polystyrene and silica respectively, and mixed the Janus NPs with proteins. The results show that different proteins can accurately adsorb on the surface of a specific material. This further illustrates the feasibility of the application of Janus NPs in the field of molecular detection.

Although a lot of work has been done to explore the synthesis and application of Janus NPs, the understanding on the effect of Janus NPs on the surrounding protein is still limited. There is still no systematic investigation on how they interact with each other exactly. Many interactions, such as the hydrophobic force, Coulomb force, hydrogen-bond, polarizability and lone-pair electrons, may contribute to the final result [18]. While in most experiments, which interaction is the most relevant factor governing a specific observation is usually not clear. Thus, a close collaboration between experimentalists and theorists is preferred [19–21]. In this work we study the adsorption process of a $\alpha+\beta$ protein on a spatially nearby Janus NP based on a coarse-grained model and molecular simulations. The coarse-grained model allows us to explore a large parameter space spanned by different surface chemical properties and NP sizes and different strengths of protein-NP interactions. In this way we are able to systematically examine the effect of NPs on proteins and seek whether there are any general principles. The conformational phase diagrams for protein-NP combination, the binding kinetics and the changes of protein structures on adsorption are investigated. The results are compared with experiments and the underlying mechanisms are then discussed.

2   Models and Methods

2.1   Models of the Proteins and Janus NP

An $\alpha+\beta$ protein GB1 (PDB ID: 3GB1) was studied to investigate how a protein is affected by the presence of a Janus NP in its proximity. The sequence length of the protein is 56, and the radius of gyration of its native tertiary structures is 1.04. The Janus NP that interacts with the proteins was treated as a rigid spherical bead with half surface hydrophobic and half surface hydrophilic.

To characterize the protein adsorption on NPs, we first define the contact between protein and NPs. A contact between residue i and NPs is deemed to be formed if the distance between the residue and the NP surface is less than $1.2d_0$, where coefficient 1.2 is used to reflect the thermal fluctuations, following the strategy in the literature [22]. We also define the fraction of NP surface covered by protein as $S = 1 - SASA/S_{NP}$, where S_{NP} is the surface area of the NP and SASA is its solvent accessible surface area that is not covered by protein, obtained by rolling a small probing bead with a radius of $1\overset{\circ}{A}$ on the NP surface.

The status of the interacting protein and the NP is denoted by a two-letter word, for example, AF, DF, AU and WU. The first letter describes the binding status of the protein on NP, which can be desorbed (D), adsorbed (A) or wrapped (W), corresponding to the parameter range $S < 0.1$, $0.1 < S < 0.8$, or $S > 0.8$, respectively. The second letter indicates the folding status of the protein C either the folded state (denoted as F, with $Q > 0.75$) or the unfolded state (denoted as U, with $Q < 0.75$). The value of 0.75 is deliberately chosen to be higher than that usually used to distinguish the folded and unfolded states, to take into account the fact that the biological function of proteins may be disrupted by a slight structure deformation. The exact values of the above parameters are adjustable to some extent; however, their changes within a range only slightly shift the conformational phase boundaries, not affecting the major conclusions drawn from the results.

To measure the magnitude of the changes of secondary structures of the protein under the influence of the NP, the relative fraction of secondary structure is calculated by normalizing the number of contacts in the secondary structure when the NP is present with respect to the corresponding value when the NP is not, with the other conditions being the same. Therefore, a value smaller than 1 suggests a destabilized secondary structure, while a value larger than 1 suggests an enhanced one by the NPs.

2.2 Molecular Dynamics Simulations

The protein was modeled with an off-lattice C_α based Go-type model; the residues were represented as beads centered at their C_α positions and interacting with each other through bonds, angles, dihedral angles, and 12-10 Lennard-Jones interactions [22]. This protein model has been extensively used in studying protein folding and dynamics and has achieved enormous success [22–26].

The interactions between the protein residue i and NP were modeled by a Lennard-Jones potential,

$$V(r_i) = \varepsilon_3 \left[5 \left(\frac{d_0}{r_i - D/2} \right)^{12} - 6 \left(\frac{d_0}{r_i - D/2} \right)^{10} \right], \tag{1}$$

if both have the same hydrophobicities or

$$V(r_i) = \varepsilon_3 \left(\frac{d_0}{r_i - D/2} \right)^{12}, \tag{2}$$

if not, where $d_0 = 2\text{Å}$, $\varepsilon_2 = 1.0\varepsilon$ and $\varepsilon_3 = \varepsilon_{npp}\varepsilon$, which determines the interaction strength between residues and the NP. r_i is the distance between the ith residue and the center of the NP, and D is the diameter of the NP.

The native contacts within proteins were determined based on the PDB structures of the proteins. Specifically, a native contact between residues i and j ($|i - j| > 4$) is defined if any distance between the heavy atoms (non-hydrogen) of two residues is smaller than a cutoff of 5Å. In post processing the trajectories after the computations finished, a contact was deemed to be formed when any distance between heavy atoms is less than 1.2 times of its native value; this is to take account of the thermal fluctuations of the structures at finite temperatures. The fraction of the formed native contacts, denoted as Q, was used to measure the closeness of the structure to the native one and characterize the folding extents of the protein; its maximum value 1 indicates the structure is the same with the native one. The interplay between protein and NP was also characterized by their contacts, here a contact between protein and the NP was deemed to be formed if the distance between the center of the residue bead and the surface of the NP was less than $1.2d_0$.

In all simulations, the protein was constrained in a finite spherical space with a soft wall, the radius of the space is set to 5 nm. The NP was fixed at the center of this space.

Molecular dynamics (MD) was employed to evolve the system. The equation of motion is described by a Langevin equation as follows [28].

$$m\ddot{x}(t) = F_c - \gamma\dot{x}(t) + \Gamma(t) \tag{3}$$

where m is the mass of the bead, $F_c = -\partial V/\partial x$ is the conformational force, γ is the friction coefficient, and Γ is the Gaussian random force, which is used to balance the energy dissipation caused by friction [28]. The random force satisfies the autocorrelation function

$$\langle \boldsymbol{\Gamma}(t)\boldsymbol{\Gamma}(t') \rangle = 2m\gamma k_B T\delta(t - t') \tag{4}$$

where k_B is the Boltzmann constant and T is the absolute temperature.

For each parameter combination, multiple long MD simulations ($>10^8$ MD steps) were carried out with each starting from different initial protein locations and at slightly different temperatures (around $0.9T_f$, where T_f is the folding temperature of the protein) to avoid possible kinetic trapping. Weighted histogram analysis method (WHAM) was used to combine these multiple trajectories and reweight them to $0.9T_f$ to calculate the thermodynamic properties [29–31].

3   Results and Discussion

3.1   Phase Diagram of $\alpha + \beta$ Protein and Janus NP

Figure 1 shows the conformational phase diagram for protein GB1 adsorbed on a Janus NP whose surface is half hydrophobic and half hydrophilic. Here the term phase diagram is borrowed from statistical physics to describe the different conformational status of the protein-NP complex; it does not necessarily imply there is a change such as heat capacity associated with the phase transition. The conformation status (or phase) of the protein is simply divided into two categories, i.e. the folded and unfolded states, since only the general effects of NPs on proteins are of interest here. There are only two phases that can be identified in the diagram which are DF and AU. According to the diagram, if both the values of interaction strength ε_{npp} between protein and NP and the diameter D of NP are small ($\varepsilon_{npp} < 7$ and $D/D_0 < 0.43$), the protein is dissociated from NP and keeps folded (the DF region). On the contrary, if both the values of ε_{npp} and D are large enough ($\varepsilon_{npp} > 7.5$ and $D/D_0 > 0.48$), the protein is adsorbed on the NP without keeping its native structure (the AU region). Different from our previous work [32], the fact that the phase diagram has only two regions results from the effects of both hydrophobic and hydrophilic sides of the NP. On one hand, the hydrophobic surface may lead to the unfolding of the protein by attacking its hydrophobic core. On the other hand, the hydrophilic surface makes the protein spread around the NP surface, which also unfolds the protein. As a result, once the protein is adsorbed on the surface of the nanoparticles, it is strongly driven to unfold. An example can be seen in AU region in Fig. 2. The structure indicates that hydrophobic residues are more likely to be adsorbed by hydrophobic surface, while the hydrophilic residues are more likely to be adsorbed by hydrophilic surface. However, because of the hydrophobicity of sequence, some hydrophobic residues are adsorbed by hydrophilic surface and some hydrophilic residues are adsorbed by hydrophobic surface. This leads to the twist of the protein and the protein is in a loose bound to the NP. Thus, the binding of protein and Janus NP is always accompanied with the unfolding of protein.

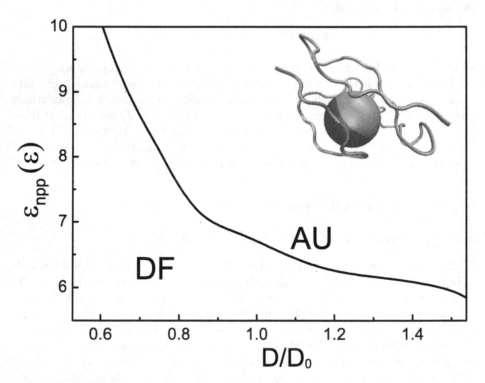

Fig. 1. Phase diagram for the adsorption and folding status of protein GB1 in close proximity to a Janus NP under different interaction strengthes (ε_{npp}) and NP diameters (D). The labels for the phases are explained in the Method section. The embedded structures provide direct pictures for the corresponding phases. The blue part of the protein chain in the structure indicates the hydrophobic residues, and the red part indicates the hydrophilic residues. The blue part of the nanoparticles represents the hydrophobic surface, and the red part represents the hydrophilic surface. (Color figure online)

The boundary of DF and AU regions are functions of both the interaction strength ε_{npp} and the diameter D. The larger ε_{npp} is, the smaller D is, and vice versa. This is due to the fact that the increase of interaction strength ε_{npp} leads to large interaction energy, meanwhile NP with large size has large surface energy [33], which may both result in the unfolding of the protein. Therefore, the two factors perform negative correlation at the boundary. The conformational phase diagram is different from our previous work where a protein adsorbed on NPs with a whole hydrophobic surface or a whole hydrophilic surface [32]. The former one has only two phases DF and AU, while the latter one has four phases DF, AF, AU and WU. The disappearance of the two phases AF and WU may due to the inconsistent distribution of the hydrophobic distribution of protein residues and the surface hydrophobicity of Janus NPs. This inconsistency makes the protein tend to unfold when it is adsorbed on the surface of Janus NPs.

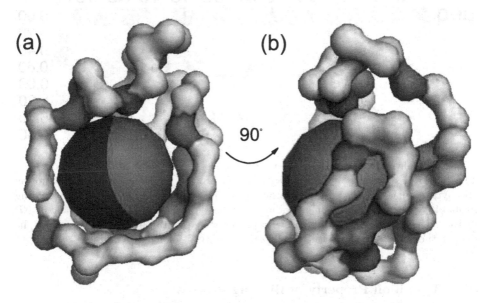

Fig. 2. The representative structure of GB1 of the largest cluster, plotted for AU phase. The structures are plotted from two view directions that are perpendicular to each other ((a) and (b)), with the parameters $\varepsilon_{npp} = 7\varepsilon$ and $D = 8\text{Å}$. The hydrophobic residues are in red and the hydrophilic residues in green. The hydrophobic surface of Janus NP is in blue and the hydrophilic surface in red. (Color figure online)

3.2 Binding Probability of Protein Residues on NP Surface

To further verify the above arguments, we calculated the binding probability of each residue upon the NP surface. As can be seen in Fig. 3, hydrophobic residues 5–7 incline to bind with the hydrophobic surface of the NP, while the residues 8–11 next to them are all hydrophilic ones and tend to bind with the hydrophilic half of the NP. Therefore, the structure is twisted to fit for the hydrophobicity.

Similarly, the residues 31–42 have high probability to bind with the hydrophilic surface, since most of them are hydrophilic residues, while residues 30, 33 and 39 around them are hydrophobic ones and have high probability to bind with the hydrophobic surface. Therefore, the structure of this sequence has also been distorted. Besides, the overall binding probability of each residue is less than 0.6, which is much lower than the binding probability of protein adsorbed on NPs with a whole hydrophobic/hydrophilic surface (the maximum value reaches over 0.9 [32]). This suggests that the protein is loosely bound to the Janus NP, which can also be verified by the structures in Fig. 2. The loosely binding may also result from the disturbing of protein structure caused by the mismatch of hydrophobicity distributions between protein residues and the Janus NP.

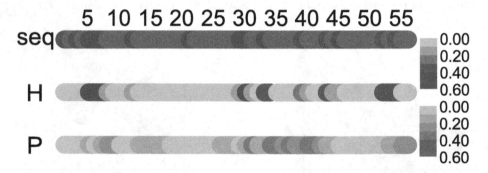

Fig. 3. The hydrophobicities of the residues and their binding probabilities on NPs. The first rod shows the hydrophobicity of the protein sequence, with blue denoting the hydrophobic residues and red otherwise. The second rod represents the binding probability of the corresponding residues and the hydrophobic surface of the Janus NP in the AU region, while the third one represents that of the hydrophilic surface. The deeper the color, the higher the binding probability. (Color figure online)

3.3   Transition Property of Binding Process

To gain further insights into the phase transition process, we calculated how the protein structure and the protein-NP contacting area S change from one phase to another at the phase boundary, as shown in Fig. 4; also shown are the typical trajectories collected at the corresponding phase boundary. In general, for a NP of fixed size (Fig. 4(a) and (b)), the Q value decreases and S increases when ε_{npp} is enlarged. This reflects the coupled adsorption and unfolding of the protein, which is consistent with the experiments that large contact areas decrease thermodynamic stabilities [8, 27]. Whereas, for a fixed interaction strength (Fig. 4(c) and (d)), the Q value gradually decreases with the increase of D, while the S value first increases and then decreases slightly after D is larger than a threshold, which is around 8Å, almost the size of hydrophobic core of the protein. The transition caused by increasing D is also a cooperativity between unfolding and binding. In the DF region, although the protein is dissociated from the NP, the structure is still affected by the NP and the protein starts to spread on the NP, since they are very close to each other. The size of NP is smaller than the protein's hydrophobic core, therefore, it cannot lead to significant structure change. In the AU region, the size of NP becomes larger than the hydrophobic core, and it makes the protein unfold with the bias to buring inside the protein. The decrease of relative contact area S value is due to that the surface area of NP increases significantly, while the contact area changes little since the protein is loosely bound to the NP, then the ratio decreases.

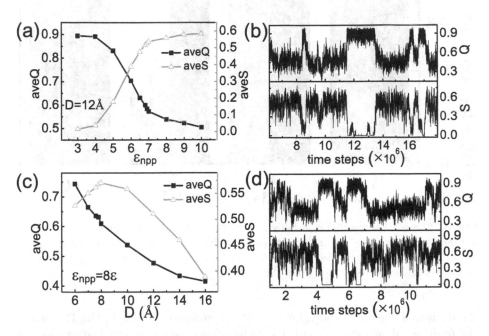

Fig. 4. The coupled adsorption and unfolding of the protein as a function of the proteinCNP interaction strength ε_{npp} on crossing the phase boundary. Black curves with solid squares give the protein nativeness Q, and blue curves with open triangles show the fraction of NP surface covered by protein S. On the right side, typical trajectories collected right at the phase boundaries are shown. The parameters $(\varepsilon_{npp}, D/D_0)$ used to calculate the trajectories are (7, 0.58) and (8, 0.38) for (b) and (d), respectively. (Color figure online)

3.4 Secondary Structures Affected by Janus NP

The presence of a nearby NP has different effects on different secondary structures of proteins. Figure 5 shows the fraction of secondary structures in each phase with respect to their values without the NP. The values are averaged over an equally spaced grid in the corresponding phase to reflect the general feature. If the value is smaller than 1, it indicates that the secondary structure is destabilized. If the value is larger than 1, it suggests that the secondary structure is

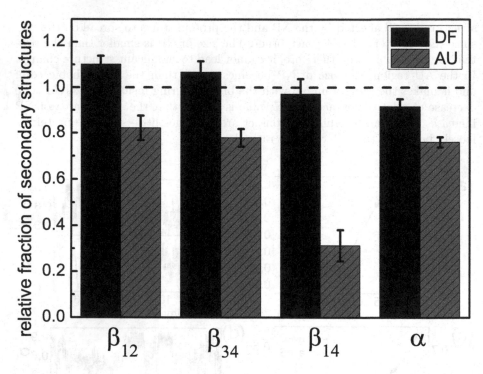

Fig. 5. The relative fraction of α-helix and β-sheets of protein GB1 when adsorbed on a Janus NP, normalised against their corresponding values obtained in simulations at the same conditions but without the NP. Error bars are shown as vertical line segments at the top of the histograms. (Color figure online)

strengthened due to the presence of NP. According to Fig. 5, in the DF phase, the fractions of hairpins β_{12} and β_{34} are increased compared with the fractions in the native structure, while the fraction of hairpin β_{14} is not sensitive to the presence of NP, as can be seen from the near-unity value. According to our previous study the instability of β-hairpin is not resulted from crowding effect [32]. In the DF region, the protein keeps folded and close to the NP. It seldom departs away from the NP, and the stability of hairpin structure is little affected by the space effect. The fraction of α-helix decreases slightly, indicating the decrease of helical structure. In the DF phase, although the protein is not adsorbed on the NP, it is still weakly attached to the NP, and hence the protein is still under the influence of the NP. The enhancement of β-structures can be tentatively attributed to its geometry properties. β-hairpin is composed of inter-strand long-order hydrogen bonds, which makes it more flexible and tolerable to the curvature of the NP. The α-helix is composed of inner-strand hydrogen bonds, which makes it more rigid and is easy to unfold when binding to NP. The above observations are consistent with the previous experiments that suggested that upon adsorption the protein underwent a change of secondary structure with a decrease of α-helices and a possible increase of β-sheet structures [33,34].

4   Conclusion

In summary, we studied how a $\alpha+\beta$ protein would be affected by a nearby Janus NP with half hydrophobic surface and half hydrophilic surface using a structure-based coarse-grained model and molecular simulations. While most previous experimental and theoretical studies have focused on NPs of size of several 10 or 100 nm, our study is interested in ultra-small NPs less than several nanometres. According to our simulation results, the conformational phase diagrams show two phases, including DF and AU. The exact phase where the protein-NP system belongs to is dependent on the protein-NP interaction strength ε_{npp} and the NP size. In general, large NPs and strong interaction strengths denature proteins to large extents, consistent with previous theoretical and experimental studies. Our simulations also show that the NP exerts different effects on different secondary structures of the protein. Although in the unfolded phases both α- and β-structures are destabilised, the β-structures are often enhanced in the folded phases and this enhancement is irrelevant to the hydrophobicity of the NP, the spatial organising pattern of the hydrophobic/hydrophilic residues or the crowding effect. This enhancement is tentatively attributed to the geometry and flexibility of the β-structures. The results may be useful for understanding the interaction of proteins with ultra-small NPs, particularly the fullerene derivatives and carbon nanotubes, considering the sizes of the NPs studied here. Our study illustrated all the possible structures of protein and Janus NP, and revealed the physical mechanism of the influence of NPs on secondary structures. This provides a deeper understanding of protein-NP system and is useful for the design of new materials.

The interactions between proteins and NPs are in fact very complex; in addition to the physical parameters considered in this work, they are also dependent on the protein and NP concentration, surface modifications of the NP, temperature, pH-value, denaturants in solvent, and etc. Further studies are ongoing in our group and they may deepen our understanding on such a system in different environments and facilitate designing new bio-nano-materials or devices.

Acknowledgements. This work was supported by Natural science fund for colleges and universities in Jiangsu Province (No. 16KJB140014, 16KJB180007, 17KJD510006), NSFC (No. 11504043), Scientific fund (No: 201710929002, 2011QDZR-11).

References

1. Mahmoudi, M., Lynch, I., Ejtehadi, M.R., et al.: Protein-nanoparticle interactions: opportunities and challenges. Chem. Rev. **111**, 5610–5637 (2011)
2. Sarikaya, M., Tamerler, C., Jen, A.K.Y., Schulten, K., Baneyx, F.: Molecular biomimetics: nanotechnology through biology. Nat. Mater. **2**, 577–585 (2003)
3. Guo, X., Zhang, J., Wang, W.: The interactions between nanomaterials and biomolecules and the microstructural features. Prog. Phys. **32**, 285–293 (2012)
4. Howes, P.D., Chandrawati, R., Stevens, M.M.: Bionanotechnology. Colloidal nanoparticles as advanced biological sensors. Science **346**, 1247390 (2014)

5. Nair, R.R., Wu, H.A., Jayaram, P.N., Grigorieva, I.V., Geim, A.K.: Unimpeded permeation of water through helium-leak-tight graphene-based membranes. Science **335**, 442 (2012)

6. Peng, Q., Mu, H.: The potential of protein-nanomaterial interaction for advanced drug delivery. J. Controlled Release Off. **225**, 121 (2016)

7. Simunovic, M., Evergren, E., Golushko, I., Prvost, C., Renard, H.F., Johannes, L., et al.: How curvature-generating proteins build scaffolds on membrane nanotubes. Proc. Natl. Acad. Sci. USA **113**, 11226 (2016)

8. Shang, W., Nuffer, J.H., Dordick, J.S., Siegel, R.W.: Unfolding of ribonuclease A on silica nanoparticle surfaces. Nano Lett. **7**, 1991–1995 (2007)

9. Gagner, J.E., Lopez, M.D., Dordick, J.S., Siegel, R.W.: Effect of gold nanoparticle morphology on adsorbed protein structure and function. Biomaterials **32**, 7241–7252 (2011)

10. Rocha, S., Thnemann, A.F., Pereira, M.C., et al.: Influence of fluorinated and hydrogenated nanoparticles on the structure and fibrillogenesis of amyloid beta-peptide. Biophys Chem. **137**, 35–42 (2008)

11. Duong, H.T.T., Nguyen, D., Neto, C., Hawkett, B.S.: Synthesis and Applications of Polymeric Janus Nanoparticles: Synthesis, Self-Assembly, and Applications (2017)

12. Kobayashi, Y., Arai, N.: Self-assembly and viscosity behavior of Janus nanoparticles in nanotube flow. Langmuir **33**, 736 (2017)

13. Lee, K., Yu, Y.: Janus nanoparticles for T cell activation: clustering ligands to enhance stimulation. J. Mater. Chem. B Mater. Biol. Med. **5**, 4410–4415 (2017)

14. Li, F., Josephson, D.P., Stein, A.: Colloidal assembly: the road from particles to colloidal molecules and crystals. Angew. Chem. Int. Ed. **50**, 360–388 (2011)

15. Yoshida, M., Roh, K.-H., Mandal, S., Bhaskar, S., Lim, D., Nandivada, H., et al.: Structurally controlled bio-hybrid materials based on unidirectional association of anisotropic microparticles with human endothelial cells. Adv. Mater. **21**, 4920–4925 (2009)

16. Roh, K.H., Martin, D.C., Lahann, J.: Biphasic Janus particles with nanoscale anisotropy. Nat. Mater. **4**, 759–763 (2005)

17. Honegger, T., Sarla, S., Lecarme, O., Berton, K., Nicolas, A., Peyrade, D.: Selective grafting of proteins on Janus particles: adsorption and covalent coupling strategies. Microelectron. Eng. **88**, 1852–1855 (2011)

18. Xia, X.R., MonteiroRiviere, N.A., Riviere, J.E.: An index for characterization of nanomaterials in biological systems. Nat. Nanotechnol. **5**, 671 (2010)

19. Nie, K., Wu, W.P., Zhang, X.L., Yang, S.M.: Molecular dynamics study on the grain size, temperature, and stress dependence of creep behavior in nanocrystalline nickel. J. Mat. Sci. **52**, 2180–2191 (2017)

20. Vilhena, J.G., Rubio-Pereda, P., Vellosillo, P., Serena, P.A., Prez, R.: Albumin (BSA) adsorption over graphene in aqueous environment: influence of orientation, adsorption protocol, and solvent treatment. Langmuir **32**, 1742 (2016)

21. Kharazian, B., Hadipour, N.L., Ejtehadi, M.R.: Understanding the nanoparticle-protein corona complexes using computational and experimental methods. Int. J. Biochem. Cell Biol. **75**, 162 (2016)

22. Clementi, C., Nymeyer, H., Onuchic, J.N.: Topological and energetic factors: what determines the structural details of the transition state ensemble and "en-route" intermediates for protein folding? an investigation for small globular proteins. J. Mol. Biol. **298**, 937 (2000)

23. Koga, N., Takada, S.: Roles of native topology and chain-length scaling in protein folding: a simulation study with a Go-like model. J. Mol. Biol. **313**, 171–180 (2001)

24. Chan, H.S., Zhang, Z., Wallin, S., Liu, Z.: Cooperativity, local-nonlocal coupling, and nonnative interactions: principles of protein folding from coarse-grained models. Annu. Rev. Phys. Chem. **62**, 301–326 (2011)
25. Wang, W., Xu, W.X., Levy, Y., et al.: Confinement effects on the kinetics and thermodynamics of protein dimerization. Proc. Natl. Acad. Sci. USA **106**, 5517–5522 (2009)
26. Guo, X., Zhang, J., Chang, L., Wang, J., Wang, W.: Effectiveness of Phi-value analysis in the binding process of Arc repressor dimer. Phys. Rev. E **84**, 011909 (2011)
27. Shang, W., Nuffer, J.H., et al.: Cytochrome C on silica nanoparticles: influence of nanoparticle size on protein structure, stability, and activity. Small **5**, 470–476 (2009)
28. Veitshans, T., Klimov, D., Thirumalai, D.: Protein folding kinetics: timescales, pathways and energy landscapes in terms of sequence-dependent properties. Fold Des. **2**, 1–22 (1997)
29. Ferrenberg, A.M., Swendsen, R.H.: New Monte Carlo technique for studying phase transitions. Phys. Rev. Lett. **61**, 2635 (1988)
30. Ferrenberg, A.M., Swendsen, R.H.: Optimized Monte Carlo data analysis. Phys. Rev. Lett. **63**, 1195 (1989)
31. Kumar, S., Rosenberg, J.M., Bouzida, D., Swendsen, R.H., Kollman, P.A.: The weighted histogram analysis method for free-energy calculations on biomolecules. I. The method. J. Comput. Chem. **13**, 1011–1021 (1992)
32. Guo, X., Wang, J., Zhang, J., Wang, W.: Conformational phase diagram for proteins absorbed on ultra-small nanoparticles studied by a structure-based coarse-grained model. Mol. Simul. **41**, 1200–1211 (2015)
33. Vertegel, A.A., Siegel, R.W., Dordick, J.S.: Silica nanoparticle size influences the structure and enzymatic activity of adsorbed lysozyme. Langmuir **20**, 6800–6807 (2004)
34. Shang, L., Wang, Y., Jiang, J., Dong, S.: pH-dependent protein conformational changes in albumin: gold nanoparticle bioconjugates: a spectroscopic study. Langmuir **23**, 2714–2721 (2007)

A Modified Bandwidth Reduction Heuristic Based on the WBRA and George-Liu Algorithm

Sanderson L. Gonzaga de Oliveira[1(✉)], Guilherme O. Chagas[1],
Diogo T. Robaina[2], Diego N. Brandão[3], and Mauricio Kischinhevsky[2]

[1] Universidade Federal de Lavras, Lavras, Minas Gerais, Brazil
`sanderson@dcc.ufla.br`, `guilherme.chagas@computacao.ufla.br`
[2] Universidade Federal Fluminense, Niterói, Rio de Janeiro, Brazil
`{drobaina,kisch}@ic.uff.br`
[3] CEFET-RJ, Nova Iguaçu, Rio de Janeiro, Brazil
`diego.brandao@eic.cefet-rj.br`

Abstract. This paper presents a modified heuristic based on the Wonder Bandwidth Reduction Algorithm with starting vertex given by the George-Liu algorithm. The results are obtained on a dataset of instances taken from the SuiteSparse matrix collection when solving linear systems using the zero-fill incomplete Cholesky-preconditioned conjugate gradient method. The numerical results show that the improved vertex labeling heuristic compares very favorably in terms of efficiency and performance with the well-known GPS algorithm for bandwidth and profile reductions.

1 Introduction

An undirected sparse graph is often used to represent a sparse symmetric matrix A. As a result, such matrices play an important role in graph theory. In order to improve cache hit rates, one can reduce processing times when using the conjugate gradient method by finding an adequate ordering to the vertices of the corresponding graph that represents the matrix A. This reduction in execution times is possible because program code and data have spatial and temporal locality. To provide more specific detail, row and column permutations of A can be obtained by reordering the vertices of the corresponding graph. A heuristic for bandwidth reduction returns an adequate ordering of graph vertices. Consequently, a heuristic for bandwidth reduction provides adequate memory location and cache coherency. Then, the use of vertex reordering algorithms is a powerful technique for reducing execution costs of linear system solvers. Thus, the computational cost of the preconditioned conjugate gradient method (i.e., the linear system solver studied here) can be reduced using appropriately the current architecture of memory hierarchy and paging policies. Hence, much attention has been given recently to the bandwidth and profile reduction problems (see [1,2,9] for discussions and lists of references). This paper considers heuristics for preprocessing matrices to reduce the running time for solving linear systems on them. Specifically, we consider the ordering of symmetric sparse positive definite matrices for small bandwidth and profile. Let $G = (V, E)$ be a connected undirected graph, where V and E are sets of vertices and edges, respectively. The bandwidth of G for a vertex labeling $S = \{s(v_1), s(v_2), \cdots, s(v_{|V|})\}$ (i.e., a bijective mapping from V to the set $\{1, 2, \cdots, |V|\}$) is defined as $\beta(G) = \max_{\{v,u\} \in E} [\|s(v) - s(u)\|]$, where $s(v)$ and $s(u)$ are labels of vertices v and u, respectively. The profile is defined as $profile(G) = \sum_{v \in V} \max_{\{v,u\} \in E} [\|s(v) - s(u)\|]$. Let $A = [a_{ij}]$ be an $n \times n$ symmetric matrix associated with a connected undirected graph $G = (V, E)$. Equivalently, the bandwidth of row i of matrix A is given by $\beta_i(A) = i - \min_{1 \leq j \leq i} [j : a_{ij} \neq 0]$, noting that a_{ij} represents the left-most non-null coefficient (i.e., in column j) in row i in matrix A. Thus, the bandwidth of a matrix A is defined as $\beta(A) = \max_{1 \leq i \leq n} [\beta_i(A)]$. The profile of a matrix A is defined as $profile(A) = \sum_{i=1}^{n} \beta_i(A)$. The bandwidth and profile minimization problems are NP-hard [10,11]. Since these problems have connections with a wide number of important applications in science and engineering, efforts should be continued to develop low-cost heuristics that are capable of producing good-quality approximate solutions. Thus, this paper gives an improved heuristic for bandwidth reduction, and our main objective here is to accelerate a preconditioned conjugate gradient method. A systematic review [9] reported the Wonder Bandwidth Reduction Algorithm (WBRA) [4] as a promising heuristic for bandwidth reduction. This present paper proposes a variant of this algorithm to provide a heuristic for bandwidth reductions with lower execution times and smaller memory requirements than the original algorithm. To be more precise, the purpose of this paper is to propose a modified WBRA with starting vertex given by the George-Liu algorithm [5]. Thereby, this paper consists of improving the Wonder Bandwidth Reduction Algorithm (WBRA) [4] for bandwidth reduction aiming at accelerating the zero-fill incomplete Cholesky-preconditioned conjugate gradient (ICCG) method.

This present work evaluates experimentally the results of the modified WBRA against the GPS algorithm [6] aiming at reducing the execution costs of the ICCG method in sequential runs applied to instances arising from real-world applications. The remainder of this paper is organized as follows. Section 2 presents the improved heuristic proposed in this work. Section 3 shows numerical experiments that compares the modified heuristic for bandwidth reduction with the original WBRA [4] and GPS ordering [6]. Finally, Sect. 4 addresses the conclusions.

2 An Improved Vertex Labeling Heuristic

Heuristics for bandwidth reduction should execute at low processing times because the main objective of bandwidth reduction is to reduce computational costs when solving linear systems [1,2]. The WBRA obtained promising bandwidth reductions in the experiments presented by Esposito *et al.* [4]. In particular, it achieved better bandwidth results than the GPS algorithm [6]. Nevertheless, in our exploratory investigations, the WBRA reached high computational times and large memory requirements. This occurs because, depending on the instance, many initial vertices may be chosen in its first step and, consequently, various structures are stored and several reordering processes are performed. Sections 2.1 and 2.2 describe the WBRA and the improved WBRA heuristic, respectively.

2.1 The WBRA

The WBRA [4] is based on graph-theoretical concepts. Let $G = (V, E)$ be a connected, simple, and undirected graph, where V and E are sets of vertices and edges, respectively. Given a vertex $v \in V$, the level structure rooted at v, with depth $\ell(v)$ (or the eccentricity of v), is a partitioning $\mathscr{L}(v) = \{L_0(v), L_1(v), \ldots, L_{\ell(v)}(v)\}$, where $L_0(v) = \{v\}$, $L_i(v) = Adj(L_{i-1}(v)) - \bigcup_{j=0}^{i-1} L_j(v)$, for $i = 1, 2, 3, \ldots, \ell(v)$ and $Adj(U) = \{w \in V : (u \in U \subseteq V) \{u, w\} \in E\}$. The width of a rooted level structure is defined as $b(\mathscr{L}(v)) = \max_{0 \leq i \leq \ell(v)} [|L_i(v)|]$. The WBRA presents two main steps. In the first step, the WBRA builds level structures rooted at each vertex of the graph, i.e., $|V|$ rooted level structures are built. Then, it reduces the width of each rooted level structure generated using a heuristic named Push_Up [4]. This process is performed level by level of a level structure, considering the bottleneck linear assignment problem. It is performed by moving some vertices from a level with a large number of vertices to adjacent levels of the level structure, satisfying the condition that, for each edge $\{v, u\} \in E$, the vertices v and u belong to the same level of the level structure or belong to adjacent levels. This can convert a rooted level structure in a level structure $\mathscr{K}(\nu, \cdots)$ that is not rooted at a specific vertex. After reducing the width of each level structure, each level structure $\mathscr{K}(\nu, \cdots)$ with width $b(\mathscr{K}(\nu, \cdots))$ smaller than the original bandwidth $\beta(A)$ [i.e., $(\nu \in V)$ $b(\mathscr{K}(\nu, \cdots)) < \beta(A)$] is stored in a priority queue organized in ascending order of width $b(\mathscr{K}(\nu, \cdots))$. Hence, in the worst case from the point of view of memory usage, the WBRA takes $O(|V|^2)$ since it can store $|V|$ level structures and a level structure grows in $\Theta(|V|)$ memory.

In its second step, the WBRA labels the vertices of the graph. In the reordering procedure, the WBRA labels the vertices of each level structure stored in the priority queue. The WBRA removes a level structure $\mathscr{K}(\nu, \cdots)$ from the priority queue and sorts the vertices of each level of the level structure in ascending-degree order. The labeling procedure reduces the bandwidths of submatrices generated by labeling the vertices of each level of the level structure. Finally, this algorithm returns the labeling with the smallest bandwidth found. Therefore, the WBRA [4] shows high computational costs because it builds a level structure rooted at each vertex of a graph and these structures are rearranged based on a bottleneck linear assignment. This strategy makes the whole procedure costly in both time and space. Thus, the WBRA for bandwidth reduction of symmetric matrices did not show competitive results in our exploratory investigations when compared with other heuristics, such as the GPS algorithm [6], when aiming at reducing the computational costs of a linear system solver applied to large instances.

2.2 An Improved Heuristic for Bandwidth Reduction

This paper proposes a modification in the first step of WBRA [4] aiming at obtaining a low-cost heuristic. The improved heuristic proposed here consists of computing only one level structure used by WBRA rooted at a carefully chosen vertex given by the George-Liu algorithm [5] instead of building level structures rooted at each vertex (i.e., $|V|$ rooted level structures) as it is performed in the original WBRA [4]. We will refer this new algorithm as ECMT-GL heuristic. The main difference between the WBRA and ECMT-GL heuristic is in their first steps.

Given a rooted level structure $\mathscr{L}(v)$, the Push-Up heuristic is also applied in the ECMT-GL heuristic to reduce the width $b(\mathscr{L}(v))$, resulting in a level structure $\mathscr{K}(\nu, \cdots)$. Then, only $\mathscr{K}(\nu, \cdots)$ is stored and no priority queue is used. Consequently, the ECMT-GL heuristic grows in $\Theta(|V|)$ memory. Subsequently, similar steps of the WBRA are performed in the ECMT-GL heuristic, with the difference that the labeling procedure is performed using only a single level structure $\mathscr{K}(\nu, \cdots)$, resulting in a low-cost heuristic for bandwidth reduction.

The original WBRA cannot have the same storage requirements than the ECMT-GL heuristic. As described, the original WBRA builds a level structure rooted at each vertex contained in V (then $|V|$ rooted level structures are built) and stores in a priority queue those rooted level structures with width smaller than the original bandwidth $\beta(A)$, which gives the memory requirements of the algorithm. After removing a level structure from the priority queue, the original WBRA labels the vertices and stores only the current level structure that provides the smallest bandwidth found. To have a memory usage of one level structure, the original WBRA would have to label the vertices according to all $|V|$ rooted level structures (instead of labeling the vertices of rooted level structures stored in the priority queue), resulting in an algorithm extremely expensive. Therefore, the variant of the WBRA proposed here improves the original algorithm in terms of processing and storage costs. Esposito *et al.* [4] performed experiments with instances up to 2,000 vertices. Moreover, the authors provided no storage cost analysis of the heuristic. Our exploratory investigations showed that the WBRA presents large memory requirements so that the WBRA is impractical to be applied even to an instance composed of appropriately 20,000 unknowns (what also depends on the number of non-null coefficients of the instance). Thus, our modification in the WBRA increases its efficiency and performance.

3 Results and Analysis

This section presents the results obtained in simulations using the ICCG method, computed after executing heuristics for vertex labeling. Thus, the results of the improved heuristic proposed in this paper are compared with the results from the use of the GPS algorithm [6].

The WBRA [4], GPS [6], and ECMT-GL heuristics were implemented using the C++ programming language. In particular, the g++ version 4.8.2 compiler was used. Additionally, a data structure based on the Compress Row Storage, Compress Column Storage, and Skyline Storage Scheme data structures was used within the implementation of the ICCG method.

The experiments were performed on an Intel® Core™ i7-2670QM CPU @ 2.20 GHz (6 MB cache, 8 GB of main memory DDR3 1333 MHz) (Intel; Santa Clara, CA, United States) workstation. The Ubuntu 16.04.3 LTS 64-bit operating system was used and the Linux kernel-version 4.4.0-97-generic is installed in this workstation. Three sequential runs, with both a reordering algorithm and with the preconditioned conjugate gradient method, were performed for each instance. A precision of 10^{-16} to the CG method using double-precision floating-point arithmetic was employed in all experiments. Table 1 shows the name and number of non-null matrix coefficients, the dimension n (or the number of unknowns) of the respective coefficient matrix of the linear system (or the number of vertices of the graph associated with the coefficient matrix), the name of the heuristic for bandwidth reduction applied, the results with respect to bandwidth and *profile* reductions, the results of the heuristics in relation to the execution costs [t(s)], in seconds (s), when applied to nine real symmetric positive definite matrices taken from the SuiteSparse matrix (SSM) collection [3]. Moreover, column % in this table shows the percentage (rounded to the nearest integer) of the execution time of the heuristics for bandwidth reduction in relation to the overall execution time of the simulation. In addition, the same table shows the number of iterations and the total running time, in seconds, of the ICCG method applied to the linear systems. The first rows in each instance in Table 1 show "—". This means that no reordering heuristic was used in these simulations. This makes it possible to check whether the use of a heuristic for bandwidth and profile reductions decreases the execution times of the linear system solver. The last column in this table shows the speed-up/down of the ICCG method. Table 1 and Figs. 1(a)–(b) reveal that the execution and memory costs of the ECMT-GL heuristic is significantly lower than the computational cost of the WBRA (that was applied to the *LFAT5000* instance). In particular, the three heuristics evaluated here obtained the same bandwidth and profile results when applied to the *LFAT5000* instance. The executions with the WBRA applied to the *cvxbqp1*, *Pres_Poisson*, and *msc10848* instances were aborted because the high consumption of time and memory. Thus, Table 1 and Figs. 1(a)–(b) show that the new ECMT-GL heuristic outperforms the WBRA in terms of running time and memory consumption.

Even though the ECMT-GL heuristic reduces bandwidth and profile to a considerable extent, Table 1 and Fig. 2 also show that the GPS algorithm [6] obtained in general better bandwidth and profile results than the ECMT-GL heuristic. The ECMT-GL heuristic achieved better bandwidth (profile) results than the GPS algorithm [6] when applied to the *cant* (*cvxbqp1*, *cant*) instance. In particular, the GPS ordering [6] increased the bandwidth and profile of the

Table 1. Results of solutions of nine linear systems (ranging from 79,966 to 4,444,880 non-null coefficients ($|E|$)) contained in the SuiteSparse matrix collection [3] using the ICCG method and vertices labeled by the GPS [6] and ECMT-GL heuristics.

Instance	$|E|$	n	Heuristic	β	Profile	t(s)	%	ICCG:iter	ICCG:t(s)	Speedup
LFAT 5000	79966	19994	—	5	84958	—	—	19994	19	—
			ECMT-GL	3	34984	0.1	1	19994	18	1.04
			GPS	3	34984	2.9	14	19994	18	0.90
			WBRA	3	34984	65.7	74	19994	23	0.21
cvxbqp1	349968	50000	—	33333	819815962	—	—	50000	485	—
			ECMT-GL	2240	53110785	6.8	2	50000	280	1.69
			GPS	1690	53398841	12.8	4	50000	332	1.41
thermo mech_TK	711558	102158	—	102138	2667823445	—	—	11121	459	—
			ECMT-GL	364	18788072	2.8	1	9090	307	1.48
			GPS	270	18153270	125.6	31	9725	284	1.12
Pres_Poisson	715804	14822	—	12583	9789525	—	—	349	9	—
			ECMT-GL	614	3166017	0.7	9	233	7	1.09
			GPS	334	2916499	23.0	70	206	10	0.27
msc23052	1142686	23052	—	23046	183660755	—	—	23052	213	—
			ECMT-GL	1992	19046925	7.3	20	1	30	5.75
			GPS	1462	17122364	27.4	54	1	23	4.20
msc10848	1229776	10848	—	10706	50044035	—	—	10848	63	—
			ECMT-GL	1963	11833479	7.8	49	1	8	4.03
			GPS	1694	6826017	14.7	57	1	11	2.45
ct20stif	2600295	52329	—	49323	162549061	—	—	52329	1063	—
			ECMT-GL	4091	107413396	46.0	22	1	159	5.18
			GPS	3329	107013694	121.2	43	1	159	3.79
cant	4007383	62451	—	275	16778583	—	—	24	272	—
			ECMT-GL	275	16778583	0.3	0	1	254	1.07
			GPS	302	16976671	1018.9	79	1	265	0.21
thread	4444880	29736	—	29339	177235110	—	—	29736	835	—
			ECMT-GL	3804	51720915	42.5	28	1	110	5.49
			GPS	3521	45119385	387.3	75	1	132	1.61

cant instance. Table 1 also shows that in general the number of ICCGM iterations was the same when using the ECMT-GL heuristic and GPS algorithm [6]. The number of ICCGM iterations was smaller using the ECMT-GL (GPS [6]) heuristic than using the GPS (ECMT-GL) algorithm when applied to the *thermomech_TK* (*Pres_Poisson*) instance. Nevertheless, the most important issue in this context is to reduce the execution time of the ICCG method. Specifically, if high cache hit rates are achieved, a large number of CGM iterations can be executed faster than a smaller number of iterations with high cache miss rates. In this scenario, Table 1 [see column ICCG:t(s)] shows lower processing times of the ICCG method in simulations in conjunction with the GPS algorithm [6] than in conjunction with the ECMT-GL heuristic only when applied to the *thermomech_TK* and *msc23052* instances. In particular, column t(s) in Table 1 and Fig. 1(a) show that the execution costs of the ECMT-GL heuristic are lower than the GPS algorithm [6]. Figure 1(b) shows that the storage costs of the ECMT-GL heuristic is similar to the GPS algorithm [6]. Moreover, both reordering algorithms shows linear expected memory requirements, but the hidden con-

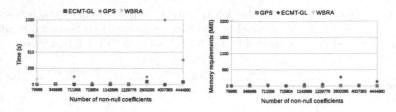

Fig. 1. Running times and memory requirements of heuristics for bandwidth and profile reductions when applied to nine instances contained in the SuiteSparse matrix collection [3].

stant in the GPS algorithm [6] is slightly smaller than the hidden constant in the ECMT-GL heuristic.

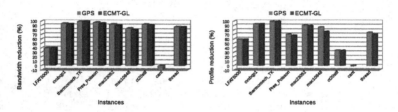

Fig. 2. Bandwidth and profile reductions (in percentage) obtained by the ECMT-GL and GPS [6] heuristics when applied to nine instances contained in the SSM collection [3].

Although the GPS algorithm [6] obtains in general better bandwidth and profile results, low execution times of the ECMT-GL heuristic pay off in reducing the running time of the ICCG method. Specifically, the ECMT-GL heuristic obtained better results (related to speedup of the ICCG method) than the GPS ordering [6] in all experiments, including when using the *thermomech_TK* and *msc23052* instances (at least when considering that only a single linear system is to be solved). As mentioned, the reason for this is that the ECMT-GL heuristic achieved similar performance to the GPS algorithm [6] at lower execution times than the GPS algorithm [6]. Specifically in the simulation using the *thermomech_TK* and *msc23052* instances (situation which could also happen in the cases of solving linear systems composed of multiple right hand side vectors and in transient FEM analysis in which linear systems are solved multiple times), the initial cost for reordering can be amortized in the iterative solution steps. In this scenario, a reordering scheme can be beneficial if it presents a reasonable cost (time and memory usage) and can reduce the runtime of the linear system solver at a higher level (such as in the case of the GPS algorithm [6] when applied to the *thermomech_TK* and *msc23052* instances).

Table 1 and Fig. 3 show the average results from the use of the ICCG method applied to nine instances taken from the SSM collection [3]. The ECMT-GL heuristic improved significantly the performance of the ICCG method when applied to the *msc23052*, *msc10848*, *ct20stif*, and *thread* instances. Table 1 and Figs. 1(a) and 3 show that on average the new ECMT-GL heuristic outpaced the GPS algorithm in terms of output quality (regarding to the speedup of the ICCG method) and running time in the simulations performed. Column % in Table 1 shows that the execution time of a heuristic for bandwidth reduction can be roughly the same order of magnitude as the ICCG computation (e.g. see results concerning the *msc10848* instance). Setting a lower precision to the CG method can let the reordering time more evident. Therefore, it is useful to parallelize the reordering and this is a next step in this work.

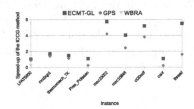

Fig. 3. Speed-ups of the ICCG method resulted when using heuristics for bandwidth and profile reductions applied to nine instances contained in the SSM collection [3].

4   Conclusions

This paper proposes a new approach to the Wonder Bandwidth Reduction Algorithm (WBRA) [4] based on the George-Liu algorithm [5] for matrix bandwidth reduction. This variant of the WBRA was termed ECMT-GL heuristic. Specifically, our approach employs a pseudo-peripheral vertex selected by the George-Liu algorithm [5] in the first step of WBRA. The results of the implementations of the WBRA [4] and GPS algorithm [6] described in this paper confirm their merit in accordance with the findings presented in the current literature, i.e., Table 1 and Fig. 2 show that these algorithms reduce the bandwidth and profile substantially. Specifically, the heuristics for bandwidth reductions evaluated in this computational experiment can enhance locality in accessing data and enable column (profile) information compression. Moreover, numerical experiments showed that the heuristic for bandwidth reduction proposed here provides further worthwhile gains when compared with the original WBRA [4] and GPS algorithm [6]. Nine model problems taken from the SuiteSparse matrix collection [3] were used to examine the efficiency of the proposed algorithm. These model problems are solved with the conjugate gradient method in conjunction with the zero-fill incomplete Cholesky preconditioner.

The performance of the proposed algorithm was compared with the original WBRA [4]. The new heuristic uses less memory and has advantageous performance properties in relation to the original algorithm. Thus, the modification in the WBRA proposed here reduces the amount of time and memory required by the algorithm to a considerable extent.

The results of the ECMT-GL heuristic were also compared with the results of the well-known GPS algorithm [6]. In experiments using nine instances (with some of them comprised of more than 4,000,000 non-null coefficients), the ECMT-GL heuristic performed best in reducing the computational cost of the ICCG method. We conclude that a high-cost heuristic for bandwidth reduction based on rooted level structures can be improved by starting the algorithm with a single vertex carefully chosen by a pseudoperipheral vertex finder (such as the George-Liu algorithm [5]). Although the original high-cost heuristic will probably yield better bandwidth results for exploring a larger domain space, low execution and storage costs of the new heuristic will pay off in reducing the execution costs of linear system solvers. This makes it possible to improve a number of heuristics developed in this field [1,7–9]. We plan to investigate parallel approaches of these algorithms and compare them along with algebraic multigrid methods in future studies.

References

1. Bernardes, J.A.B., Gonzaga de Oliveira, S.L.: A systematic review of heuristics for profile reduction of symmetric matrices. Procedia Comput. Sci. **51**, 221–230 (2015)
2. Chagas, G.O., Gonzaga de Oliveira, S.L.: Metaheuristic-based heuristics for symmetric-matrix bandwidth reduction: a systematic review. Procedia Comput. Sci. **51**, 211–220 (2015)
3. Davis, T.A., Hu, Y.: The University of Florida sparse matrix collection. ACM Trans. Math. Software **38**(1), 1–25 (2011)
4. Esposito, A., Catalano, M.S.F., Malucelli, F., Tarricone, L.: A new matrix bandwidth reduction algorithm. Oper. Res. Lett. **23**, 99–107 (1998)
5. George, A., Liu, J.W.H.: An implementation of a pseudoperipheral node finder. ACM Trans. Math. Software **5**(3), 284–295 (1979)
6. Gibbs, N.E., Poole, W.G., Stockmeyer, P.K.: An algorithm for reducing the bandwidth and profile of a sparse matrix. SIAM J. Numer. Anal. **13**(2), 236–250 (1976)
7. Gonzaga de Oliveira, S.L., Bernardes, J.A.B., Chagas, G.O.: An evaluation of low-cost heuristics for matrix bandwidth and profile reductions. Comput. Appl. Math. **37**(2), 1412–1471 (2018). https://doi.org/10.1007/s40314-016-0394-9
8. Gonzaga de Oliveira, S.L., Bernardes, J.A.B., Chagas, G.O.: An evaluation of reordering algorithms to reduce the computational cost of the incomplete Cholesky-conjugate gradient method. Comput. Appl. Math. (2017). https://doi.org/10.1007/s40314-017-0490-5
9. Gonzaga de Oliveira, S.L., Chagas, G.O.: A systematic review of heuristics for symmetric-matrix bandwidth reduction: methods not based on metaheuristics. In: Proceedings of the Brazilian Symposium on Operations Research (SBPO 2015), Sobrapo, Ipojuca, Brazil (2015)
10. Lin, Y.X., Yuan, J.J.: Profile minimization problem for matrices and graphs. Acta Mathematicae Applicatae Sinica **10**(1), 107–122 (1994)
11. Papadimitriou, C.H.: The NP-completeness of bandwidth minimization problem. Comput. J. **16**, 177–192 (1976)

Improving Large-Scale Fingerprint-Based Queries in Distributed Infrastructure

Shupeng Wang[1], Guangjun Wu[1(✉)], Binbin Li[1], Xin Jin[2], Ge Fu[2], Chao Li[2], and Jiyuan Zhang[1]

[1] Institute of Information Engineering, CAS, Beijing 100093, China
wuguangjun@iie.ac.cn
[2] National Computer Network Emergency Response Technical Team/Coordination Center of China (CNCERT/CC), Beijing 100031, China

Abstract. Fingerprints are often used in a sketching mechanism, which maps elements into concise and representative synopsis using small space. Large-scale fingerprint-based query can be used as an important tool in big data analytics, such as set membership query, rank-based query and correlationship query etc. In this paper, we propose an efficient approach to improving the performance of large-scale fingerprint-based queries in a distributed infrastructure. At initial stage of the queries, we first transform the fingerprints sketch into space constrained global rank-based sketch at query site via collecting minimal information from local sites. The time-consuming operations, such as local fingerprints construction and searching, are pushed down into local sites. The proposed approach can construct large-scale and scalable fingerprints efficiently and dynamically, meanwhile it can also supervise continuous queries by utilizing the global sketch, and run an appropriate number of jobs over distributed computing environments. We implement our approach in Spark, and evaluate its performance over real-world datasets. When compared with native SparkSQL, our approach outperforms the native routines on query response time by 2 orders of magnitude.

Keywords: Big data query · Data streams · Distributed computing
Memory computing

1 Introduction

In recent years, plenty of applications produce big and fast datasets, which are usually continuous and unlimited data sets [8,11]. Many applications have to analyze the large-scale datasets in real time and take appropriate actions [3,5, 9,13,14]. For example, a web-content service company in a highly competitive market wants to make sure that the page-view traffic is carefully monitored, such that an administer can do sophisticated load balancing, not only for better performance but also to protect against failures. A delay in detecting a response error can seriously impact customers satisfaction [10]. These applications require a continuous stream of often key-value data to be processed. Meanwhile, the data is continuously analyzed and transformed in memory before it is stored on a disk. Therefore, current analytics of big data are more focused on research for efficient processing key-value data across a cluster of servers.

The fingerprints-based structures, such as standard bloom filter (SBF) and dynamic bloom filters (DBF) [7], are usually considered as an efficient sketching mechanism for processing the key-value data, and they can map the key-value items into small and representative structure efficiently by hash functions [1,4]. Fingerprint-based queries can be used as important tools for complex queries in big data analytics, such as membership query, rank-based queries, and correlationship queries [3]. Whereas when confronting large-scale data processing, the current sketching mechanism framework not only decreases the speed of data processing because of the fixed configured policies, but also increases collisions of fingerprint-based applications for dynamic datasets [2,6,7]. In this paper, we consider the problem of deploying large-scale fingerprint-based applications over distributed infrastructure, such as Spark, and propose an efficient approach to automatically reconfigure data structure along with the continuous inputs, as well as run a reasonable number of jobs in parallel two meet the requirements of big data stream analytics. The contributions of our paper are as follows:

1. We present distributed sketching approach, which mainly constitutes global dyadic qdigest and local dynamic bloom filters (DBFs) [7], which can provide capability of data processing with high system throughput. The global dyadic qdigest is constructed via collecting the minimal rank-based qdigest structure from local sketch and can be scaled efficiently. We can also tail the operations of distributed query processing by running an appropriate number of jobs over the local sites, which contain the result tuples.
2. We present detailed theoretical and experimental evaluation of our approach in terms of query accuracy, storage space and query time. We also design and implement our approach in Spark, and compare it with the state-of-the-art sampling techniques and the native system under production environments using real-world data sets.

Spark is often considered as a general-purpose memory computing system, which can provide capability of supporting analytical queries with fault-tolerant framework. We implement prototype of our approach in Spark, and compare it with the native systems (e.g., Spark) and general-purpose sketching method (Spark with Sampling) over real-world datasets. The experimental results validate the efficiency and effectiveness of our approach. Our approach only costs 100 ms for continuously membership queries over 1.4 billion records.

2   Approach Design

2.1   Sketch Design

The data structure of our sketch includes two parts: (1) A top level dyadic qdigest, which accepts items of out-of-order data stream and compresses them into a rank-based structure. We design a hashMap-based structure to implement the dyadic qdigest to improve the speed of the data processing. (2) A precise fingerprints structure, which map keys within a range of the dyadic qdigest into DBFs. Also, we design efficient query processing techniques to boost the performance of data processing over large-scale and dynamic datasets.

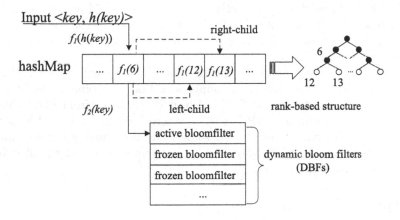

Fig. 1. Data structure for a local sketch.

We extend the traditional qdigest [12] to dyadic qdigest, which is used to divide the value space of input items into dyadic value range and compress them into a memory constrained rank-based structure for high-speed data streams processing. A dyadic qdigest can be considered as a logarithmic partition of space $[0, \phi - 1]$, and any interval $[a, b]$ can be divided into $\log_2(b - a)$ intervals. In order to improve the speed of data processing, we design a hash-based dyadic qdigest to maintain rank-based sketch structure, while maintaining the binary tree semantics of traditional qdigest [12]. Suppose the rank-based structure maintains summaries in value space $[0, \phi - 1]$. A node is represented by id, and the id is 1, iff. the node is the root node, otherwise, ids of leaf nodes equal to $value + \phi$. We can maintain a binary tree semantics for a node with id via following formulations:

1. Left child id of the node is $id \times 2$;
2. Right child id of the node is $id \times 2 + 1$;
3. Parent id of the node is $\lfloor id/2 \rfloor$.

The mapping between the hashMap and input item key can be computed by hash function f_1. A simple implementation is that we can compute the function via $f_1(h(key)) = h(key) \mod \phi$, where h is a hashcode computing function such as MD5. For example, if $\phi = 8$, $f_1(h(key)) = 6$, the right child id is $2 * f_1(h(key)) = 12$ and left child id is $2 * f_1(h(key)) + 1 = 13$. Hence, we can compute the traditional binary tree structure over domain ϕ by hash-based computing easily.

When an item with *key* inserts into the sketch structure, we first calculate the node id of the item via $f_1(h(key))$, search the corresponding node by the id, and increase the number of items in the nodes. As with the DBFs, we arrange them at each node of the dyadic qdigest to record the fingerprints of input items, such that we insert *key* into the active filter of DBF through $f_2(key)$. The basic idea of DBFs is the filters array calculated with standard bloom filters (SBF), and the bloom filter that is currently written into is called active bloom filter. If the number of keys maintained at the active filter exceeds the threshold of collisions, we freeze the active filter as a frozen filter and create a new filter as an active filter.

In general, the query and inserting efficiency for a binary tree with M nodes is $O(\log M)$. While the hash-based implementation of a binary tree structure can improve the query time to $O(1)$. Also, it can be seen from Fig. 1 that the writing time of an item into DBF is $O(k)$, where k is the number of hash functions used in the active filter. At the same time, the above structure can also be compressed and scaled flexibly to meet the requirements of the distributed memory computing framework.

2.2   Query Processing

In a distributed computing infrastructure, the driver of query application usually deployed at query site and supervise the continuous queries over distributed local sites. In our approach, the large-scale fingerprint-based queries include two stages: *the initial stage*, at which we collect information from local sites and build the global dyadic qdigest at query site using constrained space; *query processing stage*, at which we send the query to local sketches which are related to a query in a batch mode guided by the global qdigest, and push-down the query processing into each local sketch. At the end of the stage we just exchange and collect the minimal information from local sites for final results. We next present the details of the two stages.

Recall that the local sketch structure, including dyadic qdigest and DBFs attached into each range (or called node) of the dyadic structure. At the initial stage of large-scale query processing, the query site collects the dyadic qdigest from local sketches and merge them into a global dyadic qdigest, which can consume constrained space. The operation can be conducted by pairwise merging between two sketches. Since the tree merging procedure just collects and merges between high-level dyadic qdigest summaries, such that the amount of data exchanged between local sites is small. At the final stage of the merging operation, we compress the union tree according to space-constrained parameters k by constrains (1) and (2). Note that the proposed framework can transform the continuously point queries into a batch-processing mode, and run reasonable number of jobs dynamically according to data distribution. Next, we present applications of large-scale fingerprint-based queries utilizing our approach.

Now, we need to formalize the input & output of a query and extract different attributes for sketching. The problem is to search the membership of a set of keys, and returns true or false for the key existence prediction. This query method is usually used in interactive queries or as tools for users interface. The dyadic qdigest extract the hashcode of *keys* from inputs, and predict the existence in the DBFs.

The DBFs based on SBF are compact and provide probabilistic prediction and may return true for an input key. The DBF also can provide false positive error, which reports true for some keys that are not actually members of the prediction. Let m, k, n_a and d be core parameter of a SBF as the previous literature [7]. The DBFs compress the dynamic dataset D into $s \times m$ SBFs matrix. In this paper, we use $f^{SBF}_{m,k,n_a,d}$ and $f^{DBF}_{m,k,n_a,d}$ to describe the false positive error of a SBF and DBFs when the d elements maintained in the sketch. If $1 \leq d \leq n_a$, it indicates that the number of elements in the set A does not exceed the collision threshold n_a, thus $DBF(A)$ is actually a standard bloom filter, whose false positive rate can be calculated in the same way as $SBF(A)$. The error $f^{DBF}_{m,k,n_a,d}$ of a membership query can depicted as

$$f^{DBF}_{m,k,n_a,d} = f^{SBF}_{m,k,n_a,d} = (1 - e^{-k \times d/m})^k. \tag{1}$$

If $d > n_a$, there are s SBFs used in $DBF(A)$ for data set A, meanwhile there are $i(1 \leq i \leq s-1)$ SBFs which contain n_a items in the filter, and false positive rates are all $f^{SBF}_{(m,k,n_a,n_a)}$. We design an active filter for the inserting, and false positive rate of the active filter in DBF(A) is $f^{SBF}_{(m,k,n_a,t)}$, where t is $d - n_a \times \lfloor d/n_a \rfloor$. Therefore, the probability that all bits of the filters in DBF(A) are set to 1 is $(1 - f^{SBF}_{(m,k,n_a,n_a)})^{\lfloor d/n_a \rfloor}(1 - f^{SBF}_{(m,k,n_a,t)})$, and the false positive rate of DBF(A) is shown in Eq. 2. We notice that when there is only one filter in DBF(A), Eq. 2 can transform into Eq. 1.

$$
\begin{aligned}
f^{DBF}_{m,k,n_a,d} &= 1 - (1 - f^{SBF}_{(m,k,n_a,n_a)})^{\lfloor d/n_a \rfloor}(1 - f^{SBF}_{(m,k,n_a,t)}) \\
&= 1 - (1 - (1 - e^{-k \times n_a/m})^k)^{\lfloor d/n_a \rfloor} \times (1 - (1 - e^{-k \times (d - n_a \times \lfloor d/n_a \rfloor)/m})^k).
\end{aligned} \tag{2}
$$

3   Experimental Evaluation

In this paper, we implement our approach in Spark, which works on the on YARN with 11 servers. The configuration information of a server of the cluster is shown in Table 1. We use the real-word traffic of page-views nearly 100 GB uncompress datasets. We mainly focus our evaluation on query efficiency and query accuracy of our approach.

We first compare our prototype with the native system Spark. We use the rank-based queries as the testing cases. The large-scale quantiles query is a more important and complex statistical query method. For quantiles queries, Spark provides the *percentile* function to support quantiles lookups. We use the *percentile* function in SparkSQL to conduct the rank-based queries on Spark platform. The SparkSQL statement, such as "select percentile (countall, array

Table 1. Configuration information in our experiments.

Name	Configuration Information
Operating system	CentOS 6.3
CPU model	Intel(R) Xeon(R) E5-2630@2.30 GHz
CPU cores	24 × 6
Memory	32 GB
Spark version	2.1.0
JDK version	1.8.0_45-b14
Scala version	2.11.7
Hadoop version	2.7.3

(0.1, 0.2, 0.3, 0.4, 0.5, 0.6, 0.7, 0.8, 0.9, 1)) from relations", can be used to obtain the ten quantiles from data set exactly. Meanwhile, the data structure of the two approaches, such as sketching structure of our approach, and related RDDs of Spark, are all kept in memory.

The results are shown in Fig. 2(a) and (b). The large-scale rank-based fingerprints queries need to scan the dataset to obtain the global ranking quantiles, which is a time-consuming operation. Our approach can improve the query efficiency through partition and distributed sketching framework, thus it can improve the query efficiency greatly. Under the 10 GB real-world data set testing, our approach can respond a query less than 200 ms, while the memory computing framework Spark costs 35 s to respond the same query.

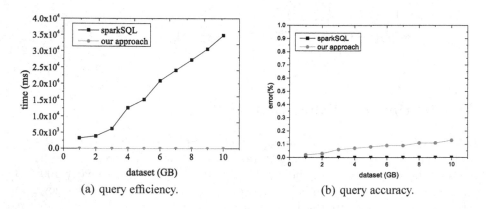

(a) query efficiency.   (b) query accuracy.

Fig. 2. Compared with native Spark.

In order to evaluate the query performance of our approach over large-scale datasets, we conduct the evaluation over 100 GB uncompressed data. When the data set is larger than the maximum space for RDDs in Spark, the data will be spilled into disk, and it impacts the query processing greatly. The Spark provides a *sampling* (denoted as Spark&Sampling) interface to conquer the real-time data processing over large-scale datasets. The Spark&Sampling is a type of Bernoulli sampling with no placement. The sampling method extracts samples from partitions and maintains samples in memory blocks. We improve the accuracy of the sampling method using adjustment weights for samples. For an input item v, we sample it with the probability of p, $p \in (0, 1)$, then the adjusted weight of the item is v/p. We configure the same memory usage for the two approaches, we compare them on three aspects: construction time, query efficiency and query accuracy. The experimental results are shown in Fig. 3(a), (b) and (c).

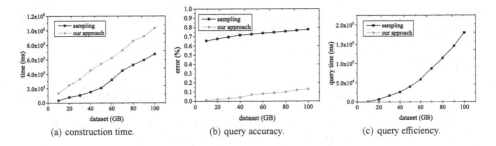

(a) construction time.   (b) query accuracy.   (c) query efficiency.

Fig. 3. Compared with Spark with sampling interface.

Our approach can extract samples from large-scale datasets and arrange them into specified sketching structure, while the Spark&Sampling extracts randomized samples from partitions and attaches them in block directly, thus the time costed in our approach is slightly higher than Spark&Sampling method.

After the sketch construction, we conduct 100 randomized rank-based fingerprints queries, and compute the average query efficiency and query accuracy of a query. The global sketch is a type of qdigest structure, which predicts the quantiles with some errors. We present the error comparisons of the two approaches. Our sketch can provide the error less than 0.1% for the rank-based quantiles estimation, while the error in Spark&sampling is larger than 0.7%. Meanwhile, our approach can improve the query response time significantly over large-scale datasets. When compared under 100 GB real-world dataset, our approach can provide an answer within 300 ms, while the Spark&sampling needs 180 s to respond the same query. Therefore, our approach is more appropriate for big and fast dataset processing and can provide real-time (or near real-time) response for large-scale fingerprint based queries

4   Conclusion

Large-scale fingerprint-based queries are often time-consuming operations. In this paper, we propose a distributed sketching framework to boost the performance of the large-scale queries, such as continuously membership queries and rank-based queries. Towards minimizing the shuffling time between the local sites, we construct a global dyadic qditest structure at query site using constrained space. For large-scale queries, the global sketch only build at initial stage of the queries, and can supervise the following continuously queries. This design enable our approach to run reasonable number of jobs under data skew scenarios. At local sites, we combine the sketching techniques, such as dyadic qdigest and dynamic bloom filters to build concise structure for dynamic data processing. The experimental results have expose the efficiency and effectiveness of our approach for large-scale queries over distributed environments. In the future, we plan to apply our approach in production environments to improve the efficiency of complex queries, such as group by queries and join queries.

Acknowledgment. This work was supported by the National Key Research and Development Program of China (2016YFB0801305).

References

1. Bloom, B.H.: Space/time trade-offs in hash coding with allowable errors. ACM (1970)
2. Corominasmurtra, B., Sol, R.V.: Universality of Zipf's law. Phys. Rev. E Stat. Nonlinear Soft Matter Phys. **82**(1 Pt 1), 011102 (2010)
3. Fan, B., Andersen, D.G., Kaminsky, M., Mitzenmacher, M.D.: Cuckoo filter: practically better than bloom. In: ACM International on Conference on Emerging NETWORKING Experiments and Technologies, pp. 75–88 (2014)
4. Fan, L., Cao, P., Almeida, J., Broder, A.Z.: Summary cache: a scalable wide-area web cache sharing protocol. IEEE/ACM Trans. Networking **8**(3), 281–293 (2000)
5. Wu, G., Yun, X., Li, C., Wang, S., Wang, Y., Zhang, X., Jia, S., Zhang, G.: Supporting real-time analytic queries in big and fast data environments. In: Candan, S., Chen, L., Pedersen, T.B., Chang, L., Hua, W. (eds.) DASFAA 2017. LNCS, vol. 10178, pp. 477–493. Springer, Cham (2017). https://doi.org/10.1007/978-3-319-55699-4_29
6. Guo, D., Wu, J., Chen, H., Luo, X.: Theory and network applications of dynamic bloom filters. In: IEEE International Conference on Computer Communications IEEE INFOCOM 2006, pp. 1–12 (2006)
7. Guo, D., Wu, J., Chen, H., Yuan, Y., Luo, X.: The dynamic bloom filters. IEEE Trans. Knowl. Data Eng. **22**(1), 120–133 (2010)
8. Guo, L., Ma, J., Chen, Z.: Learning to recommend with multi-faceted trust in social networks. In: Proceedings of the 22nd International Conference on World Wide Web Companion, WWW 2013 Companion, pp. 205–206. International World Wide Web Conferences Steering Committee, Republic and Canton of Geneva, Switzerland (2013)
9. Katsipoulakis, N.R., Thoma, C., Gratta, E.A., Labrinidis, A., Lee, A.J., Chrysanthis, P.K.: CE-Storm: confidential elastic processing of data streams. In: Proceedings of the 2015 ACM SIGMOD International Conference on Management of Data, SIGMOD 2015, pp. 859–864. ACM, New York (2015)
10. Mishne, G., Dalton, J., Li, Z., Sharma, A., Lin, J.: Fast data in the era of big data: Twitter's real-time related query suggestion architecture. In: Proceedings of the 2013 ACM SIGMOD International Conference on Management of Data, SIGMOD 2013, pp. 1147–1158. ACM, New York (2013)

11. Preis, T., Moat, H.S., Stanley, E.H.: Quantifying trading behavior in financial markets using Google trends. Sci. Rep. **3**, 1684 (2013)
12. Shrivastava, N., Buragohain, C., Agrawal, D., Suri, S.: Medians and beyond: new aggregation techniques for sensor networks. In: Proceedings of the 2nd International Conference on Embedded Networked Sensor Systems, SenSys 2004, pp. 239–249. ACM, New York (2004). https://doi.org/10.1145/1031495.1031524, https://doi.org/10.1145/1031495.1031524
13. Wang, Z., Quercia, D., Séaghdha, D.O.: Reading tweeting minds: real-time analysis of short text for computational social science. In: Proceedings of the 24th ACM Conference on Hypertext and Social Media, HT 2013, pp. 169–173. ACM (2013)
14. Xiaochun, Y., Guangjun, W., Guangyan, Z., Keqin, L., Shupeng, W.: FastRAQ: a fast approach to range-aggregate queries in big data environments. IEEE Trans. Cloud Comput. **3**(2), 206–218 (2015). https://doi.org/10.1109/TCC.2014.2338325

A Effective Truth Discovery Algorithm with Multi-source Sparse Data

Jiyuan Zhang[1,2], Shupeng Wang[1(✉)], Guangjun Wu[1(✉)], and Lei Zhang[1(✉)]

[1] Institute of Information Engineering, CAS, Beijing 100093, China
[2] School of Cyber Security, University of Chinese Academy of Sciences,
Beijing 100031, China
{zhangjiyuan,wangshupeng,wuguangjun,zhanglei1}@iie.ac.cn

Abstract. The problem to find out the truth from inconsistent information is defined as Truth Discovery. The essence of truth discovery is to estimate source quality. Therefore the measuring mechanism of data source will immensely affect the result and process of truth discovery. However the state-of-the-art algorithms dont consider how source quality is affected when null is provided by source. We propose to use the Silent Rate, True Rate and False Rate to measure source quality in this paper. In addition, we utilize Probability Graphical Model to model truth and source quality which is measured through null and real data. Our model makes full use of all claims and null to improve the accuracy of truth discovery. Compared with prevalent approaches, the effectiveness of our approach is verified on three real datasets and the recall has improved significantly.

Keywords: Truth discovery · Data fusion
Multi source data confliction

1 Introduction

With the development of information technology, the Internet has penetrated into all corner of human social life. The data on internet have accumulated sharply, and these data have been integrated into an information ocean. One of the important features of this information is diversity, so for any object, heterogeneous descriptions can be found on internet from multiple sources. The inconsistency or conflict of these diverse descriptions causes great confusion for us to identify true information from each other. Therefore, identifying the accurate and complete information from conflicting descriptions is the key factor for information integration. The problem is the Truth Discovery proposed in document [9].

In order solve the problem, this paper makes use of the Hub Authority method [2,4] to solve the problem by the quality difference of source. And we will redesign the metrics of source quality, and measure the quality of sources with three indexes, such as silent rate, true rate and false rate, to improve the accuracy of truth discovery. The main work of this paper presents is as follows:

© Springer International Publishing AG, part of Springer Nature 2018
Y. Shi et al. (Eds.): ICCS 2018, LNCS 10862, pp. 434–442, 2018.
https://doi.org/10.1007/978-3-319-93713-7_37

1. Redesign metrics for source quality. The quality of source is measured by three indexes, such as silent rate, true rate and false rate. The silent rate in the new metrics can make full use of the null data provided by the source, and can describe the source quality more comprehensively.
2. Fertilize the plate model of probabilistic graph to construct model. The relationship among the data source, the object and the truth is constructed, and a probabilistic graph model is established to deduce the truth. Combing the conditions and methods of influence propagation in probabilistic graphs, the truth probability of every claim is deduced.

2   Related Work

The problem of truth discovery is defined for the first time in document [9], and a TruthFinder algorithm is proposed for solving this kind of problem. The method is similar to the iterative mechanism of Hub Authority, which synchronously infer the truth of object and the quality of the source. Inspired by it, a series of similar methods have been developed to study various factors that affect truth discovery [2–4]. The logical criterion of this method is: the higher the source quality is, the more likely it provides truth, at the same time, the more truth it provides, the higher the source quality is. These kind of algorithm is called heuristic method.

Based on the above processing logic, recent research has transformed truth discovery into a framework for optimization. Each source is assigned a weight according to its credibility, and the optimization objective is to minimize the distance between the target value and the truth. Document [6] which is extended in [5] uses the weight to represent the distribution of the credibility of each source, and uses a variety of loss functions to deal with heterogeneous data objects, so that the truth discovery of heterogeneous data is integrated into an objective function. Document [11] builds an optimization framework based on min-max entropy to estimate the truth of objects with noise. In a word, this kind of method updates the truth and the weight of the data source iteratively until the weight converges, and obtains the truth and the weight of all the data sources.

The other method is probability method. These methods solve the problem of truth discovery in document [1,7,8,10]. The core idea is that multi-source data is considered as a mixed distribution, and the credibility of the source is integrated into the probabilistic model in the form of random variables. The probabilistic model is proposed by [10], and the quality of data sources is modeled by using two types of errors – false positive and false negative. Document [7] extends the truth discovery to the field of social group awareness. In document [8], the authors propose to use stochastic Gauss models to represent sources. So the mean represents the truth and variance represents the credibility of source. Theoretically, both solutions are proven to be contractive to an ϵ-ball around the maximum likelihood estimate.

3   Implementation

In this section, we first introduce some terms and annotations. Suppose that S is a collection of sources, and j is one of the sources; N is the set of observation objects, and n is one of the objects. If a source j can only provide a claim for an observation object, then the $n's$ claim obtained from j is denoted as x_n^j. The $n's$ truth is denoted as t_n. The $n's$ claim set is $X_n = \{x_n^j\}_{j \in S_n}$ and $N's$ claim set is $X = X_1 \cup \cdots \cup X_n$. In view of the fact that it is impossible to obtain the claims of object n from some sources, so the claims are only obtained from S_n i.e. a subset of S. We denote the collection of non-repeated claims of n as $V_n = \{v_{ni}\}, i = 1, \cdots, N'$.

In order to simplify the solution model, two hypotheses are given for the source and the object.

*Hypotheses*1 : The data sources are independent of each other, and they provide claims independently.
*Hypotheses*2 : The objects are independent of each other. The alteration of one object's claim do not affect others'.

We construct a Bayesian network model as shown in Fig. 1 to calculate the probability of truth. In the network, each node represents a random variable, the dark node represents the known variable, and the light colored node represents the unknown variable. The solid black point δ is the prior probability of the truth, and the hollow points represent the weight of the source measurement indexes. β, γ, Θ is a group of super parameters. β represents the weight of the false rate when calculating the truth. The γ is the weight of the true rate, and the Θ is the weight of the silent rate, satisfying equation $\beta + \gamma + \Theta = 1$. The directed edges that connect nodes represent dependencies among variables. | S | and | N | in the corner of the box represent the number of sources and objects.

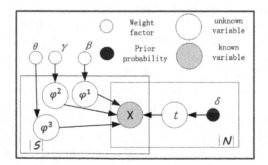

Fig. 1. Probability graphical model of FTS

3.1   Source Quality

The most important factor that affects the accuracy of truth discovery is the quality of sources, and the previous algorithm does not consider the null data how to affect source quality. In this paper, true rate, false rate to measure source quality.

$FalseRate(FR)$: The rate of all claims is not truth, which is provided by source j, i.e. $FR = \frac{Fp}{Empt+Fp+Tp}$.

$TrueRate(TR)$: The rate of all claims is truth, which is provided by source j, i.e. $TR = \frac{Tp(1-FR)}{Empt+Fp+Tp}$.

$SilentRate(SR)$: The rate of all claims is null, which is provided by source j, i.e. $SR = \frac{Empt(1-FR)}{Empt+Fp+Tp}$.

Empt is the number of null among all the claims that source j provides i.e. $Empt = \sum_{n=1}^{N} Signal(x_n^j = null)$. Fp is the expectation of false claims that the source j provides when the probability of truth is $p(t_n = v_{ni})$. Then, $Fp = p(t_n = v_{ni}) \times \sum_{n=1}^{N} Signal(x_n^j \neq v_{ni} \&\& x_n^j \neq null)$. Tp is the expectation of true claims that the source j provides when the probability of truth is $p(t_n = v_{ni})$. Then, $Tp = p(t_n = v_{ni}) \times \sum_{n=1}^{N} Signal(x_n^j == v_{ni})$. The $Signal(.)$ is an indicator function in the formula: $Signal(t) = \begin{cases} 1, & t=true \\ 0, & t=false \end{cases}$.

The quality of source j is $\phi_j = (\phi_j^1, \phi_j^2, \phi_j^3)$ which is a tri-tuple. The value of them is $\phi_j^1 = FR, \phi_j^2 = TR, \phi_j^3 = SR$.

3.2   Truth Inference

According to the hypothesis 2, all $|N|$ objects are independent of each other. From the probability graph model of Fig. 1, the probability of the observed values of all observed objects is:

$$P(X|\phi_S) = \prod_{n=1}^{|N|} P(x_n^1, \cdots, x_n^{|S|}|\phi_S) \tag{1}$$

$P(x_n^1, \cdots, x_n^{|S|}|\phi_S)$ is a joint probability density function of Object n when $|S|$ sources provide claims.

The V_n is the claim set of Object n whose truth, t_n, has $|V_n|$ possible values. Then:

$$\begin{cases} P(x_n^1, \cdots, x_n^{|S|}|\phi_S) = \sum_{i=1}^{|V_n|} \delta_{ni} p(x_n^1, \cdots, x_n^{|S|}|t_n = v_{ni}, \phi_S) \\ \sum_{i=1}^{|V_n|} \delta_{ni} = 1 \end{cases} \tag{2}$$

According to the hypothesis 1, if the sources are independent of each other to provide claims, and there is no mutual replication of claims, the probability of obtaining all the claims of object n from $|S|$ sources is a joint probability function:

$$p(x_n^1, \cdots, x_n^{|S|} | t_n = v_{ni}, \phi_S) = \prod_{j=1}^{|S|} P(x_n^j | t_n = v_{ni}, \phi_j)$$

$$= \prod_{j=1}^{|S|} (\phi_j^1)^{Signal(x_n^j \neq v_{ni} \&\& x_n^j \neq null)} \times (\phi_j^2)^{Signal(x_n^j = v_{ni})} \times (\phi_j^3)^{Signal(x_n^j = null)}$$

$$(3)$$

According to the definition of the problem, the truth probability of the object n is actually the truth probability under the condition of the current claim and the source quality, i.e.

$$p(t_n = v_{ni}) = p(t_n = v_{ni} | x_n^1, \cdots, x_n^{|S|}, \phi_S) \tag{4}$$

According to Bayes formula,

$$p(t_n = v_{ni} | x_n^1, \cdots, x_n^{|S|}, \phi_S) = \frac{p(x_n^1, \cdots, x_n^{|S|} | t_n = v_{ni}, \phi_S) \times \delta_{ni}}{P(X | \phi_S)} \tag{5}$$

In formula (5), the denominator is exactly the same for all objects. Then, the truth probability $p(t_n = v_{ni})$ is proportional to the molecular term. After substituted formula (3), formula (5) changed into formula (6).

$$p(t_n = v_{ni}) = p(t_n = v_{ni} | x_n^1, \cdots, x_n^{|S|}, \phi_S) \propto \delta_{ni} p(x_n^1, \cdots, x^{|S|} | t_n = v_{ni}, \phi_S)$$

$$(6)$$

Formula (6) is a continued product. The likelihood of the truth probability is obtained.

$$r_{ni} = \log p(t_n = v_{ni}) \propto \ln \delta_{ni}$$

$$+ \sum_{j=1}^{|S|} \{Signal(x_n^j \neq v_{ni} \&\& x_n^j \neq null) \times \ln \phi_j^1 + Signal(x_n^j == v_{ni}) \times \ln \phi_j^2$$

$$+ Signal(x_n^j == null) \times \ln \phi_j^3\}$$

$$(7)$$

3.3   Iterative Computation

The model uses silent rate, truth rate and false rate to measure source quality. β, γ and θ is the weight to adjust impact on three index. Therefore, β, γ and θ is substituted into the formula (7). The recursive formula of the final truth probability can be obtained.

$$r_{ni}^{(k+1)} = \ln \delta_{ni} + \sum_{j=1}^{|S|} \{\beta * Signal(x_n^j \neq v_{ni} \&\& x_n^j \neq null) \times \ln \phi_j^{1(k)}$$

$$+ \gamma * Signal(x_n^j == v_{ni}) \times \ln \phi_j^{2(k)} + \theta * Signal(x_n^j == null) \times \ln \phi_j^{3(k)}\}$$

$$(8)$$

Give an assumption: $f1 = \sum_{i=1}^{|X_n|} \sum_{n=1}^{N} r_{ni}^{(k)} \times Signal(x_n^j \neq v_{ni} \&\& x_n^j \neq null)$, $f2 = \sum_{n=1}^{N} Signal(x_n^j == null)$, $f3 = \sum_{i=1}^{|X_n|} \sum_{n=1}^{N} r_{ni}^{(k)} \times Signal(x_n^j == v_{ni})$ We can get the formulas of $\phi_j^{1\,(k)}, \phi_j^{2\,(k)}$ and $\phi_j^{3\,(k)}$.

$$\phi_j^{1\,(k)} = \frac{f1}{f1 + f2 + f3}, \quad \phi_j^{2\,(k)} = \frac{f3}{f2 + f3}(1 - \phi_j^{1\,(k)}), \quad \phi_j^{3\,(k)} = \frac{f2}{f2 + f3}(1 - \phi_j^{1\,(k)})$$

$$(9)$$

Algorithm 1: FTS truth discovery algorithm

---

input : X the whole claim set for all objects, the set of sources S, the set of objects N; threshold of converges α

output: The truth of all object T; The source quality of all sources ϕ_s

1 for $o_n \in N$ /*initiate the prior probability of all claims*/
2   initiate the prior probability of $o_n, \delta_{ni}, i = 1, \cdots, |V_n|$
3 end for
4 for $s \in S$ /*initiate source quality*/
5      $\phi_j = (\phi_j^1, \phi_j^2, \phi_j^3), j = 1, \cdots, |S|$
6 end for
7 $k \leftarrow 0$
8 $\phi_S' \leftarrow 0$
9 $c \leftarrow 1$
10 while $|c| > \alpha$ /* convergence conditions is not satisfied*/
11      $k \leftarrow k + 1$
12   for $o_n \in N$
13   calculate $r_{ni}^{(k)}, i = 1, \cdots, |V_n|$ from formula (9)
14   end for
15      $\phi_S' \leftarrow \phi_S$
16   for $s \in S$
17   calculate source quality from formula (10)
18          $\phi_j = (\phi_j^{1\,(k)}, \phi_j^{2\,(k)}, \phi_j^{3\,(k)}), j = 1, \cdots, |S|$
19   end for
20      $c \leftarrow \phi_S' - \phi_S$
21 end while
22 for $o_n \in N$ /*calculate truth*/
23      $i \leftarrow \max_{i=1,\cdots,|X_n|} r_{ni}^{(k)}$
24      $t_n = v_{ni}$
25 end for
26 return T, ϕ_S /*Output truth and source quality*/

The whole procedure of the FTS is shown in Algorithm 1. First, the prior probabilities of the claims of each object are initialized by uniform distribution and source quality ϕ is initialized by standard normal distribution. Then, according to the initial source quality, the whole iteration process is started. Finally, the (k+1)-th r_{ni} i.e. truth probability is calculated with k-th iteration of source quality i.e. $\phi_j{}^k$. The new source quality can be produced with new truth probability. The iterative algorithm is repeated until the source quality updates less than the threshold and the algorithm converges. The truth and source quality is calculated synchronously.

4   Experiment

In this section the truth discovery algorithm will run on three real data sets to verify the performance of the designed FTS model. As a comparison, the FTS and two state-of-art algorithms are tested under the same conditions to acquire respective recall.

4.1   Experimental Setup

The configuration of all experiments in this paper: CPU is Intel(R) Core(TM) i7-6700 3.40 GHz. Memory is 64G and OS is Windows 7. In this paper, three real datasets (http://lunadong.com/) such as *WeatherDataset*, *WeatherDataset*, and *FlightDataset* are used to verify the effect of the algorithm.

4.2   Experimental Result

In order to verify the accuracy of the algorithm, the truth discovery accuracy test was carried out on three real datasets, and the test results were listed in Table 1.

Table 1. Recall of all algorithms on different datasets.

Algorithm	Book-Author	Weather	Flight
Vote	76	70.59	54.32
TruthFinder	79	66.7	41.2
FTS	81	79.7	56.58

In the experiment, the set of ground truth is split into two parts randomly, one is used for verification, and the other is used for testing. β, γ and $\theta = 1 - \beta - \gamma$ is used to adjust the weight of silent rate, true rate and false rate. During the processes of verification, β, γ is taken from the range (0,1) and the step is 0.02 and the optimal combination of, is obtained. With the optimal β, γ, θ, recall is calculated on testing set.

From the experimental data in Table 1, we can see that our FTS method is better than the classical truth discovery algorithm on recall. It means silent rate has positive impact on truth discovery. The recall on weather and flight datasets is significantly decreased. The main reason for this phenomenon is that the number of sources in these two datasets is small, which affects the effect of truth discovery.

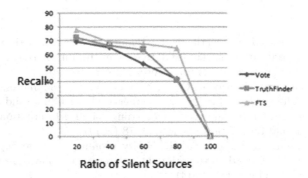

Fig. 2. Recall of different number of data source.

In order to test the influence of silent data source on the recall, the Book-Author data set are processed, and randomly selected 20%, 40%, 60%, 80% of the sources to keep silent i.e. claims is null. The experimental results are shown in Fig. 2. With the increase of silent source, the recalls of all algorithm decline steadily. If 100% of the sources remain silent, no algorithm can predict the truth, so the recall is 0. Comparing with the three algorithms, the Vote algorithm drops the fastest, which shows that the accuracy of the algorithm heavily depends on the number of sources that provide claims. The TrueFinder algorithm is also affected by the number of silent sources, and its performance on recall is lower than FTS. With comprehensive comparison, FTS algorithm is affected little by the number of silent source. The reason is that the effect of silent rate has been considered in FTS model.

5   Conclusion

First of all, the metrics of source quality has been redesigned. In FTS model, the reliability of data source quality is measured by true rate, false rate and silent rate. Thus the situation that source provides null is comprehensively comprised. Secondly, a probabilistic graph model is established to construct the relationship among the source, the object and the truth. Then the truth is deduced. In this model, the relationship among the source metrics, the truth and the claims of the source is presented in the form of figures. Using the conditions and methods of influence propagation in probabilistic graphs, the probabilities of every claim as truth are deduced. The experimental results on three datasets show that the new algorithm significantly improves the recall of truth discovery compared with the traditional classical algorithm.

Acknowledgement. This work was supported by National Natural Science Foundation of China (No. 61601458) and National Key Research and Development Program of China (No. 2016YFB0801004, 2016YFB0801305).

References

1. Blanco, L., Crescenzi, V., Merialdo, P., Papotti, P.: Probabilistic models to reconcile complex data from inaccurate data sources. In: International Conference on Advanced Information Systems Engineering, pp. 83–97 (2010)
2. Dian, Y., Hongzhao, H., Taylor, C., Ji, H., Chi, W., Shi, Z., Jiawei, H., Clare, V., Malik, M.I.: The wisdom of minority: unsupervised slot filling validation based on multi-dimensional truth-finding. In: Proceedings of 2014 International Conference on Computational Linguistics, pp. 1567–1578 (2014)
3. Furong, L., Mong Li, L., Wynne, H.: Entity profiling with varying source reliabilities. In: ACM SIGKDD International Conference on Knowledge Discovery and Data Mining, pp. 1146–1155 (2014)
4. Galland, A., Abiteboul, S., Marian, A., Senellart, P.: Corroborating information from disagreeing views, pp. 131–140 (2010)
5. Li, Q., Li, Y., Gao, J., Su, L., Zhao, B., Demirbas, M., Fan, W., Han, J.: A confidence-aware approach for truth discovery on long-tail data. Very Large Data Bases 8(4), 425–436 (2014)
6. Li, Q., Li, Y., Gao, J., Zhao, B., Fan, W., Han, J.: Resolving conflicts in heterogeneous data by truth discovery and source reliability estimation, pp. 1187–1198 (2014)
7. Wang, D., Kaplan, L.M., Le, H.K., Abdelzaher, T.F.: On truth discovery in social sensing: a maximum likelihood estimation approach, pp. 233–244 (2012)
8. Xiao, H., Gao, J., Wang, Z., Wang, S., Su, L., Liu, H.: A truth discovery approach with theoretical guarantee. In: ACM SIGKDD International Conference on Knowledge Discovery and Data Mining, pp. 1925–1934 (2016)
9. Yin, X., Han, J., Yu, P.S.: Truth discovery with multiple conflicting information providers on the web. IEEE Trans. Knowl. Data Eng. 20(6), 796–808 (2008)
10. Zhao, B., Rubinstein, B.I.P., Gemmell, J., Han, J.: A Bayesian approach to discovering truth from conflicting sources for data integration. Very Large Data Bases 5(6), 550–561 (2012)
11. Zhou, D., Basu, S., Mao, Y., Platt, J.: Learning from the wisdom of crowds by minimax entropy, pp. 2195–2203 (2012)

Blackboard Meets Dijkstra for Resource Allocation Optimization

Christian Vorhemus and Erich Schikuta[✉]

Faculty of Computer Science, University of Vienna,
Währingerstr. 29, 1090 Vienna, Austria
{christian.vorhemus,erich.schikuta}@univie.ac.at

Abstract. This paper presents the integration of Dijkstra's algorithm into a Blackboard framework to optimize the selection of web resources from service providers. The architectural framework of the implementation of the proposed Blackboard approach and its components in a real life scenario is laid out. For justification of approach, and to show practical feasibility, a sample implementation architecture is presented.

Keywords: Web-service selection · Resource allocation optimization
Blackboard method · Dijkstra algorithm

1 Introduction

With the advent of cloud computing, where resources are provisioned on demand as services on a pay-per-use basis, the proper selection of services to execute a given workflow is a crucial task. For each service or functionality, a range of concrete services may exist, having identical functional properties, but differing in their non-functional properties, such as cost, performance and availability.

In literature, the challenge of selecting service deployments respecting non-functional properties is widely known as the QoS-aware service selection problem [9]. Given an input workflow with specified abstract services (functionality), select a concrete deployment (out of several possible ones) for each abstract service in such a way that a given utility function is maximized and specified constraints are satisfied. Mathematically, this can be mapped to a multi-dimension, multi-choice knapsack problem that is known to be NP-hard in the strong sense [9]. In reality, we have also to cope with dynamic changes of services and their characteristics during the workflow execution.

In [8] we proposed a blackboard approach to automatically construct and optimize workflows. We pointed out the problem of changing conditions during the execution of the algorithm. In a distributed environment like the Web, the availability of all necessary services to complete a workflow is not guaranteed. Furthermore it is also possible that users change their configuration. To consider changed condition, we used the A-* algorithm which needs not to know all services at the beginning of the execution and allows for dynamic adaptation. A fundamental description of how services can be qualified is presented

© Springer International Publishing AG, part of Springer Nature 2018
Y. Shi et al. (Eds.): ICCS 2018, LNCS 10862, pp. 443–449, 2018.
https://doi.org/10.1007/978-3-319-93713-7_38

in [5]. Among an UML-based approach to classify QoS-Attributes, also a detailed description of how services can be combined is given.

This paper presents a novel approach for the optimization of web service selection. Hereby, we propose an artificial intelligence approach by mapping the service selection problem to a graph representation and to apply a combination of Dijkstra's algorithm and Blackboard method for optimization.

The layout of the paper is as follows: The Blackboard method and its optimization approach are presented in Sect. 2. In Sect. 3 we depict the architecture for the implementation of the proposed optimization framework for real world scenarios, where all our theoretical findings are knot together. The paper closes with a conclusion of the findings and look-out to further research.

2   The Blackboard Approach

The blackboard method [2] originally comes from artificial intelligence and uses different expert knowledge resources taking part in a stepwise process to construct solutions to given problems. The Blackboard framework consists of four different elements:

- A *global blackboard* representing shared information space considering input data and partial solutions, where different experts collect their knowledge and form the partial solutions to a global optimal solution.
- A *resource* is any kind of service which provides functionality that is needed to finish a subtask of a workflow.
- *Agents* are autonomous pieces of software. Their purpose is finding suitable resources for the Blackboard. An Agent can be a service too and therefore also be provided from external sources.
- *Controller:* There are different kinds of controlling components (see Sect. 3). Their main purpose is controlling the start of the algorithm, managing the brokers and bringing the results back to the user.

The Blackboard approach expands (combines) promising resource offerings (combinations) step by step, which are stored in the OpenList. All already used resource offerings are stored in the ClosedList. The Blackboard is divided into several regions and each region represents a subtask of a workflow. Which and how many regions exist depends on the workflow.

We give a simple example to outline the previous descriptions. Imagine, a user wants to store a video online. He also wants to convert the video from AVI to FLV and compress it to save disk space. The user normally does not care, how this workflow is completed in detail, he just wants a good, quick and cheap solution. Furthermore, the user does not want to start each subtask manually. He just defines the tasks and hands the video over to the Blackboard. Figure 1 gives a graphical representation.

The first question which shows up is: What is a good solution for the user? It is necessary to assign a numerical value to each subtask to make a comparison possible. These values are called "cost". Cost are constituted of "Quality of

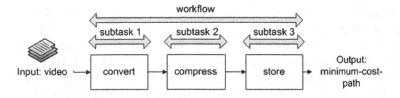

Fig. 1. Example of a workflow

Service" parameters, short QoS. The second question is: How can a user specify restrictions on the workflow? In our example, the user may need a minimum of 15 GB of disk space to store the video, so it only makes sense to search for services which provide more than 15 GB space. These rules are input parameters to the Blackboard. In our example we have the restriction, that the value for converting the video should be smaller than 60, the compression-ratio has to be greater than 20, the disk space has to be greater than 15.

Figure 2 shows a simple Blackboard consisting of 3 regions: convert, compress and store. For region "convert", three different services are available. To all services, a value is assigned. In this example we assume that there is only one cost-parameter for each service.

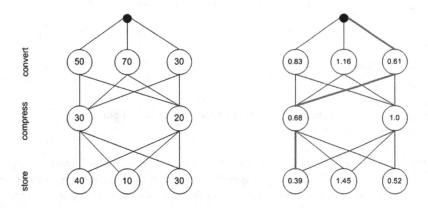

Fig. 2. Minimum cost path

We now have to find services which fulfill our restrictions, in other words, for the first region we search all services with an offer less than 60 and calculate the cost for each service. Then we look for the service with the minimal cost of each region. These are our optimal services.

2.1 Finding the Best Service Provider

In practice, there is more than one value to describe the cost of a service. For example, the user is not only interested which services offer a disk space greater than 15 GB, but he also includes the price for the storage in his calculations. To handle this scenario, we list all parameters of all providers and connect them, the result is a graph. Figure 3 shows the subtask "convert" and two providers (with ID 10 and 20). The first provider offers the conversion to AVI, the second offers the conversion to FLV and gives two more options to choose from, a faster and more expensive possibility (runtime) and a slower option with a lower price. Again, the user sets restrictions; in this example he chose FLV as output format, a runtime less than 80 and a price less than 60. Applying the formulas above to our parameters, we get the cost for each node. Note, that in case of Boolean-parameters, the cost are set to zero if the condition is true and set to infinity, if the condition is false.

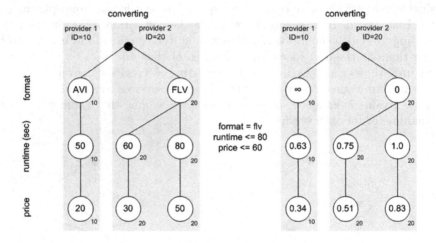

Fig. 3. Calculation of the cost of each node

To find the best provider, we use an algorithm to find the lowest cost path. The Dijkstra algorithm is an appropriate choice for this purpose. In some cases, the estimated cost for a node may be known in advance. If a good estimator is known and the risk of overestimating the cost is low, we can use the A-* algorithm instead of Dijkstra's algorithm to calculate the total cost.

2.2 Blackboard Meets Dijkstra

Our Blackboard approach using Dijkstra's algorithm is defined by Algorithm 1. The algorithm receives a list of regions (e.g. format, price and runtime) and a list of parameters as an input. Parameters are numerical values, such as price = s30. Each parameter is assigned to a service provider (serviceID), for example [price = 30, serviceID = 10].

input: List of regions, list of parameters

```
1  OpenList = [];
2  ClosedList = [];
3  path = [];
4  firstRegion = regionlist[0];
5  lastRegion = regionlist[len(regionlist)-1];

6  OpenList.add(allNodesOf(firstRegion));

7  retrace(Node)
8  |   path += Node;
9  |   if Node.region is firstregion then
10 |   |   return
11 |   else
12 |   |   retrace(Node.ancestor)
13 |   end
14 end

15 while OpenList not emtpy do
16 |   calculateCosts(OpenList);
17 |   currentNode = minimum_cost(OpenList);

18 |   if currentNode.region = lastRegion then
19 |   |   retrace(current);
20 |   end
21 |   foreach parameter in parameterlist do
22 |   |   nextRegion = regionlist.index(current.region)+1;
23 |   |   if parameter.region = nextRegion parameter not in OpenList and
       |   |   parameter not in ClosedList and parameter.serviceID =
       |   |   current.serviceID then
24 |   |   |   parameter.cost = current.cost + parameter.cost;
25 |   |   |   OpenList += parameter;
26 |   |   |   parameter.ancestor = current;
27 |   |   end
28 |   end
29 |   OpenList = OpenList \ current;
30 |   ClosedList += current;
31 end
```

Algorithm 1: Find the best provider combintation

The approach is depicted in Algorithm 1. It starts with the function calculateCosts() to determine the cost of each parameter. Then, the node with the lowest cost is added to the OpenList. The OpenList contains all known but not yet visited nodes. Then, it is checked if the current node is an "endnode" (which means, the last region of the board is reached). If this is not the case, all nodes from the next region, which are provided from the same service provider as the current node are added to the OpenList. Finally, the current node is removed from the OpenList and added to the ClosedList. The ClosedList contains all nodes, which are already visited. The algorithm is running till there are nodes in the OpenList or the exit condition is fulfilled.

3 Workflow Optimization Implementation Architecture

Computational science applications all over the world can benefit from our framework. A real-world application scenario, which we used in the past [6], is the scientific workflow environment of the ATLAS Experiment aiming at discovering new physics at the Large Hadron Collider [1]. The TAG system [3] is a distributed system composed of databases and several web services accessing them.

To describe the implementation architecture of our Blackboard based optimization framework we use the Model-View-Controller concept. A URL opened in a standard Webbrowser represents the "view". The user has the opportunity to set rules via HTML-form, all rules are stored in a shared repository to which only the user and the Blackboard have access. The GUI also displays the results of the algorithm, i.e. those service providers with the best offer. Subsequently, the workflow executes autonomously: The user receives a response with the best offer and has to confirm it. Afterwards, all tasks of the workflow are completed automatically.

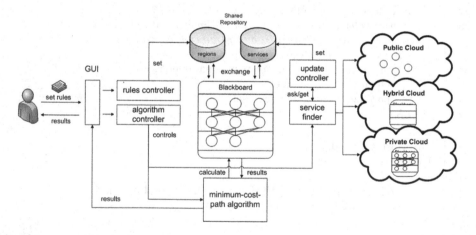

Fig. 4. The components of the sample implementation of the Blackboard approach

Figure 4 shows the graphical representation of the architecture: The left part shows the layer of the user, the right part is the service-layer. The core consists of the Blackboard, which is implemented in the sample-code as a class and several controllers that govern the process. In addition, a shared repository is used for services and rules as a cache, so that they can be accessed quickly by the Blackboard.

For justification the algorithm was implemented within the Google App Engine (GAE) [4]. The Blackboard-Application architecture of the software follows the concept shown in Fig. 4.

4   Conclusion

This paper presents an approach how the selection of services for scientific workflows on the Web can be optimized based on QoS offers of service providers. The novelty of our approach is mapping the service selection problem to a graph representation and to apply a combination of Dijkstra's algorithm and Blackboard method for optimization.

Further we present the architectural framework of the Blackboard approach and its components. The practical feasibility is shown by a use case implementation.

A further research topic is the handling of dynamically changing QoS conditions during workflow execution. The presented method can cope with this challenging situation, which is described in an extended version of this paper [7].

References

1. Aad, G., Abat, E., Abdallah, J., Abdelalim, A., Abdesselam, A., Abdinov, O., Abi, B., Abolins, M., Abramowicz, H., Acerbi, E., et al.: The ATLAS experiment at the cern large hadron collider. J. Instrum. **3**(8), S08003–S08003 (2008)
2. Corkill, D.D.: Blackboard systems. AI Expert **6**(9), 40–47 (1991)
3. Duckeck, G., Jones, R.W.: ATLAS computing. Technical design report by atlas collaboration, CERN (2005)
4. Google App Engine. https://developers.google.com/appengine/. Accessed 07 Apr 2018
5. Vinek, E., Beran, P.P., Schikuta, E.: Classification and composition of QoS attributes in distributed, heterogeneous systems. In: 11th IEEE/ACM International Symposium on Cluster, Cloud, and Grid Computing (CCGrid 2011). IEEE Computer Society Press, Newport Beach, May 2011
6. Vinek, E., Beran, P.P., Schikuta, E.: A dynamic multi-objective optimization framework for selecting distributed deployments in a heterogeneous environment. Procedia Comput. Sci. **4**, 166–175 (2011)
7. Vorhemus, C., Schikuta, E.: Blackboard meets Dijkstra for optimization of web service workflows. arXiv preprint arXiv:1801.00322 (2017)
8. Wanek, H., Schikuta, E.: Using blackboards to optimize grid workflows with respect to quality constraints. In: Fifth International Conference on Grid and Cooperative Computing Workshops (GCC 2006), pp. 290–295. IEEE Computer Society, Los Alamitos(2006)
9. Yu, T., Lin, K.-J.: Service selection algorithms for composing complex services with multiple QoS constraints. In: Benatallah, B., Casati, F., Traverso, P. (eds.) ICSOC 2005. LNCS, vol. 3826, pp. 130–143. Springer, Heidelberg (2005). https://doi.org/10.1007/11596141_11

Augmented Self-paced Learning
with Generative Adversarial Networks

Xiao-Yu Zhang[1], Shupeng Wang[1(✉)], Yanfei Lv[2(✉)], Peng Li[3(✉)],
and Haiping Wang[1]

[1] Institute of Information Engineering, Chinese Academy of Sciences,
Beijing, China
zhangxiaoyu@iie.ac.cn
[2] National Computer Network Emergency Response Technical
Team/Coordination Center of China, Beijing, China
[3] China University of Petroleum (East China), Qingdao, China

Abstract. Learning with very limited training data is a challenging but typical scenario in machine learning applications. In order to achieve a robust learning model, on one hand, the instructive labeled instances should be fully leveraged; on the other hand, extra data source need to be further explored. This paper aims to develop an effective learning framework for robust modeling, by naturally combining two promising advanced techniques, i.e. generative adversarial networks and self-paced learning. To be specific, we present a novel augmented self-paced learning with generative adversarial networks (ASPL-GANs), which consists of three component modules, i.e. a generator G, a discriminator D, and a self-paced learner S. Via competition between G and D, realistic synthetic instances with specific class labels are generated. Receiving both real and synthetic instances as training data, classifier S simulates the learning process of humans in a self-paced fashion and gradually proceeds from easy to complex instances in training. The three components are maintained in a unified framework and optimized jointly via alternating iteration. Experimental results validate the effectiveness of the proposed algorithm in classification tasks.

Keywords: Self-paced learning · Generative adversarial networks
Joint optimization · Dynamic curriculum

1 Introduction

With the evolution of devices and techniques for information creation, acquisition and distribution, all sorts of digital data emerge remarkably and have been enriching people's everyday life. In order to manipulate the large scale data effectively and efficiently, machine learning models need to be developed for automatic content analysis and understanding [1, 2]. The learning performance of a data-driven model is largely dependent on two key factors [3, 4], i.e. the number and quality of the training data, and the modeling strategy designed to explore the training data. On one hand, the acquisition of labeled instances requires intensive human effort from manual labeling. As a result, the accessible training data are usually very limited, which inevitably

© Springer International Publishing AG, part of Springer Nature 2018
Y. Shi et al. (Eds.): ICCS 2018, LNCS 10862, pp. 450–456, 2018.
https://doi.org/10.1007/978-3-319-93713-7_39

jeopardize the learning performance. On the other hand, the inference of projection function from the training data is a process that mimics human perception of the world. To bridge the gap between low-level features and high-level concepts, the sophisticated mechanism behind the learning process of humans should be formulated into the model [5–7].

The idea of automatically generating extra instances as extension of the limited training data is rather attractive, because it is relatively a much more cost-effective way to collect a large number of instances. As a deep learning [8–10] method for estimating generative models based on game theory, generative adversarial networks (GANs) [11] have aroused widespread academic concern. The main idea behind GANs is a minimax two-player game, in which a generator and a discriminator are trained simultaneously via an adversarial process with conflicting objectives. After convergence, the GANs model is capable of generating realistic synthetic instances, which have great potential as augmentation to the existing training data. As for the imitation of learning process of humans, self-paced learning (SPL) [12, 13] is a recently rising technique following the learning principle of humans, which starts by learning easier aspects of the learning task, and then gradually takes more complex instances into training. The easiness of an instances is highly related to the loss between ground truth and estimation, based on which the curriculum is dynamically constructed and the training data are progressively and effectively explored.

In this paper, we propose a novel augmented self-paced learning with generative adversarial networks (ASPL-GANs) algorithm to cope with the issues of training data and learning scheme, by absorbing the powers of two promising advanced techniques, i.e. GANs and SPL. In brief, our framework consists of three component modules: a generator G, a discriminator D, and a self-paced learner S. To extend the limited training data, realistic synthetic instances with predefined labels are generated via G vs. D rivalry. To fully explore the augmented training data, S dynamically maintains a curriculum and progressively refines the model in a self-paced fashion. The three modules are jointly optimized in a unified process, and a robust model is achieve with satisfactory experimental results.

2 Augmented Self-paced Learning with GANs

In the text that follows, we let x denote an instance, and a C-dimensional vector $y = [y_1, \ldots, y_C]^T \in \{0, 1\}^C$ denote the corresponding class label, where C is the number of classes. The i th element y_i is a class label indicator, i.e. $y_i = 1$ if instance x falls into class i, and $y_i = 0$ otherwise. $D(x)$ is a scalar indicating the probability that x comes from real data. $S(x)$ is a C-dimensional vector whose elements indicate the probabilities that x falls into the corresponding classes.

2.1 Overview

The framework and architecture of ASPL-GANs is illustrated in Fig. 1, which consists of three components, i.e. a generator G, a discriminator D and a self-paced learner S. The generator G produces synthetic instances that fall into different classes. The discriminator D and the self-paced learner S are both classifiers: the former is a binary classifier that distinguishes the synthetic instances from the real ones, and the latter is a multi-class classifier that categorizes the instances into various classes. By competing with each other, G generates more and more realist synthetic instances, and meanwhile D's discriminative capacity is constantly improved. As a self-paced learner, S embraces the idea behind the learning process of humans that gradually incorporates easy to more complex instances into training and achieves robust learning model. Moreover, the synthetic instances generated by G are leveraged to further augment the classification performance. The three components are jointly optimized in a unified framework.

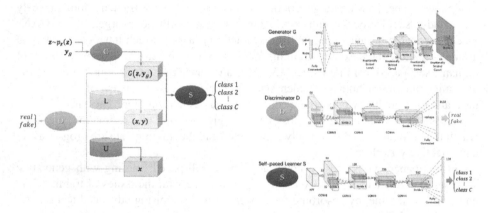

Fig. 1. The framework (left) and architecture (right) of ASPL-GANs.

2.2 Formulation

Firstly, based on the two classifiers in ASPL-GANs, i.e. D and S, we formulate two classification losses on an instance x, i.e. ℓ_d and ℓ_s, as follows.

$$
\begin{aligned}
\ell_d(x) = &- I(x \in \mathcal{X}) \log(P(\text{source}(x) = real|x)) \\
&- I(x \in \mathcal{X}_{syn}) \log(P(\text{source}(x) = synthetic|x)) \\
= &- I(x \in \mathcal{X}) \log(D(x)) - I(x \in \mathcal{X}_{syn}) \log(1 - D(x))
\end{aligned}
\tag{1}
$$

$$
\begin{aligned}
\ell_s(x) &= - \sum_{i=1}^{C} I(y_i = 1) \log(P(y_i = 1|x)) \\
&= - y^T \log(S(x))
\end{aligned}
\tag{2}
$$

where $\mathcal{X}$ and $\mathcal{X}_{syn}$ denote the collection of real and synthetic instances, respectively. Note that $\mathcal{X}$ is divided into labeled and unlabeled subsets according to whether or not the instances' labels are revealed, i.e. $\mathcal{X} = \mathcal{X}_L \bigcup \mathcal{X}_U$, whereas $\mathcal{X}_{syn}$ can be regarded as "labeled" because in the framework the class label is already predefined before a synthetic instance is generated. The indicator function is defined as:

$$I(condition) = \begin{cases} 1, & condition = true \\ 0, & condition = false \end{cases} \tag{3}$$

ℓ_d depicts the consistency between the real source and the predicted source of an instance, whereas ℓ_s measures the consistency between the real class label and the predicted label of an instance. Based on (1) and (2), the three component modules of ASPL-GANs, i.e. G, D and S, can be formulated according to their corresponding objectives, respectively.

Generator G. In ASPL-GANs, by jointly taking a random noise vector $z \sim p_{noise}$ and a class label vector $y_g \in \{0,1\}^C$ as input, G aims to generate a synthetic instance $x_g = G(z, y_g)$ that is hardly discernible from the real instances and meanwhile consistent with the given class label. The loss function for G is formulated as:

$$\begin{aligned} \mathcal{L}_G &= \sum_{x_g \in \mathcal{X}_{syn}} \left(-\ell_d(x_g) + \alpha \ell_s(x_g) \right) \\ &= \sum_{z \sim p_{noise}} \left(\log(1 - D(G(z,y_g))) - \alpha y_g^T \log(S(G(z,y_g))) \right) \end{aligned} \tag{4}$$

The first term in the summation encourages the synthetic instances that are inclined to be mistakenly identified with low discriminative probabilities from D. The second term, however, is in favor of the synthetic instances that fall into the correct categories with their given class labels on generation. α is the parameter to balance the two items.

Discriminator D. Similar to the classic GANs, D receives both real and synthetic instances as input and tries to correctly distinguish the synthetic instances from the real ones. The loss function for D is formulated as:

$$\begin{aligned} \mathcal{L}_D &= \sum_{x \in \mathcal{X} \cup \mathcal{X}_{syn}} \ell_d(x) \\ &= -\sum_{x \in \mathcal{X}} \log(D(x)) - \sum_{z \sim p_{noise}} \log(1 - D(G(z,y_g))) \end{aligned} \tag{5}$$

D aims to maximize the log-likelihood that it assigns input to the correct source. For the real instances, both labeled and unlabeled one are leveraged in modeling D, because their specific class labels are irrelevant to the fact that they are real.

Self-paced Learner S. Different from the traditional self-paced learning model, S receives both real and synthetic instances as training data. In other words, S is trained on dataset $\mathcal{X}_L \bigcup \mathcal{X}_{syn}$, and aims to correctly classify. The training data are organized adaptively w.r.t their easiness, and the model learns gradually from the easy instances to the complex ones in a self-paced way. The loss function for S is formulated as:

$$\mathcal{L}_S = \sum_{x \in \mathcal{X}_L \cup \mathcal{X}_{syn}} (v(x)u(x)\ell_d(x) + f(v(x), \lambda)) \tag{6}$$

where

$$u(x) = \begin{cases} 1, & x \in \mathcal{X}_L \\ \gamma D(x), & x \in \mathcal{X}_{syn} \end{cases} \tag{7}$$

is a weight to penalize the fake training data, and $v(x)$ is the weight reflecting the instance's importance in the objective. Based on (6) and (7), the loss function can be re-whitened as:

$$
\begin{aligned}
\mathcal{L}_S &= \frac{\sum_{x \in \mathcal{X}_L} \left(v(x)\ell_d(x) + f(v(x), \lambda) \right)}{+ \sum_{x_g \in \mathcal{X}_{syn}} \left(\gamma v(x_g) D(x_g) \ell_d(x_g) + f(v(x_g), \lambda) \right)} \\
&= \sum_{x \in \mathcal{X}_L} \left(-v(x) y^T \log(S(x)) + f(v(x), \lambda) \right) \\
&\quad + \sum_{z \sim p_{noise}} \left(\begin{array}{l} -\gamma v(G(z, y_g)) D(G(z, y_g)) y^T \log(S(G(z, y_g))) \\ + f(v(G(z, y_g)), \lambda) \end{array} \right)
\end{aligned} \tag{8}
$$

where $f(v, \lambda)$ is the self-paced regularizer, where λ is the pace age parameter controlling the learning pace. Given λ, the easy instances (with smaller losses) are preferred and leveraged for training. By jointly learning the model parameter θ_S and the latent weight v with gradually increasing λ, more instances (with larger losses) can be automatically included. In this self-paced way, the model learns from easy to complex to become a "mature" learner. S effectively simulates the learning process of intelligent human learners, by adaptively implementing a learning scheme embodied as weight $v(x)$ according to the learning pace. Apart from the real ones, the synthetic instances are leveraged as extra training data to further augment the learning performance. Prior knowledge is encoded as weight $u(x)$ imposed on the training instances. Under this mechanism, both predetermined heuristics and dynamic learning preferences are incorporated into an automatically optimized curriculum for robust learning.

3 Experiments

To validate the effectiveness of ASPL-GANs, we apply it to classification of handwritten digits and real-world images respectively. Detailed description of the datasets can be found in [2].

The proposed ASPL-GANs is compared with the follow methods:

- SL: traditional supervised learning based on labeled dataset $\mathcal{X}_L$;
- SPL: self-paced learning based on labeled dataset $\mathcal{X}_L$;
- SL-GANs: supervised learning with GANs based on labeled dataset $\mathcal{X}_L$ and synthetic dataset $\mathcal{X}_{syn}$.

Softmax regression, also known as multi-class logistic regression, is adopted to classify the images. To be fair, all the methods have access to the same number of labeled real instances. We use two distributions to determine the numbers per class. One is uniform distribution according to which the labeled instances are equally divided between classes. The other is Gaussian distribution in which the majority of labeled instances falls into only a few classes. The two settings simulate the balance and imbalance scenario of training data. For methods leveraging augmented training data, synthetic instances falling into the minority classes are inclined to be generated to alleviate the data imbalance problem.

Figure 2 illustrates the classification results of SL, SPL, SL-GANs and ASPL-GANs on both handwritten digit and real-world image datasets. The horizontal axis shows the number of initial training data.

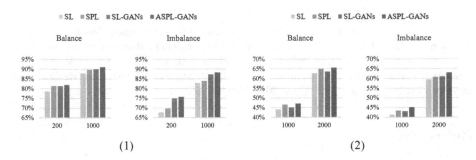

(1)   (2)

Fig. 2. The classification accuracies on (1) handwritten digit dataset and (2) real-world image dataset.

Analysis of the experimental results are as follows.

- Traditional learning method SL is trained on the limited training data, and the training data are incorporated all at once indiscriminately. As a result, the learning performance is severely hampered.
- Both SPL and SL-GANs achieved improvement compared with SL. The former explores the limited training data in a more effective way, whereas the latter leverages extra training data via GANs. As we can see, SL-GANs is especially helpful for simpler dataset such as the handwritten digit dataset, because the generated instances can be more reliable. In contrast, the synthetic real-world images is less realistic, and thus less helpful in augmenting the learning performance. SPL successfully simulates the process of human cognition, and thus achieved consistent improvement for both datasets, especially for the balance scenario. The problem of data imbalance can be alleviated by generating minority instances.
- The proposed ASPL-GANs achieved the highest classification accuracy among all the methods. By naturally combination of GANs and SPL, the problem of insufficient training data and ineffective modeling are effectively addressed.

4   Conclusion

In this paper, we have proposed the augmented self-paced learning with generative adversarial networks (ASPL-GANs) to address the issues w.r.t. limited training data and unsophisticated learning scheme. The contributions of this work are three-fold. Firstly, we developed a robust learning framework, which consists of three component modules formulated with the corresponding objectives and optimized jointly in a unified process to achieve improved learning performance. Secondly, realistic synthetic instance with predetermined class labels are generated via competition between the generator and discriminator to provide extra training data. Last but not least, both real and synthetic are incorporated in a self-paced learning scheme, which integrates prior knowledge and dynamically created curriculum to fully explore the augmented training dataset. Encouraging results are received from experiments on multiple classification tasks.

Acknowledgement. This work was supported by National Natural Science Foundation of China (Grant 61501457, 61602517), Open Project Program of National Laboratory of Pattern Recognition (Grant 201800018), Open Project Program of the State Key Laboratory of Mathematical Engineering and Advanced Computing (Grant 2017A05), and National Key Research and Development Program of China (Grant 2016YFB0801305).

References

1. Bishop, C.: Pattern Recognition and Machine Learning (Information Science and Statistics), 1st edn. Springer, New York (2007). 2006. corr. 2nd printing edn.
2. Zhang, X.Y., Wang, S., Yun, X.: Bidirectional active learning: a two-way exploration into unlabeled and labeled data set. IEEE Trans. Neural Netw. Learn. Syst. 26(12), 3034–3044 (2015)
3. Zhang, X.Y.: Simultaneous optimization for robust correlation estimation in partially observed social network. Neurocomputing. 12(205), 455–462 (2016)
4. Zhang, X.Y., Wang, S., Zhu, X., Yun, X., Wu, G., Wang, Y.: Update vs. upgrade: modeling with indeterminate multi-class active learning. Neurocomputing 25(162), 163–170 (2015)
5. Zhang, X., Xu, C., Cheng, J., Lu, H., Ma, S.: Effective annotation and search for video blogs with integration of context and content analysis. IEEE Trans. Multimedia 11(2), 272–285 (2009)
6. Liu, Y., Zhang, X., Zhu, X., Guan, Q., Zhao, X.: Listnet-based object proposals ranking. Neurocomputing 6(267), 182–194 (2017)
7. Zhang, X.: Interactive patent classification based on multi-classifier fusion and active learning. Neurocomputing 15(127), 200–205 (2014)
8. LeCun, Y., Bengio, Y., Hinton, G.: Deep learning. Nature 521(7553), 436–444 (2015)
9. Bengio, Y., Courville, A., Vincent, P.: Representation learning: a review and new perspectives. IEEE Trans. PAMI 35(8), 1798–1828 (2013)
10. Xu, G., Wu, H.Z., Shi, Y.Q.: Structural design of convolution neural networks for steganalysis. IEEE Signal Process. Lett. 23(5), 708–712 (2016)
11. Goodfellow, I., Pouget-Abadie, J., Mirza, M., Xu, B., Warde-Farley, D., Ozair, S., Courville, A., Bengio, Y.: Generative adversarial nets. In: Advances in Neural Information Processing Systems pp. 2672–2680 (2014)
12. Meng, D., Zhao, Q., Jiang, L.: What objective does self-paced learning indeed optimize? arXiv preprint arXiv:1511.06049. Accessed 19 Nov 2015
13. Kumar, M.P., Packer, B., Koller, D.: Self-paced learning for latent variable models. In: Advances in Neural Information Processing Systems pp. 1189–1197 (2010)

Benchmarking Parallel Chess Search in Stockfish on Intel Xeon and Intel Xeon Phi Processors

Pawel Czarnul[(✉)] [iD]

Faculty of Electronics, Telecommunications and Informatics,
Gdansk University of Technology, Narutowicza 11/12, 80-233 Gdańsk, Poland
pczarnul@eti.pg.edu.pl

Abstract. The paper presents results from benchmarking the parallel multithreaded Stockfish chess engine on selected multi- and many-core processors. It is shown how the strength of play for an n-thread version compares to 1-thread version on both Intel Xeon and latest Intel Xeon Phi x200 processors. Results such as the number of wins, losses and draws are presented and how these change for growing numbers of threads. Impact of using particular cores on Intel Xeon Phi is shown. Finally, strengths of play for the tested computing devices are compared.

Keywords: Parallel chess engine · Stockfish · Intel Xeon
Intel Xeon Phi

1 Introduction

For the past several years, growth in performance of computing devices has been possible mainly through increasing the number of cores, apart from other improvements such as cache organization and size, much less through increase in processor clock speed. This is especially visible in top HPC systems on the TOP500 list [14]. The top system is based on Sunway manycore processors, the second is a hybrid multicore Intel Xeon + Intel Xeon Phi coprocessor based system and the third a hybrid multicore Intel Xeon + NVIDIA P100 GPUs.

It is becoming very important to assess which computing devices perform best for particular classes of applications, especially when gains from increasing the number of threads are not obvious. We investigate performance of parallel chess game playing in the strong Stockfish engine [13], especially on the latest Intel Xeon Phi x200 processor which features upgraded internal mesh based architecture, MCDRAM memory and out of order execution. This is compared to both scalability and playing strength on server type Intel Xeon CPUs.

Partially supported by the Polish Ministry of Science and Higher Education, part of tests performed at Academic Computer Center, Gdansk, Poland, part of tests performed on hardware donated by Intel Technology Poland.

© Springer International Publishing AG, part of Springer Nature 2018
Y. Shi et al. (Eds.): ICCS 2018, LNCS 10862, pp. 457–464, 2018.
https://doi.org/10.1007/978-3-319-93713-7_40

2   Related Work

Performance of chess players, both human and engines, that play against each other is typically assessed using the Elo rating system [6,11]. Some approaches have been proposed such as the Markovian interpretation for assessment of play by various players from various eras to be able to compare strengths of play [1]. The typical algorithm for tree search in chess has been alpha-beta search. Several algorithms and approaches[1] regarding parallelization of chess playing have been proposed. In Young Brothers Wait Concept [7] the algorithm first searches the oldest brother in a search tree to obtain cutoff values and search other branches in parallel. In Lazy SMP many threads or processes search the same tree but with various depths and move orderings. It is used in many engines today such as Stockfish. Asynchronous Parallel Hierarchical Iterative Deepening (APHID) is an algorithm that is asynchronous and divides the search tree among the master (top level) which makes passes over its part of the tree and slaves which search deeper parts of the tree. Paper [3] presents speed-ups from 14.35 up to around 37.44 on 64 processors for various programs including Chinook, TheTurk, Crafty and Keyano. Monte-Carlo Tree Search, while successful for Go, suffers from issues such as difficulty to identify search traps in chess [2]. Despite optimizations, the testbed implementation could not match the strength of alpha-beta search. On the other hand, the very recent paper [12] presents AlphaZero – a program that defeated Stockfish using alpha-beta search. AlphaZero uses MCTS combined with incorporation of a non-linear function approximation based on a deep neural network. It searches fewer positions focusing on selected variations. In paper [16] the authors proposed a method called P-GPP that aimed at improving the Game Position Parallelization (GPP) that allows parallel analysis of game subtrees by various workers. P-GPP extends GPP with assignment of workers to nodes using realization probability. Implementation was tested using Stockfish for workers with communication between the master and workers using TCP sockets for up to 64 cores using two computers. The authors have demonstrated increased playing strength up to sixty workers at the win rate of 0.646.

Benchmarking performance and speed-ups was performed in several works and for engines and algorithms playing various games as well as for various computing devices – CPUs, GPUs, coprocessors such as Intel Xeon Phi. For instance, in [9] Monte Carlo Tree Search (MCTS) was benchmarked on Intel Xeon Phi and Intel Xeon processors. Speed-ups up to around 47 were achieved for Intel Xeon Phi and up to around 18 for Intel Xeon across all tested implementations including C++ 11, Cilk Plus, TBB and TPFIFO with a queue implementing work sharing through a thread pool. Furthermore, paper [10] contains data and comparison of performance of Intel Xeon CPU to Intel Xeon Phi for the MCTS algorithm useful in games such as Hex and Go. The same authors tested performance and speed-ups on both 2x Intel Xeon E5-2596v2 for a total of 24 physical cores and 48 logical processor as well as Intel Xeon Phi 7120P with

---

[1] https://chessprogramming.wikispaces.com/Parallel+Search.

61 cores and 244 logical processors. The authors, having benchmarked n-thread versions against n/2-thread versions, have determined that almost perfect speed-ups could be observed up to 16 and 64 cores for the two platforms respectively. Furthermore, they determined that the Intel Xeon Phi coprocessor offered visibly worse total performance than CPUs due to relatively higher communication/compute ratio. In paper [8] the authors proposed a general parallel game tree search algorithm on a GPU and benchmarked its performance compared to a CPU-based platform for two games: Connect6 and chess. The speed-up compared to the latter platform with pruning turned out to be 10.58x and 7.26x for the aforementioned games respectively. In terms of large scale parallelization on a cluster, paper [15] presents results obtained on a cluster for Shogi chess. The authors have investigated effects of dynamic updates in parallel searching of the alpha-beta tree which proved to offer significant improvements in performance. Speed-ups up to around 250 for branching factor 5 and depth 24 on 1536 cores of a cluster with dynamic updates and without sharing transposition tables were measured. The authors have shown that using Negascout in the master and proper windows in workers decreases the number of nodes visited and generates speed-up of up to 346 for the aforementioned configuration. Several benchmarks have been conducted for Stockfish that demonstrate visible speed-up versus the number of threads on multi-core CPUs[2,3].

The contribution of this work is as follows:

1. benchmarking the reference Stockfish chess engine on the state-of-the-art Intel Xeon Phi x200 manycore processor,
2. testing on how selection of cores (thread affinity) affects performance,
3. comparison of Intel Xeon and Intel Xeon Phi performance for Stockfish.

3   Methodology and Experiments

Similarly to the tests already performed on multicore CPUs (see footnotes 2 and 3), in this work we benchmark the Stockfish engine running with a particular number of threads against its 1 thread version. Gains allow to assess how much better a multithreaded version is and to what number of threads (and cores on which the threads run) it scales. This is especially interesting in view of the recent Intel Xeon x200 processors with up to 72 physical cores and 288 logical processors.

For the experiments performed in this work the following computing devices were used: 2 Intel Xeon E5-2680 v2 at 2.80 GHz CPUs with a total of 20 physical cores and 40 logical processors as multi-core processors and 1 Intel Xeon Phi CPU 7210 at 1.30 GHz with a total of 64 physical cores and 256 logical processors.

Each configuration included 1000 games played by an n thread version against the 1 thread version. Games were played with white and black pieces by the versions with switching colors of the pieces after every game. For the 256 thread

---

[2] http://www.fastgm.de/schach/SMP-scaling.pdf.
[3] http://www.fastgm.de/schach/SMP-scaling-SF8-C10.pdf.

configuration, the Stockfish code was slightly updated to allow such a configuration (the standard version allowed up to 128 threads). Time controls were 60 s for first 40 moves.

As a reference, Fig. 1 presents how the results changed for a configuration of an n-thread Stockfish against the 1 thread version over successive games played on the Intel Xeon Phi. The score is computed as follows from the point of view of the n-thread version:

$$s = \frac{1 \cdot n_{\text{wins}} + \frac{1}{2} \cdot n_{\text{draws}}}{n_{\text{wins}} + n_{\text{draws}} + n_{\text{losses}}} \tag{1}$$

where: n_{wins} – number of wins, n_{draws} – number of draws, n_{losses} – number of losses for the n-thread version.

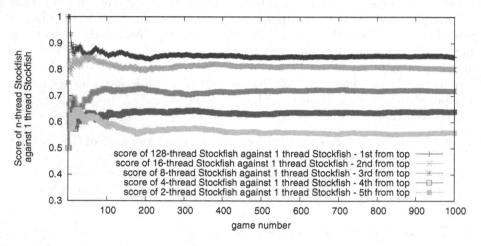

Fig. 1. Score of n-thread Stockfish against 1 thread Stockfish on Intel Xeon Phi x200

Tests were performed using tool `cutechess-cli` [4]. Firstly, tests were performed on the Intel Xeon Phi on how using particular cores affects performance. In one version, the application was instructed to use physical cores first. This was achieved with command `taskset` according to placement and identification of cores provided in file `/proc/cpuinfo`. In the other version, threads could use all available logical processors, no `taskset` command was used. Comparison of results for the Intel Xeon Phi and the two versions is shown in Fig. 2.

Following tests were performed with using physical cores first on the Intel Xeon Phi x200. Figure 3 presents numbers of games with a given result: win, loss or draw out of 1000 games played by each n thread version against the 1 thread version and the final scores for each version computed using Eq. 1. It can be seen that gain is visible up to and including 128 threads with a slight drop for 256 threads. The Stockfish code was modified (changed limits) to allow running on 256 threads as the original version limited the number to 128 threads.

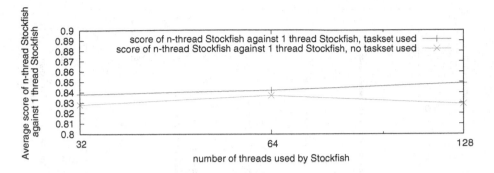

Fig. 2. How using `taskset` affects performance on Intel Xeon Phi x200

Furthermore, analogous tests were performed for a workstation with 2 Intel Xeon E5-2680 v2 2.80 GHz CPUs with a total of 20 physical cores and 40 logical processors, available to the author. Numbers of particular results and final scores are shown in Fig. 4. For this configuration, best results were obtained for 16 threads with a slight drop for 40 threads.

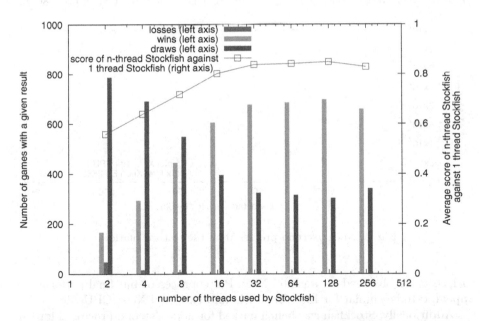

Fig. 3. n thread Stockfish against 1 thread Stockfish on Intel Xeon Phi x200

Apparently, better scalability for the Intel Xeon Phi stems from relatively lower performance of a single core and consequently better potential for improvement of the playing strength. This can be observed also for parallel computation of similarity measures between large vectors for which better speed-up compared

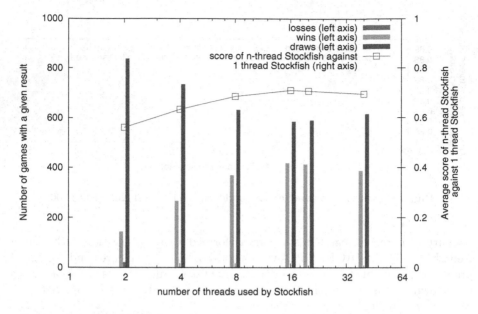

Fig. 4. n thread Stockfish against 1 thread Stockfish on 2 x Intel Xeon E5-2680 v2

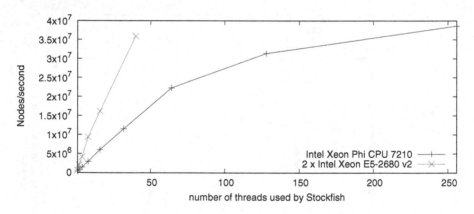

Fig. 5. Nodes/second processed on the testbed platforms

to 1 core was observed for an Intel Xeon Phi coprocessor but final performance appeared to be similar for Intel Xeon Phi and two Intel Xeon CPUs [5].

Additionally, Stockfish was benchmarked for nodes/second processed for various numbers of threads involved. Results are shown in Fig. 5. The performance of a single Intel Xeon Phi core is lower than that of a single Intel Xeon processor core. For the maximum number of threads equal to the number of logical processors on both platforms, the theoretical performance of the Intel Xeon Phi is slightly larger. It should be noted though that this is more of a theoretical benchmark for performance of processing of this particular code.

Finally, the best version on the Intel Xeon E5 CPUs using 16 threads was tested against the best version on the Intel Xeon Phi processor using 128 threads. Out of 1050 games, 38 were won on Intel Xeon Phi, 37 were lost and 975 draws were observed for a final score of 0.500047619 computed using Eq. 1.

4   Summary and Future Work

In the paper we have investigated speed-up potential of the Stockfish multi-threaded chess engine on both multi- and many-core processors such as Intel Xeon and latest Intel Xeon Phi x200 processors. It was shown that using `taskset` to select cores on an Intel Xeon Phi improved performance. Performance of two tested Intel Xeon processors appeared to be practically the same as one tested Intel Xeon Phi processor for the chess engine. We plan to test more computing devices including latest Intel Xeon CPUs as well as to conduct tests for a wider range of time controls, especially larger ones that might turn out to be more beneficial for processors with more cores.

References

1. Alliot, J.M.: Who is the master? ICGA J. **39**(1), 3–43 (2017)
2. Arenz, O.: Monte carlo chess. Bachelor thesis, Technische Universitat Darmstadt, April 2012
3. Brockington, M.G., Schaeffer, J.: APHID: asynchronous parallel game-tree search. J. Parallel Distrib. Comput. **60**, 247–273 (2000)
4. Cute Chess Website (2017). https://github.com/cutechess/cutechess
5. Czarnul, P.: Benchmarking performance of a hybrid intel xeon/xeon phi system for parallel computation of similarity measures between large vectors. Int. J. Parallel Prog. **45**(5), 1091–1107 (2017)
6. Elo, A.: The Rating of Chess Players, Past and Present. Ishi Press, Bronx (2008)
7. Feldmann, R., Monien, B., Mysliwietz, P., Vornberger, O.: Distributed game tree search. In: Kumar, V., Gopalakrishnan, P.S., Kanal, L.N. (eds.) Parallel Algorithms for Machine Intelligence and Vision, pp. 66–101. Springer, New York (1990). https://doi.org/10.1007/978-1-4612-3390-9_3
8. Li, L., Liu, H., Wang, H., Liu, T., Li, W.: A parallel algorithm for game tree search using GPGPU. IEEE Trans. Parallel Distrib. Syst. **26**(8), 2114–2127 (2015)
9. Mirsoleimani, S.A., Plaat, A., Herik, J.V.D., Vermaseren, J.: Scaling Monte Carlo tree search on Intel Xeon Phi. In: 2015 IEEE 21st International Conference on Parallel and Distributed Systems (ICPADS), pp. 666–673 (2016)
10. Mirsoleimani, S.A., Plaat, A., van den Herik, H.J., Vermaseren, J.: Parallel Monte Carlo tree search from multi-core to many-core processors. In: TrustCom/BigDataSE/ISPA, Helsinki, Finland, 20–22 August 2015, vol. 3, pp. 77–83. IEEE (2015)
11. Rydzewski, A., Czarnul, P.: A distributed system for conducting chess games in parallel. In: 6th International Young Scientists Conference in HPC and Simulation. Procedia Computer Science, Kotka, November 2017

12. Silver, D., Hubert, T., Schrittwieser, J., Antonoglou, I., Lai, M., Guez, A., Lanctot, M., Sifre, L., Kumaran, D., Graepel, T., Lillicrap, T., Simonyan, K., Hassabis, D.: Mastering Chess and Shogi by self-play with a general reinforcement learning algorithm. ArXiv e-prints, December 2017
13. Stockfish (2017). https://stockfishchess.org/
14. Strohmaier, E., Dongarra, J., Simon, H., Meuer, M.: Top500. www.top500.org/
15. Ura, A., Tsuruoka, Y., Chikayama, T.: Dynamic prediction of minimal trees in large-scale parallel game tree search. J. Inf. Process. **23**(1), 9–19 (2015)
16. Yokoyama, S., Kaneko, T., Tanaka, T.: Parameter-free tree style pipeline in asynchronous parallel game-tree search. In: Plaat, A., van den Herik, J., Kosters, W. (eds.) ACG 2015. LNCS, vol. 9525, pp. 210–222. Springer, Cham (2015). https://doi.org/10.1007/978-3-319-27992-3_19

Leveraging Uncertainty Analysis of Data to Evaluate User Influence Algorithms of Social Networks

Jianjun Wu[1,2], Ying Sha[1,2(✉)], Rui Li[1,2], Jianlong Tan[1,2], and Bin Wang[1,2]

[1] Institute of Information Engineering, Chinese Academy of Sciences, Beijing, China
[2] School of Cyber Security, University of Chinese Academy of Sciences, Beijing, China
{wujianjun,shaying,lirui,tanjianlong,wangbin}@iie.ac.cn

Abstract. Identifying of highly influential users in social networks is critical in various practices, such as advertisement, information recommendation, and surveillance of public opinion. According to recent studies, different existing user influence algorithms generally produce different results. There are no effective metrics to evaluate the representation abilities and the performance of these algorithms for the same dataset. Therefore, the results of these algorithms cannot be accurately evaluated and their limits cannot be effectively observered. In this paper, we propose an uncertainty-based Kalman filter method for predicting user influence optimal results. Simultaneously, we develop a novel evaluation metric for improving maximum correntropy and normalized discounted cumulative gain (NDCG) criterion to measure the effectiveness of user influence and the level of uncertainty fluctuation intervals of these algorithms. Experimental results validate the effectiveness of the proposed algorithm and evaluation metrics for different datasets.

Keywords: Evaluation of user influence algorithms
Influential users · Optimal estimation

1 Introduction

Recent advancements in measuring user influence have resulted in a proliferation of methods which learn various features of datasets. Even when discussing the same topic, different algorithms usually produce different results [2], because of differences in user roles and evaluation metrics, as well as because of improper application scenarios, etc.

Existing research on user influence algorithms can be divided into four categories focusing on four primary areas: (1) message content, (2) network structure, (3) both network structure and message content, and (4) user behaviors. However, these studies and evaluation criteria have not been used to assess the reliability of the algorithms or the error intervals of such reliability.

© Springer International Publishing AG, part of Springer Nature 2018
Y. Shi et al. (Eds.): ICCS 2018, LNCS 10862, pp. 465–472, 2018.
https://doi.org/10.1007/978-3-319-93713-7_41

Algorithms based on message content consider only the influence of ordered pairs, as well as pairs in the incorrect order. These algorithms have not investigate how other social behaviors influence people and information. Network structure approaches often assume that the perception of distance between users has a positive proportional relationship with the degree of influence between users, such as PageRank, Degree Centrality, IARank, KHYRank, K-truss, etc. However, not considering user interest and time for evaluation of user influence. Some studies (including TunkRank, TwitterRank [9], and LDA and its series of topic models) have considered message content and network structure. The majority of algorithms have adopted the Kendall correlation coefficient and friend recommendation scenarios. In addition to considering user behavior, Bizid et al. [1] applied supervised learning algorithms to identify prominent influencers and evaluate the effectiveness of the algorithm. However, when recall is used to evaluate the effectiveness of algorithms for a specific event, differences are not reflected with respect to the relative order of influence among individuals.

To address the above issues, this paper proposes an uncertainty-based Kalman filtering method for predicting optimal user influence result. Additionally, we propose a novel evaluation metric for improving the maximum correntropy and NDCG criterion [4] for measuring user influence effectiveness and the margin of error values for the uncertainty fluctuations of different algorithms.

To summarize, our contributions are as follows:

(1) An uncertainty-based Kalman filter method is proposed for predicting optimal user influence results. The method uses a measurement matrix, state-transition matrix, and has minimum measurement errors, allowing the method to produce the optimal approximation of (1) the true user-influence value sequence and (2) the periodic measurements of changes in user influence.

(2) We propose a metric for evaluating user influence algorithms. The metric uses impact-factors and margins of error to evaluate user influence algorithms. This is achieved by improving the maximum correntropy and NDCG criterion for measuring the effectiveness of user influence.

(3) We propose a method for comparing different influence algorithms and obtaining the error ratios for different algorithms.

2   Problem Formulation

Suppose that there are two algorithms (1 and 2) used to calculate user influence. A common method for performing such calculations is to first apply a mathematical expression for user influence. If the true value of user influence is fixed, then the true value set can be defined as $T = \{Y_n\}$, where Y_n is the true value of the measurements. The eigen function of this set can be expressed as follows:

$$G_T(y) = \begin{cases} 1 & y_i \in T \\ 0 & y_i \notin T \end{cases} \tag{1}$$

In addition, the measurements have a certain fluctuation range. Therefore, we treated the measurements as a fuzzy set of the true values, and defined it as follows:

$$\widehat{T} = \{y, u_{\widehat{T}}(y) | y \in [0, 1]\} \tag{2}$$

where $\widehat{T}$ is the fuzzy set of the true values and $u_{\widehat{T}}(y)$ is a membership function, indicating the probability that y belongs to the true value set.

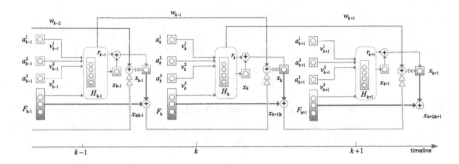

Fig. 1. Architecture of IKFE algorithm.

3   Proposed Model

This section focuses on our proposed model (improved Kalman filter estimation, IKFE); the associated framework is shown in Fig. 1. Section 3.1 describes our representation of the user influence function, among the true values (x_k), optimal estimate values ($\hat{x}_k$), predictive values ($\hat{x}_{k|k-1}$), and measurement values (z_k) for user influence produced different algorithms. Section 3.2 illustrates the optimal estimates and parameter learning for user influence.

3.1   Function of User Influence

The initial value of a user's influence, such as a_k^1, a_k^2, and a_k^3, was the result of one of the different influence algorithms at time k in Fig. 1. This value was regarded as a state variable to be estimated; the measurements of its calculated values were regarded as the measurements of its state.

(1) **True Value of User Influence:** The true value of user influence at time k can be expressed by the optimal estimated user influence value and the optimal estimation error that occurs in the computing process:

$$x_k = \widehat{x}_k + r_k \tag{3}$$

where x_k is the true value vector at time k; $\widehat{x}_k$ is the optimal estimated value vector at time k; and r_k is the estimated error vector at time k.

(2) **User Influence Prediction and Value:** We used a state-transition matrix to model changes in user influence. We could consider the process error to be the uncertainty. The true value of user influence at time k is generated from the state transition of users' influence at time $k-1$, which is expressed as

$$x_k = F_{k-1}x_{k-1} + w_{k-1} \tag{4}$$

where F_{k-1} denotes the state-transition matrix at time $k-1$ and w_{k-1} denotes the process error at time $k-1$.

The predicted value of user influence at time k, which is generated based on the users' states at time $k-1$, can be expressed as the product of the state transition matrix, as well as the optimal estimate at time $k-1$.

$$\widehat{x}_{k|k-1} = F_{k-1}\widehat{x}_{k-1} \tag{5}$$

(3) **User Influence Measurements and Values:** The following equation can be computed the relationship between the measured value and the true values of user influence, which can be expressed as follows:

$$z_k = H_k x_k + v_k \tag{6}$$

where z_k denotes the measured value of user influence at time k, H_k denotes the measurement matrix, v_k denotes the measurement error, and x_k is the true value of user influence at time k.

3.2   Optimal Estimate of User Influence

Based on Eq. (3) and the goal of achieving the minimum error for optimal estimates can be expressed as follows:

$$minJ_k = E[r_k^T r_k] \tag{7}$$

The best estimate of user influence at time k can be expressed as follows:

$$\widehat{x}_k = \widehat{x}_{k|k-1} + G_k(z_k - H_k\widehat{x}_{k|k-1}) \tag{8}$$

where G_k is the Kalman filter's gain [5].

4   Evaluation of User Influence Algorithms

In this section, we discuss our proposed metrics for evaluating user influence (improving the maximum correntropy criterion, IMCC) and the error intervals between different user influence algorithms. Section 4.1 presents our proposed criterion for evaluating user influence. In Sect. 4.2, metrics are applied to measure the margin of error of user influence algorithms.

4.1 Proposed Criterion

It can be seen from Eq. (6) that the measurement of user influence is to restore the true value of user influence through the measurement matrix (H_k). Specifically, the correntropy of the measurement sequence generated from the state-of-the-art algorithm and true value sequence is maximized (improving maximum correntropy criterion), which can be expressed as follows:

$$Sim(X,Y) = E[\ell(X,Y)] = \int \ell(X,Y) \, dP_{X,Y}(x,y) \tag{9}$$

where X is the measurement sequence, Y is the true value sequence, $P_{X,Y}(x,y)$ expresses an unknown joint probability distribution, and $\ell(X,Y)$ is a shift-invariant Mercer kernel function. $\ell(X,Y)$ can be expressed as follows:

$$\ell(X,Y) = exp\left(-\frac{e^2}{2\sigma^2}\right) \tag{10}$$

where $e = X - Y$, σ indicates the window size of the kernel function, and $\sigma > 0$. The derivation is presented in [3]. Thus, we can obtain the following optimal target:

$$argmax\frac{1}{N}\sum_{i=1}^{N} G\left(e_i\right) \tag{11}$$

where N is the number of users in the sample. The function $G\left(e_i\right)$ can be expressed as follows:

$$\sum_{i=1}^{T} \frac{\left(2^{R_i} - 1\right) + f_i}{\log_2\left(i+1\right) + \Delta l_i} \tag{12}$$

where R_i indicates the standard influence score of user i, and T is the truncation level at which $G\left(e_i\right)$ is computed. Here, Δl_i denotes the error intervals of i in the results. f_i represents the adjustment factor of i's influence, which can be expressed as follows:

$$f_i = \sum_{z=1}^{n} w_{iz} \frac{k_{iz}}{\Delta t_{iz} + 1} \tag{13}$$

where w_{iz} indicates the weighted value of user i being the maker of topic z, k_{iz} is the number of messages sent by user i regarding topic z, and Δt_{iz} denotes the length of time that user i participated in the discussion of topic z.

4.2 Evaluation of User Influence Algorithms

Substituting the measurement of user influence calculated by corresponding algorithms and the results of manual scoring in Eq. (6) yields the following proportional relationship between the measurement error of Algorithms 1 and 2. This can be expressed as follows:

$$I = \frac{\left(H_k' - H_{k(2)}\right)^{-1} v_{k(2)}}{\left(H_k' - H_{k(1)}\right)^{-1} v_{k(1)}} \implies \frac{v_{k(2)}}{v_{k(1)}} = \left(\frac{I - H_{k(2)}}{I - H_{k(1)}}\right) \qquad (14)$$

Equation (14) shows that the measurement errors of Algorithm 1 and 2 depend on the measurement matrix, and they are inversely proportional to the shift-invariant Mercer kernel function and proportional to the maximum correntropy. The detailed derivation process is not shown here due to lack of space.

5   Experiment

Experimental data were obtained from two data sets: RepLab-2014[1], and the Twitter dataset obtained from our own network spider, as listed in Table 1. The results for the top 10, top 20, top 40 user sequences computed by our proposed algorithm were compared with the results from state-of-the-art algorithms with single-feature algorithms for identifying user influence (using NDCG, the Kendall correlation coefficient, and the IMCC metric).

Table 1. Experimental datasets

Dataset	User	Following/followee	Posts/messages	Topics
RepLab-2014	39,752 (seed user 2,500)	123,867	8,535,473	Automotive and banking
Twitter dataset	1,072,954 (seed user 1,810)	3,057,162	37,435,218	Taiwan election, Diaoyu Islands dispute and Occupy Central

Table 2. Evaluation of NDCG and IMCC based on Paired Tests Bootstrap Tests and estimated difference required for satisfying achieved significance level (ASL), $ASL < \alpha$ ($\alpha = 0.05$; Twitter dataset).

Test	NDCG						IMCC					
	$\sigma = 10$			$\sigma = 20$			$\sigma = 10$			$\sigma = 20$		
Topics	a[1]	b[2]	c[3]	a[1]	b[2]	c[3]	a[1]	b[2]	c[3]	a[1]	b[2]	c[3]
Sig. (2-tailed)	0.224	0.005	0.025	0.031	0.095	0.014	0.322	0.996	0.154	0.156	0.166	0.363
Estimated diff.	0.27						0.04					

a[1] presents Diaoyu Islands dispute and Occupy Central. b[2] presents Taiwan election and Occupy Central. c[3] presents Diaoyu Islands dispute and Taiwan election.

5.1   Evaluation Criteria

To evaluate the validity of the IKFE algorithm and IMCC metric, the IKFE algorithm was compared with TwitterRank (TR) [9], Topic-Behavior Influence Tree (TBIT) [10], ProfileRank (ProR) [7] and single-feature-based algorithms for measuring user influence in the two datasets.

---

[1] http://nlp.uned.es/replab2014/.

5.2   Performance Analysis

Analysis of σ Parameter and IKFE Algorithm. Figure 2 show that the parameter σ takes different window sizes, such as 10, 20, and 40, thus impacting the performance of the algorithm. Especially, a window size of 10 results in a significantly different performance of the algorithm compared to window sizes of 20 and 40. As the window size increases, the performance of various algorithms' capacity approximates the same. For the IKFE algorithm, user influence shows a slow decrease from time k to $k+1$. Figure 3 shows that the values of single-feature algorithms show a greater change than those of other algorithms. In other words, IKFE algorithm is better able to synthesize features. Simultaneously, the fluctuation range of the IKFE algorithm is limited.

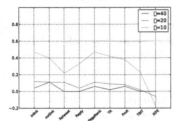

Fig. 2. Trend of algorithms for different σ based on the Kendall coefficient for the RepLab-2014 dataset.

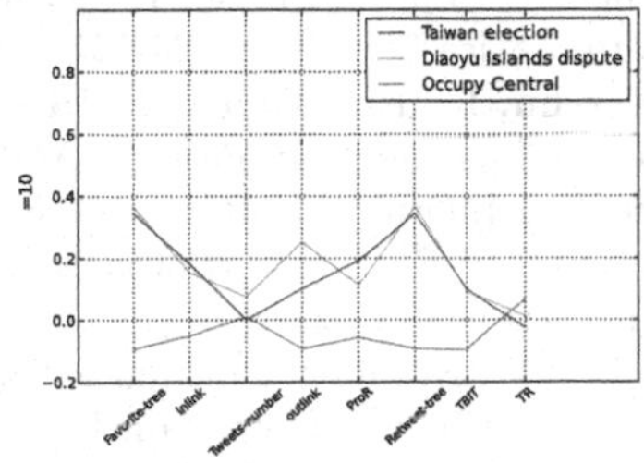

Fig. 3. Correlation of IKFE algorithm and other algorithms by the Kendall on different topics at $k+1$ time.

Comparison Metrics. As in previous work [6], we set $B = 1,000$ (B is the number of bootstrap samples). In Table 2, the p-value denoted by "Sig. (2-tailed)" is two-sided. Our results show different p-values for different window sizes. The results for the IMCC metric are not significant at the 0.05 level, whereas those for the NDCG are significant when experimenting with user sequences on c^3 (cross-topics) or different window sizes. It can be observed that the IMCC is more sensitive [6] than the NDCG. The IMCC is better that the NDCG in terms of estimated differences as the discriminative power described by [8].

6   Conclusions

We used IKFE, an uncertainty-based improved Kalman filter method, to predict the optimal user influence results. Additionally, we proposed IMCC, a metric for evaluating influence algorithms by improving the maximum correntropy and NDCG criterion. Next, we will study how to evaluate user influence algorithms of communities in social networks.

Acknowledgements. This work is supported by National Science and Technology Major Project under Grant No. 2017YFB0803003, No. 2016QY03D0505 and No. 2017YFB0803301, Natural Science Foundation of China (No. 61702508).

References

1. Bizid, I., Nayef, N., Boursier, P., Faiz, S., Morcos, J.: Prominent users detection during specific events by learning on and off-topic features of user activities. In: 2015 IEEE/ACM In-ternational Conference on Advances in Social Networks Analysis and Mining, pp. 500–503 ACM, New York (2015)
2. Cha, M., Haddadi, H., Benevenuto, F., Gummadi, K.P.: Measuring user influence in twitter: the million follower fallacy. In: International Conference on Weblogs and Social Media, Icwsm, Washington (2010)
3. Chen, B., Liu, X., Zhao, H., Principe, J.C.: Maximum correntropy kalman filter. Automatica **76**, 70–77 (2015)
4. Järvelin, K., Kekäläinen, J.: IR evaluation methods for retrieving highly relevant documents. In: International ACM SIGIR Conference on Research and Development in Information Retrieval, pp. 41–48, ACM (2000)
5. Kalman, R.E.: A new approach to linear filtering and prediction problems. J. Basic Eng. Trans. **82**, 35 (1960)
6. Sakai, T.: Evaluating evaluation metrics based on the bootstrap. In: International ACM SIGIR Conference on Research and Development in Information Retrieval, pp. 525–532. ACM (2006)
7. Silva, A., Guimaraes, S., Meira Jr, W., Zaki, M.: Profilerank: finding relevant content and influential users based on information diffusion. In: 7th Workshop on Social Network Mining and Analysis, ACM, New York (2013)
8. Wang, X., Dou, Z., Sakai, T., Wen, J.R.: Evaluating search result diversity using intent hierarchies. In: International ACM SIGIR Conference on Research and Development in Information Retrieval, pp.415–424. ACM (2016)
9. Weng, J., Lim, E.P., Jiang, J., He, Q.: Twitterrank: finding topic-sensitive influential twitterers. In: 3th ACM International Conference on Web Search and Data Mining, pp. 216–231. ACM, New York (2010)
10. Wu, J., Sha, Y., Li, R., Liang, Q., Jiang, B., Tan, J., Wang, B.: Identification of influential users based on topic-behavior influence tree in social networks. In: the 6th Conference on Natural Language Processing and Chinese Computing. Da Lian (2017)

E-Zone: A Faster Neighbor Point Query Algorithm for Matching Spacial Objects

Xiaobin Ma[1], Zhihui Du[1(✉)], Yankui Sun[1], Yuan Bai[2], Suping Wu[2],
Andrei Tchernykh[3], Yang Xu[4], Chao Wu[4], and Jianyan Wei[4]

[1] Tsinghua National Laboratory for Information Science and Technology,
Department of Computer Science and Technology, Tsinghua University,
Beijing, China
duzh@tsinghua.edu.cn
[2] College of Information Engineering, Ningxia University, Yinchuan, China
[3] CICESE Research Center, Ensenada, Mexico
[4] National Astronomical Observatories, Chinese Academy of Sciences,
Beijing, China

Abstract. Latest astronomy projects observe the spacial objects with astronomical cameras generating images continuously. To identify transient objects, the position of these objects on the images need to be compared against a reference table on the same portion of the sky, which is a complex search task called cross match. We designed Euclidean-Zone (E-Zone), a method for faster neighbor point queries which allows efficient cross match between spatial catalogs. In this paper, we implemented E-Zone algorithm utilizing euclidean distance between celestial objects with pixel coordinates to avoid the complex mathematical functions in equatorial coordinate system. Meanwhile, we surveyed on the parameters of our model and other system factors to find optimal configures of this algorithm. In addition to the sequential algorithm, we modified the serial program and implemented an OpenMP parallelized version. For serial version, the results of our algorithm achieved a speedup of 2.07 times over using equatorial coordinate system. Also, we achieved 19 ms for sequential queries and 5 ms for parallel queries for 200,000 objects on a single CPU processor over a 230,520 synthetic reference database.

Keywords: Cross match · Zone · Parallel · OpenMP

1 Introduction

Ground-based Wide Angle Cameras (GWAC) [7] in China is a telescope build for observing the sky continuously, which producing raw images every dozens of seconds. Millions of entries of celestial property catalogs will be extracted from these images. Spacial objects in the catalog flow need to be matched against reference data to identify them, subsequently observing astronomy incidents like Gamma Ray Bursts (GRBs) [6]. Cross match [11], is the procedure to identify an object by querying the distance among its neighbors in the image and find

© Springer International Publishing AG, part of Springer Nature 2018
Y. Shi et al. (Eds.): ICCS 2018, LNCS 10862, pp. 473–479, 2018.
https://doi.org/10.1007/978-3-319-93713-7_42

the nearest stars within a distance threshold. Hence, the speed of cross match and its accuracy are crucial to proceed scientific analysis of the data flow and ensure timely alerts of astronomical incidents. This procedure has to be fast enough over millions of objects on the celestial sphere. Accelerating this critical procedure, consequently, is of momentous significance.

Dozens of algorithms together with data structures, like *Hierarchical Equal-Area iso-Latitude Pixelisation (HEALPix)* [9] and *Hierarchical Triangular Mesh (HTM)* [14], have been put forward to meet different needs of a query on 2-dimensional datasets. They speed up the search procedure by decomposing and combining the search area. These methods work well on the celestial sphere coordinate system but strict distance test between these reference objects is inavoidable. So, we try to use plane coordinate system to simplify the distance calculation and speed up the search. In this paper, improvements are made based on this idea.

The major contributions of our paper are as follows: Firstly, we designed E-Zone algorithm, a memory-based neighbor points query algorithm using euclidean distance to speed up the calculation of distance between objects, which has gotten rid of the SQL database dependance. Secondly, we tested different parameters to find optimal configurations of the algorithm. Thirdly, we modified the serial algorithm with OpenMP and reached another 4 times speed up than the serial version. In this paper, we introduced the background of astronomical cross match and discussed the related works in Sect. 2. Section 3 presents the sequential E-Zone algorithm and its performance analysis. Section 4 evaluates different configurations and OpenMP to accelerate the search by lunch multiple queries. Finally, Sect. 5 concludes this paper.

2   Background and Related Work

A dominating area query algorithm called *Zone* proposed by Gray et al. [8]. It maps the celestial sphere into quantities of small horizontal zones, and reduces the search space by apportioning the search task only to these possible zones. Each zone is a declination stripe of the sphere with certain *zoneHeight*: $zoneNumber = \boldsymbol{floor}((dec + 90)/zoneHeight)$.

For given two celestial objects O_1, O_2 in spherical coordinates (ra_1, dec_1) and (ra_2, dec_2), the central angle(distance in equatorial coordinate system) between these two objects is:

$$Distance(O_1, O_2) = arccos(sin(dec_1)sin(dec_2)$$
$$+ cos(dec_1)cos(dec_2)cos(|ra_1 - ra_2|)) \tag{1}$$

But at least six trigonometric functions need to be called for calculating the distance between two celestial objects to get the distance between them. It is an nonnegligible subroutine that may consume considerable time when compared with few multiplications and additions (euclidean distance).

Hierarchical Triangular Mesh (HTM) [14] is a multilevel, recursive decomposition of the celestial sphere. Like all other algorithms accelerating the query, it tries to minimize the search space by decomposition and combination of predefined region units. By decomposing repeatedly, the celestial sphere finally will be divided into billions of little spherical triangular. The search algorithm returns a list of *HTM* triangles that cover that region, which is the minimum superset of all the query point's neighbors. Wang et al. [15] utilized both CPU and GPU to implement a similar zone divided cross match algorithm called *gridMatch*. They use a grid file to store and compute the hierarchical data structure used to store the celestial objects. Many other multicore parallel cross match algorithms for catalogs are proposed to meet different needs in various scenarios [10,13,16]. Some researchers use statistical method to improve the completeness and reliability of cross matching [12]. Multi-GPU featured astronomic catalog cross match system is proposed for workstation and cluster [5].

3   E-Zone Algorithm with Pixel Euclidean Distance

The raw images captured by GWAC are encoded with *FITS* (Flexible Image Transport System) [2], the most common digital file format designed for storage, transmission and processing astronomical images. The right ascension (*Ra*) [4] and declination (*Dec*) [1] which describe the position of the celestial object in the equatorial coordinate, were generated through this process. Thus, we can assume that there exits another projection α converting the position of the objects of the raw image $(Raw\_spher_x, Raw\_spher_y)$ into a plane coordinate (P_pixel_x, P_pixel_y), which means that the projected coordinate is certificated to calculate euclidean distance between two objects:

$$(Euclidean\_pixel_x, Euclidean\_pixel_y) = \alpha(Raw\_spher_x, Raw\_spher_y) \quad (2)$$

Equation 2 is a coordinate mapping between raw image pixel coordinate and the plane-coordinate system, where the distance can be calculated as ordinary euclidean distance. So, it is easy to express the distance between $O_1(x_1, y_1)$ and $O_2(x_2, y_2)$ using euclidean distance to avoid complex trigonometric functions: $Distance_{euc}(O_1, O_2) = \sqrt{(O_1.x - O_2.x)^2 + (O_1.y - O_2.y)^2}$.

3.1   Decompose the Celestial Sphere

Despite the approach, the calculation of the distance between two points and the definition of **zone** are different when using pixel coordinate. All the algorithms and definitions using (*ra, dec*) now need to be adapted to the new coordinate system. Similarly, we decompose the vision into horizontal strips according to its E_PIX_y. The zoneID using pixel coordinate (E_PIX_x, E_PIX_y) will be:

$$zoneID = floor(\frac{E\_PIX_y}{zoneHeight}) \quad (3)$$

We only need to consider the objects between the *maxZoneID* and *minZoneID*, when querying the objects within the circle of radius

R: $maxZoneID = floor(E\_PIX_y + R/zoneHeight)$, $minZoneID = floor(E\_PIX_y - R/zoneHeight)$.

The difference in the searching zones lies only in the unit, pixel, because the way E-Zone decompose the sphere is the same as in the original zone algorithm.

3.2   Neighbors with Pixel Distance

Without SQL database, we need to manage the data manually. The reference table needs to be preprocessed to implement the search algorithm. The reference object table is almost static. It hardly changes in a long period. Thus, this table seldom insert and delete while queries and indexing are the most frequent operations on this data structure. As a result, we do not need to be efficient at deleting or inserting elements in a B-tree. Therefore, we can implement simple arrays to meet our needs.

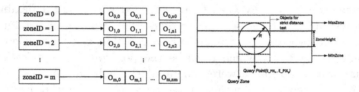

Fig. 1. The data structure and the procedure to determine the minimal strict distance test area. (Color figure online)

According to the structure shown in Fig. 1, we use a bunch of *zoneObjectList* (the arrays on the right) that is stored by E_PIX_y containing all the objects with the same *zoneID*. These arrays are indexed by another pointer array *zoneList* (the vertical array on the left), which designed for indexing zone vectors with its corresponding *zoneID* as a bucket.

We build the search tree as follows:

Step 1: Calculate all *zoneID* with formula (3) and find the object list's pointer by *zoneList[zoneID]*.

Step 2: Insert the reference objects into the object vector *∗zoneList[zoneID]* respectively.

Step 3: Sort all object vectors respectively by E_PIX_x.

The right subfigure of Fig. 1 shows, what we need to do to find the objects within a search threshold we have to find the zones between two bounds on the vertical axis. Subsequently, linear search task can find out which part of the plane need to conduct strict distance test (red dotted zone). Our optimization is mainly focused on these metrics. Any linear search algorithm can be applied to subsequent search procedure (eg. Binary search tree).

4   Experiment

In this section, we evaluate the performance of our E-Zone algorithm using pixel distance. First, we use an algorithm that is only differentiated by the distance formula, to compare and verify our speed up by euclidean distance measurement Then we feed the algorithm with different sizes of reference data to compare its time and space complexity with our analytic result. Finally, we implemented a simple parallel query program with OpenMP programming model [3] and evaluate its effectiveness.

4.1   Superiority in Using Euclidean Distance

According to the analysis in Sect. 3, angle calculation with trigonometric function is a cumbersome procedure that will slow down this program deeply. These two methods are implemented without parallelization.

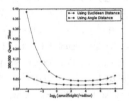

Fig. 2. Time consumption using euclidean distance and angle distance. (Serial Version)

As Fig. 2 shows, the logarithm of the ratio between *zoneHeight* and *Radius*, which varies along with the *zoneHeight* with a geometric progression from 2^{-3} to 2^8. The evaluation index is the average query time of 200,000 among 100 runs, excluding the time build the reference table and I/O. The minimum speed-up ratio is 2.069 when *zoneHeight*/*Radius* = 16. And if *zoneHeight*/*Radius* = $\frac{1}{16}$, the performance difference between two methods is the most prominent. The ratio is 5.928, but the absolute speed of this algorithm is not the optimal at this circumstance.

4.2   Performance with Parallel Queries

The catalogs obtained from raw images contains millions of objects. There is no data dependence between two queries, so higher performance could be achieved by launching these queries in parallel. We applied the simple and effective parallel model OpenMP to the outer *for* loop which invokes the search function. Great performance acceleration is achieved with OpenMP.

The left subplot of Fig. 3 shows the performance of the program written with and without OpenMP parallelization. With the growth of query size, the speed-up ratio becomes better, but becomes worse when *zoneHeight*/$R > \frac{1}{24}$. As the left subfigure of Fig. 3 shows, the ratio is higher on bigger datasets and that OpenMP works more efficiently on big zones, which agreed with that switch between threads for task dispatch consumes lots of time.

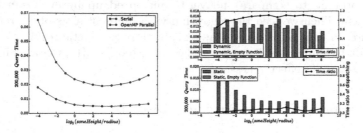

Fig. 3. Parallel performance with different environment and input parameters.

After we distribute these tasks with OpenMP on eight cores, the best average query time is reduced to around 0.0498 s for 200,000 queries over a 230,000 reference object table (Average time over 100 runs). After we adopt static dispatch strategy, we achieved a 2x speed-up over *dynamic*. We replaced the *queryPointEZone* function (seen as the code snippet above) with an empty function, which returns a constant value directly without any other statement, meanwhile, all other settings are the same. The result is shown in the right subfigure of Fig. 3. Time finishing 200,000 queries has reduced to around 5 ms. Hence, it's feasible to save time with parallel queries, and it achieved satisfying efficiency.

5   Conclusion

We find that (1) Using euclidean distance for constraint of neighbor points queries is effective in accelerating the cross match procedure of celestial queries. The formula used to compute the angle between two celestial objects in spherical coordinate is time-consuming that will slow the procedure down for over 2x. (2) Our serial cross match method can finish searching 200,000 queries over 230,520 reference objects within 0.019 s which reached 1.37x speed up over *gridMatch* algorithm. (3) The OpenMP parallelized version can finish this task within 5 ms, which achieved another 1.55x speed up on 8 cores with 16 threads. The CPU utilization is over 80%, when conducting the zone search procedure. Thus our metric is more efficient than traditional celestial angle-based metrics. For future work, we consider that it is feasible to combine the simplified coordinate system and distance measurement with GPU to achieve better performance. Moreover, a CPU/GPU hybrid algorithm has good potentials for better performance.

Acknowledgment. This research is supported in part by the National Key Research and Development Program of China (No. 2016YFB1000602 and 2017YFB0701501), the

Key Laboratory of Space Astronomy and Technology, National Astronomical Observatories, Chinese Academy of Sciences, MOE research center for online education foundation (No. 2016ZD302), and National Natural Science Foundation of China (Nos. 61440057, 61272087, 61363019).

References

1. Declination. https://en.wikipedia.org/wiki/Declination
2. Flexible image transport system. https://fits.gsfc.nasa.gov
3. openmp. http://openmp.org/wp/
4. Right ascension. https://en.wikipedia.org/wiki/Right_ascension
5. Budavari, T., Lee, M.A.: Xmatch: GPU enhanced astronomic catalog cross-matching. Astrophysics Source Code Library (2013)
6. Fishman, G.J., Meegan, C.A.: Gamma-ray bursts. Astron. Astrophys. **33**(33), 415–458 (2003)
7. Godet, O., Paul, J., Wei, J.Y., Zhang, S.-N., Atteia, J.-L., Basa, S., Barret, D., Claret, A., Cordier, B., Cuby, J.-G., et al.: The Chinese-French SVOM mission: studying the brightest astronomical explosions. In: Space Telescopes and Instrumentation 2012: Ultraviolet to Gamma Ray, vol. 8443, p. 844310. International Society for Optics and Photonics (2012)
8. Gray, J., Szalay, A.S., Thakar, A.R., Fekete, G., O'Mullane, W., Nietosantisteban, M.A., Heber, G., Rots, A.H.: There goes the neighborhood: relational algebra for spatial data search. Computer Science (2004)
9. Górski, K.M., Hivon, E.: Healpix: hierarchical equal area isolatitude pixelization of a sphere. Astrophysics Source Code Library (2011)
10. Jia, X., Luo, Q.: Multi-assignment single joins for parallel cross-match of astronomic catalogs on heterogeneous clusters. In: International Conference on Scientific and Statistical Database Management, p. 12 (2016)
11. Nietosantisteban, M.A., Thakar, A.R., Szalay, A.S.: Cross-matching very large datasets. Santisteban (2008)
12. Pineau, F.X., Derriere, S., Motch, C., Carrera, F.J., Genova, F., Michel, L., Mingo, B., Mints, A., Gómezmorán, A.N., Rosen, S.R.: Probabilistic multi-catalogue positional cross-match. Astron. Astrophys. **597**, A89 (2016)
13. Riccio, G., Brescia, M., Cavuoti, S., Mercurio, A., Di Giorgio, A.M., Molinari, S.: C3, a command-line catalogue cross-match tool for large astrophysical catalogues. Publications Astron. Soc. Pac. **129**(972), 024005 (2016)
14. Szalay, A.S., Gray, J., Fekete, G., Kunszt, P.Z., Kukol, P., Thakar, A.: Indexing the sphere with the hierarchical triangular mesh. Microsoft Research (2007)
15. Wang, S., Zhao, Y., Luo, Q., Wu, C., Yang, X.: Accelerating in-memory cross match of astronomical catalogs. In: IEEE International Conference on E-Science, pp. 326–333 (2013)
16. Zhao, Q., Sun, J., Yu, C., Cui, C., Lv, L., Xiao, J.: A paralleled large-scale astronomical cross-matching function. In: Hua, A., Chang, S.-L. (eds.) ICA3PP 2009. LNCS, vol. 5574, pp. 604–614. Springer, Heidelberg (2009). https://doi.org/10.1007/978-3-642-03095-6_57

Application of Algorithmic Differentiation for Exact Jacobians to the Universal Laminar Flame Solver

Alexander Hück[1]([✉]), Sebastian Kreutzer[1], Danny Messig[2], Arne Scholtissek[2], Christian Bischof[1], and Christian Hasse[2]

[1] Institute for Scientific Computing, Technische Universität Darmstadt, Darmstadt, Germany
{alexander.hueck,christian.bischof}@sc.tu-darmstadt.de,
sebastian.kreutzer@stud.tu-darmstadt.de
[2] Institute of Simulation of reactive Thermo-Fluid Systems, Technische Universität Darmstadt, Darmstadt, Germany
{messig,scholtissek,hasse}@stfs.tu-darmstadt.de

Abstract. We introduce algorithmic differentiation (AD) to the C++ Universal Laminar Flame (ULF) solver code. ULF is used for solving generic laminar flame configurations in the field of combustion engineering. We describe in detail the required code changes based on the operator overloading-based AD tool CoDiPack. In particular, we introduce a global alias for the scalar type in ULF and generic data structure using templates. To interface with external solvers, template-based functions which handle data conversion and type casts through specialization for the AD type are introduced. The differentiated ULF code is numerically verified and performance is measured by solving two canonical models in the field of chemically reacting flows, a homogeneous reactor and a freely propagating flame. The models stiff set of equations is solved with Newtons method. The required Jacobians, calculated with AD, are compared with the existing finite differences (FD) implementation. We observe improvements of AD over FD. The resulting code is more modular, can easily be adapted to new chemistry and transport models, and enables future sensitivity studies for arbitrary model parameters.

Keywords: Combustion engineering · Flamelet simulation
Algorithmic differentiation · Exact Jacobians · Newton method · C++

1 Introduction

The simulation of realistic combustion phenomena quickly becomes computationally expensive due to, e.g., inherent multi-scale characteristics, complex fluid flow, or detailed chemistry with many chemical species and reactions. Simulation codes for chemically reacting flows (e.g., turbulent flames) solve stiff systems of partial differential equations (PDE) on large grids, making the use of efficient

© Springer International Publishing AG, part of Springer Nature 2018
Y. Shi et al. (Eds.): ICCS 2018, LNCS 10862, pp. 480–486, 2018.
https://doi.org/10.1007/978-3-319-93713-7_43

computational strategies necessary. Here, algorithmic differentiation (AD, [3]) can help to resolve some of the computational challenges associated with chemically reacting flows. AD enables, for instance, sensitivity studies [1], or efficient optimization algorithms for key parameters [11] of these mechanisms.

In this work, we apply AD to the Universal Laminar Flame (ULF) solver [13], a C++ framework for solving generic laminar flame configurations. The code computes and tabulates the thermochemical state of these generic flames which is then parametrized by few control variables, i.e., the mixture fraction and reaction progress variable. The look-up tables obtained with ULF are used in 3D CFD simulations of chemically reacting flows, together with common chemical reduction techniques such as the flamelet concept [10]. The code is also used in other scenarios, e.g., for detailed flame structure analyses or model development, and is a key tool for studying the characteristics of chemically reacting flows.

The objective of this study is to introduce AD to ULF by using operator overloading. We focus on the technical details of this modification and how it impacts overall code performance. As an exemplary application, AD is used to compute exact Jacobians which are required by the numerical solver. The derivatives generated by AD are accurate up to machine precision, often at a lower computational cost w.r.t. finite differentiation (FD).

2   Two Canonical Models from the ULF Framework

We study the impact of AD using two canonical problems in the field of chemically reacting flows, i.e., a constant-pressure, homogeneous reactor (HR) and a freely-propagating premixed flame (FPF). The FPF is a 1D, stationary flame which burns towards a premixed stream of fresh reactants (e.g., a methane-air mixture), such that the fluid flow velocity and the burning velocity of the flame compensate each other. This yields a two-point boundary value problem described by a differential-algebraic equation (DAE) set, cf. [7]. We obtain the HR problem if all terms except the transient and the chemical source terms are omitted, resulting in an ordinary differential equation (ODE) set.

The stiff equation set is solved with an implicit time-stepping procedure based on backward-differencing formulas (BDF) with internal Newton iterations, i.e., the solvers BzzDAE [2] and CVODE [4] are used for the FPF and the HR, respectively. The discretization for the FPF is done on a 1D grid with n points. The HR is, on the other hand, solved on a single grid point. Each grid point i has a state X_i that is dependent on the temperature T_i and mass fractions $Y_{i,j}$ for species $j = 1...k$.

The internal Newton iteration of each solver requires a Jacobian. ULF uses a callback mechanism for user-defined Jacobians and computes them either numerically, or analytically for certain mechanisms. The Jacobian of the equation set $f : \mathbb{R}^N \to \mathbb{R}^N$ is typically a block tridiagonal matrix of dimension $\mathbb{R}^{N \times N}$ with $N = n(k+1)$. The main diagonal is the state X_i (Jacobian of the chemical source terms), the lower and upper diagonal describe the influence of the neighboring grid points, e.g., $i-1$ and $i+1$, determined by the transport terms.

3   Algorithmic Differentiation

AD [3] describes the semantic augmentation of scientific codes in order to compute derivatives. In the context of AD, any code is assumed to be a set of mathematical operations (e.g., +) and functions (e.g., sin) which have known analytical derivatives. Thus, the chain rule of differentiation can be applied to each statement, resulting in the propagation of derivatives through the code.

Two modes exist for AD, the forward mode (FM) and the reverse mode (RM). The FM applies the chain rule at each computational stage and propagates the derivatives of intermediate variables w.r.t. input variables along the program flow. The RM, on the other hand, propagates adjoints - derivatives of the final result w.r.t. intermediate variables - in reverse order through the program flow. This requires temporary storage, called *tape*, but computes gradients efficiently.

The semantic augmentation for AD is either done by a source transformation or by operator overloading. Due to the inherent complexity of the C++ language, there is no comprehensive source transformation tool and, thus, operator overloading is typically used in complex C++ simulation software. With operator overloading, the built-in floating point type T is re-declared to a user-defined AD type $\tilde{T}$. It stores the original value of T, called *primal value*, and overloads all required operations to perform additional derivative computations.

4   Introducing the AD Type to ULF

Introducing AD to a code typically requires 1. a type change to the AD type, 2. integration with external software packages, and 3. addition of code to initialize (*seed*) the AD type, compute, and extract the derivatives [9]. For brevity, we do not show the seeding routines. The FM seeding is analogous to the perturbation required for the existing FD implementation to compute the Jacobian. The RM, on the other hand, requires *taping* of the function and seeding of the respective function output before evaluating the tape to assemble the Jacobian.

We apply the operator overloading AD tool CoDiPack. CoDiPack uses advanced metaprogramming techniques to minimize the overhead and has been successfully used for large scale (CFD) simulations [5].

4.1   Fundamentals of Enabling Operator Overloading in ULF

We define the alias ulfScalar in a central header which, in the current design, is either set to the built-in double type or an AD type at compile time, see Fig. 1.

```
using ulfScalar = double | codi::RealForward | codi::RealReverse;
```

Fig. 1. RealForward and RealReverse are the standard CoDiPack AD types for the FM and RM, respectively. The AD types have an API for accessing the derivatives etc.

The initial design of ULF did not account for user-defined types (e.g., an AD type). This leads to compile time errors after a type change as built-in and user-defined types are treated differently [6]. Hence, we refactored several components in ULF, i.e., eliminating implicit conversions of the AD data types to some other type, handling of explicit type casts and re-designing the ULF data structures.

Generic Data Structures. The fundamental numeric data structure for computations in ULF is the `field` class. It stores, e.g., the temperature and concentration of the different chemical species. In accordance to [9], we refactored and templated this class in order to support generic scalar types, specifying two parameters, 1. the underlying vector representation type, and 2. the corresponding, underlying scalar type, see Fig. 2. We extended this principle to every other data structure in ULF, having the scalar alias as the basic type dependency.

```
1    template <typename Vector, typename Scalar>
2    class fieldTmpl : public fieldDataTmpl<Vector, Scalar> { ... };
3    using field = fieldTmpl<ulfVector, ulfScalar>;
```

Fig. 2. The class `fieldTmpl` represents the base class for fields and provides all operations. They are generically defined in the `fieldDataTmpl`. Finally, the ULF framework defines `field` as an alias for the data structure based on the `ulfScalar` alias.

Special Code Regions: External Libraries and Diagnostics. The external solver libraries and, more generically, external API calls (e.g., assert and printing statements) in ULF, do not need to be differentiated. We denote them as special regions, as they require the built-in double type. ULF, for instance, previously interfaced with external solvers by copying between the internal data representation and the different data structures of the solvers. With AD, this requires an explicit value extraction of the primal value (cf. Sect. 3). To that end, we introduced a conversion function, using template specialization, see Fig. 3. This design reduces the undue code maintenance burden of introducing user-defined types to ULF. If, e.g., a multi-precision type is required, only an additional specialization of the conversion function in a single header is required.

5   Evaluation

We evaluate the ULF AD implementation based on two reaction mechanisms, shown in Table 1. For brevity, we focus on the RM.

Timings are the median of a series of multiple runs for each mechanism. The standard deviation was less than 3% w.r.t. the median for each benchmark. All computations were conducted on a compute node of the Lichtenberg high-performance computer of TU Darmstadt, with two Intel Xeon Processor E5-2680 v3 at a fixed frequency of 2.5 GHz with 64 GB RAM.

```
1    namespace detail {
2      template <typename T>
3      struct ForSpecialization { static auto value(const T& v) { return v; } };
4    } /* namespace detail */
5    template <typename T>
6    auto value(const T& v) { return detail::ForSpecialization<T>::value(v); }
7    template <typename To, typename From>
8    auto recast(const From& v) { return static_cast<To>(value<From>(v)); }
```

Fig. 3. The functions `value` and `recast` are used for value extraction and type casting, respectively. The former makes use of the struct in the `detail` namespace which is used to specialize for user-defined types, e.g., the AD type (not shown). If built-in doubles are used, the value is simply returned (as shown).

Table 1. Mechanisms for the model evaluations.

Mechanism	Species	Reactions	Reference
ch4_USCMech (USCMech)	111	784	[12]
c3_aramco (Aramco)	253	1542	[8]

5.1 Homogeneous Reactor

Figure 4 shows the absolute timings of the solver phase for FD and the RM, respectively. The substantial speedups observed for the RM mainly result from the cheap computation of the Jacobian J. One evaluation of J is 20 to 25 times faster, depending on the mechanism. With FD, each time J is computed, the HR model function F is executed multiple times. In contrast, with the RM, F is executed once to generate a trace on the *tape*. The tape is then evaluated multiple times to generate J, avoiding costly evaluations of F. Memory overheads are negligible for the HR as the RM adds about 5 MB to 7 MB memory use.

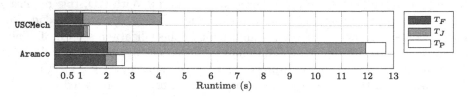

Fig. 4. For each mechanism, the top bar shows FD and the bottom bar shows AD RM measurements. The time of the solve process is divided into three phases: T_F and T_J are the cumulated time for the function and Jacobian evaluations, respectively. T_P is the time spent in CVODE.

5.2 Freely Propagating Flame

The mechanisms are solved on three different mesh resolutions on a 1D domain. As shown in Table 2, with AD, a single evaluation of F has a higher cost compared to FD. Here, the overhead ratio between FD and AD appears to be approximately constant for the different mesh configurations of both mechanisms. The evaluation of J is initially cheaper with AD but with rising mesh sizes the speedup vanishes. The total execution time with AD is slightly faster on average as the solver requires fewer steps (i.e., less invocations of F and J) for a solution.

The memory overhead is mostly constant for each mesh configuration as the tape only stores the adjoints of F to generate the Jacobian. We observe an additional main memory usage of about 100 MB to 430 MB and 180 MB to 800 MB memory from the smallest to largest mesh setup for USCMech and Aramco, respectively. We partly attribute the small variations of memory overhead to the accuracy of the measurement mechanism and due to the tape of CoDiPack which stores the data in chunks of a fixed size. Hence, the total tape memory consumption might be slightly higher than required.

Table 2. Timings for the FPF. F and J are times for a single evaluation, $\#F$ and $\#J$ are the number of invocations of each respective routine. $\mathrm{M_{AD}}/\mathrm{M_{FD}}$ is the memory ratio. Note: $\#F$ includes the evaluations required for computing J.

Mechanism	Mesh	Mode	Total time (s)	F (ms)	J (s)	$\#F$	$\#J$	$\frac{\mathrm{M_{AD}}}{\mathrm{M_{FD}}}$
USCMech	70	FD	425.009	11.194	3.842	20129	42	−
		AD	409.299	18.410	2.735	5329	42	1.64
	153	FD	1305.891	21.514	7.108	29704	58	−
		AD	1154.853	32.928	6.837	7618	55	1.69
	334	FD	2571.581	43.396	15.208	28946	67	−
		AD	2365.422	66.525	15.070	5167	65	1.7
Aramco	70	FD	1654.365	21.090	17.276	25169	25	−
		AD	1509.730	34.418	12.856	5650	24	1.26
	153	FD	5157.127	43.253	34.531	36223	40	−
		AD	4618.236	61.365	26.684	3790	40	1.26
	334	FD	11357.736	84.402	67.547	39806	47	−
		AD	11225.256	126.312	63.163	2822	42	1.27

6   Conclusion and Future Work

We presented the introduction of AD to ULF by using the operator overloading AD tool CoDiPack. In particular, we first introduced a global alias for the basic scalar type in ULF, which is set to the AD type at compile time. All other data structures were rewritten to use templates and are, subsequently, based on this alias. To interface with external APIs, template-based functions for casting and value extraction were introduced, and specialized for the AD types.

The HR model is solved on a single grid point, without transport properties. We observe substantial speedups due to the cheap computation of Jacobians with AD compared to FD. For the FPF, the underlying DAE solver typically requires less steps with AD but the evaluation of the model function is more expensive by a mostly fixed offset compared to FD.

In the future, experimentation with the ODE/DAE solver parameter settings to exploit the improved precision seems worthwhile. More importantly, the newly gained ability to calculate arbitrary derivatives up to machine precision in ULF enables us to conduct sensitivity studies not only limited to the chemical reaction rates, and model optimization experiments. In particular, advanced combustion studies such as uncertainty quantification, reconstruction of low-dimensional intrinsic manifolds or combustion regime identification become accessible.

References

1. Carmichael, G.R., Sandu, A., et al.: Sensitivity analysis for atmospheric chemistry models via automatic differentiation. Atmos. Environ. **31**(3), 475–489 (1997)
2. Ferraris, G.B., Manca, D.: Bzzode: a new C++ class for the solution of stiff and non-stiff ordinary differential equation systems. Comput. Chem. Eng. **22**(11), 1595–1621 (1998)
3. Griewank, A., Walther, A.: Evaluating Derivatives. Society for Industrial and Applied Mathematics (SIAM), 2nd edn. (2008)
4. Hindmarsh, A.C., Brown, P.N., Grant, K.E., Lee, S.L., Serban, R., Shumaker, D.E., Woodward, C.S.: SUNDIALS: suite of nonlinear and differential/algebraic equation solvers. ACM Trans. Mathe. Softw. (TOMS) **31**(3), 363–396 (2005)
5. Hück, A., Bischof, C., Sagebaum, M., Gauger, N.R., Jurgelucks, B., Larour, E., Perez, G.: A Usability Case Study of Algorithmic Differentiation Tools on the ISSM Ice Sheet Model. Optim. Methods Softw., 1–24 (2017)
6. Hück, A., Utke, J., Bischof, C.: Source transformation of C++ codes for compatibility with operator overloading. Proc. Comput. Sci. **80**, 1485–1496 (2016)
7. Kee, R.J., Grcar, J.F., Smooke, M.D., Miller, J.A., Meeks, E.: PREMIX: A Fortran Program for Modeling Steady Laminar One-Dimensional Premixed Flames. Technical report SAND85-8249, Sandia National Laboratories (1985)
8. Metcalfe, W.K., Burke, S.M., Ahmed, S.S., Curran, H.J.: A hierarchical and comparative kinetic modeling study of C1–C2 hydrocarbon and oxygenated fuels. Int. J. Chem. Kinet. **45**(10), 638–675 (2013)
9. Pawlowski, R.P., Phipps, E.T., Salinger, A.G.: Automating embedded analysis capabilities and managing software complexity in multiphysics simulation, part I: template-based generic programming. Sci. Program. **20**(2), 197–219 (2012)
10. Peters, N.: Laminar flamelet concepts in turbulent combustion. Symp. (Int.) Combust. **21**(1), 1231–1250 (1988)
11. Probst, M., Lülfesmann, M., Nicolai, M., Bücker, H., Behr, M., Bischof, C.: Sensitivity of optimal shapes of artificial grafts with respect to flow parameters. Comput. Methods Appl. Mech. Eng. **199**(17–20), 997–1005 (2010)
12. Wang, H., You, X., Joshi, A.V., Davis, S.G., Laskin, A., Egolfopoulos, F., Law, C.K.: USC Mech Version II. High-Temperature Combustion Reaction Model of H2/CO/C1-C4 Compounds (2007). http://ignis.usc.edu/USC_Mech_II.htm
13. Zschutschke, A., Messig, D., Scholtissek, A., Hasse, C.: Universal Laminar Flame Solver (ULF) (2017). https://figshare.com/articles/ULF_code_pdf/5119855

Morph Resolution Based on Autoencoders Combined with Effective Context Information

Jirong You[1,2], Ying Sha[1,2(✉)], Qi Liang[1,2], and Bin Wang[1,2]

[1] Institute of Information Engineering, Chinese Academy of Sciences, Beijing, China
{youjirong,shaying,liangqi,wangbin}@iie.ac.cn
[2] School of Cyber Security, University of Chinese Academy of Sciences, Beijing, China

Abstract. In social networks, people often create morphs, a special type of fake alternative names for avoiding internet censorship or some other purposes. How to resolve these morphs to the entities that they really refer to is very important for natural language processing tasks. Although some methods have been proposed, they do not use the context information of morphs or target entities effectively; only use the information of neighbor words of morphs or target entities. In this paper, we proposed a new approach to resolving morphs based on autoencoders combined with effective context information. First, in order to represent the semantic meanings of morphs or target candidates more precisely, we proposed a method to extract effective context information. Next, by integrating morphs or target candidates and their effective context information into autoencoders, we got the embedding representation of morphs and target candidates. Finally, we ranked target candidates based on similarity measurement of semantic meanings of morphs and target candidates. Thus, our method needs little annotated data, and experimental results demonstrated that our approach can significantly outperform state-of-the-art methods.

Keywords: Morph · Morph resolution
Effective context information · Autoencoder

1 Introduction

In social networks, people often create morphs, a special type of fake alternative names for avoiding internet censorship or some other purposes [9]. Creating morphs is very popular in Chinese social networks, such as Chinese Sina Weibo. As shown in 1, there is a piece of Chinese Sina Weibo tweet. Here a morph "Little Leo" (小李子) was created to refer to "Leonardo Wilhelm DiCaprio" (莱昂纳多)[1]. The term of "Leonardo Wilhelm DiCaprio" is called this morph's target entity.

---

[1] Leonardo Wilhelm DiCaprio is a famous actor.

© Springer International Publishing AG, part of Springer Nature 2018
Y. Shi et al. (Eds.): ICCS 2018, LNCS 10862, pp. 487–498, 2018.
https://doi.org/10.1007/978-3-319-93713-7_44

今天在电视里看了**小李子**的《泰坦尼克号》、史泰龙的《极速竞赛》，经典依然是经典，他们年轻时真帅，现在是老帅了。

Today watch the *Little Leo*'s "Titanic" and Stallone's "Speed Race" on television, the classic is still classic, they are young and handsome, and now they are old but still handsome.

Fig. 1. An example of morph use in Sina Weibo.

Morph resolution is very important in Nature Language Processing (NLP) tasks. In NLP, the first thing is to get the true meanings of words, especially including these morphs. Thus, the successful resolution of morphs is the foundation of many NLP tasks, such as word segmentation, text classification, text clustering, and machine translation.

Many approaches are proposed to solve morph resolution. Huang et al. [3] can be considered to have had the first study on this problem, but their method need a large amount of human-annotated data. Zhang et al. [16] proposed an end-to-end context-aware morph resolution system. Sha et al. [9] proposed a framework based on character-word embeddings and radical-character-word embeddings to explore the semantic links between morphs and target entities. These methods do not use the context information of morphs and target entities effectively, only use the context information of neighbor words of morphs and target entities. But there are some neighbor words are unrelated with the semantic links between morphs and target entities. There is still some room for improvement in accuracy of morphs resolution.

In this paper, we proposed a framework based on autoencoders combined with effective context information of morphs and target entities. First, we analyzed what context information are useful for morph resolution, and designed a context information filter to get effective context information by using pointwise mutual information. Second, we proposed a variant of autoencoders which can combine semantic vectors of morphs or target candidates and their effective context information, and we used the combined vectors as the semantic representations of morphs and target candidates respectively. Finally, we ranked target candidates based on similarity measurement of semantic meanings of morphs and target candidates. Using this method, we only take consider of the effective context information of morphs and target entities, and use autoencoders to get essential semantic characteristics of morphs and target entities. Experimental results show that our approach outperforms the state-of-the-art method.

Our paper offers the following contributions:

1. We proposed a new framework based on autoencoders combined with effective context information of morphs and target entities. Our approach outperforms the state-of-the-art method.
2. To get the effective context information of morphs and target entities, we leveraged pointwise mutual information between terms. This helps generate more accurate semantic representation of terms, and can improve the accuracy of morph resolution.

3. We proposed a variant of autoencoders to generate semantic representation of terms. The autoencoders can combine morphs or target entities and their effective context information and extract essential semantic characteristics of morphs and target entities.

2 Related Work

The study of morphs first appeared in some normalization work on non-formal texts using internet language. For example, Wong et al. [14] examine the phenomenon of word substitution based on phonetic patterns in Chinese chat language, such as replacing "我" (Me, pronounced 'wo') with "偶" (pronounced 'ou'), which is similar to morphs. Early normalization work on non-formal text mainly uses rules-based approaches [10,14,15]. Later, some approaches combine statistics learning with rules to work on the normalization task [2,5,12,13]. Wang et al. [13] establish a probabilistic model based on typical features of non-formal texts including phonetic, abbreviation, replacement, etc., and train it through supervised learning on large corpus.

The concept of morph first appeared in the study of Huang et al. [3]. Huang et al. [3] study the basic features of morphs, including surface features, semantic features and social features. Based on these features, a simple classification model was designed for morph resolution. Zhang et al. [16] also propose an end-to-end system including morph identification and morph resolution. Sha et al. [9] propose a framework based on character-word embedding and radical-character-word embedding to resolve morph after analyzing the common characteristic of morphs and target entities from cross-source corpora. Zhang et al. summarize eight types of patterns of generating morphs, and also study how to generate new morphs automatically based on these patterns [16].

Autoencoders are neural networks capable of learning efficient representations of the input data, without any supervision [11]. Autoencoders can act as powerful feature detectors. There have been many variations of autoencoders. The context-sensitive autoencoders [1] integrate context information into autoencoders and obtain the joint encoding of input data. In this paper, we adopted a similar model of context-sensitive autoencoders to get the semantic representation of morphs and target candidates. We don't need to prepare much annotation data since autoencoder is an unsupervised algorithm.

In this paper, aiming at making full use of effective context information of morphs and target entities, we proposed a new framework based on autoencoders combined with extracted effective context information. Compared with the current methods, our approach only incorporates the effective context information of related words, and outperforms the state-of-the-art methods.

3 Problem Formulation

Morph resolution: Given a set of morphs, our goal is to figure out a list of target candidates which are ranked on the probability of being the real target entity.

Given documents set $D = \{d_1, d_2, \ldots, d_{|D|}\}$, and morphs set $M = \{m_1, m_2, \ldots, m_{|M|}\}$. Each morph m_i in set M and their real target entities are all appeared in documents set D. Our task is to discover a list of target candidates from D for each m_i, and rank the target candidates based on the probability of being the real target entity.

As shown in Fig. 1, the morph "Little Leo" (小李子) was created to refer to "Leonardo Wilhelm DiCaprio" (莱昂纳多). Given the morph "Little Leo" and tweets set from the Sina Weibo, our goal is to discover a list target candidates from tweets and rank the target candidates based on the probability of being the real target entity. The word "Leonardo Wilhelm DiCaprio" is expected to the first result (the real target entity) in the ranked target candidates list.

4   Resolving Morphs Based on Autoencoders Combined with Effective Context Information

We designed a framework based on autoencoders combined with effective context information to solve this problem. The procedure of our algorithm is shown in Fig. 2. The procedure of morph resolution mainly consists of the following steps:

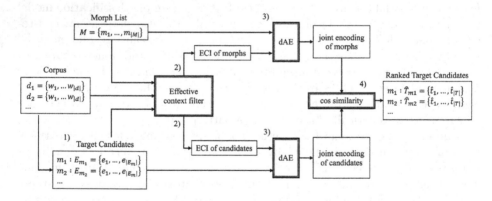

Fig. 2. The procedure of morph resolution.

1. Preprocessing

   In this step, we aim to filter out unrelated terms and extract target candidates $E_{m_i} = \{e_1, e_2, \ldots, e_{|E_{mi}|}\}$. We use two steps to extract the target candidates: (1) tweets which contain morphs are retrieved. Then we can get the published time of these tweets as these morphs' appearing time. Sha et al. discovered that morphs and target entities are highly consistent in temporal distribution [9]. Thus we set a time slot of 4 days to collect tweets which may contain target candidates of morphs; (2) since most morphs refer to named entities, such as the names of persons, organizations, locations, etc. We only need to focus on named entities in these tweets in order to find target candidates of morphs.

We can use many off-the-shelf tools working on POS (Part of Speech) and NER (Named Entities Recognition) tasks, including NLPIR [17], Standford NER [6] and so on.

2. Extracting effective context information

   We leverage effective context information (ECI) to generate semantic representation of morphs and target candidates. The effective context information are contextual terms whose semantic relationship with their target term is closer than others. The effective context information can effectively distinguish the characters of the morphs and their targets entities from other terms.

3. Autoencoders combined with effective context information

   We use deep autoencoders (dAE) to get joint encoding representation of morphs or target candidates and their effective context information. Autoencoder can fusion different types of features and embed them into an encoding, which is much more flexible than traditional word embedding methods

4. Ranking target candidates

   After creating encoding representation of morphs and target candidates, we can rank target candidate e_j by calculating cosine similarity between encodings of morph and target candidate. The larger value of cosine similarity between the morph and the target candidate, the more likely the candidate is the real target entity of the morph. The ranked target candidates sequence $\hat{T}_{mi}$ is the result of morph resolution.

In the following sections, we will focus on these two steps: "extracting effective context information" and "autoencoders combined with effective context information".

4.1 Extracting Effective Context Information

To extract the effective context information, we use the pointwise mutual information (PMI) to select right terms that are related with morphs or target entities. PMI is easy to calculate:

$$PMI(x; y) = log \frac{p(x, y)}{p(x)p(y)} \qquad (1)$$

where $p(x)$ and $p(y)$ refers to the probability of occurrence of terms x and y in the corpus respectively. $\frac{p(x,y)}{p(x)p(y)}$ represents the co-occurrence of two terms.

PMI quantifies the discrepancy between the probability of their coincidence given their joint distribution and their individual distributions, assuming independence. PMI maximizes when x and y are perfectly associated (i.e. $p(x, y) = p(x)p(y)$). We use PMI to find collocations and associations between words. Good collocation pairs have high PMI because the probability of co-occurrence is only slightly lower than the probabilities of occurrence of each word. Conversely, a pair of words whose probabilities of occurrence are considerably higher than their probability of co-occurrence gets a small PMI score.

Given a word w, we collect all contextual terms of w from preprocessed tweets which contain w as the set C_w. Note that we also need to remove auxiliary and preposition, since they are useless for our following method. Next, for each term $c_i \in C$, we will calculate PMI between w and c_i, and get the terms of top-k PMI as effective context information of w. In the same way, we can get the effective contextual terms set of all morphs and target candidates.

Table 1. Contextual terms of top-5 PMI of morphs, target entities, and non-target entities.

Terms		Words of top-5 PMI (the value of PMI)				
Morph	The flash (闪电侠) [2]	little emperor (小皇帝)	King James (詹皇)	Bosh (波什)	Dragon King (龙王)	James (詹姆斯)
	PMI	4.406	3.951	3.120	2.884	2.460
Target entity	Wade (韦德) [3]	Bosh (波什)	James (詹姆斯)	King James (詹皇)	little emperor (小皇帝)	Kobe (科比)
	PMI	9.799	9.273	5.856	2.943	2.916
Non-target	Yao (姚明) [4]	Yi Jianlian (易建联)	O'Neill (奥尼尔)	big shark (大鲨鱼)	Lin Shuhao (林书豪)	Howard (霍华德)
	PMI	4.680	4.618	3.488	2.777	2.732
Non-target	Beckham (贝克汉姆) [5]	Giggs (吉格斯)	becky (小贝)	Federer (费德勒)	Olympic Team (国奥队)	Richards (理查兹)
	PMI	4.219	3.398	2.614	2.574	2.526

Table 1 shows contextual terms of top-5 PMI of morphs, target entities, and non-target entities. Here we regard these contextual terms as effective context information. Each row shows the effective contextual terms of different words. The first and second rows show the effective contextual terms of morph "The Flash (闪电侠)" and its target entity "Wade (韦德)"; and the third and fourth rows show the effective contextual terms of non-target entities "Yao (姚明) "and "Beckham (贝克汉姆)". We can discover that the effective contextual terms of the morph and its target entity are nearly consistent, but the effective contextual terms of the morph are completely different from those of non-target entities.

This means that the effective context terms can distinguish the target entity from non-target entities. Effective contextual terms have high PMI with the morph "The flash" and its target entity "Wade", but have low PMI with those non-target entities like "Yao" (姚明) and "Beckham" (贝克汉姆).

The results mean that we can extract effective contextual terms set by using PMI. Morphs and target entities should have similar context information, so we could extract similar contextual terms set of morphs and target entities by using PMI. Through these contextual terms, we can get more accurate semantic links between morphs and target entities.

4.2   Incorporating Effective Context Information into Autoencoders

In this section, we want to get the representation of essential characters of morphs or target candidates by incorporating effective contextual terms into autoencoders.

Autoencoders neural network is an unsupervised learning algorithm, which encodes its input x into the hidden representation h, then reconstruct x with h precisely:

$$h = g(Wx + b) \tag{2}$$

$$\hat{x} = g(W'h + b') \tag{3}$$

$\hat{x}$ is the reconstruction of x. $W \in R^{d \times d'}, b \in R^{d'}, W' \in R^{d' \times d}$ are the parameters the model learned during training, d and d' means dimension of vectors before and after encoder respectively. Usually $d' \leq d$ for dimensionality reduction. Function g is the activation function in neural network. Figure 3(a) shows the structure of a basic single-layer autoencoder, it can be a cell in deep autoencoders (dAE).

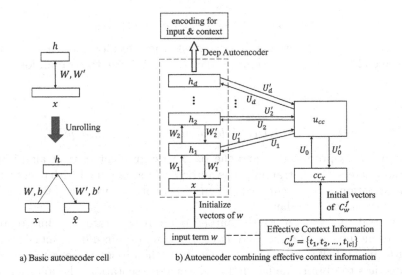

Fig. 3. (a) A basic autoencoders cell; (b) autoencoders combined with effective context information using PMI filter.

In order to incorporate effective context information into autoencoders, we need to extend the inputs of autoencoders. As Fig. 3(b) shown, besides the term w, we also input the effective context information of w. First, we extract C_w^f, the effective context information of w by using methods in Sect. 4.1. Second, we generate the word embeddings of each term in C_w^f, and set cc_x as the average of these word embeddings. There are many word embedding methods, such as word2vec [7] or GloVe [8]. Third, we generate u_{cc}, the hidden encoding representation of effective context information by using autoencoders whose input is cc_x. Finally, we can incorporate u_{cc} into deep autoencoders to generate the joint encoding for input terms and their effective context information.

For each layer k^{th} in deep autoencoders, the encoder turns $h_{k-1}(h_0 = x$ if $k = 1)$ and u_{cc} into one hidden presentation as follows:

$$h = g(W_k h_{k-1} + U_k u_{cc} + b_k) \tag{4}$$

$$\hat{h}_{k-1} = g(W'_k h + b'_k) \tag{5}$$

$$\hat{u}_{cc} = g(U'_k h + b''_k) \tag{6}$$

where $\hat{h}_{k-1}$ and $\hat{u}_{cc}$ are the reconstruction of h_{k-1} and u_{cc}. Equation 4 encodes h_{k-1} and u_{cc} into intermediate representation h; and Eqs. 5 and 6 decode h into h_{k-1} and u_{cc}. $W_k, U_k, b_k, W'_k, b'_k, U'_k$, and b''_k are the parameters the model learned during training. The whole model is composed of a stacked set of these layers. The last hidden layer h_d is the joint encoding for input terms and their effective context information.

For the whole model, the loss function must include both deviation of $(x, \hat{x})$ and $(u_{cc}, \hat{u}_{cc})$:

$$loss(x, u_{cc}) = \|x - \hat{x}\|^2 + \lambda \|u_{cc} - \hat{u}_{cc}\|^2 \tag{7}$$

where $\lambda \in [0, 1]$ is the weight that controls the effect of context information during encoding. And the optimize target is to minimize the overall loss:

$$\min_{\Theta} \sum_{i=1}^{n} loss(x^i, u_{cc}^i), \tag{8}$$

$$\Theta = \{W_k, W'_k, U_k, U'_k, b_k, b'_k, b''_k\}, \quad k \in 1, 2, ..., depth$$

we can use back-propagation and the stochastic gradient descent algorithm to learn parameters during training. The autoencoders combined with effective context information is an unsupervised neural network, so we can train the model with a little annotation data.

After training, we can use the autoencoders to generate encoding representations of morphs and target candidates. First, we obtain initial embedding vectors of terms and effective context information, then input these vectors into the autoencoders to obtain the last hidden layer representation, the joint encoding representations of morphs and target candidates respectively. Next, we can rank target candidates by calculating cosine similarity between the joint encodings of morphs and target candidates.

5   Experiments and Analysis

5.1   Datasets

We updated the datasets of Huang's work [3], and added some new morphs and tweets. At last, the datasets include 1,597,416 tweets from Chinese Sina Weibo and 25,003 tweets from Twitter. The time period of these tweets is from May, 2012 to June, 2012 and Sept, 2017 to Oct, 2017. There are 593 pairs of morphs in datasets.

5.2   Parameters Setting

In order to get the appropriate parameters in the model, we randomly selected 50,000 tweets as the verification set to adjust the parameters, including the context window wd, the number of terms for effective context information K of the PMI context filter, and the depth, the encoding dimension $d2$ and λ of the autoencoders. We choose the best parameters after the test on the verification set. During preprocessing, according to Sha's work [9], we set the time window of China Sina Weibo as one day, set the time window of Twitter as three days when we obtain the target candidates. In the initialization of vectors of terms, we choose word2vec [7] to generate 100-dimensional word vectors, which is a popular choice among studies of semantic representation of word embedding. For PMI context filter, we set the context window $wd = 20$, the number of terms for effective context information $K = 100$. For the autoencoder, set the depth as 3, the encoding dimension $d2 = 100$ and $\lambda = 0.5$. In the experiment, we use Adaptive Moment Estimation (Adam) [4] to speedup the convergence rate of SGD. Later we will discuss the effects of different parameters in the task of morph resolution.

5.3   Results

We choose indicator $Presice@K$ to evaluate the result of morph resolution since the result of this task is a ranked sequence. In this paper, $Precise@K = N_k/Q$, means for each morph m_i, if the position of e_{m_i} that is the real target of m_i in result sequence T_m is p, then N_k means the number of resolution results that $p \leq k$, and Q is the total number of morphs for the test. The performance of our approach and some other approaches are presented in Table 2 and Fig. 4. *Huang et al.* refers to work in [3], *Zhang et al.* refers to work in [16], *CW* refers to work by Sha et al. [9], while our approach is marked as *AE-ECI*. From the result we can find that our approach outperforms state-of-the-art methods.

The results show that the introduction of effective context information improves the accuracy of morph resolution. The current best method, Sha's work, just directly uses word embedding to calculate cosine similarity among words. This method only considers context information of neighbor words of morphs or target entities. But there are some neighbor words not having semantic links between morphs or target entities. In our approach, we selects terms that can effectively distinguish the characteristics of target entities from non-target entities by using PMI. Thus we can resolve the morphs more precisely.

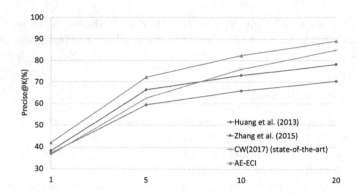

Fig. 4. Performance of several approaches on *pre@k* for morph resolution.

Table 2. Performance of several approaches on *pre@k* for morph resolution.

Precise-K (%)	Pre@1	Pre@5	Pre@10	Pre@20
Huang et al. (2013)	37.09	59.40	65.95	70.22
Zhang et al. (2015)	38.17	66.38	73.07	78.06
CW (2017) (state-of-the-art)	36.50	62.50	75.90	84.70
AE-ECI	**41.88**	**72.07**	**82.33**	**88.89**

5.4   Analysis

In this section, we discuss the effects of different parameters.

Window Size and Number of Context Terms. In PMI context filter, we select different window sizes wd and different numbers of contextual terms K to find out impact of window size and number of context terms. However, it seems that wd and K have little impact on performance. The details are shown as Table 3.

Table 3. Effects of Window size and number of context terms.

wd	5	10	10	20	20	50
K	10	10	20	10	20	10
Pre@1	40.31	41.45	**41.88**	**41.88**	41.73	41.59

Depth and Dimension of Autoencoder. Depth and dimension of autoencoders also have impact on performance. We select different combinations of depth and dimension for experimental verification, and the results show that too large or too small dimension has negative impact on performance. The possible reason may be that the ability of representation of autoencoders with too small dimension is insufficient, while autoencoders with too large dimension is hard to train. The impact of depth is similar. It seems that effect of depth is not very obvious when depth is small; but too deep model performs worse. The details are shown as Table 4.

Table 4. Effects of depth and dimension of autoencoders.

Dimension	50	100	200	300	500	100	100	100	100
Depth	3	3	3	3	3	1	2	5	10
Pre@1	39.60	**41.88**	41.59	41.02	39.31	41.59	41.31	41.45	36.89

Lambda. λ is the weight that controls effects of effective context information in encoding. We test *Pre@1* of morph resolution at different values of λ. When $\lambda = 0$ it means the effective context information is not added into the model. As shown in Table 5, we find that adding effective context information can improve the performance of model. If λ is too large, it will have negative impact on performance.

Table 5. Effects of λ.

λ	0.0	0.1	0.5	1.0
Pre@1	39.88	41.31	**41.88**	40.31

6   Conclusion

In this paper, we proposed a new approach to solve the problem of morph resolution. By analyzing the features of contextual terms of morphs and their targets, we try to extract effective context information based on PMI. We also proposed autoencoders combined with effective context information to get semantic representations of morphs and target entities. Experimental results demonstrate that our approach outperforms the state-of-the-art work on morph resolution. Next, we will try to extract topic information and integrate it to our models to improve the accuracy of morph resolution, and explore the better ways to fuse the semantic vectors of morphs or target entities and contextual terms.

Acknowledgments. This work is supported by National Science and Technology Major Project under Grant No. 2017YFB0803003, No. 2016QY03D0505 and. No. 2017YFB0803301.

References

1. Amiri, H., Resnik, P., Boyd-Graber, J., Daumé III, H.: Learning text pair similarity with context-sensitive autoencoders. In: Proceedings of the 54th Annual Meeting of the Association for Computational Linguistics, (Volume 1: Long Papers), vol. 1, pp. 1882–1892 (2016)
2. Han, B., Cook, P., Baldwin, T.: Automatically constructing a normalisation dictionary for microblogs. In: Proceedings of the 2012 Joint Conference on Empirical Methods in Natural Language Processing and Computational Natural Language Learning, pp. 421–432. Association for Computational Linguistics (2012)
3. Huang, H., Wen, Z., Yu, D., Ji, H., Sun, Y., Han, J., Li, H.: Resolving entity morphs in censored data. In: ACL (1), pp. 1083–1093 (2013)
4. Kingma, D.P., Ba, J.: Adam: a method for stochastic optimization. arXiv preprint arXiv:1412.6980 (2014)
5. Li, Z., Yarowsky, D.: Mining and modeling relations between formal and informal chinese phrases from web corpora. In: Proceedings of the Conference on Empirical Methods in Natural Language Processing, pp. 1031–1040. Association for Computational Linguistics (2008)
6. Manning, C.D., Surdeanu, M., Bauer, J., Finkel, J.R., Bethard, S., McClosky, D.: The stanford coreNLP natural language processing toolkit. In: ACL (System Demonstrations), pp. 55–60 (2014)
7. Mikolov, T., Sutskever, I., Chen, K., Corrado, G.S., Dean, J.: Distributed representations of words and phrases and their compositionality. In: Advances in Neural Information Processing Systems, pp. 3111–3119 (2013)
8. Pennington, J., Socher, R., Manning, C.: GloVe: global vectors for word representation. In: Proceedings of the 2014 Conference on Empirical Methods in Natural Language Processing (EMNLP), pp. 1532–1543 (2014)
9. Sha, Y., Shi, Z., Li, R., Liang, Q., Wang, B.: Resolving entity morphs based on character-word embedding. Procedia Comput. Sci. **108**, 48–57 (2017)
10. Sood, S.O., Antin, J., Churchill, E.F.: Using crowdsourcing to improve profanity detection. In: AAAI Spring Symposium: Wisdom of the Crowd, vol. 12, p. 06 (2012)
11. Vincent, P., Larochelle, H., Lajoie, I., Bengio, Y., Manzagol, P.A.: Stacked denoising autoencoders: learning useful representations in a deep network with a local denoising criterion. J. Mach. Learn. Res. **11**, 3371–3408 (2010)
12. Wang, A., Kan, M.Y.: Mining informal language from chinese microtext: joint word recognition and segmentation. In: ACL (1), pp. 731–741 (2013)
13. Wang, A., Kan, M.Y., Andrade, D., Onishi, T., Ishikawa, K.: Chinese informal word normalization: an experimental study. In: IJCNLP (2013)
14. Wong, K.F., Xia, Y.: Normalization of chinese chat language. Lang. Resour. Eval. **42**(2), 219–242 (2008)
15. Xia, Y., Wong, K.F., Li, W.: A phonetic-based approach to chinese chat text normalization. In: Proceedings of the 21st International Conference on Computational Linguistics and the 44th Annual Meeting of the Association for Computational Linguistics, pp. 993–1000. Association for Computational Linguistics (2006)
16. Zhang, B., Huang, H., Pan, X., Li, S., Lin, C.Y., Ji, H., Knight, K., Wen, Z., Sun, Y., Han, J., et al.: Context-aware entity morph decoding. In: ACL (1), pp. 586–595 (2015)
17. Zhou, L., Zhang, D.: NLPIR: a theoretical framework for applying natural language processing to information retrieval. J. Assoc. Inf. Sci. Technol. **54**(2), 115–123 (2003)

Old Habits Die Hard: Fingerprinting Websites on the Cloud

Xudong Zeng[1,2], Cuicui Kang[1,2], Junzheng Shi[1,2], Zhen Li[1,2(✉)], and Gang Xiong[1,2]

[1] Institute of Information Engineering, Chinese Academy of Sciences, Beijing, China
{zengxudong,kangcuicui,shijunzheng,lizhen,xionggang}@iie.ac.cn
[2] School of Cyber Security, University of Chinese Academy of Sciences, Beijing, China

Abstract. To detect malicious websites on the cloud where a variety of network traffic mixed together, precise detection method is needed. Such method ought to classify websites over composite network traffic and fit to the practical problems like unidirectional flows in ISP gateways. In this work, we investigate the website fingerprinting methods and propose a novel model to classify websites on the cloud. The proposed model can recognize websites from traffic collected with multi-tab setting and performs better than the state of the art method. Furthermore, the method keeps excellent performances with unidirectional flows and real world traffic by utilizing features only extracted from the request side.

Keywords: Website fingerprinting · Traffic analysis · Cloud platform

1 Introduction

Cyber security has become the focus of governments and public after the PRISM[1]. In the same time, encrypted communication protocols like SSL/TLS are becoming ever more popular. The percentage of encrypted requests to the google services is up to 75% [6] and still keeps increasing with the rapid development of cloud services. Nowadays, almost every cloud platform can provide users with free certificates to apply SSL/TLS and encrypt their communications. However, malicious websites are spreading among the cloud and serving with other normal websites on the same IP address [18] because of the techniques used by cloud platforms. A Chinese report [4] shows that almost 74% handled phishing websites are detected by public tip-off which embodies the need for precisely detection method.

To solve the problem, the usual ways are domain or IP blacklist. However, domain blacklist only solve the problem partially as discovering all variants isn't easy. For example, pornographic websites or online gambling websites have applied in many domains that domain blacklist could hardly gather all of them.

---

[1] https://en.wikipedia.org/wiki/PRISM_(surveillance_program).

And the IP blacklist is likely to block normal websites serving on the same IP address. Thus, traffic analysis is suggested since the superficial information is disappeared in encrypted traffic. In this field, the website fingerprinting (WFP) is popularly used in classifying websites over encrypted traffic, which utilize time, packet length, distribution and other statistical meta-data as a feature set.

In this paper, we take advantage of WFP to classify encrypted websites over HTTPS and propose a novel composite feature, termed as Request-Respond-Tuples (RRT, see Sect. 4.2). RRT is unlike the packet direction based bursts. It's defined based on a client request and the corresponding server response. After compared the performance of several machine learning algorithms, the proposed model is implemented with Random Forest [1]. And then, the proposed model is experimented with challenging scenarios where traffic is collected with simulated user behaviors. Finally, the proposed model achieves more than 20% true positive rate than the state of the art WFP model k-fingerprinting [7] in classifying websites on Content Delivery Network (CDN). And also shows promising results when being applied to real world problems.

The key contributions of this paper are listed as follows:

- This paper presents a three-phase domain collecting method, which gathers websites in the same IP address and is suitable for several cloud platforms.
- Our data sets are collected with simulated user behaviors which is more complex than previous studies.
- This paper proposed a novel WFP model and achieve a better true positive rate than k-fingerprinting [7] in recognizing websites on cloud platforms.
- The proposed model performs well with unidirectional flows and achieve 84.72% TPR with 200 positive classes.
- To the best of our knowledge, we are the first who apply WFP on traffic from ISP gateways.

The remainder of this paper is organized as follows: Sect. 2 shows the related work of WFP and Sect. 3 provides insight into the data sets. Then, data processing and RRT feature are introduced in detail in Sect. 4. The experiments are conducted in Sect. 5, where the proposed model is constructed with several the state of the art algorithms, including Naïve Bayes (NB) [22], Decision Tree (DT) [14], SVM [17] and Random Forest (RF) [1]. Furthermore, the section also discusses how to apply the proposed WFP model with realistic problems in ISP gateways. Finally, Sect. 6 concludes this paper.

2   Related Work

Deep packet inspection (DPI) [15] is a famous technique in traffic classification. But with the development of encryption, DPI faced with the great challenge that traffic analysis based on machine learning becoming another alternate method. WFP is a type of traffic analysis and it has been researched for a long time. The very first WFP models are aiming to identify pages over SSL [3,10], but more following WFP studies [?] [2,5,7,8,11–13,20] turn to focus on applying

WFP in anonymous communication networks. However, people generally don't use any proxies that most WFPs appealed to a restricted scenario. Recently, Hayes et al. [7] made well performed WFP by using the predicted results of each decision tree in a trained RF, called k-fingerprinting (KFP). KFP classified 55 webpages over 7000 webpages from Alexa top 20000 and achieved 95% true positive rate.

Liberatore et al. [?], Herrmann et al. [8], Dyer et al. [5] and many early studies adopt Naïve Bayes to learn the patterns of website. But Naïve Bayes amuse features are independent of each other which is difficult to achieve in reality. Other researchers [2,11–13] mainly focus on SVM. Panchenko et al. in 2011 [13] proposed some useful statistical features, such as burst and HTML Marker, processed WDP with SVM. And later in 2016 [11], they showed another WFP model named CUMUL with interpolants of cumulative packet lengths curve. Although previous studies obtained excellent results, WFP still need to try more machine learning algorithms and compared the difference. Juarez et al. in 2014 [9] argued that WFP studies made some naive settings such as no background traffic and ignore the difference between browser versions, user behaviors and regions. Regardless of the fact that it's hard to obtain a excellent result in complex settings, researchers still made some achievement. Wang et al. [21] applied WFP to Tor with background traffic and Panchenko et al. [12] compared results of classifying Tor hidden service between different Tor Browser Bundles.

To sum up, WFP has obtained a lot of achievement on classifying websites over anonymous communication network, but real world network is more complicated and WFP still need more breakthrough to deal with background traffic and other practical problems.

3 Data Set

We collected two data sets from different kinds of cloud platforms: App Engine and CDN. As Baidu APP Engine(BAE)[2] and Tencent CDN[3] (TCDN) are popular in China, and most of websites on them can be accessed by HTTPS. Besides the platform difference, some websites in data set **TCDN** were similar or owned by the same large website, but data set **BAE** excludes those websites manually.

3.1 Domains Collection

As we haven't found any public websites list for those two platforms. So, we come forward with a three-phased method to gather domains on cloud. First, we can build a seed list of domains which serve on specific cloud platforms by Internet search engines. Second, performing active requests to extract IP addresses for each domain in the seed list. Finally, gather domains from dns.aizhan.com or other tools which can reverse search domain by IP address. Although this three-phase method can't provide a perfect website list, it still good enough to collect numerous domains which were available on the same IP address recently.

---

[2] https://cloud.baidu.com/product/bae.html.
[3] https://cloud.tencent.com/act/event/cdn_brief.html.

3.2   Collection Settings

Based on the three-phase method, the data sets are collected by utilizing Selenium[4] to take control of Firefox and assess domains of BAE and TCDN repeatedly. The raw traffic is recorded into PCAPs[5] by Tshark[6]. For each domain, we first get its index page and then randomly perform several clicks to simulate user behaviors. Therefore, traffic is collected with multi-tab and the user behaviors are varied in each collection.

By performing random clicks in traffic collection, the generated traffic is more complicated than others with on interactions. For example, first we open the homepage of website A, and then we randomly click a hyperlink which will open a webpage of A or other websites. After performing these behaviors several times, the generated traffic behaviors will be different in each time. As a result, the target website to classify is multi-modal [19] which means the fingerprint of the target isn't stable and the classification is become more challenging.

3.3   Summary

In the data sets, **BAE** data set consists of 40 websites each with 100 instances, while the **TCDN** data set consists of 30 instances each of 200 websites and 10 instances each of 1000 websites. The summaries for both data sets are presented in Table 1. The column of different IPs describes the number of unique IP addresses. It's obvious that every IP holds more than one website in average and **TCDN** is more centralized than **BAE**. Due to the relations between websites and IP addresses are changing over time. We assume all websites of each data set serve on the same IP address.

Table 1. Summaries of BAE and TCDN

Data set	Total instances	TCP flows	Different IPs	Different SNIs
BAE	4000	52.92K	17	190
TCDN	16000	134.88K	68	2213

4   Data Processing

4.1   Preprocessing

For each trace T in the data sets, we assign $T = (SNI, P)$ where SNI is a field of SSL/TLS protocol and $P = (t, l, s)$ which stands for timestamp, packet length and packet states. In particular, when $l > 0$ indicates an incoming packets and $l < 0$ indicates an outgoing packet. And the states can be used to filter packets without payload and unused connection.

---

[4] https://www.seleniumhq.org.
[5] https://en.wikipedia.org/wiki/Pcap.
[6] https://www.wireshark.org/docs/man-pages/tshark.html.

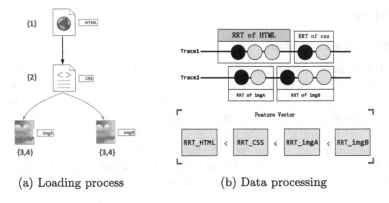

(a) Loading process   (b) Data processing

Fig. 1. In figure(a), browser first gets a CSS stylesheet and then requests two images and figure(b) demonstrates the data process where the black circles represent outgoing packets and the white are incoming.

4.2 Features

Based on the previous studies, some useful statistical features have been extracted in a new perspective. We assume that website can be identified by a set of loading patterns which consist of a partial order relation (POR) set and RRTs. In particular, the RRT is a kind of ensemble feature which describes the statistical features of the request packet(s) and the following incoming burst. And the POR in our study is based on the timing relationship that describes the start order between two RRTs. Therefore, PORs of a certain website can remain intact with background traffic. To illustrate the work more specifically, Fig. 1(a) shows the loading process of a simple webpage and the data processing is displayed in Fig. 1(b). From the figure, RRTs are slightly independent with each other which means RRTs are focused and immune to background noise. Finally, the top K RRTs are chosen to represent the loading patterns of websites. The feature set of RRT is listed as follows:

- **Time** indicates the status of server and network. So that we extract start time, time cost, distribution of packet arrival time and inter arrival time to embody this field.
- **Packet length** is the "shape" of the encrypted content. Thus, we extracted request packet length, total response packet length, last packet length and other statistical features to describe it.
- **Proportion** is the overall distribution of packets/bytes/time. According to the proportion, the local statistical feature can associated with the overall information which imply the profile of website.

5   Experiment

5.1   Experiment Setup

The websites in the experiments are recognized by traces aggregated by SNI which named as TASNI for short. However, most previous WFP models are applied on all traces belong to the same domain which is hard to achieve in reality. Furthermore, websites in WFP studies ether be regarded as monitored or unmonitored, similar to interested in or not. But we recognize websites by TASNI, that an instance may consist of several TASNIs. Thus, we assume only TASNI whose SNI equal to the domain can be regarded as monitored, because most unique resources are more likely belong to it.

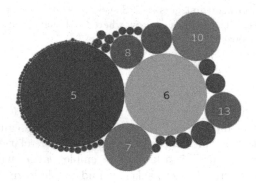

Fig. 2. The distribution of TASNI's RRT count.

It should be noted that we only conduct experiments with open-world setting [13] where the test set owns some cases that train set don't have. In order to evaluate the performance of the proposed method, True Positive Rate and False Positive Rate are used as the major evaluation metric in the experiment, which are defined as follows:

- **True Positive Rate (TPR)** is the probability that a monitored website is classified as the correct monitored page. In the following equation, $|test_{mon}|$ means the number of monitored instances for testing.

$$TPR = \frac{\sum_{i=0}^{|test_{mon}|}(Predict_i = Label_i)}{|test_{mon}|} \qquad (1)$$

- **False Positive Rate (FPR)** is probability that an unmonitored page is incorrectly classified as a monitored page. In the following equation, $|test_{unmon}|$ means the number of unmonitored instances for testing and NOISE is constant for every unmonitored instance.

$$FPR = \frac{\sum_{i=0}^{|test_{unmon}|}(Predict_i \neq NOISE)}{|test_{unmon}|} \qquad (2)$$

5.2   Model

With features extracted, several supervised machine learning algorithm are compared. As most of TASNIs in Fig. 2 have RRTs less than 6, that top 6 RRTs (K = 6) is selected. For each data set we randomly chose 60 percent of monitored TASNIs and 1000 unmonitored TASNIs for training. The rest of monitored TASNIs and 2000 randomly selected unmonitored TASNIs are used for testing. The results are displayed in Fig. 3 and Table 2, from which it can be found that the Random Forest performed much better than the others.

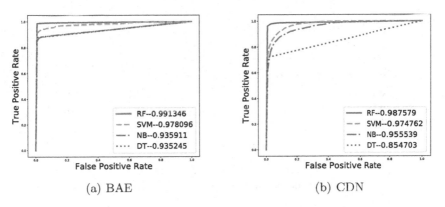

Fig. 3. The ROC curve of four classifiers on two data sets and the AUC scores of each algorithm are listed in legends. The difference between algorithms is more clear in CDN data set, as the positive kinds of CDN data set are more than BAE data set.

From the result of the comparison, the NB not perform very well. As we know, the NB algorithm assumes the features in the feature set are independent of each other. The assumption is much suitable for RRT, but it isn't very suitable for the features of RRT. The DT algorithm and SVM algorithm also not perform as well as RF. In our opinion, we assume the reason is because of the multimodal. As Wang Tao [19] hold that WFP is a kind of multi-modal classification whose class is consisted of several subclasses, where the instances of the same subclass are similar, but not similar in different subclasses. In our data set, all the traffic collected with random interaction which caused many subclasses. And the DT and SVM take all instances in a class into consideration, that the performances have been influenced. However, RF use several randomly sampled data set to build an ensemble classifier, where the influence of multi-modal would be weakened.

Therefore, Random Forest is chosen as our classifier, named as RRT+RF shortly. To elevate RRT+RF, we set up an experiment for varying the sample amount of RF, N, from 1 to 200 on **TCDN** data set. From this Fig. 4, we can see that the TPR and FPR change quickly when N is low, and become convergence when N is greater than 100. Finally, N is set to 150 where the model can achieve a nice result and training quickly as well.

Table 2. Precision, Recall, F1-score of four classifiers.

Algorithm	BAE			CDN		
	Precision	Recall	F1-score	Precision	Recall	F1-score
Random forest	98.67%	94.64%	96.32%	89.23%	88.21%	88.2%
SVM	89.6%	88.01%	88.4%	57.27%	56.53%	55.69%
Naïve Bayes	94.1%	81.64%	85.91%	41.59%	35.89%	35.3%
Decision tree	92.52%	90.41%	90.83%	73.79%	71.79%	71.63%

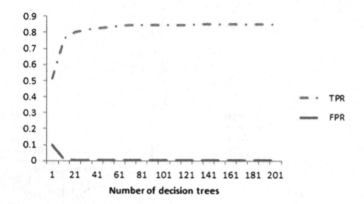

Fig. 4. TPR and FPR in different number of decision trees.

However, the number of RRTs in previous experiments is fixed. Thus, we'd like to vary the K which stands for the number of RRTs used in the model, and analyze the influence. Experiments are based on **TCDN** data set and K is varied from 1 to 10. The results of the experiment are shown in Fig. 5. As a result, we find the TPR is nearly the best when K is set to 6 which means the current WFP suffered a lot influence on default values. And when K is set to 1, the feature set degenerate into HTML Marker [13]. The proposed WFP still keeps an excellent score that means HTML document is useful for classifying websites. However, based on the results, non-HTML RRTs seems useless. Therefore, we set up our model with the K-th RRT for only and vary K from 1 to 10. The results are shown in Fig. 4 as well. From the figure, RRTs from the 2nd to 4th keep similar importance as the 1st and the performance get worse slightly when K larger than 4. The phenomenon is because of the order for the latter RRTs may change frequently as the multicore processors are used. And another reason is due to more RRTs are filled with default values when K grows up.

In order to evaluate RRT+RF, an experiment is set to contrast RRT+RF with the state of the art WFP model. As k-fingerprinting(KFP) [7] has tested on traffic from standard browser which is similar to us and built model by RF as well. So that KFP is chosen to make the comparison, and KFP is implemented

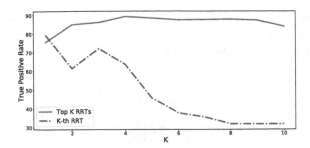

Fig. 5. TPRs of model with the top K RRTs or the K-th RRT.

by source code shared in Github[7] [7]. However, in default, KFP doesn't take advantage of length related features as all packet length of traffic from Tor are fixed. Furthermore, ACK packets which may cause noise [20]. As a result, KFP is implemented with all features without ACK packets.

The experiments performed in both data sets and the results are listed in Table 3. According to the results, RRT+RF achieves a higher TPR for BAE data set and performs much better than KFP for **TCDN** data set. To summarize, the RRT+RF achieves a better result than KFP and performs excellent in multi-class classification with cloud platforms whose servers often carry numerous websites.

Table 3. Results for RRT+RF and KFP.

Data set	TPR		FPR	
	RF+RTT	KFP	RF+RTT	KFP
BAE	98.62%	94.24%	0.95%	0.65%
TCDN	84.85%	62.89%	0.45%	5.52%

5.3 Unidirectional Flows

In an ideal situation, the WFP only needs to deal with the problems bring with encrypted technique. However, in the real world, applying WFP still has to overcome many practical difficulties. Shi et al. [16] thought perform traffic analysis will be more and more harder, with the depth of networks because of traffic aggregation. In this section, we'd like to discuss about a practical problem for applying WFP to ISP gateway. The unidirectional flow is common in ISP gateways. Its outgoing and incoming packets appear in different gateways. Faced with such problem, the WFP needs well worked with only request side or server side information as it's hard to match an outgoing trace with another incoming trace exactly. As a result, many features can't be extracted without half information. However, the response data size can be extracted base on the

---

[7] https://github.com/jhayes14/k-FP.

difference between acknowledgement number[8] of packets in the request side like Fig. 6. Finally, we select features which can be extracted in the request side, such as total outgoing bytes and total bytes.

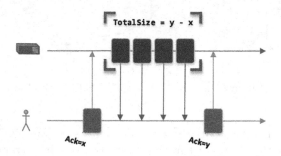

Fig. 6. Evaluate opposite consecutive packet size by acknowledgement number

Experiments conducted with traffic of request side and the results are shown in Table 4 and Fig. 7. From the results, the performance of RF+RRT is still promising on such practical problem. And the performance of The classifiers based on SVM and DT have enhanced a bit, which may because of the number of features has been decreased that reduce the difference between subclasses. According to these results, we found we can only focus on the request side traffic to implement a promising WFP when applying WFP with unidirectional flows, so that we can try to apply WFP the real world.

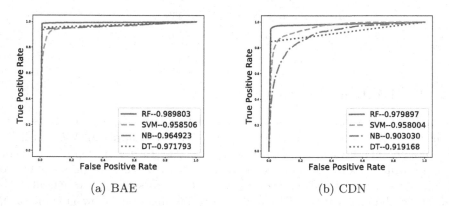

Fig. 7. The ROC curve of four classifiers on two data sets only with traffic of the request side.

---

[8] Acknowledgement number is a field of TCP protocol and used for tracing transmitted traffic volume.

Table 4. Precision, Recall, F1-score of four classifiers in unidirectional flows.

Algorithm	BAE			CDN		
	Precision	Recall	F1-score	Precision	Recall	F1-score
Random forest	99.47%	95.09%	97.15%	88.25%	86.8%	86.8%
SVM	97.47%	82.52%	77.76%	64.55%	66.04%	62.71%
Naïve Bayes	93.6%	89.43%	90.7%	15.5%	17.6%	13.51%
Decision tree	97.1%	95.38%	96.16%	79.35%	85.73%	81.28%

5.4   Real World Experiment

Base on the previous experiments, we conduct an experiment on the traffic from several gateways of CSTNet. The traffic on the ISP gateways is unlike the traffic on the local network. First, almost all of the traffic passing by the ISP gateways is unidirectional. Second, the traffic from the same client generally pass by several gateways. Finally, the situation is more open as the traffic may come from arbitrary websites. In such condition, we build a simple webpage on Amazon and collect traffic on a gateway of CSTNet.

To label ISP traffic and evaluate our method, we access our simple webpage for several times by Selenium and record the traffic as well. With the traffic collected on the client, the Client Random String (CRS) can be extracted in the SSL/TLS handshakes. As the CRS is consisted of 28 bytes, so that it's not easy to find two equal CRS. We labeled the ISP traffic's TASNI whose CRSs have occurred in client traffic, and divide all of the TASNI into timeslices for every 10 seconds. Finally, we get a labeled real world data set.

The traffic has been transformed into almost 20000 TASNIs, and about 5% of them are labeled as positive. The RF+RRT first trained with client collected data set, and then test with the ISP data set. The TPR and FPR of the purposed method are 82.88% and 4.9762%, while the ROC curve is displayed in Fig. 8. According to the results, the FPR of the purposed method isn't well, but the overall results are still promising as we are the first to apply WFP on ISP traffic.

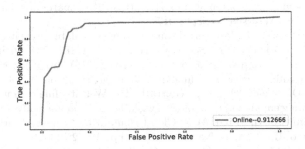

Fig. 8. The ROC curve for the RF+RRT tested on the ISP data set

6   Conclusion

In this paper, we recognize websites with traffic aggregated by SNI and propose a novel WFP model to precisely classify websites on the cloud. The proposed model consists of two parts. One is RRT, a unit to describe a pair of HTTPS request and respond. The other is Random Forest which is a well known machine learning algorithm. From the comparison of the state of the art algorithm, we discovered that a sequence of RRTs can characterize websites better than extract features from the entire traffic roughly. Finally, the purposed method deal with unidirectional flows and applied to ISP traffic, that the proposed method shows a promising performance. In the future, we will improve the feature set of RRT and practically apply to the real world.

Acknowledgment. This work is supported by The National Key Research and Development Program of China (No. 2016QY05X1000, No. 2016YFB0801200), The National Natural Science Foundation of China (No. 61702501), The CAS/SAFEA International Partnership Program for Creative Research Teams and IIE, CAS International Cooperation Project.

References

1. Breiman, L.: Random forests. Mach. Learn. **45**(1), 5–32 (2001)
2. Cai, X., Zhang, X.C., Joshi, B., Johnson, R.: Touching from a distance: website fingerprinting attacks and defenses. In: Proceedings of the ACM Conference on Computer and Communications Security, CCS 2012, Raleigh, NC, USA, 16–18 October 2012, pp. 605–616 (2012)
3. Cheng, H., Avnur, R.: Traffic analysis of SSL encrypted web browsing, project paper, University of Berkeley (1998). http://www.cs.berkeley.edu/~daw/teaching/cs261-f98/projects/final-reports/ronathan-heyning.ps
4. CNNIC: Global chinese phishing sites report, June 2016. http://www.cnnic.cn/gywm/xwzx/rdxw/20172017/201706/P020170609490614069178.pdf
5. Dyer, K.P., Coull, S.E., Ristenpart, T., Shrimpton, T.: Peek-a-Boo, I still see you: why efficient traffic analysis countermeasures fail. In: IEEE Symposium on Security and Privacy, SP 2012, 21–23 May 2012, San Francisco, California, USA, pp. 332–346 (2012)
6. Google: Google transparency report. https://transparencyreport.google.com/https/overview. Accessed 30 Sept 2017
7. Hayes, J., Danezis, G.: k-fingerprinting: a robust scalable website fingerprinting technique. In: 25th USENIX Security Symposium, USENIX Security 16, Austin, TX, USA, 10–12 August 2016, pp. 1187–1203 (2016). https://www.usenix.org/conference/usenixsecurity16/technical-sessions/presentation/hayes
8. Herrmann, D., Wendolsky, R., Federrath, H.: Website fingerprinting: attacking popular privacy enhancing technologies with the multinomial Naïve-bayes classifier. In: Proceedings of the First ACM Cloud Computing Security Workshop, CCSW 2009, Chicago, IL, USA, 13 November 2009, pp. 31–42 (2009)
9. Juárez, M., Afroz, S., Acar, G., Díaz, C., Greenstadt, R.: A critical evaluation of website fingerprinting attacks. In: Proceedings of the 2014 ACM SIGSAC Conference on Computer and Communications Security, Scottsdale, AZ, USA, 3–7 November 2014, pp. 263–274 (2014)

10. Mistry, S., Raman, B.: Quantifying traffic analysis of encrypted web-browsing, project paper, University of Berkeley (1998). http://citeseerx.ist.psu.edu/viewdoc/download?doi=10.1.1.10.5823&rep=rep1&type=pdf
11. Panchenko, A., Lanze, F., Pennekamp, J., Engel, T., Zinnen, A., Henze, M., Wehrle, K.: Website fingerprinting at internet scale. In: 23rd Annual Network and Distributed System Security Symposium, NDSS 2016, San Diego, California, USA, 21–24 February 2016 (2016). http://wp.internetsociety.org/ndss/wp-content/uploads/sites/25/2017/09/website-fingerprinting-internet-scale.pdf
12. Panchenko, A., Mitseva, A., Henze, M., Lanze, F., Wehrle, K., Engel, T.: Analysis of fingerprinting techniques for tor hidden services. In: Proceedings of the 2017 on Workshop on Privacy in the Electronic Society, Dallas, TX, USA, October 30–November 3 2017, pp. 165–175 (2017)
13. Panchenko, A., Niessen, L., Zinnen, A., Engel, T.: Website fingerprinting in onion routing based anonymization networks. In: Proceedings of the 10th Annual ACM Workshop on Privacy in the Electronic Society, WPES 2011, Chicago, IL, USA, 17 October 2011, pp. 103–114 (2011)
14. Quinlan, J.R.: Induction on decision tree. Mach. Learn. **1**(1), 81–106 (1986)
15. Sherry, J., Lan, C., Popa, R.A., Ratnasamy, S.: BlindBox: deep packet inspection over encrypted traffic. Comput. Commun. Rev. **45**(5), 213–226 (2015)
16. Shi, Y., Biswas, S.: Website fingerprinting using traffic analysis of dynamic webpages. In: IEEE Global Communications Conference, GLOBECOM 2014, Austin, TX, USA, 8–12 December 2014, pp. 557–563 (2014)
17. Suykens, J.A.K., Vandewalle, J.: Least squares support vector machine classifiers. Neural Process. Lett. **9**(3), 293–300 (1999)
18. Trevisan, M., Drago, I., Mellia, M., Munafò, M.M.: Towards web service classification using addresses and DNS. In: 2016 International Wireless Communications and Mobile Computing Conference (IWCMC), Paphos, Cyprus, 5–9 September 2016, pp. 38–43 (2016)
19. Wang, T.: Website Fingerprinting: Attacks and Defenses. Ph.D. thesis, University of Waterloo, Ontario, Canada (2015). http://hdl.handle.net/10012/10123
20. Wang, T., Cai, X., Nithyanand, R., Johnson, R., Goldberg, I.: Effective attacks and provable defenses for website fingerprinting. In: Proceedings of the 23rd USENIX Security Symposium, San Diego, CA, USA, 20–22 August 2014, pp. 143–157 (2014). https://www.usenix.org/conference/usenixsecurity14/technical-sessions/presentation/wang_tao
21. Wang, T., Goldberg, I.: On realistically attacking tor with website fingerprinting. PoPETs **2016**(4), 21–36 (2016)
22. Zolnierek, A., Rubacha, B.: The empirical study of the Naive bayes classifier in the case of Markov chain recognition task. In: Computer Recognition Systems, Proceedings of the 4th International Conference on Computer Recognition Systems, CORES 2005, 22–25 May 2005, Rydzyna Castle, Poland, pp. 329–336 (2005)

Deep Streaming Graph Representations

Minglong Lei[1], Yong Shi[2,3,4,5], Peijia Li[1], and Lingfeng Niu[2,3,4(✉)]

[1] School of Computer and Control Engineering,
University of Chinese Academy of Sciences, Beijing 100049, China
{leiminglong16,lipeijia13}@mails.ucas.ac.cn
[2] School of Economics and Management, University of Chinese Academy of Sciences,
Beijing 100190, China
{yshi,niulf}@ucas.ac.cn
[3] Key Laboratory of Big Data Mining and Knowledge Management,
Chinese Academy of Sciences, Beijing 100190, China
[4] Research Center on Fictitious Economy and Data Science,
Chinese Academy of Sciences, Beijing 100190, China
[5] College of Information Science and Technology, University of Nebraska at Omaha,
Omaha, NE 68182, USA

Abstract. Learning graph representations generally indicate mapping the vertices of a graph into a low-dimension space, in which the proximity of the original data can be preserved in the latent space. However, traditional methods that based on adjacent matrix suffered from high computational cost when encountering large graphs. In this paper, we propose a deep autoencoder driven streaming methods to learn low-dimensional representations for graphs. The proposed method process the graph as a data stream fulfilled by sampling strategy to avoid straight computation over the large adjacent matrix. Moreover, a graph regularized deep autoencoder is employed in the model to keep different aspects of proximity information. The regularized framework is able to improve the representation power of learned features during the learning process. We evaluate our method in clustering task by the features learned from our model. Experiments show that the proposed method achieves competitive results comparing with methods that directly apply deep models over the complete graphs.

Keywords: Streaming methods · Representation learning
Deep autoencoder · Graph regularization

1 Introduction

Graph representation or graph embedding [17] aims at mapping the vertices into a low-dimensional space while keeping the structural information and revealing the proximity of instances [17]. The compact representations for graph vertices is then useful for further tasks such as classification [10] and clustering [8, 15].

The most intuitive and simple idea to handle graph is only using the connection information and then representing the graph as a deterministic adjacent

© Springer International Publishing AG, part of Springer Nature 2018
Y. Shi et al. (Eds.): ICCS 2018, LNCS 10862, pp. 512–518, 2018.
https://doi.org/10.1007/978-3-319-93713-7_46

matrix. Dimension reduction techniques [12] that directly applied in the adjacent matrix can achieve superior performance in many cases.

Directly launch dimension reduction under the complete graph are efficient in many scenarios, they also have obvious disadvantages. Generally speaking, the limitations of direct matrix models are threefold. First, the direct matrix models are easily suffered from high computation complexity in large scale graphs. Since the adjacent matrix is deterministic and fixed, such methods are not flexible enough when the dataset is large. Second, the direct matrix models have not consider enough information in the model. They only provide a global view of the graph structure. However, the local information which depicts the neighborhood information should also be considered in the learned features. Finally, the success of the direct matrix models highly depend on the representation power of dimension reduction models. Methods such as spectral learning [12] and Non-negative Matrix Factorization [9] have limited representation power.

In order to solve those challenges, we propose a new deep graph representation method that based on streaming algorithm [1, 19]. The proposed method keeps the advantages of deterministic matrix methods and also introduces several new ideas to handle the limitations.

First, we introduce a streaming motivated stochastic idea into the model. Streaming methods are methods that process data streams. Specially, the input of a streaming model is organized as a sequence of data blocks. The main target of data streams is to solve memory issues. In this paper, we sample a small portion of vertices once and formulate a graph stream. With the accumulation of vertices along with the flow of data stream, more and more information will be automatically contained in the model rather in the data. Since we choose fixed small number of vertices for each time, the dimension of the input will be reduced significantly. Consequently, the streaming strategy is helpful in handling computation complexity issues.

Second, in order to combine more information in the model, we adopt a regularization framework in the proposed method. The direct matrix models only consider visible edges between vertices. The highlight point of the regularization framework is that the graph regularization term includes the vertex similarities in the model in addition to visible connections. Vertices that are similar in the original space should have similar representations in the latent low-dimensional space.

Finally, after the graph streams are obtained, we fed the data stream into a deep autoencoder [6] to learn the representations of graph vertices. The learning power of deep autoencoder assures that the learned features keep sufficient information from the original graph.

2   Related Work

Graph representation, also known as graph embedding, is a sub topic of representation learning. What representation learning [4] attempts to do is to decode data in the original space into a vector space in an unsupervised fashion so that the leaned features can be used in further tasks.

Early methods such as Laplacian Eigenmaps (LE) [3], Local Linear Embedding (LLE) [14] and are deterministic. Among those methods, the graph is denoted as an adjacent matrix and methods under the matrix is generally related to dimension reduction techniques [18]. Specially, the intuitive idea is to solve the eigenvectors of the affinity matrix. They exploit spectral properties of affinity matrices and are known as laplace methods. More recently, deep learning models are also used as dimension reduction tools for their superior ability in representation [8,15].

More recent works on graph embedding are stochastic in which the graph is no longer represented as a fixed matrix [5,13]. Methods such as Deepwalk [13] and node2vec [5] regard the graph as a vertex vocabulary where a collection node sequences are sampled from. Subsequently, language models such as skip-gram [11] can be used to obtain the ultimate representations.

The deterministic methods are not flexible [2] and the disadvantages of stochastic models are also obvious. Since stochastic models only consider local information that describes the nearest neighbors of vertices, they fail in providing a global picture under the whole graph view. The loss of global information influences the performance of such models when the graph structure is irregular.

3   Network Embedding Problem

3.1   Notations

In this paper, we denote vectors as lowercase letters with bold form and matrixes as uppercase letters in boldface. The elements of a matrix and a vector are denoted as $\mathbf{X}_{ij}$ and $\mathbf{x}_i$ respectively. Given a graph $G(V, E)$, V is the vertices set denoted as $\{v_1, ..., v_n\}$ and E is the edges set denoted as $\{v_{ij}\}_{i,j=1}^n$.

We then define the graph embedding as:

Definition 1 (Graph Embedding). *Given a N-vertex graph $G(V, E)$, the goal of graph embedding is to learn a mapping $v_i \longmapsto \mathbf{y}_i$, $\mathbf{y}_i \in \mathbb{R}^d$. The learned representations in the latent low-dimensional space should be capable to keep the structural information of the original graph.*

3.2   Streaming Strategy

In this subsection, we illustrate how to formulate the data stream from a given graph $G(V, E)$. Let K be the number of data chunks in a data stream. Denote S_k as the kth data chunk in the data stream where $k \in 1, 2, \cdots, K$. The K can be extremely large since the substantial numbers of samplings is conducive to visiting the graph completely.

Let the number of vertices that selected in one time to be $D(D \ll N)$. Obviously, the D is also the input of the embedding model since D is fixed as a constant number. In the training phase, in an arbitrary step k, we select D nodes from the vertex collection $\{v_1, ..., v_n\}$ uniformly. A subgraph is then constructed by the selected nodes. The S_k is the adjacent matrix of the subgraph. In Fig. 1

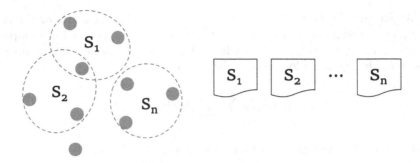

Fig. 1. The streaming strategy. Each time we choose a fixed number of vertices. The data chunks are constructed by the selected vertices.

we present the sampling process to formulate a data stream. A data stream S is denoted as $S = S_k; k \in 1, \cdots, K$.

In the embedding phase, the goal is mapping each vertex to its representations by the trained model. However, the dimension of the original data N is much higher than the input dimension of the model D. Consequently, we run a simple Principal Component Analysis (PCA) in $\mathbf{X}$ to get $\mathbf{X}^D$ with a dimension D. Then the $\mathbf{X}^D$ is served as input to obtain the compact representations for each vertex.

3.3   Graph Autoendoer

Autoencoders [16] is powerful in representation task. After getting the data stream, we use a deep graph autoencoder to get the low-dimension vectors.

Deep Autoencoder: Autoencoder paradigm attempts to copy its input to its output, which results in a code layer that may capture useful properties of the input.

Let $\mathbf{X} = \{\mathbf{x}_i : \mathbf{x}_i \in \mathbb{R}^{m \times 1}\}_{i=1}^n$ and $\mathbf{Z} = \{\mathbf{z}_i : \mathbf{z}_i \in \mathbb{R}^{m \times 1}\}_{i=1}^n$ be the input matrix and reconstruction matrix. $\mathbf{Y} = \{\mathbf{y}_i : \mathbf{y}_i \in \mathbb{R}^{d \times 1}\}_{i=1}^n$ is the code matrix where the dimension of $\mathbf{y}_i$ is usually much lower than the dimension of the original data $\mathbf{x}_i$. A layer wise interpretation of the encoder and decoder can be represented as:

$$\mathbf{Y} = f_\theta(\mathbf{X}) = \delta(W_{encoder}\mathbf{X} + b_{encoder}) \tag{1}$$

$$\mathbf{Z} = g_\theta(\mathbf{Y}) = \delta(W_{decoder}\mathbf{Y} + b_{decoder}) \tag{2}$$

For convenience, we summarize the encoder parameters as $\theta_{encoder}$, and the decoder parameters as $\theta_{decoder}$. Then the loss function can be defined as:

$$\mathcal{L} = \|\mathbf{X} - \mathbf{Z}\|_F^2 = \sum_{i=1}^n \|\mathbf{x}_i - \mathbf{z}_i\|_2^2 \tag{3}$$

Since a deep autoencoder can be thought of as a special case of feedforward networks, the parameters are optimized by backpropagate gradients through chain-rules.

Graph Regularization: In order to preserve the local structure of the data, we employ a graph regularization term derived from Laplacian Eigenmaps [3]. Suppose A is the indicator matrix where $\mathbf{A}_{ij}$ indicate if node i and node j are connected, the laplacian loss is then defined as:

$$Laplacian = \sum_{i}^{n} \sum_{j}^{n} \mathbf{A}_{ij} \|\mathbf{y}_i - \mathbf{y}_j\|_2^2 \tag{4}$$

The laplacian loss can be further written as:

$$Laplacian = \sum_{i}^{n} \sum_{j}^{n} A_{ij} \|\mathbf{y}_i - \mathbf{y}_j\|_2^2 = 2tr(\mathbf{Y}^T \mathbf{L} \mathbf{Y}) \tag{5}$$

where $tr(*)$ denotes the trace and $\mathbf{L}$ is the laplace matrix calculated by matrix $\mathbf{A}$: $\mathbf{L} = \mathbf{D} - \mathbf{A}$. $\mathbf{D}$ is a diagonal matrix where $\mathbf{D} = \sum_i^n \mathbf{A}_{ij} = \sum_i^n \mathbf{A}_{ij}$.

Combining the graph information, the optimization problem is:

$$\mathcal{L} = \|\mathbf{X} - \mathbf{Z}\|_F^2 + \alpha' \cdot 2tr(\mathbf{Y}^T \mathbf{L} \mathbf{Y}) + \beta' \cdot \frac{1}{2} \|W\|_F^2 \tag{6}$$

Merge the constant numbers into parameters α and β, the loss function is updated as:

$$\mathcal{L} = \|\mathbf{X} - \mathbf{Z}\|_F^2 + \alpha tr(\mathbf{Y}^T \mathbf{L} \mathbf{Y}) + \beta \|W\|_F^2 \tag{7}$$

where α and β are the hyperparameters that control the model complexity.

Recall that each time we have a data chunk S_k, let $\mathbf{X} = \mathbf{A} = S_k$ and then run the graph regularized autoencoder under $\mathbf{X}$ and $\mathbf{A}$. Similar to most deep neural networks, we choose gradient decent to optimize the deep autoencoder. The objective function is $\mathcal{L} = \varepsilon(f, g) + \lambda \Omega(f)$. The first term $\varepsilon(f, g)$ is the reconstruction error and the second term $\Omega(f)$ is the regularization term. The partial derivatives of $\theta_{decoder}$ only depend on the first term and the partial derivatives of $\theta_{encoder}$ depend on both terms. By using chain rules, parameters at each layer can be calculated sequentially.

4   Experiments

In this section, we conduct experiments in clustering tasks to testify the effectiveness of our method.

We use two datasets, COIL20 and ORL, to testify the our efficiency. COIL20 contains 1440 instances that belongs to 20 categories and ORL contains 400 samples that belongs to 40 classes. The KNN-graph is constructed by computing the k-nearest neighbors of each sample.

We compare our approach with several deep models to evaluate the performance of our method. Specially, we employ deep autoencoder (DAE) [7] and stacked autoencoder (SAE) [16] as baseline models.

We evaluate the learned features in clustering task. Following the general settings in most clustering procedure, we employ *purity* and *NMI* to evaluate the results.

In our experiment, we set the D to be 500 for COIL20 and 200 for ORL. The layers of deep graph autoencoders for COIL20 and ORL are 5 and 3 respectively. For COIL20, we set the dimensions as $500 - 200 - 100 - 200 - 500$. For ORL, we set the dimensions as $200 - 100 - 200$.

The clustering results of COIL20 and ORL are presented in Table 1. The results show that the streaming method has competitive representation power comparing with baseline models that utilize the complete matrices. The results also indicate that when encountering large graphs, the streaming method is relieved from computation issues and is still able to achieve superior performance.

Table 1. Results in clustering task

Methods	COIL20		ORL	
	NMI	Purity	NMI	Purity
Deep streaming + Kmeans	0.7887	0.7124	0.8425	0.7325
DAE + Kmeans	**0.8034**	**0.7241**	**0.8672**	**0.7416**
SAE + Kmeans	0.7604	0.6925	0.8390	0.7175
Kmeans	0.7301	0.6535	0.8247	0.7024

5   Conclusion

We proposed a streaming motivated embedding method to learn the low dimensional representations of the graph. The streaming strategy is used to reduce the effect of computation complexity. The deep autoencoder and graph regularization idea make sure the learned features include enough information. Experiments in clustering task verify the effectiveness of our methods. Our model achieve results as good as models that directly apply dimension reduction in the original matrix. The results can be generalized to large graphs where directly matrix models are inapplicable.

Acknowledgements. This work was supported by the National Natural Science Foundation of China (Grant No. 91546201, No. 71331005, No. 71110107026, No. 11671379, No. 11331012), UCAS Grant (No. Y55202LY00).

References

1. Aggarwal, C.C.: Data Streams: Models and Algorithms, vol. 31. Springer, New York (2007)
2. Ahmed, A., Shervashidze, N., Narayanamurthy, S., Josifovski, V., Smola, A.J.: Distributed large-scale natural graph factorization. In: Proceedings of the 22nd International Conference on World Wide Web, pp. 37–48. ACM (2013)
3. Belkin, M., Niyogi, P.: Laplacian Eigenmaps and spectral techniques for embedding and clustering. In: NIPS, vol. 14, pp. 585–591 (2001)
4. Bengio, Y., Courville, A., Vincent, P.: Representation learning: a review and new perspectives. IEEE Trans. Patt. Anal. Mach. Intell. **35**(8), 1798–1828 (2013)
5. Grover, A., Leskovec, J.: node2vec: scalable feature learning for networks. In: Proceedings of the 22nd ACM SIGKDD International Conference on Knowledge Discovery and Data Mining, pp. 855–864. ACM (2016)
6. Hinton, G.E., Osindero, S., Teh, Y.W.: A fast learning algorithm for deep belief nets. Neural Comput. **18**(7), 1527–1554 (2006)
7. Hinton, G.E., Salakhutdinov, R.R.: Reducing the dimensionality of data with neural networks. Science **313**(5786), 504–507 (2006)
8. Huang, P., Huang, Y., Wang, W., Wang, L.: Deep embedding network for clustering. In: 2014 22nd International Conference on Pattern Recognition (ICPR), pp. 1532–1537. IEEE (2014)
9. Lee, D.D., Seung, H.S.: Learning the parts of objects by non-negative matrix factorization. Nature **401**(6755), 788 (1999)
10. Lu, Q., Getoor, L.: Link-based classification. In: Proceedings of the 20th International Conference on Machine Learning (ICML2003), pp. 496–503 (2003)
11. Mikolov, T., Chen, K., Corrado, G., Dean, J.: Efficient estimation of word representations in vector space. arXiv preprint arXiv:1301.3781 (2013)
12. Ng, A.Y., Jordan, M.I., Weiss, Y.: On spectral clustering: analysis and an algorithm. In: Advances in Neural Information Processing Systems, pp. 849–856 (2002)
13. Perozzi, B., Al-Rfou, R., Skiena, S.: DeepWalk: online learning of social representations. In: Proceedings of the 20th ACM SIGKDD International Conference on Knowledge Discovery and Data Mining, pp. 701–710. ACM (2014)
14. Roweis, S.T., Saul, L.K.: Nonlinear dimensionality reduction by locally linear embedding. Science **290**(5500), 2323–2326 (2000)
15. Tian, F., Gao, B., Cui, Q., Chen, E., Liu, T.Y.: Learning deep representations for graph clustering. In: AAAI, pp. 1293–1299 (2014)
16. Vincent, P., Larochelle, H., Lajoie, I., Bengio, Y., Manzagol, P.A.: Stacked denoising autoencoders: learning useful representations in a deep network with a local denoising criterion. J. Mach. Learn. Res. **11**, 3371–3408 (2010)
17. Wang, D., Cui, P., Zhu, W.: Structural deep network embedding. In: Proceedings of the 22nd ACM SIGKDD International Conference on Knowledge Discovery and Data Mining, pp. 1225–1234. ACM (2016)
18. Yan, S., Xu, D., Zhang, B., Zhang, H.J., Yang, Q., Lin, S.: Graph embedding and extensions: a general framework for dimensionality reduction. IEEE Trans. Patt. Anal. Mach. Intell. **29**(1), 40–51 (2007)
19. Zhang, P., Zhu, X., Guo, L.: Mining data streams with labeled and unlabeled training examples. In: 2009 Ninth IEEE International Conference on Data Mining, ICDM 2009, pp. 627–636. IEEE (2009)

Adversarial Reinforcement Learning
for Chinese Text Summarization

Hao Xu[1,2], Yanan Cao[2], Yanmin Shang[2(✉)], Yanbing Liu[2],
Jianlong Tan[2], and Li Guo[2]

[1] School of Cyber Security, University of Chinese Academy of Sciences,
Beijing, China
[2] Institute of Information Engineering, Chinese Academy of Sciences,
Beijing, China
{xuhao2,caoyanan,shangyanmin,liuyanbing,tanjianlong,
guoli}@iie.ac.cn

Abstract. This paper proposes a novel *Adversarial Reinforcement Learning* architecture for Chinese text summarization. Previous abstractive methods commonly use Maximum Likelihood Estimation (MLE) to optimize the generative models, which makes auto-generated summary less incoherent and inaccuracy. To address this problem, we innovatively apply the *Adversarial Reinforcement Learning* strategy to narrow the gap between the generated summary and the human summary. In our model, we use a generator to generate summaries, a discriminator to distinguish between generated summaries and real ones, and reinforcement learning (RL) strategy to iteratively evolve the generator. Besides, in order to better tackle Chinese text summarization, we use a character-level model rather than a word-level one and append Text-Attention in the generator. Experiments were run on two Chinese corpora, respectively consisting of long documents and short texts. Experimental Results showed that our model significantly outperforms previous deep learning models on rouge score.

Keywords: Chinese text summarization · Generative adversarial network
Deep learning · Reinforcement learning

1 Introduction

With the rapid growth of the online information services, more and more data is available and accessible online. This explosion of information has resulted in a well-recognized information overload problem [1]. However, the time-cost is expensive if you want to get key information from a mass of data in an artificial way. So, it is very meaningful to build an effective automatic text summarization system which aims to automatically produce short and well-organized summaries of documents [2]. While *extractive approaches* focus on selecting representative segments directly from original text [3, 4], we aim to capture its salient idea by understanding the source text entirely, i.e. using an *abstractive approach*.

© Springer International Publishing AG, part of Springer Nature 2018
Y. Shi et al. (Eds.): ICCS 2018, LNCS 10862, pp. 519–532, 2018.
https://doi.org/10.1007/978-3-319-93713-7_47

Most recent abstractive approaches apply a sequence-to-sequence (seq2seq) framework to generate summaries and use Maximum Likelihood Estimation (MLE) to optimize the models [8, 9]. The typical seq2seq model consists of two neural networks: one for encoding the input sequence into a fixed length vector C, and another for decoding C and outputting the predicted sequence. The state-of-the-art seq2seq method uses attention mechanism to make the decoder focus on a part of the vector C selectively for connecting the target sequence with each token in the source one.

Despite the remarkable progress of previous research, Chinese text summarization still faces several challenges: (i) As mentioned above, the standard seq2seq models use MLE, i.e. maximizing the probability of the next word in summary, to optimize the objective function. Such an objective does not guarantee the generated summaries to be as natural and accurate as ground-truth ones. (ii) Different from English, the error-rate of word segmentation and the larger vocabulary in Chinese call for character-level models. Character-level summarization depends on the global contextual information of the original text. However, the decoder with attention mechanism which performed well in other natural language processing (NLP) tasks [5] just pay attention to the key parts of text.

To address these problems, we propose a novel *Adversarial Reinforcement Learning* architecture for Chinese text summarization, aiming to minimize the gap between the generated summary and the human summary. This framework consists of two models: a summary generator and an adversarial discriminator. The summary generator based on a seq2seq model is treated as an agent of reinforcement learning (RL); the state is the generated tokens so far and the action is the next token to be generated; the discriminator evaluates the generated summary and feedback the evaluation as reward to guide the learning of the generative model. In this learning process, the generated summary is evaluated by its ability to cheat the discriminator into believing that it is a human summary. Beyond the basic ARL model, in order to well capture the global contextual information of the source Chinese text, the generator introduces the text attention mechanism based on the standard seq2seq framework.

We conduct the experiments on two standard Chinese corpora, namely LCSTS (a long text corpus) and NLPCC (a short text corpus). Experiments show that our proposed model achieves better performance than the state-of-the-art systems on two corpora.

The main contributions of this paper are as follows:

- We propose a novel deep learning architecture with *Adversarial Reinforcement Learning* framework for Chinese text summarization. In this architecture, we employ a discriminator as an evaluator to teach the summary generator to generate more realistic summary.
- We introduce the attention mechanism in the source text on the intuition that the given text provides a valid context for the summary, which makes character-level summarization more accurate.

2 Related Work

Traditional abstractive works include unsupervised topic detection method, phrase-table based machine translation approaches [6], and Generative Adversarial Network approaches [7]. In recent years, more and more works employ deep neural network framework to tackle abstractive summarization problem. [8] were the first to apply seq2seq to English text summarization, achieving state-of-the-art performance on two sentence-level summarization datasets DUC-2004 and Gigaword. [13] improved this system by using encoder-decoder LSTM with attention and bidirectional neural net. Attention mechanism append to the decoder allows it to look back at parts of the encoded input sequence while the output is generated and gain better performance. [14] constructs a large-scale Chinese short text summarization dataset from the microblogging website Sina Weibo. And as far as we know, they made the first attempt to perform the seq2seq approach on a large-scale Chinese corpus, which is based on GRU encoder and decoder. In above works, the most commonly used training objective is Maximum Likelihood Estimation (MLE). However, maximizing the probability of generated summary conditioned on the source text is far from minimizing the gap between generated and human summary. This discrepancy between training and inference makes generated summaries less coherent and accuracy.

Different from MLE, reinforcement learning (RL) is a computational approach to learning whereby an agent tries to maximize the total amount of reward it receives when interacting with a complex, uncertain environment [15]. [16] proved RL methods can be adapted to text summarization problems naturally and simply on the premise of effectively selecting features and the score function.

Meanwhile, the idea of generative adversarial network (GAN) has got a huge success in computer vision [11, 12]. The adversarial training is formalized as a game between two networks: a generator network (G) to generate data, a discriminator network (D) to distinguish whether a given summary is a real one. However, discrete words are nondifferentiable and cannot provide a gradient to feed the discriminator reward back to the generator. To address this problem, Sequence Adversarial Nets with Policy Gradient (SeqGAN) [17] used the policy network as a generator, which enables the use of the adversarial network in NLP. [18] proposes to adversarial in hidden vectors of the generator rather than the output sequence.

Inspired by the successful application of RL and GAN in related tasks, we propose adversarial reinforcement learning framework for text summarization. And a discriminator is introduced as the adaptive score function. We use the discriminator as the environment or human, and output from discriminator as a reward. The updating direction of generator parameters can be obtained by using the policy gradient.

3 Adversarial Reinforcement Learning

The overall framework of our model is shown in Fig. 1. A given text sequence is denoted as $X = \{x_1, x_2, \ldots, x_n\}$ consisting of n words, where x_i is the i-th word. Summary generated by human (shown in the yellow box) is denoted as $Y = \{y_1, y_2, \ldots, y_m\}$, where y_j is the j-th word and $m < n$. The goal of this model is to generate a summary $Y' = \{y'_1, y'_2, \ldots, y'_{m'}\}$ consisting of m' words, where $m' < n$ and m maybe not equal to m'.

The *adversarial reinforcement learning* framework consists of two models: a generative model G and a discriminative model D. We use G (shown in the green box) to transform the original text X into summary Y' based on a seq2seq framework. Here, we want to make the distribution of Y' and Y overlap as much as possible. To achieve this goal, we use D (shown in the red box) based on recursive neural networks (RNN). We take the same amount of positive samples $(X, Y) \sim P_r$ and navigate samples $(X, Y') \sim P_g$ randomly to train the D, where P_r means the joint distribution of source text and real summary, and P_g means that of source text and generated summary. Meanwhile, we use strategy gradient to train G according to the reward by D.

3.1 Summary Generator

Seq2seq Model. Most recent models for text summarization and text simplification are based on the seq2seq model. In the previous work [8, 9], the encoder is a four layer Long Short-term Memory Network (LSTM) [19], which maps source texts into the hidden vector. The decoder is another LSTM, mapping from i–1 words of Y' and X to y'_i, which is formalized as $y_i \sim G(Y'_{1:i-1}|X_{1:n})$, where $Y'_{1:i}$ means the generated summary at the i-th step.

Attention mechanism is introduced to help the decoder to "attend" to different parts of the source sentence at each step of the output generation [8]. We redefine a conditional probability for seq2seq in the following:

$$G(y'_i|Y'_{1\ldots i-1}, X) = g(y'_{i-1}, s_i, c_i) \tag{1}$$

Where s_i is the hidden status unit in the decoder, and c_i is the context vector at step i. For standard LSTM decoder, at each step i, the hidden status s_i is a function of the previous step status s_{i-1}, the previous step output y'_{i-1}, and the i-th context vector:

$$s_i = f(s_{i-1}, y'_{i-1}, c_i) \tag{2}$$

$$c_i = \sum_{j=1}^{n} \alpha_{ij} h_j \tag{3}$$

The weight α is defined as follows:

$$\alpha_{ij} = \frac{exp(e_{ij})}{\sum_{k=1}^{n} exp(e_{ik})} \tag{4}$$

α_{ij} is called the alignment model, which evaluates the matching degree of the j-th word of text and the i-th word of summary.

Text-Attention. Different from the sequence transformation problem, text summarization is a mapping from original space to subspace. So, summarization models should pay attention to potential key information in the source text. From another

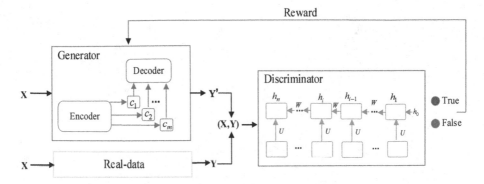

Fig. 1. Architecture of adversarial reinforcement learning for text summarization (Color figure online)

perspective, information needed by a partial summary, may be located anywhere in the source text. So, the attention should be anywhere around the text if needed. However, decoder with attention merely focuses on the latest context of the next decoded word.

As shown in Fig. 2, we introduce the Text-Attention based on IARNN-WORD [20]. In such a framework, we use attention mechanism on X, because the contextual information of X is very effective for the generated summary Y'. In order to well utilize the relevant contexts, we use attention before feeding X into the RNN model, which is formalized as follows:

$$\beta_i = \sigma(r_t m_{ti} x_i) \tag{5}$$

$$\tilde{x}_i = \beta_i * x_i \tag{6}$$

where m_{ti} is an attention matrix which transforms a text representation r_t into a word embedding representation, and β_i is a scaler between 0 and 1.

3.2 Adversarial Discriminator

The *discriminator*, called D for short, is used to distinguish generated summary from real as much as possible. This is a typical problem of binary classification. We use RNN model to capture text contextual information which is very effective for text classification, and the final layer is a 2-class softmax layer which gives the label 'Generated' or 'Real'. The framework of D is shown in Fig. 1. In order to prevent collapse mode, we use mini-batch method to train D. We sampled the same number of text-summary pairs (X, Y) and (X, Y') respectively from human and generator, where $Y' \sim G(\cdot|X)$ and the mini-batch size is k. For each text-summary pair (X_i, Y_i) sent to D, the optimization target is to minimize the cross-entropy loss for binary classification, using human summary as positive instance and generated summary as negative one.

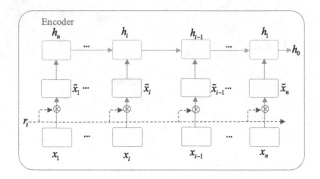

Fig. 2. Text-attention

3.3   Strategy Gradient for Training

Our goal is to encourage the generator to generate summaries that make the discriminator difficult to distinguish them from real ones. G is trained by policy gradient and reward signal is passed from D via Monte Carlo search. To be more precise, there is generally a markov decision process, performing an action y_i based on the state s_i with $Reward(s_i, y_i)$, where s_i denotes the decoding result of the previous i–1 words Y_{i-1}. A series of performed actions are called a "strategy" or "strategy path" θ^{π}. The target of RL is to find out the optimal strategy which can earn the biggest prize:

$$\theta^{\pi}_{best} = arg \max_{\theta^{\pi}} \sum_{A_i \in \theta^{\pi}_{best}}^{i} Reward(s_i, y_i) \tag{7}$$

RL can evaluate each possible action in any state through the environment feedback of reward and find out one action to maximize the expected reward $E(\sum_{y_i \in \theta^{\pi}}^{i} Reward(s_i, y_i), \theta^{\pi})$. Based on this, we assume that the generated summary is rewarded from the real summary by D, denoted as $R(X, Y')$. We denote parameters in the framework of encoder-decoder as θ, then our objective function is expressed as maximizing the expected reward of generated summary based on RL:

$$\theta^{\pi}_{best} = arg \ \max_{\theta} \mathbb{E}(R(X, Y'))$$
$$= arg \ \max_{\theta} \sum_X \sum_{Y'} P_{\theta}(X, Y')R(X, Y') \tag{8}$$
$$= arg \ \max_{\theta} \sum_X P(X) \sum_{Y'} P_{\theta}(Y'|X)R(X, Y')$$

Where $P_{\theta}(X, Y')$ denotes the joint probability of a text-summary pair (X, Y') under the parameter θ. We redefine he right-hand side of Eq. (8) as J_{θ}, which is the expectation of reward when G gets the optimal parameter. The probability distribution of each text-summary pair (X_i, Y'_i) can be regarded as a uniform distribution:

$$J_\theta = \sum_X P(X) \sum_{Y'} P_\theta(Y'|X) R(X, Y') \approx \frac{1}{n} \sum_{i=1}^n R(X_i, Y_i') \tag{9}$$

Whose gradient w.r.t. is:

$$
\begin{aligned}
\nabla J_\theta &= \sum_X P(X) \sum_{Y'} R(X, Y') \nabla P_\theta(Y'|X) \\
&= \sum_X P(X) \sum_{Y'} P_\theta(Y'|X) \frac{\nabla P_\theta(Y'|X)}{P_\theta(Y'|X)} \\
&= \sum_X P(X) \sum_{Y'} R(X, Y') P_\theta(Y'|X) \nabla \log P_\theta(Y'|X) \\
&\approx \frac{1}{n} \sum_{i=1}^n R(X_i, Y_i') \nabla \log P_\theta(Y_i'|X_i)
\end{aligned}
\tag{10}
$$

So, in this case, our optimization goal is to maximize the probability of generating a summary. That is, by updating the parameters θ, the reward will make the model improve the probability of the occurrence of the high-quality summary, while the punishment will make the model reduce the probability of the occurrence of the inferior summary. Therefore, we can use the reinforcement learning to solve the problem of GAN cannot differentiable in discrete space.

However, in all cases, mode-collapse will appear during the game. So, we adopted monte carol search to solve this problem. To be specific, when $t \neq n$, the decoding result is just a partial one whose reward is $D(X_i, Y_{i:t}')$. We use monte carol search to supplement its subsequent sequence, calculating the mean of all possible rewards.

We use the D as the reward for RL and assume the length of generated summary is m'. Then the calculation of the reward value J_θ of the generated summary is as follows:

$$J_\theta = \frac{1}{n} \sum_{i=1}^n D(X_i, Y_{1:i-1}' + y_i') \tag{11}$$

Where $Y_{1:i-1}'$ denotes the previously generated summary. Then we can have n path to get n sentences by Monte Carlo search. The *discriminator* D can give a reward for the generated summary in the whole sentence.

When updating model parameters θ, if the reward is always positive, the samples cannot cover all situations. So, we need use the baseline setting to reward. The gradient after joining the baseline is:

$$\nabla J_\theta \approx \frac{1}{n} \sum_{i=1}^n D(X_i, Y_i') \nabla \log P_\theta(Y_i'|X_i) \tag{12}$$

Equation (12) is a reward of the probability of generated summary. Unfortunately, the probability value is non-negative, which means that the *discriminator* doesn't give negative penalty term, no matter how bad the generated summary is. This will cause the generator to be unable to train effectively. Therefore, we introduced the basic value *baseline*. When we calculate the reward, we minus this *baseline* from the feedback of reward. The basic value of the reward and punishment is b, and the calculation formula of the optimization gradient in Eq. (12) is modified as follows:

$$\nabla J_\theta \approx \frac{1}{n}\sum_{i=1}^{n}(D(X_i, Y_i') - \text{b})\nabla \log P_\theta(Y_i'|X_i) \qquad (13)$$

G and D are interactive training. When we train the generator, the G continuously optimizes itself by the feedback of D. The gradient approximation is used to update θ, where α denotes the learning-rate:

$$\theta^{i+1} = \theta^i + \alpha\nabla J_{\theta^i} \qquad (14)$$

It's time to update the new D until the generated summary is indistinguishable.

As a result, the key to gradient optimization is to calculate probability of generated summary. So, as the model parameter updates, our model will gradually improve the summary and reduce the loss. The expectation of the reward is an approximation of a sample.

To sum up, our target is to approximate the distribution of generated summary to the that of real ones in a high-dimensional space. Our model works like a teacher, and the *Discriminator* directs the *Generator* to generate natural summaries. In the perfect case, the distribution of generated summaries and that of real ones will overlap completely.

4   Experiments and Results

4.1   Datasets and Evaluation Metric

We train and evaluate our framework on two datasets, one consists of short texts (on average 320 characters) and the other is long (840 characters). The short text corpus is Large Scale Chinese Short Text Summarization Dataset (LCSTS) [14], which consists of more than 2.4 million text-summary pairs, constructed from the Chinese microblogging website Sina Weibo[1]. It is split into three parts, with 2,400,591 pairs in the training set, 10,666 pairs as the development set and 1,106 pairs in the test set. The long one is NLPCC Evaluation Task 4[2], which contains text-summary pair (50k totally) for the training and the development set respectively and the test set contains 2500 text-summary pairs.

Preprocessing for Chinese Corpus. As we know, word segmentation is the first step in Chinese text processing, which is very different from English one. The accuracy of word segmentation is about 96% and more [10]. However, this tiny error-rate results in more high-frequency but wrong words and unregistered word with the growth of

---

[1] weibo.sina.com.

[2] http://tcci.ccf.org.cn/conference/2015/pages/page05_evadata.html.

corpus size, which makes the vocabulary larger. This problem will bring about more time-cost and accuracy-loss in Chinese text summarization.

Previous works generally use a 150k word vocabulary on 280k Long English corpus (CNN/Daily Mail). This vocabulary can be further reduced to 30k or lower by means of morphological reduction [21], stem reduction, and wrong word checking [22]. However, the long Chinese corpus NLPCC has a 500k word vocabulary with word frequency higher than 10. Unfortunately, in Chinese we usually directly truncate the word vocabulary, which leads to more unregistered words. Therefore, in experiments we reduce word vocabulary by representing text using characters rather than words. In previous study, the character level methods have achieved good results in English summarization [23, 24]. From intuition, character-level models for Chinese summarization are more effective because a Chinese character is meaningful, while an English letter is meaningless. This strategy also bypasses the cascade errors reduced by word segmentation.

Evaluation Metric. For evaluation, we adopt the popular evaluation metrics F1 of Rouge proposed by [25]. Rouge-1 (unigrams), Rouge-2 (bigrams) and Rouge-L (longest-common substring LCS) are all used.

4.2   Comparative Methods

To evaluate the performance of *Adversarial Reinforcement Learning*, we compare our model with some baselines and state-of-the-art methods: (i) Abs: [26] is the basic seq2seq model, which is widely used for generating texts, so it is an important baseline. (ii) Abs+: [13] is the baseline attention-based seq2seq model which relies on LSTM network encoder and decoder. It achieves 42.57 ROUGE-1 and 23.13 ROUGE-2 on English corpus Gigaword, using Google's textsum[3]. The experiment setting is 120-words text length, 4-layers bidirectional encoding and 200k vocabulary. (iii) Abs +TA: We extend Abs+ by introducing Text-Attention, referring to [20]. We compare this model to Abs+, in order to verify the effectiveness of Text-Attention. (iv) DeepRL: [27] is a new training method that combines standard supervised word prediction and reinforcement learning (RL). It uses two 200 dimensional LSTMs for the bidirectional encoder and one 400-dimensional LSTM. The input vocabulary size is limited to 150k tokens.

4.3   Model Setting

We compare our model with above baseline systems, including Abs, Abs+, Abs+TA and DeepRL. We refer to our proposed model as ARL. Experiments were conducted at word-level and character-level respectively.

In ARL model, the structure of G is based on Abs+TA. The encoder and decoder both use GRUs. In a series of experiments, we set the dimensions of GRU hidden state as 512. We start with a learning-rate of 0.5 which is an empirical value and use the Adam optimization algorithm. For D, the RNNs use LSTM units and learning rate is set

---

[3] https://github.com/tensorflow/models/tree/master/research/textsum.

as 0.2. The settings of hidden state layer and optimization algorithm in D and G are consistent. In order to successfully train the ARL model, we sampled the generated summary and the real summary randomly before training D. Due to the finiteness of generated summary, we use mini-batch strategy to feed text-summary pairs into D, in case of collapse mode. The minibatch is usually set as 64.

In LCSTS word-level experiments, to limit the vocabulary size, we prune the vocabulary to top 150k frequent words, and replace the rest words with the 'UNK' symbols. We used a random initialized 256-dimensional word2vec embeddings as input. In char-level ones, we use Chinese character sequences as both source inputs and target outputs. We limit the model vocabulary size to 12k, which covers most of the common characters. Each character is represented by a random initialized 128-dimensional word embedding.

In NLPCC word-level experiments, we set vocabulary size to 75k, and the encoder and decoder shared vocabularies. 256-dimensional word2vec embeddings are used. In char-level ones, the vocabulary size is limited to 4k and the dimensional of word2vec embeddings to 128.

All the models are trained on the GPUs Tesla V100 for about 500,000 iterations. The training process took about 3 days for our character-level model on NLPCC and LCSTS, 4 days for the NLPCC word-level model, and 6 days for the LCSTS character-level model. The training cost of comparative models varies between 6–8 days.

4.4   Training Details

As we all know, training GAN is very difficult. Therefore, in the process of implementing the model, we have applied some small tricks.

At the beginning of training, the generator's ability is still poor, even after pre-training. G are almost impossible to produce smooth and high-quality summary. And when G send these bad summaries to the D, D can only back a low reward. As previously mentioned, the training of the G can only be optimized by the feedback of the D. So, the G cannot know what a good result. Under the circumstances, the iteration training between G and D is obviously defective.

To alleviate this issue and give the generator more direct access to the gold-standard targets, we introduce the professor-forcing algorithm of [28]. We update model by human-generated responses. The most straightforward strategy is to automatically assign 1 (or other positive) rewards to the human generated response and let the *generator* use the reward to update the human generated example.

We first pre-train the generator by predicting target sequences given the text history. We followed protocols recommended by [26], such as gradient clipping, mini-batch and learning rate decay. We also pre-train the discriminator. To generate negative examples, we decode part of the training data. Half of the negative examples are generated using beam-search with mutual information and the other half is generated from sampling.

In order to keep the G and the D optimize synchronously, experimentally, we train G once every 5 steps of the D until the model converges.

4.5   Results Analysis

Results on LCSTS Corpus. The ROUGE scores of the different summarization methods are presented in Table 1. As can be seen, the character-level models always perform better than their corresponding word-level ones. And it's notable that our proposed character-level ARL model enjoys a reasonable improvement over character-level DeepRL, indicating the effectiveness of the adversarial strategy. Besides, ARL model prominently outperforms two baselines (Abs and Abs+). With respect to other methods, we found that, the MLE's training objective is flawed in text summarization task. In addition, the performance of character-level Abs+TA proved the effectiveness of Text-Attention.

Table 1. Rouge-score on LCSTS corpus

System	Rouge-1	Rouge-2	Rouge-L
Abs(word)	17.7	8.5	15.8
Abs(char)	21.5	8.9	18.6
Abs+(word)	26.8	16.1	24.1
Abs+(char)	29.9	17.4	27.2
Abs+TA(char)	30.1	18.7	28.8
DeepRL(char)	37.9	21.4	29.0
ARL(word)	31.9	17.5	27.5
ARL(char)	*39.4	*21.7	*29.1

Table 2 is an example to show the performance of our model. We can find that the results of ARL model in word-level and char-level are both closer to the main idea in semantics, while the results generated by Abs+ are incoherent. And there is a lot of "_UNK" in ABSw, even using a large vocabulary. Even more, on test set, the results of word-level models (ABSw and ARLw) have a lot of "_UNK", which are rare in the character-level models (ABSc and ARLc). This indicates that the character-level models can reduce the occurrence of rare words. To a certain extent, it improves the performance of all models referred in this section.

Results on NLPCC Corpus. Results on the long text dataset NLPCC are shown in Table 3. Our model ARL also achieves the best performance. It is worth noting that the methods character-level Abs+ is not better the word-level one. That's because attention will produce offset in long text, and our character-level ABS+TA has a good effect at the moment.

Table 2. An example of generated summaries on the test set of LCSTS corpus. **S:** the source texts, **R:** human summary, **ABSw:** Abs+ summary with word-level, **ABSc:** Abs+ summary with char-level (ABc), **ARLw:** AR summary with word-level and **ARLc:** AR summary with char-level and replacing Arabic numbers in "TAGNUM"

S:今天有传在北京某小区，一光头明星因吸毒被捕的消息。下午北京警方官方微博发布声明通报情况，证实该明星为李代沫。李代沫伙同另外6人，于17日晚在北京朝阳区三里屯某小区的暂住地内吸食毒品，6人全部被警方抓获，且当事人对犯案实施供认不讳。 Today, a bald star was arrested for drug abuse, in a Beijing neighborhood. In the afternoon, the Beijing police issued a statement, through the official microblog, confirming that the star was Daimo Li. Daimo Li, with six other people, took drugs in a temporary residence in a district of Sanlitun, Chaoyang district, Beijing, on the evening of the 17th. All six people were arrested by the police, and the parties confessed to the crime.
R: 北京警方确认李代沫吸毒被捕(图) Beijing police confirmed Daimo Li was arrested for drug abuse (photo)
ABSw: 北京警方李代沫吸毒被捕系歌手 _UNK _UNK _UNK _UNK _UNK Beijing police, Daimo Li arrested for drug as a singer _UNK*5.
ABSc:北京警方明星为李代沫吸毒被捕系谣言 Beijing police, the star Daimo Li arrested for drug was a rumor.
ARLw: 网传李代沫吸毒被抓 Internet Communication, Daimo Li was arrested for drug abuse
ARLc: 北京警方确认李代沫吸毒被捕,警方抓获TAGNUM 人 Beijing police confirmed Daimo Li was arrested for drug abuse. Police arrested TAGNUM people

Table 3. Rouge-score on NLPCC corpus

System	Rouge-1	Rouge-2	Rouge-L
Abs+(word)	11.0	6.7	14.0
Abs+(char)	14.3	5.7	13.2
ABS+TA(char)	24.5	8.7	21.8
DeepRL(char)	33.9	16.4	29.5
ARL(char)	*34.4	*17.6	*29.6

5 Conclusion

In this work, we propose an *Adversarial Reinforcement Learning* architecture for Chinese text summarization. This model got promising results in experiments which generating more natural and continuous summaries. Meanwhile, we successfully solved the word segmentation error and distant dependence of text via character-level representation and Text-Attention mechanism. In such a framework, we teach the generator to generate analogous human summary in the continuous space, which is achieved via introducing an adversarial discriminator which tries it best to distinguish the generated summarizations from the real ones.

There are several problems need to be resolved in the future work. One is that, due to the complex structure of Chinese sentences, we want to combine linguistic features (such as part-of-speech, syntax tree) with our ARL model. The other one is that, our model is still a supervised learning one relying on high-quality training datasets which is scarce. So, we will study an unsupervised or semi-supervised framework which can be applied to the text summarization task.

Acknowledgement. This work was supported by the National Key Research and Development program of China (No. 2016YFB0801300), the National Natural Science Foundation of China grants (NO. 61602466).

References

1. Mani, I., Maybury, M.T.: Advances in Automatic Text Summarization. MIT Press, Cambridge (1999)
2. Mani, I.: Automatic Summarization, vol. 3. John Benjamins Publishing, Amsterdam (2001)
3. Ruch, P., Boyer, C., et al.: Using argumentation to extract key sentences from biomedical abstracts. Int. J. Med. Inform. **76**(2–3), 195–200 (2007)
4. Erkan, G., Radev, D.R.: LexRank: graph-based lexical centrality as salience in text summarization. J. Artif. Intell. Res. **22**, 457–479 (2004)
5. Wu, Y., et al.: Google's neural machine translation system: Bridging the gap between human and machine translation. arXiv preprint arXiv:1609.08144 (2016)
6. Ma, S., Sun, X.: A semantic relevance based neural network for text summarization and text simplification. arXiv preprint arXiv:1710.02318 (2017)
7. Liu, L., et al.: Generative Adversarial Network for Abstractive Text Summarization. arXiv preprint arXiv:1711.09357 (2017)
8. Rush, A.M., et al.: A neural attention model for abstractive sentence summarization. arXiv preprint arXiv:1509.00685 (2015)
9. Nallapati, R., Zhou, B., et al.: Abstractive text summarization using sequence-to-sequence RNNS and beyond. arXiv preprint arXiv:1602.06023 (2016)
10. Peng, F., Feng, F., et al.: Chinese segmentation and new word detection using conditional random fields. In: Proceedings of the 20th International Conference on Computational Linguistics, p. 562 (2004)
11. Goodfellow, I., Pouget-Abadie, J., et al.: Generative adversarial nets. In: Advances in Neural Information Processing Systems, pp. 2672–2680 (2014)
12. Radford, A., Metz, L., et al.: Unsupervised representation learning with deep convolutional generative adversarial networks. arXiv preprint arXiv:1511.06434 (2015)
13. Liu, P., Pan, X.: Sequence-to-Sequence with Attention Model for Text Summarization (2016)
14. Hu, B., Chen, Q., et al.: LCSTS: A Large Scale Chinese Short Text Summarization Dataset (2015)
15. Sutton, R.S., Barto, A.G.: Reinforcement Learning: an Introduction, vol. 1. MIT Press, Cambridge (1998). no. 1

16. Ryang, S., Abekawa, T.: Framework of automatic text summarization using reinforcement learning. In: Proceedings of the 2012 Joint Conference on Empirical Methods in Natural Language Processing and Computational Natural Language Learning, pp. 256–265 (2012)
17. Yu, L., Zhang, W., et al.: SeqGAN: sequence generative adversarial nets with policy gradient. In: AAAI, pp. 2852–2858 (2017)
18. Makhzani, A., Shlens, J., et al.: Adversarial autoencoders. arXiv preprint arXiv:1511.05644 (2015)
19. Hochreiter, S., Schmidhuber, J.: Long short-term memory. Neural Comput. 9(8), 1735–1780 (1997)
20. Wang, B., Liu, K., et al.: Inner attention based recurrent neural networks for answer selection. In: ACL (1) (2016)
21. Tolin, B.G., et al.: Improved translation system utilizing a morphological stripping process to reduce words to their root configuration to produce reduction of database size (1996)
22. Perkins, J.: Python Text Processing with NLTK 2.0 Cookbook. Packt Publishing Ltd (2010)
23. Kim, Y., Jernite, Y., et al.: Character-aware neural language models. In: AAAI, pp. 2741–2749 (2016)
24. Zhang, X., Zhao, J., et al.: Character-level convolutional networks for text classification. In: Advances in Neural Information Processing Systems, pp. 649–657 (2015)
25. Lin, C.Y., Hovy, E.: Automatic evaluation of summaries using N-gram co-occurrence statistics. In: Proceedings of the 2003 Conference of the North American Chapter of the Association for Computational Linguistics on Human Language Technology, vol. 1, pp. 71–78 (2003)
26. Sutskever, I., Vinyals, O., et al.: Sequence to sequence learning with neural networks. In: Advances in Neural Information Processing Systems, pp. 3104–3112 (2014)
27. Li, P., Lam, W., Bing, L., et al.: Deep Recurrent Generative Decoder for Abstractive Text Summarization. arXiv preprint arXiv:1708.00625 (2017)
28. Lamb, A.M., Goyal, A.G., et al.: Professor forcing: a new algorithm for training recurrent networks. In: Advances in Neural Information Processing Systems, pp. 4601–4609 (2016)

Column Concept Determination for Chinese Web Tables via Convolutional Neural Network

Jie Xie[1,2], Cong Cao[2(✉)], Yanbing Liu[2], Yanan Cao[2], Baoke Li[1,2],
and Jianlong Tan[2]

[1] School of Cyber Security, University of Chinese Academy of Sciences,
Beijing, China
[2] Institute of Information Engineering, Chinese Academy of Sciences,
Beijing, China
{xiejie, caocong, liuyanbing, caoyanan, libaoke,
tanjianlong}@iie.ac.cn

Abstract. Hundreds of millions of tables on the Internet contain a considerable wealth of high-quality relational data. However, the web tables tend to lack explicit key semantic information. Therefore, information extraction in tables is usually supplemented by recovering the semantics of tables, where column concept determination is an important issue. In this paper, we focus on column concept determination in Chinese web tables. Different from previous research works, convolutional neural network (CNN) was applied in this task. The main contributions of our work lie in three aspects: firstly, datasets were constructed automatically based on the infoboxes in Baidu Encyclopedia; secondly, to determine the column concepts, a CNN classifier was trained to annotate cells in tables and the majority vote method was used on the columns to exclude incorrect annotations; thirdly, to verify the effectiveness, we performed the method on the real tabular dataset. Experimental results show that the proposed method outperforms the baseline methods and achieves an average accuracy of 97% for column concept determination.

Keywords: Column concept determination · Table semantic recovery
Chinese web tables

1 Introduction

The Web contains a wealth of high-quality tabular data. Cafarella et al. [1] extracted 14.1 billion HTML tables from Google's general-purpose web crawl. Lehmberg et al. [6] presented a large public corpus of web tables containing over 233 million tables. Recently, the tabular data has been utilized in knowledge base expansion [7], table searching [4, 8] and table combining.

Normally, a table may have an entity column that contains a set of entities. Each row in the table is composed of the correlation attribute values of an entity. Each column is called an attribute that describes a feature of the entity set. Cells in a single column contain similar content. Compared with free-format text, tables usually

© Springer International Publishing AG, part of Springer Nature 2018
Y. Shi et al. (Eds.): ICCS 2018, LNCS 10862, pp. 533–544, 2018.
https://doi.org/10.1007/978-3-319-93713-7_48

contribute to valuable facts about entities, concepts and relations, which can usually favor the automatic extraction of data.

However, web tables do not have any uniform schema and they tend to lack explicit key semantic information such as column headers, entity column notations and inter-column relations, which, if present, do not use controlled vocabulary. Taking the table in Fig. 1 as an example, it does not have a column header, so the information in such tables is difficult for machines to use. A key challenge is to make such information processable for machines, which usually contains but not limited to three tasks: identify entity columns, determine column concepts and annotate column relations.

萨乌丁 (Dmitry Sautin)	男 (Male)	俄罗斯 (Russia)	奥运会七枚跳水奖牌 (won seven diving medals in the Olympic Games)
高敏 (GaoMin)	女 (Female)	中国 (China)	第24、25 届奥运会女子跳水 3 米板金牌得主 (won the women's 3m springboard gold medal at the 24th and 25th Olympic Games)
田亮 (TianLiang)	男 (Male)	中国 (China)	雅典奥运会男子双人十米跳台冠军 (won the men's diving synchronized 10m platform gold medal at the Athens Olympics)
郭晶晶 (Guo Jingjing)	女 (Female)	中国 (China)	2004 年、2008 年奥运会女子 3 米板金牌 (won the women's 3m springboard gold medal in 2004 and 2008)

Fig. 1. A web table without a column header.

In this paper, we focus on column concept determination task in Chinese web tables, which determines the most appropriate concept for each column in Chinese web tables. To the best of our knowledge, this is the first work to recover the semantics of Chinese web tables. For English tables, most of the state-of-art methods were based on knowledge bases [2, 3, 7, 10, 11, 13], or databases extracted from the Web [4]. These methods can only annotate tables with facts existing in the knowledge bases, but have difficulty to discover new (or unknown) knowledge. Due to the fact that cells in Chinese tables do not have uniform specifications and may contain a certain amount of long sentences (see Fig. 1), the knowledge base-based approaches are not applicable. Therefore, we assumed column concept determination as a classification problem which we solved by leveraging convolutional neural network (CNN). In summary, we made the following contributions:

- We used the infoboxes in Baidu Encyclopedia to automatically construct datasets for text classifier.
- We trained a classifier based on CNN to annotate cells in Chinese web tables and used majority vote to exclude cells with incorrect annotations, and then we determined the concept for each column in the tables.
- We verified the effectiveness of our method on the real tabular dataset.

The rest of this paper is organized as follows. After reviewing the related works in Sect. 2, we give the problem definition in Sect. 3. In Sect. 4, we describe the proposed method in detail and experimental results are reported in Sect. 5. Finally we make a conclusion in Sect. 6.

2 Related Work

WebTables [1] showed that the World-Wide Web consisted of a huge number of data in the form of HTML tables and the research of using web tables as a high quality relational data source was initiated. Recently, a number of studies have appeared with the goal of recovering the semantics of tables to make fully use of tabular data.

For English tables, most of the state-of-art methods were based on knowledge bases [2, 3, 7, 10, 11, 13] or databases extracted from the Web [4]. Limaye et al. [3] proposed a graphical model to annotate tables based on YAGO. Wang et al. [2] used Probase [9] to generate headers for tables and identify entities in tables. Ritze et al. [7] proposed an iterative matching method (T2K) which combined schema and instance matching based on DBpedia [15]. Deng et al. [10] determined column concept by fuzzily matching its cell values to the entities within a large knowledge base. These methods have difficulty to discover new (or unknown) knowledge that do not exist in the knowledge bases.

Different from the methods mentioned above, Quercini et al. [5] utilized support vector machine (SVM) to annotate entities in English web tables. It searched information on the Web to annotate entities. However, it only focused on entity identification task in English web tables.

Considering the fact that many existing Chinese knowledge bases either are for internal use or contain insufficient knowledge for the annotation task, this paper takes the idea of text classification to deal with column concept determination task in Chinese web tables, and leverages the good feature extraction and classification performance of the convolutional neural network.

3 Problem Definition

This paper aimed to study the problem of determining column concept for Chinese web tables. The formal description of the problem will be shown in this section.

- **Web Tables:** Let T be a table with n rows and m columns. Each cell in the table can be represented as $T(i,j)$, $1 \leq i \leq n$ and $1 \leq j \leq m$ being the index of the row and column respectively. $T(i,j)$ can be a long sentence besides a word or a few words, just like the fourth column in Fig. 1. In addition, we assume that the contents in web tables are mainly Chinese. In fact, our method works as well when the table contains several English words. In this research, we model T as a bi-dimensional array of $n \times m$ cells, limiting the research scope to tables with no column branches into sub columns.
- **Column Concept Determination:** Given a table T, the method must classify a type for each cell in T and then determine the concept for each column. More formally,

for each cell $T(i,j)$, the method firstly annotates it with a type $t_{i,j}^{(k)}$. Then for the j_{th} column, if the majority of cells are annotated with type $t^{(k)}$ in the type set, we choose $t^{(k)}$ as the concept of this column.

4 Column Concept Determination

We firstly present the process of our method and then describe our model based on convolutional neural network.

Since this paper is not focus on how to identify entities in tables, we assume that the entity column is already known and presented in the first column of a table. The column concept determination problem can be viewed as a classification problem. The principle of the method is to make use of the wealthy information available on the web to enrich the scarce context of tables. Our method uses Baidu Encyclopedia to obtain related text for attributes in tables. Compared with search engine used in [5], it is easier to get useful information for attributes from Baidu Encyclopedia. The process of the method is presented in Fig. 2:

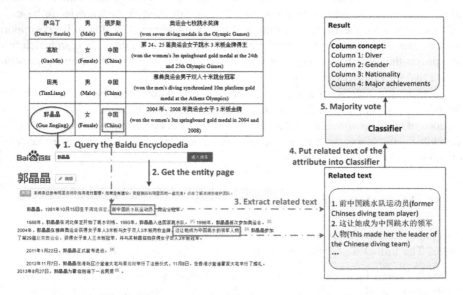

Fig. 2. The process of column concept determination.

1. Submit the entities of the table (in the entity column) to Baidu Encyclopedia.
2. Extract related text for the attribute values in the tuple from their corresponding entity pages.
3. Put the related text into classifier and find out a type for each cell.
4. Use majority vote to determine the most appropriate concept for each column.

The proposed method consists of three steps: pre-processing, annotating and post-processing. We will detail the three steps in the remainder of this section.

4.1 Pre-processing

Pre-processing enriches the context of attribute cells in tables with the related text from the Baidu Encyclopedia. Each row R_i in the table can be represented as $(e, p_1, p_2, \ldots, p_m)$, where e is the entity of the row and $p_1, p_2, \ldots, p_m$ are attribute values of e.

For each row R_i in the table, the method uses the entity e to query Baidu Encyclopedia and get the article returned. It iterates through the article and segment the document into sentences. Then we use each attribute value p_i as a keyword to extract sentences containing p_i to form its related text $RT(p_i)$. If an attribute value is composed of several sub-values or a long sentence (e.g., the last column of table in Fig. 1), we split it into several words, remove words that conflict with other attributes and then find the sentences that contain one or more of these keywords.

We are tending to solve the problem of determining column concepts for Chinese web tables. Since Chinese text does not use spaces to separate words as English text does, the method firstly uses the Chinese word segmentation technology to process the related text $RT(p_i)$ of each attribute value p_i and get a set of words L_{p_i}.

4.2 Annotating

The classification model is summarized in Fig. 3. The method feeds the word set L_{p_i} obtained from the Pre-processing step to the CNN model. The lookup table layer converts these words into word embedding. The convolutional layer extracts features of input data followed by an average pooling layer. Finally, we use a fully connected layer with dropout and Softmax classifier in our output layer. We will introduce the model layer by layer in the following parts.

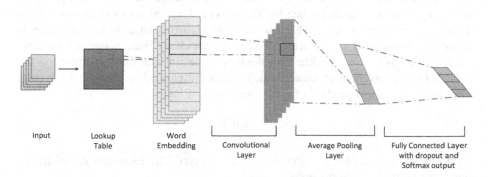

| Input | Lookup Table | Word Embedding | Convolutional Layer | Average Pooling Layer | Fully Connected Layer with dropout and Softmax output |

Fig. 3. Classification model based on CNN.

Firstly, we want to give a notation. A neural network with k layers can be considered as a composition of functions f, corresponding to each layer:

$$f_\theta(\cdot) = f_\theta^k\left(f_\theta^{k-1}\left(\cdots f_\theta^1(\cdot)\cdots\right)\right) \tag{1}$$

Lookup Table Layer. Convolutional neural network (CNN) is essentially a mathematical model. When using CNN for text classification, we firstly use word representation to convert the input words into vectors by looking up embedding. We have already got the related text of attribute p_i, which was represented by a set of words L_{p_i}. Then each word in L_{p_i} is passed through the lookup table layer to produce a numeric vector of ML_{p_i}. These numeric vectors can be viewed as the initial input of the standard CNN. More formally, the initial input numeric vector ML_{p_i} fed to the convolutional layer is given by the lookup table layer $LTF(\cdot)$:

$$f_\theta^1(\cdot) = ML_{p_i} = LTF\left(L_{p_i}\right) \tag{2}$$

There are many freely available word representation models, such as Google word2vec. We utilize word2vec to train a lookup table for representing the words.

Convolutional Layer. This layer contains several convolutional operations. Convolution is an operation between a weight vector W and the numeric vector ML_{p_i} from the Lookup Table Layer (2). The weights matrix W is regarded as the filter for the convolution:

$$f_\theta^k(\cdot) = Conv\left(f_\theta^{k-1}(\cdot), W\right) \tag{3}$$

The convolutional layer is used to extract higher level features between the attribute values and their related text.

Average Pooling Layer. The size of the convolution output depends on the number of words in L_{p_i} fed to the network. To apply subsequent standard affine layers, the features extracted by the convolutional layer have to be combined such that they are independent of the length of word set L_{p_i}. In convolutional neural networks, average or max pooling operations are often applied for this purpose. The max operation does not make much sense in our case. Since we use an attribute value to extract related sentences in the article, in general, several sentences will be matched. These sentences are complementary to each other and determine the type of the attribute value jointly. So in this work, we use an average approach, which forces the network to capture the average value of local features produced by the convolutional layer:

$$\left[f_\theta^k\right]_i = \operatorname*{mean}_t \left[f_\theta^{k-1}\right]_{i,t} \tag{4}$$

Where t is the number of output of the $k-1$ layer. The fixed size global feature vector can be then fed to the output layer.

Output Layer. The output of the average pooling layer is fed into the output layer through a fully connected network with dropout:

$$f_\theta^k(\cdot) = ReLU\left(Wf_\theta^{k-1}(\cdot) + b\right) \tag{5}$$

Where W is the weight matrix and b is the bias. We use *ReLU* as the active function. A Softmax classifier is used to compute a score of each possible type if we give the final weight matrix W and bias b. Formally, the final output can be interpreted as follow:

$$f_\theta^k(\cdot) = Softmax\left(Wf_\theta^{k-1}(\cdot) + b\right) \tag{6}$$

Softmax is a multiclass classifier. For each type in the type set $Type = \{t^{(1)}, t^{(2)}, \ldots, t^{(k)}\}$, Softmax outputs the probability that a sample belongs to different types in the form of $S = \{S^{(1)}, S^{(2)}, \ldots, S^{(k)}\}$. Then the type $t^{(k)}$ with the largest score is selected as the type of this attribute value.

4.3 Post-processing

Since the cells in a single column have similar contents, we therefore leverage the column coherence principle to rule out the cells annotated incorrectly. For the j_{th} column in a table, our method combined the annotation of the cells in column j based on majority vote. If most of the cells in a column are assigned with a type $t^{(k)}$, we choose the type $t^{(k)}$ as the concept of the j_{th} column.

5 Experiment

We performed several experiments to evaluate the proposed method. This is the first work focused on column concept determination task in Chinese web tables and it is infeasible for us to compare our method with the methods designed for English web tables for the following reasons:

- The inputs are different. We can't use the English web tables as input for our proposed method;
- The previous methods are not reproducible. It is impossible for us to reproduce the knowledge base-based method designed for English tables and then use them for our task. Since many existing Chinese knowledge bases either are for internal use or contain insufficient knowledge, it is hard for us to find a Chinese knowledge base as large as Probase [9] and DBpedia [15].

We use the Naïve Bayes classification techniques (BAYES) and support vector machine (SVM) as baselines. In Sect. 5.1, we describe the method to construct datasets and present the training and test sets obtained for classifier training. In Sect. 5.2, we evaluate the performance of three text classifiers based on BAYES, SVM and CNN separately. In Sect. 5.3, we discuss the evaluation results obtained by running our method on a set of web tables extracted from the web pages.

5.1 Dataset Construction

To make our approach scalable, we need to construct the training and test datasets that involves as little manual intervention as possible.

Inspired by [14], we found that the infoboxes in Baidu Encyclopedia contained tabular summaries of objects' key attributes. So they can be used as a source of data. We used a web crawler to extract entity pages containing infoboxes and selected the most common attributes as target attributes. For each entity page with an infobox mentioning one or more target attributes, we segmented the document into sentences using word segmentation technology. Then for each target attribute, our method used the attribute value to search for the corresponding sentences in the article. Our implementation used two heuristics to match sentences to attributes as follows.

- If an attribute value is mentioned by one or more sentences in an article, we use these sentences and the attribute name to form a positive example.
- If there is no sentence containing the attribute value exactly, we use the word segmentation technology to split the value into several words and remove words that have exactly the same value as other attribute values. Then we find the sentences containing one or more of these words, finally form a positive example.

80% of the resulting labeled sentences were used to form the training set *TR* and the remaining 20% formed test set *TE*. We used *TR* and *TE* to train CNN classifier model after the sentences were processed by word segmentation technology.

We conducted our experiment on the category of people and selected six common attribute types—Date of Birth, Nationality, Birthplace, Profession, Graduate Institution and Major Achievement. These target attributes were used to construct datasets. We automatically obtained a large number of data that have already been labeled in the end. The following Table 1 shows a summary of the datasets.

Table 1. Training and test datasets.

Type	TR	TE
Date of birth	13620	3431
Nationality	12210	3000
Birthplace	13062	3317
Profession	12302	3005
Graduate institution	8048	2018
Major achievement	7200	1774
Total	66442	16545

5.2 Setup of the Classifier

We trained and tested three text classifiers based on BAYES, SVM and CNN, following the grid-search procedure along with 10-fold cross validation to select the optimal parameters in the process of training. For the BAYES classifier, the parameter α was set to 1. For the SVM classifier, we used a RBF kernel, the parameter cost was set to 0.5 and the γ was set to 2. For the CNN classifier, the convolutional layer contained 48 convolution cores with a height of 2 and a width of the word vector. We used an average pooling to combine the local feature vectors to obtain a global feature vector. Then the vector was fed into a fully connected network with 50 neurons and 10% dropout.

Figure 4 shows the accuracy obtained while testing BAYES, SVM and CNN classifiers respectively. The results show that our classifier coupled with CNN outperforms the BAYES and SVM methods on most types. Especially, there is a significant accuracy increase in the types of birthplace and major achievement.

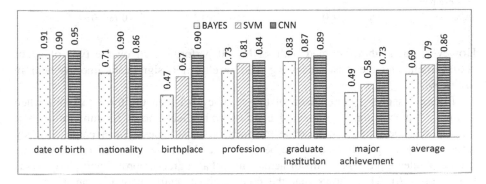

Fig. 4. Evaluation results of CNN, BAYES and SVM classifiers.

5.3 Evaluation of the Method

We randomly selected 104 tables containing entities of the category of people from a large number of tables crawled from web pages. Each row of these tables contained an entity and several attribute values. Totally we got 2820 references for the six selected attributes. There were 126 references for Date of Birth, 833 references for Nationality, 353 references for Birthplace, 346 references for Profession, 149 references for Graduate Institution and 1013 references for Major Achievement. We manually annotated these tables for our method to compare with.

We firstly ran our method without post-processing operation on these web tables to evaluate the accuracy of our classifier in handling real tabular data, and then we used the post-processing operation to rule out cells that were annotated incorrectly. The experiments were compared with two baseline methods—BAYES and SVM.

Table 2 shows a comparison of experimental results with and without post-processing operation. For all the three methods—BAYES, SVM and CNN, the post-processing dramatically increases the accuracy of the classifiers. This proves that the method used in the post-processing phase can effectively remove incorrect annotations. We can also notice that the BAYES and SVM methods have low accuracy rates on the type major achievement and their accuracy rates are not improved even after using post-processing operations. The reason is that the majority vote does not work well in the post-processing phase based on the low accuracy results given by the classifiers.

Table 2. Evaluation of the algorithm with and without post-processing.

Type	BAYES		SVM		CNN	
	BAYES	BAYES + Post-Proc	SVM	SVM + Post-Proc	CNN	CNN + Post-Proc
Date of birth	0.83	0.85	0.77	0.77	0.91	1.00
Nationality	0.67	1.00	0.74	1.00	0.71	1.00
Birthplace	0.64	0.82	0.68	0.89	0.79	0.95
Profession	0.74	0.96	0.76	0.96	0.74	0.96
Graduate institution	0.78	1.00	0.84	1.00	0.79	0.93
Major achievement	0.21	0.20	0.34	0.32	0.76	0.96
Average	0.65	0.81	0.69	0.82	0.78	0.97

However, our method coupled with CNN still performs well on the type of major achievement and the post-processing also results in a significant improvement in accuracy.

Figure 5 shows a comparison of the accuracy between the three methods when using post-processing. Our method coupled with CNN shows its superiority as it outperforms the other two baseline methods on most types. The average accuracy improves by 15% compared to the best baseline. Moreover, we can notice that the accuracy rate on the type of major achievement has a great improvement (0.96 versus 0.32 and 0.20). This shows that the convolutional neural network can effectively capture the features for attribute values from their related text, especially for the ones which consist of long sentences and are hard to classify. We observe a slight drop in the type of graduate institution, but the average accuracy of our proposed method is higher over the other two methods totally.

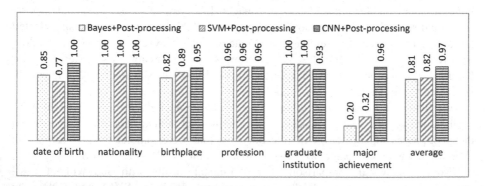

Fig. 5. Results of column concept determination in web tables (with Post-processing)

6   Conclusion

This paper described a method that determines the column concept for Chinese web tables using convolutional neural network. The proposed method can be used for the construction and expansion of the Chinese knowledge graph and can also contribute to applications such as data extraction and table searching. To the best of our knowledge, this is the first study of semantic recovery for Chinese Web tables. Another advantage which is different from the previous works is that our method is able to handle cells with long sentences. This means we can get a large amount of descriptive knowledge (e.g., major achievement) from the web tables to expand the knowledge bases. The evaluation shows our proposed method outperforms the BAYES and SVM methods and reaches an average accuracy of 97%.

For the future work, we intend to improve the scalability of our algorithm. Although our algorithm can automatically retrieve and select target attributes and training data from Baidu Encyclopedia, it is limited. We need a larger data source to get more attribute types and training data to annotate web tables.

Acknowledgement. This work was supported by the National Key R&D Program of China (No. 2017YFC0820700), the Fundamental theory and cutting edge technology Research Program of Institute of Information Engineering, CAS (Grant No. Y7Z0351101), Xinjiang Uygur Autonomous Region Science and Technology Project (No. 2016A030007-4).

References

1. Cafarella, M.J., Halevy, A.Y., Wang, D.Z., Wu, E., Zhang, Y.: WebTables: exploring the power of tables on the web. PVLDB **1**(1), 538–549 (2008)
2. Wang, J., Wang, H., Wang, Z., Zhu, Kenny Q.: Understanding tables on the web. In: Atzeni, P., Cheung, D., Ram, S. (eds.) ER 2012. LNCS, vol. 7532, pp. 141–155. Springer, Heidelberg (2012). https://doi.org/10.1007/978-3-642-34002-4_11
3. Limaye, G., Sarawagi, S., Chakrabarti, S.: Annotating and searching web tables using entities, types and relationships. PVLDB **3**(1), 1338–1347 (2010)
4. Venetis, P., Halevy, A.Y., Madhavan, J., Pasca, M., Shen, W., Fei, W., Miao, G., Chung, W.: Recovering semantics of tables on the web. PVLDB **4**(9), 528–538 (2011)
5. Quercini, G., Reynaud, C.: Entity discovery and annotation in tables. In: EDBT 2013, pp. 693–704 (2013)
6. Lehmberg, O., Ritze, D., Meusel, R., Bizer, C.: A large public corpus of web tables containing time and context metadata. In: WWW (Companion Volume) 2016, pp. 75–76 (2013)
7. Ritze, D., Lehmberg, O., Bizer, C.: Matching HTML tables to DBpedia. In: WIMS 2015, pp. 10:1–10:6 (2015)
8. Tam, N.T., Hung, N.Q.V., Weidlich, M., Aberer, K.: Result selection and summarization for web table search. In: ICDE, pp. 231–242 (2015)
9. Wu, W., Li, H., Wang, H., Zhu, K.Q.: Probase: a probabilistic taxonomy for text understanding. In: SIGMOD Conference 2012, pp. 481–492 (2012)
10. Deng, D., Jiang, Y., Li, G., Li, J., Yu, C.: Scalable column concept determination for web tables using large knowledge bases. PVLDB **6**(13), 1606–1617 (2013)
11. Ritze, D., Bizer, C.: Matching web tables to DBpedia - a feature utility study. In: EDBT 2017, pp. 210–221 (2017)
12. Hassanzadeh, O., Ward, M.J., Rodriguez-Muro, M., Srinivas, K.: Understanding a large corpus of web tables through matching with knowledge bases: an empirical study. In: OM 2015, pp. 25–34 (2015)

13. Zhang, Z.: Towards efficient and effective semantic table interpretation. In: Mika, P., Tudorache, T., Bernstein, A., Welty, C., Knoblock, C., Vrandečić, D., Groth, P., Noy, N., Janowicz, K., Goble, C. (eds.) ISWC 2014. LNCS, vol. 8796, pp. 487–502. Springer, Cham (2014). https://doi.org/10.1007/978-3-319-11964-9_31
14. Wu, F., Weld, D.S.: Autonomously semantifying Wikipedia. In: CIKM 2007, pp. 41–50 (2007)
15. Lehmann, J., Isele, R., Jakob, M., Jentzsch, A., Kontokostas, D., Mendes, P.N., Hellmann, S., Morsey, M., van Kleef, P., Auer, S., Bizer, C.: DBpedia - a large-scale, multilingual knowledge base extracted from Wikipedia. Seman. Web 6(2), 167–195 (2015)

Service-Oriented Approach for Internet of Things

Eduardo Cardoso Moraes[✉]

Federal Institute of Alagoas-IFAL, Maceió, Alagoas, Brazil
eduardo.moraes@ifal.edu.br

Abstract. The new era of industrial automation has been developed and implemented quickly, and it is impacting different areas of society. Especially in recent years, much progress has been made in this area, known as the fourth industrial revolution. Every day factories are more connected and able to communicate and interact in real time between industrial systems. There is a need to flexibilization on the shop floor to promote higher customization of products in a short life cycle and service-oriented architecture is a good option to materialize this. This paper aims to propose briefly a service-oriented model for the Internet of things in an Industry 4.0 context. Also, discusses challenges of this new revolution, also known as Industry 4.0, addressing the introduction of modern communication and computing technologies to maximize interoperability across all the different existing systems. Moreover, it will cover technologies that support this new industrial revolution and discuss impacts, possibilities, needs, and adaptation.

Keywords: Cyber-Physical Systems · Industry 4.0 · Internet of things
Services

1 Introduction

Industry 4.0 is a trendy topic today. To demonstrate the relevance of this theme, the largest meeting of the world's leading leaders involving governments, corporations, international organizations, civil society and academia met at the annual meeting of the World Economic Forum in Davos, Switzerland, in January, between 20 and 23, (2016) had as its central theme "Mastering the Fourth Industrial Revolution" (Economic 2016).

The world is evolving at speed never saw before, where new trends and technologies are developed daily and incorporated into our everyday lives. This has an impact on many different areas, the real world and virtual reality continue to merge, and allied to this modern information and communication technologies are being combined with traditional industrial processes, thus changing the various production areas. Traditional companies have realized that customers are unwilling to pay large amounts for incremental quality improvements. As a consequence, many companies, especially the industries have to adapt their production with the focus on customized products and fast market time, always with lower cost and higher quality. Especially in recent years, with the progress made in this area, it is believed that we are experiencing the fourth industrial revolution.

When talking about this new revolution, also known as Industry 4.0, we are often talking about the introduction of modern communication and information control technologies, with increasingly intelligent devices. In a factory, it is sought to maximize the interoperability between all the different existing systems. This interoperability is the backbone of making a factory more flexible and intelligent, as different subsystems are now able to communicate and interact with each other. These changes are important steps to meet most of today's industrial facility needs, such as the increasing demand for highly customized products, improving resource efficiency and higher throughput.

This article aims to propose briefly a service model for the Internet of things in an Industry 4.0 context. Therefore, cover the history of industrial evolution and to highlight that we live in a silent industrial revolution that is due to advances in several areas, especially Internet and Communication Technologies (ICT), and which areas lead these changes.

2 Service-Oriented Approach for Industrial Automation Systems

The traditional life cycle of products is decreasing specially high-technology products, with a short life on the market, a steep decline stage and the lack of a maturity stage. The change become constant and industrial companies should be ready for it. The Industry 4.0 concept brings the costumer as an active role in the life cycle of product.

To accomplish Industry 4.0 vision and concept, it is necessary to enlarge interconnectivity of Cyber-Physical Systems (CPS). According to Lee (2008), "CPS are integrations of computation and physical processes. Embedded computers and networks monitor and control the physical processes, usually with feedback loops where physical processes affect computations and vice versa". A low-coupling approach can allow these smart devices to an asymmetric communication between physical devices and with associated information counterparts or virtual devices. The vertical and rigid structure of traditional automation systems are not satisfactory anymore. SOA is an interesting approach to overcome these limitations.

The need to overcome challenges in industrial and the need for constant innovation, which must be addressed and managed with the latest and best engineering and IT practices. Companies have the challenge of adapting their planning and manufacturing systems to produce in a more integrated, flexible, reconfigurable and with better collaboration (Moraes et al. 2015).

Originally from the IT area, focusing on high-level management alignment, Service-oriented Architecture (SOA) is currently a widely accepted approach for both business and enterprise systems integration. SOA promotes discovery, low coupling, abstraction, autonomy, and service composition that is based on open web standards and which can make an essential contribution to the field of industrial automation (Colombo 2013). SOA allows customers to access services without the knowledge or control over their actual implementation because it abstracts the complexity involved.

Service Oriented Architecture (SOA) is a paradigm that has rapidly grown as a standard solution for publishing and accessing information in an increasingly ubiquitous world with a ubiquitous Internet.

This new approach, which uses intensely defined interfaces and standard protocols, allows developers to encapsulate functions and tools as services in which clients can access without knowledge or control over their application (Colombo et al. 2014). SOA establishes an architecture model that aims to improve efficiency, interoperability, agility and productivity by positioning services as the primary means throughout the logical solution. SOA enables support for achieving the associated strategic objectives that are implemented through computational services with positive impact in the shop floor.

The concept of service is defined in Fig. 1. The dissemination of SOA on the factory floor is facilitated by the installation of service-oriented protocols at equipment interfaces. With this, the devices have greater ease of integration and greater offer of composition of services.

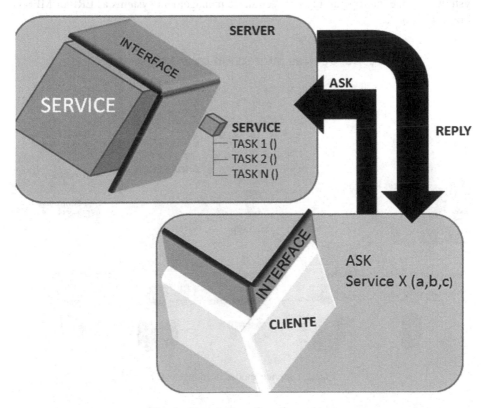

Fig. 1. Description of service concept

The types of promoted services will be classified, according to (Colombo et al. 2014), in:

- Atomic Services: Elementary services that can be promoted by a single resource.
- Composed Services: Services that require the interaction of more than one element of production and are offered as a single service to the customer.
- Configuration Services: Update services, insertion of a new production element, download of new production rules, and that do not return data to the client, being the responsibility of the production managers.

Once the service is defined, it is important to highlight the interface. Interfaces are layers that guide the registration, discovery, provisioning, and management of services. Interfaces abstract the complexity of the network and data model, and allow the client and server to communicate satisfactorily, and data exchange occurs. Data exchange may be synchronous or asynchronous. Unlike the current model of industrial automation, creating services in the devices will introduce the concept of events, where there is no predetermined cycle time, being in charge of the customer's need. The interfaces help the composition of services and reuse of components already developed.

A distributed vision of services and a new interaction between cyber-physical systems and the interoperability between these management systems as ERP or MES is shown on Fig. 2.

Industry 4.0 devices interaction based on services

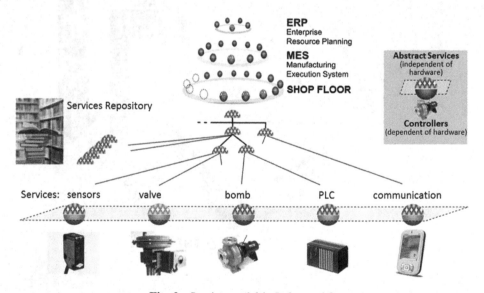

Fig. 2. Service model in Industry 4.0

Service in automation industry (shop floor) is the union of a hardware part that can be real or virtual and a logical part called abstract service that encapsulates the details and via an interface allows another devices or systems access and exchange data to execute procedures from upper-level managers.

In industry 4.0, the integration is no longer vertical or horizontal, but rather collaborative and made throughout the entire life cycle between several elements of production, inputs, machinery, process computers that aim to monitor, control, and trace all stages of production. All stages and elements exchange real-time data in an autonomous and automated mode. In this scenario orchestration of software and physical (or virtual) elements through services should be rethought. And it is a significant open challenge.

All the shop floor elements offer their functionalities through services, being able to act as client or server depending on the process and the context, which services are described in the data model, that interconnect the factory floor with the corporate systems through common interfaces.

These components contribute to the Industry 4.0 concept by abstracting the complexity of the manufacturing system by modifying the interaction between the devices, facilitating adaptations and setup changes, and allowing for less human interference. For this purpose an internal database will be used and fed by all the components in the cloud with data: for example historical data, tags, IP addresses, last revisions about devices critical to the operation. External database may contain data on failures, maintenance procedures, shutdowns, documentation, data of controllers, configuration data, or other information considered relevant.

An important advantage of CPS is the processing capability is the prediction service. The prediction can perform prognostics and analyze not only the internal database, but uses data referring to performances of similar devices seeking similarities and functions below established standards, generating alert for the management. Furthermore, it seeks to infer future behavior, seeking to obtain the optimal point to carry out some preventive action and for this will inform the responsible technical manager or responsible. It seeks to implement a more effective predictive analysis in the detection of failures, causing the maintenance by a break or the unplanned stops are reduced, with more information one can plan and perform better actions.

Computational intelligence is another interesting capability. It has strong connection to the prediction, and will be responsible for reading, analyzing and inferring key data and information from the manufacturing process using mathematical algorithms and with the support of artificial intelligence it will automatically display notifications whenever there are defined patterns, Or it may introduce learning algorithms so that a better and assertive analysis can happen with human assistance. This component has as mission to analyze the internal database, and will make inferences seeking to promote greater autonomy and with greater capacity of reasoning, benefiting from the greater capacity of processing of the devices. It can use Big Data algorithms and data mining.

Another important aspect is the information Security. In a manufacturing system that can be accessed in real time, this item has high relevance, and must be guaranteed for reliable operation. The security strategy may be associated with the data model, since some already have data encryption (e.g. OPC UA), or the control system with rules of authenticity, availability and completeness. This component can be vigilant and have proactive identification of intrusions and cyber attacks, with an action plan for an integrated system with different heterogeneous sources.

According to Schoepf (2017), the pursuit of profitably producing affordable goods that fulfill customer demands is driving industrial automation systems towards:

- Distributed control and decentralized decision-making
- A redrawing of the classical automation pyramid such that approximately 80% of discrete control is transferred to the field level
- Modular, scalable solutions
- Shorter, more flexible production cycles
- Miniaturization of equipment and smaller production lines
- Parallel communication of process data with diagnostic and condition monitoring data without impacting standard processes

The industry 4.0 will provide an innovative collaboration and rules for elements to work together to achieve the common goal, to store data in the internal database, to feed the components of computational intelligence and the prediction component. For example, in a failure situation, the collaboration module is triggered and may contain rules for replacing services with others, shutting down operation, and/or triggering external elements or persons.

CPS is revolutionizing the way manufacturing is done by connecting more smart devices and sharing the information they produce to improve existing business models and enable new ones. Thereby progressing in solutions to the problems listed in chapter 1 of this thesis, increasing productive flexibility by facilitating the (re)configuration and integrating technologies of form efficient.

In the industry 4.0, machines, production lines and storage systems will collaborate within a network composed of cyber-physical systems (CPS). These systems are capable of autonomously exchanging information, triggering actions and controlling one another.

This article is focused on the interconnectivity of the shop floor elements in an Industry 4.0 context and briefly targeted technological aspects and limitations; SOA is a promising approach to overcome some of the typical rigid and vertical automation system.

Some open questions and challenges in Industry 4.0 were discussed, service-oriented approach in industrial automation has been explained and a service model in Industry 4.0 proposed. The model is linked to a service-oriented architecture with a modularized approach for the development of interfaces in the factory floor, seeking to materialize Industry 4.0 concepts.

Towards the development of Plug & Produce concept, the term "plug-and-play" means an expectation of ease of use and reliable, foolproof operation. It seems to be easy as a plug-and-play product, where someone can simply connect and turn on – and it works. The practical extension of plug-and-play products, when applied to industrial automation, has given way to the new term: plug-and-produce.

Plug-and-produce offers a path to increase flexibility, demanded by the global market. As well as energy efficiencies and reduce costs in the way goods are produced. As the industry has been working to get products to market faster and cheaper, easy and simple solutions are needed to enable adjusts and near-immediate implementation – with no special tools or highly trained engineers or electricians required. Future factories will implement plug and produce concept and will be flexible, having modular field-level devices, facilitating quick manufacturing changes. This is a key capability of the industry 4.0 companies.

References

Colombo, A.W., Karnouskos, S., Bangemann, T.: A system of systems view on collaborative industrial automation. In: 2013 IEEE International Conference on Industrial Technology (ICIT). IEEE (2013)

Colombo, A.W., Bangemann, T., Karnouskos, S., Delsing, S., Stluka, P., Harrison, R., Jammes, F., Lastra, J.L.M.: Industrial Cloud-Based Cyber-Physical Systems. Springer (2014)

Economic, F.W.: "What is the theme of Davos 2016?" What is the theme of Davos 2016? (2016). Accessed 05 Apr 2016

Industry 4.0: The Future of Productivity and Growth in Manufacturing Industries, Boston, BCG Perspectives, Disponível em: https://www.bcgperspectives.com/content/articles/engineered_products_project_business_industry_40_future_productivity_growth_manufacturing_industries/. Accessed 14 May 2017

Lee, E.A.: Cyber physical systems: design challenges. In: 2008 11th IEEE International Symposium on Object Oriented Real-Time Distributed Computing (ISORC). IEEE (2008)

Lee, J., Bagheri, B., Kao, H.-A.: A cyber-physical systems architecture for industry 4.0-based manufacturing systems. Manufact. Lett. 3, 18–23 (2015)

Moraes, E.C., Lepikson, H.A., Colombo, A.W.: Developing interfaces based on services to the cloud manufacturing: plug and produce. In: Gen, M., Kim, Kuinam J., Huang, X., Hiroshi, Y. (eds.) Industrial Engineering, Management Science and Applications 2015. LNEE, vol. 349, pp. 821–831. Springer, Heidelberg (2015). https://doi.org/10.1007/978-3-662-47200-2_86

Moraes, E., Lepikson, H., Konstantinov, S., Wermann, J., Colombo, A.W., Ahmad, B., Harrison, R.: Improving connectivity for runtime simulation of automation systems via OPC UA. In: 2015 IEEE 13th International Conference on Industrial Informatics (INDIN), Cambridge, p. 288 (2015)

Zhang, L., et al.: Key technologies for the construction of manufacturing cloud. Comput. Integr. Manufact. Syst. 16(11), 2510–2520 (2010)

Reimer, D., Ali, A.: Engineering education and the entrepreneurial mindset at Lawrence Tech. In: Proceedings of the International Conference on Industrial Engineering and Operations Management, Istanbul, Turkey, 3–6 July 2012 (2012)

Shetty, D., Ali, A., Cummings, R.: A model to assess lean thinking manufacturing initiatives. Int. J. Lean Six Sigma 1(4), 310–334 (2010)

Schoepf, T.: Plug-and-Produce is Key for the Smart Factory of the Future – Part 1. http://www.belden.com/blog/industrialethernet/Plug-and-Produce-is-Key-for-the-Smart-Factory-of-the-Future-Part-1.cfm. Accessed 20 June 2017

Srinivasan, G., Arcelus, F.J., Pakkala, T.P.M.: A retailer's decision process when anticipating a vendor's temporary discount offer. Comput. Ind. Eng. 57, 253–260 (2009)

Adversarial Framework for General Image Inpainting

Wei Huang and Hongliang Yu$^{(\boxtimes)}$

Tsinghua University, Beijing, China
huang-w15@mails.tsinghua.edu.cn, hlyu@mail.tsinghua.edu.cn

Abstract. We present a novel adversarial framework to solve the arbitrarily sized image random inpainting problem, where a pair of convolution generator and discriminator is trained jointly to fill the relatively large but random "holes". The generator is a symmetric encoder-decoder just like an hourglass but with added skip connections. The skip connections act like information shortcut to transfer some necessary details that discarded by the "bottleneck" layer. Our discriminator is trained to distinguish whether an image is natural or not and find out the hidden holes from a reconstructed image. A combination of a standard pixel-wise L2 loss and an adversarial loss is used to guided the generator to preserve the known part of the origin image and fills the missing part with plausible result. Our experiment is conducted on over 1.24M images with uniformly random 25% missing part. We found the generator is good at capturing structure context and performs well in arbitrary size images without complex texture.

Keywords: Inpainting · GAN · Skip connections

1 Introduction

Image inpainting, or "hole filling" problem, aims to reconstruct the missing or damaged part of an input image. Classical inpainting algorithms in computer vision mainly fall into three categories: information diffusion and examplar-based filling.

Partial differential equation (PDE) is the foundation of the diffusion algorithms [2,3,12,14]. They are also referred as variational methods. Through iterations, the information outside a hole is continuously propagated into the hole, while preserving the continuity of the isophote. They can tackle cracks and small holes well, but produce blur artifacts when faced with large and textured region.

The exemplar-based algorithm, on the other hand, is able to reconstruct large region and remove large unwanted objects by patch matching and filling. The straight forward exemplar approach applies a carefully designed prioritizing filling [4,5] or a coherence optimization strategy [1,15]. The limitations are also obvious. It has difficulty in handling curved structures. When proper similar patches do not exist, it will not produce reasonable result.

© Springer International Publishing AG, part of Springer Nature 2018
Y. Shi et al. (Eds.): ICCS 2018, LNCS 10862, pp. 552–558, 2018.
https://doi.org/10.1007/978-3-319-93713-7_50

Recently, convolution network and adversarial training are also introduced into inpainting problem. Compared with the classical algorithms above, the network based algorithms are born to understand high-level semantic context, which brings it capability to tackle harder problems, like semantics required prediction. The context-encoder [13], for example, consisting of an encoder and a decoder, can predict the large squared missing center of an image.

In this paper, we aim to solve a more challenging semantic inpainting problem, the arbitrarily sized image with random holes. We adopt the adversarial training to suppress the multi-modal problem and get sharper result. Instead of predicting a single likelihood to evaluate whether an image is fake like most of other GAN works do, the discriminator provides a pixel-wise evaluation by outputting a single channel image. If the generator does not work well, the discriminator is supposed to point out the origin missing region. The output is visually explainable, as one can clearly figure out the contour of the hole mask if the inpainted image is unsatisfactory and vice versa.

In our experiment, we found the generator is good at capturing structure context and performs well in arbitrary size images without complex texture. As for the failed cases, mainly the complex texture with tiny variations in the intensity, the generator will produce reasonable but blur result.

2   Method

2.1   Adversarial Framework

The adversarial framework in this paper is based on Deep Convolutional Generative Adversarial Networks (DCGAN). A generator G and a discriminator D are trained jointly to for two opposite goals. When the training is stopped, the G is supposed to reconstruct a damaged image in high quality.

Generator. The generator G is an hourglass encoder-decoder consisting of basic convolution blocks (Conv/FullConv-BatchNorm-LeakyReLU/ ReLU), but with shortcut connections to propagate detail information in the encoder directly to the corresponding the symmetric layer of the decoder (Fig. 1).

Endoder. The encoder performs down sampling using 4*4 convolution filters with stride of 2 and padding of 1. The encoder drops out what it considered useless for reconstruction and squeezes the image information liquid into a "concept". When it passes the bottleneck layer of the encoder, the feature map size is reduced to $1*1$. The number of the filters in this the bottle layer (m), decides the channel capacity $(m*1*1)$ of the whole encoder-decoder pipeline. The activation function for the encoder is LeakyReLU with negative slope of 0.2.

Dedoder. The structure of the decoder is completely symmetric toward the encoder except the output layer. There are 3 added shortcut connection directly

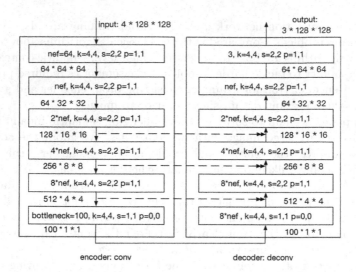

Fig. 1. Generator Architecture: an hourglass encoder-decoder with 3 added shortcut connections. The damaged image and the selected mask is passed through the encoder. The decoder then reconstructs the image without holes. k(kernel size), s(stride), p(padding) are parameters of spatial convolution/deconvolution layer.

join the 3 decoder layers closest to the bottleneck layer with their corresponding symmetric encoder layers. The final layer is supposed to output the desired reconstructed RGB image without holes. The activation function are Tanh for the final layer and ReLU for the rest layers.

Discriminator. The discriminator D is a 5-layer stack of convolution blocks (Conv-BatchNorm-LeakyReLU). All the convolution layers have the same number of 3*3 filters with stride of 1 and padding of 1. The shape of the information fluid is the same as the shape of input throughout the network. The activation layers are Sigmoid for the final layer and LeakyReLU with negative slope of 0.2 for the rest layers.

As the final step of the inpainting is to fusion the output with the origin damaged image, we specify a high-level goal, to make the "hole" indistinguishable. Instead of predicting a single likelihood to evaluate whether an image is fake like most of other GAN works do, the discriminator here is trained to find the flaw of the output of G or the hidden holes.

The discriminator is supposed to output all ones when faced with natural images and output the given hole masks (ones/white for known regions and zeroes/black for the holes) otherwise. Compared to a single number, this single channel image output is visually explainable. And it can provide more targeted guidance for each input pixel and comprehensive judgment.

2.2 Objective

The generator is trained to regress the ground truth content of the input image. It is well known that the L2 loss (Eq. 1) - and L1, prefers a blurry solution to a clear texture [10]. It is an effective way to capture and rebuild the low frequency information.

$$L_2(G) = ||x - G(x')||_2^2 \tag{1}$$

The adversarial loss is introduced to get a sharper result. The objective of a GAN can be expressed as Eq. 2. x' is the damaged input image and x is the corresponding ground truth. $\hat{M}$ is the hole mask. The holes are filled with zeroes, and the known regions are filled with ones. The all 1s mask means no holes at all. The G is trained to minimize this objective, while the D is trained to maximize it.

$$L_{GAN}(G, D) = E_x ||\hat{M} - D(G(x'))||_2^2 + E_{x'} ||1 - D(x)||_2^2 \tag{2}$$

The total loss function is a weighted average of a reconstruction loss and an adversarial loss (Eq. 3). We assign a quite large weight ($\lambda = 0.999$) upon the reconstruction loss.

$$L(G, D) = \lambda L_2(G) + (1 - \lambda)L_{GAN}(G, D) \tag{3}$$

2.3 Masks for Training

As our framework is supposed to support damaged region with arbitrary shape or position, we need to train the networks with numerous random mask. For the efficiency, the inputs within a mini-batch share the same mask and all the masks are sampled from a global pattern pool.

The global is generated as follows: (1) create a fix-sized uniform random distribution (range from 0 to 1) matrix; (2) scale it to a given large size (10000 * 10000); (3) mark the region with value less than a threshold as "holes" (ones/white) and the rest as "known region" (zeroes/black). The *scaling ratio* and the *loss threshold* are two important hyper parameters for the global pattern pool. The scaling ratio controls the continuity of the holes. Larger scaling ratio generates scatter result.

3 Experiment

3.1 Training Details

This work is implemented in Torch and trained using Intel(R) Xeon(R) CPU E5-2699 v4 @ 2.20GHz with TITAN X (Pascal). We train the G and the D jointly for 500 epochs, using stochastic gradient solver, ADAM, for optimization. The learning rate is 0.0002.

The training dataset is 100 classes of ILSVRC2010 training dataset (over 1.24M natural images). The natural images are scaled down at the same proportion so that the maximum of the width and the height is no more than 350px.

Then, 64 random crops of 128 * 128 from different images consist of a mini-batch. These crops share the same mask. During the training process, we assume the hole area of mask should be in between 20%–30%.

The G receive input with size of 128 * 128 * 4, where the first three channels are the RGB data and the last channel is a binary mask. The ones in the binary mask indicate the holes while the zeros indicate the known region. The missing region of RGB data specified by the mask will be filled with a constant mean value (R:117, G:104, B:123). We also experimented the gray value (R:127, G:127, B:127) and found no significant difference between them in improving the performance of the generator. The G consists of 10 convolution layers and the bottleneck size is 4000.

3.2 Evaluation

In prior works in GAN, the D outputs a single probability indicating whether the input is a natural image. In this random inpainting problem, we find it requires elaborate design of weight assign among the hole regions and the known regions when updating the parameters of both D and G. What's more, the output of D may be not consistent with human intuition.

Our method, on the contrary, trains D to find the pixel-wise flaw of G output. It turns out that the output of D is visual explanatory and the optimization is easier. One can clearly figure out the contour of the hole mask if the inpainted image is unsatisfying and vice versa (Fig. 2).

Fig. 2. The comparison of the G output and the D output. The output is visually explainable, because the blur or unnatural parts is darker than the normal parts.

We evaluate our inpainting framework using images from the ILSVRC2010 validation dataset (the "barn spider" and black and "gold garden spider"). As the generator only receives 128*128 images, we split the input into a batch of 128*128 crops if the input image is too large. Afterwards, the result will be tiled to create the origin-sized image. We found the G generates plausible result when faced with linear structure, curved lines and blur scenes. But it is difficult for G to handle complex texture with tiny variations in the intensity. The background regions in Fig. 3 are inpainted so well that the G successfully fools the D, while the spider body regions full of low contrast details are handled poorly.

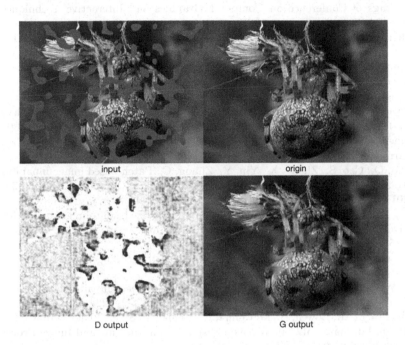

Fig. 3. Uniform random inpainting example from ILSVRC2010. The origin images are taken apart into 128 ∗ 128 crops and inpainted respectively.

4   Conclusions

In this paper, we aim to provide a unified solution for random image inpainting problems. Unlike the prior works, the output of D is visually explainable and the G is modified to adapt the general inpainting tasks. Trained in a completely unsupervised manner, without carefully designed strategy, the GAN networks learn basic common sense about natural images. The results suggest that our method is a promising approach for many inpainting tasks.

References

1. Barnes, C., Shechtman, E., Finkelstein, A., Goldman, D.B.: PatchMatch: a randomized correspondence algorithm for structural image editing. ACM Trans. Graph. **28**(3), 24:1–24:11 (2009)

2. Bertalmio, M., Bertozzi, A.L., Sapiro, G.: Navier-stokes, fluid dynamics, and image and video inpainting. In: Proceedings of the 2001 IEEE Computer Society Conference on Computer Vision and Pattern Recognition, CVPR 2001, vol. 1, pp. I-355–I-362 (2001)
3. Bertalmio, M., Sapiro, G., Caselles, V., Ballester, C.: Image inpainting. In: Proceedings of Conference on Computer Graphics and Interactive Techniques, pp. 417–424 (2000)
4. Cheng, W., Hsieh, C., Lin, S.: Robust algorithm for exemplar-based image inpainting. IEEE Trans. Image Process. **13**(9), 1200–1212 (2005)
5. Criminisi, A., Prez, P., Toyama, K.: Region filling and object removal by exemplar-based image inpainting. IEEE Trans. Image Process. **13**(9), 1200–1212 (2004)
6. Dong, W., Shi, G., Li, X.: Nonlocal image restoration with bilateral variance estimation: a low-rank approach. IEEE Trans. Image Process. **22**(2), 700–711 (2013)
7. Elad, M., Starck, J.L., Querre, P., Donoho, D.L.: Simultaneous cartoon and texture image inpainting using morphological component analysis (MCA). Appl. Comput. Harmon. Anal. **19**(3), 340–358 (2005)
8. Guo, Q., Gao, S., Zhang, X., Yin, Y., Zhang, C.: Patch-based image inpainting via two-stage low rank approximation. IEEE Trans. Vis. Comput. Graph. **2626**(c), 1 (2017)
9. He, L., Wang, Y.: Iterative support detection-based split bregman method for wavelet frame-based image inpainting. IEEE Trans. Image Process. **23**(12), 5470–5485 (2014)
10. Larsen, A.B.L., Snderby, S.K., Winther, O.: Autoencoding beyond pixels using a learned similarity metric. arXiv:1512.09300 (2015)
11. Li, W., Zhao, L., Lin, Z., Xu, D., Lu, D.: Non-local image inpainting using low-rank matrix completion. Comput. Graph. Forum **34**(6), 111–122 (2015)
12. Oliveira, M.M., Bowen, B., McKenna, R., Chang, Y.-S.: Fast Digital Image Inpainting. In: International Conference on Visualization, Imaging and Image Processing, pp. 261–266 (2001)
13. Pathak, D., Krahenbuhl, P., Donahue, J., Darrell, T., Efros, A.A.: Context encoders: feature learning by inpainting. In: Proceedings of the IEEE Conference on Computer Vision and Pattern Recognition, pp. 2536–2544 (2016)
14. Telea, Alexandru: An image inpainting technique based on the fast marching method. J. Graph. Tools **9**(1), 23–34 (2004)
15. Wexler, Y., Shechtman, E., Irani, M.: Space-time completion of video. IEEE Trans. Pattern Anal. Mach. Intell. **29**(3), 463–476 (2007)
16. Zhou, M., Chen, H., Paisley, J., Ren, L., Li, L., Xing, Z., Dunson, D., Sapiro, G., Carin, L.: Nonparametric Bayesian dictionary learning for analysis of noisy and incomplete images. IEEE Trans. Image Process. **21**(1), 5470–5485 (2012)

A Stochastic Model to Simulate the Spread of Leprosy in Juiz de Fora

Vinícius Clemente Varella[1], Aline Mota Freitas Matos[2],
Henrique Couto Teixeira[2], Angélica da Conceição Oliveira Coelho[3],
Rodrigo Weber dos Santos[1], and Marcelo Lobosco[1(✉)]

[1] Graduate Program on Computational Modeling, UFJF,
Rua José Lourenço Kelmer, s/n, Juiz de Fora, MG 36036-330, Brazil
`vcv_varella@hotmail.com`, {`rodrigo.weber`,`marcelo.lobosco`}`@ufjf.edu.br`
[2] Graduate Program on Biological Sciences, PPGCBIO, UFJF,
Rua José Lourenço Kelmer, s/n, Juiz de Fora, MG 36036-330, Brazil
`alinemotafreitas@yahoo.com.br`, `henrique.teixeira@ufjf.edu.br`
[3] Graduate Program in Nursing, UFJF, Rua José Lourenço Kelmer, s/n,
Juiz de Fora, MG 36036-330, Brazil
`angelica.fabri@ufjf.edu.br`

Abstract. This work aims to simulate the spread of leprosy in Juiz de Fora using the SIR model and considering some of its pathological aspects. SIR models divide the studied population into compartments in relation to the disease, in which S, I and R compartments refer to the groups of susceptible, infected and recovered individuals, respectively. The model was solved computationally by a stochastic approach using the Gillespie algorithm. Then, the results obtained by the model were validated using the public health records database of Juiz de Fora.

Keywords: Leprosy · Computational modelling · Epidemiology
Compartmental model · SIR model · Gillespie's algorithm
SSA algorithm

1 Introduction

Despite the decrease in number of leprosy cases in the world, some countries, like India, Indonesia and Brazil, still have difficulties in controlling this disease, which represents a big challenge to their public health systems [13]. In 2016, 22,710 new cases were registered as receiving standard multidrug therapy (MDT) in Brazil, with a registered prevalence rate of 1.08 per 10,000 population [13]. Therefore, Brazil has not yet eliminated leprosy as a public health problem: elimination is defined as the reduction of prevalence to a level below one case per 10,000 population [12].

The authors would like to thank UFJF, FAPEMIG, CAPES, CNPq and Minas Gerais Secretary of State for Health.

Mathematical and computational tools can be useful to understand the spread of leprosy. A computational model is the implementation, using programming languages, of a mathematical model that describes how a system works. Then, simulations are made with the purpose of studying the behaviour of this system in the occurrence of distinct scenarios. The main contribution of this paper is the development of a computational model that simulates, with a reasonable degree of fidelity, the spread of leprosy in a Brazilian city, Juiz de Fora, over time, using for this purpose a compartmental model, SIR (Susceptible, Infected, Recovered), solved using a stochastic approach. The results obtained from the model are then validated through a comparison with historical data of the diagnosis of the disease.

Compartmental models are frequently used to simulate the spread of diseases. For example, a SIR model was used to simulate the transmission of H1N1 virus [5], Dengue virus [2] and Cholera [3]. A recent work [10] proposed a compartmental continuous-time model to describe leprosy dynamics in Brazil. Approximate Bayesian Computation was used to fit some parameters of the model, such as the transmission coefficients and the rate of detection, using for this purpose leprosy incidence data over the period of 2000 to 2010. Then, the model was validated on incidence data from 2011 to 2012. In this work, a much simpler model was used to describe the leprosy dynamics in Juiz de Fora. The number of parameters used in our model is reduced, which allow us to fit them manually to data. Also, other work [1] used four distinct approaches (linear mixed model, back-calculation approach, deterministic compartmental model and individual-based model) to forecast the new case detection rate of leprosy in four states in Brazil (Rio Grande do Norte, Ceará, Tocantins and Amazonas). In this work, we proposed the use of a simple compartmental model using a stochastic approach. A pre-defined structure of twelve compartments was used in other work [8] to represent health conditions with respect to leprosy, and flows from these compartments are calculated according to Markov transition rates. In this work, only three compartments were used.

The remain of this work is organized as follows. First, Sect. 2 presents a very short overview of the disease. Then, Sect. 3 presents the proposed model and a draft of its computational implementation using the Gillespie algorithm. Section 4 presents the results obtained and finally Sect. 5 presents our conclusions and plans for future works.

2   Leprosy

Leprosy is an infectious disease caused by the bacterium *Mycrobacterium leprae* that affects the skin and peripheral nerves, and can reach the eyes and internal tissues of the nose. The entry route of the bacterium into the body is not definitively known, but the skin and the respiratory route are most likely [9].

It is a highly infectious disease with low pathogenicity, that is, many people are infected, however, few get sick. It is estimated that between 90% to 95% of the human population is resistant to leprosy. Also, some people, when infected, may evolve to spontaneous cure.

Leprosy has cure, although in some cases it may leave patients with physical disabilities. Access to treatment is universal in countries where it occurs and is essential for disease control because, after the start of treatment, there is a fall in the bacillary load and the patient ceases to transmit the disease. However, its control is a challenge mainly due to the possibility of long periods of incubation of the bacterium and the frequent delays in its diagnosis. For this reason, the number of reported cases is much lower than the actual number of infected individuals. Treated patients may be infected again, and relapse of the disease may also occur. Leprosy deaths are not reported in the literature, although in untreated cases the disease may evolve to physical disabilities, loss of sensitivity and impairment of neural and muscular structure.

3 Methods

In order to model the spread of leprosy in Juiz de Fora, a SIR model was used. Then, a computational model that implements it was solved using a deterministic and a stochastic approach. The deterministic implementation solves the system of ODEs that describe the SIR model using the Python's package *SciPy*. This library has a package called "integrate". One of the functions available in this package is called "odeint", and it is used to solve numerically a system of first order ODEs in the form $\frac{dy}{dt} = f(y, t)$ using the LSODA function of *odepack* package in FORTRAN. The choice of the numerical method to be used is made automatically by the function based on the characteristics of the equations. The function uses an adaptive scheme for both the integration step and the convergence order. The function can solve the ODEs system using either the BDF (Backward Differentiation Formula) or the Adams method. BDF is used for stiff equations and the implicit Adams method is used otherwise.

For the stochastic implementation the system of equations was transformed into a set of equivalents stochastic processes that were implemented using the Gillespie's Algorithm [4]. The Python programming language was also used in the implementation.

The models consider a constant population along the period of 20 years. The population was fixed in 441,816 inhabitants, which was approximately the number of inhabitants living in Juiz de Fora in 1996, according to the census [6]. Data for adjusting and validating the model was obtained from SINAN (*Sistema de Informação de Agravos de Notificação*) database. It is mandatory to register all cases of the disease in Brazil in this database. For this study, it was available all cases recorded in Juiz de Fora from 1996 to 2015. Half of data was used to adjust the parameters of the model (data from 1996 to 2004). The other half of data was used to validate it. Only the records in which the patients live all period in the city were considered, i.e., if the patient moved to another city, the record was disregarded.

3.1   Modelling the Spread of Leprosy

For simulating the spread dynamics of leprosy, it was used the SIR mathematical model [7]. SIR divides the studied population in three compartments according to their state in relation to the disease studied: susceptible (S), infected (I) and recovered(R). This model is described mathematically in Eq. 1.

$$\frac{dS}{dt} = -\beta SI, \frac{dI}{dt} = \beta SI - \mu I, \frac{dR}{dt} = \mu I, \tag{1}$$

where β represents the infection rate and μ represents the recovery rate.

The susceptible compartment is characterized by all individuals who are susceptible to the contagion of the disease or those who have been contaminated but have not yet manifested the disease and have insufficient amount of bacilli to be a possible transmitter. The infected compartment is composed by all the infected individuals that can transmit the disease, i.e., those sick.

The infection rate, β, was chosen in a way to simulate the diffusion effect observed in spatial models. In this way, it has a similar behaviour to the solution of the heat equation, given by:

$$\phi(x,t) = \frac{1}{\sqrt{4\pi tk}} \exp(\frac{-x^2}{4kt}). \tag{2}$$

In this equation, k represents the thermal conductivity of the material. Since in this work we are considering only the temporal dimension, the spacial aspects of the heat equation were ignored ($x = 0$) to define the infection rate, β, i.e., only the term $\frac{1}{\sqrt{4\pi tk}}$ was considered.

The constant values of Eqs. 1 and 2 were manually adjusted in order to fit qualitatively the number of infected and recovered cases. For fitting purposes, it was considered that the number of reported cases is less than the number of existing cases. Also, in order to reproduce the oscillatory characteristic observed in the number of infected cases, the infection rate was multiplied by the term $(sin(\frac{\pi t}{28}) + 1)$. The sum by one in the trigonometric term prevents negative values. so, the values found for the parameters were the following: $\beta = \frac{1}{\sqrt{4\pi t(4*10^{11})}}(sin(\frac{\pi t}{28}) + 1)$ and $\mu = 0.025$.

There is a tiny possibility of relapse of the disease (about 0.77% for multibacillary cases and 1.07% for paucibacillary ones [11]). For this reason, and due to the lack of notifications of relapse in Juiz de Fora, the possibility of relapse was not considered in this work. In other words, after infected, an individual recovers from the disease, and is not susceptible again.

3.2   Gillespie Implementation

The first step to implement the Gillespie algorithm is to define the equivalent reactions, as follows: (a) $S + I \rightarrow I + I$: a susceptible reacts with an infected, producing two infected; and (b) $I \rightarrow R$: an infected recovers.

Algorithm 1 presents the implementation of the SIR model. The Gillespie model works with the probabilities of a reaction to occur, one reaction per iteration. Two values are drawn from the uniform distribution in the unit interval (lines 6 and 8). The first one is used to compute the time of the next reaction (line 7). The second value is used to choose which reaction will occur in this time interval (lines 9–11). For each reaction, it is computed the probability of its occurrence (line 5). All probabilities are summed (line 5), and this value is used in the computation of the interval of the next reaction (line 7), as well as in the choice of the reaction that will occur (line 8). The second value drawn is compared to the normalized probability of occurrence of each reaction; if the drawn value is into an interval associated to a reaction, populations affected by that reaction are updated accordingly and a new iteration starts (lines 9–11).

Algorithm 1. Gillespie implementation of the SIR model

```
 1: while t < t_max do
 2:    if i==0 then
 3:       break;
 4:    end if
 5:    R1 = β * s * i; R2 = μ * i; R = R1+R2;
 6:    ran = uniformly_distributed_random(0,1);
 7:    t_n = -log (ran)/R; t = t + t_n;
 8:    if uniformly_distributed_random(0,1) < R1/R then
 9:       s = s-1; i = i+1;
10:    else
11:       i = i-1; r = r+1;
12:    end if
13: end while
```

---

4   Results

Figure 1 compares the number of infected and recovered cases registered in Juiz de Fora between 1996 to 2015, the results of the deterministic model and some of the results obtained by the stochastic approach. It's possible to notice that the Gillespie's solutions are very close to the deterministic solution. These oscillations are expected because the SSA algorithm adds noise to the solution, which may represent bacterial seasonality, changes in the treatment of disease, and so on. Figure 2 shows the CDF (cumulative distribution function) graph using 10,000 executions of the Gillespie algorithm. The graph shows that the probability of leprosy to be eradicated in the city before 2,045 is 99.21%. Therefore, the model indicates that there is no great risk of an outbreak in Juiz de Fora, if the model assumptions are kept constant. Implicitly the rates used in the model capture all aspects related to the combat of leprosy in the city. This projected scenario is in accordance with the results obtained in other works [1,10], that estimated that elimination of leprosy as a public health risk would require, on average, 44–45 years.

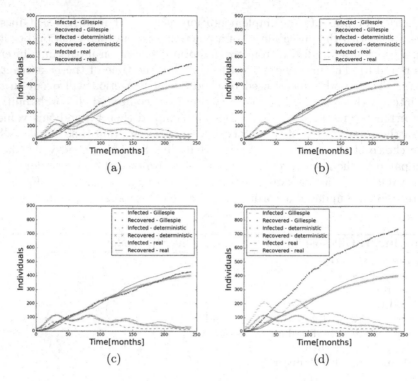

Fig. 1. Distinct results (a–d) obtained by the execution of the Gillespie algorithm. For comparison purposes, all figures also reproduces the deterministic result and the number of infected and recovered cases in Juiz de Fora.

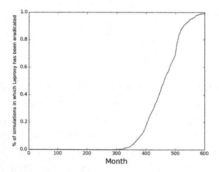

Fig. 2. CDF computed for 10,000 executions of the Gillespie algorithm. The graph presents the percentage of simulations in which leprosy has been eradicated. The probability of leprosy be eradicated after 600 months (starting in 1996) is 99,21%.

One aspect that should be highlighted is the occurrence of the so-called "hidden prevalence", i.e., cases not diagnosed and therefore not reported and registered in SINAN. The hidden prevalence occurs due to the unpreparedness or lack of knowledge about the symptoms of the disease by the health teams, so its diagnosis is made most often in advanced stages, after 5–7 years after infection. In this case, the reality may be very different from the SINAN numbers and, as consequence, our results and projections may be wrong.

5   Conclusion and Future Works

This work presented a mathematical-computational model to simulate the spread of leprosy in Juiz de Fora. The mathematical model was implemented using two approaches: a deterministic and a stochastic one. The deterministic approach used ODEs to model the spread of leprosy, while the stochastic one used the Gillespie's Stochastic Simulation Algorithm. The results of both approaches were qualitatively validated by the comparison to the historical number of diagnosis of leprosy in Juiz de Fora. Both the deterministic and the stochastic simulations obtained numbers of cases with the same order of magnitude of the registered cases, and the shapes of the curves were similar to the ones that describe the history of cases in Juiz de Fora. As future work, improvements can be made in the model to better fit its results to the historical series of leprosy cases. Also, the number of under-reporting cases needs to be verified. We plan to extend the model to a spatial domain using PDEs because the disease transmission occurs more frequently in places with vulnerability to health. Including this information in the model can be very useful and improve the quality of results.

References

1. Blok, D., Crump, R.E., Sundaresh, R.R., Ndeffo-Mbah, M., Galvani, A.A.P., Porco, T.C., de Vlas, S., Medley, G.F., Richardus, J.H.: Forecasting the new case detection rate of leprosy in four states of Brazil: a comparison of modelling approaches. Epidemics **18**, 92–100 (2017). https://doi.org/10.1016/j.epidem.2017.01.005
2. Esteva, L., Vargas, C.: Analysis of a dengue disease transmission model. Math. Biosci. **150**(2), 131–151 (1998)
3. Fister, K.R., Gaff, H., Schaefer, E., Buford, G., Norris, B.: Investigating cholera using an SIR model with age-class structure and optimal control. Involve J. Math. **9**(1), 83–100 (2015)
4. Gillespie, D.T.: A general method for numerically simulating the stochastic time evolution of coupled chemical reactions. J. Comput. Phys. **22**(4), 403–434 (1976)
5. Hattaf, K., Yousfi, N.: Mathematical model of the influenza A (H1N1) infection. Adv. Stud. Biol. **1**(8), 383–390 (2009)
6. IBGE: Juiz de Fora. http://www.cidades.ibge.gov.br/xtras/perfil.php?codmun=313670
7. Kermack, W.O., McKendrick, A.G.: A contribution to the mathematical theory of epidemics. Proc. R. Soc. Lon. Ser-A **115**(772), 700–721 (1927)
8. Meima, A., Smith, W.C.S., Van Oortmarssen, G.J., Richardus, J.H., Habbema, J.D.F.: The future incidence of leprosy: a scenario analysis. Bull. World Health Organ. **82**(5), 373–380 (2004)
9. Rees, R., McDougall, A.: Airborne infection with mycobacterium leprae in mice. J. Med. Microbiol. **10**(1), 63–68 (1977)

10. Smith, R.L.: Proposing a compartmental model for leprosy and parameterizing using regional incidence in Brazil. PLoS Negl. Trop. Dis. **10**(8), e0004925 (2016)
11. World Health Organization: Risk of relapse in leprosy. Technical report, The Leprosy Unit - Division of Control of Tropical Diseases (CTD/LEP/941 1994)
12. World Health Organization: Global strategy for the elimination of leprosy as a public health problem. Technical report, WHO (WHO/LEP/967 1996)
13. World Health Organization: Weekly Epidemiological Record. Technical report, WHO (vol. 92, no. 35, pp. 510–520, 2017)

Data Fault Identification and Repair Method of Traffic Detector

Xiao-lu Li[1], Jia-xu Chen[1], Xin-ming Yu[1], Xi Zhang[2], Fang-shu Lei[2], Peng Zhang[3], and Guang-yu Zhu[1(✉)]

[1] MOE Key Laboratory for Transportation Complex Systems Theory and Technology, Beijing Jiaotong University, Beijing 100044, China
gyzhu@bjtu.edu.cn
[2] Beijing Key Laboratory of Urban Traffic Operation Simulation and Decision Support, Beijing Transport Institute, Beijing 100073, China
[3] Transport Planning and Research Institute, Ministry of Transport, Beijing 100028, China

Abstract. The quality control and evaluation of traffic detector data are a prerequisite for subsequent applications. Considering that the PCA method is not ideal when detecting fault information with time-varying and multi-scale features, an improved MSPCA model is proposed in this paper. In combination with wavelet packet energy analysis and principal component analysis, data fault identification for traffic detectors is realized. On the basis of traditional multi-scale principal component analysis, detailed information is obtained by wavelet packet multi-scale decomposition, and a principal component analysis model is established in different scale matrices; fault data is separated by wavelet packet energy difference; according to the time characteristics and space of the detector data Correlation fixes fault data. Through case analysis, the feasibility of the method was verified.

Keywords: Fault data recognition · Fault data repair
Wavelet packet energy analysis · Principal component analysis

1 Introduction

The development of information technology and the wide application of various traffic detectors provide a large amount of traffic data for the intelligent transportation system. However, traffic detector inherent defects, disrepair, communication failures and environmental impact and other factors can produce traffic flow fault data, and reduce the credibility of data, thus affecting the reliability of traffic system [1]. Therefore, it is of great significance to identify the traffic flow fault data and to repair it reasonably and improve the quality of traffic detection data.

At present, the research on traffic detector fault data identification is mainly divided into data fault recognition based on traffic flow three-parameter law, data fault recognition based on statistical analysis and data fault recognition based on artificial intelligence [2]. Xu et al. [3] designed the method of data quality control by analyzing the influence of sampling interval of detector and intrinsic law of three parameters of

© Springer International Publishing AG, part of Springer Nature 2018
Y. Shi et al. (Eds.): ICCS 2018, LNCS 10862, pp. 567–573, 2018.
https://doi.org/10.1007/978-3-319-93713-7_52

traffic flow. Xiao et al. [4] uses wavelet analysis and least square method to study the detection of traffic flow anomaly data, and effectively reduces the misjudgment rate and false rate. Ngan et al. [5] proposes a Dirichlet process hybrid model to identify the traffic detector abnormal data, which has good robustness. Wong et al. [6] and Dang et al. [7] first identify potential outliers by clustering, and use principal component analysis (PCA) to transform ST (spatial temporal) signals into two-dimensional coordinate planes to reduce the size. Furthermore many scholars have proposed a multi-scale principal component analysis (MSPCA) model, which combines principal component analysis to remove correlation among variables, extract the decisive characteristics of wavelet analysis, and remove the advantages of measurement auto-correlation, and calculate the PCA model of wavelet coefficients at all scales. Traffic flow data restoration is one of the important measures to ensure the quality of data, and its research mainly focuses on time correlation, spatial correlation and historical correlation [8].

To summarize, principal component analysis is limited to the establishment of a fixed and single scale model. When detecting the time varying and the multi-scale characteristics of fault information, the method is not ideal. Therefore, we combine wavelet analysis with PCA, and use PCA to do multivariate statistical analysis of off-line data. Aiming at data fault recognition problem of traffic detector, a fault data identification and repair model based on improved multi-scale principal component analysis is proposed in this paper. First, the wavelet packet is used to decompose the original data with multi-scale, and the corresponding principal component analysis model is established. Then the real value of the fault data is estimated based on the temporal characteristics and spatial correlation.

2   Fault Data Recognition Model Based on Improved MSPCA

In the actual traffic data monitoring process, the distribution of noise is random. Its intensity is also time-variable. However, when dealing with wavelet coefficients beyond the statistical control limit, MSPCA uses a uniform threshold at this scale to reconstruct the wavelet without considering the time variability of the noise, so part of the noise is mistakenly identified as a fault to be separated and partially covered by the noise of the fault will be expanded, leading to false alarm phenomenon.

At the same time, in order to solve the problems of MSPCA modeling fixed, principal component subspace and SPE (Squared prediction error), and single parameter, this paper draws on the idea of adaptive PCA's principal component recursion, and modifies the following three points for traditional MSPCA:

(1) Subsection processing of traffic flow data.
(2) The wavelet decomposition is changed to wavelet packet decomposition to improve the resolution of the model.
(3) Detection of fault information by using wavelet packet energy difference method.

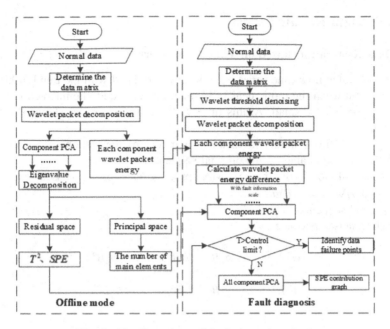

Fig. 1. The flow chart of the improved method.

Figure 1 shows the flow chart of the improved method.

Step 1: Sampling the detector to get the original data.

A sample data containing m sensors: $x \in R^m$, in the sample data, each sensor has n independent sample data, which is constructed into a data matrix X of $m \times n$ size, where each column of X represents a measurement variable, and each row represents a sample.

Step 2: By $S = \text{cov}(x) \approx \frac{X^T X}{n-1}$ calculating the co-variance matrix of X.

Step 3: Calculate the eigenvalues and eigenvectors of the related data matrix Λ.

The co-variance of the main element is Λ represents the larger eigenvalues(v) of the former A of the S.

Step 4: Calculate the main element $T = XP$.

Where $P \in R^{m \times A}$ is the load matrix, $T \in R^{n \times A}$ is the scoring matrix, and the columns of T are called principal variables and A is the number of principal components.

The principal component T represents the projection of the data matrix x in the direction of the load vector corresponding to this principal component. The larger its length, the greater the degree of coverage or variation of x in the p direction.

If $\|t_1\| > \|t_2\| > ... > \|t_m\|$, then P_1 represents the maximum direction of the data X change, and P_m represents the smallest direction of the data change.

Step 5: Calculate the principal component cumulative variance and contribution rate.

The cumulative variance contribution rate indicates that the amount of data that the former A principal can explain accounts for 6 of the total data.

According to *CPV* to calculate, normally when *CPV* reaches 85% or more, the previous principal can be assumed to explain most of the data changes.

3 Fault Data Repair Model

3.1 Data Restoration Based on Time Characteristics

The trend of traffic flow time series is positively correlated with the trend of historical time series, but when the traffic density is small and crowded, the interaction between vehicles becomes very small. At this time, traffic flow time series shows short-range correlation.

Using the ARIMA model to establish a model of the stationary sequence, and through the inverse change to the original sequence.

The general form of the ARIMA process can be expressed as follows: $\varphi(B)z_t = \phi(B)\nabla^d z_t = \theta(B)a_t$.

z_t: original sequence

a_t: white noise sequence

$$\phi(B) = 1 - \phi_1 B - \phi_2 B^2 - \ldots - \phi_p B^p \tag{1}$$

$$\theta(B) = 1 - \theta_1 B - \theta_2 B^2 - \ldots - \theta_q B^q \tag{2}$$

3.2 Data Restoration Based on Space Characteristics

In the traffic network, the traffic flow in the road section is affected by the upstream and downstream sections in the spatial characteristics, and the traffic flow sequences in the upstream and downstream sections show some correlations in time characteristics.

By statistics, correlation reflects the linear correlation between different sets of data, the greater the correlation can be linearly expressed with each other. Therefore, based on the adjacent sections of traffic flow data as an independent variable, using multiple linear regression model for traffic flow repair.

$$x_1(t) = f(x_1(t-1), \cdots, x_1(t-\tau_{\max}), x_2(t), \cdots, x_2(t-\tau_{\max}), \cdots, x_8(t), \cdots, x_8(t-\tau_{\max})) + e \tag{3}$$

$x_1(t)$, $x_1(t-1)$ means the traffic flow parameter value at the moment t and t − 1 when the detector No. 1 is at the cross-section, and so on, $f(\cdot)$ is a function to be estimated, $\tau_{\max}$ is the maximum time lag value, e is relative error.

4 Case Study

The data of the coil detector in the intersection of Chongqing is selected as the experimental data source during the week (2016-08-15 to 2016-08-20). There is a coil in front of the stop line in each lane of the intersection. There are 8 coils in total. Each detector generates about 555 data a day. The data amount every day for 555×8. In coil No. 3, two faults occur between data points 300–400. Using the correlation of the data in time and space to repair fault data.

4.1 Data Fault Recognition and Analysis

Using No. 1 detector as a typical example, Fig. 2 shows the energy difference of eight vectors decomposed by layer 3 wavelet packet of the detector data. The dashed line represents the energy difference threshold of each component. It can be seen that the node [3,0] and [3,7] found fault information with different degree of data failure near 150–200.

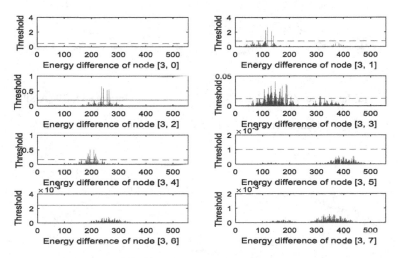

Fig. 2. Energy difference result of third layer decomposition

To validate the advantages of the proposed fault diagnosis data model, this paper will first signal to be detected in scale after wavelet packet decomposition for 3, every dimension are calculated respectively under the corresponding normal data with wavelet packet energy scale energy difference between the same below nodes. After discovering the node with obvious abnormality, that is, when the fault information is found, the node data matrix of the signal is modeled by MSPCA modeling and improved MSPCA.

Inspected after wavelet threshold in addition to the noise signal, the reconstructed signal dimension is 3 after wavelet packet decomposition, received the first scale 2 nodes energy, the second dimension for 4, the third dimension won eight node energy. Every dimension are calculated respectively under the corresponding normal data with wavelet packet energy scale with the node, the energy difference between the to find more apparent anomaly node, which found that after the location of fault information, the node data matrix of this signal PCA modeling, the result is shown in Fig. 3.

4.2 Data Recovery

For each model training, firstly, the original data sequence stability was verified by the ADF unit root, and the difference number d was determined and the time sequence was smooth and steady. Secondly, the model order number p and q are determined by AIC criterion, and the model parameters are estimated. Finally, the obtained model is used to repair and restore the difference. The fix results are shown in Fig. 4(a).

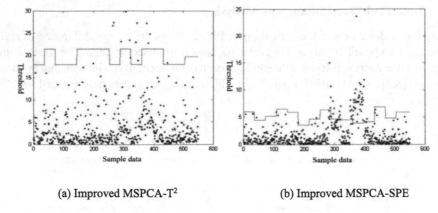

(a) Improved MSPCA-T^2 (b) Improved MSPCA-SPE

Fig. 3. Control chart of improved MSPCA fault diagnosis model

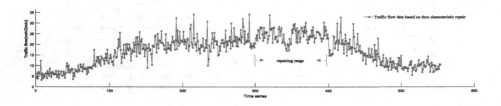

(a) Traffic flow data based on time characteristic repair

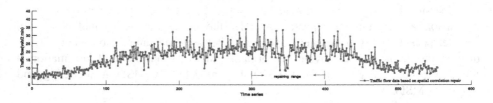

(b) Traffic flow data based on spatial correlation repair

Fig. 4. Traffic flow data of No. 3 detector

First, select the collect data of the fifth day to analyze. Calculate the rest of the detector flow data of correlation coefficients of data collected from the detector No. 3, when the time lag values are 0, 1, 2, 3, respectively. Secondly, set the correlation coefficient threshold as (0.8, 1). The sequence of conforming data is used as a preselected independent variable, corresponding detector No. 3 is a dependent variable. Spatial estimation model of traffic flow by stepwise linear regression.

$$Q_{3\_t} = 3.017 + 0.276Q_{1\_(t-2)} + 0.511Q_{2\_(t-1)} + 0.203Q_{4\_(t-1)} \tag{4}$$

Among them, $Q_{1\_(t-2)}$, $Q_{2\_(t-1)}$ and $Q_{4\_(t-1)}$, respectively represents the traffic flow of detectors No. 1, 2, 4 during t, t − 1 and t − 2 periods.

The traffic flow data collected by the detector 3 at 2016-08-08 is repaired by the formula (4), and the result is shown in Fig. 4(b).

5 Conclusion

In this paper, fault diagnosis and data restoration of traffic flow data are studied. Considering that the time-varying and multiscale features of PCA fault information are not ideal, this paper proposes an improved MSPCA model. Based on the traditional MSPCA model, using wavelet packet decomposition, and then wavelet packet energy difference method is used. Detect fault information and separate fault data to improve detection accuracy. Then use the repair model to calculate the true value according to the temporal and spatial correlation of the traffic flow data respectively. Case studies have found that the improved MSPCA fault data diagnosis model and data repair model can effectively identify abnormal data and repair it.

Acknowledgment. This work is supported by the National key research and development plan of Ministry of science and technology (2016YFB1200203-02, 2016YFC0802206-2), the National Science Foundation of China (Nos. 61572069,61503022), the Fundamental Research Funds for the Central Universities (Nos. 2017YJS308, 2017JBM301), Beijing Municipal Science and Technology Project (Z161100005116006, Z171100004417024); Shenzhen public traffic facilities construction projects (BYTD-KT-002-2).

References

1. Wang, X.Y., Zhang, J.L., Yang, X.Y.: Key Theory and Method of Traffic Flow Data Cleaning and State Identification and Optimization Control. Science Press, Beijing (2011)
2. Wen, C.L., Lv, F.Y., Bao, Z.J., et al.: A review of data driven-based incipient fault diagnosis. Acta Automatica Sinica **42**(9), 1285–1299 (2016)
3. Xu, C., Qu, Z.W., Tao, P.F., et al.: Methods of real-time screening and reconstruction for dynamic traffic abnormal data. J. Harbin Eng. Univ. **37**(2), 211–217 (2016)
4. Xiao, Q., Wang, D.J., Liu, D.: Abnormal traffic flow data detection based on wavelet analysis. In: Matec-Conferences, p. 01090 (2016)
5. Ngan, H.Y.T., Yung, N.H.C., Yeh, A.G.O.: Outlier detection in traffic data based on the Dirichlet process mixture model. Intell. Transp. Syst. IET **9**(7), 773–781 (2015)
6. Wong, C.H.M., Ngan, H.Y.T., Yung, N.H.C.: Modulo-k clustering based outlier detection for large-scale traffic data. In: Proceedings of the International Conference on IEEE Information Technology and Application. IEEE (2016)
7. Dang, T.T., Ngan, H.Y.T., Liu, W.: Distance-based k-nearest neighbors outlier detection method in large-scale traffic data. In: IEEE International Conference on Digital Signal Processing, pp. 507–510. IEEE (2015)
8. Lu, H.P., Qu, W.C., Sun, Z.Y.: Detection and repair algorithm of traffic erroneous data based on S-G filtering. Civ. Eng. J. **5**, 123–128 (2015)

The Valuation of CCIRS with a New Design

Huaying Guo and Jin Liang[✉]

School of Mathematical Sciences, Tongji University, Shanghai, China
wosghy@163.com, liang_jin@tongji.edu.cn

Abstract. This paper presents a study of pricing a credit derivatives – credit contingent interest rate swap (CCIRS) with a new design, which allows some premium to be paid later when default event doesn't happen. This item makes the contract more flexible and supplies cash liquidity to the buyer, so that the contract is more attractive. Under the reduced form framework, we provide the pricing model with the default intensity relevant to the interest rate, which follows Cox-Ingersoll-Ross (CIR) process. A semi-closed form solution is obtained, by which numerical results and parameters analysis have been carried on. Especially, it is discussed that a trigger point for the proportion of the later possible payment which causes the zero initial premium.

Keywords: Interest rate swap · CCIRS · Reduced form framework
CIR process

1 Introduction

After financial crisis, credit risk has been considered more serious, especially in over-the-counter market, which lacks margin and collateral. So many credit derivatives, such as credit default swap (CDS), collateralized debt obligation, have been created and used in financial activities to manager such risks. To manage the credit risk of interest rate swap (IRS), credit contingent interest rate swap (CCIRS) is designed and traded in the market [16].

CCIRS is a contract which provides protection to the fixed rate payer for avoiding the default risk of the floating rate payer in an IRS contract. The fixed rate payer purchases a CCIRS contract from the credit protection seller at the initial time and the protection seller will compensate the credit loss of the protection buyer in the IRS contract if the default incident happen during the life of the deal. This credit derivative offers a new way to deal with the counterparty risk of IRS. It is similar to CDS, though the value of the its underling IRS can be positive or negative.

This work is supported by National Natural Science Foundation of China (No. 11671301).

The inventions of those credit instruments provide an effective method to separate and transfer the credit risk. However, to buy them, a lot of money should be paid to the protection seller which will occupy the funds of companies and cause a corresponding increasing in liquidity strain. No doubt that this financial problem will pose a new challenge to the operation of companies.

To solve CCIRS initial cost problem, using the fact of the value of IRS might positive or negative, we design a new CCIRS with a special item, which is a later clause to reduce the initial cost of purchasing this credit derivative. Then we establish a pricing model to valuation this new product, we can even find that an appropriate item will make a zero cost of this credit instrument in the purchasing time.

To pricing a credit derivative, there are usually two frameworks: Structure and Reduced form ones. In our pricing model, the reduced form framework is used. That is, the default is assumed to be governed by a default hazard rate with parameters inferred from market data and macroeconomic variables. In the literatures, Duffie [6], Lando [8] and Jarrow [11] gave examples of research following this approach. The structure and pricing model for ordinary IRS has been presented in [2]. Duffie and Huang [7] discussed the default risk of IRS under the framework of reduced form. Li [10] studied the valuation of IRS with default risk under the contingent claim analysis framework. Brigo et al. [3] considered the Credit Valuation Adjustment of IRS with considering the wrong way risk. The pricing of single-name CCIRS was given in [12] by Liang et al., where a Partial Differential Equation (PDE) model is established with some numerical results. Using multi-factors Affine Jump Diffusion model, Liang and Xu [13] obtain a semi-closed solution of the price of single-name CCIRS.

Due to the IRS being the underlying asset, the value of the protection contract is closely connected with the stochastic interest rate. In this paper, we use a single factor model where the main factor of the default intensity is the stochastic interest rate. The model can be changed to a PDE problem. Using the PDE methods, a semi-closed form solution of the pricing model is obtained. In short words, in this paper, 1. we design a CCIRS with a new payment way; 2. under reduced framework, the new product has been valued; 3. a semi-closed form of the solution is obtained; 4. numerical examples are presented, with different parameters. The comparison of the origin and new designs are also shown.

This article is organized as follows. In Sect. 2, we give model assumptions, establish and solve the pricing model of CCIRS with the special item under the reduced form framework. In Sect. 3, numerical results are provided. The conclusion of the paper is given in Sect. 4.

2   Model Formulation

In this section, we develop a continuous time valuation framework for pricing CCIRS with the special item. First of all, let us explain the contract. Consider an IRS contract between two parties, the fixed rate payer Party A and the floating rate payer Party B. At the view point of Party A, we assume that Party A

is a default-free institution and Party B has a positive probability of default
before the final maturity. To avoid the counterparty risk, Party A buys a special
protection contract with Party C. At the initial time, A pays a premium to C.
Before the expiry time of IRS, if B defaults, A will receive compensation from
C if A has any loss. The contract is ended after A receiving the compensation.
On the contrary, if B doesn't default during the life of the contract, at the
termination time, the protection buyer A needs pay another later premium to
protection seller C. We call this particular clause a later cash flow item. The
later premium is the one predetermined in the contract, which will affect the
initial premium, and is interesting to study. Figure 1 is a conventional diagram
of the process of this product.

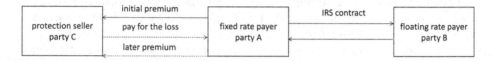

Fig. 1. Structure of CCIRS with the special item

2.1 Model Assumptions

Using the probability space $(\Omega, \mathcal{G}, \mathcal{G}_t, Q)$ to model the uncertain market, where
Q is the risk-neutral measure, and $\mathcal{G}_t$ represents all market information up to
time t. As usual, we can write $\mathcal{G}_t = \mathcal{F}_t \vee \mathcal{H}_t$, where $\mathcal{F}_t$ is the filtration contains
all the market information except defaults. $\mathcal{H}_t = \sigma\{1_{\{\tau<s\}} \mid s \leq t\}$ represents
the default information of Party B. Let τ be the default time of floating rate
payer in the swap contract, assume it a $\mathcal{G}_t$ stopping time, i.e. $\{\tau \leq t\} \in \mathcal{G}_t$. The
default time τ can be defined as

$$\tau = \inf \left\{ t; \int_0^t \lambda_s ds \geq \eta \right\},$$

where η is the unit mean exponential random variable and λ is the default
intensity. So the distributions of conditional default probability of Party B can
be given by

$$Prob\left[\tau \leq t | \mathcal{F}_t\right] = 1 - \exp\left(-\int_0^t \lambda_s ds\right).$$

We assume the risk free interest rate r_t, which is $\mathcal{F}_t$ adapted, follows the stochastic CIR process:

$$dr_t = \kappa(\theta - r_t)dt + \sigma\sqrt{r_t}dW_t,$$

where κ, θ and σ are positive constants, which represent the speed of adjustment,
the mean and the volatility of r_t respectively. The condition $\kappa\theta > \sigma^2/2$ is required
to insure r_t to be a positive process. W_t is a standard Brown motion.

Let $\tilde{P}$ be the notional principal of the IRS and r^* be the predetermined swap rate the fixed rate payer A promises to pay. The value of the IRS for Party A without considering the counterparty risk at time t before maturity T is denoted by $f(t,r)$. We approximate the discrete payments with a continuous stream of cash flows, i.e., in this IRS contract, Party A needs pay $\tilde{P}(r_t - r^*)dt$ to Party B continuously. Thus, under the risk-neutral measure Q, $f(t,r)$ can be represented as

$$f(t,r) = E^Q[\int_t^T \tilde{P}(r_s - r^*)e^{-\int_t^s r_\theta d\theta}ds|\mathcal{F}_t],$$

Due to the fact that the value of a default-free floating rate loan equals its principal (see [4]), we obtain

$$1 = E^Q[\int_t^T r_s e^{-\int_t^s r_\theta d\theta}ds + e^{-\int_t^T r_\theta d\theta}|\mathcal{F}_t].$$

So we can derive the following equality

$$f(t,r) = \tilde{P} - \tilde{P}E^Q[e^{-\int_t^T r_\theta d\theta}|\mathcal{F}_t] - \tilde{P}r^* E^Q[\int_t^T e^{-\int_t^s r_\theta d\theta}ds|\mathcal{F}_t],$$

$$= \tilde{P} - \tilde{P}B(t,T) - \tilde{P}r^* \int_t^T B(t,s)ds.$$

Here, $B(t,s)$ is the price of a s-maturity zero-coupon bond at time t, which has closed form expression within the CIR framework (see [5]).

2.2 Price of the Contract

An analysis of the cash flows of the protection contract is as follows:

- At the initial time, Party A pays an initial premium to protection seller Party C.
- Suppose at $\tau \leq T$, the Party B cannot fulfill its obligations. There are two cases: 1. the valuation of the residual payoff of the IRS contract with respect to Party A is positive, the Party C compensates the loss $(1 - R)f^+(\tau, r_\tau)$ to Party A, where $f^+(\tau, r_\tau) = \max\{f(\tau, r_\tau), 0\}$ and R is the recovery rate; 2. the valuation of IRS is non-positive, the contract CCIRS stops without any cash flow between Party A and Party C.
- If $\tau > T$, there is no default by Party B during the life of the IRS contract and the Party A has no loss. The Party A pays the later floating premium $\alpha\tilde{P}Tr_T$ to C. Here α is the adjustable factor and we call α later premium rate.

There are several reasons for setting the later premium as $\alpha\tilde{P}Tr_T$. First, we expect to reduce the initial premium for buying the protection contract through adjusting the later premium rate, which significantly makes the contract flexible.

Thus, the company can choose the appropriate contract to free up money for investment in the production of other items. Secondly, the setting makes the later premium linearly change with the life of the contract. Finally, a floating premium setting makes the later premium decreasing with the floating interest rate. Through the above analysis, under the risk-neutral measure Q, the price of the protection contract can be described as

$$E^Q[1_{\{t<\tau<T\}}f^+(\tau,r_\tau)(1-R)e^{-\int_t^\tau r_\theta d\theta} - 1_{\{\tau>T\}}\alpha\tilde{P}T r_T e^{-\int_t^T r_\theta d\theta}|\mathcal{G}_t]. \quad (1)$$

Using the results in [8], (1) can be rewritten as

$$1_{\{t<\tau\}}E^Q[\int_t^T \lambda_u f^+(u,r_u)(1-R)e^{-\int_t^u (r_\theta+\lambda_\theta)d\theta}du - \alpha\tilde{P}T r_T e^{-\int_t^T (r_\theta+\lambda_\theta)d\theta}|\mathcal{F}_t].$$

Let $(\mathcal{F}_t)_{t\geq 0}$ be the filtration generated by the process r_t and the intensity process λ is smooth function of r_t. By the strong Markov property of r_t, we obtain the following representation of the pre-default value V of the protection contract

$$V(t,r,\alpha) = E^Q[\int_t^T \lambda_u f^+(u,r_u)(1-R)e^{-\int_t^u (r_\theta+\lambda_\theta)d\theta}du - \alpha\tilde{P}T r_T e^{-\int_t^T (r_\theta+\lambda_\theta)d\theta}|r_t=r].$$

$$(2)$$

If the protection contract signed at time t, the buyer A needs to pay the initial premium $V(t,r_t,\alpha)$ to the protection seller. By Fubini theorem, we can obtain

$$V(t,r,\alpha) = \int_t^T E^Q[\lambda_u f^+(u,r_u)(1-R)e^{-\int_t^u (r_\theta+\lambda_\theta)d\theta}|r_t=r]du$$
$$- \alpha\tilde{P}T E^Q[r_T e^{-\int_t^T (r_\theta+\lambda_\theta)d\theta}|r_t=r].$$

Denote

$$\varphi_1(t,r;u) = E^Q[\lambda f^+(u,r_u)(1-R)e^{-\int_t^u (r_\theta+\lambda_\theta)d\theta}|r_t=r], \quad 0\leq t\leq u, \quad (3)$$
$$\varphi_2(t,r;T) = E^Q[r_T e^{-\int_t^T (r_\theta+\lambda_\theta)d\theta}|r_t=r], \quad 0\leq t\leq T. \quad (4)$$

Below we will use the PDE methods to solve (3) and (4). To describe the joint behavior of interest rate r_t and the default intensity of Party B, we assume they are correlated through affine dependence, i.e.

$$\lambda_t = ar_t + b, \quad (5)$$

where a, b are positive constants. In this situation, the default intensity λ_t is a monotone increasing function with respect to the interest rate r_t. So the floating rate payer will present a higher default risk as the interest rate rising up.

Suppose that φ_1, φ_2 satisfy suitable regularity conditions. Using the Feynman-Kac formula, the expectation in (3) is also a solution to the equation

$$\begin{cases} \frac{\partial\varphi_1}{\partial t} + \kappa(\theta-r)\frac{\partial\varphi_1}{\partial r} + \frac{1}{2}r\sigma^2\frac{\partial^2\varphi_1}{\partial r^2} - (ar+r+b)\varphi_1 = 0, 0<r<\infty, 0\leq t\leq u, \\ \varphi_1(u,r) = (ar+b)f^+(u,r)(1-R), \qquad\qquad\qquad 0<r<\infty, \end{cases}$$

$$(6)$$

where u is any time between 0 and T.

Referencing [14,15], (6) has a explicit solution

$$\varphi_1(t,r;u) = e^{-(p\kappa\theta + \kappa q + \sigma^2 pq + b)(u-t) - pr} r^q w(t,r;u), \tag{7}$$

where

$$w(t,r;u) = \int_0^\infty f^+(u,\xi)(1-R)(a\xi + b)e^{p\xi}\xi^{-q}G(t,r;u,\xi)d\xi,$$

$$p = \frac{-\kappa - \sqrt{\kappa^2 + 2(a+1)\sigma^2}}{\sigma^2}, \qquad q = 1 - \frac{2\kappa\theta}{\sigma^2},$$

$$G(t,r;u,\xi) = \varepsilon e^{-\phi-\varphi}\left(\frac{\psi}{\phi}\right)^{\frac{\nu}{2}} I_\nu(2(\phi\psi)^{\frac{1}{2}}), \tag{8}$$

$$\varepsilon = \frac{2(\kappa + \sigma^2 p)}{\sigma^2(1 - e^{-(\kappa+\sigma^2 p)(u-t)})}, \qquad \phi = \varepsilon r e^{-(\kappa+\sigma^2 p)(u-t)},$$

$$\psi = \varepsilon\xi, \qquad \nu = \frac{2(\kappa\theta + \sigma^2 q) - \sigma^2}{\sigma^2},$$

and $I_\nu(\cdot)$ is the modified Bessel function of the first kind of order ν, i.e.,

$$I_\nu(2(\phi\psi)^{\frac{1}{2}}) = (\phi\psi)^{\frac{\nu}{2}} \sum_{k=0}^\infty \frac{(\phi\psi)^k}{k!\Gamma(\nu+k+1)}.$$

We can also see that φ_2 is the solution of the equation

$$\begin{cases} \frac{\partial\varphi_2}{\partial t} + \kappa(\theta - r)\frac{\partial\varphi_2}{\partial r} + \frac{1}{2}r\sigma^2\frac{\partial^2\varphi_2}{\partial r^2} - (ar + r + b)\varphi_2 = 0, & 0 < r < \infty, 0 \le t \le T, \\ \varphi_2(T,r) = r, & 0 < r < \infty. \end{cases} \tag{9}$$

Using the methods in [15], we can obtain

$$\varphi_2(t,r;T) = \frac{\varepsilon^{\nu+1}e^{-\phi}\Gamma(2-q+\nu)}{(\varepsilon-p)^{2-q+\nu}\Gamma(\nu+1)}M(2-q+\nu, \nu+1, \frac{\varepsilon\phi}{\varepsilon-p}), \tag{10}$$

where $M(x,y,z) = \sum_{k=0}^\infty((x)_k/(k!(y)_k)z^k)$ is the confluent hypergeometric function and $(x)_k$ is defined by $(x)_k = x(x+1)\cdots(x+k-1)$ for $k > 0$, $(x)_0 = 1$. Then we can state the main result from the above analysis.

Theorem 1. *The pre-default value of CCIRS with the later premium item is given by*

$$V(t,r,\alpha) = \int_t^T \varphi_1(t,r;u)du - \alpha\tilde{P}T\varphi_2(t,r;T). \tag{11}$$

where φ_1 and φ_2 are given by (7) and (10) respectively.

From (4), it can be shown that $\varphi_2 > 0$. Therefore the price of the protection contract is linearly decreasing with the later premium rate α going up. If a company wants to buy a protection contract with a lower price, it can sign the contract with a higher α. Thus, this special item makes this CCIRS contract more flexible and more attractive because it has its own advantage for reducing the funding cost, that is to say, supplying liquidity at initial time.

Remark 1. (i) The intensity model (5) assumes λ_t is positive affine dependence with r_t. We can use the inverse CIR model [9] to describe the negative correlation between λ_t and r_t, i.e.

$$\lambda_t = \frac{a}{r_t} + b.$$

Using the similar methods above, we can also obtain the solutions

$$\varphi_1 = e^{-(p\kappa\theta + \kappa q + \sigma^2 pq + b)(u-t) - pr} r^q \int_0^\infty f^+(u,\xi)(1-R)(\frac{a}{\xi} + b)e^{p\xi}\xi^{-q}G(t,r;u,\xi)d\xi,$$

$$\tag{12}$$

$$\varphi_2 = \frac{\varepsilon^{\nu+1}e^{-\phi}\Gamma(2-q+\nu)}{(\varepsilon-p)^{2-q+\nu}\Gamma(\nu+1)}M(2-q+\nu,\nu+1,\frac{\varepsilon\phi}{\varepsilon-p}),$$

$$\tag{13}$$

where $G(t,r;u,\xi)$ is the fundamental solution of CIR process shown in (8). p,q are the solution of the following equations

$$q\kappa\theta + \frac{1}{2}\sigma^2 q(q-1) - a = 0, \quad p\kappa + \frac{1}{2}\sigma^2 p^2 - 1 = 0.$$

(ii) In the above model, we assume floating rate payer has a default risk. Similarly, we can price the protection contract if the protection buyer is the floating rate payer. i.e., the fixed rate payer is the one who has the default risk. The price of the protection contract can be written as

$$E^Q[1_{\{t<\tau<T\}}f^-(\tau,r_\tau)(1-R)e^{-\int_t^\tau r_\theta d\theta} - 1_{\{\tau>T\}}\alpha\tilde{P}T r_T e^{-\int_t^T r_\theta d\theta}|\mathcal{G}_t], \tag{14}$$

where $f^-(\tau,r_\tau) = \max(-f(\tau,r_\tau),0)$ is the valuation of the residual payoff of the IRS contract with respect to the floating rate payer at time τ. R is the recovery rate of IRS contract when default occurs.

(iii) The main content of our model design is to add a later payment clause in the contract to reduce the initial premium. This idea can also be used in CDS contract, whose reference assets are the corporation bonds.   None

3   Numerical Results

In this section, we provide a numerical example to illustrate how market parameters affect the value of the protection contract. Throughout the numerical analysis, unless otherwise stated, the basic parameters are given as follows:

$$\kappa = 0.3, \theta = 0.02, \sigma = 0.02, \tilde{P} = 1, T = 1, a = 9, b = 0.2, R = 0.4, r^* = 0.04.$$

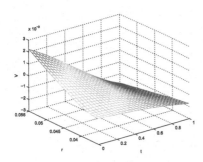

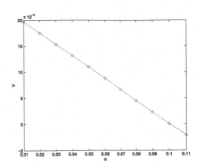

Fig. 2. V and r, t **Fig. 3.** V and α

The Fig. 2 shows the relationship between the price of the contract, interest rate r and life time T of the contract. The later premium rate $\alpha = 0.05$.

Firstly, the curve shows that the value of the protection contract is decreasing with respect to t. Under the same conditions, with t approximates to T, the value of residual payoff of the IRS contract is smaller, so the protection contract will have a lower price.

Secondly, Fig. 2 shows that the value of the protection contract is increasing with r at the initial time. Actually, according to the intensity model (5), higher r will generate a higher default intensity. In addition, with a higher initial interest rate, when default event happens, the probability of positive value of IRS is bigger. That is, the protection seller is more likely to compensate the loss.

Let $r_0 = 0.05$, we plot the price curve with different later premium rate α in Fig. 3. The value of the contract is linearly decreasing with respect to α. It is consistent with the Eq. (11). In fact, the later premium will increase with bigger α. So at the initial time, the contract will have a lower price. Especially, when α is appropriate, the price of CCIRS will be zero at initial time. That means the protection buyer should not pay anything at the signing date of the contract. Thus, it will reduce the funding costs when the company signs the CCIRS. If the fixed rate payer wants a protection for the IRS and has insufficient capital at the initial time, it could purchase a CCIRS with a proper later premium rate α.

Figures 4 and 5 show the sensitivity of the price of the contract to the intensity parameters a, b respectively. Larger a, b mean a bigger default probability. It causes the increase of the price of the protection contract.

Figure 6 shows the value of the CCIRS with new and old designs at the initial time, the below one is $\alpha = 0.05$, and the up one is $\alpha = 0$. i.e. the up and below are the values of the old and new designs respectively. r indicates the interest rate at initial time. It is clear that as the late payment condition, at initial time, the new design contract is cheaper than the traditional one for the buyer.

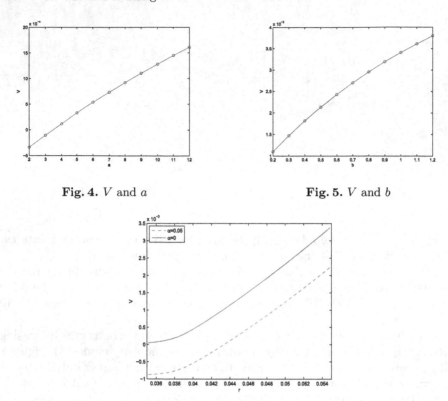

Fig. 4. V and a **Fig. 5.** V and b

Fig. 6. Comparison of the values of old and new designs

4   Conclusions

In this paper, we design a new credit contingent interest rate swap with a later payment item and provide its pricing model for valuation. Using the CIR model to describe the floating interest rate, under the reduced form framework, we calculate the price this derivative with a default intensity relevant to interest rate. The semi-closed form solutions of the pricing model are presented. We find that the later cash flow item will reduce the initial premium efficiently. At last, the numerical results show that the price of the contract is increasing with the short interest rate. A appropriate later premium rate, as in Fig. 3, will make the price of the contract be zero at the signing date. We hope that our work would be helpful for industries when they want to increase the cash liquidity in financial activities.

References

1. Brody, D.C., Hughston, L.P., Macrina, A.: Information-based asset pricing. Int. J. Theor. Appl. Financ. **11**(1), 107–142 (2008)
2. Brigo, D., Mercurio, F.: Interest Rate Models: Theory and Practice: With Smile, Inflation, and Credit. Springer, Heidelberg (2006). https://doi.org/10.1007/978-3-540-34604-3
3. Brigo, D., et al.: Counterparty Credit Risk, Collateral and Funding: With Pricing Cases for All Asset Classes. Wiley, Chichester (2013)
4. Cox, J.C., Ross, S.A.: An analysis of variable rate loan contracts. J. Financ. **35**(35), 389–403 (1980)
5. Cox, J.C., Ross, S.A.: A theory of the term structure of interest rates. Econometrica **53**(2), 385–407 (1985)
6. Duffie, D., Singleton, K.J.: Modeling term structures of defaultable bond. Soc. Sci. Electron. Publishing **12**(4), 687–720 (1999)
7. Duffie, D., Huang, M.: Swap rates and credit quality. J. Financ. **51**(3), 921–949 (1996)
8. Lando, D.: On Cox processes and credit-risky securities. Rev. Deriv. Res. **2**(2), 99C120 (1998)
9. Ge, L., et al.: Explicit formulas for pricing credit-linked notes with counterparty risk under reduced-form framework. IMA J. Manag. Math. **26**(3), 325 (2014)
10. Li, H.: Pricing of swaps with default risk. Rev. Deriv. Res. **2**(2–3), 231–250 (1998)
11. Jarrow, R.A., Turnbull, S.M.: Pricing derivatives on financial securities subject to credit risk. J. Financ. **50**(1), 53–85 (1995)
12. Liang, J., Xu, Y., Guo, G.: The pricing for credit contingent interest swap. J. Tongji Univ. **39**(2), 299–303 (2011)
13. Liang, J., Xu, Y.: Valuation of credit contingent interest rate swap. Risk Decis. Anal. **4**(1), 39–46 (2013)
14. Liang, J., Wang, T.: Valuation of loan-only credit default swap with negatively correlated default and prepayment intensities. Int. J. Comput. Math. **89**(9), 1255–1268 (2012)
15. Qian, X., et al.: Explicit formulas for pricing of callable mortgage-backed securities in a case of prepayment rate negatively correlated with interest rates. J. Math. Anal. Appl. **393**(2), 421–433 (2012)
16. Wang, Y.: Counterparty risk pricing. In: Proceedings of the China-Canada Quantitative Finance Problem Solving Workshop. Royal Bank of Canada (2008)

Method of Node Importance Measurement in Urban Road Network

Dan-qi Liu[1], Jia-lin Wang[1], Xiao-lu Li[1], Xin-ming Yu[1], Kang Song[2],
Xi Zhang[2], Fang-shu Lei[2], Peng Zhang[3], and Guang-yu Zhu[1(✉)]

[1] MOE Key Laboratory for Transportation Complex Systems Theory
and Technology, Beijing Jiaotong University, Beijing 100044, China
gyzhu@bjtu.edu.cn.com
[2] Beijing Key Laboratory of Urban Traffic Operation Simulation and Decision
Support, Beijing Transport Institute, Beijing 100073, China
[3] Transport Planning and Research Institute, Ministry of Transport,
Beijing 100028, China

Abstract. The node importance measurement plays an important role in analyzing the reliability of the urban road network. In this thesis, the topological
structure, geographic information and traffic flow characteristics of urban road
network are all considered, and methods of node importance measurement of
urban road network are proposed based on a spatially weighted degree model
and h-index from different perspectives. Experiments are given to show the
efficiency and practicability of the proposed methods.

Keywords: Urban road network · Node importance
Spatially weighted degree · The hansen index · H-index

1 Introduction

The urban road network can be abstracted into a connected graph composed of nodes
and edges. Node is an important unit of network connectivity system to find out the
important 'core nodes' in the road network, the key is to explore the method of
quantifying the importance of the nodes, namely, to study the important measurement
methods of nodes. So it is necessary through the research of methods of node important
degree, it is concluded that an effective method to measure the importance of nodes,
and then find out the important node of city road network, focus on to them, to
strengthen protection and management, to improve the reliability of urban road network, urban traffic safety and effective operation.

Node degree only considers the node information about themselves, cantona, etc.
on the basis of considering the information of neighbor nodes, think the importance of
nodes is proportional to the node and its neighbor node degree of the two. The indicators based on the global attribute of the network are involved Betweenness centrality,
Closeness centrality and eigenvector centrality. Index based on network location
attribute. Kitsak (2010) et al. proposed the indicator of the position of the node in the
network – k-shell.

2 Node Importance Measurement Based on Spatial Weighting

2.1 Spatial Weighted Model

Wan [2] proposed a space-weighted node degree model considering the road grade and the length of the road. The space weighted model can be expressed as:

$$N_d^i = \sum_{t=1}^{ec} c_t \left(1 + \omega \frac{l_t - l_{\min}}{l_{\max} - l_{\min}} \right) \tag{1}$$

ec is the number of edges connecting nodes i, c_t is the level of the first link to which the node i is connected, l_t is the length of the first link t to which the node i is connected, $l_{\min}$ and $l_{\max}$ are the minimum and maximum length of all links in the entire network, ω is the weight coefficient for the importance of link length in a particular area.

2.2 The Improvement of Space-Weighted Model

Improvement method

Traffic congestion is easily caused by the small number of lanes Therefore, in the urban road network, the number of lanes has a significant impact on node importance.

Based on the Wan model, this paper considers the influence of the number of lanes on the node importance and proposes an improved space weighted (ISWD) model, which can be expressed as:

$$k_d^i = C_d^i + \sum_{t=1}^{ec} c_t \left(\omega_1 \frac{l_t - l_{\min}}{l_{\max} - l_{\min}} + \omega_2 \frac{n_t - n_{\min}}{n_{\max} - n_{\min}} \right) \tag{2}$$

C_d^i is the traditional method of determining the node degree, c_t is the level which node i connected to the road t, n_t is the number of lanes which node i connected to the road t, ω_1 is the section length importance weight coefficient, ω_2 is the lane number importance weight coefficient, $\omega_1 + \omega_2 = 1$.

Evaluation criteria

In this paper, we use sequence difference DF to evaluate the performance of node importance measure method. The difference between the two sequences is expressed as:

$$DF(X, Y) = \frac{\sum_{i=1}^{n} (x_i - y_i)^2}{n} \tag{3}$$

X, Y are the given sequences, x_i, y_i are the sequence

$$Sum(X) = \sum_j^m DF(X, Y_j) \tag{4}$$

m is the sequence number, Y_j is the sequence which number is j.

3 H-Index Based Node Importance Measurement Method

3.1 Road Network Node Traffic Flow Correlation Analysis Theory

Due to the connectivity of the urban road network, there is often a relationship of different intensities between the traffic flows at the intersection of road networks [5].

Data Preprocessing
There are some problems in the data transmission such as errors and manual operation errors, the traffic flow data acquired from the detectors will be lacking, invalid, wrong and inaccurate, so it is necessary to carry out some pre-deal with.

Network Node Correlation Coefficient

(1) Establish the original traffic flow matrix between intersections:
(2) Data normalization
(3) find the correlation coefficient matrix

Section Cited Coefficient

$$h_{ij} = \left[(r_{ij} - \min r_{ij}) \div \frac{1 - \min r_{ij}}{m} \right] \tag{5}$$

h_{ij} is the section index for node i and node j. r_{ij} is the correlation coefficient between intersections, m is the number of intersections. Then we can get the node index matrix H between nodes:

$$H = \left(h_{ij} \right)_{m \times m} \tag{6}$$

3.2 Methods for Calculating the Importance of Urban Road Network Node Based on h Index

Firstly define the index h_r and index g_r of the node.

$$h_r^i = \max(k) : c_k^i \geq k \tag{7}$$

$$g_r^i = \max(k) : \sum_k c_k^i \geq k^2 \tag{8}$$

Evaluation criteria

(1) intersection degree

$$Sim(X, Y, k) = \frac{\mathrm{card}(X \cap Y)}{k} = \frac{\mathrm{card}\left(top_i^k \cap top_j^k\right)}{k} \tag{9}$$

(2) intersection value

$$rank_i^k|(X \cap Y) = \frac{\sum\limits_{v \subset X \cap Y} sequ_i^v}{card(X \cap Y)} \tag{10}$$

4   Case Analysis

This section chooses the importance of the regional research road network nodes within the scope of Shuiyangjiang Avenue in As shown in Fig. 1 (Table 1).

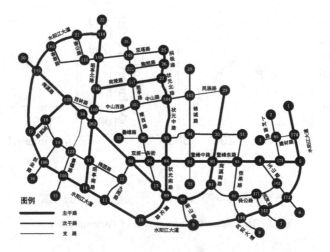

Fig. 1. The road network topology diagram within the confines of Shuiyangjiang Road

4.1   Network Node Traffic Flow Correlation Analysis

(1) data preprocessing
The traffic data of 3 different road network nodes are selected and their traffic flow statistics are plotted as shown in Fig. 2.

Table 1. Traffic volume table of lanes in intersection

Name	Type	Remarks
SSID	VARCHAR2(30)	Mount ID
CDBH	NUMBER(2)	Lane number
BEGINTIME	DATE	Statistics start time
ENDTIME	DATE	Statistics end time
Flow	NUMBER (5)	The number of vehicles counted in five minutes

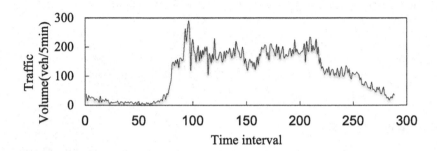

a) HK-90

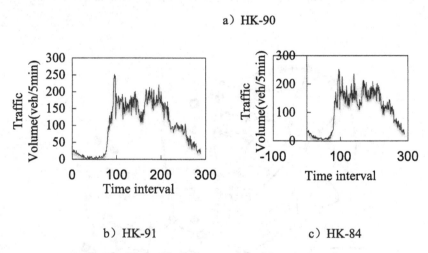

b) HK-91   c) HK-84

Fig. 2. The traffic flow sequence of three intersections

4.2   Based on the h Index Node Importance Measurement Results

h_r, g_r are shown in Table 3. Calculate the intersection of the first ten nodes of the two sorted sequences and intersection values *rank* are as follows:

$$Sim\left(top_{h_r}^{10}, top_{g_r}^{10}\right) = 0.6, \; rank_{h_r}^{10}\big|\left(top_{h_r}^{10}, top_{g_r}^{10}\right) = 2.33, \; rank_{g_r}^{10}\big|\left(top_{h_r}^{10}, top_{g_r}^{10}\right) = 1.83,$$

Table 3. h_r index and g_r index of nodes

Node number	h_r	Sort	g_r	Sort
HK-101	29	3	32	2
HK-103	27	19	30	20
HK-104	28	12	32	2
......				
HK-94	25	30	30	20
HK-95	25	30	30	20
HK-96	27	19	31	10

$\Delta rank(h_r, g_r, 10) = 2.33 - 1.83 = 0.5 < 0$, because of this, nodes based on g_r exponential identification are more important.

5 Conclusion

(1) An improved spatial weighted model is proposed for the study of the importance of urban road network nodes. This flexibility makes the model suitable for different types of spatial networks.

(2) Propose a method to calculate the importance degree of urban road network node based on Hansen index.

(3) Propose the method of calculating the degree of importance of city road network node based on h index - index and index.

Acknowledgment. This work is supported by the National key research and development plan of Ministry of science and technology (2016YFB1200203-02, 2016YFC0802206-2), the National Science Foundation of China (Nos. 61572069,61503022), the Fundamental Research Funds for the Central Universities (Nos. 2017YJS308, 2017JBM301), Beijing Municipal Science and Technology Project (Z161100005116006, Z171100004417024); Shenzhen city public traffic facilities construction projects (BYTD-KT-002-2).

References

1. Hirsch, J.E.: An index to quantify an individual's scientific research output. Proc. Natl. Acad. Sci. U.S.A. **102**(46), 16569 (2005)
2. Wan, N., Zhan, F., Cai, Z.: A spatially weighted degree model for network vulnerability analysis. Geo-spatial Inf. Sci. **14**(4), 274–281 (2011)
3. Taylor, M.A.P., Sekhar, S.V.C., D'Este, G.M.: Application of accessibility based methods for vulnerability analysis of strategic road networks. Netw. Spat. Econ. **6**(3–4), 267–291 (2006)
4. Peng, Z., Zhang, X-Y.: Management operations research course. Tsinghua University Press, Beijing, Jiaotong University Press, Beijing (2008)
5. Yu, P., Jing, Z.: Traffic flow forecasting based on correlativity of urban intersections. Traffic Comput. **23**(1), 31–34 (2005)

AdaBoost-LSTM Ensemble Learning for Financial Time Series Forecasting

Shaolong Sun[1,2], Yunjie Wei[1,3(✉)], and Shouyang Wang[1,2,3]

[1] Academy of Mathematics and Systems Science, Chinese Academy of Sciences, Beijing 100190, China
weiyunjie@amss.ac.cn
[2] School of Economics and Management, University of Chinese Academy of Sciences, Beijing 100190, China
[3] Center for Forecasting Science, Chinese Academy of Sciences, Beijing 100190, China

Abstract. A hybrid ensemble learning approach is proposed to forecast financial time series combining AdaBoost algorithm and Long Short-Term Memory (LSTM) network. Firstly, by using AdaBoost algorithm the database is trained to get the training samples. Secondly, the LSTM is utilized to forecast each training sample separately. Thirdly, AdaBoost algorithm is used to integrate the forecasting results of all the LSTM predictors to generate the ensemble results. Two major daily exchange rate datasets and two stock market index datasets are selected for model evaluation and comparison. The empirical results demonstrate that the proposed AdaBoost-LSTM ensemble learning approach outperforms some other single forecasting models and ensemble learning approaches. This suggests that the AdaBoost-LSTM ensemble learning approach is a highly promising approach for financial time series data forecasting, especially for the time series data with nonlinearity and irregularity, such as exchange rates and stock indexes.

Keywords: Financial time series forecasting
Long short-term memory network · AdaBoost algorithm · Ensemble learning

1 Introduction

Financial markets are affected by many factors, such as economic conditions, political events, traders' expectations and so on. Hence, financial time series forecasting is usually regarded as one of the most challenging tasks due to the nonlinearity and irregularity. How to forecast financial time series accurately is still an open question with respect to the economic and social organization of modern society. Many common econometric and statistical models have been applied to forecast financial time series, such as autoregressive integrated moving average (ARIMA) model [1], vector auto-regression (VAR) model [2] and error correction model (ECM) [3]. However, traditional models fail to capture the nonlinearity and complexity of financial time series which lead to poor forecasting accuracy. Hence, exploring more effective forecasting methods, which possess enough learning capacity, is really necessary for forecasting

© Springer International Publishing AG, part of Springer Nature 2018
Y. Shi et al. (Eds.): ICCS 2018, LNCS 10862, pp. 590–597, 2018.
https://doi.org/10.1007/978-3-319-93713-7_55

financial time series. Thus, nonlinear and more complex artificial intelligence methods are introduced to forecast financial time series, such as artificial neural networks (ANNs) [4, 5], support vector regression (SVR) [6] and deep learning method [7].

The forecasting accuracy of those nonlinear artificial intelligence methods are usually better than the common econometric and statistical models, while they also suffer from many problems, such as parameter optimization and overfitting. Hence, many hybrid forecasting approaches are proposed to get better forecasting performance [8–13]. So far, the decomposition ensemble learning approach has been widely used to forecast time series in many fields, such as financial time series forecasting [14, 15], crude oil price forecasting [16], nuclear energy consumption forccasting [17], PM2.5 concentration forecasting [18], etc. According to the existing literatures, ANNs are the most common used methods both in single model forecasting and hybrid model forecasting, which demonstrates that ANNs are really suitable for time series forecasting. If the advantages of different ANNs methods are combined, a better forecasting performance can be obtained. Long short-term memory (LSTM) neural network is a kind of deep neural networks, while it possesses similar properties of recurrent neural network (RNN). Therefore, LSTM is a better choice for financial time series forecasting. In addition, the above ensemble learning approach usually chooses AdaBoost to integrate different LSTM forecasters.

In this study, an AdaBoost-based LSTM ensemble learning approach is firstly proposed to forecast financial time series, combining AdaBoost ensemble algorithm and LSTM neural network. LSTM is considered as weak forecasters and AdaBoost is utilized as an ensemble tool. The rest of this paper is organized as follows: the proposed method is briefly introduced in Sect. 2. Section 3 gives the empirical results and Sect. 4 provides the conclusions.

2 AdaBoost-LSTM Ensemble Learning Approach

Suppose there is a time series, we would like to make the m-step ahead forecasting. It is noticing that the iterative forecasting strategy is implemented in this paper, which can be expressed as:

$$\hat{x}_{t+m} = f(x_t, x_{t-1}, \ldots, x_{t-(p-1)}) \tag{1}$$

where $\hat{x}$ is the forecasting value, x_t is the actual value in period t, and p denotes the lag orders.

In this study, the AdaBoost algorithm is introduced to integrate a set of LSTM predictors. An AdaBoost-LSTM ensemble learning approach is proposed for financial time series forecasting, and the flowchart is illustrated in Fig. 1. The proposed AdaBoost-LSTM ensemble learning approach consists of three main steps:

(1) The sampling weights $\{D_n^t\}$ of the training samples $\{x_t\}_{t=1}^{T}$ are calculated as follows:

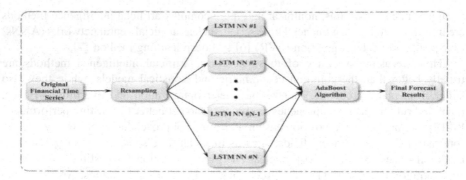

Fig. 1. The flowchart of the AdaBoost-LSTM ensemble learning approach.

$$D_n^t = \frac{1}{N}, n = (1, 2, \ldots, N; t = 1, 2, \ldots, T) \qquad (2)$$

where N is the number of LSTM predictors, T is the number of training samples.

(2) The LSTM predictor F_n is trained by the training samples which are sampled according to the sampling weights D_n^t.

(3) The foresting error $\{e_n^t\}$ and ensemble weights $\{W_n\}$ of the LSTM predictor F_n are calculated as follows:

$$e_n^t = \frac{|x_i - \hat{x}_i|}{x_i}, (n = 1, 2, \ldots, N; t = 1, 2, \ldots, T) \qquad (3)$$

$$w_n = \frac{1}{2}\ln\left(\frac{1 - \sum_{t=1}^{T} e_n^t}{\sum_{t=1}^{T} e_n^t}\right) \qquad (4)$$

(4) Update the sampling weights D_{n+1}^t of the training samples $\{x_t\}_{t=1}^T$ as follows:

$$D_{n+1}^t = \frac{D_n^t \beta_n^t}{\sum_{t=1}^{T} D_n^t \beta_n^t} \qquad (5)$$

where $\beta_n^t = exp(e_n^t)$ is the update rate of training sample x_t.

(5) Repeat the step 2–4 until all the LSTM predictors are obtained.

(6) The final forecasting result is generated by integrating the forecasting results of all the LSTM predictors with ensemble weights.

3 Empirical Study

3.1 Data Description and Evaluation Criteria

The data in this research comprises of two typical stock indexes (S&P 500 index and Shanghai composite index (SHCI)) and two main exchange rates (the euro against the US dollars (EUR/USD) and the US dollars against the China yuan (USD/CNY)). The historical data are daily data, collected from the Wind Database (http://www.wind.com.cn/). The datasets are then divided into in-sample subsets and out-of-sample subsets, as illustrated in Table 1.

Table 1. In-sample and out-of-sample dataset of the stock indexes and exchange rates.

Time Series	Sample type	From	To	Sample size
S&P 500	in-sample	January 2, 2015	December 30, 2016	504
	out-of-sample	January 3, 2017	May 31, 2017	103
SHCI	in-sample	January 5, 2015	December 30, 2016	488
	out-of-sample	January 3, 2017	May 31, 2017	97
EUR/USD	in-sample	January 1, 2015	December 30, 2016	527
	out-of-sample	January 2, 2017	May 31, 2017	108
USD/CNY	in-sample	January 5, 2015	December 30, 2016	488
	out-of-sample	January 3, 2017	May 31, 2017	97

Table 2 shows the descriptive statistics of those research data. The difference of statistics between the four series can be obviously seen from Table 2.

Table 2. The descriptive statistics of the stock indexes and exchange rates.

Time series	Minimum	Maximum	Mean	Std.*	Skewness	Kurtosis
S&P 500	1828.08	2415.82	2123.51	127.69	0.50	2.90
SHCI	2655.66	5166.35	3332.45	488.95	1.71	5.69
EURUSD	1.04	1.21	1.10	0.03	0.09	2.98
USDCNY	6.19	6.96	6.54	0.25	0.15	1.70

Note: Std.* refers to the standard deviation.

In order to evaluate the forecasting performance of the proposed AdaBoost-LSTM ensemble learning approach, mean absolute percentage error (MAPE) and directional symmetry (DS) are employed to evaluate the level forecasting accuracy and directional forecasting accuracy, respectively. MAPE and DS are defined as follows:

$$MAPE = \frac{1}{n} \sum\nolimits_{t=1}^{n} \left| \frac{Y_t - \hat{Y}_t}{Y_t} \right| * 100\% \tag{6}$$

$$DS = \frac{1}{n-1}\sum_{i=2}^{n} d_i \times 100\%, \ d_i = \begin{cases} 1, (y_i - y_{i-1})(\hat{y}_i - y_{i-1}) \geq 0 \\ 0, \text{otherwise} \end{cases} \tag{7}$$

where $\hat{y}_i$ is the forecasting value, y_i is the actual value, and n is the number of observation samples.

3.2   Forecasting Performance Comparison

The forecasting performances of the proposed AdaBoost-LSTM ensemble learning approach and benchmarks are discussed in this section. Tables 3, 4, 5 and 6 show the comparison results of MAPE and DS evaluation criteria, which show that the out-of-sample forecasting performance of the proposed approach is better than that of the benchmarks for all of the four financial time series and demonstrates that the proposed approach is an effective tool for financial time series forecasting.

Table 3. Forecasting performance of different models for stock indexes

	Models	S&P 500		SHCI	
		MAPE (%)	DS (%)	MAPE (%)	DS (%)
Single forecasts	ARIMA	4.973	52.43	5.162	51.55
	MLPNN	3.114	63.11	2.661	55.67
	SVR	2.025	66.02	2.126	60.82
	ELM	1.974	66.02	1.024	59.79
	LSTM	1.045	66.99	0.925	62.89
Ensemble forecasts	AdaBoost-MLP	1.023	70.87	0.918	67.01
	AdaBoost-SVR	0.841	72.82	1.106	71.13
	AdaBoost-ELM	0.782	71.84	0.692	70.10
	AdaBoost-LSTM	0.413	74.76	0.312	73.20

As shown in Tables 3, 4, 5 and 6, the proposed approach significantly outperforms all of the benchmark models by means of level forecasting accuracy and directional forecasting accuracy for the stock indexes and exchange rates. Overall, the ensemble learning approaches outperform the single models, while individual LSTM, ELM, SVR and MLP models consistently outperform ARIMA models in terms of MAPE and DS. Moreover, the proposed AdaBoost-LSTM ensemble learning approach produces 19.44–22.33% better directional forecasts than ARIMA models, reaching up to an accuracy rate of 76.68% in out-of-sample directional forecasting for the EUR/USD.

In summary, some interesting findings can be summarized: (1) the proposed AdaBoost-LSTM outperforms all of the benchmark models in different forecasting horizons, which implies that the AdaBoost-LSTM ensemble learning approach is a powerful learning approach for financial time series forecasting in both level accuracy and directional accuracy; (2) it clearly shows that the hybrid ensemble approach with AdaBoost is much better than the one without ensemble by means of level accuracy and directional accuracy, which reveals that AdaBoost is a more effective ensemble

Table 4. Forecasting performance of different models for exchange rates series.

	Models	EURUSD		USDCNY	
		MAPE (%)	DS (%)	MAPE (%)	DS (%)
Single forecasts	ARIMA	4.169	57.41	3.973	55.67
	MLPNN	1.973	67.59	2.034	60.82
	SVR	1.164	70.37	1.615	70.10
	ELM	1.035	68.52	0.993	67.01
	LSTM	0.917	69.44	1.024	69.07
Ensemble forecasts	AdaBoost-MLP	0.643	75.00	0.781	71.13
	AdaBoost-SVR	0.534	73.15	0.497	72.16
	AdaBoost-ELM	0.346	74.07	0.268	74.23
	AdaBoost-LSTM	0.172	76.85	0.113	76.29

Table 5. MAPE comparison with different ensemble forecasting approaches.

	Ensemble models	Number of forecasters				
		K = 10	K = 20	K = 30	K = 40	K = 50
S&P 500	AdaBoost-MLP	1.023	0.993	1.126	1.205	1.021
	AdaBoost-SVR	0.841	0.917	0.864	0.968	0.845
	AdaBoost-ELM	0.782	0.754	0.793	0.801	0.785
	AdaBoost-LSTM	0.413	0.397	0.402	0.419	0.385
SHCI	AdaBoost-MLP	0.918	1.216	1.039	1.114	1.063
	AdaBoost-SVR	1.106	0.987	1.025	1.203	1.287
	AdaBoost-ELM	0.692	0.682	0.705	0.712	0.695
	AdaBoost-LSTM	0.312	0.295	0.323	0.298	0.347
EUR/USD	AdaBoost-MLP	0.643	0.711	0.669	0.683	0.702
	AdaBoost-SVR	0.534	0.602	0.585	0.596	0.562
	AdaBoost-ELM	0.346	0.369	0.401	0.327	0.364
	AdaBoost-LSTM	0.172	0.119	0.187	0.254	0.306
USD/CNY	AdaBoost-MLP	0.781	0.816	0.798	0.833	0.778
	AdaBoost-SVR	0.497	0.506	0.485	0.523	0.519
	AdaBoost-ELM	0.268	0.314	0.296	0.337	0.274
	AdaBoost-LSTM	0.113	0.107	0.235	0.196	0.273

algorithm; (3) the forecasting performance of hybrid ensemble learning approaches are significantly better than single models. The possible reason is that the ensemble can dramatically improve the forecasting performance of single models.

Table 6. DS comparison with different ensemble forecasting approaches.

	Ensemble models	Number of forecasters				
		K = 10	K = 20	K = 30	K = 40	K = 50
S&P 500	AdaBoost-MLP	70.87	69.90	71.84	70.87	69.90
	AdaBoost-SVR	72.82	70.87	70.87	72.82	73.79
	AdaBoost-ELM	71.84	72.82	72.82	73.79	71.84
	AdaBoost-LSTM	74.76	74.76	73.79	74.76	75.73
SHCI	AdaBoost-MLP	67.01	65.98	67.01	64.95	68.04
	AdaBoost-SVR	71.13	69.07	70.10	71.13	69.07
	AdaBoost-ELM	70.10	71.13	69.07	70.10	71.13
	AdaBoost-LSTM	73.20	74.23	72.16	75.26	74.23
EUR/USD	AdaBoost-MLP	75.00	72.22	74.07	73.15	74.07
	AdaBoost-SVR	73.15	74.07	75.00	73.15	72.22
	AdaBoost-ELM	74.07	73.15	73.15	74.07	76.85
	AdaBoost-LSTM	76.85	75.93	76.85	75.93	77.78
USD/CNY	AdaBoost-MLP	71.13	70.10	72.16	70.10	74.23
	AdaBoost-SVR	72.16	75.26	73.20	74.23	74.23
	AdaBoost-ELM	74.23	73.20	74.23	72.16	72.16
	AdaBoost-LSTM	76.29	77.32	75.26	75.26	76.29

4   Conclusions

This paper proposes an AdaBoost-LSTM ensemble learning approach which employs AdaBoost algorithm to integrate the forecasting results of LSTM forecasts. Then, the proposed AdaBoost-LSTM ensemble learning approach is applied to forecast financial time series, including stock indexes and exchange rates. For model evaluation and model comparison, four typical financial time series data are collected to test the model performance. The empirical results show that the proposed AdaBoost-LSTM ensemble learning approach can significantly improve forecasting performance and outperform some other single forecasting models and some other ensemble learning approaches in terms of both level forecasting accuracy and directional forecasting accuracy, which demonstrates that the proposed approach is really a promising approach for financial time series forecasting. What's more, the proposed approach can also be employed to solve other complex time series forecasting problems, such as crude oil price forecasting, wind speed forecasting, traffic flow forecasting, etc.

References

1. Chortareas, G., Jiang, Y., Nankervis, J.C.: Forecasting exchange rate volatility using high-frequency data: Is the euro different? Int. J. Forecast. **27**(4), 1089–1107 (2011)
2. Carriero, A., Kapetanios, G., Marcellino, M.: Forecasting exchange rates with a large Bayesian VAR. Int. J. Forecast. **25**(2), 400–417 (2009)

3. Moosa, I.A., Vaz, J.J.: Cointegration, error correction and exchange rate forecasting. J. Int. Financ. Markets Institutions Money **44**, 21–34 (2016)
4. Galeshchuk, S.: Neural networks performance in exchange rate prediction. Neurocomputing **172**, 446–452 (2016)
5. Zhang, G., Hu, M.Y.: Neural network forecasting of the British pound/US dollar exchange rate. Omega **26**(4), 495–506 (1998)
6. Huang, S., Chuang, P., Wu, C., Lai, H.: Chaos-based support vector regressions for exchange rate forecasting. Expert Syst. Appl. **37**(12), 8590–8598 (2010)
7. Shen, F., Chao, J., Zhao, J.: Forecasting exchange rate using deep belief networks and conjugate gradient method. Neurocomputing **167**, 243–253 (2015)
8. Chen, A., Leung, M.T.: Regression neural network for error correction in foreign exchange forecasting and trading. Comput. Oper. Res. **31**(7), 1049–1068 (2004)
9. Nag, A.K., Mitra, A.: Forecasting daily foreign exchange rates using genetically optimized neural networks. J. Forecast. **21**(7), 501–511 (2002)
10. Sermpinis, G., Stasinakis, C., Theofilatos, K., Karathanasopoulos, A.: Modeling, forecasting and trading the EUR exchange rates with hybrid rolling genetic algorithms—Support vector regression forecast combinations. Eur. J. Oper. Res. **247**(3), 831–846 (2015)
11. Sermpinis, G., Theofilatos, K., Karathanasopoulos, A., Georgopoulos, E.F., Dunis, C.: Forecasting foreign exchange rates with adaptive neural networks using radial-basis functions and particle swarm optimization. Eur. J. Oper. Res. **225**(3), 528–540 (2013)
12. Yu, L., Wang, S., Lai, K.K.: A novel nonlinear ensemble forecasting model incorporating GLAR and ANN for foreign exchange rates. Comput. Oper. Res. **32**(10), 2523–2541 (2005)
13. Yu, L., Wang, S., Lai, K.K.: Forecasting crude oil price with an EMD-based neural network ensemble learning paradigm. Energy Econ. **30**(5), 2623–2635 (2008)
14. Plakandaras, V., Papadimitriou, T., Gogas, P.: Forecasting daily and monthly exchange rates with machine learning techniques. J. Forecast. **34**(7), 560–573 (2015)
15. Yu, L., Wang, S., Lai, K.K.: A neural-network-based nonlinear metamodeling approach to financial time series forecasting. Appl. Soft Comput. **9**(2), 563–574 (2009)
16. Yu, L., Wang, Z., Tang, L.: A decomposition-ensemble model with data-characteristic-driven reconstruction for crude oil price forecasting. Appl. Energ. **156**, 251–267 (2015)
17. Tang, L., Yu, L., Wang, S., Li, J., Wang, S.: A novel hybrid ensemble learning paradigm for nuclear energy consumption forecasting. Appl. Energ. **93**, 432–443 (2012)
18. Niu, M., Wang, Y., Sun, S., Li, Y.: A novel hybrid decomposition-and-ensemble model based on CEEMD and GWO for short-term PM2.5 concentration forecasting. Atmos. Environ. **134**, 168–180 (2016)

Analysis of Bluetooth Low Energy Detection Range Improvements for Indoor Environments

Jay Pancham[1]([⊠]), Richard Millham[1], and Simon James Fong[2]

[1] Durban University of Technology, Durban, South Africa
{panchamj, richardml}@dut.ac.za
[2] University of Macau, Taipa, Macau SAR
ccfong@umac.mo

Abstract. Real Time Location Systems (RTLS) research identifies Bluetooth Low Energy as one of the technologies that promise an acceptable response to the requirements for indoor environments. Against this background we investigate the latest developments with Bluetooth especially with regards its range and possible use in the indoor environments. Several different venues are used at the University to conduct the experiment to mimic typical indoor environments. The results indicated an acceptable range in line of sight as well as through obstacles such as glass, drywall partitions and solid brick wall. Future research will investigate methods to determine the position of Bluetooth Low Energy devices for possible location of patients and assets.

Keywords: Bluetooth low energy · BLE · Real Time Location System
RSSI · Indoor positioning

1 Introduction

Over the past several years, indoor localization has grown into an important research topic, attracting much attention in the networking research community [1]. The increase in popularity for positioning services offered by smart devices and their related technology has indicated a turning in the field of indoor localization [2]. Our ultimate goal is to design a cost effective and efficient RTLS within the constraints identified in our previous paper [3] for indoor environment in particular a Healthcare environment. Previous work by [4] also evaluated the technologies for indoor RTLS as well as identified the methods used in determining locations. This paper determines the possible range and throughput similar to quantitative technological evaluations by [5] with Bluetooth LE in different scenarios of an indoor environment. Future work will explore Bluetooth LE mesh networking for indoor localization to enhance scalability and detection range.

The rest of the paper is organized as follows. Section 2 illustrates the basic concepts of indoor localization. Section 3 defines the methodology used to conduct the experiments and obtain the results. In Sect. 4, the authors discuss the results obtained from the experiments. Thereafter conclusions and future work are discussed.

© Springer International Publishing AG, part of Springer Nature 2018
Y. Shi et al. (Eds.): ICCS 2018, LNCS 10862, pp. 598–609, 2018.
https://doi.org/10.1007/978-3-319-93713-7_56

2   Literature Review

2.1   Technologies and Techniques for RTLS

A number of different technologies have been tested for use in RTLS in the past with varied levels of success. However, due to the availability of newer technologies the best technology within the constraints need to identified for possible use for indoor RTLS. Pancham et al. evaluated the most popular technologies of RTLS published in recent peer reviewed works. The most appropriate attributes in terms of Real Time Location System (RTLS) from literature as well as from an exemplar for a typical indoor environment such as Healthcare were chosen to assess these technologies. In addition to the exemplar of a hospital, survey data of 23 US hospitals [6] was used in the evaluation process. In our previous paper review of literature we investigated technologies such as WiFi, Bluetooth and RFID and determined evaluation criteria to be cost [7], energy consumption [8], detection range [7], size and accuracy [9]. A typical domain such as Healthcare has other constraints such as electromagnetic interference [10, 11] which we now mitigate with low power transmission level but space constraints limited our selection to the most appropriate and the most common attributes.

Attempts to mitigate these constraints using popular RTLS technologies researched by [4] include Radio Frequency Identification Devices (RFID), Bluetooth classic, Bluetooth LE, Zigbee and Wi-Fi. Lee et al. compared BLE and ZigBee technologies and used a single fixed distance of 1 m and did not have conclusive results indicating which technology is better as wireless transmission is greatly affected by practical situations, such as the realistic environment interferences [5]. However this experiment did not provide measurements of aspects such as RSSI, throughput beyond this fixed distance which is needed for a proper network technology evaluation for the fixed distance.

A number of different methodologies exist to increase the accuracy, the most popular being the RSSI technique which increases accuracy to 1–2 (m) [12]. An available improvement of RSSI involves a Kamlan filter which increases Bluetooth accuracy to 0.47 m but at a cost of increased size (due to larger storage requirements) and increased power consumption due to increased computational cost [7]. As can be seen these RSSI and Kamlan filter techniques adds to the size form factor for Bluetooth and energy consumption. An example of Bluetooth system is Bluetooth Local Infotainment Point (BLIP) [13] which is a managed network offering access to LAN/ WAN via Bluetooth [14]. Such a network will require a number of BLIP nodes to which the bluetooth devices will connect to due to its limited range. These bluetooth nodes then provide access to the LAN/ WAN. With the advancement of Bluetooth LE such nodes will be minimized or eliminated depending on the environment.

Bluetooth classic also has drawbacks in crowded areas due to signal attenuation and interference. Bluetooth classic can transfer large quantities of data, but consumes battery life quickly and more costly than Bluetooth LE or other indoor localisations technologies [15]. In addition accuracy for RTLS differs at a cost in term of power consumption, size of device, and other factors. This gave birth to Bluetooth low energy (BLE) which is suitable to exchange small amounts of data consuming lower energy at a cheaper cost.

2.2   Bluetooth LE

Bluetooth Low Energy (BLE) is the power-version of Bluetooth that was built for the Internet of Things (IoT) making it perfect for devices that run for long periods on power sources, such as coin cell batteries or energy-harvesting devices [16]. One of the two systems of this version is Bluetooth low energy which transmits small packets of data whilst consuming significantly less power than the previous version of Bluetooth [8]. A BLE RTLS typically consists of a stationery anchor to detect the tags, a tag and the location engine to calculate the location [17]. BLE is an improvement and a later version of Bluetooth (BT) offering several advantages such as smaller form factor, lower cost and extended coverage. The point-to-point communication of the current BLE nodes have only limited coverage over a short range. Hence the proposal of a wireless mesh multi-hop network that has multiple nodes that are capable of communicating with each other to enable routing of packets to extend this limited coverage as a possible solution [18]. This distance can be extended further with the combination of current technologies that are more efficient.

Bluetooth® 5 released on 6 December 2016 is a transformative update on previous versions that significantly increases the range, speed and broadcast messaging capacity of Bluetooth applications. This version quadruples range and doubles speed of low energy connections while increasing the capacity of connectionless data broadcasts by eight times [19, 20]. These will impact on reliability, robustness, responsiveness. This latest version of Bluetooth will have quadruple the range, double the speed and an increased broadcasting capacity of 800% as compared to the Bluetooth Classic [21].

The earlier Bluetooth Classic version uses 79 channels with 1 MHz spacing whilst Bluetooth LE uses 40 channels with 2 MHz spacing in the unlicensed industrial, scientific and medical (ISM) band of 2.4 GHz. The range for Bluetooth LE extends from 2402 MHz (RF channel 0; logical channel 37) to 2480 MHz (RF channel 39; logical channel 39). Three channels (logical 37, 38 and 39) are so called advertising channels; logical channels 0 to 36 are data channels. The advertising channels are positioned so that they are not disturbed by the non-overlapping WLAN channels 1, 6 and 11 in the ISM band, see Fig. 1. Bluetooth LE now can provide the higher transmission speeds as a result of the increased 2402 MHz wider channels as compared to the Bluetooth classic 1 MHz channels. In addition to higher transmission speeds more data can be transmitted within these channels as a result of the higher transmission frequency.

2.3   Use of Bluetooth LE in an Indoor Environment

In order to understand the technologies used in indoor RTLS one must look at the early developments in this domain such as the RADAR system. This system was one of the first developed indoor positioning systems that use radio beacons and Received Signal Strength Indicator (RSSI) measurements for localization [2]. A number of authors have used RSSI for indoor location together with various methods such as triangulation, trilateration and fingerprinting to improve its accuracy. These different methods are required to improve the range as obstructions such as partitions, walls etc. cause degradation of the signal strength and in some cases completely blocked signals [22]. However, the determination of the indoor position of sensors is outside the scope of this paper.

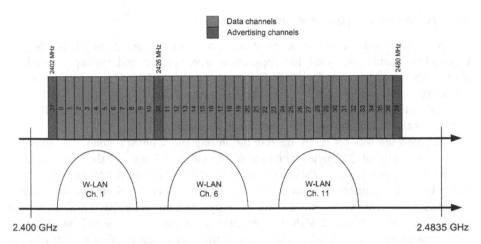

Fig. 1 Bluetooth LE channels.

3 Methodology

Our approach was to use Bluetooth LE to propose a cost effective indoor RTLS solution with low power consumption, scalability, and long detection range. In order to determine the maximum range that can be obtained within the constraints we used experimental methods to mimic and indoor environment given a Bluetooth LE v5 signal transmitted at the lowest energy level of −20 dBm. The aim of this experiment is to determine the maximum usable range indoors at clear line of sight, as well as through obstructions such as through glass door, dry wall and brick wall. Such obstructions represent partitions that would separate offices etc. in an actual indoor facility, hence representing as close as possible the actual environment. This methodology has sections that describe in detail the hardware selection and software configuration and the environment used for the experiment.

The experiment used the transmitted power level and packet size as independent variables. The power level was kept at the lowest level to establish the ranges and speed of transmission. The dependent variables were distance, obstructions resulting in different RSSI, throughput and length of time measurements. Using these variables, the following steps were used during the experiment:

Step 1: Measure and label the different predetermined distances.
Step 2: Setup the software on the Preview Development Kit (PDK)'s.
Step 3: Place the tester PDK at a fixed starting location.
Step 4: Place the responder PDK at the first measured point.
Step 5: Commence measurement of the RSSI and throughput.
Step 6: Move responder PDK to next measured point and repeat step 5.
Step 7: Stop when measurements are unusable or PDK's are disconnected.

3.1   Hardware Selection and Software Configuration

The hardware used for this experiment were two Nordic nRF 52840 PDK. Segger Embedded Studio was used for application development and testing as well as deployment onto the nRF 52840 BLE System on Chip (SoC). The selection of this latest BLE SoC was based on the many advantages identified by [20]. Nordic was selected as the preferred supplier due to its price advantage, feature set and availability over comparable features of SoC from Texas Instruments.

The software was set up to measure the throughput with Maximum Transmission Unit (MTU) size of 247 bytes, connection interval of 7.5 ms and the Physical layer (PHY) data rates was set to 2Ms/s. The Physical (PHY) layer of the Nordic nRF52832 and prior SoC's transmission was limited to 1 Ms/s as per the Nordic design specification [23]. With the advancement of technology, the latest NRF52840 SoC allows for transmission of 1 Ms/s or 2 Ms/s. Our intention is to implement the SoC in an indoor environment and hence the decision to test at the lowest transmission of −20 dBm to investigate the range and throughput. Broadcasting at the lowest level will limit the interference on other equipment and allow for more devices to be used within the same bands. One of the PDK boards was set as the tester whilst the other PDK board was set at the responder. Given limited resources, we relied on a single receiver-transmitter model. The tester sent out 1 MB of data and then queried how much of data was received by the responder. This tester PDK was connected to a laptop where Putty (a terminal emulator) was used to read the data via the USB interface. The measurements were repeated five times for each of the different distances in order to obtain an average reading. If the results showed a wide variance, the plan was to repeat the experiment multiple times. Once the data was captured the averages were calculated and reported.

3.2   Experiment Environment

The three different venues selected together with the measured distances to conduct the experiment mimicked different areas and hence is a close replica of an indoor environment similar to other research conducted [24].

The first venue selected was a multipurpose hall that is approximately 25 m² made of brick with glass doors on two opposite sides. Desks were placed at the measured intervals on which the PDK boards were placed. Data was collected at 5 m intervals up to a distance of 25 m within the hall and across obstruction such as the glass door and the brick wall where the PDK's were placed on either side of the obstruction.

The second venue was the board room that is approximately 20 m in length and made of glass panels and dry wall partitioning. Data was collected at 1 m intervals up 5 m and thereafter data was collected at 5 m intervals. Data was also collected with the glass door obstruction and the PDK's set from 2 to 6 m apart.

The third venue was an office floor of offices separated with dry wall partitioning. Tests were conducted to establish the connectivity and possible range that could be obtained through the different partitions. The different directions that were used for the measurements conducted for the office area are depicted in Fig. 5. Measurement 1 was conducted in a straight line with only the dry wall as the obstruction. These measurements were taken from 1 to 6 m at intervals of 1 m. The second measurement indicated by measurement 2 in Fig. 5 was conducted diagonally down a passage at intervals of 1 m up to 11 m. Measurement 3 was also diagonal but this time through three dry wall partitions as obstructions. This was done mainly to establish the maximum possible range. Measurement 4 was through a solid brick wall as the obstruction to confirm the loss of signal strength during its penetration through the brick wall.

4 Results

Data was collected in the hall, boardroom and the office. Figures 2, 3 and 4 indicate the RSSI, time and throughput for a distance up to 25 m. The data for the different attributes for the different venues are grouped together and indicate in their respective attribute graphs due to space constraints. The different colors in the legend indicate the different venues with their respective obstacles. In the hall the measurements were taken at 5 m intervals until the connectivity and transmission was unacceptable and data not usable. The measurements noted whilst the PDK boards were placed at different angles were not significantly different. Therefore, there additional measurements were not considered in the final analysis.

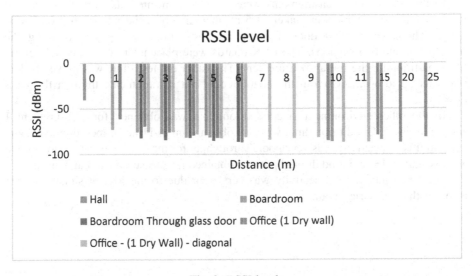

Fig. 2 RSSI levels

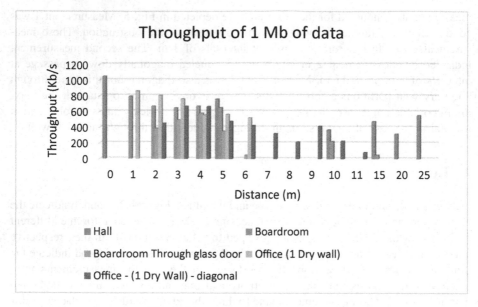

Fig. 3 Time to transmit 1 Mb of data

In the boardroom, measurements were taken at 1 m intervals from 1 to 5 m and thereafter measurements were taken at 5 m intervals up to the maximum usable distance. Thereafter a glass door, forming an obstruction, was placed dividing the boardroom into two sections. The PDK boards were placed 1 m on either side of the glass partition for the initial measurement. Thereafter the test PDK was moved at 1 m intervals up to 6 m. At 6.5 m the boards could not communicate through the glass door.

In the office environment, a good throughput was obtained for measurement 1 shown in Fig. 5. Good throughput was also obtained up to 11 m for measurement 2 and beyond this connectivity was very poor. Throughput for measurement 3 was good up to approximately 13 m. Good throughput was obtained for measurement 4 at a distance of 5 m but thereafter the connectivity was very poor due to the loss of signal strength through the solid brick wall.

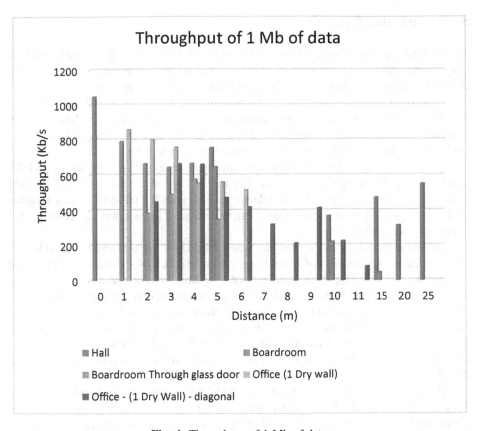

Fig. 4 Throughput of 1 Mb of data

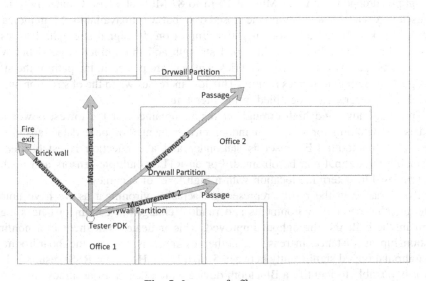

Fig. 5 Layout of office area

5 Discussion of Results

The time to transmit 1 Mb/s of data and throughput follow a nonlinear pattern which suggest that there are potential interfering variables in this experiment. Given the constraints, these interfering variables could not be isolated within this study.

A range of 25 m was obtained when transmitting at a level of −20 dBm in clear line of sight within the hall. The throughput of 759 Kbps at 5 m and 533 Kbps at 25 m indicates that data can be transmitted at longer ranges at higher speeds using Bluetooth LE v5. In the boardroom a through put of 793 Kbps at 1 m to 222 Kbps at 10 m was measured. However [1] obtained a transmission range of 2 m using Bluegiga USB dongle as a gateway and a RadBeacon Tag transmitting at the same level. This indicates that the environment delivers different results. Possible reasons for this variance could be related to the size of the boardroom as compared to the open hall as well as the makeup of the walls.

An interesting observation was that when the PDK's were placed either side of a glass door at a total distance of 2 m a lower throughput rate of 386 Kbps was measured compared to the highest throughput rate of 579 Kb/s obtained at a distance of 4 m between the PDK's with the same glass door as the obstruction. At 5 m the throughput was similar to that measured at 2 m. However, the throughput at 6 m deteriorated to 48 Kbps and at 6.5 m to an unacceptable level and in most cases disconnected completely. The RSSI measurements had little variation from 2 to 6 m. These readings across a class door are interesting as there may be reflections of the electromagnetic waves on the glass.

Measurements in the office area by Fig. 5 show that connectivity is possible up to a distance of 11 m and 13 m in the two passages respectively. This indicates that the Bluetooth LE signal transmitted at −20 dBm can penetrate a door and multiple drywall partitions. However due to the weakened signal the distance is not great. The throughput dropped from 227 Mb/s at 10 m to 82 Mb/s at 11 m. Connectivity in the fire escape was acceptable behind the closed door but was unavailable at 5 m indicating that the brick wall had a serious negative impact on the signal strength. The results indicate that in clear line of sight signal strength and throughput is good but when obstructions such as glass, partitions brick wall etc. are placed in the path of the signal the signal strength deteriorates rapidly. This loss increases when the obstruction such as a brick wall is denser as identified in the literature.

The long range and high throughput results obtained for the lowest power level used is encouraging for use in an indoor environment. For pure data transmission, given that Bluetooth LE sensor is stationary and a connection is established, an acceptable throughput can be obtained. For an RTLS, multiple sensors and methods must be used to determine location with a high level of accuracy.

The variance in the results represent an actual environment as we have noted a pattern within certain environments and random changes at certain distances e.g. at 15 m in the hall, the throughput improved. This indicates that there is a nonlinear relationship as distance increases. Another example is that in the boardroom the throughput dropped significantly between 5 m to 15 m. However, RSSI results indicate that it is possible to identify a Bluetooth device with a degree of accuracy (in an open space an RSSI level of approximately −80 dBm indicate a distance between 2 and 25 m, in an office environment an RSSI level of approximately −80 dBm indicate a distance between 2 and 13 m, whilst in the boardroom an RSSI level of approximately −80 dBm indicate a distance between 2 and 6 m. The RSSI level was measured in anticipation of future work to use this aspect as part of location determination.

6   Conclusion and Future Work

The primary focus of this paper was to test the latest Bluetooth LE v5 PDK's range and throughput in an indoor environment for future use in an RTLS. However, an accurate and reliable RTLS system within the constraints of an indoor environment such as Healthcare requires a well-designed architecture. The results obtained are promising to be used in an Indoor environment for data transmission as well as RTLS.

RTLS in Healthcare has the potential to enable efficient location of patients, employees and equipment. Although RTLS have realized benefits in some cases, further research was called for to reduce the serious technical impediments such as obstacle obstruction of signals to its implementation including asset management [6]. As a consequence, we researched the latest Bluetooth LE to establish through experimentation the possible range as well as the level of penetration through obstacles. Bluetooth LE can be configured into a low cost low energy network architecture enabling lower energy consumption [25] and extending the range. A combination of multiple methods such as triangulation, fingerprinting [26], block chain architecture and repeater tags (tags configured to forward messages) will be used to increase the location accuracy whilst minimizing energy consumption. Further research will be needed especially with regards RSSI measurements with their distances to expand on this paper's findings. The use of BLE devices, with low power consumption will extend battery life thereby reducing maintenance [5]. Due to the high volume of patients as well as the size of hospitals, especially those in the public sector, cost is an important constraint.

Some of these challenges such as network range can be realized by using mesh networks as well as intermediate sensors to link to other in the near vicinity. With the latest technology used unlike its predecessors the Bluetooth LE devices can form a mesh network to extend the network with the lowest possible energy consumption. A more detailed experiment with different values for variables such as transmission power levels, data packet size etc. will be conducted for improved and accurate performance in terms of indoor real time location. The results of this will be published in future articles. Furthermore, a prototype will be setup in a typical indoor environment such as Healthcare to test viability of the processes and newly designed architecture.

References

1. Wang, Y., Ye, Q., Cheng, J., Wang, L.: RSSI-based Bluetooth indoor localization. In: 2015 11th International Conference on Mobile Ad-Hoc and Sensor Networks (MSN), pp. 165–171. IEEE (2015)
2. Thaljaoui, A., Val, T., Nasri, N., Brulin, D.: BLE localization using RSSI measurements and iRingLA. In: 2015 IEEE International Conference on Industrial Technology (ICIT), pp. 2178–2183. IEEE (2015)
3. Pancham, J., Millham, R., Fong, S.J.: Assessment of feasible methods used by the health care industry for real time location. In: Federated Conference on Computer Science and Information Systems, Poznań, Poland (2017)
4. Pancham, J., Millham, R., Fong, S.J.: Evaluation of real time location system technologies in the health care sector. In: 2017 17th International Conference on Computational Science and Its Applications (ICCSA), pp. 1–7. IEEE (2017)
5. Lee, J.-S., Dong, M.-F., Sun, Y.-H.: A preliminary study of low power wireless technologies: ZigBee and Bluetooth low energy. In: 2015 IEEE 10th Conference on Industrial Electronics and Applications (ICIEA), pp. 135–139. IEEE (2015)
6. Fisher, J.A., Monahan, T.: Evaluation of real-time location systems in their hospital contexts. Int. J. Med. Inf. **81**(10), 705–712 (2012)
7. Tsang, Y.P., Wu, C.-H., Ip, W.H., Ho, G.T.S., Tse, Y.K.: A Bluetooth-based indoor positioning system: a simple and rapid approach. Annu. J. IIE (HK) **35**(2014), 11–26 (2015)
8. Yu, B., Lisheng, X., Li, Y.: Bluetooth low energy (BLE) based mobile electrocardiogram monitoring system. In: 2012 International Conference on Information and Automation (ICIA), pp. 763–767. IEEE (2012)
9. Zhongliang, D., Yanpei, Y., Xie, Y., Neng, W., Lei, Y.: Situation and development tendency of indoor positioning. China Commun. **10**(3), 42–55 (2013)
10. Alemdar, H., Ersoy, C.: Wireless sensor networks for healthcare: a survey. Comput. Netw. **54**(15), 2688–2710 (2010)
11. Yao, W., Chu, C.-H., Li, Z.: The adoption and implementation of RFID technologies in healthcare: a literature review. J. Med. Syst. **36**(6), 3507–3525 (2012)
12. Bal, M., Xue, H., Shen, W., Ghenniwa, H.: A 3-D indoor location tracking and visualization system based on wireless sensor networks. In: 2010 IEEE International Conference on Systems Man and Cybernetics (SMC), pp. 1584–1590. IEEE (2010)
13. Kolodziej, K.W., Hjelm, J.: Local positioning systems: LBS applications and services. CRC Press, Boca Raton (2017)
14. Deak, G., Curran, K., Condell, J.: A survey of active and passive indoor localisation systems. Comput. Commun. **35**(16), 1939–1954 (2012)
15. Zaim, D., Bellafkih, M.: Bluetooth low energy (BLE) based geomarketing system. In: 2016 11th International Conference on Intelligent Systems: Theories and Applications (SITA), pp. 1–6. IEEE (2016)
16. Bluetooth Low Energy (2016). https://www.bluetooth.com/what-is-bluetooth-technology/how-it-works/low-energy. Accessed 25 May 2017
17. Han, G., Klinker, G.J., Ostler, D., Schneider, A.: Testing a proximity-based location tracking system with Bluetooth low energy tags for future use in the OR. In: 2015 17th International Conference on E-health Networking, Application & Services (HealthCom), pp. 17–21. IEEE (2015)
18. Raza, S., Misra, P., He, Z., Voigt, T.: Building the internet of things with Bluetooth smart. Ad Hoc Networks (2016)

19. Bluetooth 5 (2016). https://www.bluetooth.com/what-is-bluetooth-technology/how-it-works/bluetooth5. Accessed 25 May 2017
20. B. S. I. Group: Bluetooth 5 Quadruples Range, Doubles Speed, Increases Data Broadcasting Capacity by 800% (2016). https://www.bluetooth.com/news/pressreleases/2016/06/16/-bluetooth-5-quadruples-rangedoubles-speedincreases-data-broadcasting-capacity-by-800
21. Schultz, B.: From cable replacement to the IoT Bluttooth 5. White Paper, December 2016
22. Abdullah, M.W., Fafoutis, X., Mellios, E., Klemm, M., Hilton, G.S.: Investigation into off-body links for wrist mounted antennas in Bluetooth systems. In: Antennas & Propagation Conference (LAPC), 2015 Loughborough, pp. 1–5. IEEE (2015)
23. nRF52832 Product Specification v1.4 (2016)
24. Larranaga, J., Muguira, L., Lopez-Garde, J.-M., Vazquez, J.-I.: An environment adaptive ZigBee-based indoor positioning algorithm. In 2010 International Conference on Indoor Positioning and Indoor Navigation (IPIN), pp. 1–8. IEEE (2010)
25. Ahmad, S., Lu, R., Ziaullah, M.: Bluetooth an optimal solution for personal asset tracking: a comparison of Bluetooth, RFID and miscellaneous anti-lost tracing technologies. Int. J. u-and e-Serv. Sci. Technol. 8(3), 179–188 (2015)
26. Jachimczyk, B., Dziak, D., Kulesza, W.J.: Using the fingerprinting method to customize RTLS based on the AoA ranging technique. Sensors 16(6), 876 (2016)

Study on an N-Parallel FENE-P Constitutive Model Based on Multiple Relaxation Times for Viscoelastic Fluid

Jingfa Li[1,2] ⬚, Bo Yu[1(✉)] ⬚, Shuyu Sun[2(✉)] ⬚,
and Dongliang Sun[1] ⬚

[1] School of Mechanical Engineering, Beijing Key Laboratory of Pipeline Critical Technology and Equipment for Deepwater Oil and Gas Development, Beijing Institute of Petrochemical Technology, Beijing 102617, China
yubobox@vip.163.com
[2] Computational Transport Phenomena Laboratory, Division of Physical Science and Engineering, King Abdullah University of Science and Technology, Thuwal 23955-6900, Saudi Arabia
shuyu.sun@kaust.edu.sa

Abstract. An N-parallel FENE-P constitutive model based on multiple relaxation times is proposed in this paper, which aims at accurately describing the apparent viscosity of viscoelastic fluid. The establishment of N-parallel FENE-P constitutive model and the numerical approach to calculate the apparent viscosity are presented in detail, respectively. To validate the performance of the proposed constitutive model, it is compared with the conventional FENE-P constitutive model (It only has single relaxation time) in estimating the apparent viscosity of two common viscoelastic fluids: polymer and surfactant solutions. The comparative results indicate the N-parallel FENE-P constitutive model can represent the apparent viscosity of polymer solutions more accurate than the traditional model in the whole range of shear rate (0.1 s^{-1}–1000 s^{-1}), and the advantage is more noteworthy especially when the shear rate is higher (10 s^{-1}–1000 s^{-1}). Despite both the proposed model and the traditional model can't capture the interesting shear thickening behavior of surfactant solutions, the proposed constitutive model still possesses advantage over the traditional one in depicting the apparent viscosity and first normal stress difference. In addition, the N-parallel FENE-P constitutive model demonstrates a better applicability and favorable adjustability of the model parameters.

Keywords: FENE-P constitutive model · N-parallel · Viscoelastic fluids
Multiple relaxation times · Apparent viscosity

1 Introduction

In 1948, Toms [1] first reported an interesting phenomenon that adding a little bit of additive, such as some kinds of polymer, into the turbulent flows would induce a drag reduction (DR) obviously in the 1st International Rheology Congress, it was later called turbulent DR effect or Toms' effect. From the 1950 to now, as two kinds of

© Springer International Publishing AG, part of Springer Nature 2018
Y. Shi et al. (Eds.): ICCS 2018, LNCS 10862, pp. 610–623, 2018.
https://doi.org/10.1007/978-3-319-93713-7_57

successful turbulent DR additives, the researches on turbulent DR mechanism and industrial applications of the polymer and surfactant attract a multitude of scholars' attentions. Among the research approaches, numerical simulation has become a significant tool to get insight into the DR mechanism of viscoelastic fluid with the rapid development of computer science in recent years. However, distinguishing from Newtonian fluid, the viscoelastic fluid shows complicated rheological properties and elastic effect. It is a prerequisite to build a constitutive model to describe the quantitative relation between elastic stress and strain in the numerical simulation of turbulent DR of viscoelastic fluids. In general, the upper convected Maxwell (UCM) model [2], Oldroyd-B model [3, 4] and Giesekus model [5] as well as FENE-P model [6] are commonly used constitutive models in a large number of literatures. For the desirable performance to represent the shear-thinning phenomenon compared with the UCM model and Oldroyd-B models, the Giesekus and FENE-P models have been applied widely.

It is well known that the rheological properties and turbulent DR effect are closely related to the microstructures (long chain structures for polymer solution or network structures for surfactant solution) formed in the viscoelastic fluids. Therefore, it is necessary to delve into the validity of the constitutive model from the perspective of relaxation-deformation of the microstructures. For the polymer solution, as shown in Fig. 1(a), the long chain structures would exert relaxation-deformation under the shear effect in flow, sometimes they even tangled with each other. Different from polymer solution, the DR effect of surfactant solution depends on the micelles composed of small surfactant molecules. As illustrated in Fig. 1(b), the spherical micells, rod-like micelles and network structures are usually formed in sequence with the increase of concentration under the shear effect in flow, which is also accompanied with relaxation-deformation of microstructures. From above all, it is evident to see that various relaxation-deformations of the microstructures will take place in the viscoelastic fluid under shear effect. In the relaxation-deformation process, the relaxation time is a key parameter for constitutive model. In polymer and surfactant solutions, the relaxation time is referred to the time consumed during a deformation period of the microstructure, it can characterize the strength of elastic effect of the viscoelastic fluid. However, the real viscoelastic fluid has a relaxation time spectrum but not only single relaxation time for the anisotropy caused by different configurations and various deformations of the microstructures under the shear in flow. In the theoretical and experimental researches of the DR effect, the relaxation time spectrum is always simplified as single relaxation time because of the sophisticated analysis when relaxation time spectrum is taken into consideration. Correspondingly, the constitutive models commonly used are characterized with only single relaxation time, which is obviously inconsistent with the actual physical process. It is the main reason responsible for the deviations between the theoretical, experimental and numerical studies of DR mechanism of viscoelastic fluid.

Based on the above analysis of the relaxation-deformation characteristics of the microstructures in viscoelastic fluid, it is apparent that the conventional constitutive models with single relaxation time can not accurately characterize the anisotropy of relaxation-deformation. Therefore, considering the idea of multiple relaxation times and the advantage of FENE-P constitutive model that the deformations are nonlinear,

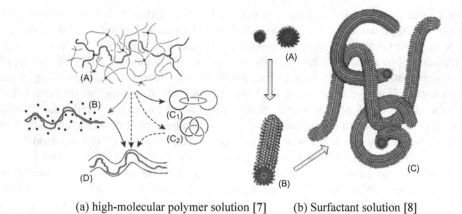

(a) high-molecular polymer solution [7]   (b) Surfactant solution [8]

Fig. 1. Schematics of microstructures formed in the viscoelastic fluids.

an N-parallel FENE-P constitutive model based on multiple relaxation times is proposed in this study.

2 The Establishment of N-Parallel FENE-P Constitutive Model Based on Multiple Relaxation Times

In this Section, the drawback of conventional FENE-P constitutive models that only has single relaxation time is taken into account and an N-parallel FENE-P constitutive model based on multiple relaxation times is proposed. The core idea of the proposed constitutive model is to put N FENE-P models in parallel to describe the rheological behaviors of viscoelastic fluids and characterize the anisotropy of relaxation-deformation of the microstructures. The establishment of the proposed N-parallel FENE-P constitutive model is presented detailedly in the following text.

To get insight into the rheological properties of the viscoelastic fluid from the microcosmic perspective, Bird et al. [6] modeled the polymer macromolecules by a discrete-element model with finitely extensible nonlinear elastic (FENE) characteristic, which is called spring-dumbbell model too. The FENE-P constitutive model is a member of the FENE model family with Peterlin's approximation [9], and its governing equation reads,

$$\tau_V + \frac{\lambda}{f(r)}\tau_V^\nabla = 2\frac{\eta_V}{f(r)}D \tag{1}$$

where τ_V is the extra elastic stress tensor; λ is the relaxation time; $f(r)$ is nonlinear factor to ensure the finite extensibility; η_V is zero-shear-rate dynamic viscosity; D is the deformation rate tensor, $D = \left(\nabla \mathbf{u} + (\nabla \mathbf{u})^\mathrm{T}\right)/2$.

As illustrated in Fig. 2, when N FENE-P models are paralleled together, the N-parallel FENE-P constitutive model satisfies the following characteristics:

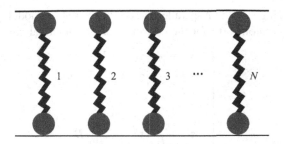

Fig. 2. Schematic of the N-parallel FENE-P model.

(1) The extra elastic stress tensor of the N-parallel FENE-P model is equal to the summation of the extra elastic stress tensors of the total N branching FENE-P models,

$$\tau_V = \tau_{v1} + \tau_{v2} + \ldots + \tau_{vn} = \sum_{i=1}^{N} \tau_{vi} \tag{2}$$

(2) The deformation rate tensor of the N-parallel FENE-P model is identical to the deformation rate tensor of each branching FENE-P model,

$$D = D_1 = D_2 = \ldots = D_N \tag{3}$$

where in the above two equations the subscript N denotes the number of the branching FENE-P models, $N \geq 2$; $\tau_{V1}, \tau_{V2}, \ldots, \tau_{VN}$ are the extra elastic stress tensors of the branching FENE-P models, respectively; $D_1, D_2, \ldots, D_N$ are the deformation rate tensors of the branching FENE-P models, respectively.

The mathematical relation between τ_{vi} and D_i of the ith branching FENE-P model can be obtained evidently based on Eq. (1),

$$\tau_{Vi} + \frac{\lambda_i}{f(r_i)} \tau_{Vi}^{\nabla} = 2 \frac{\eta_{Vi}}{f(r_i)} D_i \tag{4}$$

where $\lambda_i, f(r_i)$ respectively represent the relaxation time and nonlinear factor of the ith branching FENE-P model; η_{vi} denotes the zero-shear-rate dynamic viscosity of the ith branching FENE-P model.

Substituting Eqs. (3) – (4) into Eq. (2), the N-parallel FENE-P constitutive model can be written as follows,

$$\sum_{i=1}^{N} \tau_{Vi} + \sum_{i=1}^{N} \left(\frac{\lambda_i}{f(r_i)} \tau_{Vi}^{\nabla} \right) = 2 \sum_{i=1}^{N} \frac{\eta_{Vi}}{f(r_i)} D \tag{5}$$

From above equation we can see the N-parallel FENE-P constitutive model is a more general constitutive model. The conventional FENE-P constitutive model with single relaxation time can be regarded as an exception of the N-parallel FENE-P constitutive model when $N = 1$.

It is worth noting that the N-parallel FENE-P constitutive model can be rearranged as branching expression form for the convenience of numerical calculation,

$$
\begin{cases}
\tau_{V1} + \frac{\lambda_1}{f(r_1)}\tau_{V1}^{\nabla} = 2\frac{\eta_{V1}}{f(r_1)}D \\
\tau_{V2} + \frac{\lambda_2}{f(r_2)}\tau_{V2}^{\nabla} = 2\frac{\eta_{V2}}{f(r_2)}D \\
\quad\quad\cdot \\
\quad\quad\cdot \\
\tau_{Vi} + \frac{\lambda_i}{f(r_i)}\tau_{Vi}^{\nabla} = 2\frac{\eta_{Vi}}{f(r_i)}D \\
\quad\quad\cdot \\
\tau_{VN} + \frac{\lambda_N}{f(r_N)}\tau_{VN}^{\nabla} = 2\frac{\eta_{VN}}{f(r_N)}D
\end{cases}
\tag{6}
$$

3 Numerical Approach to Obtain the Apparent Viscosity by Solving the N-Parallel FENE-P Constitutive Model

Apparent viscosity is one of the most significant parameters to measure the rheological properties of viscoelastic fluid. However, a large body of literature reveal that the conventional constitutive model with single relaxation time show unfavorable performance in describing the apparent viscosity compared with experimental results [10]. In order to validate whether the proposed N-parallel FENE-P constitutive model gains advantage over the traditional one in representing the rheological properties of viscoelastic fluid, the numerical approach to calculate the apparent viscosity by solving the N-parallel FENE-P constitutive model is introduced in this Section.

Under a certain temperature and solution concentration, the viscosity of viscoelastic fluid is called apparent viscosity or shear viscosity for the reason that it is not a constant but has close relation to the shear rate. Generally, the apparent viscosity reads,

$$
\eta_a = \tau_{xy}/\dot{\gamma} = \left(\tau_{N,xy} + \sum_{i=1}^{N}\tau_{Vi,xy}\right)\bigg/\dot{\gamma}
\tag{7}
$$

where η_a represents the apparent viscosity; $\dot{\gamma}$ denotes the shear rate; $\tau_{N,xy}$, $\sum_{i=1}^{N}\tau_{Vi,xy}$ denote the extra viscous stress contributed by solvent and solute, respectively.

It can be seen from Eq. (7) that it is a prerequisite to obtain the mathematical relation between $\sum_{i=1}^{N}\tau_{Vi,xy}$ and $\dot{\gamma}$ before calculating the apparent viscosity. In general, water is a commonly used solvent in viscoelastic fluid and its apparent viscosity can be approximately regarded as constant under a certain temperature and solution concentration. Thus the terms $\tau_{N,xy}$ and $\dot{\gamma}$ satisfy the following relation,

$$
\tau_{N,xy} = \eta_N\dot{\gamma}
\tag{8}
$$

where η_N denotes the dynamic viscosity of solvent.

As two successfully used drag-reducing additives, the viscosities of polymer and surfactant change remarkably with the variation of shear rate. At certain temperature and solution concentration, the $\sum_{i=1}^{N} \tau_{Vi,xy}$ and $\dot{\gamma}$ meet the below equation,

$$\sum_{i=1}^{N} \tau_{Vi,xy} = \sum_{i=1}^{N} \eta_{Vi}(\dot{\gamma})\dot{\gamma} \tag{9}$$

where $\eta_{Vi}(\dot{\gamma})$ represents the dynamic viscosity of solute.

Substituting Eqs. (8) – (9) into Eq. (7), the expression of apparent viscosity of viscoelastic fluid can be obtained as below,

$$\eta_a = \eta_N + \sum_{i=1}^{N} \eta_{Vi}(\dot{\gamma}) \tag{10}$$

Therefore, the $\sum_{i=1}^{N} \tau_{Vi,xy}$ should be first computed from Eq. (6) to get $\sum_{i=1}^{N} \eta_{Vi}(\dot{\gamma})$. For the sake of concision but without loss of generality, the double-parallel FENE-P constitutive model is taken as an example to represent N-parallel FENE-P constitutive model in illustrating the numerical approach to calculate apparent viscosity. For the convenience, the present study focuses on the two-dimensional simple shear flow. Based on the above assumptions, the Eqs. (6) and (10) can be simplified as,

$$\begin{cases} \tau_{V1,xx} + \tau_{V2,xx} + \dfrac{\lambda_1}{f(r_1)}\left(\dfrac{\partial \tau_{V1,xx}}{\partial t} - 2\dfrac{\partial u}{\partial y}\tau_{V1,xy}\right) + \dfrac{\lambda_2}{f(r_2)}\left(\dfrac{\partial \tau_{V2,xx}}{\partial t} - 2\dfrac{\partial u}{\partial y}\tau_{V2,xy}\right) = 0 \\[2mm] \tau_{V1,yy} + \tau_{V2,yy} + \dfrac{\lambda_1}{f(r_1)}\left(\dfrac{\partial \tau_{V1,yy}}{\partial t}\right) + \dfrac{\lambda_2}{f(r_2)}\left(\dfrac{\partial \tau_{V2,yy}}{\partial t}\right) = 0 \\[2mm] \tau_{V1,xy} + \tau_{V2,xy} + \dfrac{\lambda_1}{f(r_1)}\left(\dfrac{\partial \tau_{V1,xy}}{\partial t} - \tau_{V1,yy}\dfrac{\partial u}{\partial y}\right) + \dfrac{\lambda_2}{f(r_2)}\left(\dfrac{\partial \tau_{V2,xy}}{\partial t} - \tau_{V2,yy}\dfrac{\partial u}{\partial y}\right) \\[2mm] \qquad\qquad\qquad = \dfrac{\eta_{V1}}{f(r_1)}\left(\dfrac{\partial u}{\partial y}\right) + \dfrac{\eta_{V2}}{f(r_2)}\left(\dfrac{\partial u}{\partial y}\right) \end{cases} \tag{11}$$

$$\eta_a = \eta_N + \eta_{V1}(\dot{\gamma}) + \eta_{V2}(\dot{\gamma}) \tag{12}$$

For two-dimensional simple shear flow, the shear rate $\dot{\gamma}$ can be expressed as,

$$\dot{\gamma} = \frac{\partial u}{\partial y} \tag{13}$$

It can be easily found that the key step to solve Eq. (11) is to discretize the unsteady term of extra elastic stress. In this paper, the second-order Adams-Bashforth scheme is adopted to discretize the term as below,

$$\frac{\tau^{n+1} - \tau^n}{\Delta t} = \frac{3}{2} F(\tau)^n - \frac{1}{2} F(\tau)^{n-1} \tag{14}$$

Then the Eq. (11) can be discretized as follows based on Eq. (14),

$$
\begin{cases}
\tau_{Vi,xx}^{n+1} = \tau_{Vi,xx}^n + \frac{3}{2} \Delta t \left[2\dot{\gamma}\tau_{Vi,xy}^n - \frac{f(r_i)^n}{\lambda_i} \tau_{Vi,xx}^n \right] \\
\qquad\qquad - \frac{1}{2} \Delta t \left[2\dot{\gamma}\tau_{Vi,xy}^{n-1} - \frac{f(r_i)^{n-1}}{\lambda_i} \tau_{Vi,xx}^{n-1} \right] \\
\tau_{Vi,yy}^{n+1} = \tau_{Vi,yy}^n - \frac{3}{2} \Delta t \left[\frac{f(r_i)^n}{\lambda_i} \tau_{Vi,yy}^n \right] + \frac{1}{2} \Delta t \left[\frac{f(r_i)^{n-1}}{\lambda_i} \tau_{Vi,yy}^{n-1} \right] \\
\tau_{Vi,xy}^{n+1} = \tau_{Vi,xy}^n + \frac{3}{2} \Delta t \left[\dot{\gamma}\tau_{Vi,yy}^n - \frac{f(r_i)^n}{\lambda_i} \tau_{Vi,xy}^n + \frac{\eta_{Vi}}{\lambda_i} \dot{\gamma} \right] \\
\qquad\qquad - \frac{1}{2} \Delta t \left[\dot{\gamma}\tau_{Vi,yy}^{n-1} - \frac{f(r_i)^{n-1}}{\lambda_i} \tau_{Vi,xy}^{n-1} + \frac{\eta_{Vi}}{\lambda_i} \dot{\gamma} \right]
\end{cases} \tag{15}
$$

where the superscript n represents time layer; the subscript i denotes the ith branching FENE-P model.

The nonlinear factor $f(r)$ in Eq. (15) is a function of conformation tensor. The trace of conformation tensor should be calculated first before calculating $f(r)$,

$$\mathrm{trace}(c_{Vi}) = c_{Vi,xx}^{n+1} + c_{Vi,yy}^{n+1} \tag{16}$$

where the conformation tensor components $c_{Vi,xx}^{n+1}$ and $c_{Vi,yy}^{n+1}$ are given as below,

$$
\begin{cases}
c_{Vi,xx}^{n+1} = \left(\frac{\lambda_i}{\eta_{Vi}} \tau_{Vi,xx}^{n+1} + 1 \right) \Big/ f(r_i)^n \\
c_{Vi,yy}^{n+1} = \left(\frac{\lambda_i}{\eta_{Vi}} \tau_{Vi,yy}^{n+1} + 1 \right) \Big/ f(r_i)^n
\end{cases} \tag{17}
$$

By solving Eqs. (16) – (17), the nonlinear factor of each branching FENE-P constitutive model can be obtained as,

$$f(r_i)^{n+1} = \frac{L^2 - 3}{L^2 - \mathrm{trace}(c_{Vi})} \tag{18}$$

where L is the maximum length of polymer molecules or surfactant micelles scaled with its equilibrium value, L is set as 100 in this study.

Hereafter we can calculate the apparent viscosity by solving the N-parallel FENE-P constitutive model based on Eqs. (12) – (18). Taking the double-parallel FENE-P constitutive model as an example, the flow chart to calculate the apparent viscosity is shown in Fig. 3.

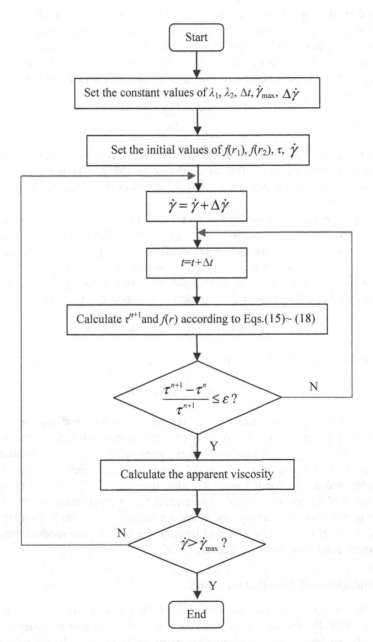

Fig. 3. Flow chart of the numerical calculation of apparent viscosity

4 Validation of the N-Parallel FENE-P Constitutive Model and Results Discussion

4.1 Determination of Model Parameters

Before calculating apparent viscosity by using the N-parallel FENE-P constitutive model, the model parameters, such as relaxation time λ_i and dynamic viscosity η_{Vi}, should be determined or given first. For the sake of following discussion, we introduce the parameter β_i, which is defined as the ratio of the dynamic viscosity of the ith branching FENE-P model (solute) to the zero-shear-rate viscosity of the solvent,

$$\beta_i = \frac{\eta_{Vi}}{\eta_N} \tag{19}$$

From the above definition, the β_i can be regarded as a dimensionless measurement of the solution concentration. The larger the β_i is, the greater the concentration of solution is. Hereafter the unknown model parameters of the N-parallel FENE-P model turn to be λ_i and β_i.

For the sake of concision but without loss of generality, the double-parallel FENE-P constitutive model is taken as an example to illustrate the determination of unknown parameters of the proposed model. When the experimental data of apparent viscosity for polymer solution or surfactant solution is given, it is easily to get the zero-shear-rate viscosity or apparent viscosity η_a with a certain initial shear rate. For the double-parallel FENE-P constitutive model, the apparent viscosity is,

$$\eta_a = \eta_N + \eta_{V1} + \eta_{V2} = (1 + \beta_1 + \beta_2)\eta_N \tag{20}$$

The above equation can also be expressed as,

$$\beta_1 + \beta_2 = \eta_a/\eta_N - 1 \tag{21}$$

In general, the experimental data of apparent viscosity and first normal stress difference can be measured by rheological experiment. Therefore, the values of apparent viscosity (or $\beta_1 + \beta_2$) and first normal stress difference can be obtained for the double-parallel FENE-P constitutive model, the unknown model parameters that need to be determined are β_1 (or β_2) and relaxation times λ_1, λ_2. Under this situation, the least square method can be utilized to determine the optimal unknown model parameters mentioned above. Similarly, the unknown parameters of the N-parallel FENE-P constitutive model can also be obtained through the least square method, but it needs more experimental data with the increase of N.

4.2 Validation and Results Discussion

Figure 4 shows the comparison of N-parallel FENE-P constitutive model ($N = 2$) and traditional FENE-P constitutive model in describing the apparent viscosity of polymer solutions. In the figure, the independent experimental data of polymer solutions with different concentrations are chosen from the works of Ptasinski et al. [11], Hashmet et al. [12] and Pumode et al. [13], respectively. It can be easily observed that the calculation results of the proposed model agree with the experimental data more accurate than the traditional model in the whole shear rate range $0.1s^{-1}$–$1000\ s^{-1}$, the advantage is more remarkable especially when the shear rate is in the range of $10\ s^{-1}$–$1000\ s^{-1}$. In addition, the N-parallel FENE-P model performs a favorable applicability for different concentrations of polymer solutions compared with the conventional model.

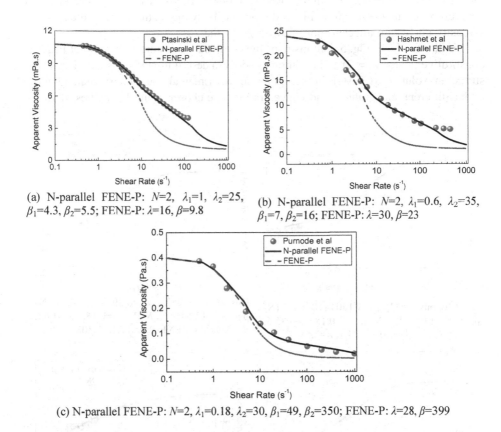

(a) N-parallel FENE-P: N=2, λ_1=1, λ_2=25, β_1=4.3, β_2=5.5; FENE-P: λ=16, β=9.8

(b) N-parallel FENE-P: N=2, λ_1=0.6, λ_2=35, β_1=7, β_2=16; FENE-P: λ=30, β=23

(c) N-parallel FENE-P: N=2, λ_1=0.18, λ_2=30, β_1=49, β_2=350; FENE-P: λ=28, β=399

Fig. 4. Comparison of N-parallel FENE-P constitutive model ($N = 2$) and traditional FENE-P model in describing the apparent viscosity of polymer solutions.

The main reason responsible for the advantages can be found from the basic idea of the N-parallel FENE-P model. From a microcosmic view, when N branching FENE-P models are adopted in constitutive model, the relaxation-deformation of the microstructures formed in the polymer solutions can be controlled and modulated by small relaxation time and large relaxation time simultaneously. It can reflect the actual relaxation-deformation characteristics of the microstructures more truly and comprehensively. However, there is only single relaxation time in the traditional constitutive model, it can not represent the small relaxation-deformation and large relaxation-deformation of the microstructures at the same time, which is not consistent with the physical reality. Therefore, the proposed constitutive model is more reasonable than the conventional one. Correspondingly, the accuracy of the proposed constitutive model is much higher.

Besides, from Fig. 4 we can also find the adjustability of model parameters of the proposed model is much better than that of the traditional model. The apparent viscosity curves with different shear-thinning rates can be obtained by modulating the model parameters of the branching FENE-P models. The increase and decrease of the apparent viscosity curves are influenced more easily by the β_i, the slope of the apparent viscosity curves are affected more obviously by the λ_i.

Similar to Fig. 4, Fig. 5 demonstrates the comparative results of N-parallel FENE-P constitutive model ($N = 2$) and traditional model in describing the apparent viscosity of surfactant solutions (CTAC). In the figure the experimental data of surfactant solutions under different temperatures and concentrations are chosen from the studies of Zhang

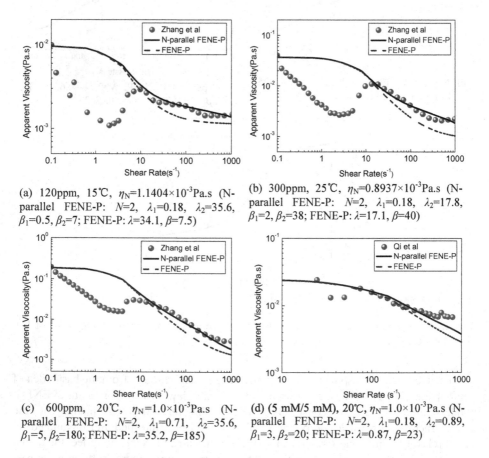

(a) 120ppm, 15℃, $\eta_N=1.1404\times10^{-3}$Pa.s (N-parallel FENE-P: $N=2$, $\lambda_1=0.18$, $\lambda_2=35.6$, $\beta_1=0.5$, $\beta_2=7$; FENE-P: $\lambda=34.1$, $\beta=7.5$)

(b) 300ppm, 25℃, $\eta_N=0.8937\times10^{-3}$Pa.s (N-parallel FENE-P: $N=2$, $\lambda_1=0.18$, $\lambda_2=17.8$, $\beta_1=2$, $\beta_2=38$; FENE-P: $\lambda=17.1$, $\beta=40$)

(c) 600ppm, 20℃, $\eta_N=1.0\times10^{-3}$Pa.s (N-parallel FENE-P: $N=2$, $\lambda_1=0.71$, $\lambda_2=35.6$, $\beta_1=5$, $\beta_2=180$; FENE-P: $\lambda=35.2$, $\beta=185$)

(d) (5 mM/5 mM), 20℃, $\eta_N=1.0\times10^{-3}$Pa.s (N-parallel FENE-P: $N=2$, $\lambda_1=0.18$, $\lambda_2=0.89$, $\beta_1=3$, $\beta_2=20$; FENE-P: $\lambda=0.87$, $\beta=23$)

Fig. 5. Comparison of N-parallel FENE-P constitutive model ($N = 2$) and traditional FENE-P model in describing the apparent viscosity of surfactant solutions.

et al. [14] and Qi et al. [15], respectively. From Fig. 5, it is a pity to see that both the N-parallel FENE-P model and the traditional model can not able to represent the unique shear thickening behavior of surfactant solution. Because for both the N-parallel FENE-P constitutive model and the traditional model, it can be proved that the FENE-P constitutive model is monotonic for the relation of apparent viscosity and share rate. The shear thickening phenomenon of the surfactant solution can be depicted by using a piecewise definition, such as the work of Galindo-Rosales [16]. However, it requires the introduction of at least 11 parameters to determine the piecewise constitutive model, which is nearly not practical in the engineering application. Fortunately, the proposed constitutive model in this paper still wins obvious advantage over the traditional one in shear rate range 10 s^{-1}–1000 s^{-1}. Furthermore, the N-parallel FENE-P model can describe all the apparent viscosities of surfactant solutions measured under different temperatures and concentrations, which indicates that the N-parallel FENE-P model has a much wider application.

The normal stress difference of surfactant solutions is not equal to zero because surfactant solution is a type of non-Newtonian fluids. Here the comparison of the first normal stress difference $(N_1(\dot{\gamma}) = \tau_{xx} - \tau_{yy})$ is illustrated in Fig. 6. The experimental data set are selected from the work of Qi et al. [15], in which the first normal stress difference of surfactant solution Arquad 16-50/NaSal was given in detail. Figure 6 indicates that the calculated first normal stress difference of the proposed constitutive model provides an excellent fit to the experimental data, the proposed model can represent the first normal stress difference more accurate than the traditional model. Especially when the shear rate is larger than 150 s^{-1}, the traditional model can't depict the first normal stress difference accurately compare to the experimental data, the maximum relative error can up to 35%.

It is worth pointing out that for the proposed N-parallel FENE-P model, although the adjustability of the model parameters becomes better and the accuracy of the calculation results becomes higher with the increase of branching number N, the

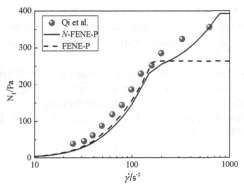

5mM/5mM, 20℃, $\eta_N = 1.0 \times 10^{-3}$Pa.s (N-parallel FENE-P: $N=2$, $\lambda_1=0.18$, $\lambda_2=0.89$, $\beta_1=3$, $\beta_2=20$; FENE-P: $\lambda=0.87$, $\beta=23$)

Fig. 6. Comparison of N-parallel FENE-P constitutive model ($N = 2$) and traditional FENE-P model in describing the first normal stress difference of surfactant solution

numerical workload also becomes heavier following the similar tendency. Therefore, it is significant to take both the computational accuracy and workload into consideration to choose the branching number. $N = 2$ and $N = 3$ were adopted in our numerical experiment and it was found that the calculation accuracy of the apparent viscosity when $N = 3$ improved slightly compared with that when $N = 2$. The calculation accuracy of the apparent viscosity and first normal stress difference has already been much higher than that of the traditional model when $N = 2$, this is the reason why we only present the comparative results when $N = 2$ in this Section.

5   Conclusions

The present study focuses on the constitutive model describing the apparent viscosity of viscoelastic fluids and an N-parallel FENE-P constitutive model is proposed based on multiple relaxation times. From our study, the following conclusions can be summarized:

(1) The proposed N-parallel FENE-P model is a more general constitutive model with better applicability. It utilizes the N branching FENE-P models to describe the rheological behaviors of viscoelastic fluid and characterize the anisotropy of relaxation-deformations of the microstructures formed in viscoelastic fluid, which is more consistent with the real physical process.

(2) Compared with the traditional FENE-P model, the proposed model demonstrates a favorable adjustability of the model parameters. The apparent viscosity curves with different shear thinning rates can be obtained by modulating the model parameters of the branching FENE-P models.

(3) The proposed N-parallel FENE-P model is shown to perform an excellent fit to several independent experimental data sets. It can represent the apparent viscosity of polymer solution more accurate than the traditional model in whole shear rate range 0.1 s^{-1}–1000 s^{-1}, the advantage is more remarkable especially when the shear rate is among 10 s^{-1}–1000 s^{-1}. Although the proposed N-parallel FENE-P model can also not capture the shear thickening behavior of surfactant solution as the conventional model, it still possesses advantages over the traditional model in representing the apparent viscosity and first normal stress difference within the shear rate range 10 s^{-1}–1000 s^{-1}.

Acknowledgements. The authors thank for support of National Natural Science Foundation of China (No. 51636006), project of Construction of Innovative Teams and Teacher Career Development for Universities and Colleges under Beijing Municipality (No. IDHT20170507), National Key R&D Program of China (Grant No. 2016YFE0204200) and the Program of Great Wall Scholar (CIT&TCD20180313).

References

1. Toms, B.A.: Some observations on the flow of linear polymer solutions through straight tubes at large Reynolds numbers. In: Proceedings of the 1st International Rheology Congress, II, Part 2, pp. 135–142. North Holland Publish Co., Netherlands (1949)
2. Renardy, M., Renardy, Y.: Linear stability of plane Couette flow of an upper convected Maxwell fluid. J. Nonnewton. Fluid Mech. **22**, 23–33 (1986)
3. Oldroyd, J.G.: On the formulation of rheological equations of state. Proc. Roy. Soc. A **200**, 523–541 (1950)
4. Oliveria, P.G.: Alternative derivation of differential constitutive equations of the Oldroyd-B type. J. Nonnewton. Fluid Mech. **160**, 40–46 (2009)
5. Giesekus, H.: A simple constitutive equation for polymer fluids based on the concept of deformation-dependent tensorial mobility. J. Nonnewton. Fluid Mech. **11**, 69–109 (1982)
6. Bird, R.B., Dotson, P.J., Johnson, N.L.: Polymer solution rheology based on a finitely extensible bead-spring chain model. J. Nonnewton. Fluid Mech. **7**(2–3), 213–235 (1980)
7. Everaers, R., Sukumaran, S.K., Grest, G.S., Svaneborg, C., Sivasubramanian, A., Kremer, K.: Rheology and microscopic topology of entangled polymeric liquids. Sciences **303**(5659), 823–826 (2004)
8. Ezrahi, S., Tuval, E., Aserin, A.: Properties, main applications and perspectives of worm micelles. Adv. Coll. Interface. Sci. **128–130**, 77–102 (2006)
9. Peterlin, A.: Streaming birefringence of soft linear macromolecules with finite chain length. Polymer **2**, 257–264 (1961)
10. Wei, J.J., Yao, Z.Q.: Rheological characteristic of drag reducing surfactant solution. J. Chem. Ind. Eng. (Chinese) **58**(2), 0335–0340 (2007)
11. Ptasinski, P.K., Nieuwstadt, F.T.M., Van Den Brule, B.H.A.A., Hulsen, M.A.: Experiments in turbulent pipe flow with polymer additives at maximum drag reduction. Flow Turbul. Combust. **66**, 159–182 (2001)
12. Hashmet, M.R., Onur, M., Tan, I.M.: Empirical correlations for viscosity of polyacrylamide solutions with the effects of concentration, molecular weight and degree of hydrolysis of polymer. J. Appl. Sci. **14**(10), 1000–1007 (2014)
13. Purnode, B., Crochet, M.J.: Polymer solution characterization with the FENE-P model. J. Nonnewton. Fluid Mech. **77**, 1–20 (1998)
14. Zhang, H.X., Wang, D.Z., Gu, W.G., Chen, H.P.: Effects of temperature and concentration on rheological characteristics of surfactant additive solutions. J. Hydrodyn. **20**(5), 603–610 (2008)
15. Qi, Y.Y., Littrell, K., Thiyagarajan, P., Talmon, Y., Schmidt, J., Lin, Z.Q.: Small-angle neutron scattering study of shearing effects on drag-reducing surfactant solutions. J. Colloid Interface Sci. **337**, 218–226 (2009)
16. Galindo-Rosalesa, F.J., Rubio-Hernández, F.J., Sevilla, A.: An apparent viscosity function for shear thickening fluids. J. Nonnewton. Fluid Mech. **166**, 321–325 (2011)

RADIC Based Fault Tolerance System with Dynamic Resource Controller

Jorge Villamayor[✉][ID], Dolores Rexachs[✉][ID], and Emilio Luque[✉][ID]

CAOS - Computer Architecture and Operating Systems,
Universidad Autónoma de Barcelona, Barcelona, Spain
{jorgeluis.villamayor,dolores.rexachs,emilio.luque}@uab.cat

Abstract. The continuously growing High-Performance Computing requirements increments the number of components and at the same time failure probabilities. Long-running parallel applications are directly affected by this phenomena, disrupting its executions on failure occurrences. MPI, a well-known standard for parallel applications follows a fail-stop semantic, requiring the application owners restart the whole execution when hard failures appear losing time and computation data. Fault Tolerance (FT) techniques approach this issue by providing high availability to the users' applications execution, though adding significant resource and time costs. In this paper, we present a Fault Tolerance Manager (FTM) framework based on RADIC architecture, which provides FT protection to parallel applications implemented with MPI, in order to successfully complete executions despite failures. The solution is implemented in the application-layer following the uncoordinated and semi-coordinated rollback recovery protocols. It uses a sender-based message logger to store exchanged messages between the application processes; and checkpoints only the processes data required to restart them in case of failures. The solution uses the concepts of ULFM for failure detection and recovery. Furthermore, a dynamic resource controller is added to the proposal, which monitors the message logger buffers and performs actions to maintain an acceptable level of protection. Experimental validation verifies the FTM functionality using two private clusters infrastructures.

Keywords: High-Performance Computing · Fault Tolerance
Application layer FT · Sender-based message logging

1 Introduction

The constantly increasing scale of High Performance Computing (HPC) platforms increments the frequency of failures in clusters and cloud environments [1]. In contemporary HPC systems the Mean Time Between Failures (MTBF)

This research has been supported by the MICINN/MINECO Spain under contracts TIN2014-53172-P and TIN2017-84875-P.

© Springer International Publishing AG, part of Springer Nature 2018
Y. Shi et al. (Eds.): ICCS 2018, LNCS 10862, pp. 624–631, 2018.
https://doi.org/10.1007/978-3-319-93713-7_58

is in range of hours, depending on the maturity and age of installation [4]. Users employing this kind of systems to run their parallel and distributed applications are directly affected. Usually, parallel and distributed applications are implemented using a Message Passing Interface (MPI), which by default follows fail-stop semantics and lacks failure mitigation, meaning the loss of user's computation time and data when failure occurs.

Fault Tolerance (FT) solutions are necessary to ensure high availability to parallel applications execution and minimize the failure impact [3]. Rollback-Recovery protocols are widely used within FT to protect application executions. The methods consist of snapshots created from the parallel execution and stored as checkpoints. In case of failures an application can recover using the last taken checkpoint, though most of the time the recovery process is not automatic, and may require human intervention. A well-known issue is that most FT solutions comes with added overhead during failure-free executions, and also with high resource consumption.

Coordinated, semi-coordinated and uncoordinated are some of the most used rollback-recovery protocols [2]. The coordinated protocol synchronizes the application processes to create a consistent state. For applications with large amount of processes, the coordination may present a source of overhead. Furthermore, when failures appear, all application processes must rollback to the last checkpoint causing waste of computation work [2]. In order to avoid this problem, the semi-coordinated and uncoordinated protocols make use of a message logger facility that allows the recovery of only affected processes when failures appear. However, the logger have to store each interchanged message during the application execution, meaning a significant source of resource usage.

In this work, a Fault Tolerance Manager (FTM) for HPC application users is presented. FTM offers automatic and transparent mechanisms to recover applications in case of failures, meaning users do not need to perform any action when failures appear. The solution uses semi-coordinated and uncoordinated rollback-recovery protocols following RADIC architecture. FTM combines application-layer checkpoints with a sender-based message logger using the concepts of ULFM for detection and recovery purposes. Furthermore, a Dynamic Resource Controller is added, it performs the monitoring of main memory usage for the logger facility, allowing to detect when its usage is reaching a limit. With this information, it invokes automatic checkpoints, in an optimistic manner, which allows freeing memory buffers used for the message logger avoiding the slowdown or stall of the application execution.

The content of this paper is organized as follows: Sect. 2 presents the design of FTM in the application-layer with the dynamic resource controller. In Sect. 3, experimental evaluation is shown, which contains the FTM functionality validation and the dynamic resource controller verification with the NAS CG benchmark application. Finally the conclusions and future work are stated in Sect. 4.

2 FTM with Dynamic Resources Controller

This section describes the design of the Fault Tolerance Manager (FTM) to provide high availability to user's applications. The traditional stack for HPC execution environment is composed of several failure prompt layers. FTM architecture isolates the user's application layer from failures. It suits the execution environment with a handler controller, which deals with failures recovering the user's application execution when failures appear. The architecture components are depicted in Fig. 1.

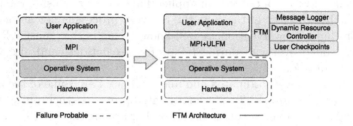

Fig. 1. FTM architecture.

The Fault Tolerance Manager uses application-layer checkpoints combined with a sender-based message logger, following the uncoordinated and semi-coordinated rollback-recovery protocols, to protect the application during failure-free executions. In order to monitor and manage the FTM resource usage for FT protection, a dynamic resource controller is also added.

Checkpointing operation is initiated by the application, hence modifications in the application's source are needed, although the application algorithm remains intact. The checkpoint operations are inserted during natural synchronization of the application processes. The checkpoints store structures containing only necessary information to restore execution in case of failures, avoiding the need to store SO particular information. The checkpoint files are used when the application is recovered from a failure.

Exchanged application's messages are stored into the message logger facility, in order to replay them to the processes affected by failures. After the processes are restarted, they directly consume messages from the logger. For the uncoordinated approach, all exchanged messages between the application processes are stored. The semi-coordinated approach stores only exchanged messages between the application processes that are in distinct nodes, as shown in Fig. 2.

When failures appear, a mechanism of detection is needed to start the recovery procedure. In this work, ULFM is used to detect failures. FTM implements an error handler, which is invoked by the ULFM detection mechanism to recovery the application execution.

The failure detection, reconfiguration and recovery procedures are implemented as a handler in FTM. To illustrate the procedures, one process per node

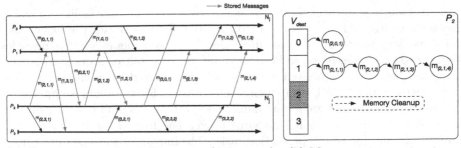

(a) Semi-coordinated stored messages (red arrows). (b) Messages storage structure.

Fig. 2. Sender-based message logger.

is used, with the uncoordinated protocol and a pessimistic sender-based message logger, shown in Fig. 3. It depicts that P_3 fails, and P_2 is the first process which detects the failure, causing the revocation of the global communicator using MPI_Comm_revoke. After the revocation, all remaining processes are notified and they shrink the global communicator, taking out the failed processes using the MPI_Comm_shrink call. Finally, the remaining processes spawn the communicator using dynamically launched processes of the application.

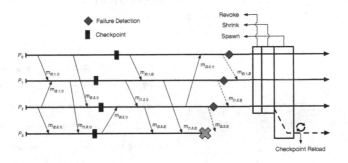

Fig. 3. Failure detection, reconfiguration and recovery procedures.

After the reconfiguration, the affected processes load the checkpoint and jump to the correct execution line in order to continue the application execution. The messages are consumed from the message logger to finish the re-execution. Meanwhile, non-failed processes continue their execution.

2.1 Dynamic Resources Controller

As previously seen, the FT protection requires resources and it comes with overhead for the user's applications. The protection of the application execution stores both, checkpoints and messages of the application processes. The uncoordinated and semi-coordinated protocols avoid the restart of all the application processes when a failure occurs. Although, they require a logger facility to replay messages to restored processes. To reduce failure-free overhead, the logger uses main memory to store processes messages. The main memory often provides high speed access compared to local hard disk or a centralized storage. However, the main memory is a limited resource, which is shared between the application processes and the FT components. The usage of FT resources is application dependent, meaning different communication pattern, size and quantity of messages, directly impacts on FT resource usage. The free available memory can rapidly ran out due to FT protection tasks. The impact of running out of main memory can result in the application execution stall.

In order to avoid the free memory ran out due to FTM protection task, the dynamic resources controller is introduced with FTM. It works on each node of the application execution. This controller constantly monitors the memory buffers usage for message logging and detects when they are reaching the limit available, triggering automatically a checkpoint invocation, storing the state of the application and freeing the memory buffers used for logging purposes, providing the application FT protection without interfering its memory usage (Fig. 4(a)). The functionality is shown in Fig. 4(b). By default the application has checkpoint moments, which are chose by the application users, though the memory may ran out meaning the lost in terms of performance. The controller detects it and automatically invokes a checkpoint creation, allowing to free the memory usage by the logging facility, therefore avoiding the application execution stall due to the lack of main memory.

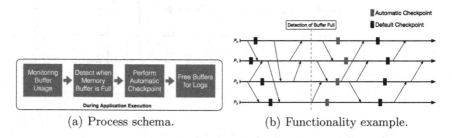

(a) Process schema.   (b) Functionality example.

Fig. 4. Dynamic resources controller

3   Experimental Results

This section presents experimental results obtained applying FTM to provide Fault Tolerance in the application-layer. The results show its automatic functionality and validate the dynamic resources controller in real execution environments and injecting failures.

The application used for the experiments is the NAS CG Benchmark. It is an implementation of the Conjugate Gradient method included in the NAS benchmark suite. The experiments are performed using Class C and D which have 150000 and 1500000 rows respectively. Two clusters were used: AOCLSB-FT, built with 2 quad-core Intel 2.66 GHz and 16 GB RAM; and AOCLSB-L suited with 8 AMD Opteron (x8) and 252GB RAM, both clusters with 30GB HDD of local disk, and a NFS shared volume of 715GB.

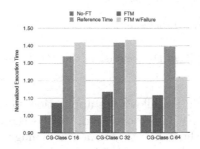

Fig. 5. CG-Class C with FTM in a failure injection scenario in AOCLSB-FT cluster.

The performance of FTM is tested applying it to the CG application. During the experiments a failure is injected to one node of the cluster at 75% of the application execution. To analyze the benefits of applying the solution, a Reference Time is calculated, which represents the scenario where a failure is injected at 75% of the application execution. As the application checkpoints at 50% of its execution, 25% of the execution is lost. This means a total execution time of around 125% in case of failures and without applying FTM. This time compared to the measured time of executing the application with FTM protection experimenting a failure (FTM w/Failure). FTM protection is setup to take checkpoints at 50% of the application execution.

Figure 5 shows the results of the execution time normalized to the execution without Fault Tolerance (No-FT). The experiments were done using 16, 32 and 64 processes with the CG Class C. It is possible to observe that having FTM protection save user time approximately 13% compared to the Reference Time when a failure appears for the 64 processes application.

An evaluation of the dynamic resource controller is also performed, executing CG Class D application in the AOCLSB-FT cluster, which has less resources compared to the AOCLSB-L, and configured to take one checkpoint at 50%. Two scenarios were evaluated, with and without the dynamic controller. Figure 6(a) shows both executions starting with a similar throughput, though when the execution without the dynamic controller starts using SWAP memory zone of the system, the throughput drastically drops, making the whole application crash. Meanwhile, the execution with the dynamic controller, optimistically invoke the checkpoints, that after their completion, release the memory buffers used for the logger facility, allowing the continuous execution of the application.

It is important to remark that the dynamic controller does not interfere in the user-defined checkpoint events, letting users the control of the checkpoint moments, though it may perform optimistic checkpoints, to free resources for

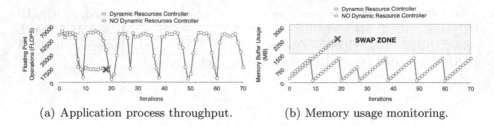

(a) Application process throughput.   (b) Memory usage monitoring.

Fig. 6. CG-Class D execution in the AOCLSB-FT cluster.

the application. The solution allows the application to continue the execution, though it may come with larger overhead, due to the automatic checkpoints invocation. Figure 6(b) shows how the memory is managed during the application execution in contrast to the execution without the management.

4   Conclusion and Future Work

This work contributes providing a novel Fault Tolerance Manager in the application-layer, allowing users to define only the necessary protection information for their applications. Furthermore, the work suits FTM with a dynamic resource controller, which monitor FT resource usage and perform actions when the usage reach boundaries where it may affect the application execution.

Experiments show the automatic functionality of the FTM applied to the NAS CG, a well-known benchmark application. Results show up to 13% of execution time benefits by applying the solution. During the experiments, throughput measurements of the application processes shows the operation of the dynamic controller, which performing optimistic checkpoints, allows the application maintain its throughput, keeping the FT protection in case of failures. Future work aims to evaluate the FTM with the dynamic resource controller for real applications in different execution environments, such as cloud and containers.

References

1. Cappello, F., Geist, A., Gropp, W., Kale, S., Kramer, B., Snir, M.: Toward exascale resilience: 2014 update. Supercomput. Front. Innov. 1(1), 5–28 (2014). https://doi. org/10.14529/jsfi140101. http://superfri.org/superfri/article/view/14
2. Castro-León, M., Meyer, H., Rexachs, D., Luque, E.: Fault tolerance at system level based on RADIC architecture. J. Parallel Distrib. Comput. 86, 98–111 (2015). https://doi.org/10.1016/j.jpdc.2015.08.005. http://www.sciencedirect.com/ science/article/pii/S0743731515001434

3. Egwutuoha, I.P., Levy, D., Selic, B., Chen, S.: A survey of fault tolerance mechanisms and checkpoint/restart implementations for high performance computing systems. J. Supercomput. **65**(3), 1302–1326 (2013). https://doi.org/10.1007/s11227-013-0884-0. http://link.springer.com/10.1007/s11227-013-0884-0
4. Wang, C., Vazhkudai, S., Ma, X., Mueller, F.: Transparent Fault Tolerance for Job Input Data in HPC Environments (2014). http://optout.csc.ncsu.edu/~mueller/ftp/pub/mueller/papers/springer14.pdf

Effective Learning with Joint Discriminative and Representative Feature Selection

Shupeng Wang[1], Xiao-Yu Zhang[1](✉), Xianglei Dang[2](✉),
Binbin Li[1](✉), and Haiping Wang[1]

[1] Institute of Information Engineering,
Chinese Academy of Sciences, Beijing, China
zhangxiaoyu@iie.ac.cn
[2] National Computer Network Emergency Response Technical
Team/Coordination Center of China, Beijing, China

Abstract. Feature selection plays an important role in various machine learning tasks such as classification. In this paper, we focus on both discriminative and representative abilities of the features, and propose a novel feature selection method with joint exploration on both labeled and unlabeled data. In particular, we implement discriminative feature selection to extract the features that can best reveal the underlying classification labels, and develop representative feature selection to obtain the features with optimal self-expressive performance. Both methods are formulated as joint $\ell_{2,1}$-norm minimization problems. An effective alternate minimization algorithm is also introduced with analytic solutions in a column-by-column manner. Extensive experiments on various classification tasks demonstrate the advantage of the proposed method over several state-of-the-art methods.

Keywords: Feature selection · Discriminative feature · Representative feature
Matrix optimization · Model learning

1 Introduction

In machine learning, high dimensional raw data are mathematically and computationally inconvenient to handle due to the curse of dimensionality [1–5]. In order to build robust learning models, feature selection is a typical and critical process, which selects a subset of relevant and informative features meanwhile removes the irrelevant and redundant ones from the input high-dimensional feature space [6, 7]. Feature selection improves both effectiveness and efficiency of the learning model in that it can enhance the generalization capability and speed up the learning process [8, 9]. The main challenge with feature selection is to select the smallest possible feature subset to achieve the highest possible learning performance.

Classic feature selection methods fall into various categories according to the involvement of classifiers in the selection procedure [10–12]. Although various feature selection methods have been proposed, the major emphases are placed on the discriminative ability of the features. That is to say, the features that achieve the highest classification performance are inclined to be selected. Since the classification labels are

© Springer International Publishing AG, part of Springer Nature 2018
Y. Shi et al. (Eds.): ICCS 2018, LNCS 10862, pp. 632–638, 2018.
https://doi.org/10.1007/978-3-319-93713-7_59

involved in feature selection, this type of feature selection methods can be severely biased to labeled data. As we know, in practical classification applications, the dataset consists of both labeled and unlabeled data. It is usually the case that there are much more unlabeled data than labeled ones. To leverage both labeled and unlabeled data for feature selection, semi-supervised feature selection methods have been studied [13, 14]. Although the information underneath unlabeled data is explored, these methods are still confined to the discriminative aspect of the features. However, a comprehensive feature selection method should further take into account the representative ability with respect to the entire dataset.

Toward this end, this paper presents a novel feature selection method to explore both discriminative and representative abilities of the features. Motivated by the previous research, discriminative feature selection is implemented on labeled data via alternate optimization. Representative feature selection is further proposed to extract the most relevant features that can best recover the entire feature set, which is formulated as a self-expressive problem in the form of $\ell_{2,1}$-norm minimization. Finally, we integrate the discriminative and representative feature selection methods into a unified process. Experimental results demonstrate that the proposed feature selection method outperforms other state-of-the-art methods in various classification tasks.

2   Discriminative Feature Selection

In this paper, we follow the conventional notations, i.e. matrices are written as boldface uppercase letters and vectors are written as boldface lowercase letters. Given a matrix $\mathbf{M} = [m_{ij}]$, its i-th row and j-th column are denoted by $\mathbf{m}^i$ and $\mathbf{m}_j$ respectively. Given the labeled dataset in the form of data matrix $\mathbf{X} = [\mathbf{x}_1, \ldots, \mathbf{x}_n] \in \mathbb{R}^{d \times n}$ and the associated label matrix $\mathbf{Y} = [\mathbf{y}_1, \ldots, \mathbf{y}_n]^T \in \mathbb{R}^{n \times c}$, where d, n and c are the numbers of features, instances (or data) and classes respectively, discriminative feature selection aims at extracting the smallest possible subset of features that can accurately reveal the underlying classification labels. This can be formulated as an optimization problem which searches for the optimal projection from the feature space to the label space with only a limited number of features involved. Denoting the projection matrix as $\mathbf{A} \in \mathbb{R}^{d \times c}$, the objective is as follows.

$$\min_{\mathbf{A}} \sum_{i=1}^{n} \left\| \mathbf{A}^T \mathbf{x}_i - \mathbf{y}_i \right\|_2 + \alpha \|\mathbf{A}\|_{2,1} \tag{1}$$

The first term in (1) is the loss of projection, and the second term is the $\ell_{2,1}$-norm regularization with parameter α to enforce several rows of $\mathbf{A}$ to be all zero. Equation (1) can be written into the matrix format:

$$\min_{\mathbf{A}} \mathcal{L}_D(\mathbf{A}) = \left\| \mathbf{X}^T \mathbf{A} - \mathbf{Y} \right\|_{2,1} + \alpha \|\mathbf{A}\|_{2,1} \tag{2}$$

According to the general half-quadratic framework [15] for regularized robust learning, an augmented cost function $\mathcal{J}_D(\mathbf{A}, \mathbf{p}, \mathbf{q})$ can be introduced for the minimization of function $\mathcal{L}_D(\mathbf{A})$ in (2).

$$\mathcal{J}_D(\mathbf{A}, \mathbf{p}, \mathbf{q}) = \mathrm{Tr}\left[(\mathbf{X}^T\mathbf{A} - \mathbf{Y})^T\mathbf{P}(\mathbf{X}^T\mathbf{A} - \mathbf{Y})\right] + \alpha\mathrm{Tr}(\mathbf{A}^T\mathbf{Q}\mathbf{A}) \qquad (3)$$

where $\mathbf{p}$ and $\mathbf{q}$ are auxiliary vectors, while $\mathbf{P}$ and $\mathbf{Q}$ are diagonal matrices defined as $\mathbf{P} = \mathrm{diag}(\mathbf{p})$ and $\mathbf{Q} = \mathrm{diag}(\mathbf{q})$ respectively. The operator $\mathrm{diag}(\cdot)$ places a vector on the main diagonal of a square matrix. The i-th diagonal element of $\mathbf{P}$ and $\mathbf{Q}$ are:

$$p_{ii} = \frac{1}{2\left\|(\mathbf{X}^T\mathbf{A} - \mathbf{Y})^i\right\|_2} = \frac{1}{2\|\mathbf{A}^T\mathbf{x}_i - \mathbf{y}_i\|_2} \qquad (4)$$

$$q_{ii} = \frac{1}{2\|\mathbf{a}^i\|_2} \qquad (5)$$

With the vectors $\mathbf{p}$ and $\mathbf{q}$ given, we take the derivative of $\mathcal{J}_D(\mathbf{A}, \mathbf{p}, \mathbf{q})$ with respect to $\mathbf{A}$, and setting the derivative to zero, and arrive at:

$$\mathbf{A}^* = \left(\mathbf{X}\mathbf{P}\mathbf{X}^T + \alpha\mathbf{Q}\right)^{-1}\mathbf{X}\mathbf{P}\mathbf{Y} \qquad (6)$$

Note that both $\mathbf{P}$ and $\mathbf{Q}$ are dependent on $\mathbf{A}$, and thus they are also unknown variables. Based on the half-quadratic optimization, the global optimal solution can be achieved iteratively in an alternate minimization way. In each iteration, $\mathbf{P}$ and $\mathbf{Q}$ are calculated with the current $\mathbf{A}$ according to (4) and (5) respectively, and then $\mathbf{A}$ is updated with the latest $\mathbf{P}$ and $\mathbf{Q}$ according to (6). The alternate optimization procedure is iterated until convergence. After obtaining the optimal $\mathbf{A}$, discriminative features can be selected accordingly. We first calculate the absolute value of the elements of $\mathbf{A}$ by $\mathrm{abs}(\mathbf{A})$, and then sort the rows of $\mathbf{A}$ by the sums along the row dimension of $\mathrm{abs}(\mathbf{A})$. Feature selection can subsequently be performed by retaining the k features corresponding to the top k rows of sorted $\mathbf{A}$.

3   Representative Feature Selection

As for unlabeled data, only the data matrix $\mathbf{X} = [\mathbf{x}_1, \ldots, \mathbf{x}_n] \in \mathbb{R}^{d \times n}$ is available, whereas the corresponding class labels are unrevealed. In this scenario, representative, rather than discriminative, feature selection is implemented to extract a limited number of informative features that are highly relevant to the rest features. The corresponding optimization problem is a self-expressive problem, which selects a relatively small subset of features that can best recover the entire feature set with linear representation. For convenience, we denote the transpose of data matrix as the feature matrix $\mathbf{F} = \mathbf{X}^T = [\mathbf{f}_1, \ldots, \mathbf{f}_d] \in \mathbb{R}^{n \times d}$, whose column vectors can be regarded as n-dimensional points in the feature space. The objective is formulated as follows to obtain the representation matrix $\mathbf{B} \in \mathbb{R}^{d \times d}$.

$$\min_{\mathbf{B}} \sum_{i=1}^{d} \|\mathbf{F}\mathbf{b}_i - \mathbf{f}_i\|_2 + \beta \|\mathbf{B}\|_{2,1} \tag{7}$$

Similar to (1), the first term in (7) is the loss of representation, and the second term is the $\ell_{2,1}$-norm regularization to ensure row sparsity of $\mathbf{B}$ for representative feature selection. Equation (7) is equivalent to

$$\min_{\mathbf{B}} \mathcal{L}_R(\mathbf{B}) = \left\|(\mathbf{F}\mathbf{B} - \mathbf{F})^T\right\|_{2,1} + \beta \|\mathbf{B}\|_{2,1} \tag{8}$$

By introducing auxiliary vectors $\mathbf{p}$ and $\mathbf{q}$, we arrive at augmented cost function:

$$\mathcal{J}_R(\mathbf{B}, \mathbf{p}, \mathbf{q}) = \mathrm{Tr}\left[(\mathbf{F}\mathbf{B} - \mathbf{F})\mathbf{P}(\mathbf{F}\mathbf{B} - \mathbf{F})^T\right] + \beta \mathrm{Tr}(\mathbf{B}^T \mathbf{Q} \mathbf{B}) \tag{9}$$

where $\mathbf{P} = \mathrm{diag}(\mathbf{p})$ and $\mathbf{Q} = \mathrm{diag}(\mathbf{q})$, with the i-th diagonal element defined as

$$p_{ii} = \frac{1}{2\left\|(\mathbf{F}\mathbf{B} - \mathbf{F})_i\right\|_2} = \frac{1}{2\|\mathbf{F}\mathbf{b}_i - \mathbf{f}_i\|_2} \tag{10}$$

$$q_{ii} = \frac{1}{2\|\mathbf{b}^i\|_2} \tag{11}$$

With the vectors $\mathbf{p}$ and $\mathbf{q}$ fixed, we set the derivative of $\mathcal{J}_R(\mathbf{B}, \mathbf{p}, \mathbf{q})$ to zero. Different from DFS, the analytic solution is not directly available. However, for each i ($1 \leq i \leq d$), the optimal representation matrix $\mathbf{B}$ can be calculated column by column with the following close form solution:

$$\mathbf{b}_i^* = p_{ii}\left(p_{ii}\mathbf{F}^T\mathbf{F} + \beta \mathbf{Q}\right)^{-1}\mathbf{F}^T\mathbf{f}_i \tag{12}$$

To achieve the global optimal solution for representative feature selection, the alternate optimization according to (10), (11) and (12) is also implemented. Similarly, representative features can be selected according to the sorted $\mathbf{B}$ with respect to the row sums of abs$(\mathbf{B})$.

4   Joint Discriminative and Representative Feature Selection

As we know, the cost associated with manually labeling often renders a fully labeled dataset infeasible, whereas acquisition of unlabeled data is relatively inexpensive. As a result, the available dataset typically consists of a very limited number of labeled data and relatively much more abundant unlabeled data. In order to fully explore and exploit both labeled and unlabeled data, the feature selection algorithms discussed above should be further integrated. In this section, we introduce the Joint Discriminative and Representative Feature Selection (JDRFS) algorithm, which implements DFS and RFS successively.

We denote labeled data as $\{\mathbf{X}_L \in \mathbb{R}^{d \times n_L}, \mathbf{Y}_L \in \mathbb{R}^{n_L \times c}\}$ and unlabeled data as $\mathbf{X}_U \in \mathbb{R}^{d \times n_U}$, where n_L and n_U stand for the numbers of labeled and unlabeled data respectively. The number of features to be selected, denoted as d_{DR} ($d_{DR} < d$), is specified by the user beforehand. Firstly, the DFS algorithm is carried out on labeled data $\{\mathbf{X}_L, \mathbf{Y}_L\}$. Based on the optimal projection matrix $\mathbf{A}$, the least discriminative features can be preliminarily filtered out from the original d features. In this way, the candidate features are effectively narrowed down. Secondly, the RFS algorithm is performed for further selection. Instead of merely confining to unlabeled data $\mathbf{X}_U$, the entire dataset $\mathbf{X} = [\mathbf{X}_L, \mathbf{X}_U] \in \mathbb{R}^{d \times n}$ ($n = n_L + n_U$) is involved. Assuming there are d_D ($d_{DR} < d_D < d$) features selected after DFS, we can trim $\mathbf{X}$ by eliminating the irrelevant features and arrive at $\mathbf{X}' \in \mathbb{R}^{d_D \times n}$, whose rows corresponds to the retained d_D features. After that, RFS is implemented on $\mathbf{X}'$ to obtain optimal representation matrix $\mathbf{B} \in \mathbb{R}^{d_D \times d_D}$. Consequently, the most representative d_{DR} features are selected out of the d_D features.

5   Experiments

In order to validate the performance of the JDRFS method, several experiments on various applications are carried out. Three classic feature extraction methods (i.e. PCA, ICA, and LDA), two sparse regularized feature selection methods (i.e. RoFS [10] and CRFS [11]), and the state-of-the-art semi-supervised feature selection method (i.e. SSFS [13]) are compared. The regularized softmax regression is used as classifier.

We evaluate different feature selection methods based on the classification performance of malwares [9], images [5], and patent documents [5].

For the classification applications, we implement two sets of experiments. In the first experiment, we employ a fixed number of training data and examine the classification performance with different numbers of features selected. In the second experiment, the number of features selected is fixed and we evaluate the classification performance with gradually increasing numbers of training data.

Fig. 1. The classification accuracy with fixed number of training data and different number of features selected.

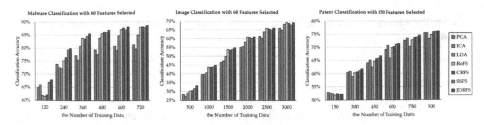

Fig. 2. The classification accuracy with fixed number of features selected and different number of training data.

Figures 1 and 2 show the classification results corresponding to the two settings respectively. In general, JDRFS and SSFS outperform the rest methods, because they take full advantage of the information from both labeled and unlabeled data. With joint exploration on both discriminative and representative abilities of the features in an explicit way, JDRFS outperforms all the competitors and receives the highest classification accuracy. We can also see that the sparse regularized feature selection methods (CRFS, and RoFS) perform better than the classic feature extraction methods (PCA, ICA, and LDA), especially in malware and image classification. This is due to the explicit incorporation of classification labels in the feature selection objective. It also explains the higher accuracy achieved by LDA, which focuses on difference between classes of data, than PCA and ICA. As for patent classification, the advantages of CRFS and RoFS over PCA, ICA, and LDA become less significant. The most probable reason is that patent, compared with malware and image, classification is highly dependent on sophisticated domain knowledge. As a result, the classification labels offer less clue for informative feature selection. For the same reason, LDA degrades severely in patent classification.

6 Conclusion

In this paper, we have explored both labeled and unlabeled data and proposed the joint discriminative and representative feature selection method. Main contributions of this work are three-fold. Firstly, both discriminative and representative abilities of the features are taken into account in a unified process, which brings about adaptive and robust performance. Secondly, representative feature selection is proposed to extract the most relevant features that can best recover the entire feature set, which is formulated as a $\ell_{2,1}$-norm self-expressive problem. Thirdly, an alternate minimization algorithm is introduced with analytic solutions in a column-by-column manner. Extensive experiments have validated the effectiveness of the proposed feature selection method and demonstrated its advantage over other state-of-the-art methods.

Acknowledgement. This work was supported by National Natural Science Foundation of China (Grant 61501457, 61602517), Open Project Program of National Laboratory of Pattern Recognition (Grant 201800018), Open Project Program of the State Key Laboratory of Mathematical Engineering and Advanced Computing (Grant 2017A05), and National Key Research and Development Program of China (Grant 2016YFB0801305).

Xiao-Yu Zhang and **Shupeng Wang** contribute equally to this paper, and are **Joint First Authors.**

References

1. Zhang, X., Xu, C., Cheng, J., Lu, H., Ma, S.: Effective annotation and search for video blogs with integration of context and content analysis. IEEE Trans. Multimedia **11**(2), 272–285 (2009)
2. Liu, H., Motoda, H.: Feature Selection for Knowledge Discovery and Data Mining. Springer, New York (2012). https://doi.org/10.1007/978-1-4615-5689-3
3. Saeys, Y., Inza, I., Larrañaga, P.: A review of feature selection techniques in bioinformatics. Bioinformatics **23**(19), 2507–2517 (2007)
4. Zhang, X.: Interactive patent classification based on multi-classifier fusion and active learning. Neurocomputing **127**, 200–205 (2014)
5. Zhang, X.Y., Wang, S., Yun, X.: Bidirectional active learning: a two-way exploration into unlabeled and labeled data set. IEEE Trans. Neural Netw. Learn. Syst. **26**(12), 3034–3044 (2015)
6. Liu, Y., Zhang, X., Zhu, X., Guan, Q., Zhao, X.: Listnet-based object proposals ranking. Neurocomputing **267**, 182–194 (2017)
7. Zhang, K., Yun, X., Zhang, X.Y., Zhu, X., Li, C., Wang, S.: Weighted hierarchical geographic information description model for social relation estimation. Neurocomputing **216**, 554–560 (2016)
8. Zhang, X.Y.: Simultaneous optimization for robust correlation estimation in partially observed social network. Neurocomputing **205**, 455–462 (2016)
9. Zhang, X.Y., Wang, S., Zhu, X., Yun, X., Wu, G., Wang, Y.: Update vs. upgrade: modeling with indeterminate multi-class active learning. Neurocomputing **162**, 163–170 (2015)
10. Nie, F., Huang, H., Cai, X., Ding, C.H.: Efficient and robust feature selection via joint $\ell_{2,1}$-norms minimization. In: Advances in Neural Information Processing Systems, pp. 1813–1821 (2010)
11. He, R., Tan, T., Wang, L., Zheng, W.S.: $l_{2,1}$ regularized correntropy for robust feature selection. In: IEEE Conference on Computer Vision and Pattern Recognition (CVPR), pp. 2504–2511 (2012)
12. He, R., Zheng, W.S., Hu, B.G.: Maximum correntropy criterion for Robust face recognition. IEEE Trans. PAMI **33**(8), 1561–1576 (2011)
13. Xu, Z., King, I., Lyu, M.R.T., Jin, R.: Discriminative semi-supervised feature selection via manifold regularization. IEEE Trans. Neural Netw. **21**(7), 1033–1047 (2010)
14. Chang, X., Nie, F., Yang, Y., Huang, H.: A convex formulation for semi-supervised multi-label feature selection. In: AAAI, pp. 1171–1177 (2014)
15. He, R., Zheng, W.S., Tan, T., Sun, Z.: Half-quadratic-based iterative minimization for robust sparse representation. IEEE Trans. Pattern Anal. Mach. Intell. **36**(2), 261–275 (2014)

Agile Tuning Method in Successive Steps for a River Flow Simulator

Mariano Trigila[1,2(✉)], Adriana Gaudiani[2,3], and Emilio Luque[4]

[1] Facultad de Informática, Universidad Nacional de La Plata, Buenos Aires, Argentina
marianotrigila@gmail.com, mariano_trigila@uca.edu.ar
[2] Facultad de Ingeniería y Ciencias Agrarias, Pontificia Universidad Católica Argentina,
Ciudad Autónoma de Buenos Aires, Argentina
agaudi@ungs.edu.ar
[3] Instituto de Ciencias, Universidad Nacional de General Sarmiento, Buenos Aires, Argentina
[4] Depto. de Arquitectura de Computadores y Sistemas Operativos,
Universidad Autònoma de Barcelona, 08193 Bellaterra (Barcelona), Spain
emilio.Luque@uab.es

Abstract. Scientists and engineers continuously build models to interpret axiomatic theories or explain the reality of the universe of interest to reduce the gap between formal theory and observation in practice. We focus our work on dealing with the uncertainty of the input data of the model to improve the quality of the simulation. To reduce this error, scientist and engineering implement techniques for model tuning and they look for ways to reduce their high computational cost. This article proposes a methodology for adjusting a simulator of a complex dynamic system that models the wave translation along rivers channels, with emphasis on the reduction of computation resources. We propose a simulator calibration by using a methodology based on successive adjustment steps of the model. We based our process in a parametric simulation. The input scenarios used to run the simulator at every step were obtained in an agile way, achieving a model improvement up to 50% in the reduction of the simulated data error. These results encouraged us to extend the adjustment process over a larger domain region.

Keywords: Parametric simulation · Tuning methodology
Flood simulation improvement · Dynamical systems · Flood model calibration

1 Introduction

The models built by scientists and engineers are often expressed in terms of processes that govern the dynamics and in terms of entities that determine the system states. They usually implement the models in a computerized simulation system. The values provided by a simulation are the model response to a certain system scenario [8]. Tuning, calibration or adjustment of the simulator are improvement process that seek the best set of input parameters to achieve the smallest difference between the output data and the reference data set [1, 6]. The automatic tuning of a simulation needs multiple instances of simulator running, one for each parameters combination. In consequence, the more parameters are considered, the more computing time is needed [8]. The main idea

© Springer International Publishing AG, part of Springer Nature 2018
Y. Shi et al. (Eds.): ICCS 2018, LNCS 10862, pp. 639–646, 2018.
https://doi.org/10.1007/978-3-319-93713-7_60

proposed in this article is an automatic tuning methodology for a simulator of a complex dynamic system that models the waves' displacement in rivers and channels. This approach exploits a local behavior of the system: Parameters of the domain of the system with spatial proximity do not change or differ very little, which allows us to reduce the search space and in consequence, the computational cost. We take advantage of the research and the results of previous works [2, 3]. Using our methodology, we were able to find input scenarios to execute the simulation that provided an improvement of up to 50% in the quality of the simulation in relation to the initial scenario (currently used for simulation and forecasting).

2   Description of the Simulator

The computational model used in our experiments is a simulation software developed in the Laboratory of Computational Hydraulics of the National Institute of Water (INA). This computer model calculates the translation of waves through a riverbed calculated by the equations of Saint Venant. It implements a one-dimensional hydrodynamic model of the Paraná River for hydrologic forecasting [4, 5]. Next, we describe the key features of the computational model.

2.1   Domain Modeling Feature

Simulator represents a hydrodynamic model consisting of two sections or filaments. Each filament represents the path of a river. See graphical representation in Fig. 1. To simulate the transport of water in a filament channel, its route is subdivided into sections. Each section (Sc) represents a specific position within the path, and it is divided into subsections (Su).

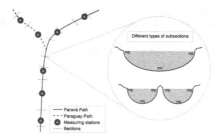

Fig. 1. Discretization of the river domain. Some types of Su in the cross Sc of the domain.

The simulator requires setting a set of input parameters values, which determines a simulation scenario. At every Su, the roughness coefficient of Manning (m) is the parameter used as an adjustment variable, which depends on the resistance offered by the main channel and the floodplain [1, 5]. We distinguish both values as Manning of plain (*mp*) and Manning of channel (*mc*). Depending on the channel geometry in each section, a greater or lesser amount is needed of *mp* and *mc*. The different forms of the sections were shown in Fig. 1.

2.2   Observed Data Measured at Monitoring Stations

A monitoring or measuring station (St) is the "physical and real" place where the river heights are surveyed and recorded. Each St is located in a city on the banks of the river channel. The data collected and recorded from the height of the river are known as observed data (OD), and they are measured daily. Data for the period from 1994 to 2011 were used to implement the experiences carried out in this work [4].

3   Proposed Methodology

We propose a search methodology to improve a simulator quality by finding the best set of parameters. Our aim is to optimize the simulation for a reduced search space, ω, such that $\omega \subset \Omega$, minimizing the use of computing resources to achieve the objective, where Ω is the whole search space with all possible combinations of the adjustment parameters and ω is the resulting reduced space [7]. Unlike the work in [3], we propose a calibration process of successive tuning steps to obtain an adjusted input parameters values from a preselected set of successive sections. Each parameters combination determines a simulation scenario and we detail its structure below. The quality of the simulated data (SD) is measured through calculating a divergence index (DI), as we explain in Sect. 3.4.

We start the method by choosing a monitoring station St_k located in an initial place k on the riverbed and selecting three contiguous sections, which are adjacent to that station. Figure 2 shows an outline of the set of possible scenarios and the selection of the best of them. This process searches the adjusted parameters set, $\widehat{X}$, for the station k, which determines the best simulation scenario $\widehat{S}_k$. This tuning method is repeated for the next station in a successive way, extending the successive adjustment process until reaching the last one, as we show in Fig. 3.

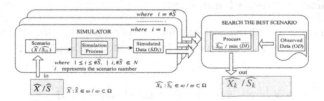

Fig. 2. Search process of the best scenario $\widehat{S}_k$ for k station.

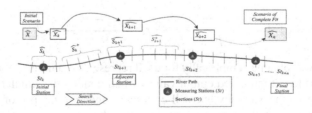

Fig. 3. Successive tuning process

3.1 Structure of the Input Scenario

We define a set of parameters for section m, subdivided into three subsections, as the 3-tupla:

$$Sc_m = (mp_m, mc_m, mp_m) \tag{1}$$

Where mp_m represent Manning value of plain and mc_m represent Manning value of channel. We remark that Eq. (1) has two independent variables, mp_m and mc_m and it takes the same mp_m value at both section ends. Initially, three contiguous and adjacent sections were chosen for station k, being its scenario $\widehat{S}_k$ defined by:

$$\widehat{S}_k = \begin{bmatrix} Sc_m \\ Sc_{m+1} \\ Sc_{m+2} \end{bmatrix} = \begin{bmatrix} mp_m & mc_m & mp_m \\ mp_{m+1} & mc_{m+1} & mp_{m+1} \\ mp_{m+2} & mc_{m+2} & mp_{m+2} \end{bmatrix} = \begin{bmatrix} mp_k & mc_k & mp_k \\ mp_k & mc_k & mp_k \\ mp_k & mc_k & mp_k \end{bmatrix} \tag{2}$$

Being a physical system, and because the sections are close together, it is assumed that the three sections have the same values of mp y mc for St_k.

We remark in Eqs. (4) and (5) that, mp_k and mc_k are independent variables. Therefore, the input scenario used to start the tuning process $\widehat{X}$ is determined by the scenarios $\widehat{S}_k$ corresponding to the sections Sc_m, and for the intermediate scenarios $\widehat{S}_k^+$ corresponding to the intermediate sections Sc_m^+ located between the stations k y $k+1$. Equation (5) represents $\widehat{X}$ structure for n stations:

$$\widehat{X} = \left\{ \widehat{S}_k, \widehat{S}_k^+, \widehat{S_{k+1}}, \widehat{S_{k+1}}^+, \ldots, \widehat{S}_n \right\}, \; with \; k = 1 \tag{3}$$

3.2 Discretization Process Parameters

The variation range of both imp and imc, and the increment step, smp and smc, are initial set values provided by INA experts. We implemented our experiences based on these values.

$$imp = \left[mp_{min}, mp_{max} \right] = [0.1, 0.71]; \; smp = 0.01 \tag{4}$$

$$imc = \left[mc_{min}, mc_{max} \right] = [0.017, 0.078]; \; smc = 0.001 \tag{5}$$

$$\#\widehat{S} = 61 \; | \frac{mp_{max} - mp_{min,}}{smp} = \#\widehat{S} \wedge \frac{mc_{max} - mc_{min,}}{smc} = \#\widehat{S} \tag{6}$$

($\#\widehat{S} = 61$) was obtained empirically for us. It represents minimum value of scenarios, which allow us to get improved output values when running the simulation. Increment $\#\widehat{S}$ could increase the accuracy but will effectively increase the use of computational resources. Equation (9) determines each scenario values $\widehat{S_{k(i)}}$:

$$
\widehat{S_{k(i)}} = \begin{bmatrix} mp_i & mc_i & mp_i \\ mp_i & mc_i & mp_i \\ mp_i & mc_i & mp_i \end{bmatrix}
$$
$$
= \begin{bmatrix} (smp \cdot i) + mp_{ini} & (smc \cdot i) + mc_{ini} & (smp \cdot i) + mp_{ini} \\ (smp \cdot i) + mp_{ini} & (smc \cdot i) + mc_{ini} & (smp \cdot i) + mp_{ini} \\ (smp \cdot i) + mp_{ini} & (smc \cdot i) + mc_{ini} & (smp \cdot i) + mp_{ini} \end{bmatrix}
$$
(7)

Where i is the number of scenario, the range $\left[i, \#\widehat{S}\right] \subset \mathbb{N}$, $where\ 1 \leq i \leq \#\widehat{S}$, mp_{ini} and mc_{ini} are the initial values. We use these values to start the search process and to run the simulator for each scenario, in order to find the best one as we describe in next section.

3.3   Search of the Best Scenario

Through a divergence index implemented with the root mean square error estimator (RMSE), the best-input scenario is determined by comparing the SD series with the OD series.

$$
DI_k^y = RSME_k^y = \sqrt[2]{\frac{\sum_{i=1}^{i=N} \left(H_k^{OD.y} - H_k^{SD.y}\right)_i^2}{N}}
$$
(8)

The index DI_k^y is the RMSE error of the series of river heights simulated $H_k^{SD.y}$ with respect to of the series of river heights observed $H_k^{OD.y}$, for a station k, and for a year y, which is the simulation time, and the number of stations, N. The best fit scenario for the k station which generates a set of output H_k^{SD} is the minimum DI_k^k, $(\min\left(\widehat{DI_k^y}\right))$ of all the simulations.

3.4   Successive Tuning Process

After obtaining the scenario that best fits for St k, the adjustment can be extended to a new St $k + 1$. We take advantage of the system locality behavior and we set the parameters with the previously calculated adjustment values. To make this possible, the scenario $\widehat{S_k}^+$ is initialized with the values of the best scenario $\widehat{S_k}$, immediately before. We took advantage of the locality behavior, which means that those sections that are close one to another have similar adjustment parameters values or they differ very little.

In the successive input scenarios, we "leave fixed the adjusted parameters values found" in the previous calibrations, and thus the previous adjustment scenarios of each section are used to find the actual adjusted parameters values. For k St the new k parameter vector is: $\widehat{X_k} = \left\{\widehat{S_k}, \widehat{S_k}^+, \widehat{S_{k+1}}, \widehat{S_{k+1}}^+, \ldots., \widehat{S_n}\right\}$

The $k + 1$ input scenario, or k + 1 parameters vector, is:

$$
\widehat{X_{k+1}} = \left\{\widehat{S_k}, \widehat{S_k}^+, \widehat{S_{k+1}}, \widehat{S_{k+1}}^+, \ldots., \widehat{S_n}\right\}, \text{ where } \widehat{S_k}^+ = \widehat{S_k}
$$

The $k + 2$ input scenario, or $k + 2$ parameters vector is:

$$\widehat{X_{k+2}} = \left\{ \widehat{S}_k, \widehat{S}_k^{+}, \widehat{S_{k+1}}, \widehat{S_{k+1}}^{+}, \dots, \widehat{S}_n \right\}, \text{ where } \widehat{S}_k^{+} = \widehat{S}_k, \widehat{S_{k+1}}^{+} = \widehat{S_{k+1}}$$

For n input scenario to the Simulator (scenario that adjusts the entire domain):

$$\widehat{X}_n = \left\{ \widehat{S}_k, \widehat{S}_k^{+}, \widehat{S_{k+1}}, \widehat{S_{k+1}}^{+}, \dots, \widehat{S}_n \right\}, \text{ where } \widehat{S}_k^{+} = \widehat{S}_k, \dots, \widehat{S_{n-1}}^{+} = \widehat{S_{n-1}} \tag{9}$$

4 Experimental Results

In search of the best scenario performed on the k St "Esquina" (ESQU), we found scenarios that improved the results up to 57% in relation to the initial scenario used by the INA's experts, determined by ratio of $DI_k^y(Fit)$ to $DI_k^y(Initial)$.

We show in Table 1 the synthesis process with the top three scenarios found for processed k St. As also, it shows the second St $k + 1$ adjusted. The best scenario was found at "La Paz", St (LAPA), which is an adjacent St to ESQU.

Table 1. Adjustment made in k St and $k + 1$ St, several years.

S_i	$\widehat{S}_{k(\infty)}$	Year	Station	Station ID	DI_k^y (I) – Initial	$DI_k^y(F)$ – Fit	Improvement $DI_k^y(F)/DI_k^y(I)$
46	(0.55, 0.062, 0.55)	2008	k	ESQU	1.55	0.66	57%
54	(0.63, 0.070, 0.63)	1999	k	ESQU	1.42	0.87	39%
38	(0.47, 0.054, 0.47)	2002	k	ESQU	1.24	0.97	22%
38	(0.47, 0.054, 0.47)	1999	$k + 1$	LAPA	1.72	0.94	45%
30	(0.39, 0.046, 0.39)	2008	$k + 1$	LAPA	1.17	0.89	24%

We show in Table 1, a synthesis process with the two best scenarios found for $k + 1$ station. Figure 4 shows a comparative graph with the observed data series (real measured), the initial simulated data series (original series loaded in the simulator) and the series of simulated data adjusted for the best fit scenarios in $(k + 1)$ station. We can see that our method achieves global better results over the whole series.

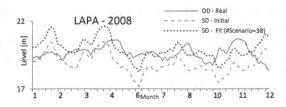

Fig. 4. Comparative OD, SD, Fit. Station k = LAPA, y = 2008

5   Conclusions

Our method "in successive steps of adjustments" was tuned by the locality simulation behavior, which provided promising results when finding scenarios that improved simulation quality and these encouraged us to continue our research in this direction. These scenarios provided numerical series of river heights closest to those observed at the measurement stations on the riverbed. The improvement percentage obtained was greater than 50%. The method is simple and manages to reduce the computational resources based on proportional successive increases of the initial scenario parameters (7). Thus, we reduced the time computing when we use the adjusted parameters obtained in the previous steps to calculate the actual one (9). We continue our work focused on finding an automatically calibration methodology of the computational model extending this methodology from a predetermined initial station to the last one at the end of the riverbed and applying the methodology described in this work. This proposal will make use of HPC techniques to decrease the execution times.

Acknowledgments. The MICINN/MINECO Spain under contracts TIN2014-53172-P and TIN2017-84875-P has supported this research. We are very grateful for the data provided by INA and we appreciate the guidance received from researchers at INA Hydraulic Laboratory.

References

1. Bladé, E., Gómez-Valentín, M., Dolz, J., Aragón-Hernández, J., Corestein, G., Sánchez-Juny, M.: Integration of 1D and 2D finite volume schemes for computations of water flow in natural channels. Adv. Water Resour. **42**, 17–29 (2012)
2. Cabrera, E., Luque, E., Taboada, M., Epelde, F., Iglesias, M.: Optimization of emergency departments by agent-based modeling and simulation. In: IEEE 13th International Conference on Information Reuse and Integration (IRI), pp. 423–430 (2012)
3. Gaudiani, A., Luque, E., García, P., Re, M., Naiouf, M., De Giusti, A.: How a computational method can help to improve the quality of river flood prediction by simulation. In: Marx Gomez, J., Sonnenschein, M., Vogel, U., Winter, A., Rapp, B., Giesen, N. (eds.) Advances and New Trends in Environmental and Energy Informatics, pp. 337–351. Springer, Cham (2016). https://doi.org/10.1007/978-3-319-23455-7_18
4. Menéndez, A.: Three decades of development and application of numerical simulation tools at INA Hydraulic lab., Mecánica Comutacional, vol. XXI, pp. 2247–2266 (2002)

5. Krauße, T., Cullmann, J.: Identification of hydrological model parameters for flood forecasting using data depth measures. Hydrol. Earth Syst. **8**, 2423–2476 (2011)
6. Sargent, R.: Verification and validation of simulation models. J. Simul. **7**, 12–24 (2013)
7. Wang, L.-F., Shi, L.-Y.: Simulation optimization: a review on theory and applications. Acta Automatica Sinica **39**(11), 1957–1968 (2013)
8. Wu, Q., Liu, S., Cai, Y., Li, X., Jiang, Y.: Improvement of hydrological model calibration by selecting multiple parameter ranges. Hydrol. Earth Syst. Sci. **21**, 393–407 (2017)

A Parallel Quicksort Algorithm on Manycore Processors in Sunway TaihuLight

Siyuan Ren, Shizhen Xu, and Guangwen Yang[(⊠)]

Tsinghua University, Beijing, China
ygw@tsinghua.edu.cn

Abstract. In this paper we present a highly efficient parallel quicksort algorithm on SW26010, a heterogeneous manycore processor that makes Sunway TaihuLight the Top-One supercomputer in the world. Motivated by the software-cache and on-chip communication design of SW26010, we propose a two-phase quicksort algorithm, with the first counting elements and the second moving elements. To make the best of such manycore architecture, we design a decentralized workflow, further optimize the memory access and balance the workload. Experiments show that our algorithm scales efficiently to 64 cores of SW26010, achieving more than 32X speedup for int32 elements on all kinds of data distributions. The result outperforms the strong scaling one of Intel TBB (Threading Building Blocks) version of quicksort on x86-64 architecture.

1 Introduction

This paper presents our design of parallel quicksort algorithm on SW26010, the heterogeneous manycore processor making the Sunway TaihuLight supercomputer currently Top-One in the world [4]. SW26010 features a cache-less design with two methods of memory access: DMA (transfer between scratchpad memory (SPM) and main memory) and Gload (transfer between register and main memory). The aggressive design of SW26010 results in an impressive performance of 3.06 TFlops, while also complicating programming design and performance optimizations.

Sorting has always been a extensively studied topic [6]. On heterogeneous architectures, prior works focus on GPGPUs. For instance, Satish et al. [9] compared several sorting algorithms on NVIDIA GPUs, including radix sort, normal quicksort, sample sort, bitonic sort and merge sort. GPU-quicksort [2] and its improvement CUDA-quicksort [8] used a double pass algorithm for parallel partition to minimize the need for communication. Leischner et al. [7] ported samplesort (a version of parallel quicksort) to GPUs, claiming significant speed improvement over GPU quicksort.

Prior works give us insights on parallel sorting algorithm, but cannot directly satisfy our need for two reasons. First, the Gload overhead is extremely high so that all the accessed memory have to be prefetched to SPM via DMA. At the same

© Springer International Publishing AG, part of Springer Nature 2018
Y. Shi et al. (Eds.): ICCS 2018, LNCS 10862, pp. 647–653, 2018.
https://doi.org/10.1007/978-3-319-93713-7_61

time, the capacity of SPM is highly limited (64 KiB). Second, SW26010 provides a customized on-chip communication mechanism, which opens new opportunities for optimization.

Based on these observations, we design and implement a new quicksort algorithm for SW26010. It alternates between parallel partitioning phase and parallel sorting phase. During first phase, the cores participate in a double-pass algorithm for parallel partitioning, where in the first pass cores count elements, and in the second cores move elements. During the second phase, the cores sort its assigned pieces in parallel.

To make the best of SW26010, we dispense with a central manager common in parallel algorithms. Instead we duplicate the metadata on SPM of all worker cores and employ a decentralized design. The tiny size of the SPM warrants special measures to maximize its utilization. Furthermore, we take advantage of the architecture by replacing memory access of value counts with register communication, and improving load balance with a simple counting scheme.

Experiments show that our algorithm performs best with int32 values, achieving more than 32 speedup (50% parallel efficiency) for sufficient array sizes and all kinds of data distributions. For double values, the lowest speedup is 20 (31% efficiency). We also compare against Intel TBB's parallel quicksort on x86-64 machines, and find that our algorithm on Sunway scales far better.

2   Architecture of SW26010

SW26010 [4] is composed of four core-groups (CGs). Each CG has one management processing element (MPE) (also referred as manager core), 64 computing processing elements (CPEs) (also referred as worker cores). The MPE is a complete 64-bit RISC core, which can run in both user and kernel modes. The CPE is also a tailored 64-bit RISC core, but it can only run in user mode. The CPE cluster is organized as an 8×8 mesh on-chip network. CPEs in one row and one column can directly communicate via register, at most 128 bit at a time. In addition, each CPE has a user-controlled scratch pad memory (SPM), of which the size is 64 KiB.

SW26010 processors provide two methods of memory access. The first is DMA, which transfers data between main memory and SPM. The second is Gload, which transfers data between main memory and register, akin to normal load/store instructions. The Gload overhead is extremely high, so it should be avoided as much as possible.

Virtual memory on one CG is usually only mapped to its own physical memory. In other words, four CGs can be regarded as four independent processors when we design algorithms. This work focuses on one core group, but we will also briefly discuss how to extend to more core groups.

3   Algorithm

As in the original quicksort, the basic idea is to recursively partition the sequence into subsequences separated by a pivot value. Values smaller than the pivot shall be moved to the left, larger to the right. Our algorithm is divided into two phases to reduce overhead. The first phase is parallel partitioning with a two pass algorithm. When the pieces are too many or small enough, we enter the second phase, when each core independently sorts its pieces. Both phases are carried out by repeated partitioning with slightly different algorithms.

3.1 Parallel Partitioning

Parallel partitioning is the core of our algorithm. We employ a two pass algorithm similar to [1, 2, 10]. In order to avoid concurrent writes. In the first pass, each core counts the total number of elements strictly smaller than and strictly larger than the pivot in its assigned subsequence. It does so by loading consecutively the values from main memory into its SPM and accumulating the count. The cores then communicate with one another about their counts, with which they can calculate the position by cumulative sum where they should write to in the next pass.

In the second pass, each core does their own partitioning again, this time directly transferring the partitioned result into their own position in the result array. This step can be done in parallel since all of the reads and writes are disjoint. After all cores commit their result, the result array is left with a middle gap to be filled by the pivot values. The cores then fill the gap in parallel with DMA writes.

The synchronization needed by the two pass algorithm is hence limited to only these places: a barrier at the end of counting pass, the communication of a small number of integers, and the barrier after the filling with pivots.

3.2 Communication of Value Counts

Because the value counts needed for calculation of target location are small in number, exchanging them through main memory among worker cores, either via DMA or Gload, would result in a great overhead. We instead decide to let the worker cores exchange the counts via register communication, with which the worker cores can transfer values at most 128 bit at a time. The smaller and larger counts are both 32-bit, so they can be concatenated into one 64-bit value and communicated in one go.

Each worker core needs only two combined values: one is the cumulative sum of counts for cores ordered before it, another is the total sum of all counts. The information flow is arranged in a zigzag fashion to deal with the restriction that cores can only communicate with one another in the same row or column.

3.3 Load Balancing

Since Sunway has 64 cores, load imbalance is a serious problem in phase II. If not all the cores finish their sorting at the same time, those that finish early will have to sit idle, wasting cycles. To reduce the imbalance, we employ a simple dynamic scheme based on an atomic counter.

To elaborate, we dedicate a small fraction of each SPM to hold the metadata of array segments that all of them are going to sort independently in parallel. When the storage of metadata is full, each core will enter phase II and choose one segment to sort. When any core finishes, it will atomically increment an counter in the main memory to get the index of next segment, until the counter exceeds the storage capacity, and the algorithm either returns to phase I or finishes.

3.4 Memory Optimization

As SPM is very small (64 KiB), any memory overhead will reduce the number of elements it can buffer at a time, thereby increasing the rounds of DMAs. Memory optimization is therefore critical to the overall performance. We employ the following tricks to further reduce memory overhead of control structures.

For one, we use an explicit stack, and during recursion of partitioning at all levels, we descend into the smaller subarray first. This bounds the memory usage of the call stack to $O(\log_2 N)$, however the pivot is chosen [5].

For another, we compress the representation of subarrays by converting 64-bit pointers to 32-bit offsets, and by reusing the sign bit to denote the base of the offset (either the original or the auxiliary array). The compression can reduce the number of bytes needed for each subarray representation from 16 bytes to 8 bytes, a 50% save.

3.5 Multiple Core Groups

To apply our algorithm to multiple core groups, we may combine the single core group algorithm with a variety of conventional parallel sorting algorithms, such as samplesort. Samplesort on n processors is composed of three steps [3]: partition the array with $n - 1$ splitters into n disjoint buckets, then distribute them onto n processors so that i-th processors have the i-th bucket, and finally sort them in parallel. To adapt our algorithm to multiple core groups, we simply regard each core group as a single processor in the sense of samplesort, and do the first step with our parallel partitioning algorithm (Sect. 3.1) with a slight modification (maintain n counts and do multi-way partitioning).

4 Experiments

To evaluate the performance of our algorithm, we test it on arrays of different sizes, different distributions, and different element types. We also test the multiple CG version against single CG version. To evaluate how our algorithm scales, we experiment with different number of worker cores active. Since there is no previous work on Sunway or similar machines to benchmark against, we instead compare our results with Intel TBB on x86-64 machines.

Sorting speed is affected by data distributions, especially for quicksort since its partitioning may be imbalanced. We test our algorithm on five different distributions of data. See Fig. 1 for the visualizations of the types of distributions.

Fig. 1. Visualizations of data distributions. The horizontal axis represents the index of element in the array, and the vertical axis the value.

For x86-64 we test on an AWS dedicated instance with 72 CPUs (Intel Xeon Platinum 8124M, the latest generation of server CPUs in 2017). The Intel TBB library is versioned 2018U1. Both the library and our test source are compiled with `-O3 -march=native` so that compiler optimizations are fully on.

4.1 Results on Sunway TaihuLight

We compare the running time of our algorithm on Sunway TaihuLight against single threaded sorting on the MPE with `std::sort`. The STL sort, as implemented on libstdc++, is a variant of quicksort called introsort.

Figure 2 shows the runtime results for sorting 32-bit integers. From the graph we can see that the distribution matters only a little. Figure 3 shows sorting different types of elements with the size fixed. The reason for the reduced efficiency with 64-bit types (int64 and double) is evident: the number of elements buffered in SPM each time is halved, and more round trips between main memory and SPM are needed. The reason for reduced efficiency of float32 values is unknown. Figure 4 shows the timings and speedups of multiple CG algorithm (adapted samplesort).

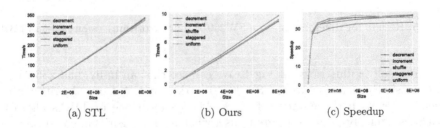

(a) STL	(b) Ours	(c) Speedup

Fig. 2. Results for int32 values

4.2 Comparison Against Intel TBB on x86-64

We compare our implementation against Intel TBB on Intel CPU. TBB is a C++ template library of generic parallel algorithms, developed by Intel, and most optimized for their own processors. For a fairer comparison, we choose a machine with one of the most powerful Intel processors available to date.

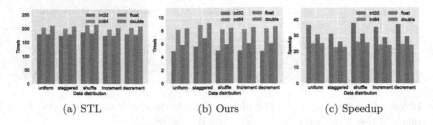

(a) STL   (b) Ours   (c) Speedup

Fig. 3. Results for different element types

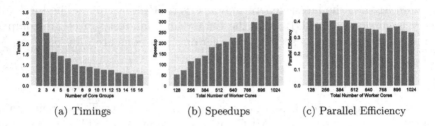

(a) Timings   (b) Speedups   (c) Parallel Efficiency

Fig. 4. Results for different number of core groups

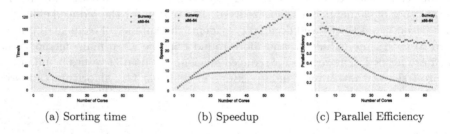

(a) Sorting time   (b) Speedup   (c) Parallel Efficiency

Fig. 5. Results for different cores on SW26010 (our algorithm) vs on x86-64 (TBB)

The result is illustrated at Fig. 5. We can see that an individual x86-64 core is about six times as fast as one SW26010 worker core, but our algorithm scales much better with the number of cores. The performance of TBB's algorithm saturates after about 20 cores are in use, whereas our algorithm could probably scale further from 64 cores, judging from the graph. Even though the comparison isn't direct since the architecture is different, it is evident that our algorithm on top of Sunway TaihuLight is much more efficient than traditional parallel sorting algorithms implemented on more common architectures.

5   Conclusion

In this paper, we present a customized parallel quicksort on SW26010 with significant speedup relatively to single core performance. It is composed of two-pass parallel partitioning algorithm with the first counting elements and the second moving elements. This design is able to leverage the on-chip communication mechanism to reduce synchronization overhead, and fast on-chip SPM to minimize the data movement overhead. Further, we design a cooperative scheduling scheme, and optimize memory usage as well as load balancing.

Experiments show that for int32 values, our algorithm achieves a speedup of more than 32 on 64 CPEs and a strong-scaling efficiency 50% for all distributions. Compared with Intel TBB's implementation of parallel quicksort on x86-64 architecture, our design scales well even when using all of 64 CPEs while TBB's implementation hardly benefit from more than 20 cores.

References

1. Blelloch, G.E.: Prefix sums and their applications. Technical report, Synthesis of Parallel Algorithms (1990). https://www.cs.cmu.edu/~guyb/papers/Ble93.pdf
2. Cederman, D., Tsigas, P.: GPU-Quicksort: a practical quicksort algorithm for graphics processors. J. Exp. Alg. **14**, 4 (2009)
3. Frazer, W.D., McKellar, A.C.: Samplesort: a sampling approach to minimal storage tree sorting. J. ACM **17**(3), 496–507 (1970)
4. Fu, H., Liao, J., Yang, J., Wang, L., Song, Z., Huang, X., Yang, C., Xue, W., Liu, F., Qiao, F., Zhao, W., Yin, X., Hou, C., Zhang, C., Ge, W., Zhang, J., Wang, Y., Zhou, C., Yang, G.: The Sunway TaihuLight supercomputer: system and applications. Sci. China Inf. Sci. **59**(7), 072001 (2016)
5. Hoare, C.A.R.: Quicksort. Comput. J. **5**(1), 10–16 (1962)
6. Knuth, D.E.: The Art of Computer Programming. Sorting and Searching, vol. 3, 2nd edn. Addison Wesley Longman Publishing Co., Inc., Redwood City (1998)
7. Leischner, N., Osipov, V., Sanders, P.: GPU sample sort. In: 2010 IEEE International Symposium on Parallel Distributed Processing, pp. 1–10, April 2010
8. Manca, E., Manconi, A., Orro, A., Armano, G., Milanesi, L.: CUDA-quicksort: an improved GPU-based implementation of quicksort. Concurr. Comput. Pract. Exp. **28**(1), 21–43 (2016)
9. Satish, N., Harris, M., Garland, M.: Designing efficient sorting algorithms for manycore GPUs. In: 2009 IEEE International Symposium on Parallel Distributed Processing, pp. 1–10, May 2009
10. Sengupta, S., Harris, M., Zhang, Y., Owens, J.D.: Scan primitives for GPU computing. In: Proceedings of the 22nd ACM SIGGRAPH/EUROGRAPHICS Symposium on Graphics Hardware, GH 2007, Eurographics Association, Aire-la-Ville, Switzerland, pp. 97–106 (2007)

How Is the Forged Certificates
in the Wild: Practice on Large-Scale SSL
Usage Measurement and Analysis

Mingxin Cui[1,2], Zigang Cao[1,2], and Gang Xiong[1,2(✉)]

[1] Institute of Information Engineering, Chinese Academy of Sciences, Beijing, China
[2] School of Cyber Security, University of Chinese Academy of Sciences,
Beijing, China
{cuimingxin,caozigang,xionggang}@iie.ac.cn

Abstract. Forged certificate is a prominent issue in the real world deployment of SSL/TLS - the most widely used encryption protocols for Internet security, which is typically used in man-in-the-middle (MITM) attacks, proxies, anonymous or malicious services, personal or temporary services, etc. It wrecks the SSL encryption, leading to privacy leakage and severe security risks. In this paper, we study forged certificates in the wild based on a long term large scale passive measurement. With the combination of certificate transparency (CT) logs and our measurement results, nearly 3 million forged certificates against the Alexa Top 10K sites are identified and studied. Our analysis reveals the causes and preference of forged certificates, as well as several significant differences from the benign ones. Finally, we discover several IP addresses used for MITM attacks by forged certificate tracing and deep behavior analysis. We believe our study can definitely contribute to research on SSL/TLS security as well as real world protocol usage.

Keywords: Forged certificate · Passive measurement · SSL MITM

1 Introduction

Secure Sockets Layer (SSL) and its successor Transport Layer Security (TLS) are security protocols that provide security and data integrity for network communications (we refer to SSL/TLS as SSL for brevity in this paper). An X.509 certificate plays an important role in SSL Public Key Infrastructure, which is the basis of the SSL encryption framework. When establishing SSL connection, the server or/and the client is required to provide a certificate to the peer to prove its identity. Since the widespread use of SSL, issues of certificate come out one after another as well, such as compromised CAs, weak public key algorithm, forged certificates, and so on. In this paper, we focus on forged certificates that mainly used in MITM attacks on HTTPS web services.

© Springer International Publishing AG, part of Springer Nature 2018
Y. Shi et al. (Eds.): ICCS 2018, LNCS 10862, pp. 654–667, 2018.
https://doi.org/10.1007/978-3-319-93713-7_62

When carrying out an SSL man-in-the-middle (MITM) attack, the attacker usually uses a forged certificate to pretend the compromised or malicious server and deceive careless users. And a victim's negligence would then lead to the privacy disclosure and property loss. Since attempts to MITM attacks on https-encrypted web sites have never stopped, it's necessary to conduct a comprehensive analysis to study the status quo of forged certificates in the real world.

Many researchers have published their work on the certificate ecosystem, providing different aspects view of X.509 certificates. And studies that try to reveal the negative side of the certificate have never been stopped. However, there're few works focused on forged certificate used by MITM attacks. In this paper, we conduct a comprehensive study of forged certificates in the wild, and the contributions of our work are as follows: First, we implement a 20-month passive measurement to collect the real-world SSL certificates on two research networks to explore the forged certificate issue, which is up to now the largest scale long term study. Second, we analyze the forged certificates against Alexa top 10 thousand web sites by combining both the passive measurement results and the public certificate transparency (CT) logs [14,18], which is highly representative and comprehensively. Third, we reveal the reasons, preferences of forged certificates, as well as distinct differences between the forged certificates and the benign ones in several attributes, offering valuable insights to researches on SSL/TLS security. Finally, several IP addresses are discovered which are probably used to carry out MITM attacks through a series of forged certificates tracing and traffic behavior analysis.

The remainder of this paper is structured as follows. Section 2 elaborates the related works. Section 3 describes our measurement and dataset used in this paper. We analyze and elaborate how forged certificates performed in the wild in Sect. 4 and compare to benign ones in Sect. 5. In Sect. 6, we try to trace and identify SSL MITM attacks and we conclude our work in Sect. 7.

2   Related Works

In recent years, many researchers have focused on the measurement of SSL encrypted traffic, and there're two ways to implement this: active measurement and passive measurement. [8] performed 110 scans of the IPv4 address space on port 443 over 14 months to study the HTTPS certificate ecosystem. [7] also implemented scans of the public IPv4 address space to collect data, with the help of ZMap [9]. And the certificate they collected could be found in Censys [1]. What's more, [19] found that a combination of Censys data and CT logs could account for more than 99% of their observed certificates. There're many other active scans which provide datasets of certificates, such as Rapid7 SSL [13]. [10] implemented both active and passive measurement to present a comprehensive analysis of X.509 certificates in the wild. The authors conducted HTTPS scans of popular HTTPS servers listed in Alexa Top 1 Million over 1.5 years from 9 locations distributed over the world. They also monitored SSL traffic on a 10 Gbps uplink of a research network.

There're also many works focused on the negative side of the certificate. [16] identified web-fraud using attributes extracted from certificates. [5] implemented an empirical study of certificates for depository institutions and showed the bad condition of bank websites in disposing SSL. [6] proposed a machine-learning approach to detect phishing websites utilizing features from their certificates. [2] studied invalid certificates in the wild, and revealed that most of the invalid certificates could be attributed to the reissues of a few types of end-user devices. Comparison between valid and invalid certificates was conducted as well. Several studies [4,11] detected SSL MITM attacks using different methods. However, they didn't focus on forged certificates used by MITM attackers. [12] implemented a method to detect the occurrence of SSL MITM attacks on Facebook, and their results indicated that 0.2% of the SSL connection they analyzed were tampered with forged SSL certificates. Their work only concentrated on Facebook, could not provide an overall view of forged certificates.

3   Measurement and Datasets

In this section, we describe our passive measurement and the datasets. The methodology of identifying forged certificates is elaborated as well.

3.1   Passive Measurement

In order to study the forged certificates, we implemented a passive measurement on two large research networks from November 2015 to June 2017. These networks could provide 100 Gbps bandwidth. Our program collected certificates and SSL sessions statistical information after an anonymous processing. Useful data would be added into the corresponding datasets, namely *DsCrt* and *DsCnn* respectively.

Table 1. Overview of certificate dataset

Cert types		#(Cert)	#(Issuers)	#(Subjects)
Forged certs	Selfsigned	107,306	922	922
	Un-selfsigned	2,759,980	215,236	3,988
	Totally	2,867,286	216,154	4,165
Benign certs		1,910,385	180	11,707
Totally		4,777,671	216,243	12,012

3.2   Datasets

Based on the measurement, we made up two datasets to store the certificates information and SSL sessions statistical information separately.

DsCrt contained all certificates we collected during the 20-month long measurement. Excluding tiny errors due to the high-speed network environment, we totally obtained 188,064,507 unique certificates, including 3,359,040 CAs (both root and intermediate) and 184,705,467 leaves. We extracted and identified these leaf certificates using the methodology mentioned in Sect. 3.3 and harvested 2,867,286 forged ones in 4,777,671 certificates that claimed to belong to Alexa Top 10k domains. After the identification, all of the gathered certificates were parsed into json format completely, referring to *Censys* data format [1]. The parsed attributes of a certificate include but are not limited to *sha1 value, signature algorithm, public key information, issuer, subject, validation period, extensions*, and so on.

DsCnn recorded the statistical information of SSL sessions detected during our measurement. For each SSL session, we stored server IP, server port, and some basic statistics such as bytes, packets, and packet interval, and of course the corresponding certificate SHA1 string. Server IP and port might help to trace the suspicious MITM attacks, and the basic statistics could be used to train machine-learning models in the future work.

3.3   Identifying Methodology

When identifying a leaf certificate was benign or not, we utilized the CAs in the Chrome root store (as of July 1, 2017). Since the measurement lasted such a long time, we ignored validation errors only due to expiration time. Thus, we recognized a leaf certificate was benign if the root CA of the corresponding certificate chain was credible. Otherwise it's not. For the latter one, we then checked if it was self-signed, and then labeled the certificate using *"is_benign"* and *"is_selfsigned"* attributes.

Since many web service providers use self-signed certificates due to the balance of cost and safety, and the compromise or abuse of root and intermediate CAs, it's really hard to identify whether a certificate was forged or not, especially for a self-signed one or a website in obscurity. Hence we chose the domains listed in Alexa Top 10k as target, and studied forged certificates of these well-known web services (if provided SSL encryption) picking the public CT logs [18] as a benchmark. For a certain certificate, if it wasn't included in any public CT logs, we regarded it as a forged one. Based on this constraint, we extracted 4,777,671 certificates which claimed to belong to Alexa Top 10k domains, and verified them with the help of CT logs included in Chrome. Finally we harvested 2,867,286 forged certificates of 4,165 different web services or domains after the verification.

3.4   Ethical Considerations

Considering the privacy and ethical issues in the passive measurement, we implement an anonymous process while dealing with the data. The client IP of each connection has been anonymized before our collection in the measurement system. Thus, we do not know the real client IP address of each SSL session. We focus on certificates and corresponding servers, but not the user privacy.

658   M. Cui et al.

Table 2. Top 20 issuers of forged certificates

No.	Issuer CN	#(Cert)	Ratio	No.	Issuer CN	#(Cert)	Ratio
1	([0-9a-z]{16})	998959	34.84%	11	UBT (EU) Ltd	15715	0.55%
2	mitmproxy	993585	34.65%	12	SSL-SG1-HK1	15350	0.54%
3	FortiGate CA	114276	3.99%	13	Lightspeed Rocket	14827	0.52%
4	(selfsigned)	107306	3.74%	14	thawte 2	14512	0.51%
5	Cisco Umbrella Secondary SubCA *-SG	52196	1.82%	15	10.1.100.51	13917	0.49%
6	Phumiiawe	34742	1.21%	16	Pifbunbaw	12630	0.44%
7	www.netspark.com	28128	0.98%	17	192.168.1.1	11597	0.40%
8	samsungsemi-prx.com	20174	0.70%	18	Essentra	11512	0.40%
9	DO_NOT_TRUST_FiddlerRoot	19921	0.69%	19	Bureau Veritas	10776	0.38%
10	(null)	18712	0.65%	20	michael.aranetworks.com	10497	0.37%

4   Forged Certificates Status in Quo

Based on the measurement and identifying methodology, we obtained 2,867,286 forged certificates of 4,165 different web services/domains. These forged certificates contained 107,306 self-signed ones of 922 different subjects. Others belonged to 215,236 different issuers of 3,988 unique subjects. Details could be seen in Table 1.

In this section, we studied the forged certificates comprehensively, including issuers, subjects, public key, validity period, lifetime, and so on. We also compared these features of forged certificates to the benign ones', tried to reveal the significant difference between them.

4.1   Issuers of Forged Certificates

We firstly analyzed the issuers of these forged certificates and tried to find out (or determine) the main causes. Table 2 lists the top 20 issuers CommonName (CN) [3] of forged certificates. No. 1 issuer CN indicated 189,912 issuers whose CNs satisfied the regular expression of [0-9a-z]{16}. No. 4 issuer CN indicated all self-signed forged certificates. No. 10 indicated the corresponding certificates didn't have the attribute of issuer CN.

These issuers could be divided into several classes. Some issuers are related to security products or anti-virus software, such as *FortiGate CA* (firewall), *Cisco Umbrella Secondary SubCA *-SG* (secure internet gateway), and www.netspark.com (content filter). Meanwhile, some others might be used for malicious services like MITM attacks, such as "[0-9a-z]{16}". According to the attributes of issuers, the certificates they've issued, and the corresponding servers, we roughly classified these issuers into 4 classes: *SecureService, Research, Proxy*, and *Suspicious*, which were presented in Table 3. Issuers classified as *SecureService* were those deployed in security products for security protection or content audit. A *Research*

Table 3. Rough classification of issuers

	SecureService	Research	Proxy	Suspicious
Examples	FortiGate CA	mitmproxy	PERSONAL Proxy CA	([0-9a-z]{16})
	Cisco Umbrella Secondary SubCA *-SG	DO_NOT_TRUST _FiddlerRoot	EBS_FG_CA _SSLProxy	
	Lightspeed Rocket	colegiomirabal.edu	ProxySchool12	thawte 2

issuer mainly claimed to belong to a research institute or a university, or indicated to a famous tool used to analyze HTTPS traffic. Actually, these tools might be used for malicious services, but we roughly classified the corresponding issuers to *Research* considering the mainly usage and the diversity of certificates faked by them. We simply considered an issuer claimed to be a proxy (mainly contained the word "proxy" in the Common Name) as *Proxy*. This category had the lowest priority due to its simplest classification basis. *Suspicious* issuers referred to those we suspected faking certificates for MITM attacks. The reason we named it *Suspicious* but not *Malicious* was that we could not directly prove that the corresponding services were malicious, and it's really hard to confirm. We determined an issuer to be a suspicious one based on three aspects: (1) the certificates faked by this issuer limited to several species, mainly for financial types; (2) the account of corresponding SSL sessions was much less than the average; (3) the account of corresponding servers for an issuer (or a series of similar issuers) was much less than the average. Examples of these classes could be seen in Table 3 as well.

4.2 Preference of Forged Certificates

In addition from the issuer's perspective, we also analyzed the forged certificate in the view of the subject, trying to figure out the preference of forged certificates. We analyzed subjects in four classes mentioned above, and found the preference of *Suspicious* issuers performed differently from the others. As showed in Fig. 1(c), more than 96% forged certificates issued by *Suspicious* issuers are related to three shopping websites which belonged to one e-commerce company Alibaba. *.tmall.com* and *.taobao.com* are mainly for domestic users, and *.aliexpress.com* mainly provides service for global consumers. Without considering *Suspicious* issuers, the top 10 forged certificates each represents a well-known web service in different fields, and they perform relatively average in the count, as showed in Fig. 1(b). The reason for this result is obvious: criminals are more interested in the wallets of victims. And the other classes of issuers do not have a clear tendency when forging certificates. Their preferences only related to the popularity of each web service.

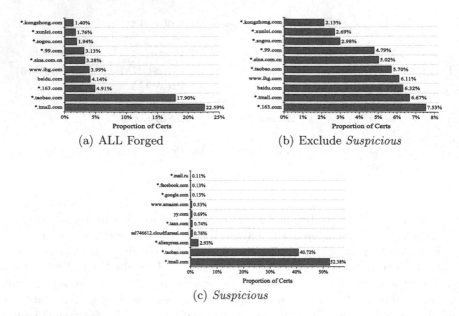

Fig. 1. Preference of Forged Certs. Abscissa axis lists the Top 10 subjects of forged certificates in different classes, vertical axis indicates the percentage of all forged certificates owned by each subject.

5 Comparison with Benign Certificates

We studied several attributes of forged certificates, including security attributes (such as certificate version, signature algorithm, and public key information), validity period, and lifetime. Compared to benign certificates, the forged ones performed extremely different in many aspects.

5.1 Security Attributes

We selected version, signature algorithm, public key algorithm and public key length to characterize the security of a certificate. Figure 2 shows the comparison of these attributes between forged and benign certificates.

Version: There're three versions of the X.509 certificate: *v1*, *v2*, and *v3*. *v1* certificates were deprecated long time ago, considering the security. And *v2* certificates were even not widely deployed on the Internet. *v3* certificate is currently the most widely used in the wild, and our measurement result confirmed this. Forged and benign certificates performed similarly in the statistical characteristics of the *version* attribute, both of which had more than 99% of *v3* certificates. The tiny difference is that compared to benign ones, more forged certificates were *v1* (nearly 1%). What's more, we find 102 benign certificates and 18 forged ones using *v4*. Since the subscript of *version* started from 0, which meant that "*version = 0*" indicated the *v1* certificates, we speculated that most of the *v4* certificates might be ascribed to misoperation.

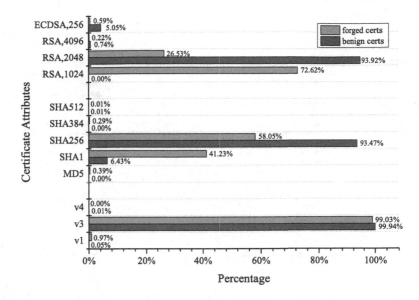

Fig. 2. Comparison of security attributes between forged and benign certs

Signature Algorithm: It's well known that MD5 and SHA1 algorithms were both cracked many years ago. Especially the SHA1 algorithm, which was once widely used, is still widely used in the wild, due to our measurement result. As shown in Fig. 2, more than 90% benign certificates used SHA256, while only 6.43% used SHA1. Well for the forged certificates, only 58.05% used SHA256, much less than the benign ones. And surprisingly to us, 41.23% of the forged certificates was still using SHA1 algorithm. It was obvious that forged certificates had a much lower security in the attribute of the signature algorithm. We then analyzed forged certificates which used SHA1 algorithm, and found out more than 80% SHA1 certificates could be attributed to *mitmproxy*. *mitmproxy* [17] is a free and open source HTTPS proxy. It's widely used for HTTPS proxies, security experiments, and of course MITM attacks. We found nearly 950,000 forged certificates signed by *mitmproxy* with the signature algorithm of SHA1 and 1024-bit RSA public key, while others used the signature algorithm of SHA256. Figure 3 is an example of certificate signed by *mitmproxy*. We found that though most of this kind of certificates used SHA1 certificates, they have changed to use SHA256 recently. We speculate that this may be attributed to version updates or source code rewrites.

Public Key Information: The situation of public key information is similar to the signature algorithm to some extent, as shown in Fig. 2. Though 1024-bit RSA key was not secure any more several years ago, 72.62% of forged certificates still use it to encrypt their SSL connection. Similarly, 45% of these insecure forged certificates can be attributed to *mitmproxy*, due to the reason mentioned above. And 48% of them were issued by *([0-9a-z]{16})*. What's more, we found that all

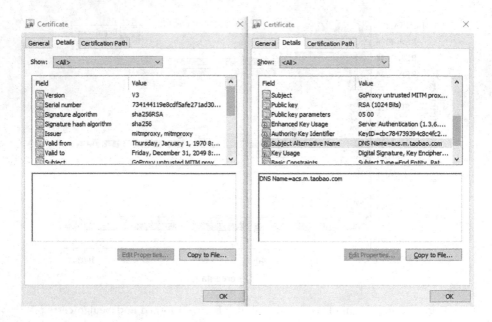

Fig. 3. An example of *mitmproxy* signed certificate

forged certificates issued by *([0-9a-z]{16})* had 1024-bit RSA public keys and were signed by SHA1 signature algorithm. For benign certificates, 2048-bit RSA public key accounts for the mainstream with a percentage of 93.92%. And different from the status of signature algorithm, 5.05% proportion of *ECDSA,256* in benign certificates indicates the trend of more secure public key algorithm. Actually, many famous companies, such as Google, Facebook, and Alibaba, have changed their public key algorithm to the more secure Elliptic curve cryptography (ECC) algorithm.

According to the results above, we can conclude that the security attributes of forged certificates performed much worse than the benign ones. Since forged certificates rarely considering security issues, the conclusion is in line with our expectation. What's more, we found that the attributes of forged certificates are closely related to the top issuers listed in Table 2. And this conclusion also applied to the attribute of the certificate validity period.

5.2   Certificate Validity Period

We calculated the validity period (the time between the certificates' *Not Before* and *Not After* attributes) of each certificate, and found a significant difference between forged certificates and the benign ones (shown in Fig. 4(a)). For benign certificates, most of their validity period were located in three intervals: 2–3 months, 6 months–1 year, and 1–2 years. While for forged ones, most of their validity period were located in two intervals: 1–2 months and 6 months–1 year. In detail, 46.07% forged certificates were valid for 32 days, and 11.86% were valid for 1 year. We then studied the three significant differences shown in Fig. 4(a), revealed that different validity periods of certificates might be caused by different issuers. We found that almost all forged certificates (more than 99.99%) which owned a 32-day validity period were issued by *mitmproxy*. What's more, 99.99% of benign certificates with the validity period of 84 day were issued by *Google Internet Authority G2*, and more than 99.96% with the validity period of 90-day were issued by *Let's Encrypt Authority X3*. Certificates validated for 2 years (730 days) cloud be attributed to issuers belonged to *DigiCert* (46.44%), *Symantec* (12.98%), *VeriSign* (7.27%), and so on.

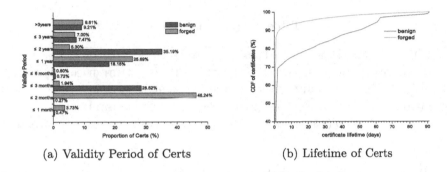

(a) Validity Period of Certs   (b) Lifetime of Certs

Fig. 4. Validity period and lifetime of certs

5.3   Certificate Lifetime

In order to compare the lifetime (the days between the first time and the last time a certificate exposed in our sight) of forged and benign certificates, we selected a three-month period, from April 1 to June 30, to implement continuous observation. During the 91-day observation, we obtained that the average lifetime of forged certificates was 3.59 days, while for authorized ones it was 12.02 days. The result demonstrated that forged certificates had a much shorter lifetime than the benign ones, as shown in Fig. 4(b). We speculated that the MITM attackers need to update their forged certificates frequently to evade the detection of security products like IDS and firewall, or to replace the blacklisted ones. Figure 4(b) also shows that more than 85% forged certificates only appeared once in our 91-day observation. This could be attributed to security tests or researches which only performed once.

5.4   Conclusion

According to the comparisons mentioned above, we cloud conclude that most forged certificates didn't care about security as the widely use of unsafe signature algorithm and public key algorithm. However, what they most concerned was evading the detection of anti-virus software. Hence the lifetime of forged certificates was much shorter than benign ones, as attackers required to update certificates frequently.

6   Tracking MITM Attacks

While the use of forged certificates can be diverse, MITM attacks directly threatened users' privacy and security. Thus tracking MITM attacks is necessary, and many researchers have focused on this issue. In this paper, we discovered a MITM attack and performed a tracking with the help of forged certificate attributes and SSL session statistics.

Table 4. Suspicious servers

Server IP	#(Sessions)	#(Ports)	#(Certs)	Lifetime
195.154.161.209	869949 (54.46%)	500 (2876-3375)	49743 (65.88%)	04/01/2017-06/30/2017
62.210.69.21	680721 (42.61%)	500 (3336-3835)	46844 (62.04%)	04/01/2017-06/30/2017
195.154.161.44	38208 (2.39%)	500 (2601-3100)	13129 (17.39%)	04/01/2017-06/30/2017
195.154.161.172	8366 (0.52%)	500 (4606-5105)	4059 (5.38%)	04/08/2017-05/29/2017

When performing a deep analysis, forged certificates with similar issuers that satisfied the regular expression of *[0-9a-z]{16}* caused our attention. According to our analysis, more than 96% certificates faked by these issuers belonged to three famous e-commerce websites in China, 52.38% for *.tmall.com*, 40.72% for *.taobao.com*, and 2.93% for *.aliexpress.com*. And all three websites belonged to the same company, Alibaba, the most famous e-commerce company in China. The first two websites mainly served domestic users, while the last one provided global online shopping services. And that's why the forged certificates of this website were far less than the former ones. According to the reasons above, we speculated that these issuers were related to the MITM attacks targeting the online shopping service of Alibaba. Thus we analyzed the statistical SSL session information of corresponding certificates to verify our suspicion.

Table 5. Information of suspicious servers

Server IP	Location		ISP	Organization	Domain
195.154.161.209	France	48.8582, 2.3387	ONLINE S.A.S	Iliad-Entreprises	poneytelecom.eu
62.210.69.21	France	48.8582, 2.3387	Free SAS	ONLINE SAS	poneytelecom.eu
195.154.161.44	France	48.8582, 2.3387	ONLINE S.A.S	Iliad-Entreprises	poneytelecom.eu
195.154.161.172	France	48.8582, 2.3387	ONLINE S.A.S	Iliad-Entreprises	poneytelecom.eu

We selected 3 months connection data from 04/01/2017 to 06/30/2017, and extracted server information of the forged certificates which met the above conditions. Finally, we obtained 230 unique servers from 1,597,532 SSL sessions.

Surprisingly, most sessions (99.98%) and certificates (99.77%) belonged to four server IPs, as showed in Table 4. We then looked up the information of these IPs with the help of MAXMIND [15], finding that they might locate in a same position and belonged to a same organization, as showed in Table 5. Thus, we suspected these IP addresses should be attributed to MITM attacks for the reasons below:

1. These IPs covered almost all forged certificates and SSL sessions.
2. Forged certificates used by these IPs are mainly related to 3 domains, which provided online shopping services. Obviously, MITM attackers cared more about the victim's wallet.
3. Each IP was served on 500 different and contiguous ports, and the number of sessions for each (*IP, port, cert*) triple per day is much less than proxy-used forged certificates.
4. These IPs belong to a same organization and locate in the same country.
5. When searching poneytelecom.eu on Google, many results indicated that this domain/organization was related to web fraud behaviors.

7   Conclusion

In this paper, we implemented a 20-month passive measurement to study the status quo of forged certificates in the wild. Based on CT logs provided by Chrome, we identified forged certificates of the web services listed in Alexa Top 10k, and finally gathered 2,867,286 forged ones. We analyzed the forged certificates in the view of both issuer and subject. Based on the analysis of issuers, we revealed the causes of forged certificates by roughly classifying them into four categories. *SecureService* certificates were mainly deployed in security products for security protection or content audit. *Research* indicated issuers that claimed to belong to a research institute or a university, or famous tools used to analyze HTTPS traffic. *Proxy* might be used for proxy servers, and *Suspicious* issuers referred to those we suspected faking certificates for MITM attacks. The study of the subject showed us the preference of forged certificates. While *Suspicious* mainly focused on financial related services, others preferences only related to the popularity of each web service. When comparing forged certificates to the benign ones, we found significant differences in security attributes, validity period, and lifetime. Benign certificates used more secure signature and public key algorithm to ensure the security of SSL encrypted connection, while forged ones performed quite terrible. Forged certificates also had a much shorter validity period and lifetime. What's more, we found the validity period of a certificate, no matter forged or benign, was related to its issuer. At last, we traced a series of *Suspicious* forged certificates and harvested four malicious server IP addresses through traffic behavior analysis.

Acknowledgments. This work is supported by The National Key Research and Development Program of China (No. 2016QY05X1000 and No. 2016YFB0801200) and The National Natural Science Foundation of China (No. 61602472). Research is also supported by the CAS/SAFEA International Partnership Program for Creative Research Teams and IIE, CAS international cooperation project.

References

1. Censys: Censys. https://censys.io/. Accessed 21 July 2017
2. Chung, T., Liu, Y., Choffnes, D.R., Levin, D., Maggs, B.M., Mislove, A., Wilson, C.: Measuring and applying invalid SSL certificates: the silent majority. In: Proceedings of the 2016 ACM on Internet Measurement Conference, IMC 2016, Santa Monica, CA, USA, 14–16 November 2016, pp. 527–541 (2016)
3. Cooper, D., Santesson, S., Farrell, S., Boeyen, S., Housley, R., Polk, W.T.: Internet X.509 public key infrastructure certificate and certificate revocation list (CRL) profile. RFC 5280, 1–151 (2008)
4. Dacosta, I., Ahamad, M., Traynor, P.: Trust no one else: detecting MITM attacks against SSL/TLS without third-parties. In: Foresti, S., Yung, M., Martinelli, F. (eds.) ESORICS 2012. LNCS, vol. 7459, pp. 199–216. Springer, Heidelberg (2012). https://doi.org/10.1007/978-3-642-33167-1_12
5. Dong, Z., Kane, K., Camp, L.: Phishing in smooth waters: the state of banking certificates in the US (2014)
6. Dong, Z., Kapadia, A., Blythe, J., Camp, L.J.: Beyond the lock icon: real-time detection of phishing websites using public key certificates. In: 2015 APWG Symposium on Electronic Crime Research, eCrime 2015, Barcelona, Spain, 26–29 May 2015, pp. 1–12 (2015)
7. Durumeric, Z., Adrian, D., Mirian, A., Bailey, M., Halderman, J.A.: A search engine backed by internet-wide scanning. In: Proceedings of the 22nd ACM SIGSAC Conference on Computer and Communications Security, Denver, CO, USA, 12–6 October 2015, pp. 542–553 (2015)
8. Durumeric, Z., Kasten, J., Bailey, M., Halderman, J.A.: Analysis of the HTTPS certificate ecosystem. In: Proceedings of the 2013 Internet Measurement Conference, IMC 2013, Barcelona, Spain, 23–25 October 2013, pp. 291–304 (2013)
9. Durumeric, Z., Wustrow, E., Halderman, J.A.: Zmap: fast internet-wide scanning and its security applications. In: Proceedings of the 22th USENIX Security Symposium, Washington, DC, USA, 14–16 August 2013, pp. 605–620 (2013)
10. Holz, R., Braun, L., Kammenhuber, N., Carle, G.: The SSL landscape: a thorough analysis of the X.509 PKI using active and passive measurements. In: Proceedings of the 11th ACM SIGCOMM Internet Measurement Conference, IMC 2011, Berlin, Germany, 2 November 2011, pp. 427–444 (2011)
11. Holz, R., Riedmaier, T., Kammenhuber, N., Carle, G.: X.509 forensics: detecting and localising the SSL/TLS men-in-the-middle. In: Foresti, S., Yung, M., Martinelli, F. (eds.) ESORICS 2012. LNCS, vol. 7459, pp. 217–234. Springer, Heidelberg (2012). https://doi.org/10.1007/978-3-642-33167-1_13
12. Huang, L., Rice, A., Ellingsen, E., Jackson, C.: Analyzing forged SSL certificates in the wild. In: 2014 IEEE Symposium on Security and Privacy, SP 2014, Berkeley, CA, USA, 18–21 May 2014, pp. 83–97 (2014)
13. Rapid7 Labs: Rapid7 Labs - SSL Certificates. https://opendata.rapid7.com/sonar.ssl/. Accessed 21 July 2017

14. Laurie, B.: Certificate transparency. ACM Commun. **57**(10), 40–46 (2014)
15. MAXMIND: Geoip2 Precision Service Demo. https://www.maxmind.com/en/geoip2-precision-demo/. Accessed 17 Sept 2017
16. Mishari, M.A., Cristofaro, E.D., Defrawy, K.M.E., Tsudik, G.: Harvesting SSL certificate data to identify web-fraud. I. J. Netw. Secur. **14**(6), 324–338 (2012)
17. mitmproxy: mitmproxy. https://mitmproxy.org/. Accessed 10 Oct 2017
18. Transparency Certificate: Certificate Transparency - Known Logs. https://www.certificate-transparency.org/known-logs, Accessed 23 July 2017
19. VanderSloot, B., Amann, J., Bernhard, M., Durumeric, Z., Bailey, M., Halderman, J.A.: Towards a complete view of the certificate ecosystem. In: Proceedings of the 2016 ACM on Internet Measurement Conference, IMC 2016, Santa Monica, CA, USA, 14–16 November 2016, pp. 543–549 (2016)

Managing Cloud Data Centers with Three-State Server Model Under Job Abandonment Phenomenon

Binh Minh Nguyen[1]([✉]), Bao Hoang[1], Huy Tran[1], and Viet Tran[2]

[1] School of Information and Communication Technology,
Hanoi University of Science and Technology, Hanoi, Vietnam
minhnb@soict.hust.edu.vn, bao.hoangnghia@gmail.com,
huydinhtran.hust@gmail.com
[2] Institute of Informatics, Slovak Academy of Sciences, Bratislava, Slovakia
viet.ui@savba.sk

Abstract. In fact, to improve the quality of system service, for user job requests, which already have waited for a long time in queues of a busy cluster, cloud vendors often migrate the jobs to other available clusters. This strategy brings about the occurrence of job abandonment phenomenon in data centers, which disturbs the server management mechanisms in the manner of decreasing effectiveness control, increasing energy consumptions, and so on. In this paper, based on the three-state model proposed in previous works, we develop a novel model and its management strategy for cloud data centers using a finite queue. Our proposed model is tested in a simulated cloud environment using CloudSim. The achieved outcomes show that our three-state server model for data centers operates well under the job abandonment phenomenon.

Keywords: Cloud computing · Three-state server queues
Job abandonment · Scheduling data center · Queuing theory
Markov chain

1 Introduction

There are thousands of jobs, which could be sent to cloud data centers at the same time. In some cases, the lack of available clusters and servers for performing these jobs is inevitable. To resolve this issue, the jobs are formed a queue to wait for processing in succession. In this way, a large number of studies that have proposed queuing models to optimize service waiting time for incoming jobs, energy consumption for data centers, and improve the quality of service (QoS) [1]. However, because jobs have different sizes and arrival times, the waiting time in the queue is also different and often not optimal.

Most studies that developed two-state models like [1,2] also exploited infinite queues. Because almost all providers offer computational resources based on capacity of their data centers, hence proposing models of finite job queues is

Y. Shi et al. (Eds.): ICCS 2018, LNCS 10862, pp. 668–674, 2018.
https://doi.org/10.1007/978-3-319-93713-7_63

essential. Nevertheless, the number of studies that dealt with the feature is quite small. We built an ON/OFF/MIDDLE/c/K model applying to a single finite-capacity queue in the work [4] for cloud data center management problem. In another aspect, although jobs abandonment has been considered in research [3] before, with the three-state approach, there are no related studies, which have addressed this problem. Hence, based on the motivation, this work continues to develop the three-state model proposed in our previous works [4] with consideration of occurring jobs abandonment when they already wait for ON servers in a long time. With this direction, our target is to reduce the mean waiting time for incoming jobs. In order to solve the job abandonment problem, we have to reduce waiting time of jobs inside the system. In this paper, we inherit the three-state model ON/OFF/MIDDLE/c/K proposed in our previous work [4] to develop a new three-state model, which operates under job abandonment phenomenon with a finite queue. In this way, the new model is called Ab(ON/OFF/MIDDLE/c/K).

The paper is organized as follows. In Sect. 2, we build a mathematical model for Ab(ON/OFF/MIDDLE/c/K). Also in this section, we propose control mechanism for the model. Section 3 dedicates to presenting our experiments with simulation dataset. The paper concludes in Sect. 4.

2   Designing Mathematical Model and Control Algorithm

2.1   Three-State Servers and Job Abandonment Phenomenon

In this research, we go further by examining the job abandonment condition with the three-state model presented in [4]. In order to build a theoretical model, jobs also are assumed to arrive at the system according to a Poisson distribution and the needed time to finish a job (service time) is an exponentially distributed random variable X with rate $\mu = \frac{1}{E[X]}$. Under abandonment condition, if a job comes to a full queue, it will be blocked. However, if a job in queue already has been waiting for an ON server for a long time that exceeds a certain threshold, the job will abandon. We assume that a job abandons from the queue with an exponential distribution having expectation: $\frac{1}{\theta}$. If the system has i ON servers and j jobs, then the abandonment rate is $(j - i)\theta$ and the number of servers in SETUP process is $min(j - i, c - i)$. Because the power supply for the turning process of servers (from OFF to MIDDLE) is assumed as a constant variable $(t_{OFF \rightarrow MIDDLE})$, we can model the system states transition for our proposed Ab(ON/OFF/MIDDLE/c/K) by a Markov chain. In which, (i, j) is a state pair, where i and j are the number of ON servers, and jobs in the system (including jobs in the queue and jobs being served) respectively.

2.2   Ab(ON/OFF/MIDDLE/c/K) Model

We inherit lemmas proved in [5], and Lemma 2 demonstrated in our previous work [4], then we improve and prove Lemma 1 in this document with job abandonment condition to build our Theorem 1 below.

Lemma 1. *In the Ab(ON/OFF/MIDDLE/c/K) model with job abandonment, at time t, system is in state (i, j) with $j > i$. At time $t + h$, probability of the system moves to a new state (i_1, j_1) $(i \neq i_1$ or $j \neq j_1)$ is:*

$$P((i,j) \to (i_1, j_1)) = \begin{cases} \min(j - i, c - i)\alpha h + o(h) & \text{where } i_1 = i + 1 \text{ and } j = j_1 \\ \lambda h + o(h) & \text{where } i_1 = i \text{ and } j_1 = j + 1 \\ (i\mu + (j - i)\theta)h + o(h) & \text{where } i_1 = i \text{ and } j_1 = j - 1 \\ o(h) & \text{in other cases} \end{cases}$$

$$(1)$$

Proof. When $j > i$, queue has $j - i$ jobs. Four event types can happen at time $(t, t + h)$, including a job arrives, a job is completed, a job leaves queue, and a server is switched from SETUP to ON. As assumptions presented above, jobs arrive according to a Poisson distribution with rate λ, this leads to the inter-arrival time (i.e. time period between two incoming jobs) being independent and conforming to an exponentially distributed random variable with expectation λ^{-1}. Otherwise, the time of execution, SETUP and abandonment processes are also considered as exponentially distributed with expectations μ^{-1}, α^{-1} and θ^{-1} respectively.

In this way, the required time to switch from an event to the next one is the minimum of the following four random variables: inter-arrival time, i execution time of i running servers, $\min(c - i, j - i)$ SETUP time of $\min(c - i, j - i)$ servers, which are switching to ON state and $j - i$ abandonment time of $j - i$ jobs in the queue. Consequently, time from t until the next event has an exponential distribution with expectation $(\lambda + \min(c - i, j - i)\alpha + i\mu + (j - i)\theta)^{-1}$, and probability that an event will occur in $(t, t + h)$ is:

$$1 - e^{(\lambda + \min(c-i,j-i)\alpha + i\mu + (j-i)\theta)} = (\lambda + \min(c - i, j - i)\alpha + i\mu + (j - i)\theta)h + o(h)$$

According to Lemma 2 defined in [4], when an event occurs, probability of a server switched to ON state is:

$$\frac{\min(c - i, j - i)\alpha}{\lambda + \min(j - i, c - i)\alpha + i\mu + (j - i)\theta}$$

In addition, because the time length required for an event occurrence and event types are independent, probability of transition occurrence $(i, j) \to (i + 1, j)$ is:

$$\begin{aligned} P((i,j) \to (i + 1, j)) &= \frac{\min(c - i, j - i)\alpha}{\lambda + \min(j - i, c - i)\alpha + i\mu + (j - i)\theta} \\ &\quad \times ((\lambda + \min(c - i, j - i)\alpha + i\mu + (j - i)\theta)h + o(h)) \\ &= \min(c - i, j - i)\alpha h + o(h) \end{aligned}$$

Similarly, we also have:

$$\begin{aligned} P((i,j) \to (i, j + 1)) &= \frac{\lambda}{\lambda + \min(j - i, c - i)\alpha + i\mu + (j - i)\theta} \\ &\quad \times ((\lambda + \min(c - i, j - i)\alpha + i\mu + (j - i)\theta)h + o(h)) \\ &= \lambda h + o(h) \end{aligned}$$

and:

$$
\begin{aligned}
P((i,j) \rightarrow (i,j-1)) &= \frac{i\mu + (j-i)\theta}{\lambda + \min(j-i, c-i)\alpha i\mu + (j-i)\theta} \\
&\quad \times ((\lambda + \min(c-i, j-i)\alpha + i\mu + (j-i)\theta)ho(h)) \\
&= (i\mu + (j-i)\theta)h + o(h)
\end{aligned}
$$

Probability of more than one event will occur in time $(t, t+h)$ is $o(h)$ with $h \rightarrow 0$. The probability thus follows $P((i,j) \rightarrow (i_1, j_1))$ in others cases.

Theorem 1. *In the Ab(ON/OFF/MIDDLE/c/K) model, expectation of the server number, which is switched from MIDDLE to ON state in time t is given by:*

$$
E[M] \approx at \sum_{j>i} \pi_{i,j} \min(c-i, j-i) \tag{2}
$$

Proof. Let K_h is the number of servers that are switched to ON state in period of time h. Therefore $K_h > 0$ when the $(i,j) \rightarrow (i_1, j)$ $(i_1 > i)$ event occurs. Based on Lemma 1, $O(K_h > 1) = o(h)$, and the total probability formula:

$$
P(K_h = 1) = \sum_{j>i} \pi_{i,j} P((i,j) \rightarrow (i_1, j)) = \sum_{j>i} \pi_{i,j}(\min(c-i, j-i)\alpha h + o(h))
$$

$$
\approx \sum_{j>i} \pi_{i,j}(\min(c-i, j-i))
$$

We have:

$$
E[K_h] \approx ah \sum_{j>i} \pi_{i,j}(\min(c-i, j-i))
$$

Dividing t into small enough time period h, assuming $K_h^{(z)}$ is the number of servers switched to ON state in time period z. We also have:

$$
E[M] = E[\sum_z K_h^{(z)}] \approx ah \sum_{j>i} \pi_{i,j}(\min(c-i, j-i))\frac{t}{h}
$$

$$
= at \sum_{j>i} \pi_{i,j}(\min(c-i, j-i))
$$

2.3 Control Algorithm

Theorem 1 puts forward a formula for calculating expectation of the server number switched from MIDDLE to ON successfully. The requirement for our strategy is that the number of servers switched from OFF to MIDDLE state must equal the expectation of server number switched from MIDDLE to ON state in any time period. For this reason, the average number of servers that must be switched to MIDDLE state is calculated by formula 2.

$$
\tau = \frac{t}{E[M]} = \frac{1}{a \sum_{j>i} \pi_{i,j}(\min(c-i, j-i))} \tag{3}
$$

Algorithm 1: Turn-on server algorithm

---
1 Calculate the τ by the formula 3
2 **while** *true* **do**
3 | Switch one server from OFF to MIDDLE
4 | Wait for a period of time τ
5 **end**

In Algorithm 1, the switching process of servers from OFF to ON is divided into two periods. Firstly, an OFF server is periodically switched to MIDDLE state after a period of time τ. Secondly, using Ab(ON/OFF/MIDDLE/c/K) strategy, MIDDLE servers are turned into ON based on the number of jobs in queue.

3 Experiment and Evaluation

3.1 Experimental Setup

For our experiments, CloudSim is used to simulate cloud environment with a data center, servers, and a finite job queue. We set the needed time to turn a server from OFF to MIDDLE state $t_{OFF \to MIDDLE} = 400(s)$, SETUP mode time with $\alpha = 0.02$, the number of servers in system $c = 200$, and queue length $K = 200$. λ is increased from 1 to 10 to assess the impact of arrival job rate on our model. While λ values are changed, the traffic intensity $\rho = \frac{\lambda}{c\mu}$ also are altered from 0.1 to 1. We also set the job service time $\mu = 0.05$ and vary θ from 0.001 to 0.02.

3.2 Ab(ON/OFF/MIDDLE/c/K) Evaluations

For the first test, Fig. 1 expresses the gained time period values. There are two important observations here: while λ has a tremendous impact on values of τ, the impacts of θ on τ are quite small. Hence, the differences of charts with diverse θ values are very small. While λ increases from 1 to 8, τ decreases from about 9.5 to 3.7. However, it raises slightly when λ exceeds 8. The phenomenon can be explained as follows: when λ is small, there are not many jobs that arrive at the data center. So the system just needs to keep a small number of MIDDLE servers. When λ augments, more jobs come into our data center, therefore, the system has to turn servers from OFF to MIDDLE more quickly. τ thus gradually decreases in inverse proportion λ. However, when λ exceeds 8, traffic intensity ρ tends to 1, almost servers are in ON state, and τ increases as shown in the Fig. 1.

To compare Ab(ON/OFF/MIDDLE/c/K) and Ab(ON/OFF/c/K), we measure three metrics, including: mean waiting time, abandonment and block proportion. The achieved results are shown by Figs. 2, 3, and 4 respectively. In Fig. 2, it is easy to see that when λ is in range (1, 6), the mean job waiting time of Ab(ON/OFF/MIDDLE/c/K) model is significantly smaller than Ab(ON/OFF/c/K). However, there is no big difference between two models

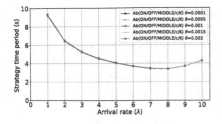

Fig. 1. Time period

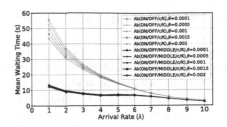

Fig. 2. Mean job waiting time

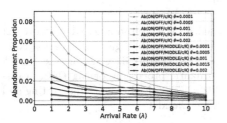

Fig. 3. Abandonment proportion

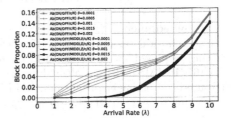

Fig. 4. Block proportion

when λ is in range of (7, 10). This could be explained as follows. While arrival rate is high ($\lambda > 6$), almost all servers are in ON state, consequently the number of MIDDLE and SETUP servers is small. In this case, our proposed control algorithm effectiveness is insignificant. On the other hand, as presented before, because λ is large, ON server quantity also is large, the mean job waiting time thus decreases and the number of leaving jobs also is small. Through this experiment, we demonstrate that our proposed model operates more effectively than the two-state model. Figure 3 shows abandonment proportion of both model with diverse values of λ and θ. The Ab(ON/OFF/MIDDLE/c/K) model thus obtains better outcomes as compared with Ab(ON/OFF/c/K) when λ is in range (1, 6). However, when λ in range (6, 10), almost all servers in this time are in ON state, so there is no big difference between two models. Like the mean waiting time results above, the job abandonment proportion decreases when λ increases. This happens because while λ augments, the mean waiting time decreases, hence jobs in queue have to wait for processing in a shorter time. This leads to the abandonment probability of a single job reduces, and the job abandonment proportion decreases. The block proportion results of both models with different values of λ and θ are described by Fig. 4. It can be seen that Ab(ON/OFF/MIDDLE/c/K) has smaller job block proportion as compared with Ab(ON/OFF/c/K). The reason for this issue is that with λ augments, traffic intensity tends to 1, so system thus also tends to reach overload point. As a result, there is a large number of jobs, which is blocked during system operation.

4   Conclusion and Future Work

In this paper, we developed a new management strategy for cloud data center under job abandonment phenomenon called Ab(ON/OFF/MIDDLE/c/K), which reduces the mean job waiting time inside the cloud system. We tested and evaluated Ab(ON/OFF/MIDDLE/c/K) by CloudSim in the simulated cloud environment. Achieved results show that our new model works well and brings good performance as compared with the two-state server model under the job abandonment phenomenon. In the near future, we will continue to evaluate our model in the aspect of energy consumption.

Acknowledgments. This research is supported by the Vietnamese MOETs project "Research on developing software framework to integrate IoT gateways for fog computing deployed on multi-cloud environment" No. B2017-BKA-32, Slovak VEGA 2/0167/16 "Methods and algorithms for the semantic processing of Big Data in distributed computing environment", and EU H2020-777536 EOSC-hub "Integrating and managing services for the European Open Science Cloud".

References

1. Gandhi, A., Harchol-Balter, M., Adan, I.: Server farms with setup costs. Perform. Eval. **67**(11), 1123–1138 (2010)
2. Kato, M., Masuyama, H., Kasahara, S., Takahashi, Y.: Effect of energy-saving server scheduling on power consumption for large scale data centers. Management **12**(2), 667–685 (2016)
3. Phung-Duc, T.: Impatient customers in power-saving data centers. In: Sericola, B., Telek, M., Horváth, G. (eds.) ASMTA 2014. LNCS, vol. 8499, pp. 79–88. Springer, Cham (2014). https://doi.org/10.1007/978-3-319-08219-6_13
4. Nguyen, B.M., Tran, D., Nguyen, G.: Enhancing service capability with multiple finite capacity server queues in cloud data centers. Cluster Comput. **19**(4), 1747–1767 (2016)
5. Phung-Duc, T.: Large-scale data center with setup time and impatient customer. In: Proceedings of the 31st UK Performance Engineering Workshop (UKPEW 2015), pp. 47–60 (2015)

The Analysis of the Effectiveness of the Perspective-Based Observational Tunnels Method by the Example of the Evaluation of Possibilities to Divide the Multidimensional Space of Coal Samples

Dariusz Jamroz[✉]

Department of Applied Computer Science,
AGH University of Science and Technology,
al. A. Mickiewicza 30, 30-059 Krakow, Poland
jamroz@agh.edu.pl

Abstract. Methods of qualitative analysis of multidimensional data using visualization of this data consist in using the transformation of a multidimensional space into a two-dimensional one. In this way, multidimensional complicated data can be presented on a two-dimensional computer screen. This allows to conduct the qualitative analysis of this data in a way which is the most natural for people, through the sense of sight. The application of complex algorithms targeted to search for multidimensional data of specific properties can be replaced with such a qualitative analysis. Some qualitative characteristics are simply visible in the two-dimensional image representing this data. The new perspective-based observational tunnels method is an example of the multidimensional data visualization method. This method was used in this paper to present and analyze the real set of seven-dimensional data describing coal samples obtained from two hard coal mines. This paper presents for the first time the application of perspective-based observational tunnels method for the evaluation of possibilities to divide the multidimensional space of coal samples by their susceptibility to fluidal gasification. This was performed in order to verify whether it will be possible to indicate the possibility of such a division by applying this method. Views presenting the analyzed data, enabling to indicate the possibility to separate areas of the multidimensional space occupied by samples with different applicability for the gasification process, were obtained as a result.

Keywords: Multidimensional data analysis · Data mining
Multidimensional visualization · Observational tunnels method
Multidimensional perspective · Fluidal gasification

© Springer International Publishing AG, part of Springer Nature 2018
Y. Shi et al. (Eds.): ICCS 2018, LNCS 10862, pp. 675–682, 2018.
https://doi.org/10.1007/978-3-319-93713-7_64

1 Introduction

The qualitative analysis of multidimensional data constitutes a valuable, practical and increasingly used tool for the analysis of real data. It enables to obtain information on characteristics which is directly visible in the two-dimensional image representing the multidimensional data, the existence of which we could not even suspect. Various methods of visualization of multidimensional data are used for such an analysis. The perspective-based observational tunnels method used in this paper was presented for the first time in the paper [1]. Its effectiveness for real data placed in the 5-dimensional space of characteristics obtained as a result of the reception of printed text was proven there. It turned out that during the construction of this type of image recognition systems, this method enables to indicate the possibility to separate individual classes in the multidimensional space of characteristics even when other methods fail. During the analysis of 7-dimensional data containing samples belonging to 3 classes of coal, the perspective-based observational tunnels method came first in the ranking of various methods in view of the readability of results [1]. The purpose of this paper is to verify whether this new method is also effective in the case of different real data. This paper presents for the first time the application of perspective-based observational tunnels method for the evaluation of possibilities to divide the multidimensional space of coal samples by their susceptibility to fluidal gasification. This was performed in order to verify whether it will be possible to indicate the possibility of such a division by applying this method. This method has never been applied for such a purpose before. Such an investigation has also a significant practical importance. Indicating the possibilities to divide the space of samples into areas with different applicability to the fluidal gasification allows to conclude that the selected characteristics of coal are sufficient for the correct recognition process of samples of coal more and less susceptible to fluidal gasification. The fluidal gasification itself is in turn significant from the perspective of the coal-based power industry which at the same time emits minimal amounts of pollution.

2 Related Papers

An example of another method of multidimensional data visualization applied during the qualitative analysis is PCA [2,3] using the orthogonal projection on vectors representing directions of the biggest variation of data. For multidimensional visualization, autoassociative neural networks [4,5] and Kohonen maps [6,7] are also used. The method of parallel coordinates [8] consists in placing n axes in parallel representing n dimensions on the plane. In the method of star graph [9], n axes going radially outward from one point are placed on the plane. Multidimensional scaling [10] transforms a multidimensional space into a two-dimensional one in such a way that the mutual distances between each pair of points in the two-dimensional image is as close as possible to their mutual distance in the multidimensional space. In the method of relevance maps [11],

n special points $F_1, F_2, ..., F_n$ representing the individual axes are placed on the plane representing the screen. These points and points belonging to the data set are distributed in the two-dimensional image in such a way that the distance from every data point to point F_k is as close as possible to the value of the k-th coordinate of a given data point.

3 Perspective-Based Observational Tunnels Method

The perspective-based observational tunnels method is a new method. It was first presented in the paper [1]. It intuitively consists in the prospective parallel projection with the local orthogonal projection. In order to understand its idea, the following terms must be introduced [1]:

Definition 1. *Observed space X is defined as any vector space, over field F of real numbers, n-dimensional, $n \geq 3$, with a scalar product.*

Definition 2. *Let $p_1, p_2 \in X$ - be linearly independent, $w \in X$. Observational plane $P \subset X$ is defined as:*

$$P = \delta(w, \{p_1, p_2\}) \tag{1}$$

where:

$$\delta(w, \{p_1, p_2\}) \overset{def}{=} \{x \in X : \exists \beta_1, \beta_2 \in F, \text{such that } x = w + \beta_1 p_1 + \beta_2 p_2\} \tag{2}$$

The two-dimensional computer screen will be represented by vectors p_1, p_2 in accordance with the above definition.

Definition 3. *The direction of projection r onto the observational plane $P = \delta(w, \{p_1, p_2\})$ is defined as any vector $r \in X$ if vectors $\{p_1, p_2, r\}$ are an orthogonal system.*

Definition 4. *The following set is called hypersurface $S_{(s,d)}$, anchored in $s \in X$ and directed towards $d \in X$:*

$$S_{(s,d)} \overset{def}{=} \{x \in X : (x - s, d) = 0\} \tag{3}$$

Definition 5. *A tunnel radius of point $a \in X$ against observational plane $P = \delta(w, \{p_1, p_2\})$ is defined as:*

$$b_a = \psi \xi r + a - w - (1 + \psi)(\beta_1 p_1 + \beta_2 p_2) \tag{4}$$

where:

$$\psi = \frac{(w - a, r)}{\xi(r, r)} \tag{5}$$

$$\beta_1 = \frac{(\psi \xi r + a - w, p_1)}{(1 + \psi)(p_1, p_1)} \tag{6}$$

$$\beta_2 = \frac{(\psi \xi r + a - w, p_2)}{(1 + \psi)(p_2, p_2)} \tag{7}$$

$r \in X$-direction of projection onto observational plane P,
$\xi \in (0, \infty)$ - coefficient of perspective.

The procedure of drawing each point a based on the perspective-based observational tunnels method consists in determining the *tunnel radius* b_a and verifying whether scalar product (b_a, b_a) is smaller than the assumed value of $b_a max$. Additionally, it must be verified whether the *distance of projection* ψ is smaller than the assumed value of ψ_{max}. If the above conditions are met, then the point should be drawn on the screen in position with coordinates β_1, β_2. In the opposite case, the point is not drawn.

4 Experiment Results

Data to be analyzed was obtained from two hard coal mines, which resulted in obtaining 99 samples in total. Thanks to the upgrading process and chemical analysis, the following 7 values were obtained for each sample: the total sulphur content, hydrogen content, nitrogen content, chlorine content, total coal content, heat of combustion and ash content. In this way, a set of 7-dimensional data was obtained. Based on the Technological applicability card for coals from among the analyzed 99 samples, only 18 samples were marked as those which can effectively be subjected to gasification. In order to conduct the qualitative analysis of the multidimensional data obtained in this way through its visualization, the computer system based on the algorithm presented in the previous point was developed. It was decided to verify whether it will be possible to indicate the possibility to divide the obtained 7-dimensional space of samples into areas with different applicability to the fluidal gasification process using the perspective-based observational tunnels method. The obtained results are presented in Figs. 1, 2 and 3.

Figure 1 presents the view of the discussed 7-dimensional data with the division into samples of coal more and less susceptible to gasification. It is clearly visible in the figure that images of points representing samples of coal more and less susceptible to gasification occupy separate areas of the figure. It is thus possible to determine the boundary dividing views of points representing different

Fig. 1. Images of 7-dimensional points representing samples of coal with lower susceptibility to gasification are marked with symbol x; samples of coal more susceptible to gasification are marked with a circle (o). All points representing samples of coal more susceptible to gasification are visible and may be easily separated from other points.

degrees of susceptibility to gasification in the figure. This in turn entails that it is possible to divide areas of the 7-dimensional space occupied by samples with different applicability to the gasification process. Such a possibility results from the existence of the representation used for the visualization, by means of which such a division is possible, as can be seen in the figure. It follows from the above that the perspective-based observational tunnels method enables to indicate the possibility to divide the space of samples into areas with different applicability to the fluidal gasification process. Figure 2 presents the view of the discussed 7-dimensional data with the division into samples of coal more and less susceptible to gasification with the omission of the condition concerning the chlorine content. Also here, despite the omission of the condition concerning the chlorine content, it is clearly visible that images of points representing samples of coal more and less susceptible to gasification occupy separate areas of the figure. Also here, it is possible to determine the boundary dividing views of points representing different degrees of susceptibility to gasification in the figure. This in turn entails that it is possible to divide areas of the 7-dimensional space occupied by samples with different applicability to the gasification process with the omission of the condition concerning the chlorine content. It follows from the above that the perspective-based observational tunnels method enables to indicate the possibility to divide the space of samples into areas with different applicability to the fluidal gasification process even with the change in conditions specifying this applicability. In this particular case, it is especially important, because the chlorine content does not influence the effectiveness of this gasification and it only influences the degree of contamination which appears as a result of gasification. However, the allocation of samples changes completely. Comparing Figs. 1 and 2, it is visible that, in Fig. 1, only 18 samples can be effectively subjected to gasification, while in Fig. 2, with the omission of the condition concerning the chlorine content, from among the same analyzed 99 samples of coal, as many as 78 samples can be effectively subjected to gasification. Figure 3 presents the view of the discussed data with the division according to the place of extraction. It is clearly visible that images of points representing samples of coal with a different place of extraction occupy separate areas of the figure. It is thus possible to determine the boundary dividing views of points representing different places of coal extraction. This in turn entails that it is possible to divide areas of the 7-dimensional space occupied by samples with different places of coal extraction. It follows from the above that the perspective-based observational tunnels method enables to indicate the possibility to divide the space of samples into areas with different places of coal extraction. Data analyzed in the paper was 7-dimensional. The perspective-based observational tunnels method can however be used on data with any large number of dimensions. The number of keys necessary to change observational parameters rapidly growing along with the number of dimensions is only a certain limitation [1]. The next papers can focus on verifying the effectiveness of the discussed method on data in the cases in which other methods fail. It can concern both real data and artificially generated multidimensional data.

Fig. 2. Images of 7-dimensional points representing samples of coal with lower susceptibility to gasification with the omission of the condition concerning the chlorine content are marked with symbol x; samples of coal more susceptible to gasification are marked with a circle (o).

Fig. 3. The view of 7-dimensional data with the division according to the place of coal extraction. Samples coming from different coal mines were marked with different symbols.

5   Conclusions

The qualitative analysis of 7-dimensional data using the perspective-based observational tunnels method enabled to draw the following conclusions:

1. It was found that images of points representing samples of coal more and less susceptible to gasification occupy separate areas of the figure. It is thus possible to determine the boundary dividing views of points representing different degrees of susceptibility to gasification in the figure. This in turn entails that it is possible to divide areas of the 7-dimensional space occupied by samples with different applicability to the gasification process. It follows from the above that the perspective-based observational tunnels method enables to indicate the possibility to divide the space of samples into areas with different applicability to the fluidal gasification process.

2. It was found that also with the omission of the condition concerning the chlorine content, images of points representing samples of coal more and less susceptible to gasification occupy separate areas of the figure. Also here, it is possible to determine the boundary dividing views of points representing different degrees of susceptibility to gasification in the figure. This in turn entails that it is possible to divide areas of the 7-dimensional space occupied by samples with different applicability to the gasification process with the omission of the condition concerning the chlorine content. It follows from the above that the perspective-based observational tunnels method enables to indicate the possibility to divide the space of samples into areas with different applicability to the fluidal gasification process even with the change in conditions specifying this applicability.

3. It was found that images of points representing samples of coal with a different place of extraction occupy separate areas of the figure. It is thus possible to determine the boundary dividing views of points representing different places of coal extraction. This in turn entails that it is possible to divide areas of the 7-dimensional space occupied by samples with different places of coal extraction. It follows from the above that the perspective-based observational tunnels method enables to indicate the possibility to divide the space of samples into areas with different places of coal extraction.

References

1. Jamroz, D.: The perspective-based observational tunnels method: a new method of multidimensional data visualization. Inf. Vis. **16**(4), 346–360 (2017)
2. Jamroz, D., Nieboba, T.: Comparison of selected methods of multi-parameter data visualization used for classification of coals. Physicochem. Probl. Mineral Process. **51**(2), 769–784 (2015)
3. Jolliffe, I.T.: Principal Component Analysis. Series: Springer Series in Statistics, 2nd edn. Springer, New York (2002)
4. Aldrich, C.: Visualization of transformed multivariate data sets with autoassociative neural networks. Pattern Recogn. Lett. **19**(8), 749–764 (1998)
5. Jamroz, D.: Application of multi-parameter data visualization by means of autoassociative neural networks to evaluate classification possibilities of various coal types. Physicochem. Probl. Mineral Process. **50**(2), 719–734 (2014)
6. Kohonen, T.: Self Organization and Associative Memory. Springer, Heidelberg (1989). https://doi.org/10.1007/978-3-642-88163-3
7. Jamroz, D., Nieboba, T.: Application of multidimensional data visualization by means of self-organizing Kohonen maps to evaluate classification possibilities of various coal types. Arch. Min. Sci. **60**(1), 39–51 (2015)
8. Inselberg, A.: Parallel Coordinates: VISUAL Multidimensional Geometry and its Applications. Springer, Heidelberg (2009). https://doi.org/10.1007/978-0-387-68628-8

9. Akers, S.B., Horel, D., Krisnamurthy, B.: The star graph: an attractive alternative to the n-cube. In: Proceedings of International Conference On Parallel Processing, pp. 393–400. Pensylvania State University Press (1987)
10. Kim, S.S., Kwon, S., Cook, D.: Interactive visualization of hierarchical clusters using MDS and MST. Metrika **51**, 39–51 (2000)
11. Assa, J., Cohen-Or, D., Milo, T.: RMAP: a system for visualizing data in multidimensional relevance space. Vis. Comput. **15**(5), 217–34 (1999)

Urban Data and Spatial Segregation: Analysis of Food Services Clusters in St. Petersburg, Russia

Aleksandra Nenko[✉], Artem Konyukhov, and Sergey Mityagin

Institute for Design and Urban Studies, ITMO University,
Saint-Petersburg, Russia
al.nenko@gmail.com

Abstract. This paper presents an approach to study spatial segregation through clusterization of food services in St. Petersburg, Russia, based on analysis of geospatial and user-generated data from open sources. We consider a food service as an urban place with social and symbolic features and we track how popularity (number of reviews) and rating of food venues in Google maps correlate with formation of food venues clusters. We also analyze environmental parameters which correlate with clusterization of food services, such as functional load of the surrounding built environment and presence of public spaces. We observe that main predictors for food services clusters formation are shops, services and offices, while public spaces (parks and river embankments) do not draw food venues. Popular and highly rated food venues form clusters in historic city centre which collocate with existing creative spaces, unpopular and low rated food venues do not form clusters and are more widely spread in peripheral city areas.

Keywords: Urban environment · Urban data · Spatial segregation
Food services · Food venue popularity · Food venue rating

1 Introduction

In the context of postindustrial economy mass consumption of services and goods is the utmost component of the everyday life of the city dwellers and the quality of services has become an unquestionable value. Contemporary urban lifestyle demands accessible, available, and variable services. Economic development follows the tendency of services complication and diversification.

Digitalization of urban life and growth of possibilities to communicate about the urban services online between the producer and consumer allows producers to promote and position their services more efficiently, clients to browse and translate feedback about the services, and researchers to trace trends in service development based on urban data coming from various data sources. Online platforms which are expressing location, type and score of urban services by expert or peer-to-peer reviews, such as Google maps, Foresquare, Instagram, become significant guides of consumption processes. Our paper lies in line with the corpus of research which digs into the possibilities of applying user-generated geolocated data to analyze urban processes.

© Springer International Publishing AG, part of Springer Nature 2018
Y. Shi et al. (Eds.): ICCS 2018, LNCS 10862, pp. 683–690, 2018.
https://doi.org/10.1007/978-3-319-93713-7_65

Service diversity and equal distribution across the urban space is considered to be a value, as far as it facilitates satisfaction of different users and improves overall subjective well-being (Jacobs 1961; Sennett 1977). At the same time urban space is segregated, while it is subject to the laws of capitalistic economy (Lefebvre 1991; Harvey 2001, 2012; Zukin 1989). For this reasons considering segregation of services in the city acquires topicality.

We pursue the thesis that an urban service is not just an economic facility or an organization which exist in vacuum, but a "place" in urban space which attracts people and proposes a certain lifestyle. Services as places contain social, economic, symbolic and environmental characteristics. In this paper to analyze classes of services we consider symbolic parameters such as popularity (number of reviews) and rating and environmental parameters of venue location. The object of this study are food services as one of the most representative FMCG (fast moving consumer goods) services spread around urban space.

2   Literature Review

Inequality of food services distribution has won attention of scholars from 1990s. Cummins and Macintyre (1999) food stores in urban areas are distributed unequally. Wrigley (2002) proves that cities and regions might even contain "food deserts" - areas with restricted access to food stores and food venues, which emerge due to unequal distribution of food stores. The latter tend to locate more in central areas of the cities, than in non-central quarters, forming "ghettos" devoid from food. Global processes of urbanization, such as gentrification, can lead to emergence of paradoxical situations, such as expensive shops and food venues next to the dwellings of the poor or disadvantaged (McDonald and Nelson 1991). Kelly and Swindel (2002) argue that sufficient diversity in services, in particular, food venues, leads to the improvement of quality of life and citizen satisfaction. Public and urban development policies should be focused on provision of the equal access to basic goods and services based on indexes of price and availability (Donkin et al. 2000). Porta et al. 2009, 2011 shows that street centralities are correlated with the location of economic activities and that the correlations are higher with secondary than primary activities.

3   Research Design and Dataset

We analyze spatial distribution of food services based on clusterization techniques and on correlation analysis with environmental characteristics described above. Formation of different classes of food venues is considered an indicator of service variety as well as of spatial segregation in the city in terms of quality of services.

The key research questions are: is there any evidence for correlation between the environmental characteristics and spatial clusterization of food services? Is there any evidence for spatial clusterization of food services according to symbolic properties of the places, in particular, parameter of venue popularity or rating?

Hypothesis 1. Clusterization of food services is correlated with characteristics of the built environment: food venues tend to collocate with (a) commercial function, (b) historical areas and (c) public spaces.

Hypothesis 2. Popular high rated venues cluster in favorable environmental conditions (collocate with objects described above) while unpopular low rated venues locate in unfavorable environmental conditions.

Hypothesis 3. Popular high rated venues tend to cluster while they "keep" the quality of service together.

The dataset on St. Petersburg food venues was parsed from Google maps open source via API and contains 4496 items. Google maps were chosen as a resource while it is well-spread in Russia: 85% of Russian smartphones run on Android system with preinstalled Google maps (Sharma 2017). Usually places records provide venue ID, its name, geographical coordinates, rating, and number of reviews. However for our dataset only 2327 records contain information on venue rating and number of reviews. We consider formation of venues clusters by analyzing their "popularity" defined through 2 parameters: (a) number of reviews given by venue clients, (b) rating of a food establishment from 1 to 5 points given by its clients. Every time client leaves th place Google asks her to leave a review and rate the venue. Google company doesn't explain how the actual calculation of the rating is processed, it might be calculated as a Bayesian average (Blumenthal 2014). Number of reviews in the dataset distribute as follows: mean - 54.24, standard deviation - 203, median - 9. During data processing venues with number of reviews beyond 3 sigma (mean average deviation) distance from the mean were removed. Ratings distribute as follows: mean - 4.26, std - 0.74, median - 4.4. It was detected that venues with rating less than 4,8 points consistently have few reviews (for 5 points ratings no more than 15 reviews) and they were removed from the dataset.

To allocate spatial clusters of food places we have applied DBSCAN (density-based spatial clustering of applications with noise) algorithm. DBSCAN allows to deliberately chose the size of the clusters and exclude single objects and is often used for spatial clusterization tasks (Ester et al. 1996; Kisilevich et al. 2010). The main parameters of the algorithm are (a) minimal number of objects in a cluster and (b) neighborhood radius. To define optimal parameters for clusterization we have allocated already existing food and drinking clusters in different parts of St. Petersburg city (Lenpoligraphmash, Loft project Etaji, Golitsyn Loft, etc.) which were to appear during clusterization procedure. Minimal number of objects in existing clusters is 5. Optimization procedure has shown the optimal radius of 100 m (when existing officially defined clusters appear on the map).

The dataset for functional objects was derived from Foursquare with its prescribed categories of venues: "Arts & Entertainment", "College & University", "Food", "Nightlife", "Office", "Residence", "Shop & Service", "Travel & Transport". The overall dataset for St. Petersburg is 166 thousand functional objects. Additionally polygons of industrial territories, rivers and parks were parsed from OpenStreetMap open source.

For each food venue functional objects in 100 m radius were defined and assigned categories (1 - objects of this category are present in the list of neighbors, 0 - objects of this category are absent).

To define probabilities of food venue location next to the functional objects the mean was calculated for each of functional categories. For each functional category Spearman correlation coefficient was calculated between venue rating and this category object presence in 100 m radius from the venue.

To define collocation of food venues with certain popularity and rating (i.e. classes of venues) we have calculated average rating for their neighboring food venues.

Figure 1 shows that at least two different classes of venues are present in the dataset. We have applied Ward's Hierarchical Clustering Method and have set "rating" and "average rating" parameters for clusterization (Ward 1963; Murtagh and Legendre 2014) and have received three classes of food venues: (1) low rated venues which collocate with low rated neighbors, (2) high rated venues which collocate with high rated neighbors, (3) high rated venues which collocate with low rated neighbors (Fig. 3).

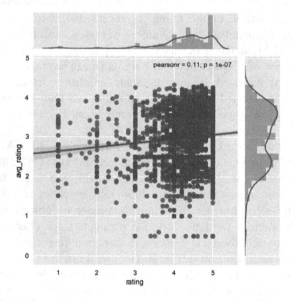

Fig. 1. Distribution of food venues rating and average rating of their neighbours

4   Results

Calculation of the proportion of food venues which collocate with functional objects give the following results: shops & services - 0.776023, offices - 0.608319, (other) food venues - 0.557829, residential areas - 0.273577, arts & entertainment venues - 0.232651, travel & transport - 0.200845, outdoor activities - 0.199066, parks - 0.169706, colleges

& universities - 0.144795, nightlife - 0.134342, industrial territories - 0.081851, river embankments - 0.051379. Hypothesis 1 has partly proved: functional objects such as shops, services and offices tend to collocate with food venues, while public spaces do not. As for the historical objects - see Fig. 4 below.

Hypothesis 2 has not proved: no correlation was detected between presence of discussed functional objects and venue rating and popularity (Fig. 2).

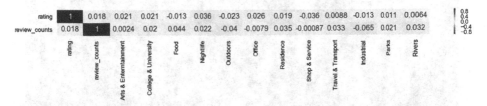

Fig. 2. Matrix of correlation between environmental parameters, food venue rating and popularity

Figure 3 shows the three classes of food venues described above and how they collocate with functional objects.

Venue class	№ 1	№ 2	№ 3
rating (mean)	2,435841	4,542263	4,316224
average rating (mean)	2,858794	3,566354	2,350592
Arts & Enterntainment	0,261062	0,297082	0,237192
College & University	0,132743	0,196286	0,145161
Food	0,615044	0,609195	0,610057
Nightlife	0,119469	0,184792	0,128083
Outdoors	0,243363	0,170645	0,225806
Office	0,588496	0,596817	0,634725
Residence	0,216814	0,263484	0,29981
Shop & Service	0,867257	0,729443	0,833966
Travel & Transport	0,234513	0,263484	0,191651
Industrial	0,053097	0,016799	0,055977
Parks	0,154867	0,167993	0,175522
Rivers	0,057522	0,056587	0,048387

Fig. 3. Venue classes and proportions of their collocation with functional objects

To check hypothesis 3 we have applied DBSCAN algorithm and have received clusters of highly rated venues (class 2) (Fig. 4) and highly rated venues with low rated neighbors (class 3). Low rated venues (class 1) do not tend to form clusters. High rated food clusters collocate with existing creative spaces (they reside on their territory) as well as shops and office zones and appear to be located mostly in historical city centre.

Their clustering might be explained by the fact that venues control quality of their services together and are controlled by their renters.

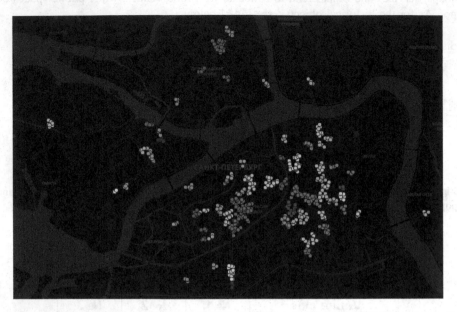

Fig. 4. Clusters of highly rated food venues (radius 100 m, minimal number of neighbors 5)

5   Conclusions

The paper shows that user-generated data on urban services together with geospatial data on functional objects can be successfully used together for analysis of spatial segregation, in particular, spatial clusterization of food services. Results received show that food services tend to collocate with certain functional objects in urban environment. The most important environmental feature for location of food venues is shops and services, second - offices and business centers. Public spaces as attractors are not significant. This hints a problem that open public space in St. Petersburg is underdeveloped, in particular, left without sterling food service. Functional objects do not impact location of venues with high (or low) ratings. Food venues tend to form clusters of popular highly rated places in historical city centre, peripheral city areas are more occupied by less popular and less rated venues. These conclusions can be interpreted as spatial segregation of urban space: monocentricity, lack of diversity.

The advantages of using different data sources to analyze food services have to be analyzed further. In this paper we have argued that Google maps has became an important datasource for Russian cities due to the abundance of Android mobile phones, however we plan to conduct a comparative survey with data from Google places, Foursquare and other location based platforms to check their applicability and resourcefulness.

The environmental characteristics should be researched further, in particular, a more detailed account should be given on *mobility* as a predictor for food services appearance and clustering. Space Syntax analysis of street network centrality and network analysis of pedestrian flows could be conducted.

A more accurate calculation is needed to define if *public spaces* (parks, streets, embankments) play any role in attracting services: while we have not detected any importance in our analysis, we are going to compose an indicator of landscape attractivity to check if high-rated popular places are clustered in locations with a good view on a river or a beautiful street.

Class formation of food venues should be also explored more for *social* parameters, such as demographic, economic, and cultural features of their users. This can be conducted based on user-specific check-in and reviews data.

Based on analysis of service-driven spatial segregation recommendation might be formed on normalization of service distribution, planning of inclusive and diverse chains of services, optimization of urban space use and improvement of the perceived quality of life.

References

Jacobs, J.: The Death and Life of Great American Cities. Random House, New York (1961)

Sennett, R.: The Fall of Public Man. Knopf., New York (1977)

Lefebvre, H.: The Production of Space. Basil Blackwell, Oxford (1991)

Harvey, D.: Spaces of Capital: Towards a Critical Geography. Edinburgh University Press, Edinburgh (2001)

Harvey, D.: Rebel Cities: From the Right to the City to the Urban Revolution. Verso, London and New York (2012)

Zukin, S.: Loft Living: Culture and Capital in Urban Change. Rutgers University Press, New Brunswick (1989)

Cummins, S., Macintyre, S.: The location of food stores in urban areas: a case study in Glasgow. Brit. Food J. **10**(7), 545–553 (1999)

Wrigley, N.: Food deserts in British cities: policy context and research priorities. Urban Stud. **39** (11), 2029–2040 (2002)

McDonald, J.M., Nelson, P.E.: Do the poor still pay more? Food price variations in large metropolitan areas. J. Urban Econ. **30**, 344–359 (1991)

Kelly, J.M., Swindel, D.: Service quality variation across urban space: first steps toward a model of citizen satisfaction. J. Urban Affairs **24**(3), 271–288 (2002)

Donkin, A.J., Dowler, E.A., Stevenson, S.J., Turner, S.A.: Mapping access to food in a deprived area: the development of price and availability indices. Public Health Nutr. **3**, 31–38 (2000)

Porta, S., Strano, E., Iacoviello, V., Messora, R., Latora, V., Cardillo, A., Wang, F., Scellato, S.: Street centrality and densities of retail and services in Bologna, Italy. Env. Plann. B Urban Anal. City Sci. **36**(3), 450–465 (2009)

Porta, S., Latora, V., Wang, F., Rueda, S., Strano, E., Scellato, S., Cardillo, A., Belli, E., Càrdenas, F., Cormenzana, B., Latora, L.: Street centrality and the location of economic activities in Barcelona. Urban Stud. **49**(7), 1471–1488 (2011)

Apple & Xiaomi Strengthen Position in Russia in Q3 2017. https://www.counterpointresearch. com/apple-posted-record-shipments-and-xiaomi-became-the-5thlarest-smartphone-brand-in-russia. Accessed 10 Jan 2018

Why Does Google Show a 4.8 Rating When I Have all 5-star Reviews? http://localu.org/blog/google-show-4-8-rating-5-star-reviews. Accessed 10 Jan 2018

Ester, M., Kriegel, H., Sander, J., Xu, X.: A Density-Based Algorithm for Discovering Clusters in Large Spatial Databases with Noise. Association for the Advancement of Artificial Intelligence. https://www.aaai.org/Papers/KDD/1996/KDD96-037.pdf. Accessed 10 Jan 2018

Kisilevich, S., Mansmann, F., Keim, D.: P-DBSCAN: a density based clustering algorithm for exploration and analysis of attractive areas using collections of geo-tagged photos. In: Proceedings of the 1st International Conference and Exhibition on Computing for Geospatial Research & Application. Association for Computer Machinery, New York (2010)

Ward, J.H.: Hierarchical grouping to optimize an objective function. J. Am. Stat. Assoc. **58**, 236–244 (1963)

Murtagh, F., Legendre, P.: Ward's hierarchical agglomerative clustering method: which algorithms implement ward's criterion? J. Classif. **31**(3), 27–295 (2014)

Control Driven Lighting Design
for Large-Scale Installations

Adam Sędziwy$^{(\boxtimes)}$, Leszek Kotulski, Sebastian Ernst, and Igor Wojnicki

Department of Applied Computer Science,
AGH University of Science and Technology,
Al. Mickiewicza 30, 30 059 Krakow, Poland
{sedziwy,kotulski,ernst,wojnicki}@agh.edu.pl

Abstract. Large-scale photometric computations carried out in the course of lighting design preparation were already subject of numerous works. They focused either on improving the quality of design, for example related to energy-efficiency, or dealt with issues concerning the computation complexity and computations as such.

However, mutual influence of the design process and dynamic dimming of luminaires has not yet been addressed. If road segments are considered separately, suboptimal results can occur in places such as junctions. Considering the entire road network at once complicates the computation procedures and requires additional processing time. This paper focuses on a method to make this more efficient approach viable by applying reversed scheme of design and control. The crucial component of both design and control modules is data inventory which role is also discussed in the paper.

Keywords: Lighting control · Lighting design · LED · GRADIS

1   Introduction

A significant part of every lighting design modernization project is the phase when the appropriate fixtures models and their parameters must be determined. This phase is often based on photometric calculations, and is called the *design phase*. Traditional approaches which rely on human-operated tools are time-consuming, especially when sensor-based dynamic dimming of lamps is considered. Then, each street needs not one, but several dozen designs, to account for different lighting classes assigned to streets at various times, as well as other parameters, such as the level of ambient light.

Preparing advanced, well suited lighting designs covering entire cities or at least whole districts, is a very demanding task. Its complexity originates from several sources: computational complexity, structural complexity of data, a need of using distributed processing supported by sophisticated heuristics and artificial intelligence-based methods. The key issue is a problem size in terms of the input data volume. An additional challenge is implementation of a lighting control system which uses pre-computed presets obtained in the result of a design

© Springer International Publishing AG, part of Springer Nature 2018
Y. Shi et al. (Eds.): ICCS 2018, LNCS 10862, pp. 691–700, 2018.
https://doi.org/10.1007/978-3-319-93713-7_66

process for all available states of roads, squares, walkways and so on. Due to the high computational complexity and practically unpredictable number of possible environment states for the case of an entire city area, the typical method assuming making designs for all possible environment conditions first and then starting control actions, is not doable. Instead we propose using the approach relying on a reversed scheme of cooperation between design and control modules.

Initially only the presets (setups computed for particular lamps) for main control patterns are precalculated. We assess that those cases cover 90–95% of a lighting installation's working time. The remaining patterns of environment's states are handled in-the fly by the control system: if it lacks appropriate response for an actual environment state (for example, some combination of traffic flow and ambient light level) then a request to the design subsystem is submitted to find suitable adjustments for relevant luminaires.

A response for such request is prepared, in turn, using AI based methods based on self-learning algorithms or prediction-based techniques (out of the scope of this work) to reduce the response time to an acceptable value. Obviously, this requires historical data stored in an inventory.

A lighting design in the precalculation phase can be generated twofold, either making the "classical" single-scene photometric computations, as made by industry-standard software [6] or applying the customized approach [17, 18].

Preparation of such a design can be aimed at determining photometric conditions for an assumed luminaire setup, but also its objective can be finding an *optimal* setup, giving the lowest power consumption for instance. Both scenarios will be discussed in the next sections.

The main difference is that in the classical approach, each street is considered separately and as a whole with adjacent row(s) of lamps. In the so-called *custom* approach, the lamps and streets are regarded as separate entities. In particular, one luminaire can illuminate several neighboring streets. Therefore, the configurations of lamps for a given lighting class on a given street must take into account the currently-assigned lighting classes for its neighbors to avoid over-lighting in overlapping regions.

In the first case (classical design), the number of presets is limited to a few dozen profiles per road, so an agent-based system such as GRADIS (formerly PhoCa [11]) can compute the design without any problems. At the same time, it must be noted that the task is already overwhelming for a human designer.

In the *custom* case, the entire combined state of an intersection consists of a million or more possible combinations. However, because the set of reachable states is much smaller, the search space can be still reduced.

The structure of the article is following. In Sect. 2 we give a brief overview on design methods and their objectives. Section 3 contains basic concepts and notions underlying lighting control. In particular, it highlights the role of an inventory in design and control actions. In Sect. 4 we discuss the method of overcoming the combinatorial explosion caused by huge number of states to be processed by a control/design system. In the last section the final conclusions are given.

2   State of Art

In this section we present the basics of design process in both *classical* and *custom* approach.

2.1   Photometric Computations for a Single Lighting Situation

Photometric computations are necessary step in preparation of a lighting infrastructure compliant with mandatory standards (see e.g., [2,7,9]) describing required illumination levels for roads, streets, pedestrian traffic zones, residential areas and so forth. In the simplest and the most frequently applied approach, a layout of each street or road is simplified in the sense that it is regarded as structurally uniform: with constant road width, lamp spacing, lamp parameters etc. Thus, the input data for a single pass of calculations made on a single road (see Fig. 1) consist of such parameters as: carriageway width, predefined reflective properties of a carriageway, number of lanes, pole setback, pole height, arm length, arm inclination, fixture model, fixture inclination, rotation and azimuth, fixture dimming (applies mainly to solid state lighting). It should be noted that to each road or walkway a row(s) is (are) ascribed. Each lamp in such a row is located with the same setback as others. We neglect here all meta-data related to database internal structure such as keys, indexes, timestamps etc.

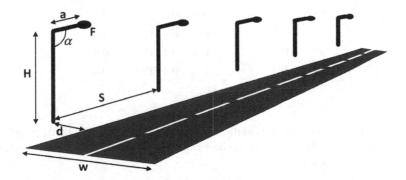

Fig. 1. The sample lighting situation with parameters being taken into account during computations: H – pole height, S – luminaire spacing, a – arm length, α – arm inclination, F – fixture model, w – carriageway width

When one deals with an optimization process which aims at finding such luminaire adjustments that the resultant power usage is minimized, for instance, then instead of single values the ranges for optimization variables appear in the above list:

– pole height → pole height[from, to, step],
– arm length → arm length[from, to, step],
– arm inclination → arm inclination[from, to, step],

- fixture model $\rightarrow$ **fix**$_1$, **fix**$_2$, ... **fix**$_N$,
- fixture inclination, rotation and azimuth $\rightarrow$ [from, to, step] for each angle type,
- fixture dimming (applies mainly to solid state lighting) $\rightarrow$ fixture dimming [from, to, step].

In other words, the input contains the Cartesian product of optimization variables. The high-level structure of output data for single pass computation (in contrast to optimization) links a set of adjustments with resultants photometric parameters. At the low level we obtain particular parameter values. For example, according to the EN 13201-2:2015 standard [7] for motorised traffic routes one has five parameters describing the lighting infrastructure performance, namely average luminance (L_{avg}), overall uniformity (U_o), longitudinal uniformity (U_l), disability glare (f_{TI}) and lighting of surroundings R_{EI}.

Table 1. M – lighting classes (for traffic routes) according to the EN 13201-2:2015 standard. L_{avg} – average luminance, U_o – overall uniformity, U_l – longitudinal uniformity, f_{TI} – disability glare, R_{EI} – lighting of surroundings

Class	L_{avg} [cd/m^2]	U_o	U_l	f_{TI} [%]	R_{EI}
M1	2.0	0.4	0.7	10	0.35
M2	1.5	0.4	0.7	10	0.35
M3	1.0	0.4	0.6	15	0.3
M4	0.75	0.4	0.6	15	0.3
M5	0.5	0.35	0.4	15	0.3
M6	0.3	0.35	0.4	20	0.3

Table 2. C – lighting classes (for conflict areas) according to the EN 13201-2:2015 standard. $\bar{E}$ – minimum allowable average horizontal illuminance, U_o – overall uniformity of horizontal illuminance

Class	$\bar{E}$ [lx]	U_o
C0	50	0.4
C1	30	0.4
C2	20	0.4
C3	15	0.4
C4	10	0.4
C5	7.5	0.4

In turn, each optimization process produces a Cartesian set (or its subset if some heuristics were applied for restricting a search space) of such output sets.

Such an approach being used by market available software [6] simplifies and thus shortens the design process flow. On the other side it yields designs which are not optimized with respect to the power usage so if an objective is energy-efficiency optimization then the customized lighting design [17] has to be applied.

2.2   Customized Computations for a Single Lighting Situation

The only but fundamental difference between regular and customized photometric computations is that a lighting situation such as street, roadway or bike lane is not regarded as uniform anymore. Instead its real layout is taken including such elements as area boundaries, locations and orientations of luminaires, individual properties of particular lamps etc. Having those data a system splits a road into multiple consecutive *segments* being lighting situations (Fig. 2). Additionally, we consider roads and luminaires as two separate sets. The lamps are ascribed to a particular segment on the basis of certain spatial conditions which have to be satisfied [4] (this assignment can be analytically derived from spatial data).

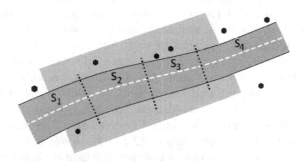

Fig. 2. The sample roadway in customized approach. The roadway area is subdivided (dotted lines) into segments $S_1, \ldots, S_4$. Hexagonal symbols denote location of luminaires and gray shaded area covers all luminaires relevant to the segment S_2.

All spatial data referencing roads and luminaires are geolocalised. This high granularity approach allows to obtain up to 15% of power usage reduction [18].

The output set structure for customized computations also diff ers from the case of regular ones. The key differences are:

1. Per segment results rather than per road (street, walkway, etc.). Individual resultant photometric parameter values are assigned to all consecutive segments which constitute a given roadway.
2. Separate, individual set of adjustments for each relevant (i.e., being ascribed to a considered segment) luminaire, instead of one set for entire row of lamps.

To support the above computation scheme one needs do deploy additional agents on the *per-segment* basis. Also the optimizing process requires using appropriate heuristics to restrict a search space size. The example is an observation that all luminaires located along a street (and thus, the corresponding segments) have the same values of most luminaire adjustments (except dimming value). Such constraints but also other, imposed by some business requirements, have to be also stored in an inventory and accessible for computing agents.

3   Lighting Control

Another use case for an inventory is a lighting control [3, 19, 20]. The concept of an adaptive control is based on the notion of a *lighting profile*. The starting point for this is the observation that an environment state is given as a convolution of various parameters such as traffic flow intensity, ambient light level, presence of pedestrians, weather conditions and so on. Those parameters are tracked by telemetric layer (e.g., rain sensors, induction loops and others). Any change of the above shifts an environment to another state. The control system performance relies on adaptation of a lighting system to such changes triggered by sensors. It should be remarked that the term *environment* used here denotes each area type (street, road, intersection, walkway, parking zone etc.). The *lighting profile* then is understood as an environment state together with the corresponding luminaires' adjustment, satisfying lighting standard requirements.

Such a control is more and more feasible due to rapidly developing IoT (Internet of Things) devices and sensor nets. It leads to broad availability of relevant data [5, 13, 16]. The main drivers are safety, convenience and energy savings [8, 10]. Currently available control systems are often based on rules and configured for particular deployments [1, 12, 14, 15]. However, they lack underlying formal models. It increases risk of not meeting lighting standards and costly adjustment to evolving requirements or deployment at new locations. Having the proposed environment model supported by photometric calculations mitigates these risks.

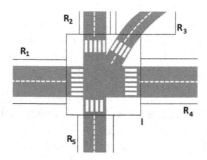

Fig. 3. The sample intersection (I) of several streets ($R_1, \ldots, R_5$). Particular calculation fields are delimited with the black lines

Let us consider a design process preparing lighting profiles for the street R_1 shown in Fig. 3. For simplicity we assume that an environment's state is defined solely by the ambient light level which is discretized to 20 levels (1– no ambient light, 20 – ambient light delivers all lighting necessary) and the traffic flow intensity. The latter parameter decides which lighting class from the series M1, . . . ,M6 (see Table 1) has to be selected. For those assumptions we obtain $6 \times 20 = 120$ possible profiles for each street. Analogously, for the intersection I for which the EN 13201-2:2015 standard specifies the lighting classes C0, C1, . . . , C5 (see Table 2) we have also 120 possible profiles. Thus for the area shown in Fig. 3, regarded as a whole, the number of states (profiles) is

$$(\text{number of states for a street/intersection})^{(\text{number of streets and intersections})} =$$
$$= 120^6 \approx 3 \times 10^{12}.$$

Remark. The above formula expressing an estimation of a number of available lighting profiles should not be confused with a number of possible lamp configurations discussed in Subsect. 2.1.

Application of heuristics such as the traffic flow conservation law or constraints imposed on ambient light correlation among particular areas allow reducing the number of states, which limits the combinatorial explosion of states to analyze and leads to both design and control optimization.

3.1   Supporting Calculations Using Inventory Data

Any automated process requires a reliable source of data to yield appropriate results. In case of lighting calculations, this involves integration of various types of data:

- *Road network.* As traffic intensity is the key factor used to alter the lighting class, and the sensors are usually sparse, it is crucial to model traffic flow using road network graphs. Also, data available in road maps can serve as an aid for selection of lighting classes.
- *Geodetic data.* For detailed calculations, it is crucial to use realistic road and sidewalk shapes. This data may be available as CAD files, or it can be regenerated in an interactive process using map data-based reasoning and aerial imagery.
- *Infrastructure data.* Obviously, all lighting point details need to be maintained, including pole and arm geometry, fixture details, etc.
- *Calculation results.* Lamp settings needed to achieve a given lighting class on a given road segments are needed by the control module.

To allow for efficient support of the design phase and dynamic control of the lamps, all this data needs to reside in a coherent, spatially-enabled repository. This allows for analysis based not only on lamp data (distance, spacing, height, etc.), but also on spatial relationships between the lamps and the lit areas. This characteristic is crucial to allow for optimizations described in Sect. 4.

4 Making Design and Control Viable

The combinatorial explosion of states described above makes the design process longer and the control process more computational resource hungry. It puts forward two goals: 1. minimize number of states in terms of combination of neighboring lighting classes to calculate photometry for; 2. minimize number of states in terms of lighting profiles for the control system to manage.

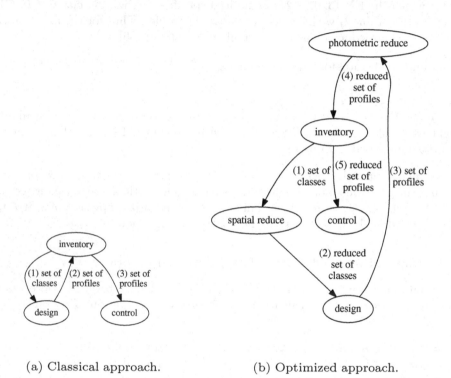

(a) Classical approach.   (b) Optimized approach.

Fig. 4. Design process upgrade to reduce combinatorial explosion of states.

As a result the design process has to be optimized as it is showed in Fig. 4. Both spatial and photometric optimizations are taken into account. The classical approach assumes that lighting classes, coupled with road parameters, are delivered to the design process. The design provides a massive set of profiles by performing photometric calculations which are stored back in the inventory. Subsequently the profiles are used by the control. The optimized approach is driven by the aforementioned goals. The set of classes is reduced thanks to spatial relationships among luminaires, traffic flow statistics, and imposed traffic laws at given locations. As a result the set of classes is significantly reduced, purging all those states which are not reachable which addresses the goal number 1. This reduced set of classes is delivered to the design process which calculates photometry, thus provides lighting profiles. Since the energy usage differences among some lighting profiles might be insignificant they are reduced further addressing the goal number 2. Such a reduced set of profiles is stored back in the inventory and subsequently passed to the control.

For the example given in Fig. 3 the number of states is reduced from 2.99×10^{12} to 54×10^6 which is 55,296 times. Such a reduction makes both the photometric design and control viable.

5   Conclusions

Pre-calculating lighting profiles to provide precise lighting design and control at intersections is a very complex task for large-scale systems. It is due to combinatorial explosion of search space. The problem is tackled twofold.

First, by changing the design-control paradigm: a design does not cover all possible control scenarios anymore but most of them. The remaining states are calculated on demand in in-the-fly mode using AI-based techniques rather than photometric computations, to reduce the response time. Those requests are submitted by a control system which plays a role of an initiator.

The second method of reducing complexity is using additional data such as a geo-spatial distribution of light points, traffic intensity statistics, and traffic law regulations. Those data impose constraints which significantly restrict a search space. On top of these there is an additional optimization performed which merges similar states together where similarity is measured by energy consumption.

Altering the design process results in the state space reduction which makes the design and control processes to be feasible.

The proposed approach is intended to be applied in the R&D project being in the development phase, co-financed by National Centre for Research and Development (Poland). Its objective is creating a high-quality (with respect to energy efficiency), large-scale, smart lighting system.

References

1. Atis, S., Ekren, N.: Development of an outdoor lighting control system using expert system. Energy Build. **130**, 773–786 (2016)
2. Australian/New Zealand Standard: AS/NZS 1158.1.1:2005 Lighting for roads and public spaces Vehicular traffic (Category V) lighting - Performance and design requirements (2005). SAI Global Limited
3. Bielecka, M., Bielecki, A., Ernst, S., Wojnicki, I.: Prediction of Traffic Intensity for Dynamic Street Lighting, September 2017. https://doi.org/10.15439/2017F389
4. CEN 13201–3, E.C.F.S.: Road lighting - part 3: Calculation of performance (2003), ref. no. EN 13201–3:2003 E
5. De Paz, J.F., Bajo, J., Rodríguez, S., Villarrubia, G., Corchado, J.M.: Intelligent system for lighting control in smart cities. Inf. Sci. **372**, 241–255 (2016)
6. DIAL: DIALux. http://goo.gl/21XOBx (2015). Accessed 28 Jan 2018

7. European Committee for Standarization: Road Lighting. Performance requirements, EN 13201-2:2015 (2015)
8. Guo, L., Eloholma, M., Halonen, L.: Intelligent road lighting control systems. Technical report, Helsinki University of Technology, Department of Electronics, Lighting Unit (2008). http://lib.tkk.fi/Diss/2008/isbn9789512296200/article2.pdf
9. Illuminating Engineering Society of North America (IESNA): American National Standard Practice For Roadway Lighting, RP-8-14. IESNA, New York (2014)
10. Kim, J.T., Hwang, T.: Feasibility study on LED street lighting with smart dimming systems in Wooi Stream, Seoul. J. Asian Archit. Build. Eng. **16**(2), 425–430 (2017)
11. Kotulski, L., Landtsheer, J.D., Penninck, S., Sędziwy, A., Wojnicki, I.: Supporting energy efficiency optimization in lighting design process. In: Proceedings of 12th European Lighting Conference Lux Europa, Krakow, 17–19 September 2013 (2013). http://goo.gl/tfbPf3. Accessed 2 Mar 2015
12. Lau, S.P., Merrett, G.V., Weddell, A.S., White, N.M.: A traffic-aware street lighting scheme for smart cities using autonomous networked sensors. Comput. Electr. Eng. **45**, 192–207 (2015)
13. Leduc, G.: Road traffic data: collection methods and applications. Working Papers Energy, Transport Climate Change **1**, 55 (2008)
14. Mahoor, M., Salmasi, F.R., Najafabadi, T.A.: A hierarchical smart street lighting system with Brute-force energy optimization. IEEE Sens. J. **17**(9), 2871–2879 (2017)
15. Marino, F., Leccese, F., Pizzuti, S.: Adaptive street lighting predictive control. Energy Procedia **111**, 790–799 (2017)
16. Merlino, G., Bruneo, D., Distefano, S., Longo, F., Puliafito, A., Al-Anbuky, A.: A smart city lighting case study on an openstack-powered infrastructure. Sensors **15**(7), 16314–16335 (2015)
17. Sędziwy, A.: A new approach to street lighting design. LEUKOS **12**(3), 151–162 (2016)
18. Sędziwy, A., Basiura, A.: Energy reduction in roadway lighting achieved with novel design approach and LEDs. LEUKOS **14**(1), 45–51 (2018)
19. Wojnicki, I., Kotulski, L.: Street lighting control, energy consumption optimization. In: Rutkowski, L., Korytkowski, M., Scherer, R., Tadeusiewicz, R., Zadeh, L.A., Zurada, J.M. (eds.) ICAISC 2017. LNCS (LNAI), vol. 10246, pp. 357–364. Springer, Cham (2017). https://doi.org/10.1007/978-3-319-59060-8_32
20. Wojnicki, I., Kotulski, L., Sędziwy, A., Ernst, S.: Application of distributed graph transformations to automated generation of control patterns for intelligent lighting systems. J. Comput. Sci. **23**, 20–30 (2017)

An OpenMP Implementation of the TVD–Hopmoc Method Based on a Synchronization Mechanism Using Locks Between Adjacent Threads on Xeon Phi (TM) Accelerators

Frederico L. Cabral[1], Carla Osthoff[1(✉)], Gabriel P. Costa[1],
Sanderson L. Gonzaga de Oliveira[2], Diego Brandão[3],
and Mauricio Kischinhevsky[4]

[1] Laboratório Nacional de Computação Científica - LNCC, Petrópolis, Brazil
{fcabral,osthoff,gcosta}@lncc.br
[2] Universidade Federal de Lavras - UFLA, Lavras, Brazil
sanderson@dcc.ufla.br
[3] Centro Federal de Educação Tecnológica Celso Suckow da Fonseca - CEFET-RJ,
Rio de Janeiro, Brazil
diego.brandao@eic.cefet-rj.br
[4] Universidade Federal Fluminense - UFF, Rio de Janeiro, Brazil
kisch@ic.uff.br

Abstract. This work focuses on the study of the 1–D TVD–Hopmoc method executed in shared memory manycore environments. In particular, this paper studies barrier costs on Intel® Xeon Phi™ (KNC and KNL) accelerators when using the OpenMP standard. This paper employs an explicit synchronization mechanism to reduce spin and thread scheduling times in an OpenMP implementation of the 1–D TVD–Hopmoc method. Basically, we define an array that represents threads and the new scheme consists of synchronizing only adjacent threads. Moreover, the new approach reduces the OpenMP scheduling time by employing an explicit work-sharing strategy. In the beginning of the process, the array that represents the computational mesh of the numerical method is partitioned among threads, instead of permitting the OpenMP API to perform this task. Thereby, the new scheme diminishes the OpenMP spin time by avoiding OpenMP barriers using an explicit synchronization mechanism where a thread only waits for its two adjacent threads. The results of the new approach is compared with a basic parallel implementation of the 1–D TVD–Hopmoc method. Specifically, numerical simulations shows that the new approach achieves promising performance gains in shared memory manycore environments for an OpenMP implementation of the 1–D TVD–Hopmoc method.

© Springer International Publishing AG, part of Springer Nature 2018
Y. Shi et al. (Eds.): ICCS 2018, LNCS 10862, pp. 701–707, 2018.
https://doi.org/10.1007/978-3-319-93713-7_67

1   Introduction

Over the last decades, since both the demand for faster computation and shared memory multicore and manycore architectures became available in large scale, an important issue has emerged: how can one obtain a speedup proportional to the number of physical cores available in a parallel architecture? Specific programming languages, libraries, and programming models has been proposed to assist programmers and researches to surmount this challenge. Among them, the OpenMP library [2] is one of the best-known standards nowadays.

Since new machines with faster clock speed are facing a certain limit because overheat and electromagnetic interference, technologies have been proposed with the objective of improving the processing capacity in computations. Multithreading, distributed processing, manycore architectures (e.g. General Purpose Graphical Processing Units (GPGPUs)), and Many Integrated Core (MIC) accelerators (such as Intel® Xeon Phi™) are examples of technologies employed to boost a computer performance. Even with these recent technologies, it is still a challenge to obtain a speedup proportional to the number of available cores in a parallel implementation due to the hardware complexity in such systems. To overcome this particular issue, the OpenMP standard offers a simple manner to convert a serial code to a parallel implementation for shared memory multicore and manycore architectures. Although a parallel implementation with the support of this API is easily reached, a basic (or naive) OpenMP implementation in general does not attain straightforwardly the expected speedup in an application. Furthermore, despite being easily implemented, the most common resources available in the OpenMP standard may generate high scheduling and synchronization running times.

High Performance Computing (HPC) is a practice widely used in computational simulations of several real-world phenomena. Numerical methods have been designed to maximize the computational capacity provided by a HPC environment. In particular, the Hopmoc method (see [3] and references therein) is a spatially decoupled alternating direction procedure for solving convection–diffusion equations. It was designed to be executed in parallel architectures (see [1] and references therein). To provide more specific detail, the unknowns are spatially decoupled, permitting message-passing minimization among threads. Specifically, the set of unknowns is decoupled into two subsets. These two subsets are calculated alternately by explicit and implicit approaches. In particular, the use of two explicit and implicit semi-steps avoids the use of a linear system solver. Moreover, this method employs a strategy based on tracking values along characteristic lines during time stepping. The two semi-steps are performed along characteristic lines by a Semi-Lagrangian scheme following concepts of the Modified Method of Characteristics. The time derivative and the advection term are combined as a direction derivative. Thus, time steps are performed in the flow direction along characteristics of the velocity field of the fluid. The Hopmoc method is a direct method in the sense that the cost per time step is previously known. To determine the value in the foot of the characteristic line, the original method uses an interpolation technique, that introduces inherent numerical errors. To overcome this limitation, the Hopmoc method was combined with a Total Variation Diminishing (TVD) scheme. This new approach, called TVD–Hopmoc, employs a flux limiter to determine the value in the foot of the characteristic line based on the Lax-Wendroff scheme [1].

We studied a basic OpenMP implementation of the TVD–Hopmoc method under the Intel® Parallel Studio XE software for Intel's Haswell/Broadwell architectures. This product showed us that the main problem in the performance of a simple OpenMP–based TVD–Hopmoc method was the use of the basic OpenMP scheduling and synchronization mechanisms. Thus, this paper employs alternative strategies to these basic OpenMP strategies. Specifically, this work uses an explicit work-sharing (EWS) strategy. The array that denotes the computational mesh of the 1–D TVD–Hopmoc method is explicitly partitioned among threads. In addition, to avoid implicit barrier costs imposed by the OpenMP standard, this paper employs an explicit synchronization mechanism to guarantee that only threads with real data dependencies participate in the synchronization. Additionally, we compare our approach along with three thread binding policies (balanced, compact, and scatter).

This paper is organized as follows. Section 2 outlines the TVD–Hopmoc method and shows how the experiments were conducted in this work. Section 3 presents the EWS strategy employed here along with our strategy to synchronize adjacent threads. Section 4 shows the experimental results that compares the new approach with a naive OpenMP–based TVD–Hopmoc method. Finally, Sect. 5 addresses the conclusions and discusses the next steps in this investigation.

2 The TVD–Hopmoc Method and Description of the Tests

Consider the advection–diffusion equation in the form

$$u_t + vu_x = du_{xx}, \tag{1}$$

with adequate initial and boundary conditions, where v is a constant positive velocity, d is the constant positive diffusivity, $0 \leq x \leq 1$ and $0 \leq t \leq T$, for T time steps. Applying the Hopmoc method to equation (1) yields $\overline{u}_i^{t+\frac{1}{2}} = \overline{\overline{u}}_i^t + \delta t \left[\theta_i^t L_h \left(\overline{\overline{u}}_i^t \right) + \theta_i^{t+1} L_h \left(\overline{u}_i^{t+\frac{1}{2}} \right) \right]$ and $u_i^{t+1} = \overline{u}_i^{t+\frac{1}{2}} + \delta t \left[\theta_i^t L_h \left(\overline{u}_i^{t+\frac{1}{2}} \right) + \theta_i^{t+1} L_h \left(u_i^{t+1} \right) \right]$, where θ_i^t is 1 (0) if $t + i$ is even (odd), $L_h \left(u_i^t \right) = d \frac{u_{i-1}^t - 2u_i^t + u_{i+1}^t}{\Delta x^2}$ is a finite-difference operator, $\overline{u}_i^{t+\frac{1}{2}}$ and u_i^{t+1} are consecutive time semi-steps, and the value of the concentration in $\overline{\overline{u}}_i^t$ is obtained by a TVD scheme to determine $\overline{\overline{u}}_{i+1}^t = u_i^t - c \left(u_i^t - u_{i-1}^t \right) \left[1 - \frac{(1-c)\phi_{i-1}}{2} + \frac{(1-c)\phi_i}{2r} \right]$, where $r = \frac{u_i^t - u_{i-1}^t}{u_{i+1}^t - u_i^t}$ [1]. The Van Leer flux limiter [4] was employed in the numerical simulations performed in this present work. This scheme delivered better results when compared with other techniques [1]. Our numerical simulations were carried out for a Gaussian pulse with amplitude 1.0, whose initial center location is 0.2, with velocity $v = 1$ and diffusion coefficient $d = \frac{2}{Re} = 10^{-3}$ (where Re stands for Reynolds number), $\Delta x = 10^{-5}$ and $\Delta x = 10^{-6}$ (i.e., 10^5 and 10^6 stencil points, respectively), and T is established as 10^4, 10^5, and 10^6.

3 EWS and Synchronization Strategies Combined with an Explicit Lock Mechanism

The main idea of our OpenMP–based TVD–Hopmoc method is to avoid the extra time caused by scheduling threads and the implicit barriers after a load sharing construct employed in the OpenMP standard. We deal with thread imbalance by partitioning explicitly the array into the team of threads. Our implementation of the TVD–Hopmoc method defines a static array that represents the unknowns. Thus, a permanent partition of this array is established for each thread in the beginning of the code, i.e., no changes are made to this partition during the execution of the process. Since the mesh is static, thread scheduling is performed only at the beginning of the execution. In addition, since each thread in the team has its required data, we do not need to use the OpenMP *parallel for* directive in our code. Thus, our OpenMP implementation of the TVD–Hopmoc method was designed to minimize synchronization in a way that a particular thread needs information only from its adjacent threads so that an implicit barrier is unnecessary. Thereby, the mechanism applied here involves a synchronization of adjacent threads, i.e., each thread waits only for two adjacent threads to reach the same synchronization point.

The strategy employed here is based on a simple lock mechanism. Using an array of booleans, a thread sets (releases) an entry in this array and, hence, informs its adjacent threads that the data cannot (can) be used by them. We will refer this approach as EWS-adSync implementation.

4 Experimental Results

This section shows the results of the new and basic approaches aforementioned in executions performed on a machine containing an Intel® Xeon Phi™ Knights-Corner (KNC) accelerator 5110P, 8GB DDR5, 1.053 GHz, 60 cores, 4 threads per core (in Sect. 4.1), and on a machine containing an Intel® Xeon Phi™ CPU 7250 @ 1.40 GHz, 68 cores, 4 threads per core (in Sect. 4.2). We evaluate the EWS-adSync implementation of the TVD–Hopmoc method along with three thread binding policies: balanced, compact, and scatter policies.

4.1 Experiments Performed on a Xeon Phi™ (Knight's Corner) Accelerator

This section shows experiments performed on an Intel® Xeon Phi™ (KNC) accelerator composed of 240 threads. Figure 1 shows that our OpenMP–based TVD–Hopmoc method using the EWS strategy in conjunction with synchronizing adjacent threads along with compact (comp.) thread binding policy (pol.)

yielded a speedup of approximately 140x (using 240 threads) in a simulation with $\Delta x = 10^{-6}$ (i.e., a mesh composed of 10^6 stencil points) and $T = 10^5$. This implementation used in conjunction with the scatter (sct.) policy delivered a speedup of 136x (using 238 threads) in a simulation with the same settings.

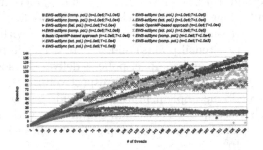

Fig. 1. Speedups obtained by two OpenMP implementations of the TVD–Hopmoc method applied to the advection–diffusion equation (1) for a Gaussian pulse with amplitude 1.0 in executions performed on a Xeon Phi^{TM} (KNC) accelerator. A basic (ou naive) implementation was employed in a simulation with $T = 10^5$ and $\Delta x = 10^{-5}$ (i.e., the mesh is composed of 10^5 stencil points). Our OpenMP–based TVD–Hopmoc method (EWS-adSync implementation) was employed with three different thread binding policies (balanced, compact, and scatter policies) in simulations with Δx set as 10^{-5} and 10^6 (i.e., meshes composed of 10^5 and 10^6 stencil points, resp.) and T specified as 10^5, 10^4, and 10^3.

The EWS-adSync implementation alongside scatter, balanced (bal.), and compact binding policies respectively achieved speedups of 134.2x, 133.8x, and 133.5x in simulations with $\Delta x = 10^{-6}$ and $T = 10^4$. These implementations dominated the basic OpenMP–based TVD-Hopmoc method, which obtained a speedup of 28x.

The EWS-adSync implementation alongside the compact policy (with speedup of 121x) achieved better results than the scatter policy (with speedup of 111x) in a simulation with $\Delta x = 10^{-5}$ and $T = 10^5$. Both implementations dominated the basic OpenMP–based TVD-Hopmoc method, which obtained a speedup of 95x. The EWS-adSync implementation alongside the compact policy (with speedup of 90x) reached slightly better results than the scatter policy (with speedup of 88x) in a simulation with $\Delta x = 10^{-5}$ and $T = 10^4$. On the other hand, the EWS-adSync implementation in conjunction with the scatter policy (with speedup of 38x) yielded better results than the compact policy (with speedup of 27x) in a simulation with $\Delta x = 10^{-5}$ and $T = 10^3$. Figure 1 shows that in general the OpenMP–based TVD–Hopmoc method obtains better speedups when setting a larger number of iterations T since it takes advantage of a higher cache hit rate.

4.2   Experiments Performed on a Xeon Phi™ (Knights Landing) Accelerator

This section shows experiments performed on an Intel® Xeon Phi™ (KNL) accelerator composed of 272 threads. Figure 2 shows that our OpenMP–based TVD–Hopmoc method using the EWS strategy in conjunction with synchronizing adjacent threads along with scatter thread binding policy yielded a speedup of approximately 91x (using 135 threads) in a simulation with $\Delta x = 10^{-5}$ (i.e., a mesh composed of 10^5 stencil points) and $T = 10^6$. This implementation used in conjunction with scatter and compact policies delivered respectively speedups of 85x and 77x (using 135 and 271 threads, respectively) with the same settings. Similarly, the EWS-adSync implementation alongside balanced policy achieved better results (with speedup of 84x) than in conjunction with both scatter (with speedup of 80x) and compact (with speedup of 69x) policies in simulations with $\Delta x = 10^{-5}$ and $T = 10^5$.

The EWS-adSync implementation alongside the scatter policy achieved similar results to the compact policy (both with speedup of 17x) in a simulation with $\Delta x = 10^{-6}$ and $T = 10^5$. It seems that the simulation with $\Delta x = 10^{-6}$ obtained a higher cache miss rate than the other experiments.

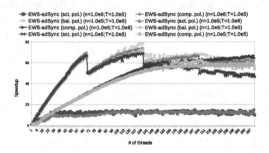

Fig. 2. Speedups of two OpenMP implementations of the TVD–Hopmoc method applied to the advection–diffusion equation (1) for a Gaussian pulse with amplitude 1.0 in runs performed on a Xeon Phi™ (KNL) accelerator. Our OpenMP–based TVD–Hopmoc method (EWS-adSync implementation) was employed with three different thread binding policies (balanced, compact, and scatter policies) in simulations with Δx established as 10^{-5} and 10^6 (i.e., meshes composed of 10^5 and 10^5 stencil points) and T was defined as 10^6 and 10^5.

5   Conclusions

Based on an explicit work-sharing strategy along with an explicit synchronization mechanism, the approach employed here to implement an OpenMP–based TVD–Hopmoc method attained reasonable speedups in manycore (Xeon Phi™ KNC and KNL accelerators) architectures. In particular, the scheduling time was profoundly reduced by replacing the effort of assigning to threads tasks at runtime with an explicit work-sharing strategy that determines *a priori* the range of the array that represents stencil points where each thread will perform its task. Moreover, using a lock array where an entry denotes a thread, the synchronization time in barriers was substituted by a strategy that only requires that each thread be synchronized with its two adjacent threads. Employing these two strategies, the team of threads presented a reasonable load balancing, where almost the total number of threads available are used simultaneously.

Our OpenMP–based TVD–Hopmoc method along with a compact thread binding policy yielded a speedup of approximately 140x when applied to a mesh composed of 10^6 stencil points in a simulation performed on an Intel® Xeon Phi™ (Knight's Corner) accelerator composed of 240 threads. Moreover, this parallel TVD–Hopmoc method alongside a balanced thread binding policy reached a speedup of approximately 91x when applied to a mesh composed of 10^5 stencil points in a simulation performed on an Intel® Xeon Phi™ (Knights Landing) accelerator composed of 272 threads. Furthermore, our OpenMP–based TVD–Hopmoc method in conjunction both with scatter and compact policies achieved a speedup of approximately 17x when applied to a mesh composed of 10^6 stencil points in a simulation performed on the same machine.

It is observed in Figs. 1 and 2 that the speedup of our OpenMP–based TVD–Hopmoc method along with scatter and balanced policies shows four trends. The speedup increases with the use of up to a number of threads that is multiple of the number of cores in the machine. We intend to provide further investigations about this characteristic in future studies.

A next step in this investigation is to implement an OpenMP–based 2–D TVD–Hopmoc method. Even in the 2–D case, we plan to use an array to represent the stencil points so that the approach employed in the 1–D case of the TVD–Hopmoc method is still valid.

Acknowledgments. This work was developed with the support of CNPq, CAPES, and FAPERJ - Fundação de Amparo à Pesquisa do Estado do Rio de Janeiro. We would like to thank the Núcleo de Computação Científica at Universidade Estadual Paulista (NCC/UNESP) for letting us execute our simulations on its heterogeneous multi-core cluster. These resources were partially funded by Intel® through the projects entitled Intel Parallel Computing Center, Modern Code Partner, and Intel/Unesp Center of Excellence in Machine Learning.

References

1. Cabral, F., Osthoff, C., Costa, G., Brandão, D.N., Kischinhevsky, M., Gonzaga de Oliveira, S.L.: Tuning up TVD HOPMOC method on Intel MIC Xeon Phi architectures with Intel Parallel Studio tools. In: Proceedings of the 8th Workshop on Applications for Multi-Core Architectures, Campinas, SP, Brazil (2017)
2. Dagum, L., Menon, R.: OpenMP: an industry standard api for shared-memory programming. Comput. Sci. Eng. IEEE **5**(1), 46–55 (1998)
3. Oliveira, S.R.F., Gonzaga de Oliveira, S.L., Kischinhevsky, M.: Convergence analysis of the Hopmoc method. Int. J. Comput. Math. **86**, 1375–1393 (2009)
4. van Leer, B.: Towards the ultimate conservative difference schemes. J. Comput. Phys. **14**, 361–370 (1974)

Data-Aware Scheduling of Scientific Workflows in Hybrid Clouds

Amirmohammad Pasdar[1($\boxtimes$)], Khaled Almi'ani[2($\boxtimes$)], and Young Choon Lee[1($\boxtimes$)]

[1] Department of Computing, Macquarie University, Sydney, NSW 2109, Australia
amirmohammad.pasdar@hdr.mq.edu.au, young.lee@mq.edu.au
[2] Al-Hussein Bin Talal University and Princess Sumaya University for Technology, Ma'an, Jordan
k.almiani@ahu.edu.jo

Abstract. In this paper, we address the scheduling of scientific workflows in hybrid clouds considering data placement and present the **Hybrid** **S**cheduling for **Hybrid** **C**louds (*HSHC)* algorithm. HSHC is a two-phase scheduling algorithm with a genetic algorithm based static phase and dynamic programming based dynamic phase. We evaluate HSHC with both a real-world scientific workflow application and random workflows in terms of makespan and costs.

1 Introduction

The cloud environment can be classified as a public, private or hybrid cloud. In a public cloud, users can acquire resources in a per-as-you-go manner wherein different pricing models exist as in Amazon EC2. The private cloud is for a particular user group and their internal usage. As the resource capacity of the latter is "fixed" and limited, the combined use of private and public clouds has been increasingly adopted, i.e., hybrid clouds [1].

In recent years, scientific and engineering communities are increasingly seeking a more cost-effective solution (i.e., hybrid cloud solutions) for running their large-scale applications [2–4]. Scientific workflows are of a particular type of such applications. However, as these workflow applications are often resource-intensive in both computation and data, the hybrid cloud alternative struggles to satisfy execution requirements, particularly of data placement efficiently.

This paper studies the data placement of scientific workflow execution in hybrid clouds. To this end, we design Hybrid Scheduling for Hybrid Clouds (HSHC) as a novel two-phase scheduling algorithm with the explicit consideration of data placement. In the *static* phase, an extended genetic algorithm is applied to simultaneously find the best place for datasets and assign their corresponding tasks accordingly. In the *dynamic* phase, intermediate data during workflow execution are dealt with to maintain the quality of schedule and execution. We evaluate HSHC in comparison with *FCFS* and *AsQ* [5]. Results show *HSHC* is a cost-effective approach that can utilize the private cloud effectively and reduce data movements in a hybrid cloud.

© Springer International Publishing AG, part of Springer Nature 2018
Y. Shi et al. (Eds.): ICCS 2018, LNCS 10862, pp. 708–714, 2018.
https://doi.org/10.1007/978-3-319-93713-7_68

Algorithm 1. Static Algorithm

Data: private VM list, task-list, dataset-list, #generation, mutation probability
Result: The optimal placement of datasets and assignment of tasks
1 Prepare the *initGeneration*;
2 Evaluate *initGeneration* via Eq. 2;
3 **while** *either the optimal is not found, or generation size is not exceeded* **do**
4   apply *tournament-selection*;
5   apply *k-way-crossover*;
6   apply *concurrent-rotation* mutation;
7   evaluate the new solution and add it the to population;
8 **end**
9 rank the population and return the best one;

---

2 Hybrid Scheduling for Hybrid Clouds (HSHC)

HSHC consists of two phases: static and dynamic. The static phase deals with finding the optimal placement for tasks and their datasets in the private cloud, using a genetic algorithm (GA, Algorithm 1). In the dynamic phase, some tasks are expected to be re-allocated due to changing execution conditions.

2.1 Static Phase

To generate the initial population, we start by placing the fixed number of tasks and their corresponding data sets to computational resources (virtual machines or VMs). Then, we randomly assign the flexible datasets and tasks to the rest of VMs in the system. The representation of a solution (chromosome) in our algorithm is shown in Fig. 1. In this structure, a cell (i) consists of task-set (TS_i), data-set (DS_i), and a VM (VM_i) that hosts the assigned data-set and task-set.

The main objective here is determining the locality of the tasks and datasets such that the overall execution time is minimized. This results in considering several factors during the representation of the fitness function. During the construction of the solution, for any given task, in order to reduce the delay in execution, this task must be assigned to the VM that results in increasing the

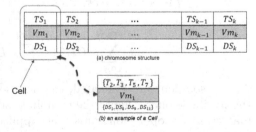

Fig. 1. Chromosome structure.

number of available data sets for this task execution. We denote the percentage of available data sets for task i at virtual machine j by $ava(t_i, VM_j)$. Moreover, for any given VM (VM_j), the dependency between data sets assigned to the VM and data sets located at different VMs must be minimized. In other words, the dependency between data sets assigned to the same VM must be maximized.

For a VM (VM_j), we refer to the data dependency between data sets assigned to VM_j as DI_j and the data dependency between its data sets and data sets of other VMs' as DO_j.

To ensure the feasibility of a solution, we use the variable ck_f to check if the assignment for the fixed data sets and tasks does not violate the locality constraints. We also use the variable ck_r to check if the assigned task can retrieve the required data sets from its current VM. Moreover, to pick up the best VMs, we use a variable termed P_{ratio}. This ratio represents how robust the selected VMs for task execution are, and it is defined as:

$$P_{ratio} = \sum_{i=0}^{M} s_i \tag{1}$$

Tasks assigned to a virtual machine might have the ability to be executed concurrently. Thus, a delay is defined to help the fitness function with the selection of solutions that have less concurrent values. To find the concurrent tasks within a VM, the workflow structure has to be considered. In other words, tasks are monitored to be realized when they will be available for execution in accordance with their required intermediate datasets. Then, they are categorized, and their execution time is examined against their assigned deadline. If within a VM, there are tasks that they do not need any intermediate datasets, they will also influence concurrent tasks. Once the priorities are ready, the amount of time they would be behind their defined deadline is evaluated based on the total amount of delay for a solution, $Tdelay$. In some situations, a solution might have virtual machines that do not have either a task-set or data-set. Thus, to increase the number of used VMs, we introduced the variable Vu_j, which denotes the percentage of the used virtual machine in the solution. Given these variables, the fitness function is defined as follows.

$$fitness = (p_r \times ck_r \times ck_f \times \sum_{j=0}^{M} vu_j) \times (\sum_{i=0;j=0}^{|T|,M} ava(t_i, VM_j)$$

$$\times (\sum_{i=0;j=0}^{|T|,M} DI_j - \sum_{i=0;j=0}^{|T|,M} DO_j) - \sum_{j=0}^{M} Tdelay_j) \tag{2}$$

As the solutions are evaluated, the new solution should be produced based on the available ones. Due to the combined structure of the chromosome, the normal crossover operation cannot be applied to the solutions. Thus, the newly proposed crossover knowns as k-way-$crossover$ is introduced. In this operation, after getting the candidates based on a tournament selection, k-worst and k-best cells of each parent are swapped with each other. By utilizing this crossover, the length of a solution may change. If either the best or worst cell has any fixed datasets, they will remain within the cell along with their corresponding tasks. *Concurrent-rotation* is introduced to mutate a solution. It creates four different ways to mutate a chromosome. For each cell within a solution, the task and dataset with least dependency are selected and by the direction-clockwise or counterclockwise- they are exchanged with the next or previous cell. If the least dependency is related to fixed datasets and its corresponding task, the next least task and dataset are selected.

The output solution is used to initially place datasets and assign their corresponding tasks to the most suitable VMs inside a private cloud.

2.2 Dynamic Phase

In the dynamic phase, based on the status of the available resources (VMs), task reallocation is done with the private cloud or public cloud. Given the ready-to-execute tasks, we map them to the VMs such that the total delay in execution is minimized. This mapping begins by trying to schedule tasks which become ready based on their required intermediate datasets in the private cloud. Then, we offload the tasks that cannot be scheduled in the private cloud to be performed in the public cloud.

In the beginning, we divide the ready-to-execute tasks into flexible and non-flexible sets. The non-flexible set contains tasks with fixed datasets, and this results in restricting the locality of the VMs. The flexible set contains the tasks that can be executed at any VMs, as long as necessary criteria like deadline and storage are met. We are mainly concerned with scheduling of the flexible tasks. We start by calculating the available capacity and workload for the current "active" VMs. This is used to determine the time in which these VMs can execute new tasks. For each task (t_i) and VM (vm_i), we maintain a value that represents the time when vm_i can finish executing t_i. We refer to this value as $T(t_i, vm_i)$. These values are stored in $FTMatrix$. Task reallocation is established by identifying the task $(t_i \in T)$ and the VM $(vm_i \in VM)$ such that the finish time $(FT(t_i, vm_i))$ is the lowest possible value in $FTMatrix$. If assigning t_i to vm_i does not violate this task deadline and its required storage, this assignment will be confirmed. In this case, we will refer to t_i and vm_i as the last confirmed assignment. Otherwise, this task will be added to an offloading list (l_{off}), where all tasks belonging to this list will be scheduled on the public cloud at a later stage. There is an exception to the list, and it is when the storage criterion would be the only violation for a task that could not be satisfied. Thus, the task would be removed from the list and would be added again in another time fraction to the ready-to-execute list. This process of task reallocation takes place for all tasks in the flexible set.

All of the offloaded tasks will be scheduled to be executed on the public cloud. Scheduling these tasks uses a strategy similar to the private cloud scheduling.

3   Evaluation

In this section, we present our evaluation results in comparison with FCFS and AsQ. The former is the traditional scheduling approach for assigning tasks to VMs through a queue-based system. The latter schedules deadline-based applications in a hybrid cloud environment in a cost-effective manner (Fig. 2).

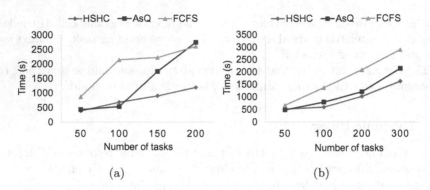

Fig. 2. Average execution time: (a) Random workflows. (b) Montage workflows.

3.1 Environment Setup

The simulation environment is composed of a private cloud and a public cloud with 20 VMs each. The public cloud has three types of VM: small, medium and large with 4, 8 and 8 VMs, respectively. The cost of public cloud is similar to the pricing of Amazon EC2, i.e., proportional pricing based on the rate of the small VM, $0.023 per hour in this study. VMs in the private cloud are with the computing power of 250 MIPS whereas that for VM types in the public cloud are 2500 MIPS, 3500 MIPS, and 4500 MIPS, respectively.

For the *static* phase, the initial population size is 50, and max generation size is 500. Mutation probability is 0.2. We have used Montage scientific workflows (http://montage.ipac.caltech.edu/docs/grid.html) and random workflows with user-defined deadlines as the input for our simulation. The random workflow is created based on a hierarchical structure that has 85 datasets which have sizes in MB from [64–512]. The input and output degrees are chosen from [3–8]. Extracted results are based on the 10% fixed datasets for the random workflows and are reported in average based on 10 simulation runs.

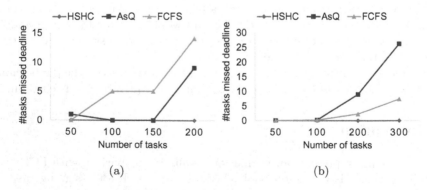

Fig. 3. Average number of tasks that missed deadline: (a) Random (b) Montage.

3.2   Results

As VMs in the homogeneous private cloud come with the low computation capabilities, consequently, the higher offloading rate to the public cloud would be noticeable to stay with the task's deadline; Fig. 5(a) and (b). Moreover, the workflow structure also influences the offloading process. Therefore, considering the deadline as well as the ability of the private cause to execute tasks in the public cloud. Also, the utilization of public cloud resources would lead having minimum execution time as it would reduce the average execution time but would increase the cost. Despite the fact that the cost for *FCFS* is almost zero for Montage shown in Fig. 6(b) it could not achieve meeting deadlines Fig. 3(b). Our proposed method executed all the tasks within the expected deadline. As it is shown in Fig. 3, missed deadlines for the other methods is considerable (Fig. 4).

Contrary, *HSHC* met all task deadlines by offloading a portion of tasks to the public cloud. For the random workflows shown in Fig. 5 *AsQ* sent fewer tasks to the public cloud in comparison to our approach, but it could not execute tasks within their deadlines. This is also true for *FCFS* as it obtained a better

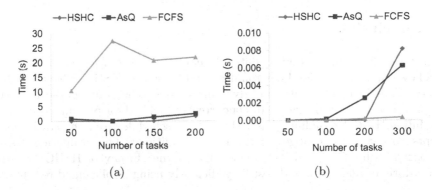

Fig. 4. Average transferring time: (a) Random (b) Montage.

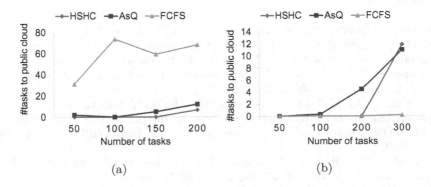

Fig. 5. Average number of tasks dispatched to public cloud: (a) Random (b) Montage.

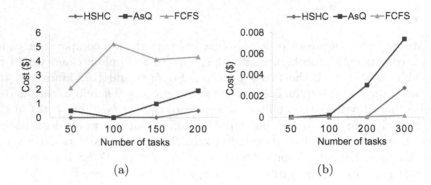

Fig. 6. Average cost: (a) Random (b) Montage.

execution time due to a higher rate of offloading but it could not also utilise the VMs properly. Thus, *HSHC* not only outperforms other approaches but also efficiently utilizes cloud VMs for task execution.

4   Conclusion

In this paper, we have studied data placement aware scheduling of scientific workflows in a hybrid cloud environment and presented HSHC. The scheduling process is divided into static and dynamic phases. The static phase leverages a customised genetic algorithm to concurrently tackle data placement and task scheduling. In the dynamic phase, the output schedule from the static phase adapts to deal with changes in execution conditions. The evaluation results compared with FCFS and AsQ demonstrated the efficacy of HSHC in terms particularly of makespan and cost by judiciously using public cloud resources.

References

1. Hoseinyfarahabady, M.R., Samani, H.R.D., Leslie, L.M., Lee, Y.C., Zomaya, A.Y.: Handling uncertainty: pareto-efficient BoT scheduling on hybrid clouds. In: International Conference on Parallel Processing (ICPP), pp. 419–428 (2013)
2. Bittencourt, L.F., Madeira, E.R., Da Fonseca, N.L.: Scheduling in hybrid clouds. IEEE Commun. Mag. **50**(9), 42–47 (2012)
3. Rahman, M., Li, X., Palit, H.: Hybrid heuristic for scheduling data analytics workflow applications in hybrid cloud environment. In: International Symposium on Parallel and Distributed Processing Workshops and Ph.d. Forum (IPDPSW), pp. 966–974. IEEE
4. Farahabady, M.R.H., Lee, Y.C., Zomaya, A.Y.: Pareto-optimal cloud bursting. IEEE Trans. Parallel Distrib. Syst. **25**(10), 2670–2682 (2014)
5. Wang, W.J., Chang, Y.S., Lo, W.T., Lee, Y.K.: Adaptive scheduling for parallel tasks with QoS satisfaction for hybrid cloud environments. J. Supercomputing **66**(2), 783–811 (2013)

Large Margin Proximal Non-parallel Support Vector Classifiers

Mingzeng Liu[1] and Yuanhai Shao[2(✉)]

[1] School of Mathematics and Physics Science,
Dalian University of Technology at Panjin,
Dalian 124221, People's Republic of China
mzliu@dlut.edu.cn

[2] School of Economics and Management, Hainan University,
Haikou 570228, People's Republic of China
shaoyuanhai21@163.com

Abstract. In this paper, we propose a novel large margin proximal non-parallel twin support vector machine for binary classification. The significant advantages over twin support vector machine are that the structural risk minimization principle is implemented and by adopting uncommon constraint formulation for the primal problem, the proposed method avoids the computation of the large inverse matrices before training which is inevitable in the formulation of twin support vector machine. In addition, the dual coordinate descend algorithm is used to solve the optimization problems to accelerate the training efficiency. Experimental results exhibit the effectiveness and the classification accuracy of the proposed method.

Keywords: Support vector machine · Non-parallel SVM
Structural risk minimization principle
Dual coordinate descend algorithm

1 Introduction

As a powerfull tool in machine learning, support vector machines (SVMs) have been gained a great deal of attention in wide variety of fields [1–5]. The classical support vector classifier (SVC) is trying to maximize the margin between two parallel hyperplanes, which results in solving a convex quadratic programming problem (QPP). Furhtermore, some non-parallel hyperplane classifiers such as the generalized eigen-value proximal support vector machine (GEPSVM) and twin support vector machine (TWSVM) have been proposed in [4,5]. TWSVM is to search two non-parallel proximal hyperplanes such that each hyperplane is closer

Supported by the Hainan Provincial Natural Science Foundation of China (No. 118QN181), the Scientific Research Foundation of Hainan University, the National Natural Science Foundation of China (Nos. 11501310, 61703370, and 61603338).

© Springer International Publishing AG, part of Springer Nature 2018
Y. Shi et al. (Eds.): ICCS 2018, LNCS 10862, pp. 715–721, 2018.
https://doi.org/10.1007/978-3-319-93713-7_69

to one class and as far as possible from the other one. In fact, as an efficient generalization of the classical SVC, TWSVMs have been studied extensively [6–14], which need to solve two small QPPs in contrast with the classical SVC. This paper proposes a novel large margin proximal non-parallel support vector machine for binary classification (PNSVM). The main contributions of PNSVM are:

- PNSVM minimizes the structural risk by imposing a regularization term.
- PNSVM is proximal both classes and maximizes the corresponding margin, while TWSVM is proximal each class and far away from the other class.
- PNSVM can be solved efficiently with dual coordinate descend method [15].

2   Related Work

Benefiting from its excellent generalization performance of twin support vector machines, the approaches of constructing the non-parallel hyperplanes have received extensive attention [6,8,9,11–14,16]. Shao et al. [6] present a variant of GEPSVM based on the difference measure, which seems to be superior in classification accuracy and computation time. For the imbalanced data classification, Shao et al. [8] suggest an efficient weighted Lagrangian twin support vector machine (WLTSVM), which is robust to outliers and overcomes the bias phenomenon in the original TWSVM. Liu et al. [9] present a support vector machine for large scale regression based on the minimization of deviation distribution. Tian et al. [11] propose a novel nonparallel SVM for binary classification, which implements the structural risk minimization and is suitable for large scale problems. Shao et al. [16] present a sparse L_q-norm least squares support vector machine, where feature selection and prediction are performed simultaneously.

3   PNSVM

3.1   Linear PNSVM

Linear PNSVM is to find two non-parallel hyperplanes $f_1(x) = w_1^T x + b_1 = 0$ and $f_2(x) = w_2^T x + b_2 = 0$ by solving the following two problems:

$$\min_{w_1,b_1,p,q_1,\rho} \quad \tfrac{1}{2}p^T p + \tfrac{1}{2}c_1(\|w_1\|^2 + b_1^2) + c_2 e_2^T q_1 + c_3\rho_1$$

$$\text{s.t.} \quad Aw_1 + e_1 b_1 = p, \tag{1}$$

$$\rho_1 e_2 \geq -(Bw_1 + e_2 b_1) + q_1 \geq e_2, \ q_1 \geq 0, \ \rho_1 \geq 1,$$

and

$$\min_{w_2,b_2,q,q_2,\rho_2} \quad \tfrac{1}{2}q^T q + \tfrac{1}{2}c_4(\|w_2\|^2 + b_2^2) + c_5 e_1^T q_2 + c_6\rho_2$$

$$\text{s.t.} \quad Bw_2 + e_2 b_2 = q, \tag{2}$$

$$\rho_2 e_1 \geq (Aw_2 + e_1 b_2) + q_2 \geq e_1, \ q_2 \geq 0, \rho_2 \geq 1,$$

where $c_i, i = 1, 2, \cdots, 6$ are parameters.

The formulation given at (1) can be understood as follows: The first term in (1) is the sum of squared distances from $f(x) = w_1 x + b_1 = 0$ to points of positive class, whose minimization means to keep $f(x) = w_1 x + b_1 = 0$ close to the positive class. The minimization of the second term in (1) implies that the structural risk principle is implemented by the term $\frac{1}{2} c_2(\|w_1^2 + b_1^2\|)$. The second constraints in (1) require the hyperplane $f(x) = w_1^T x + b_1$ to be at a distance of at least 1 and at most ρ_1 from points of negative class. The third term in (1) tries to minimize mis-classification. The last term in (1) requires the points of negative class to be a distance no far away from the hyperplane. A similar interpretation may also be given to the formulation given at (2).

The Lagrangian of the formulation (1) is given by

$$L(w_1, b_1, p, q_1, \rho_1; \alpha_1, \alpha_2, \alpha_3, \alpha_4, \beta)$$
$$= \frac{1}{2} c_1(\|w_1\|^2 + b_1^2) + \frac{1}{2} p^T p + c_2 e_2^T q_1 + c_3 \rho_1 + \alpha_1^T (A w_1 + e_1 b_1 - p)$$
$$- \alpha_2^T(-(B w_1 + e_2 b_1) + q_1 - e_2) - \alpha_3^T(\rho_1 e_2 + (B w_1 + e_2 b_1) - q_1)$$
$$- \alpha_4^T q_1 - \beta(\rho_1 - 1)$$

where $\alpha_1 \in \mathbf{R}^{m_1 \times 1}, \alpha_2 \in \mathbf{R}^{m_2 \times 1}, \alpha_3 \in \mathbf{R}^{m_2 \times 1}, \alpha_4 \in \mathbf{R}^{m_1 \times 1}, \beta \in \mathbf{R}$ are the vectors of Lagrange multipliers. The optimality conditions for w_1, b_1, p, q_1, ρ_1 are given by

$$\nabla_{w_1} L = c_1 w_1 + A^T \alpha_1 + B^T \alpha_2 - B^T \alpha_3 = 0 \tag{3}$$
$$\nabla_{b_1} L = c_1 b_1 + e_1^T \alpha_1 + e_1^T \alpha_2 - e_2^T \alpha_3 = 0 \tag{4}$$
$$\nabla_p L = \alpha_1 - p = 0 \tag{5}$$
$$\nabla_{q_1} L = c_2 e_2 - \alpha_2 + \alpha_3 - \alpha_4 = 0 \tag{6}$$
$$\nabla_{\rho_1} L = c_3 - e_2^T \alpha_3 - \beta = 0 \tag{7}$$
$$\alpha_2 \geq 0, \alpha_3 \geq 0, \alpha_4 \geq 0, \beta \geq 0. \tag{8}$$

Then substituting (3) and (7) into the Lagrangian, we obtain the dual problem of the problem

$$\min_{\alpha_1, \alpha_2, \alpha_3} f(\alpha_1, \alpha_2, \alpha_3) = \frac{1}{2}(\alpha_1^T, \alpha_2^T, \alpha_3^T) \bar{H} (\alpha_1^T, \alpha_2^T, \alpha_3^T)^T - [0, 0, -c_1 e_1](\alpha_1^T, \alpha_2^T, \alpha_3^T)^T$$
$$s.t. \qquad\qquad\qquad 0 \leq \alpha_2 \leq (c_2 + c_3) e_2 \tag{9}$$
$$0 \leq \alpha_3 \leq c_3 e_2,$$

where

$$\bar{H} = \begin{bmatrix} AA^T + c_1 I & AB^T & -AB^T \\ BA^T & BB^T & -BB^T \\ -BA^T & -BB^T & BB^T \end{bmatrix} + \begin{bmatrix} e_1 e_1^T & e_1 e_2^T & -e_1 e_2^T \\ e_2 e_1^T & e_2 e_2^T & -e_2 e_2^T \\ -e_2 e_1^T & -e_2 e_2^T & e_2 e_2^T \end{bmatrix}.$$

The dual of the problem (2) is

$$\min_{\beta_1, \beta_2, \beta_3} f(\beta_1, \beta_2, \beta_3) = \frac{1}{2}(\beta_1^T, \beta_2^T, \beta_3^T) \bar{H} (\beta_1^T, \beta_2^T, \beta_3^T)^T - [0, 0, -c_4 e_1](\beta_1^T, \beta_2^T, \beta_3^T)^T$$
$$s.t. \qquad\qquad\qquad 0 \leq \beta_2 \leq (c_5 + c_6) e_2 \tag{10}$$
$$0 \leq \beta_3 \leq c_6 e_2,$$

where

$$\tilde{H} = \begin{bmatrix} BB^T + c_4I & -BA^T & BA^T \\ -AB^T & AA^T & -AA^T \\ AB^T & -AA^T & AA^T \end{bmatrix} + \begin{bmatrix} e_2e_2^T & -e_2e_1^T & e_2e_1^T \\ -e_1e_2^T & e_1e_1^T & -e_1e_1^T \\ e_1e_2^T & -e_1e_1^T & e_1e_1^T \end{bmatrix}.$$

Once the $(\boldsymbol{w}_1, b_1)$ and $(\boldsymbol{w}_2, b_2)$ are obtained from the (9) and (10) by means of the dual coordinate descent method [15], a new input $\boldsymbol{x} \in \mathbf{R}^n$ is assigned to class i $(i = +1, -1)$ by $Class\ i = arg \min_{k=1,2} \frac{|\boldsymbol{w}_k^T\boldsymbol{x}+b_k|}{\|\boldsymbol{w}_k\|}$.

3.2   Kernel PNSVM

Kernel PNSVM searches the following two kernel-generated surfaces instead of hyperplanes $K(\boldsymbol{x}^T, \boldsymbol{C}^T)\boldsymbol{w}_1 + b_1 = 0$ and $K(\boldsymbol{x}^T, \boldsymbol{C}^T)\boldsymbol{w}_2 + b_2 = 0$, where $\boldsymbol{C}^T = [\boldsymbol{A}\ \boldsymbol{B}]^T \in \mathbf{R}^{n \times \ell}$. The optimization problems are

$$\min_{\boldsymbol{w}_1, b_1, \boldsymbol{p}, \rho, q_1} \quad \tfrac{1}{2}\boldsymbol{p}^T\boldsymbol{p} + \tfrac{1}{2}c_1(\|\boldsymbol{w}_1\|^2 + b_1^2) + c_2\boldsymbol{e}_2^T\boldsymbol{q}_1 + c_3\rho_1$$

$$s.t. \qquad K(\boldsymbol{A}, \boldsymbol{C}^T)\boldsymbol{w}_1 + \boldsymbol{e}_1 b_1 = \boldsymbol{p}, \tag{11}$$

$$\rho_1\boldsymbol{e}_2 \geq -(k(\boldsymbol{B}, \boldsymbol{C}^T)\boldsymbol{w}_1 + \boldsymbol{e}_2 b_1) + \boldsymbol{q}_1 \geq \boldsymbol{e}_2,\ \boldsymbol{q}_1 \geq 0,\ \rho_1 \geq 1,$$

and

$$\min_{\boldsymbol{w}_2, b_2, \boldsymbol{q}, \rho_2, q_2} \quad \tfrac{1}{2}\boldsymbol{q}^T\boldsymbol{q} + \tfrac{1}{2}c_4(\|\boldsymbol{w}_2\|^2 + (b_2)^2) + c_5\boldsymbol{e}_1^T\boldsymbol{q}_2 + c_6\rho_2$$

$$s.t. \qquad K(\boldsymbol{B}, \boldsymbol{C}^T)\boldsymbol{w}_2 + \boldsymbol{e}_2 b_2 = \boldsymbol{q}, \tag{12}$$

$$\rho_2\boldsymbol{e}_1 \geq (K(\boldsymbol{A}, \boldsymbol{C}^T)\boldsymbol{w}_2 + \boldsymbol{e}_1 b_2) + \boldsymbol{q}_2 \geq \boldsymbol{e}_1,\ \boldsymbol{q}_2 \geq 0, \rho_2 \geq 1.$$

where $c_i, i = 1, \cdots, 6$ are parameters.

4   Experimental Results

In this section, the UCI data sets are chosen to demonstrate the performance of our PNSVM compared with SVC, TWSVM and WLTSVM [13]. The methods are implemented by Matlab 9.0 running on a PC with an Intel(R) Core Duo i7(2.70 GHZ) with 32 GB RAM. Our PNSVM is solved by the dual coordinate descend algorithm and SVC and TWSVM are solved by the optimization toolbox QP in Matlab. The classification accuracy is measured by the standard 10-fold cross-validation.

The classification accuracy, computation time, and optimal values of $c_1(= c_2), c_4 = (c_5)$ and c_3 and c_6 in our PNSVM are listed in Table 1. The parameters from PNSVM, TWSVM, SVC and WLTSVM are searched in the range $\{2^{2i}|i = -8, \cdots, 8\}$, and the parameters c_3 and c_6 of PNSVM are selected from the set $\{0.01, 0.1, 1, 10, 100\}$. Table 1 shows the comparison results of all four methods. It can be seen from Table 1 that the accuracy of the proposed linear PNSVM is significantly better than that of the linear TWSVM on most of

Table 1. The comparison results of linear classifiers.

Datasets	PNSVM		TWSVM		SVC		WLTSVM	
	Accuracy%	Time(s)	Accuracy%	Time(s)	Accuracy%	Time(s)	Accuracy%	Time(s)
	$c_1 = c_2/c_4 = c_5$	c_3/c_6						
Hepatitis	**84.93 ± 0.03**	0.0005	82.89 ± 6.30	0.281	84.13 ± 5.58	1.170	84.39 ± 1.35	0.0062
(155 × 19)	$2^{14}/2^{12}$	0.1/0.1						
BUPA liver	**70.98 ± 0.01**	0.0346	66.40 ± 7.74	0.840	67.78 ± 5.51	3.540	68.08 ± 1.32	0.0076
(345 × 6)	$2^{10}/2^2$	10/100						
Heart-Stat	84.41 ± 0.05	0.0012	**84.44 ± 6.80**	0.454	83.12 ± 5.41	1.584	**84.96 ± 0.58**	0.0051
-log(270 × 14)	$2^{-6}/2^{16}$	10/10						
Heart-c	86.57 ± 0.07	0.0026	84.86 ± 6.27	0.516	83.33 ± 5.64	2.193	**92.05 ± 0.39**	0.0063
(303 × 14)	$2^0/2^{-8}$	0.1/100						
Votes	**96.43 ± 0.05**	0.0043	95.85 ± 2.75	1.851	95.80 ± 2.65	3.192	95.93 ± 0.21	0.0049
(435 × 16)	$2^{-6}/2^{-2}$	10/0.01						
WPBC	**84.72 ± 0.06**	0.0253	83.68 ± 5.73	0.560	83.30 ± 4.53	2.094	79.18 ± 1.73	0.0778
(198 × 34)	$2^{-14}/2^{-14}$	0.01/100						
Sonar	76.19 ± 0.15	2.4545	77.00 ± 6.10	0.375	**80.13 ± 5.43**	0.941	78.07 ± 1.41	0.0172
(208 × 60)	$2^2/2^{-12}$	100/100						
Lonosphere	**88.89 ± 0.08**	0.04	88.48 ± 5.74	0.969	88.20 ± 4.51	4.120	87.31 ± 0.64	0.0097
(351 ± 34)	$2^{16}/2^{-2}$	0.01/100						

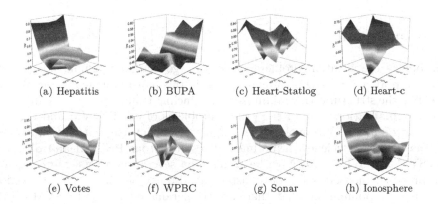

| (a) Hepatitis | (b) BUPA | (c) Heart-Statlog | (d) Heart-c |

| (e) Votes | (f) WPBC | (g) Sonar | (h) Ionosphere |

Fig. 1. The influence on Accuracy(AC) of parameters c_3 and c_6 of linear PNSVM.

data sets. And our PNSVM is the fastest on most of data sets. Figure 1 exhibits the influence on Accuracy of parameters c_3 and c_6 for linear PNSVM. It can be observed that the choice of c_3 and c_6 affects the results dramatically, which implies that adjusting the parameters c_3 and c_6 is practical selection in real applications. Table 2 is concerned with our kernel PNSVM, TWSVM ans SVC and WLTSVM. The Gaussian kernel $K(x, x') = e^{-\mu\|x-x'\|^2}$ is used. The kernel parameter μ is also searched from the sets $\{2^i | i = -8, \cdots, 8\}$. The classification accuracy and computation times for all three methods are also listed in Table 2.

Table 2. The comparison results of kernel classifiers.

Datasets	PNSVM		TWSVM		SVC		WLTSVM	
	Accuracy% $c_1 = c_2/c_4 = c_5$	Time(s) $c_3/c_6/\mu$	Accuracy%	Time(s)	Accuracy%	Time(s)	Accuracy%	Time(s)
Hepatitis (155 × 19)	**84.29 ± 0.07** $2^{-2}/2^{-14}$	0.0051 $0.01/0.01/2^2$	83.39 ± 7.31	0.797	84.13 ± 6.25	1.300	84.28 ± 0.47	0.0057
BUPA liver (345 × 6)	69.72 ± 0.01 $2^{-14}/2^8$	0.0135 $100/0.01/2^{-5}$	67.83 ± 6.49	2.700	68.32 ± 7.20	5.248	**73.18 ± 0.59**	0.0046
Heart-Stat -log(270 × 14)	**86.68 ± 0.06** $2^{-10}/2^{-10}$	0.1703 $10/1/2^1$	82.96 ± 4.67	1.130	83.33 ± 9.11	6.100	85.12 ± 0.86	0.0154
Heart-c (303 × 14)	**89.28 ± 0.05** $2^{-12}/2^4$	0.0111 $1/100/2^{-3}$	83.83 ± 5.78	2.141	83.68 ± 5.67	3.800	85.98 ± 0.62	0.0059
Votes (435 × 16)	**96.53 ± 0.03** $2^{-8}/2^0$	0.0181 $0.1/0.01/2^{-2}$	94.91 ± 4.37	3.540	95.64 ± 7.23	7.783	96.39 ± 0.14	0.0475
WPBC (198 × 34)	**84.39 ± 0.06** $2^{-10}/2^{12}$	0.0096 $10/10/2^0$	81.28 ± 5.92	1.305	80.18 ± 6.90	4.141	79.85 ± 0.43	0.0085
Sonar (208 × 60)	**90.01 ± 0.06** $2^{-8}/2^{-6}$	0.0077 $1/10/2^{-2}$	89.64 ± 6.11	2.630	88.93 ± 10.43	5.302	88.73 ± 1.27	0.0237
Lonosphere (351 ± 34)	**91.81 ± 0.03** $2^0/2^2$	0.0608 $10/100/2^{-3}$	87.46 ± 3.40	5.576	90.20 ± 4.51	15.71	90.45 ± 0.47	0.0039

5 Conclusions

For binary classification problem, a novel large margin proximal non-parallel twin support vector machine was proposed in this paper. The main contribution are that the structural risk minimization principle is implemented by introducing a regularization term in the primal problems of our PNSVM and the dual formulation of PNSVM avoids the computation of inverse matrices and speeds up the training efficiency. Experimental results of our PNSVM and SVC and TWSVM and WLTSVM, have been made on several data sets, implying that the proposed method is not only faster but also exhibits better generalization. It should be pointed out that there are six parameters in our PNSVM, so the parameter selection and more efficient algorithm [17] is a practical problem and should be addressed in the future.

References

1. Vapnik, V.N.: Statistical Learning Theory. Wiley, New York (1998)
2. Deng, N.Y., Tian, Y.J., Zhang, C.H.: Support Vector Machines: Optimization Based Theory, Algorithms, and Extensions. CRC Press, New York (2012)
3. Noble, W.S.: Support vector machine applications in computational biology. In: Kernel Methods in Computational Biology, pp. 71–92 (2004)
4. Mangasarian, O.L., Wild, E.W.: Multisurface proximal support vector machine classification via generalized eigenvalues. IEEE Trans. Pattern Anal. Mach. Intell. **28**(1), 69–74 (2006)

5. Jayadeva, R.K., Khemchandani, R., Chandra, S.: Twin support vector machines for pattern classification. IEEE Trans. Pattern Anal. Mach. Intell. **29**(5), 905–910 (2007)

6. Shao, Y.H., Zhang, C.H., Wang, X.B., Deng, N.Y.: Improvements on twin support vector machines. IEEE Trans. Neural Netw. **22**(6), 962–968 (2011)

7. Shao, Y.H., Wang, Z., Chen, W.J., Deng, N.Y.: A regularization for the projection twin support vector machine. Knowl. Based Syst. **37**, 203–210 (2013)

8. Shao, Y.H., Chen, W.J., Zhang, J.J., Wang, Z., Deng, N.Y.: An efficient weighted Largrangian twin support vector machine for imbalanced data classification. Pattern Recogn. **47**(9), 3158–3167 (2014)

9. Liu, M.Z., Shao, Y.H., Wang, Z., Li, C.N., Chen, W.J.: Minimum deviation distribution machine for large scale regression. Knowl. Based Syst. **146**, 167–180 (2018)

10. Qi, Z.Q., Tian, Y.J., Shi, Y.: Robust twin support vector machine for pattern classification. Pattern Recogn. **46**(1), 305–316 (2013)

11. Tian, Y.J., Qi, Z.Q., Ju, X.C., Shi, Y., Liu, X.H.: Nonparallel support vector machines for pattern classification. IEEE Trans. Cybern. **44**(7), 1067–1079 (2014)

12. Tian, Y.J., Ping, Y.: Large-scale linear nonparallel support vector machine solver. Neural Netw. **50**, 166–174 (2014)

13. Shao, Y.H., Chen, W.J., Wang, Z., Li, C.N., Deng, N.Y.: Weighted linear loss twin support vector machine for large-scale classification. Knowl. Based Syst. **73**, 276–288 (2015)

14. Shao, Y.H., Chen, W.J., Deng, N.Y.: Nonparallel hyperplane support vector machine for binary classification problems. Inf. Sci. **263**, 22–35 (2014)

15. Hsieh, C.J., Chang, K.W., Lin, C.J., Keerthi, S.S., Sundararajan, S.: A dual coordinate descent method for large-scale linear SVM. In: Proceedings of the 25th International Conference on Machine Learning, pp. 408–415. ACM (2008)

16. Shao, Y.H., Li, C.N., Liu, M.Z., Wang, Z., Deng, N.Y.: Sparse L_q-norm least square support vector machine with feature selection. Pattern Recogn. **78**, 167–181 (2018)

17. Wang, Z., Shao, Y.H., Bai, L., Liu, L.M., Deng, N.Y.: Stochastic gradient twin support vector machine for large scale problems. arXiv preprint arXiv:1704.05596

The Multi-core Optimization of the Unbalanced Calculation in the Clean Numerical Simulation of Rayleigh-Bénard Turbulence

Lu Li[1], Zhiliang Lin[2], and Yan Hao[1(✉)]

[1] Asia Pacific R&D Center Intel, Shanghai, China
yan.hao@intel.com
[2] Shanghai Jiaotong University, Shanghai, China

Abstract. The so-called clean numerical simulation (CNS) is used to simulate the Rayleigh-Bénard (RB) convection system. Compared with direct numerical simulation (DNS), the accuracy and reliability of investigating turbulent flows improve largely. Although CNS can well control the numerical noises, the cost of calculation is more expensive. In order to simulate the system in a reasonable period, the calculation schemes of CNS require redesign. In this paper, aiming at the CNS of the two-dimension RB system, we first propose the notions of equal difference matrix and balance point set which are crucial to model the unbalanced calculation of the system under multi-core platform. Then, according to the notions, we present algorithms to optimize the unbalanced calculation. We prove our algorithm is optimal when the core number is the power of 2 and our algorithm approaches the optimal when the core number is not the power of 2. Finally, we compare the results of our optimized algorithms with others to demonstrate the effectiveness of our optimization.

Keywords: Turbulence · Clean numerical simulation
Unbalanced calculation

1 Introduction

It is of broad interest to understand the evolution of non-equilibrium systems involves energy exchange through the system boundary with the surroundings, for example, Rayleigh-Bénard (RB) system. With the help of direct numerical simulation (DNS), we can get high resolution, both spatially and temporally. However, because of the numerical noises, e.g. truncation error and round-off error, are inevitable in DNS, the solution reliability remains controversial. Fortunately, the so-called clear numerical simulation (CNS) can well control such kind of numerical uncertainty. Aiming at investigating the laminar-turbulent transition of the two-dimension Rayleigh-Bénard (RB) system, the numerical noise of

© Springer International Publishing AG, part of Springer Nature 2018
Y. Shi et al. (Eds.): ICCS 2018, LNCS 10862, pp. 722–735, 2018.
https://doi.org/10.1007/978-3-319-93713-7_70

CNS can be well controlled even much lower than the microscopic thermal compared fluctuation [11]. Although CNS is more accurate, the cost of calculation is more expensive. In order to simulate the system in a reasonable period, the calculation schemes of CNS require optimization. In this paper, we first propose the notions of equal difference matrix and balance point set which are crucial to model the unbalanced calculation under multi-core platform. Then, according to the notions, we present algorithms to optimize the unbalanced calculation.

One significant property of our proposed optimization algorithm is provable to optimal when the core number is the power of 2 and to approach the optimal when the core number is not the power of 2 theoretically. We first model the amount of the calculation as equal difference matrix, which is the basis to understand and optimize the unbalanced calculation. The equal difference matrix reveals the relationship of the calculation amount between different grid points in spectral space quantitatively. Based on the properties of the equal difference matrix, we propose the notion of balance point set, which is the key to optimize the unbalanced calculation.

The other significant property of our proposed algorithm is high efficiency. For arbitrary cores under multi-core platform, our algorithm can complete the assignment of the calculation to different cores on the stage of the initialization procedure. On one hand, the arrangement does not disturb the calculation of CNS. It is straightforward to integrate our method into the original CNS. On the other hand, the arrangement is only done once; the time overhead of the assignment is little.

This paper is organized as follows: In Sect. 2, we discuss relevant methods in literature. In Sect. 3, first, we describe the CNS of the two-dimensional Rayleigh-Bénard system. Then, we establish the model of the calculation amount of the simulation and present the general notions of equal difference matrix and balance point set. Based on the proposed notions, we present the algorithms to optimize the unbalanced calculation under multi-core platform. In Sect. 4, we use several concrete examples to demonstrate the effectiveness of our proposed algorithms, followed by the conclusion in Sect. 5. In the Appendix, we give the proofs adopted by our algorithms.

2   Related Work

Direct numerical simulation (DNS) [1,3,15] provides an effective way to understand the evolution of non-equilibrium system involving energy exchange through the system boundary with the surroundings. However, because of the inevitable numerical noises, e.g. truncation error and round-off error, the solution reliability provided by DNS is very controversial [23]. For example, Lorenz discovered the dynamic systems governed by the Navier-Stokes equations are chaotic due to the butterfly effect no only depending on the initial conditions [12] but also on numerical algorithms [13]. Furthermore, [16,20] reported some spurious turbulence evolution cases provided by DNS.

Fortunately, the inevitable numerical noises can be well controlled by clean numerical simulation (CNS) [6–10,21]. CNS adopts arbitrary-order Taylor series method (TSM) [2] and arbitrary multiple-precision (MP) data [4] to reduce the round-off error and truncation error, respectively. Lin et al. [11] simulated Saltzman's model of Rayleigh-Bénard convection by means of CNS with considering the propagation of the inherent micro-thermal fluctuation. Compared with DNS, CNS can investigate turbulent flows with well-improved reliability and accuracy.

Numerically, introducing TSM and MP, the data and the calculation amount of CNS is much larger than DNS. In order to simulate the system in a reasonable period, CNS requires large amount of computing resources from a high performance computing (HPC) cluster. However, because of the complexity of the parallel computing there exists difficulty in fully utilizing the capacity and scalability of the HPC cluster [22, 24, 25]. In order to achieve high performance, it is necessary to re-design the CNS calculation scheme from various aspects including parallel algorithm, data arrangement, etc. Even though Lin et al. [11] have optimized the data arrangement to reduce the amount of simulation data by utilizing the symmetry of the two-dimensional Rayleigh-Bénard system.

3   Methods

3.1   2-D CNS Rayleigh-Bénard

The two-dimensional Rayleigh-Bénard system has been extensively studied [5, 14, 17–19, 26]. Following Saltzman [19], the corresponding non-dimensional governing equations in the form of stream function ψ with the Boussinesq approximation is

$$\begin{cases} \frac{\partial}{\partial t}\nabla^2\psi + \frac{\partial(\psi,\nabla^2\psi)}{\partial(x,z)} - \frac{\partial\theta}{\partial x} - C_a\nabla^4\psi = 0 \\ \frac{\partial\theta}{\partial t} + \frac{\partial(\psi,\theta)}{\partial(x,z)} - \frac{\partial\psi}{\partial x} - C_b\nabla^2\theta \end{cases} \tag{1}$$

where t denotes time, θ denotes the temperature departure from a linear variation background, x and z represent the horizontal and vertical spatial coordinates, $C_a = \sqrt{Pr/Ra}$ and $C_b = 1/\sqrt{Pr\,Ra}$ with the Prandtl number $Pr = \nu/\kappa$, where ν is the kinematic viscosity, κ is the thermal diffusivity, and the Rayleigh number $Ra = g\alpha H^3 \Delta T/\nu\kappa$, where H is the distance between the two parallel free surfaces, g is the gravity acceleration and α is the thermal expansion coefficient of the fluid, ΔT is the prescribed constant temperature difference.

As described by Saltzman [19], we use the double Fourier expansion modes to expand the stream function ψ and temperature departure θ as follows:

$$\begin{cases} \psi(x,z,t) = \sum\limits_{m=-\infty}^{+\infty}\sum\limits_{n=-\infty}^{+\infty} \Psi_{m,n}(t)\exp[2\pi Hi(\frac{m}{L}x + \frac{n}{2H}z)] \\ \theta(x,z,t) = \sum\limits_{m=-\infty}^{+\infty}\sum\limits_{n=-\infty}^{+\infty} \Theta_{m,n}(t)\exp[2\pi Hi(\frac{m}{L}x + \frac{n}{2H}z)] \end{cases} \tag{2}$$

where m and n are the wave numbers in the x and z directions, $\Psi_{m,n}(t)$ and $\Theta_{m,n}(t)$ are the expansion coefficients of the stream function and temperature components with wave numbers (m,n). Separate the real part from the imaginary part:

$$\begin{cases} \Psi_{m,n} = \Psi_{1,m,n} - i\Psi_{2,m,n} \\ \Theta_{m,n} = \Theta_{1,m,n} - i\Theta_{2,m,n} \end{cases} \tag{3}$$

Following Lin et al. [11], denote the time increment as δt and $f(j)$ as the value of $f(t)$ at $t = j\Delta t$. We use the P th-order Taylor series to expand $\Psi_{i,m,n}$ and $\Theta_{i,m,n}$ as follows:

$$\begin{cases} \Psi_{i,m,n}^{(j+1)} = \Psi_{i,m,n}(t_j + \Delta t) = \Psi_{i,m,n}^{(j)} + \sum_{k=1}^{P} \beta_{i,m,n}^{j,k}(\Delta t)^k \\ \Theta_{i,m,n}^{(j+1)} = \Theta_{i,m,n}(t_j + \Delta t) = \Theta_{i,m,n}^{(j)} + \sum_{k=1}^{P} \gamma_{i,m,n}^{j,k}(\Delta t)^k \end{cases} \tag{4}$$

where

$$\begin{aligned} &\beta_{1,m,n}^{j,k+1} \\ &= \left(\sum_{p=-M}^{M} \sum_{q=-N}^{N} C_{m,n,p,q} \frac{\alpha_{p,q}^2}{\alpha_{m,n}^2} \sum_{l=0}^{k} [\beta_{1,p,q}^{j,l} \beta_{1,m-p,n-q}^{j,k-l} \right. \\ &\quad + \beta_{2,p,q}^{j,l} \beta_{2,m-p,n-q}^{j,k-l}] + \frac{l^*m}{\alpha_{m,n}^2} \gamma_{2,m,n}^{j,k} \\ &\quad \left. - C_a \alpha_{m,n}^2 \beta_{1,m,n}^{j,k} \right) / (1+k) \end{aligned} \tag{5}$$

$$\begin{aligned} &\beta_{2,m,n}^{j,k+1} \\ &= \left(\sum_{p=-M}^{M} \sum_{q=-N}^{N} C_{m,n,p,q} \frac{\alpha_{p,q}^2}{\alpha_{m,n}^2} \sum_{l=0}^{k} [\beta_{1,p,q}^{j,l} \beta_{2,m-p,n-q}^{j,k-l} \right. \\ &\quad + \beta_{2,p,q}^{j,l} \beta_{1,m-p,n-q}^{j,k-l}] + \frac{l^*m}{\alpha_{m,n}^2} \gamma_{1,m,n}^{j,k} \\ &\quad \left. - C_a \alpha_{m,n}^2 \beta_{2,m,n}^{j,k} \right) / (1+k) \end{aligned} \tag{6}$$

$$\begin{aligned} &\gamma_{1,m,n}^{j,k+1} \\ &= \left(- \sum_{p=-M}^{M} \sum_{q=-N}^{N} C_{m,n,p,q} \sum_{l=0}^{k} [\beta_{1,p,q}^{j,l} \gamma_{1,m-p,n-q}^{j,k-l} \right. \\ &\quad - \beta_{2,p,q}^{j,l} \gamma_{2,m-p,n-q}^{j,k-l}] + l^*m\beta_{2,m,n}^{j,k} \\ &\quad \left. - C_a \alpha_{m,n}^2 \gamma_{1,m,n}^{j,k} \right) / (1+k) \end{aligned} \tag{7}$$

$$\begin{aligned} &\gamma_{2,m,n}^{j,k+1} \\ &= \left(- \sum_{p=-M}^{M} \sum_{q=-N}^{N} C_{m,n,p,q} \sum_{l=0}^{k} [\beta_{1,p,q}^{j,l} \gamma_{2,m-p,n-q}^{j,k-l} \right. \\ &\quad - \beta_{2,p,q}^{j,l} \gamma_{1,m-p,n-q}^{j,k-l}] + l^*m\beta_{1,m,n}^{j,k} \\ &\quad \left. - C_a \alpha_{m,n}^2 \gamma_{2,m,n}^{j,k} \right) / (1+k) \end{aligned} \tag{8}$$

with $C_{m,n,p,q} = \pi l^*(mq - np)$, $l^* = 2\pi H/L$ and $\alpha_{m,n}^2 = l^{*2}m^2 + \pi^2 n^2$.

Numerically, For point (p, q) in the Eqs. (5), (6), (7) and (8), $-M \leq m - p \leq M$ and $-N \leq n - q \leq N$ should be satisfied. So that let F_i, where $i = \{1, 2, 3, 4\}$, present the first term of left hand side of the four equations; $f_i(m, n)$, where $i = \{1, 2, 3, 4\}$, present the inside part of the 2-D summations, the formulas of the Eqs. (5), (6), (7) and (8) can be optimized to

$$F_i = (\sum_{p=m-M}^{M} \sum_{q=n-N}^{N} f_i(m, n))/(1 + k) \tag{9}$$

In the spectral space, to calculate $F_i, i = \{1, 2, 3, 4\}$ of the point $(0, 0)$, the 2-D summation height is from $-M$ to M and the width is from $-N$ to N. In comparison, for the point (M, N), which means that $m = M$ and $n = N$, the 2-D summation height is from 0 to M and the width is from 0 to N. The calculation amount of the 2-D summation for the point $(0, 0)$ is 4 times more than that for the point (M, N). Under multi-core platform, different gird points in Eq. (9) are assigned to different cores, the unbalanced calculation exists.

For CNS calculation, the unbalanced calculation is even worse. In one hand, the CNS calculation adopts arbitrary-precision binary floating-point computation (MPFR) [4] as the data type in order to avoid round-off error. However, the calculation amount using MPFR is much more than adopting double as the data type. In the other hand, the P th-order Taylor series aiming to avoid truncation error, also increases the amount of calculation. After adding the two new features, the amount of the calculation is much more than that of the scheme using double data type, which leads to the unbalanced calculation getting worse.

3.2   Equal Difference Matrix

Although the four equations $F_i, (i = 1, 2, 3, 4)$ are coupled, the calculations for the points in the mesh grid of two-dimensional spectral space are independent to each other because we adopt explicit calculation scheme for each sub-step in each iteration. Here the sub-step means Taylor step $(p = 1, 2, ..., P)$. In order to analyze the unbalanced calculation for F_i, we obtain the amount of the calculation of each grid point in the spectral space. Let the grid size be $M * N$, for the point (m, n), the calculation amount of $F_i, i = (1, 2, 3, 4)$ is $(2M - m) * (2N - n) * (\sum_{i=1}^{4} \sum_{p=1}^{k} t_{i,p})$, where k is the order of the Taylor expansion $(k = 1, ..., P)$, $2M - m$ and $2N - n$ are the summation times for the height and width of the point (m, n), t_i is the calculation for $f_i, i = (1, 2, 3, 4)$, which are constants for a given computing environment.

We arrange all the calculation amounts into a matrix according to each grid index. Equation (10) gives the calculation amount matrix, $t_i, i = (1, 2, 3, 4)$ are omitted so as to simplify the analysis.

$$\begin{bmatrix} 4MN & 2M(2N-1) & ... & 2M(N+1) \\ 2N(2M-1) & (2M-1)(2N-1) & ... & (N+1)(2M-1) \\ ... & ... & ... & ... \\ 2N(M+1) & (M+1)(2N-1) & ... & (N+1)(M+1) \end{bmatrix}_{m*n} \tag{10}$$

For a given row j, the row array is $\{a_n\} = \{2N(2M-j), (2N-1)(2M-j)..., (N+1)(2M-j)\}$, the difference between two adjacent items is $a_{j+1} - a_j = 2M - j$, which is a constant for the given row j. So that the row j is an equal difference array with $2M - j$ as the common difference. Similarly, for a given column i in Eq. (10), the column i is an equal difference array with $2N - i$ as the common difference. As a general extension to the equal difference array, we define the matrix of Eq. (10) as equal difference matrix.

Based on the equal difference matrix, we can model the issue of the unbalanced calculation as follows: Given an equal difference matrix EM with size $M * N$ and the core number r, the calculation of Eq. (9) under multi-core platform means dividing EM into r different sets for different r cores, the differences of the sums of the divided sets should be as small as possible.

3.3   Balance Point Set

Inspired by the Theorem 1 in the Appendix, we consider the relationship between the sums of point sets E_0 and E_1 shown in Fig. 1. $E_0 = \{a_1, a_2, a_3, a_4\}$ and $E_1 = \{b_1, b_2, b_3, b_4\}$ are in the equal difference matrix EM. $\{a_1, a_2, a_3, a_4\}$ are the four corners of the matrix. b_1 and b_2 are mirror symmetry about $n = N/2$. b_1 and b_3 are mirror symmetry about $m = M/2$. b_2 and b_4 are mirror symmetry about $m = M/2$. The 4 points form a rectangle, the center is $(M/2, N/2)$. We give point set $E_2 = \{c_1, c_2, c_3, c_4\}$ shown in Fig. 1 as an intermediate variable. c_1, c_2, b_1 and b_2 are in the same row. c_3, c_4, b_3 and b_4 are in the same row.

First we consider the relationship between the sum of E_0 and E_2. According to Theorem 1 in the Appendix,

$$a_1 + a_3 = c_1 + c_3 \tag{11}$$

$$a_2 + a_4 = c_2 + c_4 \tag{12}$$

So that

$$\sum_{i=1}^{4} a_i = \sum_{i=1}^{4} c_i \tag{13}$$

Similarly, we can get the relationship between the sum of E_1 and E_2

$$\sum_{i=1}^{4} b_i = \sum_{i=1}^{4} c_i \tag{14}$$

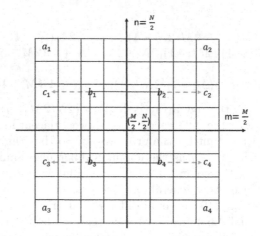

Fig. 1. The relationship between $E_0 = \{a_1, a_2, a_3, a_4\}$, $E_1 = \{b_1, b_2, b_3, b_4\}$ and $E_2 = \{c_1, c_2, c_3, c_4\}$ in equal difference matrix. E_0 is the set containing the 4 corner elements. The 4 elements of E_1 form a rectangle, the center is $(M/2, N/2)$. E_2 extends the x axis of E_1 to the border of the equal difference matrix.

So that

$$\sum_{i=1}^{4} a_i = \sum_{i=1}^{4} b_i \qquad (15)$$

Equation (15) indicates that the sum of an arbitrary 4 points in EM that form a horizontal rectangle with $(M/2, N/2)$ as center is a constant. Thus the equal difference matrix can be divided into $(M * N/4)$ sets, the sum of each set is the same. We define each set as balanced point set. The excellent property provides the basis to solve the unbalanced calculation.

Let $(M/2, N/2)$ be the origin, row $M/2$ be the horizontal axis, column $N/2$ be the vertical axis, The equal difference matrix EM is divided into four quadrants. After an arbitrary point (i, j) is assigned to the second quadrant, the balanced point set where $b_{i,j}$ can be calculated as follows:

$$E_{i,j} = \begin{cases} b_{i,j} & b_{i,N-j+1} \\ b_{M-i+1,j} & b_{M-i+1,N-j+1} \end{cases} \qquad (16)$$

where the four elements form the balanced point set $E_{i,j}$, the first row points are in the second and first quadrant respectively, the second row points are in the third and fourth quadrant respectively. Using the attribute of the equal difference array, the relationship between the 4 elements is as follows:

$$b_{i,j} > b_{i,N-j+1}, b_{M-i+1,j} > b_{M-i+1,N-j+1} \qquad (17)$$

3.4   Unbalanced Calculation Optimization

Based on the balanced point set, the unbalanced calculation of different cores under multi-core platform can be optimized in two cases. Let the equal difference matrix be EM with size $M * N$. Without loss of generality, the size M and N are powers of 2 defined as $M = 2^u$ and $N = 2^v$.

Case 1. We first consider the core number of the multi-core platform is r, where r is the power of 2. This means EM is divided into r different sets. When $r = 2^u * 2^v / 4$, the division of the balanced point sets $E_{i,j}$ satisfies, where $1 \leq i \leq M/2$ and $1 \leq j \leq N/2$. When $r = 2^u * 2^v / (4 * 2^k)$, where $1 \leq k \leq u + v - 2$, we can merge arbitrary 2^k $E_{i,j}$ together as a division part for a core because the sum of each $E_{i,j}$ is a constant. So that for each core, the calculation amount is the same. That is to say, the unbalanced calculation between different cores is solved theoretically. We develop the determined Algorithm (1) so as to programme conveniently.

Algorithm 1. Assignment strategy for case 1

Require: The equal different matrix size, 2^u and 2^v; The number of the cores under multi-core platform, 2^k;

Ensure: The set of balanced point sets for the l th core, L_l, where $1 \leq l \leq 2^k$;

 1: Arrange all the balanced point sets $\{E_{i,j}\}$ in a row-major order, $\{E_{i*2^v+j}\}$;

 2: Calculate the number of the balanced point sets in L_l, $S = 2^u * 2^v / (4 * 2^l)$;

 3: Merge the set of the balanced point set for L_l is $\{E_{S*l+1}, E_{S*l+2}, ... E_{S*(l+1)}\}$;

 4: **return** L_l;

Case 2. Case 1 demonstrates when the core number is $r = \{2, 4, 2^k, ..., 2^p * 2^q / 4\}$, the unbalanced calculation can be solved completely. When the core number r is not the power of 2, we can follow the same strategy as Algorithm (1) while handling the reminder carefully. We also arrange all the balanced point sets into a row-major order, unlike Algorithm (1) assigns continuous indexes for set L_l, where L_l represents the l th divided part for l th core, the assignment strategy changes to $L_l = \{E_l, E_{l+r}, ...\}$, where r is the number of the core. There are $(M*N)\%r$ sets with size $M*N//r+1$ and $r-(M*N)\%r$ sets with size $M*N//r$. The number of the items in L_l is not equal to each other, but the maximum difference is 1. Based our assignment strategy, we only need to consider the last $(M * N)\%r$ balanced point sets. In order to minimize the maximum difference among different L_l, these balanced point sets composed of 4 elements should be split to different cores. From the perspective of 2-D equal difference matrix, the origin is $(M/2, N/2)$, the assignment strategy mentioned above allocates the balanced point sets those are far from the origin first. As the assignment goes on, the variances of the balanced point sets are gradually lower. So that the last $(M * N)\%r$ balanced point sets have relatively low variances. If $3r/4 < (M * N)\%r$, which means that there must be 4 elements in at least one core, the algorithm that keeps as the original does not slow down the performance. If $r/2 < (M * N)\%r \leq 3 * r/4$, there must be more than $s/4$ cores are empty when processing the last $(M*N)\%r$ balanced point sets. For each of the last $(M*N)\%r$ balanced point sets, namely, E_{i_1,j_1}, based on Eq. (17) we take out the element $b_{i_1,N-j_1+1}$, every three extracted elements form a set and the set is dispatched to a free process. Based on the low variance among the elements the calculation time nearly reduces to the $3/4$ of the original. If $r/4 < (M * N)\%r \leq r/2$, these balanced point sets can be split into 2 parts, for set E_{i_1,j_1}, according to Eq. (17), one set is $\{b_{i_1,N-j_1+1}, b_{M-i+1,j}\}$, the other is $\{b_{i,j}, b_{M-i+1,N-j+1}\}$, each part contains 2 elements. For the last $(M * N)\%r$ balanced point sets the calculation time nearly halves. Similarly, if $(M * N)\%r \leq r/4$, these balanced point sets can be split into 4 parts, each element is assigned to different L_l. Algorithm (2) shows the detailed description.

Algorithm 2. Assignment strategy for case 2

Require: The equal different matrix size, M and N; The number of the cores under multi-core platform, r;
Ensure: The set of balanced point set for the lth core, L_l;
1: Arrange all the balanced point sets $\{E_{i,j}\}$ in a row-major order, $\{E_{i*N+j}\}$;
2: Calculate the remainder $(M * N)\%r$;
3: For the aliquot part, calculate the number of the balanced point set in L_l, $L_l = \{E_l, E_{l+r}, ...\}$;
4: **if** $r2 < (M * N)\%r \leq 3r/4$ **then**
5:    Split each balanced point set of E_{i_1,j_1} into 2 sets, take out the element $b_{i_1,N-j_1+1}$, every three extracted elements form new set.
6:    Merge the split E_{i_1,j_1} to L_l;
7: **end if**
8: **if** $r/4 < (M * N)\%r \leq r2$ **then**
9:    Split each balanced point set of E_{i_1,j_1} into 2 sets, one set is $\{b_{i_1,N-j_1+1}, b_{M-i+1,j}\}$, the other is $\{b_{i,j}, b_{M-i+1,N-j+1}\}$
10:    Merge the split to L_l;
11: **end if**
12: **if** $(M * N)\%r < r/4$ **then**
13:    Split each balanced point set of E_{i_1,j_1} into 4 sets, each set contains 1 elements;
14:    Merge the split E_{i_1,j_1} to L_l;
15: **end if**
16: **return** L_l;

---

4   Evaluation

4.1   Experimental Environment

Our cluster is composed of 8 homogenous nodes. The configuration of each node is shown in Table 1. We compare our algorithm with two other elementary

assignment algorithms. One assigns the EM elements $[i * \frac{N*M}{r}, (i+1) * \frac{N*M}{r})$
to the i th core (we name it "i++"), where M, N is the grid width and height, r
is the number of the cores. The other assigns the elements $\{i, i+r, ..., i+n*r\}$
to the i th core (We name it "i+r"), where $\{i+n*r|n \in N, i+n*r < M*N\}$.
According to Lin et al. [11], we set $M = N = 127$, the significant of $MPRF$ to
100-bit and the number of the Taylor expansion terms to 10.

We first compare the unbalanced calculation using the maximum elapse time
difference of the $\{F_i\}, i = (1,2,3,4)$ in Eq. (9) among the three element assignment algorithms under a fixed P th-order Taylor expansion. Then we compare
the elapsed time and the speedup ratio for the iterations of $\Psi_{i,m,n}$ and $\Theta_{i,m,n}$ in
Eq. (4).

Table 1. The configuration of the nodes.

Configuration	Setting
CPU	Intel Xeon E5-2699 v4@2.2 GHz(2*22 cores)
Memory	128 GB DDR4
Hard Disk	500 GB SSD
MPI	Intel MPI Version 5.1.3
Network	InfiniBand
Operating system	CentOS 7.2 x86_64

4.2 Unbalanced Calculation

The maximum time difference between different cores to calculate $\{F_i\}, i = (1,2,3,4)$ for different P th Taylor series can be used to quantitatively describe
the unbalanced calculation. Figures 2 and 3 show the comparison of the maxi-
mum time difference of all the cores among the three algorithms when we use
4 nodes of the cluster. For a fixed P th Taylor expansion, the maximum time
difference of our algorithm is much smaller than "i++" and "i+r" no matter
whether the core number is the power of 2 or not. In general, our algorithm is
quite effective to reduce the unbalanced calculation.

4.3 Speedup Ratio

In addition, Figs. 4 and 5 show the comparison of the elapsed time of the
calculation of $\Psi_{i,m,n}$ and $\Theta_{i,m,n}$ in Eq. (4) in a iteration among the three algorithms. For a fixed core number, the elapsed time of our algorithm is shorter
than the other two algorithms due to the more balanced calculation of our algorithm and low cost for core assignment. Table 2 gives the speedup ratios between
our algorithm and "i++", "i+r". In general, our algorithm can accelerate the
calculation.

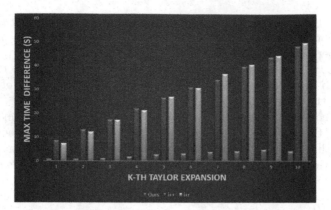

Fig. 2. The comparison of the maximum time difference among our algorithm, "i++" and "i + r". The core number is 128.

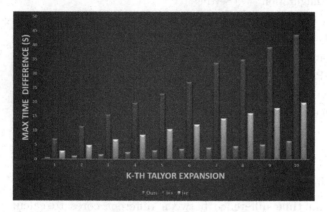

Fig. 3. The comparison of the maximum time difference among our algorithm, "i++" and "i + r". The core number is 176 which is the total CPU cores of 4 nodes.

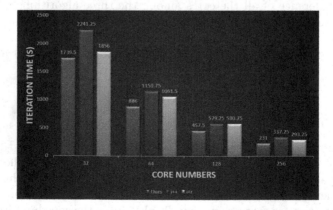

Fig. 4. The comparison of the elapsed time of an iteration among our algorithm, "i++" and "i + r". The core number is the power of 2.

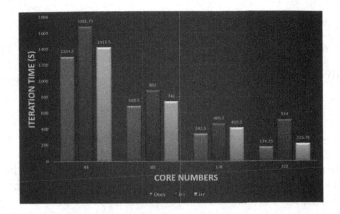

Fig. 5. The comparison of the elapsed time of an iteration among our algorithm, "i++" and "i + r". We use all the cores in the nodes.

Table 2. The speedup ratios under different core numbers.

Core number	32	44	64	88	128	176	256	352
Our algorithm VS "i++"	1.288 X	1.290 X	1.309 X	1.281 X	1.266 X	1.371 X	1.460 X	2.950 X
Our algorithm VS "i + r"	1.067 X	1.087 X	1.198 X	1.077 X	1.269 X	1.213 X	1.269 X	1.238 X

5   Conclusion

In this paper, we propose an algorithm to optimize the unbalanced calculation for the CNS calculation of the two-dimensional Rayleigh-Bénard turbulence. We first establish the model of the unbalanced calculation. Then we introduce the notions of equal difference matrix and balance point set. Based on these notions, we introduce the algorithm to optimize the unbalanced calculation under multi-core platform. We prove our algorithm is optimal when the core number is the power of 2 and our algorithm approaches to the optimal when the core number is not the power of 2. Finally, we compare our algorithms with "i++" and "i + r" algorithms and demonstrate our algorithm is effective.

A   Appendix

Theorem 1. Given an arbitrary equal difference array, namely $\{a_n\} = \{a_1, a_2, ..., a_n\}$, the common difference is d. For $i, j \in N$ and $1 \leq i, j \leq n$. $a_{n-i+1} + a_i = a_{n-j+1} + a_j$.

Use the general formula to expanse a_n:

$$a_n = a_1 + (n - 1) * d \tag{18}$$

So a_{n-i+1} is:

$$a_{n-i+1} = a_1 + (n - i) * d \tag{19}$$

So $a_{n-i+1} + a_i$ is:

$$a_{n-i+1} + a_i = a_1 + (n-i)*d + a_1 + (i-1)*d = 2*a_1 + (n-1)*d \qquad (20)$$

The Eq. (20) is independent with i. Hence we have

$$a_{n-i+1} + a_i = a_{n-j+1} + a_j \qquad (21)$$

where $i, j \in N$ and $1 \le i, j \le n$. From the perspective of the geometry, if we consider the equal difference array as a line segment, point $n - i + 1$ and point i is symmetrical about point $(n+1)/2$, which is the center of the line segment. The Eq. (21) expresses that the sums of the two symmetrical points about the center are the same.

References

1. Avila, K., Moxey, D., de Lozar, A., Avila, M., Barkley, D., Hof, B.: The onset of turbulence in pipe flow. Science **333**(6039), 192–196 (2011)
2. Barrio, R., Blesa, F., Lara, M.: VSVO formulation of the Taylor method for the numerical solution of ODEs. Comput. Math. Appl. **50**(1), 93–111 (2005)
3. Blackburn, H.M., Sherwin, S.: Formulation of a Galerkin spectral Element-Fourier method for three-dimensional incompressible flows in cylindrical geometries. J. Comput. Phys. **197**(2), 759–778 (2004)
4. Fousse, L., Hanrot, G., Lefèvre, V., Pélissier, P., Zimmermann, P.: MPFR: a multiple-precision binary floating-point library with correct rounding. ACM Trans. Math. Softw. (TOMS) **33**(2), 13 (2007)
5. Getling, A.V.: Rayleigh-Bénard Convection: Structures and Dynamics, vol. 11. World Scientific, Singapore (1998)
6. Li, X., Liao, S.: On the stability of the three classes of Newtonian three-body planar periodic orbits. Sci. China Phys. Mech. Astron. **57**(11), 2121–2126 (2014)
7. Liao, S.: On the reliability of computed chaotic solutions of non-linear differential equations. Tellus A **61**(4), 550–564 (2009)
8. Liao, S.: On the numerical simulation of propagation of micro-level inherent uncertainty for chaotic dynamic systems. Chaos Solitons Fractals **47**, 1–12 (2013)
9. Liao, S., Li, X.: On the inherent self-excited macroscopic randomness of chaotic three-body systems. Int. J. Bifurcat. Chaos **25**(09), 1530023 (2015)
10. Liao, S., Wang, P.: On the mathematically reliable long-term simulation of chaotic solutions of Lorenz equation in the interval [0, 10000]. Sci. China Phys. Mech. Astron. **57**(2), 330–335 (2014)
11. Lin, Z., Wang, L., Liao, S.: On the origin of intrinsic randomness of Rayleigh-Bénard turbulence. Sci. China Phys. Mech. Astron. **60**(1), 014712 (2017)
12. Lorenz, E.N.: Deterministic nonperiodic flow. J. Atmos. Sci. **20**(2), 130–141 (1963)
13. Lorenz, E.N.: Computational periodicity as observed in a simple system. Tellus A **58**(5), 549–557 (2006)
14. Niemela, J., Sreenivasan, K.R.: Turbulent convection at high Rayleigh numbers and aspect ratio 4. J. Fluid Mech. **557**, 411–422 (2006)
15. Orszag, S.A.: Analytical theories of turbulence. J. Fluid Mech. **41**(2), 363–386 (1970)

16. Pugachev, A.O., Ravikovich, Y.A., Savin, L.A.: Flow structure in a short chamber of a Labyrinth seal with a backward-facing step. Comput. Fluids **114**, 39–47 (2015)
17. Rayleigh, L.: Lix. on convection currents in a horizontal layer of fluid, when the higher temperature is on the under side. Lond. Edinb. Dublin Philos. Mag. J. Sci. 32(192), 529–546 (1916)
18. Roche, P.E., Castaing, B., Chabaud, B., Hébral, B.: Prandtl and Rayleigh numbers dependences in Rayleigh-Bénard convection. EPL (Europhys. Lett.) 58(5), 693 (2002)
19. Saltzman, B.: Finite amplitude free convection as an initial value problemi. J. Atmos. Sci. **19**(4), 329–341 (1962)
20. Wang, L.P., Rosa, B.: A spurious evolution of turbulence originated from round-off error in pseudo-spectral simulation. Comput. Fluids **38**(10), 1943–1949 (2009)
21. Wang, P., Li, J., Li, Q.: Computational uncertainty and the application of a high-performance multiple precision scheme to obtaining the correct reference solution of Lorenz equations. Numer. Alg. **59**(1), 147–159 (2012)
22. Yang, D., Yang, H., Wang, L., Zhou, Y., Zhang, Z., Wang, R., Liu, Y.: Performance optimization of marine science and numerical modeling on HPC cluster. PloS one **12**(1), e0169130 (2017)
23. Yao, L.S., Hughes, D.: Comment on computational periodicity as observed in a simple system, by Edward N. Lorenz (2006a). Tellus A 60(4), 803–805 (2008)
24. Zhang, L., Zhao, J., Jian-Ping, W.: Parallel computing of POP ocean model on quad-core intel xeon cluster. Comput. Eng. Appl. **45**(5), 189–192 (2009)
25. Zhao, W., Song, Z., Qiao, F., Yin, X.: High efficient parallel numerical surface wave model based on an irregular Quasi-rectangular domain decomposition scheme. Sci. China Earth Sci. **57**(8), 1869–1878 (2014)
26. Zhou, Q., Xia, K.Q.: Thermal boundary layer structure in turbulent Rayleigh-Bénard convection in a rectangular cell. J. Fluid Mech. **721**, 199–224 (2013)

ES-GP: An Effective Evolutionary Regression Framework with Gaussian Process and Adaptive Segmentation Strategy

Shijia Huang and Jinghui Zhong[(✉)]

School of Computer Science and Engineering,
South China University of Technology, Guangzhou, China
jinghuizhong@gmail.com

Abstract. This paper proposes a novel evolutionary regression framework with Gaussian process and adaptive segmentation strategy (named ES-GP) for regression problems. The proposed framework consists of two components, namely, the outer DE and the inner DE. The outer DE focuses on finding the best segmentation scheme, while the inner DE focuses on optimizing the hyper-parameters of GP model for each segment. These two components work cooperatively to find a piecewise gaussian process solution which is flexible and effective for complicated regression problems. The proposed ES-GP has been tested on four artificial regression problems and two real-world time series regression problems. The experiment results show that ES-GP is capable of improving prediction performance over non-segmented or fixed-segmented solutions.

Keywords: Gaussian process · Differential evolution

1 Introduction

Regression analysis is an active and important research topic in scientific and engineering fields. Traditional methods for regression analysis focus on choosing an appropriate model and adjusting model parameters to estimate the relationships between inputs and outputs. These methods usually make strong assumptions of data, which are ineffective if the assumptions are invalid. Gaussian Process (GP) is a powerful tool for regression analysis, which makes little assumption of data. Developed base on Statistical Learning and Bayesian theory, GP is flexible, probabilistic, and non-parametric. It has been shown quite effective in dealing with regression problems with high dimension and nonlinear complex data [1].

However, there are some drawbacks of GP. First, GP requires a matrix inversion which has a time complexity of $O(n^3)$ where n is the number of training data. Second, the covariance function and the hyper-parameters of GP model should be carefully fine-tuned to achieve satisfying performance. In the literature, many efforts have been made to solve the above problems, but most methods

© Springer International Publishing AG, part of Springer Nature 2018
Y. Shi et al. (Eds.): ICCS 2018, LNCS 10862, pp. 736–743, 2018.
https://doi.org/10.1007/978-3-319-93713-7_71

mainly focus on constructing a single type of GP model, not flexible enough for complicated regression data involving multiple significant different segments.

To address the above issues, we propose an evolutionary segmentation GP framework named ES-GP, which can automatically identify the segmentation in regression data and construct suitable GP model for each segment. In ES-GP, there is an outer DE focuses on finding a suitable segmentation scheme, while an inner DE, embedded in the outer DE, focuses on tuning the GP model associated to each segment. Once the GP model for each segment is determined, the fitness of the given segmentation scheme can be evaluated. Guided by this fitness evaluation mechanism, the proposed framework is capable of evolving both segmentation scheme and the GP model for each segment automatically. Experimental results for six regression problems show that ES-GP is capable of improving prediction performance over non-segmented or fixed-segmented solutions.

2 Preliminaries

2.1 Gaussian Process for Regression

GP is a non-parametric model that generates predictions by optimizing a Multi-variate Gaussian Distribution (MGD) over training data such that the likelihood of the outputs given the inputs is maximized [2]. Specifically, given a set of training data $s = [x, y]$ and predict output of a query input x_* is y_*, then we have:

$$\begin{bmatrix} y \\ y_* \end{bmatrix} \sim \mathcal{N} \left(\mu, \begin{bmatrix} K & K_*^T \\ K_* & K_{**} \end{bmatrix} \right) \tag{1}$$

where μ is the mean of the MGD which is commonly set to zero, T indicates matrix transposition, K, K_* and K_{**} are covariance matrixes, i.e.,

$$K = \begin{bmatrix} k(x_1, x_1) & k(x_1, x_2) & \cdots & k(x_1, x_n) \\ k(x_2, x_1) & k(x_2, x_2) & \cdots & k(x_2, x_n) \\ \vdots & \vdots & \ddots & \vdots \\ k(x_n, x_1) & k(x_n, x_2) & \cdots & k(x_n, x_n) \end{bmatrix} \tag{2}$$

$$K_* = \begin{bmatrix} k(x_*, x_1) & k(x_*, x_2) & \cdots & k(x_*, x_n) \end{bmatrix} \tag{3}$$

$$K_{**} = k(x_*, x_*) \tag{4}$$

where $k(x, x^{'})$ is the covariance function used to measure the correlation between two points. There are a number of covariance functions in the literatures, "Squared Exponential" is a common one which can be expressed as:

$$k(x, x^{'}) = \sigma_f^2 exp \left[\frac{-(x - x^{'})^2}{2l^2} \right] \tag{5}$$

where σ_f and l are hyper-parameters of the covariance function.

Based on (1) and using the marginalization property, we can get that the conditional distribution of y_* given y also follows a Gaussian-distributed, i.e.,

$$y_*|y \sim \mathcal{N}(K_*K^{-1}y, K_{**} - K_*K^{-1}K_*^T) \tag{6}$$

Hence, the best estimate of y_* is the mean of this distribution and the uncertainty of the estimate is captured by the variance.

2.2   Related Works on Enhanced GPs for Regression

Various efforts have been proposed to improve GP for regression. Generally, there are two major research directions. The first direction focuses on model calibration. Traditional methods of optimizing hyper-parameters have risks of falling into a local minima, Petelin [6] shown that evolutionary algorithms such as DE and PSO can outperform the deterministic optimization methods. Sundararajan and Keerthi [9] proposed some predictive approachs to estimate the hyper-parameters. Meanwhile, commonly used covariance functions may not model the data well, Kronberger [3] proposed a Genetic Programming to evolve composite covariance functions. Paciorek and Schervish [5] introduced a class of nonstationary covariance functions for GP regression. Seeger [7] proposed a variational Bayesian method for model selection without user interaction.

The second direction focuses on reducing the computational cost for GP model construction. Nguyen-Tuong [4] proposed the LGP which clusters data and establishes local prediction model. Williams and Seeger [10] proposed using *Nyström Method* to speed up kernel machines. Nelson and Bahamanian [8] proposed sparse GP whose covariance is parametrized by pseudo-input points.

3   The Proposed Method

3.1   General Framework

As illustrated in Fig. 1, the proposed framework consists of two components. The outer DE for finding the best segmentation scheme, and the inner DE for optimizing the GP model associated to each segment. Accordingly, the data are divided into three parts to facilitate the search. The training data is used by the inner DE to calibrate the GP model. For each segment, the commonly used covariance functions are enumerated to construct the GP model, and the hyper-parameters are optimized by Inner DE. Once the best GP model in each segment is obtained, the validation data is used to evaluate the quality of the segmentation scheme. Guided by this fitness evaluation mechanism, the outer DE evolve a group of candidate solutions iteratively, until the termination condition is met. The testing data is used to test the performance of the final solution. JADE [12] is adopted as the solver in both outer DE and inner DE.

3.2   Framework Implementation

Chromosome Representation. In this paper, we focus on dealing with one dimensional regression data. It can use a set of segment points to describe the segmentation scheme. Hence, in the proposed framework, we use an array of real numbers to represent the chromosome of the outer DE, as expressed by:

$$X_i = \{X_{i,1}, X_{i,2}, ..., X_{i,D}\} \tag{7}$$

where $\lfloor X_{i,j} \rfloor$ represents the length of the $i$ht segment and D is the maximum number of segments set by users. When the length sum of the former segments is greater than or equal to the total length of the data, the latter parts of the chromosome is ignored.

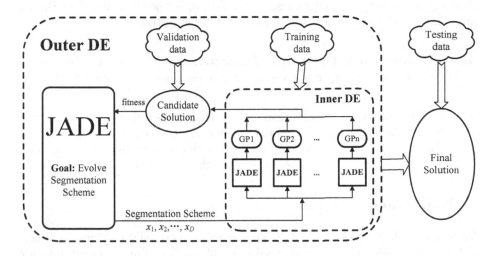

Fig. 1. Algorithm framework

Step 1 - Initialization. The first step is to form the initial population. For each chromosome X_i, the jth dimension value is randomly set by:

$$X_{i,j} = rand(L_{min}, L_{max}), \quad j = 1, 2, ..., D \tag{8}$$

where L_{min} and L_{max} are the lower bound and the upper bound of the segment length set by users, prevent producing extremely short (or long) segments.

Step 2 - Fitness Evaluation. This step aims to evaluate the fitness of the segmentation scheme. Specifically, for each segment, we enumerate commonly used covariance function and optimize the hyper-parameters by the inner DE. The GP model with optimal hyper-parameters which has the maximum marginal likelihood will be considered as the most suitable model. In the inner DE, each chromosome is a set of real numbers, with each representing one hyper-parameter of the GP model. The marginal likelihood of the GP model is used as the fitness value of the individual. Guided by this, the inner DE is capable of fine-tuning the hyper-parameter setting of the GP models associated to the segmentation.

The validation data is used to test the quality of the entire solution. For each point, we firstly determine which segment it belongs to according to its x-coordinate and make prediction by the corresponding GP model. The average error is used as the fitness value of the segmentation scheme. Root-Mean-Square-Error (REMS) is adopted to calculate the error value, i.e.,

$$f(S(\cdot)) = \sqrt{\frac{\sum_{i=1}^{N}(y_i - o_i)^2}{N}} \qquad (9)$$

where y_i is the output of current solution $S(\cdot)$, o_i is the true output of the i_{th} input data, and N is the number of the samples be tested.

Step 3 - Mutation & Crossover. The mutation and crossover is same as in JADE, so we omit the description of them, the details can be found in [12].

Step 4 - Evaluation and Selection. The selection operation selects the better one between parent vector $x_{i,g}$ and trial vector $u_{i,g}$ to become a member of the next generation. In our method, the ones that have better prediction results have a smaller fitness value and will be retained to the next generation.

4   Experiment Studies

We test the effectiveness of ES-GP on four one-dimensional artificial data sets and two real-world time series regression problems. The four artificial data are generated by combining different kinds of functions (e.g., periodic functions and linear functions). The two real time series data sets are obtained from data market.com. The first one is Ex Rate-AUS[1]. The second one is ExRate-TWI[2]. Distribution of the six experiment data sets can refer to Fig. 2.

We compare our algorithm with three other algorithms. The first one is the classic GP with single kernel function. The second one is a hybrid GP with multiple kernel functions (named FS-GP), in which data are divided into fixed length segments (set to 40 in this study). The third algorithm is SL-GEP [11], which has been show quite effective for symbolic regression.

JADE is adopted to optimize the hyper-parameters in GP for ES-GP, FS-GP and classic GP, related parameters of JADE are set according to author's recommended and the Maximum Evaluation Time is set to 5000. The kernel functions considered are: *Squared Exponential, Rational Quadratic*

---

[1] https://datamarket.com/data/set/22wv/exchange-rate-of-australian-dollar-a-for-1-us-dollar-monthly-average-jul-1969-aug-1995.

[2] https://datamarket.com/data/set/22tb/exchange-rate-twi-may-1970-aug-1995.

and *SE with Periodic Element*. Parameters setting in outer DE of ES-GP is same as in inner DE, except that MAXEVAL is 3000. Parameters of SL-GEP are set as suggested in [11].

4.1 Results

Table 1 shows the average RMSE of six data sets and the Wilcoxon's signed-rank test is conducted to check the differences. The statistical results indicate that ES-GP exhibited better performance than SLGEP, FS-GP and GP. Among them, ES-GP showed greater advantages in data set 3 and data set 4, indicating that ES-GP is very suitable for complex time series regression problem. As for the two real-world problems, ES-GP's advantage is not so obvious as in previous data sets because the segmentation characteristics are less obvious, but with the suitable segmentation scheme, the RMSE found by ES-GP is lower than other methods.

Table 1. RMSE of the six problems.

Algorithm	SLGEP [11]	GP	FS-GP	ES-GP
Artificial 1	5.5837889 -	0.0779977 -	0.1753696 -	**0.01658**
Artificial 2	10.8493016 -	1.1830659 -	1.41982 -	**1.0192136**
Artificial 3	21.4422843 -	2.2163847 -	3.2910243 -	**1.571685**
Artificial 4	23.2971078 -	4.5284973 -	5.2494532 -	**3.390701**
ExRate-AUS	12.337935 -	1.91834331 -	2.1590919 -	**1.7031436**
ExRate-TWI	9.5056589 -	1.8520972 ≈	2.0035029 -	**1.7073585**

Symbols -, ≈ and + represent that the competitor is respectively significantly worse than, similar to and better than ES-GP according to the Wilcoxon signed-rank test at $\alpha = 0.05$.

Figure 2 shows the example segmentation schemes found by ES-GP, which shows that ES-GP can find the appropriate segmentation. In artificial data set 1 and 2, the number of segments found by ES-GP is the same as we make the data and all segmentation points are almost sitting the right place. ES-GP finds more segments than originally setting in data set 3, however the original segments are within the set of these segments so the segmentation is successful. In data set 4, ES-GP finds less segments, but GP model in each segment can also perform well in such situation. The optimal segmentation is unknown for the two real-world problems. However, our method can find a promising segmentation scheme, which can help GP models perform better.

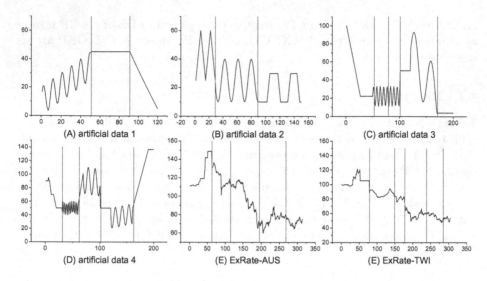

Fig. 2. Result of segmentation in experiment data sets. The blue lines represent the boundary between segments.

5   Conclusion

In this paper, we have proposed a novel evolutionary regression framework with Gaussian process and adaptive segmentation named ES-GP. In ES-GP, a new chromosome representation is proposed to represent the data segmentation scheme. An outer DE is utilized to optimize the segmentation scheme and an inner DE is utilized to optimize the Gaussian process associated to each segment. The proposed ES-GP is tested on four artificial data sets and two real-world time series regression problems. The experimental results have demonstrated that the proposed ES-GP can properly divide the data and provide promising prediction performance.

Acknowledgment. This work was supported in part by the National Natural Science Foundation of China (Grant No. 61602181), and by the Fundamental Research Funds for the Central Universities (Grant No. 2017ZD053).

References

1. Brahim-Belhouari, S., Bermak, A.: Gaussian process for nonstationary time series prediction. Comput. Stat. Data Anal. **47**(4), 705–712 (2004)
2. Rasmussen, C.E., Williams, C.K.I.: Gaussian Processes for Machine Learning. MIT Press, Cambridge (2006)
3. Kronberger, G., Kommenda, M.: Evolution of covariance functions for gaussian process regression using genetic programming. In: Moreno-Díaz, R., Pichler, F., Quesada-Arencibia, A. (eds.) EUROCAST 2013. LNCS, vol. 8111, pp. 308–315. Springer, Heidelberg (2013). https://doi.org/10.1007/978-3-642-53856-8_39

 4. Nguyen-Tuong, D., Peters, J.R., Seeger, M.: Local Gaussian process regression for real time online model learning. In: Advances in Neural Information Processing Systems, pp. 1193–1200 (2009)
 5. Paciorek, C.J., Schervish, M.J.: Nonstationary covariance functions for Gaussian process regression. In: Advances in Neural Information Processing Systems, pp. 273–280 (2004)
 6. Petelin, D., Filipič, B., Kocijan, J.: Optimization of Gaussian process models with evolutionary algorithms. In: Dobnikar, A., Lotrič, U., Šter, B. (eds.) ICANNGA 2011. LNCS, vol. 6593, pp. 420–429. Springer, Heidelberg (2011). https://doi.org/10.1007/978-3-642-20282-7_43
 7. Seeger, M.: Bayesian model selection for support vector machines, Gaussian processes and other kernel classifiers. In: Advances in Neural Information Processing Systems, pp. 603–609 (2000)
 8. Snelson, E., Ghahramani, Z.: Sparse Gaussian processes using pseudo-inputs. In: Advances in Neural Information Processing Systems, pp. 1257–1264 (2006)
 9. Sundararajan, S., Keerthi, S.S.: Predictive app roaches for choosing hyperparameters in Gaussian processes. In: Advances in Neural Information Processing Systems, pp. 631–637 (2000)
10. Williams, C.K., Seeger, M.: Using the nyström method to speed up kernel machines. In: Advances in Neural Information Processing Systems, pp. 682–688 (2001)
11. Zhong, J., Ong, Y.-S., Cai, W.: Self-learning gene expression programming. IEEE Trans. Evol. Comput. **20**(1), 65–80 (2016)
12. Zhang, J., Sanderson, A.C.: JADE: adaptive differential evolution with optional external archive. IEEE Trans. Evol. Comput. **13**(5), 945–58 (2009)

Evaluating Dynamic Scheduling of Tasks in Mobile Architectures Using ParallelME Framework

Rodrigo Carvalho[1(✉)], Guilherme Andrade[2(✉)], Diogo Santana[1(✉)],
Thiago Silveira[3(✉)], Daniel Madeira[1(✉)], Rafael Sachetto[1(✉)],
Renato Ferreira[2(✉)], and Leonardo Rocha[1(✉)]

[1] Universidade Federal de São João del Rei, São João del Rei, Brazil
{rodrigo,diogofs,dmadeira,sachetto,lcrocha}@ufsj.edu.br
[2] Universidade Federal de Minas Gerais, Belo Horizonte, Brazil
{gandrade,renato}@dcc.ufmg.br
[3] Technology, Tsinghua University, Beijing, China
zhuangzq16@mails.tsinghua.edu.cn

Abstract. Recently we observe that mobile phones stopped being just devices for basic communication to become providers of many applications that require increasing performance for good user experience. Inside today's mobile phones we find different processing units (PU) with high computational capacity, as multicore architectures and co-processors like GPUs. Libraries and run-time environments have been proposed to improve applications' performance by taking advantage of different PUs in a transparent way. Among these environments we can highlight the ParallelME. Despite the importance of task scheduling strategies in these environments, ParallelME has implemented only the First Come Firs Serve (FCFS) strategy. In this paper we extended the ParallelME framework by implementing and evaluating two different dynamic scheduling strategies, Heterogeneous Earliest Finish Time (HEFT) and Performance-Aware Multiqueue Scheduler (PAMS). We evaluate these strategies considering synthetic applications, and compare the proposals with the FCFS. For some scenarios, PAMS was proved to be up to 39% more efficient than FCFS. These gains usually imply on lower energy consumption, which is very desirable when working with mobile architectures.

Keywords: Dynamic scheduling · Parallel mobile architectures

1 Introduction

Recently we observe a growth in developing new technologies. An example is the evolution of traditional processors, which have become massively parallel and

This work was partially supported by CNPq, CAPES, Fapemig, INWEB and MAsWeb.

heterogeneous in response to the increasing demand posed to them by the new challenges in many different areas. Mobile devices as well are currently experiencing a substantial growth in processing power. They stopped being just devices for basic communication among people to be providers of many applications such as Internet access, media playing, and general purpose applications, all requiring increasing performance for good user experience. Inside today's mobile phones we find processing units with high computational capacity, as multicore architectures and co-processors like GPUs, making these devices very powerful.

Effectivetly use these devices is still a challenge. Many applications from different domains need to explore all of the available Processing Units (PUs) in a coordinated way to achieve higher performance. Faced with this requirement, libraries and run-time environments have been proposed, providing a set of ways to improve applications' performance by using the different PUs in a transparent way to mobile developers [1,3,4,9,10]. Among these libraries and run-times systems, we highlight ParallelME [4], a Parallel Mobile Engine designed to explore heterogeneity in Android devices.

At the moment ParallelME has implemented just a simple *First Come First Serve* scheduling strategy and all results reported by in recent works [4,14] used just that strategy. The purpose of this work is to extend the ParallelME, implementing and evaluating different dynamic scheduling strategies[1], whose results reported in the literature are promising in traditional architectures [5,6,15]. More specifically, we implemented two different scheduling strategies: (1) Heterogeneous Earliest Finish Time (HEFT) and; (2) Performance-Aware Multiqueue Scheduler (PAMS). HEFT was originally implemented in StarPU [7]. PAMS (Performance Aware Scheduling Technique) was proposed in [5]. Both uses knowledge of the tasks to create the task queues. In order to evaluate our strategy, we prepared a experimental set using a tunnable synthetic application, and compared our proposals with the FCFS implemented in ParallelME. With our results, we show that the new scheduling strategies, in special PAMS, achieves the best results in different scenarios, further improving the ParallelME's performance. For some scenarios, PAMS was up to 39% more efficient than FCFS.

2   Related Work

This section presents an overview of the main programming frameworks for parallel applications in mobile systems and dynamic scheduling strategies.

2.1   Parallel Mobile Frameworks

Nowadays, there are several high-level frameworks designed to facilitate the development of parallel applications in heterogeneous mobile architectures.

---

[1] Dynamic Scheduling Strategies evaluating the characteristics of the tasks at runtime, considering a limited view of the execution of entire application and thus a more challenging scenario.

Among these frameworks, we can highlight OpenCL and RenderScript, both providing tools for programming generic functions that can be executed in both GPUs and CPUs in Android OS, being the basis for several works [2,11]. OpenCL is a framework originally proposed for desktop systems which allows the execution of user code (kernels) in statically-chosen processing units. RenderScript, in turn, is a framework designed by Google to perform data-parallel computations in Android devices, transparently running user code in heterogeneous architectures. Besides the frameworks presented above, we can find others in the literature, such as Pyjama [10] and Cuckoo [13]. Pyjama focuses on multi-thread programming with an OpenMP-like programming model in Java. Cuckoo [13], provides a platform for mobile devices to offload applications in a cloud using a stub/proxy network interface.

Although the presented frameworks share the same design goal, they have different features and programming interfaces, limited by it's complex programming abstraction, preventing their popularization among mobile developers. Recently we find in literature the framework Parallel Mobile Engine (ParallelME) [4], that was designed to explore heterogeneity in Android devices. ParalleME automatically coordinates the parallel usage of computing resources keeping the programming effort similar to what sequential programmers expect. ParallelME distinguishes itself from other frameworks by its high-level programming abstraction in Java and the ability to efficiently coordinate resources in heterogeneous mobile architectures.

2.2 Dynamic Scheduling Strategies

Many proposals of dynamic schedulers are found in literature [8,12,16,17]. In [8] the authors focus on a strategy that minimizes the workload between processing units. The task distribution between the PUs is made randomly, but the inactive PUs can run tasks scheduled to another if it becames idle, using an approach called "work stealing". In [17] the authors presents Dynamic Weighted Round Robin (DWRR), which is focused on compute intensive applications. It's policy assigns a weight to each task in each PU and use this weight to sort the task queue of each PU. In [16], the authors present a strategy based on run time predictors. In this, the scheduler makes a prediction of the execution time for each task as well as the total time for a given PU to run all its tasks. Based on this prediction, the tasks are associated the less busy PUs, aiming to balance to load between the PUs. In [12] is presented a similar proposal, where such execution models are based on past run-time histories.

Another scheduling strategy that presents good results is HEFT (Heterogeneous Earliest Finish Time) [7]. HEFT uses a queue for each available processing unit and task distribution across queues is computed according to the processing capacity of each unit, based on expected execution time of previous tasks. Based on this strategy, in [5] the authors proposed another strategy called called PAMS (Performance-Aware Multiqueue Scheduler). Instead to consider the expected execution time as HEFT, PAMS takes into account performance variabilities to better utilize hybrid systems. Therefore, it uses speedup estimates for each task in order to maintain the order of tasks in the queues for each available processing unit. In this paper we implement HEFT and PAMS strategies in ParallelME and evaluate them using several synthetic applications with different characteristics.

3 Experimental Evaluation

This section presents the experimental results that were conducted to evaluate the implemented scheduling strategies in ParallelME: *FCFS HEFT*, and *PAMS*.

3.1 Workload Description

This subsection describes the workloads that were used to evaluate our dynamic scheduler. These workloads are composed of a synthetic application that allows fully control over several characteristics of the tasks. In a heterogeneous architecture a determining factor for the scheduler is the execution time ratio for the tasks on the different processing units, termed *relative speedup*. To create the workloads for our tests, first we divided our load into three groups:

- **Group 1:** Mostly CPU tasks.
- **Group 2:** Mostly GPU tasks.
- **Group 3:** Balanced CPU and GPU tasks.

In Group 1, the tasks on CPU consumes less time than on GPU. In Group 2, the inverse is observed (GPU are faster than CPU). Tasks in Group 3 are not significantly different in terms of execution time when executed on the CPU or on the GPU. For each group we varied the execution time for CPU and GPU, creating two different classes:

- **Class 1:** Tasks with high relative speedup (higher than 5x). For this, a bad decision can yield large performance hit on the application execution time.
- **Class 2:** Tasks with low relative speedup (lower than 5x). For this class, the performance penalty on the bad decisions are less significant.

Combining these three groups and the two classes above, we have created six distinct workloads, as presented in Table 1.

Table 1. Workloads used in our tests.

Name	Group	Class	Name	Group	Class
Workload 1 (WL 1)	1	1	Workload 4 (WL 4)	1	2
Workload 2 (WL 2)	2	1	Workload 5 (WL 5)	2	2
Workload 3 (WL 3)	3	1	Workload 6 (WL 6)	3	2

3.2   Experimental Results

This section presents the experimental results obtained with the new schedulers, tested with the workloads described in Sect. 3.1. All tests were performed on a **Motorola Moto E 2nd Gen. running a quad-core Cortex A7 CPU @1.2 GHz and an Adreno 302 GPU, with 1 GB of RAM**. Three tests were performed. Firstly all workloads were scheduled only in CPU and only in GPU. After these two tests, the schedulers were tested using both CPU and GPU, using the schedulies strategy FCFS, HEFT and PAMS. Each workload were composed of 100 tasks. The results presented in Fig. 1 are the average results after 10 executions, normalized by the higher execution time for each workload. Our objective is to evaluate the behavior of each scheduler policy, identifying their impact on application performance. As expected, independently of the scheduling strategy, all workloads were faster when using both CPU and GPU (2x on average). Also the better results were obtained in the workloads with higher relative speedup (workloads 1–3, all in Class 1).

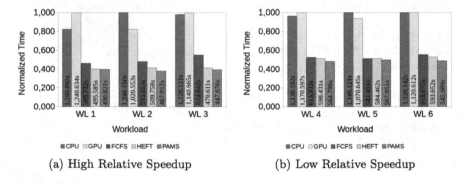

(a) High Relative Speedup   (b) Low Relative Speedup

Fig. 1. Application performance considering specific processing units and scheduling strategies. Lower is better.

When comparing each scheduler performance considering the two workload classes, we noticed that in Class 1 workloads, the performance gain of the HEFT and PAMS schedulers compared to the FCFS scheduler is greater than when we make the same comparison in Class 2 workloads. This happens because in Class 1 workloads the correct association of the task with the best PU is crucial to the performance of the application. When executing a task in the worse PU for it, the execution time is at least 5 times worse. Observing the performance of the scheduling algorithms in Class 2 tasks, the difference is much lower, that is, the average times obtained by the schedulers HEFT and PAMS are closer to those that were obtained by the scheduler FCFS. This can be explained because the relative speedup of these workloads is low. Therefore, even if the scheduler associates a task to a less appropriate PU, this does not damage too much the total execution time, since the execution times in both PUs are closer.

Finally, comparing the performance of each scheduler implemented in ParallelME, we can observe that the PAMS algorithm is more efficient than HEFT and FCFS for all workloads. Figure 1 shows that PAMS was faster than both FCFS and HEFT for all workloads and HEFT was only slower than FCFS on workload 5. PAMS and HEFT were respectively 18% and 12% more efficient than FCFS on average. The two new schedulers achieved their best when executing workload 3 (higher relative speedup and using both CPU and GPU). In this workload, PAMS was 39% and HEFT 33% more efficient than FCFS.

In order to better understand why performance differs among schedulers, we evaluate how tasks are distributed among the PUs available for each of the scheduling strategies implemented in ParallelME. The results of our studies are presented in Fig. 2. In FCFS scheduler regardless of the characteristics of the workload, approximately 50% of the tasks are executed by the CPU and 50% by the GPU, giving a poorer performance. The HEFT scheduler presents a slightly better distribution than FCFS. This happens because HEFT scheduler considers the best PU for each task according to the estimated task runtime as well as the estimated working time for each PU. Through this strategy, the tasks, for the most part, are executed by the most appropriate PU. As described in previous sections, the HEFT scheduler queues are static, that is, after a task is assigned to a PU, it will no longer be processed by another.

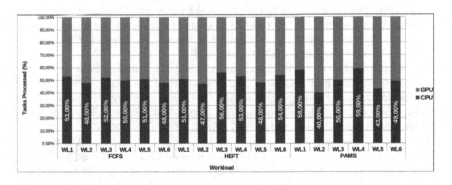

Fig. 2. Profile of tasks assignment to devices for each task executed in our application.

Finally, in PAMS algorithm the distribution of the tasks for the PUs has a more direct relation with the characteristics of each workload. Most of the workload 1 and 4 (2 and 5) tasks (approximately 60%) were processed by the CPU (GPU). We also noticed that in workloads 3 and 6 the tasks were divided evenly, with 50% of the tasks processed by the CPU and 50% by the GPU. Since PAMS uses shared queues, a PU can process jobs allocated to another PU when it is idle (no jobs in its queue). This task distribution strategy used by PAMS makes it more efficient, as it minimizes idle time.

4   Conclusion and Future Works

In this paper we extended the ParallelME framework by implementing and evaluating two different dynamic scheduling strategies, HEFT and PAMS. We performed a comparative analysis, contrasting the performance of ParallelME original scheduler (FCFS) against the new scheduling strategies. We used a synthetic application in which we could control the tasks behavior, to create the six distinct workloads. Regarding the scheduling strategies, the results shows that PAMS was faster than both FCFS and HEFT for all workloads. HEFT was only slower than FCFS in workload 6. On average, PAMS and HEFT were respectively 18% and 12% more efficient than FCFS. The best performance was achieved for workload 3, on which PAMS and HEFT were, respectively, 39% and 33% more efficient than FCFS. It is important to mention that the gains in terms of execution time usually imply on lower energy consumption, which is desirable in mobile architectures. As future work we want to evaluate more elaborate scheduling strategies that may also improve the performance of ParallelME framework.

References

1. RenderScript. https://developer.android.com/guide/topics/renderscript
2. Acosta, A., Almeida, F.: Performance analysis of paralldroid generated programs. In: Parallel, Distributed and Network-Based Processing (PDP), pp. 60–67 (2014)
3. Acosta, A., Almeida, F.: Performance analysis of paralldroid generated programs. In: 2014 22nd Euromicro International Conference on Parallel, Distributed and Network-Based Processing (PDP). IEEE (2014)
4. Andrade, G., de Carvalho, W., Utsch, R., Caldeira, P., Alburquerque, A., Ferracioli, F., Rocha, L., Frank, M., Guedes, D., Ferreira, R.: ParallelME: A Parallel Mobile Engine to Explore Heterogeneity in Mobile Computing Architectures. In: Dutot, P.-F., Trystram, D. (eds.) Euro-Par 2016. LNCS, vol. 9833, pp. 447–459. Springer, Cham (2016). https://doi.org/10.1007/978-3-319-43659-3_33
5. Andrade, G., Ferreira, R., Teodoro, G., da Rocha, L.C., Saltz, J.H., Kurç, T.M.: Efficient execution of microscopy image analysis on CPU, GPU, and MIC equipped cluster systems. In: IEEE SBAC-PAD 2014, Paris, France, pp. 89–96 (2014)
6. Andrade, G., Ramos, G., Madeira, D., Sachetto, R., Clua, E., Ferreira, R., Rocha, L.: Efficient dynamic scheduling of heterogeneous applications in hybrid architectures. ACM SAC **2014**, 866–871 (2014)
7. Augonnet, C., Thibault, S., Namyst, R., Wacrenier, P.: StarPU: a unified platform for task scheduling on heterogeneous multicore architectures (2011)
8. Blumofe, R.D., Leiserson, C.E.: Scheduling multithreaded computations by work stealing. J. ACM 46(5), 720–748 (1999). https://doi.org/10.1145/324133.324234
9. Frost, G.: Aparapi: using GPU/APUs to accelerate Java workloads (2014). https://github.com/aparapi/aparapi
10. Giacaman, N., Sinnen, O., et al.: Pyjama: OpenMP-like implementation for Java, with GUI extensions. In: Proceedings of the 2013 International Workshop on Programming Models and Applications for Multicores and Manycores. ACM (2013)
11. Gupta, K.G., Agrawal, N., Maity, S.K.: Performance analysis between Aparapi (a parallel API) and Java by implementing sobel edge detection algorithm. In: Parallel Computing Technologies (PARCOMPTECH). IEEE (2013)

12. Jooya, A., Baniasadi, A., Analoui, M.: History-aware, resource-based dynamic scheduling for heterogeneous multi-core processors. Comput. Digit. Tech. IET 5(4), 254–262 (2011). https://doi.org/10.1049/iet-cdt.2009.0045

13. Kemp, R., Palmer, N., Kielmann, T., Bal, H.: Cuckoo: A Computation Offloading Framework for Smartphones. In: Gris, M., Yang, G. (eds.) MobiCASE 2010. LNICSSITE, vol. 76, pp. 59–79. Springer, Heidelberg (2012). https://doi.org/10.1007/978-3-642-29336-8_4

14. de Moreira, W., Andrade, G.N., Caldeira, P.H., Goncalves, R.U., Ferreira, R.A., Rocha, L.C., de Sousa, R., Avelar, M.N.: Exploring heterogeneous mobile architectures with a high-level programming model. In: 29th IEEE SBAC-PAD, pp. 25–32 (2017)

15. da Rocha, L.C., Mourão, F., Andrade, G., Ferreira, R., Parthasarathy, S., Melo, D., Toledo, S., Chakrabarti, A.: D-sthark: evaluating dynamic scheduling of tasks in hybrid simulated architectures. In: ICCS 2016, California, USA, pp. 428–438 (2016)

16. Smith, W., Taylor, V., Foster, I.: Using Run-Time Predictions to Estimate Queue Wait Times and Improve Scheduler Performance. In: Feitelson, D.G., Rudolph, L. (eds.) JSSPP 1999. LNCS, vol. 1659, pp. 202–219. Springer, Heidelberg (1999). https://doi.org/10.1007/3-540-47954-6_11

17. Teodoro, G., Sachetto, R., Sertel, O., Gurcan, M., Meira Jr., W., Catalyurek, U., Ferreira, R.: Coordinating the use of GPU and CPU for improving performance of compute intensive applications. In: IEEE International Conference on Cluster Computing, September 2009

An OAuth2.0-Based Unified Authentication System for Secure Services in the Smart Campus Environment

Baozhong Gao[1], Fangai Liu[1(✉)], Shouyan Du[2(✉)],
and Fansheng Meng[1]

[1] Shandong Normal University, Shandong, China
lfa@sdnu.edu.cn
[2] Computer Network Information Center, Chinese Academy of Science,
Beijing, China
dushouyan@hotmail.com

Abstract. Based on the construction of Shandong Normal University's smart authentication system, this paper researches the key technologies of Open Authorization(OAuth) protocol, which allows secure authorization in a simple and standardized way from third-party applications accessing online services. Through the analysis of OAuth2.0 standard and the open API details between different applications, and concrete implementation procedure of the smart campus authentication platform, this paper summarizes the research methods of building the smart campus application system with existing educational resources in cloud computing environment. Through the conducting of security experiments and theoretical analysis, this system has been proved to run stably and credibly, flexible, easy to integrate with existing smart campus services, and efficiently improve the security and reliability of campus data acquisition. Also, our work provides a universal reference and significance to the authentication system construction of the smart campus.

Keywords: OAuth2.0 · Authentication and authorization · Open API
Cloud security · Smart campus · Open platform

1 Introduction

The web was proposed as a hypertext system for sharing data and information among scientists [1], and has grown into an unparalleled platform on which to develop distributed information systems [2].

Cloud computing was defined [24] by the US National Institute of Standards and Technology (NIST). They defined a cloud computing [3] as a model for enabling ubiquitous, convenient, on-demand network access to a shared pool of configurable computing resources (e.g., networks, servers, storage, applications, and services) that can be rapidly provisioned and released with minimal management effort or service provider interaction. "The data stored in the cloud needs to be confidential, preserving integrity and available" [4]. All cloud computing have to provide a secure way, including personal identification, authorization, confidentiality, and the availability of a

© Springer International Publishing AG, part of Springer Nature 2018
Y. Shi et al. (Eds.): ICCS 2018, LNCS 10862, pp. 752–764, 2018.
https://doi.org/10.1007/978-3-319-93713-7_73

certain level in order to cope with the security problem of private information exposed. On cloud-computing platforms, most of the different departments on smart campus have their own independent information systems with separate identity and authentication [9]. This has created a security issue with the uniformity of information between the different systems [5].

Google is investing in authentication using two-step verification via one-time passwords and public-key-based technology to achieve stronger user and device identification. One disadvantage of this opt in protection is that attackers who have gained access to Google accounts can enable the service with their own mobile number to impede the user restoring their account [6]. From this requirement, the Open Authorization protocol (OAuth) "was introduced as a secure and efficient method of authenticating access to cloud data APIs for authorizing third-party applications without disclosing the user's access credentials" [9].

Based on the current situation at Shandong Normal University, we use OAuth2.0 protocol to design and implement the smart campus authentication system. With this system, users do not have to provide third-party authentication credentials, in the case of using a third-party proxy to log on to a target server. Authorization allows a third-party to obtain the specified information, with a simple, convenient, safe and reliable authentication process. The release of data can be controlled, and there are also many other advantages with the system. Under the support of the unified authentication, all the third-party platforms accessed by the smart campus application are shore an interconnected entity. This further improves the security and reliability of the campus data acquisition. In addition, this promotes better campus information construction, which better serves the school affairs, which includes improvement of the life of teachers and students.

2   Related Works

2.1   OAuth2.0 Protocol

OAuth is an open license agreement, which provides a secure and reliable framework for third party applications to access HTTP services with certain authority and limitations [10]. It seeks to resolve the shortcomings of propriety authentication protocols by creating a universal and interoperable authorization mechanism between services [7]. Our smart campus system opens OAuth2.0 interface to all teachers and students of Shandong Normal University. The big advantage of using OAuth for connecting devices is that the process is well understood, and numerous libraries and API platforms provide support for API providers and client developers alike [11]. OAuth adds an additional role: the Authentication Service (AS), which is invoked by the SP to verify the identity of a user in order to grant access token [13]. OpenID Connect is an authentication protocol that is based on OAuth and adds an identity layer for applications that need it [12]. There are three main modes of participation entities in OAuth2.0:

- RO (Resource Owner): The entity that grants access control to protected resources, which is equivalent to the user defined in OAuth1.0.
- RS (Resource Server): The server that stores data resources of users and provides access to the protected resources requested.

- AS (Authorization Server): The service that verifies the identity of the resource owner and obtains the authorization, and issues the Access Token.
- UA (User-Agent): It's suitable for all non-server-side client, like Chrome, Firefox, and Safari web browsers.
- AT (Access Token): A piece of data the authorization server created that lets the client request access from the resource server [8].
- AC (Authorization Code): A piece of data that the authorization server can check, used during the transaction's request stage [8].

The standard authorization process of OAuth2.0 protocol with specified API is generally divided into six steps:

(1) User authorization: The client sends an authorization request includes the type, Client Id, and Redirect URL to RO, which begins the user authorization process.
(2) Return authorization code: RO agrees to the authorization, and returns an AC to UA.
(3) Request access token: After the user completes the authorization, the client uses AC and Redirection URL to request AT from AS.
(4) Return access token: AS authenticates client, and validates AC. If the client user's private certificate and access permissions are verified and qualified, the client will gain access to the AT from AS.
(5) Request protected resources: The client requests for the protected resources to RS through an AT.
(6) Acquire user's information: After the RS verify the validity of the AT, in response to this resource request, the client can obtain the permission to acquire protected resource using the specified information interface.

2.2 Open API Access Control with Oauth

An API is whatever the designer of the software module has specified it to be in the published API document, without any judgment regarding what functionality the API offers vis-à-vis the functionality it ought to offer [14]. The information owned by online services is made available to third-party applications in the form of public Application Programming Interfaces (APIs), typically using HTTP [15] as communication protocol and relying on the RE presentational State Transfer (REST) architectural style [12]. Our smart campus authentication system API works as following:

(1) Prerequisite description
   1. Our smart campus application system has opened the use of the Open API permissions. From the interface list of the API, it's known that some interfaces are completely open, and some interfaces need to submit applications in advance to gain access.
   2. The resources to be accessed are accessible by the user's authorization. While the site calls the Open API to read and write information about an OpenID (user), the user must have already authorized the OpenID on smart campus application system.
   3. Access Token has been successfully obtained, and is within the validity period.

(2) Call the Open API
Web sites need to send requests to a specific Open API interface to access or modify user data. When all Open API are invoked, in addition to the private parameters of each interface, all Open API need to pass generic parameters based on the OAuth2.0 protocol as following shown in Table 1 [25]:

Table 1. OAuth2.0 generic parameters

Parameters	Description
access_token	Access_Token can be obtained by using Authorization_Code and has a validity period of 3 months
oauth_consumer_key	The AppID which assigned to the app after the third-party application is successfully signed in
openid	The user ID, corresponding with Smart SDNU account

We take the library borrowing information acquisition interface as an example, the interface authority is read_personal_library, and it aims to return the number of borrowed items and the collection of borrowed information of currently logged-in user's library in the specified period.

Request: GET http://i.sdnu.edu.cn/oauth/rest/library/getborrowlist.

Request parameters are as shown in Table 2:

Table 2. /library/getborrowlist request parameters

Field	Required	Type	Description
start	false	string	Start date (formal as yyyy-MM-dd HH:mm:ss)
end	false	string	End date (formal as above)
count	false	int32	Return number (1–50, default as 10)
index	false	int32	Return page numbers (default as 1)

After successful return, we can get the user borrowing data shown as following:

```
[
    {
        "identityNumber":"2013001001",
        "bookName":"Title",
        "borrowDate":"2014-01-01T08:00:00",
        "mustReturnDate":"2014-01-31T08:00:00",
        "isRenew":false
    },
    {
        If there are any other books, the same as above.
    }
]
```

In our OAuth2.0-based smart campus authentication system, we can also get needed information through personal basic information interface, personal campus card information interface, personal library information interface, lost and found information interface, school public information interface, school news information interface, and weather information interface. Through three years' analysis chart of interface access times, we know that the three most frequently accessed interfaces are the library, card and user personal information API. During the period 2014–2016, the card and the user's personal information API vary more stable, however, the number of library API visits in 2015 increased significantly compared with 2014, and then stabilized, indicating that the construction of the new library of our school effectively improve the learning enthusiasm of teachers and students in our school, which provides a remarkable promotion significance to the study style construction of our school.

3   OAuth2.0-Based Smart Campus Authorization System

3.1   Overall Structure

In order to comply with the security and privacy requirements, based on OAuth2.0 protocol, we use APIs to put together highly distributed applications with many interconnected dependencies [16], and propose the smart campus open authentication system, which adopts the hierarchical architecture design concept. Cloud-based services, the social Web, and rapidly expanding mobile platforms will depend on identity management to provide a seamless user experience [17]. Moreover, the proposed architecture aims at minimizing the effort required by service developers to secure their services by providing a standard, configurable, and highly interoperable authorization framework [13].

The overall architecture of the system including three following layers:

- Infrastructure layer: The main work of Infrastructure Layer is to collect and process various information timely and accurately through RFID identification, infrared sensors, video capture, GPS and other technologies and equipment on the campus information collection and dynamic monitoring, and send the information collected from the hardware device to Data Layer in security.
- Application service layer: Application Service Layer's main work is to effectively integrate and management of various information, and achieve unified management of information. Based on the existing management systems, such as financial management system, student management system, staff management system, scientific research management system, equipment management system, logistics management system, through the use of cloud computing and cloud storage technologies to provide a unified management platform, which facilitates third-party applications development, the application service architecture is shown in Fig. 1.
- Information provision layer: The main work of information provision layer is to provide teachers and students with specific and effective service platform. In this platform, in accordance with the unified data specification standards, through the

identity of the open platform of the school, teachers and students' information, users can use the shared platform of teaching resources and research resources to form an interconnected shared entity.

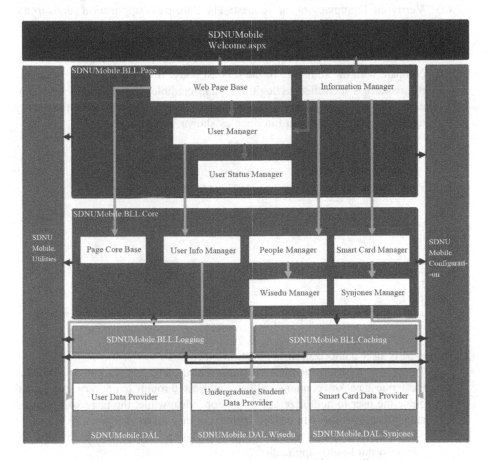

Fig. 1. Smart campus application service architecture diagram

3.2 System Workflow

(1) Third-party application access to temporary token process:

  (a) Attach the request information to the request packet: Attach the client credentials, the subsequent callback address, and the requested control information (including the value of the replay prevention single value and the timestamp of the request) to the request packet in accordance with authentication system requirements.

  (b) Request parameter signature: The HTTP request mode, HTTP protocol request packet URI, the specified request key value pairs arranged as the base string, then, through the HMAC-SHA1 or RSA-SHA1 algorithm to generate messages digest (signature), and the key that participates in the signature algorithm is the key that corresponds to the client credentials.

(c) Encapsulation: Add the signature to the HTTP request header, and finally encapsulate it as a legitimate request packet to obtain temporary token.

(d) Verify the legitimacy of the request: The third-party application sends to the OAuth2.0-based authentication system a request packet for temporary token through the client credentials. The first step of the authorization procedure is to check the validity of request packet when it receives the request, and then compare with the signature in the request body. If they are exactly the same, the request is identified as legitimate and credible. Hence, the system generates temporary token and the corresponding key, and returns to third-party application, the user login interface as shown in Fig. 2.

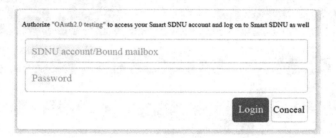

Fig. 2. User login interface

(2) Third-party user authorization application process:

(a) Temporary token authentication page: Third-party application encapsulates the request packet contains callback address through temporary token, and guide the user to authorize authentication. Meanwhile, the page will jump to authentication information page with temporary token, as shown in Fig. 3, in which the user credentials of the authentication system can be avoided for public to third-party applications.

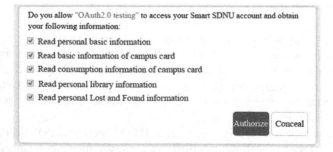

Fig. 3. User authorization interface

(b) The user agrees or denies authorization: If the user licenses, authentication system will activate the temporary token to access token, and jumps to the callback address that has previously passed to the authentication system. Then, the third-party application exchanges the temporary token for access token by triggering the callback event in the address. The corresponding temporary token is cleared if the user rejects the authorization. Therefore, the third-party application will be noticed that user is denied authorization, and the authentication system will not issue the access token.

(3) User information acquisition process:

(a) Third-party application request: After the third-party application obtains the access token and the corresponding keys, make a request with request signature which ensures that the request is credible. In order to get the user's protected information, the keys that participate in the signature algorithm must contain not only the keys that match the client's credentials, but also the keys that match the token's credentials.

(b) Server authentication: While server accepts the request for user information, it's need to verify a series of verification process as whether the request packet is legitimate, whether the requested web interface exists, whether the third-party applications have the right to call the interface, and whether the called web interface parameters are legal. After all those process passed, it can implement the business process within the server to obtain the corresponding protected resources. Among them, the protected resources are listed in the user license authority of the project.

4   System Security Testing

In order to demonstrate the effectiveness and performance of the proposed authorization system, we have conducted security experimental tests as design and injection security aspects. The operation flow is the following:

4.1   Security Testing of Design

(1) CSRF attack security testing:

Take the card data acquisition interface as an example. It obtains data normally through the website, and load JSON data from js. Then, visit http://i.sdnu.edu.cn/card/get/info interface, and check the cookie login status as well as return JSON data.

After completed the preparing work, we begin commence a CSRF attack. Try to access the web page as under the same cookie condition. If the background check request header does not contain option of X-Requested-With, it will return an error as following to prevent data leakage caused by the attack.

Error: {"status": "error", "result": "Invalid_Referer"}.

If there is an attack from third-party sites, cause the site has been prevented from cross-border attacks, it can't obtain the data as well, and will return an error as: No 'Access-Control-Allow-Origin' header is present on the requested resource.

(2) XSS attack security testing:
We process this test under the condition that there is a request tries to get data from a third-party site.

Request: >$.getJSON("http://i.sdnu.edu.cn/card/get/info?0.3132845529366785");
Response: XMLHttpRequest cannot load http://i.sdnu.edu.cn/card/get/info?Link? url1=f6LtFstZ1zpQAAbp9HC4eZtRcoFq-07mpvRYEnDQ0VcSWIm5I9qnd6HM1hhi v7Xmh2008Nd6vExMW9krveVWL:10.31324845529366785.

No 'Access-Control-Allow-Origin' header is present on the requested resource. Therefore, origin website 'http://baike.baidu.com' is not allowed to access.

It proves that the web site prevents cross-domain requests, thus, XSS attacks are unable to obtain needed data, which helps reducing the risk of user data leakage.

4.2   Security Testing of Injection

(1) Scope parameters injection testing:
We process this test under the condition that there is a process attempts to inject Scope parameters when requesting user authorization.
Request: https://i.sdnu.edu.cn/oauth/authorize_code?response_type=code&scope= 'or1=1'&client_id=00000000000000000000000000000000&oauth_version=2.0
Response: Client no permission.
The reason is that when scope in the background checking the call, there is a middle layer of the cache makes it not directly connected to the database. The injected string is simply regarded as a string rather than SQL statement processing, and the injection process is failed.

(2) Camouflage the client testing
1. User login select authorization
The attacker knows the client ID and tries to fake the client to defraud the user authorization in order to get needed data, and go on the process of user login and user authorization, the needed parameters are as shown in Table 3.
Request:https://i.sdnu.edu.cn/oauth/authorize_code?response_type= code&scope=BasicAuth,None&client_id=000000000000000000000000000000 0000&oauth_version=2.0

Table 3.

Parameters	Description
response_type	Designated as "code" in the first step
client_id	The certificate ID issued by the server to the client
redirect_uri	The redirection URI needed to return Authorize Code
scope	Scope of authority for this certification application
oauth_version	Requested authentication version (2.0)

2. Return authorize code
   Use the default callback address: https://i.sdnu.edu.cn/oauth/?authorize_code=
   YoCRIJWg932Y1NioNeO2uleyHtVN4Ps5
3. Use the authorize code to exchange for access token
   The attacker doesn't know the Client Secret while in the process of using the
   authorization code in exchange for Token. Needed parameters are as shown in
   Table 4.

Request: https://i.sdnu.edu.cn/oauth2/access_token?grant_type=authorization_
code&authorize_code=YoCRIJWg932Y1NioNeO2uleyHtVN4Ps5&client_id=000000
00000000000000000000000000

Response: Client no permission.

It proves that the third-party application should ensure that the process of accessing
to Access Token should be carried out in the server, which will not be crawled to
Secret. So that by implementing this system we can provide more security of data and
also provide efficient user authentication [18].

Table 4. Authorization parameters

Parameters	Description
grant_type	Designated as "authorization_code" in this step
authorize_code	The authorization code obtained in the previous step
client_id	The client ID

5 Performance Analysis

After a period of the OAuth2.0-based system security on-line testing, we find that the
Token within the validity period is stored in the cache database as expected. From the
process of user Authentication to obtain Token, it's certified that the whole operation
follows OAuth2.0 protocol, as well as the https protocol ensures the security of
communication process, on the whole, the smart campus unified authentication system
is running stable. In this paper, we mainly enhanced the smart campus authentication
system performance include following four aspects.

5.1 Basic User Data Management

The main characteristics of user authentication are collected through a unified data
specification standard. This forms a basic database including teacher information,
student information, school information, and class information, which helps to achieve
the independent management and verification of users between different applications.
The database is used for both customization and authentication [19]. Then, the
third-party application access providers can obtain relevant information through the
cross-platform, and compatible interface with permission [20]. It facilitates in solving
problems of user data synchronization, and updating between application systems.

5.2   Security Issues

OAuth2.0 is a protocol with authorization function to control and manage access to web services [21]. In the process of user authentication, in OAuth2.0 protocol, the user does not have to disclose user name, password, and other information to a third-party platform. Authorized HTTP communication uses digital signatures, and access tokens to replace user information. This helps to avoid leakage of sensitive user information. In user center, the user information is transmitted to the application system through the message bus with unified account management and operation no longer without an individual's explicit consent [22]. In addition, OAuth2.0 can be combined with PKI (public key infrastructure) to enrich the authentication function. It solves the problem of identity authentication, authorization problems, and user resource security under the open architecture of a cloud environment.

5.3   Cross-Platform Resource Sharing

The resource sharing platform stores only the address information of the resource and the resource token. It does not store the resource itself. The OAuth protocol has been designed to handle computation and storage overhead while providing a standard and simple authorization mechanism for resource access by third-party applications [13]. Through the security API support protocol, access can be facilitated with other applications. This is convenient in providing relevant data for their own applications, and will enhance the usability of the smart campus system. In this aspect, it solves the problem of resource-dispersants and duplicated storage.

5.4   Application Management

Through the combination of OAuth2.0 protocol and the authority control system, this system can easily access classification of applications. The administrator can allow or deny application access according to the actual situation [23]. If the application only needs simple resources, such as a user's basic information, it can be completed by the application developer self-application, and administrators post-audit. If the requested information contains sensitive resources, the developer needs to submit the main functions of the application, and the scenes that need these user resources. This will increase the application access flexibility, and solve the problem of system management cost in the process of user authentication of the smart campus system.

6   Conclusion

This paper, based on an actual situation at Shandong Normal University, proposes a smart campus unified authentication system using OAuth2.0 protocol to achieve third-party applications access and authorization. This allows users who use third-party campus applications, no longer need to provide authentication information. OAuth2.0 is the authentication method of choice by our smart campus to protect users' APIs and federate identification across domains [24]. So, it is possible for users to have safely access to the smart campus system based on cloud environment. This saves the system development costs and development cycle, which will help in successfully accessing the smart campus application system security; in addition to unified management of user information [20]. Through the testing process, it was indicated that a secure OAuth2.0 environment can be built when implemented correctly. It can also achieve the purpose of the initial design and campus information construction. As a result, this paper has a universal reference and significance to the authentication and authorization system construction of the smart campus.

Acknowledgment. This research is financially supported by the National Natural Science Foundation of China (90612003, 61602282, No. 61572301), the Natural Science Foundation of Shandong province (No. ZR2013FM008, No. ZR2016FP07), the Open Research Fund from Shandong provincial Key Laboratory of Computer Network, Grant No.: SDKLCN-2016-01, the Postdoctoral Science Foundation of China (2016M602181), and Science and technology development projects of Shandong province (2011GGH20123).

References

1. Berners-Lee, T.J.: The World-Wide Web. Comput. Netw. ISDN Syst. **25**(4), 454–459 (1992)
2. Kopecky, J., Fremantle, P., Boakes, R.: A history and future of web APIs. Inf. Technol. **56** (3), 90–97 (2014)
3. Mell, P., Grance, T.: The NIST definition of cloud computing. Commun. ACM **53**(6), 50 (2010)
4. Aldossary, S., Allen, W.: Data security, privacy, availability and integrity in cloud computing: issues and current solutions. IJACSA **7**(4), 485–498 (2016)
5. Hyeonseung, K., Chunsik, P.: Cloud computing and personal authentication service. J. Korea Inst. Inf. Secur. Cryptol. **20**(2), 11–19 (2010)
6. Grosse, E., Upadhyay, M.: Authentication at scale. IEEE Secur. Priv. **11**(1), 15–22 (2013)
7. Ferry, E., Raw, J.O., Curran, K.: Security evalution of the OAuth 2.0 Framework. Inf. Comput. Secur. **23**(1), 73–101 (2015)
8. Leiba, B.: OAuth web authorization protocol. IEEE Internet Comput. **16**, 74–77 (2012)
9. Shehab, M., Marouf, S.: Recommendation models for open authorization. IEEE Trans. Dependable Secure Comput. **9**, 1–13 (2012)
10. Huang, R.Y.: Smart Campus Construction Program and Implementation. South China University of Technology Publishing House, Guangdong (2014)
11. Phillip, J.W.: API access control with OAuth: coordinating interactions with the Internet of Things. IEEE Consum. Electron. Mag. **4**(3), 52–58 (2015)
12. Cirani, S., Picone, M., Gonizzi, P., Veltri, L., Ferrari, G.: IoT-OAS: an OAuth-based authorization service architecture for secure services in IoT scenarios. IEEE Sens. J. **15**(2), 1224–1234 (2015)
13. Sakimura, N., Bradley, J., Jones, M., Medeiros, B.D., Mortimore, C.: OpenID Connect Core 1.0 Incorporating Errata (2014). http://openid.net/specs/openid-connect-core-1_0.html
14. Rama, G.M., Kak, A.: Some structural measures of API usability. Softw. Pract. Exp. **45**(1), 75–110 (2015)
15. OpenAPI call description_OAuth2.0. http://wiki.open.qq.com/wiki/website/OpenAPI%E8% B0%83%E7%94%A8%E8%AF%B4%E6%98%8E_OAuth2.0
16. Garber, L.: The lowly API is ready to step front and center. Computer **13**, 14–17 (2013)

17. Lynch, L.: Inside the identity management game. IEEE J. Serv. Comput. **11**, 78–82 (2011)
18. Jami, S., Rao, K.S.: Providing multi user authentication and anonymous data sharing in cloud computing. IJETT **31**(1), 50–53 (2016)
19. Chess, B., Arkin, B.: Integrating user customization and authentication: the identity crisis. IEEE Secur. Priv. **8**(2), 82–85 (2012)
20. Li, X., Wang, L. Digital campus unified authentication platform research and application. JIANGXI Educ. 7–8 (2016)
21. Choi, J., Kim, J., Lee, D.K., Jang, K.S., Kim, D.J.: The OAuth2.0 web authorization protocol for the Internet Addiction Bioinformatics (IABio) database. Genom. Informatics **14**(1), 20–28 (2016)
22. Zhang, M., Shi, J.Q., Ren, E., Song, J.: OAuth2.0 in the integration of management platform for the sharing of resources research. China Chem. Trade, 182–183 (2015)
23. Wang, X.S., Du, J.B., Wang, Z.: Research and practice of OAuth authorization system in the information environment of universities. China Higher Education Information Academy, November 2014
24. Leiba, B.: OAuth web authorization protocol. IEEE Internet Comput. **16**(1), 74–77 (2012)
25. OpenID Connect Core 1.0 Incorporating Errata Set 1, vol. 8 (2014). http://openid.net/specs/openid-connect-core-1_0.html

Time Series Cluster Analysis on Electricity Consumption of North Hebei Province in China

Luhua Zhang[1], Miner Liu[2], Jingwen Xia[2], Kun Guo[3,4,5(✉)], and Jun Wang[1]

[1] Jibei Electric Power Company Limited Metering Centre,
Beijing 102208, China
[2] China University of Political Science and Law, Beijing 100088, China
[3] School of Economics and Management, University of Chinese Academy
of Sciences, Beijing 100190, China
guokun@ucas.ac.cn
[4] Research Centre on Fictitious Economy and Data Science, UCAS,
Beijing 100190, China
[5] CAS Key Laboratory of Big Data Mining and Knowledge Management,
Beijing 100190, China

Abstract. In recent years, China has vigorously promoted the building of ecological civilization and regarded green low-carbon development as one of the important directions and tasks for industrial transformation and upgrading. It calls for accelerating industrial energy conservation and consumption reduction, accelerating the implementation of cleaner production, accelerating the use of renewable resources, promoting industrial savings and cleanliness, advancing changes in low-carbon and high-efficiency production, and promoting industrial restructuring and upgrading. A series of measures have had a negative impact on the scale of industrial production in the region, thereby affecting the electricity consumption here. Based on the electricity consumption data of 31 counties in northern Hebei, this paper uses the time series clustering method to cluster the electricity consumption of 31 counties in Hebei Province. The results show that the consumption of electricity in different counties is different. The macro-control policies have different impacts on different types of counties.

Keywords: Electricity consumption · Time series clustering · Wavelet analysis

1 Introduction

In recent years, China has vigorously promoted the construction of ecological civilization. Efforts have been made to promote green development, cycle of development and low-carbon development. China seeks to create spatial patterns of resource conservation, industrial structure, mode of production and way of life, to achieve the purpose of environmental protection. The Fifth Plenary Session of the Eighth Central Committee announced that the task of reducing production capacity in the iron and steel and coal industries in 2016 has been completed. The output of raw coal fell 12.8%

© Springer International Publishing AG, part of Springer Nature 2018
Y. Shi et al. (Eds.): ICCS 2018, LNCS 10862, pp. 765–774, 2018.
https://doi.org/10.1007/978-3-319-93713-7_74

from the previous year, coke production decreased by 3.0%, and flat glass production decreased by 6.5%. Hebei made new achievement in energy saving. Hebei also has reached the goal of reducing industrial energy consumption. Hebei Province's industrial energy consumption above designated size was 210 million tons of standard coal in 2017, which was a 0.4% increase over the previous year; energy consumption per unit of industrial added value was down 4.25% from the previous year. New and old kinetic energy is being transformed from traditional industries to high-tech industries. From the perspective of investment, the investment in high-tech industries accounted for 13.8% of the provincial capital, which was an increase of 0.8% points from the first quarter. Six high-energy-consuming industries accounted for 16.3% of investment, decreasing by 0.4% points. From the perspective of output value, in the first half of the year, the proportion of the six high-energy-consuming industries accounted for 39.5% of the industry scale, which was 0.9% point lower than the same period of last year. High-tech industry accounted for 17.9%, which was an increase of 1.9% points. Investment in high-tech industries will accumulate strength for the upgrading of industrial structure in the future and will play an important role in the economic development of Hebei Province. With the decline in industrial electricity consumption and the optimization of the industrial structure, electricity consumption in Hebei counties also declines.

In order to better understand the differential development of each district and county, and to formulate a more effective macro-control policy for a certain type of county, it is necessary to analyze the characteristics of the power consumption trend in different counties and find out its commonness and characteristics. In this way, the specific members of a county and every group can have some notable characteristics, such as a similar reaction to specific events. At the same time, these groups will also support the diversity of government regulation policies. Some of these counties have similar characteristics. In order to better choose the representative counties to carry out analysis, we use a new clustering method to group the counties, and then compare and analyze the group.

2   Literatures Review

Gutiérrez-Pedrero et al., with the help of a static panel data model, found that technological advances will reduce the intensity of power consumption, material capital, and the cumulative increase in investment. However, the effect of price changes is limited. The conclusion shows that the policy on the demand side has some rigidity in changing energy intensity through price adjustments. It is necessary to supplement supply measures to improve low-carbon power generation capacity. [1]. Shahbaz et al. used a nonlinear co integration approach to investigate the impact of electricity consumption, capital formation and financial development in Portugal on economic growth. These findings show that Portugal remains an energy-dependent economy; energy is one of the major inputs to economic growth and development; and energy-saving policies should not be implemented because energy is an important engine of growth [2]. Maria et al. used panel data models and data sets from 22 European countries to analyze the impact of electricity regulation on economic growth and assess the impact of renewable energy promotion costs and network costs. The results show that these two regulatory tools have a negative impact on electricity consumption and economic growth, and estimate their growth effects from a quantitative point of view [3]. Matthew examines the balance between economic growth in the UK and the EU electricity market and the implications for policy and regulation. The UK electricity market is increasingly integrated with the European continent and is expected to be further integrated by mid-2020. This comprehensive economic benefit is estimated to be as high as about 100 lb a year, reaching 1 billion pounds [4]. The study presented by Ivan examines resident households' consumption patterns and provides near real-time categorized electricity consumption data. The results show that households that shifted their load to off-peak periods were achieved by modifying the consumption patterns for the active load of a particular consumer category. Therefore, policies on protection and demand management should be specifically formulated to stimulate the expectations of resident customers [5]. Davis et al. completed an analysis of U.S. power generation data from 2001 to 2014 in order to understand the factors that may affect the development of the power sector. This analysis shows that several "building blocks" or decarburizations strategies encouraged by the CPP are already in place in the U.S. states Utilization during analysis led to a 12% drop in CO_2 emissions [6].

Through the studies of electricity consumption in various countries, it can be seen that there is a close relationship between electricity consumption and national economic growth, but there is still relatively little research literature on electricity consumption in China. This paper analyzes the electricity consumption of 32 counties in North Hebei Province to discuss the relationship between electricity consumption and economy, policies and geographical environment.

Cuy et al. used various clustering methods to study the structure of the position marginal price on the wholesale electricity market and introduced a new correlation based on the spiky time series of event synchronization as well as the string-relatedness based on the market-provided position names another kind [7]. Rhodes, who use the data to measure the electricity in Austin, Texas 103 families, in every season, with a similar pattern of hours of electricity for household use k-means clustering algorithm are clustered into groups, and the probability of regression to determine Room Whether the main survey response can be used as a predictor of clustering results [8]. Chévez determine the impact of geographic and other man-made major social demographic factors electricity demand and electricity consumption of these homogeneous areas, using K-means clustering method, per capita consumption from the 1010 Census form a large radius of La Plata obtained the results of the analysis [9]. Bah and Azam explored the causal link between power consumption, economic growth, financial development and carbon dioxide emissions in South Africa from 1971 to 2012. The results ARDL border inspection to verify the integrity of co-existence between the included variables; Granger causality test confirmed that there is no causal relationship between electricity consumption and economic growth [10].

Therefore, the effective cluster analysis of electricity consumption can not only guide the implementation of the policy better, but also make a good review of the economic development level and industrial structure of a certain area.

In this paper, we use a new time series clustering method to cluster the electricity consumption of 32 counties in North Hebei Province. The next section will introduce our methodology briefly. The fourth part presents an empirical analysis and gives the clustering results. Finally, the conclusion constitutes Sect. 5.

3   A New Integrated Method for Time Series Clustering

As there are many effective and relatively well-clustering algorithms, we focus on how the information will be introduced to the expertise in time series mining. And we tried to combine the normal clustering algorithm with the turning point detection method based on expert experience or event mining.

There are five steps of our integrated time series clustering methodology as shown in Fig. 1.

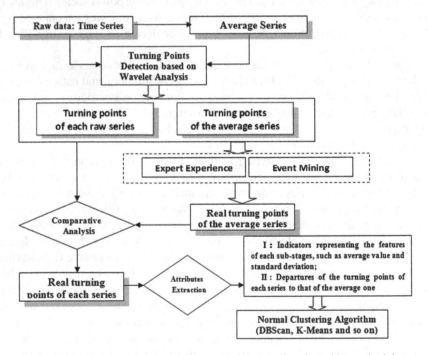

Fig. 1. Technology roadmap of the integrated time series clustering methodology

- Step 1: Detect all the turning points t_{ij} for each time series and the average series using wavelet analysis. t_{ij} is the jth turning point for series i; and for the average series i = a.
- Step 2: Based on the results of Step 1 for the average series, find several real turning points T_1, T_2, ..., T_k that can correspond to some big events using expert experiences, so that there are k + 1 stages;

- Step 3: Scan the turning points from Step 1 of each series, discard the points that far from T_1, T_2, ..., T_k and keep only k points T_{ij} like the average series.
- Step 4: In each stage, calculate the average growth rate and standard deviation. And for each series, figure out the departures from turning points Tij to the corresponding Tj. So that, there will be 2(k + 1) + k=3 k + 2 attributes of the time series.
- Step 5: Use the attributes calculated in Step 4 for clustering.

4 Empirical Analysis on Town Electricity Consumption

4.1 Data Description

In order to study the power consumption of the counties in northern Anhui, we collected electricity consumption data from January 2013 to May 2016 in 32 counties in northern Hebei Province. Due to the lack of data in Xuanhua, we only use the electricity consumption of the remaining 31 counties as samples, including: Bazhou, Changli, Wen'an, Kuancheng, Pingquan, Luanping, Ayutthaya, Fengning, Zhangbei, Qinglong, Sanhe, Gu'an, Zhulu, Shangyi, Funing, Yuxian, Huai'an, Wanquan, Chengde, Xianghe, Huailai, Yard, Chicheng, Xinglong, Kangbao, Chongli, Yangyuan, Longhua, Dachang, Yongqing and Lulong. The average power consumption of the sample and the selected three typical countries power consumption changes are shown in Fig. 2.

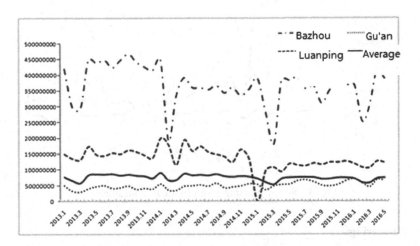

Fig. 2. Some samples of the power consumption changes.

4.2 Development Stages of Hebei Electricity Consumption

First we use wavelet decomposition and singularity detection to obtain the original turning point for each county's electricity consumption. Using the decomposition level J = 5, we find that the singularity is the most efficient at the first level. The horizontal axis k in each input signal indicates the position of this point. In our study, the horizontal axis position corresponds to the time of the event.

When location t = 1 means January 2013, t = 41 means May 2016. The obvious singularities at t = 5, 12, 17, 24, 29, 36 correspond to May 2013, December 2013, May 2014, December 2014, May 2015 and December 2015. The equidistant distribution of these singular points exactly matches the characteristics of the seasonal transformation of electricity consumption. Therefore, we have obtained seven stages throughout the period. See Fig. 2 shows that the average electricity consumption in the sample county in the different stages of the trend is broadly divided into two. In the second, fourth and sixth phases, the trend is stable and the ups and downs are small. There are obvious fluctuations in the first, third, fifth and seventh phases, and the electricity consumption in the medium term significantly reduced. However, the electricity consumption in different counties and cities also has different reactions to the changes in the phases. Taking Bazhou, Gu'an and Luanping as an example, as shown in Fig. 3, Bazhou experienced a mid-term decline in the first, third, fifth and seventh phases. However, in the second, the six stages also showed obvious ups and downs. In the first five phases, Gu'an was in line with the average level. However, the average level in the sixth phase was stable, but there was a big fluctuation in Gu'an. Luanping and the average level of roughly have the same trend.

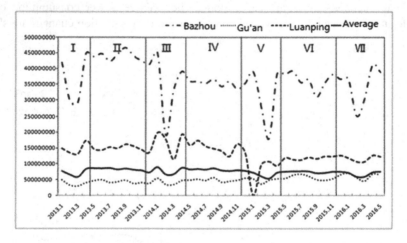

Fig. 3. Seven sub-stages of electricity consumption.

4.3 Clustering

In order to better describe the various characteristics of different stages, the indicators that represent the trend of each stage are clustered as attributes. Therefore, calculate the average growth rate, variance, and the deviations from the average of each series of turning points for each stage as attributes of the cluster analysis. Based on a total of 21 attributes in each stage, Ward's method was used to cluster 31 counties. The clustering results are shown in Table 1, 31 counties are divided into three categories.

Table 1. Results of clustering

Group no.	Number of instances	Clustered cities
1	2	Wen'an, Bazhou
2	4	Kuancheng, Pingquan, Luanping, Dacheng
3	25	Changli, Sanhe, Funing, Chengde, Chicheng, Chongli, Dachang, Fengning, Gu'an, Huai'an, Huailai, Kangbao, Longhua, Lulong, Qinglong, Shangyi, Wanquan, Weichang, Weixian, Xianghe, Xinglong, Yangyuan, Yongqing, Zhangbei

According to the results of cluster analysis, the proportions and growth rates of electricity consumption by industry in the three categories are shown in Tables 2 and 3. Figures 4, 5 and 6 show the average electricity consumption trends of primary, secondary and tertiary industries in three counties from January 2013 to May 2016.

Table 2. The proportion of electricity consumption

Group no.	Industry	2013	2014	2015	2016	Average
1	Primary industry	0.0221	0.0195	0.0214	0.0215	0.0212
	Secondary industry	0.9219	0.9171	0.9071	0.8993	0.9116
	Tertiary industry	0.0559	0.0634	0.0716	0.0792	0.0672
2	Primary industry	0.0132	0.0130	0.0193	0.0183	0.0157
	Secondary industry	0.9382	0.9411	0.9328	0.9033	0.9300
	Tertiary industry	0.0486	0.0460	0.0657	0.0783	0.0584
3	Primary industry	0.0532	0.0689	0.0833	0.0763	0.0698
	Secondary industry	0.8186	0.7884	0.7290	0.6907	0.7602
	Tertiary industry	0.1390	0.1521	0.1913	0.2331	0.1763
Average	Primary industry	0.0226	0.0222	0.0269	0.0258	0.0243
	Secondary industry	0.9164	0.9125	0.8970	0.8807	0.9024
	Tertiary industry	0.0621	0.0662	0.0817	0.0935	0.0752

The electricity consumption of the secondary industry in Group 1 accounted for an absolutely large proportion, and the ratio of electricity consumption in three industries to the average in four years was 3: 90: 7. However, the share of electricity consumption in the secondary industry dropped continuously in four years, corresponding to the ever-increasing share of electricity consumption in the tertiary industry. The proportion of primary electricity consumption has been stable at a small value.

In Group 2, the proportion of second-generation electricity consumption in the same county reaches an average of 93% within four years. The tertiary industry accounts for more electricity consumption than the first industry. Similar to the first category of counties, the share of electricity consumption in the secondary industry shows a downward trend while that of the tertiary industry shows a rising trend. The proportion of electricity consumption in the primary industry also increases.

Table 3. Electricity consumption growth rate

Group no.	Industry	2014	2015	2016
1	Primary industry	−0.1185	0.0945	0.0083
	Secondary industry	−0.0053	−0.0109	−0.0086
	Tertiary industry	0.1336	0.1292	0.1060
2	Primary industry	−0.0187	0.4869	−0.0494
	Secondary industry	0.0031	−0.0088	−0.0316
	Tertiary industry	−0.0548	0.4294	0.1925
3	Primary industry	0.2938	0.2100	−0.0845
	Secondary industry	−0.0368	−0.0754	−0.0526
	Tertiary industry	0.0944	0.2573	0.2185

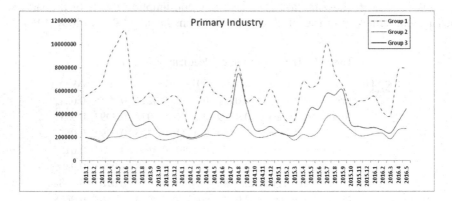

Fig. 4. Primary industry electricity consumption of three groups.

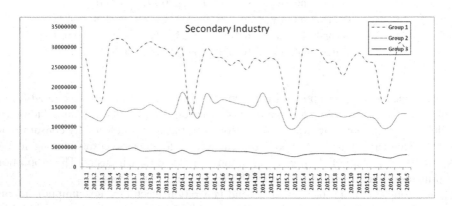

Fig. 5. Secondary industry electricity consumption of three groups

The electricity consumption of the third type of secondary industry is slightly smaller, about 80%, and the decline is most obvious in four years. The proportion of tertiary industry electricity consumption also has increased by 10% points in four years.

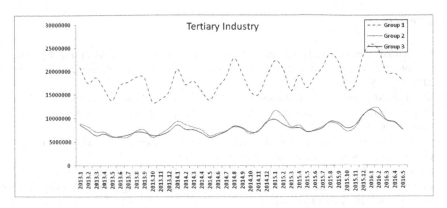

Fig. 6. Tertiary industry electricity consumption of three groups

In the past two years, the proportion of primary industry electricity consumption also increased obviously. It can be seen that the third type of county has a better industrial structure and more remarkable achievements in the transformation of the industrial structure.

In Group 3, the growth rate of electricity consumption by secondary industry in three years was almost all negative while that of the tertiary industry was all positive. It can be seen that the overall policy of industrial restructuring in Hebei Province has achieved initial success. Finally, classification has little to do with geographic information.

5 Conclusions

In this paper, we develop a new method of time series clustering. Based on the wavelet analysis, we found seven phases of electricity consumption in Hebei province from January 2013 to May 2016, and then clustered the different stages and locations of turning points as the characteristic indicators. This better reflects the classification results in different stages of change and the sensitivity of large events. The results show that 31 sample counties can be divided into three categories. Judging from the average trend of electricity consumption in each group, the progress of industrial structure optimization in each county has some differences. Group 1's primary industry is relatively stable, while Group 2 is all in an upward trend except for the secondary industry. Group 3 has the highest sensitivity to policies and the secondary industry has the most obvious drop in electricity consumption. From this we can make an effective suggestion: the policy of optimizing the industrial structure can be more targeted at certain counties, so that all counties can further implement energy conservation and emission reduction. At the same time, the first group and the second groups of counties to third types of counties can be studied to improve the policy sensitivity, optimize the industrial structure as far as possible, and reduce the energy consumption of the industry.

References

1. Gutiérrez-Pedrero, M.J., Tarancón, M.Á., Río, P.D., Alcántara, V.: Analysing the drivers of the intensity of electricity consumption of non-residential sectors in Europe. Appl. Energy **211**, 743–754 (2018)
2. Shahbaz, M., Benkraiem, R., Miloudi, A., Lahiani, A., Shahbaz, M., Benkraiem, R., et al.: Production function with electricity consumption and policy implications in portugal. MPRA Paper **110**, 588–599 (2017)
3. Costacampi, M., Garciaquevedo, J., Trujillobaute, E.: Electricity regulation and economic growth. Social Science Electronic Publishing (2018)
4. Lockwood, M., Froggatt, A., Wright, G., Dutton, J.: The implications of brexit for the electricity sector in Great Britain: trade-offs between market integration and policy influence. Energy Pol. **110**, 137–143 (2017)
5. Kantor, I., Rowlands, I.H., Parker, P.: Aggregated and disaggregated correlations of household electricity consumption with time-of-use shifting and conservation. Energy Build. **139**, 326–339 (2016)
6. Davis, C., Bollinger, L.A., Dijkema, G.P.J., Kazmerski, L.: The state of the states. Renew. Sustain. Energy Rev. **60**(3), 631–652 (2016)
7. Cuy, T., Caravelli, F., Ududec, C.: Correlations and clustering in wholesale electricity markets. Papers (2017)
8. Rhodes, J.D., Cole, W.J., Upshaw, C.R., Edgar, T.F., Webber, M.E.: Clustering analysis of residential electricity demand profiles. Appl. Energy **135**, 461–471 (2014)
9. Chévez, P., Barbero, D., Martini, I., Discoli, C.: Application of the k-means clustering method for the detection and analysis of areas of homogeneous residential electricity consumption at the Great La Plata Region, Buenos Aires, Argentina. Sustain. Cities Soc. **32**, 115–129 (2017)
10. Bah, M.M., Azam, M.: Investigating the relationship between electricity consumption and economic growth: evidence from South Africa. Renew. Sustain. Energy Rev. **80**, 531–537 (2017)

Effective Semi-supervised Learning Based on Local Correlation

Xiao-Yu Zhang[1]([✉]), Shupeng Wang[1]([✉]), Xin Jin[2]([✉]), Xiaobin Zhu[3]([✉]),
and Binbin Li[1]

[1] Institute of Information Engineering, Chinese Academy of Sciences,
Beijing, China
zhangxiaoyu@iie.ac.cn
[2] National Computer Network Emergency Response Technical
Team/Coordination Center of China, Beijing, China
[3] Beijing Technology and Business University, Beijing, China

Abstract. Traditionally, the manipulation of unlabeled instances is solely based on prediction of the existing model, which is vulnerable to ill-posed training set, especially when the labeled instances are limited or imbalanced. To address this issue, this paper investigate the local correlation based on the entire data distribution, which is leveraged as informative guidance to ameliorate the negative influence of biased model. To formulate the self-expressive property between instances within a limited vicinity, we develop the sparse self-expressive representation learning method based on column-wise sparse matrix optimization. Optimization algorithm is presented via alternating iteration. Then we further propose a novel framework, named semi-supervised learning based on local correlation, to effectively integrate the explicit prior knowledge and the implicit data distribution. In this way, the individual prediction from the learning model is refined by collective representation, and the pseudo-labeled instances are selected more effectively to augment the semi-supervised learning performance. Experimental results on multiple classification tasks indicate the effectiveness of the proposed algorithm.

Keywords: Semi-supervised learning · Local correlation · Self-expressive representation · Sparse matrix optimization · Predictive confidence

1 Introduction

Machine learning has manifested its superiority in providing effective and efficient solutions for various applications [1–5]. In order to learn a robust model, the labeled instances are indispensable in that they convey precious prior knowledge and offer informative instruction. Unfortunately, manually labeling is labor-intensive and time-consuming. The cost associated with the labeling process often renders a fully labeled training set infeasible. In contrast, the acquisition of unlabeled instances is relatively inexpensive. One can easily have access to abundant unlabeled instances. As a result, when dealing with machine learning problems, we typically have to start with very limited labeled instances and plenty of unlabeled ones [6–8].

© Springer International Publishing AG, part of Springer Nature 2018
Y. Shi et al. (Eds.): ICCS 2018, LNCS 10862, pp. 775–781, 2018.
https://doi.org/10.1007/978-3-319-93713-7_75

Recent researches indicate that the unlabeled instances, when used in conjunction with the labeled instances, can produce considerable improvement in learning performance. Semi-supervised learning [9, 10], as a machine learning mechanism that jointly explores both labeled and unlabeled instances, has aroused widespread research attention. In semi-supervised learning, the exploration into unlabeled instances is largely dependent on the model trained with the labeled instances. On one hand, the insufficient or imbalanced labeled instances are inclined to lead to ill-posed learning model, which will consequently jeopardize the learning performance of semi-supervised learning. On the other hand, pair-wise feature similarity is widely used when estimating the data distribution, which is not necessarily plausible for semantic-level recommendation of class labels.

To address the aforementioned issues, this paper proposes a novel, named semi-supervised learning based on local correlation. Robust local correlation between the instances is estimated via sparse self-expressive representation learning, which formulates the self-expressive property between instances within a limited vicinity into a column-wise sparse matrix optimization problem. Based on the local correlation, an augmented semi-supervised learning framework is implemented, which takes into account both the explicit prior knowledge and the implicit data distribution. The learning sub-stages, including individual prediction, collective refinement, and dynamic model update with pseudo-labeling, are iterated until convergence. Finally, an effective learning model is obtained with encouraging experimental results on multiple classification applications.

2   Notation

In the text that follows, we let matrix $X = [x_1, \ldots, x_n] = X_L \bigcup X_U \in \mathbb{R}^{m \times n}$ denote the entire dataset, where m is the dimension of features, and n is the total number of instances. In X, each column x_i represents a m-dimensional instance. $X_L \in \mathbb{R}^{m \times n_L}$ and $X_U \in \mathbb{R}^{m \times n_U}$ are the labeled and unlabeled dataset, respectively, where n_L and n_U are the numbers of labeled and unlabeled instances, respectively. The corresponding class labels of the instances are denoted as matrix $Y = Y_L \bigcup Y_U \in \mathbb{R}^{c \times n}$, where c is the number of classes, and $Y_L \in \mathbb{R}^{c \times n_L}$ and $Y_U \in \mathbb{R}^{c \times n_U}$ are the label matrices corresponding to the labeled and unlabeled dataset, respectively. For the labeled instance $x \in X_L$, its label $y \in Y_L$ is already known and denoted as a c-dimensional binary vector $y = [y_1, \ldots, y_c]^T \in \{0, 1\}^c$, whose ith element y_i ($1 \leq i \leq c$) is a class indicator, i.e. $y_i = 1$ if instance x falls into class i, and $y_i = 0$ otherwise. For the unlabeled instance $x \in X_U$, its label $y \in Y_U$ is unrevealed and initially evaluated as $y = 0$.

3   Robust Local Correlation Estimation

The locally linear property is widely applicable for smooth manifolds. In this scenario, an instance can be concisely represented by its close neighbors. As a result, the underlying local correlation is an effective reflection of the data distribution, and can be subsequently leveraged as instructive guidance to improve the performance of model learning. Given the instance matrix X, we develop a robust local correlation estimation method in a unsupervised fashion, which aims to infer a correlation matrix $W \in \mathbb{R}^{n \times n}$ based on the instances themselves regardless of their labels. The formulation is based on two major considerations. On one hand, an instance can be represented as a linear combination of the closely related neighbors. On the other hand, only a small number of neighbors are involved for the representation of an instance. In light of that, we estimate the robust local correlation between the instances via a novel Sparse Self-Expressive Representation Learning (SSERL), which is formulated as the follows.

$$\min_W \left\| W^T \right\|_{2,1}$$
$$\text{s.t.} X = XW, \text{diag}(W) = 0, W \geq 0 \tag{1}$$

where the minimization of $\ell_{2,1}$-norm $\left\| W^T \right\|_{2,1}$ ensures column sparsity of W.

To make the problem more flexible, the equality constraint $X = XW$ is relaxed to allow expressive errors [11], and the corresponding objective is modified as follows.

$$\min_W \mathcal{L}(W) = \left\| X - XW \right\|_F^2 + \lambda \left\| W^T \right\|_{2,1}$$
$$\text{s.t.} \text{diag}(W) = 0, W \geq 0 \tag{2}$$

In $\mathcal{L}(W)$, the first term stands for the self-expressive loss and the second term is the column sparsity regularization. λ quantifies the tradeoff between the two terms.

The optimization problem (2) is not directly solvable. According to the general half-quadratic framework for regularized robust learning [12], we introduce an augmented cost function $\mathcal{A}(W, p)$ as follows.

$$\mathcal{A}(W, p) = \left\| X - XW \right\|_F^2 + \lambda \text{Tr}\left(WPW^T \right) \tag{3}$$

where p is an auxiliary vector, and P is a diagonal matrix defined as $P = \text{diag}(p)$. The operator $\text{diag}(\cdot)$ places a vector on the main diagonal of a square matrix.

With W given, the i-th entry of p is calculated as follows.

$$p_i = \frac{1}{2 \| w_i \|_2} \tag{4}$$

With p fixed, W can be optimized in a column-by-column manner as follows.

$$w_i = \left(X^T X + \lambda p_i I \right)^{-1} X^T x_i \tag{5}$$

Based on (4) and (5), the auxiliary vector p and the correction matrix W are jointly optimized in an alternating iterative way. At the end of each iteration, the following post-processing is further implemented according to the constraints.

$$\begin{cases} W_\Omega = 0, \Omega = \{(i,j) | 1 \leq i = j \leq n\} \\ W = \max(W, 0) \end{cases} \tag{6}$$

After convergence, the optimal correlation matrix W is obtained, which can serve as an informative clue for the revelation of the underlying data distribution and the construction of the subsequent model learning.

4 Semi-supervised Learning Based on Local Correlation

Different from the traditional semi-supervised learning mechanism that solely depends on the classification model when exploring the unlabeled instances, the proposed SSL-LC takes into account both model prediction and local correlation. By iteration of the following three steps, SSL-LC is implemented in an effective way and the optimal learning model is obtained after convergence of the algorithm.

Step 1: Individual Label Prediction by Supervised Learning

As we know, for the labeled dataset $X_L \in \mathbb{R}^{m \times n_L}$, the corresponding label set $Y_L \in \mathbb{R}^{c \times n_L}$ is known beforehand. Using (X_L, Y_L) as training dataset, the classification model $\mathcal{H}_\theta$: $\mathbb{R}^m \to \mathbb{R}^c$ can be obtained with off-the-shelf optimization methods. Specifically, probabilistic model can be applied based on the posterior distribution $P(y|x; \theta)$ of label y conditioned on the input x, where θ is the optimal parameter for $\mathcal{H}_\theta$ given (X_L, Y_L). For the unlabeled instance $x \in X_U$, its label y is unknown and need to be predicted by the trained classification model $\mathcal{H}_\theta$. The prediction is given in the form of a c-dimensional vector $\tilde{y} = [P(y_1 = 1|x; \theta), \ldots, P(y_c = 1|x; \theta)]^T \in [0, 1]^c$. For the i-th entry $P(y_i = 1|x; \theta)$, larger value indicates higher probability that x falls into the i-th class with respect to $\mathcal{H}_\theta$, and vice versa. Based on the learning model $\mathcal{H}_\theta$, prediction can be made on each unlabeled instance individually. The predicted label set is collectively denoted as $\tilde{Y}_U$, which represents the classification estimation from the model point of view. With the dynamic update of model $\mathcal{H}_\theta$, the predicted label $\tilde{Y}_U$ is also dynamically renewed.

Step 2: Collective Label Refinement by Self-expressing

In addition to the posterior probability estimated by model $\mathcal{H}_\theta$, the label of an unlabeled instance $x \in X_U$ can further be concisely represented by its closely related neighbors. The local correlation W calculated via SSERL reflects the underlying relevance between instances within the vicinity, and thus can serve as an informative guidance for self-expressive representation of labels. In this way, robust label refinement is achieved against potential classification errors. To be specific, the entire label matrix can be denoted as $Y_p = [Y_L, \tilde{Y}_U]$ after inference via classification. For further refinement, the local correlation matrix W is leveraged to obtain the self-expressive representation of labels in the form of $Y_s = Y_p W$. By this means, the self-expressive property with respect to the instances is transferred to the labels, and the column-wise sparsity of W guarantees the concision of representation within a constrained vicinity. Then Y_s is normalized to obtain a legitimate probability estimation Y_n, whose j-th column is calculated as:

$$[Y_n]_j = \frac{[Y_s]_j}{\max_i [Y_s]_{ij}} \tag{7}$$

Finally, since Y_L is already known and does not need to be estimated, the refined label matrix is calculated as:

$$Y_r = [Y_L, 0^{c \times n_U}] + Y_n \odot [0^{c \times n_L}, 1^{c \times n_U}] \tag{8}$$

where $\odot$ is the element-wise product of two matrices.

Step 3: Semi-supervised Model Update by Pseudo-labeling

As discussed above, the effectiveness of semi-supervised learning stems from the comprehensive exploration on both labeled and unlabeled instances, in which the unlabeled instances with high predictive confidence are assigned with pseudo-labels and recommended to the learner as additional training data. The predictive confidence is the key measurement for selection of unlabeled instances. For the j-th instance, its predictive confidence is conveniently calculated as:

$$c_j = \max_i [Y_n \odot [0^{c \times n_L}, 1^{c \times n_U}]]_{ij} \tag{9}$$

which naturally filters out the labeled instances. Since Y_n is dependent on Y_p and W, both individual classification prediction and collective local correlation are effectively integrated in the semi-supervised learning strategy. Based on the predictive confidence defined in (9), reliable and informative unlabeled instances can be selected and recommended for model update. The pseudo-label $\hat{y}_j$ associated with the j-th instance is defined as:

$$(\hat{y}_j)^i = \begin{cases} 1, & i = \arg\max_i [Y_n \odot [0^{c \times n_L}, 1^{c \times n_U}]]_{ij} \\ 0, & i \neq \arg\max_i [Y_n \odot [0^{c \times n_L}, 1^{c \times n_U}]]_{ij} \end{cases} \tag{10}$$

Using the pseudo-labeled instances as additional training data, the learning model $\mathcal{H}_\theta$ is re-trained, which brings about updated Y_p and Y_r.

5 Experiments

To validate the effectiveness of SSL-LC, we apply it to classification tasks on malware [7] and patent [6] dataset respectively, in comparison with the following methods:

- Supervised learning (SL), which trains classifier based on the labeled dataset $T = (X_L, Y_L)$, and arrives at individual prediction Y_p accordingly.
- Supervised learning with local correlation (SL-LC), which further refines the prediction with W and obtains Y_r.
- Semi-supervised learning (SSL), which selects pseudo-labeled instances R based on unrefined prediction Y_p, and updates classifier based on $T \bigcup R$.

Experiment 1: Comparison of Different Number of Labeled Instances. Firstly, we compare the classification performance with different number of labeled instances, i.e. $|T|$. The classification performance is illustrated in Fig. 1(1).

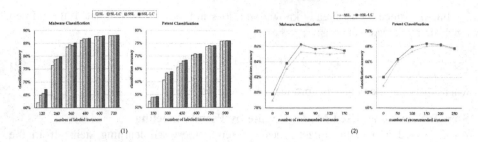

Fig. 1. The classification performance with different number of (1) labeled instances and (2) recommended instances.

Detailed analysis of experimental results are as follows, where ">" stands for "outperform(s)".

- SL-LC > SL, SSL-LC > SSL. Under the instructive guidance of local correlation, the individual prediction on a single instance can be further refined via collective representation. Therefore, the classification results are more coherent to the intrinsic data distribution and less vulnerable to overfitting with local correlation refinement.
- SSL > SL, SSL-LC > SL-LC. Compared with supervised learning, semi-supervised learning further leverages the unlabeled instances to extend the training dataset, and thus receives higher classification performance.
- When the number of labeled instances is large enough, the difference between the four methods is negligible. It is indicated that the proposed SSL-LC is especially helpful for classification problems with insufficient labeled instances.

Experiment 2: Comparison of Different Number of Recommended Instances. We further compare the classification performance with different number of recommended instances, i.e. K, where SL and SL-LC are treated as special cases of SSL and SSL-LC with $K = 0$. The classification performance is illustrated in Fig. 1(2).

As we can see, at first, the classification accuracy improves with the increase of K, because the model can learn from more and more instances. However, when K is large enough, further increase will lead to deterioration of classification performance. This results from the incorporation of the less confident pseudo-labeled instances, which inevitably brings about unreliable model.

6   Conclusion

In this paper, we have proposed an effective semi-supervised learning framework based on local correlation. Compared with traditional semi-supervised learning methods, the contributions of the work are as follows. Firstly, both the explicit prior knowledge and the implicit data distribution are integrated into a unified learning procedure, where the individual prediction from the dynamically updated learning model is refined by collective representation. Secondly, robust local correlation, rather than pair-wise similarity, is leveraged for model augment, which is formulated as a column-wise sparse matrix optimization problem. Last but not least, effective optimization is designed, in which the optimal solution is progressively reached in an iterative fashion. Experiments on multiple classification tasks indicate the effectiveness of the proposed algorithm.

Acknowledgement. This work was supported by National Natural Science Foundation of China (Grant 61501457, 61602517), Open Project Program of National Laboratory of Pattern Recognition (Grant 201800018), and Open Project Program of the State Key Laboratory of Mathematical Engineering and Advanced Computing (Grant 2017A05), and National Key Research and Development Program of China (Grant 2016YFB0801305).

References

1. Christopher, M.B.: Pattern Recognition and Machine Learning. Springer, New York (2016)
2. Witten, I.H., Frank, E., Hall, M.A., Pal, C.J.: Data Mining: Practical Machine Learning Tools and Techniques. Morgan Kaufmann, San Francisco (2016)
3. Zhang, X., Xu, C., Cheng, J., Lu, H., Ma, S.: Effective annotation and search for video blogs with integration of context and content analysis. IEEE Trans. Multimedia **11**(2), 272–285 (2009)
4. Liu, Y., Zhang, X., Zhu, X., Guan, Q., Zhao, X.: Listnet-based object proposals ranking. Neurocomputing **267**, 182–194 (2017)
5. Zhang, K., Yun, X., Zhang, X.Y., Zhu, X., Li, C., Wang, S.: Weighted hierarchical geographic information description model for social relation estimation. Neurocomputing **216**, 554–560 (2016)
6. Zhang, X.Y., Wang, S., Yun, X.: Bidirectional active learning: a two-way exploration into unlabeled and labeled data set. IEEE Trans. Neural Netw. Learn. Syst. **26**(12), 3034–3044 (2015)
7. Zhang, X.Y., Wang, S., Zhu, X., Yun, X., Wu, G., Wang, Y.: Update vs. upgrade: modeling with indeterminate multi-class active learning. Neurocomputing **162**, 163–170 (2015)
8. Zhang, X.: Interactive patent classification based on multi-classifier fusion and active learning. Neurocomputing **127**, 200–205 (2014)
9. Zhu, X., Goldberg, A.B.: Introduction to semi-supervised learning. Synth. Lect. Artif. Intell. Mach. Learn. **3**(1), 1–130 (2009)
10. Soares, R.G., Chen, H., Yao, X.: Semisupervised classification with cluster regularization. IEEE Trans. Neural Netw. Learn. Syst. **23**(11), 1779–1792 (2012)
11. Zhang, X.Y.: Simultaneous optimization for robust correlation estimation in partially observed social network. Neurocomputing **205**, 455–462 (2016)
12. He, R., Zheng, W.S., Tan, T., Sun, Z.: Half-quadratic-based iterative minimization for robust sparse representation. IEEE Trans. PAMI **36**(2), 261–275 (2014)

Detection and Prediction of House Price Bubbles: Evidence from a New City

Hanwool Jang[1], Kwangwon Ahn[1], Dongshin Kim[2], and Yena Song[3(✉)]

[1] KAIST, Daejeon 34141, Republic of Korea
[2] Pepperdine University, Malibu, CA 90263, USA
[3] Chonnam National University, Gwangju 61186, Republic of Korea
y.song@chonnam.ac.kr

Abstract. In the early stages of growth of a city, housing market fundamentals are uncertain. This could attract speculative investors as well as actual housing demand. Sejong is a recently built administrative city in South Korea. Most government departments and public agencies have moved into it, while others are in the process of moving or plan to do so. In Sejong, a drastic escalation in house prices has been noted over the last few years, but at the same time, the number of vacant housing units has increased. Using the present value model, lease-price ratio, and log-periodic power law, this study examines the bubbles in the Sejong housing market. The analysis results indicate that (i) there are significant house price bubbles, (ii) the bubbles are driven by speculative investment, and (iii) the bubbles are likely to burst earlier here than in other cities. The approach in this study can be applied to identifying pricing bubbles in other cities.

Keywords: Newly developed city · Real estate bubble
Complex system

1 Introduction

In newly developed cities, housing market fundamentals are difficult to predict. Many factors affecting the housing market, such as economic conditions, educational environment, and infrastructure, are largely uncertain. Sejong is a newly built city in South Korea, whose purpose is to function as an administrative center, similar to Washington DC in the USA. The legislative plan for the city was enacted in 2003, and government departments and public agencies started to move into it in 2012. As of 2017, the main ministry offices had completed their relocation. The key purposes of building a new administrative city were: (i) to diversify the role of a heavily laden Seoul, which worked as both an administrative capital and financial center; and (ii) to boost the local economy of Sejong and the surrounding area.

© Springer International Publishing AG, part of Springer Nature 2018
Y. Shi et al. (Eds.): ICCS 2018, LNCS 10862, pp. 782–795, 2018.
https://doi.org/10.1007/978-3-319-93713-7_76

Sejong has recently experienced a sharp rise in house (condominium[1]) prices (Fig. 1(a)). Indeed, condominium prices have increased persistently over the last few years in a national wide. Sejong has experienced a similar trend, although its price increase began later than both that of Seoul and the country as a whole. The government implemented special regulations to prevent the overheat of housing market in Sejong, but the house prices continued to rise. On the other hands, the vacancy rate indicates that in comparison with other major cities, something unusual is happening in Sejong. The vacancy rate in the Sejong housing market hit 20% in 2015, while other major cities experienced on average only that of 5.2% rate (Fig. 1(b)). This exceptional price appreciation appears that it has not been driven by housing demand while implying potential bubbles in Sejong.

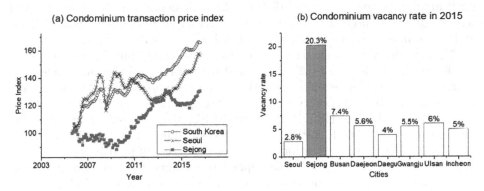

Fig. 1. Condominium price (2006 = 100) and vacancy rate are from Korea National Statistics (KNS).

Real estate prices in new cities have not been well studied in the recent literature [10, 11, 20, 23, 31]. Existing studies have focused on employment changes or the structure of a new city, rather than focusing on the housing market as their major concern. In order to bridge this gap, this paper aims to empirically evaluate the economic impacts on a new administrative city, Sejong, in terms of a real estate bubble.

First, to identify the aforementioned a real estate bubble we employed the present value model: in this calculation, the housing prices and rents with the discount rate are used. In the literatures, various approaches have been applied to detect real estate bubbles. Many of them have tried to establish the fundamental value of house price, which can be considered as the equilibrium price of

---

[1] In South Korea, the main type of housing is the condominium, as explained in the data Sect. 2.2. A condominium building consists of multiple attached units in a multi-story building, but ownership of each unit is separate. These types of condominium are referred to as apartments in South Korea. We use the term condominium (instead of apartment) throughout this paper.

supply and demand. Bourassa et al. [3] argued that house prices at 20% above their fundamental values can be seen as a sign of bubbles. Abraham [1], and Hendershott and Roche [27] constructed the statistical models to estimate fundamental market values. In both studies, the statistically significant difference between fundamental values and actual house prices was interpreted as a sign of bubbles. Conversely, Meese and Wallace [24] used the present value model and analyzed the bubble using house prices and rents, while Mikhed and Zemčík [25] used fundamental variables including real house rent, mortgage rate, personal income, building cost, stock market wealth, and population. Having with an evidence from their univariate unit root and cointegration tests, they concluded that there had been a house price bubble in the USA prior to 2006. Using data on 20 districts in Paris from 1984 to 1993, another study found that a house price bubble had spread from wealthy districts, moving to medium-priced districts, until finally reaching low-priced districts [28]. As mentioned above, in the current study we adopted the present value model which reflects true house prices and rents, in accordance with both Campbell and Shiller [5] and Wang [32].

Next, in order to analyze the cause of the real estate bubble, we employed the lease-price ratio. Lind [22] categorized house price bubbles into three categories: pure speculative bubble, irrational expectations bubble, and irrational institutions bubble. Of these, we focused on the speculative bubble in this paper.

Finally, the Log-Periodic Power Law (LPPL) was adopted to estimate the critical time of the bubble. LPPL was first developed in statistical physics, subsequently gaining a wider attention because of its successful predictions [7,13,14]. In real estate research, LPPL was applied to examine the USA and UK real estate markets which exhibited an ultimately unsustainable speculative bubble [34,35].

In summary, three approaches are applied in this research: the present value model for detecting housing bubbles, the lease-price ratio for identifying the cause of bubble and finally, the LPPL for estimating the critical time of the bubble burst.

2   Methods and Data

2.1   Methods

Present Value Model. To link the present value of an asset to its future income stream, in the way of cointegration, both Campbell and Shiller [5], and Wang [32] provided a model for testing expectations and rationality in financial markets. The present value of an asset is defined by

$$Y_t = \frac{1}{1+r} \sum_{i=0}^{\infty} \frac{1}{(1+r)^i} E_t y_{t+i}, \tag{1}$$

where Y_t is the present value of an asset as represented by the real estate price; y_t is the income as represented by rent derived from owning a real estate during the time period $(t-1, t)$; E_t is the expectations operator; and r is the discount rate. According to the present value model, if both the real estate price and rent have a unit root, they are cointegrated. This can be identified by a linear relationship. We define a new variable, called spread, as follows:

$$S_t \equiv Y_t - \theta y_t.$$

It can be seen that θ is $\frac{1}{r}$ for the dividend type of income stream. Subtracting θy_t from both sides of (1) yields

$$S_t = E_t \frac{1}{r} \sum_{i=1}^{\infty} \frac{1}{(1+r)^i} \Delta y_{t+i}. \tag{2}$$

From (2), if y_t has a unit root and Δy_t is stationary, S_t will be stationary as well. This means that Y_t and y_t have a cointegrating relation. More than that, the effect of a "rational bubble" alternative is easily observed from (2). Let this bubble term b_t satisfy

$$b_t = \frac{1}{1+r} E_t b_{t+1},$$

where b_t is a rational bubble, and thus induces explosive behavior of S_t and ΔY_t through (2). If there is a bubble, it can be noted that

$$\bar{Y}_t = \frac{1}{1+r} \sum_{i=o}^{\infty} \frac{1}{(1+r)^i} E_t y_{t+i} + b_t. \tag{3}$$

If b_t is added to the right-hand side of (1) as (3), it appears on the right-hand side of (2). Therefore, a test for the existence of a bubble is equivalent to that for cointegrating relationship between the present value Y_t and the income y_t. The implications of the above equations can be summarized: if the real estate market is rational, the house price and rent variables should be cointegrated, and the spread between the price and rent is stationary; without a cointegrating relation between the two, the spread is non-stationary and a "rational bubble," which by definition is explosive, exists in the market.

Therefore, in this study we use cointegration between price and rent as a criterion for the existence of a bubble in the market. Although the cointegration relationship can identify the existence of bubbles, it cannot fully explain the cause of bubbles. In the following, we further investigate the causality of bubbles, originating from speculation.

Lease-Price Ratio. In South Korea, the lease-price ratio is often used as a measure of speculative investment in the real estate market. There are two types of house rents in the Korean real estate market. For the purpose of simplicity, we define these as lease and rent. If a tenant pays a monthly rent with or without a deposit and the landlord keeps the monthly rent paid, it is called rent. Lease is where tenants have to make a substantial deposit (normally between 50 and 80% of the house price) for no monthly rent during their tenancy. The landlord must refund the tenant's lump sum deposit at the termination of the term, which is usually two years. The landlord receives interest income on the deposit or can invest the deposit in other assets. These returns from interest earnings can be considered as the value of monthly rents.

The lease-price ratio implies demand for speculative investment in the housing market. Yoon [33] noted that landlords might invest the deposits in the purchase of other houses for speculative purposes, thereby supplying more leases. A large proportion (approximately 70%) of landlords spends the deposits on purchasing another house or building [33]. The lease-price ratio can be a good proxy of speculative investment in a market bubble.

The KNS publishes the lease-price ratio every month. The lease-price ratio takes the form of the equation shown below:

$$\text{Lease} - \text{Price ratio} = \frac{\text{Lease}}{\text{House Price}}.$$

We can assume that if there are more speculators than people who intend to actually live in a property, the lease-price ratio will decline because speculative supply is higher than demand for leases. Thus, we can effectively identify the speculative bubble if the ratio declines or stays low compared with other regions.

Still, it remains unclear whether the lease-price ratio is driven mainly by lease supply or by house price. Identifying the relationship between lease and price is important not only for explaining the lease-price ratio itself but also for understanding the speculative investment associated with lease supply. Therefore, prior to examining the lease-price ratio we analyzed the generalized spillover effect from lease to house price in accordance with [9,18,26]. We used a generalized vector autoregressive framework with forecast-error variance decompositions $\theta_{ij}^g(H)$ for $H = 1, 2, \cdots$. Variance decompositions allowed us to split forecast error variances of each variable into parts attributable to various system shocks [8]. This helps us to ascertain the direction of volatility spillovers across major asset classes. We measured the directional volatility spillovers received by index i from all others j as follows:

$$S_{i\cdot}^g(H) = \frac{\sum_{\substack{j=1 \\ j \neq i}}^{N} \tilde{\theta}_{ij}^g(H)}{\sum_{i,j=1}^{N} \tilde{\theta}_{ij}^g(H)} \cdot 100,$$

$$\tilde{\theta}_{ij}^g(H) = \frac{\theta_{ij}^g(H)}{\sum_{j=1}^{N} \theta_{ij}^g(H)},$$

where we expressed the ratio as a percentage. In a similar fashion, the directional spillovers transmitted by index i to all others j can be measured as follows:

$$S_{\cdot i}^g(H) = \frac{\sum_{\substack{j=1 \\ j \neq i}}^{N} \tilde{\theta}_{ji}^g(H)}{\sum_{i,j=1}^{N} \tilde{\theta}_{ji}^g(H)} \cdot 100.$$

This gives us the net spillover from i to all others j as

$$S_i^g(H) = S_{\cdot i}^g(H) - S_{i\cdot}^g(H).$$

Thus, we obtain the set of directional spillover effects while providing the total and net spillover indices.

The LPPL Model. One of the key ingredients of the LPPL is a power law, which is made up of a complex system, such as the economy. The power law theory indicates that the existence of a long tail, which occurs rarely, has huge effects. There is also a short head, which occurs frequently but with much less impact. Economic systems are unstable and complex, with fewer possibilities of causing a big loss, and so there are many economic phenomena that can be explained by the power law [6, 29].

With regard to the internal mechanism of the LPPL, there is a self-organizing economy under competing influences of positive and negative feedback mechanisms [30]. This feedback leads to herding behavior in purchases during a boom and in sales during a recession. In general, during a boom, because of investors' overconfidence, imitative behavior, and cooperation among each other, investors re-invest in houses in expectation of higher prices later on, therefore this cycle goes repeatedly. Such positive feedback causes speculative bubbles and develops through the mechanism of herding behavior, which is a result of interactions between investors [34]. Collective behavior increases up to a certain point, called the critical time, from which the LPPL predicts the crash date of bubbles. Therefore, the critical time can be detected through signs of faster-than-exponential growth and its decoration by log-periodic oscillations [35]. Faster-than-exponential (super-exponential, hyperbolic, or power law) growth means that the growth rate itself is increasing while signaling an unsustainable regime.

Mathematically, these ideas are captured by the power law equation shown below:

$$\ln p(t) = A + B(t_c - t)^\beta, \tag{4}$$

where $p(t)$ is the house price or index and t_c is an estimate of the bursting of bubbles, so that $t < t_c$ and A, B, and β are the coefficients. An extension of this power law (4) takes the form of LPPL as follows

$$y_t = A + B(t_c - t)^\beta \{1 + C \cos[\omega \log(t_c - t) + \phi]\},$$

where $y_t > 0$ is the price or the log of the price at time t, $A > 0$ is the price at the critical time t_c, and $B < 0$ is the increase in y_t over time before the crash when C is close to 0; $C \in [-1, 1]$ controls the magnitude of the oscillations around the exponential trend, $t_c > 0$ is the critical time, $\beta \in [0, 1]$ is the exponent of the power law growth, $\omega > 0$ is the frequency of the fluctuations during the bubble, and $\phi \in [0, 2\pi]$ is a phase parameter.

In this study, house price index was fitted to the LPPL model and seven parameters estimated to predict the critical time. The parameter set must be such that the root mean square error (RMSE) between the observed and predicted values of the LPPL model is minimized [2]:

$$RMSE = \sqrt{\frac{1}{T} \sum_{t=1}^{T} (Y_t - y_t)^2},$$

where Y_t is the empirical value at time t. T is the number of trading dates.

2.2 Data

Condominiums are the single dominant housing type in Korea. In 2016, 48.1% of people lived in a condominium while 35.3% of people lived in single family house. In Sejong, about 60% of the housing supply was in the form of condominiums in 2015 and this figure increases up to 77% in 2017 [19]. The KNS office publishes the Condominium Transaction Price Index (CTPI) and the Rent Index (RI), a monthly measure of the price and rent changes, and they are normalized by 100 in January 2006 and June 2015, respectively. Since 2006, the CTPI has been used extensively as an authoritative indicator of house price movements in South Korea. It is based on the largest sample of housing data, especially condominiums, and provides the longest time series data compared with any other Korean house price index.

Using the datasets described in Table 1, we detected the housing bubbles, identified the types of bubbles, and estimated the critical time of bubble bursts. A series of house prices and rents are reported. The period examined was selected according to availability of the data (the RI is only available from June 2015).

Table 1. Summary statistics

	Periods	Mean	Std.	Max.	Min.	Skew	Kurtosis
CTPI and RI							
Sejong (CTPI)	(2015.06–2017.05)	124.50	3.80	130.90	118.00	0.11	1.65
South Korea (CTPI)	(2015.06–2017.05)	162.50	2.90	166.80	157.00	0.06	1.75
Sejong (RI)	(2015.06–2017.05)	98.50	3.40	100.40	90.20	−1.87	4.68
South Korea (RI)	(2015.06–2017.05)	100.10	0.20	100.30	99.80	−0.38	2.24
Lease-price ratio							
Sejong	(2014.07–2017.06)	59.10	2.06	64.20	53.30	−0.23	3.91
South Korea	(2014.07–2017.06)	72.80	1.82	74.70	69.80	−0.54	1.61
Seoul	(2014.07–2017.06)	69.50	2.54	72.00	65.30	−0.61	1.64

3 Results

3.1 Does Sejong Have a Real Estate Bubble?

The results of the unit root tests for house price and rent are presented in Table 2. The cointegration relations between house price and rent are presented in Table 3. The cointegration test identifies the stationarity in S_t, the spread (previously defined in (2)). The Dickey-Fuller (DF), Augmented Dickey-Fuller (ADF), and PP (Phillips-Perron) tests were used to examine for the presence of a unit root. Tests were carried out for house price and rent variables at various levels and on the first difference, with and without trends. The Johansen procedure was used for cointegration tests with an unrestricted constant and restricted trend. The lag length in the cointegration tests was selected using the Schwarz Bayesian information criterion (SBIC), Hannan-Quinn information criterion (HQIC), and likelihood-ratio (LR) tests. From these results, it could be concluded that both house price and rent are $I(1)$ series, i.e., they have a unit root in their levels and are stationary after the first difference operation.

Table 2. Unit root tests with PP, DF, and ADF statistics

		PP(ρ)	PP(τ)	DF	ADF
House price	No trend				
	Sejong	0.34	0.24	0.01	0.02
	South Korea	−2.14	−1.29	−1.25	−0.56
	Trend				
	Sejong	−8.51	−2.54	−2.58	−2.36
	South Korea	−8.68	−2.16	−1.69	−3.70**
Rent	No trend				
	Sejong	0.79	0.29	1.10	−1.73
	South Korea	−0.49	−0.26	0.11	−0.09
	Trend				
	Sejong	−1.77	−0.66	−0.15	−2.35
	South Korea	−3.76	−2.47	−2.27	−3.64**
First difference of house prices	No trend				
	Sejong	−22.56***	−5.01***	−4.96***	−3.79***
	South Korea	−9.59	−2.46	−2.35	−2.98**
	Trend				
	Sejong	−23.19***	−5.08***	−5.02***	−3.86**
	South Korea	−8.82	−2.24	−2.13	−2.82
First difference of rents	No trend				
	Sejong	−10.32*	−2.37	−2.18	−3.14**
	South Korea	−24.18***	−4.36***	−4.31***	−2.18
	Trend				
	Sejong	−12.40	−2.49	−2.28	−3.83**
	South Korea	−36.41***	−6.24***	−6.39***	−3.00

*, **, and *** indicate significance at the 10%, 5%, or 1% level, respectively.

The stationarity of the spread was assessed using the cointegration test, and both λ_{max} and λ_{trace} are reported in Table 3. This shows that at the national level the null hypothesis, that there is no cointegration, can be rejected. However, for Sejong we cannot reject the null hypothesis. In other words, our evaluation of the present value model for real estate in Sejong indicates that the spread between house prices and rents is non-stationary, which can be influenced by a bubble, whilst the spread obtained at the national level shows stationarity. This suggests that a housing market bubble does exist in Sejong in contrast to the picture countrywide.

Table 3. Stationarity test of S_t: cointegration between Y_t and y_t

	Unrestricted constant		Restricted trend	
	Sejong	South Korea	Sejong	South Korea
λ_{max}	4.00	21.18**	10.40	21.74**
λ_{trace}	4.09	21.32**	13.84	29.10**

** indicates rejection of the null hypothesis, i.e., there is no cointegration, at the 5% significance level. Lag lengths for Sejong and South Korea are 2 and 4, respectively.

3.2   What Is the Cause for the Real Estate Bubble?

Figure 2(a) shows the changes in lease-price ratio for the whole country, Seoul, and Sejong. The ratio for Sejong city declines significantly, while that for the country as a whole and Seoul exhibits the opposite trend. Figure 2(b) indicates that there is more supply than demand in lease (95, on average for the last five years for Sejong). Put differently, the lease-price ratio is driven by the lease supply, which is higher than demand. As shown in Fig. 1(b), the percentage of empty houses is 20% much larger than the national level of 6.5%. This can be explained by the over-supply of lease units.

To support the theory of speculative investment in lease supply, we examined the relationship between lease and price using the generalized spillover effect from lease to price in Sejong. This result is important not only for explaining the decrease in lease-price ratio but also for understanding speculative investment associated with the lease. We found a strong gross and net spillover effect from lease to price in Sejong. Lease to price explained as 38.62%. In addition, the net spillover effects from lease to price were 12.46%. Thus, we confirmed that lease had significant effects on the real estate market in terms of the gross spillover from lease to price fundamentals.

As previously discussed in Sect. 2.1, lease supply implies an increase in speculative investment; therefore, it can be concluded that speculative investment caused the bubble. Moreover, the lease-price ratio decreases due to the increase in supply in the lease market, which can result in a lower lease level and an increase in house prices as investment goods. In Sejong, it appears that the supply of leases caused a spiral effect on the house price bubble.

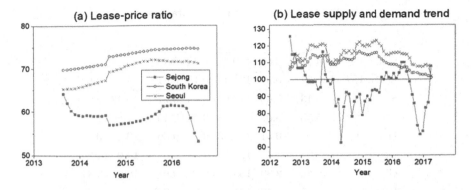

Fig. 2. Lease-price ratio and lease supply & demand trend. In (b), '100' indicates that supply and demand for condominiums are the same. Supply exceeds demand when the trend is below 100, and vice versa (KNS).

3.3 When Could Be the Probable Critical Time of the Bubble?

In order to identify the critical time of the real estate bubble in Sejong and South Korea as a whole, we fitted the LPPL model with the CTPI datasets from November 2009 to December 2016 and from December 2008 to December 2016, respectively. In accordance with [4,16], we selected the data period as follows: (i) the time window started at the end of the previous crash, which was the lowest point since the last crash; and (ii) the endpoint was the last day used to predict the future critical time of a real estate bubble. Figure 3(a) shows a monthly natural logarithm of prices sold in both Sejong and the entire country. The LPPL curve shows the best fit of the LPPL model to the data. A strong upward trend is observed in these LPPL plots, indicating a fast exponential growth in condominium prices in Sejong as well as in the wider country.

In Table 4, t_c represents the critical time estimated from the LPPL. It corresponds to the most probable time for a change in the regime or a crash to occur [14,15]. In addition, it is important to validate the LPPL calibration, i.e., to check the stylized features of the LPPL reflected by restrictions on the parameters mentioned in [2]. All the estimated parameters are within the boundaries. The two conditions $B < 0$ and $0.1 \leq \beta \leq 0.9$ ensure a faster-than-exponential acceleration of the log-price (mostly Sejong and Incheon in regard to β) [21]. The values of ω are close to the lower bound 5 (especially both Sejong and Seoul), which corroborates existing studies such as that by Johansen [17], who found that $\omega \approx 6.36 \pm 1.56$ for crashes.

To diagnose the estimation results, three robustness tests were carried out. First, relative error analysis was conducted (Fig. 3(b)). According to [14] our results suggest that the LPPL model captures the bubble precisely, as the relative errors of these two indices are well below 5%.

To check the stationarity of residuals, unit root tests were conducted. ADF and PP tests were used with one to eight lags. Both test results rejected the null

Table 4. Best fit of LPPL parameters

Region	A	B	t_c	β	C	ω	ϕ
Sejong	4.97	−0.01	110.48	0.88	0.38	5.18	0.52
South Korea	6.67	−0.97	131.15	0.13	0.01	9.72	2.68
Seoul	5.13	−0.05	163.03	0.45	0.27	5.42	2.56
Busan	5.55	−0.02	154.98	0.78	0.15	7.56	1.04
Daejeon	6.06	−0.51	148.53	0.20	0.06	10.13	0.86
Daegu	7.83	−1.45	121.58	0.17	−0.01	14.00	1.97
Gwangju	9.42	−2.80	158.87	0.11	0.01	10.04	2.47
Ulsan	6.67	−0.42	161.58	0.30	−0.03	14.95	2.06
Incheon	5.16	−0.00	183.18	0.89	−0.68	8.89	0.42

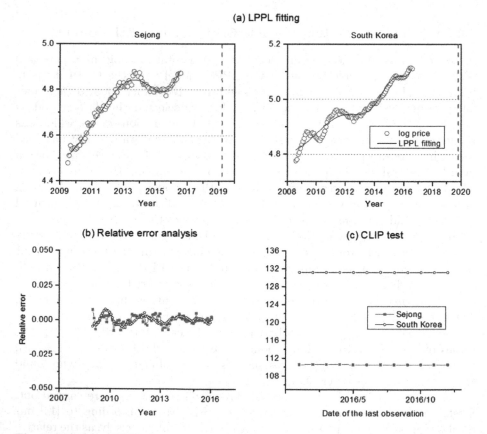

Fig. 3. Results of LPPL fitting and diagnostic tests. Vertical dash lines in (a) indicate the critical time.

hypothesis at the 1% significant level, implying that the residuals do not have a unit root but are stationary.

Finally, we carried out crash lock-in plot (hereafter CLIP) analysis in accordance with [12]. The CLIP is useful for tracking the development of a bubble and understanding whether a possible crash is imminent. The main idea of the CLIP is to plot the date of the last observation in the estimation sample on the horizontal axis and the estimated crash date t_c on the vertical axis. To implement the CLIP, we continued in changing the last observation of our estimation sample on a monthly basis for Sejong and South Korea (Fig. 3(c)). From the resulting plot we confirmed that our estimation for t_c is stable.

As such, these results indicate that the predicted t_c is a robust and precise forecast. The critical time of the bubble in Sejong is January 2019, earlier than the November 2019 for the country as a whole and that in other major cities, reflecting a relatively and probably fast growth in house prices in Sejong.

4   Conclusion

This study comprehensively examined housing market bubbles in a newly developed city: its identification, cause, and burst-timing. Our findings can be summarized as follows. First, we identified a bubble in the Sejong housing market using the present value model. House prices and rental rates were cointegrated at the national level but the result for Sejong was different, implying housing market bubbles in the new city. Second, analysis of the lease-price ratio suggests that the housing market bubbles in Sejong were caused by speculative investors. The lease-price ratio in Sejong dramatically decreased, while that for Seoul and South Korea as a whole marginally increased over the same period. Furthermore, a significantly low lease-price ratio (59.1% on average) supports our conclusion that speculative investments led to an increased lease supply in the area. Third, it is predicted that Sejong's critical bubble-burst time will be earlier than the country's critical time. The LPPL model suggests that the critical time of the bubble in Sejong will occur ten months ahead of that for the rest of the country. Additional analysis shows that our results are robust. This implies that housing price in Sejong is at a riskier stage than those in other regions in South Korea.

Our results suggest that the real estate market in Sejong, the new city of South Korea, is at a high level of bubble relative to the rest of the country. Additionally, our analysis reveals the complex relation between housing market prices and leases in South Korea, which has in part supported the creation of real estate bubbles in Sejong. Our findings have two important policy implications for urban planning and new city policies: first, the housing market should be intensively monitored to prevent and detect bubbles, especially in newly developed cities; and second, managing lease and house prices at the same time would be an effective policy approach.

The approaches used in this paper can be applied to other areas. However, it should be noted that the results might not be universally applicable.

References

1. Abraham, J.M., Hendershott, P.H.: Bubbles in metropolitan housing markets. National Bureau of Economic Research, w4774 (1994)
2. Ahn, K., Dai, B., Targia, D., Zhang, F.: Predicting the critical time of financial bubbles. PHBS Working Papers, 2016008 (2016). https://doi.org/10.1111/1540-6229.12154
3. Bourassa, S.C., Hoesli, M., Oikarinen, E.: Measuring house price bubbles. Real Estate Econ., 1–30 (2016)
4. Bree, D.S., Joseph, N.L.: Testing for financial crashes using the log-periodic power law model. Int. Rev. Finan. Anal. 30, 287–297 (2013)
5. Campbell, J.Y., Shiller, R.J.: Cointegration and tests of present value models. J. Polit. Econ. 95(5), 1062–1088 (1987)
6. Canning, D., Amaral, L.A.N., Lee, Y., Meyer, M., Stanley, H.E.: Scaling the volatility of GDP growth rates. Econ. Lett. 60(3), 335–341 (1998)
7. Clark, A.: Evidence of log-periodicity in corporate bond spreads. Phys. A Stat. Mech. Appl. 338(3), 585–595 (2004)
8. Diebold, F.X., Yilmaz, K.: Measuring financial asset return and volatility spillovers with application to global equity markets. Econ. J. 119(534), 158–171 (2009)
9. Diebold, F.X., Yilmaz, K.: Better to give than to receive: predictive directional measurement of volatility spillovers. Int. J. Forecast. 28(1), 57–66 (2012)
10. Faggio, G.: Relocation of public sector workers: Evaluating a place-based policy. University of London, October 2016
11. Faggio, G., Schluter, T., Berge, P.: The impact of public employment on private sector activity: evidence from Berlin. University of London, November 2016
12. Fantazzini, D.: Modelling bubbles and anti-bubbles in bear markets: a medium-term trading analysis. In: The Handbook of Trading, McGraw-Hill Finance and Investing, pp. 365–388. New York, U.S. (2010)
13. Filimonov, V., Sornette, D.: A stable and robust calibration scheme of the log-periodic power law model. Phys. A Stat. Mech. Appl. 392(17), 3698–3707 (2011)
14. Johansen, A., Ledoit, O., Sornette, D.: Crashes as critical points. Int. J. Theor. Appl. Finance 3(2), 219–255 (2000)
15. Johansen, A., Sornette, D.: Predicting financial crashes using discrete scale invariance. J. Risk 1(4), 5–32 (1999)
16. Johansen, A., Sornette, D.: Bubbles and anti-bubbles in Latin-American, Asian and Western stock markets: an empirical study. Int. J. Theor. Appl. Finance 4(6), 853–920 (2001)
17. Johansen, A.: Characterization of large price variations in financial markets. Phys. A Stat. Mech. Appl. 324(1), 157–166 (2003)
18. Koop, G., Pesaran, M.H., Potter, S.M.: Impulse response analysis in non-linear multivariate models. J. Econometrics 74(1), 119–147 (1996)
19. Korea National Statistics: National Census. http://kosis.kr/index/index.do
20. Kwon, Y.: Sejong Si (City): are TOD and TND models effective in planning Korea's new capital? Cities 42, 242–257 (2015)
21. Lin, L., Ren, R.E., Sornette, D.: The volatility-confined LPPL model: a consistent model of 'explosive' financial bubbles with mean-reverting residuals. Int. Rev. Financial Anal. 33, 210–225 (2014)
22. Lind, H.: Price bubbles in housing markets: Concept, theory and indicators. Int. J. Hous. Markets Anal. 2(1), 78–90 (2009)

23. Lyons, M.: Well Placed to Deliver? Independent Review of Public Sector Relocation. Shaping the Pattern of Government Service (2004)
24. Meese, R., Wallace, N.: Testing the present value relation for housing prices: should I leave my house in San Francisco? J. Urban Econ. **35**(3), 245–266 (1994)
25. Mikhed, V., Zemčík, P.: Do house prices reflect fundamentals? Aggregate and panel data evidence. J. Hous. Econ. **18**(2), 140–149 (2009)
26. Pesaran, M.H., Shin, Y.: Generalized impulse response analysis in linear multivariate models. Econ. Lett. **58**, 17–29 (1998)
27. Roche, M.J.: The rise in house prices in Dublin: bubble, fad or just fundamentals. Econ. Modell. **18**(2), 281–295 (2001)
28. Roehner, B.M.: Spatial analysis of real estate price bubbles: Paris, 1984–1993. Reg. Sci. Urban Econ. **29**, 73–88 (1999)
29. Sornette, D.: Discrete-scale invariance and complex dimensions. Phys. Rep. **297**(5), 239–270 (1998)
30. Sornette, D.: Why Stock Markets Crash: Critical Events in Complex Financial Systems. Princeton University Press, Princeton (2009)
31. Takamura, Y., Tone, K.: A comparative site evaluation study for relocating Japanese government agencies out of Tokyo. Soc. Econ. Plann. Sci. **37**(2), 85–102 (2003)
32. Wang, P.: Market efficiency and rationality in property investment. J. Real Estate Finance Econ. **21**(2), 185–201 (2000)
33. Yoon, J.: Structural changes in South Korea's rental housing market: the rise and fall of the Jeonse system. J. Comp. Asian Dev. **2**(1), 151–168 (2003)
34. Zhou, W.X., Sornette, D.: Is there a real estate bubble in the US? Phys. A Stat. Mech. Appl. **361**(1), 297–308 (2006)
35. Zhou, W.X., Sornette, D.: 2000–2003 real estate bubble in the UK but not in the USA. Phys. A Stat. Mech. Appl. **329**(1), 249–263 (2003)

A Novel Parsing-Based Automatic Domain Terminology Extraction Method

Ying Liu[1,2(✉)] (iD), Tianlin Zhang[1,2(✉)] (iD), Pei Quan[1,2], Yueran Wen[3],
Kaichao Wu[4], and Hongbo He[4]

[1] School of Computer and Control, University of Chinese Academy of Sciences,
Beijing 100190, China
Yingliu@ucas.ac.cn, zhangtianlin668@163.com
[2] Key Lab of Big Data Mining and Knowledge Management,
Chinese Academy of Sciences, Beijing 100190, China
[3] School of Labor and Human Resources, Renmin University of China,
Beijing 100872, China
[4] Computer Network Information Center, Chinese Academy of Sciences,
Beijing 100190, China

Abstract. As domain terminology plays a crucial role in the study of every domain, automatic domain terminology extraction method is in real demand. In this paper, we propose a novel parsing-based method which generates the domain compound terms by utilizing the dependent relations between the words. Dependency parsing is used to identify the dependent relations. In addition, a multi-factor evaluator is proposed to evaluate the significance of each candidate term which not only considers frequency but also includes the influence of other factors affecting domain terminology. Experimental results demonstrate that the proposed domain terminology extraction method outperforms the traditional POS-base method in both precision and recall.

Keywords: Domain terminology extraction · Dependency parsing
Multi-factor evaluation

1 Introduction

Domain terminology refers to the vocabulary of theoretical concepts in a specific domain. People can quickly understand the development of the subject through domain terminology, which is of great significance to scientific research. However, it is unaffordable to extract domain terminology manually from the massive text collections. Therefore, automatic domain terminology extraction is in real demand in various domains.

The process flow of the existing domain terminology extraction methods can be summarized into two steps: candidate term extraction and term evaluation [1]. Firstly, the candidate term extractor extracts terms that conform to the domain conditions. Secondly, the evaluation module evaluates each candidate term and filters it when necessary based on some statistical measures.

© Springer International Publishing AG, part of Springer Nature 2018
Y. Shi et al. (Eds.): ICCS 2018, LNCS 10862, pp. 796–802, 2018.
https://doi.org/10.1007/978-3-319-93713-7_77

In order to enhance the accuracy of domain terms extracted, in this paper, we propose a novel parsing-based method. The contributions of this paper can be summarized as follows:

(1) Dependency parsing is proposed to be utilized to generate candidate domain terms.
(2) A multi-factor evaluator is proposed, which evaluates and filters the candidate terms based on the linguistics rules, statistical methods, and domain-specific term characteristics.

We evaluated the performance of our proposed domain terminology extraction method with a frequency-based POS-based term extraction method. In the experiment, our method identified plentiful of accurate candidates. The recall rate has been improved. The ranking outperformed the counterpart in precision.

2 Related Work

Some automatic terminology recognition approaches have been proposed in recent years. The existing domain terminology extraction approaches can be classified into four categories [2]:

(1) Dictionary-based method. It is simple and easy to extract domain terms by matching the words with those in a domain dictionary. However, domain terminology is constantly updated so that the domain dictionaries cannot be easily maintained [3].
(2) Linguistic method. It uses the surface grammatical analysis to recognize terminology [4]. However, the linguistic rules are difficult to summarize. Linguistic method may generate lots of noise when identifying terms.
(3) Statistical method. It uses the statistical properties of the terms in corpus to identify potential terminologies. Some commonly used statistical methods are word frequency statistics, TF-IDF [5], C-Value [6], etc. Statistical methods may produce some meaningless string combinations [7], common words (non-terminology) and other noises.

3 Parsing-Based Domain Terminology Extraction Method

In this paper, we propose to use Dependency Parsing in the process of candidate domain term identification. The proposed parsing-based domain terminology extraction method consists of three steps: dependency parsing establishing, candidate term generation and candidate evaluation for ranking.

We will provide the details of each step in the following sections. In order to help you better understand our ideas, a Chinese corpus will be used as the example for explanation.

3.1   Dependency Parsing Establishment

Dependency parsing is able to reveal the syntactic structure in a given sentence by analyzing the dependencies among the components of language units. It can well explain the relationship between the adjacent words. Typical dependency parsing methods include Graph-based [8, 9] and Transition-based [10, 11].

The very first step in establishing dependency parsing is word segmentation. Since the CRF(Conditional Random Field)s-based word segmentation algorithm has been proved to be one of the best segmenter [12], we adopt CRFs-based parser as our baseline word segmenter. Next, a syntactic parse tree can be generated in the mean time. The dependency parsing represents the grammatical structure and the relationship between the words. Table 1 shows an example dependency parsing.

Table 1. Dependency parsing of "边际收益等于物品的价格。" (The marginal revenue equals to the price of the item.)

Dependent relation abbreviation	(Word-location, word-location)
amod (adjectival modifier)	(收益 (revenue)-2, 边际 (marginal)-1)
nsubj (nominal subject)	(等于 (is equal to)-3, 收益 (revenue)-2)
root (root node)	(ROOT-0, 等于 (is equal to)-3)
nmod:assmod (noun compound modifier)	(价格 (the price)-6, 物品 (the item)-4)
case (case)	(物品 (the item)-4, 的 (of)-5)
obj (object)	(等于 (is equal to)-3, 价格 (the price)-6)
punct (punctuation)	(等于 (is equal to)-3, 。(.)-7)

3.2   Candidate Term Generation

In the example sentence in the previous section, 收益 (revenue) is a nominal subject, and 边际 (marginal) serves as an adjectival modifier of 收益 (revenue). By grouping words in particular roles together, we can obtain the expected "phrases". For example, 边际收益 (marginal revenue) can be regarded as a candidate domain term.

Therefore, we propose to create grammatical rules to generate phrases, which can be regarded as domain terminologies. In this paper, we propose three grammatical rules, which may be widely accepted by different domains: Noun + Noun, (Adj| Noun) + Noun, and ((Adj | Noun) + (Adj | Noun)*(NounPrep)?)(Adj | Noun)*)Noun.

3.3   Candidates Evaluation and Ranking

It is inevitable that the candidate terms generated in Sect. 3.2 may have noise. So, in order to control the quality of the selected domain terminology, we propose a set of measures in candidate evaluation. The candidates are ranked in descending order by the evaluation score for the purpose of filtering.

3.3.1   Linguistic Rule Based Filter

In this paper, we propose to filter the candidate terms in a "backward" manner, which filters out those candidate terms that obviously cannot be terminologies by checking with the POS of the candidate terms. Word segmentation and POS tagging are performed on the candidates.

3.3.2 Multi-factor Evaluation

Traditional terminology evaluation method is based on frequency, which sorts the candidates in descending order by their frequencies in the corpus. However, as everyone knows, although frequency is an important factor, other factors, such as adhesion, etc., also play important roles in evaluation. Therefore, we propose a multi-factor evaluator. In addition to frequency, affixes (prefixes and suffixes) that often occur in phrases are considered as a factor. The affixes of hot words in a particular domain are often the same. For example, in the domain of economics, "固定成本 (constant cost)", "可变成本 (variable cost)"and "总成本 (total cost)" all contain the suffix "成本 (cost)". Table 2 shows some affixes of the hot words and the non-terms in the candidate set in the economics corpus.

Table 2. Some affixes of the hot words and non-terms in economics

Hot words prefix	Hot words suffix	Non-terms prefix	Non-terms suffix
供给 (supply)	市场 (market)	可以 (could)	进行 (in progress)
福利 (welfare)	价格 (price)	处理 (deal with)	有关 (about)
货币 (currency)	竞争 (competition)	进行 (in progress)	基础 (base)
平均 (average)	成本 (cost)	十分 (very)	重要 (important)

Based on the observations in Table 2, affixes can either bring positive or negative impacts to domain terminology. Therefore, we propose an influence factor which indicates the impact of the affixes.

Equation 1 denotes the relationship between the frequency and the influence factor of non-terminology affixes, a is adjustment threshold.

$$\alpha = \frac{f_{word}}{a} \tag{1}$$

Equation 2 denotes the relationship between the average frequency and the influence factor of the hot-word affixes. The number of the candidate terms which occurs only once, $C_{(1)}$, is excluded, b is adjustment threshold.

$$\beta = \left\lceil b \frac{\sum_{i=2}^{n} f_{(i)}}{C - C_{(1)}} \right\rceil \tag{2}$$

Equation 3 denotes the relationship between the frequency and other factors, named as the evaluation score.

$$v = f_{word} - \alpha + \beta \tag{3}$$

The candidates are ranked in descending order by their evaluation scores. The higher the value, the more consistent with the characteristics of the domain terminology. By experiment, when a is $1/2$ and b is 2, the effect is the best. The notations in Eqs. 1, 2 and 3 are listed in Table 3.

Table 3. Notations used in the multi-factor evaluator

Notation	Indication
f_{word}	The frequency of a candidate term
α	The influence factor of non-terminology affixes
$f_{(i)}$	The sum of the frequencies of the words with frequency i
$C_{(1)}$	The total number of candidate terms each occurring only once
C	The total number of the candidate terms
β	The influence factor of hot word affixes in a given domain
v	The evaluation score

4   Performance Analysis

4.1   Datasets and Experiments Settings

For the purpose of evaluation, we use the well-known textbook Macroeconomics (Chinese Edition) [13] as the corpus, whose domain terminology has already been labeled by domain experts. The total number of the domain terms labeled is 349.

Two different parsers are explored for comparison: Stanford parser [14], LTP parser [15]. In order to evaluate the performance of our proposed automatic parsing-based terminology extraction method, we implement the traditional POS-based method for a fair comparison. Four measures are studied in the experiments: *precision (P)*, *recall (R)*, *n-precision (P(n))* and *n-recall (R(n))* as defined in Eqs. 4, 5, 6 and 7. *n-precision* considers the top-n entries as well as *n-recall*.

$$P = \frac{total\ number\ of\ the\ extracted\ domain\ terms}{total\ number\ of\ extracted\ words} \times 100\% \tag{4}$$

$$R = \frac{total\ number\ of\ the\ extracted\ domain\ terms}{total\ number\ of\ the\ labeled\ domain\ terms} \times 100\% \tag{5}$$

$$P(n) = \frac{total\ number\ of\ extracted\ terminologies\ in\ top - n\ results}{n} \times 100\% \tag{6}$$

$$R(n) = \frac{total\ number\ of\ extracted\ terminologies\ in\ top - n\ results}{total\ number\ of\ the\ labeled\ domain\ terms} \times 100\% \tag{7}$$

4.2 Experimental Results and Discussion

Table 4 presents the precision and recall of our proposed domain terminology extraction method when using different parsers, the traditional POS, Stanford Parser and the LTP parser. The LTP parser contributes to the best precision.

Table 4. Total precision and recall of different methods

Method	Number of candidates	Precision	Recall
POS	1117	12.0%	38.4%
Stanford parser	1367	17.6%	69.1%
LTP parser	1654	18.7%	88.5%

In order to verify the effectiveness of the proposed multi-factor evaluator and the rationality of the ranking, n-precision and n-recall are used as the measures. The n-precision and n-recall of the extracted terms is shown in Table 5. When including the multi-factor evaluator for filtering and reordering, the n-precision rise significantly, the n-recall is higher than that of the POS-based method.

Table 5. Precision and recall of different methods in top-n results

Method	Top 50 P(n)/R(n)	Top 100 P(n) R(n)	Top 200 P(n)/R(n)	Top 500 P(n)/R(n)
POS	56.0%/8.0%	41.0%/11.7%	29.0%/16.6%	15.0%/21.5%
Stanford parser	50.0%/7.2%	25.0%/7.2%	19.0%/10.9%	11.6%/16.6%
LTP parser	40.0%/5.7%	31.0%/8.9%	20.5%/11.7%	12.4%/17.8%
POS + evaluator	56.0%/8.0%	42.0%/12.0%	30.0%/17.2%	18.2%/26.1%
Stanford parser + evaluator	48.0%/6.9%	41.0%/11.7%	35.0%/20.0%	22.6%/32.4%
LTP-parser + evaluator	58.0%/8.3%	50.0%/14.3%	41.0%/23.5%	27.6%/39.5%

5 Conclusion

Domain terminology is important in the study of every domain. Thus, an automatic domain terminology extraction method is in real demand. In this paper, we presented a novel automatic domain terminology extraction method. It generates the candidate domain terms by using dependency parsing. In addition, a multi-factor evaluator is proposed to evaluate the significance of each candidate term which not only considers frequency but also includes the influence of other factors affecting domain terminology. A Chinese corpus in economics is used in the performance evaluation. Experimental results demonstrate that the proposed domain terminology extraction method outperforms the traditional POS-based method in both precision and recall.

Acknowledgements. This project was partially supported by Grants from Natural Science Foundation of China #71671178/#91546201/#61202321, and the open project of the Key Lab of Big Data Mining and Knowledge Management. It was also supported by Hainan Provincial Department of Science and Technology under Grant No. ZDKJ2016021, and by Guangdong Provincial Science and Technology Project 2016B010127004.

References

1. Nakagawa, H., Mori, T.: Automatic term recognition based on statistics of compound nouns and their components. Terminology **9**, 201–219 (2003)
2. Korkontzelos, I., Klapaftis, I.P., Manandhar, S.: Reviewing and evaluating automatic term recognition techniques. In: 6th International Conference on Advances in Natural Language Processing, pp. 248–259 (2008)
3. Krauthammer, M., Nenadic, G.: Term identification in the biomedical literature. J. Biomed. Inform. **37**(6), 512–526 (2004)
4. Bourigault, D.: Surface grammatical analysis for the extraction of terminological noun phrases. In: Proceedings of the 14th Conference on Computational Linguistics, Stroudsburg, PA, USA, pp. 977–981 (1992)
5. Rezgui, Y.: Text-based domain ontology building using tf-idf and metric clusters techniques. Knowl. Eng. Rev. **22**, 379–403 (2007)
6. Frantzi, K., Ananiadou, S., Mima, H.: Automatic recognition of multi-word terms: the c-value/nc-value method. Int. J. Digit. Libr. **3**(2), 115–130 (2000)
7. Damerau, F.J.: Generating and evaluating domain-oriented multi-word terms from texts. Inf. Process. Manage. **29**(4), 433–447 (1993)
8. Eisner, J.: Three new probabilistic models for dependency parsing: an exploration. In: Proceedings of the 16th International Conference on Computational Linguistics (COLING-96), Copenhagen, pp. 340–345 (1996). http://cs.jhu.edu/~jason/papers/#coling96
9. McDonald, R., Pereira, F., Ribarov, K., Hajic, J.: Non-projective dependency parsing using spanning tree algorithms. In: Proceedings of Human Language Technology Conference and Conference on Empirical Methods in Natural Language Processing, pp. 523–530. Association for Computational Linguistics, Vancouver (2005). http://www.aclweb.org/anthology/H/H05/H05-1066
10. Kubler, S., McDonald, R., Nivre, J.: Dependency parsing. Synthesis Lectures on Human Language Technologies. Morgan & Claypool, San Rafael (2009). http://books.google.com/books?id=k3iiup7HB9UC
11. Nivre, J., Hall, J., Nilsson, J., Chanev, A., Eryigit, G., Kubler, S., Marinov, S., Marsi, E.: MaltParser: a language-independent system for data-driven dependency parsing. Nat. Lang. Eng. **13**, 95–135 (2007)
12. Yang, D., Pan, Y., Furui, S.: Automatic Chinese abbreviation generation using conditional random field. In: NAACL 2009, pp. 273–276 (2009)
13. Mankiw, N.G.: Macroeconomics, 4th ed. China Renmin University Press (2002)
14. Klein, D., Manning, C.D.: Fast exact inference with a factored model for natural language parsing. In: Advances in Neural Information Processing Systems (NIPS 2002), vol. 15, pp. 3–10. MIT Press, Cambridge (2003)
15. Che, W., Li, Z., Liu, T.: LTP: a Chinese language technology platform. In: Proceedings of the Coling 2010: Demonstrations, pp. 13–16, Beijing, China (2010)

Remote Procedure Calls for Improved Data Locality with the Epiphany Architecture

James A. Ross[1]([⊠]) and David A. Richie[2]

[1] U.S. Army Research Laboratory,
Aberdeen Proving Ground, MD 21005, USA
`james.a.ross176.civ@mail.mil`
[2] Brown Deer Technology, Forest Hill, MD 21050, USA
`drichie@browndeertechnology.com`

Abstract. This paper describes the software implementation of an emerging parallel programming model for partitioned global address space (PGAS) architectures. Applications with irregular memory access to distributed memory do not perform well on conventional symmetric multiprocessing (SMP) architectures with hierarchical caches. Such applications tend to scale with the number of memory interfaces and corresponding memory access latency. Using a remote procedure call (RPC) technique, these applications may see reduced latency and higher throughput compared to remote memory access or explicit message passing. The software implementation of a remote procedure call method detailed in the paper is designed for the low-power Adapteva Epiphany architecture.

Keywords: Remote procedure call (RPC) · Network-on-chip (NoC)
Distributed computing · Partitioned global address space (PGAS)
Programming model

1 Introduction and Motivation

Many high performance computing (HPC) applications often rely on computer architectures optimized for dense linear algebra, large contiguous datasets, and regular memory access patterns. Architectures based on a partitioned global address space (PGAS) are enabled by a higher degree of memory locality than conventional symmetric multiprocessing (SMP) with hierarchical caches and unified memory access. SMP architectures excel at algorithms with regular, contiguous memory access patterns and a high degree of data re-use; however, many applications are not like this. A certain class of applications may express irregular memory access patterns, are "data intensive" (bandwidth-heavy), or express "weak locality" where relatively small blocks of memory are associated. For these applications, memory latency and bandwidth drive application performance. These applications may benefit from PGAS architectures and the re-emerging

© Springer International Publishing AG, part of Springer Nature 2018
Y. Shi et al. (Eds.): ICCS 2018, LNCS 10862, pp. 803–810, 2018.
https://doi.org/10.1007/978-3-319-93713-7_78

remote procedure call (RPC) concept. By exporting the execution of a program to the core closely associated with the data, an application may reduce the total memory latency and network congestion associated with what would be remote direct memory access (RDMA).

2 Background and Related Work

The 16-core Epiphany-III coprocessor is included within the inexpensive ARM-based single-board computer "Parallella" [1]. All of the software tools and firmware are open source, enabling rigorous study of the processor architecture and the exploration of new programming models. Although not discussed in detail in this paper, the CO-PRocessing Threads (COPRTHR) 2.0 SDK [2] further simplifies the execution model to the point where the host code is significantly simplified, supplemental, and even not required depending on the use case. We also use the *ARL OpenSHMEM for Epiphany* library in this work [3]. Currently, a full implementation of OpenSHMEM 1.4 is available under a BSD open source license [4]. The combination of the COPRTHR SDK and the OpenSHMEM library enabled further exploration of hybrid programming models [5], high-level C++ templated metaprogramming techniques for distributed shared memory systems [6].

The middleware and library designs for Epiphany emphasize a reduced memory footprint, high performance, and simplicity, which are often competing goals. The OpenSHMEM communications library is designed for computer platforms using PGAS programming models [7]. Historically, these were large Cray supercomputers and then commodity clusters. But now the Adapteva Epiphany architecture represents a divergence in computer architectures typically used with OpenSHMEM. In some ways, the architecture is much more capable than the library can expose. The architecture presents a challenge in identifying the most effective and optimal programming models to exploit it. While OpenSHMEM does reasonably well at exposing the capability of the Epiphany cores, the library does not provide any mechanism for RPCs.

Recent publications on new computer architectures and programming models have rekindled an interest in the RPC concept to improve performance on PGAS architectures with non-uniform memory access to non-local memory spaces. In particular, the Emu System Architecture is a newly developed scalable PGAS architecture that uses hardware-accelerated "migrating threads" to offload execution to the remote processor with local access to application memory [8]. The Emu programming model is based on a partial implementation of the C language extension, Cilk. Cilk abandons C semantics and the partial implementation is used for little or no improvement in code quality over a simple C API. The Emu software and hardware RPC implementation details are not publicly documented, and a proprietary, closed source compiler is used so that the software details are not open for inspection. This paper discusses the Epiphany-specific RPC implementation details in Sect. 3, the performance evaluation in Sect. 4, and a discussion of future work in Sect. 5.

3   Remote Procedure Call Technique

Although the RPC implementation described in this paper is designed for Epiphany, the techniques may be generally applicable to other PGAS architectures. The GNU Compiler Collection toolchain is used, without modification, to enable the RPC capability on Epiphany. In order to keep the interface as simple as possible, decisions were made to use a direct call method rather than passing function and arguments through a library call. This abstraction hides much of the complexity, but has some limitations at this time. The RPC dispatch routine (Algorithm 1) uses a global address pointer passed in the first function argument to select the remote core for execution. Up to four 32-bit function arguments may be used and are registers in the Epiphany application binary interface (ABI). In the case of 64-bit arguments, the ABI uses two consecutive registers. For the purposes of this work, any RPC prototype can work as long as the ABI does not exceed four 32-bit arguments and one 32-bit return value.

Algorithm 1. RPC dispatch routine

---

function RPC_DISPATCH($a1, a2, a3, a4$)
    rpc_call← ip
    $high\_addr \leftarrow mask(a1)$
    if $high\_addr = my\_addr$ **then**
        return RPC_CALL($a1, a2, a3, a4$)
    end if
    $remote\_lock \leftarrow high\_addr | lock\_addr$
    $remote\_queue \leftarrow high\_addr | queue$
    ACQUIRE_LOCK($remote\_lock$)
    if $remote\_queue$ is full **then**
        RELEASE_LOCK($remote\_lock$)
        return RPC_CALL($a1, a2, a3, a4$)
    end if
    $p\_event \leftarrow my\_addr | \&event$
    $remote\_queue$.push($\{a1, a2, a3, a4, rpc\_call, p\_event\}$)
    RELEASE_LOCK($remote\_lock$)
    if $remote\_queue$ initially empty **then**
        SIGNAL_REMOTE_INTERRUPT($high\_addr$)
    end if
    repeat
    until $event.status =$ rpc_complete
    return $event.val$
end function

An overview of the specialized RPC interrupt service request (ISR) appears in Algorithm 2. The user-defined ISR precludes other applications from using it, but it is sufficiently generalized and exposed so that applications can easily make use of it. The ISR operates at the lowest priority level after every other interrupt or exception. It may also be interrupted, but the RPC queue and the RPC dispatch method are designed so the ISR need only be signalled when the first work item is added to the queue.

Algorithm 2. RPC interrupt service request

---

function RPC_ISR
    ACQUIRE_LOCK(my_lock)
    while $queue$ is not empty **do**
        $work \leftarrow queue.\text{pop}()$
        RELEASE_LOCK(my_lock)
        $work.event.val \leftarrow work.\text{RPC\_CALL}(work.a1, work.a2, work.a3, work.a4)$
        $work.evevent.status = \text{rpc\_complete}$
        ACQUIRE_LOCK(my_lock)
    end while
    RELEASE_LOCK(my_lock)
end function

Setting up code to use the developed RPC methods is easy, but there are some restrictions. The subroutine should localize the global-local addresses to improve performance. A convenient inline subroutine has been made for this. If one of the addresses is non-local, it will not modify the pointer and default to RDMA. Listing 1 shows creating a dot product routine, a corresponding routine without a return value, and using the RPC macro to set up the RPC dispatch jump table.

```
float dotprod(float* a, float* b, int n)
{
        a = localize(a); // translate global addresses to local
        b = localize(b);
        float sum = 0.0f;
        for (int i = 0; i < n; i++) sum += a[i] * b[i];
        return sum;
}
RPC(dotprod) // dotprod_rpc symbol and jump table entry
```

List. 1. Example code for RPC function with symbol registration and jump table entry.

Using the RPC method is also very easy. The RPC calls made with the RPC macro have a _rpc suffix and are called like regular functions, but with the first pointer as a global address on a remote core. An example of application setup with mixed OpenSHMEM and RPC calls is presented in Listing 2. OpenSHMEM with symmetric allocation is not required, but it is convenient for demonstration.

```
float* A = shmem_malloc(n * sizeof(*A)); // symmetric allocation
float* B = shmem_malloc(n * sizeof(*B));
float* A1 = shmem_ptr(A, 1); // address of 'A' on PE #1
float* B1 = shmem_ptr(B, 1);
float res = dotprod_rpc(A1, B1, n); // RPC on PE #1
```

List. 2. Application code example for mixed usage of OpenSHMEM and RPC. The address translation for the B vector is necessary in case RDMA is required.

4   Results

The results presented include performance figures for an optimized single precision floating point RPC dot product operation using a stack-based RPC work queue. The dot product subroutine was chosen because it has a tunable work size parameter, n, relatively low arithmetic intensity at 0.25 FLOPS/byte—representing the challenging "data-intensive" operations—and reduces to a single 32-bit value result. Dot product performance for a single Epiphany core executing on local memory approaches the core peak performance of 1.2 GFLOPS and 4.8 GB/s. This corresponds to a dual-issue fused multiply-add and double-word (64-bit) load per clock cycle at 600 MHz. The small bump in the results around $n = 16$ on Figs. 1 and 2 is the result of the subroutine using a different code path for larger arrays. Figure 1 shows the total on-chip bandwidth performance for various execution configurations. The highest performance is achieved with a

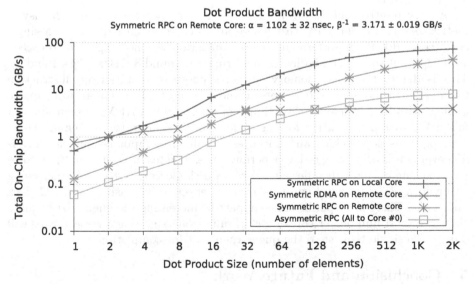

Fig. 1. Symmetric, or load-balanced, RPC with a stack-based queue can achieve over 60% of the bandwidth performance as if execution were accessing local scratchpad data (throughput up to 2.95 GB/s vs 4.8 GB/s per core). However, there must be sufficient work on the remote core to mitigate the overhead of the RPC dispatch versus RDMA.

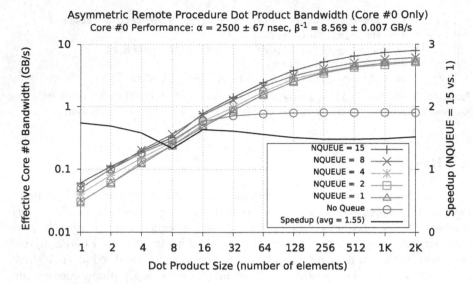

Fig. 2. Effect of RPC queue size for an asymmetric workload shows a speedup of about 1.5x from a queue size of one to 15. The greatest improvement comes from having a single extra workload enqueued (NQUEUE = 1) compared to no queue at all.

symmetric load executing a dot product on local data, without address translation (localization for array pointers a and b within the subroutine), which adds a small overhead.

A very positive and initially unexpected result occurred during the asymmetric loading for the RPC test where all 16 cores made requests to a single core (core #0). Peak performance of the operation was not expected to exceed 4.8 GB/s, but the timing indicated performance around 8 GB/s (Figs. 1 and 2). This is due to the local memory system supporting simultaneous instruction fetching, data fetching, and remote memory requests. If a remote work queue is filled with RPC requests, the calling core will perform RDMA execution as a fallback rather than waiting for the remote core resources to become available. This prevents deadlocking and improves overall throughput because no core is idle even if it is operating at lower performance. The result is that multiple cores may execute on data in different banks on a single core, effectively increasing bandwidth performance. Figure 2 shows the effect of increasing the RPC work queue size. There is no performance impact by increasing the queue size to more than the total number of cores on-chip minus one since each remote core will only add a single request to the queue then wait for completion.

5   Conclusion and Future Work

The combination of fast message passing with OpenSHMEM to handle symmetric application execution and the RPC techniques described here for handling asymmetric workloads remote procedure calls creates a very flexible and high-performance programming paradigm. This combination creates potential for good performance on diverse applications with both regular and irregular data layouts, memory access patterns, and program execution on the Epiphany architecture. We hope that developers on similar memory-mapped parallel architectures may use this paper as a guide for exploring the inter-processor RPC concept.

The developments in this paper will be built into the COPRTHR 2.0 SDK as low-level operating system services. It may also be used by some of the non-blocking subroutines in the *ARL OpenSHMEM for Epiphany* software stack for particular remote subroutines to enable higher performance. We will extend this work to support asynchronous RPC requests so programs do not block on remote operations. Additional reductions in instruction overhead may be found through low-level optimization of the RPC dispatch and software interrupt routines by transforming the high-level C code to optimized Epiphany assembly. The software interrupt appears to be overly conservative in saving the state and the dispatch method is overly conservative in assumptions of address locations and memory alignment, so these routines should be able to be substantially optimized. Since no considerations are made for load balancing and quality of service in this work, future development may allow for remote cores to defer servicing RPCs with tunable priority.

References

1. Olofsson, A., Nordström, T., Ul-Abdin, Z.: Kickstarting high-performance energy-efficient manycore architectures with Epiphany. In 2014 48th Asilomar Conference on Signals, Systems and Computers, pp. 1719–1726, November 2014
2. COPRTHR-2 Epiphany/Parallella Developer Resources. http://www.browndeertechnology.com/resources_epiphany_developer_coprthr2.htm. Accessed 01 July 2016
3. Ross, J., Richie, D.: An OpenSHMEM Implementation for the Adapteva Epiphany Coprocessor. In: Gorentla Venkata, M., Imam, N., Pophale, S., Mintz, T.M. (eds.) OpenSHMEM 2016. LNCS, vol. 10007, pp. 146–159. Springer, Cham (2016). https://doi.org/10.1007/978-3-319-50995-2_10
4. GitHub - US Army Research Lab/openshmem-epiphany - ARL OpenSHMEM for Epiphany. https://github.com/USArmyResearchLab/openshmem-epiphany/. Accessed 06 Feb 2018
5. Richie, D.A., Ross, J.A.: OpenCL + OpenSHMEM Hybrid Programming Model for the Adapteva Epiphany Architecture. In: Gorentla Venkata, M., Imam, N., Pophale, S., Mintz, T.M. (eds.) OpenSHMEM 2016. LNCS, vol. 10007, pp. 181–192. Springer, Cham (2016). https://doi.org/10.1007/978-3-319-50995-2_12
6. Richie, D., Ross, J., Infantolino, J.: A distributed shared memory model and C++ templated meta-programming interface for the epiphany RISC array processor. In: ICCS, 2017 (2017)
7. Chapman, B., Curtis, T., Pophale, S., Poole, S., Kuehn, J., Koelbel, C., Smith, L.: Introducing OpenSHMEM: SHMEM for the PGAS community. In: Proceedings of the Fourth Conference on Partitioned Global Address Space Programming Model, PGAS 2010, pp. 2:1–2:3. ACM, New York (2010)

8. Dysart, T., Kogge, P., Deneroff, M., Bovell, E., Briggs, P., Brockman, J., Jacobsen, K., Juan, Y., Kuntz, S., Lethin, R., McMahon, J., Pawar, C., Perrigo, M., Rucker, S., Ruttenberg, J., Ruttenberg, M., Stein, S.: Highly scalable near memory processing with migrating threads on the Emu System Architecture. In: Proceedings of the Sixth Workshop on Irregular Applications: Architectures and Algorithms, IA³ 2016, pp. 2–9. IEEE Press, Piscataway (2016)

Identifying the Propagation Sources
of Stealth Worms

Yanwei Sun[1,2,3], Lihua Yin[1], Zhen Wang[4(✉)], Yunchuan Guo[2,3],
and Binxing Fang[5]

[1] Cyberspace Institute of Advanced Technology (CIAT),
Guangzhou University, Guangzhou, China
[2] State Key Laboratory of Information Security,
Institute of Information Engineering, Chinese Academy of Sciences, Beijing, China
[3] School of Cyber Security, University of Chinese Academy of Sciences,
Beijing, China
[4] School of Cyberspace, Hangzhou Dianzi University, Hangzhou, China
wangzhen@hdu.edu.cn
[5] Institute of Electronic and Information Engineering of UESTC in Guangdong,
Dongguan, China

Abstract. Worm virus can spread in various ways with great destructive power, which poses a great threat to network security. One example is the WannaCry worm in May 2017. By identifying the sources of worms, we can better understand the causation of risks, and then implement better security measures. However, the current available detection system may not be able to fully detect the existing threats when the worms with the stealth characteristics do not show any abnormal behaviors. This paper makes two key contributions toward the challenging problem of identifying the propagation sources: (1) A modified algorithm of observed results based on Bayes rule has been proposed, which can modify the results of possible missed nodes, so as to improve the accuracy of identifying the propagation sources. (2) We have applied the method of branch and bound, effectively reduced the traversal space and improved the efficiency of the algorithm by calculating the upper and lower bounds of the infection probability of nodes. Through the experiment simulation in the real network, we verified the accuracy and high efficiency of the algorithm for tracing the sources of worms.

Keywords: Stealth worm · Propagation sources · Bayes rule

This work was supported by the National Key R&D Program of China (No. 2016YFB0800702), Natural Science Foundation of Zhejiang Province (Grant Nos. LY18F030007 and LY18F020017), and DongGuan Innovative Research Team Program (No. 201636000100038).

Y. Shi et al. (Eds.): ICCS 2018, LNCS 10862, pp. 811–817, 2018.
https://doi.org/10.1007/978-3-319-93713-7_79

1   Introduction

Worms are spreading rapidly via emails, social networks and self-scanning etc. Moreover, they are also very destructive. In May 2017, the WannaCry worm broke out worldwide via MS17-010 bug, infected at least 200,000 users in 150 countries[1], and resulted in the losses of almost 4 billion USD[2]. In order to effectively prevent the spreading of worms, the most critical means is to identify the source of spreading [1]. However, there is high false negative rate of the monitoring results because some worms are exploiting zero-day vulnerabilities and some are changing their own characteristics to avoid the detection [2]. So it is a great challenge to identify the sources of stealth worms in the case of high false negative rate.

To infer the origin of the propagation, one of the principles is to employing the maximum likelihood estimation on each potential source, and then select the most likely one as the propagation source. But these studies ignored the stealth characteristic, which may cause a false negative rate for the observing results, for instance, the false negative rate of honeycyber [3] reached about 0.92%. In this case, the results acquired by the existing identifying methods may have deviation.

Aiming at this problem, this paper mainly discusses the methods for identifying the sources of stealth worms. We use Bayesian Theory to correct the observed results of each node, and then propose an efficient algorithm based on branch and bound. Experimental results on three real-world data sets empirically demonstrate that our method consistently achieves an improvement in accuracy.

2   Related Work

There are many representative studies on the issue of identifying the propagation source. According to the differences in the observations, we can divide the study into complete observation [4,5] and snapshot [6–8]. In order to find the rumor source, Shah et al. [4] constructed a maximum likelihood estimator based on SIR model, and then proposed a computationally efficient algorithm to calculate the rumor centrality for each node. Fioriti et al. [5] focused on locating the multiple origins of a disease outbreak. When a node had been removed, the larger the reduction of the eigenvalue, the more likely this node was the origin. Compared with complete observation, snapshot provided less information and attracted a lot research. Prakash et al. [6] proposed a two step approach to identify the number of seed nodes based on SI model. They first found the high-quality seeds and then calculated the minimum description length score to identify the best set of seeds. Lokhov et al. [7] defined the snapshot as the following case: there was only single source at initial time t and the observation was conducted at t_0 where $t_0 - t$ was unknown. By discussing the propagation dynamic equations, the DMP method chose the node which had the highest probabilities that could

---

[1] http://www.straitstimes.com/tech/accidental-hero-halts-global-ransomware-attack-but-warns-this-is-not-over.

[2] https://www.cbsnews.com/news/wannacry-ransomware-attacks-wannacry-virus-losses.

produce the snapshot. Luo et al. [8] dealt with the single source at SIS model, and showed that the source estimator was a Jordan infection center. However, all these works ignored the stealth characteristic. In this paper, we mainly discuss the methods for identifying the sources of stealth worms.

3   Identify the Propagation Resource

3.1   Basic Assumptions

Worm propagation in our study follows SI model, also we use discrete time model and assume that it takes one time tick to infect a suspectable node. After the end of each time tick, we record the monitor result and record the infected time if the node is infected. We use the directed graph $G = (V, E)$ to represent the network topology in which $V = \{1, 2, \ldots, n\}$ is the set of nodes and E is the set of edges. More specifically, we use V_S for suspectable node set and V_I for infected node set. If $(i, j) \in E$ and $i \in V_I$, $j \in V_S$, we use r_{ij} to denote the probability that node j is infected by node i. We assume r_{ij} is a fixed value, the quantization process is beyond the scope of this article, we assume that this value is known.

The network is observed over a time period $[0, T]$. For the uninfected nodes in the observation, the real status may be uninfected, or may be infected but undetected. For the infected nodes in the observation, we assume that the real state is infected. However, the infection time recorded in the observation result only indicates that the node is found infected at that time, which may not be the actual infection time of the node. Altogether, we consider the situation that the detection technique may has false negative rate and has no false positive rate.

3.2   Identify the Propagation Source

The Process of Correction. Let's illustrate the correction process through an example. The network shown in Fig. 1 has total 9 nodes. At time tick t, the node 2,3,6,7 are detected infected. According to the network connectivity, we conclude that at this time, node 8 (labeled yellow) has a high probability of being a false negative (the probability calculation will be introduced at next subsection). Since a new node is considered to be a infected node and has the ability to infect other nodes, we have to re-traverse the remaining uninfected nodes. In the next traversal process, because of the influence of adding node 8, it is estimated that the probability of node 5 being infected also exceeds the threshold, so node 5 is considered as the infected node. The above process is repeated until no new node is found infected and then the traversal at time t ends.

At time $t + 1$, observations show that node 4 is found to be infected, so we traverse node 1 and node 9, finding that the probabilities of false negative of both two nodes are pretty low, so we believe node 1 and node 9 are not infected at time $t + 1$. The traversal at time $t + 1$ ends.

At time $t + 2$, it is observed that node 8 is infected. Since node 8 has previously been identified as an infected node, this shows that there is a delay in

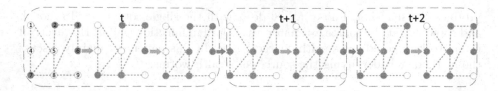

Fig. 1. An illustrative example

the observation results in terms of node 8. At this point, the observation results tend to be stable, i.e. nodes 1, 9 are uninfected nodes, node 5 is infected but undetected nodes, and the remaining nodes are infected and detected nodes.

Calculate the False Negative Probability. We use j_{obv}^t to represent the observation at time tick t for node j. For each $j_{obv}^t \in V_S^t$, we fist compute the probability of being infected:

$$P(j \in V_I^t) = 1 - \prod_{(i,j)\in E \wedge i \in V_I^t} (1 - r_{ij}) \tag{1}$$

After obtaining the above probability, we calculate the probability that node j is in an infected state under the condition that its observation result is uninfected by using the Bayesian formula:

$$
\begin{aligned}
P(j \in V_I^t | j_{obv}^t \in V_S^t) &= \frac{P(j \in V_I^t \wedge j_{obv}^t \in V_S^t)}{P(j_{obv}^t \in V_S^t)} \\
&= \frac{P(j \in V_I^t) \cdot P(j_{obv}^t \in V_S^t | j \in V_I^t)}{P(j \in V_I^t) \cdot P(j_{obv}^t \in V_S^t | j \in V_I^t) + P(j \in V_S^t) \cdot P(j_{obv}^t \in V_S^t | j \in V_S^t)} \\
&= \frac{P(j \in V_I^t) \cdot P_{FN}}{P(j \in V_I^t) \cdot P_{FN} + (1 - P(j \in V_I^t)) \cdot (1 - P_{FN})}
\end{aligned}
\tag{2}
$$

We assume that P_{FN} is a fixed value and is known. This assumption is reasonable, because this value can be obtained from the statistics of past observations and real results. So we first compute $P(j \in V_I^t)$ and then $P(j \in V_I^t | j_{obv}^t \in V_S^t)$. If the above probability exceeds our preset threshold Th, for example 80%, then we think that the observation of the state of node j is wrong.

After correcting the observation, we use DMP algorithm [7] to infer the origin of the propagation. As for the algorithm itself, this article will not go into details.

4 An Efficient Traversal Algorithm for Correction Process

During the process of correction, every time a missed node is found, it is necessary to re-execute the iteration. If the algorithm is directly applied to large-scale

Algorithm 1. Revising the observed result

Input:
    Network G; the infection probability r_{ij}; observed result set; the threshold Th.
Output:
    A set of revised result.
1: Initialize V_S^0 and V_I^0 based on observed result; Initialize $V_{FN}^t = V_{Remove}^t = \varnothing$
2: **for** each time point $t \in [0, T]$ **do**
3:     **while** repeat time $t_r \leq K$ **do**
4:         **for** each node $j \in V_S^t$ **do**
5:             Calculating $P(j \in V_I^t)$ and $P(j \in V_I^t | j_{obv}^t \in V_S^t)$
6:             **if** $P(j \in V_I^t | j_{obv}^t \in V_S^t) \geq Th$ **then**
7:                 Set $V_I^t = V_I^t \bigcup j$ and $V_S^t = V_S^t \setminus j$ and $V_{FN}^t = V_{FN}^t \bigcup j$
8:                 Record the infected time of node j
9:             **else**
10:                 Calculating $P_{max}(j \in V_I^t)$ and $P_{max}(j \in V_I^t | j_{obv}^t \in V_S^t)$
11:                 **if** $P_{max}(j \in V_I^t | j_{obv}^t \in V_S^t) \leq Th$ **then**
12:                     Set $V_S^t = V_S^t \setminus j$ and $V_{Remove}^t = V_{Remove}^t \bigcup j$
13:                 **end if**
14:             **end if**
15:         **end for**
16:         **if** The number of infected nodes is larger **then**
17:             Sort the V_S^t according to the number of infected neighbors DESC.
18:         **else**
19:             Sort the V_S^t according to the number of neighbors ASC.
20:         **end if**
21:     **end while**
22: **end for**
23: **return** V_I^t and V_S^t and V_{FN}^t and V_{Remove}^t

---

networks, its efficiency is not satisfactory. Therefore, we optimize the iterative process of the algorithm based on branch and bound:

Algorithm 1 shows the efficient traversal method for correction process. The optimization idea is as follows: at time t, for the suspectable nodes in the observation result, if any node satisfies the following condition, the node must be an uninfected node:

$$P_{max}(j \in V_I^t | j_{obv}^t \in V_S^t) = \frac{P_{max}(j \in V_I^t \wedge j_{obv}^t \in V_S^t)}{P_{max}(j_{obv}^t \in V_S^t)}$$
$$= \frac{P_{max}(j \in V_I^t) \cdot P_{FN}}{P_{max}(j \in V_I^t) \cdot P_{FN} + (1 - P_{max}(j \in V_I^t)) \cdot (1 - P_{FN})} \leq Th \tag{3}$$

where:
$$P_{max}(j \in V_I^t) = 1 - \prod_{(i,j) \in E} (1 - r_{ij}) \tag{4}$$

It can be seen that in the calculation, the number of neighbors around node j is relaxed. The idea is that even if all its neighbors are infected, the probability of the node j being infected is still small, so that the $P_{max}(j \in V_I^t | j_{obv}^t \in V_S^t)$ is less than the pre-set threshold. It can be concluded that this node is an uninfected node, regardless of its neighbors' real state.

Also, in order to reduce the iteration round as much as possible, we do not terminate the traversal immediately after discovering an missing node at each iteration, but move the node from set V_S^t to V_I^t and then continue traversing subsequent nodes. Inspired by this idea, we need to adjust the traversal order of these two traversals. More specifically, the node which has more infected neighbors has the higher priority to traverse, because it is more likely to be the false negative node compared with other nodes. Meanwhile, we could also traverse the node which has less neighbors, because this node is more likely to be the real uninfected one. Which way to choose is depend on the propagation situation. If the number of infected node is larger than the suspectable node, that means the worm spreads rapidly, and we should choose the first way to traverse.

5   Experiment

The method proposed in this paper was tested on three real world networks, include the power grid network[3], the enron email network[4] and AS-level network[5]. For the sake of discussion, the infection probability between nodes in the above networks were generated randomly, and it was assumed that $r_{ij} = r_{ji}$. All experiments were subject to independent performance test in windows7 system. The test computer was configured as an Intel Core i7-6700 3.4 GHz processor, 8 GB memory and 4G virtual memory allocated by ECLIPSE.

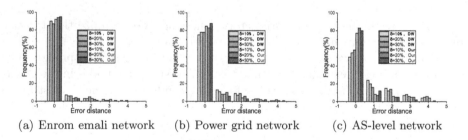

(a) Enrom emali network   (b) Power grid network   (c) AS-level network

Fig. 2. Accuracy comparison with the existing work.

Accuracy comparison with the existing work. The accuracy between this work and [9] was compared. We used the same configurations with that work. The false negative rate was not considered in [9], so when the false negative rate was

---

[3] http://www-personal.umich.edu/~mejn/netdata/.

[4] http://www.cs.cmu.edu/~enron/.

[5] http://data.caida.org/datasets/as-relationships/serial-1/.

higher, the accuracy of [9] was decreased significantly, and the effect of this work was significantly better in this case. It can be seen that, when the false negative rate was close to 20%, the probability of error distance = 0 for [9] was only 50%, while it was remained at about 70% in our algorithm.

6 Conclusion

This paper presents the first work on identifying the propagation source of stealth worm. We propose a modified algorithm of observed results based on bayes formula, which can modify the results of possible false negative nodes, so as to improve the accuracy of identifying the propagation sources. After that, we have applied the method of branch and bound, effectively reduced the traversal space and improved the efficiency of the algorithm by calculating the upper and lower bounds of the infection probability of nodes. We test our algorithm on three real networks, and the results show the accuracy of the algorithm.

References

1. Jiang, J., Wen, S., Shui, Y., Xiang, Y., Zhou, W.: Identifying propagation sources in networks: state-of-the-art and comparative studies. IEEE Commun. Surv. Tutorials **19**(1), 465–481 (2017)
2. Kaur, R., Singh, M.: A survey on zero-day polymorphic worm detection techniques. IEEE Commun. Surv. Tutorials **16**(3), 1520–1549 (2014)
3. Mohammed, M.M.Z.E., Chan, H.A., Ventura, N.: Honeycyber: automated signature generation for zero-day polymorphic worms. In: Military Communications Conference, MILCOM 2008, pp. 1–6. IEEE (2008)
4. Shah, D., Zaman, T.: Rumors in a network: who's the culprit? IEEE Trans. Inf. Theory **57**(8), 5163–5181 (2011)
5. Fioriti, V., Chinnici, M.: Predicting the sources of an outbreak with a spectral technique. arXiv preprint arXiv:1211.2333 (2012)
6. Prakash, B.A., Vreeken, J., Faloutsos, C.: Efficiently spotting the starting points of an epidemic in a large graph. Knowl. Inf. Syst. **38**(1), 35–59 (2014)
7. Lokhov, A.Y., Mézard, M., Ohta, H., Zdeborová, L.: Inferring the origin of an epidemic with a dynamic message-passing algorithm. Phys. Rev. E **90**(1), 012801 (2014)
8. Luo, W., Tay, W.P.: Finding an infection source under the sis model. In: 2013 IEEE International Conference on Acoustics, Speech and Signal Processing (ICASSP), pp. 2930–2934. IEEE (2013)
9. Wang, D., Wen, S., Xiang, Y., Zhou, W., Zhang, J., Nepal, S.: Catch me if you can: detecting compromised users through partial observation on networks. In: 2017 IEEE 37th International Conference on Distributed Computing Systems (ICDCS), pp. 2417–2422. IEEE (2017)

Machine Learning Based Text Mining in Electronic Health Records: Cardiovascular Patient Cases

Sergey Sikorskiy[1]([⊠]), Oleg Metsker[1], Alexey Yakovlev[2], and Sergey Kovalchuk[1]

[1] ITMO University, Saint Petersburg, Russia
sikorskiy.s@hotmail.com, olegmetsker@gmail.com,
sergey.v.kovalchuk@gmail.com
[2] Almazov National Medical Research Centre, Saint Petersburg, Russia
alex.yakovlev@mail.ru

Abstract. This article presents the approach and experimental study results of machine learning based text mining methods with application for EHR analysis. It is shown how the application of ML-based text mining methods to identify classes and features correlation to increases the possibility of prediction models. The analysis of the data in EHR has significant importance because it contains valuable information that is crucial for the decision-making process during patient treatment. The preprocessing of EHR using regular expressions and the means of vectorization and clustering medical texts data is shown. The correlation analysis confirms the dependence between the found classes of diagnosis and individual characteristics of patients and episodes. The medical interpretation of the findings is also presented with the support of physicians from the specialized medical center, which confirms the effectiveness of the shown approach.

Keywords: Text mining · Cardiology · Machine learning · Decision support
Treatment process analysis · Acute coronary syndrome

1 Introduction

The developing methods of electronic health record (EHR) analysis is a relevant scientific problem because EHR contains critical information about the treatment process. In this regard, the automation of EHR texts processing could significantly expand and improve the diseases classification, the treatment duration, and cost prediction as well as prediction other important events. However, the difficulties of EHR analysis are associated with the semi-structuring, specific stylistic and grammatical features, abbreviations, clinician terms, etc. Pattern-based methods are often used to solving this problem [1]. These methods are characterized by high accuracy but they do not provide high flexibility and identification of various combinations of speech turns which limits their application. On the other hand, the machine learning (ML) based methods show high flexibility in the analysis of EHR and have a relatively good accuracy [2–4].

Y. Shi et al. (Eds.): ICCS 2018, LNCS 10862, pp. 818–824, 2018.
https://doi.org/10.1007/978-3-319-93713-7_80

This research is demonstrating the capabilities of using ML-based methods of text mining to extend EHR analysis. The experimental study is focused on data extraction and classification of EHR of cardiovascular patients in Alamazov Centre (one of the leading cardiological centers in Russia). The proposed approach enables improvement of the accuracy of events and parameters predicting in the course of patient treatment.

2 Related Work

The text-mining methods are widely used in a various domains [5–9]. Also, there are a lot of applications in healthcare. For example, a task of extraction of associations of diseases and genes associated with them is considered in [10]. The proposed approach is based on the method of named object recognition (NOR) using a dictionary of names and synonyms. Also, to analyze text on associations the analysis of the EHR semantics was applied to identify the links between medical terms with disease and treatment. For example, semantic analysis based on the ML method to identify clinical terms is presented in [11]. There are known problems of determining the sequence of events (treatment, examination, operation) and identifying cause-and-effect relationships in semi-structured EHR in the healthcare domain. The semantic analysis allows defining the relationship between events and causes. For example, solving this problem is possible with the semantic analysis using name recognition, Bayesian statistics, and logical rules to identify the risk factors [12]. It is possible to extract cause-and-effect relationships from EHR with using text mining based on ML methods. For example, a random forest is used to classify the descriptions of allergic reactions to drugs. Such method provides sufficient accuracy (90%) in comparison with the pattern based method (82%) [13].

Considering healthcare in Russia, it worth to mention that the Russian language has own features. To analyze EHR in the Russian language, the pattern based methods [1] are used more often. The pattern based methods demonstrate good accuracy in EHR analysis, but it does not give flexibility comparable to ML methods.

3 EHR Analysis: Cardiovascular Patients

Within the study, the analysis of diagnoses performed to identify implicit connections between patients EHR that do not fit into the basic clinician categories. The analyzed EHR dataset contains information about 8865 cardiovascular patients, different age categories from 25 to 96 years and various outcomes of treatment (died or not), which is not reflected in the texts of diagnoses. The diagnoses were taken from electronic medical records of the patients of the Almazov Centre treated from 2010 to 2017. The general study group (n = 8865) included several categories of the patients:

- Patients with the acute coronary syndrome (ACS), admitted to hospital urgently by Ambulance or by transfer from other hospitals (n = 4955).
- Patients with a stable course of coronary heart disease, which is a routine performed angioplasty and stenting of coronary arteries (n = 2760).

- Patients with heart rhythm disorders, which was performed by the arrhythmic interventions in emergency and planned order or cardioversion (n = 619).
- Other patients with emergency cardiac conditions requiring treatment in intensive care units and surgery patients (n = 531).

The study analyzed cases of medical care, which accumulated a sufficient amount of text data (5500 patients) containing a detailed description of clinical diagnosis (underlying disease, associated conditions, complications, comorbidities with detailed characteristics and stages, the name and date of invasive interventions and surgical operations, ICD-10 codes). Analyzed EHRs include only manual entry of the text (without templates). The comparison of the selected group with the general database of cardiovascular patients by average indicators (gender, age, indicators, analyses, death rate, the average length of stay, etc.) do not reveal differences. It can be concluded that the selected cases are representative.

EHR preprocessing involves bringing the text to a more readable form because the diagnoses contain an abundance of abbreviations and various stylistic methods of writing medical texts. The preprocessing is to find and unify terms and acronyms. Regular expressions and other procedural methods collected in the Python script enabled unification of terms within the texts with replacement of various occurrence of the terms with a single one. The complete list contains more than 1000 regular expressions in 12 main groups: (1) abbreviation of diseases and synonyms; (2) ranks, stages of disease, functional classes; (3) removing unnecessary words; (4) general condition of the patient; (5) drugs; (6) locations and type of pain; (7) breathing and dyspnea; (8) edemas; (9) urogenital system; (10) blood pressure; (11) numerals; (12) removing special characters.

Further EHR processing is based on the methods of texts vectorization and bringing them to binary values and identify groups of the patients. This stage includes converting of texts to the matrix of token (keywords) counts using CountVectorizer from scikit-learn[1] library. Within the analysis 1060 keywords were used. Top keywords include: disease (6064); ischemic (5912); heart (5463); acute (3607); coronary (2477); heart attack (2301); myocardium (1739) heart (1502); angina (1265); hypertonic (1084).

The developed pre-processing routines were generalized to enable reusing of the script in various analysis scenarios.

On the next step ML methods were hired to get deeper understanding of patient variability. The reducing of dimensions of the binary vectors using the t-SNE [14] method from the scikit-learn package discovers the 10 clusters (Fig. 1). The configuration of the t-SNE method to obtain clusters of patients eliminates the random initialization of the model and the coefficient of perplexity 30 which gives reasonable distinction between clusters. t-SNE method gives clearer cluster boundaries even in 2d space, while, for example, principal component analysis (PCA) widely used for dimension reduction shows a weak distinction between clusters with 2 principal components. As a result, t-SNE was selected for further analysis and interpretation.

---

[1] http://scikit-learn.org/.

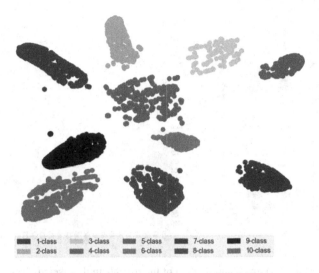

Fig. 1. The clusters of diagnoses descriptions.

From a practical point of view, interpretation of different clusters can have different meanings. Class of the patient can be considered as a predictor of an event (e.g., re-hospitalization). To get deeper insight on clusters interpretation it is needed to analyze the patient data and individual characteristics in depth. The obtained 10 classes of patients during the analysis of individual parameters of patients and episodes revealed various meaning of classes. For example, Class 5 and Class 10 differ in the duration of treatment comparing to other classes (Fig. 2a). Also, the correlation analysis showed correlations by class variable (C1–C10, Boolean) with individual characteristics of patients and episodes: age; ischemic chronic disease (IHD); essential hypertension (EH); angina (Ang); Q-wave infarction (QInf); treatment duration in intensive care (TIC); treatment duration in hospital (THosp); hemoglobin minimum (HGB); troponin maximum (Trop); glucose maximum (Gluc); leukocytes maximum (Lkc); thrombocytes maximum (PLT); Repetition (Rep); cholesterol (Ch) (Fig. 2b).

E.g., there is notable correlation between C1 and duration of treatment in the hospital; C3 and presence of hypertension in patients; C4 and myocardial infarction, C5 and repeatability, duration of treatment in intensive care, angina; C8 and cholesterol, maximum leukocyte level, maximum troponin level, q heart attack, angina pectoris, and duration; C10 and leukocytes, angina pectoris, and duration.

It is possible to expand the idea that a combination of text characteristics associated with repeated hospitalizations has been found. E.g., repetition of hospitalization is an essential indicator of value-based medicine related to high cost of treatment.

In general, the diagnosis is based on individual symptoms, syndromes, laboratory and instrumental studies, as well as the results of assessing the dynamics of these manifestations. During the observation of the patient, a clinician forms an idea of the nature of the disease and formulates a diagnosis. The presence of the disease implies the probable presence of certain risk factors that contributed to its development. The role of well-known pathogenetic mechanisms in its occurrence and progression,

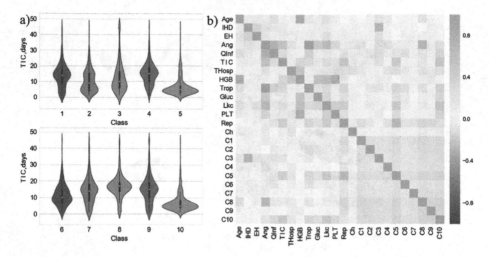

Fig. 2. EHR analysis (a) treatment duration of the patients in discovered classes; (b) correlation matrix of text classes with individual characteristics of the patients

characteristics of its course, the need for and a specific effect of therapy, the probable prognosis, is considered as a single logical structure of the patient with a particular disease. The classes obtained earlier were analyzed with using the clinical method associated with indication of most frequent tokens in EHR texts:

- **Class 1.** (n = 592) Patients with ACS in the duration of hospital stay is slightly above average (14 K/d), in-hospital mortality of 1.8%. **Tokens:** acute, coronary.
- **Class 2.** Lighter, sharper, more heavy routine, or massive intervention in stable patients. Hospitalization 10 days, mortality of 1.2%. **Tokens:** ischemic, chronic, rheumatic.
- **Class 3.** Mostly scheduled patients with significant heart failure complicating various cardiac diseases, duration of admission is above average and relatively high mortality (2.7%). **Tokens:** atherosclerosis, mitral.
- **Class 4.** Patients with the most severe myocardial infarction, including transmural (with Q), with prolonged hospitalization (15/d), relatively high mortality of 3.1%. **Tokens:** ischemic, acute, infarction.
- **Class 5.** These are planned subsequent stages of revascularization in ACS or planned interventions (including stenting, reconstructive vascular surgery) with a favorable course, but requiring a subsequent step of early hospital rehabilitation, almost no mortality, the duration of treatment is small (mortality 0.4%, bed-day 7). **Tokens:** ischemic, hypertension, angina.
- **Class 6.** Planned stenting or patients with unstable angina, mortality is almost there, stay short light patients. **Tokens:** ischemic, unstable.
- **Class 7.** A variety of emergency patients with stay above average, but almost without lethality and severe emergency pathology with a favorable prognosis. **Tokens:** coronary, acute, syndrome.

- **Class 8.** Young patients with severe transmural heart attacks, with pronounced risk factors, even longer hospitalization than in 4 Class, but with a more favorable prognosis. **Tokens:** infarction, myocardium, acute.
- **Class 9.** Patients with ACS, hospitalized at a later stage of the disease. **Tokens:** coronary, ischemic, acute.
- **Class 10.** The most stable planned patients. **Tokens:** heart, failure, cardiac.

Based on this, one can draw conclusions about the impact of certain words in the diagnosis on the length of stay and the probability of death (for example, ischemic, action, infarction to increase the mortality rate). In the same time, this classification does not correspond to the nosological forms or type of operation or category of patients. It reflects the severity of the patient's condition, the seriousness of intervention, unique features, and overall treatment strategy. Also, it may coincide in patients with various diseases and vary in patients with the same diseases (depending on the characteristics of the patient and the course of the disease). The classification does not coincide with the principles of construction of medical nosological classifications, closer to the prognostic scales, but more fully and multifaceted (with characteristics' combinations). From the cost analysis or predict future outcomes should be more accurate than the tradition nosological classification and the scale. Clinical statistical groups (flexible classes) must form not on nosology but on clusters with cost accounting.

4 Discussion and Conclusion

Medical processes have many aspects to be considered. For example, the diagnosis of anamnesis and patient characteristics may be different from pathway or event classification. So one need to understand how the different classifications may be compared from the point of view of medical knowledge. For this purpose, it is necessary to have accurate predictive models. From medical point of view, this approach does not allow to plan the patient's treatment strategy for the long term, but enables assessing the characteristics of the episode of care and outcomes in the short term. It is relevant for a large medical center where a lot of patients receiving different treatment, which may have a similar set of random and unrelated characteristics. The interpretation of these combinations to a certain extent conditional, in fact, is the search for matches between clusters and groups selected by the clinical approach.

Using ML methods for data processing enables selection of combinations of features to be divided into classes outside the logical framework of the clinical presentation of the patient. It needs extraordinary efforts to integrate this information into the structure of the representation of the patient, with similar interpretation, some non-obvious characteristics of the groups identified in the analysis may be lost. The logical structure of the clinical presentation of the patient is the basis for the formation of treatment strategies and clinical decision-making in the conditions of data shortage.

The current study is still in progress. It includes development of a generalized toolbox for classifying, processing, and analyzing of EHR text data. Based on the early results of the analysis of texts, it can be concluded that the proposed approach to clustering of text data is useful. Future work includes several directions of development. For example, having information about which group a patient belongs to, it may be possible to efficiently solve the problem of prognosis (required tests, duration or type of disease), as well as to improve the model of prediction of treatment processes.

Acknowledgements. This work financially supported by Ministry of Education and Science of the Russian Federation, Agreement #14.575.21.0161 (26/09/2017). Unique Identification RFMEFI57517X0161.

References

1. Metsker, O., Bolgova, E., Yakovlev, A., Funkner, A., Kovalchuk, S.: Pattern-based mining in electronic health records for complex clinical process analysis. Procedia Comput. Sci. **119**, 197–206 (2017)
2. Rakocevic, G., Djukic, T., Filipovic, N., Milutinović, V.: Computational Medicine in Data Mining and Modeling. Springer, New York (2013). https://doi.org/10.1007/978-1-4614-8785-2
3. Thompson, P., Batista-Navarro, R.T., Kontonatsios, G., Carter, J., Toon, E., McNaught, J., Timmermann, C., Worboys, M., Ananiadou, S.: Text mining the history of medicine. PLoS ONE **11**, e0144717 (2016)
4. Pereira, L., Rijo, R., Silva, C., Martinho, R.: Text mining applied to electronic medical records. Int. J. E-Health Med. Commun. **6**, 1–18 (2015)
5. Gupta, A., Simaan, M., Zaki, M.J.: Investigating bank failures using text mining. In: 2016 IEEE Symposium Series on Computational Intelligence (SSCI), pp. 1–8. IEEE (2016)
6. Suh-Lee, C., Jo, J.-Y., Kim, Y.: Text mining for security threat detection discovering hidden information in unstructured log messages. In: 2016 IEEE Conference on Communications and Network Security (CNS), pp. 252–260. IEEE (2016)
7. Septiana, I., Setiowati, Y., Fariza, A.: Road condition monitoring application based on social media with text mining system: case study: East Java. In: 2016 International Electronics Symposium (IES), pp. 148–153. IEEE (2016)
8. Landge, M.A., Rajeswari, K.: GPU accelerated Chemical Text mining for relationship identification between chemical entities in heterogeneous environment. In: 2016 International Conference on Computing Communication Control and Automation (ICCUBEA), pp. 1–6. IEEE (2016)
9. Mahmoud, M.A., Ahmad, M.S.: A prototype for context identification of scientific papers via agent-based text mining. In: 2016 2nd International Symposium on Agent, Multi-Agent Systems and Robotics (ISAMSR), pp. 40–44. IEEE (2016)
10. Pletscher-Frankild, S., Pallejà, A., Tsafou, K., Binder, J.X., Jensen, L.J.: DISEASES: text mining and data integration of disease–gene associations. Methods **74**, 83–89 (2015)
11. Bino Patric Prakash, G., Jacob, S.G., Radhameena, S.: Mining semantic representation from medical text: a Bayesian approach. In: 2014 International Conference on Recent Trends in Information Technology. pp. 1–4. IEEE (2014)
12. Urbain, J.: Mining heart disease risk factors in clinical text with named entity recognition and distributional semantic models. J. Biomed. Inform. **58**, S143–S149 (2015)
13. Casillas, A., Gojenola, K., Perez, A., Oronoz, M.: Clinical text mining for efficient extraction of drug-allergy reactions. In: Proceedings of the 2016 IEEE International Conference on Bioinformatics and Biomedicine, BIBM 2016, pp. 946–952 (2017)
14. Platzer, A.: Visualization of SNPs with t-SNE. PLoS ONE **8**, e56883 (2013)

Evolutionary Ensemble Approach
for Behavioral Credit Scoring

Nikolay O. Nikitin[✉], Anna V. Kalyuzhnaya, Klavdiya Bochenina,
Alexander A. Kudryashov, Amir Uteuov, Ivan Derevitskii,
and Alexander V. Boukhanovsky

ITMO University, 49 Kronverksky Pr., St. Petersburg 197101, Russian Federation
nikolay.o.nikitin@gmail.com

Abstract. This paper is concerned with the question of potential quality of
scoring models that can be achieved using not only application form data but also
behavioral data extracted from the transactional datasets. The several model types
and a different configuration of the ensembles were analyzed in a set of experiments. Another aim of the research is to prove the effectiveness of evolutionary
optimization of an ensemble structure and use it to increase the quality of default
prediction. The example of obtained results is presented using models for
borrowers default prediction trained on the set of features (purchase amount,
location, merchant category) extracted from a transactional dataset of bank
customers.

Keywords: Credit scoring · Credit risk modeling · Financial behavior
Ensemble modeling · Evolutionary algorithms

1 Introduction

Scoring tasks and associated scoring models vary a lot depending on application area
and objectives. For example, application form-based scoring [1] is used by lenders to
decide which credit applicants are good or bad. Collection scoring techniques [2] are
used for segmentation of defaulted borrowers to optimize debts recovery, and profit
scoring approach [3] is used to estimate profit on specific credit product.

In this work, we consider scoring prediction problem for behavioral data in several
aspects. First of all, the set of experiments were conducted to determine the potential
quality of default prediction using different types of scoring models for the behavioral
dataset. Then, the possible impact of the evolutionary approach to improving the quality
of ensemble of different models by optimization of its structure was analyzed in comparison with the un-optimized ensemble.

This paper follows in Sect. 2 with a review of works in the same domain, in Sect. 3
we introduce the problem statement and the approaches for scoring task. Section 4
describes the dataset used as a case study and presents the conducted experiments. In
Sect. 5 we provide the summary of results; conclusion and future ways of increasing the
scoring model are placed in Sect. 6.

© Springer International Publishing AG, part of Springer Nature 2018
Y. Shi et al. (Eds.): ICCS 2018, LNCS 10862, pp. 825–831, 2018.
https://doi.org/10.1007/978-3-319-93713-7_81

2   Related Work

Credit scoring problem is usually considered within a framework of supervised learning. Thus, all common machine learning methods are used to deal with it: Bayesian methods, logistic regression, neural networks, k-nearest neighbor, etc. (a review of popular existing methods for credit scoring problems can be found in [4]).

A good and yet relatively simple solution to improve the predictive power of machine learning model is to use the ensemble methods. The key idea of this approach is to train different estimators (probably on different regions of input space) and then combine their predictions. In [5] authors performed a comparison of three common ensemble techniques on the datasets for credit scoring problem: bagging, boosting and stacking. Stacking and bagging on decision trees were reported as two best ensemble techniques. The Kaggle platform for machine learning competitions published a practical review of ensemble methods, illustrated on real word problems [6].

The current trend appears to be the enrichment of primary application form features with information about dynamics of financial and social behavior extracted from bank transactional bases and open data sources. According to some studies, the involvement of transactional data allows increasing the quality of scoring prediction significantly [7].

It is worth to mention that in the vast majority of the studies on credit scoring models are aimed to the resulting quality of classification and do not study in detail the possible effect of optimization the structure of ensemble of models. In contrast, in this paper we are aimed to investigate, how good the prediction for behavioral data can be and how much the ensemble structure and parameters can be evolutionary improved to increase the reliability of the scoring prediction.

3   Problem Statement and Approaches for Behavioral Scoring

The widely used approach for making a credit-granting (underwriting) decision is the application form-based scoring. It's based on demographic and static features like age, gender, education, employment history, financial statement, credit history. The application form data allows to create sufficiently effective scoring model, but this approach isn't possible in some cases. For example, pre-approved credit card proposal to debit card clients can be based only on a limited behavioral dataset, that bank can extract from the transactional history of a customer.

3.1   Predictive Models for Scoring Task

The credit default prediction result is binary, so the two-classes classification algorithms potentially applicable approach for this task. The set of behavioral characteristics of every client can be used as predictor variables, and default flag as the response variable. The several methods were chosen to build an ensemble: K-nearest neighbors classifier, linear (LDA) and quadratic separating surface (QDA) classifiers, feed-forward neural network with one single hidden layer, XGboost-based predictive model, Random Forest classifier.

An ensemble approach to scoring model allows to combine the advantages of different classifiers and to improve the quality of prediction of default. The probability vectors obtained at the output of each model included in the ensemble used as an input of a metamodel constructed using an algorithm that performs the maximization of the quality metrics and generates the optimal set of ensemble weights. While the total number of models combinations is 2^7, we implement the evolutionary algorithm using the DEoptim [8] package, which performs fast multidimensional optimization in weights space using the algorithm of differential evolution.

3.2 Metrics for Quality Estimation of Classification-Based Models

The standard accuracy metric is not suitable for the scoring task due to the very unbalanced sample of profiles with many "good" profiles (>97%) and a small amount of "bad." Therefore, threshold-independence metric AUC (the area under the receiver operating characteristic curve – ROC, that describes the diagnostic ability of a binary classifier) was selected to compare models.

Kolmogorov-Smirnov statistic allows estimating the value of threshold by comparison of probability distributions of original and predicted datasets. The probability which corresponds to the maximum of KS coefficient can be chosen as optimal in general case.

4 Case Study

4.1 Transactional Dataset

To provide the experiments with different configurations of scoring model, totally depersonalized transactional dataset was used. We obtained it for research purposes from one of the major banks in Russia. The dataset contains details for more than 10M anonymized transactions that were done by cardholders before they applied for a credit card and bank's application underwriting procedure accepted them. The time range of transactions starts on January 1, 2014, and covers the range up to December 31, 2016.

Each entity in the dataset is assigned to indicator variable of default, that corresponds to the payment delinquency for 90 or more days. The delinquency rate for the profiles from this dataset is 3.02%

The set of parameters of transactions included in the dataset and the summary of behavioral profile parameters that can be used as predictor variables in scoring models presented in Table 1.

This data allows identifying the profiles of bank clients as a set of some derived parameters, that characterize their financial behavior pattern, obtained from transactions structure. Also, the date variable can be used to take macroeconomic variability into account.

Since some profile variables have a lognormal distribution, the logarithmic transformation for one-side-restricted values and additional scaling to [0, 1] range was applied.

Table 1. Variables from the transactional dataset

Variable group	Transactional variables	Behavioral profile parameters
Attributes of transaction	IDs of client and contract, date of the transaction, date of contract signing	The numbers of actual and closed contracts
MCC (merchant category code)	Amount of transaction (in roubles), the location of The terminal used for operation (if known), transaction type (payment/cash withdrawal/ transfer), Merchant Category Code (if known)	Common frequency and quantitative characteristics of transactions; Merchant category-specific characteristics of transactions
Geo	Address of payment terminal	Spatial-based characteristics of transactions
Default mark	Binary flag of default	

4.2   Evolutionary Ensemble Model

The comparison of performance for scoring models is presented in Fig. 1.

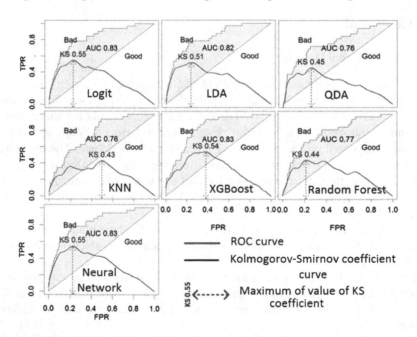

Fig. 1. The AUC and KS performance metrics for scoring models

The maximum value of Kolmogorov-Smirnov coefficient can be interpreted as an optimal value for probability threshold for each model.

The ensemble of these models can have a different configuration, and it's unnecessary to include all models to the ensemble. To measure the effect from every new model in the ensemble, we conduct a set of experiments and compare the quality of the scoring prediction for evolutionary-optimized ensembles with a different structure (from 2 to 7 models with separate optimization procedure for every size value). The logit regression was chosen as the base model. The structure of the ensemble is presented in Fig. 2a, the summary plot displaying the results is shown in Fig. 2b.

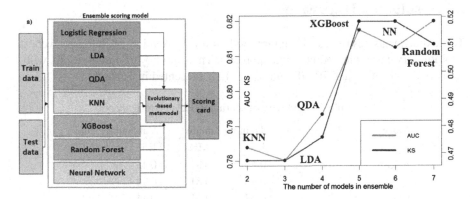

Fig. 2. (a) Structure of the ensemble of heterogeneous scoring models (b) Dependence of quality metrics AUC and KS on the number of models in optimized configuration the ensemble

It can be seen that the overall quality of the scoring score increases with the number of models used, but the useful effect isn't similar - for example, the neural network model does not enhance the ensemble quality.

The set of predictors of ensemble scoring models includes variables with different predictive power. The redundant variables make the development of interpretable scoring card difficult and can cause the re-training effect. Therefore, the evolutionary

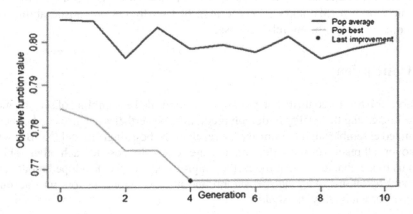

Fig. 3. The convergence of the evolutionary algorithm with an AUC-based fitness function

approach based on kofnGA algorithm [9] was used to create an optimal subset of input variables. The results of execution are presented in Fig. 3.

The convergence is achieved in 4 generations where experimentally determined population size equals 50 individuals; mutation probability equals 0.7 and variables subset size equals 14. The optimal variable set contains 8 variables from "MCC" group, 4 financial parameters and 2 geo parameters.

5   Results and Discussions

The experiments results can be interpreted as a confirmation of the effectiveness of evolutionary ensemble optimization approach. The summary of model results with 10-fold cross-validation and 70-30 train/test ratio is presented in Table 2.

Table 2. Summary of scoring models performance

Model	Training sample		Validation sample	
	KS	AUC	KS	AUC
Logistic regression	0.46	0.81	0.45	0.79
KNN	0.46	0.81	0.34	0.72
LDA	0.67	0.81	0.44	0.79
QDA	0.52	0.82	0.48	0.74
Random forest	0.97	0.99	0.41	0.78
XGBoost	0.6	0.88	0.49	0.81
Neural network	0.46	0.81	0.45	0.79
Base ensemble	0.74	0.94	0.49	0.80
Optimized ensemble	0.75	0.95	**0.51**	**0.82**

It can be seen that some best of single models provide similar quality of scoring predictions. The simple "blended" ensemble with equal weights for every model cannot improve the final quality, but the evolutionary optimization allows to increase the result of the scoring prediction slightly. The problem for the case study is the limited access to additional data (like applications forms), that's why the prognostic ability of the applied models can't be entirely disclosed.

6   Conclusion

The obtained results confirm that evolutionary-controlled ensembling of scoring models allows increasing the quality of default prediction. Nevertheless, it also can be seen that optimized ensemble slightly improve the result of the best single model (XGBoost) and, moreover, all results of individual models are relatively close to each other. This fact leads us to the conclusion that the further improvement of the developed model can be achieved by taking additional behavioral and non-behavioral factors into account to increase current quality threshold.

Acknowledgments. This research is financially supported by The Russian Science Foundation, Agreement № 17-71-30029 with co-financing of Bank Saint Petersburg.

References

1. Abdou, H.A., Pointon, J.: Credit scoring, statistical techniques and evaluation criteria: a review of the literature. Intell. Syst. Account. Fin. Manag. **18**(2–3), 59–88 (2011)
2. Ha, S.H.: Behavioral assessment of recoverable credit of retailer's customers. Inf. Sci. (Ny) **180**(19), 3703–3717 (2010)
3. Serrano-Cinca, C., Gutiérrez-Nieto, B.: The use of profit scoring as an alternative to credit scoring systems in peer-to-peer (P2P) lending. Decis. Support Syst. **89**, 113–122 (2016)
4. Lessmann, S., et al.: Benchmarking state-of-the-art classification algorithms for credit scoring: an update of research. Eur. J. Oper. Res. **247**(1), 124–136 (2015)
5. Wang, G., et al.: A comparative assessment of ensemble learning for credit scoring. Expert Syst. Appl. **38**(1), 223–230 (2011)
6. Kaggle Ensembling Guide [Electronic resource]
7. Westley, K., Theodore, I.: Transaction Scoring: Where Risk Meets Opportunity [Electronic resource]
8. Mullen, K.M., et al.: DEoptim: an R package for global optimization by differential evolution. J. Stat. Softw. **40**(6), 1–26 (2009)
9. Wolters, M.A.: A genetic algorithm for selection of fixed-size subsets with application to design problems. J. Stat. Softw. **68**(1), 1–18 (2015)

Detecting Influential Users
in Customer-Oriented Online Communities

Ivan Nuzhdenko$^{(\boxtimes)}$, Amir Uteuov, and Klavdiya Bochenina

ITMO University, Saint Petersburg, Russia
ivanbor38@niuitmo.ru

Abstract. Every year the activity of users in various social networks is increasing. Different business entities can analyze in more detail the behavior of the audience and adapt their products and services to its needs. Social network data allow not only to find the influential individuals according to their local topological properties, but also to investigate their preferences, and thus to personalize strategies of interaction with opinion leaders. However, information channels of organizations (e.g., community of a bank in a social network) include not only target audience but also employees and fake accounts. This lowers the applicability of network-based methods of identifying influential nodes. In this study, we propose an algorithm of discovering influential nodes which combines topological metrics with the individual characteristics of users' profiles and measures of their activities. The algorithm is used along with preliminary clustering procedure, which is aimed at the identification of groups of users with different roles, and with the algorithm of profiling the interests of users according to their subscriptions. The applicability of approach is tested using the data from a community of large Russian bank in the vk.com social network. Our results show that: (i) it is important to consider user's role in the leader detection algorithm, (ii) the roles of poorly described users may be effectively identified using roles of its neighbors, (iii) proposed approach allows for finding users with high values of actual informational influence and for distinguishing their key interests.

Keywords: Social network analysis · Opinion leaders · Topic modeling
Opinion mining

1 Introduction

The popularity of online social networks (OSNs) has led to the development of a wide variety of algorithms and tools to analyze different aspects of human activities and behavior in online context. Digital traces of individuals can give us useful insights on their habits, preferences, emotional state, structure and dynamics of social contacts and their involvement in information spreading. One of the most studied fields along with modeling cascades of information messages (review in [1]) is the detection of influential users in OSN (e.g. [2, 3]).

The vast majority of studies on finding influential users is focused on topological properties of nodes in a network. The restrictions of pure network-based methods lead to a necessity of data-driven algorithms development which combine topological and

© Springer International Publishing AG, part of Springer Nature 2018
Y. Shi et al. (Eds.): ICCS 2018, LNCS 10862, pp. 832–838, 2018.
https://doi.org/10.1007/978-3-319-93713-7_82

individual characteristics aiming to solve a domain problem. In this study, we show an example of such approach for customer relationship management via specialized enterprise communities in OSN. We are focused on what we call customer-oriented online communities – communities which are created by a representative of an enterprise to inform the clients about the news, to answer their questions and to provide them any desirable support.

There are different ways to find opinion leaders in a social graph (i.e. to determine the users which information messages may have a strong impact on their audience). These approaches are: (i) using degree centrality, (ii) grouping local topological measures (e.g. different centrality measures [2]), (iii) using connectivity properties [4], (iv) exploiting both topology and semantic (for instance, [3] combines PageRank and sentiment analysis), (v) exploiting history of users' feedback (e.g. [5]). Existing algorithms mostly do not account for the functional role of a user within a community; however, there exist communities in which this role clearly influences the level of involvement of users within the context. In this study we propose an algorithm which exploits different kinds of data available in customer-oriented online communities to identify influential users who are not affiliated with community owner and belong to the target audience of a domain community. The paper is organized as follows. Section 2 gives a description of a problem and of proposed method. Section 3 describes a dataset. Finally, Sect. 4 demonstrates the results.

2   Method

By the customer-oriented community in online social network we mean a group in a social network which is owned by a particular stakeholder (e.g. a bank or a retailer) to inform the clients about news of organization, to provide real-time support, to answer the questions, to promote campaigns etc. In the customer-oriented community (in contrast to, e.g., entertainment community) the goal of the stakeholder is to interact only with the target audience to increase their loyalty and lifetime value.

The definition of a leader in a customer-oriented community also changes compared to ordinary communities. The leader of the customer-oriented online community is not only a person with high impact on their audience, but also the one who belongs to the target audience of community stakeholder (for a bank it will be a client or potential customer, not an employee and not a bot). After the opinion leaders in the customer-oriented community are detected, a stakeholder may suggest them personalized offers with account of their interests (this is the case that we consider in frames of this study) or to consider the interests of groups of influential users while developing strategies of customer relationship management. In this study, we use information from community, topology of network of subscribers and user profile data to identify the influential users among the people with a required role ("customer").

We obtain the data from the largest Russian online social network vk.com (denoted as VK). It supports automated collection of: (i) a list of community subscribers, (ii) a list of subscribers' friends, (iii) reactions of users to community posts (likes, shares, comments), and (iv) for each user – sex, age, place of work. Moreover, users in VK have personal page including the following additional information: (i) "wall", which means the chronologically sorted list of user posts and shares (information from a wall may also be commented and shared by the friends of a user), (ii) list of user subscriptions which may be used to estimate their interests.

All these data may be used to estimate target properties of opinion leaders (Table 1, Algorithm 1). By target property we mean the parameter of a leader which is important in a context of customer-oriented community. For example, the level of user involvement in a community "life" influences the potential informational influence on this user by messages generated by this community (if a user has several hundred subscriptions, it will likely miss the information from a single one).

Table 1. Algorithms: (i) influential users' detection, (ii) user affiliation detection

(i) Algorithm 1. Influential users detection	(ii) Algorithm 2. User affiliation detection
Input: Followers (list of followers) 1 **for** f **in** Followers: 2 **if** f.workplace != bank 3 **if** f.friends_number > M 4 **if** f.friends_inside_comm > N 5 **if** f.posts_number > P 6 **if** f.avg_likes_per_post > Q 7 then: 8 f.is_influential = **True** 9 **if** f.is_influential 10 interests = f.get_interests()	Input: G (network of subscribers) 1 **for** cluster **in** G.get_clusters(): 2 label = cluster.workplace.most_common() 3 **if** label.frequency() > threshold 4 then: 5 **for** follower **in** cluster 6 follower.affiliation = label

Algorithm 1 is organized as a system of filters. It takes into account the potential information impact and behavioral characteristics forming a certain level of trust in users. Values M, N, P and Q may be chosen as k-th (e.g. 0.9) quantile of the corresponding distribution or to be set according to a desired threshold. The majority of users do not specify information about their place of work in the OSN which is needed by Algorithm 1. To address this, we use procedure of user affiliation detection described in Algorithm 2. To identify the interests of users (Algorithm 1, step 10), the information on users' subscriptions was processed (see the details in Sect. 4.2). The output of Algorithm 1 is a list of opinion leaders with their personal interests.

3   Data Description

To perform the study, we collected the data of the community of a large Russian bank in VK OSN for a period 26.04.2016–20.09.2017. The page of a community contains 400 posts with 29139 followers, 10682 likes, 1850 comments and 1330 shares in total. For each of the followers we also collected data required by Algorithms 1, 2 (see Table 1). To check the actual information impact of influential users, we also collected data on likes, comments and shares on all posts from users' personal pages ("walls"). The size of the resulting dataset amounted to 23 GB. It contained 973 000 posts with information about likes, shares, comments and date of the publication (Table 2).

To study local topological properties characterizing user behavior a network of community subscribers was created. A node in the network represents community user

Table 2. Descriptive statistics of dataset with personal pages of community followers

Target property	Mean	Median	Max
Average likes per post	3.6	0.48	850
Average shares per post	0.12	0	65.5
Posts number	59.7	15	16599
Friends number	337.8	170	10000
Friends inside community	2.6	1	708
Subscriptions number	244.7	102	5008

and an edge represents friendly link between users. Thus, a resulting network contains only friend relationships between subscribers and do not contain relationships with people who are not members of a community. The resulting graph has 17580 nodes and 38593 edges, and average clustering coefficient equals to 0.09.

4 Results

4.1 User Affiliation Recovery

Figure 1 represents a visualization of the giant component of a network of subscribers (15000 nodes) after clustering (see Algorithm 2). Different colors represent different clusters, a size of a circle represents a number of friends inside the community. As it was expected, the information about user affiliation was available for a low percentage of users (9%). In total, 2083 different occupations were found. As a result, from 2524 users with known occupation 199 (8%) were labeled as affiliated with a bank.

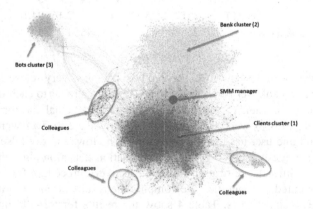

Fig. 1. Giant component of a community of a bank (cluster 1 – aquamarine, cluster 2 – yellow, cluster 3 – green) (Color figure online)

To assign labels to clusters, we calculate a percentage of users with a bank and non-bank affiliation for each cluster. Although the percentage of users with known workplace for clusters 1 and 2 is similar (11% and 15%, respectively), the concentration of bank employees in a cluster 2 is extremely high (49%). At the same time, cluster 2 contains only 2% of users with known occupation from the bank. This suggests that cluster 1 is a cluster of clients, and cluster 2 is a cluster of bank employees. Cluster 3 was marked as cluster of bots by analysis of the similarity network of users. The smaller clusters of users from the same organizations can also be distinguished (the examples are shown in Fig. 1).

4.2   Detection of Influential Users and Their Interests

For this chapter, we used the following values of filters: (a) more than 200 total friends, (b) more than 20 friends inside the community, (c) less than 100 subscriptions to other groups, (d) more than 10 posts on a personal page. After the filtration process, the algorithm divided extracted followers on four clusters which we denote as bank_possible, bank_verified (true positive), ok_possible, ok_verified (true negative), see Table 3. Bank_verified means that the follower has an affiliation with a bank verified by the workplace field on the personal page and the detection algorithm assigns this follower to the bank cluster. Bank_possible means that the algorithm assigns a follower to the bank cluster but there is no information about the workplace on his or her page. The same logic holds for ok_verified and ok_possible clusters. There was only one false negative from 45 users, and there were no false positive cases.

Table 3. Characteristics of groups (user affiliation detection algorithm): 1 – avg friends count (total), 2 – avg friends count (inside community), 3 – avg likes count, 4 – avg shares count, 5 – avg friends count from "bank" cluster, 6 – avg friends count from "non-bank" cluster

Cluster (size)	1	2	3	4	5	6
bank_possible (23)	372	32	14.15	0.2	30	2
bank_verified (10)	413	40	11.42	0.14	35	5
ok_verified (6)	3152	26.5	33.54	3	2.16	24.16
ok_possible (5)	2364	38.8	31.1	1.48	1.2	39

Table 3 demonstrates that ok_verified cluster has very close parameters to ok_possible while bank_verified and bank_possible are similar to each other. From the 23 users within the cluster, 16 (69.5%) were classified as actual and former employees of the bank, 4 (17.4%) were classified as "unknown", 2 (8.7%) were classified as "non-bank" and one user has deleted the profile. The low count of false positive cases (only 2 of 23) suggests the good quality of affiliation detection algorithm.

To show the importance of user affiliation recovery procedure for leader detection in customer-oriented communities, we compare the results of our algorithm with basic topological-based approaches. Table 4 show the results for top-500 influential users. 33% of important nodes determined by degree centrality were affiliated with a bank and 14% was marked as bots. In case of betweenness centrality – 12% of followers were in

Table 4. Quality of target audience detection for topological-based approaches

Metric	Ok (% of total)	Bank (% of total)	Bots (% of total)	% of non-target audience
Degree	53%	33%	14%	47%
PageRank	75%	20%	5%	25%
Betweenness	87%	12%	1%	13%

the bank cluster. 20% of users provided by PageRank was affiliated with bank and 5% was marked as bots. It means that these algorithms may provide from 10 to 50% of non-target audience in the resulting list of the opinion leaders.

Figure 2 gives the tornado diagrams for the number of extracted followers and average shares which show effect of input on output parameters. Median values were used to calculate a baseline. Border values corresponds to 25 and 75 percentiles. The most important parameters are number of friends within community/in total.

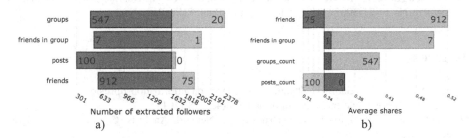

Fig. 2. Tornado chart for: (a) extracted followers, (b) average shares

To detect leaders' interests, we applied topic modelling for their subscriptions (12K communities). In this study, ARTM model was used as it showed better results compared to LDA [6]. Topic extraction algorithm created 32 different clusters. After that, we have found the preferred topics for particular users according to their subscriptions (Fig. 3). Two interests with high frequency can be distinguished for the leaders: beauty salons and theaters/museums.

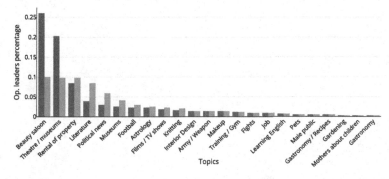

Fig. 3. Comparison of interests of leaders and ordinary users (blue – opinion leaders, orange – ordinary users) (Color figure online)

5 Conclusion

The recent trend in approaches to influential user detection in online social networks incorporates different types of available information while deciding on the potential impact of a user. In this study, as an example of such a problem we consider detection of leaders in customer-oriented online communities. The detection procedure is organized as a system of filters accounting for different target parameters of potential leaders. We account for different roles of users inside a community by introducing user affiliation recovery algorithm. Finally, we supplement leader detection algorithm with a tool for identifying interests of users according to their subscriptions. The experimental part of the study was conducted using the data on a banking community from the largest Russian social network, vk.com and showed the acceptable accuracy of affiliation detection and the restricted applicability of pure network-based approaches for customer-oriented communities.

Acknowledgements. This research is financially supported by The Russian Science Foundation, Agreement No 17-71-30029 with co-financing of Bank Saint Petersburg.

References

1. Li, M., Wang, X., Gao, K., Zhang, S.: A survey on information diffusion in online social networks: models and methods. Information **8**(4), 118 (2017)
2. Identifying Key Opinion Leaders Using Social Network Analysis. Cogniz. 20-20 Insights, June 2015
3. Zhu, M., Lin, X., Lu, T., Wang, H.: Identification of opinion leaders in social networks based on sentiment analysis: evidence from an automotive forum. Adv. Comput. Sci. Res. **58**, 412–416 (2016)
4. Helal, N.A., Ismail, R.M., Badr, N.L., Mostafa, M.G.M.: A novel social network mining approach for customer segmentation and viral marketing. Wiley Interdiscip. Rev. Data Min. Knowl. Discov. **6**(5), 177–189 (2016)
5. Sheikhahmadi, A., Nematbakhsh, M.A., Zareie, A.: Identification of influential users by neighbors in online social networks. Phys. A Stat. Mech. Appl. **486**, 517–534 (2017)
6. Vorontsov, K., Potapenko, A.: Additive regularization of topic models. Mach. Learn. **101**(1–3), 303–323 (2015)

GeoSkelSL: A Python High-Level DSL for Parallel Computing in Geosciences

Kevin Bourgeois[1,2]([⊠]), Sophie Robert[1], Sébastien Limet[1], and Victor Essayan[2]

[1] Univ. Orléans, INSA Centre Val de Loire, LIFO EA4022, Orléans, France
{kevin.bourgeois,sophie.robert,sebastien.limet}@univ-orleans.fr
[2] Géo-Hyd (Antea Group), Olivet, France
{kevin.bourgeois,victor.essayan}@anteagroup.com

Abstract. This paper presents GeoSkelSL a Domain Specific Language (DSL) dedicated to Geosciences that helps non experts in computer science to write their own parallel programs. This DSL is embedded in Python language which is widely used in Geosciences. The program written by the user is derived to an efficient C++/MPI parallel program using implicit parallel patterns. The tools associated to the DSL also generate scripts that allow the user to automatically compile and run the resulting program on the targeted computer.

Keywords: GIS · DSL · Implicit parallelism · Performance

1 Introduction

In the last decades, in almost every sciences, the amount of data to process have grown dramatically because of the technological progress that improved the resolution of the measuring tools and also because of the emergence of new technologies such as sensor networks. These progress allow scientists to refine their theoretical models to make them more precise which increases the need of computation power to compute them. Geosciences are particularly affected by these trends. Indeed, geosciences cover an area at the edge of the computer science and the earth sciences and aim at gathering, storing, processing and delivering geographic information. The global warming and the pollution or water resource problems became global concerns which reinforce the need for geosciences. For example, many countries impose regulations that command to collect and analyze some environmental data to provide indicators to the citizens.

On the other hand, during the same period, parallel computers became widespread since nowadays almost all computers have several processing units. It is now quite easy to any scientist to access a powerful parallel computer like a cluster. However, writing programs that efficiently exploit the computing power of such computers is not an easy task and requires high expertise in computer science. Unfortunately, very few people have great skills in both their scientific domain and computer science.

© Springer International Publishing AG, part of Springer Nature 2018
Y. Shi et al. (Eds.): ICCS 2018, LNCS 10862, pp. 839–845, 2018.
https://doi.org/10.1007/978-3-319-93713-7_83

A first solution, form a team composed of geoscientists and computer-scientists expert in parallel programming, may be difficult to implement because it could take a long time to make understand them each others. It may be a problem when programs become too complicated and the scientist loose the expertise on his codes. This could be also financially too expensive for small scientific units.

A second solution, provide tools to help non computer-scientists to produce efficient parallel program, is more attractive since it tends to make the geoscientist independent from the technicalities of parallel programming which allows him to master his programs. However, providing such tools needs to resolve three main issues, first, providing an easy-to-use programming language that is accepted by the scientist, then, being able to derive an efficient parallel program from the one written by the user and providing tools to easily run the generated programs on parallel machines.

According to their domain, the geoscientists are familiar with Python as GIS like ArcGIS or QGIS use it as script language. Therefore, the proposed programming language should be close to -or embedded in- Python.

Using implicit parallel patterns allow to hide some points of the parallelism. But using libraries as ScaLAPACK remains difficult because, programs are dependent of the provided routines which makes them difficult to evolve. The use of parallel patterns address this last issue however, they are usually based on a low-level language so they are hard to use for non computer scientists.

To provide a user-friendly tool that abstracts scientists from all the worries associated with parallelization, we propose the Geoskel framework. It relies on parallel patterns associated to a *Domain-Specific Language* (DSL) embedded in Python language. Thus, it is split into three layers: from a high-level programming language used to write algorithms, to a low-level data system to efficiently manage data on disks, with an implicit parallelism pattern layer in-between.

The GeoSkel heart is the implicit parallel patterns aimed to cover the recurring computations on rasters in geosciences [1]. This layer is written in C++ using template classes and the MPI parallel library. GeoSkelSL is the DSL top-level layer. It is a DSL embedded in Python allowing geoscientists to have a classical view of their GIS and to write their programs in a sequential way knowing the available predefined parallel patterns. This program is either executable in a Python context or can be transformed in a parallel program which can be automatically launched on a cluster. GeoSkelSL is the main contribution of the paper and is detailed Sect. 2 as well as the parallel program generation.

At the low-level layer, the datasets are stored in a distributed file system and the main objective of this layer in GeoSkel is to provide an efficient way to select the data required by the program and to distribute them according to the parallel execution.

The main tools used by geoscientists rely on Geographical Information Systems (GIS), like ArcGIS, QGIS [11] or GrassGIS [6]. These GISs were designed from sequential algorithms and focused on dealing with data of different formats as well as providing relevant user interfaces. They were not originally designed to be used on huge data sets. For several years now, some projects extend them with tools to perform parallel computations on large volume of data. SAGA-GIS has a module library and proposes parallel versions of some classical algorithms in hydrology. Thanks to the possibility to add external modules, QGIS and ArcGIS allow to include some optimized parallel computations. For example, TauDEM [10] a tool set to analyze a Digital Elevation Model and based on parallel processing can be used both by QGIS and ArcGIS.

All these systems strongly depend on external contributions for parallel processing and for geoscientists who are not specialists of parallel computing, it is very difficult to implement a new algorithm that is not included in the used toolkit.

Implicit parallelism aims at helping non specialists to write parallel programs. The user writes the program in a sequential way and the transformation into a parallel program is realized thanks to automatic tools which tends to hide the technicalities of data distribution, data communication or task division.

One approach to propose implicit parallelism is to provide parallel containers that are automatically distributed among the nodes and that can be handled as sequential containers. The Standard Adaptive Parallel Library is a C++ library similar and compatible with the STL [8]. The user builds programs using View and pAlgorithms. The View is equivalent to the iterator in the STL library, it is used to access the pContainers, which are parallel data structures. The pAlgorithms are the parallel equivalent to the algorithms of the STL.

The second approach to provide implicit parallelism is to write the program in a specific programming language. In this context, DSL [2] can be used. In general, the DSL's role is to hide low-level tools to users while allowing them to develop their applications by mean of the features provided by these tools. For example, in geosciences, the DSL [5] aims to specify visualization of large scale geospatial datasets. Instead of writing the visualization code using low-level API as Google Maps or Javascript libraries a DSL is proposed to describe the application as data properties, data treatments and visualization settings. Then the DSL source code is transformed into the appropriate visualization code.

In the implicit parallelism context, many DSLs are proposed either to be suitable for a scientific domain or for a class of parallel algorithms. In the machine learning domain, OptiML [9] is an implicit parallel DSL built on Scala [7] which design allows to take advantage of heterogeneous hardware.

The approaches described in [4] propose a DSL to write programs based on classical parallel patterns. In [4], the DSL is composed of simple expressions to describe the operation sequences. the DSL code is transformed into an executable program using rewriting rules and refactoring code which introduces parallel patterns. The DSLs presented above are not suitable for our purpose since none of them is both dedicated to geosciences and provides implicit parallelism. Hence, we describe GeoSkelSL a DSL embedded in Python and detail the DSL source code transformation into parallel patterns in the C++ layer.

2   GeoSkelSL

In this section, we present the main contribution of the paper i.e. the DSL called GeoSkelSL. It is the top layer of GeoSkel framework. The first objective of this high-level programming language is to be accessible to geoscientists to allow them to write their own programs in an usual way. The DSL source code will be transformed into a parallel C++/MPI program that will be compile to be run on the targeted computer. Therefore, the original program needs to contain the useful information for this transformation which must be transparent for the user. First, the main GeoSkelSL features are described. Then, the whole derivation process that transforms the DSL source code to a parallel program is detailed.

2.1   GeoSkelSL Features

GeoSkel is the interface with users. For its design, we have worked with geoscientists to understand their needs and expectations. This allowed us to extract the main features wanted in the DSL. They can be summarized in three points. The DSL must rely on a well-known language in geosciences, promote the expressiveness of the data they deal with, and hide the technical concerns related to the code parallelization. Our DSL is based on Python. It is a very common language in the geoscience domain and it is used in a lot of GIS tools such as ArcGIS, QGIS or GrassGIS. Therefore, Python is a well-known language to geoscientists, making it a good language to build a DSL on it. Moreover, embedding GeoSkelSL in Python language favors its use in GIS tools.

The Data. Our DSL deals with rasters which are matrices describing terrains with metadata as the projection used, the coordinates, the resolution, the color interpretation. It can have multiple bands and each of them can have its own datatype. A raster can depict the elevation of a terrain, soil pollutant concentrations at various depths, air pollutant concentrations. The rasters are used in many applications as watershed delineation, pollutant spreading and heat diffusion.

GeoSkelSL provides a `Mesh` class to handle rasters. Therefore a mesh is used to store each band of a raster. This class is also extended with basic operators corresponding to classical computations on a mesh as the addition or the subtraction. Thanks to a bracket operator for the cell access, a mesh is also usable as a standard 2D matrix. Regarding the metadata, GeoSkelSL uses GDAL [3] and its Python API to be able to read them. Therefore, `load_data` and `write_data` are the only functions necessary for the data management. They support the reading and the writing of the metadata information on the raster.

The Computation. The computation on rasters are based on the implicit parallel patterns implemented as a C++ library in our framework. These patterns allow to separate the writing of the computation to realize on the raster and the parallelization. According to the chosen pattern the user only needs to write some functions in Python to describe the computation to apply on the raster cells in a sequential way. For example, applying a median filter on a raster consists in using the stencil pattern. Thus, in GeoSkelSL the main program consists in few lines to describe how to load the data, which pattern to use and finally where the result is saved.

2.2 The Program Derivation

The program derivation consists in using the GeoSkelSL source code to concretely instantiate the parallel patterns. The main issues are the data types, the data distribution and the data dependencies that will define the exchanges necessary to the computation. The derivation process is based on a partial execution of the GeoSkelSL source code in order to guess the parameters of the parallelization. The steps illustrated Fig. 1 allow to build the C++ main program with the relevant parameters to instantiate correctly the parallel pattern and to launch its execution on a cluster.

As GeoSkelSL is based on Python, the user does not explicitly type variables or functions. However, the targeted program is a C++ program where all variables are statically typed. The derivation process has to type each Python variable. Choosing the right type is very important regarding performance. For example, the run-time of a program can be much longer using **double** rather than **float**.

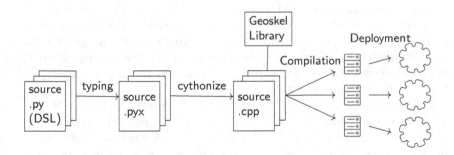

Fig. 1. Derivation process from the DSL source code to the parallel program.

Python has only two types to store numbers: **int** for integer and **float** to approximate real numbers. In C++, the programmer can control the precision of both integer and float numbers using different types like **short**, **int** or **long** for integers or **float** and **double** for real numbers. During the derivation from Python to C++, all variables and functions must be statically typed with the smallest equivalent in C++ for best performance. To do the type guessing the user must give at least the type of the incoming mesh. This can be done either using a parameter of the **load_data** function, or it can be guess by reading the metadata of the raster performing a partial execution of **load_data**. Each variable assignment of the Python program is then executed once to determine its type. NumPy is used to determine the smallest type needed in C++. NumPy is a Python library for scientific computing. NumPy types are very similar to C++ types and the execution of a variable assignment returns the smallest corresponding type.

The data distribution on the cluster nodes is based on a round-robin distribution which consists in splitting the mesh into sub-meshes in various shapes and sizes. For example, for the stencil pattern, a distribution per block of lines is chosen and the size of the block is defined according to the mesh size. The size of the raster is again guessed thanks to the partial execution of load_data.

The data exchanges depend on the data dependencies in the computation functions. Then, the size of the ghosts needs to be defined. In our patterns the computation of a raster cell can be dependent of a set of neighboring cells. As the data are distributed on different nodes the neighborhood of cells on edges is not local. These ghost cells need to be sent before the computation. The size of the ghosts can be guessed from the Python functions written by the user. Indeed, from the mesh accesses the neighborhood size can be defined as a distance with the studied cell. When multiple parallel patterns are called, all meshes share the larger ghost size found. This neighborhood size is necessary to the load_mesh function in the C++ main program.

The derivation from Python to C++ is based on the Cython library. This is a language very close to Python but it supports a subset of C/C++, like the typing, the variable declarations or the function calls. A Cython code (.pyx) can produce external modules than can be used in a standard C++ program. This feature is very useful to integrate the Python functions written by the user and which are the parameters of the parallel pattern. After the partial GeoSkelSL source code execution, a Cython typed code is generated with annotations to add the parameters related to the data distribution and the ghost size. The functions written by the user are also translated in Cython code. Then we use Cython associated to predefined rules to transform the original main program into a new main program in C++.

The programs are likely to be written on the desktop computer of geoscientists. The program derivation above generates a C++ program on this computer. It remains several steps that could be very tricky for non computer scientists, namely the compilation of this C++ program and the execution on a cluster. To overcome these issues, at the end of the derivation process, a script is generated. It automatically pushes and compiles C++ sources to the desired cluster thanks to a configuration file and finally launches the program.

Some experiments, not presented here for lack of space, show a good scalability of the programs generated from our DSL. These experiments show also an overhead of about 10% of these programs with regard to equivalent ones directly written in C++.

3   Conclusion and Future Work

In this paper, we introduced GeoSkelSL, an efficient and simple DSL intended for geoscientists. GeoSkelSL is embedded into Python as it is a widely used language in geosciences that can be easily integrated into popular GIS such as ArcGIS or QGIS. GeoSkelSL requires no skills in parallel programming and produces efficient and scalable programs. GeoSkelSL is the top level of the GeoSkel framework. It is used to derive the C++ program from the original Python program written by the user.

In the future, we plan to extend GeoSkelSL to handle vector data which are very common data structures used in geosciences. Vector data are made off geometric features such as points, lines or polygons representing roads, rivers, forests etc. Usually, vector data is not as huge as raster data, therefore it is possible to broadcast such data instead of split them as the rasters. However, new patterns have to be implemented to be able to handle them. In the current implementation, it is possible to write programs that call several patterns but no real optimization of the workflow is done. An analysis of the program workflow would allow us to better distribute the data among the nodes to reduce communications and improve performance of the generated programs.

References

1. Bourgeois, K., Robert, S., Limet, S., Essayan, V.: Efficient implicit parallel patterns for geographic information system. In: International Conference on Computational Science, ICCS, pp. 545–554 (2017)
2. Van Deursen, A., Klint, P., Visser, J.: Domain-specific languages: an annotated bibliography. ACM Sigplan Not. **35**(6), 26–36 (2000)
3. GDAL/OGR contributors. The GDAL/OGR Geospatial Data Abstraction software Library. The Open Source Geospatial Foundation (2018)
4. Janjic, V., Brown, C., Mackenzie, K., Hammond, K., Danelutto, M., Aldinucci, M., Daniel García, J.: RPL: a domain-specific language for designing and implementing parallel C++ applications. In: 24th Euromicro International Conference on Parallel, Distributed, and Network-Based Processing, PDP, pp. 288–295 (2016)
5. Ledur, C., Griebler, D., Manssour, I., Fernandes, L.G.: Towards a domain-specific language for geospatial data visualization maps with big data sets. In: 2015 IEEE/ACS 12th International Conference of Computer Systems and Applications (AICCSA), pp. 1–8. IEEE (2015)
6. Neteler, M., Bowman, H.M., Landa, M., Metz, M.: Grass gis: a multi-purpose open source gis. Environ. Model. Softw. **31**, 124–130 (2012)
7. Odersky, M., Micheloud, S., Mihaylov, N., Schinz, M., Stenman, E., Zenger, M., et al.: An overview of the scala programming language. Technical report (2004)
8. Rauchwerger, L., Arzu, F., Ouchi, K.: Standard templates adaptive parallel library (STAPL). In: O'Hallaron, D.R. (ed.) LCR 1998. LNCS, vol. 1511, pp. 402–409. Springer, Heidelberg (1998). https://doi.org/10.1007/3-540-49530-4_32
9. Sujeeth, A., Lee, H., Brown, K., Rompf, T., Chafi, H., Wu, M., Atreya, A., Odersky, M., Olukotun, K.: Optiml: an implicitly parallel domain-specific language for machine learning. In: Proceedings of the 28th International Conference on Machine Learning (ICML-2011), pp. 609–616 (2011)
10. Tarboton, D.G.: Terrain Analysis Using Digital Elevation Models (TauDEM). Utah State University, Utah Water Research Laboratory (2005)
11. QGIS Development Team, et al.: QGIS geographic information system. open source geospatial foundation project (2012)

Precedent-Based Approach
for the Identification of Deviant Behavior
in Social Media

Anna V. Kalyuzhnaya$^{(\boxtimes)}$, Nikolay O. Nikitin, Nikolay Butakov,
and Denis Nasonov

ITMO University, 49 Kronverksky Pr., St. Petersburg 197101,
Russian Federation
kalyuzhnaya.ann@gmail.com

Abstract. The current paper is devoted to a problem of deviant users' identification in social media. For this purpose, each user of social media source should be described through a profile that aggregates open information about him/her within the special structure. Aggregated user profiles are formally described in terms of multivariate random process. The special emphasis in the paper is made on methods for identifying of users with certain on a base of few precedents and control the quality of search results. Experimental study shows the implementation of described methods for the case of commercial usage of the personal account in social media.

Keywords: Deviant user · Social media · Behavior pattern
Precedent-based search

1 Introduction

Nowadays increasing the popularity of social media can be observed. As a result, more and more people have their digital reflection on the Internet. This situation gives new opportunities for analysis of the real-life behavior of person using his digital trace, on the one hand. On the other hand, it creates new behavioral patterns that exist only on the Internet and differs from real-life patterns. Investigation of behavioral patterns of social media users put before us the first task to divide normal (or typical) and deviant behavior, and more than this to identify different types of deviations.

In a frame of this research, we define deviant behavior as behavior that differs from some categorical or quantitative norm. And, therefore, we can distinguish deviations in a broad sense and semantic-normative deviations (in a narrow sense). Deviation in a broad sense (or statistical deviation) can be defined on the basis of behavioral factors that represent a statistical minority of the population. The semantically-normative deviation is defined on the basis of the postulated norm, which explicitly or implicitly divides behavior into conformal (corresponding to expectations) and deviant (not satisfying expectations). Unlike statistical deviation, this form of deviation operates categorical variables. The definition of semantically-normative deviation is based both on the observed behavioral patterns and on the tasks of a specific subject area for which an analysis of the behavior of social media users is conducted. Other words, we can identify the user with semantically-normative deviation if we know how looks like such user and what is the target population for this, or we can find precedents (examples of deviant profile). The main research question of this paper is how to identify users with certain semantically-normative deviation on a base of few precedents. This question is highly relevant because normally identification of similar objects requires large labeled samples for search algorithms training. Although, labeling of social media data is an enormously time/human resources consuming procedure. And whether we can find a solution for identification of profiles similar to few labeled ones, the secondary question is how we can control the quality of search results.

2 Related Work

The area of user behavior profiling studied in several works in different domains. The most widespread approaches are either profiling based on analysis of user posts and comments texts or based on statistical aggregating different types of activities. Text analysis approaches [1–3] represented mostly by generative stochastic models based on LDA and by recurrent neural networks while the second class of approaches [4–6] use vectors built on aggregated users' features to find outliers using supervised and unsupervised methods. Aggregated features may include topological, temporal, and other user's behavior characteristics, but all of them represented in profile as aggregated value or set of values. The advantage of this class is a generalized representation of user's features and activities. It should be noticed that mentioned works use user's profiles for specific goals in certain domains. E.g., works [1, 2, 5] use users profiles for cyber-bullying detection and employ only those features that may help in this task. That reduces the ability of such approaches to be used in other areas.

Discussed works also use supervised and unsupervised methods for outlier detection. Supervised methods need labeled data, unsupervised, in their own turn, needs results interpretation after the moment when separated clusters are found and outliers detected, which may be uninterpretable. In contrary, the suggested approach is intended to be used as semi-supervised, which means that for training we use both: labeled samples and information about structural differences in the users' profiles, represented as features vectors. Despite the variety of existing approaches like [8], there are no methods of unification for approaches and algorithms that can be used to different forms of deviant behavior and different tasks of detection.

3 The Identification of Deviant Users in Social Media

3.1 Aggregated Social Media Profile Model and Its Components

From formal point of view, the task of designing a model of behavioral aggregated user profiles can be designed in terms of a multidimensional random function.

$X = \{X1, \ldots, Xn\}$ – n-dimensional random process, defined in the n-dimensional space of attributes (features) of the aggregated user profile, for which the mathematical model is formalized. For a random process X there is a family of n-dimensional distribution functions

$$\{F_t(X,t)\} = \{F_{t1}[(X1,\ldots,Xn)_{t1}],\ldots,F_{tM}[(X1,\ldots,Xn)_{tM}]\} \qquad (1)$$

that are defined on quasi-stationary intervals $t = t1\ldots tM$. Within the quasi-stationary interval, the realization of the n-dimensional random process X can be considered as an n-dimensional random variable (regardless of time). Then, the time aggregated profile can also be represented as a sequence of profiles on quasi-stationary intervals. On the basis of the general probabilistic model can be constructed aggregated n-dimensional profile.

For correct building an aggregated behavior profile it is necessary to look on the problem from two different sides: how user's state drives the user to leave traces in social media and how these traces can be used to restore user's state. For clarity let introduce the following definitions. User behavior profile is an aggregation of events in user's trace in a way that can be used to (a) characterize user's main aspects of behavior; (b) make users comparable and distinguishable. An event is an elementary action performed by the user in social network or media. Trace is a set of events generated by a certain user for a defined interval of time. The behavior of users in social networks is a reflection of activities and processes taking place in the real world. The user interacts with social network by creating posts on important for his topics, commenting existing posts and discussing different things with other users – e.g., the user generates events. These events are combined into an explicit digital trace of implicit internal state of the user which stays behind each event.

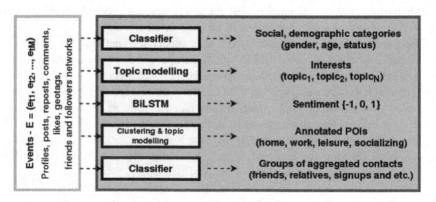

Fig. 1. Aggregation of main aspects of user behavior profile

User behavior is conditioned by two main groups of factors internal (or individual, which is specific for a concrete user) and external (or social, which depend on how user's relation with external for him real world). External factors can be represented as an environment where the user lives, including cultural, social, political and other contexts. This environment influences user's activities as in the real world as in social networks. These factors can be seen as latent variables having specific values for individual users. To estimate values of the hidden factors mentioned above, available digital traces have to be processed and aggregated into components. These components represent user behavior too but as a result of available observations. Components can be organized in four main aspects of the way they are being aggregated (static information, sentiment-semantic, topological and geo-temporal, see Fig. 1), starting with data collecting from social networks. User behavior can change over time and may be addressed by aggregating user's events only for time intervals of a certain length with overlapping to catch his evolution and development trends. But this topic is out of the scope for the current work.

3.2 Precedent-Based Algorithm for Deviant Users Identification

To identify deviant users, two methods have been developed, applied depending on the setting of a specific task. The first method was developed to identify deviants at the population level (unsupervised). This method is applicable to the task of searching for deviant users and subpopulations, considering the unknown form of their deviation in a given population. The first method directly follows from the descriptive model of ordinary users.

More interesting and complicated is the second method that is designed for the identification of profiles with specific deviation, described as a range of aggregated profile features. Since the concrete features values, associated with deviation, are not always known, the approach based on initial set of expertly-confirmed deviant profile examples can be more suitable.

The small number of confirmed deviants is a common problem for this task. A manual search of deviant profiles in a social network is quite difficult, so identification process can be started from 2–3 confirmed profiles. For this reason, a stage of preliminary semiautomatic profile set extension can be added. The main idea is to find the subset of profiles feature space, where the known deviants are similar to each other and differ from non-deviant profiles.

The search for an optimal subset of profile features is a complex task. When we have 48 features, and the problem is to found a subset with unknown size with the best quality of deviations identification, the number of combinations to check will be 2^{48}, that is hard to compute. Therefore, the evolutionary approach based on kofnGA algorithm [7] was applied to reduce the time of optimization, with the size of the population set to 30 and mutation probability is 0.3. Since the algorithm deals with the fixed size of the subset, it's performing for every variant of size is needed. Then, comparison of obtained quality metrics was performed. The additional penalty was added to subspace when deviants or normal profiles are indistinguishable (to avoid the trivial cases with space with insignificant dimensions).

To identify the additional deviants, that are similar to already known, we develop the iterative algorithm, based on the several k-nearest neighbors classifiers. It's presented in Fig. 2.

The generative classifier G, which trained on the manually pre-labeled deviant profiles subsample ("old" deviants), that mixed with random sample the unlabeled profiles (to solve the problem of only positive markup [9]), separates the whole set of

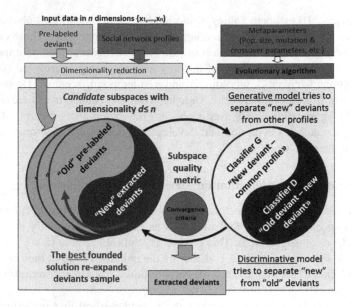

Fig. 2. Algorithm for deviant's identification based on expertly confirmed profiles

profiles as deviant and non-deviant, in order to found the group of "new" deviants. For this model, the evolutionary algorithm tries to maximize the quality of classification.

Otherwise, a discriminative model D tries to separate expertly-confirmed deviant profiles and profiles that are recognized as deviant by the model G. Evolutionary algorithm tries to minimize the quality of classification, that means that the automatically extracted "new" deviant profiles must be indistinguishable from pre-approved "old" deviant profiles. The quality of every classifier is measured as AUC (the area under the receiver operating characteristic curve – ROC, that describes the effectiveness of a binary classifier). While the approach is iterative, the obtained deviants for every cycle can be used to extend the base deviant set and then repeat the classification if needed, that allow controlling the expected quality and size of result sample.

4   Experimental Study

To provide the experiments with profiling and user class matching, we parse the data from public user pages of VK social network. The obtained dataset contains behavioral features for 48K user accounts aggregated for an entire lifetime.

The case study of profiling is devoted to the analysis of social network profiles, that are intended for commercial purposes – for example, as an online clothing store. First of all, we manually labeled several examples of such pages. Then previously-described iterative algorithm for profile set extension was applied to this task. The initial set of commercial accounts contains 17 entities. The example of commercial accounts localization in some 3-dimensional space is presented in Fig. 3a.

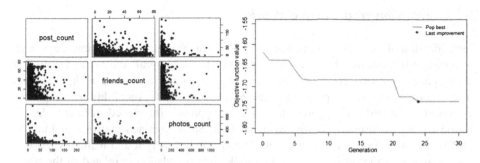

Fig. 3. (a) The subspace of accounts sample (red dots in commercial accounts) (b) The convergence of evolutionary algorithm of optimal dimensions' search (Color figure online)

To verify the results of deviants' identification, the dictionary of domain-specific key phrases was created. Then, it was used to check the correctness of automated deviants markup and measure the population quality – the ratio of correctly recognized deviants to total deviant sample size (that can be changed from 0 to 1).

The optimization problem is to determine the optimal subset of behavioral features, that allows finding the accounts with similar deviation. The experiment was conducted with the dimensionality of space is varied from 5 to 20. The convergence of evolutionary optimization algorithm was achieved in 24 epochs (Fig. 3b).

The founded optimal space contains 10 dimensions (statistics of posts, friends, followers, photos, likes, comments, emotions, etc.). Then, since the quality of extracted accounts depends on the expected size of the sample, the sensitivity analysis of deviant population was provided. When the initial expertly-confirmed sample is 100% correct, after the first iteration only 60% of accounts founded are really online shops, and the other are fans of sales, photographers and artists, active travelers. The further expansion of the sample tends to lower quality. The dependency of the quality metric from deviant sample size is presented in Fig. 4.

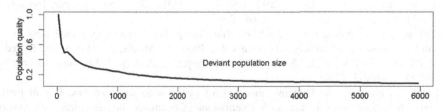

Fig. 4. Quality of extended population

In this case, the quality decreases rapidly, that can be explained by the significant similarity of commercial accounts with some other.

5   Conclusion and Future Works

Identification of deviant users in social media is highly relevant task nowadays. Relevance can be explained by increasing necessity for behavioral analysis and control in cyberspace, from one point of view, and the possibility to explore additional open information about the real person to analyze his/her integrity, reliability or compliance with some standards. This paper discusses an approach for precedent-based identification of deviant users in a targeted population. Such approach allows searching for profiles of users similar to few examples which can be easily found manually. Also, it was shown how the quality of searched look-alike population is related to the population size.

Current results make possible next research step – prediction of future deviant behavior. This ambitious task can be subdivided into two research directions: prediction of the next (the nearest) deviant or even delinquent action of the deviant user (on the level of population), and the probabilistic forecast with different horizons of deviant changes in user behavior.

Acknowledgments. This research financially supported by Ministry of Education and Science of the Russian Federation, Agreement #14.578.21.0196 (03.10.2016). Unique Identification RFMEFI57816X0196.

References

1. Raisi, E., Huang, B.: Cyberbullying identification using participant-vocabulary consistency, pp. 46–50 (2016)
2. Sax, S.: Flame Wars: Automatic Insult Detection
3. Wang, Y., et al.: Topic-level influencers identification in the Microblog sphere, pp. 4–5 (2016)
4. Angeletou, S., Rowe, M., Alani, H.: Modelling and analysis of user behaviour in online communities. In: Aroyo, L., Welty, C., Alani, H., Taylor, J., Bernstein, A., Kagal, L., Noy, N., Blomqvist, E. (eds.) ISWC 2011. LNCS, vol. 7031, pp. 35–50. Springer, Heidelberg (2011). https://doi.org/10.1007/978-3-642-25073-6_3
5. Dadvar, M., Ordelman, R., de Jong, F., Trieschnigg, D.: Towards user modelling in the combat against cyberbullying. In: Bouma, G., Ittoo, A., Métais, E., Wortmann, H. (eds.) NLDB 2012. LNCS, vol. 7337, pp. 277–283. Springer, Heidelberg (2012). https://doi.org/10.1007/978-3-642-31178-9_34
6. Galal, A., Elkorany, A.: Dynamic modeling of twitter users dynamic modeling of twitter users. In: Proceedings if the 17th International Conference on Enterprise Information Systems, vol. 2, pp. 585–593 (2015)
7. Wolters, M.A.: A genetic algorithm for selection of fixed-size subsets with application to design problems. J. Stat. Softw. **68**(1), 1–18 (2015)
8. Ma, Q., et al.: A sub-linear, massive-scale look-alike audience extension system. In: Proceedings of the 5th International Workshop on Big Data, Streams and Heterogeneous Source Mining: Algorithms, Systems, Programming Models and Applications (2016)
9. Elkan, C., Noto, K.: Learning classifiers from only positive and unlabeled data. In: Proceedings of the 14th ACM SIGKDD International Conference on Knowledge Discovery and Data Mining, pp. 213–220. ACM (2008)

Performance Analysis of 2D-compatible 2.5D-PDGEMM on Knights Landing Cluster

Daichi Mukunoki[1,2(✉)] and Toshiyuki Imamura[1]

[1] RIKEN Center for Computational Science, 7-1-26 Minatojima-minami-machi,
Chuo-ku, Kobe, Hyogo 650-0047, Japan
{daichi.mukunoki,imamura.toshiyuki}@riken.jp
[2] Tokyo Woman's Christian University,
2-6-1 Zempukuji, Suginami-ku, Tokyo 167-8585, Japan

Abstract. This paper discusses the performance of a parallel matrix multiplication routine (PDGEMM) that uses the 2.5D algorithm, which is a communication-reducing algorithm, on a cluster based on the Xeon Phi 7200-series (codenamed Knights Landing), Oakforest-PACS. Although the algorithm required a 2.5D matrix distribution instead of the conventional 2D distribution, it performed computations of 2D distributed matrices on a 2D process grid by redistributing the matrices (2D-compatible 2.5D-PDGEMM). Our use of up to 8192 nodes (8192 Xeon Phi processors) demonstrates that in terms of strong scaling, our implementation performs better than conventional 2D implementations.

Keywords: Parallel matrix multiplication · 2.5D algorithm
Xeon Phi · Knights landing

1 Introduction

Toward the Exa-scale computing era, the degree of parallelism (i.e., the numbers of nodes, cores, and processes) of HPC systems is increasing. On such highly parallel systems, computations can become communication-bound when the size of a problem is insufficiently large, even if the computation is a compute-intensive task, such as parallel matrix multiplication (the so-called PDGEMM in ScaLA-PACK). Consequently, communication-avoiding techniques have been the focus of research to improve performance of computations in terms of strong scaling on highly parallel systems.

For PDGEMM, the 2.5D algorithm (2.5D-PDGEMM) has been proposed as a communication-avoiding algorithm [4] that assumes a 2D distribution of matrices stacked and duplicated vertically in a 3D process grid (the 2.5D distribution). The 2.5D algorithm decreases the number of the computational steps of the 2D algorithms (e.g., Cannon and SUMMA) by parallelizing the steps by utilizing the redundancy of the matrices in the 2.5D distribution, unlike the conventional

© Springer International Publishing AG, part of Springer Nature 2018
Y. Shi et al. (Eds.): ICCS 2018, LNCS 10862, pp. 853–858, 2018.
https://doi.org/10.1007/978-3-319-93713-7_85

PDGEMM, which uses 2D algorithms that are computed in parallel only by utilizing the 2D data parallelism of the matrices. Thus, if the 2.5D algorithm is used to compute matrices distributed in a 2D process grid with a 2D distribution, as executed by ScaLAPACK PDGEMM, the matrices must be redistributed from 2D to 2.5D. The implementation and performance of 2.5D-PDGEMM have been featured in several studies [1,3,4]; however, so far, these studies have not addressed the 2D compatibility.

We expect that such a 2D compatibility would be required so that, in the future, applications using the conventional PDGEMM would be able to achieve good strong scalability on highly parallel systems. Our previous study proposed a 2D-compatible 2.5D-PDGEMM implementation that computes matrices distributed on a 2D process grid with a 2D distribution and analyzed the performance of up to 16384 nodes on the K computer [2]. This implementation outperformed conventional 2D implementations, including the ScaLAPACK PDGEMM, in terms of strong scaling, even when the cost of the matrix redistribution between 2D and 2.5D was included.

This paper presents the results of our 2D-compatible 2.5D-PDGEMM implementation on the Oakforest-PACS system, which is a Xeon Phi 7200-series (codenamed Knights Landing) based cluster hosted by the Joint Center for Advanced High Performance Computing (JCAHPC), Japan. The system is equipped with 8208 Xeon Phi processors and was ranked numer six on the TOP500 list in November 2016. Our study used 8192 of the processors to assess the performance and effectiveness of the 2D-compatible 2.5D-PDGEMM on Xeon Phi-based supercomputers.

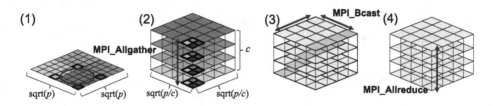

Fig. 1. Implementation of 2D-compatible 2.5D-PDGEMM

2   Implementation

Our 2D-compatible 2.5D-PDGEMM is based on the SUMMA algorithm [5] and computes $C = \alpha AB + \beta C$, where α and β are scalar values, and whereas A, B, and C are dense matrices distributed on a 2D process grid with a 2D block distribution. For simplicity, our current implementation only supports square matrices, a square process grid, and a 2D block distribution. Figure 1 summarizes our implementation. p corresponds to the total number of processes joining the computation and c corresponds to the stack size (duplication factor) of the 2.5D algorithm. Thus, the matrices are initially distributed on a 2D process grid of $p = \sqrt{p} \times \sqrt{p}$ processes with a 2D distribution.

The computation is executed as follows: (1) the MPI_Comm_split creates the 3D logical process grid from a 2D process grid by dividing the original 2D process grid to form the levels of the 3D process grid; (2) the MPI_Allgather redistributes and duplicates matrices A and B; (3) the 2.5D algorithm executes $1/c$ of the SUMMA algorithm's steps at each level of the 3D process grid using DGEMM and MPI_Bcast; and (4) the MPI_Allreduce computes the final result for matrix C by reducing and redistributing the temporal results of the matrix on each level of the 3D process grid.

Table 1. Environment and conditions of evaluation

Processor	Intel Xeon Phi 7250 (Knights Landing, 1.4 GHz, 68 cores)
Memory	MCDRAM (16 GB) + DDR4 (96 GB)
Interconnect	Intel Omni-Path Architecture (100 Gbps, Full-bisection Fat Tree)
Compiler	Intel compiler 18.0.1
MKL	Intel MKL 2018.1
MPI	Intel MPI 2018.1.163
MPI options	OMP_NUM_THREADS = 16, I_MPI_PIN_DOMAIN = 64
	I_MPI_PIN_PROCESSOR_EXCLUDE_LIST = 0,1,68,69,136,137,204,205
	I_MPI_PERHOST = 4, KMP_AFFINITY = scatter,
	KMP_HW_SUBSET = 1t, I_MPI_FABRICS = tmi:tmi,
	HFI_NO_CPUAFFINITY = 1

3   Results

We evaluated the performance of our implementation using 8192 nodes on the Oakforest-PACS system. Table 1 summarizes the environment and conditions of the evaluation. Each node is equipped with one processor; therefore, the number of nodes is equal to the number of processors. The parallel execution model was a hybrid of the MPI and the OpenMP; however, hyperthreading was not used (1 OpenMP thread per core). We assigned 4 MPI processes per node when the number of the nodes was 256, 1024, and 4096 for performance reasons; however, due to a limitation in our implementation, we assigned 2 MPI processes per node when the number of the nodes was 128, 512, 2048, and 8192. On the Oakforest-PACS system, the tickless mode was set for the core number 0 only to receive timer interrupts. Therefore, the logical cores 0 and 1 were excluded to avoid the effects of OS jitter (the logical core 1 was also excluded, as both belong to the same core group).

We evaluated the performance of our implementation with stack sizes of $c = 1, 4$, and 16. Our implementation was designed to perform equivalently to the conventional 2D-SUMMA when $c = 1$. In addition, we measured the performance of the ScaLAPACK PDGEMM for reference (the block size $nb = 512$ at maximum). We excluded the MPI sub-communicator setup cost from the execution time, because, on ScaLAPACK, such a communicator setup process becomes separated from the PDGEMM routine.

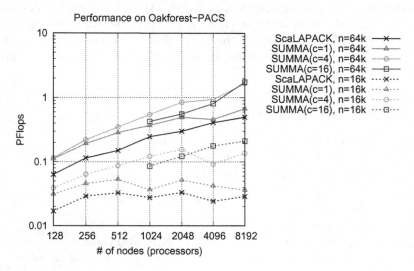

Fig. 2. Strong scaling performances for matrix sizes n = 16384 (16 k) and n = 65536 (64 k)

Figure 2 shows the strong scaling performances when the matrix size n = 16384 (16 k) and n = 65536 (64 k). Figure 3 shows the breakdown of the performances when the matrix size n = 65536. Bcast corresponds to the communication cost of using the SUMMA algorithm for the 2.5D matrix multiplication whereas Allgather and Allreduce correspond to the communication costs for redistribution and reduction.

Overall, the results show that the effectiveness of the 2.5D algorithm is higher than that we observed in our previous work on the K computer [2]. The factor that may most strongly cause the difference between the results of the Oakforest-PACS and the K computer is the ratio of the computation performance to the communication performance. Whereas the K computer has a relatively richer network compared with the floating-point performance per node, i.e., $20\,[\text{GB/s}]/128\,[\text{GFlops}] \approx 0.16$, the Oakforest-PACS system is a typical example of modern supercomputers, which has a relatively huge floating-point performance per node compared with the network's performance, i.e., $25\,[\text{GB/s}]/3046.4\,[\text{GFlops}] \approx 0.0082$. Thus, the Oakforest-PACS is approximately 20 times more a "Flops-oriented" system than the K computer is. The evaluation indicates that the 2.5D-PDGEMM is more effective as a communication-avoiding technique in such environments.

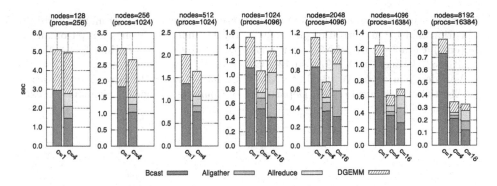

Fig. 3. Performance breakdown (matrix size n=65536)

4   Conclusions

This paper presented the evaluation of the performance of our 2D-compatible 2.5D-PDGEMM, which was designed to execute computations of 2D distributed matrices by using up to 8192 Xeon Phi Knights Landing processors on the Oakforest-PACS system. The results demonstrated that, on recent HPC systems, such as the Oakforest-PACS, which provide huge floating-point performance as compared with the network's performance, a 2D-compatible 2.5D-PDGEMM was quite effective as a substitute for the conventional 2D-PDGEMM. Beyond this study, we will further analyze and estimate the performance of the 2.5D-PDGEMM on future Exa-scale systems by creating a performance model and using a system simulator.

Acknowledgment. The computational resource of the Oakforest-PACS was awarded by the "Large-scale HPC Challenge" Project, Joint Center for Advanced High Performance Computing (JCAHPC). This study is supported by the FLAGSHIP2020 project.

References

1. Georganas, E., González-Domínguez, J., Solomonik, E., Zheng, Y., Touriño, J., Yelick, K.: Communication Avoiding and Overlapping for Numerical Linear Algebra. In: Proceedings of the International Conference on High Performance Computing, Networking, Storage and Analysis (SC 2012), pp. 100:1–100:11 (2012)
2. Mukunoki, D., Imamura, T.: Implementation and performance analysis of 2.5D-PDGEMM on the K computer. In: Wyrzykowski, R., Dongarra, J., Deelman, E., Karczewski, K. (eds.) PPAM 2017. LNCS, vol. 10777, pp. 348–358. Springer, Cham (2018). https://doi.org/10.1007/978-3-319-78024-5_31
3. Schatz, M., Van de Geijn, R.A., Poulson, J.: Parallel matrix multiplication: a systematic journey. SIAM J. Sci. Comput. **38**(6), C748–C781 (2016)

4. Solomonik, E., Demmel, J.: Communication-optimal parallel 2.5D matrix multiplication and LU factorization algorithms. In: Jeannot, E., Namyst, R., Roman, J. (eds.) Euro-Par 2011. LNCS, vol. 6853, pp. 90–109. Springer, Heidelberg (2011). https://doi.org/10.1007/978-3-642-23397-5_10
5. Van de Geijn, R.A., Watts, J.: SUMMA: Scalable Universal Matrix Multiplication Algorithm, Technical report, Department of Computer Science, University of Texas at Austin (1995)

Author Index